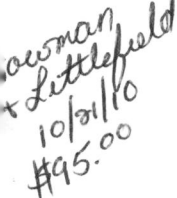

WITHDRAWN

The Who, What, *and* Where *of* America

The Who, What, *and* Where *of* America

Understanding the American Community Survey

edited by Deirdre A. Gaquin

 **Bernan** Press

Lanham, Maryland

Published in the United States of America
by Bernan Press, a wholly owned subsidiary of
The Rowman & Littlefield Publishing Group, Inc.
4501 Forbes Boulevard, Suite 200
Lanham, Maryland 20706

Bernan Press
800-865-3457
info@bernan.com
www.bernan.com

ISBN 13: 978-1-59888-398-5
E-ISBN: 978-1-59888-399-2

∞ ™ The paper used in this publication meets the minimum requirements of
American National Standard for Information Sciences—Permanence of
Paper for Printed Library Materials, ANSI/NISO Z39.48-1992.
Manufactured in the United States of America.

Contents

Preface

As the nation prepares for the 2010 census, a major change is taking place. All American households will answer a simple questionnaire with 10 questions. No longer will some people get the "long form" with dozens of detailed questions about employment, education, income, previous residence, housing characteristics, and more. The data gleaned from these important questions have long been used by federal, state, and local governments to evaluate their populations and program needs; by large and small businesses and non-profit organizations for a variety of planning and location purposes; and by academic researchers to study trends in social and economic conditions. The "long form" has been replaced by the American Community Survey (ACS). Under development for more than a decade, the ACS is an ongoing survey of the American people that is ushering in a new era in social and economic data analysis. The census "long form" provided detailed estimates of social and economic characteristics every ten years. The ACS collects this same information on a rolling basis. It takes five years of ACS responses to accumulate a sample almost as large as the census "long form" collected at a single point in time. But data users will now have the ability to study these characteristics and trends throughout the decade.

Because the ACS is a sample survey, large numbers of sample cases are needed before reliable estimates can be made for small populations. Each year's sample is large enough to produce estimates for the nation, all the states, all metropolitan areas, and many counties and cities. This book contains a selection of data from the first 3-year estimates released from the ACS for all states and metropolitan areas, and for counties and cities with populations of 20,000 or more. In the near future, 5-year estimates will be released for all geographic entities in the United States.

This book is designed to include a sampling of key information, but also to guide users through the process of using the Census Bureau's Web site to expand on the information included here. The state tables in this book include over 300 data items. The metropolitan area, county, and city tables include 48 data items. The data in the tables are a small selection that shows what is available for the smaller counties and citie. Every column includes an ACS Table Number that enables users to find the original data on the Census Bureau's Web site. The selection in this book is limited because there is a great deal of suppression in the county and city data. Much more information is likely to be available for analysis of larger cities and counties or for analysis of specific racial or ethnic groups if those groups have large populations in a particular city or county.

One of the most notable differences between the census "long form" and the ACS is the time frame of the estimates. We are accustomed to the census data that give us specific information every ten years, a snapshot of the country on April 1. The ACS multi-year estimates are different. The data in this book are all from the 2005–2007 3-year estimates. They are not averages, nor do they represent 2006, the midpoint. They are period estimates with data spread evenly throughout the three years. To help in the understanding of these estimates, we have included a measure of population change for each geographic area. These are from the Census Bureau's Population Estimates Program which provides the official population counts that underlie the ACS sample. If an area experienced unusually large population growth or decline during those three years, we should recognize the variations that may be hidden in the ACS estimates—perhaps a lot of people moving into a new development, a city annexing a large tract of land, or a lot of people leaving the area because of a plant closing.

Because the years 2005 through 2007 preceded the economic downturn, the data in this book generally represent the social and economic picture before increases in unemployment and decreases in housing values. In a few years, we will be able to compare these numbers with 2008–2010 estimates. In the meantime, annual estimates will continue to let us analyze the larger areas with populations of 65,000 or more, and new 3-year estimates will be released every year. But each year's 3-year estimates will include overlap with earlier estimates so they will be of limited use for comparison until a completely new 3-year period is available.

Finally, it is always critical to remember that all estimates are subject to sampling error. On the Census Bureau's Web site, every ACS number is accompanied by its margin of error. In the interests of space and simplicity, this book does not include the margins of error, but all users are encouraged to consult the Census Bureau's Web site and to understand some basics: small differences are very likely to represent no difference at all; do not draw conclusions from small numbers; use these numbers as a starting point to explore the wealth of information from the ACS.

Introduction

The American Community Survey (ACS) is ushering in the most substantial change in the decennial census in more than 60 years. It will replace the decennial census long form in 2010 and collect long-form-type information annually rather than only once every 10 years, providing more current data throughout the decade. The new ACS estimates combine three years of survey responses (2005–2007) to produce data for midsize communities. This is the first update for communities with populations between 20,000 and 65,000 since the 2000 decennial census.

The ACS, part of the 2010 Decennial Census Program, gathers demographic, social, economic, housing, and financial information about the nation's people and communities on a continuous basis. The ACS is an ongoing survey conducted by the U.S. Census Bureau in every county, American Indian and Alaska Native Area, and Hawaiian Home Land in the United States. The ACS is also conducted as the Puerto Rico Community Survey in every municipio in Puerto Rico. As the largest survey in the United States, it is the only source of small-area data on a wide range of important social and economic characteristics for all communities in the country. After years of planning, development, and a demonstration period, the ACS began nationwide full implementation in 2005.

Data from the ACS are available on the Census Bureau's Web site. The ACS main page is <http://www.census.gov/acs/www/>.

There is a vast amount of information collected in the ACS. In this publication, a selection of this data has been collected in various tables by subject and geography type.

Volume Organization

The data tables in this book contain a representative selection of information from the ACS.

Part A. Who contains the following subjects: age, race/ethnicity, and household structure, among others.
Part B. What contains the following subject areas: education, employment, and income.

Part C. Where comprises data on: migration, housing, and transportation.

Within each part are four tables. Table 1 covers the 50 states and the District of Columbia; Table 2 contains all counties with populations of 20,000 or more. Table 3 has all the nation's metropolitan statistical areas; and Table 4 comprises all cities with populations of 20,000 or more. Counties and cities are listed alphabetically by state. Metropolitan areas are listed alphabetically, except that metropolitan divisions are listed alphabetically within the metropolitan statistical area of which they are components.

In addition, each part is preceded by highlights and ranking tables that show how areas diverge from the national norm, as well as showing the differences among small areas. These research aids are invaluable for helping researchers understand what the census data tell us about who we are, what we do, and where we live.

In the following sections, information about the ACS and how to use the data is included, much of it excerpted from the wealth of information available on the Census Bureau's Web site. Especially helpful are the instructions, definitions, and guidelines on using the data in the Compass series of handbooks. Readers are encouraged to explore the Census Bureau's Web site to expand on the information contained here and to keep up to date with this constantly changing dataset.

Deirdre A. Gaquin has been a data use consultant to private organizations, government agencies, and universities for over 25 years. Prior to that, she was Director of Data Access Services at Data Use & Access Laboratories, a pioneer in private sector distribution of federal statistical data. A former President of the Association of Public Data Users, Ms. Gaquin has served on numerous boards, panels, and task forces concerned with federal statistical data and has worked on four decennial censuses. She holds a Master of Urban Planning (MUP) degree from Hunter College. Ms. Gaquin is also an editor of Bernan Press's *County and City Extra*; *The Who, What, and Where of America: Understanding the Census Results*; *Places, Towns and Townships*; and *The Almanac of American Education*.

Understanding the American Community Survey

Every 10 years since 1790, Congress has authorized funds to conduct a national census of the U.S. population, as required by the U.S. Constitution. From 1960 through 2000, censuses have consisted of:

- a "short form," which included basic questions about age, sex, race, Hispanic origin, household relationship, and owner/renter status, and

- a "long form" used for only a sample of households that included not only the basic short-form questions but also detailed questions about socioeconomic and housing characteristics.

The American Community Survey (ACS) will replace the decennial census long form in 2010 and thereafter by collecting long-form-type information annually rather than only once every 10 years, providing more current data throughout the decade. The 2010 Census will continue to count the population to support the constitutional mandate—to provide population counts needed to apportion the seats in the U. S. House of Representatives. The ACS data will provide, for the first time, a regular stream of updated information for states and local areas, and will revolutionize the way we use data to understand our communities. It produces social, housing, and economic characteristics for demographic groups, eventually for geographic areas as small as census tracts and block groups.

Some Key Facts About the ACS:

- The ACS will annually provide the same kind of detailed information previously available only every 10 years from the census. The ACS is conducted under the authority of Title 13, United States Code, Sections 141 and 193.

- All answers are confidential. Any Census Bureau employee who violates that confidentiality is subject to a jail term, a fine, or both.

- The Census Bureau may use the information it collects only for statistical purposes.

- Addresses are selected at random to represent similar households in their area. The survey is conducted by mail, telephone, and personal visit. Response to this survey is required by Section 221 of Title 13.

- Approximately 2.5 percent of U.S. households are surveyed per year. A sample of group quarters (nursing homes, college dormitories, etc.) is included in the ACS as well.

Data from the ACS can be extremely valuable for a variety of purposes that include: to monitor the well-being of America's children and families, to investigate the characteristics of the U.S. workforce, to determine the economic well-being of working-poor families, or to track social, economic, and demographic changes in the general U.S. population. Many people are being cautious in their approach to the ACS, and rightly so. This is a relatively new survey with a new approach to measuring change in our communities. The ACS has great potential, particularly as a source of annual data for local areas. By providing data each year, the ACS will provide critical information for communities when they need it most.

New Opportunities

The main benefits of the ACS are timeliness and access to annual data for states, local areas, and small population subgroups. The ACS will deliver useful, relevant data, similar to data from previous census long forms, but updated every year instead of every 10 years. The ACS provides comparable information across and within states for program evaluation and use in funding formulas.

- ACS information is often used to determine the location of new schools, hospitals, and highways.

- ACS provides information for tracking the well-being of children, families, and the elderly.

- The data will aid federal, state, and local governments in distributing benefits fairly. About $300 billion in federal program funds are distributed each year based, in whole or in part, on census and ACS data.

- The data are used by community programs, such as those for the elderly, libraries, hospitals, banks, and other organizations.

- The data are used by transportation planners to evaluate peak volumes of traffic in order to reduce congestion, plan for parking, and develop plans for carpooling and flexible work schedules.

- Corporations, small businesses, and individuals can use these data to develop business plans, to set strategies for expansion or starting a business, and to determine trends in their service areas to meet current and future needs.

- Small towns and rural communities have much to gain from the ACS. Lacking the staff and resources to conduct their own research, many local communities rely on decennial census information that becomes increasingly outdated throughout the decade, or use local administrative records that are not comparable with information collected in neighboring areas.

- The ACS also provides tools for those who want to conduct their own research. The ACS includes a Public Use Microdata Sample (PUMS) file each year that enables researchers to create custom universes and tabulations from individual ACS records that have been stripped of personally identifiable information.

- The use of professional, highly trained, permanent interviewers has improved the accuracy of ACS data compared with those from the decennial census long-form sample. This strategy has effectively reduced the number of refusals to complete the ACS questionnaire. ACS interviewers also obtain more complete information than decennial census interviewers.

New Challenges

The main challenges for ACS data users are understanding and using multiyear estimates and the relatively large confidence intervals associated with ACS data for smaller geographic areas and subgroups of the population.

- ACS data will be produced every year, but the sample size of the ACS is smaller than that of the Census 2000 long form sample. Data users need to pay more attention to the margin of error.

- By 2010, data users will have access to 5-year estimates of ACS data. The sample size based on 5-year period estimates of ACS data is still smaller than the long-form sample in the decennial census, resulting in larger standard errors in the ACS 5-year estimates.

- Because the ACS will produce 1-year, 3-year, and 5-year estimates, data users will have to decide which ones are appropriate to their needs.

- Data users will need to be aware of the implications of multiyear estimates, particularly in analyzing employment and income data that will span a full year or even a 5-year period.

The ACS includes several questions that are very similar to those collected in other federal surveys— especially the Current Population Survey (CPS), the American Housing Survey, and the Survey of Income and Program Participation. In some cases, there are clear guidelines about which data to use. For example, the CPS is the official source of income and poverty data. It includes detailed questions on these topics and should be used in reporting national trends in these subject areas. The Census Bureau recommends that ACS information on income and poverty be used to supplement CPS data for areas below the state level and for population subgroups (such as age, sex, race, Hispanic origin, type of household) at the state level. For an explanation of various income and poverty data sources, see the Census Bureau's guidelines at <http://www.census.gov/hhes/www/poverty/description.html>. For states, generally the Census Bureau recommends using the ACS, though the CPS is still valuable as a source for examining historical state income and poverty trends.

The ACS Sample

The ACS is sent each month to a sample of roughly 250,000 addresses in the United States and Puerto Rico, or 3 million a year, resulting in nearly 2 million final interviews. The sample represents all housing units and group quarters in the United States and Puerto Rico. (Group quarters include places such as college dormitories, prisons, military barracks, and nursing homes.) The addresses are selected from the Census Bureau's Master Address File (MAF), which is also the basis for the decennial census.

The annual ACS sample is smaller than that of the Census 2000 long-form sample, which included about 18 million housing units. As a result, the ACS needs to combine population or housing data from multiple years to produce reliable numbers for small counties, neighborhoods, and other local areas. To provide information for communities each year, the ACS will provide 1-, 3-, and 5-year estimates.

The ACS sample is not spread evenly across all areas but includes a larger proportion of addresses in sparsely populated rural communities and American Indian reservations and a lower proportion in densely populated areas. Over a 5-year period, the ACS will sample about 15 million addresses and complete interviews for about 11 million. This sample is sufficient to produce estimates for small geographic areas, such as neighborhoods and sparsely-populated rural counties. In a 5-year period no address will be selected for the ACS more than once, and many addresses will never be selected for the survey.

Geography

The ACS data are tabulated for a variety of geographic areas ranging in size from broad geographic regions (Northeast, Midwest, South, and West) to cities, towns, neighborhoods, and census block groups. Prior to December 2008, ACS data were only available for geographic areas with at least 65,000 people, including regions, divisions, states, the District of Columbia, Puerto Rico, congressional districts, Public Use Microdata Areas (PUMAs)—census-constructed geographic areas, each with approximately a population of 100,000—and many large counties, metropolitan areas, cities, school districts, and American Indian areas. Starting in December 2008, 3-year estimates became available for all areas with at least 20,000 people, and by 2010, 5-year estimates for geographic areas down to the block group level will be available. By 2010 there will be 1-, 3-, and 5-year estimates—three sets of numbers—available. Less populous areas will receive only 5-year estimates. The vast majority of areas will receive only 5-year estimates.

All the tables in this book contain data from 2005–2007, the first release of 3-year estimates. The population cutoff of 20,000 yields data for 1,817 of the 3,141 counties in the United States, and for 2,065 cities, as well as all states and metropolitan areas. More information about geography can be found in Appendix C.

Data Comparability

Since ACS data are collected continuously, they are not always comparable with data collected from the decennial census. For example, both surveys ask about employment status during the week prior to the survey. However, data from the decennial census are typically collected between March and August, whereas data from the ACS are collected nearly every day and reflect employment throughout the year. Other factors that may also have an impact on the data include seasonal variation in population and minor differences in question wording and question order. In 2006, the ACS began including samples of the population living in group quarters (e.g., jails, college dormitories, and nursing homes) for the first time. As a result, 2006 ACS data may not be comparable with data from earlier ACS surveys. This is especially true for estimates of young adults and the elderly, who are more likely than other groups to be living in group quarters facilities.

One of the most important uses of the ACS estimates is to make comparisons between estimates. Several key types of comparisons are of general interest to users:

- Comparisons of estimates from different geographic areas within the same time period (e.g., comparing the proportion of people below the poverty level in two counties).

- Comparisons of estimates for the same geographic area across time periods (e.g., comparing the proportion of people below the poverty level in a county for 2006 and 2007).

- Comparisons of ACS estimates with the corresponding estimates from past decennial census samples (e.g., comparing the proportion of people below the poverty level in a county for 2006 and 2000).

A number of conditions must be met when comparing survey estimates. Of primary importance is that the comparison takes into account the sampling error associated with each estimate, thus determining whether the observed differences between estimates are statistically significant. Statistical significance means that there is statistical evidence that a true difference exists within the full population, and that the observed difference is unlikely to have occurred by chance due to sampling. A method for determining statistical significance when making comparisons, as well as considerations associated with the various types of comparisons, can be found in Appendix 4 of the *ACS General Handbook*: <http://www.census.gov/acs/www/Downloads/ACSGeneralHandbook.pdf>.

Subjects Covered

The topics covered by the ACS focus on demographic, social, economic, and housing characteristics. These topics are virtually the same as those covered by the Census 2000 long form sample data.

Demographic Characteristics
Age, Sex, Hispanic Origin, Race, Relationship to Householder (e.g., spouse)

Social Characteristics
Marital Status and Marital History, Fertility, Grandparents as Caregivers, Ancestry, Place of Birth, Citizenship and Year of Entry, Language Spoken at Home, Educational Attainment and School Enrollment, Residence One Year Ago, Veteran Status, Period of Military Service, and VA Service-Connected Disability Rating, Disability

Economic Characteristics
Income, Food Stamps Benefit, Labor Force Status, Industry, Occupation, Class of Worker, Place of Work and Journey to Work, Work Status Last Year, Vehicles Available, Health Insurance Coverage

Housing Characteristics
Year Structure Built, Units in Structure, Year Moved Into Unit, Rooms, Bedrooms, Kitchen Facilities, Plumbing

Facilities, House Heating Fuel, Telephone Service Available, Farm Residence

Financial Characteristics
Tenure (Owner/Renter), Housing Value, Rent, Selected Monthly Owner Costs

Note: Marital History, VA Service-Connected Disability Rating, and Health Insurance Coverage are new for 2008 and are not available for the years included in this book.

ACS Estimates Availability

The ACS began in 1996 and has expanded each subsequent year. From 2000 through 2004, the sample included between 740,000 and 900,000 addresses annually. In 2005, the ACS shifted from a demonstration program to the full sample size and design. It became the largest household survey in the United States, with an annual sample size of about 3 million addresses. The 2005, 2006, and 2007 ACS single year estimates are available for geographic areas with a population of 65,000 or more. For the first time, data are available for areas of 20,000 or more, as a 3-year period estimate (2005–2007). The ACS will accumulate sample over 3-year and 5-year intervals to produce estimates for smaller geographic areas including census tracts and block groups. For small areas with populations less than 20,000, it will take 5 years to accumulate a large enough sample to provide estimates with accuracy similar to the decennial census. Beginning in 2010, and every year thereafter, the nation will have this five-year period estimate available, a resource that will show the most up-to-date estimates annually for neighborhoods and rural areas. Even with the accumulated 5-year averages of 15 million sample households, the ACS will not achieve the sample size of the decennial census long form, which included about 18 million households in 2000.

Annually, the ACS produces updated, single-year estimates of demographic, housing, social, and economic char-acteristics for all states, as well as for larger counties, cities, metropolitan and urban areas, and congressional districts. Geographic areas must have a minimum population of 65,000 to qualify for estimates based on a single year's sample. Every congressional district meets this threshold and therefore new single year estimates are released each year for every congressional district. Some school districts, townships, and American Indian and Alaska Native areas also meet this population threshold.

For areas with populations of at least 20,000, the Census Bureau will produce estimates using data collected over 3 years. For rural areas and city neighborhoods (including census tracts and block groups) with fewer than 20,000 people, the Census Bureau plans to produce estimates using data collected over 5 years, with plans to update these multiyear estimates every year. ACS data are released every year, about 8 months after the end of each calendar year of data collection.

For some geographic areas—including three-quarters of all counties, most school districts, and most cities, towns, and American Indian reservations—only 3-year or 5-year estimates will be available because of their population size. Because some federal grant programs allocate funds directly to these areas, Congress can use the 3- and 5-year estimates to evaluate needs at the relevant geographic level, compare characteristics between areas within and among states, and analyze how various formulas distribute funds. The vast majority of areas will receive only 5-year estimates. In partnership with the states, the Census Bureau created Public Use Microdata Areas (PUMAs), which are special, nonoverlapping areas within a state, each with a population of about 100,000

Definitions of these geographic areas are at <http://www.census.gov/acs/www/UseData/geo.htm>.

Using the ACS

The ACS data are complex and cover a broad range of topics and geographic areas. Because this is a relatively new survey, many people do not fully understand how to interpret and use the ACS data. The key points are summarized below.

- Use caution in comparing ACS data with data from the decennial census or other sources. Every survey uses different methods, which could affect the comparability of the numbers.

- The ACS was designed to provide estimates of the characteristics of the population, not to provide counts of the population in different geographic areas or population subgroups.

- Be careful in drawing conclusions about small differences between two estimates because they may not be statistically different.

- Data users need to be careful not to interpret annual fluctuations in the data as long-term trends.

- Use caution in comparing data from 2006 and later surveys with data from the 2000–2005 surveys. Unlike earlier surveys, the 2006 ACS survey includes samples of the population living in group quarters (e.g., college dorms and nursing homes), so the data may not be comparable, especially for young adults and the elderly, who are more likely than other age groups to be living in group quarters facilities.

- Data users should not interpret or refer to 3- year or 5-year period estimates as estimates of the middle year or last year in the series. For example, a 2005–2007 estimate is not a "2006 average."

- Data users should *not* rely on overlapping confidence intervals as a test for statistical significance because this method will not always provide an accurate result.

Differences Between the ACS and the Decennial Census

While the main function of the decennial census is to provide *counts* of people for the purpose of congressional apportionment and legislative redistricting, the primary purpose of the ACS is to measure the changing social and economic *characteristics* of the U.S. population. As a result, the ACS does not provide official counts of the population in between censuses. Instead, the Census Bureau's Population Estimates Program will continue to be the official source for annual population totals, by age, race, Hispanic origin, and sex. ACS estimates are controlled to match the Census Bureau's annual population estimates, by age, sex, race, and Hispanic origin. For more information about population estimates, visit the Census Bureau's Web site at <http://www.census.gov/popest/estimates.php>.

There are many similarities between the methods used in the decennial census sample and the ACS. Both the ACS and the decennial census sample data are based on information from a sample of the population. The data from the Census 2000 sample of about one-sixth of the population were collected using a "long-form" questionnaire, whose content was the model for the ACS. While some differences exist in the specific Census 2000 question wording and that of the ACS, most questions are identical or nearly identical. Differences in the design and implementation of the two surveys are noted below with references provided to a series of evaluation studies that assess the degree to which these differences are likely to impact the estimates. The ACS produces period estimates and these estimates do not measure characteristics for the same time frame as the decennial census estimates, which are interpreted to be a snapshot of April 1 of the census year.

Some data items were collected by both the ACS and the Census 2000 long form with slightly different definitions that could affect the comparability of the estimates for these items. One example is annual costs for a mobile home. Census 2000 included installment loan costs in the total annual costs but the ACS does not. In this example, the ACS could be expected to yield smaller estimates than Census 2000.

While some differences were a part of the census and survey design objectives, other differences observed between ACS and census results were not by design, but due to nonsampling error—differences related to how well the surveys were conducted. The ACS and the census experience different levels and types of coverage error, different levels and treatment of unit and item nonresponse, and different instances of measurement and processing error. Both Census 2000 and the ACS had similar high levels of survey coverage and low levels of unit nonresponse. Higher levels of unit nonresponse were found in the nonresponse follow-up stage of Census 2000. Higher item nonresponse rates were also found in Census 2000.

Census Bureau analysts have compared sample estimates from Census 2000 with 1-year ACS estimates based on data collected in 2000 and 3-year ACS estimates based on data collected in 1999–2001 in selected counties. In general, ACS estimates were found to be quite similar to those produced from decennial census data.

A series of reports summarize their findings and can be found at <http://www.census.gov/acs/www/AdvMeth/Reports.htm>.

Residence Rules

The fundamentally different purposes of the ACS and the census, and their timing, led to important differences in the choice of data collection methods. For example, the residence rules for a census or survey determine the sample unit's occupancy status and household membership. Defining the rules in a dissimilar way can affect those two very important estimates. The Census 2000 residence rules, which determined where people should be counted, were based on the principle of "usual residence" on April 1, 2000, in keeping with the focus of the census on the requirements of congressional apportionment and state redistricting. To accomplish this, the decennial census attempts to restrict and determine a principal place of residence on one specific date for everyone enumerated. The ACS residence rules are based on a "current residence" concept since data are collected continuously throughout the entire year with responses provided relative to the continuously changing survey interview dates. This method is consistent with the goal that the ACS produce estimates that reflect annual averages of the characteristics of all areas.

Residence rules determine which individuals are considered to be residents of a particular housing unit or group quarters. While many people have definite ties to a single housing unit or group quarters, some people may stay in different places for significant periods of time over the course of the year. For example, migrant workers move with crop seasons and do not live in any one location for the entire year. Differences in treatment of these populations in the census and ACS can lead to differences in estimates of the characteristics of some areas.

For the past several censuses, decennial census residence rules were designed to produce an accurate count of the population as of Census Day, April 1, while the ACS residence rules were designed to collect representative information to produce annual average estimates of the characteristics of all kinds of areas. When interviewing the population living in housing units, the decennial census uses a "usual residence" rule to enumerate people at the place where they live or stay most of the time as of April 1. The ACS uses a "current residence" rule to interview people who are currently living or staying in the sample

housing unit as long as their stay at that address will exceed 2 months. The residence rules governing the census enumerations of people in group quarters depend on the type of group quarter and, where permitted, whether people claim a "usual residence" elsewhere. The ACS applies a straight de facto residence rule to every type of group quarter. Everyone living or staying in a group quarter on the day it is visited by an ACS interviewer is eligible to be sampled and interviewed for the survey.

Further information on residence rules can be found at <http://www.census.gov/acs/www/AdvMeth/CollProc/CollProc1.htm>.

The differences in the ACS and census data as a consequence of the different residence rules are most likely minimal for most areas and most characteristics. However, for certain segments of the population the usual and current residence concepts could result in different residence decisions. Appreciable differences may occur in areas where large proportions of the total population spend several months of the year in what would not be considered their residence under decennial census rules. In particular, data for areas that include large beach, lake, or mountain vacation areas may differ appreciably between the census and the ACS if populations live there for more than 2 months.

Reference Periods

Estimates produced by the ACS are not measuring exactly what decennial samples have been measuring. The ACS yearly samples, spread over 12 months, collect information that is anchored to the day on which the sampled unit was interviewed, whether it is the day that a mail questionnaire is completed or the day that an interview is conducted by telephone or personal visit. Individual questions with time references such as "last week" or "the last 12 months" all begin the reference period as of this interview date. Even the information on types and amounts of income refers to the 12 months prior to the day the question is answered. ACS interviews are conducted just about every day of the year, and all of the estimates that the survey releases are considered to be averages for a specific time period. The 1-year estimates reflect the full calendar year; 3-year and 5-year estimates reflect the full 36- or 60-month period.

Most decennial census sample estimates are anchored in this same way to the date of enumeration. The most obvious difference between the ACS and the census is the overall time frame in which they are conducted. The census enumeration time period is less than half the time period used to collect data for each single-year ACS estimate. But a more important difference is that the distribution of census enumeration dates are highly clustered in March and

April (when most census mail returns were received) with additional, smaller clusters seen in May and June (when nonresponse follow-up activities took place).

This means that the data from the decennial census tend to describe the characteristics of the population and housing in the March through June time period (with an overrepresentation of March/April), while the ACS characteristics describe the characteristics nearly every day over the full calendar year. For employment and income estimates, the decennial census referred to the prior calendar year for all respondents, while the ACS asks about the 12 months preceding the interview.

Those who are interested in more information about differences in reference periods should refer to the Census Bureau's guidance on comparisons that contrasts for each question the specific reference periods used in Census 2000 with those used in the ACS: <http://www.census.gov/acs/www/UscData/compACS.htm>.

Some specific differences in reference periods between the ACS and the decennial census are described below. Users should consider the potential impact these different reference periods could have on distributions when comparing ACS estimates with Census 2000.

Income Data

To estimate annual income, the Census 2000 long-form sample used the calendar year prior to Census Day as the reference period, and the ACS uses the 12 months prior to the interview date as the reference period. Thus, while Census 2000 collected income information for calendar year 1999, the ACS collects income information for the 12 months preceding the interview date. The responses are a mixture of 12 reference periods ranging from, in the case of the 2006 ACS single-year estimates, the full calendar year 2005 through November 2006. The ACS income responses for each of these reference periods are individually inflation-adjusted to represent dollar values for the ACS collection year. Further inflation adjustments are made to the 3- and 5-year estimates to reflect dollar values of the final year of the estimate.

School Enrollment

The school enrollment question on the ACS asks if a person had "at any time in the last 3 months attended a school or college." A consistent 3-month reference period is used for all interviews. In contrast, Census 2000 asked if a person had "at any time since February 1 attended a school or college." Since Census 2000 data were collected from mid-March to late-August, the reference period could have been as short as about 6 weeks or as long as 7 months.

Utility Costs

The reference periods for two utility cost questions—gas and electricity—differ between Census 2000 and the ACS. The census asked for annual costs, while the ACS asks for the utility costs in the previous month.

Period Estimates

The ACS produces period estimates of socioeconomic and housing characteristics. It is designed to provide estimates that describe the average characteristics of an area over a specific time period. In the case of ACS single-year estimates, the period is the calendar year (e.g., the 2007 ACS covers January through December 2007). In the case of ACS multiyear estimates, the period is either 3 or 5 calendar years (e.g., the 2005– 2007 ACS estimates cover January 2005 through December 2007, and the 2006–2010 ACS estimates cover January 2006 through December 2010). The ACS multiyear estimates are similar in many ways to the ACS single-year estimates, but they encompass a longer time period. The differences in time periods between single-year and multiyear ACS estimates affect decisions about which set of estimates should be used for a particular analysis. While one may think of these estimates as representing average characteristics over a single calendar year or multiple calendar years, it must be remembered that the 1-year estimates are not calculated as an average of 12 monthly values and the multiyear estimates are not calculated as the average of either 36 or 60 monthly values. Nor are the multiyear estimates calculated as the average of 3 or 5 single-year estimates. Rather, the ACS collects survey information continuously nearly every day of the year and then aggregates the results over a specific time period—1 year, 3 years, or 5 years. The data collection is spread evenly across the entire period represented so as not to over-represent any particular month or year within the period.

Because ACS estimates provide information about the characteristics of the population and housing for areas over an entire time frame, ACS single-year and multiyear estimates contrast with "point-in-time" estimates, such as those from the decennial census long-form samples or monthly employment estimates from the Current Population Survey (CPS), which are designed to measure characteristics as of a certain date or narrow time period. For example, Census 2000 was designed to measure the characteristics of the population and housing in the United States based upon data collected around April 1, 2000, and thus its data reflect a narrower time frame than ACS data. The monthly CPS collects data for an even narrower time frame, the week containing the 12th of each month.

Most areas have consistent population characteristics throughout the calendar year, and their period estimates may not look much different from estimates that would be obtained from a "point-in-time" survey design. However, some areas may experience changes in the estimated characteristics of the population, depending on when in the calendar year measurement occurred. For these areas, the ACS period estimates (even for a single-year) may noticeably differ from "point-in-time" estimates. The impact will be more noticeable in smaller areas where changes such as a factory closing can have a large impact on population characteristics, and in areas with a large physical event such as Hurricane Katrina's impact on the New Orleans area. This logic can be extended to better interpret 3- year and 5-year estimates where the periods involved are much longer. If, over the full period of time (for example, 36 months), there have been major or consistent changes in certain population or housing characteristics for an area, a period estimate for that area could differ markedly from estimates based on a "point-in-time" survey. For example, the 5-year estimates for 2006–2010 will be affected by the volatility in the economy and the housing market during those years.

All the tables in this book include 3-year estimates from 2005 through 2007. Some of the cities experienced strong growth during that time due to housing development. According to the population estimates, Maricopa city, Arizona (near Phoenix), more than tripled its population between 2005 and 2007, from 10,500 to 37,863. Because it has fewer than 65,000 people, there are no ACS 1-year estimates, but it is safe to assume that the 3-year estimates include shifting characteristics. North Las Vegas, Nevada, is a larger city that grew by 20 percent—from 176,520 in 2005 to 212,114 in 2007. In column 6 of Table C-4, we can see that owner occupants of North Las Vegas paid a median 31.6 percent of their incomes for selected owner costs, well above the 24.7 percent median for the United States. Because we can look at the 1-year estimates for North Las Vegas, we can see how this median fluctuated during the 3-year period.

The important thing to keep in mind is that ACS single-year estimates describe the population and characteristics of an area for the full year, not for any specific day or period within the year, while ACS multiyear estimates describe the population and characteristics of an area for the full 3- or 5-year period, not for any specific day, period, or year within the multiyear time period.

Deciding Which ACS Estimate to Use

Three primary uses of ACS estimates are:

- to understand the characteristics of the population of an area for local planning needs

- to make comparisons across areas

- To assess change over time in an area

Local planning could include making local decisions such as where to locate schools or hospitals, determining the need for services or new businesses, and carrying out transportation or other infrastructure analysis. In the past, decennial census sample data provided the most comprehensive information. However, the currency of those data suffered through the intercensal period, and the ability to assess change over time was limited. ACS estimates greatly improve the currency of data for understanding the characteristics of housing and population and enhance the ability to assess change over time.

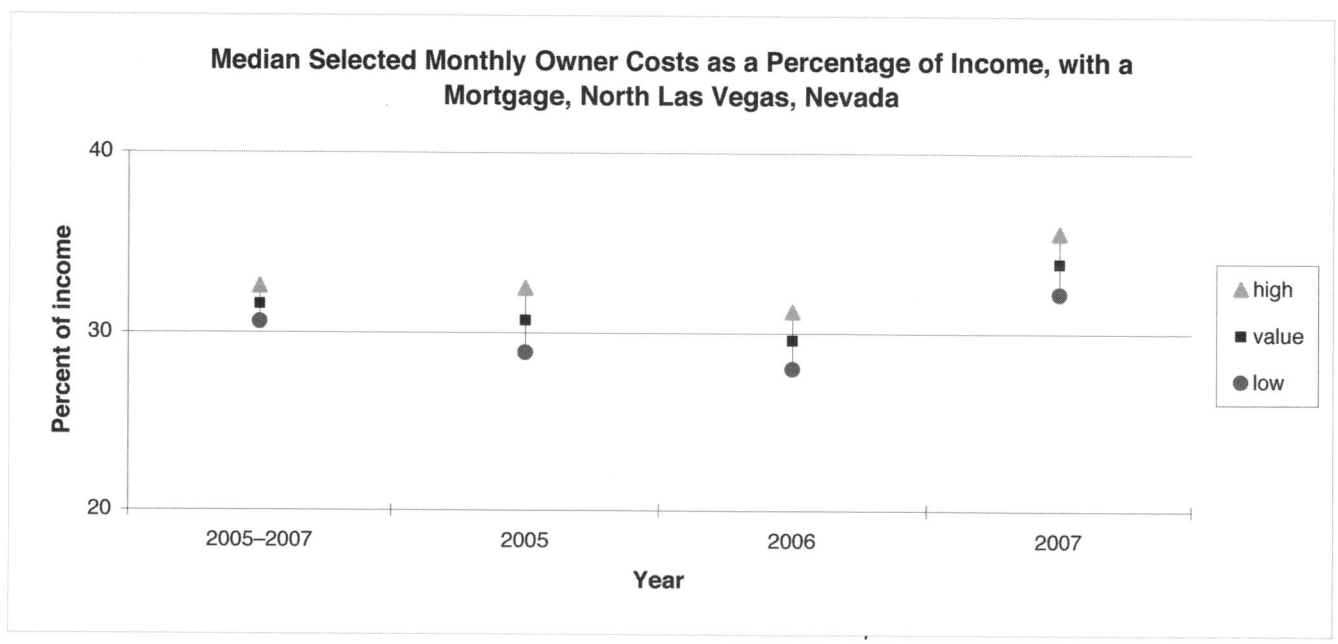

Several key factors can guide users trying to decide whether to use single-year or multiyear ACS estimates for areas where both are available:

- intended use of the estimates

- precision of the estimates

- currency of the estimates

All of these factors, along with an understanding of the differences between single-year and multiyear ACS estimates, should be taken into consideration when deciding which set of estimates to use.

For users interested in obtaining estimates for small geographic areas, multiyear ACS estimates will be the only option. For the very smallest of these areas (less than 20,000 population), the only option will be to use the 5-year ACS estimates. Users have a choice of two sets of multiyear estimates when analyzing data for small geographic areas with populations of at least 20,000. Both 3-year and 5-year ACS estimates will be available. Only the largest areas with populations of 65,000 and more receive all three data series.

The key trade-off to be made in deciding whether to use single-year or multiyear estimates is between currency and precision. In general, the single-year estimates are preferred, as they will be more relevant to the current conditions. However, the user must take into account the level of uncertainty present in the single-year estimates, which may be large for small subpopulation groups and rare characteristics. While single-year estimates offer more current estimates, they also have higher sampling variability. One measure, the coefficient of variation (CV) can help you determine the fitness for use of a single-year estimate in order to assess if you should opt instead to use the multiyear estimate (or if you should use a 5-year estimate rather than a 3-year estimate). The CV is calculated as the ratio of the standard error of the estimate to the estimate, times 100. A single-year estimate with a small CV is usually preferable to a multiyear estimate as it is more up to date. However, multiyear estimates are an alternative option when a single-year estimate has an unacceptably high CV. Single-year estimates for small subpopulations (e.g., families with a female householder, no husband, and related children less than 18 years) will typically have larger CVs. In general, multiyear estimates are preferable to single-year estimates when looking at estimates for small subpopulations.

For the complete discussion on deciding which estimates to use and on calculating the CV, see Appendix 1 of the *ACS General Handbook*: <http://www.ccnsus.gov/acs/www/Downloads/ACSGeneralHandbook.pdf>.

Single-year estimates provide more current information

Single-year estimates provide more current information about areas that have changing population and/or housing characteristics because they are based on the most current data—data from the past year. In contrast, multiyear estimates provide less current information because they are based on both data from the previous year and data that are 2 and 3 years old. As noted earlier, for many areas with minimal change taking place, using the "less current" sample used to produce the multiyear estimates may not have a substantial influence on the estimates. However, in areas experiencing major changes over a given time period, the multiyear estimates may be quite different from the single-year estimates for any of the individual years. Single-year and multiyear estimates are not expected to be the same because they are based on data from two different time periods. This will be true even if the ACS single year is the midyear of the ACS multiyear period (e.g., 2007 single year, 2006–2008 multiyear).

Multiyear estimates are based on larger sample sizes and will therefore be more reliable

The 3-year estimates are based on three times as many sample cases as the 1-year estimates. For some characteristics this increased sample is needed for the estimates to be reliable enough for use in certain applications. For other characteristics the increased sample may not be necessary.

Multiyear estimates are the only type of estimates available for geographic areas with populations of less than 65,000. Users may think that they only need to use multiyear estimates when they are working with small areas, but this isn't the case. Estimates for large geographic areas benefit from the increased sample resulting in more precise estimates of population and housing characteristics, especially for subpopulations within those areas. In addition, users may determine that they want to use single-year estimates, despite their reduced reliability, as building blocks to produce estimates for meaningful higher levels of geography. These aggregations will similarly benefit from the increased sample sizes and gain reliability.

Often users want to compare the characteristics of one area to those of another area. These comparisons can be in the form of rankings or of specific pairs of comparisons. Whenever you want to make a comparison between two different geographic areas you need to take the type of estimate into account. It is important that comparisons be made within the same estimate type. That is, 1-year estimates should only be compared with other 1-year estimates, 3-year estimates should only be compared with other 3-year estimates, and 5-year estimates should only be compared with other 5-year estimates.

You certainly can compare characteristics for areas with populations of 30,000 to areas with populations of 100,000 but you should use the data set that they have in common. In this example you could use the 3-year or the 5-year estimates because they are available for areas of 30,000 and areas of 100,000. For that reason, this book includes only the 3-year estimates for 2005 through 2007, though 1-year estimates are available for many of the areas in the book.

Users are encouraged to make comparisons between sequential single-year estimates. In American FactFinder (AFF), comparison profiles are available beginning with the 2007 single-year data. These profiles identify statistically significant differences between the 2007 ACS and the 2006 ACS.

Caution is needed when using multiyear estimates for estimating year-to-year change in a particular characteristic. This is because roughly two-thirds of the data in a 3-year estimate overlap with the data in the next year's 3-year estimate (the overlap is roughly four-fifths for 5-year estimates). When comparing 2006–2008 3-year estimates with 2007–2009 3-year estimates, the differences in overlapping multiyear estimates are driven by differences in the non-overlapping years. A data user interested in comparing 2009 with 2008 will not be able to isolate those differences using these two successive 3-year estimates. While the interpretation of this difference is difficult, these comparisons can be made with caution.

Users who are interested in comparing overlapping multiyear period estimates should refer to Appendix 4 of the *ACS General Handbook* for more information: <http://www.census.gov/acs/www/Downloads/ACSGeneral Handbook.pdf>.

Multiyear estimates are likely to confuse some data users, in part because of their statistical properties, and in part because this is a new product from the Census Bureau. The ACS will provide all states and communities that have at least 65,000 residents with single-year estimates of demographic, housing, social, and economic characteristics—a boon to government agencies that need to budget and plan for public services like transportation, medical care, and schools. For geographic areas with smaller populations, the ACS samples too few households to provide reliable single-year estimates. For these communities, several years of data will be pooled together to create reliable 3-year or 5-year estimates.

Single-year, 3-year, and 5-year estimates from the ACS are all "period" estimates that represent data collected over a period of time (as opposed to "point-in-time" estimates, such as the decennial census, that approximate the characteristics of an area on a specific date). While a single-year estimate includes information collected over a 12-month period, a 3-year estimate represents data collected over a 36-month period, and a 5-year estimate includes data collected over a 60-month period. Therefore, ACS estimates based on data collected from 2005–2007 should not be called "2006" or "2007" estimates. Nor should 2005–2009 period estimates be labeled "2007" estimates, even though that is the midpoint of the 5-year period. Multiyear estimates should be labeled to indicate clearly the full period of time (e.g., "The child poverty rate in 2005–2007 was X percent"). The primary advantage of using multiyear estimates is the increased statistical reliability of the data for less populated areas and small population subgroups.

Multiyear estimates should, in general, be used when single-year estimates have large CVs or when the precision of the estimates is more important than the currency of the data. Multiyear estimates should also be used when analyzing data for smaller geographies and smaller populations in larger geographies. Multiyear estimates are also of value when examining change over nonoverlapping time periods and for smoothing data trends over time.

Single-year estimates should, in general, be used for larger geographies and populations when currency is more important than the precision of the estimates. Single-year estimates should be used to examine year-to-year change for estimates with small CVs. Given the availability of a single-year estimate, calculating the CV provides useful information to determine if the single-year estimate should be used. For areas believed to be experiencing rapid changes in a characteristic, single-year estimates should generally be used rather than multiyear estimates as long as the CV for the single-year estimate is reasonable for the specific usage.

Local area variations may occur due to rapidly occurring changes. Multiyear estimates will tend to be insensitive to such changes when they first occur. Single-year estimates, if associated with sufficiently small CVs, can be very valuable in identifying and studying such phenomena.

Data users also need to use caution in looking at trends involving income or other measures that are adjusted for inflation, such as rental costs, home values, and energy costs. Note that inflation adjustment is based on a national-level consumer price index: it does not adjust for differences in costs of living across different geographic areas.

Appendix 5 of the *ACS General Handbook* provides information on the adjustment of single-year and multi-year ACS estimates for inflation: <http://www.census.gov/acs/www/Downloads/ACSGeneralHandbook.pdf>.

Margin of Error

All data that are based on samples, such as the ACS and the census long-form samples, include a range of uncertainty. Two broad types of error can occur: sampling error and nonsampling error. Nonsampling errors can result from mistakes in how the data are reported or coded, problems in the sampling frame or survey questionnaires, or problems related to nonresponse or interviewer bias. The Census Bureau tries to minimize nonsampling errors by using trained interviewers and by carefully reviewing the survey's sampling methods, data processing techniques, and questionnaire design.

Appendix 6 of the *ACS General Handbook* includes a more detailed description of different types of errors in the ACS and other measures of ACS quality: <http://www.census.gov/acs/www/Downloads/ACSGeneral Handbook.pdf>.

Sampling error occurs when data are based on a sample of a population rather than the full population. Sampling error is easier to measure than nonsampling error and can be used to assess the statistical reliability of survey data. For any given area, the larger the sample and the more months included in the data, the greater the confidence in the estimate. The Census Bureau reported the 90-percent confidence interval on all ACS estimates produced for 2005 and earlier. With the release of the 2006 ACS data, *margins of error* are now provided for every ACS estimate. Ninety percent confidence intervals define a range expected to contain the *true* value of an estimate with a level of confidence of 90 percent. Margins of error are easily converted into these confidence ranges. By adding and subtracting the margin of error from the point estimate, we can calculate the 90-percent confidence interval for an estimate. Therefore, we can be 90 percent confident that the true number of falls between the lower-bound interval and the upper-bound interval.

Detailed information about sampling error and instructions for calculating confidence intervals and margins of error are included in Appendix 3 of the *ACS General Handbook*: <http://www.census.gov/acs/www/Downloads/ACSGeneral Handbook.pdf>.

The margin of error around an estimate is important because it helps one draw conclusions about the data. Small differences between two estimates may not be statistically significant if the confidence intervals of those estimates overlap. However, the Census Bureau cautions data users not to rely on overlapping confidence intervals as a test for statistical significance, because this method will not always produce accurate results. Instead, the Census Bureau recommends following the detailed instructions for conducting statistical significance tests in Appendix 4 the *ACS General Handbook*.

In some cases, data users will need to construct custom ACS estimates by combining data across multiple geographic areas or population subgroups or it may be necessary to derive a new percentage, proportion, or ratio from published ACS data. In such cases, additional calculations are needed to produce confidence intervals and margins of error for the derived estimates. Appendix 3 of the *ACS General Handbook* provides detailed instructions on how to make these calculations. Note that these error measures do not tell us about the magnitude of nonsampling errors.

Some advanced data users will also want to construct custom ACS estimates from the Census Bureau's Public Use Microdata Samples (PUMS). There are separate instructions for conducting significance tests for PUMS estimates, available on the Census Bureau's American FactFinder (AFF) Web site at: <http://www.ccnsus.gov/acs/www/Downloads/2005-2007/AccuracyPUMS.pdf>.

Accessing ACS Data Online

All ACS data are available through the Census Bureau's American FactFinder (AFF) Web site at <http://factfinder.census.gov>. From the AFF home page, click on *Data Sets*, and then choose the *American Community Survey* from the list of options in the drop-down menu.

For the 2007 ACS, two data sets are shown—the 1-year estimates (based on the 2007 ACS) and the 3-year estimates (based on the 2005–2007 ACS). All the tables in this book were produced from these 3-year estimates for 2005–2007. Tabs also index 2005 and 2006 ACS data sets. The AFF will default to the most recent data set but users can choose from any of these data sets. Once a data set is selected, the accessed tables will all correspond to this specific data set. All tables are clearly labeled, identifying the data set.

The *2007 Quick Guide* provides detailed descriptions of the different ACS data products that are available. It can be found at <http://factfinder.census.gov/home/saff/aff_acs2007_quickguide.pdf>. Additional assistance can be found at FactFinder Help (online help, census data information, glossary, and tutorial): <http://factfinder.census.gov/home/en/epss/main.html>. The set of ACS data products are described below.

• **Data profiles, ranking tables, and narrative profiles.** The *data profiles* and *ranking tables* are good places to start for novice data users. *Data profiles* provide separate fact sheets on the social, economic, demographic, and housing characteristics for different geographic areas, while *ranking tables* provide state-level rankings of key ACS variables. *Narrative profiles* also provide clear, concise textual descriptions of the data included in the *data profiles*. They must be accessed by selecting *data profiles* from the menu.

• **Geographic comparison tables.** The *geographic comparison tables* allow comparison of ACS data across a variety of geographic areas, including metropolitan areas, cities, counties, and congressional districts.

• **Thematic maps.** The *thematic maps* provide graphic displays of the data available through the *geographic comparison tables*. Different shades of color are used to display variations in the data. Data users can also highlight areas with statistically different values from a selected state, county, or metropolitan area of interest.

• **Subject tables.** For information about a particular topic (e.g., employment, education, and income), start with the *subject tables*, which provide pretabulated numbers and percentages for a wide variety of topics, often available separately by age, gender, or race/ethnicity.

• **Selected population profiles.** The most detailed race/ethnic data are available through the *selected population profiles*, which provide summary tables separately for over 100 detailed race, ethnic, and tribal groups. Beginning with the 2007 ACS, the *selected population profiles* also include country of birth. Data are currently unavailable for many of these tables because the ACS does not publish single-year estimates for groups with fewer than 65,000 people in a given area. However, more of these data tables will be available with the release of 3- and 5-year estimates.

• **Comparison profiles.** The *comparison profiles* show data side-by-side from the 2006 ACS and the 2007 ACS, indicating where there is a statistically significant difference between the two sets of estimates. Comparison profiles are only available for 1-year estimates.

• **Detailed tables and summary files.** The *detailed tables* are the best source for advanced data users or those who want access to the most comprehensive ACS tables. Advanced users can download *detailed tables* through the ACS *Summary File* on the Census Bureau's FTP Web site: <http://www.census.gov/acs/www/Special/acsftp.html>.

• **Public Use Microdata Sample files.** Those with expertise in using SAS, SPSS, or STATA may also be interested in the *Public Use Microdata Sample (PUMS) files*, which contain a sample of individual records of people and households that responded to the survey (stripped of all identifying information). The PUMS files permit analysis of specific population groups and custom variables that are not available through AFF. For example, PUMS data users can look at the proportion of children ages 5 to 11 living in low-income working families, or the number of scientists and engineers earning more than $75,000. Data users can also combine multiple years of PUMS data to produce data for relatively small population subgroups (e.g., American Indian physicians). More information about the PUMS is available in the PUMS Handbook.

• **Custom tables.** The *custom tables* option allows someone to customize specific detailed tables to meet his or her needs. You can extract selected rows of data from one or more detailed tables to create a table with just the estimates you want to include. The tables in this book were developed through this option.

More ACS Resources

There is a wealth of information about the ACS on the Web, and new information becomes available on a regular basis. Each year, the ACS data release represents a new stage in a new process. Consequently, many new documents are required to explain the survey and how to use it. These resources cover many of the topics discussed in this book, but in greater detail.

The best place to start is the Census Bureau's ACS main page:

<http://www.census.gov/acs/>.

Background and Overview Information

American Community Survey Web Page Site Map:

<http://www.census.gov/acs/www/Site_Map.html>

This link is the site map for the ACS Web page. It provides an overview of the links and materials that are available online, including numerous reference documents.

What Is the ACS?

<http://www.census.gov/acs/www/SBasics/What/What1.htm>

This Web page includes basic information about the ACS and has links to additional information including background materials.

ACS Design, Methodology, Operations

The Design and Methodology Report contains descriptions of the basic design of the ACS and details of the full set of methods and procedures. This version, issued April 2009, includes updated information reflecting survey changes, modifications, improvements, and the methods used to produce the first 2005–2007 ACS 3-year estimates.

<http://www.census.gov/acs/www/Downloads/dm1.pdf>

About the Data (Methodology):

<http://www.census.gov/acs/www/AdvMeth/>

This Web page contains links to information on ACS data collection and processing, evaluation reports, multiyear estimates study, and related topics.

Accuracy of the Data (2007)

<http://www.census.gov/acs/www/Downloads/ACS/accuracy2007.pdf>

This document provides data users with a basic understanding of the sample design, estimation methodology, and accuracy of the 2007 ACS data.

ACS Sample Size

<http://www.census.gov/acs/www/SBasics/SSizes/SSizes06.htm>

This link provides sample size information for the counties that were published in the 2006 ACS. The initial sample size and the final completed interviews are provided. The sample sizes for all published counties and county equivalents starting with the 2007 ACS will only be available in the B98 series of detailed tables on American FactFinder.

ACS Quality Measures

<http://www.census.gov/acs/www/UseData/sse/>

This Web page includes information about the steps taken by the Census Bureau to improve the accuracy of ACS data. Four indicators of survey quality are described and measures are provided at the national and state level.

Guidance on Data Products and Using the Data

How to Use the Data:

<http://www.census.gov/acs/www/UseData/>

This Web page includes links to many documents and materials that explain the ACS data products.

Comparing ACS Data to other sources:

<http://www.census.gov/acs/www/UseData/compACS.htm>

Tables are provided with guidance on comparing the 2007 ACS data products to 2006 ACS data and Census 2000 data.

Information on Using Different Sources of Data for Income and Poverty:

<http://www.census.gov/hhes/www/income/factsheet.html>
<http://www.census.gov/prod/2008pubs/acs-09.pdf>

This fact sheet highlights the sources that should be used for data on income and poverty, focusing on comparing the ACS and the Current Population Survey (CPS).

Public Use Microdata Sample (PUMS):

<http://www.census.gov/acs/www/Products/PUMS/>

This Web page provides guidance in accessing ACS microdata.

FactFinder Help (online help, census data information, glossary, and tutorial):

<http://factfinder.census.gov/home/en/epss/main.html>

2007 Guide to the Data Products (Web page):

<http://www.census.gov/acs/www/Products/users_guide/>

The *A Compass for Understanding and Using American Community Survey Data: What General Data Users Need to Know* provides a complete overview:

<http://www.census.gov/acs/www/Downloads/ACSGeneral Handbook.pdf>

An excellent overview of the ACS, complete with several chapters of useful information for data users, is *Using the American Community Survey: Benefits and Challenges*, edited by Constance F. Citro and Graham Kalton (The National Academies Press, 2007). The book is available for purchase and is also available to read online at no charge.

<http://books.nap.edu/catalog.php?record_id=11901>

Who
Age, Race/Ethnicity, and Households

Who: Age, Race/Ethnicity, and Household Structure

The American population is changing in fundamental ways, and the American Community Survey (ACS) provides information to show how Americans really look and function. The new ACS estimates combine three years of survey responses (2005–2007) to produce data for communities with populations of 20,000 or more, providing a regular stream of updated social, housing, and economic characteristics for demographic groups.

One of this survey's most valuable aspects is that it allows users to compare their city or town against other local areas or against the United States. It highlights the differences among small areas within the United States. National trends are not mirrored in every community. Some places are changing even faster than the national picture; others are lagging or even going in a different direction. It is important for people to know how their locality fits into the national picture. These tables offer Americans information needed to compare various areas to see how they differ and how they are similar.

Population

Although the ACS is replacing the census long form as the key source of detailed social and economic characteristics, the official population estimates are still developed through the Census Bureau's Population Estimates Program. After the 2010 census, these estimates, and all ACS estimates, will be adjusted to reflect the new population count.

Eight states had populations of ten million or more, led by California and Texas. Over 48 percent of the nation's population lived in these eight states. Another eight states had populations of less than one million, representing about two percent of the nation's population. During the 2005–2007 period, the United States' population increased by 1.9 percent. Four states, located in the West, had population growth exceeding five percent during this period. Overall, 22 states had population growth above the national average. Ten states had population growth less than 0.5 percent, including three—Michigan, Rhode Island, and Louisiana—that lost population during this period.

Nearly 37 percent of the U.S. population resided in the 75 most populous counties. Thirty-seven of these counties had populations exceeding one million. Los Angeles County was, by far, the most populous county in the nation, with nearly 10 million residents. Forty-two counties had population growth exceeding 20 percent from 2005 to 2007. Ten of these counties were in Texas and nine in Georgia. Of these 42 counties, 20 had populations less than 100,000 and the remaining 22 had populations between 100,000 and 1 million. Wake County, NC, with about 794,000 residents was the most populous county with a growth rate over 10 percent. During the 2005–2007 period, 429 counties experienced population losses. Seven counties had population losses exceeding 5 percent. Four of those counties were located in Louisiana and two in Mississippi, all of which experienced high out-migration after Hurricane Katrina.

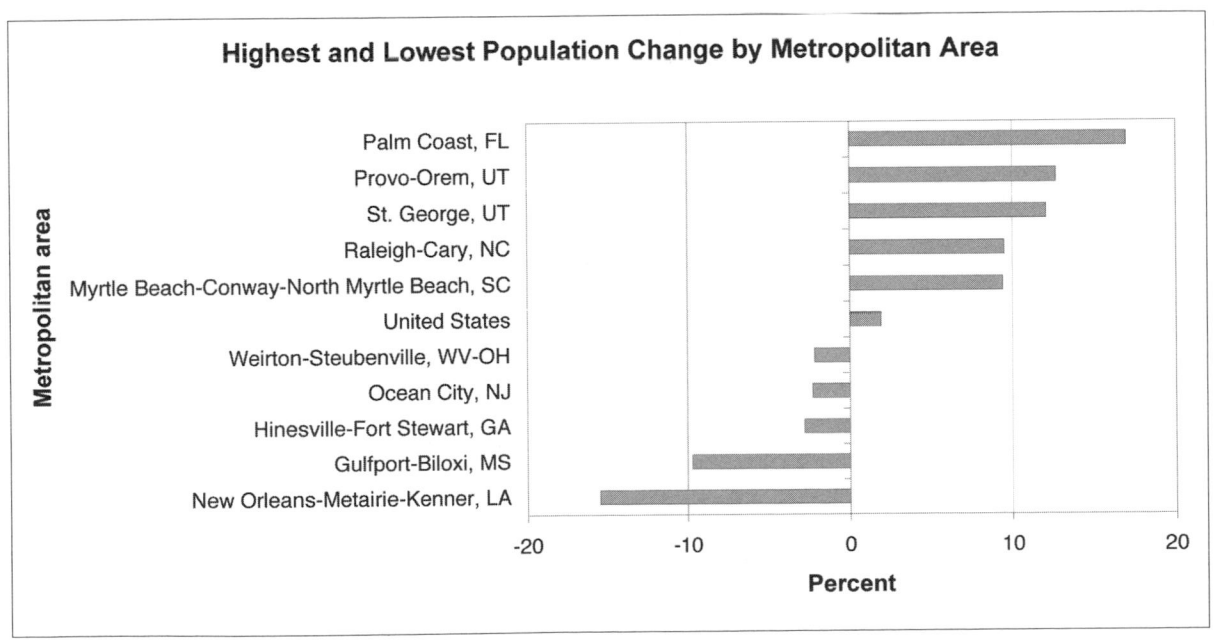

Highest and Lowest Population Change by Metropolitan Area

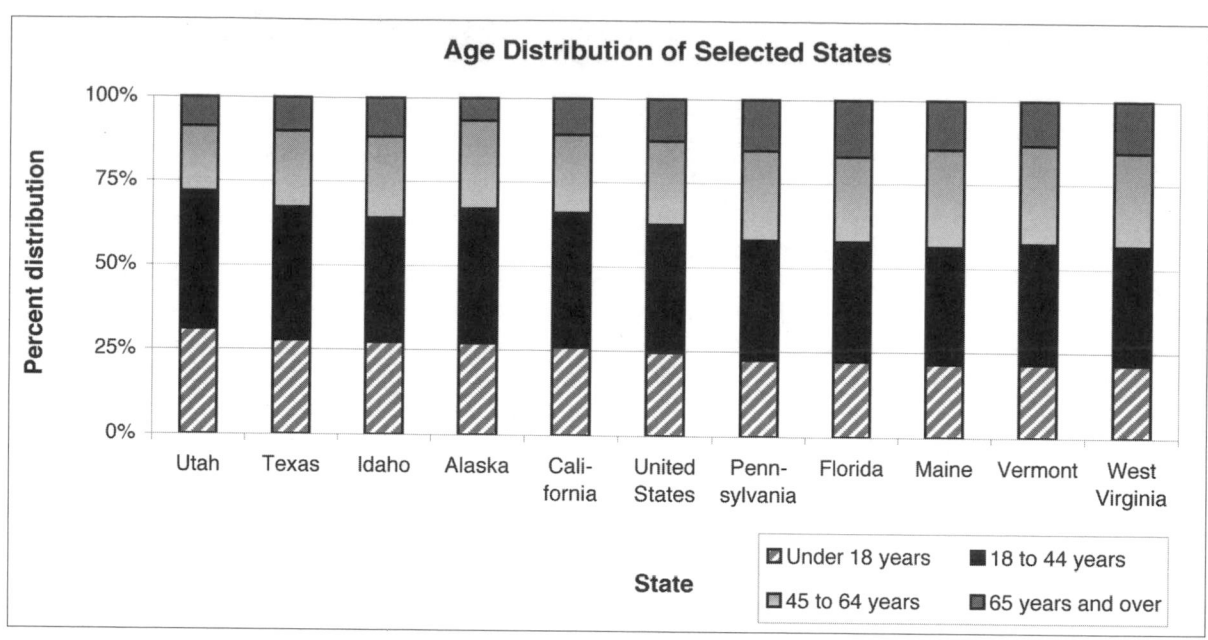

Age Distribution of Selected States

Among the more populous counties, Cuyahoga County, OH, and Wayne County, MI, had the highest rates of population loss during the period, both over a 2.0 percent drop. Since the ACS includes only counties with populations of 20,000 or more, gains and losses in smaller counties are not included in this discussion.

Nearly 250 million people, or about 83 percent of the population, lived in the nation's 363 metropolitan statistical areas. Just over 26 percent of the U.S. population resided in the 10 most populous metropolitan areas. Fifty-one metropolitan areas had populations of one million or more. Three metropolitan areas—Palm Coast, FL; Provo-Orem, UT; St. George, UT—had growth rates exceeding 10 percent from 2005 to 2007. Among metropolitan areas of more than a million people, six had growth rates above 6 percent. The largest of these were Phoenix-Mesa-Scottsdale, AZ, and Atlanta-Sandy-Springs-Marietta, GA. The Raleigh-Cary, NC, metropolitan area grew by 9.5 percent, the highest growth rate among metropolitan areas of a million or more people. About 49 percent of metropolitan areas had growth rates exceeding the national rate of 1.9 percent.

Thirty-three cities have populations of 500,000 or more, including eight with populations of a million or more. With more than 8 million people, New York is, by far, the largest city. Los Angeles is second, with 3.8 million people, and Chicago's 2.7 million people still outnumber the fast-growing Houston's 2 million. Of the 2,065 cities[1] with populations of 20,000 or more, 269 have populations exceeding 100,000,

representing about 27 percent of the nation's population. From 2005 to 2007, 99 of these more populous cities had growth rates exceeding the national rate of 1.9 percent. Surprise, AZ, and North Las Vegas, NV, had the highest growth of these cities, with over 20 percent. Among all 2,065 cities included in this publication, 31 had population growth rates exceeding 20 percent. Nine are cities located in Texas and five each are located in Arizona and California.

Age

During the 2005–2007 time period, the United States' median age was 36.4 years. Maine, Vermont, and West Virginia had the highest median ages among the states, all over 40 years. Utah had the lowest median age with 28.6 years. Thirty-one percent of Utah's population was under age 18. Florida, West Virginia, and Pennsylvania had the highest proportions of population 65 years and over. North Dakota had the highest proportion (2.4 percent) of population 85 years old and over.

Five metropolitan areas had one in three residents under the age of 18. Three were located in Texas, one in Georgia, and one in Utah. Fifteen metropolitan areas had at least one in five residents who were over age 65. Ten were located in Florida. Punta Gorda, FL, had the highest proportion with 31.5 percent.

Three counties had median ages over 50, with two in Florida and one in Oregon. Over 64 percent of the over 1,800 counties included in this book had median ages that exceeded the U.S. average of 36.4 years. There were 13 counties with at least one in four residents age 65 years or over. The most populous was Sarasota County, FL, and seven more of these older counties were in Florida. In 11

---

1. Of these cities, 386 are Census Designated Places (CDPs). CDPs are included in the ACS but not in the Population Estimates Program, so no growth rates are calculated for these CDPs. See Appendix A for more information. Six CDPs had populations over 100,000,

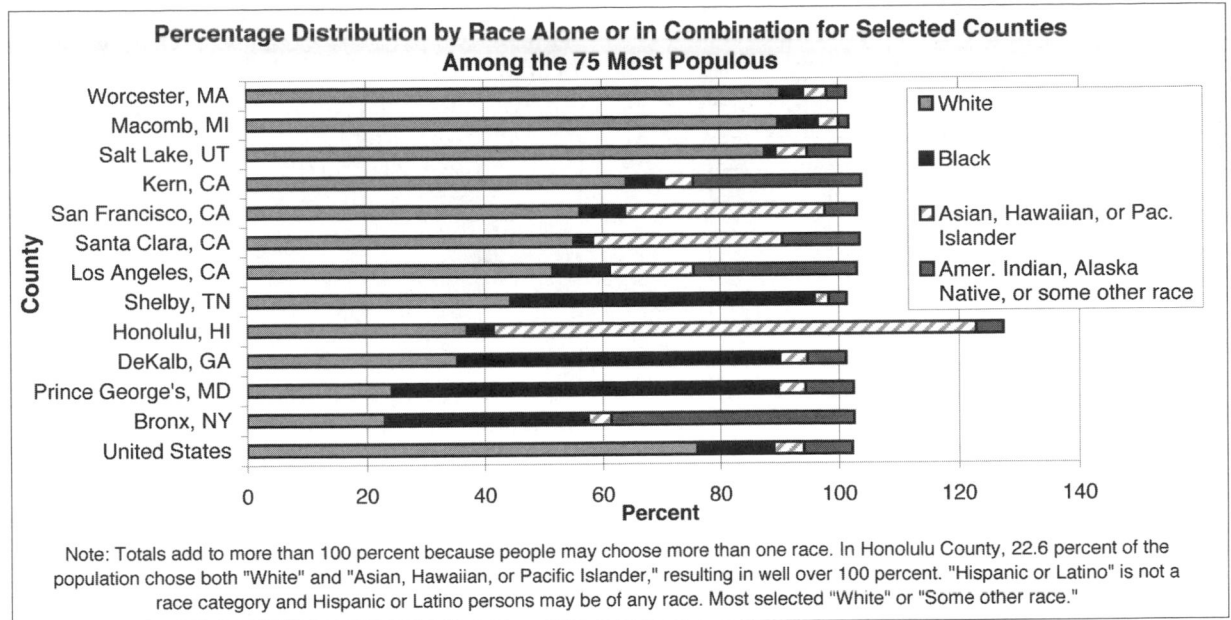

Percentage Distribution by Race Alone or in Combination for Selected Counties Among the 75 Most Populous

Note: Totals add to more than 100 percent because people may choose more than one race. In Honolulu County, 22.6 percent of the population chose both "White" and "Asian, Hawaiian, or Pacific Islander," resulting in well over 100 percent. "Hispanic or Latino" is not a race category and Hispanic or Latino persons may be of any race. Most selected "White" or "Some other race."

counties, one-third of the population was under age 18. Six of these younger counties were in Texas.

Thirteen cities had median ages of 50 years or more. All were located in three states: Florida, Arizona, and California. Three age-restricted communities in Arizona had median ages over 70. Ninety-six cities had 20 percent or more of their populations consisting of people 65 years and older. Nationally, this age group accounted for 12.5 percent of the population. In 44 cities, more than 35 percent of the population was under 18 years old. Most of these cities could be found in California, Utah, and Texas. Fifty-one cities, predominantly college towns, had median ages of 25 years or less.

The working-age population is generally considered to include people between the ages of 25 and 64. Nationally, 53 percent of the population was in this category. Sixty-four cities had proportions of working-age population that exceeded 60 percent. Three of these cities were among the 75 most populous—San Francisco, Seattle, and Portland.

Race/Ethnicity

Probably the most visible place-based demographic difference is in racial and ethnic composition. Seen from afar, the U.S. population may be a melting pot, but at close range it varies widely. Among the states, New Jersey came the closest to matching the national portrait of race and Hispanic origin, followed by Illinois and New York, though each state differed along one or more dimensions. The other states showed a wide range of racial and ethnic composition. For example, about 95 percent of the population of Vermont and Maine was non-Hispanic White. In contrast, Hawaii, the District of Columbia, New Mexico,

California, and Texas are all "majority minority" states, with non-Hispanic Whites making up less that 50 percent of their populations. About 56 percent of the District of Columbia's population was Black. Over 18 percent of Alaska residents were American Indian or Alaska Native alone or in combination. Close to four in five Hawaiian residents were Asian, Native Hawaiian, or Pacific Islander. In New Mexico, more than 44 percent of the population was Hispanic.

Thirty-three metropolitan areas had populations consisting 95 percent or more of Whites alone or in combination. In the Honolulu metropolitan area, more than 81 percent of the population was Asian, Native Hawaiian, or Pacific Islander. Fifty percent of the population of Albany, GA, was Black, the closest to majority Black of any metropolitan area. Hispanic or Latino residents[2] make up a majority in 12 metropolitan areas, the largest of which is San Antonio, TX, with nearly two million residents.

Among smaller geography types, the racial and ethnic characteristics of a population varied even more widely. Over 75 percent of the 1,817 counties or county equivalents included in American Community Survey 2005–2007 estimates were majority White. Of these counties, 541 had White populations of 95 percent or more. Thirty-nine were found in Ohio, 45 in Indiana, and 37 were located in Pennsylvania. However, many counties had a majority population that was some other race or ethnic group. Among the 48 counties with majority Black populations, 11 can be found in Mississippi. Four U.S. counties had majority Asian, Native Hawaiian, or Pacific Islander populations. All were located in Hawaii. Four more counties had populations with 25

---

2. Hispanic or Latino persons may be of any race. Most self-identify as "White" or "some other race."

Cities with Large American Indian or Alaska Native Populations

City	Percent
Farmington city, NM	21.9
Lumberton city, NC	17.8
Juneau city and borough, AK	17.1
Muskogee city, OK	16.8
Shawnee city, OK	16.3
Ardmore city, OK	14.4
Sapulpa city, OK	14.1
Rapid City city, SD	12.5
Flagstaff city, AZ	12.4
Fairbanks city, AK	11.6
Bartlesville city, OK	11.5
Anchorage municipality, AK	10.4
Ponca City city, OK	10.2

Source: ACS Table B01003

percent of this race group, led by San Francisco, with 33.8 percent. The other three were also located in California. Six counties had majority Native American, Alaska Native, or some other race populations. They were located in Arizona, New Mexico, Texas, and Oklahoma. Some of these counties contained (or were contained in) tribal reservations. Twenty-eight counties had populations that were majority Hispanic (of any race). Counties in the Southwest that were originally settled by the Spanish had populations with higher proportions of Hispanic residents.

Just over 500 cities had 90 percent White populations. The most populous of these cities were Lincoln, NE, and Scott-

sdale, AZ, both with less than a quarter of a million people. With 247,246 people, Lincoln was the only city among the 75 most populous (ranked 72). Over 100 cities were majority Black, with thirty-one having Black populations of three-quarters or more. Eight of these cities were in Maryland, and five were in Illinois. Detroit, MI, (84 percent Black) was, by far, the most populous, with about 837,000 residents. Twenty-three cities were majority Asian, Native Hawaiian, and Pacific Islander. All were located in either California or Hawaii. Honolulu was the most populous of the 23 cities. In the city table in this section, the American Indian or Alaska Native population was combined with those who answered "some other race" because most cities had too few respondents in either category. However, 13 cities have American Indian or Alaska Native populations of 10 percent or more.

Foreign-Born Population and Foreign Languages

Nationally, 12.5 percent of the population was foreign born. Over 27 percent of California's population was foreign born. The only other state that exceeded 20 percent was New York, while 18 to 20 percent of the populations in New Jersey, Florida, and Nevada were foreign born. West Virginia (1.3 percent) and Mississippi (1.7 percent) had the lowest proportions of foreign-born residents.

In 10 counties, more than one-third of the residents were foreign born. Six of these counties were among the 75 most populous, led by Miami-Dade County, FL, with 50.4 percent and Queens County, NY, with 48.3 percent. More than 90 percent of the counties included in this publication had foreign-born proportions less than the U.S. average of 12.5

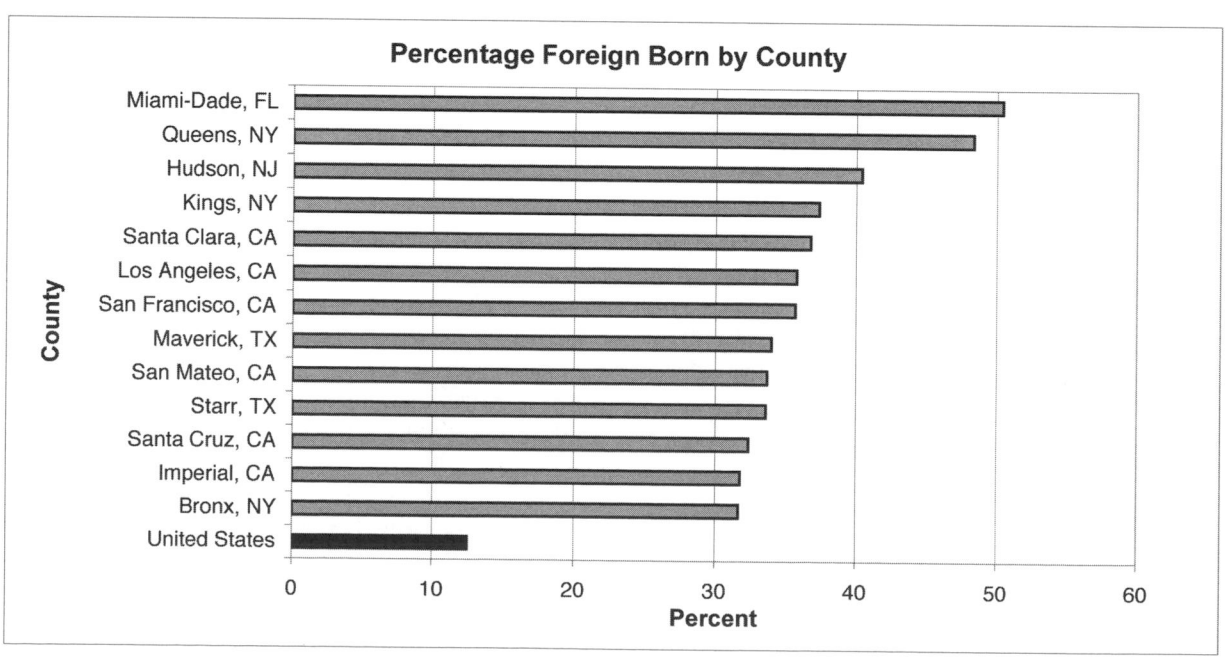

6   **The Who, What, and Where of America**

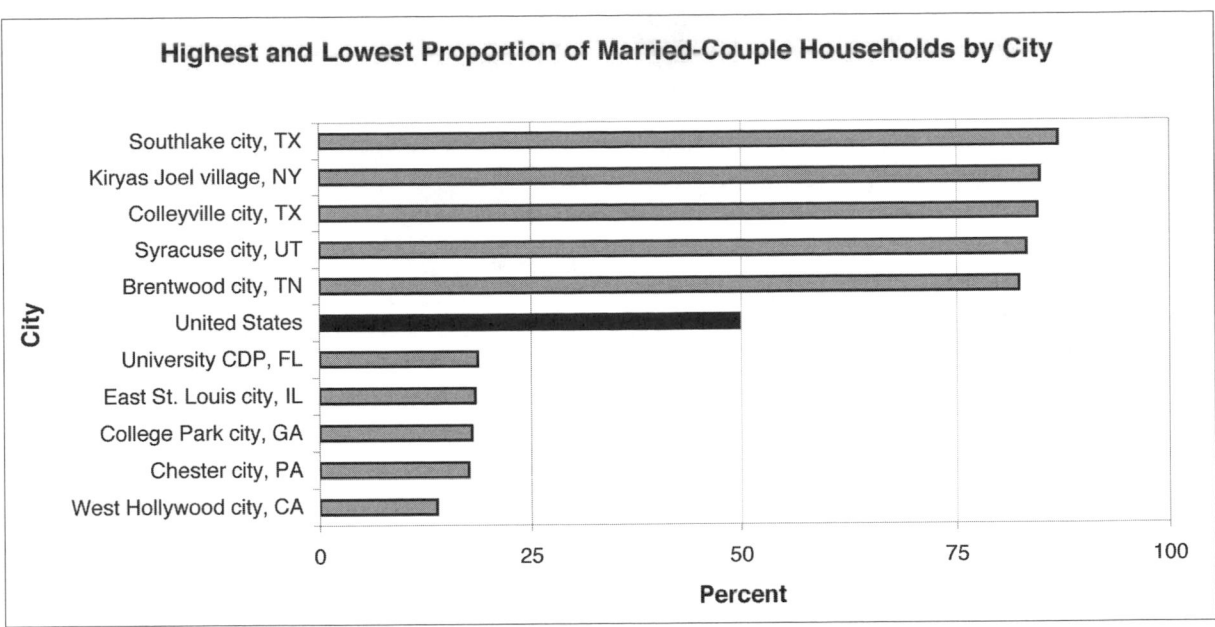

Highest and Lowest Proportion of Married-Couple Households by City

percent, including eight counties with over a million people. Twenty-eight metropolitan areas had foreign-born populations of 20 percent or more. Miami-Fort Lauderdale-Pompano Beach, FL, and San Jose-Sunnyvale-Santa Clara, CA, had the highest proportions, both over 36 percent.

Of the 2,065 cities, just over 900 had foreign-born proportions that exceeded the U.S. average. Thirty cities had majority foreign-born residents. Florida had the most with 14 such cities, followed by California with 13. Among the most populous cities, Miami, FL, and Santa Ana, CA, had the highest proportions, both exceeding 50 percent.

Nearly 20 percent of American households spoke a language other than English (in addition to or instead of English). States with the highest proportions of Spanish-speaking households were New Mexico (32.2 percent), Texas (28.3 percent), and California (24.4 percent). In about 10 percent of California households, no adult spoke English well. West Virginia and Mississippi had the lowest proportions of households speaking a language other than English.

Household Structure

Places that differ from the national age portrait also differ from the nation's household portrait. Two-thirds of the nation's households were family households (people related by birth, marriage, or adoption). Nonfamily households included people living alone or with unrelated people. About half of all households were married-couple family households. In some areas, people lived predominantly in married-couple households, while others were dominated by male- and female-

headed family households (no spouse present) or by nonfamily households.

Nearly a third of the nation's households are made up of nonfamily households—people living alone, or with other, unrelated adults. Nine states and the District of Columbia had proportions of nonfamily households that exceeded this national level of one-third. More than half of the District of Columbia's households were nonfamily households, most of them one-person households. Although there were large numbers of single-person households in every age group, Pennsylvania and West Virginia had the highest proportion of persons over 65 years old living alone. Among all ages, Utah had the lowest proportion of single-person households, with 19.3 percent. Nationally, 27.3 percent of households consisted of a person living alone.

The District of Columbia (54.0 percent), New York (35.7 percent), Massachusetts (34.5 percent), and California (34.1 percent) had the highest proportions of never married residents. Idaho (58.9 percent) and Utah (58.3 percent) had the highest percentages of currently married residents.

In five metropolitan areas—Albany, GA; Laredo, TX; Hinesville-Fort Stewart, GA; El Centro, CA; El Paso, TX—20 percent or more of households were female-headed families. Four of the five metropolitan areas with the highest rates of male-headed family households were in California. Provo-Orem, UT, had the lowest proportion of one-person households among all the MSAs, at just 12.9 percent.

Among the 75 most populous cities, 8 exceeded the national average of 49.8 percent of married-couple households. Plano, TX, had the highest proportion with 59.7 percent. Sixty of these most populous cities had above average rates of one-person households. Three cities—Washington, DC; Atlanta, GA; and Cincinnati, OH—had rates exceeding 45 percent of householders living alone.

Utah had the highest average household size—3.12 persons per household. The District of Columbia (2.20 persons) and North Dakota (2.25 persons) had the lowest average household sizes. The national average was 2.60 persons per household.

Over 66 percent of children lived in married-couple family households. Utah had the highest proportion—78.9 percent—and Mississippi had the lowest proportion with 56.7 percent of children living in married-couple family households.

Six metropolitan areas—three in Texas and three in California—had someone under age 18 in more than 50 per-cent of their households. Nationally, 34.6 percent of households included children. More than 58 percent of metropolitan areas had a lower proportion than the U.S. average.

In 13 counties, 50 percent or more of households included children under age 18. About 44 percent of the counties included in this publication exceeded the U.S. proportion of 34.6 percent of households with children. Among the 75 most populous counties, San Bernardino, CA, had the highest proportion of households with children, with 47.8 percent. Among the 75 most populous counties, New York and San Francisco had the lowest proportions of households with children.

Nationally, 30.9 percent of households included someone 60 years old or older. Half of the states had higher proportions, led by Florida and Hawaii. In 10 counties, more than half of the households included someone age 60 or over. Among the largest counties, 43.8 percent of households in Palm Beach County, FL, included someone age 60 years or over.

State Rankings, 2005–2007
Selected Rankings

Population rank	State	Total population [A-1, col 1]	Per-cent change rank	State	Percent change 2005–2007 [A-1, col 2]	Percent Non-Hispanic White rank	State	Percent Non-Hispanic White alone or in combination [A-1, col 3]
	United States	298,757,310		United States	1.9		United States	66.3
1	California	36,264,467	1	Arizona	6.5	1	Vermont	95.4
2	Texas	23,385,340	1	Nevada	6.5	2	Maine	94.8
3	New York	19,280,753	3	Utah	5.6	3	West Virginia	93.7
4	Florida	18,014,927	4	Idaho	5.2	4	New Hampshire	93.4
5	Illinois	12,783,049	5	Georgia	4.8	5	Iowa	90.9
6	Pennsylvania	12,400,959	6	Texas	4.6	6	North Dakota	90.2
7	Ohio	11,463,403	7	North Carolina	4.4	7	Montana	88.3
8	Michigan	10,094,027	8	Colorado	4.0	8	Kentucky	88.1
9	Georgia	9,331,515	9	South Carolina	3.6	9	Wyoming	87.7
10	North Carolina	8,869,861	10	Oregon	3.2	10	South Dakota	86.5
11	New Jersey	8,669,815	10	Washington	3.2	11	Idaho	86.0
12	Virginia	7,636,644	10	Wyoming	3.2	12	Minnesota	85.9
13	Massachusetts	6,437,759	13	Delaware	2.9	13	Wisconsin	85.6
14	Washington	6,371,390	13	Florida	2.9	14	Nebraska	84.8
15	Indiana	6,301,687	15	New Mexico	2.8	15	Indiana	83.7
16	Arizona	6,152,175	15	Tennessee	2.8	16	Ohio	82.8
17	Tennessee	6,073,646	17	Montana	2.4	16	Utah	82.8
18	Missouri	5,834,644	18	Arkansas	2.3	18	Missouri	82.4
19	Maryland	5,597,843	18	Oklahoma	2.3	19	Pennsylvania	82.0
20	Wisconsin	5,571,593	20	Alaska	2.1	20	Kansas	81.0
21	Minnesota	5,155,344	20	South Dakota	2.1	21	Oregon	80.8
22	Colorado	4,767,161	22	Virginia	2.0	22	Massachusetts	79.4
23	Alabama	4,585,900	23	Alabama	1.9	23	Rhode Island	79.0
24	Louisiana	4,344,053	24	Kentucky	1.7	24	Michigan	77.6
25	South Carolina	4,330,933	25	California	1.6	25	Tennessee	77.4
26	Kentucky	4,205,648	25	Minnesota	1.6	26	Arkansas	76.3
27	Oregon	3,689,498	25	Missouri	1.6	26	Washington	76.3
28	Oklahoma	3,576,929	28	Indiana	1.4	28	Connecticut	74.6
29	Connecticut	3,494,851	29	Kansas	1.3	29	Oklahoma	72.1
30	Iowa	2,972,066	30	Hawaii	1.2	30	Colorado	71.5
31	Mississippi	2,906,118	30	Nebraska	1.2	31	Delaware	69.1
32	Arkansas	2,805,353	32	District of Columbia	1.1	32	Alabama	68.8
33	Kansas	2,757,827	32	Iowa	1.1	33	North Carolina	67.8
34	Utah	2,576,626	32	Wisconsin	1.1	34	Virginia	67.5
35	Nevada	2,488,917	35	Illinois	1.0	35	Alaska	66.1
36	New Mexico	1,942,847	35	New Hampshire	1.0	36	Illinois	65.3
37	West Virginia	1,808,787	37	Maryland	0.8	36	South Carolina	65.3
38	Nebraska	1,764,131	38	Mississippi	0.6	38	New Jersey	62.5
39	Idaho	1,463,059	38	North Dakota	0.6	39	Louisiana	62.1
40	Maine	1,314,780	40	Connecticut	0.5	40	Florida	61.2
41	New Hampshire	1,310,254	40	Pennsylvania	0.5	41	New York	60.3
42	Hawaii	1,276,534	42	Maine	0.4	42	Arizona	59.6
43	Rhode Island	1,062,065	42	West Virginia	0.4	43	Mississippi	59.2
44	Montana	946,815	44	Massachusetts	0.3	44	Georgia	59.0
45	Delaware	852,689	44	New Jersey	0.3	45	Nevada	58.9
46	South Dakota	788,241	46	New York	0.2	46	Maryland	58.5
47	Alaska	676,778	46	Vermont	0.2	47	Texas	48.3
48	North Dakota	637,709	48	Ohio	0.1	48	California	43.0
49	Vermont	620,589	49	Michigan	-0.4	49	New Mexico	42.4
50	District of Columbia	585,267	50	Rhode Island	-0.8	50	District of Columbia	31.4
51	Wyoming	514,044	51	Louisiana	-4.5	51	Hawaii	24.5

State Rankings, 2005–2007
Selected Rankings

Percent Black rank	State	Percent Black alone or in combination [A-1, col 4]	Percent Amer. Indian or Alaska Native rank	State	Percent Amer. Indian or Alaska Native alone or in combination [A-1, col 5]	Percent Asian and Native Hawaiian or Pacific Islander rank	State	Percent Asian and Native Hawaiian or Pac. Islander alone or in combination [A-1, cols 6 + 7]
	United States	13.1		United States	1.5		United States	5.2
1	District of Columbia	56.4	1	Alaska	18.2	1	Hawaii	78.7
2	Mississippi	37.5	2	Oklahoma	11.6	2	California	13.9
3	Louisiana	32.5	3	New Mexico	10.4	3	Washington	8.5
4	Georgia	30.2	4	South Dakota	9.4	4	Nevada	7.8
5	Maryland	29.8	5	Montana	7.7	4	New Jersey	7.8
6	South Carolina	29.2	6	North Dakota	5.9	6	New York	7.2
7	Alabama	26.7	7	Arizona	5.2	7	Alaska	7.0
8	North Carolina	22.1	8	Wyoming	3.2	8	Maryland	5.5
9	Delaware	21.3	9	Oregon	3.1	9	Virginia	5.4
10	Virginia	20.5	10	Washington	2.7	10	Massachusetts	5.2
11	Tennessee	17.2	11	Idaho	2.3	11	Oregon	4.8
12	New York	16.5	12	Hawaii	2.2	12	Illinois	4.6
13	Arkansas	16.1	13	Nevada	2.0	13	Minnesota	3.9
14	Florida	16.0	14	Kansas	1.9	14	Connecticut	3.8
15	Illinois	15.4	15	Colorado	1.8	15	District of Columbia	3.7
16	Michigan	14.9	16	North Carolina	1.7	15	Texas	3.7
17	New Jersey	14.3	17	California	1.6	17	Colorado	3.5
18	Ohio	12.6	17	Maine	1.6	17	Utah	3.5
19	Missouri	12.0	17	Minnesota	1.6	19	Delaware	3.3
19	Texas	12.0	17	Nebraska	1.6	20	Arizona	3.1
21	Pennsylvania	11.1	17	Utah	1.6	20	Georgia	3.1
22	Connecticut	10.4	22	Arkansas	1.5	20	Rhode Island	3.1
23	Indiana	9.4	23	Michigan	1.3	23	Florida	2.7
24	Oklahoma	8.6	23	Wisconsin	1.3	23	Michigan	2.7
25	Nevada	8.3	25	Missouri	1.2	25	Kansas	2.6
26	Kentucky	8.1	26	Vermont	1.1	25	Pennsylvania	2.6
27	California	7.0	27	Alabama	1.0	27	Oklahoma	2.3
28	Massachusetts	6.8	27	Louisiana	1.0	27	Wisconsin	2.3
29	Kansas	6.7	27	Rhode Island	1.0	29	North Carolina	2.2
30	Rhode Island	6.4	27	Texas	1.0	30	Nebraska	2.1
30	Wisconsin	6.4	31	Delaware	0.8	30	New Hampshire	2.1
32	Alaska	5.0	31	Indiana	0.8	32	Idaho	1.9
32	Minnesota	5.0	31	Maryland	0.8	32	Iowa	1.9
34	Nebraska	4.8	31	Mississippi	0.8	32	Ohio	1.9
35	Colorado	4.6	31	Tennessee	0.8	35	Missouri	1.8
36	Washington	4.4	31	Virginia	0.8	35	New Mexico	1.8
37	Arizona	4.1	37	Connecticut	0.7	37	Louisiana	1.7
38	West Virginia	3.9	37	District of Columbia	0.7	38	Indiana	1.6
39	Hawaii	3.5	37	Florida	0.7	38	Tennessee	1.6
40	Iowa	2.9	37	Iowa	0.7	40	South Carolina	1.5
41	New Mexico	2.7	37	New Hampshire	0.7	41	Arkansas	1.4
42	Oregon	2.4	37	New York	0.7	42	Kentucky	1.3
43	New Hampshire	1.4	37	Ohio	0.7	42	North Dakota	1.3
43	South Dakota	1.4	37	South Carolina	0.7	42	Vermont	1.3
43	Utah	1.4	45	Georgia	0.6	45	Alabama	1.2
46	Maine	1.3	45	Kentucky	0.6	45	Maine	1.2
46	Wyoming	1.3	45	Massachusetts	0.6	45	Montana	1.2
48	North Dakota	1.2	45	West Virginia	0.6	45	South Dakota	1.2
49	Vermont	1.1	49	Illinois	0.5	45	Wyoming	1.2
50	Idaho	1.0	49	New Jersey	0.5	50	Mississippi	1.0
51	Montana	0.9	51	Pennsylvania	0.4	51	West Virginia	0.9

State Rankings, 2005–2007
Selected Rankings

Percent Hispanic or Latino rank	State	Percent Hispanic or Latino [A-1, col 9]	Median age rank	State	Median age (years) [A-1, col 23]	Average household size rank	State	Average household size [A-1, col 43]
	United States	14.7		United States	36.4		United States	2.60
1	New Mexico	44.1	1	Maine	41.1	1	Utah	3.12
2	California	35.7	2	Vermont	40.4	2	California	2.92
3	Texas	35.5	3	West Virginia	40.3	3	Hawaii	2.86
4	Arizona	29.0	4	Florida	39.8	4	Texas	2.82
5	Nevada	24.3	5	Pennsylvania	39.5	5	Alaska	2.80
6	Florida	20.1	6	Montana	39.3	6	Arizona	2.73
7	Colorado	19.6	6	New Hampshire	39.3	7	New Jersey	2.70
8	New York	16.2	8	Connecticut	38.9	8	Georgia	2.69
9	New Jersey	15.6	9	Massachusetts	38.3	9	Illinois	2.64
10	Illinois	14.6	9	Rhode Island	38.3	10	Louisiana	2.63
11	Connecticut	11.2	11	New Jersey	38.2	10	Nevada	2.63
12	Utah	11.1	12	Iowa	37.9	10	New York	2.63
13	Rhode Island	10.9	13	Hawaii	37.7	13	Idaho	2.62
14	Oregon	10.2	13	Wisconsin	37.7	13	Maryland	2.62
15	Idaho	9.5	15	Delaware	37.6	15	New Mexico	2.61
16	Washington	9.1	15	Ohio	37.6	16	Mississippi	2.60
17	Kansas	8.5	15	Oregon	37.6	17	Delaware	2.57
18	District of Columbia	8.3	18	New York	37.4	18	Connecticut	2.55
19	Hawaii	8.1	19	Kentucky	37.3	18	Michigan	2.55
20	Massachusetts	8.0	19	Michigan	37.3	20	Massachusetts	2.54
21	Georgia	7.4	19	Missouri	37.3	20	New Hampshire	2.54
22	Nebraska	7.3	19	Wyoming	37.3	20	Virginia	2.54
23	Wyoming	7.2	23	Maryland	37.2	23	Colorado	2.53
24	Oklahoma	6.9	23	Tennessee	37.2	23	Rhode Island	2.53
25	North Carolina	6.7	25	Alabama	37.1	25	South Carolina	2.52
26	Delaware	6.3	25	South Dakota	37.1	25	Washington	2.52
26	Virginia	6.3	27	North Dakota	37.0	27	Indiana	2.50
28	Maryland	6.0	27	South Carolina	37.0	27	Oklahoma	2.50
29	Alaska	5.5	29	Minnesota	36.9	29	Arkansas	2.49
30	Arkansas	5.0	30	Arkansas	36.8	29	Florida	2.49
31	Indiana	4.7	30	Virginia	36.8	29	Montana	2.49
31	Wisconsin	4.7	30	Washington	36.8	29	Oregon	2.49
33	Pennsylvania	4.3	33	North Carolina	36.6	33	Alabama	2.48
34	Michigan	3.9	34	Indiana	36.3	33	North Carolina	2.48
35	Iowa	3.8	35	Kansas	36.1	33	Ohio	2.48
35	Minnesota	3.8	36	Nebraska	36.0	33	Tennessee	2.48
37	South Carolina	3.6	36	Oklahoma	36.0	37	Kansas	2.47
38	Tennessee	3.3	38	Illinois	35.7	37	Kentucky	2.47
39	Louisiana	3.0	39	Nevada	35.6	39	Minnesota	2.46
40	Missouri	2.9	39	New Mexico	35.6	39	Missouri	2.46
41	Alabama	2.5	41	Colorado	35.5	39	Pennsylvania	2.46
41	Montana	2.5	41	Louisiana	35.5	42	Nebraska	2.45
43	New Hampshire	2.4	43	Mississippi	35.1	43	South Dakota	2.43
43	Ohio	2.4	44	District of Columbia	35.0	43	Wyoming	2.43
45	Kentucky	2.1	45	Arizona	34.8	45	Wisconsin	2.42
45	South Dakota	2.1	46	Georgia	34.6	46	Vermont	2.39
47	Mississippi	1.8	47	California	34.5	46	West Virginia	2.39
48	North Dakota	1.6	48	Idaho	34.2	48	Iowa	2.38
49	Vermont	1.3	49	Alaska	33.4	49	Maine	2.35
50	Maine	1.1	50	Texas	33.1	50	North Dakota	2.25
51	West Virginia	1.0	51	Utah	28.3	51	District of Columbia	2.20

State Rankings, 2005–2007
Selected Rankings

Never married rank	State	Percent never married [A-1, col 33]	Now married rank	State	Percent now married [A-1, col 34]	Divorced rank	State	Percent divorced [A-1, col 36]
	United States	30.4		United States	52.7		United States	10.5
1	District of Columbia	54.0	1	Idaho	58.9	1	Nevada	13.4
2	New York	35.7	2	Utah	58.3	2	Wyoming	12.9
3	Massachusetts	34.5	3	Iowa	56.5	3	Oklahoma	12.7
4	California	34.1	4	Kansas	56.4	3	Oregon	12.7
5	Rhode Island	33.6	5	Wyoming	56.3	5	Tennessee	12.6
6	Maryland	32.5	6	Nebraska	56.2	6	Maine	12.5
7	Alaska	32.4	7	Arkansas	55.9	7	Vermont	12.4
7	Illinois	32.4	8	West Virginia	55.6	8	Kentucky	12.3
9	Louisiana	32.0	9	North Carolina	55.1	8	Washington	12.3
10	Hawaii	31.5	9	South Dakota	55.1	10	Arkansas	12.2
11	New Jersey	31.4	11	Minnesota	55.0	10	Florida	12.2
12	New Mexico	31.3	11	New Hampshire	55.0	10	Montana	12.2
13	Georgia	31.1	13	North Dakota	54.9	10	New Mexico	12.2
14	Connecticut	30.8	14	Kentucky	54.7	14	Arizona	12.1
14	Mississippi	30.8	14	Oklahoma	54.7	15	Alaska	11.8
16	Michigan	30.7	16	Virginia	54.6	15	Colorado	11.8
17	Pennsylvania	30.6	17	Indiana	54.4	15	Indiana	11.8
18	Delaware	30.5	17	Maine	54.4	18	Alabama	11.7
19	Minnesota	30.1	17	Montana	54.4	19	Idaho	11.6
20	Arizona	30.0	17	Texas	54.4	19	Missouri	11.6
21	North Dakota	29.9	21	Colorado	54.2	19	West Virginia	11.6
22	South Carolina	29.8	21	Wisconsin	54.2	22	Ohio	11.5
22	Wisconsin	29.8	23	Alabama	54.0	23	Georgia	11.3
24	Virginia	29.7	24	Missouri	53.9	23	New Hampshire	11.3
25	Texas	29.4	24	Tennessee	53.9	25	Louisiana	11.0
25	Vermont	29.4	26	New Jersey	53.6	25	Michigan	11.0
27	Colorado	29.3	27	Washington	53.4	27	Kansas	10.9
28	Ohio	29.2	28	Oregon	53.3	28	Mississippi	10.7
29	Washington	29.0	29	South Carolina	53.1	29	Texas	10.6
30	Utah	28.9	30	Connecticut	52.9	30	Delaware	10.5
31	South Dakota	28.5	30	Florida	52.9	31	Rhode Island	10.4
32	Nevada	28.3	32	Hawaii	52.8	32	North Carolina	10.1
32	North Carolina	28.3	33	Nevada	52.7	33	Iowa	9.9
34	Oregon	28.2	33	Pennsylvania	52.7	33	South Carolina	9.9
35	New Hampshire	27.9	35	Ohio	52.4	33	Wisconsin	9.9
36	Missouri	27.7	36	Alaska	52.3	36	South Dakota	9.8
36	Nebraska	27.7	36	Delaware	52.3	37	Connecticut	9.7
38	Florida	27.5	38	Vermont	52.2	37	Nebraska	9.7
39	Indiana	27.4	39	Arizona	52.1	39	California	9.6
40	Montana	27.2	40	Michigan	52.0	39	Virginia	9.6
41	Alabama	26.8	41	Maryland	51.9	41	Maryland	9.5
41	Iowa	26.8	42	Illinois	51.8	42	District of Columbia	9.4
43	Tennessee	26.6	43	Georgia	51.7	42	Hawaii	9.4
44	Maine	26.4	44	California	50.9	44	Illinois	9.3
45	Kansas	26.3	45	Mississippi	50.8	44	Minnesota	9.3
46	Kentucky	25.7	46	New Mexico	50.5	46	Massachusetts	9.0
47	Oklahoma	25.5	47	Massachusetts	50.0	47	Pennsylvania	8.9
48	Wyoming	25.2	48	Louisiana	49.5	47	Utah	8.9
49	West Virginia	24.7	49	New York	49.2	49	New York	8.4
50	Arkansas	24.4	50	Rhode Island	49.0	50	North Dakota	8.3
51	Idaho	24.2	51	District of Columbia	30.0	51	New Jersey	8.1

State Rankings, 2005–2007
Selected Rankings

Foreign born rank	State	Percent foreign-born population [A-1, col 37]	Spanish-speaking households rank	State	Percent of households speaking Spanish with or without English [A-1, col 39]	Households where no adult speaks English well rank	State	Percent of households where no adult speaks English well [A-1, col 41]
	United States	12.5		United States	11.2		United States	4.8
1	California	27.2	1	New Mexico	32.2	1	California	10.7
2	New York	21.6	2	Texas	28.3	2	Texas	8.6
3	New Jersey	19.7	3	California	24.4	3	New York	8.2
4	Florida	18.7	4	Arizona	19.9	4	Florida	7.2
5	Nevada	18.5	5	Florida	18.0	5	New Jersey	7.1
6	Hawaii	16.9	6	Nevada	16.9	6	Nevada	7.0
7	Texas	15.8	7	New York	13.6	7	Arizona	6.8
8	Arizona	15.0	8	New Jersey	13.3	8	New Mexico	6.4
9	Massachusetts	14.2	9	Colorado	12.0	9	Hawaii	5.9
10	Illinois	13.7	10	Illinois	10.9	10	Massachusetts	5.6
11	District of Columbia	12.7	11	Utah	10.1	11	Illinois	5.5
12	Connecticut	12.6	12	Connecticut	9.5	11	Rhode Island	5.5
12	Rhode Island	12.6	13	Rhode Island	9.3	13	Connecticut	5.0
14	Washington	12.2	14	Idaho	8.0	14	Colorado	4.2
15	Maryland	12.1	15	Oregon	7.8	14	Washington	4.2
16	Colorado	10.1	16	District of Columbia	7.7	16	Oregon	3.5
16	Virginia	10.1	17	Massachusetts	7.1	16	Utah	3.5
18	Oregon	9.7	18	Washington	6.9	18	Georgia	3.2
19	New Mexico	9.4	19	Georgia	6.6	19	Maryland	3.1
20	Georgia	9.0	20	Kansas	6.4	20	District of Columbia	3.0
21	Utah	8.0	21	Delaware	6.2	21	Virginia	2.8
22	Delaware	7.6	22	North Carolina	6.0	22	North Carolina	2.7
23	North Carolina	6.8	23	Maryland	5.9	23	Alaska	2.6
24	Alaska	6.7	23	Nebraska	5.9	24	Kansas	2.5
25	Minnesota	6.5	25	Virginia	5.8	24	Nebraska	2.5
26	Kansas	6.0	26	Oklahoma	5.4	26	Delaware	2.4
26	Michigan	6.0	27	Wyoming	5.2	26	Idaho	2.4
28	Idaho	5.6	28	Indiana	4.7	28	Minnesota	2.1
28	Nebraska	5.6	29	Wisconsin	4.6	28	Oklahoma	2.1
30	New Hampshire	5.4	30	Alaska	4.3	30	Pennsylvania	2.0
31	Pennsylvania	5.2	30	Arkansas	4.3	31	Michigan	1.9
32	Oklahoma	4.9	32	Pennsylvania	4.1	32	Indiana	1.8
33	Wisconsin	4.3	33	Iowa	3.9	33	Louisiana	1.7
34	South Carolina	4.2	33	Minnesota	3.9	34	South Carolina	1.6
35	Indiana	4.1	33	South Carolina	3.9	34	Wisconsin	1.6
36	Tennessee	4.0	36	Louisiana	3.6	36	Arkansas	1.5
37	Arkansas	3.9	36	Michigan	3.6	36	Iowa	1.5
38	Iowa	3.8	38	Tennessee	3.4	38	New Hampshire	1.4
39	Vermont	3.7	39	Missouri	3.2	38	Tennessee	1.4
40	Ohio	3.6	40	Hawaii	2.9	40	Ohio	1.3
41	Missouri	3.5	41	Alabama	2.8	41	Maine	1.2
42	Maine	3.2	41	Ohio	2.8	41	Missouri	1.2
43	Louisiana	3.1	43	New Hampshire	2.7	43	South Dakota	1.1
44	Alabama	2.9	44	Kentucky	2.6	44	Alabama	1.0
45	Kentucky	2.7	45	Mississippi	2.4	44	Kentucky	1.0
45	Wyoming	2.7	45	Montana	2.4	44	North Dakota	1.0
47	North Dakota	2.3	45	South Dakota	2.4	47	Vermont	0.8
48	South Dakota	2.1	48	North Dakota	1.9	47	Wyoming	0.8
49	Montana	1.9	49	Vermont	1.5	49	Mississippi	0.7
50	Mississippi	1.7	49	West Virginia	1.5	50	Montana	0.4
51	West Virginia	1.3	51	Maine	1.4	51	West Virginia	0.3

State Rankings, 2005–2007
Selected Rankings

Married-couple family households rank	State	Percent of households married-couple family [A-1, col 45]	Female householder rank	State	Percent of households female householder [A-1, col 43]	One-person households	State	One-person households [A-1, col 49]
	United States	49.8		United States	12.5		United States	27.3
1	Utah	62.2	1	Mississippi	18.2	1	District of Columbia	47.9
2	Idaho	57.0	2	District of Columbia	17.5	2	North Dakota	31.0
3	New Hampshire	54.3	3	Louisiana	16.5	3	Rhode Island	29.5
4	Iowa	52.8	4	South Carolina	15.1	4	New York	29.4
4	Kansas	52.8	5	Georgia	14.7	5	Massachusetts	29.0
4	Nebraska	52.8	6	New York	14.6	6	Ohio	28.9
7	South Dakota	52.7	7	Alabama	14.5	6	Pennsylvania	28.9
8	Montana	52.6	8	Maryland	13.8	8	Montana	28.7
8	Wyoming	52.6	9	Texas	13.5	9	South Dakota	28.6
10	Minnesota	52.3	10	Delaware	13.2	10	Missouri	28.4
11	New Jersey	52.2	10	New Mexico	13.2	10	Nebraska	28.4
12	Hawaii	52.1	12	Tennessee	13.1	12	Colorado	28.3
12	West Virginia	52.1	13	North Carolina	13.0	12	Iowa	28.3
14	Texas	51.7	14	California	12.8	12	Wisconsin	28.3
15	Indiana	51.6	15	Arkansas	12.7	15	Oregon	28.1
16	Arkansas	51.3	15	New Jersey	12.7	15	Washington	28.1
16	Wisconsin	51.3	15	Rhode Island	12.7	17	Kentucky	28.0
18	Connecticut	51.2	18	Hawaii	12.6	17	New Mexico	28.0
18	Maine	51.2	19	Illinois	12.5	17	Oklahoma	28.0
20	Alaska	51.1	19	Ohio	12.5	17	West Virginia	28.0
21	North Dakota	51.0	21	Florida	12.3	21	Florida	27.9
22	Kentucky	50.8	21	Kentucky	12.3	21	Illinois	27.9
22	Virginia	50.8	21	Michigan	12.3	21	Kansas	27.9
24	Oklahoma	50.6	24	Connecticut	12.1	21	Michigan	27.9
25	Colorado	50.3	24	Virginia	12.1	21	Minnesota	27.9
26	Michigan	50.2	26	Massachusetts	12.0	21	Vermont	27.9
27	Missouri	50.0	26	Oklahoma	12.0	27	Wyoming	27.8
28	Delaware	49.9	28	Missouri	11.9	28	North Carolina	27.7
28	Illinois	49.9	29	Arizona	11.8	28	Tennessee	27.7
28	Pennsylvania	49.9	30	Pennsylvania	11.7	30	Alabama	27.5
28	Washington	49.9	31	Alaska	11.6	31	Maine	27.4
32	California	49.8	31	Nevada	11.6	32	South Carolina	27.3
32	Oregon	49.8	33	Indiana	11.5	32	Virginia	27.3
32	Tennessee	49.8	34	West Virginia	10.9	34	Arkansas	27.2
35	Alabama	49.7	35	Washington	10.2	34	Louisiana	27.2
36	Arizona	49.5	36	Kansas	10.1	36	Connecticut	27.1
36	North Carolina	49.5	36	Vermont	10.1	37	Indiana	27.0
36	Vermont	49.5	38	Oregon	10.0	37	Maryland	27.0
39	Ohio	49.2	39	Maine	9.8	39	Arizona	26.8
40	Georgia	49.0	40	Colorado	9.7	40	Nevada	26.7
41	Maryland	48.7	40	Wisconsin	9.7	41	Georgia	26.4
42	South Carolina	48.5	42	Nebraska	9.5	42	Mississippi	26.3
43	Florida	48.4	43	New Hampshire	9.3	43	Delaware	26.2
44	Massachusetts	47.9	43	South Dakota	9.3	44	New Jersey	25.7
44	Nevada	47.9	45	Iowa	9.2	45	New Hampshire	24.8
46	New Mexico	47.3	45	Minnesota	9.2	45	Texas	24.8
47	Rhode Island	47.1	45	Utah	9.2	47	California	24.7
48	Mississippi	46.9	48	Idaho	9.0	48	Alaska	24.5
49	Louisiana	46.8	49	Montana	8.4	49	Idaho	23.7
50	New York	45.2	50	Wyoming	8.2	50	Hawaii	23.5
51	District of Columbia	21.7	51	North Dakota	7.4	51	Utah	19.3

County Rankings, 2005–2007
Selected Rankings

Population rank	County	Total population [A-2, col 1]	Percent change rank	County	Percent change 2005–2007 [A-2, col 2]	Foreign born rank	County	Percent foreign-born population [A-2, col 15]
	United States	298,757,310		United States	1.9		United States	12.5
1	Los Angeles County, CA	9,883,649	1	Pinal County, AZ	26.1	1	Miami-Dade County, FL	50.4
2	Cook County, IL	5,288,161	2	Kendall County, IL	22.5	2	Queens County, NY	48.3
3	Harris County, TX	3,854,245	3	Rockwall County, TX	18.9	3	Hudson County, NJ	40.4
4	Maricopa County, AZ	3,768,449	4	Flagler County, FL	17.2	4	Kings County, NY	37.4
5	Orange County, CA	2,988,407	5	Paulding County, GA	15.1	5	Santa Clara County, CA	36.8
6	San Diego County, CA	2,954,960	6	Union County, NC	14.8	6	Los Angeles County, CA	35.8
7	Kings County, NY	2,520,835	7	Forsyth County, GA	14.6	7	San Francisco County, CA	35.7
8	Miami-Dade County, FL	2,373,297	8	Jackson County, GA	14.0	8	Maverick County, TX	34.0
9	Dallas County, TX	2,336,012	9	Sumter County, FL	13.8	9	San Mateo County, CA	33.7
10	Queens County, NY	2,263,858	10	Barrow County, GA	13.0	10	Starr County, TX	33.6
11	Wayne County, MI	2,008,238	11	Lyon County, NV	12.5	11	Santa Cruz County, AZ	32.4
12	Riverside County, CA	2,002,663	12	Williamson County, TX	12.4	12	Imperial County, CA	31.8
13	San Bernardino County, CA	1,982,845	13	Brunswick County, NC	12.2	13	Bronx County, NY	31.7
14	King County, WA	1,832,835	13	Washington County, UT	12.2	14	Alameda County, CA	30.5
15	Clark County, NV	1,774,086	15	Lincoln County, SD	12.0	14	Orange County, CA	30.5
16	Broward County, FL	1,767,681	16	Newton County, GA	11.9	16	Colusa County, CA	30.1
17	Santa Clara County, CA	1,722,819	17	Hays County, TX	11.8	17	Monterey County, CA	30.0
18	Tarrant County, TX	1,668,042	18	Cherokee County, GA	11.6	18	Broward County, FL	29.9
19	New York County, NY	1,613,257	19	Sandoval County, NM	11.5	19	Montgomery County, MD	29.4
20	Bexar County, TX	1,555,168	20	Henry County, GA	11.3	20	Hendry County, FL	29.2
21	Middlesex County, MA	1,468,419	21	Ascension Parish, LA	11.2	21	Fairfax city, VA	28.9
22	Suffolk County, NY	1,457,115	22	Comal County, TX	11.0	22	Hidalgo County, TX	28.5
23	Philadelphia County, PA	1,454,382	22	Franklin County, WA	11.0	22	Webb County, TX	28.5
24	Alameda County, CA	1,454,159	24	Collin County, TX	10.9	24	Bergen County, NJ	28.4
25	Sacramento County, CA	1,373,773	24	Fort Bend County, TX	10.9	24	New York County, NY	28.4
26	Bronx County, NY	1,369,859	26	Douglas County, GA	10.7	26	Seward County, KS	28.2
27	Nassau County, NY	1,313,526	27	Broomfield County, CO	10.6	27	Passaic County, NJ	28.1
28	Cuyahoga County, OH	1,310,905	27	Osceola County, FL	10.6	28	Union County, NJ	28.0
29	Palm Beach County, FL	1,264,012	29	Dallas County, IA	10.5	29	Fairfax County, VA	27.7
30	Allegheny County, PA	1,226,174	29	Dorchester County, SC	10.5	29	Middlesex County, NJ	27.7
31	Oakland County, MI	1,207,603	29	Iron County, UT	10.5	31	Suffolk County, MA	27.4
32	Hillsborough County, FL	1,157,007	32	Douglas County, CO	10.4	32	El Paso County, TX	27.0
33	Hennepin County, MN	1,130,110	33	Montgomery County, TX	10.3	33	Ford County, KS	25.6
34	Franklin County, OH	1,109,535	33	York County, SC	10.3	34	Cameron County, TX	25.4
35	Orange County, FL	1,050,676	35	Kendall County, TX	10.2	34	Merced County, CA	25.4
36	Contra Costa County, CA	1,011,372	35	Matanuska-Susitna Borough, AK	10.2	36	Alexandria city, VA	25.3
37	Fairfax County, VA	1,006,576	35	Wake County, NC	10.2	36	Franklin County, WA	25.3
38	St. Louis County, MO	998,368	38	Guadalupe County, TX	10.1	38	Arlington County, VA	25.1
39	Salt Lake County, UT	987,913	38	Pearl River County, MS	10.1	39	Yuma County, AZ	24.9
40	Fulton County, GA	963,676	38	Walton County, GA	10.1	40	DeSoto County, FL	24.4
41	Milwaukee County, WI	951,026	41	Denton County, TX	10.0	40	Harris County, TX	24.4
42	Westchester County, NY	949,041	41	Nye County, NV	10.0	42	Westchester County, NY	24.1
43	Pima County, AZ	947,626	43	Christian County, MO	9.9	43	Dallas County, TX	24.0
44	Travis County, TX	940,517	43	Kaufman County, TX	9.9	43	Val Verde County, TX	24.0
45	DuPage County, IL	928,086	43	King George County, VA	9.9	45	Essex County, NJ	23.7
46	Montgomery County, MD	925,719	43	Loudoun County, VA	9.9	45	San Joaquin County, CA	23.7
47	Pinellas County, FL	922,147	47	DeSoto County, MS	9.8	47	Collier County, FL	23.6
48	Erie County, NY	919,112	47	Rutherford County, TN	9.8	48	Contra Costa County, CA	23.4
49	Shelby County, TN	908,701	49	Canyon County, ID	9.7	49	Manassas city, VA	23.2
50	Honolulu County, HI	904,783	49	St. Lucie County, FL	9.7	50	San Diego County, CA	23.0
51	Fairfield County, CT	894,724	51	Cabarrus County, NC	9.5	51	Gwinnett County, GA	22.9
52	Bergen County, NJ	894,299	52	Effingham County, GA	9.4	52	Tulare County, CA	22.7
53	Fresno County, CA	886,074	53	Fayette County, TN	9.3	53	Fort Bend County, TX	22.6
54	Hartford County, CT	874,545	53	Horry County, SC	9.3	53	Santa Barbara County, CA	22.6
55	Marion County, IN	872,842	53	Lake County, FL	9.3	55	Riverside County, CA	22.4
56	Hamilton County, OH	845,647	53	St. Johns County, FL	9.3	56	Napa County, CA	22.3
57	New Haven County, CT	843,571	53	Tooele County, UT	9.3	57	Finney County, KS	22.1
58	Duval County, FL	841,077	53	Wasatch County, UT	9.3	58	Ventura County, CA	22.0
59	Mecklenburg County, NC	834,932	53	Williamson County, TN	9.3	59	Fresno County, CA	21.7
60	Prince George's County, MD	833,862	60	Coweta County, GA	9.2	59	Texas County, OK	21.7
61	Macomb County, MI	828,972	60	Dawson County, GA	9.2	61	San Benito County, CA	21.6
62	Ventura County, CA	794,412	60	Deschutes County, OR	9.2	61	Somerset County, NJ	21.6
63	Wake County, NC	794,316	60	Scott County, KY	9.2	61	Yolo County, CA	21.6
64	Baltimore County, MD	786,547	64	Campbell County, WY	9.1	64	San Bernardino County, CA	21.4
65	Middlesex County, NJ	785,479	65	Culpeper County, VA	9.0	65	Moore County, TX	21.3
66	Worcester County, MA	779,386	66	Lee County, FL	8.9	66	Clark County, NV	21.2
67	Essex County, NJ	779,203	67	Hall County, GA	8.8	66	Palm Beach County, FL	21.2
68	Montgomery County, PA	774,424	67	Pender County, NC	8.8	68	Sutter County, CA	21.1
69	Kern County, CA	771,347	69	Benton County, AR	8.6	69	Cook County, IL	20.9
70	Pierce County, WA	762,223	69	Ellis County, TX	8.6	69	Richmond County, NY	20.9
71	San Francisco County, CA	757,604	69	Lincoln County, MO	8.6	71	Rockland County, NY	20.7
72	Gwinnett County, GA	748,715	69	Pasco County, FL	8.6	72	Madera County, CA	20.6
73	Essex County, MA	731,841	69	Tangipahoa Parish, LA	8.6	73	Kings County, CA	20.5
74	Monroe County, NY	730,215	74	Garfield County, CO	8.5	74	Kern County, CA	20.4
75	DeKalb County, GA	728,987	74	Livingston Parish, LA	8.5	75	Titus County, TX	20.1

County Rankings, 2005–2007
Selected Rankings

Married-couple family rank	County	Percent married-couple families [A-2, col 18]	Female householders rank	County	Percent female householders [A-2, col 20]	One-person households	County	Percent one-person households [A-2, col 22]
	United States	49.8		United States	12.5		United States	27.3
1	Goochland County, VA	83.4	1	Coahoma County, MS	33.3	1	New York County, NY	49.9
2	Holmes County, OH	72.0	2	Holmes County, MS	33.1	2	District of Columbia, DC	47.9
3	Jefferson County, ID	71.8	3	Sunflower County, MS	31.8	3	Alexandria city, VA	46.7
4	Box Elder County, UT	71.5	4	Bronx County, NY	30.9	4	Arlington County, VA	44.2
5	Utah County, UT	70.3	5	Leflore County, MS	30.0	5	St. Louis city, MO	43.9
6	Rockwall County, TX	70.1	6	Washington County, MS	28.1	6	Charlottesville city, VA	43.4
7	Sanpete County, UT	70.0	7	Marlboro County, SC	25.9	7	Richmond city, VA	42.6
8	Douglas County, CO	69.7	8	Bolivar County, MS	25.7	8	Fredericksburg city, VA	42.3
9	Williamson County, TN	69.6	8	Dallas County, AL	25.7	9	San Francisco County, CA	42.2
10	Dawson County, GA	69.5	10	Williamsburg County, SC	25.4	10	Denver County, CO	42.1
11	Davis County, UT	69.3	11	Fairfield County, SC	25.3	11	Baltimore city, MD	39.8
11	Elbert County, CO	69.3	12	Marion County, SC	25.1	12	Jackson County, IL	39.3
13	Kendall County, IL	69.2	13	Clay County, MS	25.0	13	Orleans Parish, LA	38.8
14	Morrow County, OH	68.8	14	Hertford County, NC	24.8	14	Philadelphia County, PA	38.7
15	Oldham County, KY	68.6	15	Dillon County, SC	24.5	15	Suffolk County, MA	38.1
16	George County, MS	68.4	16	Barnwell County, SC	24.1	16	Macon County, AL	37.5
16	LaGrange County, IN	68.4	16	Gadsden County, FL	24.1	17	Roanoke city, VA	37.4
18	Wasatch County, UT	68.2	16	McDuffie County, GA	24.1	18	Dodge County, GA	36.7
19	Forsyth County, GA	68.1	19	Dougherty County, GA	23.8	18	Fulton County, GA	36.7
20	Oconee County, GA	68.0	20	Adams County, MS	23.7	20	Davidson County, TN	36.5
21	Miami County, KS	67.3	20	Hinds County, MS	23.7	21	Taos County, NM	36.4
21	Uintah County, UT	67.3	20	Phillips County, AK	23.7	22	Teton County, WY	36.2
23	Cache County, UT	67.1	23	Apache County, AZ	23.4	23	Staunton city, VA	36.0
23	Wilson County, TX	67.1	24	Clayton County, GA	23.3	24	Stutsman County, ND	35.9
25	Carver County, MN	66.8	25	Crisp County, GA	23.1	25	Winchester city, VA	35.8
26	Washington County, UT	66.7	25	Macon County, AL	23.1	26	Northampton County, NC	35.7
27	Cass County, NE	66.6	27	Baltimore city, MD	23.0	26	Pinellas County, FL	35.7
27	Delaware County, OH	66.6	28	Crittenden County, AK	22.6	28	Danville city, VA	35.6
27	Medina County, TX	66.6	29	Yazoo County, MS	22.3	29	Hamilton County, OH	35.4
30	Fort Bend County, TX	66.4	30	Richmond County, GA	21.9	30	Cuyahoga County, OH	35.3
31	Tooele County, UT	66.1	31	Sumter County, GA	21.8	31	Milwaukee County, WI	35.2
32	Columbia County, GA	66.0	32	Mitchell County, GA	21.6	31	Sheridan County, WY	35.2
32	Sioux County, IA	66.0	33	Petersburg city, VA	21.5	33	Multnomah County, OR	35.1
32	Spencer County, IN	66.0	33	Webb County, TX	21.5	34	Monongalia County, WV	34.8
32	York County, VA	66.0	35	Butler County, AL	21.4	35	Allegheny County, PA	34.5
36	Fayette County, GA	65.6	35	Kings County, NY	21.4	35	Ramsey County, MN	34.5
36	Livingston County, MI	65.6	35	Robeson County, NC	21.4	37	McDonough County, IL	34.4
38	Sherburne County, MN	65.5	38	Muscogee County, GA	21.2	38	Monroe County, IN	34.3
39	Carroll County, MD	65.3	38	Philadelphia County, PA	21.2	39	Albany County, NY	34.2
40	Harrison County, IN	65.2	40	Danville city, VA	21.1	39	Durham County, NC	34.2
41	Hanover County, VA	65.1	40	Liberty County, GA	21.1	41	Allegany County, MD	34.1
41	Plymouth County, IA	65.1	42	Edgecombe County, NC	21.0	41	Ohio County, WV	34.1
43	Rogers County, OK	65.0	42	Panola County, MS	21.0	43	Lynchburg city, VA	33.9
44	Calumet County, WI	64.8	44	Marengo County, AL	20.9	44	Franklin County, KY	33.8
44	Davie County, NC	64.8	45	Monroe County, MS	20.8	44	Hennepin County, MN	33.8
46	Bingham County, ID	64.6	46	Iberville County, LA	20.7	44	Lawrence County, SD	33.8
46	Chambers County, TX	64.6	46	Orangeburg County, SC	20.7	47	Dickinson County, MI	33.7
46	Hancock County, IN	64.6	48	Orleans County, LA	20.6	47	Greene County, NY	33.7
46	Hunterdon County, NJ	64.6	49	St. Louis city, MO	20.5	49	Boyle County, KY	33.6
46	Saunders County, NE	64.6	50	St. Landry County, LA	20.4	49	Hopewell city, VA	33.6
46	Scott County, MN	64.6	51	Imperial County, CA	20.3	49	Lewis and Clark County, MT	33.6
46	Stafford County, VA	64.6	51	Laurens County, GA	20.3	52	Clarke County, GA	33.5
53	Ottawa County, MI	64.5	51	Washington County, GA	20.3	52	Jefferson County, KY	33.5
53	Summit County, UT	64.5	54	Burke County, GA	20.2	52	Lincoln County, OR	33.5
55	Putnam County, OH	64.4	54	Florence County, SC	20.2	55	DeKalb County, GA	33.4
56	Butler County, KS	64.3	54	Hopewell city, VA	20.2	55	Fayette County, KY	33.4
56	Hamilton County, IN	64.3	54	Shelby County, TN	20.2	55	Lafayette County, MS	33.4
56	Putnam County, WV	64.3	54	St. Francis County, AK	20.2	55	Marion County, IN	33.4
59	Geauga County, OH	64.2	54	St. Mary County, LA	20.2	55	Petersburg city, VA	33.4
59	Union County, NC	64.2	60	Scott County, MS	20.1	60	Cass County, ND	33.2
59	Warrick County, IN	64.2	60	Tippah County, MS	20.1	61	Bibb County, GA	33.1
62	Morgan County, IN	64.1	62	Caddo County, LA	20.0	61	Broome County, NY	33.1
62	Will County, IL	64.1	62	De Soto County, LA	20.0	63	Alachua County, FL	32.9
64	Madison County, NC	63.8	62	El Paso County, TX	20.0	63	Jefferson County, WA	32.9
65	Leelanau County, MI	63.7	62	Halifax County, NC	20.0	63	Montgomery County, OH	32.9
65	Medina County, OH	63.7	62	Pike County, AL	20.0	63	Vanderburgh County, IN	32.9
65	Parker County, TX	63.7	62	Vance County, NC	20.0	63	Whitman County, WA	32.9
68	Bremer County, IA	63.6	68	Scotland County, NC	19.9	68	Leon County, FL	32.8
68	Lapeer County, MI	63.6	69	Bee County, TX	19.8	68	Travis County, TX	32.8
68	Lincoln County, SD	63.6	69	Wayne County, MI	19.8	70	Clatsop County, OR	32.7
68	St. Clair County, AL	63.6	71	Lauderdale County, MS	19.7	70	Crawford County, KS	32.7
68	Sussex County, NJ	63.6	71	Portsmouth city, VA	19.7	70	Garland County, AR	32.7
73	Botetourt County, VA	63.5	73	Marshall County, MS	19.6	70	Harrisonburg city, VA	32.7
73	McHenry County, IL	63.5	73	Sumter County, SC	19.6	70	King County, WA	32.7
73	Paulding County, GA	63.5	75	Cameron County, TX	19.5	70	Richland County, SC	32.7
73	Wise County, TX	63.5	75	Jefferson County, AK	19.5			
			75	Jim Wells County, TX	19.5			
			75	Lowndes County, MS	19.5			

Metropolitan Area Rankings, 2005–2007
Selected Rankings

Population rank	Area name	Total population [A-3, col 1]	Percent change rank	Area name	Percent change 2005–2007 [A-3, col 2]
	United States	298,757,310		United States	1.9
1	New York-Northern New Jersey-Long Island, NY-NJ-PA	18,785,319	1	Palm Coast, FL	17.0
2	Los Angeles-Long Beach-Santa Ana, CA	12,872,056	2	Provo-Orem, UT	12.7
3	Chicago-Naperville-Joliet, IL-IN-WI	9,463,477	3	St. George, UT	12.1
4	Dallas-Fort Worth-Arlington, TX	5,979,240	4	Raleigh-Cary, NC	9.5
5	Philadelphia-Camden-Wilmington, PA-NJ-DE-MD	5,810,526	5	Myrtle Beach-Conway-North Myrtle Beach, SC	9.4
6	Houston-Sugar Land-Baytown, TX	5,485,720	6	Bend, OR	9.1
7	Miami-Fort Lauderdale-Pompano Beach, FL	5,404,990	7	Austin-Round Rock, TX	8.7
8	Washington-Arlington-Alexandria, DC-VA-MD-WV	5,263,322	7	Cape Coral-Fort Myers, FL	8.7
9	Atlanta-Sandy Springs-Marietta, GA	5,122,275	9	Charlotte-Gastonia-Concord, NC-SC	8.4
10	Detroit-Warren-Livonia, MI	4,488,815	10	Gainesville, GA	8.3
11	Boston-Cambridge-Quincy, MA-NH	4,467,781	11	Boise City-Nampa, ID	7.8
12	San Francisco-Oakland-Fremont, CA	4,171,627	12	Phoenix-Mesa-Scottsdale, AZ	7.6
13	Phoenix-Mesa-Scottsdale, AZ	4,036,744	13	Ocala, FL	7.5
14	Riverside-San Bernardino-Ontario, CA	3,985,508	13	Prescott, AZ	7.5
15	Seattle-Tacoma-Bellevue, WA	3,259,078	15	Las Vegas-Paradise, NV	7.3
16	Minneapolis-St. Paul-Bloomington, MN-WI	3,172,801	16	Grand Junction, CO	7.2
17	San Diego-Carlsbad-San Marcos, CA	2,954,960	16	Greeley, CO	7.2
18	St. Louis, MO-IL	2,790,203	18	Wilmington, NC	7.1
19	Tampa-St. Petersburg-Clearwater, FL	2,687,027	19	Fayetteville-Springdale-Rogers, AR-MO	6.6
20	Baltimore-Towson, MD	2,660,496	20	Lakeland, FL	6.5
21	Denver-Aurora, CO	2,413,844	21	Atlanta-Sandy Springs-Marietta, GA	6.4
22	Pittsburgh, PA	2,364,622	21	Idaho Falls, ID	6.4
23	Portland-Vancouver-Beaverton, OR-WA	2,133,931	23	Port St. Lucie, FL	6.2
24	Cincinnati-Middletown, OH-KY-IN	2,118,212	24	Coeur d'Alene, ID	5.9
25	Cleveland-Elyria-Mentor, OH	2,106,901	24	Dover, DE	5.9
26	Sacramento–Arden-Arcade–Roseville, CA	2,063,900	26	Dallas-Fort Worth Arlington, TX	5.8
27	Orlando-Kissimmee, FL	1,990,388	27	McAllen-Edinburg-Mission, TX	5.7
28	Kansas City, MO-KS	1,962,412	27	Sioux Falls, SD	5.7
29	San Antonio, TX	1,936,735	29	Houston-Sugar Land-Baytown, TX	5.6
30	San Jose-Sunnyvale-Santa Clara, CA	1,777,616	29	San Antonio, TX	5.6
31	Las Vegas-Paradise, NV	1,774,086	29	Yuba City, CA	5.6
32	Columbus, OH	1,734,721	32	Baton Rouge, LA	5.5
33	Indianapolis-Carmel, IN	1,670,070	33	Greenville, NC	5.4
34	Virginia Beach-Norfolk-Newport News, VA-NC	1,654,563	33	Lake Havasu City-Kingman, AZ	5.4
35	Providence-New Bedford-Fall River, RI-MA	1,605,211	35	Ogden-Clearfield, UT	5.3
36	Charlotte-Gastonia-Concord, NC-SC	1,586,202	35	Yuma, AZ	5.3
37	Milwaukee-Waukesha-West Allis, WI	1,539,985	37	Tucson, AZ	5.2
38	Austin-Round Rock, TX	1,533,263	38	Bakersfield, CA	5.1
39	Nashville-Davidson–Murfreesboro–Franklin, TN	1,486,442	38	Hattiesburg, MS	5.1
40	Jacksonville, FL	1,276,323	40	Riverside-San Bernardino-Ontario, CA	5.0
41	Memphis, TN-MS-AR	1,269,637	41	Charleston-North Charleston, SC	4.9
42	Louisville-Jefferson County, KY-IN	1,220,992	41	El Centro, CA	4.9
43	Richmond, VA	1,194,021	41	Nashville-Davidson–Murfreesboro–Franklin, TN	4.9
44	Hartford-West Hartford-East Hartford, CT	1,185,150	44	Midland, TX	4.8
45	Oklahoma City, OK	1,175,167	44	Orlando-Kissimmee, FL	4.8
46	Buffalo-Niagara Falls, NY	1,134,280	44	Savannah, GA	4.8
47	New Orleans-Metairie-Kenner, LA	1,110,265	44	Springfield, MO	4.8
48	Birmingham-Hoover, AL	1,098,834	48	Killeen-Temple-Fort Hood, TX	4.7
49	Salt Lake City, UT	1,075,530	48	Laredo, TX	4.7
50	Rochester, NY	1,031,480	48	Olympia, WA	4.7
51	Raleigh-Cary, NC	1,001,313	48	Salt Lake City, UT	4.7
52	Tucson, AZ	947,626	52	Huntsville, AL	4.6
53	Honolulu, HI	904,783	52	Las Cruces, NM	4.6
54	Bridgeport-Stamford-Norwalk, CT	894,724	54	Albuquerque, NM	4.5
55	Tulsa, OK	893,734	55	Durham, NC	4.4
56	Fresno, CA	886,074	55	Hagerstown-Martinsburg, MD-WV	4.4
57	Albany-Schenectady-Troy, NY	850,506	55	Kennewick-Richland-Pasco, WA	4.4
58	New Haven-Milford, CT	843,571	55	Winchester, VA-WV	4.4
59	Dayton, OH	838,165	59	Auburn-Opelika, AL	4.3
60	Omaha-Council Bluffs, NE-IA	820,725	60	Ames, IA	4.2
61	Albuquerque, NM	819,576	60	Athens-Clarke County, GA	4.2
62	Allentown-Bethlehem-Easton, PA-NJ	794,961	60	Des Moines-West Des Moines, IA	4.2
63	Oxnard-Thousand Oaks-Ventura, CA	794,412	60	Tyler, TX	4.2
64	Worcester, MA	779,386	64	Clarksville, TN-KY	4.1
65	Grand Rapids-Wyoming, MI	772,963	64	Greenville-Mauldin-Easley, SC	4.1
66	Bakersfield, CA	771,347	64	Longview, WA	4.1
67	Baton Rouge, LA	753,299	64	Odessa, TX	4.1
68	El Paso, TX	724,217	64	Warner Robins, GA	4.1
69	Columbia, SC	703,807	69	Brunswick, GA	4.0
70	Akron, OH	700,134	69	Denver-Aurora, CO	4.0
71	McAllen-Edinburg-Mission, TX	689,929	69	Fort Collins-Loveland, CO	4.0
72	Greensboro-High Point, NC	686,727	69	Jacksonville, FL	4.0
73	Springfield, MA	683,262	69	Madera, CA	4.0
74	Sarasota-Bradenton-Venice, FL	678,880	74	Bellingham, WA	3.9
75	Knoxville, TN	669,962	74	Bowling Green, KY	3.9
			74	Logan, UT-ID	3.9

Metropolitan Area Rankings, 2005–2007
Selected Rankings

Foreign born rank	Area name	Percent foreign-born population [A-3, col 15]	One-person households rank	Area name	One-person households [A-3, col 22]
	United States	12.5		United States	27.3
1	Miami-Fort Lauderdale-Pompano Beach, FL	36.9	1	Hot Springs, AR	32.7
2	San Jose-Sunnyvale-Santa Clara, CA	36.3	2	Gainesville, FL	32.3
3	Los Angeles-Long Beach-Santa Ana, CA	34.6	3	Bloomington, IN	32.0
4	El Centro, CA	31.8	4	Buffalo-Niagara Falls, NY	31.9
5	Salinas, CA	30.0	5	Durham, NC	31.8
6	San Francisco-Oakland-Fremont, CA	29.5	6	Pittsfield, MA	31.7
7	Laredo, TX	28.5	7	Champaign-Urbana, IL	31.6
7	McAllen-Edinburg-Mission, TX	28.5	7	Cleveland-Elyria-Mentor, OH	31.6
9	New York-Northern New Jersey-Long Island, NY-NJ-PA	28.1	9	Fargo, ND-MN	31.5
10	El Paso, TX	27.0	9	Lawrence, KS	31.5
11	Brownsville-Harlingen, TX	25.4	9	Morgantown, WV	31.5
11	Merced, CA	25.4	9	Scranton–Wilkes-Barre, PA	31.5
13	Yuma, AZ	24.9	13	Pittsburgh, PA	31.4
14	Stockton, CA	23.7	14	Springfield, IL	31.3
15	Naples-Marco Island, FL	23.6	15	Tallahassee, FL	31.1
16	San Diego-Carlsbad-San Marcos, CA	23.0	16	Binghamton, NY	31.0
17	Visalia-Porterville, CA	22.7	16	Charlottesville, VA	31.0
18	Santa Barbara-Santa Maria-Goleta, CA	22.6	16	Duluth, MN-WI	31.0
19	Napa, CA	22.3	16	Grand Forks, ND-MN	31.0
20	Oxnard-Thousand Oaks-Ventura, CA	22.0	16	Tuscaloosa, AL	31.0
21	Riverside-San Bernardino-Ontario, CA	21.9	21	Greenville, NC	30.9
22	Fresno, CA	21.7	22	Santa Fe, NM	30.8
23	Houston-Sugar Land-Baytown, TX	21.3	23	Milwaukee-Waukesha-West Allis, WI	30.7
24	Las Vegas-Paradise, NV	21.2	23	Roanoke, VA	30.7
25	Madera, CA	20.6	23	Tampa-St. Petersburg-Clearwater, FL	30.7
26	Hanford-Corcoran, CA	20.5	23	Tucson, AZ	30.7
27	Bakersfield, CA	20.4	27	Auburn-Opelika, AL	30.6
28	Washington-Arlington-Alexandria, DC-VA-MD-WV	20.1	27	Cumberland, MD-WV	30.6
29	Modesto, CA	19.9	27	Ithaca, NY	30.6
30	Bridgeport-Stamford-Norwalk, CT	19.4	27	Pine Bluff, AR	30.6
31	Las Cruces, NM	19.3	31	Deltona-Daytona Beach-Ormond Beach, FL	30.5
32	Vallejo-Fairfield, CA	18.9	31	Iowa City, IA	30.5
33	Honolulu, HI	18.7	33	Madison, WI	30.4
34	Yakima, WA	18.4	34	Albany-Schenectady-Troy, NY	30.3
35	Trenton-Ewing, NJ	18.2	35	Carson City, NV	30.2
36	Gainesville, GA	18.1	35	Davenport-Moline-Rock Island, IA-IL	30.2
37	Dallas-Fort Worth-Arlington, TX	17.7	37	Bismarck, ND	30.1
38	Chicago-Naperville-Joliet, IL-IN-WI	17.6	37	Dayton, OH	30.1
38	Yuba City, CA	17.6	37	Oshkosh-Neenah, WI	30.1
40	Sacramento–Arden-Arcade–Roseville, CA	17.4	37	Springfield, MA	30.1
41	Santa Cruz-Watsonville, CA	17.1	41	Albuquerque, NM	30.0
41	Santa Rosa-Petaluma, CA	17.1	41	Danville, VA	30.0
43	Phoenix-Mesa-Scottsdale, AZ	16.8	41	Sarasota-Bradenton-Venice, FL	30.0
44	Boston-Cambridge-Quincy, MA-NH	15.9	41	Wheeling, WV-OH	30.0
45	Orlando-Kissimmee, FL	15.7	45	Seattle-Tacoma-Bellevue, WA	29.9
46	Seattle-Tacoma-Bellevue, WA	15.3	45	Shreveport-Bossier City, LA	29.9
47	Reno-Sparks, NV	15.1	45	State College, PA	29.9
48	Dalton, GA	14.9	48	Ann Arbor, MI	29.8
49	Kennewick-Richland-Pasco, WA	14.5	48	South Bend-Mishawaka, IN-MI	29.8
50	Cape Coral-Fort Myers, FL	14.4	50	Johnson City, TN	29.7
51	Atlantic City, NJ	14.2	50	Lexington-Fayette, KY	29.7
52	Austin-Round Rock, TX	14.1	50	San Francisco-Oakland-Fremont, CA	29.7
52	Port St. Lucie, FL	14.1	50	Toledo, OH	29.7
54	Wenatchee, WA	13.7	50	Wilmington, NC	29.7
55	Tucson, AZ	13.4	55	Decatur, IL	29.6
56	Salem, OR	13.3	55	Spokane, WA	29.6
57	Ithaca, NY	13.0	55	Syracuse, NY	29.6
58	Santa Fe, NM	12.9	58	Johnstown, PA	29.5
59	Atlanta-Sandy Springs-Marietta, GA	12.6	58	Lincoln, NE	29.5
59	Providence-New Bedford-Fall River, RI-MA	12.6	58	Louisville-Jefferson County, KY-IN	29.5
61	Denver-Aurora, CO	12.5	58	Missoula, MT	29.5
61	Palm Coast, FL	12.5	58	Reno-Sparks, NV	29.5
63	Durham, NC	12.1	63	Anderson, IN	29.4
63	Portland-Vancouver-Beaverton, OR-WA	12.1	63	Denver-Aurora, CO	29.4
65	Sarasota-Bradenton-Venice, FL	12.0	63	Macon, GA	29.4
65	Tampa-St. Petersburg-Clearwater, FL	12.0	66	Detroit-Warren-Livonia, MI	29.3
67	Bellingham, WA	11.7	66	Rocky Mount, NC	29.3
68	Boulder, CO	11.6	66	Youngstown-Warren-Boardman, OH-PA	29.3
68	Hartford-West Hartford-East Hartford, CT	11.6	69	Asheville, NC	29.2
70	Carson City, NV	11.5	69	Barnstable Town, MA	29.2
70	College Station-Bryan, TX	11.5	69	Billings, MT	29.2
72	Ann Arbor, MI	11.4	69	Blacksburg-Christiansburg-Radford, VA	29.2
72	Salt Lake City, UT	11.4	69	Columbia, MO	29.2
74	New Haven-Milford, CT	11.0	69	La Crosse, WI-MN	29.2
74	San Antonio, TX	11.0	69	Terre Haute, IN	29.2
			69	Utica-Rome, NY	29.2
			69	Weirton-Steubenville, WV-OH	29.2

Population rank	City	Total population [A-4, col 1]	Percent change rank	City	Percent change 2005–2007 [A-4, col 2]	Foreign born rank	City	Percent foreign-born population [A-4, col 15]
	United States	298,757,310		United States	1.9		United States	12.5
1	New York city, NY	8,246,310	1	Maricopa city, AZ	260.6	1	Fountainbleau CDP, FL	76.2
2	Los Angeles city, CA	3,770,590	2	Beaumont city, CA	49.4	2	Hialeah city, FL	70.8
3	Chicago city, IL	2,740,224	3	Queen Creek town, AZ	42.8	3	Westchester CDP, FL	69.4
4	Houston city, TX	2,034,749	4	Spring Hill city, TN	39.9	4	University Park CDP, FL	67.1
5	Philadelphia city, PA	1,454,382	5	Little Elm city, TX	31.6	5	Coral Terrace CDP, FL	65.1
6	Phoenix city, AZ	1,440,018	6	Kyle city, TX	31.2	6	Tamiami CDP, FL	64.4
7	San Antonio city, TX	1,267,984	7	Leander city, TX	30.2	7	Doral city, FL	62.2
8	San Diego city, CA	1,264,263	8	North Port city, FL	29.3	8	West New York town, NJ	59.1
9	Dallas city, TX	1,187,603	9	Lincoln city, CA	29.2	9	Kendall West CDP, FL	58.4
10	San Jose city, CA	898,901	10	Homestead city, FL	28.4	9	Miami city, FL	58.4
11	Detroit city, MI	837,711	11	Goodyear city, AZ	28.2	9	Union City city, NJ	58.4
12	Jacksonville city, FL	797,966	12	Wake Forest town, NC	25.8	12	Rosemead city, CA	56.2
13	Indianapolis city (balance), IN	790,815	12	Lake Elsinore city, CA	25.8	13	Glendale city, CA	54.0
14	San Francisco city, CA	757,604	14	Frisco city, TX	25.5	14	Miami Beach city, FL	53.9
15	Austin city, TX	725,306	15	Plainfield village, IL	25.1	15	Alhambra city, CA	53.7
16	Columbus city, OH	724,095	16	Oswego village, IL	24.6	16	Monterey Park city, CA	53.6
17	Charlotte city, NC	649,578	17	Wentzville city, MO	24.4	17	Rowland Heights CDP, CA	53.5
18	Memphis city, TN	649,443	18	San Jacinto city, CA	24.3	18	Daly City city, CA	53.4
19	Baltimore city, MD	639,493	19	Huntley village, IL	24.1	19	San Gabriel city, CA	53.2
20	Fort Worth city, TX	635,612	20	Surprise city, AZ	23.6	20	The Hammocks CDP, FL	53.1
21	Boston city, MA	600,980	21	Meridian city, ID	22.3	21	Lennox CDP, CA	52.8
22	El Paso city, TX	592,627	22	Canton city, GA	21.6	22	Huntington Park city, CA	52.1
23	Nashville-Davidson (balance), TN	586,214	23	Pflugerville city, TX	21.5	23	El Monte city, CA	51.8
24	Washington, DC	585,267	23	Marana town, AZ	21.5	24	Kendale Lakes CDP, FL	51.6
25	Milwaukee city, WI	584,007	25	Cedar Park city, TX	21.3	25	Bailey's Crossroads CDP, VA	51.5
26	Denver city, CO	576,842	26	Pearland city, TX	21.1	26	Milpitas city, CA	51.3
27	Seattle city, WA	565,809	27	Coachella city, CA	20.7	27	Santa Ana city, CA	51.0
28	Louisville/Jefferson County (balance), KY	560,454	28	Castle Rock town, CO	20.4	28	South Miami Heights CDP, FL	50.9
29	Las Vegas city, NV	558,892	29	Wylie city, TX	20.2	29	South El Monte city, CA	50.6
30	Portland city, OR	541,550	29	North Las Vegas city, NV	20.2	30	North Miami Beach city, FL	50.0
31	Oklahoma City city, OK	540,321	31	Commerce City city, CO	20.0	31	Arcadia city, CA	49.6
32	Tucson city, AZ	520,482	32	Riverton city, UT	19.9	32	Bell Gardens city, CA	49.5
33	Albuquerque city, NM	505,578	32	McKinney city, TX	19.9	33	North Miami city, FL	48.8
34	Mesa city, AZ	478,014	34	Desert Hot Springs city, CA	19.7	34	Spring Valley village, NY	48.7
35	Fresno city, CA	471,722	35	South Jordan city, UT	19.5	35	Richmond West CDP, FL	48.5
36	Long Beach city, CA	463,838	36	Indio city, CA	19.0	36	Maywood city, CA	48.4
37	Sacramento city, CA	446,721	37	Lehi city, UT	18.6	37	Bell city, CA	48.1
38	Atlanta city, GA	439,275	37	Perris city, CA	18.6	38	East Los Angeles CDP, CA	48.0
39	Virginia Beach city, VA	436,903	39	Syracuse city, UT	18.3	39	Cupertino city, CA	47.8
40	Kansas City city, MO	436,562	39	Newnan city, GA	18.3	39	Fort Lee borough, NJ	47.8
41	Cleveland city, OH	405,014	41	Victorville city, CA	17.9	41	Cudahy city, CA	47.6
42	Colorado Springs city, CO	390,397	41	Georgetown city, TX	17.9	42	Baldwin Park city, CA	47.5
43	Tulsa city, OK	384,040	43	Palm Coast city, FL	17.1	43	Union City city, CA	47.2
44	Omaha city, NE	379,851	44	Woodstock city, GA	16.9	44	Elizabeth city, NJ	46.4
45	Oakland city, CA	372,247	45	Huntersville town, NC	16.8	45	South Gate city, CA	46.1
46	Minneapolis city, MN	362,513	46	Rockwall city, TX	16.6	46	Golden Glades CDP, FL	45.9
47	Honolulu CDP, HI	359,694	46	Port St. Lucie city, FL	16.6	47	Passaic city, NJ	45.8
48	Arlington city, TX	356,764	48	Mansfield city, TX	16.3	48	Westminster city, CA	45.5
49	Wichita city, KS	356,564	49	Rio Rancho city, NM	16.0	49	Cicero town, IL	45.4
50	St. Louis city, MO	352,389	50	Delano city, CA	15.8	49	San Luis city, AZ	45.4
51	Miami city, FL	352,064	51	Casa Grande city, AZ	15.5	51	Calexico city, CA	45.3
52	Raleigh city, NC	341,891	52	Fishers town, IN	15.4	52	Lauderdale Lakes city, FL	45.2
53	Anaheim city, CA	336,471	52	Kiryas Joel village, NY	15.4	52	Temple City city, CA	45.2
54	Santa Ana city, CA	333,236	54	Caldwell city, ID	15.2	54	Bergenfield borough, NJ	45.1
55	Tampa city, FL	325,265	55	Cornelius town, NC	15.1	54	Cerritos city, CA	45.1
56	Bakersfield city, CA	312,478	55	Sanger city, CA	15.1	54	Port Chester village, NY	45.1
57	Riverside city, CA	305,568	55	Avondale city, AZ	15.1	57	Walnut city, CA	44.8
58	Cincinnati city, OH	302,471	58	Harker Heights city, TX	15.0	58	Florence-Graham CDP, CA	44.5
59	New Orleans city, LA	301,016	59	Summerville town, SC	14.9	58	Miami Lakes town, FL	44.5
60	Aurora city, CO	296,999	60	Adelanto city, CA	14.4	60	Country Club CDP, FL	44.4
61	Pittsburgh city, PA	296,324	61	Gilbert town, AZ	14.3	60	Golden Gate CDP, FL	44.4
62	Toledo city, OH	289,103	62	Lacey city, WA	13.9	62	The Crossings CDP, FL	44.2
63	Stockton city, CA	288,166	62	Pasco city, WA	13.9	63	Chillum CDP, MD	44.0
64	Corpus Christi city, TX	284,435	64	Prescott Valley town, AZ	13.8	64	Cliffside Park borough, NJ	43.8
65	Anchorage municipality, AK	278,735	64	West Fargo city, ND	13.8	64	Elmont CDP, NY	43.8
66	Lexington-Fayette urban county, KY	275,726	66	La Quinta city, CA	13.7	66	Fremont city, CA	43.4
67	St. Paul city, MN	271,203	67	Buckeye town, AZ	13.6	67	Garden Grove city, CA	43.3
68	Newark city, NJ	265,375	68	Burleson city, TX	13.5	68	Sunnyvale city, CA	43.0
69	Buffalo city, NY	263,030	69	Redmond city, OR	13.3	69	Kearny town, NJ	42.8
70	Plano city, TX	255,591	70	Bentonville city, AR	13.2	70	Kendall CDP, FL	42.7
71	Fort Wayne city, IN	249,830	71	Corinth city, TX	13.1	71	Diamond Bar city, CA	42.6
72	Lincoln city, NE	247,246	72	Rogers city, AR	13.0	72	Miramar city, FL	42.4
73	St. Petersburg city, FL	240,507	72	Cary town, NC	13.0	73	Coachella city, CA	42.3
74	Glendale city, AZ	239,178	74	Issaquah city, WA	12.8	73	Wheaton-Glenmont CDP, MD	42.3
75	Greensboro city, NC	237,423	74	St. Cloud city, FL	12.8	75	San Pablo city, CA	42.2
			74	Cedar City city, UT	12.8			

Table A-1. States — Who: Age, Race/Ethnicity, and Household Structure, 2005–2007

State code	STATE	Total population	Percent change 2005–2007	Race alone or in combination (percent)						Percent Hispanic or Latino	Percent two or more races	Percent White alone, not Hispanic or Latino
				White	Black	American Indian or Alaska Native	Asian	Native Hawaiian or Pacific Islander	Some other race			
	ACS table number:	B01003	Population estimates	B02008	B02009	B02010	B02011	B02012	B02013	C03002	B02001	B01001H
		1	2	3	4	5	6	7	8	9	10	11

Table A-1. States — Who: Age, Race/Ethnicity, and Household Structure, 2005–2007—*Continued*

STATE	Total population	Population by age (percent)								+/- U.S. percent under 18 years	+/- U.S. percent 65 years and over	Percent female
		Under 5 years	5 to 17 years	18 to 24 years	25 to 44 years	45 to 64 years	65 to 84 years	85 years and over			
ACS table number:	B01003	B01001	B01001	B01001	B01001	B01001	B01001	B01001	B01001	B01001	B01001
	12	13	14	15	16	17	18	19	20	21	22

Table A-1. States — Who: Age, Race/Ethnicity, and Household Structure, 2005–2007—*Continued*

STATE	Total population	Median age							
		White alone, not Hispanic or Latino	Black	American Indian or Alaska Native	Asian	Native Hawaiian or Pacific Islander	Some other race	Two or more races	Hispanic or Latino
ACS table number:	B01002	B01002H	B01002B	B01002C	B01002D	B01002E	B01002F	B01002G	B01002I
	23	24	25	26	27	28	29	30	31

Table A-1. States — Who: Age, Race/Ethnicity, and Household Structure, 2005–2007—*Continued*

STATE	Total population 15 years and over	Marital status of population 15 years and over (percent)				Percent foreign born	Languages spoken (percent of households)			
		Never married	Now married	Widowed	Divorced		English only	Spanish, with or without English	Other languages, with or without English	No adult speaks English well
ACS table number:	B12001	B12001	B12001	B12001	B12001	C05002	B16002	B16002	B16002	B16002
	32	33	34	35	36	37	38	39	40	41

Table A-1. States — Who: Age, Race/Ethnicity, and Household Structure, 2005–2007—*Continued*

STATE			Household type (percent)							
			Family households				Nonfamily households			
									One-person household	House-holder not alone
	Total households	Average household size	Total family households	Married-couple families	Male householder families	Female householder families	Total nonfamily households	Total	65 years and over	
ACS table number:	B11001	B25010	B11001	B11001	B11001	B11001	B11001	B11001	C11010	B11001
	42	43	44	45	46	47	48	49	50	51

Table A-1. States — Who: Age, Race/Ethnicity, and Household Structure, 2005–2007—*Continued*

STATE	Households with people under 18 years old				Households with people 60 years and over				
	Total households with children	Household type (percent)			Total households with people 60 years and over	Household type (percent)			
		Married-couple families	Male householder families	Female householder families		Married-couple families	Male householder families	Female householder families	Nonfamily households
ACS table number:	C11005	C11005	C11005	C11005	B11006	B11006	B11006	B11006	B11006
	52	53	54	55	56	57	58	59	60

Table A-2. Counties — Who: Age, Race/Ethnicity, and Household Structure, 2005–2007

STATE County code	STATE County			Population by age (percent)							Race alone or in combination (percent)				
		Total population	Percent change 2005–2007	Under 5 years	5 to 17 years	18 to 24 years	25 to 44 years	45 to 64 years	65 years and over	Median age	White	Black	Asian Hawaiian or Pacific Islander	American Indian, Alaska Native, or some other race	Percent Hispanic or Latino
ACS table number:		B01003	Population estimates	B01001	B01001	B01001	B01001	B01001	B01001	B01002	B02008	B02009	B02011 + B02012	B02010 + B02013	C03002
		1	2	3	4	5	6	7	8	9	10	11	12	13	14

Table A-2. Counties — Who: Age, Race/Ethnicity, and Household Structure, 2005–2007—*Continued*

STATE County			Household type (percent)						Percent of households with people under 18 years	Percent of households with people 60 years and over
			Family households				Nonfamily households			
	Percent foreign born	Total households	Total family households	Married-couple families	Male householder families	Female householder families	Total nonfamily households	One-person households		
ACS table number:	C05002	B11001	B11001	B11001	B11001	B11001	B11001	B11001	C11005	B11006
	15	16	17	18	19	20	21	22	23	24

Table A-3. Metropolitan Areas — Who: Age, Race/Ethnicity, and Household Structure, 2005–2007

Metro area or division code	Area name		Percent change 2005–2007	Population by age (percent)						Median age	Race alone or in combination (percent)				Percent Hispanic or Latino
		Total population		Under 5 years	5 to 17 years	18 to 24 years	25 to 44 years	45 to 64 years	65 years and over		White	Black	Asian Hawaiian or Pacific Islander	Amer. Indian, Alaska Native, or some other race	
ACS table number:		B01003	Population estimates	B01001	B01001	B01001	B01001	B01001	B01001	B01002	B02008	B02009	B02011 + B02012	B02010 + B02013	C03002
		1	2	3	4	5	6	7	8	9	10	11	12	13	14

Table A-3. Metropolitan Areas — Who: Age, Race/Ethnicity, and Household Structure, 2005–2007—*Continued*

Area name	Percent foreign born	Total households	Household type (percent)							Percent of households with people under 18 years	Percent of households with people 60 years and over
			Family households				Nonfamily households				
			Total family households	Married-couple families	Male householder families	Female householder families	Total nonfamily households	One-person households			
ACS table number:	C05002	B11001	B11001	B11001	B11001	B11001	B11001	B11001	C11005	B11006
	15	16	17	18	19	20	21	22	23	24

Table A-4. Cities — Who: Age, Race/Ethnicity, and Household Structure, 2005–2007

STATE Place code	STATE City		Percent change 2005–2007	Population by age (percent)						Median age	Race alone or in combination (percent)				Percent Hispanic or Latino
		Total population		Under 5 years	5 to 17 years	18 to 24 years	25 to 44 years	45 to 64 years	65 years and over		White	Black	Asian Hawaiian or Pacific Islander	Amer. Indian, Alaska Native, or some other race	
	ACS table number:	B01003	Population estimates	B01001	B01001	B01001	B01001	B01001	B01001	B01002	B02008	B02009	B02011 + B02012	B02010 + B02013	C03002
		1	2	3	4	5	6	7	8	9	10	11	12	13	14

Table A-4. Cities — Who: Age, Race/Ethnicity, and Household Structure, 2005–2007—*Continued*

STATE City	Percent foreign born	Total households	Household type (percent)							Percent of households with people under 18 years	Percent of households with people 60 years and over
			Family households				Nonfamily households				
			Total family households	Married-couple families	Male householder families	Female householder families	Total nonfamily households	One-person households			
ACS table number:	C05002	B11001	B11001	B11001	B11001	B11001	B11001	B11001	C11005	B11006
	15	16	17	18	19	20	21	22	23	24

Table A-1. States — Who: Age, Race/Ethnicity, and Household Structure, 2005–2007

State code	STATE	Total population	Percent change 2005–2007	Race alone or in combination (percent)						Percent Hispanic or Latino	Percent two or more races	Percent White alone, not Hispanic or Latino
				White	Black	American Indian or Alaska Native	Asian	Native Hawaiian or Pacific Islander	Some other race			
ACS table number:		B01003	Population estimates	B02008	B02009	B02010	B02011	B02012	B02013	C03002	B02001	B01001H
		1	2	3	4	5	6	7	8	9	10	11
00	United States	298,757,310	1.9	75.9	13.1	1.5	4.9	0.3	6.7	14.7	2.1	66.3
01	Alabama	4,585,900	1.9	71.3	26.7	1.0	1.1	0.1	0.9	2.5	1.1	68.8
02	Alaska	676,778	2.1	75.2	5.0	18.2	6.1	0.9	2.3	5.5	7.2	66.1
04	Arizona	6,152,175	6.5	78.5	4.1	5.2	2.8	0.3	11.7	29.0	2.4	59.6
05	Arkansas	2,805,353	2.3	80.1	16.1	1.5	1.3	0.1	2.5	5.0	1.6	76.3
06	California	36,264,467	1.6	63.1	7.0	1.6	13.4	0.5	17.9	35.7	3.3	43.0
08	Colorado	4,767,161	4.0	85.5	4.6	1.8	3.3	0.2	7.5	19.6	2.6	71.5
09	Connecticut	3,494,851	0.5	81.6	10.4	0.7	3.7	0.1	5.6	11.2	1.9	74.6
10	Delaware	852,689	2.9	74.1	21.3	0.8	3.2	0.1	2.3	6.3	1.6	69.1
11	District of Columbia	585,267	1.1	35.5	56.4	0.7	3.6	0.1	5.3	8.3	1.5	31.4
12	Florida	18,014,927	2.9	77.8	16.0	0.7	2.6	0.1	4.6	20.1	1.7	61.2
13	Georgia	9,331,515	4.8	63.4	30.2	0.6	3.0	0.1	4.1	7.4	1.3	59.0
15	Hawaii	1,276,534	1.2	41.7	3.5	2.2	55.9	22.8	2.5	8.1	21.3	24.5
16	Idaho	1,463,059	5.2	94.1	1.0	2.3	1.6	0.3	3.0	9.5	2.2	86.0
17	Illinois	12,783,049	1.0	72.5	15.4	0.5	4.5	0.1	8.6	14.6	1.5	65.3
18	Indiana	6,301,687	1.4	87.2	9.4	0.8	1.5	0.1	2.7	4.7	1.6	83.7
19	Iowa	2,972,066	1.1	94.1	2.9	0.7	1.8	0.1	1.8	3.8	1.3	90.9
20	Kansas	2,757,827	1.3	87.6	6.7	1.9	2.5	0.1	3.9	8.5	2.5	81.0
21	Kentucky	4,205,648	1.7	90.4	8.1	0.6	1.2	0.1	1.0	2.1	1.2	88.1
22	Louisiana	4,344,053	-4.5	65.0	32.5	1.0	1.6	0.1	1.1	3.0	1.1	62.1
23	Maine	1,314,780	0.4	97.0	1.3	1.6	1.2	0.0	0.5	1.1	1.6	94.8
24	Maryland	5,597,843	0.8	62.6	29.8	0.8	5.4	0.1	3.3	6.0	1.9	58.5
25	Massachusetts	6,437,759	0.3	84.5	6.8	0.6	5.1	0.1	4.7	8.0	1.7	79.4
26	Michigan	10,094,027	-0.4	81.1	14.9	1.3	2.6	0.1	1.9	3.9	1.8	77.6
27	Minnesota	5,155,344	1.6	89.5	5.0	1.6	3.8	0.1	1.8	3.8	1.6	85.9
28	Mississippi	2,906,118	0.6	60.9	37.5	0.8	0.9	0.1	0.8	1.8	0.9	59.2
29	Missouri	5,834,644	1.6	85.6	12.0	1.2	1.7	0.1	1.2	2.9	1.8	82.4
30	Montana	946,815	2.4	91.6	0.9	7.7	1.0	0.2	0.8	2.5	2.1	88.3
31	Nebraska	1,764,131	1.2	90.4	4.8	1.6	1.9	0.2	3.0	7.3	1.7	84.8
32	Nevada	2,488,917	6.5	77.2	8.3	2.0	7.0	0.8	8.1	24.3	3.1	58.9
33	New Hampshire	1,310,254	1.0	96.0	1.4	0.7	2.1	0.0	0.9	2.4	1.0	93.4
34	New Jersey	8,669,815	0.3	70.9	14.3	0.5	7.7	0.1	8.1	15.6	1.5	62.5
35	New Mexico	1,942,847	2.8	71.4	2.7	10.4	1.7	0.1	16.8	44.1	3.1	42.4
36	New York	19,280,753	0.2	67.8	16.5	0.7	7.1	0.1	9.6	16.2	1.7	60.3
37	North Carolina	8,869,861	4.4	71.7	22.1	1.7	2.1	0.1	4.0	6.7	1.5	67.8
38	North Dakota	637,709	0.6	92.3	1.2	5.9	1.2	0.1	0.8	1.6	1.4	90.2
39	Ohio	11,463,403	0.1	85.4	12.6	0.7	1.8	0.1	1.2	2.4	1.5	82.8
40	Oklahoma	3,576,929	2.3	80.6	8.6	11.6	2.1	0.2	3.1	6.9	6.0	72.1
41	Oregon	3,689,498	3.2	89.1	2.4	3.1	4.4	0.4	3.9	10.2	3.1	80.8
42	Pennsylvania	12,400,959	0.5	85.0	11.1	0.4	2.5	0.1	2.2	4.3	1.2	82.0
44	Rhode Island	1,062,065	-0.8	84.5	6.4	1.0	3.0	0.1	7.3	10.9	2.1	79.0
45	South Carolina	4,330,933	3.6	68.3	29.2	0.7	1.4	0.1	1.5	3.6	1.2	65.3
46	South Dakota	788,241	2.1	89.0	1.4	9.4	1.1	0.1	0.9	2.1	1.8	86.5
47	Tennessee	6,073,646	2.8	80.3	17.2	0.8	1.5	0.1	1.5	3.3	1.2	77.4
48	Texas	23,385,340	4.6	72.1	12.0	1.0	3.6	0.1	13.0	35.5	1.8	48.3
49	Utah	2,576,626	5.6	91.1	1.4	1.6	2.5	1.0	4.2	11.1	1.8	82.8
50	Vermont	620,589	0.2	97.6	1.1	1.1	1.3	0.0	0.4	1.3	1.5	95.4
51	Virginia	7,636,644	2.0	72.4	20.5	0.8	5.3	0.1	2.9	6.3	1.9	67.5
53	Washington	6,371,390	3.2	83.8	4.4	2.7	7.8	0.7	4.4	9.1	3.4	76.3
54	West Virginia	1,808,787	0.4	95.5	3.9	0.6	0.8	0.1	0.3	1.0	1.2	93.7
55	Wisconsin	5,571,593	1.1	88.7	6.4	1.3	2.2	0.1	2.7	4.7	1.3	85.6
56	Wyoming	514,044	3.2	93.8	1.3	3.2	1.1	0.1	2.8	7.2	2.3	87.7

STATE	Total population	Population by age (percent)							+/- U.S. percent under 18 years	+/- U.S. percent 65 years and over	Percent female
		Under 5 years	5 to 17 years	18 to 24 years	25 to 44 years	45 to 64 years	65 to 84 years	85 years and over			
ACS table number:	B01003	B01001	B01001	B01001	B01001	B01001	B01001	B01001	B01001	B01001	B01001
	12	13	14	15	16	17	18	19	20	21	22
United States	298,757,310	6.9	17.8	9.9	28.0	25.0	10.8	1.7	0.0	0.0	50.8
Alabama..................................	4,585,900	6.7	17.7	9.9	26.9	25.5	11.8	1.6	-0.3	0.9	51.6
Alaska....................................	676,778	7.3	19.7	11.2	28.8	26.3	6.0	0.7	2.3	-5.8	48.1
Arizona..................................	6,152,175	7.8	18.6	9.4	28.3	23.1	11.3	1.5	1.7	0.3	49.9
Arkansas................................	2,805,353	7.0	17.8	9.5	26.8	25.0	12.1	1.8	0.1	1.4	51.0
California................................	36,264,467	7.3	18.7	10.4	29.5	23.3	9.4	1.4	1.2	-1.7	50.0
Colorado	4,767,161	7.2	17.5	9.7	30.1	25.5	8.8	1.2	0.0	-2.5	49.6
Connecticut	3,494,851	6.1	17.6	9.1	27.0	26.7	11.3	2.2	-1.0	1.0	51.3
Delaware	852,689	6.8	17.1	9.8	27.2	25.7	11.8	1.7	-0.8	0.9	51.5
District of Columbia.................	585,267	6.1	13.4	12.5	32.7	23.4	10.3	1.6	-5.2	-0.6	52.8
Florida	18,014,927	6.3	16.0	8.8	26.7	25.4	14.6	2.3	-2.4	4.4	50.9
Georgia	9,331,515	7.7	18.8	9.8	29.9	24.0	8.6	1.1	1.8	-2.7	50.8
Hawaii....................................	1,276,534	6.4	15.9	9.7	28.2	25.7	12.1	2.0	-2.4	1.5	49.6
Idaho.....................................	1,463,059	7.8	19.4	10.0	26.9	24.2	10.0	1.6	2.6	-0.9	49.8
Illinois	12,783,049	7.0	18.1	10.0	28.4	24.5	10.3	1.7	0.4	-0.5	50.8
Indiana...................................	6,301,687	6.9	18.2	9.7	27.6	25.2	10.8	1.7	0.4	-0.1	50.8
Iowa......................................	2,972,066	6.5	17.4	10.4	25.4	25.6	12.3	2.3	-0.8	2.2	50.7
Kansas...................................	2,757,827	7.1	18.1	10.5	26.5	24.9	10.9	2.0	0.5	0.5	50.5
Kentucky................................	4,205,648	6.6	17.2	9.3	28.1	25.9	11.2	1.6	-0.8	0.3	51.1
Louisiana................................	4,344,053	7.0	18.4	10.9	26.8	24.9	10.6	1.5	0.7	0.5	51.4
Maine.....................................	1,314,780	5.4	16.2	8.7	26.0	29.2	12.7	1.9	-3.2	2.2	51.2
Maryland	5,597,843	6.7	17.7	9.5	28.3	26.1	10.2	1.5	-0.3	-0.9	51.7
Massachusetts	6,437,759	5.9	16.6	9.9	28.2	26.1	11.2	2.1	-2.2	0.8	51.6
Michigan	10,094,027	6.4	18.2	9.7	27.0	26.1	10.9	1.7	-0.1	0.1	50.8
Minnesota	5,155,344	6.7	17.7	9.9	27.8	25.7	10.3	1.9	-0.2	-0.3	50.2
Mississippi..............................	2,906,118	7.4	19.0	10.7	26.3	24.3	10.8	1.5	1.6	-0.1	51.5
Missouri..................................	5,834,644	6.7	17.7	9.7	27.0	25.6	11.5	1.8	-0.3	0.9	51.2
Montana.................................	946,815	6.1	17.1	10.1	24.7	28.2	11.9	1.9	-1.5	1.3	50.0
Nebraska	1,764,131	7.3	18.0	10.6	26.1	24.8	11.2	2.1	0.6	0.8	50.5
Nevada	2,488,917	7.5	18.3	8.3	30.0	24.9	10.1	1.1	1.1	-1.4	49.1
New Hampshire	1,310,254	5.8	17.3	9.1	27.3	28.1	10.7	1.7	-1.6	-0.1	50.7
New Jersey..............................	8,669,815	6.5	17.5	8.7	28.3	26.0	11.2	1.8	-0.7	0.5	51.1
New Mexico............................	1,942,847	7.2	18.4	10.5	26.5	24.9	10.9	1.6	0.9	0.0	50.6
New York................................	19,280,753	6.2	16.9	10.1	28.1	25.5	11.3	1.8	-1.5	0.6	51.5
North Carolina.........................	8,869,861	7.0	17.4	9.6	28.5	25.3	10.7	1.4	-0.3	-0.4	51.1
North Dakota...........................	637,709	6.1	16.4	13.0	24.6	25.4	12.1	2.4	-2.2	2.0	49.7
Ohio......................................	11,463,403	6.5	17.7	9.5	26.8	26.1	11.6	1.8	-0.5	0.9	51.3
Oklahoma...............................	3,576,929	7.1	17.8	10.5	26.5	24.9	11.6	1.6	0.2	0.7	50.6
Oregon...................................	3,689,498	6.3	17.0	9.1	27.8	26.9	11.1	1.9	-1.5	0.4	50.4
Pennsylvania	12,400,959	5.9	16.7	9.6	25.9	26.7	13.0	2.2	-2.1	2.7	51.4
Rhode Island	1,062,065	5.8	16.5	10.7	27.3	25.9	11.7	2.1	-2.4	1.4	51.7
South Carolina.........................	4,330,933	6.7	17.5	9.9	27.2	25.8	11.4	1.4	-0.5	0.3	51.3
South Dakota...........................	788,241	7.0	17.8	10.6	25.1	25.4	11.9	2.3	0.1	1.7	50.1
Tennessee	6,073,646	6.7	17.4	9.1	28.3	25.9	11.2	1.5	-0.6	0.2	51.2
Texas.....................................	23,385,340	8.3	19.4	10.3	29.2	22.7	8.8	1.2	3.0	-2.5	50.2
Utah	2,576,626	9.7	21.3	12.8	28.2	19.4	7.6	1.1	6.2	-3.8	49.6
Vermont	620,589	5.2	16.4	9.9	25.7	29.4	11.7	1.6	-3.1	0.8	50.9
Virginia	7,636,644	6.7	17.2	10.0	28.8	25.7	10.2	1.4	-0.8	-0.9	51.0
Washington	6,371,390	6.5	17.5	9.4	28.7	26.4	10.0	1.6	-0.8	-0.9	50.2
West Virginia	1,808,787	5.8	15.7	9.0	26.2	27.9	13.4	2.0	-3.2	2.9	51.1
Wisconsin	5,571,593	6.4	17.4	9.9	27.1	26.1	11.2	1.9	-0.9	0.6	50.3
Wyoming................................	514,044	6.6	17.4	10.5	25.5	27.8	10.7	1.4	-0.7	-0.3	49.4

Table A-1. States — Who: Age, Race/Ethnicity, and Household Structure, 2005–2007—*Continued*

STATE / ACS table number:	Total population B01002	White alone, not Hispanic or Latino B01002H	Black B01002B	American Indian or Alaska Native B01002C	Asian B01002D	Native Hawaiian or Pacific Islander B01002E	Some other race B01002F	Two or more races B01002G	Hispanic or Latino B01002I
	23	24	25	26	27	28	29	30	31
United States	36.4	40.6	31.3	31.5	35.3	30.2	27.4	18.7	27.3
Alabama	37.1	40.2	31.1	37.1	33.2	22.9	25.2	22.7	24.9
Alaska	33.4	36.8	27.2	29.1	37.0	26.8	27.2	17.0	24.8
Arizona	34.8	42.4	29.6	26.5	33.9	31.1	26.5	16.4	25.6
Arkansas	36.8	40.1	29.4	32.7	31.3	25.9	23.3	19.1	23.8
California	34.5	42.5	32.9	35.2	36.9	32.4	27.3	18.7	26.6
Colorado	35.5	39.1	31.1	33.7	33.8	31.0	28.2	17.7	27.1
Connecticut	38.9	42.3	31.3	34.7	33.4	29.1	28.0	17.6	27.7
Delaware	37.6	41.6	32.2	38.7	33.4	-	26.6	14.7	25.5
District of Columbia	35.0	34.4	37.1	46.1	31.7	-	30.0	25.7	30.3
Florida	39.8	45.1	29.8	39.5	35.7	30.3	28.6	22.0	33.3
Georgia	34.6	38.4	30.7	36.9	33.7	24.1	25.9	18.0	25.9
Hawaii	37.7	40.4	26.8	37.8	46.2	31.4	30.9	23.7	25.1
Idaho	34.2	36.4	20.4	32.1	32.6	31.8	27.4	17.8	23.7
Illinois	35.7	40.2	31.0	37.8	34.3	27.6	26.8	16.7	26.5
Indiana	36.3	38.3	30.4	39.6	31.5	29.5	26.2	17.0	25.9
Iowa	37.9	39.6	26.4	29.3	29.9	32.8	25.0	14.7	24.0
Kansas	36.1	38.9	29.6	31.2	31.9	27.7	27.2	17.4	25.4
Kentucky	37.3	38.5	31.4	38.5	33.1	31.3	23.6	15.8	25.3
Louisiana	35.5	38.9	29.4	36.2	32.6	38.1	29.1	19.8	30.4
Maine	41.1	41.9	19.6	33.8	28.2	-	25.6	23.0	25.8
Maryland	37.2	40.9	33.7	39.2	35.9	32.4	27.5	18.5	28.1
Massachusetts	38.3	41.0	30.4	36.7	32.3	24.4	27.8	19.5	26.9
Michigan	37.3	39.7	31.5	34.6	32.3	27.9	27.1	18.1	25.9
Minnesota	36.9	39.4	26.2	30.4	28.5	35.5	26.6	15.2	25.1
Mississippi	35.1	39.6	29.0	28.8	31.5	23.8	24.5	19.2	25.4
Missouri	37.3	39.2	30.9	36.9	32.7	23.2	26.4	18.9	25.6
Montana	39.3	41.3	19.0	26.2	26.2	23.6	28.0	21.3	24.4
Nebraska	36.0	38.7	27.9	25.0	31.3	24.0	26.2	16.0	24.6
Nevada	35.6	41.7	31.4	33.3	38.6	31.5	26.9	16.9	26.2
New Hampshire	39.3	40.3	24.8	35.6	32.4	33.3	27.4	16.0	26.3
New Jersey	38.2	42.3	33.0	33.8	35.4	30.0	29.1	20.7	30.4
New Mexico	35.6	44.6	28.0	28.0	35.0	-	30.4	19.3	29.7
New York	37.4	41.3	33.0	36.0	35.4	32.3	30.0	21.5	30.4
North Carolina	36.6	40.1	32.8	33.2	32.7	25.3	25.6	17.1	25.6
North Dakota	37.0	39.1	21.8	24.7	28.0	24.6	22.9	14.4	22.8
Ohio	37.6	39.4	31.6	37.8	32.9	27.0	27.0	16.2	26.2
Oklahoma	36.0	40.1	29.1	29.5	31.7	29.3	26.0	23.9	24.5
Oregon	37.6	41.1	30.0	30.5	34.2	28.6	26.2	20.3	25.2
Pennsylvania	39.5	41.8	31.9	39.0	32.7	28.6	25.9	16.0	25.8
Rhode Island	38.3	41.5	28.7	29.8	29.6	29.0	26.2	19.7	25.9
South Carolina	37.0	40.3	32.2	37.5	34.3	35.0	25.8	16.4	26.0
South Dakota	37.1	39.9	22.7	23.2	27.4	-	26.1	15.9	23.7
Tennessee	37.2	39.7	30.6	38.7	33.8	28.2	25.4	17.3	25.4
Texas	33.1	39.8	30.7	34.6	33.7	27.2	27.3	18.9	26.9
Utah	28.3	29.2	22.3	25.7	31.8	25.0	25.3	13.7	24.8
Vermont	40.4	41.0	20.9	41.0	29.9	27.6	29.1	21.1	28.4
Virginia	36.8	39.8	33.2	36.7	34.9	27.6	27.0	17.3	27.3
Washington	36.8	40.2	30.5	30.4	35.3	29.8	25.6	18.7	24.5
West Virginia	40.3	40.9	35.7	42.7	36.1	18.5	24.4	18.0	25.5
Wisconsin	37.7	40.2	27.1	31.6	26.8	26.0	25.8	15.8	25.2
Wyoming	37.3	39.2	24.6	26.4	29.7	-	30.0	18.3	26.7

	Total population 15 years and over	Marital status of population 15 years and over (percent)				Percent foreign born	Languages spoken (percent of households)			
		Never married	Now married	Widowed	Divorced		English only	Spanish, with or without English	Other languages, with or without English	No adult speaks English well
STATE										
ACS table number:	B12001	B12001	B12001	B12001	B12001	C05002	B16002	B16002	B16002	B16002
	32	33	34	35	36	37	38	39	40	41
United States	237,984,051	30.4	52.7	6.4	10.5	12.5	80.4	11.2	8.4	4.8
Alabama...............................	3,664,025	26.8	54.0	7.5	11.7	2.9	94.8	2.8	2.4	1.0
Alaska.................................	527,857	32.4	52.3	3.6	11.8	6.7	82.1	4.3	13.6	2.6
Arizona...............................	4,793,083	30.0	52.1	5.8	12.1	15.0	72.9	19.9	7.3	6.8
Arkansas.............................	2,228,889	24.4	55.9	7.5	12.2	3.9	93.5	4.3	2.2	1.5
California............................	28,500,813	34.1	50.9	5.4	9.6	27.2	59.8	24.4	15.7	10.7
Colorado	3,788,497	29.3	54.2	4.7	11.8	10.1	81.8	12.0	6.1	4.2
Connecticut........................	2,818,404	30.8	52.9	6.6	9.7	12.6	78.0	9.5	12.5	5.0
Delaware	684,434	30.5	52.3	6.7	10.5	7.6	86.8	6.2	7.0	2.4
District of Columbia	490,250	54.0	30.0	6.5	9.4	12.7	82.9	7.7	9.4	3.0
Florida	14,710,306	27.5	52.9	7.5	12.2	18.7	74.1	18.0	7.9	7.2
Georgia	7,272,856	31.1	51.7	5.9	11.3	9.0	88.0	6.6	5.4	3.2
Hawaii	1,042,119	31.5	52.8	6.3	9.4	16.9	69.1	2.9	28.0	5.9
Idaho.................................	1,132,127	24.2	58.9	5.3	11.6	5.6	88.2	8.0	3.8	2.4
Illinois	10,129,259	32.4	51.8	6.4	9.3	13.7	78.8	10.9	10.3	5.5
Indiana	4,993,573	27.4	54.4	6.4	11.8	4.1	91.3	4.7	4.0	1.8
Iowa	2,388,847	26.8	56.5	6.8	9.9	3.8	92.6	3.9	3.5	1.5
Kansas................................	2,184,649	26.3	56.4	6.4	10.9	6.0	89.3	6.4	4.3	2.5
Kentucky............................	3,375,926	25.7	54.7	7.2	12.3	2.7	94.8	2.6	2.6	1.0
Louisiana............................	3,435,720	32.0	49.5	7.5	11.0	3.1	87.6	3.6	8.8	1.7
Maine.................................	1,087,583	26.4	54.4	6.7	12.5	3.2	89.1	1.4	9.5	1.2
Maryland	4,478,066	32.5	51.9	6.2	9.5	12.1	83.7	5.9	10.4	3.1
Massachusetts	5,255,659	34.5	50.0	6.5	9.0	14.2	77.7	7.1	15.1	5.6
Michigan	8,067,620	30.7	52.0	6.3	11.0	6.0	89.5	3.6	6.9	1.9
Minnesota	4,120,980	30.1	55.0	5.6	9.3	6.5	89.4	3.9	6.7	2.1
Mississippi	2,273,913	30.8	50.8	7.7	10.7	1.7	95.7	2.4	1.9	0.7
Missouri..............................	4,665,795	27.7	53.9	6.8	11.6	3.5	93.0	3.2	3.8	1.2
Montana.............................	769,225	27.2	54.4	6.2	12.2	1.9	93.4	2.4	4.2	0.4
Nebraska............................	1,396,158	27.7	56.2	6.5	9.7	5.6	90.2	5.9	3.9	2.5
Nevada...............................	1,950,254	28.3	52.7	5.5	13.4	18.5	73.5	16.9	9.7	7.0
New Hampshire	1,066,026	27.9	55.0	5.8	11.3	5.4	88.3	2.7	9.0	1.4
New Jersey..........................	6,957,696	31.4	53.6	6.9	8.1	19.7	71.2	13.3	15.5	7.1
New Mexico.........................	1,533,059	31.3	50.5	6.0	12.2	9.4	59.9	32.2	7.9	6.4
New York............................	15,629,723	35.7	49.2	6.8	8.4	21.6	70.7	13.6	15.7	8.2
North Carolina	7,069,945	28.3	55.1	6.6	10.1	6.8	90.1	6.0	3.8	2.7
North Dakota.......................	521,038	29.9	54.9	6.9	8.3	2.3	91.9	1.9	6.2	1.0
Ohio	9,185,985	29.2	52.4	6.9	11.5	3.6	92.2	2.8	5.0	1.3
Oklahoma...........................	2,840,872	25.5	54.7	7.0	12.7	4.9	90.8	5.4	3.8	2.1
Oregon...............................	2,906,644	28.2	53.3	5.8	12.7	9.7	85.7	7.8	6.6	3.5
Pennsylvania	10,123,094	30.6	52.7	7.7	8.9	5.2	89.2	4.1	6.7	2.0
Rhode Island	868,986	33.6	49.0	7.0	10.4	12.6	78.0	9.3	12.7	5.5
South Carolina.....................	3,468,817	29.8	53.1	7.2	9.9	4.2	93.0	3.9	3.0	1.6
South Dakota.......................	627,309	28.5	55.1	6.7	9.8	2.1	91.9	2.4	5.7	1.1
Tennessee...........................	4,866,479	26.6	53.9	7.0	12.6	4.0	93.6	3.4	3.0	1.4
Texas..................................	17,950,511	29.4	54.4	5.6	10.6	15.8	66.2	28.3	5.5	8.6
Utah	1,903,305	28.9	58.3	3.9	8.9	8.0	82.8	10.1	7.1	3.5
Vermont	513,999	29.4	52.2	6.0	12.4	3.7	92.3	1.5	6.3	0.8
Virginia	6,131,514	29.7	54.6	6.1	9.6	10.1	86.1	5.8	8.1	2.8
Washington	5,119,583	29.0	53.4	5.3	12.3	12.2	82.8	6.9	10.3	4.2
West Virginia	1,490,866	24.7	55.6	8.2	11.6	1.3	96.5	1.5	1.9	0.3
Wisconsin............................	4,488,815	29.8	54.2	6.1	9.9	4.3	90.6	4.6	4.8	1.6
Wyoming.............................	412,898	25.2	56.3	5.7	12.9	2.7	91.3	5.2	3.5	0.8

Table A-1. States — Who: Age, Race/Ethnicity, and Household Structure, 2005–2007—Continued

			Household type (percent)							
			Family households				Nonfamily households			
								One-person household		
STATE	Total households	Average household size	Total family households	Married-couple families	Male householder families	Female householder families	Total nonfamily households	Total	65 years and over	Householder not alone
ACS table number:	B11001	B25010	B11001	B11001	B11001	B11001	B11001	B11001	C11010	B11001
	42	43	44	45	46	47	48	49	50	51
United States	111,609,629	2.60	66.9	49.8	4.6	12.5	33.1	27.3	9.2	5.9
Alabama	1,798,304	2.48	68.4	49.7	4.2	14.5	31.6	27.5	9.9	4.1
Alaska	233,861	2.80	68.3	51.1	5.7	11.6	31.7	24.5	4.5	7.2
Arizona	2,215,761	2.73	66.3	49.5	5.0	11.8	33.7	26.8	8.7	6.9
Arkansas	1,096,622	2.49	68.4	51.3	4.3	12.7	31.6	27.2	10.0	4.5
California	12,140,888	2.92	68.3	49.8	5.8	12.8	31.7	24.7	8.0	7.0
Colorado	1,838,303	2.53	64.5	50.3	4.4	9.7	35.5	28.3	7.3	7.2
Connecticut	1,323,431	2.55	67.3	51.2	4.0	12.1	32.7	27.1	10.2	5.6
Delaware	321,748	2.57	67.7	49.9	4.7	13.2	32.3	26.2	9.2	6.1
District of Columbia	249,805	2.20	42.9	21.7	3.8	17.5	57.1	47.9	10.5	9.2
Florida	7,077,123	2.49	65.3	48.4	4.6	12.3	34.7	27.9	10.8	6.8
Georgia	3,364,749	2.69	68.2	49.0	4.6	14.7	31.8	26.4	7.1	5.4
Hawaii	433,664	2.86	70.0	52.1	5.3	12.6	30.0	23.5	7.5	6.4
Idaho	545,171	2.62	70.1	57.0	4.1	9.0	29.9	23.7	7.8	6.2
Illinois	4,724,462	2.64	66.8	49.9	4.4	12.5	33.2	27.9	9.5	5.3
Indiana	2,447,887	2.50	67.5	51.6	4.4	11.5	32.5	27.0	9.3	5.5
Iowa	1,206,848	2.38	65.5	52.8	3.5	9.2	34.5	28.3	10.8	6.2
Kansas	1,083,868	2.47	66.8	52.8	3.9	10.1	33.2	27.9	9.6	5.3
Kentucky	1,654,119	2.47	67.3	50.8	4.2	12.3	32.7	28.0	9.7	4.6
Louisiana	1,605,203	2.63	67.9	46.8	4.7	16.5	32.1	27.2	9.2	4.9
Maine	542,424	2.35	65.3	51.2	4.3	9.8	34.7	27.4	10.6	7.2
Maryland	2,082,573	2.62	67.0	48.7	4.6	13.8	33.0	27.0	8.4	6.0
Massachusetts	2,448,608	2.54	64.0	47.9	4.1	12.0	36.0	29.0	10.3	7.1
Michigan	3,864,307	2.55	66.8	50.2	4.3	12.3	33.2	27.9	9.5	5.3
Minnesota	2,041,466	2.46	65.4	52.3	4.0	9.2	34.6	27.9	9.0	6.7
Mississippi	1,079,584	2.60	69.8	46.9	4.7	18.2	30.2	26.3	9.5	3.9
Missouri	2,300,211	2.46	66.1	50.0	4.1	11.9	33.9	28.4	9.8	5.5
Montana	369,329	2.49	64.7	52.6	3.7	8.4	35.3	28.7	10.1	6.6
Nebraska	698,163	2.45	65.9	52.8	3.7	9.5	34.1	28.4	10.0	5.7
Nevada	932,715	2.63	65.5	47.9	6.0	11.6	34.5	26.7	7.4	7.8
New Hampshire	500,671	2.54	67.7	54.3	4.0	9.3	32.3	24.8	8.6	7.5
New Jersey	3,143,408	2.70	69.5	52.2	4.6	12.7	30.5	25.7	9.7	4.8
New Mexico	728,508	2.61	65.9	47.3	5.4	13.2	34.1	28.0	9.1	6.0
New York	7,096,035	2.63	64.7	45.2	4.9	14.6	35.3	29.4	10.4	5.9
North Carolina	3,471,751	2.48	66.9	49.5	4.3	13.0	33.1	27.7	8.7	5.4
North Dakota	271,131	2.25	61.9	51.0	3.5	7.4	38.1	31.0	10.6	7.1
Ohio	4,500,621	2.48	65.9	49.2	4.2	12.5	34.1	28.9	10.1	5.3
Oklahoma	1,386,849	2.50	67.1	50.6	4.4	12.0	32.9	28.0	10.0	4.9
Oregon	1,447,409	2.49	64.0	49.8	4.1	10.0	36.0	28.1	9.1	7.9
Pennsylvania	4,858,509	2.46	65.8	49.9	4.2	11.7	34.2	28.9	11.4	5.3
Rhode Island	404,549	2.53	63.9	47.1	4.1	12.7	36.1	29.5	10.6	6.6
South Carolina	1,664,561	2.52	67.7	48.5	4.2	15.1	32.3	27.3	9.0	5.0
South Dakota	311,644	2.43	65.7	52.7	3.8	9.3	34.3	28.6	10.5	5.7
Tennessee	2,382,975	2.48	67.4	49.8	4.5	13.1	32.6	27.7	9.1	5.0
Texas	8,095,025	2.82	70.2	51.7	4.9	13.5	29.8	24.8	7.2	5.0
Utah	812,604	3.12	75.5	62.2	4.0	9.2	24.5	19.3	6.0	5.2
Vermont	250,871	2.39	64.0	49.5	4.5	10.1	36.0	27.9	9.8	8.1
Virginia	2,909,223	2.54	67.0	50.8	4.1	12.1	33.0	27.3	8.4	5.7
Washington	2,472,477	2.52	64.5	49.9	4.4	10.2	35.5	28.1	8.3	7.4
West Virginia	738,943	2.39	67.2	52.1	4.1	10.9	32.8	28.0	11.4	4.9
Wisconsin	2,235,246	2.42	65.2	51.3	4.2	9.7	34.8	28.3	9.6	6.6
Wyoming	205,422	2.43	65.6	52.6	4.8	8.2	34.4	27.8	8.7	6.5

STATE	Households with people under 18 years old				Households with people 60 years and over				
	Total households with children	Household type (percent			Total households with people 60 years and over	Household type (percent)			
		Married-couple families	Male householder families	Female householder families		Married-couple families	Male householder families	Female householder families	Nonfamily households
ACS table number:	C11005	C11005	C11005	C11005	B11006	B11006	B11006	B11006	B11006
	52	53	54	55	56	57	58	59	60
United States	38,635,678	66.5	7.6	24.9	34,542,072	48.2	3.3	8.8	39.7
Alabama	617,576	62.7	6.9	29.6	584,119	47.0	3.2	10.2	39.6
Alaska	91,608	66.0	9.7	22.9	50,523	52.5	4.3	8.5	34.7
Arizona	757,904	65.1	9.3	24.6	713,044	52.1	2.9	7.4	37.5
Arkansas	374,127	64.5	7.7	26.6	362,540	49.9	2.8	7.9	39.4
California	4,673,148	68.2	8.7	22.3	3,627,937	47.5	4.6	10.4	37.6
Colorado	623,413	69.9	8.2	20.9	465,321	50.6	2.8	6.2	40.4
Connecticut	455,229	69.7	6.0	23.5	433,939	47.4	3.2	8.1	41.3
Delaware	109,438	63.4	8.3	27.0	105,355	49.9	2.9	8.0	39.1
District of Columbia	54,072	37.0	8.2	53.7	70,427	25.7	5.0	16.2	53.1
Florida	2,155,851	63.2	8.2	27.3	2,655,936	50.4	3.1	7.9	38.6
Georgia	1,255,958	64.0	6.9	28.2	891,964	48.1	3.5	10.9	37.5
Hawaii	153,242	70.0	7.3	21.8	159,542	51.8	5.7	13.3	29.2
Idaho	201,294	73.1	7.7	18.1	157,224	55.5	2.1	5.6	36.7
Illinois	1,667,015	68.2	6.9	24.1	1,420,586	46.2	3.6	9.5	40.8
Indiana	845,194	66.5	8.2	23.9	722,930	49.1	2.7	7.4	40.8
Iowa	382,230	70.5	7.2	21.1	379,622	50.7	1.9	4.9	42.6
Kansas	371,792	69.9	7.4	21.6	320,260	50.1	2.0	6.1	41.8
Kentucky	556,263	66.3	7.1	25.5	513,173	47.2	3.1	8.3	41.4
Louisiana	575,195	59.5	7.1	32.4	497,492	45.0	4.0	11.6	39.4
Maine	164,998	65.9	9.4	22.9	180,255	49.7	2.2	5.6	42.4
Maryland	738,777	65.3	7.4	26.3	627,282	47.6	3.6	10.4	38.4
Massachusetts	795,080	68.8	6.4	24.0	786,753	44.9	3.6	8.7	42.8
Michigan	1,299,543	66.3	7.4	25.2	1,189,046	48.0	3.0	8.2	40.8
Minnesota	679,725	71.2	7.7	20.0	570,643	50.4	2.3	5.0	42.3
Mississippi	404,283	56.7	7.3	34.9	344,109	44.9	3.4	12.8	38.9
Missouri	766,091	65.8	7.5	25.5	718,089	48.6	2.8	7.5	41.2
Montana	110,080	70.2	8.1	20.7	119,564	51.3	2.3	4.7	41.8
Nebraska	234,166	71.6	6.6	20.9	206,201	50.1	2.1	5.2	42.6
Nevada	320,689	64.4	10.6	23.7	278,800	48.7	4.3	8.8	38.3
New Hampshire	168,143	72.1	7.4	19.3	150,918	52.5	2.7	5.6	39.2
New Jersey	1,145,923	70.8	6.5	21.9	1,043,773	47.5	4.0	9.9	38.6
New Mexico	253,883	61.0	10.0	27.7	227,302	48.2	3.4	9.1	39.3
New York	2,370,249	63.6	7.4	28.2	2,357,472	43.1	4.1	11.2	41.6
North Carolina	1,180,307	64.3	7.3	27.3	1,034,919	49.1	3.0	8.8	39.1
North Dakota	79,857	73.4	6.5	18.7	81,145	49.4	2.5	4.2	43.8
Ohio	1,488,887	64.6	7.6	26.6	1,411,865	47.1	2.9	8.0	42.0
Oklahoma	470,716	65.2	8.0	25.7	439,126	49.0	2.7	7.5	40.8
Oregon	455,068	67.7	8.4	22.6	445,724	50.3	2.3	6.5	40.9
Pennsylvania	1,518,769	67.3	7.3	24.2	1,683,290	46.5	3.2	8.5	41.9
Rhode Island	128,102	65.1	6.3	27.8	132,977	45.7	3.1	8.1	43.0
South Carolina	560,674	60.9	7.0	31.3	531,772	48.3	3.0	10.6	38.2
South Dakota	98,806	68.9	8.0	21.8	96,164	51.5	2.2	5.0	41.4
Tennessee	805,576	63.9	7.8	27.2	737,104	48.0	3.3	9.0	39.7
Texas	3,227,311	67.1	7.3	24.7	2,186,897	50.3	3.7	10.2	35.8
Utah	350,840	78.9	5.7	14.7	204,375	58.3	2.7	7.6	31.4
Vermont	77,775	65.9	9.5	23.3	79,367	48.6	2.5	6.0	42.9
Virginia	994,348	67.9	6.9	24.4	854,124	49.2	3.1	9.2	38.5
Washington	819,545	68.1	8.4	22.3	709,090	50.1	2.8	6.3	40.9
West Virginia	223,650	68.8	7.4	22.5	261,327	47.7	2.9	8.3	41.0
Wisconsin	719,316	68.7	8.2	21.9	660,272	50.0	2.4	5.5	42.1
Wyoming	63,952	68.5	10.5	19.9	60,393	52.1	2.2	4.7	41.0

Table A-2. Counties — Who: Age, Race/Ethnicity, and Household Structure, 2005–2007

STATE County code	STATE County	Total population	Percent change 2005–2007	Population by age (percent)						Median age	Race alone or in combination (percent)				Percent Hispanic or Latino
				Under 5 years	5 to 17 years	18 to 24 years	25 to 44 years	45 to 64 years	65 years and over		White	Black	Asian Hawaiian or Pacific Islander	Amer. Indian, Alaska Native, or some other race	
	ACS table number:	B01003	Population estimates	B01001	B01001	B01001	B01001	B01001	B01001	B01002	B02008	B02009	B02011 + B02012	B02010 + B02013	C03002
		1	2	3	4	5	6	7	8	9	10	11	12	13	14
00 000	**United States**	298,757,310	1.9	6.9	17.8	9.9	28.0	25.0	12.5	36.4	75.9	13.1	5.1	8.1	14.7
01 000	**Alabama**	4,585,900	1.9	6.7	17.7	9.9	26.9	25.5	13.4	37.1	71.3	26.7	1.2	1.9	2.5
01 001	Autauga	48,995	4.3	6.9	20.0	8.7	28.5	25.0	10.9	35.9	80.4	18.0	1.1	2.0	1.8
01 003	Baldwin	167,421	5.9	6.3	17.2	8.3	26.3	25.5	16.4	39.5	87.5	10.4	0.6	2.3	2.5
01 005	Barbour	28,123	-1.3	6.1	17.1	9.0	29.6	25.2	13.0	37.2	51.2	47.7	-	1.5	-
01 007	Bibb	21,424	0.6	6.3	17.8	9.5	30.9	23.3	12.1	35.9	77.1	22.6	-	0.5	-
01 009	Blount	55,803	3.0	7.0	17.7	8.0	28.2	25.5	13.5	37.1	96.6	1.8	-	2.2	6.6
01 013	Butler	20,241	-1.0	6.7	17.8	9.7	23.4	26.4	16.1	39.5	57.8	42.2	-	0.7	-
01 015	Calhoun	112,620	0.9	6.5	16.7	10.4	25.6	26.3	14.4	38.2	78.2	20.1	1.0	2.0	2.2
01 017	Chambers	34,916	-1.1	6.2	17.6	7.5	26.2	26.5	16.0	39.2	62.3	38.2	-	0.5	-
01 019	Cherokee	24,451	1.2	5.3	16.2	6.8	26.2	28.9	16.6	41.0	92.6	6.1	-	0.7	-
01 021	Chilton	41,844	2.0	6.6	18.2	8.2	29.4	24.8	12.9	36.2	87.8	10.8	0.4	2.1	4.0
01 025	Clarke	26,662	-0.9	6.5	19.3	10.4	23.5	25.5	14.8	37.7	54.8	44.6	-	-	-
01 031	Coffee	45,881	3.6	6.5	17.4	8.5	27.1	26.0	14.5	37.5	79.3	18.7	1.5	1.9	3.7
01 033	Colbert	54,505	0.3	5.5	16.7	8.7	25.4	27.4	16.2	41.1	82.7	16.8	0.4	1.0	1.4
01 039	Covington	36,815	1.1	6.2	16.3	8.5	25.6	25.2	18.3	40.6	85.6	12.7	-	2.3	1.1
01 043	Cullman	79,904	1.5	6.3	16.9	8.5	27.7	25.4	15.2	38.1	96.9	1.7	0.4	2.1	3.4
01 045	Dale	48,158	-0.3	7.7	19.1	8.9	26.4	25.1	12.8	36.3	76.2	21.6	1.8	2.4	3.8
01 047	Dallas	43,258	-0.8	7.9	19.3	9.9	22.9	25.6	14.4	37.1	32.2	67.3	0.4	0.3	-
01 049	DeKalb	67,346	1.9	7.2	17.6	7.9	28.1	25.4	13.9	37.0	94.7	1.8	0.4	4.0	9.3
01 051	Elmore	75,436	5.8	6.8	18.2	9.9	29.8	24.4	11.0	35.4	75.9	22.1	0.7	2.1	1.6
01 053	Escambia	37,617	-0.2	6.6	16.5	9.3	27.3	26.0	14.3	38.2	64.3	31.9	-	5.1	1.3
01 055	Etowah	102,885	0.7	6.3	16.9	8.3	26.4	26.3	15.8	39.0	83.7	15.1	0.6	1.6	2.6
01 059	Franklin	30,531	-0.3	7.1	17.0	8.9	27.4	23.8	15.8	38.2	87.0	5.1	0.1	8.3	-
01 061	Geneva	25,687	0.4	6.1	16.2	8.0	25.5	26.9	17.3	41.7	88.1	10.8	-	2.4	-
01 069	Houston	95,366	3.8	7.0	18.2	8.1	26.3	25.9	14.4	38.1	72.2	25.8	0.9	1.8	1.7
01 071	Jackson	53,020	0.1	5.9	16.8	7.5	26.9	27.8	15.0	40.4	95.6	3.1	1.4	3.7	1.6
01 073	Jefferson	659,065	0.0	6.9	17.3	9.4	26.8	26.3	13.3	37.7	56.6	41.3	1.5	1.4	2.7
01 077	Lauderdale	88,029	1.2	5.5	15.7	11.3	25.1	26.2	16.1	39.2	89.1	10.6	0.6	1.3	1.4
01 079	Lawrence	34,160	-0.3	5.7	17.4	8.1	29.3	26.6	12.9	38.7	83.3	13.0	-	8.0	1.5
01 081	Lee	127,940	4.2	6.0	16.6	21.8	26.7	20.4	8.5	28.5	74.3	23.4	2.1	1.4	1.8
01 083	Limestone	71,833	5.8	6.2	17.7	8.9	29.7	25.6	11.9	37.3	83.6	13.5	0.8	3.1	3.7
01 087	Macon	22,549	-1.8	5.2	16.9	18.9	20.8	23.4	14.9	34.1	16.3	82.9	-	1.3	-
01 089	Madison	306,224	4.4	6.3	18.2	10.0	27.5	25.8	12.1	37.4	72.3	24.6	2.8	2.3	2.6
01 091	Marengo	21,326	-0.6	6.7	19.4	9.3	23.5	26.2	14.8	38.9	46.8	53.1	-	0.5	-
01 093	Marion	29,585	0.2	5.8	15.4	7.5	27.2	26.7	17.5	40.9	94.8	3.6	0.7	2.1	1.6
01 095	Marshall	86,372	3.0	8.1	17.5	7.4	28.3	24.5	14.2	37.0	95.4	2.0	0.6	2.9	9.2
01 097	Mobile	401,616	1.5	7.3	19.2	9.5	26.3	25.4	12.3	35.8	62.6	34.7	2.1	1.7	1.6
01 099	Monroe	22,991	-1.9	6.5	19.6	9.7	23.5	26.6	14.1	38.2	58.0	41.0	-	1.6	-
01 101	Montgomery	224,542	1.6	7.5	18.5	11.6	26.1	24.5	11.8	34.7	45.1	53.2	1.6	1.2	1.7
01 103	Morgan	113,988	2.0	6.7	17.5	8.1	27.5	26.6	13.7	38.9	84.6	12.4	0.8	4.1	5.2
01 109	Pike	29,881	0.7	6.6	16.5	16.5	25.2	22.5	12.6	32.6	61.1	36.9	1.1	2.0	1.6
01 111	Randolph	22,466	-0.3	6.0	18.0	9.4	25.0	25.2	16.5	38.8	77.3	22.7	-	1.7	-
01 113	Russell	49,634	2.3	6.7	18.9	8.0	27.2	25.4	13.8	38.0	56.6	42.3	0.9	2.1	2.2
01 115	St. Clair	75,011	8.4	6.5	17.7	8.5	29.9	25.4	12.0	36.6	90.3	9.4	-	1.2	1.4
01 117	Shelby	176,636	6.8	7.8	18.9	8.7	29.8	25.9	8.8	35.3	87.2	10.0	1.6	1.9	3.4
01 121	Talladega	80,113	0.4	6.4	17.3	8.7	27.5	26.5	13.6	37.6	66.8	31.8	0.4	1.6	1.3
01 123	Tallapoosa	40,637	0.8	5.8	17.0	7.7	24.9	27.4	17.3	41.2	73.3	25.9	0.7	1.3	0.9
01 125	Tuscaloosa	174,823	4.1	6.5	16.5	15.8	27.2	23.1	10.9	32.2	67.3	30.7	1.6	1.4	1.7
01 127	Walker	69,051	-0.6	6.2	16.6	7.7	27.3	26.7	15.5	39.0	93.2	6.8	0.4	1.0	1.3
01 133	Winston	24,261	0.0	5.7	16.6	8.1	27.0	27.1	15.5	41.4	98.3	-	0.8	2.5	-
02 000	**Alaska**	676,778	2.1	7.3	19.7	11.2	28.8	26.3	6.7	33.4	75.2	5.0	7.0	20.5	5.5
02 020	Anchorage	278,735	1.1	7.6	19.3	10.6	30.5	25.6	6.4	33.2	77.4	8.4	9.9	13.6	7.7
02 090	Fairbanks North Star	95,600	3.1	8.1	20.0	13.7	30.3	22.4	5.5	29.7	81.8	7.3	4.3	12.7	6.0
02 110	Juneau	30,850	-1.0	5.4	17.8	11.1	27.1	31.3	7.3	38.2	81.3	1.5	7.0	19.1	4.3
02 122	Kenai Peninsula	52,281	3.0	6.1	18.9	9.9	25.1	30.8	9.2	38.0	90.6	1.0	2.3	11.1	3.0
02 170	Matanuska-Susitna	79,078	10.2	6.9	19.9	12.7	26.5	27.0	7.0	34.0	93.2	0.9	2.3	10.8	3.3
04 000	**Arizona**	6,152,175	6.5	7.8	18.6	9.4	28.3	23.1	12.8	34.8	78.5	4.1	3.1	16.9	29.0
04 001	Apache	69,250	2.5	8.1	23.9	12.1	21.9	23.9	10.1	30.8	23.6	0.4	-	76.8	5.0
04 003	Cochise	126,701	1.9	7.0	17.7	9.7	22.4	26.8	16.4	39.8	85.9	5.5	3.1	9.4	31.3
04 005	Coconino	126,087	2.2	7.4	18.3	14.9	26.1	25.5	7.8	31.6	64.2	1.5	1.7	34.8	11.8
04 007	Gila	51,441	2.2	6.5	16.8	7.9	19.9	27.7	21.2	43.6	79.8	0.7	0.6	21.1	16.7
04 009	Graham	33,640	6.0	6.8	19.8	13.4	25.9	21.2	12.9	31.8	70.6	1.8	0.7	29.2	27.6
04 012	La Paz	20,046	1.1	5.4	13.3	6.0	19.2	25.8	30.3	49.9	72.1	0.2	1.1	28.9	22.6
04 013	Maricopa	3,768,449	6.4	8.3	19.0	9.1	30.2	22.4	11.1	33.7	81.1	4.8	3.6	12.8	29.7
04 015	Mohave	190,623	5.2	6.2	16.2	6.9	23.7	26.2	20.9	42.5	92.6	1.3	1.7	7.4	13.6
04 017	Navajo	109,130	4.0	7.8	22.9	11.0	24.5	22.4	11.4	31.3	48.5	1.4	0.8	52.4	9.2
04 019	Pima	947,626	4.3	6.9	17.0	10.5	26.5	24.5	14.6	36.7	72.9	3.9	3.3	23.3	32.3
04 021	Pinal	268,295	26.1	7.4	18.0	9.6	29.1	21.8	14.1	34.0	74.8	3.9	1.9	22.8	29.6
04 023	Santa Cruz	42,020	4.1	6.3	25.9	9.4	22.0	24.1	12.3	34.6	83.0	-	1.1	16.7	-
04 025	Yavapai	205,684	7.6	5.3	14.8	8.3	22.6	26.9	22.2	44.4	91.7	0.9	1.5	7.9	12.5
04 027	Yuma	185,658	5.5	8.8	20.0	9.8	23.8	19.7	17.8	34.7	74.5	2.6	1.7	23.4	55.0

STATE County	Percent foreign born	Total households	Household type (percent)						Percent of households with people under 18 years	Percent of households with people 60 years and over
			Family households				Nonfamily households			
			Total family households	Married-couple families	Male householder families	Female householder families	Total nonfamily households	One-person households		
ACS table number:	C05002	B11001	B11001	B11001	B11001	B11001	B11001	B11001	C11005	B11006
	15	16	17	18	19	20	21	22	23	24
United States............................	12.5	111,609,629	66.9	49.8	4.6	12.5	33.1	27.3	34.6	30.9
Alabama............................	2.9	1,798,304	68.4	49.7	4.2	14.5	31.6	27.5	34.3	32.5
Autauga	1.4	18,275	72.3	57.2	3.9	11.3	27.7	24.7	40.1	28.7
Baldwin	3.1	68,495	72.5	57.7	3.3	11.5	27.5	22.4	33.8	36.4
Barbour	2.5	10,491	68.4	45.4	4.8	18.2	31.6	28.0	35.5	33.5
Bibb..........................	0.3	7,394	71.2	57.5	3.6	10.1	28.8	26.8	31.5	35.9
Blount.......................	4.0	18,931	74.5	61.8	3.6	9.1	25.5	23.9	35.7	35.9
Butler........................	-	7,830	66.3	41.4	3.6	21.4	33.7	30.3	27.4	38.1
Calhoun.....................	2.3	46,849	67.5	47.7	5.0	14.7	32.5	27.8	33.7	34.6
Chambers...................	0.4	13,612	69.0	51.5	3.9	13.5	31.0	29.5	33.1	37.5
Cherokee....................	0.5	10,038	74.8	59.3	4.8	10.7	25.2	23.0	32.9	36.6
Chilton......................	3.0	16,069	74.9	61.1	4.1	9.7	25.1	23.4	36.2	33.9
Clarke.......................	0.2	9,605	65.7	48.9	1.2	15.6	34.3	31.8	32.3	40.4
Coffee.......................	4.6	18,673	70.2	53.0	5.3	11.9	29.8	25.8	35.1	34.4
Colbert......................	1.6	22,666	70.0	54.8	3.4	11.8	30.0	26.8	32.0	38.0
Covington...................	1.4	14,461	69.7	52.6	4.8	12.3	30.3	27.5	33.2	42.4
Cullman.....................	2.3	30,793	71.2	56.0	4.9	10.3	28.8	24.9	33.2	34.4
Dale..........................	3.3	18,856	73.0	55.2	4.7	13.1	27.0	23.5	38.3	32.6
Dallas........................	0.6	17,022	66.4	34.5	6.1	25.7	33.6	30.9	37.9	35.8
DeKalb.......................	5.4	24,971	70.3	55.3	4.3	10.7	29.7	26.3	35.7	34.7
Elmore.......................	1.5	25,229	75.0	59.3	3.5	12.2	25.0	20.0	40.0	29.7
Escambia....................	0.8	14,151	70.1	49.9	5.4	14.8	29.9	27.0	33.6	36.0
Etowah......................	2.2	43,059	70.2	50.2	6.5	13.5	29.8	26.7	34.7	36.1
Franklin.....................	8.1	12,192	69.9	51.9	5.6	12.4	30.1	25.1	34.0	36.1
Geneva......................	1.4	10,308	68.2	53.2	4.1	10.9	31.8	28.8	31.8	40.1
Houston.....................	1.6	36,562	68.1	50.0	3.8	14.3	31.9	28.6	33.7	33.1
Jackson......................	1.3	21,129	71.1	55.7	4.9	10.5	28.9	27.4	32.5	38.4
Jefferson....................	3.6	266,554	65.8	44.6	3.9	17.3	34.2	29.8	34.4	31.3
Lauderdale..................	1.3	36,002	68.3	53.1	3.5	11.7	31.7	28.8	29.7	35.9
Lawrence....................	1.0	13,246	77.5	61.6	3.9	12.1	22.5	19.7	38.8	34.4
Lee...........................	3.9	52,996	58.8	41.8	4.2	12.8	41.2	30.6	34.1	21.0
Limestone...................	3.3	26,097	72.0	58.9	3.6	9.4	28.0	23.4	36.5	29.8
Macon........................	1.6	7,883	59.7	31.2	5.4	23.1	40.3	37.5	29.4	38.9
Madison.....................	5.0	121,186	67.0	50.1	4.0	12.9	33.0	28.6	32.4	29.5
Marengo.....................	-	8,319	64.4	41.4	2.2	20.9	35.6	31.3	32.0	35.0
Marion.......................	1.1	12,929	68.5	51.9	3.5	13.1	31.5	28.7	32.5	39.2
Marshall.....................	6.2	32,853	69.8	52.7	4.5	12.6	30.2	26.4	36.7	34.5
Mobile.......................	3.1	150,853	69.8	46.4	4.9	18.5	30.2	26.5	36.4	31.9
Monroe	0.5	9,474	66.9	45.5	4.6	16.8	33.1	28.0	35.5	36.1
Montgomery................	3.1	88,590	64.2	40.3	4.6	19.3	35.8	32.3	35.2	28.8
Morgan......................	4.4	45,632	70.3	54.8	4.0	11.5	29.7	26.5	32.9	34.2
Pike..........................	2.2	12,708	62.7	37.7	5.0	20.0	37.3	30.6	34.2	30.0
Randolph....................	0.7	7,870	74.5	57.8	3.0	13.7	25.5	21.3	34.4	36.4
Russell......................	1.9	20,729	63.8	42.5	4.1	17.3	36.2	31.9	33.7	31.0
St. Clair.....................	1.4	25,338	76.1	63.6	2.6	9.9	23.9	21.4	35.0	34.8
Shelby.......................	3.9	68,254	72.2	59.7	3.6	8.9	27.8	23.9	37.0	23.4
Talladega....................	1.6	29,931	70.9	51.2	4.3	15.4	29.1	25.7	34.9	33.9
Tallapoosa..................	1.1	16,048	69.8	52.2	4.1	13.4	30.2	26.8	33.2	40.3
Tuscaloosa..................	3.5	70,196	60.9	44.2	3.7	13.0	39.1	30.7	29.7	26.1
Walker.......................	1.0	27,054	71.9	53.7	4.1	14.1	28.1	25.9	33.7	36.7
Winston.....................	-	9,559	70.2	57.2	2.8	10.1	29.8	25.9	31.6	38.6
Alaska	6.7	233,861	68.3	51.1	5.7	11.6	31.7	24.5	39.2	21.6
Anchorage..................	8.6	102,476	67.9	50.9	5.0	12.0	32.1	24.4	39.1	20.4
Fairbanks North Star	5.1	32,550	67.8	51.4	5.5	10.9	32.2	25.4	38.9	19.1
Juneau......................	6.4	11,618	65.8	50.0	5.9	9.8	34.2	26.6	35.6	23.2
Kenai Peninsula............	2.4	19,339	67.1	55.2	3.8	8.1	32.9	26.6	32.7	26.0
Matanuska-Susitna	3.5	21,724	73.7	55.9	6.0	11.8	26.3	20.2	41.0	20.8
Arizona	15.0	2,215,761	66.3	49.5	5.0	11.8	33.7	26.8	34.2	32.2
Apache......................	1.1	18,678	72.6	44.6	4.5	23.4	27.4	25.2	40.4	37.5
Cochise......................	12.3	48,308	67.3	52.6	4.3	10.4	32.7	28.6	33.1	40.7
Coconino....................	5.6	43,286	66.5	48.8	4.7	13.0	33.5	23.7	34.4	24.6
Gila..........................	3.1	18,685	64.7	47.4	4.8	12.5	35.3	30.6	25.0	51.6
Graham......................	4.7	10,447	77.3	57.9	4.0	15.5	22.7	19.5	45.4	36.3
La Paz.......................	10.5	8,932	66.3	47.8	6.4	12.1	33.7	29.2	25.6	57.5
Maricopa....................	17.2	1,318,623	66.0	49.4	5.2	11.4	34.0	26.7	35.4	28.9
Mohave......................	6.8	75,033	68.6	52.5	4.6	11.5	31.4	24.7	28.7	45.5
Navajo.......................	2.1	34,143	74.1	51.7	5.4	17.0	25.9	21.8	41.4	34.9
Pima.........................	13.4	370,126	62.4	45.3	4.7	12.4	37.6	30.7	30.8	33.9
Pinal.........................	10.6	102,648	72.5	54.9	6.1	11.5	27.5	21.3	37.8	33.8
Santa Cruz..................	32.4	10,877	80.6	60.2	4.5	15.9	19.4	17.6	48.1	35.4
Yavapai......................	7.7	84,352	64.0	51.7	3.5	8.8	36.0	29.0	23.5	45.6
Yuma.........................	24.9	68,857	73.7	56.5	3.8	13.4	26.3	21.5	39.4	39.4

STATE County code	STATE County	Total population	Percent change 2005–2007	Population by age (percent)						Median age	Race alone or in combination (percent)				Percent Hispanic or Latino
				Under 5 years	5 to 17 years	18 to 24 years	25 to 44 years	45 to 64 years	65 years and over		White	Black	Asian Hawaiian or Pacific Islander	Amer. Indian, Alaska Native, or some other race	
	ACS table number:	B01003	Population estimates	B01001	B01001	B01001	B01001	B01001	B01001	B01002	B02008	B02009	B02011 + B02012	B02010 + B02013	C03002
		1	2	3	4	5	6	7	8	9	10	11	12	13	14
05 000	**Arkansas**	2,805,353	2.3	7.0	17.8	9.5	26.8	25.0	13.9	36.8	80.1	16.1	1.4	4.0	5.0
05 003	Ashley	22,587	-2.2	5.9	18.8	8.3	25.3	26.8	14.9	39.4	69.3	27.6	-	4.0	-
05 005	Baxter	41,129	4.1	5.1	14.1	6.7	21.4	26.4	26.4	46.9	98.5	0.6	0.5	2.1	1.4
05 007	Benton	195,082	8.6	8.1	19.2	8.4	29.5	22.7	12.0	34.5	87.6	1.6	2.3	10.2	13.3
05 009	Boone	36,016	3.5	5.8	16.9	7.4	26.7	25.7	17.5	40.2	98.8	0.6	0.2	2.0	1.3
05 015	Carroll	27,143	2.2	6.6	16.6	7.0	26.1	27.4	16.3	40.3	90.6	0.6	3.4	6.4	13.7
05 019	Clark	23,421	1.7	5.0	16.1	19.8	26.4	18.3	14.4	33.0	74.8	20.0	3.5	2.5	3.8
05 023	Cleburne	25,245	1.3	5.4	15.1	7.2	23.6	26.7	21.9	44.4	98.0	-	-	2.0	-
05 027	Columbia	24,530	-1.0	6.2	16.5	13.3	23.6	24.6	15.8	37.8	61.3	37.2	0.9	0.3	1.6
05 029	Conway	20,566	1.4	6.2	17.7	8.6	25.2	26.1	16.2	38.3	86.4	13.2	-	1.1	2.6
05 031	Craighead	89,603	4.6	7.1	17.4	12.4	28.9	22.6	11.6	33.6	87.8	10.9	0.9	1.4	3.2
05 033	Crawford	58,039	3.6	6.8	19.5	8.3	27.8	25.8	11.9	36.4	93.9	1.6	1.6	5.6	4.8
05 035	Crittenden	51,798	1.3	8.5	21.8	9.3	26.2	24.2	10.0	33.5	50.1	49.3	-	2.1	1.8
05 045	Faulkner	101,906	6.3	7.0	17.7	15.9	28.7	21.1	9.5	31.1	88.2	10.4	1.4	1.8	2.6
05 051	Garland	94,967	3.3	5.9	15.6	7.8	24.4	25.2	20.9	41.9	88.2	8.8	0.8	3.9	3.5
05 055	Greene	39,831	3.1	7.1	17.9	7.6	28.8	24.8	13.8	36.9	98.3	0.3	0.5	2.3	1.5
05 057	Hempstead	23,151	0.7	7.0	18.7	9.6	25.5	25.9	13.5	37.0	65.8	30.3	-	2.4	-
05 059	Hot Spring	31,512	2.6	5.7	17.5	7.1	27.1	27.6	15.0	39.0	87.9	11.3	-	2.2	2.0
05 063	Independence	34,439	0.8	6.6	16.7	8.8	26.1	26.6	15.2	39.2	95.5	2.6	1.1	2.0	2.6
05 069	Jefferson	80,054	-2.3	6.9	17.9	10.6	25.8	26.0	12.7	36.4	46.3	52.2	1.1	1.8	1.3
05 071	Johnson	24,312	3.6	8.0	17.7	9.0	26.9	24.0	14.4	36.6	95.6	1.8	-	3.8	10.0
05 083	Logan	22,588	0.0	6.0	18.1	7.5	25.9	25.9	16.7	40.0	96.6	1.5	1.0	2.1	2.0
05 085	Lonoke	61,719	6.4	7.0	19.8	8.8	29.7	24.1	10.6	35.0	91.1	7.2	1.0	2.8	2.4
05 091	Miller	42,577	0.8	6.5	19.0	7.9	27.8	25.2	13.6	37.7	73.5	25.2	0.2	2.4	2.1
05 093	Mississippi	46,900	-1.1	8.1	20.3	8.7	25.2	25.3	12.5	35.4	64.5	34.6	-	2.0	2.7
05 103	Ouachita	26,354	-2.2	6.5	17.1	9.5	22.0	28.1	16.8	41.7	58.9	40.7	-	1.1	1.1
05 107	Phillips	22,638	-5.4	8.9	21.5	8.9	21.7	24.5	14.6	34.9	38.2	61.8	-	-	-
05 111	Poinsett	24,960	-1.0	7.0	18.3	7.9	27.5	25.2	14.2	37.2	91.7	7.7	-	0.9	2.0
05 113	Polk	20,147	0.9	6.4	17.7	7.6	24.0	26.1	18.3	41.1	95.9	-	-	5.2	-
05 115	Pope	58,216	3.0	6.6	17.5	12.9	26.0	24.0	13.1	35.0	95.2	3.4	1.1	2.8	4.1
05 119	Pulaski	371,973	1.2	7.8	17.9	8.5	27.7	26.3	11.8	36.5	62.5	34.8	2.1	2.5	3.8
05 123	St. Francis	27,175	-2.1	7.6	18.9	9.0	27.7	25.0	11.9	35.1	45.9	53.1	-	1.5	3.1
05 125	Saline	93,213	6.5	5.9	17.9	8.2	28.2	26.4	13.4	37.9	93.7	4.3	1.0	2.2	2.0
05 131	Sebastian	120,235	2.7	7.6	18.5	8.1	27.4	25.7	12.7	36.7	84.1	7.4	4.0	8.2	10.2
05 139	Union	43,487	-1.0	6.6	17.5	8.0	25.2	26.8	15.9	40.4	65.1	33.5	0.5	1.6	1.8
05 143	Washington	189,610	5.5	8.4	17.8	13.1	29.9	21.5	9.4	31.4	83.8	3.6	3.2	11.4	12.5
05 145	White	72,488	2.9	6.6	17.1	12.7	26.0	23.6	14.0	35.5	93.9	4.9	0.3	2.5	2.6
05 149	Yell	21,560	2.7	7.6	18.5	10.2	25.1	24.0	14.6	37.5	92.4	1.5	1.5	6.6	18.1
06 000	**California**	36,264,467	1.6	7.3	18.7	10.4	29.5	23.3	10.8	34.5	63.1	7.0	13.9	19.5	35.7
06 001	Alameda	1,454,159	1.2	6.8	16.9	9.3	30.5	25.8	10.6	36.7	49.5	14.4	27.2	13.1	21.1
06 005	Amador	38,244	2.2	3.8	13.5	8.2	26.5	29.9	18.0	43.6	91.3	2.2	1.9	9.2	10.2
06 007	Butte	217,191	1.7	5.5	15.9	15.9	24.4	23.5	14.9	34.7	88.1	2.1	5.3	9.7	12.3
06 009	Calaveras	46,389	2.4	3.8	15.2	9.3	22.7	31.0	18.0	44.5	93.6	0.4	1.7	6.3	9.5
06 011	Colusa	21,022	3.0	9.0	20.3	10.5	27.2	21.6	11.4	31.1	70.6	1.0	1.3	29.6	49.9
06 013	Contra Costa	1,011,372	1.4	6.5	18.5	9.1	27.1	27.2	11.7	37.7	63.7	10.2	15.7	14.7	21.8
06 015	Del Norte	28,738	1.7	4.7	15.8	11.4	30.7	23.8	13.6	37.4	79.7	3.6	3.1	17.7	15.6
06 017	El Dorado	174,835	1.2	5.4	17.0	9.6	26.3	30.2	11.5	39.7	90.3	1.4	4.9	6.2	11.2
06 019	Fresno	886,074	3.0	8.6	21.5	11.7	28.0	20.5	9.7	30.1	64.9	5.9	9.7	23.2	47.6
06 021	Glenn	27,846	2.0	7.6	20.3	10.6	27.0	22.5	11.9	34.2	71.4	1.0	3.5	27.5	33.8
06 023	Humboldt	129,080	-0.2	5.6	14.8	13.5	27.0	26.6	12.5	35.6	87.6	2.0	3.6	12.7	7.9
06 025	Imperial	157,829	5.2	9.2	20.3	12.6	27.6	19.9	10.4	30.7	72.6	3.9	2.8	23.3	75.5
06 029	Kern	771,347	5.3	8.8	21.4	11.3	29.6	20.1	8.9	29.9	64.1	6.4	4.9	28.4	45.1
06 031	Kings	146,308	3.5	8.2	19.2	12.8	34.5	17.8	7.4	30.0	70.9	8.6	4.5	19.6	47.4
06 033	Lake	64,555	0.7	5.6	16.6	9.0	24.0	28.1	16.7	41.7	90.1	2.9	1.9	8.6	14.9
06 035	Lassen	34,406	2.8	4.4	11.9	12.5	38.4	24.4	8.4	35.2	73.4	10.3	1.7	17.4	15.0
06 037	Los Angeles	9,883,649	-0.1	7.3	19.2	10.4	30.2	22.7	10.2	34.1	51.6	9.6	14.2	27.6	47.1
06 039	Madera	143,656	4.3	8.1	19.9	10.8	29.2	21.8	10.3	32.3	80.7	4.6	2.6	15.7	49.3
06 041	Marin	246,507	1.2	5.6	14.1	7.1	24.9	33.3	15.0	43.8	84.1	3.6	7.1	8.0	13.2
06 045	Mendocino	86,680	-1.0	5.9	16.5	9.4	24.4	29.1	14.7	40.1	89.9	1.2	2.2	9.4	19.7
06 047	Merced	242,173	2.8	8.9	23.0	11.5	27.9	19.4	9.3	29.0	65.9	4.2	7.9	25.1	51.7
06 053	Monterey	407,534	-0.3	8.5	19.0	11.2	29.3	22.0	10.0	32.2	66.0	4.0	8.3	25.4	51.4
06 055	Napa	131,505	1.6	6.2	16.6	10.1	26.2	26.5	14.4	38.5	83.7	1.9	7.1	10.0	28.6
06 057	Nevada	96,841	0.4	4.1	14.8	8.7	22.4	32.3	17.6	44.9	94.6	0.8	2.0	5.0	7.3
06 059	Orange	2,988,407	0.5	7.1	18.7	9.7	29.6	24.0	10.8	35.5	65.3	2.1	17.4	17.8	33.0
06 061	Placer	324,133	5.6	5.9	16.6	9.4	28.6	25.1	14.4	37.8	87.1	1.9	6.8	7.3	11.4
06 063	Plumas	20,793	-1.8	3.6	14.6	7.8	21.4	33.4	19.2	46.0	90.9	-	-	10.8	-
06 065	Riverside	2,002,663	7.6	7.9	20.5	10.6	30.0	19.7	11.4	31.6	65.4	6.8	6.5	25.1	42.1
06 067	Sacramento	1,373,773	1.8	7.3	19.0	9.6	30.0	23.1	11.0	34.1	64.8	11.5	16.0	12.3	19.2
06 069	San Benito	54,797	-0.8	7.8	22.1	9.7	28.2	24.0	8.3	32.7	61.0	1.0	6.7	39.8	51.9
06 071	San Bernardino	1,982,845	2.8	8.1	22.0	11.4	29.6	20.8	8.2	30.2	64.0	9.8	7.2	22.7	45.7
06 073	San Diego	2,954,960	1.1	7.4	17.7	11.5	29.6	22.8	11.1	34.2	72.6	6.1	12.5	12.6	29.9
06 075	San Francisco	757,604	1.8	5.1	9.1	7.6	38.2	25.5	14.5	39.5	56.3	7.6	33.8	5.4	14.0
06 077	San Joaquin	664,423	2.0	8.1	21.2	10.6	28.8	21.5	9.8	31.6	64.2	8.6	16.0	15.9	35.7
06 079	San Luis Obispo	260,278	1.6	4.9	14.3	15.5	25.2	25.9	14.2	37.8	87.3	2.5	4.4	8.9	18.4
06 081	San Mateo	701,985	1.3	6.7	15.7	8.1	28.6	27.8	13.0	39.7	63.5	3.7	27.2	9.4	22.8

STATE County	Percent foreign born	Total households	Household type (percent)						Percent of households with people under 18 years	Percent of households with people 60 years and over
			Family households				Nonfamily households			
			Total family households	Married-couple families	Male householder families	Female householder families	Total nonfamily households	One-person households		
ACS table number:	C05002	B11001	B11001	B11001	B11001	B11001	B11001	B11001	C11005	B11006
	15	16	17	18	19	20	21	22	23	24
Arkansas...........	3.9	1,096,622	68.4	51.3	4.3	12.7	31.6	27.2	34.1	33.1
Ashley...............	2.5	9,279	73.3	58.1	4.2	10.9	26.7	24.2	39.8	37.3
Baxter...............	1.5	18,139	65.5	55.4	2.2	7.9	34.5	30.1	25.9	49.4
Benton..............	9.8	71,918	74.1	60.7	5.0	8.3	25.9	21.9	37.9	29.6
Boone...............	0.9	13,946	68.7	58.4	4.0	6.2	31.3	25.5	33.4	38.4
Carroll..............	8.6	10,845	69.4	52.8	4.3	12.4	30.6	25.3	35.1	37.2
Clark................	3.9	8,818	60.4	47.8	2.1	10.5	39.6	29.4	26.8	33.8
Cleburne...........	0.2	9,802	73.1	60.0	2.1	10.9	26.9	24.7	27.3	48.5
Columbia...........	2.4	10,639	66.8	44.8	5.1	17.0	33.2	31.0	33.3	35.1
Conway.............	1.7	8,371	71.1	54.2	3.6	13.3	28.9	26.9	32.9	37.3
Craighead...........	2.9	34,095	67.6	49.1	4.2	14.4	32.4	27.3	33.7	27.9
Crawford...........	3.4	21,041	75.8	60.8	3.7	11.3	24.2	20.5	38.6	32.4
Crittenden.........	0.7	19,899	69.8	41.8	5.4	22.6	30.2	26.0	40.5	28.4
Faulkner...........	2.3	37,487	69.9	56.4	3.5	10.0	30.1	24.1	35.7	25.5
Garland............	3.9	38,796	63.3	47.8	3.6	11.9	36.7	32.7	26.8	42.9
Greene.............	0.7	16,192	70.6	56.1	3.2	11.2	29.4	23.9	35.6	32.6
Hempstead.........	7.6	8,839	76.4	52.4	7.8	16.2	23.6	19.8	44.1	29.5
Hot Spring.........	0.9	11,476	66.9	51.8	5.2	10.0	33.1	29.4	30.7	35.5
Independence......	1.9	14,064	70.9	55.5	5.3	10.0	29.1	26.3	32.9	33.9
Jefferson...........	1.8	30,446	64.4	40.5	4.5	19.5	35.6	31.7	34.3	32.9
Johnson............	6.3	8,814	67.9	52.0	4.9	11.0	32.1	27.4	32.4	34.1
Logan...............	1.1	9,087	69.5	60.1	2.5	6.9	30.5	27.8	33.1	41.1
Lonoke..............	1.8	22,120	74.8	59.5	3.1	12.2	25.2	21.9	39.7	28.1
Miller...............	1.1	16,533	68.2	48.1	5.6	14.5	31.8	27.2	35.3	33.3
Mississippi.........	1.1	18,081	72.3	44.5	8.6	19.1	27.7	25.7	39.0	24.3
Ouachita............	1.0	10,648	68.8	45.3	4.8	18.7	31.2	28.1	33.7	37.2
Phillips.............	-	8,861	71.7	42.4	5.6	23.7	28.3	25.5	38.7	39.2
Poinsett............	0.7	10,019	70.2	51.5	4.8	14.0	29.8	26.3	33.1	34.2
Polk.................	2.6	7,957	69.7	56.6	5.9	7.3	30.3	27.0	34.6	40.0
Pope................	2.6	21,852	67.6	53.5	3.2	10.9	32.4	26.3	32.8	31.3
Pulaski..............	4.4	153,273	62.8	43.7	3.7	15.4	37.2	31.9	32.8	28.4
St. Francis.........	1.7	10,026	63.3	39.7	3.4	20.2	36.7	30.7	33.1	30.8
Saline...............	2.2	35,766	72.7	57.9	3.3	11.4	27.3	21.8	35.7	31.4
Sebastian...........	8.5	46,730	65.1	48.2	4.4	12.5	34.9	30.4	32.8	31.5
Union...............	1.2	18,325	71.1	48.4	5.0	17.7	28.9	27.2	34.6	35.1
Washington.........	10.0	73,409	65.1	49.4	5.7	10.1	34.9	26.4	35.1	24.1
White...............	1.8	27,075	73.3	57.2	3.3	12.8	26.7	22.8	35.8	34.1
Yell.................	12.7	7,757	71.3	55.7	6.9	8.7	28.7	25.6	36.5	33.2
California............	27.2	12,140,888	68.3	49.8	5.8	12.8	31.7	24.7	38.5	29.9
Alameda............	30.5	519,056	64.1	46.4	5.3	12.4	35.9	28.0	35.3	28.3
Amador.............	4.1	14,563	71.4	59.1	3.3	9.0	28.6	20.9	28.7	40.6
Butte...............	7.5	84,607	58.6	43.3	4.3	11.0	41.4	29.0	29.6	33.8
Calaveras...........	4.5	18,393	70.1	54.9	5.6	9.6	29.9	23.6	31.4	42.5
Colusa..............	30.1	6,700	75.3	59.4	4.9	11.1	24.7	20.1	44.5	32.8
Contra Costa........	23.4	362,362	70.4	54.3	5.1	11.1	29.6	23.4	37.4	31.3
Del Norte...........	7.8	9,662	63.7	45.8	4.6	13.3	36.3	31.2	32.7	39.3
El Dorado...........	7.6	65,310	70.8	59.0	4.4	7.4	29.2	22.1	32.8	29.8
Fresno..............	21.7	276,929	72.8	50.1	6.6	16.2	27.2	21.9	44.7	28.9
Glenn...............	17.1	9,450	75.5	58.4	3.6	13.5	24.5	21.2	41.1	34.7
Humboldt...........	4.8	52,112	56.0	41.0	4.2	10.8	44.0	31.8	27.2	30.3
Imperial............	31.8	45,561	80.5	54.5	5.6	20.3	19.5	17.7	51.7	32.3
Kern................	20.4	235,842	74.3	51.6	6.9	15.9	25.7	20.7	47.6	26.6
Kings...............	20.5	38,808	78.6	56.6	8.5	13.5	21.4	18.2	51.4	25.3
Lake................	7.5	24,896	65.3	47.4	4.2	13.6	34.7	26.4	31.7	39.4
Lassen..............	7.0	10,324	66.4	52.3	3.5	10.6	33.6	24.6	37.3	27.3
Los Angeles.........	35.8	3,176,441	67.3	45.8	6.5	15.0	32.7	26.0	39.1	29.3
Madera.............	20.6	41,849	79.3	60.2	8.1	11.0	20.7	17.6	45.8	32.4
Marin...............	18.5	100,489	60.8	48.7	3.7	8.4	39.2	31.5	29.3	37.1
Mendocino..........	11.6	33,749	63.9	45.7	5.9	12.3	36.1	27.3	31.0	37.0
Merced.............	25.4	72,599	78.6	56.7	6.6	15.2	21.4	17.2	51.4	27.0
Monterey...........	30.0	124,146	71.4	53.7	5.7	11.9	28.6	22.9	41.5	31.0
Napa................	22.3	48,312	64.8	51.1	5.0	8.7	35.2	28.2	31.4	38.2
Nevada.............	5.1	39,376	69.5	56.1	3.9	9.5	30.5	23.6	29.8	39.2
Orange.............	30.5	972,040	70.6	53.9	5.6	11.1	29.4	22.8	38.4	30.8
Placer..............	10.5	123,247	71.5	57.3	4.3	9.9	28.5	22.5	36.7	32.8
Plumas.............	6.2	10,012	56.7	47.2	2.1	7.4	43.3	32.2	22.0	36.7
Riverside...........	22.4	636,755	73.4	55.4	5.9	12.0	26.6	20.5	44.1	31.5
Sacramento.........	19.6	500,777	65.6	46.0	5.5	14.1	34.4	26.7	37.0	27.9
San Benito..........	21.6	16,647	79.8	61.6	6.0	12.2	20.2	16.5	49.1	29.7
San Bernardino......	21.4	591,141	76.4	53.8	7.3	15.4	23.6	18.7	47.8	26.4
San Diego...........	23.0	1,041,790	65.7	49.2	4.9	11.6	34.3	25.8	35.5	28.9
San Francisco.......	35.7	321,692	44.1	32.2	3.8	8.0	55.9	42.2	18.8	30.3
San Joaquin........	23.7	207,792	74.2	53.2	7.2	13.9	25.8	20.3	45.9	28.8
San Luis Obispo.....	9.5	103,026	62.4	49.2	4.1	9.1	37.6	25.9	28.8	30.7
San Mateo..........	33.7	252,648	67.9	53.1	4.6	10.2	32.1	25.7	33.9	32.9

Table A-2. Counties — Who: Age, Race/Ethnicity, and Household Structure, 2005–2007—*Continued*

STATE County code	STATE County	Total population	Percent change 2005–2007	Population by age (percent)						Median age	Race alone or in combination (percent)				Percent Hispanic or Latino
				Under 5 years	5 to 17 years	18 to 24 years	25 to 44 years	45 to 64 years	65 years and over		White	Black	Asian Hawaiian or Pacific Islander	Amer. Indian, Alaska Native, or some other race	
	ACS table number:	B01003	Population estimates	B01001	B01001	B01001	B01001	B01001	B01001	B01002	B02008	B02009	B02011 + B02012	B02010 + B02013	C03002
		1	2	3	4	5	6	7	8	9	10	11	12	13	14
	California—Cont.														
06 083	Santa Barbara	402,968	0.4	7.1	16.8	14.4	26.2	22.7	12.8	33.9	78.2	2.6	5.9	17.0	38.0
06 085	Santa Clara	1,722,819	3.0	7.3	16.8	8.9	31.7	24.7	10.5	36.4	55.2	3.2	32.2	12.9	25.4
06 087	Santa Cruz	250,877	0.6	6.5	15.5	12.9	26.5	28.3	10.3	37.0	88.7	1.5	5.6	8.1	28.5
06 089	Shasta	178,539	1.0	5.7	16.9	10.2	25.6	26.5	15.1	38.5	91.5	1.3	3.1	7.2	7.5
06 093	Siskiyou	44,360	-0.4	4.9	14.7	10.0	20.8	30.7	18.9	44.6	92.9	1.8	2.1	8.3	9.3
06 095	Solano	408,388	0.1	6.9	19.2	9.9	28.2	25.3	10.6	35.4	56.4	16.6	17.6	14.9	21.5
06 097	Sonoma	463,544	0.2	6.1	16.6	10.0	26.0	28.6	12.8	39.1	82.2	2.0	5.3	13.8	21.9
06 099	Stanislaus	506,405	2.0	8.0	21.1	10.7	28.5	21.6	10.1	31.6	75.6	3.3	6.7	17.9	38.2
06 101	Sutter	90,075	4.6	7.5	19.2	10.2	28.5	22.5	12.0	33.6	70.8	2.9	14.1	18.0	26.4
06 103	Tehama	60,441	2.4	6.4	18.2	9.4	26.9	23.9	15.3	37.1	84.2	0.4	1.9	17.5	19.3
06 107	Tulare	413,933	3.7	9.5	22.6	11.1	27.6	19.7	9.4	28.8	76.4	2.0	4.2	20.1	55.9
06 109	Tuolumne	56,083	-0.9	4.4	13.0	8.9	26.8	28.1	18.9	43.0	90.5	3.0	2.0	7.0	9.5
06 111	Ventura	794,412	0.9	7.2	19.3	10.2	27.2	25.2	10.9	35.5	72.2	2.7	8.0	20.7	36.7
06 113	Yolo	191,159	4.7	6.3	17.0	19.1	27.7	20.7	9.3	29.6	72.0	3.1	14.1	15.6	27.9
06 115	Yuba	69,801	7.5	8.8	20.4	11.6	29.2	20.9	9.1	30.1	74.6	3.8	9.6	19.7	21.8
08 000	**Colorado**	4,767,161	4.0	7.2	17.5	9.7	30.1	25.5	10.0	35.5	85.5	4.6	3.5	9.3	19.6
08 001	Adams	411,462	5.7	8.9	19.7	8.7	33.1	21.6	7.9	32.1	79.9	3.5	4.1	15.7	34.6
08 005	Arapahoe	535,523	3.4	7.4	18.2	8.5	29.3	26.7	9.9	36.1	79.9	10.4	5.7	6.8	16.6
08 013	Boulder	286,471	2.6	5.9	15.4	13.4	29.8	27.1	8.3	35.5	89.2	1.4	4.6	7.2	12.8
08 014	Broomfield	51,235	10.6	7.1	19.4	9.4	32.2	25.1	6.8	34.2	90.4	1.5	6.2	5.3	10.9
08 029	Delta	29,924	2.7	5.7	16.5	7.0	24.7	26.5	19.7	41.6	94.1	0.8	0.8	6.2	12.8
08 031	Denver	576,842	3.9	8.7	15.3	8.1	34.5	22.8	10.6	35.1	74.5	10.8	3.9	13.5	34.2
08 035	Douglas	259,427	10.4	8.3	21.0	7.7	33.5	24.5	5.0	33.6	92.4	2.1	4.5	3.4	6.8
08 037	Eagle	49,772	6.6	8.2	15.4	8.1	41.1	23.2	3.8	33.4	94.7	-	-	5.6	-
08 039	Elbert	22,596	1.4	4.5	19.8	9.4	24.9	33.4	8.0	41.1	95.1	1.1	1.0	4.0	5.3
08 041	El Paso	578,779	3.4	7.3	18.9	10.0	30.1	24.4	9.2	34.1	83.9	8.1	4.6	8.2	12.9
08 043	Fremont	47,198	0.8	4.2	13.3	8.0	32.0	27.1	15.4	40.6	83.9	4.7	0.7	11.9	12.2
08 045	Garfield	51,539	8.5	8.4	18.1	8.3	30.4	25.9	9.0	34.7	94.4	0.8	1.1	5.7	-
08 059	Jefferson	526,008	1.1	5.8	17.3	8.8	26.6	30.4	11.1	39.8	89.9	1.7	3.3	7.5	13.2
08 067	La Plata	48,733	3.6	4.8	14.9	14.1	27.3	28.6	10.3	36.5	89.1	0.5	1.0	12.1	10.5
08 069	Larimer	281,742	4.2	6.0	15.8	13.8	28.9	25.3	10.2	34.3	93.4	1.5	2.6	5.6	9.6
08 075	Logan	20,970	0.8	5.9	16.2	11.8	26.7	25.4	14.2	37.7	91.2	2.7	0.9	5.9	-
08 077	Mesa	134,258	7.3	6.5	16.4	9.9	26.8	25.2	15.2	37.1	92.4	1.2	1.2	7.9	11.4
08 083	Montezuma	24,902	2.9	6.2	18.1	7.4	25.3	27.6	15.4	40.0	83.0	-	-	17.1	-
08 085	Montrose	38,254	6.5	6.5	17.5	8.3	26.1	25.2	16.4	38.5	95.3	-	0.7	6.4	-
08 087	Morgan	27,884	0.7	7.8	20.6	9.4	25.4	23.6	13.3	35.8	84.5	-	1.3	15.5	-
08 101	Pueblo	152,216	3.0	6.5	17.8	9.9	26.7	24.2	14.8	36.6	85.2	2.8	1.1	14.4	38.8
08 107	Routt	21,820	4.9	5.6	13.9	9.2	33.6	31.7	6.0	37.1	97.0	-	1.8	0.8	-
08 117	Summit	25,991	4.3	6.9	12.0	7.7	44.9	23.8	4.7	33.7	94.4	1.4	2.0	3.5	-
08 119	Teller	21,562	2.4	4.9	15.7	7.6	23.8	36.8	11.2	43.8	94.9	-	1.7	5.0	5.0
08 123	Weld	235,328	7.4	8.3	18.8	12.4	30.8	21.6	8.0	31.0	87.4	0.7	2.3	11.5	27.5
09 000	**Connecticut**	3,494,851	0.5	6.1	17.6	9.1	27.0	26.7	13.5	38.9	81.6	10.4	3.7	6.3	11.2
09 001	Fairfield	894,724	0.0	6.6	18.7	8.0	26.6	27.0	13.0	39.0	79.2	10.7	4.5	7.0	14.4
09 003	Hartford	874,545	0.5	6.1	17.4	8.9	26.8	26.7	14.1	39.4	76.9	13.3	3.8	8.2	13.1
09 005	Litchfield	188,165	0.2	5.2	17.2	7.4	25.9	29.9	14.4	41.8	96.2	1.8	1.8	1.8	3.4
09 007	Middlesex	163,215	1.3	5.5	16.7	8.5	26.9	28.5	13.9	40.6	91.3	5.5	2.4	2.7	3.8
09 009	New Haven	843,571	0.4	6.1	17.4	9.6	27.4	25.8	13.7	38.1	79.4	13.1	3.7	6.1	12.3
09 011	New London	267,029	0.7	5.9	17.1	9.1	28.9	25.9	13.0	38.2	85.7	7.0	4.1	6.4	6.2
09 013	Tolland	147,390	1.1	4.9	15.7	16.3	25.6	26.9	10.7	37.1	92.2	3.7	3.2	2.7	3.5
09 015	Windham	116,212	1.6	5.8	16.9	10.7	28.8	25.8	12.0	37.1	92.0	2.8	1.4	6.3	7.9
10 000	**Delaware**	852,689	2.9	6.8	17.1	9.8	27.2	25.7	13.4	37.6	74.1	21.3	3.3	3.1	6.3
10 001	Kent	147,974	6.0	7.3	18.4	10.3	27.5	24.0	12.5	35.5	73.7	23.2	3.0	3.6	4.1
10 003	New Castle	524,682	1.4	6.8	17.4	10.4	27.8	26.0	11.6	36.9	71.9	23.2	4.1	2.3	6.9
10 005	Sussex	180,033	4.8	6.4	15.4	7.5	25.2	26.0	19.6	42.1	80.9	14.3	1.0	5.1	6.2
11 000	**District of Columbia**	585,267	1.1	6.1	13.4	12.5	32.7	23.4	11.9	35.0	35.5	56.4	3.7	6.1	8.3
11 001	District of Columbia	585,267	1.1	6.1	13.4	12.5	32.7	23.4	11.9	35.0	35.5	56.4	3.7	6.1	8.3
12 000	**Florida**	18,014,927	2.9	6.3	16.0	8.8	26.7	25.4	16.9	39.8	77.8	16.0	2.7	5.4	20.1
12 001	Alachua	236,308	3.5	5.5	13.4	23.0	26.2	21.9	10.0	29.9	74.0	20.5	5.1	2.4	7.1
12 003	Baker	25,081	5.3	7.9	17.3	12.1	28.5	24.1	10.1	34.3	84.7	14.0	0.7	1.2	1.8
12 005	Bay	163,256	1.5	6.8	16.3	8.0	27.4	27.6	13.9	39.5	85.0	11.9	2.7	2.9	3.3
12 007	Bradford	28,408	2.7	5.7	14.6	14.0	27.4	25.6	12.7	36.5	78.0	20.7	1.1	2.1	2.6
12 009	Brevard	531,642	1.8	5.1	15.4	8.1	24.1	27.2	20.0	43.2	86.0	10.1	2.7	3.0	6.5
12 011	Broward	1,767,681	-0.6	6.5	17.3	7.9	28.0	26.1	14.2	39.0	67.8	25.3	3.5	5.9	22.7
12 015	Charlotte	153,063	-0.3	3.8	12.2	5.9	20.1	26.5	31.5	51.3	91.7	5.6	1.5	2.6	4.8
12 017	Citrus	136,729	5.4	3.9	12.7	6.3	20.9	25.9	30.3	50.0	94.7	3.3	1.5	2.1	3.9
12 019	Clay	175,534	8.2	6.6	18.2	9.7	27.7	27.7	10.1	37.0	86.1	9.7	3.9	3.2	6.3
12 021	Collier	311,926	3.0	6.4	14.3	6.7	24.5	23.6	24.5	43.6	85.6	6.0	1.1	8.2	24.9
12 023	Columbia	66,244	6.3	6.4	16.8	10.1	27.0	25.3	14.4	36.9	79.3	18.5	0.9	2.5	3.8
12 027	DeSoto	34,497	1.1	6.9	15.5	10.9	29.2	21.1	16.4	34.8	83.0	12.4	0.5	5.4	32.1
12 031	Duval	841,077	2.1	7.6	18.4	8.9	29.1	25.6	10.4	35.9	64.8	30.0	4.0	3.1	5.8
12 033	Escambia	305,214	1.3	6.5	16.0	12.2	25.2	26.0	14.3	37.6	73.7	22.9	3.5	3.5	3.5

STATE County	Percent foreign born	Total households	Household type (percent)						Percent of households with people under 18 years	Percent of households with people 60 years and over
			Family households				Nonfamily households			
			Total family households	Married-couple families	Male householder families	Female householder families	Total nonfamily households	One-person households		
ACS table number:	C05002	B11001	B11001	B11001	B11001	B11001	B11001	B11001	C11005	B11006
	15	16	17	18	19	20	21	22	23	24
California—Cont.										
Santa Barbara	22.6	140,137	64.1	49.1	4.7	10.3	35.9	25.1	34.1	32.2
Santa Clara	36.8	582,108	69.8	54.4	5.2	10.3	30.2	24.3	38.5	28.1
Santa Cruz	17.1	93,518	61.5	47.1	4.7	9.7	38.5	27.5	32.7	28.9
Shasta	4.1	68,762	68.1	50.2	5.3	12.6	31.9	26.2	33.2	36.5
Siskiyou	5.5	19,766	63.5	49.7	4.5	9.3	36.5	29.2	28.7	40.7
Solano	18.9	135,704	73.0	52.3	6.1	14.6	27.0	21.7	41.3	30.4
Sonoma	17.1	177,331	63.7	49.3	4.8	9.6	36.3	27.7	32.7	32.9
Stanislaus	19.9	158,836	74.2	54.1	6.3	13.8	25.8	20.4	44.0	29.4
Sutter	21.1	30,431	74.2	57.2	5.1	11.8	25.8	21.3	41.2	33.3
Tehama	10.3	22,817	68.4	45.9	6.6	15.9	31.6	25.2	35.5	37.4
Tulare	22.7	121,457	78.2	56.0	8.2	14.0	21.8	18.0	49.5	29.1
Tuolumne	3.9	22,161	64.0	50.3	3.0	10.8	36.0	28.1	26.9	43.1
Ventura	22.0	255,527	73.8	58.0	4.9	10.9	26.2	20.8	40.7	31.5
Yolo	21.6	66,828	60.9	47.2	3.9	9.8	39.1	25.1	33.7	25.5
Yuba	13.0	23,801	70.1	51.6	5.3	13.2	29.9	23.1	43.6	29.1
Colorado	10.1	1,838,303	64.5	50.3	4.4	9.7	35.5	28.3	33.9	25.3
Adams	15.5	144,492	70.8	53.3	6.1	11.5	29.2	22.9	41.0	21.9
Arapahoe	14.7	208,881	65.3	49.0	4.8	11.5	34.7	28.5	35.6	24.8
Boulder	11.6	113,419	59.7	47.1	4.4	8.2	40.3	29.0	32.3	22.5
Broomfield	7.3	17,507	68.3	53.5	4.3	10.4	31.7	25.7	39.6	19.9
Delta	4.6	11,583	69.7	58.3	3.1	8.2	30.3	25.9	31.1	44.8
Denver	18.3	244,261	48.9	34.2	4.4	10.2	51.1	42.1	25.8	25.4
Douglas	6.0	91,557	78.6	69.7	3.1	5.9	21.4	16.5	45.6	16.0
Eagle	19.0	15,207	63.0	49.4	3.3	10.3	37.0	26.8	36.5	13.5
Elbert	2.1	8,035	78.7	69.3	1.8	7.5	21.3	15.1	37.6	26.4
El Paso	7.8	217,217	67.2	52.4	4.2	10.6	32.8	27.0	36.8	24.0
Fremont	4.9	16,401	66.8	52.6	4.1	10.2	33.2	29.3	30.0	40.4
Garfield	16.3	18,765	71.9	60.5	5.5	5.9	28.1	19.7	35.4	24.0
Jefferson	6.4	213,324	66.7	52.6	4.5	9.6	33.3	26.8	32.0	27.1
La Plata	3.5	20,639	61.3	48.2	6.2	6.9	38.7	28.0	28.4	25.9
Larimer	5.2	111,524	62.7	50.1	3.7	8.8	37.3	27.1	31.1	23.6
Logan	4.3	8,065	65.9	53.1	4.0	8.8	34.1	30.0	34.1	32.6
Mesa	3.9	53,533	66.9	51.3	5.0	10.6	33.1	25.9	32.4	33.9
Montezuma	1.9	10,132	71.8	56.2	4.4	11.2	28.2	25.2	38.3	35.5
Montrose	6.1	15,540	66.0	54.6	2.6	8.9	34.0	30.3	29.2	35.2
Morgan	12.7	10,014	70.0	56.2	4.5	9.3	30.0	24.3	37.7	31.2
Pueblo	3.4	58,819	67.2	47.8	4.8	14.6	32.8	27.7	34.0	33.0
Routt	4.2	10,001	61.4	53.8	2.3	5.3	38.6	27.8	29.5	16.5
Summit	12.3	9,880	59.4	51.1	5.1	3.2	40.6	26.7	26.6	14.0
Teller	2.2	9,143	73.0	63.1	3.2	6.8	27.0	19.3	33.2	24.4
Weld	9.8	81,024	70.1	56.9	4.0	9.3	29.9	23.0	40.2	22.7
Connecticut	12.6	1,323,431	67.3	51.2	4.0	12.1	32.7	27.1	34.4	32.8
Fairfield	19.4	324,360	70.1	54.2	4.0	11.9	29.9	25.0	37.4	33.2
Hartford	13.4	337,494	65.7	48.1	4.0	13.6	34.3	28.9	33.6	33.4
Litchfield	6.5	74,026	68.8	56.0	3.5	9.4	31.2	26.6	32.9	34.5
Middlesex	6.9	65,162	67.4	54.8	4.0	8.6	32.6	26.3	32.8	32.8
New Haven	11.0	322,561	65.8	48.2	3.9	13.6	34.2	28.4	33.7	33.0
New London	7.3	104,132	66.1	52.0	3.9	10.2	33.9	27.4	33.0	30.9
Tolland	6.0	52,777	69.9	58.5	3.8	7.6	30.1	22.4	33.4	28.6
Windham	4.1	42,919	66.1	49.3	5.6	11.2	33.9	27.4	32.8	30.5
Delaware	7.6	321,748	67.7	49.9	4.7	13.2	32.3	26.2	34.0	32.7
Kent	4.8	55,685	71.1	52.7	4.2	14.3	28.9	24.2	37.8	31.4
New Castle	8.9	193,434	66.6	48.4	4.7	13.4	33.4	26.8	34.7	29.8
Sussex	5.9	72,629	68.2	51.7	4.8	11.6	31.8	25.8	29.3	41.6
District of Columbia	12.7	249,805	42.9	21.7	3.8	17.5	57.1	47.9	21.6	28.2
District of Columbia	12.7	249,805	42.9	21.7	3.8	17.5	57.1	47.9	21.6	28.2
Florida	18.7	7,077,123	65.3	48.4	4.6	12.3	34.7	27.9	30.5	37.5
Alachua	9.6	95,850	52.6	36.9	3.9	11.9	47.4	32.9	24.8	24.9
Baker	1.2	7,560	75.2	56.2	4.2	14.9	24.8	22.4	38.5	30.8
Bay	5.4	71,417	65.5	48.1	3.9	13.6	34.5	26.7	31.2	31.5
Bradford	1.2	8,217	72.8	54.1	4.7	14.0	27.2	25.0	31.1	35.2
Brevard	8.2	217,708	65.5	51.0	3.8	10.7	34.5	28.6	27.1	41.8
Broward	29.9	676,384	62.7	44.5	4.7	13.5	37.3	30.2	32.2	34.6
Charlotte	9.9	70,376	67.6	55.7	3.6	8.3	32.4	26.7	21.9	53.7
Citrus	5.6	58,905	67.9	56.6	3.2	8.1	32.1	26.4	21.5	53.8
Clay	5.1	63,858	76.3	58.5	5.6	12.2	23.7	18.6	41.1	29.0
Collier	23.6	119,883	67.0	56.4	3.5	7.1	33.0	27.3	25.4	49.8
Columbia	3.1	22,161	70.2	47.3	6.0	17.0	29.8	25.1	36.6	37.8
DeSoto	24.4	10,906	69.8	52.1	5.1	12.6	30.2	23.6	35.7	45.6
Duval	7.9	335,842	63.6	44.2	4.5	14.9	36.4	29.7	33.2	26.7
Escambia	4.3	117,990	65.1	46.8	4.1	14.2	34.9	28.8	30.9	34.9

Table A-2. Counties — Who: Age, Race/Ethnicity, and Household Structure, 2005–2007—*Continued*

STATE County code	STATE County	Total population	Percent change 2005–2007	Population by age (percent)						Median age	Race alone or in combination (percent)				Percent Hispanic or Latino
				Under 5 years	5 to 17 years	18 to 24 years	25 to 44 years	45 to 64 years	65 years and over		White	Black	Asian Hawaiian or Pacific Islander	Amer. Indian, Alaska Native, or some other race	
	ACS table number:	B01003	Population estimates	B01001	B01001	B01001	B01001	B01001	B01001	B01002	B02008	B02009	B02011 + B02012	B02010 + B02013	C03002
		1	2	3	4	5	6	7	8	9	10	11	12	13	14
	Florida—Cont.														
12 035	Flagler	82,085	17.2	4.8	13.7	7.8	24.6	24.8	24.3	44.3	86.4	10.2	2.1	2.7	7.6
12 039	Gadsden	46,539	2.5	7.6	16.8	9.8	27.4	25.6	12.7	36.6	40.2	55.4	0.3	4.6	8.2
12 049	Hardee	28,314	3.5	8.4	18.7	8.9	31.4	18.8	13.8	33.4	82.3	7.4	3.0	8.7	40.7
12 051	Hendry	39,128	2.8	9.9	19.0	12.3	28.9	20.1	9.9	30.8	66.6	14.6	-	20.1	46.6
12 053	Hernando	162,975	8.1	5.0	14.2	7.5	22.9	24.2	26.2	45.3	92.4	5.2	1.2	2.6	8.2
12 055	Highlands	97,392	4.3	5.1	13.8	6.7	21.7	21.3	31.4	47.2	85.2	9.8	1.4	4.3	15.6
12 057	Hillsborough	1,157,007	3.6	7.2	17.8	9.3	29.1	25.1	11.5	36.2	76.1	16.5	3.5	5.9	21.8
12 061	Indian River	129,401	4.0	5.3	13.7	7.5	22.8	24.9	25.9	45.5	88.4	8.8	1.3	2.5	9.3
12 063	Jackson	49,043	1.1	5.7	14.8	9.9	28.5	25.7	15.3	37.9	70.7	26.9	0.6	3.7	3.4
12 069	Lake	288,580	9.3	5.7	14.2	6.9	24.1	21.8	27.2	44.2	84.5	9.1	1.8	5.7	9.8
12 071	Lee	567,711	8.9	6.1	14.7	7.0	25.2	24.6	22.4	42.8	85.6	7.7	1.5	6.1	15.8
12 073	Leon	257,630	2.7	6.1	14.6	19.8	27.2	23.7	8.6	31.1	64.7	31.6	3.0	2.3	4.3
12 075	Levy	38,307	4.4	5.9	16.1	8.7	23.9	27.3	18.0	41.5	87.3	11.0	0.8	3.7	5.2
12 081	Manatee	310,764	3.3	6.2	15.2	7.1	24.3	24.9	22.3	43.1	84.4	8.9	1.8	5.8	12.5
12 083	Marion	313,658	7.6	5.5	14.9	7.7	24.2	23.8	23.9	43.4	84.3	11.8	1.5	3.3	8.6
12 085	Martin	138,675	0.5	4.2	13.7	7.0	22.1	26.7	26.3	47.0	88.7	6.1	1.2	5.1	9.7
12 086	Miami-Dade	2,373,297	1.3	6.6	16.6	9.7	28.1	24.5	14.4	38.2	73.2	20.2	1.8	6.4	61.4
12 087	Monroe	74,534	-3.6	4.5	11.8	5.3	25.3	37.9	15.2	46.5	90.4	5.6	1.5	3.5	18.0
12 089	Nassau	66,506	6.0	5.7	16.3	8.1	26.2	28.8	15.0	41.2	90.3	8.1	1.1	1.6	2.3
12 091	Okaloosa	182,644	-1.1	7.1	16.9	8.6	27.1	27.4	12.9	38.7	85.3	10.6	4.3	2.9	5.4
12 093	Okeechobee	39,888	2.4	7.2	17.2	10.0	26.4	22.6	16.6	36.7	84.6	9.1	1.1	6.7	22.3
12 095	Orange	1,050,676	3.5	7.6	17.7	10.1	31.3	23.8	9.5	34.6	66.3	20.4	4.9	10.7	23.7
12 097	Osceola	243,872	10.6	7.6	18.5	9.0	30.7	22.9	11.3	34.5	77.1	11.5	3.7	10.9	39.1
12 099	Palm Beach	1,264,012	0.6	6.0	15.3	7.4	24.8	24.9	21.5	42.5	74.3	16.0	2.5	8.3	16.7
12 101	Pasco	444,898	8.6	5.7	15.3	7.5	26.0	24.2	21.4	42.1	92.3	4.0	2.1	3.0	9.2
12 103	Pinellas	922,147	-0.9	5.0	14.2	6.8	24.3	28.9	20.8	44.8	85.4	10.6	3.3	2.3	6.7
12 105	Polk	557,184	6.7	7.0	17.2	8.5	26.3	23.6	17.4	38.2	78.7	14.7	1.7	7.1	14.5
12 107	Putnam	73,324	1.5	6.6	17.3	8.5	23.1	25.6	18.9	40.4	79.4	17.7	0.7	3.0	7.9
12 109	St. Johns	168,125	9.3	5.4	15.7	8.9	26.3	29.1	14.5	41.0	90.7	6.7	2.5	1.8	4.2
12 111	St. Lucie	249,687	9.7	6.4	16.1	8.1	25.7	23.6	20.1	40.5	78.1	17.3	1.8	4.2	13.9
12 113	Santa Rosa	144,681	3.2	6.1	17.5	8.4	27.9	28.1	11.9	38.8	91.1	5.6	2.9	3.0	3.6
12 115	Sarasota	368,116	2.2	4.4	12.1	6.0	21.4	26.7	29.5	49.7	91.9	4.8	1.4	3.0	6.7
12 117	Seminole	407,260	1.6	6.0	17.4	8.9	28.2	28.5	11.0	38.5	81.2	11.5	4.1	5.8	14.6
12 119	Sumter	67,942	13.8	4.0	12.1	5.6	31.1	24.9	22.3	43.5	84.5	12.8	0.9	3.0	8.0
12 121	Suwannee	38,763	4.0	6.4	16.5	8.5	24.0	26.7	17.9	40.5	84.3	12.0	0.6	4.0	7.6
12 127	Volusia	494,198	2.9	5.3	14.6	9.0	24.6	26.1	20.5	42.5	85.7	10.5	1.8	3.5	9.7
12 129	Wakulla	28,765	7.2	5.8	16.0	8.0	29.3	28.3	12.7	38.3	85.8	13.0	-	1.7	2.8
12 131	Walton	51,355	6.5	5.8	15.1	7.2	28.3	28.8	14.8	41.1	88.0	7.3	0.9	5.2	3.2
12 133	Washington	22,382	4.5	6.2	16.0	8.6	27.1	27.5	14.6	39.7	83.9	14.5	-	3.0	2.7
13 000	**Georgia**	9,331,515	4.8	7.7	18.8	9.8	29.9	24.0	9.8	34.6	63.4	30.2	3.1	4.7	7.4
13 009	Baldwin	45,729	1.1	6.0	14.2	18.6	26.9	23.2	11.0	34.7	55.8	43.3	1.5	-	1.4
13 013	Barrow	63,245	13.0	8.7	20.4	8.2	34.9	19.2	8.6	32.0	83.1	11.5	2.9	4.1	6.6
13 015	Bartow	90,489	5.2	8.6	20.0	7.6	31.1	23.0	9.7	33.7	85.6	9.9	0.9	4.3	5.6
13 021	Bibb	154,664	0.2	7.8	19.2	9.9	25.5	24.8	12.7	35.8	47.7	50.2	1.5	1.3	1.7
13 029	Bryan	28,915	8.3	7.9	21.0	9.1	29.8	24.9	7.3	34.5	81.6	15.8	1.7	2.7	2.8
13 031	Bulloch	64,837	4.1	6.2	15.4	26.4	24.3	18.7	9.0	26.4	68.7	29.0	1.5	2.2	2.5
13 033	Burke	22,759	-0.5	8.8	21.6	10.9	23.6	24.5	10.6	34.4	47.9	52.3	-	-	-
13 035	Butts	23,113	5.7	6.9	16.8	8.8	32.1	24.0	11.3	35.4	71.1	27.3	-	-	-
13 039	Camden	47,244	5.8	8.0	22.6	11.2	30.7	20.1	7.4	30.2	77.7	20.6	2.2	2.8	3.2
13 045	Carroll	108,252	7.1	7.6	18.8	11.4	30.7	21.6	10.0	32.3	79.7	17.4	0.9	3.1	4.3
13 047	Catoosa	60,961	4.2	6.9	18.4	7.8	30.1	24.5	12.3	36.1	95.6	2.6	1.1	2.1	1.8
13 051	Chatham	244,296	3.4	7.6	17.7	11.2	27.3	23.9	12.3	34.7	55.8	40.9	2.6	1.9	2.9
13 055	Chattooga	26,282	3.3	5.8	16.9	8.7	30.6	24.0	14.0	35.7	86.8	11.0	-	1.6	-
13 057	Cherokee	193,843	11.6	8.6	20.2	8.3	31.6	24.2	7.1	33.8	86.5	5.9	2.1	7.1	8.3
13 059	Clarke	111,691	4.3	6.5	12.4	28.3	28.7	15.9	8.3	26.4	67.0	26.4	4.1	3.4	8.6
13 063	Clayton	268,960	2.5	8.6	21.5	9.0	32.3	21.8	6.7	32.1	26.6	61.5	5.3	8.3	10.8
13 067	Cobb	678,711	4.3	7.9	18.4	8.8	31.0	25.8	8.1	35.5	65.3	22.9	4.4	8.7	10.9
13 069	Coffee	39,689	2.3	8.0	19.7	10.5	28.4	22.9	10.6	33.9	68.3	26.6	-	4.9	-
13 071	Colquitt	44,160	3.1	8.1	19.1	9.7	28.6	22.0	12.6	33.8	65.8	23.3	0.4	11.1	14.6
13 073	Columbia	105,694	6.6	7.2	20.5	9.6	26.5	27.3	9.1	36.2	80.3	15.1	4.1	2.5	3.0
13 077	Coweta	114,004	9.2	7.9	20.4	7.7	31.8	23.2	9.0	34.3	78.6	17.7	1.4	3.6	5.2
13 081	Crisp	21,937	1.6	7.7	20.1	10.5	23.3	24.7	13.6	34.7	53.0	45.3	-	1.9	-
13 085	Dawson	20,578	9.2	7.3	18.0	7.5	31.4	24.8	11.1	36.1	97.5	-	-	1.9	-
13 087	Decatur	28,293	2.0	7.2	19.8	9.0	26.9	24.2	12.9	35.3	57.2	40.3	-	2.8	-
13 089	DeKalb	728,987	2.5	7.5	16.8	9.4	33.3	24.7	8.4	35.4	35.3	54.8	4.6	6.5	9.7
13 091	Dodge	19,838	2.2	6.5	18.4	11.6	26.0	23.7	13.8	35.6	68.5	30.4	-	1.2	-
13 095	Dougherty	95,348	0.5	7.9	19.4	11.8	25.1	23.3	12.4	33.4	34.7	63.5	1.2	1.5	1.4
13 097	Douglas	118,591	10.7	8.0	20.9	9.0	31.2	23.7	7.2	32.8	64.0	32.8	1.7	3.4	5.2
13 103	Effingham	48,527	9.4	7.4	20.8	9.2	30.3	23.8	8.4	33.9	84.3	15.2	-	-	-
13 105	Elbert	20,601	-0.6	6.3	17.8	8.4	26.9	26.0	14.7	38.1	67.0	30.3	-	2.1	-
13 107	Emanuel	22,309	1.9	8.1	17.3	11.2	26.1	24.3	13.0	34.6	64.2	33.3	-	2.6	-
13 111	Fannin	22,201	3.7	5.7	14.4	7.2	25.8	26.5	20.3	42.5	97.6	-	-	1.9	-
13 113	Fayette	104,545	3.4	5.1	19.6	9.8	23.1	31.6	10.8	40.1	76.5	18.5	3.7	2.9	3.8
13 115	Floyd	94,979	1.5	7.4	17.5	10.0	26.8	24.3	14.1	36.4	81.9	14.0	1.5	4.0	7.5

Table A-2. Counties — Who: Age, Race/Ethnicity, and Household Structure, 2005–2007—*Continued*

STATE County	Percent foreign born	Total households	Household type (percent)						Percent of households with people under 18 years	Percent of households with people 60 years and over
			Family households				Nonfamily households			
			Total family households	Married-couple families	Male householder families	Female householder families	Total nonfamily households	One-person households		
ACS table number:	C05002	B11001	B11001	B11001	B11001	B11001	B11001	B11001	C11005	B11006
	15	16	17	18	19	20	21	22	23	24
Florida—Cont.										
Flagler	12.5	37,601	69.5	57.2	3.5	8.9	30.5	21.3	26.7	44.7
Gadsden	6.1	15,656	70.0	41.1	4.8	24.1	30.0	25.7	36.0	36.3
Hardee	19.5	8,644	81.1	55.0	11.0	15.1	18.9	14.5	49.9	34.7
Hendry	29.2	10,964	80.1	56.6	7.7	15.8	19.9	14.7	47.8	30.7
Hernando	6.4	66,252	69.3	57.9	3.1	8.3	30.7	25.3	26.6	50.7
Highlands	11.7	40,152	66.1	52.8	3.9	9.3	33.9	28.5	23.8	56.8
Hillsborough	14.6	453,926	64.1	45.7	5.0	13.4	35.9	28.5	33.5	28.1
Indian River	10.3	58,175	65.6	51.5	4.0	10.1	34.4	27.2	27.6	47.1
Jackson	3.3	16,916	68.3	48.2	6.7	13.4	31.7	26.8	36.1	33.6
Lake	8.3	114,906	70.2	57.6	3.7	9.0	29.8	25.0	27.3	50.7
Lee	14.4	243,673	66.2	53.2	3.9	9.0	33.8	26.3	26.5	43.6
Leon	5.5	107,535	55.2	37.7	4.1	13.4	44.8	32.8	28.1	21.9
Levy	3.9	14,341	71.6	54.9	4.6	12.1	28.4	22.5	32.4	42.2
Manatee	11.9	131,981	65.3	50.6	4.4	10.3	34.7	27.9	27.3	43.7
Marion	6.0	127,764	67.9	53.3	3.9	10.7	32.1	26.5	26.8	48.0
Martin	10.7	58,784	65.9	53.0	4.0	8.8	34.1	28.4	25.4	48.7
Miami-Dade	50.4	830,844	68.7	45.5	5.9	17.3	31.3	25.9	35.4	36.3
Monroe	16.1	31,925	59.4	48.3	4.2	6.9	40.6	31.2	20.6	37.5
Nassau	3.1	25,521	74.8	59.1	4.9	10.8	25.2	20.3	34.8	36.8
Okaloosa	5.5	74,771	67.2	52.9	3.5	10.9	32.8	26.8	32.1	31.3
Okeechobee	14.1	12,732	72.4	53.0	4.9	14.6	27.6	22.1	35.1	43.3
Orange	18.6	393,502	65.0	44.9	5.2	14.8	35.0	25.7	35.4	24.8
Osceola	19.4	89,369	75.4	54.0	5.3	16.2	24.6	18.1	42.6	29.3
Palm Beach	21.2	507,904	62.1	47.6	4.2	10.4	37.9	31.1	27.1	43.8
Pasco	8.7	179,419	66.4	52.4	4.3	9.7	33.6	26.7	28.7	42.7
Pinellas	11.5	410,560	57.1	42.9	3.9	10.3	42.9	35.7	23.1	41.7
Polk	10.1	222,196	70.7	53.5	5.2	12.1	29.3	23.4	33.6	38.0
Putnam	3.9	27,661	65.6	46.4	5.3	14.0	34.4	29.1	28.9	43.0
St. Johns	6.0	65,874	67.8	56.0	2.6	9.1	32.2	25.3	32.2	33.6
St. Lucie	16.0	98,889	69.1	52.8	5.2	11.1	30.9	25.0	31.2	43.0
Santa Rosa	4.1	50,026	75.7	60.5	3.8	11.4	24.3	19.3	35.6	31.6
Sarasota	12.1	168,014	61.2	50.5	3.0	7.7	38.8	31.6	20.7	51.7
Seminole	11.4	154,503	68.1	51.0	5.0	12.0	31.9	25.4	33.7	28.8
Sumter	6.6	32,090	76.7	60.7	6.7	9.3	23.3	16.9	35.9	43.7
Suwannee	6.1	12,527	69.8	50.3	5.8	13.7	30.2	25.6	32.8	45.9
Volusia	7.6	201,368	62.3	47.6	3.9	10.8	37.7	30.5	26.7	42.6
Wakulla	1.0	10,605	70.5	58.4	3.3	8.9	29.5	23.1	33.2	32.2
Walton	4.1	21,458	65.2	50.7	2.6	11.9	34.8	26.7	24.5	35.1
Washington	2.6	8,209	67.7	53.6	2.4	11.7	32.3	29.4	31.5	39.1
Georgia	9.0	3,364,749	68.2	49.0	4.6	14.7	31.8	26.4	37.3	26.5
Baldwin	2.6	14,374	63.5	41.5	3.8	18.1	36.5	30.6	29.0	33.0
Barrow	5.2	21,730	76.2	59.6	5.7	10.9	23.8	20.6	44.7	25.3
Bartow	4.1	32,966	73.8	58.9	4.6	10.3	26.2	22.0	39.3	26.5
Bibb	2.3	58,801	61.9	39.0	3.8	19.2	38.1	33.1	31.8	32.2
Bryan	4.2	10,068	78.2	60.9	3.3	14.0	21.8	17.6	48.8	22.6
Bulloch	2.4	23,229	60.0	43.0	3.8	13.2	40.0	29.2	33.4	22.7
Burke	0.3	7,814	68.4	42.6	5.5	20.2	31.6	28.6	41.4	33.1
Butts	1.5	7,538	78.0	60.6	3.7	13.7	22.0	17.4	39.5	31.9
Camden	2.4	17,498	71.1	56.3	3.1	11.8	28.9	23.0	42.5	22.0
Carroll	4.7	39,697	69.4	52.6	4.0	12.7	30.6	23.9	37.6	26.8
Catoosa	2.5	23,550	72.7	56.8	4.9	10.9	27.3	22.6	39.3	30.8
Chatham	4.6	96,627	63.4	42.5	5.0	15.9	36.6	29.7	31.2	30.8
Chattooga	2.5	9,107	73.8	51.1	6.7	16.0	26.2	23.3	36.9	34.9
Cherokee	8.5	70,142	76.4	62.6	4.1	9.6	23.6	19.5	43.1	20.5
Clarke	9.9	42,540	49.9	31.6	4.7	13.7	50.1	33.5	26.3	20.2
Clayton	14.0	88,190	68.3	39.2	5.8	23.3	31.7	26.5	42.3	20.8
Cobb	15.1	248,741	68.2	52.0	4.4	11.7	31.8	25.9	37.6	21.9
Coffee	5.3	14,270	72.5	50.8	6.4	15.3	27.5	24.4	41.1	31.7
Colquitt	10.3	15,902	72.7	47.9	6.2	18.6	27.3	25.0	43.0	31.4
Columbia	4.9	38,232	78.8	66.0	3.7	9.1	21.2	17.5	40.5	25.5
Coweta	4.6	39,864	78.6	62.1	4.3	12.2	21.4	17.6	42.5	24.9
Crisp	0.9	8,257	68.1	39.3	5.6	23.1	31.9	30.3	37.7	34.9
Dawson	2.2	7,343	81.2	69.5	5.7	6.0	18.8	13.7	35.5	30.4
Decatur	1.8	11,269	69.9	48.9	4.7	16.3	30.1	27.8	39.7	28.1
DeKalb	16.3	267,301	57.9	36.1	5.0	16.9	42.1	33.4	32.0	22.7
Dodge	1.1	6,681	59.3	42.4	4.7	12.2	40.7	36.7	30.7	40.0
Dougherty	1.8	36,920	64.1	36.4	3.9	23.8	35.9	31.4	35.5	30.0
Douglas	5.8	41,939	73.2	52.9	5.2	15.0	26.8	20.4	41.5	21.6
Effingham	1.3	16,568	78.4	61.9	4.2	12.4	21.6	19.6	42.7	24.5
Elbert	2.3	7,930	69.8	51.1	4.5	14.2	30.2	26.8	36.7	36.2
Emanuel	5.3	8,161	66.6	46.5	4.9	15.2	33.4	29.7	35.8	34.8
Fannin	3.0	10,861	69.1	56.1	3.4	9.6	30.9	26.2	33.1	38.0
Fayette	7.3	36,591	78.4	65.6	2.9	9.9	21.6	18.6	42.3	31.1
Floyd	6.4	34,506	68.6	49.8	5.2	13.6	31.4	27.4	33.5	35.2

Table A-2. Counties — Who: Age, Race/Ethnicity, and Household Structure, 2005–2007—Continued

STATE County code	STATE County	Total population	Percent change 2005–2007	Population by age (percent)							Race alone or in combination (percent)			
				Under 5 years	5 to 17 years	18 to 24 years	25 to 44 years	45 to 64 years	65 years and over	Median age	White	Black	Asian Hawaiian or Pacific Islander	Amer. Indian, Alaska Native, or some other race	Percent Hispanic or Latino
	ACS table number:	B01003	Population estimates	B01001	B01001	B01001	B01001	B01001	B01001	B01002	B02008	B02009	B02011 + B02012	B02010 + B02013	C03002
		1	2	3	4	5	6	7	8	9	10	11	12	13	14
	Georgia—Cont.														
13 117	Forsyth	148,637	14.6	8.8	20.6	6.9	33.4	22.6	7.6	34.0	92.5	2.9	3.8	2.3	7.7
13 119	Franklin	21,641	1.4	6.7	17.3	8.4	27.2	24.6	15.8	38.4	90.5	8.4	1.4	-	1.7
13 121	Fulton	963,676	6.2	7.3	17.7	9.2	32.6	25.4	7.9	35.2	49.1	43.1	4.4	4.5	7.9
13 123	Gilmer	27,889	4.2	6.8	17.6	7.6	29.5	24.4	14.1	36.2	93.7	-	-	7.9	-
13 127	Glynn	73,276	4.8	7.2	18.0	8.8	25.7	26.0	14.2	37.8	71.8	26.3	1.1	1.7	4.3
13 129	Gordon	50,856	4.9	8.5	18.5	8.4	31.3	22.7	10.7	34.0	86.0	4.0	1.2	9.8	12.7
13 131	Grady	24,681	3.1	7.7	18.9	9.4	27.0	24.2	12.8	35.6	63.7	30.3	-	6.8	8.8
13 135	Gwinnett	748,715	7.8	8.9	20.2	8.3	32.7	24.0	6.0	33.6	63.0	20.4	9.6	8.7	16.3
13 137	Habersham	40,852	7.3	7.2	16.9	10.9	26.6	23.7	14.7	37.6	88.4	4.6	2.1	6.4	10.8
13 139	Hall	172,729	8.8	9.2	19.4	8.6	31.7	21.7	9.5	32.6	85.3	6.9	1.9	6.9	25.2
13 143	Haralson	28,378	2.1	8.1	17.5	8.0	27.9	24.5	13.9	36.6	93.4	5.6	-	-	-
13 145	Harris	28,250	6.2	6.0	18.1	9.0	27.1	27.9	11.8	37.7	78.7	19.6	1.0	2.2	1.9
13 147	Hart	24,091	1.5	6.5	16.8	7.1	27.2	25.9	16.5	40.6	78.6	20.1	-	2.0	-
13 151	Henry	176,870	11.3	8.3	21.8	8.5	32.9	21.4	7.1	32.1	66.3	29.2	3.1	3.2	4.5
13 153	Houston	128,345	4.0	7.5	19.9	9.8	28.3	24.2	10.2	34.6	69.1	27.4	2.8	3.0	3.7
13 157	Jackson	55,598	14.0	7.9	19.2	8.3	31.7	22.3	10.6	33.6	89.8	8.0	1.6	1.9	4.4
13 169	Jones	26,949	2.1	6.6	18.5	9.4	27.7	26.2	11.7	37.0	74.8	24.9	0.7	1.0	-
13 175	Laurens	47,095	1.8	7.5	18.5	8.7	27.0	24.6	13.8	36.2	63.2	35.2	1.1	1.2	1.4
13 177	Lee	32,025	7.1	6.2	20.8	11.1	28.5	26.6	6.8	33.8	81.3	18.7	1.0	0.5	1.5
13 179	Liberty	61,333	-4.0	10.7	22.9	13.6	31.6	16.1	5.1	26.3	51.2	43.2	3.4	5.4	6.8
13 185	Lowndes	100,243	3.3	7.8	18.4	14.7	29.2	20.7	9.2	30.5	63.1	34.4	1.7	2.9	2.9
13 187	Lumpkin	25,762	7.0	6.1	17.4	15.6	27.9	22.8	10.3	32.5	95.0	1.5	1.5	3.0	4.6
13 189	McDuffie	21,508	0.7	7.5	18.9	8.2	29.6	23.5	12.4	36.3	60.2	38.8	-	-	-
13 195	Madison	27,618	2.8	6.1	19.1	8.2	28.4	25.6	12.6	37.0	89.3	9.3	-	2.2	-
13 199	Meriwether	22,859	-0.4	6.9	18.7	8.5	26.4	25.6	13.7	36.6	59.0	40.8	-	0.8	-
13 205	Mitchell	23,796	2.8	7.1	18.3	11.1	27.7	23.5	12.2	36.0	51.8	46.5	-	1.3	-
13 207	Monroe	24,359	6.6	5.4	18.7	12.1	25.8	26.9	11.2	37.7	73.2	27.0	-	1.0	-
13 213	Murray	40,501	1.2	7.9	20.1	7.9	32.6	22.7	8.8	33.5	91.7	1.1	-	8.4	11.1
13 215	Muscogee	189,173	-0.8	7.8	19.2	12.4	25.4	23.5	11.5	33.4	50.1	46.3	2.9	3.2	4.0
13 217	Newton	90,847	11.9	9.0	20.7	8.8	32.5	19.9	9.0	31.3	64.3	33.8	1.3	2.5	3.5
13 219	Oconee	30,339	7.0	6.0	21.0	9.4	25.2	29.2	9.3	37.4	89.4	7.4	2.3	1.4	3.6
13 223	Paulding	119,645	15.1	8.9	22.2	6.7	36.7	19.6	5.9	32.2	84.0	14.9	0.6	2.3	4.0
13 225	Peach	25,134	4.6	7.0	17.8	16.8	24.0	23.1	11.2	33.7	52.0	44.5	-	4.2	-
13 227	Pickens	29,298	8.2	6.2	16.8	6.9	29.9	25.1	15.1	38.9	95.9	2.5	-	2.5	-
13 233	Polk	40,893	2.9	8.5	18.3	9.1	27.5	23.8	12.8	35.2	83.4	13.3	-	4.4	-
13 237	Putnam	19,942	3.0	6.5	16.1	8.8	25.2	25.8	17.5	40.0	67.5	32.5	-	-	-
13 245	Richmond	197,206	0.2	8.0	18.8	11.3	26.9	23.5	11.5	33.5	45.3	52.3	2.5	2.3	2.7
13 247	Rockdale	79,933	5.2	7.2	20.1	9.8	27.2	26.2	9.5	35.4	58.3	36.1	3.3	3.7	9.0
13 255	Spalding	61,969	2.8	7.7	19.7	8.1	28.5	24.3	11.7	35.2	66.0	32.1	1.0	2.3	2.4
13 257	Stephens	25,183	0.8	6.6	17.1	9.0	25.7	24.9	16.7	38.1	87.3	13.0	0.5	-	1.4
13 261	Sumter	32,484	0.4	7.1	19.5	12.9	24.8	23.4	12.4	34.0	46.9	49.5	0.7	3.4	3.4
13 267	Tattnall	23,065	1.3	7.6	15.3	13.1	31.4	21.4	11.2	33.4	65.6	28.4	1.4	5.5	-
13 275	Thomas	44,735	2.2	7.1	18.1	9.1	25.7	25.3	14.8	38.3	61.0	38.0	0.6	1.6	2.0
13 277	Tift	41,156	2.8	8.1	19.2	11.5	26.6	22.9	11.7	34.1	65.7	28.5	0.6	5.3	-
13 279	Toombs	27,352	3.3	8.3	19.7	11.9	22.5	24.9	12.8	33.5	66.7	23.6	0.7	9.7	11.1
13 285	Troup	62,855	2.0	8.0	19.1	9.5	27.8	23.7	12.0	34.4	65.3	33.4	0.9	1.4	2.3
13 291	Union	20,396	5.8	4.9	14.3	6.8	25.1	25.2	23.7	43.8	98.8	0.2	-	2.3	-
13 293	Upson	27,513	0.3	6.3	18.1	8.5	27.2	25.4	14.5	37.8	71.2	28.4	-	-	-
13 295	Walker	63,885	2.1	6.3	17.5	8.0	28.9	25.5	13.8	37.3	94.7	4.8	0.3	1.3	1.2
13 297	Walton	79,251	10.1	7.6	19.9	7.7	31.8	22.4	10.6	34.8	81.0	17.2	1.1	1.3	1.1
13 299	Ware	35,424	2.5	7.2	17.1	10.3	25.9	24.5	15.0	37.1	70.5	28.0	-	2.1	-
13 303	Washington	20,483	5.0	6.4	18.2	10.0	26.9	25.2	13.3	37.9	46.9	52.5	-	-	-
13 305	Wayne	28,649	2.6	7.1	18.0	8.7	30.8	23.7	11.7	35.5	76.8	20.3	0.5	3.5	4.4
13 311	White	24,435	5.2	6.5	16.9	10.5	25.5	24.8	15.8	38.3	95.4	4.5	-	1.6	-
13 313	Whitfield	91,915	3.2	9.9	19.9	7.9	28.5	23.6	10.2	33.8	73.6	3.7	1.3	22.7	29.0
13 321	Worth	21,396	-0.7	6.9	19.0	9.0	24.7	26.8	13.5	37.8	69.4	30.3	-	0.3	-
15 000	**Hawaii**	1,276,534	1.2	6.4	15.9	9.7	28.2	25.7	14.0	37.7	41.7	3.5	78.7	4.7	8.1
15 001	Hawaii	169,082	5.0	5.8	16.8	9.4	26.3	28.3	13.5	38.6	53.9	1.5	72.4	6.4	10.8
15 003	Honolulu	904,783	0.4	6.6	15.6	10.3	28.5	24.6	14.5	37.3	37.0	4.5	81.4	4.5	7.4
15 007	Kauai	62,162	1.9	5.8	16.9	7.6	26.4	28.8	14.6	40.0	50.8	0.9	75.4	3.0	9.5
15 009	Maui	140,415	2.0	6.1	16.5	7.6	29.9	28.2	11.7	38.2	53.2	1.3	70.4	4.6	8.8
16 000	**Idaho**	1,463,059	5.2	7.8	19.4	10.0	26.9	24.2	11.6	34.2	94.1	1.0	1.9	5.3	9.5
16 001	Ada	360,789	7.5	7.6	19.0	8.8	30.8	24.3	9.5	34.3	94.2	1.6	3.1	3.4	6.2
16 005	Bannock	79,340	1.6	8.9	19.4	12.9	25.8	22.9	10.2	30.5	93.7	1.0	2.1	5.5	5.4
16 011	Bingham	43,148	1.3	9.1	22.9	9.8	23.6	23.5	11.0	31.0	86.0	1.4	1.0	14.1	14.8
16 013	Blaine	21,364	2.1	6.6	15.8	8.2	27.6	31.7	10.2	39.7	94.8	-	1.4	4.6	-
16 017	Bonner	40,455	2.8	5.3	17.0	7.1	23.4	33.0	14.2	43.4	98.0	-	0.9	2.4	2.2
16 019	Bonneville	93,620	6.3	9.7	20.8	9.2	26.0	23.8	10.5	32.0	95.8	0.9	1.2	3.7	8.8
16 027	Canyon	171,498	9.7	9.5	21.7	9.0	29.7	19.9	10.2	30.5	91.4	1.0	1.7	8.6	20.3
16 031	Cassia	20,879	0.2	9.4	22.9	9.1	22.4	23.2	13.0	33.7	89.3	0.5	1.1	11.6	-
16 039	Elmore	28,625	0.8	8.1	20.9	9.8	33.7	19.0	8.5	32.6	89.5	4.5	3.1	7.4	13.1

STATE County	Percent foreign born	Total households	Household type (percent)						Percent of households with people under 18 years	Percent of households with people 60 years and over
			Family households				Nonfamily households			
			Total family households	Married-couple families	Male householder families	Female householder families	Total nonfamily households	One-person households		
ACS table number:	C05002	B11001	B11001	B11001	B11001	B11001	B11001	B11001	C11005	B11006
	15	16	17	18	19	20	21	22	23	24
Georgia—Cont.										
Forsyth	10.2	51,314	79.7	68.1	4.0	7.6	20.3	15.5	44.4	22.0
Franklin	2.1	7,965	71.2	54.1	4.7	12.4	28.8	25.3	34.8	40.4
Fulton	12.1	348,215	56.0	37.4	3.9	14.8	44.0	36.7	31.4	22.3
Gilmer	6.7	11,553	65.1	52.8	4.4	7.9	34.9	25.5	31.6	32.6
Glynn	4.5	28,652	64.6	45.7	4.4	14.4	35.4	30.5	30.9	34.6
Gordon	8.9	18,663	71.6	56.9	3.8	10.9	28.4	25.0	39.2	28.8
Grady	6.6	9,141	67.0	46.0	4.6	16.3	33.0	29.9	35.4	33.7
Gwinnett	22.9	252,872	74.4	57.3	5.3	11.7	25.6	20.2	44.3	19.2
Habersham	7.3	14,549	73.0	57.6	4.0	11.3	27.0	23.0	36.2	36.8
Hall	18.1	54,184	74.4	56.0	5.6	12.8	25.6	21.2	40.7	27.6
Haralson	1.0	10,531	75.5	56.8	5.5	13.2	24.5	21.6	34.1	33.8
Harris	2.9	10,676	78.8	62.3	2.6	14.0	21.2	19.1	37.8	33.1
Hart	0.8	8,884	75.0	55.4	3.1	16.4	25.0	22.3	39.6	34.9
Henry	6.2	61,139	78.5	59.9	5.7	12.9	21.5	17.4	46.8	21.7
Houston	3.8	48,519	68.4	48.5	4.8	15.1	31.6	27.9	41.7	25.7
Jackson	3.7	20,080	73.3	55.4	5.1	12.8	26.7	22.8	41.7	31.7
Jones	-	9,493	75.4	57.5	6.3	11.6	24.6	20.8	41.9	31.6
Laurens	1.0	17,048	69.0	44.9	3.8	20.3	31.0	28.1	38.5	30.7
Lee	1.5	10,605	79.4	63.4	2.2	13.8	20.6	16.4	46.4	22.7
Liberty	5.9	20,465	73.0	48.5	3.4	21.1	27.0	23.2	47.1	15.5
Lowndes	3.6	38,206	69.0	46.7	4.6	17.7	31.0	24.2	37.6	23.9
Lumpkin	4.8	9,514	66.6	53.5	4.0	9.1	33.4	27.3	34.5	25.6
McDuffie	1.7	8,403	72.0	43.9	4.0	24.1	28.0	25.5	37.0	33.3
Madison	2.5	10,070	76.9	57.3	6.7	12.8	23.1	20.0	39.2	32.2
Meriwether	1.1	8,783	71.4	48.8	3.6	19.0	28.6	23.0	36.8	33.3
Mitchell	1.5	8,277	66.6	42.9	2.2	21.6	33.4	30.1	35.7	30.2
Monroe	2.0	9,028	77.3	57.2	6.2	13.8	22.7	18.7	37.9	30.0
Murray	6.9	13,604	72.2	57.7	4.2	10.2	27.8	23.1	40.4	28.2
Muscogee	3.9	71,365	66.4	40.2	5.1	21.2	33.6	29.5	36.9	29.6
Newton	5.9	32,095	75.5	55.1	5.3	15.2	24.5	20.4	44.5	25.8
Oconee	6.8	11,097	80.4	68.0	2.9	9.5	19.6	16.0	41.9	26.8
Paulding	3.4	43,715	78.0	63.5	3.4	11.1	22.0	18.0	48.3	16.9
Peach	3.5	8,385	70.5	47.9	4.3	18.2	29.5	25.5	33.5	30.3
Pickens	2.4	11,501	72.8	60.6	4.1	8.1	27.2	23.1	35.6	35.9
Polk	5.8	15,110	70.7	49.3	4.4	17.0	29.3	25.2	36.4	31.8
Putnam	1.2	8,014	70.8	49.8	5.0	16.0	29.2	21.3	29.0	36.5
Richmond	3.5	75,266	63.6	37.4	4.4	21.9	36.4	32.1	35.3	29.8
Rockdale	11.1	27,104	73.4	54.2	4.9	14.3	26.6	21.0	39.8	28.1
Spalding	2.7	22,197	72.2	48.1	5.7	18.5	27.8	23.4	38.2	31.0
Stephens	1.7	8,825	71.8	55.8	5.9	10.2	28.2	24.2	32.9	39.6
Sumter	3.7	11,917	65.0	38.4	4.8	21.8	35.0	27.9	35.1	33.6
Tattnall	7.8	7,073	74.1	51.7	8.4	14.0	25.9	21.5	35.9	30.9
Thomas	1.4	17,350	66.1	46.4	5.5	14.2	33.9	29.8	32.0	37.2
Tift	6.9	14,997	70.8	47.0	6.1	17.7	29.2	24.9	37.7	32.0
Toombs	6.0	9,768	64.6	40.6	6.1	17.9	35.4	30.5	37.9	33.9
Troup	2.5	22,907	69.2	47.3	4.2	17.6	30.8	25.6	37.7	30.5
Union	1.1	9,154	71.2	60.9	5.1	5.2	28.8	23.8	24.3	45.8
Upson	1.7	10,485	68.4	49.6	4.1	14.6	31.6	26.6	32.9	37.1
Walker	1.0	25,181	72.0	54.1	5.1	12.8	28.0	23.5	34.8	32.6
Walton	2.6	27,098	78.3	62.0	4.5	11.8	21.7	16.5	41.6	28.3
Ware	1.9	13,245	64.5	45.3	4.3	15.0	35.5	31.9	31.8	33.9
Washington	1.5	7,211	67.0	44.0	2.7	20.3	33.0	28.9	35.5	35.0
Wayne	4.1	9,544	73.1	58.3	3.1	11.7	26.9	24.4	37.4	33.5
White	2.0	9,369	69.3	59.9	1.8	7.5	30.7	25.7	32.5	37.2
Whitfield	18.5	31,274	73.8	54.9	6.0	13.0	26.2	22.3	39.5	27.8
Worth	0.4	7,750	74.0	50.3	5.6	18.1	26.0	23.7	40.3	37.8
Hawaii	16.9	433,664	70.0	52.1	5.3	12.6	30.0	23.5	35.3	36.8
Hawaii	10.4	62,069	70.2	50.2	6.7	13.2	29.8	22.0	34.0	36.0
Honolulu	18.7	301,189	70.4	52.6	5.1	12.7	29.6	23.8	35.3	37.6
Kauai	12.0	21,739	74.0	53.8	6.1	14.1	26.0	19.5	39.3	36.8
Maui	15.7	48,586	66.2	50.5	4.9	10.8	33.8	25.5	35.6	32.6
Idaho	5.6	545,171	70.1	57.0	4.1	9.0	29.9	23.7	36.9	28.8
Ada	5.2	139,341	66.7	54.1	3.8	8.8	33.3	25.5	36.1	24.1
Bannock	2.6	28,927	68.9	54.1	4.3	10.5	31.1	24.7	37.7	25.4
Bingham	6.8	14,025	77.4	64.6	4.8	8.0	22.6	20.2	41.4	32.4
Blaine	14.6	8,508	65.7	55.2	1.4	9.2	34.3	23.2	35.8	27.7
Bonner	2.9	15,318	70.0	58.1	3.2	8.8	30.0	24.4	29.2	34.2
Bonneville	4.6	33,864	72.6	59.9	3.4	9.3	27.4	22.7	39.1	28.6
Canyon	9.1	59,557	75.1	58.7	5.4	11.0	24.9	20.0	43.9	26.0
Cassia	11.6	7,321	76.8	63.4	3.8	9.5	23.2	20.4	43.6	34.3
Elmore	7.8	9,978	75.4	63.1	5.2	7.1	24.6	20.6	48.2	20.6

STATE County code	STATE County	Total population B01003	Percent change 2005–2007 Population estimates	Under 5 years B01001	5 to 17 years B01001	18 to 24 years B01001	25 to 44 years B01001	45 to 64 years B01001	65 years and over B01001	Median age B01002	White B02008	Black B02009	Asian Hawaiian or Pacific Islander B02011 + B02012	Amer. Indian, Alaska Native, or some other race B02010 + B02013	Percent Hispanic or Latino C03002
		1	2	3	4	5	6	7	8	9	10	11	12	13	14
	Idaho—Cont.														
16 051	Jefferson	22,007	7.5	9.5	23.2	10.7	25.5	22.0	9.1	29.2	93.0	-	-	7.5	-
16 053	Jerome	19,660	4.2	9.0	22.0	10.3	24.0	23.3	11.3	33.2	94.3	1.0	-	5.7	-
16 055	Kootenai	130,668	6.0	6.5	18.6	8.7	26.7	26.0	13.5	37.1	97.7	0.7	1.2	3.0	3.2
16 057	Latah	36,142	0.8	5.6	13.8	24.7	25.0	21.5	9.5	28.5	95.1	1.2	3.3	2.9	2.7
16 065	Madison	35,897	5.2	11.0	17.3	31.7	20.3	14.0	5.7	22.2	97.2	0.4	2.4	1.4	4.3
16 069	Nez Perce	38,521	2.2	5.8	16.3	9.2	24.7	26.2	17.7	40.8	94.5	1.2	1.5	6.1	2.3
16 075	Payette	22,199	4.8	7.2	21.3	8.5	24.6	24.5	13.8	36.0	91.2	-	1.5	9.5	14.0
16 083	Twin Falls	71,190	5.5	7.8	18.9	9.9	25.7	23.3	14.4	34.9	95.3	0.4	2.3	4.0	11.5
17 000	**Illinois**	12,783,049	1.0	7.0	18.1	10.0	28.4	24.5	12.0	35.7	72.5	15.4	4.6	9.2	14.6
17 001	Adams	67,053	0.1	6.2	16.9	10.0	24.9	24.8	17.3	39.0	96.0	4.0	0.7	1.1	1.0
17 007	Boone	51,622	7.8	7.2	20.4	10.4	29.0	22.7	10.2	33.7	91.1	2.2	1.5	6.4	18.4
17 011	Bureau	34,946	0.6	6.1	16.6	8.6	24.5	26.6	17.7	40.6	95.9	0.9	0.8	3.1	6.2
17 019	Champaign	188,474	1.9	6.0	14.2	23.5	27.1	19.4	9.8	28.3	78.5	12.3	8.9	2.4	4.0
17 021	Christian	34,668	-0.9	5.9	17.0	7.7	26.6	25.7	17.1	40.2	96.7	2.1	1.0	1.9	1.1
17 027	Clinton	36,280	1.2	5.6	16.6	10.1	28.1	24.3	15.3	39.0	95.1	4.4	0.7	0.8	2.2
17 029	Coles	51,157	-0.5	5.2	13.4	23.1	23.2	21.4	13.8	31.4	95.0	3.4	1.4	0.8	1.9
17 031	Cook	5,288,161	-0.3	7.2	17.9	9.6	29.5	24.1	11.7	35.5	53.2	26.3	6.1	16.1	22.5
17 037	DeKalb	101,275	5.1	6.2	15.8	22.0	27.7	19.0	9.3	28.1	87.4	6.1	3.1	5.1	9.0
17 043	DuPage	928,086	0.2	6.6	18.7	9.0	27.8	27.4	10.4	37.4	82.4	4.6	10.3	4.3	11.8
17 049	Effingham	34,317	-0.6	6.7	19.0	9.4	25.8	24.6	14.6	37.6	98.7	-	1.0	1.2	-
17 051	Fayette	21,487	-0.3	5.6	16.2	9.7	28.6	24.3	15.6	38.6	99.2	0.4	-	0.2	-
17 055	Franklin	39,468	0.2	6.2	16.4	8.2	25.4	25.4	18.3	40.3	98.9	0.5	0.3	0.9	1.0
17 057	Fulton	36,987	-0.8	5.4	15.2	8.5	27.6	25.7	17.7	41.3	95.7	3.3	-	1.2	2.3
17 063	Grundy	45,412	8.4	7.2	17.9	9.3	30.6	24.0	10.9	34.6	96.4	2.0	0.9	2.1	7.2
17 073	Henry	49,707	-0.5	5.6	17.0	9.0	23.8	28.0	16.7	40.9	96.7	1.6	0.5	2.5	3.8
17 075	Iroquois	30,307	-0.4	5.9	17.1	8.3	23.8	23.7	21.3	42.1	95.8	1.2	0.4	3.5	5.2
17 077	Jackson	58,990	-0.4	5.5	12.6	26.9	25.8	18.2	10.9	27.2	80.6	13.6	4.8	2.7	3.1
17 081	Jefferson	40,153	0.1	6.0	16.1	8.6	28.2	25.9	15.2	39.4	89.9	8.7	0.9	1.6	1.6
17 083	Jersey	22,335	1.1	6.2	16.5	11.3	25.5	25.4	15.1	37.6	98.3	1.4	-	1.0	0.4
17 085	Jo Daviess	22,345	0.0	4.7	15.0	7.9	24.4	27.9	20.1	43.5	96.3	0.8	-	2.4	-
17 089	Kane	489,641	4.7	8.8	21.0	9.2	30.3	22.6	8.2	32.3	80.5	6.3	3.3	11.6	27.8
17 091	Kankakee	109,276	2.6	7.0	18.7	9.9	27.2	24.2	12.9	35.4	81.8	15.5	1.1	2.8	6.8
17 093	Kendall	87,808	22.5	8.7	20.0	9.6	33.6	20.9	7.1	31.5	88.1	4.9	2.7	6.9	14.5
17 095	Knox	52,306	-1.7	5.3	15.7	9.4	25.8	26.2	17.7	40.5	89.4	7.8	1.0	2.7	3.8
17 097	Lake	703,706	1.9	7.4	20.9	9.5	27.8	25.3	9.2	34.9	80.9	7.2	6.1	7.5	18.6
17 099	LaSalle	112,165	0.9	6.2	17.7	9.0	25.7	25.5	15.9	39.1	96.0	2.0	0.9	3.2	6.7
17 103	Lee	35,349	0.4	5.1	17.1	8.5	27.5	26.4	15.5	40.1	94.0	5.2	1.1	2.8	4.1
17 105	Livingston	38,428	-1.1	5.8	16.4	9.4	26.7	26.7	15.0	39.5	93.1	5.6	0.7	2.0	2.8
17 107	Logan	30,161	-1.4	5.4	14.1	12.6	28.6	24.6	14.6	38.3	90.3	7.8	0.6	2.2	-
17 109	McDonough	32,016	-0.3	4.2	11.3	30.3	19.7	20.3	14.2	27.6	91.5	4.8	4.2	1.2	1.9
17 111	McHenry	309,448	4.4	7.2	20.5	8.7	29.5	24.8	9.3	35.4	91.7	1.3	3.0	5.5	10.5
17 113	McLean	162,031	2.8	6.6	16.3	18.3	27.7	21.2	9.9	30.8	88.6	7.9	3.2	2.1	3.3
17 115	Macon	109,101	-0.7	6.3	16.9	10.1	23.8	27.2	15.7	39.3	84.0	15.8	1.2	1.3	1.2
17 117	Macoupin	48,293	-0.4	6.0	16.4	9.6	25.2	25.8	16.9	39.7	98.6	1.1	0.5	0.9	0.8
17 119	Madison	266,142	0.9	6.3	17.2	10.2	27.0	25.3	13.9	37.1	90.2	8.5	1.0	1.6	2.0
17 121	Marion	39,696	-0.4	6.3	17.2	8.5	24.6	25.9	17.5	40.3	95.7	5.0	0.5	1.0	1.1
17 133	Monroe	31,864	3.4	6.2	17.3	9.9	28.4	25.4	12.8	37.7	98.1	0.6	1.0	0.9	-
17 135	Montgomery	29,916	-0.5	5.3	16.0	8.8	27.6	25.3	17.0	39.4	95.4	4.2	-	1.0	1.2
17 137	Morgan	35,378	-0.7	5.7	15.5	11.8	25.2	25.8	16.0	38.6	94.2	6.1	0.9	1.4	1.6
17 141	Ogle	54,543	1.9	5.8	18.9	9.2	25.5	26.8	13.8	38.1	96.0	1.2	0.9	4.1	8.2
17 143	Peoria	182,461	0.6	7.2	17.6	10.8	25.5	25.1	13.9	36.0	79.0	18.2	2.7	2.0	2.7
17 145	Perry	22,632	-0.3	5.5	14.1	12.0	27.8	25.3	15.2	38.2	90.1	8.5	0.3	1.0	2.7
17 157	Randolph	32,885	-0.7	5.5	15.2	9.7	29.2	25.3	15.1	38.1	88.9	8.6	-	2.9	2.8
17 161	Rock Island	146,820	0.4	6.5	16.3	10.2	25.7	25.7	15.5	38.3	85.2	9.0	2.0	5.8	10.0
17 163	St. Clair	260,185	1.0	7.1	19.0	9.8	27.2	24.4	12.5	35.6	69.1	29.9	1.7	1.4	2.6
17 165	Saline	26,028	0.4	6.5	16.1	8.7	24.5	25.5	18.7	40.6	94.5	5.7	-	1.1	-
17 167	Sangamon	193,460	0.7	6.6	17.2	8.5	27.2	26.9	13.6	38.6	87.9	11.4	1.7	1.4	1.3
17 173	Shelby	21,907	-1.4	5.5	16.7	9.0	23.7	26.5	18.6	41.9	98.4	-	0.8	0.6	-
17 177	Stephenson	46,972	-1.7	5.8	17.6	8.5	24.7	26.4	17.1	41.2	89.4	8.8	1.1	2.3	2.2
17 179	Tazewell	130,128	1.5	6.2	16.7	8.5	26.9	26.5	15.3	38.9	97.8	1.4	0.8	1.4	1.4
17 183	Vermilion	81,566	-0.8	6.6	17.5	8.9	25.5	25.3	16.2	38.3	85.1	12.2	0.9	3.3	3.5
17 195	Whiteside	59,246	-0.1	6.3	17.0	8.7	25.0	26.2	16.8	40.2	94.0	1.8	0.7	6.0	9.6
17 197	Will	654,540	6.5	8.0	20.9	9.4	31.2	22.6	8.0	32.8	78.5	11.3	4.0	8.0	13.6
17 199	Williamson	63,956	1.7	6.0	15.8	9.0	28.1	24.6	16.5	38.5	94.2	5.0	0.9	0.7	0.3
17 201	Winnebago	294,171	3.0	6.9	18.5	8.7	28.2	24.9	12.8	36.4	82.7	11.9	2.4	4.4	9.7
17 203	Woodford	37,496	2.6	6.0	18.5	10.3	24.5	26.6	14.1	37.9	98.6	0.9	0.6	0.7	1.1
18 000	**Indiana**	6,301,687	1.4	6.9	18.2	9.7	27.6	25.2	12.4	36.3	87.2	9.4	1.6	3.4	4.7
18 001	Adams	33,659	-0.2	8.9	21.4	8.8	24.6	23.0	13.3	34.1	98.7	-	0.5	1.5	3.4
18 003	Allen	346,248	1.9	7.7	19.5	8.8	27.5	25.0	11.4	35.5	83.6	12.7	2.5	3.9	5.6
18 005	Bartholomew	73,987	2.1	6.9	18.7	7.3	27.5	26.2	13.4	38.0	94.4	2.5	2.9	1.6	3.7
18 011	Boone	52,838	5.2	7.6	19.3	7.8	27.3	26.3	11.7	37.4	97.1	1.6	1.7	0.8	1.7
18 017	Cass	39,483	-1.5	6.7	18.0	7.3	26.9	26.9	14.2	38.6	90.1	2.6	0.4	6.8	-
18 019	Clark	103,411	3.5	6.7	17.3	7.6	30.0	25.9	12.5	37.3	90.1	7.6	0.9	2.9	2.7
18 021	Clay	26,745	-0.8	6.4	18.1	8.3	26.6	25.9	14.7	37.7	98.2	-	-	1.6	-

STATE County	Percent foreign born	Total households	Household type (percent)						Percent of households with people under 18 years	Percent of households with people 60 years and over
			Family households				Nonfamily households			
			Total family households	Married-couple families	Male householder families	Female householder families	Total nonfamily households	One-person households		
ACS table number:	C05002	B11001	B11001	B11001	B11001	B11001	B11001	B11001	C11005	B11006
	15	16	17	18	19	20	21	22	23	24
Idaho—Cont.										
Jefferson	5.1	7,046	82.3	71.8	3.2	7.3	17.7	15.1	45.0	25.9
Jerome	15.1	6,553	75.9	61.0	4.4	10.6	24.1	20.8	39.7	30.0
Kootenai	2.5	50,628	68.5	54.1	4.0	10.4	31.5	25.1	33.6	32.2
Latah	3.6	13,625	58.7	50.3	2.9	5.5	41.3	29.6	28.9	23.1
Madison	2.9	9,582	73.1	62.9	2.0	8.2	26.9	13.8	39.6	21.4
Nez Perce	1.8	15,844	66.8	50.9	5.9	10.0	33.2	25.8	32.2	33.6
Payette	3.8	7,966	73.0	59.2	4.8	9.0	27.0	23.7	37.1	34.0
Twin Falls	6.7	26,912	70.5	55.9	3.5	11.0	29.5	23.7	37.3	33.0
Illinois	13.7	4,724,462	66.8	49.9	4.4	12.5	33.2	27.9	35.3	30.1
Adams	0.7	27,362	64.9	52.0	2.8	10.1	35.1	29.7	31.2	35.9
Boone	9.8	16,632	77.3	62.0	4.2	11.2	22.7	19.5	42.6	29.0
Bureau	3.4	14,750	69.1	55.5	3.1	10.5	30.9	28.3	31.6	34.4
Champaign	9.4	75,038	54.6	41.6	3.2	9.8	45.4	32.4	27.1	22.5
Christian	1.5	14,011	66.2	51.9	4.8	9.5	33.8	30.4	31.3	37.8
Clinton	1.5	13,546	71.5	58.3	3.8	9.4	28.5	23.8	36.3	33.6
Coles	2.1	20,639	57.1	45.5	3.3	8.3	42.9	28.2	31.1	25.2
Cook	20.9	1,935,764	63.4	42.7	5.1	15.6	36.6	31.1	34.1	30.7
DeKalb	7.5	35,451	63.7	49.3	3.9	10.4	36.3	24.9	35.1	22.9
DuPage	18.4	335,292	71.1	59.0	3.4	8.7	28.9	24.4	37.6	27.4
Effingham	1.1	13,237	68.5	57.0	4.0	7.6	31.5	27.8	34.8	32.5
Fayette	0.9	8,005	70.0	52.3	7.5	10.1	30.0	26.9	34.0	35.6
Franklin	0.6	16,141	66.4	51.0	4.8	10.7	33.6	29.8	30.9	40.5
Fulton	1.5	14,777	68.4	54.2	3.3	10.9	31.6	28.1	31.5	38.0
Grundy	3.3	16,696	72.7	57.1	4.8	10.7	27.3	22.3	37.7	27.3
Henry	1.1	19,825	68.5	57.1	2.6	8.8	31.5	28.1	28.6	36.5
Iroquois	2.9	11,645	70.8	58.6	3.9	8.3	29.2	24.3	36.0	28.4
Jackson	5.6	24,471	48.8	36.7	2.2	9.9	51.2	39.3	23.5	24.8
Jefferson	1.3	15,841	66.9	52.8	4.1	9.9	33.1	26.3	32.4	35.4
Jersey	0.3	8,633	70.5	56.7	2.8	11.0	29.5	24.3	37.1	34.5
Jo Daviess	4.3	10,240	66.1	51.4	5.0	9.8	33.9	26.9	28.3	38.8
Kane	18.3	160,402	75.4	59.7	5.3	10.4	24.6	20.3	44.0	24.5
Kankakee	4.6	40,249	69.4	51.5	4.3	13.6	30.6	25.1	38.2	30.9
Kendall	8.8	28,793	79.9	69.2	3.5	7.2	20.1	16.3	46.6	21.6
Knox	1.3	21,637	63.1	47.6	5.1	10.4	36.9	32.4	30.2	38.3
Lake	18.1	233,617	74.3	60.8	3.8	9.7	25.7	21.5	42.2	26.1
LaSalle	3.6	45,375	66.7	53.0	3.8	9.9	33.3	28.9	32.5	32.2
Lee	2.5	13,490	70.2	57.0	3.9	9.3	29.8	25.5	35.1	29.2
Livingston	1.5	14,730	66.8	53.3	3.6	9.9	33.2	27.3	33.2	31.6
Logan	0.9	10,927	65.7	52.8	3.0	9.9	34.3	29.6	30.9	36.7
McDonough	4.4	12,883	54.2	42.1	3.1	9.0	45.8	34.4	22.1	31.6
McHenry	10.4	105,901	76.0	63.5	4.1	8.3	24.0	19.2	41.8	25.7
McLean	4.4	61,177	63.9	51.5	3.0	9.4	36.1	26.5	33.3	22.9
Macon	1.9	46,343	65.5	49.3	4.1	12.1	34.5	29.6	30.8	32.9
Macoupin	0.6	19,569	67.4	54.4	3.0	9.9	32.6	28.9	32.4	36.2
Madison	2.0	107,271	67.1	51.2	3.7	12.2	32.9	26.1	33.4	31.2
Marion	0.8	16,373	67.6	50.6	3.6	13.3	32.4	27.6	32.2	34.4
Monroe	2.3	11,741	75.2	62.8	3.3	9.0	24.8	20.9	38.9	29.6
Montgomery	1.4	11,285	69.2	56.9	3.8	8.5	30.8	28.1	32.9	34.9
Morgan	1.1	13,700	63.3	50.5	4.9	7.9	36.7	31.7	28.6	35.0
Ogle	4.9	20,282	70.7	56.7	5.9	8.2	29.3	24.7	36.1	33.8
Peoria	3.6	74,136	62.1	45.1	3.4	13.6	37.9	32.1	31.1	30.9
Perry	1.2	8,603	66.9	49.6	3.7	13.6	33.1	28.9	32.5	37.0
Randolph	1.2	12,252	68.4	53.7	3.4	11.2	31.6	29.4	32.9	36.1
Rock Island	5.6	60,173	62.8	47.8	3.6	11.5	37.2	32.5	29.5	33.5
St. Clair	2.3	101,362	67.9	46.5	4.5	16.9	32.1	27.8	36.8	30.5
Saline	0.7	11,310	66.9	50.6	3.5	12.8	33.1	31.1	31.5	37.1
Sangamon	2.2	81,172	61.7	45.0	4.2	12.5	38.3	32.1	32.5	29.7
Shelby	0.8	9,084	69.9	57.2	3.7	8.9	30.1	27.0	31.5	37.8
Stephenson	1.7	19,336	65.3	51.1	2.7	11.5	34.7	29.7	30.0	36.1
Tazewell	1.5	52,692	70.3	57.0	3.7	9.6	29.7	25.4	32.5	32.2
Vermilion	1.7	32,857	66.1	48.0	4.9	13.2	33.9	28.8	32.5	36.9
Whiteside	2.3	23,855	67.0	52.1	3.7	11.2	33.0	28.1	33.7	37.6
Will	11.1	210,889	77.6	64.1	3.8	9.7	22.4	18.5	45.6	23.9
Williamson	1.4	25,852	66.2	52.2	3.1	11.0	33.8	29.4	32.6	34.3
Winnebago	8.3	110,162	67.4	50.6	4.5	12.3	32.6	28.0	34.6	30.9
Woodford	1.5	13,896	74.3	61.5	3.9	8.8	25.7	22.1	35.8	32.2
Indiana	4.1	2,447,887	67.5	51.6	4.4	11.5	32.5	27.0	34.5	29.5
Adams	0.5	12,088	70.4	57.8	5.5	7.1	29.6	26.6	38.1	31.3
Allen	4.9	135,553	66.4	50.3	4.1	11.9	33.6	27.9	35.7	26.1
Bartholomew	5.9	27,992	71.8	57.4	4.3	10.1	28.2	22.8	36.8	30.4
Boone	2.1	19,743	72.9	63.0	2.2	7.8	27.1	22.5	39.3	29.4
Cass	6.8	15,853	71.1	57.0	5.4	8.7	28.9	23.3	37.2	34.9
Clark	2.1	43,463	65.1	47.4	5.6	12.1	34.9	29.2	33.4	28.6
Clay	0.4	10,429	72.0	59.0	2.1	10.9	28.0	23.3	36.5	32.4

Table A-2. Counties — Who: Age, Race/Ethnicity, and Household Structure, 2005–2007—*Continued*

STATE County code	STATE County	Total population	Percent change 2005–2007	Population by age (percent)						Median age	Race alone or in combination (percent)				Percent Hispanic or Latino
				Under 5 years	5 to 17 years	18 to 24 years	25 to 44 years	45 to 64 years	65 years and over		White	Black	Asian Hawaiian or Pacific Islander	Amer. Indian, Alaska Native, or some other race	
ACS table number:		B01003	Population estimates	B01001	B01001	B01001	B01001	B01001	B01001	B01002	B02008	B02009	B02011 + B02012	B02010 + B02013	C03002
		1	2	3	4	5	6	7	8	9	10	11	12	13	14
	Indiana—Cont.														
18 023	Clinton	33,757	0.3	7.4	19.0	8.4	27.5	23.7	14.0	35.7	95.7	0.9	-	4.0	-
18 027	Daviess	29,997	-0.1	8.3	20.1	7.8	26.1	23.8	14.0	35.2	97.8	-	-	2.9	-
18 029	Dearborn	49,205	2.3	6.7	18.7	8.0	27.3	27.4	11.8	38.2	98.7	1.4	-	0.5	0.7
18 031	Decatur	25,007	-0.4	7.5	18.5	7.4	27.9	25.3	13.3	36.7	98.9	1.1	-	1.3	-
18 033	DeKalb	41,585	0.9	6.9	19.5	8.0	28.4	25.2	11.9	36.1	97.6	0.4	0.5	6.9	2.0
18 035	Delaware	115,939	-1.1	5.4	15.4	17.2	24.1	23.8	14.1	34.9	91.2	7.5	1.3	1.4	1.3
18 037	Dubois	41,013	1.1	6.8	18.7	7.8	27.5	25.6	13.7	38.0	97.2	0.5	0.4	3.0	-
18 039	Elkhart	195,987	2.3	8.5	20.1	8.1	29.3	23.3	10.8	33.9	86.2	6.3	1.4	7.8	13.1
18 041	Fayette	24,420	-1.3	6.3	16.8	6.8	27.7	26.5	15.8	39.2	97.8	2.1	0.5	-	-
18 043	Floyd	72,426	1.7	6.0	18.2	8.8	26.3	28.1	12.6	38.7	93.9	5.6	0.8	1.0	1.6
18 047	Franklin	23,082	1.2	6.2	19.3	8.1	27.6	25.6	13.2	38.1	99.8	-	-	-	-
18 049	Fulton	20,290	0.1	6.2	17.8	6.9	26.6	26.5	15.9	40.2	96.7	1.1	0.6	3.1	-
18 051	Gibson	32,890	-0.6	6.4	17.3	8.4	26.6	26.5	14.8	39.2	96.8	2.5	0.8	0.5	0.9
18 053	Grant	69,470	-1.7	5.6	16.3	12.1	23.4	26.8	15.8	38.6	90.8	8.3	0.3	2.0	2.7
18 055	Greene	32,896	-1.1	6.1	17.5	7.9	26.8	26.6	15.2	41.0	99.4	0.7	0.5	1.6	-
18 057	Hamilton	251,873	8.1	8.0	22.1	7.5	31.1	23.7	7.6	34.0	91.4	4.0	4.0	2.1	2.7
18 059	Hancock	64,436	6.2	6.9	18.4	8.3	27.1	27.1	12.2	37.9	96.7	2.4	0.9	1.2	1.3
18 061	Harrison	36,632	1.0	6.2	17.6	8.6	28.4	27.4	11.9	37.9	98.0	0.7	1.1	1.1	-
18 063	Hendricks	130,455	6.4	6.5	19.9	8.3	30.5	24.9	9.8	35.4	93.7	4.1	1.7	1.3	2.0
18 065	Henry	47,331	-0.3	5.5	16.4	7.5	27.6	27.2	15.8	40.3	97.5	1.8	-	1.1	-
18 067	Howard	84,015	-0.7	6.7	18.0	7.0	26.9	26.9	14.5	38.7	91.1	7.6	1.4	1.4	2.0
18 069	Huntington	37,875	-0.7	6.2	17.6	9.5	26.2	25.7	14.7	38.2	98.8	0.5	0.6	1.0	1.1
18 071	Jackson	42,057	0.6	7.8	17.0	7.7	29.2	24.2	14.0	36.9	98.4	0.9	0.8	0.9	4.4
18 073	Jasper	31,808	3.1	6.5	18.8	10.6	26.7	24.3	13.2	35.8	98.2	1.1	-	1.3	3.8
18 075	Jay	21,460	0.5	7.2	19.4	6.5	26.5	25.0	15.4	38.3	97.9	2.2	-	1.4	-
18 077	Jefferson	32,617	0.9	6.0	17.4	11.0	26.0	25.9	13.6	38.1	96.6	2.0	0.8	1.8	1.3
18 079	Jennings	28,051	0.1	6.9	19.4	7.1	29.4	25.6	11.6	37.2	99.0	1.6	0.4	0.6	-
18 081	Johnson	132,592	5.2	6.6	19.2	9.2	29.4	24.4	11.2	35.5	95.8	1.6	1.5	1.6	2.0
18 083	Knox	38,053	-0.5	5.9	15.5	13.4	24.4	25.0	15.9	38.3	97.0	2.6	0.7	1.1	1.1
18 085	Kosciusko	75,796	0.9	7.1	19.0	7.9	28.0	25.5	12.5	36.2	93.4	1.0	0.9	5.9	6.6
18 087	LaGrange	36,691	1.9	9.6	22.8	8.1	27.7	20.8	11.0	30.8	99.0	-	0.3	1.9	-
18 089	Lake	490,093	0.8	7.1	19.0	9.0	25.6	26.4	12.8	37.2	64.2	26.4	1.4	10.0	14.0
18 091	LaPorte	109,440	0.5	6.1	17.2	8.2	27.9	26.9	13.7	38.7	88.0	11.1	0.6	2.3	4.0
18 093	Lawrence	45,969	0.1	6.0	17.3	6.6	27.3	27.0	15.7	40.2	98.6	0.7	0.6	0.7	1.0
18 095	Madison	131,085	0.4	6.1	16.8	8.6	27.1	26.1	15.3	38.9	90.1	8.9	0.6	1.6	2.1
18 097	Marion	872,842	0.9	8.3	18.4	8.2	30.5	23.9	10.8	35.2	69.2	26.3	2.1	4.7	6.5
18 099	Marshall	46,577	0.7	7.2	19.3	8.5	26.3	25.5	13.2	36.6	93.6	0.9	0.6	6.8	8.4
18 103	Miami	36,802	-0.5	6.0	17.7	8.0	28.9	26.1	13.4	38.5	94.6	4.3	0.6	3.6	1.6
18 105	Monroe	127,126	2.6	5.0	12.5	26.8	26.6	19.3	9.7	27.8	90.9	4.1	5.2	1.9	2.2
18 107	Montgomery	37,817	0.1	6.1	18.4	8.7	26.4	25.4	15.0	37.9	98.5	1.2	0.6	1.0	-
18 109	Morgan	69,561	1.0	6.3	18.8	8.0	27.9	27.4	11.4	37.9	98.6	0.9	0.5	1.1	0.9
18 113	Noble	47,449	0.5	7.3	19.9	8.3	28.8	24.5	11.2	35.4	93.8	0.2	0.1	7.7	-
18 119	Owen	22,368	0.1	6.1	17.5	7.8	27.2	27.6	13.8	39.3	98.4	0.7	-	1.5	-
18 127	Porter	158,169	3.1	6.2	17.8	10.4	26.3	28.0	11.4	37.2	94.3	2.8	1.5	2.8	6.2
18 129	Posey	26,385	-1.0	4.9	18.4	9.0	24.4	30.5	12.8	40.8	99.1	0.8	0.6	-	-
18 133	Putnam	36,914	0.3	5.6	16.2	13.5	28.4	23.8	12.6	35.8	94.6	4.8	0.2	1.5	1.0
18 135	Randolph	26,072	-1.5	5.8	17.4	7.2	25.5	27.5	16.7	40.5	98.1	0.3	0.7	2.1	-
18 137	Ripley	27,363	0.2	6.8	19.7	7.4	27.3	24.7	14.1	37.8	98.1	-	1.0	1.0	-
18 141	St. Joseph	265,507	0.4	7.1	18.3	11.7	25.3	24.6	13.0	35.5	82.4	13.1	2.1	4.7	5.9
18 143	Scott	23,639	0.2	6.5	18.0	7.4	30.7	25.3	12.0	36.7	99.0	0.5	0.5	0.7	-
18 145	Shelby	43,759	1.3	6.5	18.1	8.0	27.4	26.9	13.1	38.2	96.4	1.4	1.0	2.6	2.5
18 147	Spencer	20,325	0.1	5.9	17.5	8.1	26.0	28.4	14.1	40.3	97.8	1.2	-	1.4	-
18 149	Starke	23,496	0.5	6.3	18.5	8.1	25.9	25.9	15.3	38.6	97.6	-	0.3	2.5	2.6
18 151	Steuben	33,523	-0.3	6.2	17.8	10.0	26.9	26.6	12.5	37.2	97.4	-	0.7	8.4	2.8
18 153	Sullivan	21,424	-0.8	5.5	15.6	9.3	30.2	25.7	13.8	37.9	97.3	2.6	-	0.3	-
18 157	Tippecanoe	160,369	3.9	6.3	14.7	24.0	27.0	18.8	9.2	27.8	89.1	3.8	5.7	2.6	6.8
18 163	Vanderburgh	173,942	0.6	6.8	16.4	11.1	26.0	25.2	14.5	37.3	89.6	9.5	1.3	1.2	1.2
18 167	Vigo	104,792	0.3	6.3	15.9	14.9	24.9	24.4	13.6	35.3	91.5	7.0	1.9	1.1	1.3
18 169	Wabash	33,346	-1.8	5.9	16.2	10.9	23.8	26.3	16.9	40.3	97.4	0.8	-	2.4	1.3
18 173	Warrick	56,305	2.6	6.1	18.4	8.3	26.3	29.0	11.9	39.4	96.9	1.5	1.2	1.3	1.1
18 175	Washington	27,799	1.0	6.2	18.4	8.2	28.7	25.9	12.6	37.1	98.1	0.4	0.6	1.4	-
18 177	Wayne	68,571	-0.9	6.4	16.6	9.1	25.5	26.0	16.4	39.4	93.0	6.2	0.8	1.6	1.9
18 179	Wells	27,867	0.5	6.0	18.2	8.4	25.9	26.8	14.7	39.2	98.8	0.5	-	1.1	1.7
18 181	White	23,976	-1.3	6.2	17.7	7.7	24.7	27.2	16.6	41.1	97.3	-	-	3.1	7.3
18 183	Whitley	32,354	2.0	6.8	18.0	8.2	26.8	27.1	13.0	37.5	99.0	0.5	0.5	1.5	-
19 000	**Iowa**	2,972,066	1.1	6.5	17.4	10.4	25.4	25.6	14.7	37.9	94.1	2.9	1.8	2.5	3.8
19 011	Benton	26,591	-0.4	6.1	18.7	8.3	27.0	25.7	14.2	38.8	98.9	0.6	-	0.8	0.7
19 013	Black Hawk	127,180	0.5	6.6	16.0	15.1	24.1	24.4	13.9	35.0	89.4	8.8	1.5	1.9	2.5
19 015	Boone	26,358	0.1	5.9	17.2	8.5	25.9	26.9	15.6	39.9	98.1	1.1	-	1.2	-
19 017	Bremer	23,595	1.2	5.5	16.2	14.1	21.2	26.5	16.6	39.0	98.4	0.8	0.9	0.5	0.6
19 019	Buchanan	20,852	0.7	7.3	18.7	9.0	24.5	25.5	15.0	36.9	98.6	-	0.5	-	0.9
19 027	Carroll	20,901	-0.1	6.6	17.3	8.8	22.1	25.9	19.7	41.6	99.4	-	0.5	0.4	-
19 033	Cerro Gordo	44,183	-0.8	5.7	16.2	8.5	24.4	27.0	18.1	41.8	96.6	2.0	0.6	2.2	3.0
19 045	Clinton	49,198	-0.5	5.9	17.9	9.0	24.1	27.0	16.1	40.5	97.3	2.7	0.7	1.8	1.6

STATE County	Percent foreign born	Total households	Household type (percent)						Percent of households with people under 18 years	Percent of households with people 60 years and over
			Family households				Nonfamily households			
			Total family households	Married-couple families	Male householder families	Female householder families	Total nonfamily households	One-person households		
ACS table number:	C05002	B11001	B11001	B11001	B11001	B11001	B11001	B11001	C11005	B11006
	15	16	17	18	19	20	21	22	23	24
Indiana—Cont.										
Clinton	7.0	12,203	72.6	58.8	5.4	8.3	27.4	23.6	34.9	30.6
Daviess	2.4	10,949	71.0	56.1	3.9	11.0	29.0	26.1	36.8	34.1
Dearborn	1.0	18,143	76.4	62.3	5.0	9.2	23.6	19.8	37.2	29.4
Decatur	0.7	9,838	72.8	55.1	6.1	11.7	27.2	23.3	36.6	30.0
DeKalb	2.0	15,613	71.0	56.2	5.0	9.8	29.0	25.3	35.7	29.7
Delaware	2.2	46,513	62.5	46.1	4.7	11.7	37.5	28.8	27.9	31.4
Dubois	2.9	15,590	72.3	61.0	3.4	7.9	27.7	24.2	36.7	30.6
Elkhart	9.5	70,835	72.3	55.1	5.4	11.8	27.7	22.2	40.3	27.6
Fayette	1.4	10,071	67.8	53.6	4.5	9.6	32.2	28.3	32.9	34.5
Floyd	1.9	28,236	70.4	54.1	3.2	13.1	29.6	25.7	36.4	29.6
Franklin	0.4	7,967	76.0	61.9	6.7	7.4	24.0	19.2	35.9	29.8
Fulton	2.1	8,363	72.2	54.8	4.7	12.7	27.8	23.9	37.3	34.8
Gibson	0.6	12,986	66.5	54.5	4.8	7.2	33.5	28.9	31.7	33.5
Grant	1.1	27,649	66.1	49.8	3.5	12.9	33.9	29.5	30.6	35.2
Greene	1.1	13,881	68.0	53.6	3.4	11.0	32.0	28.8	31.3	33.3
Hamilton	6.2	88,941	75.9	64.3	3.4	8.3	24.1	18.8	44.5	20.8
Hancock	1.6	24,834	76.9	64.6	4.2	8.0	23.1	18.1	38.4	30.7
Harrison	0.8	13,505	78.7	65.2	4.9	8.5	21.3	17.4	39.3	28.2
Hendricks	3.1	49,755	74.6	62.6	3.8	8.2	25.4	20.5	39.9	24.8
Henry	0.3	18,981	68.4	56.3	3.3	8.9	31.6	27.6	32.9	36.0
Howard	2.4	34,683	70.2	52.8	4.2	13.2	29.8	25.5	33.7	31.2
Huntington	1.0	14,435	72.4	59.9	2.9	9.6	27.6	24.2	34.3	33.7
Jackson	3.7	17,005	71.7	59.8	3.4	8.5	28.3	24.2	34.8	32.0
Jasper	2.3	11,984	72.4	60.6	3.1	8.7	27.6	24.2	36.2	33.0
Jay	1.0	8,437	68.6	53.4	4.8	10.4	31.4	28.2	33.0	35.1
Jefferson	0.9	12,502	67.4	51.9	4.4	11.1	32.6	29.9	35.8	33.5
Jennings	1.3	11,654	74.3	55.6	5.7	13.0	25.7	21.6	41.1	29.4
Johnson	2.7	50,241	73.1	59.1	4.2	9.8	26.9	21.8	38.2	27.4
Knox	0.7	15,077	67.9	52.7	2.9	12.3	32.1	28.0	33.4	36.8
Kosciusko	4.5	29,822	71.4	57.4	5.5	8.5	28.6	23.2	37.4	28.3
LaGrange	2.4	12,117	79.9	68.4	3.6	7.9	20.1	17.5	40.5	29.5
Lake	6.6	184,254	68.1	46.5	5.1	16.6	31.9	27.4	35.0	32.2
LaPorte	3.1	41,694	68.3	51.0	4.6	12.7	31.7	26.8	33.3	33.5
Lawrence	1.3	18,719	69.9	55.7	4.3	9.8	30.1	26.5	33.0	35.4
Madison	1.1	51,392	65.6	48.7	4.4	12.4	34.4	29.4	31.0	34.5
Marion	6.7	357,445	59.7	39.0	5.0	15.7	40.3	33.4	32.9	25.4
Marshall	4.9	16,839	75.9	62.2	5.8	7.9	24.1	21.1	37.6	33.5
Miami	0.5	13,448	68.1	54.2	3.7	10.2	31.9	29.6	29.8	34.1
Monroe	6.5	46,657	52.7	41.8	2.6	8.3	47.3	34.3	26.1	24.0
Montgomery	2.7	14,712	67.7	57.3	2.3	8.1	32.3	28.9	31.9	33.4
Morgan	1.1	24,933	76.3	64.1	2.7	9.6	23.7	20.0	36.1	30.1
Noble	5.2	17,378	75.7	60.6	6.0	9.1	24.3	19.6	37.4	28.5
Owen	0.6	8,363	70.3	58.9	4.6	6.8	29.7	24.3	32.6	35.5
Porter	3.0	61,024	69.8	55.9	3.2	10.6	30.2	25.1	32.9	29.4
Posey	1.2	10,435	71.0	60.7	2.7	7.5	29.0	26.6	33.4	30.4
Putnam	1.4	12,674	71.6	58.6	4.4	8.7	28.4	23.4	36.4	32.6
Randolph	1.6	10,779	70.8	53.7	5.0	12.0	29.2	25.3	33.2	37.3
Ripley	1.7	10,588	73.5	59.2	6.2	8.1	26.5	24.1	38.3	35.4
St. Joseph	5.6	100,719	64.0	48.2	3.7	12.0	36.0	30.7	31.9	30.8
Scott	0.5	9,711	69.3	52.5	6.0	10.8	30.7	24.9	39.5	28.2
Shelby	1.9	17,008	72.0	60.1	4.0	7.9	28.0	24.8	33.8	32.3
Spencer	1.7	8,306	74.8	66.0	3.3	5.5	25.2	18.6	37.1	31.5
Starke	2.8	9,015	71.0	54.3	4.6	12.1	29.0	25.0	36.2	37.1
Steuben	2.0	14,455	69.5	55.2	5.7	8.6	30.5	25.0	33.7	28.8
Sullivan	-	8,221	63.1	49.3	3.8	10.0	36.9	29.5	30.4	34.8
Tippecanoe	10.0	60,326	58.7	43.3	4.8	10.6	41.3	29.1	31.3	22.8
Vanderburgh	2.2	72,465	61.7	45.9	4.6	11.2	38.3	32.9	31.0	30.8
Vigo	2.7	41,443	60.8	45.5	3.4	11.9	39.2	31.3	29.9	30.9
Wabash	1.0	13,312	70.8	56.4	4.3	10.0	29.2	26.6	32.4	36.1
Warrick	1.9	21,648	78.0	64.2	4.8	9.0	22.0	18.7	39.0	30.6
Washington	0.8	10,657	69.1	54.6	3.8	10.7	30.9	26.4	35.2	30.3
Wayne	1.8	27,410	66.8	50.6	6.2	10.0	33.2	28.3	32.2	35.9
Wells	2.0	10,959	66.2	56.6	2.2	7.4	33.8	28.6	31.8	30.4
White	5.9	9,945	72.5	56.9	6.2	9.4	27.5	23.9	33.3	35.4
Whitley	0.7	12,836	68.6	59.6	2.8	6.2	31.4	25.6	32.7	30.1
Iowa	3.8	1,206,848	65.5	52.8	3.5	9.2	34.5	28.3	31.7	31.5
Benton	0.8	10,110	71.5	60.1	1.7	9.7	28.5	24.6	36.3	30.7
Black Hawk	5.0	50,964	63.0	48.2	3.6	11.2	37.0	28.7	30.0	30.8
Boone	0.7	10,759	69.1	56.8	3.6	8.6	30.9	25.1	31.9	33.4
Bremer	1.9	9,651	73.2	63.6	2.5	7.0	26.8	21.3	31.7	35.2
Buchanan	1.0	8,591	69.7	57.2	4.7	7.9	30.3	24.3	35.4	29.8
Carroll	0.8	8,570	64.0	55.8	3.1	5.1	36.0	32.6	28.9	39.0
Cerro Gordo	1.1	19,113	61.8	50.8	2.9	8.1	38.2	32.5	28.5	35.0
Clinton	1.1	20,708	65.0	53.9	2.3	8.8	35.0	29.6	30.5	35.5

Table A-2. Counties — Who: Age, Race/Ethnicity, and Household Structure, 2005–2007—*Continued*

STATE County code	STATE County (ACS table number)	Total population B01003 [1]	Percent change 2005–2007 (Population estimates) [2]	Under 5 years B01001 [3]	5 to 17 years B01001 [4]	18 to 24 years B01001 [5]	25 to 44 years B01001 [6]	45 to 64 years B01001 [7]	65 years and over B01001 [8]	Median age B01002 [9]	White B01002 [10]	Black B02008 [11]	Asian Hawaiian or Pacific Islander B02011 + B02012 [12]	Amer. Indian, Alaska Native, or some other race B02010 + B02013 [13]	Percent Hispanic or Latino C03002 [14]
	Iowa—Cont.														
19 049	Dallas	54,599	10.5	7.3	19.3	9.0	32.6	22.9	8.9	33.3	94.2	1.4	1.8	3.3	6.1
19 057	Des Moines	40,661	0.1	6.3	16.8	8.6	23.7	28.0	16.5	41.3	94.8	4.8	0.9	1.4	2.2
19 061	Dubuque	91,626	1.5	6.6	17.7	10.6	24.6	25.5	15.0	38.3	97.1	2.0	1.1	1.0	1.6
19 065	Fayette	20,713	-2.6	5.2	17.0	9.7	21.6	26.6	19.9	42.5	97.8	1.0	0.7	0.6	1.8
19 087	Henry	20,139	-0.3	6.4	17.0	9.3	26.8	25.4	15.1	38.4	96.1	2.1	2.4	1.6	2.0
19 097	Jackson	20,068	-0.2	5.2	17.8	8.0	23.7	27.4	17.9	41.9	99.6	-	0.2	1.0	-
19 099	Jasper	36,887	-0.8	5.9	16.8	7.6	26.3	27.4	15.9	41.0	97.6	1.5	0.4	1.1	1.4
19 103	Johnson	123,549	3.5	6.2	14.3	21.6	29.2	20.8	7.8	29.3	89.4	4.4	5.3	2.2	3.2
19 105	Jones	20,359	0.4	5.2	16.8	8.7	26.7	26.7	16.0	41.0	97.0	1.5	1.4	1.8	1.0
19 111	Lee	35,894	-1.5	5.2	17.5	7.9	23.9	28.9	16.7	41.9	95.8	3.9	0.6	2.0	2.6
19 113	Linn	202,949	2.7	7.0	18.1	9.2	28.2	24.9	12.6	36.5	93.8	4.2	2.3	1.5	2.0
19 123	Mahaska	22,239	0.1	6.2	17.6	9.9	25.0	25.5	15.7	38.8	96.6	1.2	1.7	1.3	1.3
19 125	Marion	32,627	1.3	6.0	17.6	11.3	24.4	25.2	15.4	38.1	98.0	0.8	1.3	1.0	1.0
19 127	Marshall	39,167	0.5	7.4	17.2	8.3	23.4	27.1	16.6	40.4	91.7	2.0	1.3	6.3	13.1
19 139	Muscatine	42,241	0.9	7.4	18.9	9.1	25.9	26.7	12.0	37.9	94.3	1.4	1.2	4.4	13.4
19 149	Plymouth	24,490	-0.9	6.2	19.0	9.2	22.6	27.5	15.5	39.3	97.6	0.4	1.1	1.2	-
19 153	Polk	410,952	3.7	8.0	18.4	8.3	29.9	24.5	10.9	35.6	88.8	5.9	3.4	3.9	6.1
19 155	Pottawattamie	89,281	0.4	7.2	17.7	8.6	26.8	26.2	13.5	37.9	96.3	1.4	0.9	2.6	4.1
19 163	Scott	161,533	1.5	7.2	18.5	9.6	25.8	26.7	12.3	37.3	88.9	7.6	2.2	3.3	4.6
19 167	Sioux	32,137	1.3	7.4	17.9	16.0	21.7	22.0	14.9	33.0	97.4	0.4	1.4	1.3	4.9
19 169	Story	83,553	3.2	5.4	12.8	27.6	25.0	19.0	10.3	27.3	90.6	2.3	6.4	1.7	2.0
19 179	Wapello	35,711	-0.7	6.6	17.0	9.0	24.2	26.3	16.9	39.7	93.5	1.4	1.0	4.8	6.4
19 181	Warren	43,747	3.5	6.1	18.1	11.1	25.9	26.1	12.6	36.9	98.3	0.7	0.5	0.9	1.4
19 183	Washington	21,199	1.3	7.1	18.2	7.4	24.1	26.0	17.3	40.2	96.6	0.6	0.7	2.9	-
19 187	Webster	38,636	-0.1	6.2	17.0	9.9	24.0	26.2	16.8	38.6	95.2	4.6	1.0	1.2	2.8
19 191	Winneshiek	20,899	0.0	4.8	14.8	18.6	20.6	24.6	16.7	37.8	98.6	0.5	0.6	0.8	1.7
19 193	Woodbury	101,995	0.7	7.7	19.8	9.6	25.3	24.6	13.0	35.8	88.7	3.2	2.7	7.4	11.1
20 000	**Kansas**	2,757,827	1.3	7.1	18.1	10.5	26.5	24.9	13.0	36.1	87.6	6.7	2.6	5.7	8.5
20 009	Barton	27,822	-0.5	6.2	17.4	10.3	21.3	27.1	17.7	40.8	90.7	1.5	0.8	9.7	11.0
20 015	Butler	62,396	2.2	6.5	18.9	10.4	25.3	26.3	12.6	36.7	96.3	2.0	0.8	2.8	2.6
20 021	Cherokee	21,377	-0.3	5.7	18.1	8.7	26.0	26.3	15.2	39.5	96.0	0.7	-	7.8	1.3
20 035	Cowley	34,317	-0.7	6.0	18.3	10.1	25.1	25.8	14.7	38.8	91.0	3.6	1.8	6.1	5.5
20 037	Crawford	38,714	0.8	6.3	15.8	17.0	25.5	21.3	14.1	31.9	94.5	2.9	1.9	3.4	3.2
20 045	Douglas	112,522	1.8	5.5	13.7	24.0	28.5	19.5	8.6	28.2	88.1	5.3	4.6	4.7	3.8
20 051	Ellis	27,324	1.2	6.9	13.4	18.3	24.0	22.7	14.8	33.0	97.0	2.6	1.3	1.4	1.3
20 055	Finney	38,475	-0.9	9.4	23.7	10.8	27.0	21.8	7.2	30.4	81.6	1.4	2.9	14.9	43.9
20 057	Ford	33,126	0.8	9.6	21.8	9.4	28.9	20.2	10.1	31.2	80.5	1.6	2.1	17.2	46.6
20 059	Franklin	26,280	1.8	6.6	19.1	8.8	27.7	24.4	13.3	36.6	96.8	3.0	-	3.6	3.0
20 061	Geary	25,318	-0.8	10.3	19.6	10.8	28.6	20.3	10.4	30.1	74.1	19.3	5.3	4.1	7.8
20 079	Harvey	33,406	0.3	6.1	18.1	10.1	23.8	25.2	16.8	37.9	92.8	2.7	0.8	6.3	9.3
20 091	Johnson	516,370	4.0	7.4	18.9	8.5	29.3	25.8	10.1	36.0	90.0	4.7	4.3	3.1	5.6
20 099	Labette	21,971	0.1	6.4	17.4	9.5	24.5	26.0	16.2	39.9	92.8	6.5	-	5.0	3.5
20 103	Leavenworth	72,670	2.5	6.3	18.8	9.5	29.4	26.3	9.8	36.1	86.0	11.2	1.7	3.8	3.7
20 111	Lyon	35,860	0.3	7.2	16.3	17.3	24.6	22.8	11.8	32.1	90.8	3.6	2.4	6.6	19.3
20 113	McPherson	29,170	-0.2	5.7	16.6	11.2	22.8	26.6	17.1	40.1	98.0	1.6	0.5	2.0	2.5
20 121	Miami	30,451	3.8	7.1	18.8	9.0	26.6	27.2	11.4	37.7	98.0	1.4	1.1	2.2	1.8
20 125	Montgomery	34,383	0.7	6.6	16.4	8.8	23.2	27.2	17.7	41.8	90.4	7.1	-	6.1	3.3
20 155	Reno	63,274	-0.3	6.4	16.6	9.3	25.0	26.0	16.7	39.8	94.2	3.4	0.8	4.7	6.3
20 161	Riley	68,492	2.5	6.5	13.1	30.9	26.4	15.3	7.7	24.8	87.9	7.8	4.6	3.3	6.3
20 169	Saline	54,258	1.1	7.2	17.8	8.9	26.3	25.4	14.4	37.7	93.1	4.1	2.3	3.4	4.9
20 173	Sedgwick	470,217	2.3	8.0	19.7	9.2	27.7	24.2	11.3	34.6	80.9	10.3	4.3	7.9	10.2
20 175	Seward	22,885	1.7	11.4	21.5	9.9	28.3	20.7	8.2	30.1	69.0	3.4	2.8	28.2	50.8
20 177	Shawnee	172,529	1.1	7.1	17.5	8.8	26.3	26.4	13.8	38.0	82.9	10.5	1.5	7.8	8.5
20 191	Sumner	24,154	-2.2	7.1	18.8	8.8	22.1	28.7	14.5	39.7	95.9	1.3	-	4.6	3.6
20 209	Wyandotte	153,989	-0.3	8.8	19.8	9.0	28.3	23.5	10.6	33.6	60.5	28.4	1.9	11.8	21.7
21 000	**Kentucky**	4,205,648	1.7	6.6	17.2	9.3	28.1	25.9	12.8	37.3	90.4	8.1	1.3	1.5	2.1
21 005	Anderson	20,737	5.1	6.1	19.0	7.1	30.4	26.1	11.4	38.0	97.0	3.4	0.4		
21 009	Barren	40,607	2.9	6.3	17.1	7.0	28.2	26.1	15.3	39.5	94.6	4.4	0.7	0.5	1.2
21 013	Bell	29,121	-0.9	6.0	16.6	8.8	27.6	26.5	14.6	39.0	95.8	4.2		0.5	1.2
21 015	Boone	109,075	6.5	7.9	19.9	8.5	31.3	23.9	8.6	34.2	94.4	3.1	2.1		2.8
21 019	Boyd	48,665	-0.7	6.2	15.6	7.7	26.7	28.1	15.8	41.4	96.4	3.0	0.6	1.3	-
21 021	Boyle	28,471	1.3	5.5	16.4	11.1	26.8	25.6	14.6	38.6	89.7	10.1		1.7	2.0
21 029	Bullitt	72,516	4.0	6.1	19.0	8.2	31.0	26.4	9.3	36.1	98.2	1.2	0.5	1.2	0.9
21 035	Calloway	35,899	1.9	4.8	13.5	20.7	23.8	22.6	14.5	34.1	92.7	5.6	1.3	1.7	1.7
21 037	Campbell	86,899	-0.2	6.4	17.7	10.1	27.1	26.0	12.8	37.7	96.1	3.2	0.9	0.7	0.2
21 043	Carter	27,401	0.3	6.2	17.3	9.3	28.7	25.3	13.2	36.5	99.4	0.4		0.8	-
21 047	Christian	79,159	3.5	9.6	21.8	12.3	27.2	19.2	10.0	29.7	72.8	23.3	2.0	4.4	5.2
21 049	Clark	35,101	2.6	6.6	16.6	7.4	29.2	27.6	12.7	37.7	94.3	5.1	0.5	0.5	1.4
21 051	Clay	23,828	-0.9	5.6	18.8	7.5	31.9	24.7	11.4	37.4	94.1	5.8		0.4	-
21 059	Daviess	93,118	1.4	7.1	17.6	8.8	25.8	26.1	14.5	38.0	93.6	5.4	0.7	1.5	1.3
21 067	Fayette	275,726	2.5	6.8	15.0	12.7	31.0	24.0	10.4	34.7	80.8	14.6	3.4	2.9	5.2
21 071	Floyd	42,009	0.0	6.3	16.0	8.4	28.9	27.5	12.9	39.0	97.9	1.2	1.3		0.4
21 073	Franklin	48,423	0.0	6.2	15.7	9.4	28.0	28.1	12.6	39.2	87.1	11.1	1.2	1.6	2.0
21 081	Grant	24,800	2.9	7.4	19.4	7.8	32.5	23.2	9.6	34.0	99.1			-	-

STATE County	Percent foreign born	Total households	Household type (percent)						Percent of households with people under 18 years	Percent of households with people 60 years and over
			Family households				Nonfamily households			
			Total family households	Married-couple families	Male householder families	Female householder families	Total nonfamily households	One-person households		
ACS table number:	C05002	B11001	B11001	B11001	B11001	B11001	B11001	B11001	C11005	B11006
	15	16	17	18	19	20	21	22	23	24
Iowa—Cont.										
Dallas	7.0	20,115	70.3	57.6	3.3	9.4	29.7	23.5	38.8	22.6
Des Moines	1.9	17,223	68.0	50.9	3.5	13.7	32.0	27.4	30.9	36.3
Dubuque	1.9	36,520	66.8	55.1	3.0	8.7	33.2	27.7	31.8	31.8
Fayette	1.7	8,653	66.5	55.5	3.9	7.1	33.5	29.6	30.5	38.5
Henry	2.6	8,093	69.0	54.1	1.6	13.3	31.0	29.0	32.4	34.5
Jackson	1.2	8,374	64.7	51.2	3.9	9.6	35.3	30.0	29.4	36.0
Jasper	0.8	15,256	65.5	53.1	3.4	9.1	34.5	27.3	29.7	32.1
Johnson	7.1	50,082	54.0	43.9	2.4	7.6	46.0	31.1	28.4	18.2
Jones	0.6	7,759	69.1	59.4	4.3	5.5	30.9	26.8	29.2	35.2
Lee	1.5	14,802	67.6	51.3	3.7	12.6	32.4	28.6	29.9	36.2
Linn	2.7	84,535	62.7	48.8	3.6	10.3	37.3	29.4	32.9	27.4
Mahaska	1.5	9,053	69.1	56.8	3.6	8.6	30.9	25.5	31.7	34.5
Marion	1.6	12,563	71.0	60.5	2.7	7.8	29.0	25.1	32.3	32.6
Marshall	7.8	15,723	65.3	52.7	3.1	9.4	34.7	26.9	33.8	33.5
Muscatine	6.0	16,302	69.5	54.7	4.8	10.0	30.5	24.9	35.9	29.4
Plymouth	1.7	9,740	73.7	65.1	2.6	6.0	26.3	23.9	33.3	34.3
Polk	6.9	167,421	64.4	50.0	3.7	10.7	35.6	29.3	34.4	25.9
Pottawattamie	2.8	36,094	69.4	53.0	4.3	12.1	30.6	24.8	33.0	30.9
Scott	3.6	64,373	64.7	49.0	3.7	11.9	35.3	29.5	31.7	29.7
Sioux	5.1	11,132	72.8	66.0	1.5	5.3	27.2	25.6	35.6	33.2
Story	8.8	31,467	56.4	47.7	2.4	6.4	43.6	29.1	26.4	22.5
Wapello	4.4	14,987	63.2	50.6	3.3	9.4	36.8	29.9	30.2	37.6
Warren	1.3	16,362	72.6	60.1	3.0	9.5	27.4	23.3	37.6	28.5
Washington	2.8	8,447	69.3	55.4	3.1	10.8	30.7	26.6	33.3	35.6
Webster	1.7	15,776	66.1	49.0	6.9	10.2	33.9	29.2	31.9	36.8
Winneshiek	1.7	7,952	68.6	60.5	3.3	4.9	31.4	26.6	29.1	35.9
Woodbury	7.5	38,702	66.2	49.8	5.3	11.1	33.8	27.4	32.3	30.9
Kansas	6.0	1,083,868	66.8	52.8	3.9	10.1	33.2	27.9	34.3	29.5
Barton	5.0	11,640	67.3	53.1	2.9	11.3	32.7	28.3	29.8	38.3
Butler	1.0	23,111	76.5	64.3	4.5	7.8	23.5	20.6	38.0	27.8
Cherokee	-	9,007	65.4	52.6	2.6	10.2	34.6	30.4	33.1	32.6
Cowley	3.1	13,632	70.5	55.1	2.4	13.0	29.5	25.7	36.3	35.0
Crawford	4.3	16,058	58.0	46.5	2.7	8.8	42.0	32.7	25.6	29.8
Douglas	6.9	42,996	55.2	41.5	3.2	10.5	44.8	31.5	29.5	22.0
Ellis	1.1	11,468	61.3	49.4	4.9	6.9	38.7	31.1	28.1	30.4
Finney	22.1	12,146	73.9	56.6	5.2	12.1	26.1	21.2	45.2	24.2
Ford	25.6	10,846	74.0	55.0	3.9	15.1	26.0	20.3	47.6	22.5
Franklin	0.6	10,225	72.2	57.2	5.3	9.7	27.8	25.0	37.3	30.9
Geary	7.6	10,816	71.8	54.6	4.1	13.1	28.2	25.8	41.4	24.6
Harvey	4.4	13,170	68.3	57.3	4.8	6.2	31.7	27.6	32.3	33.8
Johnson	7.2	198,333	68.1	56.3	3.6	8.2	31.9	26.0	36.6	24.4
Labette	0.2	8,897	66.6	49.7	3.8	13.1	33.4	30.3	33.1	36.8
Leavenworth	2.8	25,023	76.3	59.9	4.2	12.1	23.7	20.5	40.2	28.0
Lyon	11.4	14,226	64.0	46.7	4.8	12.5	36.0	27.2	33.2	25.8
McPherson	1.6	11,838	71.2	59.6	2.6	9.1	28.8	25.4	33.6	32.5
Miami	1.1	11,480	77.1	67.3	3.3	6.5	22.9	18.6	40.5	29.4
Montgomery	1.4	14,799	66.9	52.5	3.4	11.1	33.1	28.4	33.3	36.6
Reno	1.7	25,627	65.9	52.5	3.5	9.9	34.1	29.3	29.3	34.7
Riley	5.3	23,362	56.8	46.1	2.5	8.2	43.2	31.0	28.4	20.3
Saline	3.6	21,754	64.3	48.4	5.3	10.7	35.7	31.1	32.0	32.0
Sedgwick	7.4	184,433	65.8	49.5	4.6	11.7	34.2	29.3	35.7	27.4
Seward	28.2	7,511	70.8	48.7	7.7	14.4	29.2	22.6	45.0	23.1
Shawnee	3.9	72,004	64.4	47.8	3.9	12.7	35.6	30.7	32.0	31.2
Sumner	0.9	9,445	71.8	59.8	4.2	7.8	28.2	25.0	36.4	31.2
Wyandotte	12.5	58,112	64.4	41.8	5.6	17.0	35.6	30.2	36.8	27.6
Kentucky	2.7	1,654,119	67.3	50.8	4.2	12.3	32.7	28.0	33.6	31.0
Anderson	0.5	7,917	77.8	59.4	5.2	13.2	22.2	20.2	38.0	25.3
Barren	1.7	16,226	69.2	54.0	2.9	12.3	30.8	26.6	33.8	35.3
Bell	0.3	11,275	65.6	45.4	6.4	13.7	34.4	30.2	30.2	37.4
Boone	4.0	39,646	71.9	55.7	4.2	12.0	28.1	22.7	41.3	21.3
Boyd	1.0	19,831	68.0	52.5	3.8	11.7	32.0	27.3	30.0	36.7
Boyle	2.3	10,875	64.7	51.0	3.2	10.5	35.3	33.6	30.1	37.4
Bullitt	0.7	27,038	76.9	60.6	5.4	11.0	23.1	17.9	39.4	27.1
Calloway	1.6	14,537	61.6	49.8	3.4	8.4	38.4	32.6	27.6	32.7
Campbell	1.8	35,156	62.4	47.1	3.6	11.7	37.6	32.1	32.0	30.6
Carter	0.4	10,534	71.7	54.4	6.9	10.3	28.3	24.7	32.8	28.2
Christian	2.2	25,079	72.1	50.1	3.9	18.1	27.9	25.4	43.0	29.1
Clark	1.1	14,518	69.6	52.6	4.5	12.5	30.4	23.8	37.5	29.6
Clay	1.2	7,283	71.7	53.8	6.8	11.1	28.3	25.8	36.9	34.3
Daviess	1.3	38,862	68.5	51.0	3.8	13.7	31.5	28.0	34.8	33.5
Fayette	7.8	117,478	57.0	42.2	3.9	10.9	43.0	33.4	29.2	24.0
Floyd	0.5	16,004	69.4	50.1	6.5	12.8	30.6	27.8	32.5	32.3
Franklin	2.9	21,146	62.1	45.1	3.0	14.0	37.9	33.8	30.1	30.8
Grant	3.0	8,735	74.8	55.6	7.0	12.1	25.2	22.0	42.3	28.9

STATE County code	STATE County ACS table number	Total population B01003	Percent change 2005–2007 Population estimates	Population by age (percent)						Median age	Race alone or in combination (percent)				Percent Hispanic or Latino
				Under 5 years B01001	5 to 17 years B01001	18 to 24 years B01001	25 to 44 years B01001	45 to 64 years B01001	65 years and over B01001	B01002	White B02008	Black B02009	Asian Hawaiian or Pacific Islander B02011 + B02012	Amer. Indian, Alaska Native, or some other race B02010 + B02013	C03002
		1	2	3	4	5	6	7	8	9	10	11	12	13	14
	Kentucky—Cont.														
21 083	Graves	37,388	0.7	6.5	17.3	8.4	25.6	26.0	16.2	39.9	91.6	5.1	-	3.5	-
21 085	Grayson	25,226	1.0	6.3	17.0	7.4	28.4	26.3	14.6	39.1	99.4	-	-	1.8	-
21 089	Greenup	37,115	0.7	5.7	16.0	7.5	25.5	28.9	16.4	41.3	98.6	1.3	0.4	0.8	-
21 093	Hardin	97,289	1.2	7.5	18.7	10.0	27.3	25.3	11.2	35.9	84.8	12.2	3.1	2.3	3.7
21 095	Harlan	31,085	-0.1	5.8	16.9	8.2	26.1	28.9	13.9	39.9	96.6	2.2	1.1	2.0	0.9
21 101	Henderson	45,211	0.3	6.6	17.0	7.8	27.2	27.9	13.4	38.8	91.2	8.0	0.6	1.2	1.4
21 107	Hopkins	46,289	0.1	6.3	16.9	7.4	26.4	27.8	15.2	40.1	92.6	6.8	0.5	1.1	1.1
21 111	Jefferson	704,648	1.2	6.9	17.2	8.3	27.4	26.8	13.3	38.4	77.0	20.6	2.2	1.8	2.8
21 113	Jessamine	44,446	5.4	7.4	17.8	10.2	29.0	25.3	10.2	34.3	95.5	4.5	0.4	1.3	1.5
21 115	Johnson	23,907	1.0	6.6	16.5	8.4	28.4	27.2	12.9	38.0	98.9	0.8	1.0	0.5	-
21 117	Kenton	155,104	2.1	7.5	18.4	8.5	28.9	26.0	10.7	36.1	94.0	5.2	1.1	1.2	1.7
21 121	Knox	32,310	1.4	7.4	18.2	8.5	27.8	25.0	13.1	36.3	97.1	2.8	-	-	-
21 125	Laurel	56,712	2.3	6.8	17.8	8.0	29.9	25.5	11.9	36.6	97.6	1.5	0.6	0.8	0.2
21 133	Letcher	24,111	-0.8	6.0	15.5	7.8	28.3	28.6	13.9	39.5	98.7	0.7	-	0.9	-
21 137	Lincoln	25,093	1.2	6.7	18.1	7.5	29.9	24.4	13.5	37.0	96.6	2.5	-	1.5	-
21 141	Logan	26,990	1.0	6.6	16.2	8.4	28.2	26.4	14.2	38.7	93.6	4.5	-	2.2	-
21 145	McCracken	64,572	0.5	6.2	16.2	8.1	24.8	28.9	15.8	41.1	87.9	11.6	0.8	1.1	1.2
21 151	Madison	80,022	3.0	6.5	15.8	16.6	29.3	21.4	10.4	31.3	94.5	4.1	1.2	2.3	1.2
21 157	Marshall	31,006	1.7	5.0	15.1	8.2	25.3	28.3	18.1	42.4	98.9	-	1.0	0.8	-
21 163	Meade	27,558	-2.2	5.3	20.7	8.2	31.6	24.7	9.4	34.8	92.9	4.8	0.6	2.6	2.4
21 167	Mercer	21,667	1.3	6.3	17.3	6.8	28.1	26.9	14.6	39.7	95.7	5.1	0.6	-	1.8
21 173	Montgomery	24,766	4.1	6.9	17.8	7.1	29.1	26.4	12.9	36.9	96.3	3.2	-	-	-
21 177	Muhlenberg	31,387	-0.3	5.6	16.1	7.9	27.6	27.2	15.5	39.9	96.4	3.7	0.8	1.5	-
21 179	Nelson	41,712	4.0	6.9	19.2	8.2	29.1	25.4	11.2	36.5	93.7	5.9	0.4	0.3	1.1
21 183	Ohio	23,463	0.6	6.7	16.9	7.8	27.4	26.6	14.5	38.7	98.2	1.3	-	1.3	-
21 185	Oldham	54,395	6.0	5.6	18.9	8.9	28.7	30.0	7.9	38.0	93.3	5.2	1.0	1.6	2.1
21 193	Perry	29,190	0.3	7.1	16.6	8.9	27.2	27.8	12.4	37.8	97.5	2.3	0.6	-	-
21 195	Pike	65,656	-0.3	5.7	16.3	8.0	28.2	28.8	13.0	39.4	98.9	0.6	0.5	0.5	0.7
21 199	Pulaski	59,556	2.0	6.4	16.1	7.9	27.1	26.0	16.4	39.4	97.0	1.5	0.6	1.4	1.2
21 205	Rowan	22,378	1.8	6.2	16.0	20.9	24.6	20.6	11.8	29.5	96.3	2.4	3.2	-	-
21 209	Scott	41,227	9.2	7.8	18.9	10.9	31.3	22.4	8.8	32.9	93.4	5.9	1.0	1.2	2.0
21 211	Shelby	39,267	6.6	7.9	17.2	10.0	29.0	25.6	10.3	35.9	85.9	9.3	0.8	4.9	8.0
21 217	Taylor	23,773	1.3	5.9	16.2	10.7	24.9	25.8	16.6	39.4	93.7	5.6	0.4	1.3	-
21 227	Warren	101,973	4.4	6.8	16.2	14.8	28.2	23.3	10.7	33.3	88.6	9.2	1.6	1.6	3.5
21 231	Wayne	20,519	0.9	6.2	17.6	8.3	28.7	25.3	13.9	37.3	96.2	2.2	0.6	1.5	-
21 235	Whitley	38,017	1.6	6.3	17.8	10.1	27.8	24.1	13.9	35.7	98.4	0.4	1.0	1.5	-
21 239	Woodford	24,155	1.4	6.6	17.0	8.7	25.8	30.3	11.6	39.8	93.9	5.2	-	1.5	-
22 000	**Louisiana**	4,344,053	-4.5	7.0	18.4	10.9	26.8	24.9	12.0	35.5	65.0	32.5	1.6	2.1	3.0
22 001	Acadia	59,502	2.0	7.8	20.2	10.4	25.4	23.7	12.5	34.7	80.2	19.5	-	1.0	1.1
22 003	Allen	25,327	2.5	7.1	17.8	9.9	31.5	21.5	12.2	34.7	70.5	24.9	-	6.0	4.7
22 005	Ascension	94,520	11.2	8.3	20.6	10.2	30.1	22.7	8.1	32.1	76.0	21.2	0.8	2.6	3.6
22 007	Assumption	22,972	0.6	6.0	18.9	11.2	27.3	24.9	11.8	38.0	67.1	31.9	-	-	-
22 009	Avoyelles	41,948	2.0	7.4	18.0	9.8	27.8	23.8	13.2	36.2	67.0	31.7	0.4	1.4	0.3
22 011	Beauregard	34,587	1.5	6.4	19.5	9.0	27.9	24.8	12.4	36.0	84.6	14.3	0.9	2.1	2.3
22 015	Bossier	107,233	3.2	7.7	19.3	10.2	28.1	23.6	11.2	34.2	74.9	22.3	2.0	2.1	4.3
22 017	Caddo	252,163	0.9	7.2	18.3	10.2	26.0	24.8	13.5	35.7	51.1	47.2	1.2	1.7	2.1
22 019	Calcasieu	184,162	0.0	7.2	18.5	10.2	26.7	24.9	12.5	35.5	73.8	25.2	1.0	1.8	1.8
22 031	De Soto	26,102	1.1	6.8	19.1	9.5	25.5	25.8	13.3	37.1	58.3	40.7	-	0.9	2.0
22 033	East Baton Rouge	424,597	4.4	6.9	18.0	14.4	26.2	24.0	10.5	32.8	53.0	44.3	2.7	1.3	2.6
22 037	East Feliciana	20,802	1.3	6.2	16.9	9.0	29.4	26.6	11.9	37.4	53.6	45.0	-	1.2	-
22 039	Evangeline	35,602	1.9	7.3	20.4	9.8	27.0	23.0	12.5	34.6	68.4	29.1	0.4	2.2	2.3
22 041	Franklin	20,107	-0.5	7.1	18.5	8.3	26.6	23.4	16.2	37.5	68.2	32.3	-	0.6	-
22 045	Iberia	74,436	1.8	7.6	20.2	9.4	26.7	24.1	11.9	34.2	64.5	32.7	2.4	1.1	1.8
22 047	Iberville	32,526	0.8	6.8	17.0	10.8	29.5	24.6	11.2	36.1	49.1	50.5	-	1.1	-
22 051	Jefferson	431,350	-5.8	6.5	17.3	9.2	26.2	27.4	13.3	38.8	66.9	26.8	4.0	3.8	8.7
22 053	Jefferson Davis	31,121	0.8	7.4	20.0	9.5	25.7	23.4	14.0	35.4	80.4	19.2	-	1.1	-
22 055	Lafayette	201,909	3.8	7.4	18.6	11.6	28.3	24.0	10.1	33.4	71.8	26.1	1.6	1.6	2.3
22 057	Lafourche	92,341	1.4	6.4	18.5	10.1	28.7	24.4	11.8	36.1	82.6	13.9	0.7	3.9	2.0
22 061	Lincoln	42,619	-0.4	6.3	14.9	26.6	21.9	18.6	11.6	26.5	57.0	41.9	0.5	1.5	-
22 063	Livingston	112,445	8.5	7.5	19.9	9.8	30.3	23.4	9.1	33.3	93.5	5.6	0.6	1.3	1.6
22 067	Morehouse	29,166	-2.2	6.9	18.4	8.4	26.0	24.8	15.5	36.7	54.2	45.5	-	-	-
22 069	Natchitoches	39,233	1.8	7.4	17.4	16.9	24.7	21.4	12.1	30.1	57.6	39.8	0.8	3.2	1.7
22 071	Orleans	301,016	-47.3	6.1	15.2	12.8	26.0	27.6	12.3	38.2	32.3	64.1	3.0	1.8	4.0
22 073	Ouachita	149,175	0.8	7.5	19.2	11.5	26.6	23.1	12.1	33.6	63.5	35.2	1.1	1.4	1.6
22 075	Plaquemines	23,918	-24.7	6.8	20.5	10.1	27.0	23.9	11.7	36.0	70.3	27.5	-	0.9	-
22 077	Pointe Coupee	22,212	2.6	6.6	17.6	10.0	24.9	26.2	14.6	38.2	60.3	38.8	-	-	-
22 079	Rapides	129,147	2.1	7.3	18.5	9.7	26.4	24.8	13.3	36.2	66.0	31.8	1.1	2.0	2.0
22 083	Richland	20,420	0.7	7.0	18.5	9.4	26.4	24.8	13.9	35.3	61.2	38.3	-	0.6	-
22 085	Sabine	23,571	1.1	7.0	17.7	8.6	25.3	25.5	15.9	39.0	75.7	17.1	-	9.9	3.2
22 089	St. Charles	51,392	3.7	6.8	20.2	10.2	26.5	26.6	9.8	36.8	70.3	27.7	1.2	1.9	3.7
22 093	St. James	21,340	2.8	7.1	19.1	10.5	25.6	25.4	12.3	37.2	48.7	51.3	-	-	-
22 095	St. John the Baptist	46,993	4.6	7.8	21.2	11.1	26.8	24.7	8.3	32.9	48.0	49.4	0.9	2.8	4.1
22 097	St. Landry	90,272	3.0	7.6	19.8	10.0	25.1	23.6	13.9	35.3	56.5	42.7	0.4	0.4	1.1
22 099	St. Martin	50,968	3.2	7.1	19.7	9.2	28.7	24.8	10.4	34.4	67.3	31.4	1.1	0.8	1.1

Table A-2. Counties — Who: Age, Race/Ethnicity, and Household Structure, 2005–2007—*Continued*

STATE County	Percent foreign born	Total households	Household type (percent) Family households — Total family households	Married-couple families	Male householder families	Female householder families	Nonfamily households — Total nonfamily households	One-person households	Percent of households with people under 18 years	Percent of households with people 60 years and over
ACS table number:	C05002	B11001	B11001	B11001	B11001	B11001	B11001	B11001	C11005	B11006
	15	16	17	18	19	20	21	22	23	24
Kentucky—Cont.										
Graves	3.4	14,528	72.0	59.0	2.9	10.1	28.0	24.9	32.2	37.1
Grayson	0.4	9,404	70.2	54.4	3.0	12.8	29.8	25.4	34.5	36.4
Greenup	0.8	14,560	71.7	58.3	2.4	11.0	28.3	25.5	31.5	38.3
Hardin	4.1	37,133	73.3	56.8	4.4	12.1	26.7	22.6	37.1	27.6
Harlan	-	12,101	69.3	51.5	2.9	14.9	30.7	29.0	29.3	38.7
Henderson	1.3	18,528	69.0	53.0	2.9	13.1	31.0	29.1	31.9	31.9
Hopkins	1.0	18,403	67.6	54.6	2.6	10.4	32.4	28.5	30.1	35.1
Jefferson	4.9	293,129	60.9	42.2	4.2	14.4	39.1	33.5	30.6	30.4
Jessamine	1.5	16,645	73.7	54.7	5.5	13.5	26.3	21.4	39.2	25.2
Johnson	-	8,772	74.2	60.7	3.4	10.0	25.8	23.8	36.0	34.8
Kenton	2.2	61,452	66.0	49.4	4.5	12.1	34.0	28.4	35.3	26.4
Knox	-	12,754	67.7	52.7	2.8	12.3	32.3	28.2	33.3	34.2
Laurel	0.7	20,047	71.9	57.4	4.2	10.3	28.1	24.6	37.6	30.8
Letcher	0.6	9,996	70.6	54.2	4.3	12.2	29.4	26.4	33.5	34.6
Lincoln	0.8	10,305	70.4	53.9	3.1	13.4	29.6	24.4	36.6	31.5
Logan	5.3	10,468	71.6	54.7	3.9	13.1	28.4	23.4	31.7	37.4
McCracken	1.6	27,927	65.9	50.3	2.9	12.6	34.1	30.7	31.1	35.6
Madison	2.6	29,164	66.3	50.9	3.7	11.6	33.7	27.4	32.0	27.1
Marshall	1.1	13,003	70.9	57.5	3.5	9.9	29.1	27.9	30.2	37.6
Meade	1.1	9,543	72.4	54.9	6.4	11.1	27.6	23.8	40.9	25.8
Mercer	1.7	8,815	70.1	52.2	6.3	11.7	29.9	24.2	30.8	33.1
Montgomery	0.9	9,664	64.8	51.4	2.3	11.1	35.2	31.9	32.1	29.1
Muhlenberg	0.7	13,061	72.1	58.7	2.3	11.1	27.9	24.7	33.4	36.0
Nelson	1.3	15,636	72.0	58.0	2.9	11.2	28.0	24.9	36.6	26.6
Ohio	0.7	8,816	71.8	58.2	3.9	9.7	28.2	25.8	36.1	33.5
Oldham	2.3	18,889	81.2	68.6	4.7	7.9	18.8	14.8	45.8	24.8
Perry	0.6	10,926	70.8	51.9	3.7	15.2	29.2	26.9	32.1	34.9
Pike	0.7	28,102	71.6	54.9	4.0	12.8	28.4	26.7	35.6	32.4
Pulaski	1.7	23,521	69.8	54.6	3.3	11.9	30.2	26.7	31.9	35.3
Rowan	2.6	7,885	69.0	52.0	2.8	14.2	31.0	25.7	31.7	29.9
Scott	2.0	14,875	72.8	57.8	4.4	10.6	27.2	22.0	37.9	24.8
Shelby	5.7	14,565	70.6	55.5	3.1	12.0	29.4	24.0	36.3	27.0
Taylor	1.2	9,728	65.7	48.0	4.2	13.6	34.3	30.9	31.8	34.6
Warren	5.7	39,948	65.3	48.4	4.2	12.6	34.7	26.9	33.2	26.3
Wayne	2.0	8,117	69.4	54.4	3.2	11.8	30.6	26.2	31.2	34.4
Whitley	0.8	13,196	72.2	54.3	3.6	14.4	27.8	24.5	36.0	36.3
Woodford	4.1	9,679	73.6	60.5	4.6	8.5	26.4	21.3	36.0	30.2
Louisiana	3.1	1,605,203	67.9	46.8	4.7	16.5	32.1	27.2	35.8	31.0
Acadia	0.8	21,900	72.3	51.0	3.4	17.0	27.7	24.8	38.7	32.4
Allen	2.9	8,428	69.8	49.9	3.7	16.2	30.2	26.6	39.9	32.4
Ascension	2.5	33,532	73.8	56.2	4.6	13.0	26.2	22.2	42.4	22.8
Assumption	0.8	8,499	74.3	48.5	7.8	17.9	25.7	20.9	40.8	34.1
Avoyelles	0.3	15,673	69.9	45.6	5.8	18.4	30.1	25.5	40.7	31.1
Beauregard	0.9	13,051	74.2	55.8	6.5	11.9	25.8	22.2	40.1	31.0
Bossier	3.6	41,472	69.3	50.5	4.4	14.4	30.7	25.2	36.4	27.7
Caddo	1.8	97,241	63.0	38.6	4.4	20.0	37.0	32.4	33.2	33.1
Calcasieu	1.8	72,001	68.3	48.2	5.4	14.7	31.7	27.3	35.9	31.4
De Soto	1.1	9,693	73.0	46.6	6.4	20.0	27.0	24.6	37.0	34.2
East Baton Rouge	4.5	164,450	63.3	41.1	5.0	17.2	36.7	29.4	32.8	26.6
East Feliciana	-	6,933	74.7	51.2	4.1	19.3	25.3	22.8	40.1	34.7
Evangeline	2.5	12,823	71.6	50.7	5.4	15.6	28.4	25.9	39.7	32.0
Franklin	-	7,716	65.1	42.8	4.5	17.8	34.9	29.7	35.4	38.6
Iberia	2.7	25,892	72.9	51.9	3.8	17.2	27.1	22.5	39.0	32.0
Iberville	0.6	11,615	70.1	45.2	4.2	20.7	29.9	25.5	36.2	33.6
Jefferson	9.3	159,117	66.3	45.9	5.6	14.8	33.7	28.4	33.0	34.0
Jefferson Davis	0.4	11,790	71.4	51.2	4.8	15.4	28.6	25.7	39.5	34.3
Lafayette	3.1	80,141	65.0	44.9	4.6	15.5	35.0	27.4	36.1	23.6
Lafourche	2.1	32,872	73.0	57.5	3.1	12.4	27.0	21.4	39.7	29.4
Lincoln	1.9	16,005	57.5	40.8	4.2	12.5	42.5	30.9	29.1	28.4
Livingston	1.1	38,099	73.6	57.6	3.9	12.2	26.4	22.9	40.7	27.5
Morehouse	-	10,852	69.4	45.9	4.6	18.9	30.6	28.3	32.5	37.2
Natchitoches	1.3	14,590	63.7	42.4	4.0	17.4	36.3	29.6	35.3	30.2
Orleans	5.3	101,221	54.4	29.9	3.9	20.6	45.6	38.8	25.9	32.2
Ouachita	1.2	54,511	67.9	45.2	3.8	19.0	32.1	29.1	36.9	30.6
Plaquemines	1.7	7,501	79.3	58.8	2.9	17.6	20.7	17.3	32.0	34.7
Pointe Coupee	-	8,756	69.0	49.9	1.9	17.1	31.0	25.6	37.0	35.4
Rapides	2.3	49,046	67.5	46.6	4.0	16.8	32.5	28.7	36.6	32.7
Richland	-	7,671	73.7	54.0	4.2	15.5	26.3	24.3	38.2	32.3
Sabine	0.6	10,023	68.5	52.3	3.2	13.0	31.5	29.1	33.9	36.8
St. Charles	3.8	17,658	78.4	53.5	7.1	17.7	21.6	18.3	42.5	27.8
St. James	-	7,528	76.5	54.8	3.4	18.3	23.5	20.7	41.3	34.8
St. John the Baptist	2.5	15,609	74.7	48.5	7.1	19.0	25.3	21.5	39.5	25.0
St. Landry	0.9	32,007	67.7	42.8	4.5	20.4	32.3	29.1	36.2	35.3
St. Martin	1.3	19,295	71.7	48.7	5.3	17.7	28.3	24.9	39.9	29.1

STATE County code	STATE County	Total population	Percent change 2005–2007	Population by age (percent)						Median age	Race alone or in combination (percent)				Percent Hispanic or Latino
				Under 5 years	5 to 17 years	18 to 24 years	25 to 44 years	45 to 64 years	65 years and over		White	Black	Asian Hawaiian or Pacific Islander	Amer. Indian, Alaska Native, or some other race	
	ACS table number:	B01003	Population estimates	B01001	B01001	B01001	B01001	B01001	B01001	B01002	B02008	B02009	B02011 + B02012	B02010 + B02013	C03002
		1	2	3	4	5	6	7	8	9	10	11	12	13	14
	Louisiana—Cont.														
22 101	St. Mary	51,282	0.8	7.3	19.3	9.0	26.4	25.4	12.7	36.5	63.7	33.2	1.4	3.1	2.9
22 103	St. Tammany	222,801	4.2	6.8	19.5	9.5	25.7	27.1	11.4	36.9	85.5	12.4	1.6	2.4	3.5
22 105	Tangipahoa	111,598	8.6	7.4	18.9	12.7	26.9	23.2	10.7	31.5	70.0	29.4	0.6	0.9	2.0
22 109	Terrebonne	107,612	2.0	7.6	19.1	10.0	28.3	24.1	10.9	34.7	74.2	18.9	1.2	6.7	2.3
22 111	Union	22,787	0.1	7.1	17.4	8.9	25.6	25.4	15.7	38.7	70.7	27.6	-	1.5	3.1
22 113	Vermilion	55,351	1.4	7.1	18.8	9.8	27.1	23.7	13.5	36.1	82.7	15.0	2.5	0.8	1.9
22 115	Vernon	48,723	-5.8	9.4	21.4	12.6	29.0	18.4	9.3	29.5	78.2	16.0	3.6	6.5	7.8
22 117	Washington	44,311	2.2	7.1	18.6	9.9	25.9	24.4	14.0	36.2	67.6	32.0	-	1.1	1.1
22 119	Webster	40,930	0.1	6.2	17.3	9.6	24.4	25.9	16.7	39.4	65.3	33.2	0.9	1.2	1.2
22 121	West Baton Rouge	22,126	5.1	7.1	18.3	10.7	26.7	26.9	10.3	35.0	62.9	36.4	-	3.0	-
23 000	**Maine**	1,314,780	0.4	5.4	16.2	8.7	26.0	29.2	14.7	41.1	97.0	1.3	1.2	2.1	1.1
23 001	Androscoggin	106,837	0.1	6.2	16.8	8.9	27.5	26.5	14.2	39.4	95.0	3.8	0.9	8.5	1.4
23 003	Aroostook	72,176	-0.4	4.8	15.1	8.9	23.9	29.8	17.6	43.4	97.3	1.0	0.9	2.1	1.0
23 005	Cumberland	274,712	0.4	5.6	16.4	8.6	27.0	28.9	13.5	40.5	95.3	2.3	2.1	1.3	1.6
23 007	Franklin	29,840	0.7	4.6	15.5	12.1	24.6	28.8	14.3	40.0	98.9	0.2	-	1.7	-
23 009	Hancock	53,208	0.3	5.1	14.8	8.4	24.4	31.3	16.0	43.4	97.9	0.6	0.9	1.1	0.9
23 011	Kennebec	120,559	0.5	5.2	16.2	8.8	26.0	29.4	14.4	41.1	97.9	0.8	0.9	1.5	1.0
23 013	Knox	40,879	-0.5	5.0	15.0	7.1	25.1	30.5	17.3	43.5	98.5	0.5	0.6	0.9	0.8
23 015	Lincoln	34,837	-0.3	4.7	15.1	6.6	23.5	31.3	18.7	45.0	98.6	0.5	0.5	0.8	0.7
23 017	Oxford	56,486	0.9	5.1	16.1	7.5	25.6	30.0	15.8	42.4	98.8	0.5	0.6	0.9	0.8
23 019	Penobscot	147,971	1.2	5.4	15.5	11.6	26.3	27.8	13.4	39.3	97.2	1.0	1.1	1.8	0.9
23 023	Sagadahoc	36,402	0.1	5.6	17.5	7.2	26.0	29.8	13.8	40.5	98.4	1.8	1.6	0.8	1.7
23 025	Somerset	51,381	1.3	5.4	16.7	7.4	26.1	29.4	15.0	41.8	97.7	0.6	1.1	1.3	0.6
23 027	Waldo	38,385	0.9	5.4	16.4	8.1	25.8	30.1	14.3	42.0	98.7	0.2	0.4	2.0	0.8
23 029	Washington	32,801	-0.4	5.1	15.4	7.9	24.5	29.1	18.0	43.0	94.8	0.7	0.7	5.5	1.4
23 031	York	201,075	0.2	5.4	17.1	7.7	26.3	29.6	14.0	40.9	97.7	0.9	1.1	1.0	1.1
24 000	**Maryland**	5,597,843	0.8	6.7	17.7	9.5	28.3	26.1	11.6	37.2	62.6	29.8	5.5	4.1	6.0
24 001	Allegany	72,661	-0.3	4.8	14.3	12.5	25.9	24.6	17.9	39.7	93.2	6.5	0.8	0.8	1.0
24 003	Anne Arundel	510,824	0.4	6.7	17.7	9.0	28.9	26.9	10.8	37.5	80.1	15.8	3.8	2.7	3.9
24 005	Baltimore	786,547	0.8	6.1	16.7	9.6	27.1	26.2	14.4	38.7	69.9	25.0	4.5	2.0	2.7
24 009	Calvert	87,539	1.6	6.1	19.8	8.9	28.9	26.8	9.5	37.1	84.2	14.5	1.6	2.1	2.3
24 011	Caroline	32,240	4.4	7.0	17.9	9.1	27.5	25.7	12.7	37.1	82.6	14.1	2.1	2.6	4.2
24 013	Carroll	168,195	1.4	6.0	19.0	8.9	27.1	27.7	11.4	38.3	94.0	4.1	1.9	1.2	1.7
24 015	Cecil	98,358	3.1	6.5	18.7	8.3	30.6	25.3	10.6	36.3	92.7	5.9	1.3	1.4	2.1
24 017	Charles	139,006	2.3	7.1	20.0	9.0	31.0	24.9	8.0	35.0	59.8	37.3	3.2	3.0	3.4
24 019	Dorchester	31,468	2.3	5.6	16.3	7.7	25.7	27.4	17.4	41.3	70.0	28.1	1.1	1.9	1.9
24 021	Frederick	222,034	2.4	7.1	19.1	8.8	29.5	25.7	9.8	36.5	85.5	9.0	3.9	3.5	5.1
24 023	Garrett	29,649	-0.2	5.3	16.9	8.1	26.7	26.9	16.1	40.1	99.3	-	-	1.1	-
24 025	Harford	238,960	1.1	6.4	19.3	8.5	28.0	26.8	11.1	37.2	84.8	12.4	2.8	2.1	2.5
24 027	Howard	270,651	2.2	6.5	19.6	8.2	28.8	28.1	8.9	37.6	70.5	17.6	11.7	3.0	4.4
24 031	Montgomery	925,719	1.1	7.1	17.5	8.1	27.5	27.8	12.0	38.7	63.0	17.0	14.1	8.3	14.0
24 033	Prince George's	833,862	-1.1	7.2	18.2	10.9	30.0	25.0	8.7	34.8	24.2	65.6	4.6	8.0	11.3
24 035	Queen Anne's	45,826	3.4	5.8	17.8	8.4	26.6	28.4	13.1	39.6	89.5	8.5	1.3	1.4	1.8
24 037	St. Mary's	98,650	3.5	7.3	19.0	10.3	30.7	23.3	9.5	34.3	81.9	15.3	2.9	1.8	2.7
24 039	Somerset	25,798	1.8	4.9	12.7	16.4	29.1	23.5	13.4	35.8	56.4	42.0	0.5	2.3	2.0
24 041	Talbot	35,970	1.6	4.7	15.3	7.1	23.8	27.0	22.2	44.5	85.1	14.7	1.1	1.4	2.9
24 043	Washington	143,233	2.7	6.4	16.5	8.2	31.0	24.1	13.7	37.7	88.5	10.1	1.5	1.3	2.2
24 045	Wicomico	92,172	3.5	6.6	16.9	12.5	26.5	24.3	13.1	35.6	73.1	24.2	2.0	2.3	3.1
24 047	Worcester	49,123	1.1	4.8	14.3	6.9	26.8	25.3	21.8	43.1	84.0	14.9	1.1	0.7	2.0
24 510	Baltimore city	639,493	-0.4	7.2	17.2	11.1	27.9	24.6	12.0	35.4	32.4	64.6	2.3	2.1	2.4
25 000	**Massachusetts**	6,437,759	0.3	5.9	16.6	9.9	28.2	26.1	13.3	38.3	84.5	6.8	5.2	5.3	8.0
25 001	Barnstable	223,574	-1.3	4.3	14.0	7.1	23.0	28.2	23.4	46.0	95.6	2.7	1.1	2.0	1.7
25 003	Berkshire	130,346	-0.9	4.7	15.2	10.2	23.5	28.4	18.0	42.4	95.6	3.1	1.6	1.1	2.4
25 005	Bristol	543,146	-0.1	5.9	17.3	8.9	28.6	25.8	13.6	38.2	91.6	4.0	2.0	4.3	4.6
25 009	Essex	731,841	0.3	6.2	17.8	8.8	26.4	27.2	13.6	39.2	84.6	3.9	3.3	9.9	13.6
25 011	Franklin	71,740	-0.4	4.8	15.1	9.7	25.4	31.1	13.9	41.7	96.1	1.7	1.8	1.9	2.5
25 013	Hampden	458,549	-0.3	6.2	18.2	10.4	26.0	25.4	13.9	37.4	80.9	9.0	2.0	10.1	17.6
25 015	Hampshire	152,973	0.2	4.0	13.0	20.8	24.2	25.7	12.4	35.6	91.8	2.7	4.2	3.3	4.0
25 017	Middlesex	1,468,419	0.6	5.9	16.0	9.5	29.5	26.4	12.8	38.5	84.4	4.5	8.8	3.8	5.4
25 021	Norfolk	652,932	0.5	6.0	16.9	8.4	26.8	27.9	14.0	40.2	86.5	5.2	8.0	1.5	2.5
25 023	Plymouth	488,878	0.5	6.3	18.6	8.8	26.3	27.8	12.2	39.1	88.1	8.0	1.6	4.1	2.8
25 025	Suffolk	710,119	0.8	6.2	13.7	13.4	35.2	20.7	10.9	33.9	62.0	22.9	8.0	10.3	17.4
25 027	Worcester	779,386	0.5	6.2	18.0	9.3	28.2	26.0	12.3	37.8	90.3	3.9	3.9	3.3	7.8
26 000	**Michigan**	10,094,027	-0.4	6.4	18.2	9.7	27.0	26.1	12.6	37.3	81.1	14.9	2.7	3.2	3.9
26 005	Allegan	112,398	0.6	6.7	19.3	8.5	28.0	26.0	11.4	36.5	93.4	1.7	0.9	5.5	6.5
26 007	Alpena	29,902	-1.6	5.0	15.6	9.0	23.0	28.7	18.7	43.7	99.4	0.4	0.5	1.1	-
26 009	Antrim	24,278	0.2	5.2	16.6	7.5	25.0	26.5	19.1	41.9	98.2	-	-	3.1	1.6
26 015	Barry	59,042	0.3	5.9	18.4	8.3	26.6	28.0	12.7	38.7	97.9	0.8	0.5	1.8	1.8
26 017	Bay	108,059	-1.0	5.7	16.9	8.7	25.1	28.1	15.5	40.7	96.1	2.0	0.7	3.0	4.0
26 021	Berrien	159,806	-0.4	6.6	18.1	8.5	24.8	26.9	15.0	39.6	81.7	15.6	1.6	2.9	3.7
26 023	Branch	46,278	-0.3	6.2	17.3	7.9	29.4	25.9	13.3	37.9	93.6	4.1	0.2	4.0	4.1
26 025	Calhoun	137,452	-1.1	6.8	18.1	9.0	26.4	25.9	13.8	37.7	86.1	11.5	1.9	2.4	3.7

STATE County	Percent foreign born	Total households	Household type (percent)						Percent of households with people under 18 years	Percent of households with people 60 years and over
			Family households				Nonfamily households			
			Total family households	Married-couple families	Male householder families	Female householder families	Total nonfamily households	One-person households		
ACS table number:	C05002	B11001	B11001	B11001	B11001	B11001	B11001	B11001	C11005	B11006
	15	16	17	18	19	20	21	22	23	24
Louisiana—Cont.										
St. Mary	2.8	19,362	72.6	47.3	5.2	20.2	27.4	21.2	39.9	33.3
St. Tammany	2.8	79,727	74.1	57.9	4.7	11.6	25.9	21.1	38.2	31.2
Tangipahoa	0.8	40,510	70.5	50.5	3.9	16.1	29.5	25.2	38.1	29.7
Terrebonne	1.8	38,060	73.7	53.0	5.1	15.6	26.3	21.1	40.8	29.9
Union	1.5	8,614	75.2	53.8	4.7	16.8	24.8	23.6	38.2	35.1
Vermilion	2.8	20,445	73.1	54.2	3.9	15.1	26.9	22.5	40.0	33.0
Vernon	3.6	18,503	74.2	56.6	4.6	13.0	25.8	22.1	42.8	24.6
Washington	0.5	17,177	70.4	45.9	5.3	19.1	29.6	28.2	37.7	37.1
Webster	0.8	16,691	66.0	44.1	4.7	17.3	34.0	29.5	34.0	37.8
West Baton Rouge	1.8	8,639	70.1	47.7	4.4	17.9	29.9	27.4	39.1	28.7
Maine	3.2	542,424	65.3	51.2	4.3	9.8	34.7	27.4	30.4	33.2
Androscoggin	4.0	43,450	66.1	50.0	5.8	10.3	33.9	26.7	32.1	30.7
Aroostook	5.2	31,114	65.6	52.2	5.3	8.0	34.4	29.5	29.0	36.9
Cumberland	5.1	112,705	62.4	48.8	3.6	10.0	37.6	28.9	30.6	31.0
Franklin	2.0	12,477	65.6	50.6	5.6	9.4	34.4	27.5	28.0	34.6
Hancock	2.7	22,229	64.9	53.3	3.9	7.6	35.1	29.1	27.0	34.9
Kennebec	2.3	50,657	66.1	51.2	4.5	10.4	33.9	26.1	30.6	33.0
Knox	1.9	17,289	63.6	50.7	3.5	9.5	36.4	28.9	28.1	38.0
Lincoln	1.4	14,639	63.6	51.6	4.3	7.7	36.4	30.9	26.8	42.2
Oxford	1.7	23,189	67.7	53.5	4.5	9.7	32.3	27.5	30.9	33.3
Penobscot	2.4	60,477	62.7	48.6	3.9	10.3	37.3	28.9	29.2	31.1
Sagadahoc	2.0	14,510	67.0	54.7	2.6	9.7	33.0	26.7	28.1	32.9
Somerset	2.3	21,689	66.4	48.5	5.7	12.2	33.6	26.7	32.7	34.2
Waldo	1.2	15,629	68.6	55.0	4.8	8.8	31.4	24.9	30.4	33.7
Washington	4.8	14,322	64.3	50.5	4.5	9.4	35.7	30.3	28.4	38.1
York	2.8	80,437	69.0	54.5	4.4	10.1	31.0	23.7	33.1	32.9
Maryland	12.1	2,082,573	67.0	48.7	4.6	13.8	33.0	27.0	35.5	30.1
Allegany	1.1	29,305	59.5	45.0	4.2	10.3	40.5	34.1	27.2	40.2
Anne Arundel	6.1	189,828	69.9	54.6	4.2	11.1	30.1	24.3	35.5	29.7
Baltimore	9.2	309,808	64.4	46.7	4.5	13.1	35.6	29.2	32.1	33.4
Calvert	3.3	29,383	75.5	59.4	3.7	12.4	24.5	18.7	43.6	28.5
Caroline	5.5	12,059	73.2	53.8	5.1	14.4	26.8	22.7	38.8	31.8
Carroll	3.3	58,795	77.2	65.3	3.8	8.1	22.8	18.6	39.8	29.6
Cecil	2.7	35,920	73.2	56.9	5.3	11.0	26.8	21.7	39.2	29.1
Charles	4.1	48,669	75.5	55.0	4.7	15.8	24.5	20.4	41.4	24.7
Dorchester	2.9	13,020	68.4	46.7	3.7	18.0	31.6	26.1	34.7	37.8
Frederick	7.6	80,360	71.1	58.0	3.8	9.2	28.9	22.7	38.4	26.2
Garrett	0.4	12,741	70.9	59.2	2.6	9.0	29.1	23.2	34.7	36.1
Harford	4.0	88,958	73.0	58.6	4.1	10.3	27.0	22.1	38.8	29.5
Howard	15.6	98,093	73.9	60.5	3.6	9.8	26.1	20.9	42.3	24.8
Montgomery	29.4	342,617	69.3	54.7	4.0	10.5	30.7	25.2	36.7	30.7
Prince George's	18.3	298,271	66.0	41.0	6.1	18.9	34.0	27.7	37.3	25.5
Queen Anne's	2.7	17,166	72.0	59.4	3.5	9.0	28.0	20.3	33.9	33.1
St. Mary's	4.1	36,258	70.9	54.3	4.0	12.5	29.1	22.3	41.5	25.1
Somerset	3.5	7,991	65.6	44.8	4.5	16.3	34.4	28.5	30.2	42.0
Talbot	3.6	16,206	69.0	53.7	5.3	9.9	31.0	25.4	30.0	42.4
Washington	3.5	55,310	67.7	51.2	4.0	12.5	32.3	26.6	35.5	30.3
Wicomico	4.6	35,678	64.1	44.6	5.4	14.1	35.9	26.5	33.3	32.6
Worcester	4.7	22,290	66.6	53.7	3.8	9.1	33.4	29.6	31.3	42.6
Baltimore city	5.9	235,734	53.0	24.8	5.2	23.0	47.0	39.8	28.6	31.7
Massachusetts	14.2	2,448,608	64.0	47.9	4.1	12.0	36.0	29.0	32.5	32.1
Barnstable	7.8	98,989	63.9	51.6	3.8	8.6	36.1	29.2	25.7	44.8
Berkshire	3.5	55,127	62.4	45.5	5.2	11.8	37.6	31.7	28.6	38.9
Bristol	12.5	208,881	67.6	49.5	4.0	14.2	32.4	27.0	35.0	32.7
Essex	13.7	273,755	66.5	48.8	4.5	13.2	33.5	28.2	34.7	32.8
Franklin	3.9	29,774	63.0	47.5	4.7	10.8	37.0	27.6	30.4	31.1
Hampden	8.5	175,132	63.7	43.5	4.6	15.6	36.3	30.3	32.5	32.8
Hampshire	7.8	56,913	58.5	46.2	3.2	9.1	41.5	30.9	27.9	31.0
Middlesex	17.8	556,748	64.3	51.1	3.5	9.8	35.7	28.3	32.5	31.2
Norfolk	14.6	250,997	66.2	53.1	3.2	9.8	33.8	27.7	33.8	33.4
Plymouth	7.8	173,356	71.4	54.9	4.8	11.7	28.6	23.1	36.9	33.5
Suffolk	27.4	271,713	49.5	28.3	4.6	16.6	50.5	38.1	25.7	26.7
Worcester	9.9	287,535	67.3	51.9	4.2	11.2	32.7	26.6	35.3	30.4
Michigan	6.0	3,864,307	66.8	50.2	4.3	12.3	33.2	27.9	33.6	30.8
Allegan	3.1	41,815	74.0	59.6	4.5	9.8	26.0	20.6	37.4	28.0
Alpena	1.0	12,996	67.0	50.9	5.1	10.9	33.0	28.3	29.4	39.3
Antrim	1.4	9,878	71.3	57.6	4.0	9.7	28.7	24.0	30.8	40.8
Barry	1.5	22,525	74.8	61.0	5.9	7.9	25.2	20.3	35.7	31.0
Bay	1.9	44,733	66.6	52.0	3.6	11.1	33.4	28.4	30.6	34.2
Berrien	5.5	63,400	67.1	50.0	4.3	12.7	32.9	28.3	32.1	34.1
Branch	2.3	16,578	69.4	55.3	6.1	8.0	30.6	26.8	33.8	33.4
Calhoun	3.1	54,257	67.2	48.0	5.0	14.2	32.8	28.7	33.9	32.8

STATE County code	STATE County ACS table number:	Total population B01003	Percent change 2005–2007 Population estimates	Under 5 years B01001	5 to 17 years B01001	18 to 24 years B01001	25 to 44 years B01001	45 to 64 years B01001	65 years and over B01001	Median age B01002	White B02008	Black B02009	Asian Hawaiian or Pacific Islander B02011 + B02012	Amer. Indian, Alaska Native, or some other race B02010 + B02013	Percent Hispanic or Latino C03002
		1	2	3	4	5	6	7	8	9	10	11	12	13	14
Michigan—Cont.															
26 027	Cass	50,728	-0.8	5.3	17.7	8.1	25.4	29.6	13.9	40.5	91.9	6.7	0.8	3.7	2.7
26 029	Charlevoix	26,242	-0.8	5.5	17.5	7.3	24.9	28.4	16.3	42.0	97.5	0.5	-	2.9	1.2
26 031	Cheboygan	26,958	-1.3	5.1	16.2	7.1	25.2	27.7	18.7	42.4	97.7	0.1	-	4.9	0.9
26 033	Chippewa	38,724	0.8	4.8	14.7	12.0	29.8	25.2	13.5	38.5	80.6	6.5	0.9	15.7	2.1
26 035	Clare	30,990	-1.7	5.3	17.0	7.9	24.9	26.6	18.3	41.6	97.7	1.1	-	2.4	1.2
26 037	Clinton	69,358	1.2	6.0	18.9	9.3	26.3	27.9	11.6	37.7	96.7	1.9	1.2	2.2	2.8
26 041	Delta	37,650	-1.3	5.3	15.9	9.2	22.5	29.0	18.1	43.4	97.2	-	0.4	3.8	0.4
26 043	Dickinson	27,068	-1.1	5.2	17.0	7.9	22.8	27.9	19.2	43.3	98.8	-	0.8	1.2	0.8
26 045	Eaton	107,331	0.1	5.8	17.4	10.2	25.7	28.6	12.2	37.9	90.8	6.9	1.8	2.8	3.7
26 047	Emmet	33,387	0.2	5.6	17.1	8.5	24.9	28.3	15.7	40.5	95.8	0.6	0.8	4.6	0.3
26 049	Genesee	437,405	-1.1	6.9	19.1	8.6	27.2	26.0	12.3	36.7	77.8	20.7	1.2	2.5	2.4
26 051	Gladwin	26,579	-1.7	5.1	15.8	7.2	24.8	27.1	20.1	43.2	98.3	0.3	-	2.3	1.2
26 055	Grand Traverse	84,493	2.3	5.6	16.9	8.5	27.3	27.6	14.1	39.4	96.6	1.2	0.8	2.6	1.8
26 057	Gratiot	42,128	0.2	6.8	17.2	11.1	27.0	24.1	13.8	36.6	94.5	4.1	0.8	4.3	4.7
26 059	Hillsdale	46,847	-0.2	6.2	17.8	9.8	25.9	26.2	14.2	37.4	98.0	0.8	0.6	1.3	1.4
26 061	Houghton	35,370	-1.0	5.4	14.8	20.7	22.2	22.4	14.5	32.8	95.2	2.2	1.7	1.2	1.0
26 063	Huron	33,963	-2.4	5.0	16.2	7.3	22.7	28.1	20.7	44.2	98.0	0.3	0.7	1.8	1.9
26 065	Ingham	280,097	-0.6	6.3	16.1	18.8	25.9	23.1	9.8	31.5	82.1	12.4	4.9	3.5	5.9
26 067	Ionia	64,021	0.3	6.7	18.1	10.3	30.1	24.6	10.2	35.0	93.0	5.7	0.6	3.8	3.1
26 069	Iosco	26,429	-1.1	4.2	15.3	7.0	21.7	28.7	23.2	46.1	97.4	1.0	0.8	2.6	1.2
26 073	Isabella	66,500	0.7	5.2	13.4	30.1	22.9	18.8	9.4	25.6	91.8	3.3	2.3	4.9	2.6
26 075	Jackson	162,934	0.2	6.4	17.8	8.8	27.9	26.3	12.8	37.9	89.4	9.3	0.9	2.4	2.6
26 077	Kalamazoo	244,153	1.0	6.4	16.9	14.9	26.1	24.0	11.6	34.0	85.9	11.0	2.6	2.7	3.2
26 081	Kent	600,659	1.2	7.8	19.6	9.8	29.0	23.6	10.3	34.2	83.8	10.1	2.5	6.0	9.0
26 087	Lapeer	92,232	-0.3	5.9	18.9	8.8	27.3	28.3	10.9	38.3	97.5	1.2	0.6	2.2	3.6
26 089	Leelanau	21,880	0.1	4.3	16.6	7.3	21.1	31.4	19.3	45.5	93.8	-	-	6.6	5.6
26 091	Lenawee	101,230	0.2	6.2	18.1	9.5	26.0	26.7	13.5	37.8	94.0	2.6	1.0	4.4	7.3
26 093	Livingston	181,710	2.0	5.8	19.5	8.8	27.7	28.6	9.5	37.8	97.5	1.0	1.2	1.4	1.7
26 099	Macomb	828,972	0.6	6.1	17.4	8.1	28.9	26.0	13.4	38.3	89.9	6.7	3.5	1.7	2.0
26 101	Manistee	24,917	-0.7	5.0	14.7	7.8	25.6	28.1	18.7	42.7	93.8	3.5	0.6	2.8	3.1
26 103	Marquette	65,187	0.1	4.6	14.0	15.0	24.3	28.0	14.1	39.5	96.1	1.7	0.8	2.7	0.9
26 105	Mason	28,763	0.2	5.5	16.2	8.1	24.1	27.6	18.6	43.0	97.2	1.0	0.5	2.5	3.4
26 107	Mecosta	42,268	-0.6	5.7	15.1	19.7	23.4	22.2	14.0	31.5	93.6	5.0	1.4	2.1	1.5
26 109	Menominee	24,414	-1.5	4.8	16.4	8.2	23.6	29.2	17.8	43.2	97.1	0.4	-	3.3	-
26 111	Midland	83,017	-0.5	5.7	18.6	9.9	25.1	27.4	13.4	38.6	96.6	1.4	2.3	1.6	1.8
26 115	Monroe	153,098	0.8	5.8	18.7	9.1	27.3	27.3	11.8	37.8	96.5	2.8	0.8	1.6	2.6
26 117	Montcalm	63,058	-0.2	6.4	18.5	8.5	27.7	25.8	13.1	37.1	96.2	1.4	0.7	3.7	2.7
26 121	Muskegon	174,236	0.2	6.7	18.9	9.2	27.2	25.5	12.5	36.5	82.9	14.5	0.8	3.6	4.2
26 123	Newaygo	49,241	-0.5	6.4	19.7	8.5	25.5	26.3	13.5	37.7	95.8	1.4	0.6	3.9	4.9
26 125	Oakland	1,207,603	-0.2	6.2	18.1	8.0	27.1	28.8	11.8	39.3	81.2	12.4	5.8	2.3	3.0
26 127	Oceana	27,884	-0.3	7.2	18.4	9.0	24.7	26.1	14.5	37.2	89.8	0.8	-	10.8	14.1
26 129	Ogemaw	21,481	-1.4	5.1	16.0	8.0	22.9	27.4	20.6	43.5	99.0	0.3	-	2.4	1.4
26 133	Osceola	23,275	-1.1	6.4	18.0	8.3	25.2	26.1	15.9	39.2	98.8	0.9	-	1.7	1.2
26 137	Otsego	24,287	-0.3	6.0	17.8	7.9	26.8	26.2	15.3	39.6	99.1	0.4	0.7	2.2	-
26 139	Ottawa	256,976	1.8	6.9	19.5	12.4	27.1	23.4	10.7	33.4	92.1	1.8	2.8	5.4	7.9
26 143	Roscommon	25,665	-1.0	4.4	14.3	7.1	21.1	28.4	24.6	46.9	98.2	1.0	-	1.7	0.9
26 145	Saginaw	204,612	-2.1	6.4	18.4	9.7	24.6	26.8	14.0	38.1	77.4	19.7	1.3	3.6	7.1
26 147	St. Clair	170,060	0.3	6.1	18.2	8.4	27.5	26.9	12.8	38.3	96.1	2.9	0.7	1.9	2.5
26 149	St. Joseph	62,434	0.0	7.7	18.7	8.4	26.6	25.5	13.1	37.0	94.2	2.9	0.8	3.5	6.1
26 151	Sanilac	43,897	-0.9	6.3	18.1	8.3	24.9	26.4	16.0	39.3	97.9	0.6	0.6	2.4	3.0
26 155	Shiawassee	72,096	-0.8	6.1	18.2	8.6	26.7	27.6	12.9	38.5	98.3	0.6	0.5	1.5	2.0
26 157	Tuscola	57,143	-1.3	5.7	18.1	9.1	25.0	28.0	14.0	39.5	96.8	1.3	0.8	2.6	2.5
26 159	Van Buren	78,012	-0.1	6.8	19.0	8.5	25.5	27.4	12.7	37.5	91.1	5.5	0.7	4.8	8.9
26 161	Washtenaw	347,670	1.4	6.1	15.6	16.6	29.6	23.3	8.7	32.8	77.7	13.5	8.8	2.6	3.3
26 163	Wayne	2,008,238	-2.1	6.9	20.1	8.4	27.6	25.3	11.7	36.2	53.3	42.1	2.7	3.6	4.8
26 165	Wexford	31,695	0.6	6.7	17.5	8.2	27.0	25.5	15.1	38.7	98.2	0.7	0.4	2.5	1.2
27 000	**Minnesota**	5,155,344	1.6	6.7	17.7	9.9	27.8	25.7	12.2	36.9	89.5	5.0	3.9	3.4	3.8
27 003	Anoka	323,611	1.8	6.9	19.9	8.5	30.7	25.9	8.2	35.6	91.2	4.0	4.2	2.6	2.5
27 005	Becker	31,778	1.3	6.5	16.9	8.8	24.4	27.0	16.4	40.1	92.7	0.5	0.5	9.4	1.0
27 007	Beltrami	43,162	2.1	7.3	18.2	14.5	24.8	22.8	12.4	31.7	79.9	0.8	1.0	21.0	1.5
27 009	Benton	39,054	2.2	7.4	18.1	10.5	32.3	21.5	10.2	32.8	96.8	2.1	1.9	1.7	1.3
27 013	Blue Earth	59,235	2.2	5.8	14.1	20.2	27.1	21.0	11.8	31.1	94.3	2.5	2.6	2.0	2.1
27 015	Brown	26,073	-0.3	5.3	16.5	10.4	22.2	27.0	18.5	42.1	97.7	0.5	0.6	2.1	3.0
27 017	Carlton	33,765	0.6	6.0	16.7	10.1	25.4	27.1	14.6	39.2	92.6	1.1	0.7	7.2	1.1
27 019	Carver	86,297	5.3	7.6	21.4	8.9	30.5	24.0	7.5	34.5	94.8	1.7	2.5	2.4	3.6
27 021	Cass	28,741	0.1	6.0	16.0	8.1	23.9	27.4	18.6	42.0	88.6	0.6	0.5	11.9	1.0
27 025	Chisago	49,417	3.0	7.3	19.2	8.8	31.6	23.5	9.7	34.8	96.1	2.2	0.6	1.5	1.9
27 027	Clay	54,110	2.8	6.1	16.4	18.6	24.0	22.4	12.5	32.4	95.6	0.9	1.5	3.5	3.4
27 035	Crow Wing	60,724	3.2	6.2	16.7	8.4	26.0	25.4	17.3	40.0	97.7	0.8	0.6	1.8	0.9
27 037	Dakota	385,971	2.3	7.1	20.1	8.5	30.0	26.1	8.2	35.6	89.4	4.8	4.6	3.1	4.2
27 041	Douglas	35,600	2.5	5.8	15.3	10.0	25.5	24.8	18.6	40.0	98.5	0.8	0.5	1.0	0.8
27 045	Fillmore	21,047	-0.4	6.6	17.4	8.1	23.2	26.3	18.3	41.7	99.1	0.3	0.4	0.3	0.7
27 047	Freeborn	31,398	-0.9	6.2	15.9	7.7	23.6	27.5	19.2	42.3	97.0	0.8	0.8	1.8	6.9
27 049	Goodhue	45,539	1.2	6.0	17.1	9.4	24.8	27.4	15.2	40.0	96.3	1.1	0.8	2.0	1.7

STATE County	Percent foreign born	Total households	Household type (percent) Family households Total family households	Married-couple families	Male householder families	Female householder families	Nonfamily households Total nonfamily households	One-person households	Percent of households with people under 18 years	Percent of households with people 60 years and over
ACS table number:	C05002	B11001	B11001	B11001	B11001	B11001	B11001	B11001	C11005	B11006
	15	16	17	18	19	20	21	22	23	24
Michigan—Cont.										
Cass	1.8	20,897	69.9	55.1	5.1	9.8	30.1	25.6	33.2	33.3
Charlevoix	1.7	11,707	69.5	56.9	4.4	8.2	30.5	25.3	32.0	34.4
Cheboygan	1.1	11,744	69.7	55.8	5.9	8.0	30.3	24.5	30.3	37.2
Chippewa	2.8	14,663	64.8	50.0	3.4	11.4	35.2	27.9	32.3	31.8
Clare	0.4	12,766	67.2	53.9	4.0	9.3	32.8	27.3	29.3	39.4
Clinton	1.8	27,361	72.5	60.9	3.5	8.1	27.5	21.1	34.8	28.3
Delta	1.0	16,571	64.0	52.1	4.5	7.3	36.0	30.5	28.1	34.5
Dickinson	1.0	11,415	62.1	48.7	3.5	9.9	37.9	33.7	27.4	40.5
Eaton	3.4	42,291	66.4	52.8	4.2	9.4	33.6	28.3	30.9	30.3
Emmet	1.2	13,790	63.0	48.9	4.6	9.6	37.0	30.8	30.4	35.3
Genesee	2.3	173,622	66.1	46.1	4.6	15.4	33.9	29.1	34.0	30.3
Gladwin	0.8	11,537	71.0	57.0	3.9	10.1	29.0	23.3	30.5	41.3
Grand Traverse	1.7	34,386	62.9	50.7	3.9	8.4	37.1	29.0	29.8	30.6
Gratiot	1.6	14,317	73.2	58.6	5.0	9.7	26.8	22.8	37.1	31.7
Hillsdale	1.8	18,206	69.3	55.9	4.5	9.0	30.7	25.0	30.8	34.6
Houghton	2.8	14,086	57.0	44.2	3.7	9.0	43.0	32.5	25.0	33.7
Huron	1.6	15,062	65.2	53.8	3.4	8.0	34.8	31.2	28.2	40.4
Ingham	8.3	107,929	59.4	43.4	3.6	12.5	40.6	30.8	30.3	25.0
Ionia	1.8	21,847	72.9	57.9	5.1	9.8	27.1	22.0	38.1	28.0
Iosco	1.5	12,216	67.6	54.7	4.9	8.0	32.4	28.5	27.8	44.8
Isabella	3.1	24,078	56.5	42.9	3.4	10.2	43.5	24.2	28.0	24.5
Jackson	1.7	60,667	68.3	51.9	4.1	12.4	31.7	26.8	35.1	31.8
Kalamazoo	4.4	97,600	60.2	45.6	4.1	10.6	39.8	29.8	31.2	27.6
Kent	8.1	225,252	67.0	50.8	4.2	12.0	33.0	26.9	36.6	25.6
Lapeer	3.0	33,228	76.2	63.6	3.5	9.1	23.8	20.1	36.7	29.5
Leelanau	3.8	9,559	72.8	63.7	2.8	6.3	27.2	21.9	28.6	38.6
Lenawee	2.2	37,726	72.8	59.1	4.8	8.9	27.2	23.2	35.8	33.1
Livingston	3.0	66,492	75.9	65.6	3.4	6.8	24.1	19.8	37.5	26.4
Macomb	9.6	327,282	66.7	52.2	3.9	10.6	33.3	29.0	32.6	31.7
Manistee	1.4	10,373	66.1	52.3	3.7	10.1	33.9	27.9	28.8	41.8
Marquette	2.0	25,423	64.5	52.4	3.2	8.9	35.5	28.7	26.9	32.8
Mason	1.9	12,328	67.3	55.3	3.0	9.0	32.7	29.0	31.8	40.6
Mecosta	1.8	16,360	60.3	48.1	3.3	8.9	39.7	29.6	28.3	31.4
Menominee	1.1	10,692	66.4	54.9	4.0	7.5	33.6	29.0	29.4	33.9
Midland	2.9	32,842	69.4	57.0	3.3	9.1	30.6	25.7	33.6	30.8
Monroe	2.0	57,946	71.8	58.6	3.9	9.3	28.2	22.9	36.4	29.8
Montcalm	1.0	22,779	70.1	53.6	5.8	10.8	29.9	24.0	34.5	31.1
Muskegon	2.0	65,259	67.6	49.6	4.8	13.2	32.4	28.0	35.7	31.5
Newaygo	2.2	18,950	73.2	58.0	5.5	9.7	26.8	21.4	37.4	31.9
Oakland	11.5	480,435	66.3	52.5	3.8	10.0	33.7	29.0	33.0	29.5
Oceana	5.9	10,364	71.9	56.9	4.1	11.0	28.1	22.3	36.3	33.2
Ogemaw	1.0	8,479	70.0	56.9	3.6	9.5	30.0	25.3	27.3	43.7
Osceola	0.7	8,665	71.2	56.9	3.8	10.5	28.8	23.7	33.2	36.8
Otsego	1.9	9,508	70.2	58.1	2.8	9.3	29.8	22.3	34.9	31.7
Ottawa	5.3	90,396	74.9	64.5	3.3	7.1	25.1	20.3	39.1	26.9
Roscommon	1.0	11,987	60.7	49.3	3.0	8.4	39.3	31.2	21.7	45.9
Saginaw	1.8	77,707	68.8	49.4	4.1	15.3	31.2	26.6	34.7	33.4
St. Clair	2.1	66,121	70.2	55.5	4.2	10.5	29.8	25.2	34.3	31.6
St. Joseph	4.3	22,810	71.1	54.2	4.5	12.4	28.9	24.5	33.7	32.4
Sanilac	1.2	17,173	71.1	57.8	3.5	9.8	28.9	25.1	34.6	34.7
Shiawassee	1.0	27,942	72.3	55.8	5.0	11.5	27.7	23.9	35.1	30.5
Tuscola	1.3	21,716	74.1	60.4	4.1	9.6	25.9	22.0	35.7	34.6
Van Buren	4.8	29,437	71.4	54.9	4.5	12.0	28.6	24.0	34.5	30.9
Washtenaw	11.4	132,861	59.9	46.8	3.4	9.7	40.1	29.8	30.6	23.0
Wayne	7.8	716,137	64.7	39.7	5.2	19.8	35.3	31.2	35.5	31.4
Wexford	1.3	12,877	66.5	53.2	4.2	9.0	33.5	27.3	34.0	32.3
Minnesota	6.5	2,041,466	65.4	52.3	4.0	9.2	34.6	27.9	33.3	28.0
Anoka	6.4	118,098	73.3	58.6	4.5	10.3	26.7	20.7	39.4	22.8
Becker	1.0	13,180	67.3	55.8	3.8	7.7	32.7	28.4	30.3	35.7
Beltrami	1.6	15,527	67.9	51.3	3.9	12.7	32.1	26.5	34.2	30.6
Benton	0.7	14,834	63.8	52.4	3.7	7.7	36.2	27.5	32.5	22.5
Blue Earth	4.4	23,233	57.7	45.6	3.7	8.4	42.3	28.8	30.0	27.2
Brown	1.4	10,818	68.7	57.7	2.6	8.3	31.3	27.5	33.3	34.3
Carlton	1.2	13,565	69.3	56.0	4.2	9.1	30.7	25.3	33.3	31.7
Carver	5.4	31,431	76.1	66.8	2.6	6.7	23.9	18.7	42.3	20.3
Cass	0.7	13,025	68.5	56.5	4.2	7.9	31.5	26.9	30.3	37.2
Chisago	1.2	17,840	74.4	62.4	4.0	8.0	25.6	17.7	41.4	24.8
Clay	2.8	20,615	65.0	52.7	3.9	8.5	35.0	26.6	32.3	28.2
Crow Wing	1.0	26,180	64.9	55.0	2.7	7.2	35.1	27.3	30.2	33.5
Dakota	7.3	146,728	70.6	55.0	4.8	10.7	29.4	23.5	39.8	21.7
Douglas	1.2	15,902	65.6	54.0	3.4	8.3	34.4	28.6	28.6	34.7
Fillmore	1.2	8,474	67.3	58.1	3.1	6.2	32.7	28.6	29.5	37.7
Freeborn	3.5	12,961	67.1	56.9	3.3	6.9	32.9	28.5	28.1	39.6
Goodhue	2.0	18,438	69.4	57.3	3.8	8.3	30.6	26.4	33.1	33.5

Table A-2. Counties — Who: Age, Race/Ethnicity, and Household Structure, 2005–2007—*Continued*

STATE County code	STATE County	Total population	Percent change 2005–2007	Population by age (percent) Under 5 years	5 to 17 years	18 to 24 years	25 to 44 years	45 to 64 years	65 years and over	Median age	Race alone or in combination (percent) White	Black	Asian Hawaiian or Pacific Islander	Amer. Indian, Alaska Native, or some other race	Percent Hispanic or Latino
	ACS table number:	B01003	Population estimates	B01001	B01001	B01001	B01001	B01001	B01001	B01002	B02008	B02009	B02011 + B02012	B02010 + B02013	C03002
		1	2	3	4	5	6	7	8	9	10	11	12	13	14
	Minnesota—Cont.														
27 053	Hennepin	1,130,110	1.0	7.0	16.6	8.9	30.0	26.6	10.8	37.2	80.4	11.6	6.0	4.6	5.9
27 059	Isanti	38,097	4.5	6.5	18.0	9.1	31.0	24.9	10.4	35.4	98.2	0.5	0.9	1.8	1.4
27 061	Itasca	44,269	1.1	5.3	15.9	9.5	22.1	29.6	17.6	43.4	95.8	0.5	0.3	4.9	0.7
27 067	Kandiyohi	40,859	-0.4	6.8	17.2	9.9	24.3	26.6	15.2	37.5	94.6	0.8	0.6	4.5	9.2
27 079	Le Sueur	27,605	3.2	5.9	18.2	9.1	26.7	26.1	14.0	38.5	98.5	0.7	0.7	0.8	4.7
27 083	Lyon	24,709	0.1	6.0	17.9	13.8	23.8	24.0	14.5	35.5	95.0	1.0	2.8	1.7	4.8
27 085	McLeod	36,824	2.4	7.2	18.5	8.3	27.0	25.1	13.9	36.8	96.1	0.3	1.3	2.9	4.8
27 091	Martin	20,568	-1.3	5.1	16.6	8.3	20.7	28.5	20.8	44.2	98.5	-	0.7	0.5	2.8
27 093	Meeker	23,171	0.6	6.7	17.8	8.7	24.2	26.4	16.1	39.4	97.7	0.3	0.7	1.4	2.9
27 095	Mille Lacs	25,957	3.3	6.7	17.3	8.7	27.8	23.8	15.5	37.4	94.1	0.6	0.6	6.3	1.3
27 097	Morrison	32,576	0.8	6.6	18.2	8.8	25.8	25.3	15.3	37.9	98.6	0.5	0.6	1.2	0.8
27 099	Mower	38,134	-0.5	7.0	17.5	8.7	24.1	24.2	18.4	39.5	94.8	1.4	1.8	2.8	7.1
27 103	Nicollet	31,370	2.4	6.6	15.8	17.3	24.2	24.5	11.7	34.0	96.1	1.8	1.6	0.8	-
27 105	Nobles	20,155	-0.6	7.7	18.4	8.8	23.1	25.6	16.5	39.1	87.8	0.9	4.2	5.8	-
27 109	Olmsted	137,514	3.3	7.6	18.1	8.3	29.5	24.9	11.6	36.3	90.7	4.1	5.6	1.0	2.9
27 111	Otter Tail	57,112	-0.1	5.2	16.3	9.2	22.2	27.5	19.6	43.0	97.8	0.7	0.6	1.1	1.9
27 115	Pine	28,036	0.7	5.7	17.1	8.4	28.1	25.2	15.5	39.2	95.1	1.8	0.6	4.0	1.9
27 119	Polk	30,733	-0.2	5.7	16.7	11.8	22.6	26.3	16.9	39.7	94.7	0.7	0.6	5.1	4.9
27 123	Ramsey	498,692	0.3	6.9	17.6	10.2	27.4	25.5	12.5	36.8	78.3	10.7	9.6	4.2	6.2
27 131	Rice	61,336	2.2	6.4	16.4	16.9	25.8	23.2	11.3	33.0	95.1	1.8	1.7	2.2	7.0
27 137	St. Louis	196,606	0.0	5.2	14.7	13.3	22.9	28.2	15.7	40.4	95.8	1.6	1.0	2.9	0.9
27 139	Scott	122,721	6.8	8.9	21.2	8.2	34.1	21.4	6.2	32.7	91.0	2.5	5.3	2.2	3.7
27 141	Sherburne	83,914	6.3	8.0	20.2	10.7	32.2	21.7	7.2	31.3	96.7	1.7	1.4	1.5	1.8
27 145	Stearns	144,404	2.3	6.4	16.8	15.9	26.5	22.7	11.7	32.8	95.3	1.9	2.1	1.7	1.7
27 147	Steele	35,965	2.4	7.4	18.7	9.0	27.3	24.6	13.1	36.7	95.4	2.5	1.1	1.9	5.1
27 153	Todd	24,008	-0.1	6.2	17.5	10.3	22.7	27.1	16.2	40.0	98.3	-	0.7	1.9	-
27 157	Wabasha	21,816	0.0	6.0	17.2	8.9	24.4	27.5	15.9	40.9	98.2	-	0.4	1.8	2.2
27 163	Washington	222,031	4.1	6.8	20.1	8.7	28.3	27.6	8.6	36.5	91.3	3.7	4.6	2.2	2.6
27 169	Winona	49,717	0.4	5.4	14.7	19.8	22.8	23.8	13.5	34.1	96.5	1.1	2.4	0.5	1.4
27 171	Wright	113,666	7.0	8.6	20.3	8.5	31.5	22.6	8.5	33.4	96.6	1.2	1.1	1.9	1.9
28 000	**Mississippi**	2,906,118	0.6	7.4	19.0	10.7	26.3	24.3	12.4	35.1	60.9	37.5	1.0	1.6	1.8
28 001	Adams	31,886	-0.2	6.7	17.9	9.7	21.2	27.7	16.8	41.2	42.8	56.9	-	0.3	-
28 003	Alcorn	35,357	1.5	6.8	17.5	7.4	26.6	26.1	15.6	39.5	88.1	11.8	0.2	-	-
28 011	Bolivar	37,652	0.1	8.1	18.8	15.5	23.6	23.0	11.0	31.7	32.8	65.7	0.6	1.4	1.4
28 025	Clay	21,056	-0.7	7.0	19.3	9.0	25.2	25.4	14.0	36.0	43.2	57.3	-	-	-
28 027	Coahoma	27,932	-2.6	8.9	22.4	10.2	23.2	23.3	11.9	32.1	24.4	75.0	-	0.3	-
28 029	Copiah	29,168	1.3	7.5	17.9	12.3	24.7	24.9	12.7	35.1	47.3	51.2	-	1.1	-
28 031	Covington	20,226	1.5	7.4	19.7	8.7	26.9	23.7	13.6	35.2	63.0	36.0	1.1	-	-
28 033	DeSoto	143,112	9.8	7.9	21.2	8.5	30.0	23.0	9.4	33.6	78.6	19.7	1.3	1.3	3.7
28 035	Forrest	77,097	3.4	7.3	17.1	17.5	26.4	20.5	11.2	29.8	62.0	35.4	1.5	2.2	1.8
28 039	George	21,449	5.2	7.7	21.2	8.4	26.7	24.1	11.8	34.0	89.5	9.3	-	1.0	2.2
28 043	Grenada	22,951	1.5	6.7	19.3	7.8	27.5	24.4	14.3	37.2	57.6	41.8	-	-	-
28 045	Hancock	41,567	-14.0	5.8	17.8	8.1	24.8	28.7	14.8	41.5	91.7	6.8	1.1	1.5	2.3
28 047	Harrison	181,764	-10.1	7.2	18.9	9.5	27.1	25.4	11.9	36.5	72.4	23.5	3.7	3.2	3.6
28 049	Hinds	249,874	0.0	7.9	19.5	12.0	25.5	24.3	10.8	33.3	33.4	65.4	0.9	1.4	1.2
28 051	Holmes	20,568	-0.7	9.0	20.7	13.0	24.2	21.0	12.0	30.5	18.5	81.5	-	0.5	-
28 057	Itawamba	23,026	0.0	6.0	17.4	10.8	26.7	24.6	14.5	37.6	91.9	7.0	-	0.7	-
28 059	Jackson	130,863	-3.2	7.3	19.2	8.8	26.3	26.8	11.7	37.0	75.0	22.7	2.0	1.5	3.0
28 067	Jones	66,270	1.5	7.7	17.7	9.9	26.1	24.3	14.3	36.3	70.1	27.7	-	2.7	4.0
28 071	Lafayette	42,076	3.4	5.9	14.0	25.8	24.7	19.4	10.2	26.8	72.6	24.6	2.1	1.5	1.3
28 073	Lamar	45,959	7.9	8.0	19.7	11.0	28.1	23.4	9.9	32.9	83.1	15.2	0.9	1.8	1.3
28 075	Lauderdale	77,049	-0.1	7.5	18.6	10.3	25.4	24.2	14.0	36.3	57.7	41.2	0.7	0.4	1.5
28 079	Leake	22,636	1.9	7.7	21.2	10.8	24.1	22.1	14.0	33.9	54.1	37.1	-	7.0	-
28 081	Lee	79,343	2.7	7.8	19.6	8.4	27.6	24.5	12.2	36.1	72.9	26.6	0.7	1.0	1.5
28 083	Leflore	35,229	-0.7	8.1	19.9	13.1	25.4	22.0	11.5	31.1	27.2	72.5	-	-	-
28 085	Lincoln	34,169	2.5	6.9	18.3	8.2	27.5	24.8	14.3	37.1	68.9	30.9	-	0.6	-
28 087	Lowndes	59,559	0.2	7.5	19.7	10.3	25.7	24.6	12.3	35.6	55.4	44.4	0.2	-	1.6
28 089	Madison	87,033	5.8	7.6	20.7	9.7	28.1	23.6	10.2	34.3	59.8	38.1	1.6	0.8	1.5
28 091	Marion	25,450	2.6	7.7	19.1	9.4	25.7	23.6	14.4	36.1	66.2	33.5	0.4	-	-
28 093	Marshall	36,200	2.5	7.1	18.2	10.6	27.4	24.7	12.1	35.0	49.3	48.3	1.0	2.5	1.6
28 095	Monroe	37,179	-0.5	6.8	18.3	8.7	25.9	25.2	15.1	38.5	69.3	31.5	-	0.3	-
28 099	Neshoba	30,004	1.7	8.4	19.9	9.7	24.6	23.3	14.1	34.6	65.1	21.7	-	14.1	1.5
28 101	Newton	22,155	1.4	7.7	18.6	12.0	23.3	23.7	14.6	35.1	64.5	31.2	-	4.2	0.6
28 105	Oktibbeha	43,229	3.4	6.6	14.5	28.3	23.2	18.0	9.3	25.2	59.8	37.1	3.4	0.7	0.7
28 107	Panola	35,192	1.2	8.0	19.9	9.7	26.8	23.3	12.3	34.3	50.7	48.1	-	0.8	-
28 109	Pearl River	55,084	10.1	6.6	18.5	9.5	26.1	25.8	13.5	36.7	85.9	12.8	0.5	1.9	1.8
28 113	Pike	39,480	2.9	8.3	19.0	9.3	24.5	24.4	14.5	35.9	50.1	48.5	1.4	-	-
28 115	Pontotoc	28,573	2.4	7.3	19.4	9.2	27.4	24.8	12.0	35.7	85.4	14.0	-	2.7	-
28 117	Prentiss	25,501	-0.9	6.2	17.6	11.8	25.9	23.8	14.8	36.4	85.2	14.5	-	-	-
28 121	Rankin	135,092	5.3	7.4	18.3	9.7	29.5	24.6	10.5	35.0	78.8	19.8	1.0	1.1	1.9
28 123	Scott	28,743	1.0	7.8	19.8	10.1	26.3	23.8	12.2	33.9	56.0	39.1	-	4.8	-
28 127	Simpson	27,863	-0.1	7.2	19.6	8.9	26.4	24.7	13.2	35.7	63.7	36.3	-	-	-
28 133	Sunflower	31,149	-1.5	7.2	18.5	13.9	29.2	21.5	9.6	31.9	27.4	71.1	0.5	1.6	1.8

STATE County	Percent foreign born	Total households	Household type (percent)						Percent of households with people under 18 years	Percent of households with people 60 years and over
			Family households				Nonfamily households			
			Total family households	Married-couple families	Male householder families	Female householder families	Total nonfamily households	One-person households		
ACS table number:	C05002	B11001	B11001	B11001	B11001	B11001	B11001	B11001	C11005	B11006
	15	16	17	18	19	20	21	22	23	24
Minnesota—Cont.										
Hennepin	12.1	463,097	58.4	44.4	4.1	9.9	41.6	33.8	30.4	25.5
Isanti	1.5	14,579	72.7	58.5	5.9	8.3	27.3	21.5	41.2	24.0
Itasca	0.9	19,221	68.6	56.1	5.2	7.3	31.4	23.0	28.1	34.9
Kandiyohi	4.6	16,115	68.6	57.9	2.6	8.1	31.3	26.3	31.1	30.9
Le Sueur	2.6	10,516	68.7	56.3	3.2	9.2	31.3	25.4	35.1	29.5
Lyon	4.8	10,195	62.9	52.2	3.9	6.8	37.1	29.9	31.8	28.0
McLeod	3.0	14,178	69.4	58.1	3.8	7.5	30.6	25.6	34.4	30.9
Martin	2.7	9,225	64.6	53.9	3.0	7.7	35.4	32.0	29.8	39.2
Meeker	1.9	9,230	70.1	60.3	4.1	5.7	29.9	24.5	33.7	32.0
Mille Lacs	1.1	9,998	64.8	54.0	4.3	6.6	35.2	29.3	30.7	33.7
Morrison	0.8	13,411	69.7	56.7	5.1	7.9	30.3	25.0	36.0	32.5
Mower	4.9	15,651	65.5	50.4	5.4	9.8	34.5	27.9	29.0	37.9
Nicollet	3.1	12,009	66.8	55.6	3.2	8.1	33.2	26.7	32.2	27.5
Nobles	10.6	8,080	67.9	54.2	2.9	10.8	32.1	28.9	34.9	34.0
Olmsted	8.5	54,279	65.4	54.2	3.0	8.1	34.6	28.7	34.9	25.9
Otter Tail	2.5	24,584	66.5	55.6	3.8	7.1	33.5	28.0	29.3	37.8
Pine	1.6	10,795	67.7	52.0	3.6	12.1	32.3	25.2	29.9	34.4
Polk	1.9	12,399	64.3	53.3	2.8	8.3	35.7	29.0	30.8	34.5
Ramsey	11.2	199,541	58.0	41.6	4.2	12.2	42.0	34.5	29.7	28.6
Rice	5.2	21,180	69.3	56.9	2.8	9.6	30.7	24.0	34.6	29.4
St. Louis	1.9	84,582	59.9	47.1	3.8	9.1	40.1	32.2	26.4	33.5
Scott	7.4	42,063	76.0	64.6	4.0	7.4	24.0	17.5	44.4	18.5
Sherburne	2.3	28,316	76.3	65.5	4.6	6.2	23.7	17.6	44.6	19.5
Stearns	3.5	54,438	66.2	54.8	4.3	7.0	33.8	24.4	34.5	26.5
Steele	3.0	13,709	71.7	59.7	3.2	8.7	28.3	24.8	35.5	29.3
Todd	3.4	9,975	70.6	60.3	5.3	5.0	29.4	24.5	34.2	35.5
Wabasha	1.6	8,958	68.6	58.1	4.6	5.9	31.4	26.4	30.3	36.5
Washington	6.0	82,901	73.6	61.3	3.6	8.7	26.4	21.3	39.3	23.8
Winona	3.2	19,237	61.0	52.3	2.6	6.2	39.0	30.7	28.4	30.9
Wright	2.5	42,939	74.0	61.1	4.4	8.6	26.0	19.3	42.8	21.2
Mississippi	1.7	1,079,584	69.8	46.9	4.7	18.2	30.2	26.3	37.4	31.9
Adams	0.5	12,768	66.7	38.8	4.1	23.7	33.3	30.1	34.4	39.5
Alcorn	0.8	13,758	68.0	52.6	2.8	12.6	32.0	29.3	32.3	35.9
Bolivar	0.7	13,425	65.0	34.1	5.3	25.7	35.0	29.9	36.9	32.7
Clay	-	8,100	72.4	43.8	3.5	25.0	27.6	25.6	36.4	28.6
Coahoma	0.4	10,263	71.5	34.9	3.3	33.3	28.5	25.5	42.6	33.8
Copiah	1.5	10,204	67.5	43.8	5.6	18.1	32.5	28.1	32.8	31.2
Covington	-	7,865	78.6	56.0	3.2	19.4	21.4	19.7	48.7	32.2
DeSoto	3.1	52,195	75.7	57.8	4.3	13.6	24.3	19.2	42.8	23.5
Forrest	2.6	29,243	60.2	37.4	4.0	18.9	39.8	32.2	31.8	27.3
George	1.4	6,785	82.7	68.4	3.6	10.7	17.3	15.4	41.6	33.3
Grenada		8,887	66.1	45.4	5.4	15.3	33.9	28.8	39.2	34.7
Hancock	1.7	17,398	74.6	58.2	6.2	10.2	25.4	21.8	38.0	35.2
Harrison	4.6	68,755	68.5	46.6	5.6	16.3	31.5	26.0	37.0	30.1
Hinds	1.3	91,291	64.4	35.7	5.0	23.7	35.6	31.3	36.4	28.2
Holmes	-	7,128	67.3	31.0	3.1	33.1	32.7	29.2	37.5	35.3
Itawamba	0.5	9,179	74.4	56.3	3.6	14.5	25.6	22.3	37.1	30.5
Jackson	2.9	48,286	74.0	51.7	5.9	16.5	26.0	21.7	39.3	32.2
Jones	2.6	25,758	73.4	50.3	5.7	17.5	26.6	24.1	38.7	34.6
Lafayette	4.4	14,932	56.4	40.1	2.8	13.5	43.6	33.4	24.2	27.1
Lamar	1.5	14,991	72.3	59.0	2.2	11.1	27.7	22.4	40.2	27.0
Lauderdale	1.3	30,884	67.4	42.7	5.0	19.7	32.6	29.6	37.3	31.4
Leake	3.3	7,254	74.8	48.7	7.5	18.7	25.2	24.0	38.9	39.4
Lee	1.1	29,086	69.9	49.6	4.6	15.7	30.1	26.8	36.2	30.9
Leflore	0.4	13,057	66.8	32.7	4.1	30.0	33.2	31.0	39.1	29.8
Lincoln	0.5	13,250	75.2	56.8	5.7	12.7	24.8	22.3	38.2	34.0
Lowndes	1.3	23,161	71.1	46.9	4.7	19.5	28.9	25.4	39.9	27.2
Madison	2.6	33,106	67.8	49.7	2.9	15.2	32.2	26.9	37.8	26.8
Marion	0.7	8,830	70.4	49.2	3.7	17.5	29.6	25.2	36.1	38.4
Marshall	2.0	12,214	74.4	51.0	3.8	19.6	25.6	22.9	39.0	34.1
Monroe	0.6	15,104	75.4	51.3	3.4	20.8	24.6	22.5	37.3	34.4
Neshoba	0.5	10,346	70.7	47.3	5.7	17.7	29.3	26.9	40.2	31.6
Newton	0.5	8,081	72.8	50.7	5.3	16.8	27.2	26.1	36.1	38.7
Oktibbeha	3.1	16,619	55.8	37.8	3.3	14.7	44.2	30.3	31.1	22.1
Panola	-	11,934	73.5	47.1	5.4	21.0	26.5	22.8	35.8	36.5
Pearl River	1.2	20,942	70.0	53.8	5.4	10.7	30.0	23.9	38.3	35.4
Pike	1.5	14,287	66.7	43.9	4.4	18.4	33.3	30.8	35.9	36.1
Pontotoc	2.1	9,869	76.4	58.3	4.2	13.9	23.6	20.6	39.8	30.5
Prentiss	0.9	9,816	74.2	53.4	4.5	16.4	25.8	23.8	36.4	37.6
Rankin	1.4	48,951	71.6	55.1	3.8	12.7	28.4	24.8	37.6	28.2
Scott	5.3	9,806	74.1	47.9	6.2	20.1	25.9	23.1	37.7	35.0
Simpson	-	10,181	69.1	53.9	2.1	13.1	30.9	27.4	36.5	35.1
Sunflower	1.4	9,592	73.2	35.3	6.0	31.8	26.8	25.0	44.2	33.8

Table A-2. Counties — Who: Age, Race/Ethnicity, and Household Structure, 2005–2007—*Continued*

STATE County code	STATE County	Total population	Percent change 2005–2007	Under 5 years	5 to 17 years	18 to 24 years	25 to 44 years	45 to 64 years	65 years and over	Median age	White	Black	Asian Hawaiian or Pacific Islander	Amer. Indian, Alaska Native, or some other race	Percent Hispanic or Latino
	ACS table number:	B01003	Population estimates	B01001	B01001	B01001	B01001	B01001	B01001	B01002	B02008	B02009	B02011 + B02012	B02010 + B02013	C03002
		1	2	3	4	5	6	7	8	9	10	11	12	13	14
	Mississippi—Cont.														
28 137	Tate	26,648	2.2	7.6	18.5	12.1	25.3	25.0	11.5	34.5	68.6	31.2	-	1.3	-
28 139	Tippah	21,101	0.5	7.0	17.8	8.6	28.2	25.1	13.4	35.9	84.2	17.6	-	1.3	-
28 145	Union	26,802	1.1	6.8	19.0	9.2	27.3	23.9	13.7	36.2	82.1	16.0	-	1.9	2.8
28 149	Warren	48,877	0.5	7.9	19.8	8.9	24.9	26.9	11.6	36.3	51.4	46.5	0.8	1.6	1.4
28 151	Washington	56,605	-3.4	8.4	21.1	9.9	23.7	25.1	11.9	34.3	32.2	67.4	0.4	1.5	-
28 153	Wayne	20,994	0.9	7.1	19.8	9.8	26.6	24.8	11.9	37.1	60.9	38.2	-	-	-
28 163	Yazoo	27,245	-0.5	7.7	19.1	9.6	27.5	23.6	12.4	35.0	40.9	58.7	0.3	1.4	-
29 000	**Missouri**	5,834,644	1.6	6.7	17.7	9.7	27.0	25.6	13.4	37.3	85.6	12.0	1.8	2.5	2.9
29 001	Adair	24,627	0.3	5.6	12.5	29.3	21.1	19.5	11.9	26.3	95.8	2.7	1.3	-	1.7
29 007	Audrain	25,917	0.2	6.8	17.1	7.2	28.4	24.7	15.8	38.8	91.6	7.6	-	2.3	-
29 009	Barry	35,867	2.2	7.1	18.6	7.5	25.9	25.2	15.6	38.3	95.3	0.5	1.0	4.8	7.5
29 019	Boone	149,563	4.1	6.5	15.9	18.6	28.6	21.4	9.0	30.4	86.5	9.7	3.7	2.5	2.3
29 021	Buchanan	85,698	1.4	6.6	16.9	10.2	27.6	24.2	14.6	37.6	93.9	5.4	0.8	2.3	3.0
29 023	Butler	41,348	0.1	6.8	16.9	8.0	26.2	25.6	16.4	39.3	92.6	7.8	0.4	0.5	-
29 027	Callaway	42,980	2.1	6.2	17.6	11.5	28.9	24.7	11.2	35.7	92.7	5.8	1.1	1.9	1.3
29 029	Camden	39,873	3.5	6.0	14.5	7.3	23.2	29.7	19.2	44.1	98.2	0.7	-	2.8	1.6
29 031	Cape Girardeau	72,047	2.2	6.2	16.2	13.5	26.0	24.5	13.6	35.9	92.2	6.5	1.2	1.7	1.2
29 037	Cass	94,877	4.6	6.8	19.8	8.7	27.7	25.3	11.6	36.1	94.2	3.4	1.0	2.6	3.2
29 043	Christian	69,761	9.9	7.5	18.8	8.8	30.6	23.4	10.9	34.0	97.4	1.0	0.7	2.5	2.0
29 047	Clay	206,691	5.3	7.4	18.4	8.6	29.6	25.3	10.7	35.9	92.7	4.8	2.4	2.8	4.6
29 049	Clinton	20,578	2.2	7.0	17.7	9.3	26.1	26.3	13.7	37.7	97.9	0.9	-	3.0	-
29 051	Cole	73,172	1.5	6.6	17.0	10.0	27.4	27.3	11.7	37.7	87.4	10.3	1.5	2.5	1.7
29 055	Crawford	23,859	1.9	7.2	18.4	7.7	26.5	24.6	15.6	38.0	99.3	-	-	2.2	-
29 069	Dunklin	31,838	-1.4	7.1	18.5	7.8	24.7	25.5	16.5	38.6	89.2	9.6	-	2.0	4.0
29 071	Franklin	99,132	1.8	6.6	18.6	8.4	27.8	25.7	12.9	37.4	98.0	1.2	0.5	1.1	1.0
29 077	Greene	259,450	3.6	6.4	15.7	12.9	27.7	23.7	13.6	35.5	94.5	3.3	1.7	2.5	2.4
29 083	Henry	22,371	0.4	6.0	16.4	6.9	26.1	25.6	19.0	41.4	97.4	1.4	0.4	2.5	1.2
29 091	Howell	38,370	1.4	6.5	17.7	8.4	25.1	24.9	17.4	39.0	98.0	0.5	0.6	2.4	1.4
29 095	Jackson	664,676	0.6	7.6	18.0	8.2	28.4	25.6	12.2	36.8	72.1	23.8	2.1	4.4	7.2
29 097	Jasper	113,140	3.8	7.8	18.2	9.4	28.0	23.2	13.4	34.8	93.9	2.0	1.4	4.7	5.3
29 099	Jefferson	213,600	2.5	6.8	18.8	8.7	29.2	26.5	10.1	36.2	97.9	1.4	1.0	1.1	1.3
29 101	Johnson	51,699	0.9	7.6	16.8	17.7	27.0	20.9	10.0	29.6	92.1	4.7	3.1	3.1	3.3
29 105	Laclede	34,848	3.4	7.2	18.0	8.0	27.6	24.3	14.9	36.9	97.4	1.0	0.7	2.6	1.6
29 107	Lafayette	32,785	-0.7	6.2	17.7	8.2	25.6	26.3	16.0	39.6	96.8	2.8	0.5	0.9	1.4
29 109	Lawrence	37,226	2.2	6.6	19.3	7.8	26.8	24.1	15.4	36.7	97.3	-	0.2	4.1	4.8
29 113	Lincoln	49,540	8.6	7.3	20.2	9.0	30.6	23.2	9.7	33.6	97.5	2.6	1.0	1.9	1.6
29 119	McDonald	22,772	1.3	7.9	20.4	7.2	27.9	25.2	11.4	35.8	92.1	1.0	0.7	9.3	12.9
29 127	Marion	28,198	0.1	6.9	17.9	9.2	25.7	24.4	15.9	37.8	93.5	6.6	0.5	1.7	0.5
29 131	Miller	24,761	1.3	6.5	17.7	8.2	27.6	24.7	15.3	37.7	98.3	0.9	0.4	1.4	1.2
29 141	Morgan	20,602	2.2	6.3	16.5	7.5	23.2	26.0	20.6	42.8	98.6	-	1.1	1.3	-
29 145	Newton	55,505	1.9	6.6	18.7	8.7	25.9	26.2	13.9	37.5	94.8	1.1	1.6	5.1	3.1
29 147	Nodaway	22,080	0.2	4.9	12.7	26.2	22.2	20.3	13.7	29.6	96.6	2.0	0.9	1.6	1.9
29 159	Pettis	40,472	1.8	7.3	18.3	8.7	26.4	23.7	15.5	36.6	92.9	3.6	1.1	4.0	6.4
29 161	Phelps	42,352	1.2	6.4	16.0	14.9	25.1	23.6	14.0	34.3	93.2	2.3	3.7	1.2	1.6
29 165	Platte	83,442	3.3	6.4	18.2	8.2	30.0	27.6	9.6	37.2	91.7	5.1	2.8	3.2	3.9
29 167	Polk	29,664	3.9	6.5	17.6	13.1	25.5	21.9	15.4	34.1	97.9	1.2	0.2	9.0	1.8
29 169	Pulaski	44,012	1.0	7.0	19.5	19.0	28.2	18.6	7.8	27.3	80.1	12.5	4.0	7.0	7.3
29 175	Randolph	25,527	0.5	6.7	17.2	8.3	29.0	24.7	14.0	37.2	92.3	7.0	-	2.6	1.4
29 177	Ray	23,537	0.0	6.2	18.7	8.9	25.7	27.5	12.9	38.7	98.4	1.3	-	1.0	2.0
29 183	St. Charles	335,967	5.0	7.0	19.8	9.3	29.1	25.0	9.9	35.4	93.6	4.5	2.0	1.4	2.2
29 187	St. Francois	62,206	1.9	6.2	15.7	9.7	30.8	23.5	14.1	36.5	94.8	3.6	0.6	1.5	1.1
29 189	St. Louis	998,368	-0.6	6.0	17.7	9.2	24.6	28.4	14.1	40.1	74.5	22.0	3.4	1.4	2.1
29 195	Saline	22,771	-0.8	6.6	16.7	12.1	24.4	25.1	15.2	38.1	88.2	5.6	0.9	5.6	6.9
29 201	Scott	40,693	0.2	7.1	19.0	7.8	25.9	26.3	14.0	37.6	87.8	11.4	0.5	1.3	1.4
29 207	Stoddard	29,779	-0.2	5.8	16.7	7.8	26.2	26.0	17.6	40.7	98.3	1.7	-	1.1	1.1
29 209	Stone	31,085	3.5	5.2	15.3	6.8	23.5	28.2	21.0	44.5	98.9	-	0.5	8.9	-
29 213	Taney	44,346	6.1	6.7	16.0	9.4	26.2	24.8	16.9	38.0	97.7	0.9	0.2	4.3	3.4
29 215	Texas	23,238	1.0	6.4	16.3	8.3	23.9	26.8	18.3	42.1	97.7	1.8	-	1.7	1.3
29 217	Vernon	20,107	-1.2	6.8	18.7	8.3	25.0	25.1	16.1	37.9	98.1	0.7	0.7	1.8	1.1
29 219	Warren	29,538	6.5	7.1	18.3	8.4	27.9	25.1	13.3	36.1	96.1	2.9	0.5	1.9	2.1
29 221	Washington	24,088	2.0	7.3	18.2	8.5	29.1	24.8	12.1	35.7	96.9	3.1	0.6	1.9	-
29 225	Webster	35,090	4.7	7.7	19.4	8.2	28.8	23.7	12.1	35.4	97.9	0.7	-	3.2	1.5
29 510	St. Louis city	352,389	-0.5	7.4	17.8	9.5	28.9	24.5	11.9	35.8	47.2	50.4	2.4	1.7	2.6
30 000	**Montana**	946,815	2.4	6.1	17.1	10.1	24.7	28.2	13.8	39.3	91.6	0.9	1.2	8.5	2.5
30 013	Cascade	81,832	-0.1	7.2	17.9	8.2	25.3	26.6	14.8	39.2	91.9	2.4	1.7	6.7	3.1
30 029	Flathead	84,693	5.1	6.3	17.3	8.2	25.7	29.6	13.0	39.6	96.5	0.6	0.8	3.8	0.8
30 031	Gallatin	84,199	8.2	6.8	14.8	16.4	29.8	24.0	8.4	31.9	95.9	0.6	1.5	3.3	2.4
30 047	Lake	28,275	1.6	6.5	18.2	8.7	23.2	27.8	15.6	39.0	77.2	0.7	0.6	26.5	2.9
30 049	Lewis and Clark	59,050	3.2	5.8	17.3	9.4	24.2	30.5	12.7	40.4	95.9	0.7	1.1	4.0	2.0
30 063	Missoula	103,986	3.3	5.6	15.5	14.2	28.4	25.9	10.4	34.1	95.2	0.9	2.0	4.2	2.3
30 081	Ravalli	39,833	2.9	5.8	17.3	7.8	22.6	29.8	16.6	42.2	98.1	-	-	3.2	-
30 093	Silver Bow	32,705	-0.4	5.5	16.7	9.9	23.0	28.2	16.6	41.5	96.4	0.8	0.2	4.1	3.1
30 111	Yellowstone	138,198	2.5	6.8	17.5	9.0	26.4	26.8	13.5	38.3	92.6	1.5	1.5	6.3	4.7

STATE County	Percent foreign born	Total households	Household type (percent)						Percent of households with people under 18 years	Percent of households with people 60 years and over
			Family households				Nonfamily households			
			Total family households	Married-couple families	Male householder families	Female householder families	Total nonfamily households	One-person households		
ACS table number:	C05002	B11001	B11001	B11001	B11001	B11001	B11001	B11001	C11005	B11006
	15	16	17	18	19	20	21	22	23	24
Mississippi—Cont.										
Tate	0.6	9,738	73.2	53.9	3.5	15.9	26.8	23.2	38.7	34.4
Tippah	2.4	7,971	77.3	53.7	3.5	20.1	22.7	20.0	42.0	32.1
Union	2.7	9,781	71.6	53.3	3.3	15.1	28.4	26.8	34.8	35.8
Warren	1.7	19,461	68.0	44.1	5.3	18.6	32.0	28.7	36.8	28.7
Washington	0.5	21,118	68.8	34.3	6.4	28.1	31.2	28.6	39.1	32.6
Wayne	1.1	8,630	68.8	48.9	3.3	16.6	31.2	29.5	33.9	35.1
Yazoo	1.5	9,066	70.3	39.4	8.6	22.3	29.7	26.3	40.9	38.5
Missouri	3.5	2,300,211	66.1	50.0	4.1	11.9	33.9	28.4	33.3	31.2
Adair	2.0	9,565	56.5	46.3	3.1	7.1	43.5	32.3	27.4	24.4
Audrain	1.2	10,058	69.6	52.1	5.9	11.6	30.4	27.2	32.0	35.9
Barry	3.9	14,411	70.4	56.7	3.8	9.9	29.6	22.1	33.8	34.8
Boone	5.4	62,559	58.5	44.0	4.2	10.3	41.5	29.2	30.8	20.7
Buchanan	1.6	33,242	65.4	48.9	5.4	11.1	34.6	28.8	33.9	32.4
Butler	0.9	16,938	66.7	48.5	5.1	13.2	33.3	29.3	32.7	35.4
Callaway	1.3	15,559	73.1	56.4	4.5	12.3	26.9	21.7	36.8	28.8
Camden	0.5	16,206	69.5	56.1	4.7	8.6	30.5	23.1	26.6	42.1
Cape Girardeau	1.6	29,178	66.7	50.0	4.6	12.1	33.3	26.9	33.1	29.9
Cass	1.8	35,443	75.5	60.0	4.3	11.2	24.5	20.0	39.0	29.6
Christian	1.3	26,380	76.9	63.1	4.3	9.5	23.1	18.3	40.6	25.1
Clay	4.1	77,965	68.4	54.0	3.6	10.8	31.6	25.7	35.7	26.0
Clinton	1.6	8,126	67.5	55.4	3.5	8.7	32.5	26.5	33.9	33.3
Cole	3.0	28,671	64.2	51.3	3.2	9.7	35.8	30.4	33.1	25.4
Crawford	0.4	8,598	70.3	57.4	3.6	9.3	29.7	24.5	33.0	35.5
Dunklin	2.2	13,208	64.8	45.0	4.9	14.8	35.2	30.4	34.3	37.7
Franklin	0.8	37,778	71.8	57.2	5.2	9.5	28.2	24.0	36.5	31.4
Greene	2.4	109,183	60.6	47.1	3.7	9.8	39.4	31.3	28.8	29.5
Henry	0.8	9,397	66.5	53.0	3.2	10.3	33.5	28.4	29.6	37.6
Howell	1.8	15,105	70.8	56.4	4.4	10.0	29.2	25.2	33.3	38.9
Jackson	5.5	272,761	61.1	42.0	4.3	14.8	38.9	32.6	32.4	29.2
Jasper	3.6	43,507	65.9	50.5	3.9	11.5	34.1	28.2	35.1	32.6
Jefferson	1.7	78,867	74.3	58.1	4.7	11.5	25.7	20.4	38.9	26.9
Johnson	3.2	18,299	66.1	54.4	3.2	8.5	33.9	26.8	33.5	27.6
Laclede	1.5	14,061	71.4	57.2	4.3	9.9	28.6	23.9	36.0	34.6
Lafayette	0.9	13,151	68.7	56.5	3.2	9.0	31.3	28.0	33.7	37.2
Lawrence	2.9	13,789	72.1	55.0	4.6	12.5	27.9	25.5	38.2	34.1
Lincoln	1.0	15,309	77.6	60.0	3.4	14.2	22.4	18.7	43.0	25.5
McDonald	6.9	8,046	72.9	59.7	3.6	9.5	27.1	21.5	36.0	35.9
Marion	0.4	11,615	66.1	50.4	2.8	12.9	33.9	29.7	34.7	32.7
Miller	0.9	9,887	67.9	49.4	8.7	9.8	32.1	27.3	36.1	31.9
Morgan	2.4	7,975	74.4	58.8	4.2	11.4	25.6	19.8	33.7	35.8
Newton	2.1	20,779	75.0	57.6	6.7	10.7	25.0	22.9	37.6	33.8
Nodaway	1.4	7,978	61.3	49.7	5.2	6.4	38.7	29.6	26.2	31.2
Pettis	4.6	15,512	66.3	51.7	5.2	9.4	33.7	28.8	32.2	34.3
Phelps	3.7	16,927	60.4	47.0	4.7	8.7	39.6	30.2	29.6	29.3
Platte	4.4	33,131	67.1	53.6	3.7	9.8	32.9	26.9	34.2	25.8
Polk	1.7	10,756	70.2	56.0	4.4	9.8	29.8	25.6	36.1	37.4
Pulaski	5.3	14,127	71.6	55.5	4.5	11.6	28.4	24.7	44.7	24.1
Randolph	0.8	9,535	67.7	52.6	4.7	10.4	32.3	28.1	32.3	33.4
Ray	0.7	9,246	71.4	59.7	2.0	9.7	28.6	24.7	35.6	32.0
St. Charles	3.2	124,517	73.0	60.9	3.1	8.9	27.0	21.4	38.6	26.3
St. Francois	1.0	22,679	66.9	52.1	3.7	11.2	33.1	25.5	33.8	31.4
St. Louis	5.9	403,291	65.6	48.4	3.9	13.3	34.4	29.8	32.5	32.3
Saline	4.9	8,992	64.6	47.2	6.1	11.2	35.4	28.7	36.1	34.4
Scott	0.5	16,084	68.0	49.6	4.7	13.8	32.0	28.7	31.5	35.8
Stoddard	0.2	12,162	68.2	52.5	6.6	9.0	31.8	27.9	31.4	37.6
Stone	0.9	11,787	70.7	60.9	1.9	7.8	29.3	25.8	24.3	45.7
Taney	2.3	19,241	65.5	52.1	4.3	9.1	34.5	28.4	29.2	39.3
Texas	1.4	9,327	70.1	57.8	2.8	9.5	29.9	26.7	34.1	41.1
Vernon	0.3	8,069	67.0	51.5	3.3	12.2	33.0	30.2	32.7	35.4
Warren	1.3	11,058	73.7	62.0	2.6	9.1	26.3	19.4	35.3	31.7
Washington	0.1	8,346	73.1	57.1	5.6	10.4	26.9	22.2	36.2	33.8
Webster	0.3	12,068	74.5	60.3	4.9	9.3	25.5	22.2	40.1	31.1
St. Louis city	6.5	140,934	50.0	24.3	5.2	20.5	50.0	43.9	27.1	28.4
Montana	1.9	369,329	64.7	52.6	3.7	8.4	35.3	28.7	29.8	32.4
Cascade	1.9	32,190	66.5	52.2	4.7	9.6	33.5	28.6	33.0	33.3
Flathead	1.5	30,521	66.4	54.7	3.7	8.0	33.6	27.0	30.3	31.8
Gallatin	3.1	31,890	61.1	53.3	2.7	5.1	38.9	26.5	29.4	20.8
Lake	2.0	10,632	72.6	55.9	5.4	11.3	27.4	23.3	33.0	38.3
Lewis and Clark	1.9	23,068	61.3	50.1	3.6	7.5	38.7	33.6	27.2	30.9
Missoula	2.5	40,636	58.5	45.8	4.1	8.6	41.5	29.5	27.3	26.0
Ravalli	1.4	14,896	68.4	57.5	3.8	7.2	31.6	26.9	27.5	40.1
Silver Bow	1.4	14,280	58.7	44.0	3.3	11.3	41.3	32.1	26.1	33.0
Yellowstone	1.9	55,196	63.5	51.6	2.9	9.0	36.5	29.5	30.6	30.7

Table A-2. Counties — Who: Age, Race/Ethnicity, and Household Structure, 2005–2007—*Continued*

STATE County code	STATE County	Total population	Percent change 2005–2007	Population by age (percent)						Median age	Race alone or in combination (percent)				Percent Hispanic or Latino
				Under 5 years	5 to 17 years	18 to 24 years	25 to 44 years	45 to 64 years	65 years and over		White	Black	Asian Hawaiian or Pacific Islander	Amer. Indian, Alaska Native, or some other race	
	ACS table number:	B01003	Population estimates	B01001	B01001	B01001	B01001	B01001	B01001	B01002	B02008	B02009	B02011 + B02012	B02010 + B02013	C03002
		1	2	3	4	5	6	7	8	9	10	11	12	13	14
31 000	**Nebraska**	1,764,131	1.2	7.3	18.0	10.6	26.1	24.8	13.3	36.0	90.4	4.8	2.1	4.6	7.3
31 001	Adams	32,990	-0.1	6.4	17.6	12.1	23.5	25.2	15.3	36.8	95.7	0.8	2.4	2.5	6.3
31 019	Buffalo	44,542	2.0	7.1	16.8	17.6	25.4	21.8	11.4	30.8	95.1	1.2	1.0	3.9	5.3
31 025	Cass	25,487	0.7	6.4	19.2	8.2	26.5	27.5	12.2	38.8	98.7	-	1.2	0.9	-
31 043	Dakota	20,174	1.3	8.9	21.8	9.0	27.5	23.1	9.7	32.6	76.4	1.2	4.1	20.0	28.7
31 047	Dawson	24,610	1.5	8.7	21.0	8.2	24.7	24.8	12.4	35.6	79.4	1.4	-	19.8	30.3
31 053	Dodge	35,933	0.4	6.7	16.9	9.9	23.5	25.3	17.7	39.9	94.8	0.5	0.8	4.9	6.3
31 055	Douglas	492,524	2.0	8.2	18.5	10.1	28.7	23.9	10.6	34.1	81.7	12.4	2.9	5.6	9.1
31 067	Gage	23,146	0.7	6.0	15.9	8.8	24.4	25.7	19.2	42.2	98.1	0.4	0.5	1.5	1.3
31 079	Hall	55,028	2.3	8.6	18.7	8.0	26.3	24.7	13.7	35.9	92.6	1.2	1.4	5.8	18.5
31 109	Lancaster	272,010	2.6	7.3	16.3	14.1	29.4	22.8	10.1	32.5	91.5	4.0	3.7	2.7	4.4
31 111	Lincoln	35,394	0.9	6.9	17.8	8.3	25.5	26.8	14.6	38.7	96.1	0.4	0.7	4.9	5.7
31 119	Madison	34,933	-3.7	7.8	18.6	11.1	23.4	24.8	14.3	35.8	92.5	1.6	1.4	5.9	11.4
31 141	Platte	31,477	2.2	7.2	19.3	8.7	24.6	25.3	15.0	38.1	94.9	-	1.2	4.5	9.7
31 153	Sarpy	142,905	5.4	8.6	20.5	10.5	30.0	22.5	7.8	31.8	92.3	4.4	3.3	3.0	5.6
31 155	Saunders	20,172	-0.2	6.4	18.4	8.4	24.4	27.7	14.7	40.1	98.6	0.5	-	1.6	-
31 157	Scotts Bluff	36,286	0.2	7.3	17.7	8.3	23.9	25.5	17.3	38.9	91.0	0.7	0.9	9.2	18.5
32 000	**Nevada**	2,488,917	6.5	7.5	18.3	8.3	30.0	24.9	11.1	35.6	77.2	8.3	7.8	10.1	24.3
32 001	Churchill	24,676	1.8	8.3	19.4	7.4	25.4	25.6	13.8	36.7	86.2	1.9	4.8	10.6	9.7
32 003	Clark	1,774,086	7.5	7.8	18.4	8.0	31.3	24.0	10.4	35.0	74.3	10.6	9.1	9.6	26.9
32 005	Douglas	45,558	-0.7	4.5	14.7	7.7	22.4	32.5	18.2	45.5	94.2	0.9	2.8	4.1	8.7
32 007	Elko	45,745	5.7	6.9	21.3	9.8	27.7	26.5	7.7	34.0	89.7	1.2	1.5	9.1	21.5
32 019	Lyon	49,824	12.5	6.2	23.6	8.7	23.8	24.6	13.1	34.9	89.6	1.1	0.8	11.6	14.0
32 023	Nye	42,180	10.0	4.9	16.7	8.3	23.4	25.2	21.5	42.8	89.7	2.4	2.0	8.5	11.4
32 031	Washoe	398,348	3.9	7.2	17.3	9.4	28.1	26.8	11.4	36.7	80.9	3.0	6.4	12.6	20.2
32 510	Carson City	55,244	-1.3	7.3	16.5	8.5	24.9	27.0	15.8	40.8	85.7	2.1	2.5	11.8	18.8
33 000	**New Hampshire**	1,310,254	1.0	5.8	17.3	9.1	27.3	28.1	12.4	39.3	96.0	1.4	2.2	1.6	2.4
33 001	Belknap	60,948	0.3	4.9	16.2	7.2	26.7	29.8	15.2	41.5	97.8	0.5	1.0	1.3	1.0
33 003	Carroll	47,089	1.4	4.7	15.5	6.6	24.8	30.0	18.4	43.9	98.8	0.4	0.3	1.3	0.8
33 005	Cheshire	77,566	0.5	5.1	15.3	13.1	25.1	27.4	14.1	38.9	97.5	0.8	1.1	1.7	1.2
33 007	Coos	32,995	-1.3	4.7	15.2	7.2	25.1	29.2	18.6	43.2	98.4	0.2	-	1.9	1.0
33 009	Grafton	85,215	0.9	4.8	14.6	14.5	24.9	26.5	14.7	38.7	96.4	1.1	2.5	1.3	1.5
33 011	Hillsborough	400,855	0.8	6.4	18.5	8.0	28.6	27.5	11.0	38.4	93.4	2.2	3.4	2.2	4.5
33 013	Merrimack	147,439	1.3	5.4	17.0	9.6	27.3	28.4	12.3	39.5	97.0	1.2	1.5	1.0	1.4
33 015	Rockingham	295,098	1.1	6.0	18.3	7.3	27.2	30.2	11.0	40.2	96.8	1.1	1.9	1.3	1.9
33 017	Strafford	120,494	2.1	6.1	16.2	13.6	28.3	24.6	11.2	35.8	96.7	1.4	2.2	1.3	1.5
33 019	Sullivan	42,555	0.8	5.8	16.4	6.8	26.8	28.6	15.6	40.9	98.0	0.9	0.7	0.7	0.9
34 000	**New Jersey**	8,669,815	0.3	6.5	17.5	8.7	28.3	26.0	13.0	38.2	70.9	14.3	7.8	8.6	15.6
34 001	Atlantic	269,774	0.7	6.5	17.7	8.5	28.3	25.2	13.6	38.2	67.2	17.5	6.8	10.5	14.1
34 003	Bergen	894,299	0.2	5.6	16.8	7.8	26.9	28.2	14.8	40.9	75.1	6.2	14.3	6.0	13.9
34 005	Burlington	447,101	0.0	6.0	17.5	8.5	28.8	26.3	12.9	38.5	76.9	17.3	4.5	3.7	5.2
34 007	Camden	513,147	0.3	6.7	18.6	9.1	27.7	25.7	12.2	37.1	68.2	19.8	4.9	9.1	11.7
34 009	Cape May	97,555	-2.2	4.9	15.6	7.3	24.2	27.5	20.5	43.8	92.0	6.3	0.2	2.6	4.1
34 011	Cumberland	154,086	2.0	7.2	17.3	8.8	31.0	23.3	12.4	35.9	68.1	22.1	1.3	10.4	22.7
34 013	Essex	779,203	-0.9	7.3	18.4	9.3	28.8	24.6	11.6	36.1	42.5	42.1	4.6	12.6	18.0
34 015	Gloucester	281,218	3.3	6.0	17.9	10.2	28.3	26.1	11.5	37.3	86.2	10.7	2.6	2.2	3.5
34 017	Hudson	600,129	-0.7	6.6	15.4	9.2	35.3	22.6	10.9	35.7	58.4	14.5	11.7	17.3	40.6
34 019	Hunterdon	129,111	0.4	5.6	18.1	7.6	25.7	31.9	11.1	41.3	92.0	3.1	3.5	2.6	4.1
34 021	Mercer	364,567	0.5	6.2	17.0	10.8	28.4	25.5	12.1	37.0	67.2	20.7	8.2	5.7	12.3
34 023	Middlesex	785,479	0.5	6.4	16.7	9.7	30.3	24.8	12.0	36.9	63.3	10.1	18.6	9.6	16.7
34 025	Monmouth	641,721	0.0	6.0	18.5	8.3	25.7	28.7	12.7	40.0	83.7	8.4	5.4	4.0	8.1
34 027	Morris	487,123	0.6	6.2	18.0	7.8	26.7	28.9	12.5	40.0	84.9	3.5	8.8	4.0	10.2
34 029	Ocean	561,394	1.5	6.7	16.5	7.3	25.6	23.1	20.8	40.7	92.1	3.7	2.0	3.2	6.6
34 031	Passaic	492,301	-0.1	7.5	18.5	9.5	28.2	24.4	12.0	36.2	59.5	12.9	4.9	24.4	34.0
34 033	Salem	65,789	0.8	5.9	17.3	9.2	26.4	27.3	13.9	39.2	81.2	15.9	1.0	3.3	4.9
34 035	Somerset	320,213	2.1	6.7	18.6	7.0	28.5	27.8	11.5	39.0	75.8	9.0	12.3	4.2	11.7
34 037	Sussex	151,174	0.4	5.6	19.2	8.7	26.1	30.4	9.9	39.6	94.7	2.0	2.0	2.3	5.4
34 039	Union	524,992	-0.2	7.0	18.0	8.7	27.8	25.9	12.7	38.1	61.0	22.0	4.8	13.5	24.5
34 041	Warren	109,439	0.5	6.0	18.4	7.7	27.4	27.5	12.8	39.4	92.1	3.4	2.6	3.3	5.9
35 000	**New Mexico**	1,942,847	2.8	7.2	18.4	10.5	26.5	24.9	12.5	35.6	71.4	2.7	1.8	27.2	44.1
35 001	Bernalillo	618,845	3.5	7.5	17.3	10.2	28.3	24.9	11.9	35.5	71.7	3.8	2.9	25.0	44.8
35 005	Chaves	61,832	2.1	7.8	18.9	10.6	24.5	23.5	14.7	35.1	79.5	1.5	1.2	26.2	47.8
35 006	Cibola	27,164	0.3	7.2	19.3	10.5	26.9	23.4	12.7	35.5	46.8	-	0.6	55.6	33.6
35 009	Curry	45,602	-1.1	9.7	20.6	10.0	27.4	20.7	11.5	30.9	63.2	9.3	3.3	27.1	34.4
35 013	Dona Ana	194,181	4.7	8.3	19.2	13.7	26.5	20.7	11.6	30.9	86.3	2.2	1.4	11.6	64.6
35 015	Eddy	50,824	1.6	6.9	18.9	9.5	24.6	26.1	14.0	37.6	77.9	2.4	0.8	22.8	41.3
35 017	Grant	29,459	1.4	5.8	15.9	11.2	20.0	27.9	19.1	43.8	70.2	1.1	0.8	31.3	48.2
35 025	Lea	56,998	3.5	8.4	20.0	11.3	25.9	22.7	11.8	32.3	84.7	5.3	-	11.0	45.6
35 027	Lincoln	20,768	0.6	5.5	15.4	9.5	19.7	30.3	19.6	44.9	90.5	1.0	-	15.0	-
35 029	Luna	26,563	3.4	7.0	20.8	7.9	23.5	21.1	19.7	37.5	89.8	1.0	0.5	11.0	59.6
35 031	McKinley	70,385	-0.8	8.0	24.5	11.9	24.4	22.1	9.2	29.9	22.2	1.0	0.8	77.5	13.1
35 035	Otero	63,076	-0.3	6.5	19.6	10.5	26.4	23.6	13.4	36.1	73.9	5.3	2.5	21.5	33.9
35 039	Rio Arriba	40,700	0.7	8.0	18.4	9.7	25.0	26.4	12.5	36.9	78.0	0.8	0.2	22.1	72.2

Table A-2. Counties — Who: Age, Race/Ethnicity, and Household Structure, 2005–2007—*Continued*

STATE County	Percent foreign born	Total households	Household type (percent)						Percent of households with people under 18 years	Percent of households with people 60 years and over
			Family households				Nonfamily households			
			Total family households	Married-couple families	Male householder families	Female householder families	Total nonfamily households	One-person households		
ACS table number:	C05002	B11001	B11001	B11001	B11001	B11001	B11001	B11001	C11005	B11006
	15	16	17	18	19	20	21	22	23	24
Nebraska.................	5.6	698,163	65.9	52.8	3.7	9.5	34.1	28.4	33.5	29.5
Adams.................	5.3	12,556	68.1	54.5	2.5	11.0	31.9	26.7	34.9	33.6
Buffalo.................	3.5	17,278	62.3	53.0	2.4	7.0	37.7	28.8	30.5	26.1
Cass.................	0.9	9,451	76.6	66.6	4.2	5.9	23.4	19.9	37.6	29.8
Dakota.................	16.1	7,464	71.4	54.0	6.5	11.0	28.6	23.5	42.9	27.4
Dawson.................	18.3	8,842	65.2	56.5	2.0	6.6	34.8	31.0	32.3	32.2
Dodge.................	3.7	14,223	68.2	54.5	3.2	10.6	31.8	28.0	32.4	36.0
Douglas.................	7.8	192,075	62.6	45.9	4.2	12.5	37.4	30.8	33.8	25.5
Gage.................	1.2	9,596	63.2	51.0	3.7	8.5	36.8	32.5	31.1	38.3
Hall.................	11.1	20,985	68.8	51.7	2.8	14.2	31.2	27.2	36.9	28.8
Lancaster.................	6.9	107,799	62.0	49.5	3.7	8.8	38.0	29.4	32.9	23.4
Lincoln.................	1.9	14,820	67.4	54.7	5.2	7.5	32.6	25.7	34.0	31.6
Madison.................	6.5	13,364	63.1	53.4	2.8	6.9	36.9	32.0	31.2	32.4
Platte.................	6.4	12,639	70.6	57.9	2.5	10.1	29.4	25.9	34.4	31.7
Sarpy.................	4.3	53,313	73.8	60.6	3.5	9.7	26.2	20.6	41.3	20.2
Saunders.................	1.0	7,773	74.3	64.6	3.3	6.5	25.7	21.0	38.5	30.9
Scotts Bluff.................	3.3	15,183	64.5	50.2	3.0	11.3	35.5	31.1	30.8	37.9
Nevada.................	18.5	932,715	65.5	47.9	6.0	11.6	34.5	26.7	34.4	29.9
Churchill.................	5.9	8,888	66.5	56.5	1.9	8.1	33.5	28.2	32.7	36.8
Clark.................	21.2	662,025	65.7	46.9	6.5	12.4	34.3	26.2	35.4	28.7
Douglas.................	6.8	18,673	74.0	62.0	5.1	7.0	26.0	20.7	32.3	39.5
Elko.................	10.7	17,003	69.0	57.8	3.4	7.9	31.0	25.6	38.1	24.1
Lyon.................	3.0	14,974	72.1	56.5	5.7	9.9	27.9	23.9	31.4	38.5
Nye.................	7.3	14,187	68.4	57.0	3.8	7.6	31.6	26.0	25.0	50.8
Washoe.................	15.2	155,567	61.9	46.7	5.1	10.1	38.1	29.5	31.8	29.7
Carson City.................	11.5	21,330	64.6	46.8	5.6	12.1	35.4	30.2	31.9	37.5
New Hampshire.................	5.4	500,671	67.7	54.3	4.0	9.3	32.3	24.8	33.6	30.1
Belknap.................	3.6	23,909	69.2	55.1	3.6	10.5	30.8	22.6	30.6	34.7
Carroll.................	1.9	19,269	63.6	51.6	4.0	8.0	36.4	30.0	29.6	40.1
Cheshire.................	2.7	29,687	65.6	52.9	4.7	8.0	34.4	25.1	30.7	34.0
Coos.................	3.2	14,267	65.9	52.5	5.5	7.9	34.1	28.2	29.2	39.3
Grafton.................	4.8	32,536	63.4	51.4	4.1	8.0	36.6	28.6	27.5	34.7
Hillsborough.................	8.6	149,761	68.5	53.9	4.6	10.1	31.5	24.2	35.6	27.4
Merrimack.................	3.7	55,379	67.8	54.2	3.9	9.7	32.2	24.9	34.6	29.7
Rockingham.................	5.1	113,033	69.7	57.7	3.2	8.8	30.3	23.2	35.4	28.6
Strafford.................	3.8	45,177	65.1	51.7	3.9	9.5	34.9	26.2	32.7	26.4
Sullivan.................	2.5	17,653	68.7	55.2	3.4	10.1	31.3	23.3	32.3	34.6
New Jersey.................	19.7	3,143,408	69.5	52.2	4.6	12.7	30.5	25.7	36.5	33.2
Atlantic.................	14.2	102,672	65.9	45.4	5.0	15.5	34.1	28.8	35.4	32.3
Bergen.................	28.4	332,605	70.6	57.0	3.7	9.9	29.4	25.5	34.9	36.6
Burlington.................	8.6	164,400	71.0	55.9	4.0	11.1	29.0	24.2	36.3	32.3
Camden.................	9.0	191,148	68.7	47.3	5.2	16.2	31.3	26.0	37.3	31.5
Cape May.................	3.0	47,229	65.4	48.9	4.8	11.6	34.6	28.0	31.2	39.7
Cumberland.................	8.3	50,165	69.0	46.0	6.0	17.0	31.0	25.8	37.5	34.0
Essex.................	23.7	278,402	66.1	40.5	6.2	19.4	33.9	29.5	38.3	31.5
Gloucester.................	4.3	99,708	72.9	57.0	3.9	12.0	27.1	22.6	40.1	29.9
Hudson.................	40.4	226,987	60.4	37.8	6.2	16.5	39.6	31.9	32.2	28.0
Hunterdon.................	8.4	46,256	73.3	64.6	2.5	6.3	26.7	21.8	36.2	31.4
Mercer.................	18.2	127,253	68.5	49.6	5.0	13.9	31.5	26.3	36.4	32.6
Middlesex.................	27.7	269,888	72.2	56.2	4.4	11.6	27.8	23.0	38.9	30.3
Monmouth.................	12.3	231,344	71.0	56.9	3.8	10.3	29.0	24.7	37.0	33.9
Morris.................	18.2	173,978	72.7	62.0	3.0	7.7	27.3	23.2	37.9	32.9
Ocean.................	7.6	221,305	68.4	56.0	3.9	8.5	31.6	27.2	31.4	44.1
Passaic.................	28.1	160,505	71.6	49.6	5.7	16.3	28.4	24.0	38.0	32.6
Salem.................	2.8	25,073	69.4	52.7	4.6	12.0	30.6	25.8	31.9	35.5
Somerset.................	21.6	113,495	73.0	60.7	3.2	9.1	27.0	22.8	38.9	30.7
Sussex.................	6.5	54,830	76.2	63.6	4.3	8.3	23.8	19.3	39.8	28.9
Union.................	28.0	183,634	70.7	49.8	6.1	14.8	29.3	25.4	38.0	33.5
Warren.................	7.7	42,531	69.8	55.2	4.4	10.2	30.2	25.7	35.9	33.0
New Mexico.................	9.4	728,508	65.9	47.3	5.4	13.2	34.1	28.0	34.8	31.2
Bernalillo.................	10.7	251,101	60.9	43.0	5.3	12.6	39.1	32.1	32.4	28.2
Chaves.................	11.3	22,742	70.4	48.5	6.0	15.9	29.6	24.7	38.1	36.4
Cibola.................	2.5	8,121	72.3	45.3	9.5	17.5	27.7	24.1	37.5	35.0
Curry.................	6.8	17,542	65.3	47.7	5.2	12.4	34.7	29.0	37.6	28.6
Dona Ana.................	19.3	68,164	69.9	50.8	3.9	15.3	30.1	23.1	38.2	28.9
Eddy.................	4.6	19,789	69.7	51.3	6.8	11.6	30.3	23.6	37.1	34.1
Grant.................	3.9	12,083	71.9	55.1	4.4	12.4	28.1	24.1	31.5	42.3
Lea.................	12.2	21,101	75.5	55.6	4.5	15.4	24.5	21.2	40.0	30.0
Lincoln.................	8.2	7,989	61.9	50.4	3.5	8.0	38.1	31.9	23.9	48.6
Luna.................	18.5	9,842	64.7	45.7	4.7	14.3	35.3	32.0	37.7	44.5
McKinley.................	3.0	19,029	70.3	44.7	7.1	18.5	29.7	25.1	44.1	30.1
Otero.................	9.3	24,552	70.7	54.6	4.2	11.8	29.3	25.2	37.1	34.1
Rio Arriba.................	5.2	13,995	73.5	50.9	8.8	13.8	26.5	21.2	42.1	32.6

Table A-2. Counties — Who: Age, Race/Ethnicity, and Household Structure, 2005–2007—*Continued*

STATE County code	STATE County	Total population	Percent change 2005–2007	Population by age (percent)						Median age	Race alone or in combination (percent)				Percent Hispanic or Latino
				Under 5 years	5 to 17 years	18 to 24 years	25 to 44 years	45 to 64 years	65 years and over		White	Black	Asian Hawaiian or Pacific Islander	Amer. Indian, Alaska Native, or some other race	
	ACS table number:	B01003	Population estimates	B01001	B01001	B01001	B01001	B01001	B01001	B01002	B02008	B02009	B02011 + B02012	B02010 + B02013	C03002
		1	2	3	4	5	6	7	8	9	10	11	12	13	14
	New Mexico—Cont.														
35 043	Sandoval	111,855	11.5	6.6	19.5	9.6	27.7	25.8	10.8	35.7	71.5	3.0	1.8	27.0	32.1
35 045	San Juan	122,056	0.4	7.8	20.2	11.2	26.8	23.7	10.2	32.6	57.5	1.4	0.7	43.2	17.0
35 047	San Miguel	28,846	-1.5	6.1	17.6	12.2	24.4	26.4	13.4	38.3	63.5	1.8	2.1	38.8	77.3
35 049	Santa Fe	141,207	2.4	5.7	15.8	8.8	27.1	30.0	12.6	40.0	77.4	1.2	1.5	22.5	50.0
35 055	Taos	31,398	1.3	5.5	15.6	9.7	22.8	30.8	15.5	42.9	61.5	1.0	0.3	42.3	55.2
35 061	Valencia	69,784	4.3	6.6	20.0	10.1	27.1	25.2	11.1	35.5	58.7	2.1	0.9	43.3	55.5
36 000	**New York**	19,280,753	0.2	6.2	16.9	10.1	28.1	25.5	13.1	37.4	67.8	16.5	7.2	10.4	16.2
36 001	Albany	299,268	0.1	5.2	15.6	13.1	26.6	26.0	13.6	37.7	82.4	12.9	4.2	2.4	3.8
36 003	Allegany	49,718	-0.4	5.2	15.7	18.0	22.5	24.2	14.5	34.9	96.9	1.5	1.3	1.2	1.1
36 005	Bronx	1,369,859	0.7	7.9	20.5	10.6	29.4	21.1	10.4	32.3	23.0	34.5	3.9	41.1	50.7
36 007	Broome	196,212	-0.2	5.1	15.6	12.6	24.7	25.7	16.4	39.2	90.8	5.0	3.9	1.8	2.4
36 009	Cattaraugus	80,674	-1.6	5.8	17.2	10.9	24.1	27.1	14.9	39.0	95.4	1.6	0.8	3.6	1.1
36 011	Cayuga	80,352	-0.7	5.0	16.5	9.7	27.4	27.0	14.4	39.4	94.0	4.8	0.6	2.0	2.1
36 013	Chautauqua	134,474	-0.9	5.2	16.6	11.9	24.1	26.4	15.8	38.9	95.8	2.9	0.6	2.1	4.7
36 015	Chemung	88,199	-0.4	5.7	16.6	10.0	25.9	26.5	15.3	39.0	92.6	6.6	1.4	1.6	2.0
36 017	Chenango	51,141	0.3	5.1	17.5	8.7	25.6	27.8	15.2	40.4	97.8	1.2	0.5	1.2	1.4
36 019	Clinton	82,048	0.5	4.6	15.0	13.4	28.9	25.3	12.8	37.1	94.6	3.6	1.2	1.9	2.7
36 021	Columbia	62,632	-0.9	5.1	16.2	8.1	24.6	29.3	16.5	42.8	91.9	5.4	1.7	1.9	3.1
36 023	Cortland	48,407	-0.1	5.6	16.3	16.6	24.5	24.6	12.5	34.4	97.0	2.3	-	1.5	1.6
36 025	Delaware	46,555	-1.3	4.7	15.5	10.3	23.1	27.8	18.7	42.7	96.3	1.7	1.0	2.3	2.7
36 027	Dutchess	292,322	0.2	5.5	17.5	11.3	26.7	26.6	12.4	38.1	82.1	10.9	3.7	5.8	8.5
36 029	Erie	919,112	-1.3	5.4	16.9	10.5	25.0	26.7	15.5	39.7	82.5	14.1	2.1	2.6	3.7
36 031	Essex	38,243	-0.5	4.5	14.4	9.4	27.6	27.4	16.8	41.0	94.8	3.5	0.3	2.3	2.3
36 033	Franklin	50,431	0.1	4.7	15.4	10.6	30.1	26.2	13.0	38.2	84.4	6.6	0.6	9.1	4.1
36 035	Fulton	55,022	0.2	5.5	16.5	8.4	27.1	27.0	15.6	40.8	96.2	3.0	1.0	1.5	2.2
36 037	Genesee	58,445	-1.1	5.3	17.5	9.5	25.2	27.4	15.1	40.4	95.7	2.8	0.8	2.1	2.0
36 039	Greene	49,203	0.4	5.6	16.0	10.6	26.1	26.6	15.2	39.1	90.2	6.8	0.5	3.9	5.0
36 043	Herkimer	62,694	-0.6	5.2	16.4	9.7	25.2	27.2	16.3	40.4	97.6	1.1	0.8	1.4	1.3
36 045	Jefferson	116,804	1.0	6.9	18.0	11.7	30.9	21.0	11.4	32.3	90.9	6.1	2.1	3.4	4.3
36 047	Kings	2,520,835	0.7	7.5	18.0	10.1	29.2	23.2	12.1	34.9	43.7	36.2	9.3	12.4	19.6
36 049	Lewis	26,374	0.9	5.9	17.8	9.3	25.8	26.7	14.5	38.6	97.7	1.0	0.5	1.0	0.9
36 051	Livingston	63,381	-0.6	5.0	14.9	16.4	25.2	26.2	12.3	37.0	95.2	3.4	1.4	1.4	2.4
36 053	Madison	69,719	0.3	5.0	16.4	15.2	24.1	26.3	13.1	37.0	96.2	2.2	1.0	1.4	1.4
36 055	Monroe	730,215	-0.2	5.8	17.6	11.4	25.4	26.5	13.3	38.0	80.5	15.3	3.3	2.8	5.7
36 057	Montgomery	48,738	0.0	6.2	16.7	8.5	24.8	26.4	17.3	39.9	93.3	2.3	1.1	4.9	8.6
36 059	Nassau	1,313,526	-1.1	5.7	17.7	9.4	23.5	28.7	14.9	40.8	76.2	11.5	7.0	6.7	12.1
36 061	New York	1,613,257	0.9	6.0	10.8	8.8	38.0	23.9	12.5	37.3	56.8	16.7	11.4	17.7	25.1
36 063	Niagara	215,168	-0.4	5.3	16.9	10.0	25.1	27.5	15.2	40.3	91.3	7.3	1.0	2.1	1.6
36 065	Oneida	232,361	-0.1	5.3	16.5	10.4	25.9	26.0	15.8	39.5	91.2	6.8	1.7	2.4	3.7
36 067	Onondaga	455,126	-0.5	5.9	17.7	11.1	25.9	25.8	13.7	37.8	85.9	11.1	3.1	2.3	2.8
36 069	Ontario	103,657	0.5	5.4	17.1	10.4	25.1	28.1	14.0	40.0	95.3	3.0	1.1	1.8	2.7
36 071	Orange	374,066	1.7	6.9	20.3	10.5	27.7	24.8	9.9	34.6	79.5	10.5	2.7	9.9	15.3
36 073	Orleans	42,584	-1.0	5.2	17.7	9.9	27.4	26.6	13.2	38.5	91.4	7.5	0.5	2.0	4.2
36 075	Oswego	121,752	-0.5	5.4	17.7	13.0	26.0	26.0	11.7	36.8	97.6	1.0	0.8	1.6	1.5
36 077	Otsego	62,561	-0.5	4.3	14.5	17.8	22.0	26.1	15.3	38.0	95.9	2.6	1.2	1.9	2.3
36 079	Putnam	99,405	0.0	5.7	18.5	8.2	26.6	30.2	10.7	39.9	91.7	3.0	2.0	6.1	9.7
36 081	Queens	2,263,858	0.6	6.2	15.4	9.1	31.0	25.1	13.2	37.7	45.8	20.3	21.7	14.2	26.2
36 083	Rensselaer	154,719	0.8	5.5	16.6	11.5	26.6	26.6	13.1	38.2	92.7	5.7	2.6	2.4	2.7
36 085	Richmond	478,501	1.4	6.0	18.0	9.4	28.3	26.4	11.9	37.4	76.6	10.6	7.6	6.4	14.7
36 087	Rockland	295,682	0.6	7.4	19.5	9.7	23.7	26.8	12.9	37.4	78.7	12.0	6.7	3.9	12.7
36 089	St. Lawrence	109,939	-0.3	5.4	15.3	15.8	25.4	24.7	13.3	36.1	95.1	2.6	1.1	2.4	1.9
36 091	Saratoga	214,608	1.2	5.6	16.9	9.2	29.0	27.4	11.9	38.3	96.0	2.2	2.0	1.2	1.9
36 093	Schenectady	149,921	1.4	6.1	17.1	9.6	25.5	26.4	15.4	39.4	84.0	9.3	3.9	4.2	4.2
36 095	Schoharie	31,990	0.3	4.5	15.5	12.7	24.7	27.4	15.2	40.1	96.9	1.5	0.4	1.8	2.1
36 099	Seneca	34,279	-0.4	5.4	15.5	10.1	27.9	26.6	14.5	39.3	93.1	5.3	1.3	1.7	2.9
36 101	Steuben	97,109	-0.6	5.5	17.3	8.8	25.6	27.3	15.4	40.0	96.8	1.8	1.3	0.9	1.1
36 103	Suffolk	1,457,115	-0.6	6.5	18.5	9.0	26.6	26.8	12.5	38.5	85.1	7.9	3.7	4.9	13.0
36 105	Sullivan	75,817	1.2	5.8	17.2	8.7	27.1	27.4	13.8	39.9	85.1	9.9	1.8	5.3	11.2
36 107	Tioga	50,588	-0.6	5.7	17.9	8.6	25.5	28.2	14.1	40.2	98.6	1.2	1.0	0.7	1.3
36 109	Tompkins	100,590	0.8	4.1	11.7	28.2	25.7	20.8	9.5	28.4	84.9	4.8	10.9	2.4	3.9
36 111	Ulster	181,755	0.2	5.0	16.1	10.7	26.5	28.3	13.4	40.0	90.5	7.1	2.1	2.6	7.2
36 113	Warren	65,840	0.9	4.9	16.0	8.8	27.2	27.2	16.0	40.3	97.6	1.2	0.9	1.2	1.5
36 115	Washington	62,439	1.0	5.0	16.2	9.6	28.1	26.6	14.5	39.5	95.3	4.0	0.6	1.0	2.3
36 117	Wayne	91,643	-0.8	5.9	18.6	8.3	26.1	28.3	12.9	39.7	94.9	3.8	0.7	2.5	3.0
36 119	Westchester	949,041	0.4	6.4	18.1	8.6	26.0	27.0	14.0	39.3	69.6	14.6	6.1	11.4	18.5
36 121	Wyoming	42,133	-0.9	4.9	15.5	9.3	29.4	28.2	12.8	39.4	91.7	6.1	0.3	2.5	3.2
36 123	Yates	24,497	0.1	5.5	18.3	11.9	22.3	26.0	16.1	37.8	97.9	0.9	-	0.6	1.5
37 000	**North Carolina**	8,869,861	4.4	7.0	17.4	9.6	28.5	25.3	12.1	36.6	71.7	22.1	2.2	5.7	6.7
37 001	Alamance	142,392	3.9	6.6	17.3	9.8	27.6	24.9	13.8	37.4	72.4	18.9	1.5	8.6	10.3
37 003	Alexander	36,015	2.1	6.1	18.3	7.4	28.5	26.8	13.0	38.6	90.1	6.4		2.6	-
37 007	Anson	25,323	-1.0	6.1	16.9	8.6	28.8	25.5	14.2	38.9	49.1	48.6	1.3	1.7	1.4
37 009	Ashe	25,327	1.5	5.2	14.2	6.6	26.5	28.3	19.2	43.2	96.3	0.8		2.3	-
37 013	Beaufort	45,669	0.7	6.6	16.3	7.9	23.8	28.5	16.9	41.4	69.7	28.1		2.6	-

STATE County	Percent foreign born	Total households	Household type (percent)						Percent of households with people under 18 years	Percent of households with people 60 years and over
			Family households				Nonfamily households			
			Total family households	Married-couple families	Male householder families	Female householder families	Total nonfamily households	One-person households		
ACS table number:	C05002	B11001	B11001	B11001	B11001	B11001	B11001	B11001	C11005	B11006
	15	16	17	18	19	20	21	22	23	24
New Mexico—Cont.										
Sandoval	4.8	38,606	71.1	53.9	5.2	11.9	28.9	22.8	38.1	29.2
San Juan	2.7	38,466	74.5	53.6	7.1	13.8	25.5	21.8	39.5	28.3
San Miguel	2.3	10,727	62.0	38.8	8.4	14.9	38.0	31.8	35.5	35.2
Santa Fe	12.9	52,956	60.6	45.0	4.4	11.2	39.4	30.8	29.8	32.7
Taos	3.1	12,775	59.6	40.3	5.3	14.0	40.4	36.4	28.0	35.9
Valencia	6.3	24,193	74.3	51.0	6.9	16.4	25.7	21.1	39.3	31.0
New York	21.6	7,096,035	64.7	45.2	4.9	14.6	35.3	29.4	33.4	33.2
Albany	7.1	122,538	57.3	41.7	3.8	11.9	42.7	34.2	28.7	30.8
Allegany	2.1	18,574	64.8	52.1	4.8	8.0	35.2	28.3	30.8	35.1
Bronx	31.7	468,735	66.6	28.3	7.4	30.9	33.4	29.5	42.3	29.8
Broome	5.8	80,870	60.1	44.1	4.2	11.8	39.9	33.1	29.2	35.5
Cattaraugus	1.8	32,394	65.5	48.1	4.7	12.7	34.5	28.3	32.3	34.0
Cayuga	1.9	31,438	67.1	50.9	4.8	11.4	32.9	27.4	31.8	33.8
Chautauqua	1.6	54,351	64.7	48.9	4.5	11.4	35.3	28.5	32.1	34.1
Chemung	2.1	34,767	65.7	48.1	3.8	13.7	34.3	28.7	34.7	34.5
Chenango	2.4	19,783	67.9	51.3	7.2	9.4	32.1	26.3	33.4	34.2
Clinton	4.1	30,088	64.2	49.3	4.5	10.4	35.8	27.2	32.0	31.4
Columbia	5.0	25,275	65.5	49.7	5.8	10.0	34.5	26.2	30.6	35.1
Cortland	1.8	18,034	64.9	49.5	4.2	11.3	35.1	27.7	34.1	31.7
Delaware	3.9	19,030	64.9	48.5	5.2	11.2	35.1	27.9	30.2	40.6
Dutchess	9.7	102,218	69.4	54.0	4.8	10.6	30.6	24.6	35.6	32.2
Erie	5.2	378,698	61.6	44.3	4.0	13.3	38.4	32.4	30.2	34.4
Essex	3.7	15,542	66.2	52.3	4.7	9.2	33.8	28.2	30.9	36.9
Franklin	4.2	19,071	66.6	50.5	6.1	10.1	33.4	26.6	33.7	33.1
Fulton	1.4	23,126	67.5	47.1	6.5	14.0	32.5	26.5	35.1	36.1
Genesee	1.9	22,893	68.5	52.6	4.8	11.1	31.5	27.0	34.3	33.5
Greene	5.6	18,609	60.7	45.8	4.6	10.3	39.3	33.7	28.3	38.3
Herkimer	2.7	25,238	66.9	50.5	4.6	11.8	33.1	27.7	31.3	37.0
Jefferson	2.7	43,512	71.3	53.0	4.9	13.3	20.7	24.4	35.6	27.1
Kings	37.4	877,714	64.2	36.8	6.0	21.4	35.8	29.9	34.7	33.1
Lewis	1.5	11,078	69.0	56.4	3.4	9.1	31.0	24.8	33.3	31.2
Livingston	2.3	22,644	66.4	53.8	3.4	9.2	33.6	24.5	32.6	30.1
Madison	2.4	25,967	67.7	52.4	4.7	10.6	32.3	25.3	32.8	33.4
Monroe	7.6	284,888	63.3	45.9	4.2	13.2	36.7	30.1	32.2	31.5
Montgomery	3.5	19,760	64.5	45.4	5.9	13.1	35.5	29.0	29.9	38.6
Nassau	20.0	435,464	76.6	62.0	3.9	10.7	23.4	20.1	37.8	40.0
New York	28.4	735,382	40.9	26.0	3.1	11.7	59.1	49.9	19.6	27.7
Niagara	3.6	87,249	65.0	48.1	4.1	12.9	35.0	30.0	29.8	34.3
Oneida	5.7	92,393	64.7	46.6	4.6	13.5	35.3	29.6	31.5	35.7
Onondaga	5.8	181,325	61.5	44.8	3.9	12.9	38.5	31.0	32.0	31.4
Ontario	2.9	40,709	67.1	52.5	4.1	10.6	32.9	26.8	33.2	33.8
Orange	11.0	123,112	72.9	56.0	5.1	11.9	27.1	22.6	41.4	29.7
Orleans	2.3	15,119	67.6	52.1	5.8	9.7	32.4	24.4	34.6	35.0
Oswego	1.8	46,183	65.1	50.5	5.0	9.6	34.9	26.5	34.1	30.0
Otsego	3.1	25,129	63.4	49.0	4.5	9.9	36.6	26.6	29.8	36.6
Putnam	10.8	33,513	76.4	62.8	4.8	8.9	23.6	19.3	37.6	32.7
Queens	48.3	774,251	67.8	45.1	6.6	16.2	32.2	26.7	34.2	35.0
Rensselaer	5.1	60,591	63.2	46.1	4.5	12.6	36.8	28.4	30.5	31.0
Richmond	20.9	166,069	75.0	56.3	4.7	14.0	25.0	21.4	40.1	33.5
Rockland	20.7	93,564	75.0	61.4	3.8	9.9	25.0	21.4	38.1	37.1
St. Lawrence	3.6	40,172	66.7	51.0	4.5	11.3	33.3	26.2	33.5	32.4
Saratoga	3.7	83,936	66.5	54.0	3.4	9.1	33.5	26.4	33.3	29.4
Schenectady	8.4	58,134	64.2	47.5	4.4	12.3	35.8	30.5	31.0	34.8
Schoharie	2.3	12,338	67.6	52.5	3.9	11.1	32.4	25.6	32.1	37.8
Seneca	3.2	11,862	71.8	53.0	4.6	14.2	28.2	22.8	33.4	35.9
Steuben	2.1	38,950	65.7	51.2	5.3	9.2	34.3	29.1	32.4	35.0
Suffolk	13.1	480,627	75.7	60.6	4.5	10.7	24.3	19.7	39.7	35.6
Sullivan	8.2	29,091	66.2	48.9	4.4	13.0	33.8	27.7	33.0	35.1
Tioga	2.3	19,761	72.6	55.9	6.8	10.0	27.4	22.5	33.3	32.7
Tompkins	13.0	37,374	52.3	42.8	2.4	7.0	47.7	30.6	24.0	24.4
Ulster	7.1	69,354	63.7	48.9	3.7	11.0	36.3	28.0	30.3	33.7
Warren	2.7	27,257	64.5	47.4	4.4	12.6	35.5	28.0	30.7	36.7
Washington	1.6	23,853	66.9	53.0	3.8	10.1	33.1	26.3	34.4	34.8
Wayne	2.5	36,171	71.3	56.7	4.2	10.4	28.7	23.3	37.3	31.4
Westchester	24.1	335,848	69.0	53.2	4.3	11.6	31.0	26.8	35.9	34.8
Wyoming	1.9	15,140	69.7	56.1	4.4	9.2	30.3	24.3	33.1	32.9
Yates	2.5	9,298	67.8	54.3	3.8	9.7	32.2	25.3	34.3	38.4
North Carolina	6.8	3,471,751	66.9	49.5	4.3	13.0	33.1	27.7	34.0	29.8
Alamance	8.1	56,608	69.6	49.1	5.4	15.0	30.4	24.9	35.0	31.6
Alexander	3.3	13,026	67.6	55.7	2.4	9.4	32.4	27.8	31.6	32.6
Anson	1.6	8,558	68.0	44.0	5.4	18.5	32.0	29.5	31.1	41.6
Ashe	3.0	11,145	68.4	55.2	5.5	7.7	31.6	28.4	29.1	39.6
Beaufort	3.4	18,908	71.1	55.6	2.3	13.2	28.9	24.9	32.6	37.6

Table A-2. Counties — Who: Age, Race/Ethnicity, and Household Structure, 2005–2007—Continued

STATE County code	STATE County	Total population	Percent change 2005–2007	Population by age (percent)							Race alone or in combination (percent)				Percent Hispanic or Latino
				Under 5 years	5 to 17 years	18 to 24 years	25 to 44 years	45 to 64 years	65 years and over	Median age	White	Black	Asian Hawaiian or Pacific Islander	Amer. Indian, Alaska Native, or some other race	
	ACS table number:	B01003	Population estimates	B01001	B01001	B01001	B01001	B01001	B01001	B01002	B02008	B02009	B02011 + B02012	B02010 + B02013	C03002
		1	2	3	4	5	6	7	8	9	10	11	12	13	14
North Carolina—Cont.															
37 017	Bladen	32,426	-0.9	7.3	17.2	9.4	25.4	26.8	13.8	38.0	57.8	36.4	0.4	5.6	5.5
37 019	Brunswick	93,887	12.2	5.7	15.4	8.1	26.6	25.9	18.2	41.0	86.1	10.4	0.2	6.8	3.6
37 021	Buncombe	222,881	3.6	6.0	15.6	8.5	27.1	27.7	15.2	40.5	90.9	7.8	1.2	1.8	4.0
37 023	Burke	88,828	0.3	5.6	17.2	8.4	27.1	27.0	14.7	39.8	85.8	7.0	3.6	4.8	4.9
37 025	Cabarrus	155,970	9.5	7.9	18.9	8.1	29.9	24.5	10.7	35.6	81.7	14.4	1.6	3.6	8.1
37 027	Caldwell	79,113	0.8	5.9	17.0	7.2	28.0	27.4	14.4	39.6	90.7	6.0	0.6	3.5	3.7
37 031	Carteret	62,974	1.3	5.3	14.3	7.5	25.0	30.8	17.1	43.9	90.5	7.6	0.9	2.8	2.2
37 033	Caswell	23,332	-0.4	4.9	16.5	7.8	27.2	29.0	14.6	40.9	64.5	34.8	-	1.5	2.4
37 035	Catawba	153,246	3.1	6.7	17.4	7.7	29.2	26.0	12.9	37.8	83.1	8.8	3.0	6.5	8.3
37 037	Chatham	59,811	5.7	6.4	16.5	7.8	29.1	26.3	13.8	38.7	76.7	15.4	2.0	6.8	12.3
37 039	Cherokee	26,049	3.8	5.2	14.9	6.6	24.5	28.3	20.5	43.9	95.1	2.2	-	3.7	1.4
37 045	Cleveland	97,920	0.9	6.1	18.1	8.1	26.9	26.5	14.3	38.9	77.1	21.1	1.1	1.7	1.8
37 047	Columbus	53,971	0.4	6.9	17.7	8.9	25.4	26.4	14.6	38.7	63.3	31.2	0.1	6.3	2.9
37 049	Craven	96,008	1.8	8.0	17.6	10.5	24.7	24.7	14.5	36.2	71.9	24.4	1.7	4.3	3.8
37 051	Cumberland	306,503	0.3	8.3	20.0	11.6	28.1	23.0	8.9	32.8	57.2	37.7	3.5	6.1	6.1
37 053	Currituck	23,468	4.5	6.4	17.0	8.2	29.2	28.3	11.0	39.0	91.6	7.6	0.8	1.8	2.0
37 055	Dare	33,766	0.2	6.0	15.6	6.6	27.6	31.0	13.2	41.7	94.5	3.3	0.7	2.4	3.3
37 057	Davidson	154,922	2.1	6.3	17.5	7.7	28.4	26.8	13.3	38.6	88.2	9.7	1.2	2.2	5.4
37 059	Davie	39,642	4.6	5.7	17.9	8.3	27.0	26.4	14.7	39.2	91.4	6.9	0.7	2.6	5.8
37 061	Duplin	52,364	2.5	7.6	18.5	8.0	28.6	24.6	12.8	35.7	57.0	27.4	-	16.2	
37 063	Durham	250,407	4.9	7.9	16.3	11.0	32.6	23.0	9.3	34.1	49.6	38.0	4.7	10.2	11.3
37 065	Edgecombe	53,053	-1.4	6.9	18.6	8.8	25.5	28.1	12.0	38.1	39.9	56.3	-	4.3	3.8
37 067	Forsyth	331,984	4.2	7.2	17.3	9.4	27.9	25.8	12.5	37.1	66.6	25.9	1.6	7.0	9.7
37 069	Franklin	55,667	5.3	6.5	17.9	9.2	30.4	25.5	10.6	36.4	67.7	27.9	0.8	5.1	6.6
37 071	Gaston	198,494	3.9	6.7	17.6	7.7	29.1	26.1	12.8	37.7	80.3	14.7	1.4	4.8	5.1
37 077	Granville	54,061	3.5	6.0	17.6	10.1	30.0	25.5	10.9	37.1	60.8	34.2	0.7	5.6	5.9
37 079	Greene	20,191	3.1	7.0	16.4	10.2	28.6	25.6	12.2	35.0	49.9	38.9	-	9.8	
37 081	Guilford	455,983	4.4	6.7	17.1	10.6	28.2	25.6	11.8	36.6	62.5	31.6	3.4	4.2	5.6
37 083	Halifax	55,293	-0.9	6.4	18.1	8.3	25.4	26.4	15.5	40.2	42.4	54.0	1.0	4.4	1.2
37 085	Harnett	105,825	5.5	7.4	19.3	10.1	31.4	22.1	9.6	33.4	69.8	23.1	1.4	7.5	8.0
37 087	Haywood	56,149	1.0	5.1	14.8	6.7	25.7	27.9	19.8	43.1	97.2	2.1	-	1.0	1.8
37 089	Henderson	98,657	4.4	5.9	15.3	6.9	24.2	26.0	21.7	43.0	91.1	3.6	0.9	5.4	8.0
37 091	Hertford	23,229	-0.3	6.3	15.9	12.0	23.4	27.5	14.9	39.8	37.0	62.0	0.6	3.3	1.9
37 093	Hoke	41,102	6.8	9.4	21.4	10.4	31.9	19.5	7.3	30.9	50.2	36.3	1.9	15.9	10.1
37 097	Iredell	145,967	8.0	6.9	18.3	8.0	28.9	25.6	12.2	36.9	82.9	13.2	1.7	3.1	5.1
37 099	Jackson	36,243	3.0	4.3	13.2	18.9	24.0	26.0	13.6	35.9	85.8	2.8	0.6	12.7	2.0
37 101	Johnston	151,330	8.2	7.9	19.2	7.6	32.5	23.4	9.3	34.9	80.1	16.6	0.6	4.2	10.4
37 105	Lee	56,768	4.5	8.0	18.0	8.6	26.6	25.0	13.9	38.4	68.4	20.4	0.9	11.2	15.2
37 107	Lenoir	57,079	-1.1	6.8	17.7	7.9	24.5	27.3	15.8	40.6	55.7	41.2	0.5	3.8	4.5
37 109	Lincoln	71,155	5.7	6.3	18.1	7.6	29.2	26.7	12.0	37.7	86.6	6.8	0.2	7.2	-
37 111	McDowell	43,261	1.1	5.8	16.5	7.4	28.2	27.0	15.1	39.4	92.8	4.6	1.2	1.9	4.2
37 113	Macon	32,193	2.7	5.3	14.5	7.2	22.3	27.7	22.9	45.9	90.0	2.8	-	7.8	8.8
37 115	Madison	20,141	1.5	5.7	14.6	10.9	25.3	26.8	16.6	40.2	96.4	1.3	-	2.1	-
37 117	Martin	23,845	-1.7	6.3	17.3	7.7	24.1	28.2	16.3	42.0	53.5	44.8	-	2.9	-
37 119	Mecklenburg	834,932	8.1	8.2	18.1	8.9	32.2	24.3	8.2	34.8	62.5	30.2	4.2	4.8	9.6
37 123	Montgomery	27,305	1.1	7.0	18.3	10.0	25.7	25.6	13.3	37.1	65.4	20.3	1.8	13.1	14.6
37 125	Moore	82,650	4.3	6.0	16.1	7.6	25.0	24.4	21.0	42.3	80.6	15.3	0.9	3.9	5.4
37 127	Nash	91,636	2.7	6.7	18.0	8.8	26.0	27.0	13.5	38.0	58.7	36.9	0.9	4.1	4.3
37 129	New Hanover	186,708	4.4	6.3	15.1	11.5	28.7	25.5	13.0	37.0	80.2	16.3	1.3	3.2	3.1
37 131	Northampton	20,924	-1.2	5.7	16.2	9.0	22.3	27.9	19.0	43.3	40.8	58.8	-	1.1	-
37 133	Onslow	161,524	1.8	9.4	17.9	21.6	26.3	17.8	7.0	25.4	76.2	19.0	3.4	6.5	6.6
37 135	Orange	122,117	3.7	5.5	13.9	18.7	27.0	25.5	9.4	33.7	77.1	14.2	6.2	4.5	5.8
37 139	Pasquotank	39,424	6.1	7.4	16.9	12.8	26.1	24.0	12.9	35.1	58.5	39.3	1.3	2.0	2.0
37 141	Pender	47,863	8.8	5.9	16.2	8.2	27.4	27.3	14.9	39.7	76.6	20.3	0.5	3.4	4.8
37 145	Person	37,142	1.0	6.5	16.8	7.7	28.0	27.5	13.4	39.5	69.5	28.5	0.6	2.8	2.8
37 147	Pitt	148,337	5.3	7.2	16.7	16.6	27.8	22.1	9.6	31.5	62.6	34.5	1.4	3.5	4.3
37 151	Randolph	138,586	2.3	6.5	18.0	7.5	28.6	26.5	13.0	38.3	87.2	6.3	0.9	6.8	9.6
37 153	Richmond	45,990	-0.2	6.7	18.4	9.3	27.0	24.7	13.8	36.5	63.5	31.4	0.8	5.6	4.1
37 155	Robeson	127,155	1.5	7.6	19.8	10.2	28.0	24.0	10.4	33.6	34.3	25.0	0.6	41.8	7.7
37 157	Rockingham	92,158	0.6	5.9	16.7	7.1	26.9	28.1	15.4	40.7	77.6	19.0	0.5	4.4	4.6
37 159	Rowan	135,596	2.6	6.2	17.6	8.6	27.7	25.8	14.1	38.4	79.9	15.8	1.3	4.4	6.0
37 161	Rutherford	62,963	0.3	6.1	17.3	7.6	26.3	26.4	16.4	40.1	86.7	12.0	0.7	1.5	2.1
37 163	Sampson	63,033	1.9	7.2	18.6	8.5	28.7	24.2	12.8	36.0	58.3	29.3	0.5	14.7	15.0
37 165	Scotland	36,370	-0.2	6.4	18.7	10.2	26.3	26.6	11.7	36.5	50.7	39.7	-	10.7	0.4
37 167	Stanly	58,740	1.3	6.2	17.5	8.6	26.6	26.2	14.8	39.4	83.5	12.9	0.9	3.2	3.2
37 169	Stokes	45,765	1.4	5.6	17.1	7.1	27.5	28.5	14.2	40.6	94.6	4.7	-	1.4	2.2
37 171	Surry	72,212	0.4	6.1	17.6	6.9	27.1	26.4	16.0	40.0	93.5	4.2	0.6	2.8	8.7
37 175	Transylvania	29,709	1.8	4.6	14.3	9.9	20.1	27.4	23.7	45.9	92.7	5.7	0.8	1.4	-
37 179	Union	172,597	14.8	8.3	19.8	9.0	31.2	23.3	8.4	33.5	82.7	12.8	1.4	4.3	9.2
37 181	Vance	43,012	0.1	7.6	19.9	7.7	26.8	25.2	12.8	36.4	45.4	49.9	-	4.9	-
37 183	Wake	794,316	10.2	7.9	18.1	10.0	32.1	24.3	7.6	34.4	70.2	21.0	4.9	5.8	8.0
37 189	Watauga	44,070	2.4	3.9	10.7	29.1	21.3	23.2	11.9	30.0	96.8	1.8	1.0	2.2	2.0
37 191	Wayne	113,268	0.2	7.6	18.2	9.0	27.2	25.7	12.3	36.7	62.6	33.4	1.2	4.4	6.5
37 193	Wilkes	66,675	0.4	6.0	16.3	7.1	27.9	27.3	15.4	39.6	91.3	5.2	0.8	3.9	5.0

STATE County	Percent foreign born	Total households	Household type (percent)						Percent of households with people under 18 years	Percent of households with people 60 years and over
			Family households				Nonfamily households			
			Total family households	Married-couple families	Male householder families	Female householder families	Total nonfamily households	One-person households		
ACS table number:	C05002	B11001	B11001	B11001	B11001	B11001	B11001	B11001	C11005	B11006
	15	16	17	18	19	20	21	22	23	24
North Carolina—Cont.										
Bladen	2.5	12,773	68.4	45.4	6.0	17.0	31.6	29.6	32.6	34.4
Brunswick	3.4	42,315	66.3	53.0	4.4	8.8	33.7	26.7	28.9	38.7
Buncombe	5.1	94,052	62.0	47.9	3.6	10.4	38.0	30.2	28.6	33.7
Burke	4.9	34,093	68.4	51.0	5.5	11.9	31.6	27.7	33.2	35.6
Cabarrus	6.4	59,766	71.0	55.2	4.5	11.3	29.0	23.6	36.6	26.7
Caldwell	2.4	31,032	70.4	54.6	4.0	11.8	29.6	26.2	31.8	33.8
Carteret	3.1	27,277	66.7	51.9	3.3	11.5	33.3	27.6	25.3	38.7
Caswell	1.0	8,572	67.4	50.5	7.1	9.8	32.6	27.1	31.0	34.2
Catawba	7.4	58,797	67.2	51.1	5.0	11.0	32.8	27.7	33.9	31.6
Chatham	10.7	22,499	67.9	53.3	4.0	10.5	32.1	25.3	31.0	33.8
Cherokee	2.0	11,019	72.1	59.2	3.8	9.0	27.9	23.7	30.4	42.7
Cleveland	1.7	37,206	70.9	51.4	4.3	15.2	29.1	25.2	33.9	34.1
Columbus	1.8	21,124	70.9	50.5	4.1	16.4	29.1	25.6	36.1	36.0
Craven	4.1	38,862	70.0	52.3	3.9	13.9	30.0	25.3	34.8	32.9
Cumberland	4.9	117,517	69.2	46.4	4.0	18.7	30.8	25.2	40.8	24.2
Currituck	3.6	9,203	74.3	58.9	5.7	9.7	25.7	18.2	32.8	30.3
Dare	4.0	15,568	65.3	48.5	6.3	10.5	34.7	25.6	31.4	29.3
Davidson	4.5	61,027	70.5	53.8	5.3	11.4	29.5	25.6	33.8	33.2
Davie	5.2	15,249	78.4	64.8	5.7	7.9	21.6	19.8	36.2	33.1
Duplin	13.5	17,038	65.4	47.5	4.1	13.8	34.6	29.1	34.5	35.3
Durham	14.0	100,830	58.1	40.0	3.6	14.5	41.9	34.2	31.4	23.1
Edgecombe	2.3	21,313	67.1	39.8	6.3	21.0	32.9	28.6	34.5	33.6
Forsyth	7.8	133,900	65.4	46.9	4.0	14.5	34.6	29.8	33.6	29.2
Franklin	4.3	20,324	68.5	52.4	3.4	12.7	31.5	27.8	35.9	28.4
Gaston	4.4	75,619	69.2	51.2	4.9	13.1	30.8	26.6	34.7	31.8
Granville	5.0	18,915	70.0	50.1	7.3	12.6	30.0	26.3	37.6	29.5
Greene	7.4	6,439	68.2	45.7	5.3	17.2	31.8	29.3	33.0	38.1
Guilford	8.4	184,357	63.0	44.7	4.4	14.0	37.0	30.5	32.8	27.6
Halifax	1.4	21,391	68.8	44.2	4.6	20.0	31.2	28.9	33.8	37.2
Harnett	6.5	38,030	71.2	50.2	5.2	15.8	28.8	24.7	39.4	25.4
Haywood	1.5	24,839	68.2	56.2	2.6	9.4	31.8	28.0	26.7	40.9
Henderson	7.7	42,205	67.8	54.1	3.8	9.9	32.2	28.3	28.4	42.7
Hertford	2.2	8,478	66.2	38.8	2.6	24.8	33.8	30.8	34.7	40.2
Hoke	5.3	13,363	72.0	49.1	6.4	16.5	28.0	23.0	42.7	23.2
Iredell	4.2	55,700	70.9	56.6	3.8	10.5	29.1	24.2	35.2	31.1
Jackson	3.7	14,770	64.2	49.5	3.9	10.8	35.8	25.5	25.2	32.4
Johnston	7.1	54,695	73.0	56.1	5.6	11.3	27.0	23.5	40.6	26.2
Lee	10.8	21,011	73.0	51.9	5.9	15.2	27.0	24.4	36.7	33.8
Lenoir	3.2	24,779	63.6	43.5	4.1	16.0	36.4	32.1	31.4	35.2
Lincoln	5.4	27,191	75.7	59.0	4.4	12.4	24.3	20.0	35.9	30.1
McDowell	3.1	16,848	66.9	51.9	3.5	11.4	33.1	27.6	29.6	36.9
Macon	7.8	14,671	67.0	54.8	2.8	9.4	33.0	28.6	27.7	45.8
Madison	1.3	8,020	71.9	63.8	4.0	4.1	28.1	24.9	28.3	39.8
Martin	1.5	9,781	70.0	47.2	5.5	17.3	30.0	27.9	29.4	37.8
Mecklenburg	12.3	337,700	62.5	44.5	4.5	13.4	37.5	30.4	34.3	21.7
Montgomery	8.7	10,044	64.2	47.7	4.5	12.1	35.8	31.7	34.0	33.6
Moore	4.3	30,317	68.9	56.8	3.5	8.5	31.1	27.7	28.5	45.8
Nash	4.3	35,760	66.4	47.2	3.8	15.4	33.6	29.8	32.8	32.8
New Hanover	4.2	81,514	58.5	44.2	3.3	11.1	41.5	32.2	26.8	29.6
Northampton	0.5	7,954	60.2	38.9	3.8	17.6	39.8	35.7	29.1	46.5
Onslow	4.6	54,259	74.4	56.5	3.0	14.9	25.6	20.9	41.3	21.9
Orange	11.7	48,932	57.2	44.9	2.6	9.7	42.8	32.3	30.4	24.9
Pasquotank	2.1	14,278	73.4	49.5	5.6	18.3	26.6	24.0	38.2	33.4
Pender	4.2	19,107	69.6	50.1	7.8	11.7	30.4	25.5	33.4	35.0
Person	2.6	14,788	73.1	52.0	5.1	16.0	26.9	23.0	34.8	33.3
Pitt	4.2	61,572	59.6	40.9	3.6	15.0	40.4	31.0	33.3	23.4
Randolph	7.2	53,334	70.3	54.0	4.8	11.5	29.7	26.2	36.3	33.3
Richmond	3.3	18,074	69.2	43.9	8.2	17.1	30.8	26.2	36.0	35.2
Robeson	5.6	43,510	69.0	41.8	5.8	21.4	31.0	27.0	39.2	31.1
Rockingham	3.8	37,378	69.9	49.8	4.9	15.2	30.1	26.4	36.4	35.9
Rowan	5.0	52,027	70.6	53.5	5.1	12.0	29.4	25.5	34.7	34.0
Rutherford	1.9	25,926	68.6	52.6	2.3	13.6	31.4	28.0	31.3	36.0
Sampson	9.5	22,427	70.2	48.7	6.1	15.4	29.8	25.6	38.8	33.4
Scotland	0.8	12,968	68.8	43.8	5.1	19.9	31.2	27.5	38.3	34.7
Stanly	3.4	21,960	69.6	56.8	3.7	9.1	30.4	26.5	33.4	36.1
Stokes	1.6	17,478	74.6	60.0	4.2	10.4	25.4	22.4	34.8	34.7
Surry	5.7	28,194	70.7	54.1	5.9	10.7	29.3	26.4	31.1	37.2
Transylvania	2.5	12,498	66.6	55.4	2.2	9.1	33.4	30.7	23.7	45.0
Union	7.8	60,277	79.0	64.2	4.1	10.7	21.0	17.3	45.9	24.5
Vance	3.6	16,437	68.3	43.0	5.2	20.0	31.7	29.7	35.4	33.2
Wake	11.5	299,587	65.4	51.3	3.7	10.3	34.6	28.4	36.4	20.7
Watauga	2.8	18,350	54.2	44.6	2.0	7.6	45.8	30.3	22.6	27.2
Wayne	4.8	44,116	70.4	50.1	4.9	15.3	29.6	25.5	37.5	29.5
Wilkes	4.0	26,205	71.0	57.5	4.4	9.2	29.0	24.1	28.9	36.9

Table A-2. Counties — Who: Age, Race/Ethnicity, and Household Structure, 2005–2007—*Continued*

STATE County code	STATE County	Total population	Percent change 2005–2007	Population by age (percent)						Median age	Race alone or in combination (percent)				Percent Hispanic or Latino
				Under 5 years	5 to 17 years	18 to 24 years	25 to 44 years	45 to 64 years	65 years and over		White	Black	Asian Hawaiian or Pacific Islander	Amer. Indian, Alaska Native, or some other race	
	ACS table number:	B01003	Population estimates	B01001	B01001	B01001	B01001	B01001	B01001	B01002	B02008	B02009	B02011 + B02012	B02010 + B02013	C03002
		1	2	3	4	5	6	7	8	9	10	11	12	13	14
	North Carolina—Cont.														
37 195	Wilson	76,069	1.6	6.9	18.0	8.7	26.6	26.3	13.4	38.0	54.2	39.2	0.8	7.0	8.3
37 197	Yadkin	37,587	1.2	5.9	17.7	7.3	27.3	26.3	15.5	39.7	90.5	4.2	-	5.5	-
38 000	**North Dakota**	637,709	0.6	6.1	16.4	13.0	24.6	25.4	14.5	37.0	92.3	1.2	1.3	6.7	1.6
38 015	Burleigh	75,728	4.2	6.3	15.8	12.5	27.3	25.1	13.0	36.3	94.2	0.7	0.8	5.2	1.2
38 017	Cass	135,109	3.8	6.8	15.9	15.6	30.7	21.4	9.5	31.2	94.7	2.3	2.0	2.6	2.0
38 035	Grand Forks	66,902	0.6	6.5	15.0	22.3	25.5	21.0	9.7	28.7	93.2	2.0	1.7	4.8	2.7
38 059	Morton	25,591	2.6	6.0	17.7	10.2	23.9	27.8	14.3	38.8	96.3	-	1.5	3.5	0.4
38 089	Stark	22,245	1.5	5.5	16.3	14.8	22.0	25.3	16.1	37.2	96.7	0.5	1.3	1.8	-
38 093	Stutsman	20,684	-1.6	5.0	14.9	12.3	22.2	28.3	17.4	41.7	97.0	0.5	0.8	2.6	1.0
38 101	Ward	56,192	-1.1	8.1	17.7	13.0	25.1	22.9	13.1	33.9	94.0	2.8	1.5	3.9	2.8
39 000	**Ohio**	11,463,403	0.1	6.5	17.7	9.5	26.8	26.1	13.4	37.6	85.4	12.6	1.8	1.9	2.4
39 001	Adams	28,203	-0.2	6.8	18.3	8.4	28.7	24.3	13.4	36.0	98.9	0.4	-	1.7	-
39 003	Allen	105,391	-0.4	6.8	18.1	10.1	25.0	25.5	14.4	37.1	85.8	12.8	0.8	2.1	1.7
39 005	Ashland	54,435	1.6	6.3	17.5	11.6	25.2	25.1	14.3	37.0	98.0	1.1	1.2	0.7	0.7
39 007	Ashtabula	101,577	-0.9	6.0	17.9	7.4	26.8	27.3	14.5	39.3	95.5	3.9	0.5	1.9	2.9
39 009	Athens	63,265	0.0	4.5	12.4	32.6	22.2	18.6	9.6	25.2	94.5	3.2	2.7	1.4	1.3
39 011	Auglaize	46,516	-0.5	6.4	18.9	8.7	25.1	26.2	14.7	38.0	98.6	0.8	0.7	1.0	0.8
39 013	Belmont	68,315	-1.2	5.1	14.9	8.5	25.6	28.3	17.4	42.0	94.9	4.8	0.6	0.9	0.5
39 015	Brown	43,815	0.6	6.5	19.1	7.9	28.7	25.3	12.6	36.8	98.3	1.3	-	1.0	-
39 017	Butler	353,310	2.6	6.9	18.1	11.7	27.6	24.7	10.9	35.0	90.5	7.1	2.3	1.6	2.4
39 019	Carroll	28,732	-1.3	5.4	17.0	7.7	25.8	29.2	14.8	40.4	98.5	0.8	-	1.2	-
39 021	Champaign	39,385	0.8	6.6	17.6	8.2	27.0	27.2	13.4	38.6	97.3	3.1	-	1.5	-
39 023	Clark	141,122	-0.8	6.2	17.5	9.0	25.1	26.7	15.4	39.0	89.6	9.9	0.9	1.5	1.6
39 025	Clermont	191,285	2.4	7.2	19.2	8.3	29.0	25.8	10.5	36.0	97.7	1.6	1.0	1.0	1.1
39 027	Clinton	42,685	2.3	7.2	18.0	9.4	28.3	24.5	12.7	36.3	96.2	3.1	0.7	1.6	1.3
39 029	Columbiana	109,192	-0.8	5.5	16.5	8.3	26.4	27.9	15.3	40.0	96.5	2.6	0.4	1.3	1.3
39 031	Coshocton	36,524	-0.9	6.4	17.8	8.3	26.3	26.5	14.7	38.8	97.4	2.1	-	0.5	-
39 033	Crawford	44,655	-2.2	6.1	17.0	7.4	26.1	27.0	16.3	39.7	98.8	1.2	0.5	0.7	1.0
39 035	Cuyahoga	1,310,905	-2.4	6.2	17.7	8.3	25.7	26.9	15.1	39.8	66.7	29.6	2.6	2.7	4.0
39 037	Darke	52,399	-0.9	6.6	17.9	8.0	25.6	26.2	15.7	39.5	98.9	0.9	0.5	1.2	1.0
39 039	Defiance	38,607	-0.2	6.8	17.6	8.6	26.0	27.1	13.9	38.7	95.6	2.0	0.4	4.1	7.8
39 041	Delaware	155,231	7.7	8.0	19.7	9.2	31.8	23.2	8.1	33.4	91.8	4.3	4.3	1.4	1.7
39 043	Erie	77,566	-0.7	5.9	16.7	7.9	23.9	29.2	16.4	41.3	88.8	9.8	0.7	2.4	2.4
39 045	Fairfield	139,519	2.7	6.4	18.8	8.9	29.0	25.8	11.1	36.0	92.9	6.4	1.2	1.0	1.2
39 047	Fayette	28,261	0.2	7.0	17.4	7.7	27.4	26.0	14.5	37.5	96.3	2.8	0.9	1.8	1.7
39 049	Franklin	1,109,535	1.5	7.6	17.8	10.5	31.0	23.4	9.7	34.2	74.9	20.6	4.4	2.2	3.6
39 051	Fulton	42,598	-0.2	6.4	19.1	8.5	25.8	26.8	13.3	38.6	96.9	0.5	1.1	2.3	6.5
39 053	Gallia	30,874	-0.3	6.5	16.9	9.6	25.5	27.1	14.3	37.6	95.7	3.4	-	1.6	0.5
39 055	Geauga	94,722	0.7	6.0	19.1	8.4	22.0	30.5	14.0	40.7	97.8	1.8	0.7	0.7	0.8
39 057	Greene	153,921	1.0	5.8	16.3	15.1	24.3	26.3	12.2	36.2	89.8	7.6	3.1	1.8	1.7
39 059	Guernsey	40,503	-0.6	6.1	18.7	7.8	26.2	26.3	15.0	38.7	96.5	1.7	0.5	2.3	0.9
39 061	Hamilton	845,647	-0.6	6.7	17.9	9.8	26.2	26.0	13.4	37.8	72.6	25.4	2.3	1.6	1.6
39 063	Hancock	73,758	1.2	6.3	17.8	10.3	26.6	25.6	13.3	36.8	94.0	1.6	2.1	3.6	3.5
39 065	Hardin	31,695	-0.3	6.5	16.4	15.8	24.8	23.7	12.9	34.0	97.7	1.5	0.5	0.9	1.0
39 069	Henry	29,133	-1.0	5.8	18.6	7.2	27.5	26.6	14.2	38.5	96.2	1.1	-	4.0	-
39 071	Highland	42,453	1.2	7.5	18.5	7.8	27.8	24.8	13.6	36.2	97.8	2.4	-	1.3	-
39 073	Hocking	28,810	0.7	5.9	18.1	8.0	27.0	27.5	13.4	38.2	98.1	1.4	0.7	1.4	-
39 075	Holmes	41,350	0.2	10.1	24.1	7.5	28.5	19.0	10.7	29.0	98.8	0.6	-	0.8	-
39 077	Huron	59,871	-0.2	7.1	19.5	8.0	27.3	25.4	12.7	36.4	95.3	1.3	1.0	3.4	5.0
39 079	Jackson	33,289	0.0	6.6	17.9	7.9	28.0	25.7	14.0	38.0	98.6	0.7	-	1.7	1.2
39 081	Jefferson	69,428	-2.0	5.0	15.1	9.5	22.9	28.8	18.8	43.4	93.5	6.3	0.7	0.8	0.8
39 083	Knox	58,489	1.6	6.3	16.7	12.3	25.3	25.1	14.2	36.6	97.8	1.5	0.4	0.9	0.9
39 085	Lake	232,722	0.5	5.6	17.0	8.0	26.0	28.7	14.7	40.7	94.8	3.1	1.4	1.5	2.7
39 087	Lawrence	62,589	0.2	6.1	17.0	8.1	27.5	26.5	14.7	38.2	96.8	2.9	0.4	0.3	0.6
39 089	Licking	155,503	1.9	6.7	18.0	9.5	26.8	26.6	12.4	37.5	96.1	3.3	1.1	1.1	1.0
39 091	Logan	46,237	-0.1	6.4	18.7	7.9	26.6	26.5	14.0	38.0	96.8	2.6	0.9	1.2	0.9
39 093	Lorain	300,659	1.1	6.2	18.4	9.1	26.8	26.4	13.0	37.7	87.6	9.5	1.1	4.3	7.3
39 095	Lucas	444,370	-1.1	6.9	18.3	10.1	26.6	25.3	12.7	36.2	78.1	18.9	1.8	3.8	5.1
39 097	Madison	41,134	1.6	6.1	17.0	9.5	30.2	25.5	11.6	37.3	92.4	6.9	0.9	1.3	0.9
39 099	Mahoning	243,289	-2.2	5.5	16.8	9.0	23.7	27.9	17.2	41.5	82.3	16.6	0.8	1.5	3.4
39 101	Marion	65,501	-0.8	5.8	17.1	8.1	29.1	26.2	13.7	38.2	93.6	5.2	0.8	3.3	1.4
39 103	Medina	167,893	2.4	6.3	19.0	8.4	27.6	27.4	11.4	37.9	97.4	1.7	1.2	0.6	1.2
39 105	Meigs	22,976	-0.9	6.4	16.3	8.0	27.0	27.4	14.9	40.0	98.0	1.5	0.3	0.9	0.7
39 107	Mercer	40,838	0.2	7.1	19.7	8.8	24.4	25.5	14.5	36.8	98.6	0.4	0.4	1.3	1.3
39 109	Miami	100,890	0.4	6.0	17.9	8.2	25.9	27.5	14.4	39.3	96.7	2.9	1.3	0.9	1.1
39 113	Montgomery	541,502	-1.3	6.5	17.3	9.6	26.1	26.0	14.5	38.5	76.9	21.2	1.9	1.7	1.7
39 117	Morrow	34,262	1.4	6.6	18.3	8.1	28.1	27.0	11.8	37.3	99.1	0.4	0.3	1.8	0.9
39 119	Muskingum	85,347	0.1	6.3	18.0	9.1	26.2	25.5	14.9	37.9	96.0	5.4	0.2	1.3	-
39 123	Ottawa	41,198	-0.5	5.2	15.7	8.0	24.6	30.1	16.4	42.5	97.4	1.1	0.3	2.2	-
39 127	Perry	34,832	0.1	6.6	19.5	8.3	27.9	25.4	12.3	36.7	98.9	0.5	-	1.3	-
39 129	Pickaway	53,142	2.7	6.0	17.4	9.2	29.2	26.1	12.1	37.0	94.9	5.4	0.4	1.1	0.8
39 131	Pike	27,902	0.4	6.7	19.0	7.5	28.8	24.0	14.0	36.5	97.5	1.4	-	1.9	0.7
39 133	Portage	155,373	0.4	5.2	16.3	14.9	26.5	25.6	11.4	35.6	94.2	4.3	1.4	1.2	0.9

STATE County	Percent foreign born	Total households	Household type (percent)						Percent of households with people under 18 years	Percent of households with people 60 years and over
			Family households				Nonfamily households			
			Total family households	Married-couple families	Male householder families	Female householder families	Total nonfamily households	One-person households		
ACS table number:	C05002	B11001	B11001	B11001	B11001	B11001	B11001	B11001	C11005	B11006
	15	16	17	18	19	20	21	22	23	24
North Carolina—Cont.										
Wilson	5.9	29,586	65.9	43.7	3.8	18.5	34.1	29.3	33.2	31.8
Yadkin	4.9	14,728	68.7	56.6	3.4	8.7	31.3	27.5	29.9	36.4
North Dakota	2.3	271,131	61.9	51.0	3.5	7.4	38.1	31.0	29.5	29.9
Burleigh	1.6	31,251	62.3	50.9	3.1	8.3	37.7	30.0	30.1	27.1
Cass	3.7	59,718	55.4	43.8	2.7	8.9	44.6	33.2	29.6	19.7
Grand Forks	2.7	26,989	55.9	45.6	3.0	7.3	44.1	31.9	27.6	23.2
Morton	1.0	10,281	64.4	54.6	3.0	6.7	35.6	30.3	29.6	32.4
Stark	2.2	9,231	62.8	52.8	2.9	7.0	37.2	30.3	28.3	32.2
Stutsman	1.3	8,853	60.1	50.1	4.2	5.8	39.9	35.9	27.0	35.8
Ward	2.8	23,635	64.7	54.0	4.3	6.5	35.3	29.7	33.0	27.9
Ohio	3.6	4,500,621	65.9	49.2	4.2	12.5	34.1	28.9	33.1	31.4
Adams	0.4	9,853	73.6	58.9	4.2	10.5	26.4	22.8	38.1	35.6
Allen	1.5	40,596	68.0	52.2	3.3	12.5	32.0	27.2	35.0	33.4
Ashland	1.4	19,672	69.2	57.8	3.7	7.7	30.8	25.8	31.8	34.3
Ashtabula	1.8	39,272	66.6	50.0	5.0	11.5	33.4	27.0	33.4	34.6
Athens	4.6	21,970	54.1	42.1	3.1	9.0	45.9	30.7	26.5	26.7
Auglaize	0.7	18,163	72.8	60.2	4.0	8.6	27.2	24.5	36.6	32.7
Belmont	0.9	28,232	68.6	51.6	5.2	11.8	31.4	27.7	30.6	36.3
Brown	0.2	16,063	73.9	57.9	5.7	10.4	26.1	22.2	36.9	32.1
Butler	4.1	129,731	69.3	53.5	4.1	11.7	30.7	24.9	36.1	26.9
Carroll	0.4	11,197	73.2	61.6	4.0	7.6	26.8	23.3	32.3	33.7
Champaign	0.9	15,446	74.3	60.2	5.3	8.8	25.7	22.5	37.1	32.2
Clark	1.8	55,422	67.0	49.3	4.2	13.6	33.0	28.4	32.5	35.2
Clermont	2.0	71,769	72.7	58.2	4.3	10.1	27.3	22.3	38.9	27.7
Clinton	1.5	16,547	70.3	55.8	5.0	9.4	29.7	26.3	38.3	30.1
Columbiana	1.1	41,746	70.5	55.1	4.1	11.3	29.5	25.4	33.5	36.3
Coshocton	0.5	14,225	69.0	52.6	5.5	11.0	31.0	27.6	31.8	35.8
Crawford	1.1	18,657	68.1	54.9	4.1	9.1	31.9	27.6	32.2	36.7
Cuyahoga	6.9	542,856	60.1	39.9	4.1	16.1	39.9	35.3	30.5	33.8
Darke	1.2	20,889	71.7	58.2	5.8	7.7	28.3	24.4	34.1	35.7
Defiance	1.1	15,061	70.6	58.0	4.0	8.5	29.4	24.1	32.9	33.4
Delaware	4.3	56,607	76.3	66.6	3.7	6.1	23.7	19.2	41.8	21.3
Erie	2.2	31,874	67.9	54.5	3.5	9.9	32.1	27.3	30.1	35.9
Fairfield	2.4	51,069	74.7	61.2	3.5	10.1	25.3	21.0	38.9	29.5
Fayette	1.3	11,466	71.1	52.8	5.5	12.8	28.9	25.7	35.0	32.9
Franklin	8.3	449,236	59.8	41.5	4.8	13.5	40.2	32.2	33.4	23.9
Fulton	2.6	15,841	72.5	59.9	4.5	8.2	27.5	22.6	32.9	33.2
Gallia	0.4	11,782	70.0	55.5	4.1	10.4	30.0	25.7	34.0	34.6
Geauga	2.9	33,028	76.1	64.2	3.9	8.0	23.9	20.3	37.1	35.5
Greene	3.8	59,914	68.8	54.1	3.7	11.1	31.2	24.7	33.5	28.5
Guernsey	1.3	16,474	68.4	53.2	3.6	11.6	31.6	28.4	33.1	34.7
Hamilton	4.3	331,706	59.9	41.3	3.8	14.8	40.1	35.4	31.2	31.0
Hancock	2.6	30,848	65.6	53.0	4.0	8.6	34.4	28.2	32.3	28.2
Hardin	0.6	11,883	65.9	51.1	4.6	10.1	34.1	28.5	32.7	31.2
Henry	1.3	11,172	73.2	59.3	4.5	9.4	26.8	23.7	35.1	33.2
Highland	0.7	15,405	68.9	54.4	4.0	10.5	31.1	26.5	36.1	32.6
Hocking	0.5	10,730	72.3	55.3	4.9	12.1	27.7	22.8	36.9	32.1
Holmes	1.3	11,588	82.5	72.0	2.3	8.1	17.5	15.9	46.3	28.4
Huron	2.8	23,104	71.5	57.5	3.8	10.1	28.5	23.0	37.2	31.0
Jackson	0.6	13,017	68.2	53.1	5.1	10.0	31.8	29.4	34.9	32.8
Jefferson	1.1	29,535	65.6	48.2	4.2	13.2	34.4	29.3	29.9	39.9
Knox	1.3	21,265	71.7	58.8	4.2	8.8	28.3	23.3	33.2	33.8
Lake	5.8	92,949	67.4	51.8	4.4	11.1	32.6	28.2	31.3	33.5
Lawrence	0.5	24,657	68.9	50.5	4.0	14.4	31.1	28.4	34.7	35.4
Licking	1.4	59,291	71.4	56.3	4.5	10.6	28.6	22.9	34.9	29.9
Logan	1.4	18,886	69.7	52.9	4.1	12.7	30.3	25.7	35.2	33.4
Lorain	2.4	110,452	69.9	52.8	4.1	13.1	30.1	25.8	35.4	32.2
Lucas	3.5	178,247	62.1	42.4	4.6	15.1	37.9	31.5	32.9	29.9
Madison	1.0	14,480	70.3	53.6	5.7	11.0	29.7	25.1	35.6	31.4
Mahoning	2.8	99,678	65.9	47.2	4.1	14.6	34.1	29.9	30.6	38.0
Marion	1.4	24,866	67.4	50.8	5.0	11.6	32.6	28.4	34.1	33.8
Medina	3.0	61,084	76.0	63.7	3.2	9.1	24.0	20.0	37.7	28.6
Meigs	0.5	9,451	68.9	53.2	5.0	10.7	31.1	27.0	32.1	34.9
Mercer	0.8	15,092	75.5	60.0	4.4	11.1	24.5	22.0	36.5	33.6
Miami	1.4	39,306	71.3	57.0	3.6	10.7	28.7	24.5	33.4	33.3
Montgomery	2.9	224,650	61.2	42.8	4.0	14.3	38.8	32.9	30.5	32.0
Morrow	0.4	12,005	78.4	68.8	4.0	5.6	21.6	17.1	39.6	33.0
Muskingum	0.3	32,385	68.4	51.0	4.6	12.7	31.6	27.2	32.8	34.6
Ottawa	1.1	18,125	66.5	53.8	3.8	8.8	33.5	26.4	30.4	35.7
Perry	0.1	12,438	73.5	57.6	3.5	12.4	26.5	21.9	38.4	34.0
Pickaway	0.9	17,888	73.5	61.1	2.4	10.0	26.5	21.3	36.8	34.3
Pike	0.3	10,939	72.6	52.0	5.1	15.4	27.4	25.1	36.4	32.6
Portage	2.5	59,426	65.7	52.3	3.2	10.2	34.3	25.3	31.5	28.4

Table A-2. Counties — Who: Age, Race/Ethnicity, and Household Structure, 2005–2007—*Continued*

STATE County code	STATE County	Total population	Percent change 2005–2007	Population by age (percent)						Median age	Race alone or in combination (percent)				Percent Hispanic or Latino
				Under 5 years	5 to 17 years	18 to 24 years	25 to 44 years	45 to 64 years	65 years and over		White	Black	Asian Hawaiian or Pacific Islander	Amer. Indian, Alaska Native, or some other race	
	ACS table number:	B01003	Population estimates	B01001	B01001	B01001	B01001	B01001	B01001	B01002	B02008	B02009	B02011 + B02012	B02010 + B02013	C03002
		1	2	3	4	5	6	7	8	9	10	11	12	13	14
	Ohio—Cont.														
39 135	Preble	41,852	-0.4	6.1	17.5	8.0	26.5	27.5	14.4	40.2	98.6	0.6	0.4	1.3	0.6
39 137	Putnam	34,651	-0.1	6.9	20.0	10.0	24.4	24.8	13.9	37.2	96.3	-	0.7	3.5	-
39 139	Richland	126,369	-1.1	6.0	17.1	8.6	26.1	27.0	15.2	39.3	89.2	10.6	0.8	1.2	1.1
39 141	Ross	75,137	0.7	5.9	16.4	8.2	30.4	26.1	13.0	37.7	93.6	5.4	0.6	2.8	0.7
39 143	Sandusky	61,146	-0.5	6.7	17.7	8.4	24.9	27.3	14.9	39.1	92.7	3.7	0.5	5.2	7.6
39 145	Scioto	76,090	-0.4	6.2	16.7	9.5	27.4	25.2	15.0	37.8	96.6	3.1	0.5	1.6	0.7
39 147	Seneca	56,954	-1.0	6.3	17.4	10.4	25.4	26.4	14.2	38.2	95.6	2.8	0.7	2.2	3.9
39 149	Shelby	48,639	0.7	7.6	19.5	7.8	27.5	25.2	12.4	36.4	96.0	2.5	1.3	1.4	1.1
39 151	Stark	378,691	0.0	5.9	17.4	8.6	25.1	27.5	15.4	40.1	91.3	8.4	0.9	1.1	1.1
39 153	Summit	544,761	-0.4	6.1	17.8	8.7	26.5	26.9	13.9	38.8	83.5	14.6	2.1	1.2	1.1
39 155	Trumbull	215,398	-1.8	5.5	16.9	8.2	24.7	28.3	16.4	41.2	90.9	8.7	0.6	0.8	0.9
39 157	Tuscarawas	91,330	0.0	6.4	17.2	7.7	26.2	26.8	15.7	39.3	98.0	1.1	0.4	1.2	1.0
39 159	Union	46,395	4.0	7.2	19.9	7.8	31.9	24.2	9.1	35.3	96.0	3.4	1.4	2.2	1.1
39 161	Van Wert	29,004	-0.6	6.3	17.9	8.3	25.9	26.5	15.1	38.4	98.3	1.4	0.2	1.4	-
39 165	Warren	199,626	4.9	7.2	19.6	8.1	31.6	23.9	9.6	35.1	93.2	3.6	3.3	1.1	1.6
39 167	Washington	61,773	-0.7	5.6	16.2	9.4	24.7	28.0	16.1	40.3	98.1	1.7	0.8	0.9	0.6
39 169	Wayne	113,471	0.3	7.0	18.4	9.9	25.8	25.6	13.2	36.8	97.1	1.9	1.0	0.8	1.1
39 171	Williams	38,379	-0.1	5.9	17.3	8.0	26.9	26.9	15.0	39.6	98.0	1.0	-	1.7	-
39 173	Wood	124,732	1.0	5.5	15.9	18.7	23.9	24.5	11.5	33.2	95.7	2.2	1.4	2.3	3.8
39 175	Wyandot	22,571	-1.0	6.4	16.9	7.8	27.0	26.0	15.9	39.1	98.2	-	0.9	0.7	-
40 000	**Oklahoma**	3,576,929	2.3	7.1	17.8	10.5	26.5	24.9	13.2	36.0	80.6	8.6	2.2	14.7	6.9
40 001	Adair	21,801	1.2	8.1	20.3	9.3	27.1	23.7	11.6	33.8	56.1	-	1.2	50.0	3.7
40 013	Bryan	38,708	4.9	6.8	16.8	11.9	25.6	23.9	14.9	36.2	91.3	2.3	0.9	17.6	3.7
40 015	Caddo	29,543	-1.4	6.8	19.6	11.3	23.9	23.9	14.5	36.3	68.1	4.0	0.1	31.6	7.7
40 017	Canadian	100,275	6.6	6.7	18.8	10.0	28.0	26.4	10.2	35.5	89.1	3.3	3.1	8.8	5.0
40 019	Carter	47,142	1.9	6.9	18.2	8.3	25.2	26.0	15.4	39.0	80.9	8.3	0.5	12.7	3.6
40 021	Cherokee	44,990	2.0	5.9	17.3	17.8	24.2	22.7	12.0	31.2	60.1	3.2	0.8	41.3	5.9
40 027	Cleveland	231,544	4.7	6.0	16.7	15.3	28.9	24.1	9.1	32.8	86.3	5.5	4.6	10.0	5.3
40 031	Comanche	112,719	1.7	8.8	20.3	12.0	27.1	21.3	10.6	31.8	69.1	21.0	4.5	12.5	9.2
40 037	Creek	68,505	1.4	6.3	18.2	8.4	25.5	27.1	14.5	39.3	89.7	3.2	0.5	14.5	2.3
40 039	Custer	25,832	2.2	6.4	15.5	18.5	23.9	21.3	14.4	32.8	80.6	3.8	1.7	15.3	10.8
40 041	Delaware	39,724	3.6	5.3	17.1	8.3	24.0	26.6	18.7	41.2	77.6	0.4	0.9	27.7	2.3
40 047	Garfield	57,326	1.1	7.4	17.8	8.1	25.1	26.0	15.7	38.2	88.9	4.1	2.8	7.9	6.1
40 049	Garvin	27,012	0.9	6.4	17.2	7.5	25.8	25.4	17.7	39.8	88.3	3.4	-	11.9	4.2
40 051	Grady	49,900	3.3	6.6	18.5	10.5	26.8	25.5	12.1	35.8	90.0	3.4	0.7	8.7	3.7
40 065	Jackson	26,161	-2.6	8.1	21.3	10.3	24.3	24.0	12.1	34.4	79.6	8.2	1.6	13.6	19.0
40 071	Kay	45,796	-1.0	6.9	18.1	9.0	22.8	26.4	16.7	40.3	87.4	2.3	1.1	13.8	5.3
40 079	Le Flore	49,309	1.6	7.1	17.9	8.7	27.0	25.2	14.1	36.6	87.3	2.7	0.2	18.4	5.9
40 081	Lincoln	32,191	0.8	5.9	18.9	9.2	24.8	26.8	14.3	38.1	90.3	2.9	0.5	11.3	2.1
40 083	Logan	35,895	2.8	5.8	18.8	10.1	26.2	26.8	12.4	36.8	84.6	9.3	0.7	7.3	4.0
40 087	McClain	30,856	6.5	6.8	17.8	11.2	24.5	26.8	12.9	37.6	90.8	0.7	-	12.2	5.5
40 089	McCurtain	33,527	0.1	6.9	19.1	7.6	26.5	25.9	14.0	38.0	73.8	9.4	0.3	20.2	4.0
40 097	Mayes	39,343	1.5	6.2	18.0	8.5	26.5	25.5	15.3	38.3	90.1	0.7	0.2	27.8	2.2
40 101	Muskogee	70,715	1.2	6.7	17.2	10.1	25.9	24.9	15.2	37.3	69.9	13.7	0.9	22.1	3.7
40 109	Oklahoma	694,506	2.1	8.4	17.8	9.7	28.0	23.8	12.2	34.6	74.4	16.6	4.0	11.3	11.8
40 111	Okmulgee	39,278	-0.1	6.6	18.3	10.6	23.8	25.9	14.8	37.3	78.2	11.2	0.4	19.8	2.3
40 113	Osage	45,209	1.2	5.0	17.5	9.8	25.3	28.9	13.3	39.8	74.8	12.0	-	20.7	2.5
40 115	Ottawa	32,615	-0.1	5.7	18.4	9.9	24.4	24.7	16.8	38.3	79.7	1.5	2.0	23.5	4.1
40 119	Payne	78,338	5.5	5.7	12.8	26.3	25.6	19.2	10.5	27.7	87.3	4.8	4.2	8.1	2.6
40 121	Pittsburg	44,359	1.7	5.6	16.1	8.8	26.5	25.7	17.3	40.6	84.1	4.6	0.5	18.6	2.7
40 123	Pontotoc	35,980	3.0	6.5	16.8	13.3	24.9	24.0	14.4	35.7	81.1	3.1	1.0	21.8	2.9
40 125	Pottawatomie	68,350	1.9	6.5	17.8	11.4	25.8	24.5	14.1	36.3	84.3	4.3	1.1	16.6	3.0
40 131	Rogers	81,370	4.3	5.9	19.3	9.7	26.6	26.4	12.1	36.9	87.3	1.1	0.8	18.6	2.9
40 133	Seminole	24,163	0.2	7.1	17.7	9.4	23.4	26.2	16.3	39.2	77.0	6.6	-	23.6	2.6
40 135	Sequoyah	40,694	1.8	6.2	18.6	10.6	24.3	26.2	14.1	38.1	81.2	2.3	-	27.3	2.6
40 137	Stephens	42,909	1.7	6.6	17.1	9.1	23.5	26.3	17.3	41.4	89.9	3.0	0.7	9.8	5.0
40 139	Texas	19,994	0.5	9.4	20.0	11.3	27.8	21.4	10.1	31.6	69.1	2.8	-	29.8	39.1
40 143	Tulsa	577,727	2.5	8.0	18.3	9.1	27.8	24.9	12.0	35.7	78.6	12.4	2.5	12.0	8.9
40 145	Wagoner	65,185	6.4	6.3	19.2	9.6	27.6	27.0	10.2	36.2	83.4	4.8	1.3	15.6	3.6
40 147	Washington	49,173	2.5	5.5	17.2	9.4	22.6	27.6	17.8	40.8	86.4	3.1	1.3	16.0	3.8
41 000	**Oregon**	3,689,498	3.2	6.3	17.0	9.1	27.8	26.9	12.9	37.6	89.1	2.4	4.8	7.0	10.2
41 003	Benton	80,470	2.2	4.9	13.7	20.7	24.3	25.4	11.0	33.1	88.9	1.6	6.9	5.5	5.7
41 005	Clackamas	371,340	2.7	5.6	17.6	8.5	26.5	29.8	12.0	38.9	93.8	1.4	4.7	3.9	6.8
41 007	Clatsop	36,976	2.2	5.4	15.7	9.5	23.5	29.4	16.6	42.2	93.2	0.8	2.8	6.5	6.0
41 009	Columbia	48,086	4.1	5.3	18.3	8.5	26.7	29.8	11.6	39.5	96.0	0.3	1.9	4.3	3.6
41 011	Coos	63,655	-0.4	4.9	14.2	7.6	22.6	30.2	20.4	45.5	94.6	0.6	1.6	5.8	4.4
41 013	Crook	22,383	5.5	5.2	18.1	7.6	27.0	26.0	16.2	39.4	97.6	1.1	0.3	2.0	-
41 015	Curry	21,941	-1.5	3.1	13.5	6.2	18.7	31.4	27.1	50.1	96.7	0.8	0.5	4.5	-
41 017	Deschutes	148,052	9.2	6.0	16.7	8.1	28.6	27.2	13.5	38.6	95.9	0.8	1.9	3.4	5.6
41 019	Douglas	103,656	1.1	5.1	15.8	7.7	23.4	28.6	19.4	43.4	95.5	0.5	1.7	5.3	3.9
41 027	Hood River	21,177	1.2	7.4	19.2	7.4	29.6	24.4	12.1	36.6	85.9	-	3.1	12.9	25.8
41 029	Jackson	196,866	2.5	5.6	16.4	9.0	24.9	27.8	16.3	40.8	95.5	1.0	2.1	4.4	8.4
41 031	Jefferson	20,179	4.8	7.6	20.3	9.1	25.6	24.8	12.6	35.3	79.8	-	0.4	22.0	-

64 The Who, What, and Where of America

Table A-2. Counties — Who: Age, Race/Ethnicity, and Household Structure, 2005–2007—*Continued*

STATE County	Percent foreign born	Total households	Household type (percent)						Percent of households with people under 18 years	Percent of households with people 60 years and over
			Family households				Nonfamily households			
			Total family households	Married-couple families	Male householder families	Female householder families	Total nonfamily households	One-person households		
ACS table number:	C05002	B11001	B11001	B11001	B11001	B11001	B11001	B11001	C11005	B11006
	15	16	17	18	19	20	21	22	23	24
Ohio—Cont.										
Preble	1.1	16,546	70.3	56.8	5.2	8.4	29.7	25.5	31.8	35.0
Putnam	1.0	12,430	76.6	64.4	4.6	7.6	23.4	21.3	37.7	33.0
Richland	1.5	49,720	67.8	52.4	2.9	12.4	32.2	27.3	31.8	34.5
Ross	1.1	27,203	68.3	52.2	4.5	11.7	31.7	26.8	33.0	33.5
Sandusky	1.4	23,915	69.7	54.1	4.3	11.3	30.3	26.4	33.0	33.8
Scioto	0.6	30,660	68.2	49.1	4.7	14.4	31.8	27.5	34.6	36.2
Seneca	1.3	22,311	68.5	53.0	5.2	10.3	31.5	25.6	33.6	33.4
Shelby	2.1	18,561	72.4	58.0	4.7	9.7	27.6	24.7	36.4	28.9
Stark	2.2	149,953	68.0	51.2	4.3	12.5	32.0	27.4	32.6	34.1
Summit	3.6	220,092	64.7	48.0	4.2	12.5	35.3	29.8	31.1	31.6
Trumbull	1.3	87,595	66.2	48.3	4.2	13.7	33.8	29.1	29.4	36.0
Tuscarawas	0.9	35,500	68.3	55.5	3.5	9.3	31.7	27.1	32.2	35.5
Union	2.5	16,946	73.9	63.3	3.3	7.3	26.1	19.3	41.2	24.4
Van Wert	0.4	11,725	71.9	58.0	3.5	10.3	28.1	23.2	34.2	35.2
Warren	4.5	69,694	75.7	62.9	3.2	9.6	24.3	19.7	42.4	24.4
Washington	0.7	25,200	68.0	56.1	2.4	9.5	32.0	27.7	28.7	36.0
Wayne	1.6	42,432	71.2	57.9	4.3	8.9	28.8	24.1	34.5	32.8
Williams	1.2	15,301	69.3	56.0	4.4	9.0	30.7	26.6	34.0	32.3
Wood	3.0	48,712	64.0	51.7	4.3	8.1	36.0	26.6	30.5	26.8
Wyandot	2.3	9,043	71.6	58.1	4.6	8.8	28.4	22.8	34.8	31.9
Oklahoma	4.9	1,386,849	67.1	50.6	4.4	12.0	32.9	28.0	33.9	31.7
Adair	1.9	7,569	70.1	59.3	4.5	14.3	21.9	20.0	42.5	31.3
Bryan	3.3	15,130	70.0	50.9	4.7	14.3	30.0	27.0	35.2	35.0
Caddo	3.5	10,713	71.6	53.9	5.0	12.7	28.4	25.1	36.9	37.2
Canadian	4.0	36,150	76.2	62.4	3.6	10.2	23.8	21.0	40.0	28.0
Carter	1.8	18,607	67.6	49.6	4.0	14.0	32.4	28.0	33.8	33.4
Cherokee	2.6	16,247	64.0	48.8	3.6	11.6	36.0	29.0	31.8	33.0
Cleveland	5.7	89,659	66.6	52.2	5.5	8.9	33.4	26.0	34.2	23.4
Comanche	4.7	41,060	71.1	50.7	3.5	16.8	28.9	24.6	38.9	20.7
Creek	1.5	26,252	71.9	55.5	5.8	10.6	28.1	25.7	34.9	34.8
Custer	7.0	10,438	66.2	47.4	4.4	14.5	33.8	25.9	34.3	30.7
Delaware	2.0	15,372	72.2	58.4	3.2	10.6	27.8	23.8	31.0	43.1
Garfield	4.1	22,791	67.1	53.0	3.6	10.6	32.9	27.0	31.9	32.0
Garvin	1.4	10,110	72.2	56.6	3.3	12.4	27.8	26.0	35.3	41.8
Grady	1.8	17,847	73.4	58.6	4.9	9.9	26.6	23.8	37.0	31.6
Jackson	6.0	10,039	69.2	54.0	2.6	12.6	30.8	26.4	34.2	30.6
Kay	3.2	18,541	68.9	51.4	4.8	12.6	31.1	28.5	33.1	36.4
Le Flore	3.5	17,873	73.1	54.6	4.1	14.4	26.9	24.8	38.8	33.5
Lincoln	1.2	12,497	75.3	60.3	5.4	9.6	24.7	21.9	37.0	35.5
Logan	1.5	12,759	72.8	58.9	3.8	10.1	27.2	23.9	33.3	31.2
McClain	2.9	10,900	77.8	60.9	5.1	11.9	22.2	18.3	39.3	32.0
McCurtain	0.8	13,862	67.8	47.3	4.5	16.0	32.2	29.2	37.4	34.4
Mayes	0.9	15,427	69.8	56.0	4.0	9.8	30.2	25.2	34.9	36.0
Muskogee	2.5	26,303	66.5	49.4	4.4	12.7	33.5	28.9	35.0	36.9
Oklahoma	9.1	279,582	61.7	43.5	4.7	13.6	38.3	32.2	32.3	29.3
Okmulgee	1.0	15,479	72.1	51.8	4.8	15.6	27.9	24.5	35.6	34.5
Osage	1.3	16,880	74.2	58.2	5.3	10.8	25.8	23.3	36.9	35.5
Ottawa	2.7	12,825	68.1	50.8	4.0	13.4	31.9	28.8	32.2	40.2
Payne	6.1	26,484	55.5	43.7	4.4	7.4	44.5	31.9	25.0	27.7
Pittsburg	1.4	18,278	66.0	50.2	4.0	11.8	34.0	29.8	30.1	39.6
Pontotoc	1.4	14,466	63.6	48.7	5.2	9.7	36.4	28.7	30.8	31.8
Pottawatomie	1.8	24,772	70.1	53.4	4.7	12.0	29.9	25.5	35.6	33.3
Rogers	1.6	28,231	76.5	65.0	2.0	9.5	23.5	19.9	38.6	30.6
Seminole	1.0	9,204	69.6	47.3	7.6	14.6	30.4	27.0	36.9	37.5
Sequoyah	1.3	14,785	73.1	56.9	5.3	10.9	26.9	22.7	36.0	36.3
Stephens	0.8	17,466	68.3	53.8	5.1	9.4	31.7	27.4	29.1	35.9
Texas	21.7	6,980	71.0	59.4	2.9	8.8	29.0	22.7	39.4	30.2
Tulsa	7.1	233,204	63.5	45.9	4.7	12.9	36.5	31.1	33.5	28.2
Wagoner	2.3	24,838	79.0	62.5	4.1	12.3	21.0	17.2	40.7	27.2
Washington	2.8	19,878	66.4	52.5	2.9	10.9	33.6	30.0	30.1	38.5
Oregon	9.7	1,447,409	64.0	49.8	4.1	10.0	36.0	28.1	31.4	30.8
Benton	8.8	32,517	58.1	45.6	3.9	8.6	41.9	28.0	27.9	26.2
Clackamas	8.0	139,137	68.8	56.1	3.6	9.1	31.2	24.6	33.9	30.6
Clatsop	4.6	16,076	61.2	47.0	5.6	8.7	38.8	32.7	29.6	36.7
Columbia	3.0	18,182	71.5	57.7	4.0	9.9	28.5	23.1	33.6	32.8
Coos	3.8	27,364	61.8	49.4	3.6	8.8	38.2	31.9	23.4	43.3
Crook	4.4	8,927	72.4	62.0	3.9	6.5	27.6	21.4	33.5	36.7
Curry	4.1	10,364	66.2	54.4	3.2	8.5	33.8	28.5	24.7	51.0
Deschutes	5.1	60,302	68.1	57.3	3.4	7.4	31.9	22.7	31.9	29.6
Douglas	2.7	42,024	68.0	53.8	4.5	9.7	32.0	27.4	28.3	41.6
Hood River	16.1	7,706	72.1	58.6	3.6	9.9	27.9	24.3	40.1	29.9
Jackson	5.4	80,058	63.5	48.6	4.1	10.8	36.5	29.0	29.8	36.5
Jefferson	10.0	7,368	73.7	58.1	4.2	11.5	26.3	19.8	37.8	31.7

STATE County code	STATE County ACS table number:	Total population B01003	Percent change 2005–2007 Population estimates	Population by age (percent)						Median age B01002	Race alone or in combination (percent)				Percent Hispanic or Latino C03002
				Under 5 years B01001	5 to 17 years B01001	18 to 24 years B01001	25 to 44 years B01001	45 to 64 years B01001	65 years and over B01001		White B02008	Black B02009	Asian Hawaiian or Pacific Islander B02011 + B02012	Amer. Indian, Alaska Native, or some other race B02010 + B02013	
		1	2	3	4	5	6	7	8	9	10	11	12	13	14
	Oregon—Cont.														
41 033	Josephine	80,607	1.4	4.9	16.0	6.9	23.2	28.5	20.5	44.3	96.3	0.8	1.2	4.9	5.2
41 035	Klamath	65,983	1.6	6.0	17.6	9.7	23.6	27.6	15.4	39.0	92.8	1.1	1.3	8.5	8.6
41 039	Lane	339,869	2.3	5.3	15.2	11.6	26.7	27.2	13.9	38.1	92.0	1.5	4.0	5.4	5.9
41 041	Lincoln	45,650	0.9	4.7	14.7	7.1	22.6	32.0	18.9	45.5	93.3	0.3	2.4	6.5	6.8
41 043	Linn	110,893	4.4	6.4	17.5	8.4	26.2	26.3	15.1	38.4	94.0	0.7	1.8	6.0	5.7
41 045	Malheur	31,037	0.3	7.1	18.8	10.6	25.5	23.8	14.2	35.8	79.9	2.3	1.5	22.5	27.5
41 047	Marion	307,056	2.9	7.5	19.0	9.5	28.3	23.7	11.9	34.6	86.0	1.6	3.3	12.4	21.2
41 051	Multnomah	688,923	3.6	6.8	15.9	8.1	31.9	26.9	10.4	36.9	82.9	6.9	7.7	6.2	10.0
41 053	Polk	72,748	7.2	5.8	16.7	12.6	24.9	24.7	15.3	36.8	90.2	1.0	2.6	9.9	10.8
41 057	Tillamook	24,981	0.6	5.0	15.2	7.1	22.4	30.6	19.8	45.3	93.2	-	2.3	6.7	7.5
41 059	Umatilla	73,243	0.6	7.2	19.2	9.5	26.8	25.3	12.1	35.8	90.6	1.4	1.4	10.5	18.5
41 061	Union	24,560	1.1	5.7	17.1	12.7	21.1	27.7	15.6	40.3	94.7	0.9	2.8	4.0	3.2
41 065	Wasco	23,593	1.4	5.9	17.4	8.5	22.1	28.9	17.2	42.1	90.5	-	2.5	9.9	11.3
41 067	Washington	511,861	4.5	7.5	18.8	7.8	32.0	25.0	8.9	35.0	82.4	2.4	10.1	8.9	14.2
41 071	Yamhill	93,901	5.7	6.4	17.9	11.9	27.4	24.7	11.8	34.9	89.1	1.1	2.2	10.9	13.3
42 000	**Pennsylvania**	12,400,959	0.5	5.9	16.7	9.6	25.9	26.7	15.2	39.5	85.0	11.1	2.6	2.7	4.3
42 001	Adams	99,914	1.9	5.6	17.1	10.3	27.2	25.7	14.0	38.1	94.3	2.0	0.9	3.9	5.0
42 003	Allegheny	1,226,174	-1.2	5.3	15.7	9.6	24.5	28.0	17.0	41.5	83.9	13.8	2.6	1.3	1.3
42 005	Armstrong	69,424	-1.2	5.0	15.6	7.4	24.9	29.0	18.2	43.2	98.4	1.0	0.4	0.6	0.5
42 007	Beaver	174,189	-1.4	5.1	15.8	8.0	23.9	28.8	18.3	43.4	93.2	7.0	0.5	0.8	0.9
42 009	Bedford	49,650	0.1	5.5	16.4	7.1	26.2	27.6	17.3	41.3	98.7	0.6	0.4	1.0	0.7
42 011	Berks	398,155	2.1	6.4	17.5	9.6	26.9	25.5	14.1	38.2	87.7	5.3	1.4	7.1	12.8
42 013	Blair	125,711	-0.3	5.7	15.6	8.9	25.6	27.1	17.1	40.9	97.8	1.8	0.6	0.7	0.6
42 015	Bradford	61,626	-0.6	6.0	17.4	7.3	24.7	27.8	16.8	41.9	98.5	0.6	0.8	1.0	0.7
42 017	Bucks	619,093	0.7	5.7	17.8	8.4	25.8	29.0	13.3	40.2	92.0	4.0	3.6	1.4	3.1
42 019	Butler	181,082	1.0	5.8	17.3	9.5	25.8	27.2	14.4	39.8	98.1	1.3	1.0	0.6	0.8
42 021	Cambria	145,984	-1.3	5.1	14.5	9.8	23.8	28.0	18.8	42.5	95.6	3.7	0.6	0.7	1.1
42 025	Carbon	62,326	2.7	5.0	15.8	7.5	27.5	26.8	17.5	42.2	97.2	1.7	0.6	1.4	2.4
42 027	Centre	143,557	2.0	4.5	12.0	28.2	24.8	19.6	10.8	28.6	90.7	3.4	5.6	1.4	2.1
42 029	Chester	478,821	3.2	6.5	18.3	9.3	26.3	27.6	12.0	38.3	88.8	7.0	3.3	2.2	4.5
42 031	Clarion	40,100	-0.1	5.1	15.0	14.3	23.8	25.1	16.7	39.0	98.6	1.0	0.5	0.7	0.5
42 033	Clearfield	81,802	-0.7	4.8	15.2	8.6	26.8	27.2	17.5	41.5	97.1	2.5		0.6	0.7
42 035	Clinton	37,234	0.0	5.5	14.4	13.8	24.5	25.2	16.6	38.2	97.6	1.6	0.5	0.6	0.9
42 037	Columbia	64,661	0.2	4.8	14.1	15.1	24.4	25.5	16.1	38.3	97.4	1.3	0.8	0.9	1.4
42 039	Crawford	88,884	-0.5	5.7	16.8	9.7	24.9	26.8	16.0	39.6	97.3	2.2	0.5	0.8	0.8
42 041	Cumberland	225,536	2.3	5.2	15.4	11.3	26.1	26.9	15.0	39.7	93.9	3.6	2.5	1.2	1.9
42 043	Dauphin	254,277	1.0	6.4	17.2	7.5	27.2	27.8	13.8	39.4	77.4	18.5	2.7	3.3	5.2
42 045	Delaware	553,511	0.4	6.2	18.0	10.6	24.7	26.3	14.3	39.0	76.7	18.4	4.7	1.3	2.0
42 047	Elk	32,914	-2.0	4.7	16.4	7.6	25.0	28.1	18.2	42.5	98.9	0.3	0.6	0.5	0.5
42 049	Erie	279,252	0.0	5.9	17.5	11.2	25.0	26.2	14.3	38.1	91.6	7.2	1.0	1.7	2.6
42 051	Fayette	144,962	-0.6	5.1	15.8	7.9	26.2	27.5	17.5	41.5	95.2	4.6	0.4	0.7	0.4
42 055	Franklin	139,459	3.4	6.3	16.8	7.6	27.6	25.4	16.3	39.2	95.4	3.4	1.0	1.3	2.8
42 059	Greene	39,717	-1.3	5.0	15.6	9.5	27.0	27.9	15.0	39.5	95.6	4.0	0.7	0.5	1.0
42 061	Huntingdon	45,547	-0.1	4.8	14.8	9.6	28.6	26.8	15.4	40.1	94.1	5.3	0.4	1.1	1.3
42 063	Indiana	87,888	-0.4	4.8	13.6	18.1	22.5	25.5	15.5	37.7	96.4	2.1	1.2	0.7	0.6
42 065	Jefferson	45,151	-0.1	5.4	16.0	8.0	25.1	27.2	18.2	41.9	98.9	0.4	0.5	0.5	0.6
42 067	Juniata	23,163	0.0	6.6	17.2	7.1	27.3	25.4	16.5	39.4	97.7	0.7	0.5	1.6	2.0
42 069	Lackawanna	209,223	0.1	5.3	15.5	10.0	24.4	26.6	18.1	41.1	96.0	2.3	1.1	1.3	2.6
42 071	Lancaster	493,910	1.8	6.9	18.5	8.8	26.4	25.0	14.3	37.3	92.2	4.1	1.9	3.1	6.7
42 073	Lawrence	91,456	-1.1	5.3	16.2	8.9	23.4	27.7	18.4	42.1	95.8	5.0	-	0.7	-
42 075	Lebanon	126,426	2.4	6.2	16.5	8.2	26.7	26.1	16.3	39.7	92.8	2.2	1.1	5.0	6.5
42 077	Lehigh	333,423	2.5	6.3	17.3	8.5	26.5	26.2	15.1	39.1	84.3	5.5	3.0	8.8	14.2
42 079	Luzerne	311,938	0.2	5.1	15.0	9.2	25.4	27.0	18.3	42.0	95.2	2.9	0.9	1.7	3.2
42 081	Lycoming	117,311	-0.8	5.6	15.9	10.7	24.5	27.2	16.2	40.5	94.3	5.2	0.6	1.1	0.9
42 083	McKean	43,858	-0.7	5.2	16.3	8.4	26.2	27.0	16.8	40.5	96.3	2.4	0.6	1.5	1.3
42 085	Mercer	117,517	-1.2	5.3	16.5	9.4	24.4	26.7	17.8	41.2	93.7	5.9	0.7	0.7	0.8
42 087	Mifflin	46,609	2.1	6.3	16.8	7.0	26.8	25.5	17.6	40.4	98.6	0.7	0.5	0.5	0.7
42 089	Monroe	162,612	2.8	5.4	19.3	10.6	26.7	26.4	11.6	37.6	83.5	12.0	2.4	3.7	10.9
42 091	Montgomery	774,424	0.4	6.2	17.3	8.1	26.2	27.5	14.7	40.2	85.4	9.0	5.6	1.4	2.9
42 095	Northampton	289,773	2.7	5.6	16.6	10.3	26.2	26.7	14.6	39.1	89.7	4.8	2.3	5.5	8.4
42 097	Northumberland	91,214	-0.6	5.3	14.9	7.5	26.1	27.6	18.7	42.5	96.8	2.2	0.4	1.3	1.6
42 099	Perry	44,852	1.4	6.2	17.3	7.6	27.5	28.9	12.5	39.7	98.9	0.8	0.4	0.7	0.9
42 101	Philadelphia	1,454,382	-0.7	7.3	17.9	10.8	27.7	23.3	13.0	35.3	43.9	44.9	5.8	7.3	10.3
42 103	Pike	57,101	5.8	4.4	19.1	7.5	27.7	26.8	14.5	39.8	91.0	5.9	1.3	3.0	7.5
42 107	Schuylkill	146,838	0.7	4.9	14.5	7.8	27.1	27.3	18.4	42.2	96.0	2.8	0.7	1.1	1.7
42 109	Snyder	37,983	0.8	6.1	16.2	12.3	25.7	25.6	14.1	38.2	97.4	1.5	0.7	1.0	1.3
42 111	Somerset	78,192	-0.8	4.8	15.0	7.7	26.1	27.9	18.5	42.5	97.4	2.4	0.4	0.3	0.9
42 115	Susquehanna	41,389	-1.2	5.5	17.1	7.9	24.8	28.5	16.2	42.1	99.0	0.5	0.5	0.6	1.0
42 117	Tioga	40,838	-1.0	5.1	16.2	11.1	23.6	26.9	17.1	40.5	98.5	1.0	0.5	1.2	0.7
42 119	Union	43,354	2.2	4.8	12.7	14.6	29.6	24.5	13.8	38.0	88.1	7.7	1.7	3.8	4.6
42 121	Venango	55,161	-1.4	5.3	16.6	7.6	24.1	29.4	17.0	42.5	98.4	1.6	0.4	0.8	0.7
42 123	Warren	41,250	-1.5	5.0	16.4	7.1	23.4	30.4	17.6	44.0	99.1	0.4	0.4	0.6	0.5
42 125	Washington	205,302	0.2	5.1	15.6	9.0	24.5	28.5	17.2	42.1	95.7	4.0	0.7	0.8	0.8
42 127	Wayne	51,142	3.1	4.8	16.3	7.1	26.2	27.9	17.7	42.4	96.0	3.0	0.6	1.1	2.7

Table A-2. Counties — Who: Age, Race/Ethnicity, and Household Structure, 2005–2007—*Continued*

STATE County	Percent foreign born	Total households	Household type (percent)						Percent of households with people under 18 years	Percent of households with people 60 years and over
			Family households				Nonfamily households			
			Total family households	Married-couple families	Male householder families	Female householder families	Total nonfamily households	One-person households		
ACS table number:	C05002	B11001	B11001	B11001	B11001	B11001	B11001	B11001	C11005	B11006
	15	16	17	18	19	20	21	22	23	24
Oregon—Cont.										
Josephine	3.7	33,545	67.6	53.6	4.1	10.0	32.4	27.4	29.5	43.3
Klamath	4.6	26,048	66.9	50.6	5.4	10.8	33.1	25.8	30.9	35.7
Lane	6.1	137,630	61.0	47.1	4.0	9.8	39.0	28.5	28.5	30.4
Lincoln	6.1	19,623	58.1	46.7	2.7	8.7	41.9	33.5	22.1	43.6
Linn	3.5	42,994	68.4	53.5	4.4	10.5	31.6	25.5	33.3	34.9
Malheur	9.7	10,413	67.6	52.2	4.9	10.5	32.4	27.3	37.2	34.9
Marion	14.9	110,417	69.3	52.0	5.3	11.9	30.7	24.0	37.6	30.8
Multnomah	13.7	286,953	54.6	39.8	4.0	10.8	45.4	35.1	27.5	25.2
Polk	6.5	25,586	69.0	54.4	3.9	10.7	31.0	25.5	31.7	37.2
Tillamook	5.8	10,792	64.7	54.8	2.0	7.8	35.3	31.5	25.0	42.1
Umatilla	9.6	26,065	70.2	51.5	6.5	12.2	29.8	24.3	37.5	32.3
Union	2.4	9,782	65.9	54.1	2.9	9.0	34.1	27.1	29.2	34.7
Wasco	7.0	9,002	64.4	48.5	4.7	11.1	35.6	29.4	29.0	39.0
Washington	16.8	189,280	66.4	52.8	4.1	9.5	33.6	25.9	36.5	23.7
Yamhill	7.6	32,833	71.1	54.7	4.8	11.6	28.9	24.2	37.6	29.4
Pennsylvania	5.2	4,858,509	65.8	49.9	4.2	11.7	34.2	28.9	31.3	34.6
Adams	3.9	37,131	70.7	58.1	3.6	9.0	29.3	23.7	35.0	31.9
Allegheny	4.5	520,849	60.1	44.5	3.7	11.9	39.9	34.5	27.2	35.9
Armstrong	0.9	28,803	67.3	54.6	3.3	9.4	32.7	29.4	30.2	37.9
Beaver	2.0	71,290	68.0	52.2	4.7	11.1	32.0	28.5	29.0	39.0
Bedford	0.7	19,956	70.1	59.0	3.1	8.0	29.9	26.0	30.2	36.8
Berks	6.0	149,410	70.0	54.0	4.9	11.1	30.0	23.9	34.9	33.1
Blair	1.0	51,384	66.5	51.6	3.6	11.3	33.5	29.0	30.4	37.3
Bradford	0.8	24,853	67.7	54.2	3.9	9.6	32.3	26.5	31.3	37.2
Bucks	7.6	227,650	71.4	59.1	3.8	8.5	28.6	24.2	34.6	33.4
Butler	1.8	70,878	70.8	58.9	3.0	9.0	29.2	24.1	32.4	31.6
Cambria	1.6	59,305	67.0	51.2	3.9	11.9	33.0	29.5	27.8	41.5
Carbon	1.7	24,781	67.7	53.0	4.1	10.7	32.3	26.3	29.1	37.7
Centre	6.0	51,319	57.0	40.0	2.4	5.7	43.0	29.9	26.1	26.6
Chester	6.9	173,518	70.9	59.3	3.7	7.9	29.1	23.1	35.9	29.7
Clarion	1.0	15,969	66.2	53.2	3.4	9.6	33.8	28.5	29.7	36.1
Clearfield	0.6	33,214	67.0	52.9	4.1	10.0	33.0	28.0	29.5	36.4
Clinton	1.5	14,971	65.2	50.2	5.3	9.7	34.8	27.4	29.2	35.8
Columbia	1.9	25,589	66.5	51.9	4.6	9.9	33.5	26.5	30.0	36.2
Crawford	1.0	34,847	68.1	54.0	4.2	9.9	31.9	27.2	30.4	36.5
Cumberland	4.2	89,331	65.5	53.8	3.2	8.6	34.5	27.7	29.5	32.9
Dauphin	5.1	104,500	62.8	45.9	4.0	12.8	37.2	31.2	31.2	31.0
Delaware	8.2	204,448	66.4	48.3	4.7	13.4	33.6	29.0	33.3	34.7
Elk	0.9	13,803	67.9	52.7	6.6	8.6	32.1	28.3	30.6	37.0
Erie	3.7	107,218	65.3	48.7	3.4	13.2	34.7	29.1	32.1	32.6
Fayette	0.9	58,801	67.4	49.3	4.6	13.5	32.6	29.1	29.5	39.5
Franklin	3.3	56,376	70.3	58.9	3.2	8.2	29.7	24.2	33.2	33.3
Greene	0.9	14,509	71.1	52.1	4.6	14.4	28.9	25.2	32.3	37.8
Huntingdon	1.3	16,717	67.4	55.6	4.5	7.3	32.6	28.6	29.6	37.5
Indiana	1.6	34,699	66.1	53.4	3.6	9.1	33.9	26.3	27.8	35.5
Jefferson	0.7	18,792	70.1	56.4	4.6	9.1	29.9	27.2	30.2	38.0
Juniata	1.3	8,862	73.1	62.8	4.9	5.3	26.9	24.2	32.1	34.9
Lackawanna	3.4	86,218	63.5	47.1	4.3	12.2	36.5	31.5	28.9	40.5
Lancaster	4.0	185,001	70.3	57.8	3.6	8.9	29.7	24.1	34.7	31.4
Lawrence	1.2	36,349	69.7	55.6	3.4	10.8	30.3	27.3	32.1	39.9
Lebanon	2.7	49,465	68.7	54.6	4.0	10.1	31.3	26.0	31.5	36.2
Lehigh	8.3	129,391	67.0	51.0	4.2	11.8	33.0	27.1	33.1	34.5
Luzerne	2.9	129,840	63.5	47.4	4.3	11.7	36.5	32.2	28.3	38.8
Lycoming	1.1	47,719	66.7	50.9	4.7	11.1	33.3	27.0	30.2	35.2
McKean	1.4	17,376	65.9	51.0	5.0	9.9	34.1	30.4	30.4	36.5
Mercer	1.6	46,671	67.2	53.7	3.0	10.6	32.8	28.4	29.0	37.5
Mifflin	0.7	18,927	66.3	53.0	5.3	8.1	33.7	29.4	31.7	39.9
Monroe	8.4	59,036	74.5	58.8	4.5	11.2	25.5	19.9	39.0	31.6
Montgomery	8.3	296,231	69.1	55.5	3.5	10.0	30.9	26.0	34.2	33.5
Northampton	6.0	109,164	70.9	55.5	4.2	11.1	29.1	24.2	34.1	34.3
Northumberland	1.0	38,270	65.1	50.8	4.8	9.5	34.9	30.1	27.9	39.7
Perry	0.8	17,282	73.5	59.7	5.2	8.6	26.5	21.8	33.1	31.6
Philadelphia	10.9	557,985	55.2	28.4	5.6	21.2	44.8	38.7	29.9	32.1
Pike	7.0	22,611	73.7	58.2	4.2	11.4	26.3	20.4	37.8	35.7
Schuylkill	1.9	60,311	66.0	49.1	5.7	11.3	34.0	29.7	29.0	39.1
Snyder	1.5	13,994	71.6	61.8	3.0	6.8	28.4	23.3	33.0	34.2
Somerset	0.8	30,995	68.4	56.0	4.1	8.4	31.6	27.3	28.8	40.0
Susquehanna	1.5	17,384	70.6	54.4	6.3	9.9	29.4	25.1	32.5	36.5
Tioga	1.2	16,610	68.2	54.3	4.9	9.1	31.8	25.3	29.7	36.8
Union	4.6	13,549	68.4	58.3	2.3	7.8	31.6	26.9	32.5	36.3
Venango	0.6	22,699	68.6	52.7	4.6	11.3	31.4	26.9	31.6	36.9
Warren	1.1	17,758	65.6	53.6	4.3	7.7	34.4	29.3	28.2	36.9
Washington	1.1	82,946	65.6	51.9	3.7	9.9	34.4	29.2	28.6	37.5
Wayne	3.8	20,552	68.6	55.1	3.4	10.0	31.4	26.8	32.5	40.0

STATE County code	STATE County	Total population	Percent change 2005–2007	Population by age (percent)						Median age	Race alone or in combination (percent)					Percent Hispanic or Latino
				Under 5 years	5 to 17 years	18 to 24 years	25 to 44 years	45 to 64 years	65 years and over		White	Black	Asian Hawaiian or Pacific Islander	Amer. Indian, Alaska Native, or some other race		
	ACS table number:	B01003	Population estimates	B01001	B01001	B01001	B01001	B01001	B01001	B01002	B02008	B02009	B02011 + B02012	B02010 + B02013		C03002
		1	2	3	4	5	6	7	8	9	10	11	12	13		14
	Pennsylvania—Cont.															
42 129	Westmoreland	363,489	-0.6	4.7	15.4	8.1	24.1	29.5	18.2	43.4	96.7	2.8	0.8	0.5		0.7
42 131	Wyoming	27,881	-0.4	5.6	17.2	8.9	25.4	28.3	14.5	39.4	98.4	0.9	0.6	0.3		1.0
42 133	York	414,023	3.6	6.2	17.1	8.0	27.9	27.2	13.6	39.3	92.2	5.4	1.3	2.2		4.0
44 000	**Rhode Island**	1,062,065	-0.8	5.8	16.5	10.7	27.3	25.9	13.9	38.3	84.5	6.4	3.0	8.3		10.9
44 001	Bristol	50,302	-1.0	4.9	15.2	11.4	23.7	28.2	16.6	41.5	97.3	1.4	2.0	0.3		1.5
44 003	Kent	169,578	-1.2	5.2	16.3	8.0	27.1	28.9	14.5	41.0	95.1	1.9	2.2	1.9		2.6
44 005	Newport	83,007	-0.2	4.9	15.5	8.7	27.1	28.4	15.4	41.6	93.9	4.6	2.0	1.5		3.2
44 007	Providence	631,933	-0.9	6.4	16.9	11.1	28.3	24.0	13.4	36.5	77.1	9.2	3.6	12.7		16.8
44 009	Washington	127,245	-0.6	4.7	16.0	13.0	24.1	28.6	13.5	40.0	95.7	1.7	2.2	2.3		1.9
45 000	**South Carolina**	4,330,933	3.6	6.7	17.5	9.9	27.2	25.8	12.8	37.0	68.3	29.2	1.5	2.2		3.6
45 001	Abbeville	25,550	-0.9	5.8	17.4	10.0	25.1	26.7	15.0	39.0	70.3	29.3	-	-		1.0
45 003	Aiken	150,409	2.4	6.3	17.8	8.9	25.7	26.9	14.3	38.9	71.7	26.4	0.9	2.4		3.1
45 007	Anderson	177,151	3.2	6.5	17.6	8.1	27.2	26.4	14.2	38.2	82.5	17.2	0.9	1.2		1.8
45 011	Barnwell	23,011	-0.3	7.1	18.6	10.4	24.3	26.4	13.1	37.4	54.9	44.6	-	1.7		-
45 013	Beaufort	143,421	5.7	7.6	16.6	9.8	25.2	22.8	17.9	37.5	75.3	21.8	1.5	2.8		9.3
45 015	Berkeley	158,365	7.0	7.2	19.2	10.5	28.7	25.2	9.2	34.3	68.8	27.4	2.7	3.5		3.5
45 019	Charleston	340,326	1.7	7.0	16.4	11.1	27.8	25.7	12.0	36.2	65.0	32.1	1.8	2.3		3.4
45 021	Cherokee	53,797	0.9	6.5	18.4	7.1	29.4	26.2	12.3	36.6	78.2	21.3	-	1.3		2.6
45 023	Chester	32,698	-1.1	6.5	18.5	7.8	26.5	27.2	13.4	38.7	60.0	38.3	-	2.2		1.0
45 025	Chesterfield	42,711	0.0	6.3	18.6	8.0	27.2	27.2	12.8	38.7	65.5	34.3	0.5	1.1		3.0
45 027	Clarendon	32,783	0.2	6.1	17.2	11.7	22.6	26.5	15.8	38.8	47.8	51.1	-	1.6		-
45 029	Colleton	38,918	-0.2	7.1	19.7	8.3	25.0	26.3	13.5	37.9	57.6	41.2	-	1.7		2.0
45 031	Darlington	66,878	-0.1	6.3	18.6	8.2	26.4	27.2	13.2	37.9	57.0	42.2	0.4	1.7		1.2
45 033	Dillon	30,710	-0.1	7.7	20.1	8.4	26.3	25.2	12.4	35.5	51.3	46.4	-	3.3		2.6
45 035	Dorchester	117,660	10.5	6.9	19.7	9.6	28.7	25.6	9.5	35.4	71.5	26.2	2.0	2.0		2.8
45 037	Edgefield	25,337	0.1	5.2	16.3	10.4	30.2	27.0	11.0	37.4	56.9	40.8	0.9	2.1		2.5
45 039	Fairfield	23,554	-1.6	6.4	17.9	9.0	25.1	27.9	13.6	39.2	44.5	56.9	-	0.7		-
45 041	Florence	130,887	1.5	7.3	17.8	9.7	26.3	26.4	12.4	36.9	58.1	40.7	1.1	1.2		1.4
45 043	Georgetown	60,013	1.6	6.2	16.6	8.8	23.9	27.4	17.1	40.3	63.7	34.3	1.0	1.2		-
45 045	Greenville	417,138	5.3	7.0	17.5	9.0	28.4	26.2	12.0	37.2	77.1	18.8	2.2	3.0		6.3
45 047	Greenwood	67,980	0.8	6.7	18.0	10.2	26.1	24.7	14.4	37.4	64.5	31.9	1.3	3.4		4.4
45 049	Hampton	21,108	1.0	6.9	18.8	11.4	25.0	25.1	12.7	36.3	42.3	55.0	0.3	3.4		-
45 051	Horry	239,419	9.3	6.3	15.2	8.2	28.5	25.4	16.3	39.3	81.4	15.1	1.3	3.2		4.0
45 053	Jasper	21,569	3.6	7.5	18.2	10.3	29.3	21.7	13.0	35.4	41.3	49.1	-	9.0		-
45 055	Kershaw	57,022	4.2	6.6	18.2	8.8	25.9	27.3	13.2	38.5	71.2	26.8	0.5	2.1		2.2
45 057	Lancaster	71,646	5.1	6.0	17.9	8.5	28.4	26.4	12.9	37.5	72.4	27.0	0.5	0.9		3.0
45 059	Laurens	69,493	0.1	5.7	17.8	9.4	27.1	26.5	13.6	38.6	73.5	25.9	0.4	1.2		3.0
45 063	Lexington	238,299	4.3	6.8	18.2	8.5	27.6	27.4	11.4	37.7	82.6	14.9	1.5	2.3		3.3
45 067	Marion	34,148	-1.6	6.7	18.3	9.2	25.6	27.2	13.0	37.7	44.1	55.9	-	0.6		-
45 069	Marlboro	28,460	4.4	5.9	17.1	9.6	28.9	26.2	12.4	37.2	44.3	52.8	-	4.5		1.1
45 071	Newberry	37,350	1.8	6.2	17.2	9.5	26.9	25.5	14.6	37.7	63.3	31.8	-	5.0		-
45 073	Oconee	70,016	2.1	5.7	16.2	7.6	26.0	26.8	17.6	41.2	90.0	8.7	0.5	1.3		3.4
45 075	Orangeburg	90,176	-0.9	7.1	17.4	12.5	23.6	25.4	14.1	36.6	36.7	62.2	0.7	1.3		1.2
45 077	Pickens	114,772	2.0	5.6	15.7	16.0	26.4	23.6	12.6	34.5	91.1	7.1	1.8	1.1		2.5
45 079	Richland	351,355	3.6	6.8	17.3	14.3	27.8	24.3	9.6	34.0	50.8	46.4	2.7	2.1		3.5
45 083	Spartanburg	270,368	3.7	6.6	17.6	8.8	28.0	26.0	13.1	37.4	75.8	21.2	2.1	1.9		4.3
45 085	Sumter	104,295	-0.9	7.6	19.4	9.8	25.6	24.9	12.6	36.3	50.6	47.8	1.3	1.0		2.2
45 087	Union	28,032	-1.8	5.8	17.1	7.3	25.4	28.0	16.3	41.0	67.2	32.1	-	0.5		-
45 089	Williamsburg	35,215	1.8	6.6	18.0	10.6	23.6	27.0	14.2	38.6	32.7	66.9	-	0.5		-
45 091	York	198,886	10.3	6.9	18.3	9.8	28.5	25.7	10.8	36.1	77.9	19.9	1.4	2.4		3.3
46 000	**South Dakota**	788,241	2.1	7.0	17.8	10.6	25.1	25.4	14.2	37.1	89.0	1.4	1.2	10.3		2.1
46 011	Brookings	28,939	2.6	5.8	13.0	26.6	23.5	20.6	10.6	27.7	96.0	0.9	2.3	2.1		1.1
46 013	Brown	34,970	0.6	6.3	16.0	11.6	23.7	25.8	16.6	38.7	95.5	-	0.7	5.1		0.2
46 029	Codington	26,142	1.8	7.5	17.2	9.1	26.6	24.8	14.8	37.5	97.1	-	0.4	2.5		-
46 081	Lawrence	23,017	2.8	5.6	14.6	15.5	21.7	27.2	15.4	38.1	97.0	-	2.3	2.4		2.2
46 083	Lincoln	35,738	12.0	9.0	19.5	10.1	31.5	22.7	7.1	30.9	98.4	1.6	1.0	1.7		-
46 093	Meade	24,274	-2.1	7.6	18.8	9.6	25.6	27.5	10.9	36.9	93.2	2.6	2.1	4.5		3.4
46 099	Minnehaha	171,316	5.0	7.7	18.0	9.4	29.3	24.1	11.6	35.3	92.1	3.1	1.4	4.7		3.6
46 103	Pennington	94,904	2.8	7.6	17.6	10.2	26.0	26.0	12.6	36.3	89.2	2.1	1.6	10.9		3.4
46 135	Yankton	21,644	0.0	5.5	17.1	9.8	25.5	27.1	15.2	40.4	94.7	1.8	-	4.0		2.3
47 000	**Tennessee**	6,073,646	2.8	6.7	17.4	9.1	28.3	25.9	12.7	37.2	80.3	17.2	1.5	2.3		3.3
47 001	Anderson	72,715	2.3	5.9	16.1	7.4	25.9	28.3	16.4	41.3	93.4	4.5	1.4	1.8		1.6
47 003	Bedford	43,042	5.0	7.8	18.1	8.3	30.6	23.5	11.6	34.3	83.4	9.1	-	8.2		-
47 009	Blount	117,683	4.0	5.9	16.2	8.5	27.8	27.1	14.5	39.8	95.0	3.4	1.2	1.7		1.6
47 011	Bradley	93,820	3.4	6.3	16.7	9.5	29.4	25.0	13.1	36.7	92.5	4.5	0.9	3.0		3.1
47 013	Campbell	40,601	0.8	6.0	16.6	6.6	28.5	25.7	16.6	38.8	99.2	-	-	2.1		-
47 017	Carroll	28,826	0.7	6.1	16.0	8.2	26.6	25.7	17.4	40.2	87.3	11.3	0.3	1.6		1.5
47 019	Carter	58,960	0.9	5.1	14.6	9.2	29.3	26.4	15.4	39.3	97.6	2.2	0.4	1.8		1.2
47 021	Cheatham	38,567	2.8	6.3	19.3	7.4	29.2	27.7	10.1	37.8	95.6	2.6	0.5	1.7		1.9
47 025	Claiborne	31,054	1.4	5.9	16.6	8.3	28.3	26.7	14.3	38.5	98.0	1.7	-	0.6		-
47 029	Cocke	35,043	1.7	5.8	16.2	6.5	28.8	28.3	14.4	39.3	96.1	2.8	-	1.1		0.3
47 031	Coffee	51,258	2.1	6.5	17.7	8.0	27.3	25.0	15.5	38.2	94.9	2.5	1.1	4.2		3.2

STATE County	Percent foreign born	Total households	Household type (percent)						Percent of households with people under 18 years	Percent of households with people 60 years and over
			Family households				Nonfamily households			
			Total family households	Married-couple families	Male householder families	Female householder families	Total nonfamily households	One-person households		
ACS table number:	C05002	B11001	B11001	B11001	B11001	B11001	B11001	B11001	C11005	B11006
	15	16	17	18	19	20	21	22	23	24
Pennsylvania—Cont.										
Westmoreland	1.6	150,612	67.7	54.7	3.8	9.3	32.3	28.1	28.1	38.7
Wyoming	1.5	11,074	71.6	55.1	6.6	10.0	28.4	23.0	32.7	37.0
York	2.9	162,264	70.3	56.3	4.6	9.4	29.7	23.8	33.4	31.8
Rhode Island	12.6	404,549	63.9	47.1	4.1	12.7	36.1	29.5	31.7	32.9
Bristol	9.9	18,783	68.0	57.4	1.5	9.1	32.0	26.6	29.5	39.2
Kent	5.7	68,696	64.1	49.4	4.0	10.7	35.9	30.3	31.7	33.8
Newport	5.6	33,675	64.0	51.2	3.1	9.6	36.0	31.3	29.5	35.7
Providence	17.3	233,792	62.8	43.5	4.5	14.8	37.2	30.3	32.5	31.7
Washington	3.7	49,603	66.9	54.3	3.8	8.8	33.1	24.4	30.2	33.0
South Carolina	4.2	1,664,561	67.7	48.5	4.2	15.1	32.3	27.3	33.7	31.9
Abbeville	1.6	9,468	70.9	50.1	2.5	18.2	29.1	27.2	36.5	33.5
Aiken	3.0	58,988	70.1	50.8	4.1	15.2	29.9	26.6	34.7	33.6
Anderson	2.4	68,821	71.7	53.5	4.6	13.7	28.3	23.7	35.0	34.1
Barnwell	1.1	8,590	72.0	42.3	5.5	24.1	28.0	25.2	35.8	34.8
Beaufort	8.3	56,539	70.2	55.3	3.8	11.1	29.8	24.1	32.0	39.4
Berkeley	4.1	55,150	72.2	52.1	5.1	15.0	27.8	23.6	38.0	26.9
Charleston	4.8	137,878	60.3	40.9	3.5	15.9	39.7	31.9	28.5	30.0
Cherokee	2.4	20,532	67.9	49.1	4.1	14.8	32.1	28.0	33.4	31.7
Chester	2.0	12,700	67.6	44.1	4.7	18.7	32.4	28.4	31.4	34.9
Chesterfield	2.2	16,110	66.5	47.4	4.0	15.1	33.5	29.7	34.0	35.7
Clarendon	1.7	12,994	69.4	46.8	5.6	17.0	30.6	25.2	34.3	36.3
Colleton	1.0	14,257	68.7	47.1	4.6	17.1	31.3	27.2	36.9	36.1
Darlington	1.7	24,122	67.9	48.2	4.6	15.2	32.1	29.3	31.6	32.3
Dillon	2.0	11,579	65.7	36.1	5.1	24.5	34.3	28.4	40.6	35.9
Dorchester	3.3	41,571	72.7	53.9	4.4	14.5	27.3	23.6	39.4	27.5
Edgefield	2.6	8,877	75.3	52.3	4.0	19.0	24.7	21.0	37.2	31.0
Fairfield	1.4	8,075	64.7	37.0	2.4	25.3	35.3	31.7	35.5	39.4
Florence	2.5	48,556	71.1	47.6	3.3	20.2	28.9	25.9	36.8	32.0
Georgetown	2.8	22,541	68.8	52.3	3.0	13.5	31.2	26.1	31.8	43.5
Greenville	7.3	162,936	67.1	49.9	4.6	12.6	32.9	28.6	32.6	29.8
Greenwood	4.3	25,726	66.3	47.3	3.6	15.4	33.7	28.5	31.2	34.8
Hampton	3.0	7,261	67.9	47.3	4.9	15.7	32.1	30.5	34.3	34.5
Horry	5.7	105,192	63.9	46.6	4.5	12.8	36.1	27.4	29.2	34.7
Jasper	8.1	7,306	71.4	47.0	6.3	18.0	28.6	25.5	40.8	36.0
Kershaw	2.4	22,082	71.6	49.9	6.0	15.6	28.4	24.2	35.2	31.9
Lancaster	2.7	25,393	70.3	51.6	3.6	15.1	29.7	25.7	34.8	33.1
Laurens	3.1	26,163	69.4	48.9	4.2	16.2	30.6	26.1	36.0	31.8
Lexington	4.2	93,870	69.5	53.7	3.5	12.3	30.5	25.2	34.7	28.3
Marion	2.4	12,684	72.7	42.1	5.5	25.1	27.3	23.8	37.0	40.0
Marlboro	0.6	9,685	66.9	36.6	4.4	25.9	33.1	30.1	33.6	38.7
Newberry	5.5	13,647	71.3	50.2	3.8	17.3	28.7	24.4	35.4	37.4
Oconee	3.6	28,990	67.7	56.2	3.2	8.4	32.3	28.0	27.4	38.9
Orangeburg	1.1	34,122	66.1	40.5	4.9	20.7	33.9	28.8	33.5	35.1
Pickens	4.2	43,954	69.1	55.6	3.6	9.9	30.9	23.9	33.4	31.5
Richland	4.9	134,542	61.7	42.0	3.6	16.1	38.3	32.7	33.1	25.1
Spartanburg	5.4	104,536	69.2	50.6	4.4	14.2	30.8	27.4	35.1	32.0
Sumter	2.4	38,817	68.3	43.7	5.0	19.6	31.7	28.0	36.7	32.8
Union	0.3	11,286	69.0	46.5	6.7	15.9	31.0	27.5	38.4	38.1
Williamsburg	1.0	12,140	68.8	39.6	3.8	25.4	31.2	27.6	34.5	39.6
York	3.7	74,915	70.9	53.5	3.6	13.8	29.1	23.8	37.0	28.4
South Dakota	2.1	311,644	65.7	52.7	3.8	9.3	34.3	28.6	31.7	30.9
Brookings	4.1	11,710	52.9	44.9	2.0	5.9	47.1	30.9	24.2	23.7
Brown	1.0	14,669	62.3	50.1	3.3	8.9	37.7	32.1	27.7	31.8
Codington	0.4	11,128	64.6	52.9	3.7	7.9	35.4	29.0	35.1	32.3
Lawrence	1.4	10,035	57.4	44.9	3.8	8.7	42.6	33.8	25.6	33.2
Lincoln	1.5	10,779	75.3	63.6	3.3	8.4	24.7	20.8	39.0	19.5
Meade	2.5	9,741	71.5	59.7	2.4	9.4	28.5	23.3	36.7	24.1
Minnehaha	4.6	67,415	64.8	50.4	3.5	10.9	35.2	29.0	33.5	25.9
Pennington	2.4	37,678	65.7	50.1	4.7	11.0	34.3	27.9	31.5	28.7
Yankton	1.7	8,716	67.2	54.3	4.5	8.4	32.8	29.8	33.2	30.5
Tennessee	4.0	2,382,975	67.4	49.8	4.5	13.1	32.6	27.7	33.8	30.9
Anderson	2.1	30,844	66.5	50.6	2.7	13.2	33.5	29.1	30.9	36.5
Bedford	9.0	15,561	66.8	49.1	6.5	11.2	33.2	27.9	38.0	30.8
Blount	2.5	46,279	71.1	55.8	3.8	11.5	28.9	24.7	33.2	33.7
Bradley	3.4	37,402	70.9	57.0	4.4	9.6	29.1	24.3	33.9	31.7
Campbell	0.8	15,509	67.6	49.6	4.7	13.3	32.4	28.4	32.2	39.6
Carroll	1.7	11,529	70.3	53.8	5.4	11.1	29.7	26.1	36.4	39.4
Carter	1.4	23,549	67.0	51.8	4.1	11.1	33.0	28.1	29.4	35.3
Cheatham	2.7	14,054	75.1	57.7	5.1	12.4	24.9	21.3	42.8	26.4
Claiborne	-	12,445	71.4	57.8	3.2	10.4	28.6	26.1	31.7	34.5
Cocke	1.1	14,068	67.8	53.5	4.0	10.4	32.2	27.6	31.7	33.9
Coffee	3.2	20,309	71.4	52.1	6.4	12.8	28.6	24.9	37.5	36.0

STATE County code	STATE County	Total population	Percent change 2005–2007	Population by age (percent)						Median age	Race alone or in combination (percent)				Percent Hispanic or Latino
				Under 5 years	5 to 17 years	18 to 24 years	25 to 44 years	45 to 64 years	65 years and over		White	Black	Asian Hawaiian or Pacific Islander	Amer. Indian, Alaska Native, or some other race	
	ACS table number:	B01003	Population estimates	B01001	B01001	B01001	B01001	B01001	B01001	B01002	B02008	B02009	B02011 + B02012	B02010 + B02013	C03002
		1	2	3	4	5	6	7	8	9	10	11	12	13	14
	Tennessee—Cont.														
47 035	Cumberland	52,003	4.2	5.4	15.5	6.8	24.8	24.1	23.5	43.2	98.4	0.5	0.5	1.8	1.5
47 037	Davidson	613,632	2.0	7.4	16.0	9.4	31.3	24.9	10.9	36.0	66.6	28.0	3.3	3.1	7.1
47 043	Dickson	46,480	3.6	6.9	18.7	7.6	29.3	25.2	12.4	37.2	92.8	4.8	-	2.9	1.8
47 045	Dyer	37,656	0.2	6.4	18.6	7.6	27.1	26.4	13.9	38.7	84.9	15.1	-	0.8	-
47 047	Fayette	35,663	9.3	6.7	17.9	8.3	29.6	24.8	12.7	35.6	69.7	28.8	1.4	0.3	1.8
47 051	Franklin	40,861	1.6	6.0	16.1	10.6	25.6	26.2	15.6	38.4	94.8	3.8	0.6	5.0	2.1
47 053	Gibson	48,193	1.4	6.4	16.9	8.5	25.4	25.8	17.0	40.9	80.2	19.8	-	0.8	1.4
47 055	Giles	29,075	-0.3	5.3	17.4	8.3	26.9	26.8	15.3	39.4	86.9	12.8	0.3	0.8	-
47 057	Grainger	22,333	2.0	5.9	16.1	7.0	30.0	27.1	13.8	39.7	98.2	-	-	1.1	-
47 059	Greene	65,424	1.7	6.0	16.2	7.7	27.4	26.7	15.9	40.3	97.1	2.6	0.4	1.2	1.9
47 063	Hamblen	60,865	3.0	6.9	16.5	8.7	27.7	25.4	14.8	38.1	92.8	4.2	1.1	3.9	9.8
47 065	Hamilton	327,138	2.1	6.1	16.4	9.5	26.1	27.7	14.1	39.1	76.7	20.8	1.7	2.0	2.7
47 069	Hardeman	27,823	0.0	5.6	16.4	9.4	30.7	24.9	13.0	37.5	58.6	41.2	-	0.8	-
47 071	Hardin	25,934	1.0	5.2	16.6	7.6	26.2	27.4	17.0	40.3	95.1	4.4	-	1.2	-
47 073	Hawkins	56,534	1.9	5.9	16.7	6.7	28.7	27.3	14.7	40.0	97.5	1.7	0.4	1.3	1.0
47 077	Henderson	26,478	2.2	7.0	17.2	7.6	28.8	25.7	13.8	37.1	91.6	8.6	-	1.8	-
47 079	Henry	31,486	1.0	6.2	15.2	6.9	25.6	27.5	18.5	42.0	90.6	9.2	-	1.4	1.2
47 081	Hickman	23,562	1.6	5.6	18.5	7.7	29.9	25.0	13.3	37.0	93.8	4.9	-	2.1	-
47 089	Jefferson	49,069	4.8	5.7	16.4	10.3	27.7	25.7	14.3	37.8	96.7	2.3	0.6	1.2	2.2
47 093	Knox	416,447	3.6	6.1	16.1	11.1	27.9	26.2	12.6	37.3	88.7	9.5	1.9	1.4	2.0
47 097	Lauderdale	26,625	0.5	6.9	17.3	9.8	29.6	24.1	12.3	36.6	64.7	35.7	-	0.6	-
47 099	Lawrence	40,736	0.5	7.2	18.0	7.9	27.2	24.4	15.4	37.8	97.7	2.0	0.3	1.3	1.3
47 103	Lincoln	32,441	1.8	6.3	16.6	8.5	25.9	26.5	16.3	40.7	94.1	6.0	-	3.6	-
47 105	Loudon	44,351	5.1	6.7	15.2	7.3	25.5	25.9	19.4	41.9	97.0	1.6	0.5	1.0	3.9
47 107	McMinn	51,609	2.1	5.8	16.7	7.0	28.4	27.3	14.7	40.1	94.2	4.8	1.4	1.3	2.3
47 109	McNairy	25,358	2.0	6.7	17.0	7.2	26.4	25.9	16.8	39.6	92.3	7.3	-	1.2	-
47 111	Macon	21,410	1.5	6.5	17.8	7.4	30.6	25.4	12.5	36.3	98.7	-	-	1.1	-
47 113	Madison	95,880	1.7	7.0	18.4	10.4	26.9	25.1	12.2	35.8	64.8	34.0	0.9	1.3	2.6
47 115	Marion	27,955	1.4	5.9	16.6	7.5	27.7	28.4	13.9	39.5	96.1	3.1	0.2	2.3	-
47 117	Marshall	28,607	4.0	6.7	17.6	7.3	29.6	26.5	12.3	37.3	88.7	8.1	-	3.4	4.0
47 119	Maury	77,684	5.9	6.9	17.9	8.5	28.1	26.4	12.2	37.2	83.2	13.4	0.6	3.9	4.4
47 123	Monroe	43,865	4.5	6.4	17.6	8.3	29.1	24.5	14.2	36.5	95.9	3.3	-	1.8	-
47 125	Montgomery	150,045	4.6	8.3	20.6	10.1	31.3	21.4	8.3	32.0	75.3	20.9	3.1	3.5	5.5
47 129	Morgan	20,175	1.5	5.6	15.9	8.2	31.0	26.3	13.0	38.6	96.8	1.8	-	1.2	-
47 131	Obion	31,716	-0.7	6.3	16.4	7.6	26.5	26.8	16.2	40.3	88.1	10.4	-	2.3	2.9
47 133	Overton	20,727	2.5	6.1	16.1	7.6	27.4	26.5	16.3	40.3	98.8	0.7	-	1.4	-
47 141	Putnam	68,593	4.2	6.8	15.7	13.8	27.0	22.7	14.0	34.6	95.5	2.3	1.4	1.8	4.5
47 143	Rhea	30,044	2.0	6.4	16.8	9.2	26.7	26.6	14.2	39.1	96.7	2.3	0.7	2.7	2.2
47 145	Roane	53,033	1.5	5.2	15.7	7.5	25.4	29.6	16.7	42.3	95.9	3.0	0.6	1.5	0.9
47 147	Robertson	61,660	5.7	7.7	18.2	8.4	29.4	25.2	11.0	35.8	90.1	8.3	0.6	1.7	5.5
47 149	Rutherford	230,760	9.8	7.7	18.8	11.9	31.8	21.9	7.8	32.1	82.7	12.0	3.0	3.6	4.9
47 151	Scott	21,828	1.3	7.7	18.5	7.6	29.4	24.7	12.0	35.7	98.1	-	-	1.7	-
47 155	Sevier	81,592	4.9	6.3	16.1	7.2	29.0	26.8	14.6	39.7	97.7	1.2	0.7	1.6	2.0
47 157	Shelby	908,701	0.5	7.7	19.8	9.6	27.5	25.4	9.9	34.9	44.4	51.5	2.4	3.0	3.9
47 163	Sullivan	152,711	0.9	5.2	15.7	7.1	26.1	28.8	17.1	42.0	96.9	2.4	0.6	1.2	0.9
47 165	Sumner	148,382	6.1	6.6	18.2	8.4	28.5	27.0	11.3	37.5	91.2	7.0	1.0	1.6	2.8
47 167	Tipton	56,442	4.5	6.6	19.5	9.0	29.0	25.2	10.7	36.1	79.5	19.3	1.0	1.3	1.6
47 177	Warren	39,466	1.1	7.0	16.7	7.2	29.6	24.9	14.5	38.5	94.3	4.6	0.8	2.7	5.1
47 179	Washington	114,719	3.5	5.8	15.4	10.7	27.9	25.6	14.6	38.0	94.9	4.5	1.0	0.8	2.0
47 183	Weakley	33,358	-0.9	5.9	15.2	14.7	25.0	24.3	14.8	35.9	90.4	9.2	0.6	0.9	1.6
47 185	White	24,561	2.6	6.4	16.7	7.9	27.5	25.9	15.6	39.8	96.7	1.8	-	1.7	1.3
47 187	Williamson	159,095	9.3	6.6	19.9	8.6	26.9	29.4	8.6	37.4	91.6	5.6	2.4	2.0	3.6
47 189	Wilson	103,111	6.6	6.8	18.4	8.6	28.1	27.5	10.6	37.4	91.6	7.3	0.8	1.3	2.2
48 000	**Texas**	23,385,340	4.6	8.3	19.4	10.3	29.2	22.7	10.0	33.1	72.1	12.0	3.7	14.0	35.5
48 001	Anderson	56,454	1.2	5.9	14.1	10.6	33.9	23.9	11.6	36.4	72.9	23.0	0.8	4.5	13.6
48 005	Angelina	82,067	2.0	7.8	19.1	9.4	26.9	23.2	13.6	35.0	78.5	14.9	1.1	6.6	17.3
48 007	Aransas	24,521	1.3	5.5	16.8	7.4	23.2	25.2	21.8	43.5	89.3	1.8	3.4	9.6	22.3
48 013	Atascosa	43,032	2.6	7.9	20.9	10.4	25.9	23.7	11.2	34.0	85.9	2.2	0.5	15.0	-
48 015	Austin	26,172	3.2	6.3	18.7	9.9	24.8	25.3	15.0	37.2	84.9	11.5	-	5.6	19.9
48 019	Bandera	19,807	3.5	5.4	17.0	9.9	22.3	28.8	16.7	43.0	93.6	0.9	0.8	6.3	16.3
48 021	Bastrop	70,501	4.9	7.0	19.8	9.2	28.7	25.0	10.3	34.8	81.0	8.9	0.9	11.3	28.1
48 025	Bee	32,555	0.6	4.7	16.4	14.3	34.3	20.6	10.6	34.7	78.0	10.7	0.4	12.5	55.3
48 027	Bell	268,188	5.8	10.3	20.8	9.7	31.1	19.0	9.0	30.3	70.5	22.5	4.7	6.8	18.7
48 029	Bexar	1,555,168	5.2	8.4	19.8	10.6	28.7	22.3	10.2	32.8	67.7	7.7	2.7	24.5	57.0
48 037	Bowie	90,928	1.7	6.5	17.2	9.8	28.5	24.8	13.2	36.4	72.1	24.8	0.8	4.0	5.4
48 039	Brazoria	284,363	7.1	8.1	19.8	9.3	29.9	24.0	9.0	33.9	78.5	10.8	4.2	8.1	25.4
48 041	Brazos	167,823	4.1	7.1	14.6	29.8	26.1	15.4	7.1	24.4	77.1	10.8	5.4	9.0	20.4
48 049	Brown	38,434	1.0	6.1	18.2	10.4	25.1	23.7	16.5	37.5	89.7	5.4	-	6.8	17.6
48 053	Burnet	42,353	6.6	6.5	16.1	8.4	24.9	23.2	20.9	41.1	94.2	2.1	0.6	3.7	16.6
48 055	Caldwell	36,401	1.3	7.4	19.4	9.9	29.0	22.7	11.6	34.3	64.7	8.5	0.8	27.5	43.3
48 057	Calhoun	20,330	0.4	7.4	19.8	8.2	25.3	24.9	14.4	37.8	75.6	1.5	5.4	20.7	43.4
48 061	Cameron	379,874	3.9	11.4	22.8	10.8	25.1	18.8	11.1	28.8	86.6	0.6	0.7	13.2	86.0
48 067	Cass	29,408	-0.4	5.9	16.3	8.7	23.2	27.3	18.6	42.3	80.1	19.5	-	1.4	2.5

STATE County	Percent foreign born	Total households	Household type (percent)							Percent of households with people under 18 years	Percent of households with people 60 years and over
			Family households				Nonfamily households				
			Total family households	Married-couple families	Male householder families	Female householder families	Total nonfamily households	One-person households		
ACS table number:	C05002	B11001	B11001	B11001	B11001	B11001	B11001	B11001	C11005	B11006
	15	16	17	18	19	20	21	22	23	24
Tennessee—Cont.										
Cumberland	2.0	20,418	73.0	58.9	6.2	7.9	27.0	22.2	31.7	46.5
Davidson	10.1	248,006	56.7	37.9	3.8	14.9	43.3	36.5	28.9	26.2
Dickson	2.2	18,161	70.5	55.1	4.4	10.9	29.5	25.4	35.5	30.9
Dyer	0.5	14,849	69.6	50.2	6.0	13.4	30.4	25.9	35.1	32.7
Fayette	2.4	12,060	76.7	57.3	6.3	13.1	23.3	19.8	33.8	34.7
Franklin	2.1	15,747	69.3	56.3	4.0	8.9	30.7	26.6	33.1	35.9
Gibson	1.1	20,148	65.9	46.0	6.1	13.7	34.1	32.1	32.5	38.2
Giles	1.4	11,712	68.6	53.8	3.5	11.3	31.4	27.2	32.1	35.6
Grainger	0.2	8,186	72.7	61.0	2.6	9.1	27.3	24.7	33.5	35.8
Greene	0.9	26,906	69.9	53.1	5.0	11.8	30.1	25.2	34.5	34.5
Hamblen	8.3	24,358	69.8	52.8	6.1	10.9	30.2	26.4	35.5	33.9
Hamilton	4.0	132,102	64.4	48.1	3.9	12.4	35.6	29.9	29.7	32.9
Hardeman	0.9	9,518	76.2	50.8	6.5	18.8	23.8	21.3	40.6	35.3
Hardin	0.8	10,402	70.4	53.1	5.5	11.8	29.6	26.5	33.7	39.3
Hawkins	1.1	22,513	73.2	57.4	4.7	11.1	26.8	24.4	33.2	34.0
Henderson	1.0	10,582	72.5	57.0	3.9	11.6	27.5	24.1	36.6	35.6
Henry	0.9	13,348	71.0	51.3	4.7	15.0	29.0	25.9	31.0	39.4
Hickman	1.1	8,382	72.0	57.5	3.2	11.3	28.0	24.1	35.2	35.9
Jefferson	2.0	19,077	71.2	57.4	4.2	9.6	28.8	24.8	37.0	33.6
Knox	3.9	173,713	63.4	48.5	3.9	11.0	36.6	30.4	30.6	29.3
Lauderdale	-	9,225	69.9	49.6	2.4	17.9	30.1	25.4	37.1	35.0
Lawrence	0.9	15,131	72.7	58.7	5.2	8.8	27.3	24.7	35.2	38.6
Lincoln	0.9	13,236	67.7	55.1	4.7	7.9	32.3	28.1	31.0	37.7
Loudon	3.3	17,845	72.7	61.4	3.1	8.2	27.3	23.8	29.1	42.7
McMinn	2.8	20,503	67.5	51.7	4.0	11.8	32.5	28.2	31.3	32.5
McNairy	0.5	9,946	72.0	56.6	4.8	10.6	28.0	25.3	33.8	42.4
Macon	2.2	8,064	69.7	56.2	4.4	9.1	30.3	25.6	33.6	30.3
Madison	2.8	38,374	68.2	46.9	4.7	16.6	31.8	28.1	36.6	29.1
Marion	0.8	11,855	72.4	54.0	7.3	11.1	27.6	24.6	33.3	35.1
Marshall	3.2	11,362	73.6	53.2	8.8	11.7	26.4	22.5	39.4	29.5
Maury	3.6	30,989	69.9	53.5	2.8	13.6	30.1	24.2	37.7	28.9
Monroe	1.4	16,197	71.9	56.3	5.5	10.2	28.1	24.3	35.7	37.0
Montgomery	4.5	57,090	74.3	55.8	3.9	14.5	25.7	19.9	43.4	21.2
Morgan	0.9	7,425	72.1	57.8	3.9	10.5	27.9	24.2	34.8	32.4
Obion	2.6	13,014	67.6	52.5	3.7	11.4	32.4	28.6	30.9	35.6
Overton	0.5	8,680	71.2	57.1	3.0	11.1	28.8	26.2	35.4	37.9
Putnam	5.2	26,813	65.1	51.2	3.9	10.0	34.9	29.3	32.4	33.3
Rhea	2.2	11,718	69.5	55.7	3.1	10.8	30.5	26.3	32.6	33.9
Roane	1.4	21,318	72.2	57.2	5.3	9.8	27.8	24.4	31.7	48.8
Robertson	4.5	22,876	73.4	57.8	5.2	10.5	26.6	22.8	38.1	29.4
Rutherford	5.7	87,993	69.7	52.1	4.7	13.0	30.3	21.7	40.4	21.7
Scott	0.7	8,600	64.4	49.5	3.4	11.5	35.6	32.2	33.5	29.7
Sevier	2.7	31,401	72.7	57.6	4.4	10.7	27.3	22.3	33.7	32.7
Shelby	5.2	345,026	64.5	38.7	5.6	20.2	35.5	30.6	35.6	26.4
Sullivan	1.5	66,667	66.5	51.6	4.2	10.7	33.5	29.0	29.6	36.8
Sumner	3.4	56,519	73.7	59.1	3.8	10.8	26.3	22.0	36.8	29.3
Tipton	1.4	20,788	75.0	55.2	4.4	15.4	25.0	18.5	41.7	26.2
Warren	3.7	14,833	69.1	54.6	4.1	10.4	30.9	27.9	34.5	33.0
Washington	2.8	45,726	63.6	48.7	4.1	10.7	36.4	30.5	29.7	33.2
Weakley	1.8	13,349	67.4	52.4	3.3	11.8	32.6	25.9	33.4	34.8
White	1.8	9,457	69.3	55.7	3.9	9.7	30.7	27.9	32.1	39.2
Williamson	5.2	56,624	79.8	69.6	2.9	7.2	20.2	16.6	41.5	25.0
Wilson	2.4	38,816	74.2	59.9	4.7	9.5	25.8	19.9	38.5	30.1
Texas	15.8	8,095,025	70.2	51.7	4.9	13.5	29.8	24.8	39.9	27.0
Anderson	4.1	15,676	66.9	50.8	5.1	11.0	33.1	29.1	35.8	34.7
Angelina	9.1	29,985	72.8	55.1	4.1	13.7	27.2	23.8	36.5	34.4
Aransas	5.2	9,917	70.2	55.0	4.8	10.4	29.8	26.4	29.2	45.9
Atascosa	5.0	13,371	75.7	57.6	6.0	12.1	24.3	21.8	43.8	34.4
Austin	7.6	9,077	77.9	59.7	8.6	9.6	22.1	18.8	37.5	36.9
Bandera	2.7	7,323	76.7	59.7	3.0	14.0	23.3	20.7	33.9	38.9
Bastrop	9.9	21,345	74.4	55.9	7.9	10.6	25.6	22.1	39.6	29.0
Bee	4.8	9,222	73.5	46.1	7.6	19.8	26.5	18.3	40.6	32.3
Bell	7.7	94,849	71.4	52.9	4.3	14.1	28.6	24.6	42.5	24.0
Bexar	12.3	531,371	68.8	47.8	4.9	16.1	31.2	26.0	39.1	28.0
Bowie	3.9	34,064	68.5	47.5	5.6	15.4	31.5	27.8	34.6	33.3
Brazoria	11.0	97,781	75.9	59.9	5.6	10.3	24.1	20.0	43.3	25.3
Brazos	12.5	60,804	54.6	40.0	4.3	10.3	45.4	28.5	31.0	18.0
Brown	3.1	13,826	69.0	53.8	5.5	9.7	31.0	26.5	34.0	39.4
Burnet	6.2	15,627	69.6	56.9	3.0	9.6	30.4	26.9	33.4	45.3
Caldwell	5.8	11,287	74.0	53.5	10.8	9.7	26.0	22.1	41.1	30.3
Calhoun	12.4	7,972	68.2	51.4	5.0	11.7	31.8	26.4	38.2	35.3
Cameron	25.4	114,787	81.2	57.3	4.4	19.5	18.8	16.6	51.1	34.5
Cass	1.4	12,425	71.3	52.9	3.7	14.7	28.7	26.7	32.6	42.2

STATE County code	STATE County	Total population	Percent change 2005–2007	Population by age (percent)						Median age	Race alone or in combination (percent)				Percent Hispanic or Latino
				Under 5 years	5 to 17 years	18 to 24 years	25 to 44 years	45 to 64 years	65 years and over		White	Black	Asian Hawaiian or Pacific Islander	Amer. Indian, Alaska Native, or some other race	
	ACS table number:	B01003	Population estimates	B01001	B01001	B01001	B01001	B01001	B01001	B01002	B02008	B02009	B02011 + B02012	B02010 + B02013	C03002
		1	2	3	4	5	6	7	8	9	10	11	12	13	14
	Texas—Cont.														
48 071	Chambers	28,384	2.6	6.4	19.3	8.2	30.8	26.2	9.1	36.2	80.8	11.3	-	7.7	15.3
48 073	Cherokee	47,933	0.9	7.9	18.2	10.1	27.1	22.9	13.9	35.8	79.9	16.0	0.5	4.1	17.6
48 085	Collin	695,317	10.9	8.1	20.2	8.1	34.0	23.2	6.5	33.7	79.6	7.7	10.1	4.7	13.5
48 089	Colorado	20,558	1.1	6.3	16.9	9.9	22.4	25.7	18.8	40.6	81.0	14.8	-	5.0	
48 091	Comal	100,008	11.0	6.7	17.6	9.1	27.1	25.7	13.9	37.3	89.6	2.4	1.3	9.0	24.5
48 097	Cooke	38,393	0.4	7.0	18.8	9.6	24.7	25.1	14.8	36.8	85.9	3.5	0.8	12.3	13.4
48 099	Coryell	72,283	-1.4	6.5	24.1	15.1	31.6	16.3	6.4	27.3	73.6	21.7	3.6	5.8	13.0
48 113	Dallas	2,336,012	2.7	8.9	19.2	9.1	32.4	22.0	8.4	32.8	60.7	20.8	4.8	15.3	37.1
48 121	Denton	585,139	10.0	8.2	19.4	10.8	33.9	22.3	5.5	31.8	83.2	8.1	5.9	5.7	16.1
48 135	Ector	126,914	4.1	9.0	20.5	10.8	26.0	22.7	11.0	31.7	84.6	3.8	1.2	14.9	48.4
48 139	Ellis	137,820	8.6	7.9	20.1	10.7	28.6	23.6	9.2	32.7	79.1	9.4	0.7	12.4	21.9
48 141	El Paso	724,217	3.1	9.8	21.4	11.4	26.0	21.1	10.4	31.0	77.9	3.3	1.5	19.4	81.3
48 143	Erath	35,174	3.2	6.8	16.5	19.9	24.1	20.1	12.6	30.5	88.4	2.3	0.6	10.2	
48 147	Fannin	32,875	1.2	6.2	15.8	9.3	27.3	25.0	16.5	39.0	88.3	8.3	-	4.7	7.2
48 149	Fayette	22,419	0.9	6.7	14.8	8.1	22.9	26.0	21.4	43.2	87.1	7.2	0.6	6.0	15.6
48 157	Fort Bend	484,948	10.9	7.3	21.2	10.3	29.3	25.6	6.4	32.8	56.8	21.3	14.7	8.8	23.3
48 167	Galveston	279,604	3.2	7.3	18.5	9.5	27.5	26.1	11.0	36.1	76.6	14.8	3.3	7.2	20.5
48 171	Gillespie	23,143	3.5	5.6	14.8	4.7	24.9	24.9	25.0	44.9	95.4	-	-	5.6	
48 179	Gray	21,718	3.1	5.6	17.7	7.7	24.5	26.1	18.3	39.2	83.2	7.0	0.4	12.6	17.8
48 181	Grayson	117,179	2.5	6.9	17.5	9.1	26.6	25.1	14.9	37.1	87.0	6.4	0.9	7.7	9.3
48 183	Gregg	115,927	2.2	8.1	18.2	9.9	26.4	23.9	13.5	35.1	71.8	20.7	1.0	7.9	12.3
48 185	Grimes	25,321	2.1	6.2	16.9	9.9	28.4	25.0	13.6	36.8	75.6	19.2	-	7.1	
48 187	Guadalupe	107,632	10.1	6.8	19.3	10.6	27.6	23.9	11.8	35.0	78.2	6.0	1.8	15.2	34.3
48 189	Hale	35,783	-0.1	8.3	19.9	12.4	25.9	21.1	12.5	32.7	81.2	6.4	-	14.1	52.1
48 199	Hardin	51,013	1.8	6.4	18.6	9.1	27.3	26.2	12.5	37.3	91.2	7.0	0.6	1.9	3.6
48 201	Harris	3,854,245	4.9	8.8	20.0	9.5	30.8	23.2	7.7	32.6	61.1	18.9	5.9	15.6	37.9
48 203	Harrison	63,127	1.6	6.8	18.2	11.0	24.9	26.4	12.6	36.8	72.5	23.5	0.7	4.1	7.9
48 209	Hays	133,710	11.8	7.0	17.0	20.2	27.8	20.3	7.6	27.6	71.4	4.7	1.4	24.5	31.6
48 213	Henderson	78,814	0.4	6.3	17.3	8.3	25.5	24.8	17.8	38.8	86.8	6.7	0.6	7.0	9.3
48 215	Hidalgo	689,929	6.1	12.0	23.7	11.1	26.8	16.9	9.5	27.1	67.0	0.7	0.9	32.4	89.3
48 217	Hill	35,023	1.9	6.7	18.2	9.3	25.1	23.7	17.0	36.7	88.3	7.7	-	5.5	17.0
48 219	Hockley	22,424	-1.8	7.5	18.3	14.7	23.1	23.7	12.7	34.2	87.9	3.9	0.3	9.8	41.1
48 221	Hood	48,035	4.9	5.9	16.4	8.2	25.2	25.5	18.8	40.9	90.2	0.4	0.4	9.7	9.2
48 223	Hopkins	33,422	1.9	7.2	17.7	8.9	27.7	24.6	13.9	36.2	88.6	7.9	0.5	3.6	12.4
48 225	Houston	22,796	-0.3	5.6	16.0	8.9	26.6	25.0	18.0	39.9	69.2	27.1	-	4.3	
48 227	Howard	32,113	0.7	7.0	16.1	9.9	28.6	24.1	14.4	37.0	73.4	4.8	0.7	25.2	40.9
48 231	Hunt	82,324	1.6	6.8	17.9	10.9	27.5	24.3	12.7	35.4	86.2	9.4	0.9	4.7	10.9
48 233	Hutchinson	21,907	-0.4	7.2	18.3	10.1	22.1	26.4	15.9	38.5	82.0	3.3	-	16.0	17.9
48 241	Jasper	34,679	-1.4	6.9	17.9	8.6	25.7	24.8	16.2	38.6	81.4	17.7	0.6	2.0	4.8
48 245	Jefferson	243,300	-1.8	6.8	17.8	10.3	27.1	24.8	13.3	36.4	55.4	34.9	3.0	7.9	13.1
48 249	Jim Wells	40,843	1.1	7.9	21.3	11.1	24.6	22.7	12.4	33.4	88.0	1.0	-	10.6	
48 251	Johnson	146,663	4.0	7.2	19.3	9.9	29.2	24.2	10.2	34.5	91.5	3.7	1.1	5.7	15.3
48 257	Kaufman	91,906	9.9	7.8	19.6	9.4	30.3	23.2	9.6	33.2	82.3	10.8	0.9	7.1	15.6
48 259	Kendall	29,878	10.2	6.3	18.3	9.0	25.3	26.5	14.5	39.0	94.6	1.5	0.7	3.5	
48 265	Kerr	47,074	3.6	5.9	15.8	8.5	21.2	24.0	24.7	43.7	92.8	3.0	0.9	4.8	22.1
48 273	Kleberg	30,553	-1.1	8.6	17.5	16.9	24.1	20.5	12.4	30.5	80.3	5.6	1.0	14.8	
48 277	Lamar	49,173	0.2	6.7	18.3	9.4	25.7	23.7	16.3	37.9	84.0	13.6	0.6	3.5	4.8
48 281	Lampasas	20,269	6.7	6.0	19.2	9.0	25.0	25.1	15.8	37.3	90.0	3.5	1.3	7.9	16.0
48 291	Liberty	74,917	1.2	7.1	18.9	9.6	30.0	23.6	10.7	34.5	80.4	12.8	0.7	7.4	14.0
48 293	Limestone	22,450	0.0	6.6	17.7	8.9	27.4	24.0	15.3	37.8	73.5	20.4	-	6.9	
48 303	Lubbock	258,255	2.2	7.8	17.5	15.9	26.7	21.0	11.2	30.7	80.4	7.9	1.7	11.8	29.7
48 309	McLennan	226,260	1.6	7.5	18.4	14.8	25.2	21.8	12.3	31.8	78.4	15.4	1.8	5.8	20.8
48 321	Matagorda	37,176	-1.0	7.5	20.1	9.6	23.7	25.4	13.6	36.1	74.6	12.4	2.4	12.9	35.5
48 323	Maverick	50,980	2.8	10.0	24.6	10.9	23.8	20.3	10.4	29.3	46.4	-	0.5	54.4	
48 325	Medina	43,142	3.4	6.8	20.1	9.9	26.7	23.7	12.8	35.0	86.5	2.9	0.5	11.3	47.0
48 329	Midland	123,532	4.8	8.1	20.1	10.7	24.6	24.7	11.8	34.0	85.3	7.1	1.4	7.9	34.9
48 331	Milam	24,875	0.0	7.0	19.0	9.6	25.4	24.6	17.1	38.8	74.1	10.6	0.4	17.1	21.2
48 339	Montgomery	393,363	10.3	7.5	20.0	9.2	29.5	24.6	9.2	33.5	86.9	4.7	2.0	7.6	16.9
48 341	Moore	20,031	0.9	10.8	22.7	8.7	26.5	21.1	10.3	30.5	60.2	1.9	-	38.5	51.8
48 347	Nacogdoches	61,842	1.9	7.4	16.6	20.5	23.2	20.3	12.0	29.4	79.8	16.9	1.0	3.8	14.8
48 349	Navarro	48,942	2.2	7.1	19.0	10.5	27.7	21.8	13.9	34.9	72.2	17.1	-	12.4	21.1
48 355	Nueces	319,854	1.0	7.7	19.4	10.6	26.2	24.6	11.5	34.5	78.6	4.7	1.7	17.2	58.7
48 361	Orange	82,844	-1.1	6.3	18.2	9.3	25.8	26.3	14.0	37.9	88.6	9.2	1.1	2.8	4.4
48 363	Palo Pinto	27,377	0.2	6.7	18.2	8.4	25.7	25.3	15.6	38.9	87.9	3.1	-	9.7	15.9
48 365	Panola	22,990	0.6	6.0	16.8	11.1	22.8	26.3	17.1	39.9	79.8	17.8	-	3.3	5.3
48 367	Parker	104,935	7.2	6.1	18.3	10.0	28.7	25.9	10.9	36.2	92.8	2.6	0.7	5.5	9.1
48 373	Polk	46,221	0.8	5.7	16.0	9.4	26.7	22.3	19.9	38.7	83.4	13.1	-	5.2	10.6
48 375	Potter	120,603	0.9	9.2	19.5	9.5	29.0	21.2	11.5	32.4	70.3	10.5	2.6	19.1	32.2
48 381	Randall	111,339	2.9	6.5	18.2	12.6	26.4	25.6	10.7	34.6	89.8	2.7	1.6	8.2	13.6
48 397	Rockwall	68,025	18.9	8.0	19.8	9.4	30.7	23.6	8.5	33.0	85.3	5.7	2.9	8.0	14.9
48 401	Rusk	48,110	1.9	6.4	16.7	9.0	27.6	25.1	15.2	38.2	76.2	19.0	0.2	5.6	10.9
48 407	San Jacinto	24,517	1.9	5.6	17.7	9.2	24.5	26.4	16.6	40.1	84.9	12.5	-	3.8	7.1
48 409	San Patricio	68,550	-0.1	8.1	20.9	10.8	24.6	23.8	11.7	33.9	74.0	3.0	1.2	24.5	51.8
48 419	Shelby	26,242	1.8	7.7	18.7	8.7	27.2	22.3	15.5	36.0	74.9	18.0	-	6.3	14.5

STATE County	Percent foreign born	Total households	Household type (percent)						Percent of households with people under 18 years	Percent of households with people 60 years and over
			Family households				Nonfamily households			
			Total family households	Married-couple families	Male householder families	Female householder families	Total nonfamily households	One-person households		
ACS table number:	C05002	B11001	B11001	B11001	B11001	B11001	B11001	B11001	C11005	B11006
	15	16	17	18	19	20	21	22	23	24
Texas—Cont.										
Chambers	6.2	11,343	78.6	64.6	3.6	10.4	21.4	16.3	49.5	23.9
Cherokee	8.4	15,867	73.3	56.0	3.8	13.5	26.7	24.7	40.7	33.4
Collin	16.5	245,691	72.1	59.8	3.9	8.4	27.9	22.9	42.3	18.6
Colorado	7.0	7,614	68.5	52.7	4.7	11.1	31.5	26.5	33.1	39.1
Comal	5.9	36,583	74.7	62.3	4.1	8.3	25.3	19.4	37.0	33.5
Cooke	7.9	14,003	75.4	60.1	4.6	10.7	24.6	21.2	38.2	32.9
Coryell	5.4	19,236	75.8	58.5	2.9	14.4	24.2	21.6	47.5	22.0
Dallas	24.0	819,749	66.0	45.3	5.8	14.9	34.0	28.7	39.1	23.5
Denton	13.1	196,453	69.9	56.1	4.1	9.6	30.1	23.4	41.5	16.8
Ector	10.9	45,434	70.1	51.8	4.1	14.1	29.9	24.8	39.8	28.4
Ellis	7.4	45,019	77.3	62.0	4.2	11.1	22.7	19.4	44.0	27.1
El Paso	27.0	229,655	76.9	51.5	5.4	20.0	23.1	19.9	47.4	30.0
Erath	6.8	12,750	60.4	50.7	3.4	6.3	39.6	29.3	29.8	28.7
Fannin	4.1	11,499	74.6	60.4	3.4	10.8	25.4	23.1	37.8	37.2
Fayette	5.2	9,232	68.0	55.1	5.6	7.2	32.0	26.7	32.2	42.2
Fort Bend	22.6	133,209	83.2	66.4	4.9	11.9	16.8	14.3	50.3	22.4
Galveston	10.1	105,249	67.3	49.6	4.6	13.2	32.7	27.0	36.5	29.3
Gillespie	6.5	9,154	73.8	63.0	3.0	7.8	26.2	23.9	29.3	45.9
Gray	6.2	8,201	76.0	59.7	3.1	13.2	24.0	20.1	34.1	40.1
Grayson	5.2	43,845	69.5	52.5	4.5	12.5	30.5	25.8	34.5	35.2
Gregg	7.5	44,083	67.5	48.9	4.3	14.3	32.5	27.9	37.1	32.4
Grimes	6.7	7,479	72.1	55.2	2.4	14.4	27.9	24.1	34.5	34.5
Guadalupe	7.7	36,322	76.0	61.0	4.4	10.6	24.0	21.1	39.9	31.9
Hale	8.8	11,964	73.0	54.4	4.4	14.2	27.0	21.1	40.5	34.9
Hardin	1.3	18,469	75.2	59.6	3.3	12.3	24.8	19.4	37.5	30.9
Harris	24.4	1,323,191	68.7	48.6	5.6	14.5	31.3	26.0	41.0	22.9
Harrison	5.8	23,209	71.4	54.3	2.4	14.6	28.6	25.2	37.3	35.1
Hays	4.9	43,153	64.6	51.3	4.4	8.9	35.4	25.1	35.5	21.3
Henderson	5.6	29,987	74.8	56.2	4.9	13.7	25.2	22.5	35.1	39.1
Hidalgo	28.5	201,366	83.1	59.9	4.2	19.0	16.9	14.6	54.9	30.1
Hill	7.5	12,235	73.6	57.1	4.1	12.4	26.4	23.8	34.9	40.8
Hockley	6.5	8,170	75.9	60.8	2.4	12.7	24.1	22.0	40.6	34.1
Hood	5.5	17,460	71.0	56.5	4.7	9.7	29.0	23.3	31.7	43.4
Hopkins	7.7	12,497	74.6	56.2	6.4	12.1	25.4	22.4	39.1	31.4
Houston	5.7	8,041	67.0	45.7	4.5	16.8	33.0	30.5	33.9	43.6
Howard	15.5	11,247	67.3	48.1	7.5	11.6	32.7	29.0	37.5	35.4
Hunt	5.9	29,282	70.4	53.7	5.1	11.7	29.6	24.1	35.0	33.3
Hutchinson	7.1	8,796	73.2	57.5	3.9	11.8	26.8	23.6	37.2	37.2
Jasper	2.3	13,399	72.3	52.4	5.4	14.4	27.7	25.3	38.7	38.1
Jefferson	8.9	90,823	66.2	44.4	5.0	16.8	33.8	29.0	35.2	33.2
Jim Wells	3.6	13,192	76.4	51.1	5.7	19.5	23.6	21.7	44.5	36.3
Johnson	6.4	46,920	77.3	59.4	5.9	12.0	22.7	18.6	41.5	28.3
Kaufman	7.3	27,968	80.9	63.0	4.7	13.2	19.1	16.5	42.8	27.8
Kendall	7.6	11,129	73.6	60.2	4.3	9.1	26.4	20.6	38.1	33.6
Kerr	6.7	18,931	74.4	57.6	4.8	12.0	25.6	20.7	32.6	43.2
Kleberg	4.4	11,016	66.3	47.3	6.1	12.9	33.7	25.4	38.8	31.5
Lamar	4.8	18,622	71.7	54.6	2.8	14.3	28.3	25.6	35.0	37.5
Lampasas	5.8	6,890	73.3	60.3	2.0	11.0	26.7	23.4	38.2	32.4
Liberty	6.5	23,944	72.4	56.1	5.5	10.7	27.6	25.0	37.9	35.1
Limestone	8.0	7,929	72.2	50.1	6.7	15.3	27.8	24.4	37.9	40.1
Lubbock	3.7	99,875	64.3	46.9	4.6	12.8	35.7	26.9	34.4	26.2
McLennan	8.3	80,973	66.6	47.7	4.2	14.7	33.4	27.3	36.2	29.2
Matagorda	12.2	14,172	72.7	53.9	5.8	13.0	27.3	23.7	37.0	31.9
Maverick	34.0	12,938	80.6	60.4	5.0	15.1	19.4	18.3	52.0	34.9
Medina	5.0	12,809	77.9	66.6	2.7	8.6	22.1	18.8	39.4	39.8
Midland	8.7	46,331	69.4	54.6	3.3	11.4	30.6	26.3	38.6	28.2
Milam	6.5	9,419	69.4	57.6	5.2	6.5	30.6	26.8	34.3	37.3
Montgomery	10.9	132,350	76.3	61.3	4.6	10.4	23.7	20.0	42.0	26.0
Moore	21.3	6,607	80.3	61.2	5.7	13.4	19.7	18.7	54.8	28.7
Nacogdoches	7.8	22,619	61.6	46.9	3.4	11.3	38.4	29.8	31.1	30.1
Navarro	9.8	16,261	69.7	51.6	4.1	14.0	30.3	26.9	39.0	38.5
Nueces	7.4	115,713	69.6	47.1	6.5	16.0	30.4	25.0	38.1	30.1
Orange	1.6	32,448	74.3	55.4	4.1	14.8	25.7	21.9	35.8	34.3
Palo Pinto	6.4	10,324	67.6	50.8	5.8	11.0	32.4	29.0	34.6	35.8
Panola	1.7	8,568	71.1	57.6	2.4	11.0	28.9	25.9	34.3	38.8
Parker	3.6	34,787	78.5	63.7	5.1	9.7	21.5	18.3	39.9	30.7
Polk	5.3	16,632	68.5	50.0	4.3	14.2	31.5	26.2	31.8	42.9
Potter	11.5	41,868	65.8	44.4	5.2	16.2	34.2	29.1	37.1	29.4
Randall	3.6	42,577	67.7	54.4	3.7	9.6	32.3	25.8	36.0	25.4
Rockwall	8.3	22,417	82.7	70.1	3.4	9.2	17.3	12.2	48.3	24.3
Rusk	5.6	17,275	74.5	60.3	3.9	10.3	25.5	22.7	36.1	38.3
San Jacinto	2.9	8,385	73.3	57.4	3.8	12.1	26.7	22.3	32.4	42.4
San Patricio	4.0	23,450	75.3	56.6	5.6	13.2	24.7	22.3	42.3	32.2
Shelby	10.9	9,953	70.2	47.4	8.4	14.4	29.8	27.9	37.7	34.1

Table A-2. Counties — Who: Age, Race/Ethnicity, and Household Structure, 2005–2007—*Continued*

STATE County code	STATE County	Total population	Percent change 2005–2007	Population by age (percent)						Median age	Race alone or in combination (percent)				Percent Hispanic or Latino
				Under 5 years	5 to 17 years	18 to 24 years	25 to 44 years	45 to 64 years	65 years and over		White	Black	Asian Hawaiian or Pacific Islander	Amer. Indian, Alaska Native, or some other race	
	ACS table number:	B01003	Population estimates	B01001	B01001	B01001	B01001	B01001	B01001	B01002	B02008	B02009	B02011 + B02012	B02010 + B02013	C03002
		1	2	3	4	5	6	7	8	9	10	11	12	13	14
	Texas—Cont.														
48 423	Smith	194,613	4.4	7.6	18.1	10.3	26.4	23.3	14.2	35.2	72.9	18.7	1.0	8.9	14.6
48 427	Starr	60,751	3.6	12.1	24.5	11.3	24.5	17.7	9.9	26.0	60.5	-	0.5	38.9	-
48 439	Tarrant	1,668,042	6.1	8.5	19.6	9.4	31.0	23.1	8.4	33.2	70.2	14.2	4.8	12.7	24.6
48 441	Taylor	126,192	0.4	7.9	18.3	13.3	26.0	21.7	12.9	32.9	81.0	7.5	2.0	12.0	20.0
48 449	Titus	28,776	4.4	9.4	21.1	9.4	27.9	20.4	11.9	32.2	79.6	10.3	1.1	11.0	35.7
48 451	Tom Green	105,770	1.2	7.5	17.7	12.9	24.9	23.3	13.8	34.4	81.2	4.8	1.6	14.5	33.6
48 453	Travis	940,517	7.6	8.1	16.7	12.0	35.0	21.6	6.7	32.0	67.3	8.9	6.2	19.8	32.0
48 457	Tyler	20,284	0.8	5.2	14.7	7.9	25.8	28.6	17.7	40.8	83.0	15.0	-	1.4	-
48 459	Upshur	37,655	1.3	6.4	18.1	8.2	26.6	25.6	15.0	38.7	86.7	10.1	0.4	3.5	4.7
48 463	Uvalde	26,587	0.0	8.5	21.7	10.8	24.2	21.4	13.4	33.7	81.5	0.7	0.8	17.4	67.4
48 465	Val Verde	47,537	1.8	9.6	21.1	9.6	24.7	20.4	14.6	33.1	84.7	2.1	0.7	13.8	77.6
48 467	Van Zandt	51,785	1.2	6.1	17.6	8.4	25.4	24.7	17.7	39.8	93.2	3.8	-	3.5	8.9
48 469	Victoria	85,545	1.4	7.8	19.8	9.6	25.1	24.7	12.9	35.7	74.0	6.9	1.3	22.0	41.0
48 471	Walker	64,111	-0.8	4.7	12.1	20.9	31.6	21.4	9.4	33.0	68.5	23.8	1.3	8.0	15.3
48 473	Waller	35,207	3.9	7.5	17.6	17.3	25.1	22.9	9.6	30.2	69.3	26.4	1.1	5.0	23.2
48 477	Washington	31,774	1.8	6.6	15.3	12.6	23.6	24.8	17.0	38.5	78.3	18.1	1.6	2.9	11.4
48 479	Webb	227,578	5.0	13.0	24.2	11.3	26.4	17.1	8.0	26.2	75.6	0.6	0.6	24.4	94.7
48 481	Wharton	40,947	-0.1	8.0	19.1	9.9	24.6	24.9	13.6	36.5	70.2	15.4	0.8	14.7	34.8
48 485	Wichita	128,936	-1.2	7.2	17.9	13.1	26.8	22.4	12.6	33.6	81.2	11.1	2.9	7.2	14.2
48 489	Willacy	20,439	0.9	9.1	21.0	11.5	24.3	21.9	12.1	31.6	86.1	2.3	-	12.8	-
48 491	Williamson	352,134	12.4	8.3	20.4	8.9	32.3	21.8	8.2	33.1	82.5	6.7	4.6	9.0	20.3
48 493	Wilson	38,068	6.3	6.4	19.7	9.9	26.7	25.8	11.6	36.6	85.5	2.5	-	13.9	-
48 497	Wise	56,715	3.2	6.8	19.4	9.1	28.3	25.4	11.0	35.9	90.9	1.8	0.6	9.5	13.7
48 499	Wood	41,388	3.4	5.9	15.0	9.5	23.5	24.6	21.5	41.9	91.8	6.4	0.4	2.1	7.2
49 000	**Utah**	2,576,626	5.6	9.7	21.3	12.8	28.2	19.4	8.7	28.3	91.1	1.4	3.5	5.9	11.1
49 003	Box Elder	46,835	4.1	8.8	23.3	10.9	25.3	20.9	10.7	29.4	93.7	0.4	1.6	5.7	7.2
49 005	Cache	106,688	3.9	10.8	20.3	19.8	26.5	15.2	7.4	24.7	93.2	1.0	3.0	4.6	8.3
49 011	Davis	278,992	6.8	9.8	22.9	12.1	27.5	19.9	7.7	27.7	94.1	1.9	3.1	3.4	6.9
49 021	Iron	41,570	10.5	9.8	20.4	19.0	24.8	16.9	9.3	25.6	94.2	-	1.8	5.8	5.6
49 035	Salt Lake	987,913	4.8	9.1	20.3	10.9	30.0	21.4	8.4	30.5	87.6	-	5.3	7.3	15.1
49 039	Sanpete	24,145	3.6	8.0	22.4	16.3	23.8	18.6	11.0	27.1	94.4	-	2.2	4.5	8.1
49 043	Summit	35,092	2.3	7.0	19.3	10.3	28.6	28.6	6.1	34.6	96.2	0.7	1.5	2.4	11.0
49 045	Tooele	52,525	9.3	10.2	23.5	9.5	31.9	17.8	7.1	28.3	94.1	1.9	1.7	5.2	9.6
49 047	Uintah	27,972	7.6	8.7	21.7	10.9	26.6	22.2	9.9	29.6	88.2	-	1.0	11.4	-
49 049	Utah	470,154	6.3	11.7	22.6	17.8	27.4	14.2	6.3	24.2	93.5	0.8	2.9	4.8	8.8
49 051	Wasatch	19,747	9.3	9.3	21.7	10.2	30.1	19.5	9.2	29.6	98.2	-	0.4	1.4	-
49 053	Washington	126,775	12.2	9.2	19.7	11.4	26.9	15.7	17.1	29.6	93.5	0.8	2.5	4.4	7.1
49 057	Weber	217,641	3.6	9.0	20.9	10.9	28.2	20.9	10.2	30.0	93.4	1.9	2.1	4.2	15.0
50 000	**Vermont**	620,589	0.2	5.2	16.4	9.9	25.7	29.4	13.3	40.4	97.6	1.1	1.4	1.5	1.3
50 001	Addison	36,638	0.6	5.0	16.9	13.2	24.2	29.0	11.8	38.8	97.7	0.6	1.1	1.6	1.3
50 003	Bennington	36,529	-0.3	4.9	16.0	8.4	23.0	30.0	17.8	43.8	99.1	0.8	0.4	1.5	1.3
50 005	Caledonia	30,587	0.8	5.5	16.0	10.2	24.7	29.1	14.5	40.5	98.8	0.6	0.4	1.5	0.9
50 007	Chittenden	151,105	1.0	5.4	16.4	12.9	27.8	27.2	10.2	36.9	95.3	2.0	3.0	1.4	1.6
50 011	Franklin	47,754	0.8	6.4	19.3	7.4	28.8	27.1	11.1	38.1	98.3	0.7	0.5	2.3	0.9
50 015	Lamoille	24,588	0.8	5.5	16.8	10.2	26.8	28.2	12.4	38.3	98.4	0.8	0.7	1.2	1.0
50 017	Orange	29,028	0.1	5.0	16.7	9.0	25.2	30.6	13.5	41.5	99.1	0.5	0.7	1.3	0.9
50 019	Orleans	27,266	0.1	5.3	16.4	7.8	26.1	29.0	15.5	40.9	98.0	0.9	0.6	2.3	1.0
50 021	Rutland	63,332	-0.2	4.9	15.5	9.6	24.0	30.4	15.7	42.8	98.5	0.4	1.0	1.0	1.0
50 023	Washington	58,995	-0.2	5.4	15.7	9.7	25.4	30.3	13.6	41.0	98.6	0.9	1.0	1.5	1.6
50 025	Windham	43,624	-0.6	4.8	15.9	8.2	24.1	32.6	14.3	43.0	97.7	1.2	1.3	1.4	1.5
50 027	Windsor	57,098	-0.8	4.9	15.4	7.0	23.9	32.4	16.4	44.4	97.9	0.8	1.1	1.0	1.2
51 000	**Virginia**	7,636,644	2.0	6.7	17.2	10.0	28.8	25.7	11.6	36.8	72.4	20.5	5.4	3.7	6.3
51 001	Accomack	38,614	-0.7	5.3	18.0	7.1	26.8	26.6	16.3	38.8	67.9	29.5	0.4	3.6	8.3
51 003	Albemarle	91,927	2.9	5.6	16.4	14.0	26.5	25.2	12.3	36.0	84.0	10.4	5.2	2.0	3.6
51 009	Amherst	32,081	0.9	4.9	16.4	11.5	25.1	26.5	15.6	39.8	79.0	19.9	0.4	1.3	1.3
51 013	Arlington	201,798	2.4	6.4	11.3	7.4	40.6	25.2	9.1	36.9	73.1	8.8	10.0	10.6	16.2
51 015	Augusta	70,031	2.8	5.5	16.2	7.6	28.3	29.3	13.2	40.1	94.4	4.7	-	1.7	1.7
51 019	Bedford	65,561	3.8	5.4	16.6	7.9	26.8	30.3	13.1	41.4	91.5	7.2	0.9	1.1	1.1
51 023	Botetourt	31,801	1.5	4.8	15.9	7.9	25.5	31.9	14.0	42.7	93.3	5.7	0.9	0.7	0.2
51 027	Buchanan	24,182	-2.4	4.6	14.3	8.6	27.3	31.0	14.2	42.2	97.3	2.2	-	-	-
51 031	Campbell	52,444	1.7	5.6	16.5	8.1	27.9	27.4	14.4	39.9	85.7	14.4	1.0	2.1	1.1
51 033	Caroline	26,336	7.9	7.5	16.6	8.9	28.9	25.9	12.1	37.5	69.7	31.1	0.9	1.5	3.2
51 035	Carroll	29,144	-0.1	4.8	15.7	6.4	27.5	27.6	18.0	41.9	98.1	0.9	-	1.7	-
51 041	Chesterfield	293,265	4.7	6.5	19.3	10.1	27.7	28.7	7.7	36.0	74.7	21.6	3.4	1.9	5.0
51 047	Culpeper	43,945	9.0	7.1	17.6	8.5	32.4	23.3	11.0	35.6	80.0	17.2	1.9	3.5	6.7
51 053	Dinwiddie	25,452	2.2	5.6	17.5	8.6	28.2	28.5	11.6	39.5	66.7	32.9	0.5	-	1.5
51 059	Fairfax	1,006,576	0.5	6.9	17.8	8.3	27.7	30.2	9.2	38.6	69.4	9.9	16.9	5.9	13.3
51 061	Fauquier	65,417	3.2	5.7	19.3	8.6	26.9	28.7	10.9	38.7	88.3	9.5	1.6	2.6	5.0
51 065	Fluvanna	24,879	3.5	7.3	16.2	6.8	30.6	25.4	13.7	38.7	80.8	17.2	-	2.2	-
51 067	Franklin	50,430	2.7	5.5	15.5	8.9	26.5	28.5	15.0	41.4	89.8	9.3	-	1.1	-
51 069	Frederick	70,766	6.3	6.6	18.2	8.8	30.3	25.2	10.9	36.5	93.0	4.3	1.4	2.1	5.1

STATE County	Percent foreign born	Total households	Household type (percent) Family households Total family households	Married-couple families	Male householder families	Female householder families	Nonfamily households Total nonfamily households	One-person households	Percent of households with people under 18 years	Percent of households with people 60 years and over
ACS table number:	C05002	B11001	B11001	B11001	B11001	B11001	B11001	B11001	C11005	B11006
	15	16	17	18	19	20	21	22	23	24
Texas—Cont.										
Smith	8.4	69,168	69.5	52.7	4.0	12.9	30.5	26.3	35.8	33.9
Starr	33.6	14,980	83.9	63.2	4.2	16.5	16.1	14.8	52.3	37.5
Tarrant	15.5	591,745	69.2	51.4	4.8	13.0	30.8	25.5	40.1	23.0
Taylor	4.1	48,995	67.1	50.5	3.6	13.1	32.9	27.5	34.7	30.1
Titus	20.1	9,924	78.0	57.0	7.8	13.3	22.0	20.7	43.7	34.5
Tom Green	5.6	40,887	66.0	48.9	4.1	13.0	34.0	29.2	35.5	31.0
Travis	17.5	368,578	56.7	41.1	4.7	11.0	43.3	32.8	32.0	17.7
Tyler	2.2	8,267	71.3	57.6	1.4	12.3	28.7	25.7	31.8	42.0
Upshur	2.7	13,391	73.4	57.3	4.2	11.9	26.6	24.1	34.9	36.7
Uvalde	7.6	8,480	78.8	57.9	2.6	18.3	21.2	17.9	40.7	35.4
Val Verde	24.0	14,789	78.2	60.6	2.0	15.6	21.8	20.1	45.5	38.1
Van Zandt	4.6	18,991	75.9	62.0	3.4	10.4	24.1	21.7	40.9	37.4
Victoria	5.3	31,531	72.2	51.1	5.5	15.6	27.8	24.0	39.0	30.1
Walker	10.3	19,226	61.1	44.7	4.2	12.3	38.9	24.7	30.9	25.8
Waller	12.6	12,511	77.6	52.7	9.7	15.2	22.4	19.3	42.7	26.0
Washington	6.7	12,167	68.4	55.8	3.7	8.8	31.6	26.7	31.7	33.3
Webb	28.5	60,889	83.5	56.1	5.9	21.5	16.5	14.1	57.4	29.0
Wharton	6.6	15,031	70.7	53.5	6.1	11.1	29.3	25.9	38.5	33.1
Wichita	5.7	48,641	67.0	51.1	3.1	12.8	33.0	27.6	36.6	30.1
Willacy	15.3	5,836	80.5	58.0	3.6	18.9	19.5	16.8	47.2	35.3
Williamson	10.1	116,012	74.3	60.5	3.7	10.1	25.7	20.7	43.4	21.6
Wilson	4.9	11,502	80.5	67.1	3.7	9.7	19.5	16.8	43.3	29.8
Wise	6.8	17,829	79.0	63.5	5.1	10.4	21.0	17.9	40.4	32.8
Wood	3.6	15,054	75.6	60.9	6.6	8.2	24.4	20.1	32.4	44.0
Utah	8.0	812,604	75.5	62.2	4.0	9.2	24.5	19.3	43.2	25.2
Box Elder	3.0	14,789	83.1	71.5	4.2	7.4	16.9	15.3	44.9	28.1
Cache	6.8	31,340	76.4	67.1	2.2	7.2	23.6	16.1	44.5	22.6
Davis	4.3	84,524	81.7	69.3	3.5	8.9	18.3	15.6	47.5	22.7
Iron	3.0	13,774	74.8	63.2	3.6	8.0	25.2	15.7	42.5	23.7
Salt Lake	11.9	324,945	70.8	55.4	4.8	10.5	29.2	23.4	40.6	24.0
Sanpete	5.4	6,886	78.9	70.0	2.1	6.8	21.1	15.8	44.1	36.0
Summit	8.9	11,740	74.0	64.5	2.8	6.7	26.0	18.5	41.7	21.7
Tooele	3.3	15,980	81.1	66.1	4.3	10.6	18.9	14.4	53.8	21.7
Uintah	0.7	9,143	81.6	67.3	4.2	10.0	18.4	16.1	42.7	28.5
Utah	6.7	125,843	80.7	70.3	2.9	7.5	19.3	12.9	49.0	21.3
Wasatch	7.4	6,604	77.6	68.2	2.3	7.1	22.4	14.2	46.3	24.5
Washington	5.4	43,121	76.3	66.7	3.1	6.6	23.7	19.1	36.9	37.8
Weber	8.0	73,435	75.5	59.8	4.8	10.9	24.5	21.1	41.6	27.6
Vermont	3.7	250,871	64.0	49.5	4.5	10.1	36.0	27.9	31.0	31.6
Addison	3.7	13,463	68.0	54.3	5.3	8.4	32.0	24.7	32.3	32.2
Bennington	2.4	15,420	67.9	55.2	2.9	9.8	32.1	27.6	30.7	36.4
Caledonia	1.7	12,622	61.7	46.2	5.6	9.9	38.3	30.1	33.0	32.2
Chittenden	5.7	59,159	59.4	46.3	3.7	9.4	40.6	29.4	30.9	25.4
Franklin	2.9	18,219	71.5	54.2	5.1	12.2	28.5	22.5	36.1	29.1
Lamoille	3.9	10,072	63.1	46.8	6.2	10.1	36.9	28.2	31.7	30.7
Orange	1.9	11,544	67.0	54.4	4.1	8.5	33.0	26.2	29.7	32.0
Orleans	4.8	10,540	67.2	52.4	4.6	10.2	32.8	27.2	32.4	36.5
Rutland	1.8	25,987	63.4	48.1	5.5	9.8	36.6	28.6	27.8	36.1
Washington	3.8	24,371	62.6	47.8	3.7	11.1	37.4	28.5	30.0	31.9
Windham	3.1	18,847	61.3	45.1	5.1	11.1	38.7	31.2	31.6	35.4
Windsor	3.1	24,884	66.7	52.0	4.1	10.6	33.3	26.2	29.6	34.3
Virginia	10.1	2,909,223	67.0	50.8	4.1	12.1	33.0	27.3	34.2	29.4
Accomack	6.0	14,921	67.8	44.5	5.6	17.7	32.2	29.8	33.2	39.4
Albemarle	7.8	37,012	64.2	51.9	3.4	8.9	35.8	28.7	31.2	28.0
Amherst	1.8	12,728	69.8	51.0	4.1	14.7	30.2	25.4	34.2	36.1
Arlington	25.1	89,525	45.2	35.0	3.4	6.8	54.8	44.2	21.0	21.0
Augusta	1.1	27,368	73.9	59.4	4.8	9.7	26.1	23.2	33.0	34.1
Bedford	1.9	27,002	71.6	61.7	2.7	7.2	28.4	24.4	31.7	31.7
Botetourt	1.7	12,772	75.8	63.5	4.2	8.0	24.2	21.2	31.4	36.0
Buchanan	0.8	9,193	67.9	51.1	5.4	11.3	32.1	30.7	27.7	40.0
Campbell	1.8	21,802	68.9	51.7	3.5	13.7	31.1	25.7	32.6	33.6
Caroline	2.0	9,729	70.2	54.8	4.0	11.5	29.8	26.5	35.9	33.9
Carroll	1.3	12,746	70.6	58.8	4.2	7.6	29.4	26.3	31.0	36.8
Chesterfield	7.1	108,690	75.1	58.9	4.2	12.1	24.9	19.8	40.0	24.0
Culpeper	6.7	16,344	74.0	59.9	5.2	8.9	26.0	20.6	38.4	28.1
Dinwiddie	1.2	9,454	72.3	53.8	6.8	11.6	27.7	22.3	31.4	30.1
Fairfax	27.7	365,093	69.2	56.1	3.8	9.2	30.8	25.5	35.5	27.4
Fauquier	5.7	22,118	71.0	58.5	3.7	8.8	29.0	23.1	33.4	31.7
Fluvanna	2.5	9,332	69.5	56.3	1.6	11.7	30.5	24.0	29.7	33.2
Franklin	1.9	20,702	71.9	57.3	4.0	10.6	28.1	24.0	31.0	34.8
Frederick	4.6	26,544	72.9	57.6	5.1	10.2	27.1	20.5	39.8	28.6

STATE County code	STATE County	Total population	Percent change 2005–2007	Population by age (percent) Under 5 years	5 to 17 years	18 to 24 years	25 to 44 years	45 to 64 years	65 years and over	Median age	Race alone or in combination (percent) White	Black	Asian Hawaiian or Pacific Islander	Amer. Indian, Alaska Native, or some other race	Percent Hispanic or Latino
	ACS table number:	B01003	Population estimates	B01001	B01001	B01001	B01001	B01001	B01001	B01002	B02008	B02009	B02011 + B02012	B02010 + B02013	C03002
		1	2	3	4	5	6	7	8	9	10	11	12	13	14
	Virginia—Cont.														
51 073	Gloucester..................	37,780	2.8	5.6	17.1	8.5	26.8	29.3	12.7	41.1	87.1	10.7	1.3	2.0	2.1
51 075	Goochland.................	19,947	7.1	5.4	15.1	7.7	30.2	28.8	12.8	41.4	68.6	27.5	1.4	2.1	2.4
51 083	Halifax......................	35,622	-0.4	6.1	16.6	7.9	22.8	28.1	18.6	43.0	61.2	38.0	-	1.6	-
51 085	Hanover....................	97,857	2.5	5.9	18.5	9.4	25.8	28.7	11.6	39.1	88.5	10.3	1.5	1.2	1.4
51 087	Henrico....................	285,657	2.9	6.8	17.7	7.9	29.9	25.5	12.2	37.4	66.0	28.1	5.4	2.2	3.4
51 089	Henry......................	55,665	-0.5	5.3	15.3	8.1	26.3	28.2	16.9	41.9	72.5	22.9	0.6	5.2	5.9
51 093	Isle of Wight............	34,018	6.4	5.8	17.3	8.7	26.7	28.5	12.9	39.2	74.0	26.3	0.7	0.6	1.5
51 095	James City...............	59,345	6.9	5.0	15.9	9.0	27.3	24.9	17.8	40.5	82.4	14.4	2.4	2.5	2.8
51 099	King George	21,619	9.9	7.6	19.1	9.6	30.8	23.5	9.4	33.7	81.7	18.7	1.7	1.8	2.8
51 105	Lee	23,404	0.5	5.3	16.0	8.3	26.8	27.9	15.6	40.0	97.0	2.5	0.1	0.2	-
51 107	Loudoun...................	266,087	9.9	9.6	20.5	7.3	35.4	21.5	5.6	32.7	75.5	9.1	12.6	5.5	9.7
51 109	Louisa.....................	30,957	7.0	6.2	16.8	7.0	29.4	26.8	13.8	38.8	80.1	19.9	-	1.6	1.2
51 117	Mecklenburg............	32,013	0.4	5.9	14.7	7.8	26.0	25.9	19.5	42.0	61.4	38.6	0.5	-	1.8
51 121	Montgomery.............	88,146	2.4	4.6	11.4	31.7	26.0	17.6	8.8	25.9	89.8	4.6	5.8	1.1	2.0
51 137	Orange....................	31,374	8.0	6.4	15.9	8.7	27.8	24.3	17.0	39.9	84.2	14.6	1.3	-	1.4
51 139	Page.......................	23,953	1.7	5.5	15.9	7.3	28.4	26.9	16.0	41.2	97.1	2.8	0.5	-	1.4
51 143	Pittsylvania..............	60,940	-0.3	5.6	15.9	8.3	25.7	30.0	14.6	41.6	74.9	22.7	0.3	2.4	1.9
51 145	Powhatan.................	27,153	5.8	5.6	16.5	4.0	36.8	27.4	9.7	37.5	74.7	23.4	-	1.7	-
51 147	Prince Edward...........	21,074	2.6	3.7	14.9	25.7	22.1	19.7	13.8	30.4	64.1	36.3	0.4	0.3	-
51 149	Prince George...........	36,080	-1.3	4.1	17.5	17.9	29.9	23.8	6.7	33.6	60.6	35.5	2.8	2.0	6.4
51 153	Prince William..........	352,773	4.4	9.1	20.6	8.9	32.6	22.8	6.0	32.3	63.3	20.3	8.0	11.1	18.3
51 155	Pulaski....................	34,882	1.0	5.1	14.5	7.4	27.1	29.6	16.3	42.0	92.2	7.4	-	-	1.8
51 161	Roanoke...................	89,501	2.2	5.8	16.4	8.2	24.5	29.5	15.6	41.9	92.2	5.3	2.3	1.3	1.8
51 163	Rockbridge...............	21,312	1.6	6.0	14.8	7.9	25.0	29.0	17.3	42.4	95.4	4.3	-	-	-
51 165	Rockingham..............	72,551	2.6	6.0	17.3	9.3	26.8	26.8	14.0	39.2	96.2	2.5	0.7	1.9	4.4
51 167	Russell	28,677	0.8	5.1	15.7	7.7	27.1	29.2	15.2	41.5	98.6	1.0	-	-	-
51 169	Scott.......................	22,840	-0.1	5.2	14.4	7.3	26.3	28.1	18.7	42.6	97.8	2.1	-	0.6	-
51 171	Shenandoah	39,741	3.8	6.2	15.9	6.7	27.5	26.2	17.3	41.2	94.7	2.3	0.7	3.2	4.8
51 173	Smyth	32,189	-0.5	5.2	15.9	6.7	27.4	27.6	17.2	42.0	98.0	2.3	0.4	-	1.2
51 177	Spotsylvania.............	117,330	3.7	7.6	20.2	8.6	31.2	24.1	8.3	34.0	80.7	15.9	2.8	3.8	5.9
51 179	Stafford	118,551	3.6	7.2	21.3	10.1	31.3	24.3	5.9	33.1	76.1	17.5	3.9	5.7	7.4
51 185	Tazewell	43,885	-0.1	5.1	15.0	8.0	25.9	30.0	16.1	42.1	96.3	3.8	0.8	-	-
51 187	Warren	35,692	3.7	6.9	17.9	8.7	29.5	25.0	12.0	37.3	92.1	6.1	0.7	2.0	3.0
51 191	Washington	52,295	1.4	5.1	14.3	9.0	27.0	28.1	16.4	41.5	97.9	2.2	-	0.6	-
51 195	Wise	41,692	-0.2	6.0	14.7	11.2	28.0	26.7	13.4	37.1	93.9	5.5	0.4	1.1	-
51 197	Wythe.....................	28,332	1.4	5.7	15.4	7.1	28.0	27.1	16.8	41.3	95.8	3.9	0.6	-	-
51 199	York........................	61,016	0.8	5.0	19.3	10.3	25.9	28.4	11.1	38.7	80.1	14.3	4.7	2.5	3.9
51 510	Alexandria city	138,621	1.8	8.2	11.2	5.9	39.6	24.6	10.5	37.2	68.4	22.4	6.6	5.5	13.3
51 540	Charlottesville city........	41,015	1.0	5.6	11.0	25.3	27.5	17.5	13.1	28.9	71.9	22.4	5.3	3.1	3.3
51 550	Chesapeake city............	218,145	1.2	6.8	19.6	9.9	28.1	26.0	9.5	35.8	66.1	30.7	3.0	2.6	2.8
51 590	Danville city	45,307	-1.6	6.1	15.8	8.1	23.0	26.1	20.8	42.4	52.2	46.1	0.4	2.2	-
51 600	Fairfax city	22,743	6.0	5.4	14.2	9.2	29.3	27.6	14.2	40.6	75.1	6.6	16.1	5.4	13.3
51 630	Fredericksburg city	21,918	5.2	8.4	13.1	20.5	25.6	17.5	14.9	30.7	71.7	21.3	2.7	5.1	7.1
51 650	Hampton city.............	146,672	-0.4	6.5	16.8	12.6	29.3	23.7	11.1	35.1	48.1	48.3	2.7	3.1	3.5
51 660	Harrisonburg city........	43,430	3.2	5.7	10.6	39.1	20.6	15.0	9.0	22.6	87.7	7.0	4.8	2.1	12.7
51 670	Hopewell city	22,764	2.2	8.9	18.9	8.0	28.5	21.6	14.0	34.3	59.5	38.2	1.0	2.8	3.8
51 680	Lynchburg city...........	69,784	4.7	6.5	14.4	18.5	23.2	20.9	16.5	33.9	68.3	29.6	2.1	1.8	1.8
51 683	Manassas city............	36,133	-4.0	8.8	20.3	8.7	31.5	23.1	7.6	33.2	67.6	13.8	4.3	17.4	25.9
51 700	Newport News city........	180,079	-0.9	8.4	20.0	9.8	28.9	22.4	10.4	33.3	53.3	42.8	3.5	3.2	4.7
51 710	Norfolk city...............	237,309	-0.7	8.2	17.3	16.5	28.5	19.6	9.9	29.4	49.8	45.6	4.0	3.3	4.6
51 730	Petersburg city...........	32,672	1.4	8.2	16.8	9.0	25.7	24.2	16.1	38.4	20.8	77.4	1.5	0.3	2.6
51 740	Portsmouth city...........	101,856	1.1	7.9	18.1	11.5	26.7	22.7	13.0	34.4	45.6	52.7	1.9	2.3	2.4
51 760	Richmond city............	198,869	1.1	7.4	14.9	12.4	29.1	22.2	14.0	35.3	42.9	54.1	1.9	3.6	4.2
51 770	Roanoke city.............	92,475	0.2	6.1	16.6	6.7	28.5	25.2	17.0	39.9	70.4	27.7	1.5	2.3	2.3
51 775	Salem city.................	25,048	1.8	4.8	14.7	13.4	24.7	25.7	16.7	40.3	91.9	7.4	1.6	-	1.3
51 790	Staunton city	23,525	1.8	5.7	14.6	8.9	24.7	26.0	20.0	41.7	87.0	13.0	0.9	1.1	1.5
51 800	Suffolk city...............	79,849	4.3	7.7	19.3	9.1	29.7	23.6	10.7	34.9	55.3	41.5	1.8	2.6	2.3
51 810	Virginia Beach city.........	436,903	-0.8	7.0	19.0	9.4	30.7	24.1	9.8	35.2	73.0	21.0	6.8	2.6	5.4
51 820	Waynesboro city	21,407	2.5	7.3	17.4	6.1	25.3	25.1	18.8	40.7	85.3	11.8	0.5	3.8	4.6
51 840	Winchester city...........	25,744	0.4	7.4	15.1	10.7	28.5	21.9	16.3	35.7	82.3	12.3	2.0	4.0	10.6
53 000	**Washington**	6,371,390	3.2	6.5	17.5	9.4	28.7	26.4	11.6	36.8	83.8	4.4	8.5	7.1	9.1
53 003	Asotin.....................	21,027	0.9	6.4	16.3	8.9	24.2	26.1	18.0	40.5	98.4	1.2	-	1.8	-
53 005	Benton.....................	157,742	2.0	7.1	19.8	8.9	27.4	26.0	10.9	35.6	85.9	1.6	3.2	11.0	15.3
53 007	Chelan	70,029	2.8	6.5	18.7	9.4	23.9	26.1	15.4	38.6	92.2	1.1	1.2	7.9	22.0
53 009	Clallam	69,670	2.4	4.5	14.9	8.2	22.5	27.4	22.5	44.9	91.0	1.2	2.4	8.2	4.2
53 011	Clark.......................	409,306	4.4	7.0	19.5	8.4	29.7	25.3	10.2	35.1	90.5	2.7	5.4	5.0	6.2
53 015	Cowlitz....................	98,547	4.3	6.4	18.1	8.8	26.3	26.9	13.4	38.0	95.1	1.0	2.1	5.1	5.9
53 017	Douglas...................	35,287	5.1	7.1	19.9	9.6	25.3	24.7	13.4	35.7	80.5	0.8	1.9	20.5	23.5
53 021	Franklin...................	66,125	11.0	11.0	22.6	10.8	29.8	18.8	7.0	28.0	66.5	2.6	2.2	31.4	48.4
53 025	Grant......................	81,433	3.9	8.9	21.7	9.8	26.6	21.6	11.4	31.5	73.8	1.4	1.4	25.7	34.8
53 027	Grays Harbor	70,793	1.6	5.7	16.7	9.3	26.1	27.2	15.0	39.4	89.9	1.3	2.4	10.5	6.6
53 029	Island......................	80,622	2.1	5.9	16.7	10.3	24.8	24.6	17.7	39.2	90.9	2.7	6.4	3.5	4.3

Table A-2. Counties — Who: Age, Race/Ethnicity, and Household Structure, 2005–2007—*Continued*

STATE County	Percent foreign born	Total households	Household type (percent)						Percent of households with people under 18 years	Percent of households with people 60 years and over
			Family households				Nonfamily households			
			Total family households	Married-couple families	Male householder families	Female householder families	Total nonfamily households	One-person households		
ACS table number:	C05002	B11001	B11001	B11001	B11001	B11001	B11001	B11001	C11005	B11006
	15	16	17	18	19	20	21	22	23	24
Virginia—Cont.										
Gloucester	1.6	14,379	76.1	57.6	7.9	10.6	23.9	19.3	38.9	28.7
Goochland	2.8	7,027	88.1	83.4	1.6	3.0	11.9	8.8	27.5	35.0
Halifax	1.3	14,467	67.2	47.2	4.2	15.8	32.8	30.9	31.1	42.6
Hanover	2.5	35,484	78.7	65.1	3.8	9.8	21.3	17.5	39.7	30.4
Henrico	9.7	116,621	64.1	46.5	3.4	14.2	35.9	29.8	34.5	26.9
Henry	4.7	22,956	68.5	49.8	4.4	14.4	31.5	28.3	29.9	39.5
Isle of Wight	1.5	13,576	75.0	59.0	4.6	11.4	25.0	21.6	35.9	32.5
James City	5.8	24,569	72.0	61.7	2.2	8.1	28.0	22.5	32.7	35.6
King George	2.2	7,693	75.6	60.0	3.5	12.1	24.4	17.4	44.7	25.7
Lee	0.2	9,413	67.6	51.4	4.0	12.2	32.4	29.9	26.9	42.0
Loudoun	19.2	85,657	70.0	60.7	2.6	6.7	30.0	25.9	42.4	16.9
Louisa	2.1	12,783	68.6	54.8	2.9	10.9	31.4	26.7	36.2	31.0
Mecklenburg	1.5	12,755	68.7	48.1	3.7	16.9	31.3	29.5	32.6	40.9
Montgomery	6.9	32,106	55.6	45.3	2.4	7.8	44.4	28.0	26.0	22.2
Orange	3.8	12,114	69.4	55.4	3.1	10.8	30.6	26.3	29.9	36.9
Page	1.8	9,755	66.9	48.7	5.4	12.8	33.1	30.1	31.1	36.2
Pittsylvania	1.9	25,419	71.8	56.8	3.2	11.8	28.2	25.6	32.1	35.8
Powhatan	1.6	-	-	-	-	-	-	-	-	-
Prince Edward	3.1	6,721	62.8	45.2	3.1	14.5	37.2	30.4	26.8	34.5
Prince George	5.2	10,532	81.4	62.1	5.9	13.4	18.6	15.3	43.2	23.5
Prince William	20.0	121,993	76.6	58.2	5.8	12.6	23.4	18.3	46.3	20.4
Pulaski	1.0	14,887	65.0	48.7	5.4	10.9	35.0	30.4	25.8	36.5
Roanoke	4.3	36,831	65.5	54.5	3.2	7.8	34.5	30.8	30.2	33.8
Rockbridge	2.0	9,296	69.3	55.0	5.0	9.2	30.7	23.7	31.3	37.5
Rockingham	4.1	28,507	74.1	60.1	5.7	8.3	25.9	23.0	36.1	32.7
Russell	0.8	12,224	70.5	58.9	2.4	9.2	29.5	24.9	33.7	36.6
Scott	-	10,057	65.7	53.2	3.6	8.9	34.3	29.3	30.7	38.5
Shenandoah	4.2	16,749	66.8	53.4	4.5	8.9	33.2	26.9	31.7	38.5
Smyth	1.6	13,355	69.0	50.3	6.4	12.3	31.0	27.0	28.7	40.4
Spotsylvania	5.8	40,856	76.3	60.0	5.3	11.1	23.7	17.9	44.4	23.9
Stafford	8.4	38,866	80.2	64.6	5.0	10.6	19.8	16.1	47.9	20.7
Tazewell	0.8	17,756	71.1	55.2	3.6	12.3	28.9	25.8	29.3	37.4
Warren	2.9	13,470	69.1	53.7	5.1	10.4	30.9	25.2	36.9	29.9
Washington	0.8	22,136	70.7	55.3	3.5	11.8	29.3	24.4	31.0	35.4
Wise	0.9	16,025	68.9	54.8	3.8	10.3	31.1	27.6	31.5	32.8
Wythe	0.9	11,986	70.5	56.4	3.9	10.1	29.5	22.8	31.5	34.8
York	6.8	22,816	78.2	66.0	2.6	9.6	21.8	17.2	39.6	28.8
Alexandria city	25.3	62,309	44.8	33.5	3.8	7.6	55.2	46.7	19.9	22.4
Charlottesville city	10.6	16,694	42.2	26.5	2.5	13.3	57.8	43.4	21.5	27.9
Chesapeake city	3.8	77,808	75.3	56.2	4.5	14.6	24.7	21.3	42.1	27.8
Danville city	1.8	19,972	59.8	35.0	3.7	21.1	40.2	35.6	29.9	39.9
Fairfax city	28.9	8,311	61.9	46.7	6.0	9.2	38.1	30.2	26.4	33.3
Fredericksburg city	6.2	8,560	48.9	31.1	4.8	13.0	51.1	42.3	26.6	35.1
Hampton city	4.7	54,650	62.5	42.7	3.7	16.1	37.5	30.6	33.6	27.8
Harrisonburg city	13.3	13,920	45.9	33.1	5.5	7.3	54.1	32.7	21.1	24.1
Hopewell city	3.0	8,740	60.4	34.0	6.2	20.2	39.6	33.6	26.9	31.6
Lynchburg city	3.6	25,903	59.5	40.2	3.4	15.9	40.5	33.9	28.8	36.4
Manassas city	23.2	11,703	77.4	56.6	6.2	14.6	22.6	18.1	50.4	24.7
Newport News city	6.2	73,274	65.5	42.4	5.3	17.8	34.5	29.6	36.2	26.0
Norfolk city	5.6	85,129	59.9	36.0	4.7	19.3	40.1	32.3	33.1	26.2
Petersburg city	2.3	12,447	58.2	30.3	6.3	21.5	41.8	33.4	28.0	38.3
Portsmouth city	1.9	38,848	63.6	38.5	5.3	19.7	36.4	31.4	33.4	31.6
Richmond city	5.5	81,611	48.7	25.5	4.2	19.1	51.3	42.6	25.9	31.3
Roanoke city	4.4	41,822	55.7	36.6	4.4	14.8	44.3	37.4	26.8	34.1
Salem city	3.7	9,680	65.1	45.0	6.0	14.2	34.9	29.7	30.5	37.9
Staunton city	2.5	9,712	57.6	41.6	3.7	12.2	42.4	36.0	27.8	35.4
Suffolk city	3.1	29,858	76.8	56.1	3.5	17.2	23.2	18.8	43.8	27.8
Virginia Beach city	8.4	161,814	69.5	52.2	3.8	13.4	30.5	23.9	38.3	25.3
Waynesboro city	2.5	8,595	62.3	46.2	4.0	12.0	37.7	31.1	27.7	35.4
Winchester city	10.4	10,026	55.8	39.1	3.9	12.8	44.2	35.8	26.3	35.3
Washington	12.2	2,472,477	64.5	49.9	4.4	10.2	35.5	28.1	33.1	28.7
Asotin	1.9	8,561	65.1	51.0	3.4	10.8	34.9	29.4	30.6	38.2
Benton	10.1	56,720	69.3	53.7	5.3	10.3	30.7	25.7	36.0	29.3
Chelan	13.1	25,901	69.6	55.2	3.8	10.6	30.4	25.8	33.8	38.1
Clallam	4.5	30,593	65.9	51.2	5.5	9.2	34.1	28.0	26.4	44.5
Clark	9.6	147,270	69.6	53.5	4.9	11.1	30.4	24.2	38.6	27.0
Cowlitz	4.4	37,931	69.2	51.5	5.2	12.5	30.8	25.5	36.1	32.3
Douglas	15.0	13,177	71.2	56.5	3.5	11.2	28.8	22.0	39.9	33.0
Franklin	25.3	19,766	78.1	60.1	7.4	10.6	21.9	17.6	52.1	23.0
Grant	17.7	27,484	73.6	58.0	4.3	11.3	26.4	21.7	40.8	30.7
Grays Harbor	4.9	27,786	65.4	48.3	5.5	11.7	34.6	27.3	31.1	37.3
Island	6.7	30,360	70.2	58.3	3.0	9.0	29.8	24.2	30.5	40.2

STATE County code	STATE County	Total population	Percent change 2005–2007	Population by age (percent)						Median age	Race alone or in combination (percent)					Percent Hispanic or Latino
				Under 5 years	5 to 17 years	18 to 24 years	25 to 44 years	45 to 64 years	65 years and over		White	Black	Asian Hawaiian or Pacific Islander	Amer. Indian, Alaska Native, or some other race	
	ACS table number:	B01003	Population estimates	B01001	B01001	B01001	B01001	B01001	B01001	B01002	B02008	B02009	B02011 + B02012	B02010 + B02013	C03002
		1	2	3	4	5	6	7	8	9	10	11	12	13	14
	Washington—Cont.														
53 031	Jefferson	28,880	2.8	3.5	13.1	7.0	20.8	32.8	22.9	48.6	93.5	0.6	2.2	5.5	2.6
53 033	King	1,832,835	3.0	6.2	15.5	8.4	31.4	27.9	10.6	38.1	76.3	7.0	15.5	5.3	7.2
53 035	Kitsap	238,449	-1.3	6.1	17.9	9.0	26.9	28.3	11.8	38.3	89.0	3.7	7.6	4.9	4.7
53 037	Kittitas	37,924	3.5	4.8	13.4	24.3	23.5	22.6	11.4	29.5	91.5	0.4	4.7	5.8	6.3
53 039	Klickitat	19,780	3.4	6.1	16.7	7.0	24.1	29.9	16.2	43.0	90.0	-	2.0	9.7	9.0
53 041	Lewis	72,699	2.7	6.2	17.6	9.0	24.8	26.6	15.9	39.5	95.2	0.8	1.1	5.8	7.0
53 045	Mason	54,864	5.8	5.5	16.0	8.5	26.5	26.4	17.0	40.0	91.0	1.5	2.4	7.8	6.0
53 047	Okanogan	39,325	1.4	6.3	17.8	9.1	22.8	28.2	15.8	40.4	78.1	0.7	1.1	22.2	15.6
53 049	Pacific	21,385	1.1	4.4	14.5	7.4	21.4	29.3	23.0	47.1	90.8	-	2.5	9.0	6.5
53 053	Pierce	762,223	3.1	6.9	18.7	9.4	29.5	25.1	10.4	35.4	81.8	8.8	9.2	5.5	7.0
53 057	Skagit	114,372	3.7	6.3	17.7	9.5	26.4	25.4	14.7	37.5	87.4	1.1	2.8	10.1	13.7
53 061	Snohomish	664,020	4.0	6.6	18.8	8.6	29.8	26.7	9.4	36.4	85.7	3.1	9.6	5.7	6.6
53 063	Spokane	448,018	3.6	6.3	17.4	10.7	27.4	25.7	12.5	36.1	93.7	2.6	3.5	3.8	3.6
53 065	Stevens	41,321	2.5	5.7	17.9	9.3	21.4	30.7	14.9	41.6	92.3	0.2	1.3	8.7	2.3
53 067	Thurston	233,113	4.8	5.8	16.8	9.7	28.3	27.6	11.9	37.5	87.4	3.7	7.1	5.5	5.5
53 071	Walla Walla	57,541	0.7	6.4	16.5	14.0	25.6	22.8	14.7	35.2	87.8	2.2	2.2	10.3	17.6
53 073	Whatcom	189,110	4.0	5.6	16.3	14.3	26.8	24.9	12.1	35.0	90.1	1.4	4.7	5.9	6.2
53 075	Whitman	41,344	-0.4	4.6	11.7	33.9	23.4	17.4	9.0	24.9	88.1	2.6	9.1	3.2	3.8
53 077	Yakima	230,907	1.9	9.0	21.8	9.4	26.1	22.5	11.3	32.3	76.3	1.3	1.8	22.8	39.9
54 000	**West Virginia**	1,808,787	0.4	5.8	15.7	9.0	26.2	27.9	15.4	40.3	95.5	3.9	0.9	1.0	1.0
54 003	Berkeley	96,396	7.7	7.2	18.7	7.6	31.1	24.7	10.6	35.7	92.5	6.8	0.9	2.1	2.9
54 005	Boone	25,231	-0.5	6.1	16.3	7.0	27.5	29.6	13.6	40.4	98.8	1.4	-	-	-
54 009	Brooke	23,945	-2.5	4.8	14.5	9.3	22.9	29.7	18.9	43.6	98.1	1.0	1.4	1.2	-
54 011	Cabell	94,412	0.0	6.0	14.3	13.0	25.2	25.3	16.1	38.1	93.9	5.4	1.1	1.0	0.8
54 019	Fayette	46,348	0.0	6.1	15.3	9.0	25.5	28.0	16.0	40.7	93.6	5.6	0.8	1.0	0.8
54 025	Greenbrier	34,573	0.1	5.7	15.2	7.7	24.4	29.0	18.0	43.4	95.4	4.1	-	1.2	-
54 027	Hampshire	22,189	3.9	5.4	17.4	7.7	27.2	28.0	14.3	39.3	98.2	-	-	1.5	-
54 029	Hancock	30,599	-2.6	5.4	14.9	6.3	24.6	30.3	18.6	44.3	97.1	2.9	-	0.5	-
54 033	Harrison	68,282	0.2	5.9	16.2	8.0	25.3	28.1	16.5	41.4	97.5	2.1	0.9	0.4	1.1
54 035	Jackson	28,147	0.6	5.9	16.6	7.3	26.3	26.8	17.1	41.3	99.1	-	0.9	-	-
54 037	Jefferson	49,695	4.7	6.7	18.1	8.7	28.7	27.0	10.9	37.5	90.9	7.5	1.2	2.3	3.4
54 039	Kanawha	192,057	-0.9	6.1	15.2	7.3	25.7	29.3	16.5	42.0	91.1	8.3	1.4	0.7	1.3
54 043	Lincoln	22,331	-0.1	6.3	16.5	7.3	29.1	27.0	13.9	38.5	99.6	-	-	1.2	-
54 045	Logan	35,713	-0.4	6.3	15.4	7.2	27.4	29.4	14.3	40.8	96.6	2.8	0.6	0.5	0.6
54 047	McDowell	23,392	-3.4	6.1	15.2	7.2	23.7	31.7	16.1	43.6	88.0	11.7	-	-	-
54 049	Marion	56,548	0.6	5.4	14.6	10.6	25.7	26.8	16.8	40.5	95.9	4.0	0.6	0.6	0.8
54 051	Marshall	33,519	-2.2	5.0	16.0	7.6	24.2	30.6	16.6	42.6	99.1	0.9	0.4	0.6	0.8
54 053	Mason	25,557	-0.1	5.6	15.7	7.3	26.5	28.4	16.5	41.5	99.2	1.6	-	0.9	-
54 055	Mercer	61,238	0.2	5.9	15.4	8.1	25.5	27.8	17.3	41.2	93.0	6.2	0.7	1.1	0.6
54 057	Mineral	26,761	-0.5	5.5	15.8	9.5	25.4	29.2	14.5	40.3	96.7	3.5	0.3	0.3	-
54 059	Mingo	26,742	-0.1	7.0	15.4	7.9	27.6	29.3	12.7	39.4	96.3	3.3	-	-	-
54 061	Monongalia	86,881	1.4	5.3	12.6	24.5	25.8	21.6	10.3	30.0	93.0	4.3	2.8	1.3	1.4
54 067	Nicholas	26,152	0.2	5.5	15.4	7.7	26.2	29.0	16.3	41.6	99.6	-	-	-	-
54 069	Ohio	44,660	-1.2	5.3	15.1	10.3	22.0	28.6	18.8	43.4	94.8	4.5	1.3	0.3	0.7
54 077	Preston	30,066	1.5	5.4	15.9	7.7	27.5	28.3	15.3	40.5	97.9	1.8	-	0.5	-
54 079	Putnam	54,440	2.1	6.1	17.4	7.6	27.0	29.1	12.7	39.8	98.0	1.8	0.4	0.1	-
54 081	Raleigh	78,843	0.7	5.6	15.2	7.8	27.0	28.3	16.0	40.8	90.3	8.7	1.0	1.0	1.1
54 083	Randolph	28,341	-0.3	6.0	15.7	7.8	27.5	27.7	15.4	41.0	98.6	1.1	0.5	-	-
54 097	Upshur	23,460	0.5	5.9	15.5	12.0	24.3	26.9	15.4	39.6	98.1	0.9	0.7	0.9	0.6
54 099	Wayne	41,558	-1.7	5.4	16.6	7.9	27.5	27.7	15.0	39.4	99.2	-	0.5	0.6	-
54 107	Wood	86,342	-0.7	5.7	16.2	7.5	26.2	28.3	16.1	41.3	98.0	1.2	1.3	1.0	0.9
54 109	Wyoming	23,903	-1.9	5.7	15.1	7.0	25.3	32.7	14.2	42.8	99.0	0.8	0.6	-	-
55 000	**Wisconsin**	5,571,593	1.1	6.4	17.4	9.9	27.1	26.1	13.1	37.7	88.7	6.4	2.3	4.0	4.7
55 001	Adams	20,654	0.0	4.2	13.5	6.4	28.1	27.4	20.3	44.0	93.4	3.6	1.1	2.4	3.0
55 005	Barron	45,652	0.0	5.8	16.2	8.9	25.1	27.1	17.1	41.4	97.7	0.7	0.6	2.0	1.3
55 009	Brown	240,801	1.9	6.8	18.0	9.7	29.0	25.4	11.0	36.2	89.9	2.3	2.7	6.8	5.5
55 015	Calumet	44,225	0.5	7.2	19.1	8.0	29.2	26.1	10.4	36.6	95.9	0.4	2.7	1.6	1.9
55 017	Chippewa	59,862	1.8	6.3	16.9	9.2	27.6	25.9	14.1	38.3	98.0	0.6	1.0	1.0	0.7
55 019	Clark	33,557	-0.4	7.9	20.0	8.2	24.4	23.8	15.7	36.7	98.2	0.4	0.5	1.5	1.7
55 021	Columbia	54,949	1.2	6.0	16.8	8.1	27.4	27.3	14.4	39.6	97.0	1.3	0.6	1.7	1.9
55 025	Dane	469,709	3.0	6.3	15.7	13.2	30.4	24.9	9.4	34.7	88.9	5.2	4.9	3.1	4.6
55 027	Dodge	87,633	0.7	5.5	16.0	8.8	29.6	26.2	13.8	38.6	95.5	3.2	0.2	2.0	3.2
55 029	Door	27,965	-0.9	4.3	14.6	6.7	22.8	31.3	20.4	45.7	97.5	0.9	0.5	1.8	0.5
55 031	Douglas	43,803	-0.4	5.7	16.6	9.8	26.2	27.5	14.2	39.1	96.2	1.4	0.5	2.4	0.9
55 033	Dunn	42,068	1.5	5.8	15.4	19.7	25.1	22.9	11.2	32.0	96.5	0.6	1.4	1.4	1.1
55 035	Eau Claire	96,364	2.1	5.9	15.8	16.6	25.8	23.6	12.2	33.5	95.7	1.1	3.1	1.2	1.2
55 039	Fond du Lac	98,755	0.7	5.8	17.3	9.6	26.8	26.2	14.3	38.6	95.9	1.5	1.1	2.9	3.1
55 043	Grant	48,890	-0.6	5.8	15.3	15.3	22.8	24.7	16.2	37.9	97.9	1.3	0.7	0.7	0.7
55 045	Green	35,311	2.6	6.3	17.7	8.1	26.3	27.2	14.4	39.9	99.0	0.6	0.5	1.1	1.3
55 049	Iowa	23,496	0.7	6.6	17.9	8.0	26.6	27.7	13.2	39.6	98.6	0.6	0.6	0.8	0.7
55 055	Jefferson	79,449	1.9	6.5	16.6	10.5	28.0	25.9	12.5	37.7	97.8	0.6	0.7	2.1	5.3
55 057	Juneau	26,513	0.4	5.9	17.3	7.9	26.5	26.2	16.3	40.0	94.6	2.3	0.9	3.1	2.0

STATE County	Percent foreign born	Total households	Household type (percent)						Percent of households with people under 18 years	Percent of households with people 60 years and over
			Family households				Nonfamily households			
			Total family households	Married-couple families	Male householder families	Female householder families	Total nonfamily households	One-person households		
ACS table number:	C05002	B11001	B11001	B11001	B11001	B11001	B11001	B11001	C11005	B11006
	15	16	17	18	19	20	21	22	23	24
Washington—Cont.										
Jefferson	5.2	12,778	60.5	53.0	2.2	5.3	39.5	32.9	21.5	47.1
King	19.0	753,780	58.5	45.7	3.9	8.9	41.5	32.7	29.7	25.8
Kitsap	6.2	91,579	67.8	54.4	4.2	9.3	32.2	25.6	32.9	30.1
Kittitas	5.9	15,669	56.5	46.1	3.5	7.0	43.5	28.4	26.3	28.4
Klickitat	6.8	8,193	65.0	51.7	4.5	8.9	35.0	28.9	26.9	39.8
Lewis	4.5	27,791	69.5	54.5	5.6	9.4	30.5	25.0	33.6	37.1
Mason	4.3	19,909	63.4	52.8	1.7	8.9	36.6	31.4	27.5	37.4
Okanogan	8.5	15,689	67.0	50.3	6.1	10.6	33.0	27.7	30.7	38.4
Pacific	7.7	9,752	66.5	52.2	3.3	11.0	33.5	27.3	29.1	41.3
Pierce	8.7	285,724	66.9	49.3	5.2	12.4	33.1	26.3	36.0	27.3
Skagit	10.9	42,982	67.9	52.2	4.5	11.2	32.1	25.2	33.2	35.7
Snohomish	12.7	255,031	67.2	52.4	4.8	10.1	32.8	25.4	35.6	25.1
Spokane	4.7	178,952	63.2	48.4	4.2	10.6	36.8	29.6	32.2	29.2
Stevens	2.9	15,459	72.8	58.8	5.4	8.6	27.2	23.0	32.4	38.5
Thurston	7.1	91,918	67.2	51.6	3.6	12.0	32.8	25.5	35.0	28.7
Walla Walla	9.4	20,817	64.6	48.9	3.2	12.6	35.4	28.4	33.9	31.9
Whatcom	11.7	74,831	61.5	50.4	3.1	8.1	38.5	27.6	30.3	28.6
Whitman	10.0	15,772	51.6	44.9	1.3	5.4	48.4	32.9	23.9	22.6
Yakima	18.4	76,698	77.7	53.3	6.5	12.9	27.3	21.6	43.1	30.9
West Virginia	1.3	738,943	67.2	52.1	4.1	10.9	32.8	28.0	30.3	35.4
Berkeley	2.9	37,329	67.8	52.3	5.2	10.3	32.2	25.7	36.8	26.1
Boone	0.3	10,317	71.4	59.1	4.5	7.8	28.6	26.0	31.3	31.7
Brooke	1.0	9,953	68.4	54.0	3.3	11.2	31.6	28.8	28.6	40.3
Cabell	1.6	39,236	61.7	46.1	3.9	11.6	38.3	31.8	26.8	35.4
Fayette	0.6	18,848	67.0	50.5	3.6	13.0	33.0	28.9	29.9	38.6
Greenbrier	0.5	15,342	65.7	49.4	4.6	11.6	34.3	28.2	28.7	39.0
Hampshire	1.3	8,364	70.8	55.5	4.0	11.3	29.2	25.4	29.2	38.0
Hancock	1.1	13,588	67.0	51.1	5.5	10.5	33.0	29.3	30.1	37.5
Harrison	1.0	28,028	69.0	54.2	3.5	11.3	31.0	27.2	30.6	38.5
Jackson	0.9	11,363	76.1	61.6	5.1	9.4	23.9	18.3	35.9	34.2
Jefferson	2.9	18,704	71.6	57.5	5.7	8.4	28.4	21.9	35.5	31.9
Kanawha	1.6	82,401	63.0	47.3	3.3	12.4	37.0	32.3	27.0	35.9
Lincoln	-	8,601	71.0	55.7	5.1	10.2	29.0	25.6	36.2	33.5
Logan	0.5	14,894	73.6	49.8	5.6	18.1	26.4	22.7	32.7	35.1
McDowell	0.6	9,296	66.7	47.0	4.0	15.7	33.3	31.5	28.3	36.4
Marion	1.0	22,813	64.7	50.0	3.4	11.3	35.3	28.5	27.0	35.9
Marshall	0.8	14,102	67.4	52.4	4.5	10.5	32.6	28.9	32.1	35.8
Mason	0.6	11,038	68.8	51.0	5.5	12.4	31.2	26.9	35.3	36.5
Mercer	1.3	25,606	64.7	48.6	4.6	11.4	35.3	30.9	29.4	39.0
Mineral	0.9	11,065	72.8	58.3	5.6	8.9	27.2	21.5	34.7	33.4
Mingo	-	11,408	69.2	53.5	4.7	11.0	30.8	26.9	32.0	32.6
Monongalia	4.3	31,378	55.8	44.6	3.4	7.8	44.2	34.8	26.5	24.7
Nicholas	-	10,149	73.3	62.6	4.7	6.0	26.7	25.4	29.3	41.4
Ohio	2.0	20,037	61.1	47.2	2.4	11.4	38.9	34.1	26.9	35.6
Preston	0.8	11,543	72.4	57.5	2.9	12.0	27.6	22.6	32.7	37.7
Putnam	0.8	21,090	77.4	64.3	3.8	9.3	22.6	19.5	36.4	30.2
Raleigh	1.2	31,642	67.6	48.9	5.6	13.1	32.4	28.6	30.2	36.6
Randolph	1.4	11,336	67.2	53.5	2.9	10.8	32.8	27.5	30.7	38.0
Upshur	1.1	9,547	66.3	56.0	3.4	7.0	33.7	27.0	29.3	37.9
Wayne	0.7	16,639	72.6	57.5	3.3	11.8	27.4	25.1	35.2	37.0
Wood	1.3	37,005	66.0	50.7	4.0	11.3	34.0	28.6	28.9	34.9
Wyoming	0.9	9,823	72.6	58.0	5.0	9.7	27.4	24.8	30.8	34.2
Wisconsin	4.3	2,235,246	65.2	51.3	4.2	9.7	34.8	28.3	32.2	29.5
Adams	3.1	9,306	68.6	54.5	5.7	8.4	31.4	26.1	27.3	39.7
Barron	1.6	19,590	65.5	51.5	3.3	10.7	34.5	28.3	28.9	33.4
Brown	5.0	95,165	65.8	50.7	4.5	10.6	34.2	27.6	35.7	25.5
Calumet	3.2	17,364	72.2	64.8	1.8	5.6	27.8	20.5	37.8	24.0
Chippewa	0.9	23,435	70.7	59.0	3.5	8.2	29.3	23.7	34.4	31.1
Clark	1.7	12,518	70.2	60.0	4.8	5.4	29.8	26.2	34.6	35.8
Columbia	2.6	22,304	68.1	56.0	4.5	7.6	31.9	26.5	29.8	32.4
Dane	7.1	187,852	58.4	47.7	3.4	7.3	41.6	31.2	29.8	22.3
Dodge	1.9	33,596	70.1	56.6	4.5	9.0	29.9	25.1	33.7	31.0
Door	1.6	13,464	66.1	54.4	5.9	5.8	33.9	29.1	26.0	39.2
Douglas	1.4	18,244	64.3	48.4	4.8	11.1	35.7	29.5	30.4	33.4
Dunn	2.2	15,439	65.8	54.7	4.9	6.2	34.2	23.8	31.7	26.7
Eau Claire	2.5	38,661	61.3	48.5	4.0	8.9	38.7	29.6	29.9	27.9
Fond du Lac	2.5	39,184	66.5	54.1	4.6	7.9	33.5	27.9	31.1	30.5
Grant	1.1	19,093	64.7	54.7	2.9	7.1	35.3	28.5	28.9	34.8
Green	1.5	14,591	66.1	54.4	3.9	7.9	33.9	27.7	31.5	30.4
Iowa	1.2	9,555	70.3	57.7	5.3	7.3	29.7	24.6	33.5	30.1
Jefferson	3.5	30,801	70.5	58.9	4.3	7.3	29.5	24.4	34.1	31.2
Juneau	1.8	11,103	67.4	53.3	4.1	10.0	32.6	23.9	32.7	33.9

Table A-2. Counties — Who: Age, Race/Ethnicity, and Household Structure, 2005–2007—*Continued*

STATE County code	STATE County	Total population	Percent change 2005–2007	Population by age (percent)						Median age	Race alone or in combination (percent)				Percent Hispanic or Latino
				Under 5 years	5 to 17 years	18 to 24 years	25 to 44 years	45 to 64 years	65 years and over		White	Black	Asian Hawaiian or Pacific Islander	Amer. Indian, Alaska Native, or some other race	
	ACS table number:	B01003	Population estimates	B01001	B01001	B01001	B01001	B01001	B01001	B01002	B02008	B02009	B02011 + B02012	B02010 + B02013	C03002
		1	2	3	4	5	6	7	8	9	10	11	12	13	14
	Wisconsin—Cont.														
55 059	Kenosha	161,254	2.1	6.9	19.4	9.3	28.3	24.8	11.2	36.3	87.6	6.5	1.7	6.2	9.0
55 061	Kewaunee	20,532	0.2	6.1	16.5	9.1	26.6	26.4	15.2	39.8	98.7	-	0.8	1.1	1.5
55 063	La Crosse	110,494	1.6	5.8	16.0	15.1	26.1	24.2	12.7	35.0	94.9	1.4	3.5	1.0	1.0
55 067	Langlade	20,360	-0.7	5.2	16.3	7.8	24.6	26.9	19.2	42.7	97.6	0.4	-	2.3	1.1
55 069	Lincoln	29,771	-0.8	5.0	17.2	8.0	25.3	27.1	17.4	41.3	98.0	-	0.7	2.0	1.1
55 071	Manitowoc	81,009	-0.2	5.6	16.8	8.9	24.9	28.1	15.7	41.1	96.6	0.7	2.4	1.4	2.3
55 073	Marathon	128,952	1.7	6.0	18.2	8.6	26.8	27.1	13.3	38.7	94.3	0.6	4.9	1.2	1.2
55 075	Marinette	42,729	-0.8	5.0	15.6	9.4	23.0	28.5	18.5	43.2	98.3	0.4	0.2	1.9	0.9
55 079	Milwaukee	951,026	0.2	7.7	18.6	9.5	28.0	24.3	11.8	35.4	63.7	26.4	3.4	8.5	11.2
55 081	Monroe	42,650	2.2	7.2	18.6	8.5	25.9	26.4	13.5	37.6	97.3	1.0	0.8	1.8	2.5
55 083	Oconto	37,364	0.6	5.4	16.9	8.0	26.5	27.9	15.3	40.9	97.7	0.1	0.4	2.3	0.8
55 085	Oneida	36,444	-1.2	4.3	15.0	7.6	23.1	29.8	20.2	45.0	97.7	0.7	0.6	2.0	1.0
55 087	Outagamie	171,906	2.1	6.7	18.7	9.1	28.9	25.1	11.5	36.6	94.0	1.1	2.6	3.3	2.6
55 089	Ozaukee	85,345	0.5	5.2	18.1	9.3	22.2	31.2	14.0	42.1	96.9	1.7	1.7	0.7	1.7
55 093	Pierce	39,296	1.6	5.8	16.2	16.7	26.7	25.0	9.6	33.9	97.7	0.3	1.5	1.0	1.0
55 095	Polk	44,155	0.8	6.0	17.5	7.9	25.8	27.9	15.0	40.3	98.1	0.6	0.5	1.8	0.9
55 097	Portage	67,898	1.0	5.4	16.0	16.4	26.0	25.0	11.2	34.6	95.9	0.7	2.7	1.5	1.7
55 101	Racine	194,522	0.6	6.7	18.8	8.8	26.9	26.6	12.2	37.6	83.9	11.3	1.1	5.6	9.6
55 105	Rock	158,104	2.0	6.7	18.4	8.4	27.8	25.8	12.8	37.1	91.3	5.1	1.3	3.9	5.7
55 109	St. Croix	78,978	5.8	7.4	18.8	8.6	30.4	25.6	9.3	35.6	97.0	0.9	1.5	1.3	1.3
55 111	Sauk	57,962	1.8	6.5	17.3	7.8	27.4	26.3	14.6	39.0	96.9	0.7	0.5	2.7	2.3
55 115	Shawano	41,008	0.3	5.8	17.2	8.0	25.9	26.0	17.1	40.8	92.8	0.5	0.5	7.4	1.5
55 117	Sheboygan	114,053	0.7	6.1	17.4	8.5	27.2	26.8	14.0	38.6	91.2	1.7	4.1	4.2	4.6
55 121	Trempealeau	27,712	0.8	6.1	17.5	7.7	26.2	26.4	16.2	40.2	97.6	0.5	0.4	2.0	1.7
55 123	Vernon	28,875	0.9	7.1	18.4	8.2	22.9	26.9	16.3	39.8	98.8	0.5	0.3	0.8	0.9
55 125	Vilas	22,096	0.0	4.2	13.9	6.7	22.6	27.6	25.0	46.5	91.6	0.5	-	10.3	-
55 127	Walworth	100,140	1.6	6.1	16.7	12.7	26.4	25.3	12.8	36.4	94.0	1.1	1.1	4.8	8.4
55 131	Washington	126,636	2.5	6.3	18.2	8.2	28.0	27.3	12.1	38.6	98.0	1.2	1.1	1.2	1.7
55 133	Waukesha	376,978	1.1	5.8	18.0	8.6	24.5	30.0	13.2	40.7	95.1	1.6	2.6	1.7	3.3
55 135	Waupaca	52,048	0.0	5.5	17.3	7.8	25.9	27.0	16.5	41.2	98.1	0.4	0.5	1.8	1.8
55 137	Waushara	24,698	0.7	4.8	15.9	9.0	25.5	26.6	18.2	41.8	94.0	2.1	1.3	3.1	5.0
55 139	Winnebago	161,074	1.4	5.7	16.1	11.6	28.4	25.6	12.5	37.2	94.9	1.8	2.1	2.2	2.7
55 141	Wood	74,196	-0.8	5.7	17.2	8.1	24.8	27.3	16.9	41.4	96.8	0.7	1.7	1.5	1.2
56 000	**Wyoming**	514,044	3.2	6.6	17.4	10.5	25.5	27.8	12.2	37.3	93.8	1.3	1.2	6.1	7.2
56 001	Albany	32,427	-1.0	5.7	12.2	28.2	25.4	20.3	8.2	26.9	91.9	1.4	3.7	6.1	7.6
56 005	Campbell	38,655	9.1	8.0	19.8	9.9	28.6	28.1	5.6	32.9	95.5	0.6	0.7	4.3	4.6
56 013	Fremont	36,869	3.2	7.3	18.1	8.9	23.1	27.9	14.6	39.0	78.8	0.6	0.7	21.7	5.0
56 021	Laramie	85,841	1.1	7.5	18.0	8.9	28.3	25.5	11.8	36.1	90.2	4.2	1.9	8.1	11.3
56 025	Natrona	70,493	3.3	7.1	17.5	10.1	26.0	26.8	12.5	36.9	94.8	1.6	0.9	5.0	5.4
56 029	Park	26,726	2.6	4.8	16.3	10.7	21.5	30.5	16.1	42.8	97.4	-	1.7	0.7	-
56 033	Sheridan	27,546	3.1	5.7	16.3	8.7	23.2	30.6	15.5	41.9	96.6	-	0.8	4.0	2.8
56 037	Sweetwater	38,218	5.3	8.0	18.1	10.3	25.7	29.2	8.7	35.6	96.1	1.7	1.1	4.8	10.8
56 039	Teton	19,662	3.5	3.2	16.4	6.7	36.6	29.2	8.0	37.7	99.4	-	-	-	-
56 041	Uinta	19,788	3.8	7.5	21.6	8.6	25.5	29.2	7.8	34.8	98.4	-	-	3.6	-

STATE County	Percent foreign born	Total households	Household type (percent)							Percent of households with people under 18 years	Percent of households with people 60 years and over
			Family households				Nonfamily households				
			Total family households	Married-couple families	Male householder families	Female householder families	Total nonfamily households	One-person households			
ACS table number:	C05002	B11001	B11001	B11001	B11001	B11001	B11001	B11001	C11005	B11006
	15	16	17	18	19	20	21	22	23	24
Wisconsin—Cont.										
Kenosha	6.1	59,838	67.5	51.5	4.2	11.8	32.5	27.4	37.1	25.9
Kewaunee	1.6	8,272	69.9	59.7	4.3	5.9	30.1	25.2	32.9	35.9
La Crosse	2.9	44,452	60.5	48.7	2.8	9.0	39.5	30.2	30.2	27.0
Langlade	1.2	8,565	68.0	54.2	6.0	7.9	32.0	28.2	31.8	37.9
Lincoln	1.0	12,753	68.7	55.9	4.6	8.1	31.3	26.6	31.0	34.9
Manitowoc	3.1	33,704	66.3	55.6	3.7	7.0	33.7	29.1	30.2	33.0
Marathon	3.6	52,251	69.1	57.4	4.8	6.9	30.9	25.2	33.3	29.4
Marinette	1.2	18,814	66.2	50.8	5.0	10.5	33.8	29.1	31.8	34.7
Milwaukee	8.2	377,310	58.0	36.7	4.8	16.5	42.0	35.2	31.6	28.0
Monroe	2.1	17,411	65.9	51.1	4.6	10.2	34.1	28.3	33.6	30.8
Oconto	0.8	15,975	71.1	56.9	5.5	8.7	28.9	23.6	33.6	33.2
Oneida	1.6	17,494	65.4	54.8	2.8	7.8	34.6	27.6	27.2	36.7
Outagamie	3.4	67,707	67.9	56.6	3.4	7.9	32.1	26.4	35.6	26.2
Ozaukee	4.2	33,385	71.8	63.0	2.9	5.9	28.2	23.8	31.7	33.6
Pierce	1.5	14,706	67.7	56.8	3.4	7.5	32.3	24.5	34.3	23.4
Polk	1.0	17,569	69.3	58.3	3.6	7.5	30.7	25.3	32.5	33.0
Portage	2.5	26,459	63.5	52.7	3.5	7.3	36.5	24.9	29.2	27.9
Racine	4.9	75,140	69.1	50.6	5.8	12.7	30.9	25.8	34.1	27.7
Rock	4.6	62,035	66.9	51.7	4.3	11.0	33.1	28.3	34.1	30.4
St. Croix	2.6	30,910	72.0	59.4	4.3	8.3	28.0	20.4	37.5	22.2
Sauk	2.9	24,910	67.2	53.5	4.8	8.8	32.8	27.2	32.9	30.3
Shawano	1.0	16,884	69.3	53.0	5.1	11.2	30.7	25.1	33.8	36.1
Sheboygan	5.0	46,278	66.4	56.1	3.7	6.6	33.6	28.1	31.1	30.4
Trempealeau	1.7	11,489	67.2	54.8	4.5	7.9	32.8	26.8	30.5	36.1
Vernon	1.3	12,126	65.6	55.9	3.2	6.4	34.4	28.2	31.8	35.9
Vilas	1.6	10,849	72.3	63.0	3.7	5.7	27.7	22.2	26.9	43.4
Walworth	6.3	38,579	63.6	52.9	3.6	7.1	36.4	28.7	31.4	30.6
Washington	2.1	50,050	71.6	58.9	3.5	9.3	28.4	22.5	34.8	28.1
Waukesha	4.3	146,942	72.1	62.5	3.4	6.3	27.9	23.4	33.7	31.7
Waupaca	1.2	21,304	66.6	54.8	3.3	8.4	33.4	27.8	32.9	32.9
Waushara	2.9	10,423	69.4	56.4	4.2	8.8	30.6	24.8	27.4	38.4
Winnebago	2.8	65,897	61.0	49.5	3.5	8.0	39.0	30.1	30.4	28.9
Wood	2.1	31,367	66.4	55.1	3.9	7.5	33.6	27.5	29.9	35.1
Wyoming	2.7	205,422	65.6	52.6	4.8	8.2	34.4	27.8	31.1	29.4
Albany	5.0	13,890	53.2	41.6	4.9	6.7	46.8	32.0	24.7	17.0
Campbell	1.3	13,344	74.4	58.8	6.6	9.0	25.6	20.7	38.4	18.9
Fremont	1.1	14,296	68.1	53.4	5.4	9.4	31.9	27.2	31.0	36.9
Laramie	3.1	33,640	66.1	50.4	4.6	11.1	33.9	28.8	32.2	28.6
Natrona	1.7	27,359	64.4	49.5	4.6	10.3	35.6	28.9	32.8	28.8
Park	2.0	11,603	65.2	56.8	3.4	5.1	34.8	28.4	25.9	35.1
Sheridan	1.6	11,929	57.1	48.8	3.4	5.0	42.9	35.2	25.9	33.0
Sweetwater	5.0	15,107	71.4	55.6	7.9	7.9	28.6	22.8	37.1	24.6
Teton	8.5	7,942	49.0	43.1	3.2	2.6	51.0	36.2	15.7	23.2
Uinta	2.9	7,208	75.2	60.9	2.7	11.6	24.8	19.2	41.3	21.5

Metro area or division code	Area name	Total population	Percent change 2005–2007	Population by age (percent)						Median age	Race alone or in combination (percent)				Percent Hispanic or Latino
				Under 5 years	5 to 17 years	18 to 24 years	25 to 44 years	45 to 64 years	65 years and over		White	Black	Asian Hawaiian or Pacific Islander	Amer. Indian, Alaska Native, or some other race	
	ACS table number:	B01003	Population estimates	B01001	B01001	B01001	B01001	B01001	B01001	B01002	B02008	B02009	B02011 + B02012	B02010 + B02013	C03002
		1	2	3	4	5	6	7	8	9	10	11	12	13	14
10180	Abilene, TX	159,005	0.3	7.1	17.9	12.6	26.4	22.4	13.5	34.2	81.1	7.5	1.9	12.0	19.4
10420	Akron, OH	700,134	-0.2	5.9	17.5	10.1	26.5	26.7	13.3	38.0	85.9	12.4	2.0	1.2	1.1
10500	Albany, GA	164,253	1.3	7.5	19.5	11.3	25.6	24.6	11.5	34.4	48.7	50.2	0.9	1.3	1.4
10580	Albany-Schenectady-Troy, NY	850,506	0.6	5.5	16.4	11.2	26.9	26.6	13.4	38.4	88.5	7.8	3.1	2.4	3.1
10740	Albuquerque, NM	819,576	4.5	7.3	17.9	10.1	28.0	25.1	11.6	35.5	70.6	3.5	3.1	26.9	43.9
10780	Alexandria, LA	149,875	3.8	7.2	18.4	9.4	26.8	24.9	13.2	36.2	68.6	29.3	1.0	2.1	2.0
10900	Allentown-Bethlehem-Easton, PA-NJ	794,961	2.3	5.9	17.1	9.0	26.6	26.6	14.8	39.4	88.3	4.7	2.5	6.2	10.0
11020	Altoona, PA	125,711	-0.4	5.7	15.6	8.9	25.6	27.1	17.1	40.9	97.8	1.8	0.6	0.7	0.6
11100	Amarillo, TX	240,338	1.9	7.8	18.8	10.9	27.5	23.5	11.4	33.7	80.1	6.5	2.2	13.6	22.7
11180	Ames, IA	83,553	4.2	5.4	12.8	27.6	25.0	19.0	10.3	27.3	90.6	2.3	6.4	1.7	2.0
11260	Anchorage, AK	357,813	2.6	7.5	19.4	11.1	29.6	25.9	6.6	33.4	80.6	6.7	8.3	13.0	6.7
11300	Anderson, IN	131,085	0.4	6.1	16.8	8.6	27.1	26.1	15.3	38.9	90.1	8.9	0.6	1.6	2.1
11340	Anderson, SC	177,151	3.3	6.5	17.6	8.1	27.2	26.4	14.2	38.2	82.5	17.2	0.9	1.2	1.8
11460	Ann Arbor, MI	347,670	1.1	6.1	15.6	16.6	29.6	23.3	8.7	32.8	77.7	13.5	8.8	2.6	3.3
11500	Anniston-Oxford, AL	112,620	0.8	6.5	16.7	10.4	25.6	26.3	14.4	38.2	78.2	20.1	1.0	2.0	2.2
11540	Appleton, WI	216,131	1.7	6.8	18.8	8.9	29.0	25.3	11.3	36.6	94.4	1.0	2.7	3.0	2.4
11700	Asheville, NC	397,828	3.3	5.8	15.4	7.9	26.1	27.2	17.6	41.4	92.1	5.6	1.0	2.6	4.5
12020	Athens-Clarke County, GA	183,351	4.2	6.4	15.3	20.6	28.1	20.4	9.3	29.5	74.9	20.2	3.0	2.8	6.4
12060	Atlanta-Sandy Springs-Marietta, GA	5,122,275	6.4	7.9	19.1	8.8	32.0	24.3	8.0	34.5	59.8	31.4	4.4	5.8	8.9
12100	Atlantic City, NJ	269,774	0.7	6.5	17.7	8.5	28.3	25.2	13.6	38.2	67.2	17.5	6.8	10.5	14.1
12220	Auburn-Opelika, AL	127,940	4.3	6.0	16.6	21.8	26.7	20.4	8.5	28.5	74.3	23.4	2.1	1.4	1.8
12260	Augusta-Richmond County, GA-SC	522,913	2.2	7.2	18.9	10.1	26.6	25.5	11.8	35.8	61.2	36.2	2.2	2.2	2.7
12420	Austin-Round Rock, TX	1,533,263	8.7	8.0	17.8	11.8	33.3	21.7	7.4	32.1	71.7	8.0	5.0	17.5	29.4
12540	Bakersfield, CA	771,347	5.1	8.8	21.4	11.3	29.6	20.1	8.9	29.9	64.1	6.4	4.9	28.4	45.1
12580	Baltimore-Towson, MD	2,660,496	0.6	6.5	17.7	9.5	27.9	26.3	12.1	37.5	66.1	29.3	4.2	2.2	2.9
12620	Bangor, ME	147,971	1.1	5.4	15.5	11.6	26.3	27.8	13.4	39.3	97.2	1.0	1.1	1.8	0.9
12700	Barnstable Town, MA	223,574	-1.3	4.3	14.0	7.1	23.0	28.2	23.4	46.0	95.6	2.7	1.1	2.0	1.7
12940	Baton Rouge, LA	753,299	5.5	7.1	18.5	12.5	27.7	24.1	10.2	33.6	62.2	35.6	1.8	1.5	2.3
12980	Battle Creek, MI	137,452	-1.3	6.8	18.1	9.0	26.4	25.9	13.8	37.7	86.1	11.5	1.9	2.4	3.7
13020	Bay City, MI	108,059	-1.1	5.7	16.9	8.7	25.1	28.1	15.5	40.7	96.1	2.0	0.7	3.0	4.0
13140	Beaumont-Port Arthur, TX	377,157	-1.0	6.6	18.0	9.9	26.8	25.3	13.4	36.9	67.6	25.5	2.3	6.0	9.9
13380	Bellingham, WA	189,110	3.9	5.6	16.3	14.3	26.8	24.9	12.1	35.0	90.1	1.4	4.7	5.9	6.2
13460	Bend, OR	148,052	9.1	6.0	16.7	8.1	28.6	27.2	13.5	38.6	95.9	0.8	1.9	3.4	5.6
13740	Billings, MT	147,923	2.2	6.6	17.5	8.9	26.1	27.2	13.7	38.8	92.9	1.4	1.4	6.0	4.6
13780	Binghamton, NY	246,800	-0.4	5.2	16.0	11.8	24.8	26.2	15.9	39.5	92.4	4.2	3.3	1.6	2.2
13820	Birmingham-Hoover, AL	1,098,834	1.9	6.9	17.6	9.0	27.8	26.0	12.6	37.2	69.7	28.4	1.3	1.5	2.8
13900	Bismarck, ND	101,319	3.8	6.2	16.3	11.9	26.5	25.8	13.3	36.7	94.7	0.6	1.0	4.8	1.0
13980	Blacksburg-Christiansburg-Radford, VA	156,112	1.9	4.7	12.3	25.1	25.6	20.8	11.5	30.3	91.0	5.4	3.6	1.0	1.7
14020	Bloomington, IN	182,390	1.5	5.4	14.0	21.1	26.7	21.6	11.2	30.9	93.4	3.1	3.8	1.8	1.9
14060	Bloomington-Normal, IL	162,031	2.7	6.6	16.3	18.3	27.7	21.2	9.9	30.8	88.6	7.9	3.2	2.1	3.3
14260	Boise City-Nampa, ID	566,760	7.8	8.1	19.9	8.8	30.1	23.1	10.0	33.4	93.4	1.3	2.6	5.2	10.8
14460	Boston-Cambridge-Quincy, MA-NH	4,467,781	0.8	6.0	16.5	9.7	29.0	26.2	12.6	38.1	82.8	7.5	6.2	5.3	7.6
14460 14484	•Boston-Quincy, MA Division	1,851,929	1.2	6.1	16.1	10.4	29.9	25.1	12.3	37.1	77.5	12.7	6.3	5.5	8.3
14460 15764	•Cambridge-Newton-Framingham, MA Division	1,468,419	0.5	5.9	16.0	9.5	29.5	26.4	12.8	38.5	84.4	4.5	8.8	3.8	5.4
14460 37764	•Peabody, MA Division	731,841	0.3	6.2	17.8	8.8	26.4	27.2	13.6	39.2	84.6	3.9	3.3	9.9	13.6
14460 40484	•Rockingham County-Strafford County, NH Division	415,592	1.3	6.0	17.7	9.1	27.5	28.6	11.1	39.0	96.8	1.2	2.0	1.3	1.8
14500	Boulder, CO	286,471	2.4	5.9	15.4	13.4	29.8	27.1	8.3	35.5	89.2	1.4	4.6	7.2	12.8
14540	Bowling Green, KY	113,904	3.9	6.7	16.2	14.0	28.3	23.7	11.1	33.8	89.8	8.3	1.5	1.4	3.2
14740	Bremerton-Silverdale, WA	238,449	0.9	6.1	17.9	9.0	26.9	28.3	11.8	38.3	89.0	3.7	7.6	4.9	4.7
14860	Bridgeport-Stamford-Norwalk, CT	894,724	-0.1	6.6	18.7	8.0	26.6	27.0	13.0	39.0	79.2	10.7	4.5	7.0	14.4
15180	Brownsville-Harlingen, TX	379,874	3.6	11.4	22.8	10.8	25.1	18.8	11.1	28.8	86.6	0.6	0.7	13.2	86.0
15260	Brunswick, GA	99,809	4.0	6.7	18.5	8.7	26.1	26.1	13.8	37.7	74.6	24.0	0.9	1.5	3.6
15380	Buffalo-Niagara Falls, NY	1,134,380	-1.2	5.4	16.9	10.4	25.0	26.9	15.4	39.8	84.1	12.8	1.9	2.5	3.3
15500	Burlington, NC	142,392	3.8	6.6	17.3	9.8	27.6	24.9	13.8	37.4	72.4	18.9	1.5	8.6	10.3
15540	Burlington-South Burlington, VT	206,437	0.9	5.6	17.1	11.4	28.0	27.4	10.5	37.4	96.1	1.7	2.3	1.7	1.4
15940	Canton-Massillon, OH	407,423	0.0	5.9	17.4	8.6	25.2	27.6	15.4	40.1	91.8	7.8	0.8	1.2	1.0
15980	Cape Coral-Fort Myers, FL	567,711	8.7	6.1	14.7	7.0	25.2	24.6	22.4	42.8	85.6	7.7	1.5	6.1	15.8
16180	Carson City, NV	55,244	-1.5	7.3	16.5	8.5	24.9	27.0	15.8	40.8	85.7	2.1	2.5	11.8	18.8
16220	Casper, WY	70,493	3.4	7.1	17.5	10.1	26.0	26.8	12.5	36.9	94.8	1.6	0.9	5.0	5.4
16300	Cedar Rapids, IA	249,899	2.2	6.7	18.0	9.1	28.0	25.2	13.0	37.0	94.6	3.6	2.0	1.4	1.8
16580	Champaign-Urbana, IL	219,045	2.3	6.0	14.6	21.4	26.7	20.5	10.8	29.8	81.3	10.8	7.8	2.1	3.6
16620	Charleston, WV	304,169	-0.3	6.1	15.8	7.4	26.3	29.0	15.3	41.0	93.9	5.7	1.0	0.6	1.0
16700	Charleston-North Charleston, SC	616,351	4.9	7.0	17.7	10.7	28.2	25.6	10.8	35.6	67.2	29.8	2.1	2.6	3.3
16740	Charlotte-Gastonia-Concord, NC-SC	1,586,202	8.4	7.8	18.3	8.8	31.0	24.6	9.5	35.3	70.5	23.8	2.9	4.3	7.9
16820	Charlottesville, VA	190,560	2.4	5.8	15.4	14.2	27.5	24.1	13.0	35.1	81.5	14.0	3.9	2.3	3.1
16860	Chattanooga, TN-GA	508,031	2.4	6.2	16.9	9.0	27.1	27.0	13.8	38.4	83.4	14.6	1.4	2.1	2.2
16940	Cheyenne, WY	85,841	1.4	7.5	18.0	8.9	28.3	25.5	11.8	36.1	90.2	4.2	1.9	8.1	11.3
16980	Chicago-Naperville-Joliet, IL-IN-WI	9,463,477	1.1	7.3	18.7	9.6	29.1	24.5	10.8	35.3	65.5	18.5	5.6	12.1	19.1
16980 16974	•Chicago-Naperville-Joliet, IL Division	7,904,371	1.1	7.3	18.5	9.6	29.5	24.2	10.8	35.2	63.0	19.6	6.0	13.0	20.0

Table A-3. Metropolitan Areas — Who: Age, Race/Ethnicity, and Household Structure, 2005–2007—*Continued*

Area name	Percent foreign born	Total households	Family households — Total family households	Married-couple families	Male householder families	Female householder families	Nonfamily households — Total nonfamily households	One-person households	Percent of households with people under 18 years	Percent of households with people 60 years and over
ACS table number:	C05002	B11001	B11001	B11001	B11001	B11001	B11001	B11001	C11005	B11006
	15	16	17	18	19	20	21	22	23	24
Abilene, TX	3.9	60,536	67.7	51.7	3.3	12.6	32.3	27.3	34.5	31.5
Akron, OH	3.4	279,518	64.9	49.0	4.0	12.0	35.1	28.9	31.2	30.9
Albany, GA	1.6	60,574	68.9	43.5	3.9	21.5	31.1	27.2	38.1	30.0
Albany-Schenectady-Troy, NY	5.9	337,537	62.2	46.9	3.9	11.4	37.8	30.3	30.7	31.4
Albuquerque, NM	9.4	320,462	63.3	45.1	5.4	12.8	36.7	30.0	33.7	28.6
Alexandria, LA	2.2	57,460	68.9	48.3	4.0	16.7	31.1	27.4	37.6	32.2
Allentown-Bethlehem-Easton, PA-NJ	6.9	305,867	68.8	53.4	4.2	11.3	31.2	25.8	33.5	34.5
Altoona, PA	1.0	51,384	66.5	51.6	3.6	11.3	33.5	29.0	30.4	37.3
Amarillo, TX	7.5	87,799	67.0	50.0	4.3	12.6	33.0	27.3	36.3	27.7
Ames, IA	8.8	31,467	56.4	47.7	2.4	6.4	43.6	29.1	26.4	22.5
Anchorage, AK	7.4	124,200	68.9	51.7	5.2	12.0	31.1	23.7	39.5	20.5
Anderson, IN	1.1	51,392	65.6	48.7	4.4	12.4	34.4	29.4	31.0	34.5
Anderson, SC	2.4	68,821	71.7	53.5	4.6	13.7	28.3	23.7	35.0	34.1
Ann Arbor, MI	11.4	132,861	59.9	46.8	3.4	9.7	40.1	29.8	30.6	23.0
Anniston-Oxford, AL	2.3	46,849	67.5	47.7	5.0	14.7	32.5	27.8	33.7	34.6
Appleton, WI	3.4	85,071	68.8	58.3	3.1	7.4	31.2	25.2	36.1	25.8
Asheville, NC	5.0	169,116	64.8	51.4	3.5	9.9	35.2	29.2	28.3	37.3
Athens-Clarke County, GA	7.7	68,554	60.1	42.6	4.8	12.7	39.9	28.4	31.3	23.9
Atlanta-Sandy Springs-Marietta, GA	12.6	1,820,162	67.9	49.6	4.6	13.7	32.1	26.1	38.3	22.7
Atlantic City, NJ	14.2	102,672	65.9	45.4	5.0	15.5	34.1	28.8	35.4	32.3
Auburn-Opelika, AL	3.9	52,996	58.8	41.8	4.2	12.8	41.2	30.6	34.1	21.0
Augusta-Richmond County, GA-SC	3.4	197,580	69.6	48.1	4.2	17.3	30.4	26.7	36.5	30.4
Austin-Round Rock, TX	14.1	560,375	62.0	46.7	4.7	10.6	38.0	29.1	35.1	19.5
Bakersfield, CA	20.4	235,842	74.3	51.6	6.9	15.9	25.7	20.7	47.6	26.6
Baltimore-Towson, MD	7.5	998,382	65.3	46.8	4.4	14.1	34.7	28.5	34.0	30.9
Bangor, ME	2.4	60,477	62.7	48.6	3.9	10.3	37.3	28.9	29.2	31.1
Barnstable Town, MA	7.8	98,989	63.9	51.6	3.8	8.6	36.1	29.2	25.7	44.8
Baton Rouge, LA	3.1	279,761	67.0	46.2	4.6	16.2	33.0	27.2	35.7	27.3
Battle Creek, MI	3.1	54,257	67.2	48.0	5.0	14.2	32.8	28.7	33.9	32.8
Bay City, MI	1.9	44,733	66.6	52.0	3.6	11.1	33.4	28.4	30.6	34.2
Beaumont-Port Arthur, TX	6.3	141,740	69.3	48.9	4.6	15.7	30.7	26.1	35.6	33.1
Bellingham, WA	11.7	74,831	61.5	50.4	3.1	8.1	38.5	27.6	30.3	28.6
Bend, OR	5.1	60,302	68.1	57.3	3.4	7.4	31.9	22.7	31.9	29.6
Billings, MT	1.8	59,100	63.9	52.2	2.9	8.8	36.1	29.2	30.7	31.0
Binghamton, NY	5.1	100,631	62.6	46.4	4.7	11.5	37.4	31.0	30.0	35.0
Birmingham-Hoover, AL	3.3	429,594	68.6	50.3	3.8	14.6	31.4	27.6	34.9	31.0
Bismarck, ND	1.5	41,532	62.8	51.8	3.1	7.9	37.2	30.1	30.0	28.4
Blacksburg-Christiansburg-Radford, VA	4.6	59,507	58.6	45.9	3.3	9.3	41.4	29.2	26.5	27.8
Bloomington, IN	4.8	68,901	57.9	46.2	3.0	8.7	42.1	32.0	28.0	27.3
Bloomington-Normal, IL	4.4	61,177	63.9	51.5	3.0	9.4	36.1	26.5	33.3	22.9
Boise City-Nampa, ID	6.5	212,275	69.4	55.9	4.2	9.3	30.6	23.8	38.3	25.3
Boston-Cambridge-Quincy, MA-NH	15.9	1,684,779	63.7	48.2	3.9	11.6	36.3	28.9	32.6	31.0
•Boston-Quincy, MA Division	17.7	696,066	61.0	43.9	4.2	13.0	39.0	30.6	31.4	30.8
•Cambridge-Newton-Framingham, MA Division	17.8	556,748	64.3	51.1	3.5	9.8	35.7	28.3	32.5	31.2
•Peabody, MA Division	13.7	273,755	66.5	48.8	4.5	13.2	33.5	28.2	34.7	32.8
•Rockingham County-Strafford County, NH Division	4.7	158,210	68.4	56.0	3.4	9.0	31.6	24.1	34.6	28.0
Boulder, CO	11.6	113,419	59.7	47.1	4.4	8.2	40.3	29.0	32.3	22.5
Bowling Green, KY	5.1	44,622	66.1	49.5	4.4	12.1	33.9	26.6	33.2	27.0
Bremerton-Silverdale, WA	6.2	91,579	67.8	54.4	4.2	9.3	32.2	25.6	32.9	30.1
Bridgeport-Stamford-Norwalk, CT	19.4	324,360	70.1	54.2	4.0	11.9	29.9	25.0	37.4	33.2
Brownsville-Harlingen, TX	25.4	114,787	81.2	57.3	4.4	19.5	18.8	16.6	51.1	34.5
Brunswick, GA	3.6	39,019	66.0	47.9	4.3	13.7	34.0	28.7	32.1	33.4
Buffalo-Niagara Falls, NY	4.9	465,947	62.3	45.0	4.0	13.2	37.7	31.9	30.1	34.4
Burlington, NC	8.1	56,608	69.6	49.1	5.4	15.0	30.4	24.9	35.0	31.6
Burlington-South Burlington, VT	5.0	80,394	62.6	48.4	4.2	10.0	37.4	27.6	32.2	26.5
Canton-Massillon, OH	2.1	161,150	68.4	51.9	4.3	12.2	31.6	27.2	32.5	34.0
Cape Coral-Fort Myers, FL	14.4	243,673	66.2	53.2	3.9	9.0	33.8	26.3	26.5	43.6
Carson City, NV	11.5	21,330	64.6	46.8	5.6	12.1	35.4	30.2	31.9	37.5
Casper, WY	1.7	27,359	64.4	49.5	4.6	10.3	35.6	28.9	32.8	28.8
Cedar Rapids, IA	2.3	102,404	64.1	50.7	3.5	9.9	35.9	28.7	33.0	28.3
Champaign-Urbana, IL	8.3	87,476	56.9	43.9	3.4	9.6	43.1	31.6	28.3	23.8
Charleston, WV	1.2	126,252	66.9	51.9	3.7	11.3	33.1	28.9	29.8	34.5
Charleston-North Charleston, SC	4.3	234,599	65.3	45.8	4.0	15.4	34.7	28.5	32.7	28.8
Charlotte-Gastonia-Concord, NC-SC	9.0	616,835	66.8	49.4	4.4	13.0	33.2	27.2	36.0	24.8
Charlottesville, VA	6.8	76,147	60.7	47.3	3.3	10.1	39.3	31.0	29.0	29.6
Chattanooga, TN-GA	3.2	202,514	67.1	50.4	4.3	12.3	32.9	27.8	31.8	32.9
Cheyenne, WY	3.1	33,640	66.1	50.4	4.6	11.1	33.9	28.8	32.2	28.6
Chicago-Naperville-Joliet, IL-IN-WI	17.6	3,385,546	67.4	49.4	4.7	13.4	32.6	27.5	36.6	29.0
•Chicago-Naperville-Joliet, IL Division	18.8	2,829,188	66.7	48.4	4.8	13.6	33.3	28.1	36.4	29.1

Table A-3. Metropolitan Areas — Who: Age, Race/Ethnicity, and Household Structure, 2005–2007—*Continued*

Metro area or division code	Area name	Total population	Percent change 2005–2007	Under 5 years	5 to 17 years	18 to 24 years	25 to 44 years	45 to 64 years	65 years and over	Median age	White	Black	Asian Hawaiian or Pacific Islander	Amer. Indian, Alaska Native, or some other race	Percent Hispanic or Latino
						Population by age (percent)						Race alone or in combination (percent)			
	ACS table number:	B01003	Population estimates	B01001	B01001	B01001	B01001	B01001	B01001	B01002	B02008	B02009	B02011 + B02012	B02010 + B02013	C03002
		1	2	3	4	5	6	7	8	9	10	11	12	13	14
16980 23844	•Gary, IN Division	694,146	1.3	6.8	18.7	9.4	25.9	26.7	12.5	37.2	73.3	19.4	1.3	7.8	11.5
16980 29404	•Lake County-Kenosha County, IL-WI Division	864,960	1.7	7.3	20.6	9.4	27.9	25.2	9.6	35.1	82.1	7.1	5.3	7.2	16.8
17020	Chico, CA	217,191	1.5	5.5	15.9	15.9	24.4	23.5	14.9	34.7	88.1	2.1	5.3	9.7	12.3
17140	Cincinnati-Middletown, OH-KY-IN	2,118,212	2.0	7.0	18.4	9.5	27.9	25.4	11.8	36.5	85.6	12.6	2.0	1.3	1.6
17300	Clarksville, TN-KY	255,401	4.1	8.4	20.7	10.5	29.5	21.3	9.6	31.9	76.4	19.9	2.6	3.6	5.0
17420	Cleveland, TN	109,555	2.8	6.3	16.5	9.0	29.2	25.4	13.6	37.2	93.3	4.0	0.8	2.9	2.8
17460	Cleveland-Elyria-Mentor, OH	2,106,901	-1.0	6.2	17.9	8.4	25.9	27.3	14.4	39.5	76.7	20.3	2.1	2.5	3.9
17660	Coeur d'Alene, ID	130,668	5.9	6.5	18.6	8.7	26.7	26.0	13.5	37.1	97.7	0.7	1.2	3.0	3.2
17780	College Station-Bryan, TX	200,407	3.5	7.0	15.3	26.4	25.8	16.9	8.7	25.8	76.9	12.1	4.6	8.6	19.8
17820	Colorado Springs, CO	600,341	3.3	7.3	18.8	9.9	29.9	24.9	9.2	34.4	84.3	7.8	4.5	8.1	12.7
17860	Columbia, MO	159,467	3.7	6.5	15.9	18.4	28.2	21.6	9.4	30.8	86.9	9.4	3.5	2.6	2.4
17900	Columbia, SC	703,807	3.6	6.7	17.7	11.4	27.4	25.9	10.8	35.9	63.3	34.0	1.9	2.3	3.5
17980	Columbus, GA-AL	287,208	-0.4	7.4	19.1	11.6	26.5	23.7	11.6	34.3	55.0	42.1	2.3	3.1	3.8
18020	Columbus, IN	73,987	2.1	6.9	18.7	7.3	27.5	26.2	13.4	38.0	94.4	2.5	2.9	1.6	3.7
18140	Columbus, OH	1,734,721	2.4	7.4	18.1	10.0	30.4	24.1	10.0	34.7	81.8	14.8	3.5	1.9	2.7
18580	Corpus Christi, TX	412,925	0.6	7.7	19.5	10.5	25.8	24.5	12.1	35.0	78.5	4.2	1.7	18.0	55.4
18700	Corvallis, OR	80,470	2.1	4.9	13.7	20.7	24.3	25.4	11.0	33.1	88.9	1.6	6.9	5.5	5.7
19060	Cumberland, MD-WV	99,422	-0.2	5.0	14.7	11.7	25.8	25.8	17.0	39.9	94.2	5.7	0.8	0.7	0.9
19100	Dallas-Fort Worth-Arlington, TX	5,979,240	5.8	8.4	19.5	9.3	32.0	22.7	8.1	33.1	70.8	14.5	5.1	11.5	26.3
19100 19124	•Dallas-Plano-Irving, TX Division	4,002,885	5.8	8.5	19.4	9.3	32.6	22.4	7.8	32.9	69.4	15.5	5.6	11.4	28.0
19100 23104	•Fort Worth-Arlington, TX Division	1,976,355	5.8	8.2	19.5	9.4	30.7	23.4	8.7	33.5	73.6	12.4	4.2	11.7	22.8
19140	Dalton, GA	132,416	2.3	9.3	20.0	7.9	29.7	23.3	9.8	33.7	79.1	2.9	0.9	18.3	23.5
19180	Danville, IL	81,566	-0.7	6.6	17.5	8.9	25.5	25.3	16.2	38.3	85.1	12.2	0.9	3.3	3.5
19260	Danville, VA	106,247	-0.6	5.8	15.8	8.2	24.5	28.4	17.2	42.0	65.2	32.7	0.4	2.3	1.9
19340	Davenport-Moline-Rock Island, IA-IL	374,605	0.7	6.6	17.3	9.7	25.4	26.6	14.3	38.3	88.9	7.0	1.8	4.1	6.5
19380	Dayton, OH	838,165	-0.5	6.3	17.2	10.4	25.7	26.3	14.0	38.3	82.7	15.5	2.0	1.6	1.6
19460	Decatur, AL	148,148	1.4	6.4	17.5	8.1	27.9	26.6	13.5	38.9	84.3	12.5	0.6	5.0	4.3
19500	Decatur, IL	109,101	-0.9	6.3	16.9	10.1	23.8	27.2	15.7	39.3	84.0	15.8	1.2	1.3	1.2
19660	Deltona-Daytona Beach-Ormond Beach, FL	494,198	2.9	5.3	14.6	9.0	24.6	26.1	20.5	42.5	85.7	10.5	1.8	3.5	9.7
19740	Denver-Aurora, CO	2,413,844	4.0	7.7	17.8	8.4	31.1	25.6	9.3	35.6	82.7	6.1	4.3	9.6	21.7
19780	Des Moines-West Des Moines, IA	535,598	4.2	7.7	18.4	8.6	29.6	24.6	11.1	35.6	90.6	4.7	2.9	3.5	5.5
19820	Detroit-Warren-Livonia, MI	4,488,815	-0.9	6.5	18.9	8.3	27.7	26.6	12.0	37.6	71.9	23.6	3.5	2.7	3.5
19820 19804	•Detroit-Livonia-Dearborn, MI Division	2,008,238	-2.1	6.9	20.1	8.4	27.6	25.3	11.7	36.2	53.3	42.1	2.7	3.6	4.8
19820 47644	•Warren-Troy-Farmington Hills, MI Division	2,480,577	0.1	6.1	18.0	8.2	27.8	27.7	12.2	38.8	86.9	8.6	4.1	2.0	2.6
20020	Dothan, AL	137,579	2.8	6.7	17.7	8.5	25.8	26.1	15.2	39.1	74.5	23.9	0.7	1.8	1.7
20100	Dover, DE	147,974	5.9	7.3	18.4	10.3	27.5	24.0	12.5	35.5	73.7	23.2	3.0	3.6	4.1
20220	Dubuque, IA	91,626	1.5	6.6	17.7	10.6	24.6	25.5	15.0	38.3	97.1	2.0	1.1	1.0	1.6
20260	Duluth, MN-WI	274,174	-0.1	5.3	15.2	12.4	23.8	28.0	15.3	40.1	95.5	1.5	1.1	3.4	0.9
20500	Durham, NC	469,477	4.4	7.0	15.7	12.4	30.3	24.4	10.2	34.9	61.8	28.2	4.4	7.7	9.3
20740	Eau Claire, WI	156,226	1.8	6.1	16.2	13.8	26.5	24.5	12.9	35.7	96.6	0.9	2.3	1.1	1.0
20940	El Centro, CA	157,829	4.9	9.2	20.3	12.6	27.6	19.9	10.4	30.7	72.6	3.9	2.8	23.3	75.5
21060	Elizabethtown, KY	110,878	1.3	7.3	18.5	9.8	27.3	25.5	11.7	36.2	85.9	11.3	2.7	2.2	3.3
21140	Elkhart-Goshen, IN	195,987	2.2	8.5	20.1	8.1	29.3	23.3	10.8	33.9	86.2	6.3	1.4	7.8	13.1
21300	Elmira, NY	88,199	-0.5	5.7	16.6	10.0	25.9	26.5	15.3	39.0	92.6	6.6	1.4	1.6	2.0
21340	El Paso, TX	724,217	2.8	9.8	21.4	11.4	26.0	21.1	10.4	31.0	77.9	3.3	1.5	19.4	81.3
21500	Erie, PA	279,252	0.2	5.9	17.5	11.2	25.0	26.2	14.3	38.1	91.6	7.2	1.0	1.7	2.6
21660	Eugene-Springfield, OR	339,869	2.2	5.3	15.2	11.6	26.7	27.2	13.9	38.1	92.0	1.5	4.0	5.4	5.9
21780	Evansville, IN-KY	348,645	0.6	6.5	17.1	9.7	26.1	26.7	13.9	38.5	92.5	6.6	1.1	1.2	1.3
21820	Fairbanks, AK	95,600	3.6	8.1	20.0	13.7	30.3	22.4	5.5	29.7	81.8	7.3	4.3	12.7	6.0
22020	Fargo, ND-MN	189,219	3.4	6.6	16.0	16.5	28.8	21.7	10.4	31.5	94.9	1.9	1.9	2.9	2.4
22140	Farmington, NM	122,056	0.3	7.8	20.2	11.2	26.8	23.7	10.2	32.6	57.5	1.4	0.7	43.2	17.0
22180	Fayetteville, NC	347,605	1.8	8.4	20.2	11.5	28.5	22.6	8.7	32.5	56.4	37.6	3.3	7.3	6.6
22220	Fayetteville-Springdale-Rogers, AR-MO	422,626	6.6	8.2	18.6	10.4	29.4	22.4	11.0	33.2	86.4	2.4	2.6	10.5	12.6
22380	Flagstaff, AZ	126,087	2.2	7.4	18.3	14.9	26.1	25.5	7.8	31.6	64.2	1.5	1.7	34.8	11.8
22420	Flint, MI	437,405	-1.2	6.9	19.1	8.6	27.2	26.0	12.3	36.7	77.8	20.7	1.2	2.5	2.4
22500	Florence, SC	197,765	0.9	7.0	18.1	9.2	26.3	26.7	12.7	37.2	57.7	41.2	0.8	1.4	1.3
22520	Florence-Muscle Shoals, AL	142,534	0.9	5.5	16.1	10.3	25.2	26.7	16.2	39.8	86.6	13.0	0.5	1.3	1.4
22540	Fond du Lac, WI	98,755	0.7	5.8	17.3	9.6	26.8	26.2	14.3	38.6	95.9	1.5	1.1	2.9	3.1
22660	Fort Collins-Loveland, CO	281,742	4.0	6.0	15.8	13.8	28.9	25.3	10.2	34.3	93.4	1.5	2.6	5.6	9.6
22900	Fort Smith, AR-OK	286,346	2.3	7.1	18.6	8.6	26.8	25.7	13.3	37.0	87.1	4.2	2.1	11.9	6.8
23020	Fort Walton Beach-Crestview-Destin, FL	182,644	-1.2	7.1	16.9	8.6	27.1	27.4	12.9	38.7	85.3	10.6	4.3	2.9	5.4
23060	Fort Wayne, IN	406,469	1.8	7.5	19.3	8.8	27.4	25.3	11.8	35.9	85.9	10.9	2.2	3.5	4.9
23420	Fresno, CA	886,074	2.8	8.6	21.5	11.7	28.0	20.5	9.7	30.1	64.9	5.9	9.7	23.2	47.6
23460	Gadsden, AL	102,885	0.6	6.3	16.9	8.3	26.4	26.3	15.8	40.0	83.7	15.1	0.6	1.6	2.6
23540	Gainesville, FL	252,927	3.6	5.6	13.5	22.5	26.0	22.1	10.4	30.2	75.2	19.6	4.8	2.5	6.8
23580	Gainesville, GA	172,729	8.3	9.2	19.4	8.6	31.7	21.7	9.5	32.6	85.3	6.9	1.9	6.9	25.2
24020	Glens Falls, NY	128,279	0.8	4.9	16.1	9.2	27.6	26.9	15.3	39.9	96.5	2.6	0.8	1.1	1.9
24140	Goldsboro, NC	113,268	0.2	7.6	18.2	9.0	27.2	25.7	12.3	36.7	62.6	33.4	1.2	4.4	6.5

Area name	Percent foreign born	Total households	Household type (percent)						Percent of households with people under 18 years	Percent of households with people 60 years and over
			Family households				Nonfamily households			
			Total family households	Married-couple families	Male householder families	Female householder families	Total nonfamily households	One-person households		
ACS table number:	C05002	B11001	B11001	B11001	B11001	B11001	B11001	B11001	C11005	B11006
	15	16	17	18	19	20	21	22	23	24
•Gary, IN Division	5.5	262,903	68.7	49.6	4.5	14.7	31.3	26.7	34.6	31.7
•Lake County-Kenosha County, IL-WI Division	15.8	293,455	72.9	58.9	3.9	10.1	27.1	22.7	41.1	26.1
Chico, CA	7.5	84,607	58.6	43.3	4.3	11.0	41.4	29.0	29.6	33.8
Cincinnati-Middletown, OH-KY-IN	3.5	803,129	66.3	49.6	4.1	12.6	33.7	28.7	35.0	28.6
Clarksville, TN-KY	3.5	92,608	73.1	54.1	3.9	15.1	26.9	22.3	41.9	25.2
Cleveland, TN	3.1	44,083	70.4	55.5	4.8	10.2	29.6	24.8	32.7	33.4
Cleveland-Elyria-Mentor, OH	5.6	840,369	64.0	45.6	4.1	14.3	36.0	31.6	32.0	33.2
Coeur d'Alene, ID	2.5	50,628	68.5	54.1	4.0	10.4	31.5	25.1	33.6	32.2
College Station-Bryan, TX	11.5	73,853	57.4	41.9	4.6	11.0	42.6	28.0	31.8	21.8
Colorado Springs, CO	7.6	226,360	67.4	52.9	4.2	10.4	32.6	26.7	36.7	24.0
Columbia, MO	5.2	66,342	59.0	44.6	4.1	10.3	41.0	29.2	30.8	21.6
Columbia, SC	4.4	271,279	65.6	47.0	3.8	14.8	34.4	29.1	33.7	27.7
Columbus, GA-AL	3.4	108,447	67.1	43.3	4.5	19.3	32.9	28.9	36.6	30.0
Columbus, IN	5.9	27,992	71.8	57.4	4.3	10.1	28.2	22.8	36.8	30.4
Columbus, OH	6.2	677,522	64.6	48.2	4.5	11.9	35.4	28.4	35.1	25.3
Corpus Christi, TX	6.7	149,080	70.5	49.1	6.2	15.2	29.5	24.7	38.2	31.5
Corvallis, OR	8.8	32,517	58.1	45.6	3.9	8.6	41.9	28.0	27.9	26.2
Cumberland, MD-WV	1.0	40,370	63.1	48.6	4.6	9.9	36.9	30.6	29.2	38.3
Dallas-Fort Worth-Arlington, TX	17.7	2,080,056	69.3	51.5	5.1	12.7	30.7	25.5	40.3	22.8
•Dallas-Plano-Irving, TX Division	19.5	1,388,775	68.6	50.9	5.1	12.7	31.4	26.0	40.3	22.2
•Fort Worth-Arlington, TX Division	13.9	691,281	70.5	52.9	4.9	12.7	29.5	24.5	40.2	24.0
Dalton, GA	14.9	44,878	73.3	55.7	5.4	12.2	26.7	22.5	39.8	28.0
Danville, IL	1.7	32,857	66.1	48.0	4.9	13.2	33.9	28.8	32.5	36.9
Danville, VA	1.9	45,391	66.5	47.2	3.4	15.9	33.5	30.0	31.1	37.6
Davenport-Moline-Rock Island, IA-IL	3.9	151,011	64.7	50.1	3.5	11.1	35.3	30.2	30.6	32.2
Dayton, OH	2.8	340,416	64.1	47.1	4.0	13.0	35.9	30.1	31.5	31.7
Decatur, AL	3.6	58,878	72.0	56.4	4.0	11.6	28.0	25.0	34.2	34.3
Decatur, IL	1.9	46,343	65.5	49.3	4.1	12.1	34.5	29.6	30.8	32.9
Deltona-Daytona Beach-Ormond Beach, FL	7.6	201,368	62.3	47.6	3.9	10.8	37.7	30.5	26.7	42.6
Denver-Aurora, CO	12.5	941,502	63.6	49.0	4.6	10.1	36.4	29.4	34.0	24.1
Des Moines-West Des Moines, IA	6.1	214,297	66.0	52.1	3.6	10.3	34.0	28.0	35.1	26.0
Detroit-Warren-Livonia, MI	8.6	1,689,695	66.4	47.9	4.4	14.1	33.6	29.3	34.3	30.7
•Detroit-Livonia-Dearborn, MI Division	7.8	716,137	64.7	39.7	5.2	19.8	35.3	31.2	35.5	31.4
•Warren-Troy-Farmington Hills, MI Division	9.3	973,558	67.7	53.9	3.8	10.0	32.3	27.8	33.4	30.2
Dothan, AL	1.5	53,191	68.6	50.8	3.7	14.1	31.4	28.4	32.9	35.5
Dover, DE	4.8	55,685	71.1	52.7	4.2	14.3	28.9	24.2	37.8	31.4
Dubuque, IA	1.9	36,520	66.8	55.1	3.0	8.7	33.2	27.7	31.8	31.8
Duluth, MN-WI	1.7	116,391	61.7	48.4	4.0	9.4	38.3	31.0	27.9	33.3
Durham, NC	12.1	187,049	60.2	43.8	3.5	12.9	39.8	31.8	31.4	25.7
Eau Claire, WI	1.9	62,096	64.9	52.5	3.8	8.6	35.1	27.4	31.6	29.1
El Centro, CA	31.8	45,561	80.5	54.5	5.6	20.3	19.5	17.7	51.7	32.3
Elizabethtown, KY	3.6	42,038	73.4	57.6	4.2	11.6	26.6	22.8	36.5	28.4
Elkhart-Goshen, IN	9.5	70,835	72.3	55.1	5.4	11.8	27.7	22.2	40.3	27.6
Elmira, NY	2.1	34,767	65.7	48.1	3.8	13.7	34.3	28.7	34.7	34.5
El Paso, TX	27.0	229,655	76.9	51.5	5.4	20.0	23.1	19.9	47.4	30.0
Erie, PA	3.7	107,218	65.3	48.7	3.4	13.2	34.7	29.1	32.1	32.6
Eugene-Springfield, OR	6.1	137,630	61.0	47.1	4.0	9.8	39.0	28.5	28.5	30.4
Evansville, IN-KY	1.8	141,508	66.7	51.9	4.4	10.4	33.3	29.1	32.6	31.4
Fairbanks, AK	5.1	32,550	67.8	51.4	5.5	10.9	32.2	25.4	38.9	19.1
Fargo, ND-MN	3.5	80,333	57.9	46.1	3.0	8.7	42.1	31.5	30.3	21.9
Farmington, NM	2.7	38,466	74.5	53.6	7.1	13.8	25.5	21.8	39.5	28.3
Fayetteville, NC	4.9	130,880	69.5	46.7	4.2	18.5	30.5	25.0	41.0	24.1
Fayetteville-Springdale-Rogers, AR-MO	9.5	158,750	70.1	55.7	5.2	9.2	29.9	23.8	36.4	27.5
Flagstaff, AZ	5.6	43,286	66.5	48.8	4.7	13.0	33.5	23.7	34.4	24.6
Flint, MI	2.3	173,622	66.1	46.1	4.6	15.4	33.9	29.1	34.0	30.3
Florence, SC	2.2	72,678	70.1	47.8	3.7	18.6	29.9	27.0	35.1	32.1
Florence-Muscle Shoals, AL	1.4	58,668	69.0	53.8	3.4	11.7	31.0	28.0	30.6	36.7
Fond du Lac, WI	2.5	39,184	66.5	54.1	4.6	7.9	33.5	27.9	31.1	30.5
Fort Collins-Loveland, CO	5.2	111,524	62.7	50.1	3.7	8.8	37.3	27.1	31.1	23.6
Fort Smith, AR-OK	5.1	107,262	69.6	53.3	4.2	12.0	30.4	26.5	35.4	33.2
Fort Walton Beach-Crestview-Destin, FL	5.5	74,771	67.2	52.9	3.5	10.9	32.8	26.8	32.1	31.3
Fort Wayne, IN	4.4	159,348	66.5	51.5	3.9	11.2	33.5	27.8	35.2	26.7
Fresno, CA	21.7	276,929	72.8	50.1	6.6	16.2	27.2	21.9	44.7	28.9
Gadsden, AL	2.2	43,059	70.2	50.2	6.5	13.5	29.8	26.7	34.7	36.1
Gainesville, FL	9.3	101,425	53.7	38.0	4.0	11.7	46.3	32.3	25.1	25.6
Gainesville, GA	18.1	54,184	74.4	56.0	5.6	12.8	25.6	21.2	40.7	27.6
Glens Falls, NY	2.1	51,110	65.6	50.0	4.1	11.4	34.4	27.2	32.4	35.8
Goldsboro, NC	4.8	44,116	70.4	50.1	4.9	15.3	29.6	25.5	37.5	29.5

Metro area or division code	Area name	Total population	Percent change 2005–2007	Under 5 years	5 to 17 years	18 to 24 years	25 to 44 years	45 to 64 years	65 years and over	Median age	White	Black	Asian Hawaiian or Pacific Islander	Amer. Indian, Alaska Native, or some other race	Percent Hispanic or Latino
	ACS table number:	B01003	Population estimates	B01001	B01001	B01001	B01001	B01001	B01001	B01002	B02008	B02009	B02011 + B02012	B02010 + B02013	C03002
		1	2	3	4	5	6	7	8	9	10	11	12	13	14
24220	Grand Forks, ND-MN	97,635	-0.5	6.3	15.5	19.0	24.6	22.7	12.0	31.6	93.7	1.6	1.4	4.9	3.4
24300	Grand Junction, CO	134,258	7.2	6.5	16.4	9.9	26.8	25.2	15.2	37.1	92.4	1.2	1.2	7.9	11.4
24340	Grand Rapids-Wyoming, MI	772,963	0.9	7.4	19.4	9.6	28.7	24.2	10.7	34.8	86.4	8.4	2.1	5.4	7.7
24500	Great Falls, MT	81,832	0.0	7.2	17.9	8.2	25.3	26.6	14.8	39.2	91.9	2.4	1.7	6.7	3.1
24540	Greeley, CO	235,328	7.2	8.3	18.8	12.4	30.8	21.6	8.0	31.0	87.4	0.7	2.3	11.5	27.5
24580	Green Bay, WI	298,697	1.6	6.6	17.8	9.5	28.6	25.8	11.8	36.9	91.5	1.9	2.3	5.8	4.7
24660	Greensboro-High Point, NC	686,727	3.3	6.5	17.2	9.5	28.1	26.1	12.5	37.4	69.5	24.8	2.5	4.8	6.3
24780	Greenville, NC	168,528	5.4	7.2	16.7	15.8	27.9	22.5	10.0	32.1	61.1	35.0	1.3	4.4	5.1
24860	Greenville-Mauldin-Easley, SC	601,403	4.1	6.6	17.2	10.4	27.9	25.7	12.3	36.9	79.3	17.4	2.0	2.4	5.2
25060	Gulfport-Biloxi, MS	238,611	-9.7	6.9	18.8	9.4	26.8	25.8	12.3	37.0	76.1	20.4	3.1	2.7	3.2
25180	Hagerstown-Martinsburg, MD-WV	255,762	4.4	6.7	17.3	7.8	30.8	24.6	12.7	37.1	90.7	8.3	1.3	1.6	2.4
25260	Hanford-Corcoran, CA	146,308	3.3	8.2	19.2	12.8	34.5	17.8	7.4	30.0	70.9	8.6	4.5	19.6	47.4
25420	Harrisburg-Carlisle, PA	524,665	1.6	5.9	16.4	9.2	26.8	27.5	14.2	39.6	86.3	10.6	2.5	2.1	3.4
25500	Harrisonburg, VA	115,981	2.9	5.9	14.7	20.5	24.5	22.3	12.1	32.0	93.0	4.2	2.3	2.1	7.5
25540	Hartford-West Hartford-East Hartford, CT	1,185,150	0.7	5.9	17.1	9.7	26.6	27.0	13.7	39.3	80.8	11.0	3.5	6.7	10.6
25620	Hattiesburg, MS	135,128	5.1	7.5	18.2	14.2	27.5	21.8	10.9	31.4	70.4	27.4	1.2	2.0	1.5
25860	Hickory-Lenoir-Morganton, NC	357,202	1.7	6.2	17.3	7.8	28.4	26.6	13.7	38.8	86.2	7.5	2.4	5.1	5.9
25980	Hinesville-Fort Stewart, GA	72,255	-2.8	10.4	23.1	13.6	31.0	16.8	5.0	26.6	53.7	40.8	2.9	5.5	7.7
26100	Holland-Grand Haven, MI	256,976	1.7	6.9	19.5	12.4	27.1	23.4	10.7	33.4	92.1	1.8	2.8	5.4	7.9
26180	Honolulu, HI	904,783	0.1	6.6	15.6	10.3	28.5	24.6	14.5	37.3	37.0	4.5	81.4	4.5	7.4
26300	Hot Springs, AR	94,967	3.3	5.9	15.6	7.8	24.4	25.2	20.9	41.9	88.2	8.8	0.8	3.9	3.5
26380	Houma-Bayou Cane-Thibodaux, LA	199,953	1.8	7.0	18.8	10.1	28.5	24.3	11.3	35.3	78.1	16.6	0.9	5.4	2.1
26420	Houston-Sugar Land-Baytown, TX	5,485,720	5.6	8.4	20.0	9.6	30.3	23.7	8.1	32.9	64.9	17.3	6.0	13.3	32.8
26580	Huntington-Ashland, WV-KY-OH	284,339	-0.2	5.9	15.7	9.5	26.3	26.9	15.6	39.5	96.4	3.2	0.7	0.9	0.8
26620	Huntsville, AL	378,057	4.6	6.3	18.2	9.8	27.9	25.8	12.1	37.4	74.5	22.5	2.4	2.4	2.8
26820	Idaho Falls, ID	115,627	6.4	9.7	21.3	9.5	25.9	23.5	10.3	31.4	95.2	0.8	1.1	4.5	9.0
26900	Indianapolis-Carmel, IN	1,670,070	3.0	7.7	19.1	8.3	30.0	24.5	10.5	35.4	81.3	15.1	2.1	3.2	4.4
26980	Iowa City, IA	144,748	3.1	6.3	14.9	19.6	28.5	21.6	9.2	30.6	90.5	3.8	4.6	2.3	3.3
27060	Ithaca, NY	100,590	0.5	4.1	11.7	28.2	25.7	20.8	9.5	28.4	84.9	4.8	10.9	2.4	3.9
27100	Jackson, MI	162,934	0.1	6.4	17.8	8.8	27.9	26.3	12.8	37.9	89.4	9.3	0.9	2.4	2.6
27140	Jackson, MS	529,030	2.4	7.7	19.3	10.9	27.0	24.3	10.8	34.1	51.7	46.9	1.0	1.1	1.4
27180	Jackson, TN	111,893	1.6	6.8	18.4	10.6	26.8	25.0	12.4	35.7	68.2	30.7	0.9	1.1	2.4
27260	Jacksonville, FL	1,276,523	4.0	7.1	17.9	9.1	28.4	26.5	11.1	36.9	72.9	22.7	3.6	2.8	5.4
27340	Jacksonville, NC	161,524	2.8	9.4	17.9	21.6	26.3	17.8	7.0	25.4	76.2	19.0	3.4	6.5	6.6
27500	Janesville, WI	158,104	1.9	6.7	18.4	8.4	27.8	25.8	12.8	37.1	91.3	5.1	1.3	3.9	5.7
27620	Jefferson City, MO	144,663	1.2	6.6	17.3	10.3	27.9	25.9	11.9	37.1	90.8	7.3	1.2	2.2	1.7
27740	Johnson City, TN	191,320	2.4	5.5	15.1	9.9	28.2	26.1	15.2	39.0	96.2	3.4	0.8	1.1	1.8
27780	Johnstown, PA	145,984	-1.2	5.1	14.5	9.8	23.8	28.0	18.8	42.5	95.6	3.7	0.6	0.7	1.1
27860	Jonesboro, AR	114,563	2.7	7.0	17.6	11.4	28.6	23.2	12.2	34.3	88.7	10.2	0.8	1.4	2.9
27900	Joplin, MO	168,645	3.1	7.4	18.3	9.2	27.3	24.2	13.6	35.7	94.2	1.7	1.5	4.8	4.6
28020	Kalamazoo-Portage, MI	322,165	0.6	6.5	17.4	13.4	26.0	24.8	11.9	35.0	87.2	9.7	2.2	3.2	4.6
28100	Kankakee-Bradley, IL	109,276	2.9	7.0	18.7	9.9	27.2	24.2	12.9	35.4	81.8	15.5	1.1	2.8	6.8
28140	Kansas City, MO-KS	1,962,412	2.3	7.4	18.6	8.5	28.6	25.6	11.3	36.3	82.7	13.0	2.5	4.1	6.7
28420	Kennewick-Richland-Pasco, WA	223,867	4.4	8.2	20.6	9.5	28.1	23.9	9.7	32.8	80.2	1.9	3.0	17.0	25.1
28660	Killeen-Temple-Fort Hood, TX	360,740	4.7	9.3	21.4	10.8	30.9	18.8	8.9	29.9	72.2	21.3	4.3	6.6	17.4
28700	Kingsport-Bristol-Bristol, TN-VA	301,803	1.1	5.3	15.6	7.4	26.7	28.1	16.9	41.6	96.9	2.6	0.4	1.1	0.9
28740	Kingston, NY	181,755	0.1	5.0	16.1	10.7	26.5	28.3	13.4	40.0	90.5	7.1	2.1	2.6	7.2
28940	Knoxville, TN	669,962	3.5	6.1	16.1	9.9	27.5	26.6	13.8	38.5	91.2	7.1	1.6	1.6	2.0
29020	Kokomo, IN	100,172	-0.9	6.6	17.7	7.3	26.6	27.2	14.6	39.2	92.3	6.5	1.2	1.3	1.9
29100	La Crosse, WI-MN	130,094	1.4	5.8	16.3	14.1	25.8	24.7	13.3	35.8	95.5	1.3	3.2	0.8	1.0
29140	Lafayette, IN	189,237	3.2	6.3	15.2	21.5	26.9	20.0	10.1	29.2	90.6	3.3	4.9	2.4	6.3
29180	Lafayette, LA	252,877	3.7	7.3	18.8	11.1	28.4	24.2	10.2	33.5	70.9	27.2	1.5	1.4	2.1
29340	Lake Charles, LA	191,253	-1.1	7.1	18.7	10.0	26.8	24.9	12.5	35.7	74.7	24.3	0.9	1.7	1.8
29420	Lake Havasu City-Kingman, AZ	190,623	5.4	6.2	16.2	6.9	23.7	26.2	20.9	42.5	92.6	1.3	1.7	7.4	13.6
29460	Lakeland, FL	557,184	6.5	7.0	17.2	8.5	26.3	23.6	17.4	38.2	78.7	14.7	1.7	7.1	14.5
29540	Lancaster, PA	493,910	1.9	6.9	18.5	8.8	26.4	25.0	14.3	37.3	92.2	4.1	1.9	3.1	6.7
29620	Lansing-East Lansing, MI	456,786	-0.3	6.1	16.8	15.3	25.9	25.2	10.7	34.3	86.4	9.5	3.7	3.1	4.9
29700	Laredo, TX	227,578	4.7	13.0	24.2	11.3	26.4	17.1	8.0	26.2	75.6	0.6	0.6	24.4	94.7
29740	Las Cruces, NM	194,181	4.6	8.3	19.2	13.7	26.5	20.7	11.6	30.9	86.3	2.2	1.4	11.6	64.6
29820	Las Vegas-Paradise, NV	1,774,086	7.3	7.8	18.4	8.0	31.3	24.0	10.4	35.0	74.3	10.6	9.1	9.6	26.9
29940	Lawrence, KS	112,522	1.7	5.5	13.7	24.0	28.5	19.5	8.6	28.2	88.1	5.3	4.6	4.7	3.8
30020	Lawton, OK	112,719	1.9	8.8	20.3	12.0	27.1	21.3	10.6	31.8	69.1	21.0	4.5	12.5	9.2
30140	Lebanon, PA	126,426	2.4	6.2	16.5	8.2	26.7	26.1	16.3	39.7	92.8	2.2	1.1	5.0	6.5
30300	Lewiston, ID-WA	59,548	1.6	6.0	16.3	9.1	24.5	26.2	17.8	40.7	95.9	1.2	1.5	4.7	2.3
30340	Lewiston-Auburn, ME	106,837	0.1	6.2	16.8	8.9	27.5	26.5	14.2	39.4	95.0	3.8	0.9	8.5	1.4
30460	Lexington-Fayette, KY	440,380	3.2	6.9	16.0	11.4	30.3	24.7	10.7	35.2	85.7	11.2	2.4	2.3	4.2
30620	Lima, OH	105,391	-0.4	6.8	18.1	10.1	25.0	25.5	14.4	37.1	85.8	12.8	0.8	2.1	1.7
30700	Lincoln, NE	288,637	2.3	7.2	16.3	14.3	28.9	22.9	10.4	32.7	91.9	3.8	3.5	2.6	4.2
30780	Little Rock-North Little Rock-Conway, AR	656,501	3.2	7.2	18.1	9.6	28.1	25.3	11.6	35.8	75.0	22.7	1.6	2.3	3.2
30860	Logan, UT-ID	118,774	3.9	10.6	20.8	18.7	26.3	15.9	7.8	25.0	93.5	0.9	2.7	4.5	8.1

Area name	Percent foreign born	Total households	Household type (percent)						Percent of households with people under 18 years	Percent of households with people 60 years and over
			Family households				Nonfamily households			
			Total family households	Married-couple families	Male householder families	Female householder families	Total nonfamily households	One-person households		
ACS table number:	C05002	B11001	B11001	B11001	B11001	B11001	B11001	B11001	C11005	B11006
	15	16	17	18	19	20	21	22	23	24
Grand Forks, ND-MN	2.4	39,388	58.5	48.0	3.0	7.6	41.5	31.0	28.6	26.8
Grand Junction, CO	3.9	53,533	66.9	51.3	5.0	10.6	33.1	25.9	32.4	33.9
Grand Rapids-Wyoming, MI	6.7	288,574	68.5	52.7	4.5	11.4	31.5	25.7	36.7	26.6
Great Falls, MT...........................	1.9	32,190	66.5	52.2	4.7	9.6	33.5	28.6	33.0	33.3
Greeley, CO	9.8	81,024	70.1	56.9	4.0	9.3	29.9	23.0	40.2	22.7
Green Bay, WI	4.2	119,412	66.8	52.2	4.6	10.0	33.2	26.9	35.2	27.3
Greensboro-High Point, NC	7.5	275,069	65.4	47.2	4.5	13.6	34.6	29.1	34.0	29.9
Greenville, NC	4.6	68,011	60.4	41.4	3.8	15.3	39.6	30.9	33.3	24.8
Greenville-Mauldin-Easley, SC	6.3	233,053	67.7	50.9	4.3	12.5	32.3	27.4	33.2	30.4
Gulfport-Biloxi, MS	3.8	91,367	70.2	49.4	5.4	15.3	29.8	24.8	37.5	30.9
Hagerstown-Martinsburg, MD-WV....	3.1	99,509	67.8	51.9	4.4	11.5	32.2	26.2	35.8	29.0
Hanford-Corcoran, CA.....................	20.5	38,808	78.6	56.6	8.5	13.5	21.4	18.2	51.4	25.3
Harrisburg-Carlisle, PA	4.4	211,113	64.8	50.4	3.8	10.7	35.2	29.0	30.6	31.8
Harrisonburg, VA	7.5	42,427	64.8	51.2	5.6	7.9	35.2	26.2	31.1	29.9
Hartford-West Hartford-East Hartford, CT	11.6	455,433	66.4	50.3	4.0	12.2	33.6	27.8	33.5	32.8
Hattiesburg, MS	2.1	49,040	65.3	46.2	3.5	15.5	34.7	28.5	35.4	28.0
Hickory-Lenoir-Morganton, NC	5.3	136,948	68.2	52.3	4.7	11.3	31.8	27.4	33.0	33.2
Hinesville-Fort Stewart, GA	5.7	24,081	73.0	48.5	3.6	20.9	27.0	23.1	47.1	15.7
Holland-Grand Haven, MI	5.3	90,396	74.9	64.5	3.3	7.1	25.1	20.3	39.1	26.9
Honolulu, HI	18.7	301,189	70.4	52.6	5.1	12.7	29.6	23.8	35.3	37.6
Hot Springs, AR	3.9	38,796	63.3	47.8	3.6	11.9	36.7	32.7	26.8	42.9
Houma-Bayou Cane-Thibodaux, LA...	1.9	70,937	73.4	55.1	4.2	14.1	26.6	21.3	40.3	29.7
Houston-Sugar Land-Baytown, TX.....	21.3	1,857,040	70.8	51.7	5.5	13.6	29.2	24.3	41.6	23.9
Huntington-Ashland, WV-KY-OH.......	1.0	114,923	67.1	51.4	3.6	12.2	32.9	28.5	30.9	36.3
Huntsville, AL.............................	4.6	147,283	67.9	51.6	3.9	12.3	32.1	27.7	33.1	29.6
Idaho Falls, ID	4.7	40,910	74.3	62.0	3.4	9.0	25.7	21.4	40.1	28.1
Indianapolis-Carmel, IN	5.2	651,395	66.5	49.6	4.4	12.5	33.5	27.6	36.1	25.8
Iowa City, IA	6.4	58,529	56.2	45.6	2.5	8.1	43.8	30.5	29.1	20.7
Ithaca, NY................................	13.0	37,374	52.3	42.8	2.4	7.0	47.7	30.6	24.0	24.4
Jackson, MI................................	1.7	60,667	68.3	51.9	4.1	12.4	31.7	26.8	35.1	31.8
Jackson, MS...............................	1.5	193,661	67.2	44.4	4.2	18.6	32.8	28.5	36.8	28.5
Jackson, TN...............................	2.6	44,360	68.6	47.7	4.9	16.0	31.4	27.4	36.1	29.5
Jacksonville, FL...........................	6.9	498,655	66.5	48.6	4.4	13.6	33.5	27.1	34.3	28.5
Jacksonville, NC	4.6	54,259	74.4	56.5	3.0	14.9	25.6	20.9	41.3	21.9
Janesville, WI	4.6	62,035	66.9	51.7	4.3	11.0	33.1	28.3	34.1	30.4
Jefferson City, MO	2.1	54,568	68.1	54.1	3.7	10.3	31.9	26.8	34.9	28.2
Johnson City, TN	2.3	76,443	65.0	50.5	4.0	10.6	35.0	29.7	29.5	34.3
Johnstown, PA............................	1.6	59,305	67.0	51.2	3.9	11.9	33.0	29.5	27.8	41.5
Jonesboro, AR............................	2.4	44,114	68.2	49.6	4.4	14.3	31.8	27.1	33.6	29.4
Joplin, MO................................	3.1	64,286	68.9	52.8	4.8	11.3	31.1	26.5	35.9	33.0
Kalamazoo-Portage, MI..................	4.5	127,037	62.8	47.7	4.2	10.9	37.2	28.5	32.0	28.4
Kankakee-Bradley, IL	4.6	40,249	69.4	51.5	4.3	13.6	30.6	25.1	38.2	30.9
Kansas City, MO-KS	5.6	767,120	66.2	50.3	4.0	11.9	33.8	28.1	35.1	27.7
Kennewick-Richland-Pasco, WA........	14.5	76,486	71.6	55.3	5.8	10.4	28.4	23.6	40.1	27.7
Killeen-Temple-Fort Hood, TX...........	7.1	120,975	72.2	54.2	4.0	14.0	27.8	24.1	43.0	24.1
Kingsport-Bristol-Bristol, TN-VA........	1.1	129,524	67.8	52.4	4.4	11.1	32.2	27.9	30.2	36.6
Kingston, NY	7.1	69,354	63.7	48.9	3.7	11.0	36.3	28.0	30.3	33.7
Knoxville, TN	3.3	276,343	65.7	50.9	3.7	11.1	34.3	28.8	31.1	31.7
Kokomo, IN	2.3	41,471	70.4	53.6	4.2	12.6	29.6	25.5	33.1	31.5
La Crosse, WI-MN	2.7	52,240	62.5	50.5	3.0	9.0	37.5	29.2	30.5	28.3
Lafayette, IN	8.8	72,091	60.8	46.4	4.6	9.7	39.2	28.3	31.7	24.8
Lafayette, LA..............................	2.7	99,436	66.3	45.7	4.7	15.9	33.7	26.9	36.9	24.6
Lake Charles, LA	1.7	74,958	68.6	48.9	5.3	14.4	31.4	27.2	36.2	31.4
Lake Havasu City-Kingman, AZ	6.8	75,033	68.6	52.5	4.6	11.5	31.4	24.7	28.7	45.5
Lakeland, FL...............................	10.1	222,196	70.7	53.5	5.2	12.1	29.3	23.4	33.6	38.0
Lancaster, PA..............................	4.0	185,001	70.3	57.8	3.6	8.9	29.7	24.1	34.7	31.4
Lansing-East Lansing, MI	6.1	177,581	63.1	48.3	3.7	11.1	36.9	28.7	31.1	26.8
Laredo, TX	28.5	60,859	83.5	56.1	5.9	21.5	16.5	14.1	57.4	29.0
Las Cruces, NM	19.3	68,164	69.9	50.8	3.9	15.3	30.1	23.1	38.2	28.9
Las Vegas-Paradise, NV	21.2	662,025	65.7	46.9	6.5	12.4	34.3	26.2	35.4	28.7
Lawrence, KS..............................	6.9	42,996	55.2	41.5	3.2	10.5	44.8	31.5	29.5	22.0
Lawton, OK...............................	4.7	41,060	71.1	50.7	3.5	16.8	28.9	24.6	38.9	29.7
Lebanon, PA	2.7	49,465	68.7	54.6	4.0	10.1	31.3	26.0	31.5	36.2
Lewiston, ID-WA	1.9	24,405	66.2	50.9	5.0	10.3	33.8	27.1	31.6	35.2
Lewiston-Auburn, ME	4.0	43,450	66.1	50.0	5.8	10.3	33.9	26.7	32.1	30.7
Lexington-Fayette, KY	5.6	181,595	62.2	46.6	4.2	11.4	37.8	29.7	32.1	25.3
Lima, OH	1.5	40,596	68.0	52.2	3.3	12.5	32.0	27.2	35.0	33.4
Lincoln, NE................................	6.5	114,228	62.2	50.0	3.6	8.5	37.8	29.5	32.7	24.0
Little Rock-North Little Rock-Conway, AR................................	3.4	259,043	66.9	49.5	3.6	13.7	33.1	28.0	34.5	28.5
Logan, UT-ID	6.5	35,397	77.0	67.0	2.8	7.1	23.0	16.2	44.7	23.7

Table A-3. Metropolitan Areas — Who: Age, Race/Ethnicity, and Household Structure, 2005–2007—*Continued*

Metro area or division code	Area name	Total population	Percent change 2005–2007	Population by age (percent)						Median age	Race alone or in combination (percent)				Percent Hispanic or Latino
				Under 5 years	5 to 17 years	18 to 24 years	25 to 44 years	45 to 64 years	65 years and over		White	Black	Asian Hawaiian or Pacific Islander	Amer. Indian, Alaska Native, or some other race	
	ACS table number:	B01003	Population estimates	B01001	B01001	B01001	B01001	B01001	B01001	B01002	B02008	B02009	B02011 + B02012	B02010 + B02013	C03002
		1	2	3	4	5	6	7	8	9	10	11	12	13	14
30980	Longview, TX	201,692	1.9	7.4	17.8	9.4	26.7	24.5	14.2	36.2	75.7	18.3	0.7	6.5	10.6
31020	Longview, WA	98,547	4.1	6.4	18.1	8.8	26.3	26.9	13.4	38.0	95.1	1.0	2.1	5.1	5.9
31100	Los Angeles-Long Beach-Santa Ana, CA	12,872,056	-0.2	7.2	19.1	10.2	30.0	23.0	10.4	34.4	54.8	7.9	14.9	25.3	43.9
31100 31084	•Los Angeles-Long Beach-Glendale, CA Division	9,883,649	-0.4	7.3	19.2	10.4	30.2	22.7	10.2	34.1	51.6	9.6	14.2	27.6	47.1
31100 42044	•Santa Ana-Anaheim-Irvine, CA Division	2,988,407	0.2	7.1	18.7	9.7	29.6	24.0	10.8	35.5	65.3	2.1	17.4	17.8	33.0
31140	Louisville-Jefferson County, KY-IN	1,220,992	2.1	6.7	17.7	8.4	28.1	26.8	12.3	37.8	84.1	13.9	1.6	1.9	2.5
31180	Lubbock, TX	264,705	2.1	7.7	17.5	15.7	26.6	21.1	11.3	30.8	80.4	7.9	1.7	11.9	30.2
31340	Lynchburg, VA	239,546	3.3	5.8	16.0	11.5	25.6	26.1	15.0	39.1	80.6	18.3	1.1	1.6	1.3
31420	Macon, GA	226,689	1.0	7.2	19.1	9.9	26.2	25.4	12.1	36.3	55.2	43.1	1.1	1.5	1.6
31460	Madera, CA	143,656	4.0	8.1	19.9	10.8	29.2	21.8	10.3	32.3	80.7	4.6	2.6	15.7	49.3
31540	Madison, WI	548,154	2.7	6.3	15.9	12.5	30.0	25.2	10.1	35.4	90.1	4.6	4.3	2.9	4.2
31700	Manchester-Nashua, NH	400,855	0.7	6.4	18.5	8.0	28.6	27.5	11.0	38.4	93.4	2.2	3.4	2.2	4.5
31900	Mansfield, OH	126,369	-0.8	6.0	17.1	8.6	26.1	27.0	15.2	39.3	94.2	10.6	0.8	1.2	1.1
32580	McAllen-Edinburg-Mission, TX	689,929	5.7	12.0	23.7	11.1	26.8	16.9	9.5	27.1	67.0	0.7	0.9	32.4	89.3
32780	Medford, OR	196,866	2.4	5.6	16.4	9.0	24.9	27.8	16.3	40.8	95.5	1.0	2.1	4.4	8.4
32820	Memphis, TN-MS-AR	1,269,637	2.1	7.7	19.9	9.5	27.9	25.0	10.0	34.7	51.3	45.4	2.0	2.6	3.5
32900	Merced, CA	242,173	2.6	8.9	23.0	11.5	27.9	19.4	9.3	29.0	65.9	4.2	7.9	25.1	51.7
33100	Miami-Fort Lauderdale-Pompano Beach, FL	5,404,990	0.3	6.4	16.5	8.6	27.3	25.1	16.0	39.4	71.7	20.9	2.6	6.7	38.3
33100 22744	•Fort Lauderdale-Pompano Beach-Deerfield Beach, FL Division	1,767,681	-0.8	6.5	17.3	7.9	28.0	26.1	14.2	39.0	67.8	25.3	3.5	5.9	22.7
33100 33124	•Miami-Miami Beach-Kendall, FL Division	2,373,297	1.1	6.6	16.6	9.7	28.1	24.5	14.4	38.2	73.2	20.2	1.8	6.4	61.4
33100 48424	•West Palm Beach-Boca Raton-Boynton Beach, FL Division	1,264,012	0.4	6.0	15.3	7.4	24.8	24.9	21.5	42.5	74.3	16.0	2.5	8.3	16.7
33140	Michigan City-La Porte, IN	109,440	1.0	6.1	17.2	8.2	27.9	26.9	13.7	38.7	88.0	11.1	0.6	2.3	4.0
33260	Midland, TX	123,532	4.8	8.1	20.1	10.7	24.6	24.7	11.8	34.0	85.3	7.1	1.4	7.9	34.9
33340	Milwaukee-Waukesha-West Allis, WI	1,539,985	0.6	7.0	18.4	9.2	26.8	26.3	12.3	37.2	76.0	16.9	2.9	5.8	7.9
33460	Minneapolis-St. Paul-Bloomington, MN-WI	3,172,801	2.1	7.1	18.4	9.1	29.8	25.7	9.8	36.0	85.9	7.3	5.4	3.4	4.4
33540	Missoula, MT	103,986	3.4	5.6	15.5	14.2	28.4	25.9	10.4	34.1	95.2	0.9	2.0	4.2	2.3
33660	Mobile, AL	401,616	1.6	7.3	19.2	9.5	26.3	25.4	12.3	35.8	62.6	34.7	2.1	1.7	1.6
33700	Modesto, CA	506,405	1.8	8.0	21.1	10.7	28.5	21.6	10.1	31.6	75.6	3.3	6.7	17.9	38.2
33740	Monroe, LA	171,962	0.8	7.4	18.9	11.2	26.5	23.4	12.5	34.2	64.4	34.2	1.0	1.5	1.8
33780	Monroe, MI	153,098	0.7	5.8	18.7	9.1	27.3	27.3	11.8	37.8	96.5	2.8	0.8	1.6	2.6
33860	Montgomery, AL	361,759	2.8	7.3	18.7	10.8	27.2	24.6	11.5	35.1	55.7	42.6	1.3	1.5	1.6
34060	Morgantown, WV	116,947	1.4	5.3	13.4	20.2	26.2	23.3	11.5	33.0	94.2	3.6	2.2	1.1	1.2
34100	Morristown, TN	132,267	3.4	6.3	16.4	9.0	28.1	25.8	14.4	38.2	95.2	2.9	0.9	2.5	5.5
34580	Mount Vernon-Anacortes, WA	114,372	3.5	6.3	17.7	9.5	26.4	25.4	14.7	37.5	87.4	1.1	2.8	10.1	13.7
34620	Muncie, IN	115,939	-1.2	5.4	15.4	17.2	24.1	23.8	14.1	34.9	91.2	7.5	1.3	1.4	1.3
34740	Muskegon-Norton Shores, MI	174,236	0.1	6.7	18.9	9.2	27.2	25.5	12.5	36.5	82.9	14.5	0.8	3.6	4.2
34820	Myrtle Beach-Conway-North Myrtle Beach, SC	239,419	9.4	6.3	15.2	8.2	28.5	25.4	16.3	39.3	81.4	15.1	1.3	3.2	4.0
34900	Napa, CA	131,505	1.3	6.2	16.6	10.1	26.2	26.5	14.4	38.5	83.7	1.9	7.1	10.0	28.6
34940	Naples-Marco Island, FL	311,926	2.7	6.4	14.3	6.7	24.5	23.6	24.5	43.6	85.6	6.0	1.1	8.2	24.9
34980	Nashville-Davidson–Murfreesboro–Franklin, TN	1,486,442	4.9	7.1	17.6	9.3	30.1	25.5	10.4	35.9	80.2	15.9	2.3	2.6	4.9
35300	New Haven-Milford, CT	843,571	0.5	6.1	17.4	9.6	27.4	25.8	13.7	38.1	79.4	13.1	3.7	6.1	12.3
35380	New Orleans-Metairie-Kenner, LA	1,110,265	-15.5	6.5	17.5	10.5	26.1	27.2	12.2	37.8	61.3	34.5	2.9	2.7	5.7
35620	New York-Northern New Jersey-Long Island, NY-NJ-PA	18,785,319	0.6	6.6	17.1	9.1	29.0	25.4	12.8	37.5	60.9	18.4	9.5	12.8	21.1
35620 20764	•Edison, NJ Division	2,308,807	0.7	6.4	17.4	8.4	27.6	25.9	14.3	38.8	77.7	7.9	10.0	5.7	11.2
35620 35004	•Nassau-Suffolk, NY Division	2,770,641	0.2	6.1	18.2	9.2	25.2	27.7	13.6	39.6	80.9	9.6	5.3	5.8	12.5
35620 35084	•Newark-Union, NJ-PA Division	2,128,704	-0.2	6.7	18.3	8.6	27.6	26.8	12.0	38.2	64.7	22.1	5.3	9.2	15.8
35620 35644	•New York-White Plains-Wayne, NY-NJ Division	11,577,167	0.8	6.7	16.6	9.4	30.4	24.4	12.5	36.6	52.1	22.0	11.3	16.6	26.1
35660	Niles-Benton Harbor, MI	159,806	-0.4	6.6	18.1	8.5	24.8	26.9	15.0	39.6	81.7	15.6	1.6	2.9	3.7
35980	Norwich-New London, CT	267,029	-0.5	5.9	17.1	9.1	28.9	25.9	13.0	38.2	85.7	7.0	4.1	6.4	6.2
36100	Ocala, FL	313,658	7.5	5.5	14.9	7.7	24.2	23.8	23.9	43.4	84.3	11.8	1.5	3.3	8.6
36140	Ocean City, NJ	97,555	-2.3	4.9	15.6	7.3	24.2	27.5	20.5	43.8	92.0	6.3	0.2	2.6	4.1
36220	Odessa, TX	126,914	4.1	9.0	20.5	10.8	26.0	22.7	11.0	31.7	84.6	3.8	1.2	14.9	48.4
36260	Ogden-Clearfield, UT	504,616	5.3	9.4	22.0	11.6	27.7	20.4	8.8	28.8	93.9	1.9	2.6	3.7	10.3
36420	Oklahoma City, OK	1,175,167	3.0	7.5	17.8	10.9	27.9	24.4	11.5	34.6	79.8	11.7	3.6	10.6	8.9
36500	Olympia, WA	233,113	4.7	5.8	16.8	9.7	28.3	27.6	11.9	37.5	87.4	3.7	7.1	5.5	5.5
36540	Omaha-Council Bluffs, NE-IA	820,725	2.2	7.9	18.8	9.9	28.3	24.4	10.8	34.6	87.1	8.4	2.5	4.3	7.0
36740	Orlando-Kissimmee, FL	1,990,388	4.8	7.0	17.3	9.3	29.6	24.4	12.6	36.4	73.3	15.8	4.1	9.0	21.7
36780	Oshkosh-Neenah, WI	161,074	1.2	5.7	16.1	11.6	28.4	25.6	12.5	37.2	94.9	1.8	2.1	2.2	2.7
36980	Owensboro, KY	111,444	1.1	7.0	17.7	8.6	26.0	26.3	14.4	38.2	94.5	4.6	0.6	1.4	1.2
37100	Oxnard-Thousand Oaks-Ventura, CA	794,412	0.5	7.2	19.3	10.2	27.2	25.2	10.9	35.5	72.2	2.7	8.0	20.7	36.7
37340	Palm Bay-Melbourne-Titusville, FL	531,642	1.7	5.1	15.4	8.1	24.1	27.2	20.0	43.2	86.0	10.1	2.7	3.0	6.5
37380	Palm Coast, FL	82,085	17.0	4.8	13.7	7.8	24.6	24.8	24.3	44.3	86.4	10.2	2.1	2.7	7.6

Area name	Percent foreign born	Total households	Household type (percent)						Percent of households with people under 18 years	Percent of households with people 60 years and over
			Family households				Nonfamily households			
			Total family households	Married-couple families	Male householder families	Female householder families	Total nonfamily households	One-person households		
ACS table number:	C05002	B11001	B11001	B11001	B11001	B11001	B11001	B11001	C11005	B11006
	15	16	17	18	19	20	21	22	23	24
Longview, TX	6.1	74,749	70.2	53.0	4.2	12.9	29.8	26.0	36.5	34.6
Longview, WA	4.4	37,931	69.2	51.5	5.2	12.5	30.8	25.5	36.1	32.3
Los Angeles-Long Beach-Santa Ana, CA	34.6	4,148,481	68.1	47.7	6.3	14.1	31.9	25.2	38.9	29.7
•Los Angeles-Long Beach-Glendale, CA Division	35.8	3,176,441	67.3	45.8	6.5	15.0	32.7	26.0	39.1	29.3
•Santa Ana-Anaheim-Irvine, CA Division......	30.5	972,040	70.6	53.9	5.6	11.1	29.4	22.8	38.4	30.8
Louisville-Jefferson County, KY-IN......	3.6	489,689	65.3	47.9	4.4	13.1	34.7	29.5	34.5	29.3
Lubbock, TX.....................	3.7	102,286	64.5	47.1	4.7	12.7	35.5	26.9	31.7	26.4
Lynchburg, VA	2.3	95,650	67.2	50.8	3.3	13.1	32.8	27.7	33.8	34.8
Macon, GA	2.0	84,844	66.2	45.0	4.2	17.0	33.8	29.4	33.8	32.0
Madera, CA	20.6	41,849	79.3	60.2	8.1	11.0	20.7	17.6	45.8	32.4
Madison, WI	6.4	219,711	59.9	49.0	3.6	7.3	40.1	30.4	30.0	23.6
Manchester-Nashua, NH	8.6	149,761	68.5	53.9	4.6	10.1	31.5	24.2	35.6	27.4
Mansfield, OH.....................	1.5	49,720	67.8	52.4	2.9	12.4	32.2	27.3	31.8	34.5
McAllen-Edinburg-Mission, TX	28.5	201,366	83.1	59.9	4.2	19.0	16.9	14.6	54.9	30.1
Medford, OR.....................	5.4	80,058	63.5	48.6	4.1	10.8	36.5	29.0	29.8	36.5
Memphis, TN-MS-AR	4.3	475,835	67.1	42.7	5.4	19.1	32.9	28.0	37.0	26.9
Merced, CA	25.4	72,599	78.6	56.7	6.6	15.2	21.4	17.2	51.4	27.0
Miami-Fort Lauderdale-Pompano Beach, FL	36.9	2,015,132	65.0	45.7	5.1	14.3	35.0	28.6	32.2	37.6
•Fort Lauderdale-Pompano Beach-Deerfield Beach, FL Division...............	29.9	676,384	62.7	44.5	4.7	13.5	37.3	30.2	32.2	34.6
•Miami-Miami Beach-Kendall, FL Division.....................	50.4	830,844	68.7	45.5	5.9	17.3	31.3	25.9	35.4	36.3
•West Palm Beach-Boca Raton-Boynton Beach, FL Division...............	21.2	507,904	62.1	47.6	4.2	10.4	37.9	31.1	27.1	43.8
Michigan City-La Porte, IN.................	3.1	41,694	68.3	51.0	4.6	12.7	31.7	26.8	33.3	33.5
Midland, TX.....................	8.7	46,331	69.4	54.6	3.3	11.4	30.6	26.3	38.6	28.2
Milwaukee-Waukesha-West Allis, WI.....................	6.5	607,687	63.3	46.2	4.2	12.9	36.7	30.7	32.4	29.2
Minneapolis-St. Paul-Bloomington, MN-WI.....................	8.7	1,233,149	65.1	51.0	4.2	9.9	34.9	27.9	34.9	24.4
Missoula, MT	2.5	40,636	58.5	45.8	4.1	8.6	41.5	29.5	27.3	26.0
Mobile, AL.....................	3.1	150,853	69.8	46.4	4.9	18.5	30.2	26.5	36.4	31.9
Modesto, CA.....................	19.9	158,856	74.2	54.1	6.3	13.8	25.8	20.4	44.0	29.4
Monroe, LA	1.3	63,125	68.9	46.4	3.9	18.7	31.1	28.4	37.1	31.3
Monroe, MI	2.0	57,946	71.8	58.6	3.9	9.3	28.2	22.9	36.4	29.8
Montgomery, AL.....................	2.5	136,874	67.7	46.2	4.3	17.3	32.3	28.6	36.9	29.2
Morgantown, WV.....................	3.4	42,921	60.3	48.1	3.3	8.9	39.7	31.5	28.2	28.2
Morristown, TN.....................	4.6	51,621	70.8	55.8	4.8	10.1	29.2	25.6	35.7	34.1
Mount Vernon-Anacortes, WA.........	10.9	42,982	67.9	52.2	4.5	11.2	32.1	25.2	33.2	35.7
Muncie, IN.....................	2.2	46,513	62.5	46.1	4.7	11.7	37.5	28.8	27.9	31.4
Muskegon-Norton Shores, MI	2.0	65,259	67.6	49.6	4.8	13.2	32.4	28.0	35.7	31.5
Myrtle Beach-Conway-North Myrtle Beach, SC	5.7	105,192	63.9	46.6	4.5	12.8	36.1	27.4	29.2	34.7
Napa, CA.....................	22.3	48,312	64.8	51.1	5.0	8.7	35.2	28.2	31.4	38.2
Naples-Marco Island, FL	23.6	119,883	67.0	56.4	3.5	7.1	33.0	27.3	25.4	49.8
Nashville-Davidson-Murfreesboro-Franklin, TN	6.5	574,448	66.1	49.6	4.1	12.5	33.9	27.8	34.6	26.6
New Haven-Milford, CT	11.0	322,561	65.8	48.2	3.9	13.6	34.2	28.4	33.7	33.0
New Orleans-Metairie-Kenner, LA	6.0	392,659	66.0	45.0	5.1	15.9	34.0	28.6	32.9	32.3
New York-Northern New Jersey-Long Island, NY-NJ-PA...............	28.1	6,717,007	66.5	46.6	5.0	14.9	33.5	28.3	34.9	33.4
•Edison, NJ Division.....................	17.7	836,032	71.0	56.9	4.0	10.1	29.0	24.5	36.4	35.0
•Nassau-Suffolk, NY Division............	16.4	916,091	76.1	61.2	4.2	10.7	23.9	19.9	38.8	37.7
•Newark-Union, NJ-PA Division	20.9	759,711	70.1	51.3	5.0	13.8	29.9	25.6	38.1	32.2
•New York-White Plains-Wayne, NY-NJ Division.....................	34.2	4,205,173	62.8	40.5	5.3	17.0	37.2	31.4	33.2	32.4
Niles-Benton Harbor, MI.................	5.5	63,400	67.1	50.0	4.3	12.7	32.9	28.3	32.1	34.1
Norwich-New London, CT.................	7.3	104,132	66.1	52.0	3.9	10.2	33.9	27.4	33.0	30.9
Ocala, FL.....................	6.0	127,764	67.9	53.3	3.9	10.7	32.1	26.5	26.8	48.0
Ocean City, NJ.....................	3.0	47,229	65.4	48.9	4.8	11.6	34.6	28.0	31.2	39.7
Odessa, TX.....................	10.9	45,434	70.1	51.8	4.1	14.1	29.9	24.8	39.8	28.4
Ogden-Clearfield, UT	5.9	160,434	78.9	65.0	4.1	9.8	21.1	18.1	44.8	25.0
Oklahoma City, OK	7.1	459,390	65.3	48.5	4.7	12.0	34.7	28.9	33.8	28.5
Olympia, WA.....................	7.1	91,918	67.2	51.6	3.6	12.0	32.8	25.5	35.0	28.7
Omaha-Council Bluffs, NE-IA	5.8	317,650	66.5	51.1	4.0	11.4	33.5	27.4	35.2	25.8
Orlando-Kissimmee, FL.....................	15.7	752,280	67.7	49.2	5.0	13.5	32.3	24.6	34.7	30.1
Oshkosh-Neenah, WI.....................	2.8	65,897	61.0	49.5	3.5	8.0	39.0	30.1	30.4	28.9
Owensboro, KY	1.1	45,945	69.2	52.2	3.6	13.4	30.8	27.2	34.9	33.0
Oxnard-Thousand Oaks-Ventura, CA.....................	22.0	255,527	73.8	58.0	4.9	10.9	26.2	20.8	40.7	31.5
Palm Bay-Melbourne-Titusville, FL	8.2	217,708	65.5	51.0	3.8	10.7	34.5	28.6	27.1	41.8
Palm Coast, FL.....................	12.5	37,601	69.5	57.2	3.5	8.9	30.5	21.3	26.7	44.7

Metro area or division code	Area name	Total population	Percent change 2005–2007	Population by age (percent)						Median age	Race alone or in combination (percent)				Percent Hispanic or Latino
				Under 5 years	5 to 17 years	18 to 24 years	25 to 44 years	45 to 64 years	65 years and over		White	Black	Asian Hawaiian or Pacific Islander	Amer. Indian, Alaska Native, or some other race	
	ACS table number:	B01003	Population estimates	B01001	B01001	B01001	B01001	B01001	B01001	B01002	B02008	B02009	B02011 + B02012	B02010 + B02013	C03002
		1	2	3	4	5	6	7	8	9	10	11	12	13	14
37460	Panama City-Lynn Haven, FL	163,256	1.3	6.8	16.3	8.0	27.4	27.6	13.9	39.5	85.0	11.9	2.7	2.9	3.3
37620	Parkersburg-Marietta-Vienna, WV-OH	161,492	-0.6	5.7	16.1	8.5	25.6	28.1	16.0	40.9	98.1	1.3	1.0	1.0	0.7
37700	Pascagoula, MS	152,312	-1.9	7.4	19.5	8.7	26.3	26.4	11.7	36.5	77.0	20.8	2.1	1.5	2.9
37860	Pensacola-Ferry Pass-Brent, FL	449,895	1.5	6.4	16.5	11.0	26.0	26.6	13.5	38.0	79.3	17.3	3.4	3.3	3.5
37900	Peoria, IL	369,121	0.9	6.6	17.3	9.8	25.8	25.9	14.6	37.6	88.6	9.6	1.8	1.6	2.0
37980	Philadelphia-Camden-Wilmington, PA-NJ-DE-MD	5,810,526	0.6	6.5	17.8	9.6	27.1	26.0	13.0	37.8	71.9	21.2	4.6	4.0	6.2
37980 15804	•Camden, NJ Division	1,241,466	0.9	6.3	18.0	9.1	28.3	26.0	12.3	37.7	75.4	16.8	4.3	5.6	7.5
37980 37964	•Philadelphia, PA Division	3,880,231	0.4	6.5	17.8	9.7	26.5	26.0	13.4	38.0	70.1	22.7	4.9	3.7	5.8
37980 48864	•Wilmington, DE-MD-NJ Division	688,829	1.4	6.7	17.6	10.0	28.1	26.0	11.7	37.0	75.7	20.0	3.4	2.3	6.0
38060	Phoenix-Mesa-Scottsdale, AZ	4,036,744	7.6	8.3	18.9	9.1	30.1	22.3	11.3	33.8	80.6	4.8	3.5	13.5	29.7
38220	Pine Bluff, AR	102,243	-2.0	6.5	17.2	10.7	26.7	25.9	13.0	37.2	52.2	46.4	0.9	1.6	1.3
38300	Pittsburgh, PA	2,364,622	-0.8	5.2	15.8	9.0	24.6	28.3	17.1	41.9	89.8	8.9	1.7	1.0	1.0
38340	Pittsfield, MA	130,346	-0.9	4.7	15.2	10.2	23.5	28.4	18.0	42.4	95.6	3.1	1.6	1.1	2.4
38540	Pocatello, ID	87,021	1.7	8.8	19.5	12.6	25.8	22.9	10.3	30.8	93.6	0.9	1.9	5.7	7.2
38860	Portland-South Portland-Biddeford, ME	512,189	0.2	5.5	16.8	8.2	26.6	29.2	13.7	40.6	96.5	1.7	1.7	1.2	1.4
38900	Portland-Vancouver-Beaverton, OR-WA	2,133,931	3.8	6.7	17.7	8.4	30.2	26.6	10.4	36.3	86.8	3.6	6.9	6.4	9.7
38940	Port St. Lucie, FL	388,362	6.2	5.6	15.3	7.7	24.4	24.7	22.3	42.8	81.8	13.3	1.6	4.5	12.4
39100	Poughkeepsie-Newburgh-Middletown, NY	666,388	1.0	6.3	19.1	10.8	27.2	25.6	11.0	36.2	80.7	10.7	3.2	8.1	12.3
39140	Prescott, AZ	205,684	7.5	5.3	14.8	8.3	22.6	26.9	22.2	44.4	91.7	0.9	1.5	7.9	12.5
39300	Providence-New Bedford-Fall River, RI-MA	1,605,211	-0.7	5.8	16.8	10.1	27.7	25.8	13.8	38.3	86.9	5.6	2.7	6.9	8.8
39340	Provo-Orem, UT	479,368	12.7	11.6	22.6	17.6	27.4	14.3	6.4	24.3	93.5	0.8	2.9	4.7	8.7
39380	Pueblo, CO	152,216	3.3	6.5	17.8	9.9	26.7	24.2	14.8	36.6	85.2	2.8	1.1	14.4	38.8
39460	Punta Gorda, FL	153,063	-0.4	3.8	12.2	5.9	20.1	26.5	31.5	51.3	91.7	5.6	1.5	2.6	4.8
39540	Racine, WI	194,522	1.1	6.7	18.8	8.8	26.9	26.6	12.2	37.6	83.9	11.3	1.1	5.6	9.6
39580	Raleigh-Cary, NC	1,001,313	9.5	7.8	18.2	9.6	32.0	24.3	8.1	34.6	71.5	20.7	4.0	5.5	8.3
39660	Rapid City, SD	119,178	1.9	7.6	17.8	10.1	25.9	26.3	12.3	36.4	90.1	2.2	1.7	9.6	3.4
39740	Reading, PA	398,155	2.1	6.4	17.5	9.6	26.9	25.5	14.1	38.2	87.7	5.3	1.4	7.1	12.8
39820	Redding, CA	178,539	0.9	5.7	16.9	10.2	25.6	26.5	15.1	38.5	91.5	1.3	3.1	7.2	7.5
39900	Reno-Sparks, NV	401,463	3.8	7.2	17.2	9.4	28.0	26.9	11.4	36.7	81.0	3.0	6.4	12.5	20.1
40060	Richmond, VA	1,194,021	3.2	6.6	17.5	9.6	28.7	26.2	11.4	37.0	65.6	31.0	3.0	2.2	3.6
40140	Riverside-San Bernardino-Ontario, CA	3,985,508	5.0	8.0	21.2	11.0	29.8	20.2	9.8	30.8	64.7	8.3	6.8	23.9	43.9
40220	Roanoke, VA	294,422	1.6	5.7	16.1	8.2	26.3	28.0	15.8	41.1	85.2	13.2	1.5	1.4	1.7
40340	Rochester, MN	178,766	2.5	7.4	18.2	8.4	28.7	25.2	12.1	36.7	92.5	3.2	4.5	1.2	2.9
40380	Rochester, NY	1,031,480	-0.2	5.7	17.5	11.3	25.5	26.8	13.3	38.3	84.6	12.0	2.6	2.6	4.9
40420	Rockford, IL	345,793	3.6	6.9	18.8	9.0	28.4	24.5	12.4	36.0	84.0	10.4	2.3	4.7	11.0
40580	Rocky Mount, NC	144,689	1.1	6.8	18.2	8.8	25.9	27.4	13.0	38.0	51.8	44.0	0.7	4.2	4.1
40660	Rome, GA	94,979	1.2	7.4	17.5	10.0	26.8	24.3	14.1	36.4	81.9	14.0	1.5	4.0	7.5
40900	Sacramento–Arden-Arcade–Roseville, CA	2,063,900	2.5	6.8	18.3	10.5	29.3	23.8	11.4	34.7	71.1	8.4	13.4	11.3	18.1
40980	Saginaw-Saginaw Township North, MI	204,612	-2.0	6.4	18.4	9.7	24.6	26.8	14.0	38.1	77.4	19.7	1.3	3.6	7.1
41060	St. Cloud, MN	183,458	2.3	6.6	17.1	14.8	27.8	22.4	11.3	32.8	95.6	1.9	2.0	1.7	1.7
41100	St. George, UT	126,775	12.1	9.2	19.7	11.4	26.9	15.7	17.1	29.6	93.5	0.8	2.5	4.4	7.1
41140	St. Joseph, MO-KS	122,442	1.8	6.3	16.7	10.1	27.8	24.8	14.2	37.8	94.2	5.2	0.8	2.2	2.5
41180	St. Louis, MO-IL	2,790,203	1.2	6.5	18.1	9.4	26.9	26.3	12.8	37.6	79.1	18.8	2.2	1.4	2.0
41420	Salem, OR	379,804	3.6	7.2	18.6	10.1	27.7	23.9	12.6	34.9	86.8	1.5	3.1	11.9	19.2
41500	Salinas, CA	407,534	-0.6	8.5	19.0	11.2	29.3	22.0	10.0	32.2	66.0	4.0	8.3	25.4	51.4
41540	Salisbury, MD	117,970	3.0	6.2	16.0	13.4	27.1	24.1	13.2	35.6	69.5	28.1	1.7	2.3	2.9
41620	Salt Lake City, UT	1,075,530	4.7	9.1	20.4	10.8	30.0	21.4	8.2	30.5	88.2	1.8	5.0	7.1	14.7
41660	San Angelo, TX	107,185	1.6	7.4	17.7	12.8	25.0	23.3	13.8	34.7	81.4	4.7	1.6	14.4	33.4
41700	San Antonio, TX	1,936,735	5.6	8.0	19.6	10.5	28.3	22.8	10.7	33.4	71.3	6.9	2.4	22.0	52.6
41740	San Diego-Carlsbad-San Marcos, CA	2,954,960	1.0	7.4	17.7	11.5	29.6	22.8	11.1	34.2	72.6	6.1	12.5	12.6	29.9
41780	Sandusky, OH	77,566	-0.8	5.9	16.7	7.9	23.9	29.2	16.4	41.3	88.8	9.8	0.7	2.4	2.4
41860	San Francisco-Oakland-Fremont, CA	4,171,627	1.4	6.3	15.5	8.6	30.4	26.9	12.3	38.4	58.6	9.7	24.4	11.2	19.8
41860 36084	•Oakland-Fremont-Hayward, CA Division	2,465,531	1.1	6.7	17.5	9.2	29.1	26.4	11.1	37.1	55.4	12.7	22.5	13.8	21.4
41860 41884	•San Francisco-San Mateo-Redwood City, CA Division	1,706,096	1.9	5.8	12.5	7.7	32.3	27.6	14.0	40.1	63.3	5.4	27.3	7.4	17.5
41940	San Jose-Sunnyvale-Santa Clara, CA	1,777,616	2.5	7.3	17.0	8.9	31.6	24.7	10.5	36.3	55.3	3.1	31.4	13.7	26.2
42020	San Luis Obispo-Paso Robles, CA	260,278	1.5	4.9	14.3	15.5	25.2	25.9	14.2	37.8	87.3	2.5	4.4	8.9	18.4
42060	Santa Barbara-Santa Maria-Goleta, CA	402,968	0.1	7.1	16.8	14.4	26.2	22.7	12.8	33.9	78.2	2.6	5.9	17.0	38.0
42100	Santa Cruz-Watsonville, CA	250,877	0.4	6.5	15.5	12.9	26.5	28.3	10.3	37.0	88.7	1.5	5.6	8.1	28.5
42140	Santa Fe, NM	141,207	2.3	5.7	15.8	8.8	27.1	30.0	12.6	40.0	77.4	1.2	1.5	22.5	50.0
42220	Santa Rosa-Petaluma, CA	463,544	0.0	6.1	16.6	10.0	26.0	28.6	12.8	39.1	82.2	2.0	5.3	13.8	21.9

Area name	Percent foreign born	Total households	Household type (percent)						Percent of households with people under 18 years	Percent of households with people 60 years and over
			Family households				Nonfamily households			
			Total family households	Married-couple families	Male householder families	Female householder families	Total nonfamily households	One-person households		
ACS table number:	C05002	B11001	B11001	B11001	B11001	B11001	B11001	B11001	C11005	B11006
	15	16	17	18	19	20	21	22	23	24
Panama City-Lynn Haven, FL	5.4	71,417	65.5	48.1	3.9	13.6	34.5	26.7	31.2	31.5
Parkersburg-Marietta-Vienna, WV-OH	1.0	67,453	67.1	53.4	3.4	10.3	32.9	28.1	28.8	35.4
Pascagoula, MS	2.7	55,071	75.1	53.7	5.6	15.7	24.9	20.9	39.6	32.4
Pensacola-Ferry Pass-Brent, FL	4.2	168,016	68.3	50.9	4.0	13.3	31.7	26.0	32.3	33.9
Peoria, IL	2.5	148,604	66.3	51.4	3.5	11.4	33.7	28.7	32.0	31.8
Philadelphia-Camden-Wilmington, PA-NJ-DE-MD	8.6	2,169,515	65.8	47.3	4.6	13.9	34.2	28.8	34.0	32.1
•Camden, NJ Division	7.8	455,256	70.5	52.6	4.5	13.4	29.5	24.6	37.6	31.4
•Philadelphia, PA Division	9.0	1,459,832	64.0	45.2	4.6	14.3	36.0	30.7	32.7	32.7
•Wilmington, DE-MD-NJ Division	7.5	254,427	67.8	50.1	4.8	12.9	32.2	26.0	35.1	30.3
Phoenix-Mesa-Scottsdale, AZ	16.8	1,421,271	66.5	49.8	5.3	11.4	33.5	26.3	35.5	29.2
Pine Bluff, AR	1.6	38,057	66.0	44.1	4.1	17.8	34.0	30.6	34.0	33.5
Pittsburgh, PA	3.0	984,179	63.7	48.8	3.8	11.1	36.3	31.4	28.2	36.6
Pittsfield, MA	3.5	55,127	62.4	45.5	5.2	11.8	37.6	31.7	28.6	38.9
Pocatello, ID	3.4	31,690	69.5	54.7	4.4	10.4	30.5	24.5	38.5	25.7
Portland-South Portland-Biddeford, ME	4.0	207,652	65.3	51.4	3.9	10.0	34.7	26.7	31.4	31.9
Portland-Vancouver-Beaverton, OR-WA	12.1	817,906	63.5	49.1	4.2	10.3	36.5	28.5	33.2	26.4
Port St. Lucie, FL	14.1	157,673	67.9	52.9	4.8	10.2	32.1	26.3	29.0	45.1
Poughkeepsie-Newburgh-Middletown, NY	10.5	225,330	71.3	55.1	5.0	11.3	28.7	23.5	38.8	30.9
Prescott, AZ	7.7	94,352	64.0	51.7	3.5	8.8	36.0	29.0	23.5	45.6
Providence-New Bedford-Fall River, RI-MA	12.6	613,430	65.2	47.9	4.1	13.2	34.8	28.7	32.8	32.8
Provo-Orem, UT	6.6	128,810	80.6	70.3	2.9	7.5	19.4	12.9	48.9	21.5
Pueblo, CO	3.4	58,819	67.2	47.8	4.8	14.6	32.8	27.7	34.0	33.0
Punta Gorda, FL	9.9	70,376	67.6	55.7	3.6	8.3	32.4	26.7	21.9	53.7
Racine, WI	4.9	75,140	69.1	50.6	5.8	12.7	30.9	25.8	34.1	27.7
Raleigh-Cary, NC	10.4	374,606	66.7	52.1	4.0	10.6	33.3	27.7	37.0	21.9
Rapid City, SD	2.4	47,419	66.9	52.1	4.2	10.7	33.1	27.0	32.6	27.7
Reading, PA	6.0	149,410	70.0	54.0	4.9	11.1	30.0	23.9	34.9	33.1
Redding, CA	4.1	68,762	68.1	50.2	5.3	12.6	31.9	26.2	33.2	36.5
Reno-Sparks, NV	15.1	157,000	61.9	46.7	5.1	10.1	38.1	29.5	31.7	29.8
Richmond, VA	5.9	459,039	66.8	49.1	4.0	13.8	33.2	27.2	34.4	28.9
Riverside-San Bernardino-Ontario, CA	21.9	1,227,896	74.8	54.7	6.6	13.6	25.2	19.7	45.9	29.0
Roanoke, VA	3.5	123,888	64.5	49.1	4.2	11.2	35.5	30.7	29.4	34.6
Rochester, MN	6.9	70,452	66.6	55.7	3.4	7.5	33.4	27.6	34.7	27.5
Rochester, NY	6.1	399,531	64.8	48.2	4.2	12.3	35.2	28.6	32.9	31.8
Rockford, IL	8.5	126,794	68.7	52.1	4.5	12.1	31.3	26.9	35.7	30.7
Rocky Mount, NC	3.6	57,073	66.7	44.4	4.8	17.5	33.3	29.3	33.4	33.1
Rome, GA	6.4	34,506	68.6	49.8	5.2	13.6	31.4	27.4	33.5	35.2
Sacramento-Arden-Arcade-Roseville, CA	17.4	756,162	66.6	49.1	5.1	12.4	33.4	25.5	36.3	28.7
Saginaw-Saginaw Township North, MI	1.8	77,707	68.8	49.4	4.1	15.3	31.2	26.6	34.7	33.4
St. Cloud, MN	2.9	69,272	65.7	54.3	4.2	7.2	34.3	25.1	34.0	25.6
St. George, UT	5.4	43,121	76.3	66.7	3.1	6.6	23.7	19.1	36.9	37.8
St. Joseph, MO-KS	1.6	46,675	67.3	51.8	5.0	10.4	32.7	27.9	34.4	32.9
St. Louis, MO-IL	4.0	1,090,503	66.2	48.7	4.1	13.4	33.8	28.6	33.9	30.4
Salem, OR	13.3	136,003	69.2	52.5	5.1	11.7	30.8	24.3	36.5	32.0
Salinas, CA	30.0	124,146	71.4	53.7	5.7	11.9	28.6	22.9	41.5	31.0
Salisbury, MD	4.4	43,669	64.4	44.6	5.2	14.5	35.6	26.8	32.7	34.3
Salt Lake City, UT	11.4	352,665	71.4	56.2	4.7	10.4	28.6	22.8	41.2	23.8
San Angelo, TX	5.5	41,514	66.1	49.2	4.1	12.9	33.9	29.1	35.5	31.0
San Antonio, TX	11.0	660,410	70.2	50.6	4.8	14.8	29.8	24.8	39.1	29.1
San Diego-Carlsbad-San Marcos, CA	23.0	1,041,790	65.7	49.2	4.9	11.6	34.3	25.8	35.5	28.9
Sandusky, OH	2.2	31,874	67.9	54.5	3.5	9.9	32.1	27.3	30.1	35.9
San Francisco-Oakland-Fremont, CA	29.5	1,556,247	61.8	46.6	4.7	10.6	38.2	29.7	31.8	30.7
•Oakland-Fremont-Hayward, CA Division	27.6	881,418	66.7	49.7	5.2	11.8	33.3	26.1	36.2	29.5
•San Francisco-San Mateo-Redwood City, CA Division	32.4	674,829	55.5	42.5	4.1	8.9	44.5	34.4	26.0	32.3
San Jose-Sunnyvale-Santa Clara, CA	36.3	598,755	70.1	54.6	5.2	10.3	29.9	24.1	38.8	28.2
San Luis Obispo-Paso Robles, CA	9.5	103,026	62.4	49.2	4.1	9.1	37.6	25.9	28.8	30.7
Santa Barbara-Santa Maria-Goleta, CA	22.6	140,137	64.1	49.1	4.7	10.3	35.9	25.1	34.1	32.2
Santa Cruz-Watsonville, CA	17.1	93,518	61.5	47.1	4.7	9.7	38.5	27.5	32.7	28.9
Santa Fe, NM	12.9	52,956	60.6	45.0	4.4	11.2	39.4	30.8	29.8	32.7
Santa Rosa-Petaluma, CA	17.1	177,331	63.7	49.3	4.8	9.6	36.3	27.7	32.7	32.9

Metro area or division code	Area name ACS table number	Total population B01003	Percent change 2005–2007 Population estimates	Under 5 years B01001	5 to 17 years B01001	18 to 24 years B01001	25 to 44 years B01001	45 to 64 years B01001	65 years and over B01001	Median age B01002	White B02008	Black B02009	Asian Hawaiian or Pacific Islander B02011 + B02012	Amer. Indian, Alaska Native, or some other race B02010 + B02013	Percent Hispanic or Latino C03002
		1	2	3	4	5	6	7	8	9	10	11	12	13	14
42260	Sarasota-Bradenton-Venice, FL	678,880	2.6	5.2	13.5	6.5	22.7	25.8	26.2	46.6	88.5	6.7	1.5	4.3	9.4
42340	Savannah, GA	321,738	4.8	7.6	18.4	10.7	28.0	24.0	11.3	34.6	62.4	34.8	2.2	1.8	2.7
42540	Scranton–Wilkes-Barre, PA	548,942	0.1	5.2	15.3	9.5	25.0	26.9	18.0	41.6	95.7	2.5	1.0	1.5	2.9
42660	Seattle-Tacoma-Bellevue, WA	3,259,078	3.2	6.4	16.9	8.7	30.6	27.0	10.3	37.1	79.5	6.6	12.8	5.4	7.0
42660 42644	•Seattle-Bellevue-Everett, WA Division	2,496,855	3.1	6.3	16.4	8.5	31.0	27.6	10.3	37.6	78.8	5.9	13.9	5.4	7.0
42660 45104	•Tacoma, WA Division	762,223	3.2	6.9	18.7	9.4	29.5	25.1	10.4	35.4	81.8	8.8	9.2	5.5	7.0
42680	Sebastian-Vero Beach, FL	129,401	3.8	5.3	13.7	7.5	22.8	24.9	25.9	45.5	88.4	8.8	1.3	2.5	9.3
43100	Sheboygan, WI	114,053	0.5	6.1	17.4	8.5	27.2	26.8	14.0	38.6	91.2	1.7	4.1	4.2	4.6
43300	Sherman-Denison, TX	117,179	2.2	6.9	17.5	9.1	26.6	25.1	14.9	37.1	87.0	6.4	0.9	7.7	9.3
43340	Shreveport-Bossier City, LA	385,498	1.6	7.3	18.6	10.1	26.5	24.5	12.8	35.3	58.2	39.8	1.3	1.8	2.7
43580	Sioux City, IA-NE-SD	141,983	1.1	7.6	19.9	9.4	25.3	24.9	12.8	35.9	87.9	2.6	2.8	8.5	12.6
43620	Sioux Falls, SD	221,210	5.7	7.7	18.2	9.4	29.2	24.1	11.3	34.9	93.5	2.7	1.3	4.0	3.1
43780	South Bend-Mishawaka, IN-MI	316,235	0.2	6.8	18.2	11.1	25.4	25.4	13.1	36.2	83.9	12.1	1.9	4.6	5.4
43900	Spartanburg, SC	270,368	3.8	6.6	17.6	8.8	28.0	26.0	13.1	37.4	75.8	21.2	2.1	1.9	4.3
44060	Spokane, WA	448,018	3.5	6.3	17.4	10.7	27.4	25.7	12.5	36.1	93.7	2.6	3.5	3.8	3.6
44100	Springfield, IL	205,874	0.6	6.5	17.2	8.5	27.1	27.1	13.6	38.8	88.5	10.8	1.6	1.4	1.3
44140	Springfield, MA	683,262	0.1	5.5	16.7	12.6	25.5	26.1	13.5	37.5	84.9	6.8	2.4	7.7	13.0
44180	Springfield, MO	410,464	4.8	6.7	16.8	11.7	27.9	23.6	13.2	35.2	95.7	2.4	1.2	3.1	2.2
44220	Springfield, OH	141,122	-0.9	6.2	17.5	9.0	25.1	26.7	15.4	39.0	89.6	9.9	0.9	1.5	1.6
44300	State College, PA	143,557	1.6	4.5	12.0	28.2	24.8	19.6	10.8	28.6	90.7	3.4	5.6	1.4	2.1
44700	Stockton, CA	664,423	1.8	8.1	21.2	10.6	28.8	21.5	9.8	31.6	64.2	8.6	16.0	15.9	35.7
44940	Sumter, SC	104,295	-0.7	7.6	19.4	9.8	25.6	24.9	12.6	36.3	50.6	47.8	1.3	1.0	2.2
45060	Syracuse, NY	646,597	-0.4	5.7	17.5	11.9	25.7	25.9	13.2	37.5	89.2	8.3	2.4	2.1	2.4
45220	Tallahassee, FL	349,727	3.5	6.3	14.9	17.2	27.2	24.7	9.6	32.9	62.8	33.7	2.3	2.5	4.6
45300	Tampa-St. Petersburg-Clearwater, FL	2,687,027	3.0	6.0	15.9	8.1	26.6	26.2	17.2	40.7	83.0	11.7	3.1	4.0	13.7
45460	Terre Haute, IN	169,407	0.6	6.2	16.2	12.5	25.9	25.3	14.0	36.7	94.0	4.8	1.2	1.2	1.1
45500	Texarkana, TX-Texarkana, AR	133,505	1.5	6.5	17.8	9.2	28.3	24.9	13.3	36.7	72.6	24.9	0.7	3.5	4.3
45780	Toledo, OH	652,898	-0.5	6.5	17.8	11.5	25.9	25.5	12.8	36.2	83.9	13.4	1.6	3.3	4.9
45820	Topeka, KS	228,381	0.6	6.8	17.7	8.9	25.8	26.8	14.0	38.5	86.3	8.2	1.3	6.8	6.9
45940	Trenton-Ewing, NJ	364,567	0.4	6.2	17.0	10.8	28.4	25.5	12.1	37.0	67.2	20.7	8.2	5.7	12.3
46060	Tucson, AZ	947,626	5.2	6.9	17.0	10.5	26.5	24.5	14.6	36.7	72.9	3.9	3.3	23.3	32.3
46140	Tulsa, OK	893,734	2.6	7.3	18.4	9.2	27.1	25.7	12.3	36.4	80.6	9.9	2.0	13.9	6.7
46220	Tuscaloosa, AL	202,097	3.2	6.5	16.9	15.2	26.8	23.3	11.3	32.7	62.8	35.3	1.4	1.4	1.6
46340	Tyler, TX	194,613	4.2	7.6	18.1	10.3	26.4	23.3	14.2	35.2	72.9	18.7	1.0	8.9	14.6
46540	Utica-Rome, NY	295,059	-0.3	5.3	16.5	10.2	25.8	26.3	15.9	39.7	92.6	5.5	1.6	2.2	3.2
46660	Valdosta, GA	128,225	3.0	7.6	18.5	13.7	28.9	21.3	10.0	31.4	63.8	33.1	1.7	3.4	3.7
46700	Vallejo-Fairfield, CA	408,388	-0.1	6.9	19.2	9.9	28.2	25.3	10.6	35.4	56.4	16.6	17.6	14.9	21.5
47020	Victoria, TX	113,259	1.2	7.5	19.8	9.4	24.9	24.9	13.5	36.6	75.2	5.9	2.0	20.7	41.5
47220	Vineland-Millville-Bridgeton, NJ	154,086	1.9	7.2	17.3	8.8	31.0	23.3	12.4	35.9	68.1	22.1	1.3	10.4	22.7
47260	Virginia Beach-Norfolk-Newport News, VA-NC	1,654,563	0.6	7.1	18.4	11.2	28.7	23.9	10.8	34.8	63.3	32.6	4.0	2.7	3.9
47300	Visalia-Porterville, CA	413,933	3.5	9.5	22.6	11.1	27.6	19.7	9.4	28.8	76.4	2.0	4.2	20.1	55.9
47380	Waco, TX	226,260	1.7	7.5	18.4	14.8	25.2	21.8	12.3	31.8	78.4	15.4	1.8	5.8	20.8
47580	Warner Robins, GA	128,345	4.1	7.5	19.9	9.8	28.3	24.2	10.2	34.6	69.1	27.4	2.8	3.0	3.7
47900	Washington-Arlington-Alexandria, DC-VA-MD-WV	5,263,322	1.5	7.2	17.5	9.2	30.5	26.1	9.5	36.2	59.1	27.2	9.2	6.9	11.5
47900 13644	•Bethesda-Gaithersburg-Frederick, MD Division	1,147,753	1.4	7.1	17.8	8.3	27.9	27.4	11.5	38.3	67.3	15.5	12.1	7.3	12.3
47900 47894	•Washington-Arlington-Alexandria, DC-VA-MD-WV Division	4,115,569	1.6	7.2	17.4	9.5	31.2	25.7	9.0	35.7	56.8	30.4	8.4	6.7	11.3
47940	Waterloo-Cedar Falls, IA	162,996	0.5	6.3	16.1	14.5	23.5	25.0	14.6	36.5	91.4	7.0	1.4	1.6	2.1
48140	Wausau, WI	128,952	1.7	6.0	18.2	8.6	26.8	27.1	13.3	38.7	94.3	0.6	4.9	1.2	1.2
48260	Weirton-Steubenville, WV-OH	123,972	-2.2	5.1	14.9	8.7	23.3	29.3	18.7	43.6	95.3	4.4	0.8	0.8	0.7
48300	Wenatchee, WA	105,316	3.4	6.7	19.1	9.5	24.3	25.6	14.8	37.8	88.3	1.0	1.5	12.1	22.5
48540	Wheeling, WV-OH	146,494	-1.1	5.1	15.2	8.9	24.2	28.9	17.6	42.5	95.8	3.8	0.8	0.7	0.6
48620	Wichita, KS	590,173	2.0	7.7	19.5	9.3	27.0	24.7	11.9	35.3	83.8	8.7	3.6	7.1	9.1
48660	Wichita Falls, TX	149,168	-1.2	7.0	17.9	12.6	26.5	23.2	12.9	34.6	83.1	9.7	2.7	6.8	13.0
48700	Williamsport, PA	117,311	-0.7	5.6	15.9	10.7	24.5	27.2	16.2	40.5	94.3	5.2	0.6	1.1	0.9
48900	Wilmington, NC	328,458	7.1	6.1	15.4	10.0	27.9	25.9	14.7	38.3	81.4	15.2	0.9	4.2	3.5
49020	Winchester, VA-WV	118,699	4.4	6.6	17.4	9.0	29.3	25.0	12.7	37.0	91.7	5.4	1.4	2.7	5.3
49180	Winston-Salem, NC	454,978	3.6	6.8	17.3	8.9	27.7	26.2	13.1	37.9	73.5	20.4	1.3	5.9	8.5
49340	Worcester, MA	779,386	0.6	6.2	18.0	9.3	28.2	26.0	12.3	37.8	90.3	3.9	3.9	3.3	7.8
49420	Yakima, WA	230,907	1.7	9.0	21.8	9.4	26.1	22.5	11.3	32.3	76.3	1.3	1.8	22.8	39.9
49620	York-Hanover, PA	414,023	3.5	6.2	17.1	8.0	27.9	27.2	13.6	39.3	92.2	5.4	1.3	2.2	4.0
49660	Youngstown-Warren-Boardman, OH-PA	576,204	-1.8	5.4	16.8	8.8	24.2	27.8	17.0	41.4	87.8	11.5	0.7	1.1	1.9
49700	Yuba City, CA	159,876	5.6	8.1	19.7	10.8	28.8	21.8	10.8	31.8	72.4	3.3	12.1	18.7	24.4
49740	Yuma, AZ	185,658	5.3	8.8	20.0	9.8	23.8	19.7	17.8	34.7	74.5	2.6	1.7	23.4	55.0

Area name	Percent foreign born	Total households	Family households				Nonfamily households		Percent of households with people under 18 years	Percent of households with people 60 years and over
			Total family households	Married-couple families	Male householder families	Female householder families	Total nonfamily households	One-person households		
ACS table number:	C05002	B11001	B11001	B11001	B11001	B11001	B11001	B11001	C11005	B11006
	15	16	17	18	19	20	21	22	23	24
Sarasota-Bradenton-Venice, FL	12.0	299,995	63.0	50.5	3.7	8.8	37.0	30.0	23.6	48.2
Savannah, GA	4.1	123,263	66.6	46.6	4.7	15.3	33.4	27.3	34.2	29.3
Scranton–Wilkes-Barre, PA	3.0	227,132	63.9	47.7	4.4	11.8	36.1	31.5	28.7	39.4
Seattle-Tacoma-Bellevue, WA	15.3	1,294,535	62.1	47.8	4.4	9.9	37.9	29.9	32.3	26.0
•Seattle-Bellevue-Everett, WA Division	17.4	1,008,811	60.7	47.4	4.1	9.2	39.3	30.9	31.2	25.6
•Tacoma, WA Division	8.7	285,724	66.9	49.3	5.2	12.4	33.1	26.3	36.0	27.3
Sebastian-Vero Beach, FL	10.3	58,175	65.6	51.5	4.0	10.1	34.4	27.2	27.6	47.1
Sheboygan, WI	5.0	46,278	66.4	56.1	3.7	6.6	33.6	28.1	31.1	30.4
Sherman-Denison, TX	5.2	43,845	69.5	52.5	4.5	12.5	30.5	25.8	34.5	35.2
Shreveport-Bossier City, LA	2.3	148,406	65.4	42.4	4.5	18.4	34.6	29.9	34.3	31.6
Sioux City, IA-NE-SD	8.0	54,302	66.9	51.4	5.3	10.2	33.1	26.6	33.6	30.9
Sioux Falls, SD	3.8	83,973	66.3	52.6	3.5	10.2	33.7	27.9	33.8	26.0
South Bend-Mishawaka, IN-MI	5.0	121,616	65.0	49.4	4.0	11.6	35.0	29.8	32.1	31.2
Spartanburg, SC	5.4	104,536	69.2	50.6	4.4	14.2	30.8	27.4	35.1	32.0
Spokane, WA	4.7	178,952	63.2	48.4	4.2	10.6	36.8	29.6	32.2	29.2
Springfield, IL	2.1	86,365	62.5	46.0	4.1	12.4	37.5	31.3	33.1	29.8
Springfield, MA	7.9	261,819	62.5	44.5	4.3	13.6	37.5	30.1	31.3	32.3
Springfield, MO	1.9	164,626	65.3	51.6	3.9	9.9	34.7	27.8	32.3	29.7
Springfield, OH	1.8	55,422	67.0	49.3	4.2	13.6	33.0	28.4	32.5	35.2
State College, PA	6.8	51,319	57.0	49.0	2.4	5.7	43.0	29.9	26.1	26.6
Stockton, CA	23.7	207,792	74.2	53.2	7.2	13.9	25.8	20.3	45.9	28.8
Sumter, SC	7.4	38,817	68.3	43.7	5.0	19.6	31.7	28.0	36.7	32.8
Syracuse, NY	4.7	253,475	62.8	46.6	4.2	12.0	37.2	29.6	32.4	31.4
Tallahassee, FL	5.0	138,401	58.5	40.1	4.1	14.2	41.5	31.1	29.7	24.7
Tampa-St. Petersburg-Clearwater, FL	12.0	1,110,157	62.2	46.5	4.4	11.3	37.8	30.7	28.5	36.9
Terre Haute, IN	1.8	66,964	63.7	49.2	3.2	11.3	36.3	29.2	31.5	31.4
Texarkana, TX-Texarkana, AR	3.0	50,597	68.4	47.7	5.6	15.1	31.6	27.6	34.8	33.3
Toledo, OH	3.2	260,925	63.4	46.0	4.5	12.9	36.6	29.7	32.2	29.9
Topeka, KS	3.1	93,869	66.6	50.9	3.8	11.9	33.4	28.8	32.4	32.0
Trenton-Ewing, NJ	18.2	127,253	68.5	49.6	5.0	13.9	31.5	26.3	36.4	32.6
Tucson, AZ	13.4	370,126	62.4	45.3	4.7	12.4	37.6	30.7	30.8	33.9
Tulsa, OK	5.2	350,732	67.4	50.4	4.5	12.4	32.6	28.0	34.8	29.5
Tuscaloosa, AL	3.1	80,443	61.6	43.5	3.8	14.3	38.4	31.0	30.8	27.6
Tyler, TX	8.4	69,168	69.5	52.7	4.0	12.9	30.5	26.3	35.8	33.9
Utica-Rome, NY	5.1	117,631	65.2	47.4	4.6	13.1	34.8	29.2	31.4	36.0
Valdosta, GA	4.1	48,739	70.4	47.5	5.3	17.6	29.6	24.0	38.8	25.1
Vallejo-Fairfield, CA	18.9	135,704	73.0	52.3	6.1	14.6	27.0	21.7	41.3	30.4
Victoria, TX	6.3	42,288	71.6	51.9	5.3	14.4	28.4	24.3	38.4	31.9
Vineland-Millville-Bridgeton, NJ	8.3	50,165	69.0	46.0	6.0	17.0	31.0	25.8	37.5	34.0
Virginia Beach-Norfolk-Newport News, VA-NC	5.5	620,138	68.5	49.1	4.3	15.1	31.5	25.7	36.8	27.7
Visalia-Porterville, CA	22.7	121,457	78.2	56.0	8.2	14.0	21.8	18.0	49.5	29.1
Waco, TX	8.3	80,973	66.6	47.7	4.2	14.7	33.4	27.3	36.2	29.2
Warner Robins, GA	3.8	48,519	68.4	48.5	4.8	15.1	31.6	27.9	37.6	25.7
Washington-Arlington-Alexandria, DC-VA-MD-WV	20.1	1,949,715	64.6	48.0	4.4	12.3	35.4	29.1	34.9	26.3
•Bethesda-Gaithersburg-Frederick, MD Division	25.2	422,977	69.6	55.4	4.0	10.3	30.4	24.8	37.0	29.9
•Washington-Arlington-Alexandria, DC-VA-MD-WV Division	18.6	1,526,738	63.3	46.0	4.5	12.8	36.7	30.3	34.3	25.3
Waterloo-Cedar Falls, IA	4.2	65,857	65.2	51.8	3.4	10.0	34.8	27.3	30.1	31.9
Wausau, WI	3.6	52,251	69.1	57.4	4.8	6.9	30.9	25.2	33.3	29.4
Weirton-Steubenville, WV-OH	1.1	53,076	66.5	50.0	4.4	12.1	33.5	29.2	29.7	39.4
Wenatchee, WA	13.7	39,078	70.2	55.6	3.7	10.8	29.8	24.5	35.9	36.4
Wheeling, WV-OH	1.2	62,371	65.9	50.4	4.1	11.4	34.1	30.0	29.7	36.0
Wichita, KS	6.3	230,159	67.3	51.9	4.6	10.8	32.7	28.1	35.8	28.0
Wichita Falls, TX	5.2	56,573	68.7	53.4	3.3	12.0	31.3	26.4	36.7	31.0
Williamsport, PA	1.1	47,719	66.7	50.9	4.7	11.1	33.3	27.0	30.2	35.2
Wilmington, NC	4.0	142,936	62.3	47.6	4.2	10.5	37.7	29.7	28.3	33.0
Winchester, VA-WV	5.2	44,934	68.7	53.1	4.7	11.0	31.3	24.8	34.8	31.8
Winston-Salem, NC	6.7	181,355	67.7	50.5	4.1	13.1	32.3	28.0	33.7	30.6
Worcester, MA	9.9	287,535	67.3	51.9	4.2	11.2	32.7	26.6	35.3	30.4
Yakima, WA	18.4	76,698	72.7	53.3	6.5	12.9	27.3	21.6	43.1	30.9
York-Hanover, PA	2.9	162,264	70.3	56.3	4.6	9.4	29.7	23.8	33.4	31.8
Youngstown-Warren-Boardman, OH-PA	2.0	233,944	66.3	48.9	3.9	13.5	33.7	29.3	29.8	37.2
Yuba City, CA	17.6	54,232	72.4	54.8	5.2	12.4	27.6	22.1	42.3	31.4
Yuma, AZ	24.9	68,857	73.7	56.5	3.8	13.4	26.3	21.5	39.4	39.4

Table A-4. Cities — Who: Age, Race/Ethnicity, and Household Structure, 2005–2007

STATE Place code	STATE City (ACS table number:)	Total population B01003	Percent change 2005–2007 Population estimates	Under 5 years B01001	5 to 17 years B01001	18 to 24 years B01001	25 to 44 years B01001	45 to 64 years B01001	65 years and over B01001	Median age B01002	White B02008	Black B02009	Asian Hawaiian or Pacific Islander B02011+B02012	Amer. Indian, Alaska Native, or some other race B02010+B02013	Percent Hispanic or Latino C03002
		1	2	3	4	5	6	7	8	9	10	11	12	13	14
00 00000	United States	298,757,310	1.9	6.9	17.8	9.9	28.0	25.0	12.5	36.4	75.9	13.1	5.1	8.1	14.7
01 00000	Alabama	4,585,900	1.9	6.7	17.7	9.9	26.9	25.5	13.4	37.1	71.3	26.7	1.2	1.9	2.5
01 00820	Alabaster	28,938	4.6	9.2	19.1	8.7	30.0	24.8	8.2	34.1	83.1	14.7	0.7	1.8	-
01 01852	Anniston	22,368	0.2	8.0	15.0	8.4	24.1	27.3	17.3	40.4	46.5	52.2	1.2	1.2	1.5
01 02956	Athens	20,498	8.7	6.6	14.8	9.5	27.5	24.5	17.1	37.9	73.1	21.6	1.4	4.6	6.1
01 03076	Auburn	50,093	5.1	4.5	11.2	39.3	22.8	14.3	7.9	23.5	79.0	16.6	4.0	1.4	1.8
01 05980	Bessemer	28,113	-1.5	8.6	16.9	9.3	26.3	25.0	14.0	36.7	26.6	72.1	-	1.4	1.8
01 07000	Birmingham	218,090	-0.9	7.1	16.7	11.0	27.2	25.3	12.7	36.2	23.3	75.2	1.1	1.2	2.6
01 20104	Decatur	54,309	2.1	6.7	18.2	8.4	26.7	25.3	14.7	37.8	74.3	21.2	0.7	6.0	8.0
01 21184	Dothan	62,151	5.0	7.2	17.8	8.1	25.8	26.2	14.9	37.6	66.6	31.3	1.2	1.6	1.9
01 24184	Enterprise	21,797	7.4	6.0	18.7	8.3	27.6	24.5	14.9	36.2	71.3	25.6	2.3	2.1	4.6
01 26896	Florence	35,754	2.2	5.0	13.4	15.4	23.4	23.4	19.4	38.2	79.1	20.1	1.3	1.8	1.3
01 28696	Gadsden	38,121	-0.7	6.9	16.3	9.6	26.3	23.8	17.2	37.2	63.6	35.2	0.3	1.7	5.4
01 35800	Homewood	27,050	-0.9	7.9	13.3	19.3	29.4	19.1	11.0	30.4	81.3	13.9	3.9	1.9	6.8
01 35896	Hoover	72,596	3.4	6.7	18.4	6.7	29.9	28.1	10.2	37.6	82.3	12.5	4.7	1.6	5.6
01 37000	Huntsville	166,550	3.0	5.8	16.1	12.3	25.9	25.3	14.5	37.8	63.7	32.5	3.2	2.4	3.1
01 45784	Madison	37,412	5.4	8.0	22.4	7.6	27.6	27.5	6.9	35.5	81.9	14.7	4.4	0.5	3.4
01 50000	Mobile	194,091	0.7	7.4	18.5	10.8	25.8	24.1	13.5	35.1	48.3	48.9	2.2	1.5	1.6
01 51000	Montgomery	200,993	1.7	7.7	18.7	12.1	26.3	23.6	11.7	33.8	43.4	54.9	1.7	1.2	1.7
01 51696	Mountain Brook	21,345	1.0	5.5	22.4	5.1	21.3	29.4	16.2	42.6	99.0	-	0.9	-	-
01 55200	Northport	22,385	5.6	8.0	16.9	11.1	27.7	23.2	13.1	34.1	69.7	27.6	2.5	0.7	2.0
01 57048	Opelika	24,988	1.6	8.2	17.5	9.1	26.7	26.8	11.5	35.8	53.5	46.5	0.8	1.8	2.0
01 57576	Oxford	21,530	1.9	7.4	17.7	6.1	30.7	25.9	12.2	37.2	87.4	9.1	0.7	3.4	3.4
01 58848	Pelham	18,318	6.6	7.9	18.4	8.3	32.2	23.7	9.5	33.2	86.9	7.2	3.2	3.1	9.0
01 59472	Phenix	30,901	4.5	7.3	19.3	8.4	29.1	22.2	13.7	34.9	48.7	48.7	1.6	1.7	2.8
01 62328	Prattville	28,094	6.7	6.9	20.7	8.4	27.9	24.4	11.7	36.2	81.5	16.2	1.2	3.1	2.9
01 62496	Prichard	25,621	0.5	6.6	21.4	11.6	22.7	24.8	12.9	33.5	15.5	84.5	0.4	0.6	0.4
01 77256	Tuscaloosa	79,584	7.2	6.0	13.6	24.0	24.9	20.0	11.5	27.9	53.1	44.1	2.0	1.7	2.6
01 78552	Vestavia Hills	33,507	-0.5	6.6	18.2	5.9	24.7	27.8	16.8	40.7	92.1	5.0	2.8	0.4	1.1
02 00000	Alaska	676,778	2.1	7.3	19.7	11.2	28.8	26.3	6.7	33.4	75.2	5.0	7.0	20.5	5.5
02 03000	Anchorage municipality	278,735	1.1	7.6	19.3	10.6	30.5	25.6	6.4	33.2	77.4	8.4	9.9	13.6	7.7
02 24230	Fairbanks	33,593	1.7	9.8	18.5	19.6	29.0	18.1	5.0	26.2	73.0	15.3	4.2	15.3	7.8
02 36400	Juneau city and borough	30,850	-1.0	5.4	17.8	11.1	27.1	31.3	7.3	38.2	81.3	1.5	7.0	19.1	4.3
04 00000	Arizona	6,152,175	6.5	7.8	18.6	9.4	28.3	23.1	12.8	34.8	78.5	4.1	3.1	16.9	29.0
04 02830	Apache Junction	44,422	-1.4	6.3	18.2	7.8	23.8	21.2	22.7	39.2	94.9	1.2	2.3	3.5	15.8
04 04720	Avondale	67,876	15.1	10.2	24.1	9.4	33.6	18.0	4.6	28.5	68.4	6.9	4.2	23.7	50.6
04 07940	Buckeye town	27,004	13.6	11.2	19.9	9.6	36.7	17.5	5.1	28.4	77.0	5.3	3.4	16.6	44.0
04 08220	Bullhead	39,640	5.9	5.8	16.1	5.8	25.5	26.0	20.8	42.4	89.4	1.7	2.5	8.8	21.5
04 10530	Casa Grande	41,093	15.4	7.6	22.2	10.0	28.3	20.1	11.8	30.2	69.3	5.0	1.5	27.2	40.7
04 10670	Casas Adobes CDP	57,574	-	6.1	16.7	8.6	27.0	25.8	15.9	39.6	84.1	2.9	3.8	11.9	19.6
04 11230	Catalina Foothills CDP	56,986	-	4.8	15.5	6.7	18.1	33.9	21.0	48.0	90.4	1.4	5.3	4.3	7.9
04 12000	Chandler	236,726	6.1	8.3	20.6	8.5	34.6	21.8	6.2	32.8	80.3	5.2	8.5	9.0	20.8
04 20540	Drexel Heights CDP	26,755	-	8.2	23.6	8.3	27.4	22.9	9.5	30.9	56.5	3.4	1.4	43.9	60.9
04 22220	El Mirage	32,666	9.5	12.2	26.4	9.4	35.4	12.3	4.4	25.8	53.4	11.0	2.0	36.9	45.4
04 23260	Flagstaff	63,434	3.5	6.8	16.0	21.7	27.1	21.9	6.6	27.7	76.3	2.3	2.2	21.4	17.3
04 25030	Fortuna Foothills CDP	27,223	-	6.6	9.5	2.6	16.3	21.5	43.5	62.5	83.7	2.0	0.7	15.7	23.4
04 25300	Fountain Hills town	23,182	6.9	3.7	13.0	3.7	22.0	35.4	22.2	49.7	97.9	-	2.1	0.3	-
04 27400	Gilbert town	183,848	13.9	10.4	23.9	7.3	33.2	20.0	5.2	31.0	85.4	4.0	5.7	7.4	14.2
04 27820	Glendale	239,178	3.5	9.0	20.4	9.7	29.8	23.3	7.7	31.9	79.1	6.1	4.0	14.3	34.1
04 28380	Goodyear	52,179	28.2	8.5	20.8	7.0	33.2	22.4	8.1	33.4	79.9	6.2	3.9	13.8	27.1
04 29710	Green Valley CDP	21,206	-	0.9	1.6	0.4	3.6	23.7	69.7	71.1	97.9	0.6	1.0	1.2	3.8
04 37620	Kingman	29,219	9.5	8.1	15.3	10.8	25.4	21.9	18.5	35.9	95.6	-	0.8	5.5	10.7
04 39370	Lake Havasu	51,934	3.3	5.4	15.3	6.7	22.2	26.8	23.5	45.2	95.0	-	0.6	5.2	14.2
04 44270	Marana town	26,116	21.5	7.7	17.7	5.6	30.1	26.0	12.9	38.2	79.9	3.2	3.3	15.3	23.9
04 44410	Maricopa	18,603	260.6	10.2	16.2	9.3	43.7	17.8	2.7	29.1	71.9	7.2	5.5	20.3	22.1
04 46000	Mesa	478,014	2.1	8.3	18.4	10.0	28.9	21.3	13.2	33.6	86.0	3.1	2.6	10.6	25.6
04 49360	New River CDP	25,037	-	7.2	20.7	4.4	27.5	32.6	7.7	39.2	97.0	0.9	2.0	1.8	7.5
04 51600	Oro Valley town	39,856	3.6	5.2	16.7	5.3	19.8	30.5	22.5	46.9	91.3	3.0	3.9	5.2	9.3
04 54050	Peoria	145,891	9.0	7.5	20.1	7.2	28.1	23.3	13.8	37.0	88.3	3.8	3.2	6.9	18.7
04 55000	Phoenix	1,440,018	5.4	9.0	20.1	9.4	32.2	21.5	7.8	31.5	76.7	6.0	2.9	16.4	41.5
04 57380	Prescott	42,900	5.2	3.8	10.8	9.9	18.9	28.6	27.9	49.9	93.2	0.6	2.7	4.6	6.7
04 57450	Prescott Valley town	36,366	13.9	6.9	17.2	10.3	26.6	21.0	18.0	37.6	88.0	0.7	1.5	11.6	15.7
04 58150	Queen Creek town	38,135	42.8	15.8	22.8	4.3	38.4	15.1	3.6	28.5	77.4	6.3	3.8	14.9	20.4
04 63470	San Luis	15,433	10.4	9.6	25.0	13.6	28.1	17.9	5.8	25.8	84.0	2.0	-	15.4	-
04 65000	Scottsdale	215,723	3.3	5.5	13.0	6.7	26.5	30.6	17.7	43.8	92.7	2.0	3.6	3.1	8.2
04 66820	Sierra Vista	39,080	2.9	7.8	16.2	12.6	26.0	22.0	15.5	33.9	81.9	11.0	5.1	6.5	16.3
04 66845	Sierra Vista Southeast CDP	20,254	-	5.6	23.0	9.0	21.9	28.8	11.7	38.8	87.5	4.9	4.3	7.5	24.6
04 70320	Sun CDP	41,431	-	0.8	0.4	0.2	3.0	27.1	68.5	71.6	96.8	1.1	0.6	0.6	2.7
04 70355	Sun West CDP	27,136	-	-	-	-	-	-	-	74.4	99.0	0.5	0.2	-	-
04 71510	Surprise	102,456	23.6	10.7	15.5	5.8	27.5	22.7	17.8	36.8	81.9	4.5	2.9	13.5	20.3
04 73000	Tempe	167,141	4.2	5.1	15.1	22.0	31.3	19.4	7.2	28.3	83.2	4.6	7.4	7.8	22.0
04 77000	Tucson	520,482	1.7	7.6	16.5	13.4	29.2	21.7	11.7	32.8	67.3	5.0	3.5	27.7	39.5
04 85540	Yuma	95,419	4.5	9.7	20.4	11.8	26.2	17.9	14.1	30.9	71.5	4.0	2.3	24.7	52.5

STATE City	Percent foreign born	Total households	Household type (percent)							Percent of households with people under 18 years	Percent of households with people 60 years and over
			Family households				Nonfamily households				
			Total family households	Married-couple families	Male householder families	Female householder families	Total nonfamily households	One-person households			
ACS table number:	C05002	B11001	B11001	B11001	B11001	B11001	B11001	B11001	C11005	B11006
	15	16	17	18	19	20	21	22	23	24
United States..............	12.5	111,609,629	66.9	49.8	4.6	12.5	33.1	27.3	34.6	30.9
Alabama......................	2.9	1,798,304	68.4	49.7	4.2	14.5	31.6	27.5	34.3	32.5
Alabaster.....................	2.7	10,380	77.9	63.7	4.6	9.7	22.1	20.3	42.1	21.0
Anniston......................	2.6	10,241	59.8	37.3	5.2	17.3	40.2	35.4	28.7	37.4
Athens........................	5.5	8,249	65.3	49.8	3.8	11.7	34.7	30.7	33.2	35.9
Auburn........................	7.1	21,965	43.3	32.0	3.8	7.5	56.7	37.5	22.7	16.1
Bessemer	1.0	11,490	65.1	30.1	5.7	29.3	34.9	32.2	36.0	36.0
Birmingham..................	3.3	90,641	57.8	28.0	4.8	24.9	42.2	36.2	31.9	29.9
Decatur.......................	6.4	22,268	66.6	49.1	3.5	14.0	33.4	30.2	31.2	34.9
Dothan........................	1.9	24,611	65.5	46.6	4.0	14.9	34.5	31.1	32.9	32.1
Enterprise	7.3	9,029	70.7	51.7	6.0	13.0	29.3	23.6	35.8	32.7
Florence......................	2.2	15,677	59.0	40.4	2.8	15.8	41.0	36.4	25.1	36.6
Gadsden......................	3.1	16,531	62.9	38.1	6.4	18.5	37.1	33.5	33.7	36.5
Homewood...................	10.4	11,048	57.1	42.7	3.7	10.7	42.9	34.2	32.0	27.7
Hoover........................	8.5	29,676	69.5	56.9	3.7	9.0	30.5	26.2	35.7	25.7
Huntsville....................	6.1	69,229	60.8	41.5	3.9	15.3	39.2	33.7	27.7	32.1
Madison......................	7.0	13,875	73.8	59.5	2.3	12.0	26.2	23.5	41.6	22.4
Mobile........................	3.8	74,912	64.4	37.9	4.6	21.8	35.6	31.2	33.9	33.5
Montgomery..................	3.2	80,441	62.9	38.4	4.8	19.7	37.1	33.5	35.0	28.2
Mountain Brook.............	2.7	8,028	77.9	71.9	1.1	4.9	22.1	20.6	38.7	36.6
Northport	3.2	9,347	64.8	47.2	2.4	15.3	35.2	27.5	33.3	24.6
Opelika.......................	2.5	10,916	60.4	36.5	3.4	20.5	39.6	36.6	34.7	30.3
Oxford........................	2.9	8,570	75.4	55.0	5.2	15.2	24.6	21.5	38.4	31.4
Pelham........................	7.9	7,614	63.6	51.9	2.8	8.9	36.4	31.0	34.3	26.1
Phenix........................	2.3	12,869	63.5	39.0	4.8	19.7	36.5	31.6	35.9	29.3
Prattville.....................	2.0	10,705	71.4	54.5	4.2	12.8	28.6	25.1	41.0	28.0
Prichard......................	0.6	9,327	67.2	28.2	7.4	31.6	32.8	29.9	39.7	33.5
Tuscaloosa...................	4.8	33,039	50.2	31.7	3.8	14.7	49.8	37.6	23.1	26.4
Vestavia Hills................	5.0	13,973	66.4	55.2	1.8	9.4	33.6	30.4	33.8	33.6
Alaska	6.7	233,861	68.3	51.1	5.7	11.6	31.7	24.5	39.2	21.6
Anchorage municipality	8.6	102,476	67.9	50.9	5.0	12.0	32.1	24.4	39.1	20.4
Fairbanks	4.9	11,320	58.1	38.8	4.3	15.0	41.9	33.4	37.5	16.6
Juneau city and borough....	6.4	11,618	65.8	50.0	5.9	9.8	34.2	26.6	35.6	23.2
Arizona	15.0	2,215,761	66.3	49.5	5.0	11.8	33.7	26.8	34.2	32.2
Apache Junction	9.0	19,542	65.4	49.1	6.7	9.5	34.6	28.2	30.1	42.2
Avondale	10.8	19,505	78.1	53.7	7.0	17.4	21.9	16.0	53.3	16.9
Buckeye town	15.1	7,357	72.7	53.9	6.3	12.5	27.3	24.1	49.3	15.6
Bullhead	13.1	16,449	65.3	49.5	3.9	11.8	34.7	27.8	26.5	45.7
Casa Grande..................	10.6	16,384	71.6	48.8	7.4	15.5	28.4	23.2	43.6	30.7
Casas Adobes CDP	8.1	23,565	61.8	45.0	4.0	12.7	38.2	32.1	29.0	34.2
Catalina Foothills CDP........	9.1	24,558	65.7	55.9	3.1	6.8	34.3	30.1	25.4	43.1
Chandler......................	14.0	82,288	69.7	54.2	4.3	11.2	30.3	22.8	41.6	18.5
Drexel Heights CDP...........	15.5	8,265	78.3	56.9	5.6	15.8	21.7	17.3	47.3	29.9
El Mirage	20.1	8,699	81.1	55.5	5.6	20.0	18.9	12.3	59.5	15.3
Flagstaff......................	8.2	22,256	61.4	44.5	5.2	11.6	38.6	25.6	31.6	19.8
Fortuna Foothills CDP........	13.3	12,369	71.8	65.3	1.8	4.8	28.2	21.8	16.6	67.9
Fountain Hills town	6.8	10,364	70.9	64.8	2.2	3.9	29.1	24.0	19.0	49.1
Gilbert town	9.0	57,609	78.4	63.0	4.3	11.1	21.6	16.0	49.9	17.8
Glendale......................	18.0	77,990	69.8	48.5	7.0	14.4	30.2	23.3	41.3	23.8
Goodyear......................	12.8	16,032	82.3	67.6	4.3	10.3	17.7	13.8	43.2	28.7
Green Valley CDP	7.4	12,775	55.1	52.6	0.8	1.7	44.9	41.5	2.3	89.6
Kingman......................	3.6	11,011	73.4	53.1	6.8	13.5	26.6	20.3	35.3	36.7
Lake Havasu..................	6.7	21,869	67.2	52.7	3.4	11.0	32.8	27.5	26.9	45.8
Marana town..................	9.8	9,847	73.7	64.9	2.6	6.1	26.3	19.1	33.4	33.7
Maricopa	9.9	7,491	73.1	60.2	6.1	6.8	26.9	17.5	45.2	9.5
Mesa..........................	15.5	170,023	65.8	49.5	5.0	11.3	34.2	27.4	33.7	32.3
New River CDP................	4.4	8,903	78.5	71.0	1.2	6.3	21.5	19.2	37.9	27.0
Oro Valley town	6.9	16,058	74.2	64.6	3.1	6.5	25.8	22.2	28.0	47.6
Peoria	9.1	51,333	70.4	55.6	5.0	9.8	29.6	24.2	36.7	33.8
Phoenix.......................	23.7	483,915	63.8	43.8	6.2	13.7	36.2	28.4	38.1	22.4
Prescott	6.6	19,079	57.8	47.8	3.4	6.5	42.2	34.5	16.9	48.5
Prescott Valley town..........	8.3	14,061	68.9	54.0	4.8	10.1	31.1	22.7	31.1	39.6
Queen Creek town	10.3	11,192	81.1	66.8	5.0	9.3	18.9	10.7	57.5	11.1
San Luis	45.4	3,622	90.6	58.6	4.2	27.9	9.4	9.4	73.9	29.5
Scottsdale....................	10.3	95,783	56.8	46.7	3.5	6.6	43.2	34.6	21.9	36.5
Sierra Vista...................	8.8	15,716	69.2	54.1	3.7	11.4	30.8	28.1	34.4	35.8
Sierra Vista Southeast CDP...	7.3	6,879	75.4	62.9	3.0	9.5	24.6	17.8	39.8	37.0
Sun CDP	5.4	24,383	51.5	46.4	0.8	4.4	48.5	45.1	0.9	92.3
Sun West CDP	5.2	15,383	61.8	57.1	1.8	2.9	38.2	35.1	-	95.4
Surprise	11.6	37,324	74.5	64.7	3.1	6.6	25.5	21.0	31.3	42.3
Tempe.........................	17.1	60,024	52.5	36.3	6.4	9.8	47.5	31.3	26.3	19.9
Tucson........................	16.6	205,563	56.5	36.6	5.2	14.7	43.5	35.3	30.8	27.9
Yuma..........................	20.2	36,235	70.3	50.7	4.3	15.3	29.7	24.6	40.6	31.7

Table A-4. Cities — Who: Age, Race/Ethnicity, and Household Structure, 2005–2007—*Continued*

STATE Place code	STATE / City	Total population	Percent change 2005–2007	Under 5 years	5 to 17 years	18 to 24 years	25 to 44 years	45 to 64 years	65 years and over	Median age	White	Black	Asian Hawaiian or Pacific Islander	Amer. Indian, Alaska Native, or some other race	Percent Hispanic or Latino
	ACS table number:	B01003	Population estimates	B01001	B01001	B01001	B01001	B01001	B01001	B01002	B02008	B02009	B02011 + B02012	B02010 + B02013	C03002
		1	2	3	4	5	6	7	8	9	10	11	12	13	14
05 00000	**Arkansas**	2,805,353	2.3	7.0	17.8	9.5	26.8	25.0	13.9	36.8	80.1	16.1	1.4	4.0	5.0
05 05290	Benton	24,361	10.4	5.3	20.4	10.6	28.5	22.6	12.6	34.6	93.3	3.9	0.5	3.3	-
05 05320	Bentonville	30,227	13.2	9.8	20.6	10.1	36.0	16.6	7.0	29.9	87.9	4.8	3.6	6.5	6.8
05 10300	Cabot	21,015	11.7	8.9	21.1	7.8	32.6	20.9	8.7	31.7	96.8	1.1	2.4	2.1	1.6
05 15190	Conway	55,166	9.8	8.1	16.2	22.6	28.3	16.9	8.0	26.7	83.3	15.3	1.7	1.4	3.3
05 23290	Fayetteville	69,000	4.7	6.8	13.3	22.7	30.7	19.0	7.4	28.1	85.8	7.3	3.3	5.6	5.0
05 24550	Fort Smith	83,575	2.3	8.0	18.0	8.9	27.7	25.0	12.4	35.3	78.7	10.2	5.0	9.8	13.3
05 33400	Hot Springs	38,458	3.0	5.8	15.9	9.2	26.3	22.1	20.7	39.1	78.4	17.3	0.6	5.6	-
05 34750	Jacksonville	28,570	1.5	9.9	19.2	12.2	27.8	22.3	8.6	30.9	62.9	32.6	4.1	2.8	4.1
05 35710	Jonesboro	61,447	5.4	7.3	16.7	14.5	28.7	21.4	11.4	32.0	82.8	15.6	1.3	1.3	3.7
05 41000	Little Rock	190,142	0.8	7.7	17.9	8.7	28.9	25.1	11.7	35.5	53.7	42.7	2.5	2.7	4.7
05 50450	North Little Rock	58,264	0.2	7.0	17.6	8.2	26.8	27.3	13.2	38.0	60.2	38.8	1.3	2.7	4.2
05 53390	Paragould	23,494	3.7	7.4	16.7	9.5	28.7	22.5	15.2	35.4	98.5	-	-	2.2	-
05 55310	Pine Bluff	50,166	-2.8	8.0	18.2	12.1	24.8	24.1	12.8	34.0	26.6	71.8	0.9	2.1	1.6
05 60410	Rogers	47,082	13.1	10.4	20.5	7.7	31.1	20.9	9.4	31.4	82.5	0.8	3.5	14.2	26.3
05 61670	Russellville	26,777	3.3	6.8	16.4	16.5	25.8	21.5	13.0	31.7	90.7	7.1	2.3	3.3	6.6
05 63020	Searcy	21,087	2.5	6.9	14.7	24.7	22.4	18.3	12.9	27.0	88.6	11.2	0.6	0.7	2.9
05 63800	Sherwood	24,057	3.1	8.0	17.2	7.4	28.2	26.8	12.4	38.4	82.6	15.1	1.1	1.2	1.9
05 66080	Springdale	63,837	8.4	10.5	21.3	9.0	30.4	20.4	8.4	30.3	72.2	2.1	4.7	23.5	30.0
05 68810	Texarkana	30,163	0.6	6.6	19.4	8.3	28.5	23.0	14.2	36.3	64.9	33.7	0.3	2.7	2.5
05 71480	Van Buren	20,862	4.7	8.0	19.6	11.4	28.1	23.2	9.8	32.6	88.2	3.3	3.4	8.6	10.3
05 74540	West Memphis	27,769	-1.1	8.4	21.6	11.0	24.4	24.1	10.6	32.6	40.2	59.9	-	1.4	1.0
06 00000	**California**	36,264,467	1.6	7.3	18.7	10.4	29.5	23.3	10.8	34.5	63.1	7.0	13.9	19.5	35.7
06 00296	Adelanto	25,718	14.4	8.9	26.5	11.6	34.2	15.8	3.0	26.8	51.7	20.8	2.6	27.8	52.4
06 00394	Agoura Hills	20,493	-1.2	4.4	22.8	7.6	24.5	33.1	7.5	38.9	84.5	3.6	9.5	4.7	9.1
06 00562	Alameda	74,142	0.1	5.9	15.2	7.2	29.6	29.3	12.8	40.6	58.8	6.8	32.6	7.9	11.2
06 00884	Alhambra	85,075	-0.8	6.2	14.3	9.3	30.7	25.6	13.9	38.3	27.1	2.9	52.8	20.5	32.9
06 00947	Aliso Viejo	46,451	0.0	10.0	16.7	6.3	41.3	22.5	3.1	34.9	74.9	4.9	15.4	8.6	18.9
06 01290	Altadena CDP	42,373	-	6.0	19.1	8.0	26.3	29.9	10.7	39.0	54.7	29.9	6.3	12.6	23.5
06 02000	Anaheim	336,471	0.4	8.5	20.5	10.5	31.0	20.2	9.1	32.0	65.5	2.9	14.3	19.7	52.3
06 02252	Antioch	100,432	0.2	7.8	22.0	11.7	26.6	24.2	7.8	32.3	51.3	17.9	12.2	24.3	29.2
06 02364	Apple Valley town	68,831	8.7	7.4	22.0	9.6	25.4	22.5	13.2	33.1	72.2	10.5	3.1	17.2	27.4
06 02462	Arcadia	58,345	0.6	4.1	18.4	8.5	25.5	28.2	15.3	41.5	37.4	1.0	56.1	7.3	11.4
06 02553	Arden-Arcade CDP	92,056	-	7.0	13.8	9.4	27.6	25.9	16.3	39.2	79.4	8.3	7.8	9.1	15.2
06 02980	Ashland CDP	21,112	-	8.0	20.0	10.8	30.6	22.5	8.1	31.5	47.2	22.2	19.8	14.1	37.5
06 03064	Atascadero	27,014	2.1	5.2	18.1	8.3	28.1	29.2	11.2	39.0	87.0	3.3	2.5	9.9	14.9
06 03162	Atwater	30,414	0.4	9.4	21.9	10.1	29.3	18.4	10.9	29.4	64.3	5.4	6.9	25.8	47.6
06 03386	Azusa	48,296	-0.7	8.6	19.7	15.5	30.8	17.3	8.1	29.0	47.2	4.1	8.9	41.1	65.6
06 03526	Bakersfield	312,478	7.6	9.4	21.6	10.9	30.3	19.3	8.4	29.5	59.6	9.0	6.7	29.0	40.8
06 03666	Baldwin Park	79,980	-0.9	9.1	22.4	11.8	29.2	19.4	8.1	30.1	31.2	1.8	12.5	56.7	81.3
06 03820	Banning	27,774	0.2	6.2	16.6	8.9	22.0	19.5	26.8	42.2	77.5	8.4	4.4	15.1	34.5
06 04030	Barstow	24,395	-0.6	8.4	24.9	9.5	26.8	21.1	9.2	29.2	49.9	18.9	4.0	31.6	39.5
06 04415	Bay Point CDP	20,374	-	9.7	21.2	9.8	31.0	20.1	8.3	30.7	49.9	11.1	9.8	32.1	45.2
06 04758	Beaumont	21,291	49.4	9.7	22.8	10.0	33.8	16.1	7.7	28.4	75.2	3.7	6.3	20.2	47.1
06 04870	Bell	36,983	-1.3	9.3	22.5	10.0	33.7	18.5	5.9	29.1	51.8	1.3	-	47.1	-
06 04982	Bellflower	76,986	-1.1	8.1	22.8	11.2	29.1	20.3	8.5	30.8	38.6	12.5	12.6	39.5	51.0
06 04996	Bell Gardens	44,721	-0.2	9.9	26.1	11.2	30.9	17.3	4.6	26.5	53.5	1.1	0.6	46.2	-
06 05108	Belmont	25,239	0.7	6.8	15.5	8.0	29.1	29.2	11.3	39.9	77.7	0.8	21.7	4.0	12.5
06 05290	Benicia	25,050	0.2	4.6	18.7	8.4	21.6	34.7	12.0	43.0	81.1	4.1	12.2	6.9	11.3
06 06000	Berkeley	107,268	0.8	4.1	8.5	24.5	26.5	25.1	11.3	34.8	66.7	12.3	19.0	6.7	10.0
06 06308	Beverly Hills	35,049	-0.9	3.7	16.9	7.9	24.9	28.4	18.2	42.7	88.1	2.9	8.3	0.9	4.2
06 07064	Bloomington CDP	22,233	-	6.3	25.7	11.8	27.3	21.9	7.0	30.0	71.3	2.8	2.0	26.5	73.3
06 07218	Blythe	21,125	3.0	5.9	13.3	13.3	42.4	18.5	6.6	32.4	62.5	17.4	2.7	19.7	47.7
06 08058	Brawley	24,248	2.1	13.2	20.6	10.9	27.0	18.8	9.6	30.4	71.6	3.4	1.8	26.1	77.0
06 08100	Brea	38,921	0.0	4.7	19.3	8.5	27.2	27.9	12.4	38.2	71.2	2.1	15.9	13.3	21.2
06 08142	Brentwood	43,750	12.0	8.2	25.3	6.1	30.5	19.6	10.3	34.2	77.0	5.1	8.5	15.1	27.2
06 08786	Buena Park	82,649	0.3	8.0	20.2	9.7	29.2	23.1	9.7	33.5	43.3	4.8	25.5	28.8	38.8
06 08954	Burbank	102,770	-0.3	6.1	15.8	7.9	32.5	25.7	12.1	38.5	70.3	3.8	11.0	18.0	25.3
06 09066	Burlingame	30,018	0.8	8.4	13.7	5.3	30.6	28.4	13.7	40.6	73.1	2.3	20.4	8.4	9.1
06 09598	Calabasas	21,365	2.2	3.9	25.4	8.0	21.4	31.8	9.6	41.0	88.6	0.7	9.7	1.3	-
06 09710	Calexico	32,562	6.2	7.3	23.1	14.5	24.3	20.6	10.0	30.7	79.4	-	2.1	19.6	-
06 10046	Camarillo	61,068	3.0	6.4	16.4	8.0	26.1	27.2	16.0	40.0	76.2	2.5	10.8	14.6	21.5
06 10345	Campbell	36,199	1.8	6.3	13.6	8.1	30.7	29.5	11.8	39.1	75.0	3.0	16.9	10.9	15.9
06 11194	Carlsbad	94,581	4.6	6.7	18.5	6.1	28.9	26.8	13.1	39.4	86.9	1.2	8.6	5.8	12.8
06 11390	Carmichael CDP	53,023	-	4.6	18.8	10.1	22.6	27.4	16.5	40.2	85.2	4.1	7.8	6.2	8.7
06 11530	Carson	95,420	-0.7	7.0	18.5	11.2	26.2	24.4	12.6	35.5	26.9	28.2	28.2	20.9	36.5
06 11964	Castro Valley CDP	55,484	-	5.8	18.5	7.1	23.6	31.3	13.7	42.6	73.0	7.3	18.5	5.0	15.9
06 12048	Cathedral	44,529	2.2	6.5	18.8	9.0	29.5	22.6	13.5	34.9	78.9	3.0	3.2	18.9	55.0
06 12524	Ceres	43,590	6.2	7.9	23.5	11.5	30.2	19.6	7.3	29.5	58.6	5.3	8.1	32.0	50.9
06 12552	Cerritos	53,370	-1.3	3.4	19.5	9.8	23.6	29.5	14.2	40.6	23.9	10.2	60.9	7.3	10.4
06 13014	Chico	85,224	1.7	5.8	13.5	28.1	27.0	16.4	9.2	26.1	88.7	2.9	6.3	8.2	11.9
06 13210	Chino	76,664	8.0	6.4	18.1	12.7	35.0	21.5	6.2	31.1	56.9	7.8	8.7	30.4	50.7
06 13214	Chino Hills	78,373	-1.1	6.8	22.0	9.4	31.6	24.0	6.2	33.2	51.5	5.3	31.1	14.9	26.1
06 13392	Chula Vista	221,413	2.8	8.5	21.4	9.4	29.4	20.7	10.6	33.0	61.0	5.1	17.1	21.5	54.6

STATE City	Percent foreign born	Total households	Household type (percent)							Percent of households with people under 18 years	Percent of households with people 60 years and over
			Family households				Nonfamily households				
			Total family households	Married-couple families	Male householder families	Female householder families	Total nonfamily households	One-person households		
ACS table number:	C05002	B11001	B11001	B11001	B11001	B11001	B11001	B11001	C11005	B11006
	15	16	17	18	19	20	21	22	23	24
Arkansas	3.9	1,096,622	68.4	51.3	4.3	12.7	31.6	27.2	34.1	33.1
Benton	2.5	9,741	66.6	48.3	2.7	15.6	33.4	23.8	37.3	28.5
Bentonville	6.9	10,717	67.9	54.4	3.9	9.6	32.1	26.1	43.6	18.0
Cabot	1.8	7,582	74.9	61.0	1.9	12.0	25.1	21.0	44.7	23.3
Conway	3.2	19,918	63.7	49.4	2.9	11.5	36.3	27.5	35.6	20.4
Fayetteville	6.9	29,564	49.6	35.9	3.9	9.8	50.4	34.3	26.9	16.9
Fort Smith	11.5	32,924	61.1	43.2	4.7	13.2	38.9	33.3	32.5	31.0
Hot Springs	5.1	16,261	52.4	33.1	4.2	15.1	47.6	41.9	27.1	40.8
Jacksonville	4.5	10,693	70.0	48.1	4.6	17.3	30.0	26.2	41.8	23.1
Jonesboro	3.9	23,418	65.3	45.2	3.5	16.6	34.7	29.0	32.9	26.2
Little Rock	6.1	79,573	58.6	38.2	3.6	16.7	41.4	34.8	31.5	26.8
North Little Rock	3.1	25,538	61.1	41.3	4.1	15.8	38.9	35.6	29.0	30.5
Paragould	0.8	9,731	67.0	51.7	3.4	11.9	33.0	26.3	33.8	32.2
Pine Bluff	2.0	19,245	59.5	32.9	4.6	22.0	40.5	36.0	35.0	32.0
Rogers	18.2	16,924	73.1	56.0	8.2	8.8	26.9	23.7	43.8	26.5
Russellville	4.4	10,382	60.7	44.8	2.9	12.9	39.3	31.5	30.8	27.6
Searcy	3.3	7,691	61.2	43.5	4.4	13.2	38.8	32.8	29.0	29.4
Sherwood	1.2	10,016	69.1	52.3	3.2	13.5	30.9	28.2	35.2	30.7
Springdale	20.5	21,653	78.0	55.7	10.5	11.8	22.0	18.6	46.8	24.3
Texarkana	1.4	11,933	64.4	42.3	5.1	17.0	35.6	30.5	34.1	31.7
Van Buren	7.5	7,443	71.7	50.5	4.9	16.2	28.3	24.1	38.9	27.3
West Memphis	0.4	10,847	66.3	33.9	5.2	27.2	33.7	28.6	39.2	29.7
California	27.2	12,140,888	68.3	49.8	5.8	12.8	31.7	24.7	38.5	29.9
Adelanto	23.9	6,576	80.7	47.8	9.4	23.5	19.3	15.5	61.0	16.7
Agoura Hills	15.9	7,108	74.2	65.0	2.2	7.0	25.8	20.3	41.3	23.6
Alameda	28.9	29,287	60.9	41.8	6.4	12.6	39.1	31.6	31.0	30.9
Alhambra	53.7	28,535	71.0	49.8	6.6	14.6	29.0	22.5	34.2	34.2
Aliso Viejo	24.2	18,009	62.6	48.6	3.0	11.0	37.4	29.3	37.1	12.2
Altadena CDP	15.5	14,559	69.4	48.8	6.1	14.5	30.6	25.4	37.2	33.7
Anaheim	38.6	96,930	74.7	52.1	6.6	15.9	25.3	19.2	46.1	29.2
Antioch	21.9	32,217	76.0	56.4	6.3	13.2	24.0	18.2	45.6	24.2
Apple Valley town	11.0	22,697	77.6	55.9	7.5	14.2	22.4	18.9	42.0	34.3
Arcadia	49.6	19,618	74.2	59.2	4.7	10.3	25.8	21.3	39.6	37.2
Arden-Arcade CDP	15.2	41,184	55.0	37.7	4.0	13.2	45.0	36.8	27.0	33.4
Ashland CDP	34.2	6,623	64.2	32.9	9.2	22.0	35.8	26.7	46.7	22.0
Atascadero	5.4	10,531	67.7	52.7	4.6	10.4	32.3	24.2	34.4	26.2
Atwater	21.8	9,187	73.8	55.2	3.5	15.1	26.2	17.5	50.9	28.0
Azusa	35.1	13,123	72.3	49.1	9.3	13.9	27.7	20.4	46.3	26.9
Bakersfield	17.8	100,108	73.7	51.4	5.6	16.7	26.3	21.7	48.2	23.9
Baldwin Park	47.5	17,557	88.0	60.8	8.2	18.9	12.0	8.3	59.7	32.4
Banning	18.4	11,048	63.5	47.6	3.4	12.5	36.5	31.0	29.1	51.0
Barstow	10.9	8,158	71.8	43.6	4.7	23.5	28.2	22.0	45.4	24.9
Bay Point CDP	32.4	6,370	77.8	55.8	5.9	16.1	22.2	17.2	50.1	21.9
Beaumont	24.1	6,612	75.0	55.5	7.9	11.6	25.0	17.2	50.8	18.8
Bell	48.1	8,869	86.3	55.3	10.2	20.8	13.7	11.9	57.6	25.6
Bellflower	30.0	23,701	73.3	43.7	7.8	21.7	26.7	20.9	46.7	26.6
Bell Gardens	49.5	9,741	87.9	62.0	6.0	19.9	12.1	8.7	66.3	18.7
Belmont	23.6	10,490	64.0	51.9	4.3	7.9	36.0	28.3	32.8	28.0
Benicia	11.3	9,882	71.4	55.5	3.2	12.7	28.6	23.5	33.6	32.9
Berkeley	19.1	43,132	43.4	31.2	3.7	8.5	56.6	39.3	18.4	29.1
Beverly Hills	39.0	14,557	56.6	45.3	3.3	7.9	43.4	38.3	25.8	40.9
Bloomington CDP	34.3	5,276	83.7	56.0	14.5	13.2	16.3	13.8	56.9	25.3
Blythe	13.2	4,712	70.9	38.8	8.5	23.6	29.1	25.1	42.8	27.0
Brawley	24.7	7,367	81.9	53.7	4.0	24.3	18.1	15.1	54.0	29.3
Brea	19.3	14,415	72.1	56.1	5.4	10.6	27.9	23.4	33.7	29.7
Brentwood	17.4	14,001	80.4	69.6	2.9	7.9	19.6	16.3	51.6	27.1
Buena Park	35.5	23,641	79.5	56.7	8.0	14.8	20.5	16.0	45.7	30.4
Burbank	30.2	40,930	58.5	42.4	4.5	11.6	41.5	33.2	31.2	29.4
Burlingame	27.5	12,221	59.6	45.9	6.9	6.8	40.4	33.9	31.0	26.6
Calabasas	27.4	7,814	70.9	58.9	4.7	7.2	29.1	21.6	39.1	26.5
Calexico	45.3	8,688	83.7	55.6	4.2	23.8	16.3	14.7	57.7	33.3
Camarillo	14.6	22,581	69.0	54.6	5.1	9.2	31.0	26.6	32.8	40.8
Campbell	19.6	15,541	58.1	41.3	5.6	11.3	41.9	34.4	27.3	24.3
Carlsbad	12.4	37,759	66.4	54.7	2.9	8.8	33.6	26.2	34.9	29.3
Carmichael CDP	15.3	20,507	64.6	49.7	3.3	11.6	35.4	29.2	34.3	34.9
Carson	31.1	25,425	81.1	55.0	6.0	20.1	18.9	15.3	44.9	41.6
Castro Valley CDP	18.6	20,834	69.4	51.2	6.0	12.2	30.6	27.1	36.2	34.5
Cathedral	30.4	16,371	63.8	46.6	7.0	10.2	36.2	26.9	36.4	34.6
Ceres	24.7	11,845	85.6	59.4	7.6	18.7	14.4	10.9	55.1	23.5
Cerritos	45.1	15,889	85.6	71.1	4.0	10.5	14.4	12.2	41.8	45.4
Chico	7.9	33,401	47.8	32.0	3.6	12.1	52.2	31.0	28.0	21.9
Chino	21.4	19,661	81.8	58.1	6.7	17.0	18.2	14.5	51.5	25.9
Chino Hills	26.6	22,801	84.0	71.1	4.5	8.4	16.0	12.7	50.1	19.4
Chula Vista	30.9	71,189	77.7	55.1	6.2	16.4	22.3	18.2	47.2	28.9

STATE Place code	STATE City ACS table number:	Total population B01003	Percent change 2005–2007 Population estimates	Population by age (percent)						Median age B01002	Race alone or in combination (percent)				Percent Hispanic or Latino C03002
				Under 5 years B01001	5 to 17 years B01001	18 to 24 years B01001	25 to 44 years B01001	45 to 64 years B01001	65 years and over B01001		White B02008	Black B02009	Asian Hawaiian or Pacific Islander B02011 + B02012	Amer. Indian, Alaska Native, or some other race B02010 + B02013	
		1	2	3	4	5	6	7	8	9	10	11	12	13	14
	California—Cont.														
06 13588	Citrus Heights	85,146	-1.0	5.7	18.2	10.5	28.3	23.8	13.5	35.6	85.1	4.3	5.4	7.6	12.5
06 13756	Claremont	34,390	-0.1	3.6	15.7	18.2	23.2	24.3	15.1	37.9	78.4	5.0	12.3	9.7	19.1
06 14218	Clovis	87,525	4.9	8.1	19.9	12.0	28.6	22.2	9.3	32.5	77.2	3.6	10.2	15.1	25.2
06 14260	Coachella	30,782	20.7	10.7	25.1	13.8	29.9	16.1	4.3	25.2	71.4	0.5	-	28.5	
06 14890	Colton	52,421	-0.7	9.2	22.6	11.1	32.6	18.3	6.2	27.5	51.7	13.0	5.2	33.2	65.6
06 15044	Compton	97,299	-0.8	9.9	25.9	12.5	28.5	16.5	6.8	25.9	22.0	34.7	2.1	42.9	63.8
06 16000	Concord	120,737	-0.7	6.5	16.1	10.1	29.9	25.8	11.6	36.6	68.6	3.7	13.0	19.8	28.5
06 16224	Corcoran	24,124	4.3	4.1	11.7	10.3	45.8	22.3	5.8	36.1	46.9	13.4	2.9	41.6	60.0
06 16350	Corona	153,064	1.7	7.9	21.4	10.3	34.7	19.9	5.8	30.5	69.5	6.7	10.6	17.0	40.9
06 16378	Coronado	22,202	-3.8	3.4	13.8	19.5	26.2	21.3	15.8	35.7	91.4	5.0	3.0	3.0	13.1
06 16532	Costa Mesa	107,820	-0.6	7.1	15.4	11.6	35.6	21.6	8.7	33.7	73.3	1.7	9.8	17.4	33.0
06 16742	Covina	51,873	-0.8	6.7	21.0	9.7	28.4	24.5	9.6	34.7	56.9	6.9	11.8	29.0	47.1
06 17498	Cudahy	25,338	-1.5	10.3	28.1	12.7	31.9	13.3	3.6	24.2	56.3	-	1.4	42.5	-
06 17568	Culver	40,677	-1.5	6.7	13.6	7.0	30.9	27.4	14.4	40.5	61.6	11.1	15.4	15.8	22.4
06 17610	Cupertino	56,592	2.2	6.3	21.5	5.6	27.9	27.2	11.6	39.5	39.6	1.8	57.3	2.9	4.0
06 17750	Cypress	48,861	-0.2	5.9	19.6	8.5	26.2	27.8	12.0	38.9	59.9	3.0	30.7	10.1	14.7
06 17918	Daly	98,230	0.8	5.2	14.1	10.5	29.0	27.9	13.3	39.5	30.9	4.1	56.7	11.5	23.2
06 17946	Dana Point	32,018	-0.3	5.6	11.6	6.9	26.1	32.4	17.4	44.9	88.1	0.6	4.9	9.1	12.2
06 17988	Danville town	42,534	-0.9	5.6	20.9	6.1	21.9	33.4	12.1	42.8	85.4	1.3	13.7	3.1	4.6
06 18100	Davis	66,310	2.0	4.4	12.9	32.6	24.6	17.7	7.8	25.0	72.6	3.2	21.7	6.8	11.2
06 18394	Delano	46,079	15.8	7.4	19.9	12.3	33.9	18.4	8.0	29.5	54.0	5.2	16.2	27.7	71.5
06 18996	Desert Hot Springs	23,516	19.7	7.3	27.0	9.5	29.6	17.5	9.1	29.2	63.4	6.8	0.7	31.7	56.0
06 19192	Diamond Bar	56,462	-0.6	4.8	19.2	9.1	25.9	31.6	9.4	39.9	38.3	4.2	52.3	8.1	19.0
06 19318	Dinuba	19,104	4.8	10.1	24.9	11.7	29.3	15.4	8.6	26.3	74.7	-	3.9	22.6	-
06 19766	Downey	112,255	-1.0	7.9	22.9	8.6	29.5	21.2	9.9	31.7	64.1	3.9	8.7	25.8	66.3
06 19990	Duarte	23,034	-0.8	6.1	18.5	8.2	25.4	23.6	18.2	38.5	58.5	10.4	11.9	20.7	50.0
06 20018	Dublin	41,637	11.9	7.1	15.9	10.6	37.4	23.5	5.6	34.6	61.2	10.2	24.1	9.3	12.8
06 20802	East Los Angeles CDP	125,999	-	9.4	22.5	11.6	30.8	16.5	9.1	29.0	62.3	0.5	0.8	37.4	97.6
06 20956	East Palo Alto	25,788	2.9	10.7	22.6	12.5	30.4	16.5	7.4	27.3	55.6	20.3	15.8	9.0	54.6
06 21712	El Cajon	94,676	-0.5	8.8	19.6	10.1	29.2	21.6	10.8	33.3	79.0	8.1	6.1	10.3	30.1
06 21782	El Centro	41,672	1.7	10.4	20.8	11.5	25.2	21.1	10.9	29.9	73.7	3.0	3.3	21.9	76.4
06 21796	El Cerrito	25,659	-1.5	4.2	12.1	5.9	29.6	28.4	19.8	44.2	60.1	9.2	26.9	7.5	11.3
06 21880	El Dorado Hills CDP	32,436	-	7.1	21.6	8.1	27.8	28.3	7.1	36.9	82.8	1.9	13.2	2.9	8.4
06 22020	Elk Grove	140,242	4.8	8.3	23.7	7.8	31.8	21.5	6.8	32.6	49.8	12.1	29.5	13.1	16.2
06 22230	El Monte	111,335	0.2	8.6	20.8	10.7	31.2	19.9	8.9	31.2	37.8	1.0	24.6	38.1	68.7
06 22300	El Paso de Robles (Paso Robles)	27,868	3.0	9.1	18.6	11.0	25.7	23.8	11.8	33.2	81.9	4.0	3.1	14.5	33.0
06 22678	Encinitas	58,792	0.2	6.5	16.7	6.5	29.3	29.8	11.2	39.6	88.7	0.6	6.3	8.2	16.7
06 22804	Escondido	138,267	1.0	8.1	19.8	10.1	29.9	21.1	11.0	33.8	75.7	2.9	7.2	16.7	43.3
06 23042	Eureka	26,799	-1.3	6.5	13.8	13.7	28.6	25.5	11.8	34.0	84.6	3.1	5.4	16.8	12.9
06 23182	Fairfield	105,332	0.6	8.4	20.5	10.7	30.6	20.8	9.0	31.8	51.1	18.3	17.6	18.9	25.9
06 23294	Fair Oaks CDP	27,439	-	5.1	17.4	8.3	22.1	30.5	16.6	43.5	90.5	0.8	5.4	4.5	7.2
06 23462	Fallbrook CDP	29,787	-	7.1	20.1	8.1	26.9	22.9	14.9	36.1	68.9	1.8	2.0	29.4	39.9
06 24477	Florence-Graham CDP	65,780	-	11.6	24.7	11.8	31.7	15.1	5.0	25.7	52.5	10.1	-	38.5	-
06 24498	Florin CDP	25,071	-	9.8	19.0	10.0	27.4	19.3	14.4	31.8	48.8	19.4	19.4	13.3	28.8
06 24638	Folsom	71,094	3.8	7.5	18.0	7.1	36.4	23.1	7.9	35.6	76.8	7.0	11.5	7.1	10.1
06 24680	Fontana	184,223	4.3	8.9	25.0	11.3	32.5	17.6	4.7	27.8	63.3	12.0	7.3	21.3	62.8
06 25338	Foster	30,290	0.8	7.5	15.7	6.0	33.2	27.6	9.9	38.8	54.0	2.4	46.0	3.0	6.0
06 25380	Fountain Valley	55,394	-0.6	5.4	14.5	8.8	25.7	29.3	16.3	42.3	61.5	1.0	32.6	7.4	11.6
06 26000	Fremont	208,455	0.6	7.4	18.0	6.7	32.3	25.7	10.0	36.6	40.2	4.0	49.2	10.5	15.4
06 27000	Fresno	471,722	2.4	9.0	21.9	12.1	28.9	19.3	8.8	28.8	56.3	9.2	12.7	25.5	44.0
06 28000	Fullerton	133,958	-0.3	7.4	17.8	11.8	29.2	23.2	10.6	34.5	53.4	2.6	22.7	23.8	31.1
06 28112	Galt	22,791	4.4	10.6	24.3	7.6	26.2	22.4	8.9	31.5	68.4	3.0	3.4	28.6	41.6
06 28168	Gardena	58,436	-1.1	6.2	17.4	8.3	29.4	24.9	13.9	37.4	23.3	26.3	30.2	23.0	34.1
06 29000	Garden Grove	169,511	-0.1	7.4	19.8	9.8	29.1	23.3	10.7	34.6	39.2	1.4	34.4	26.8	39.0
06 29504	Gilroy	46,956	7.4	9.2	20.8	11.3	27.4	20.8	10.5	32.4	67.9	2.0	7.4	26.2	57.5
06 30000	Glendale	194,004	-1.1	4.6	15.3	8.9	28.9	27.5	14.7	40.6	72.7	1.9	16.0	10.9	17.0
06 30014	Glendora	50,331	-1.2	4.8	19.2	10.1	22.6	28.3	15.0	40.9	76.3	2.9	9.5	14.9	25.0
06 30378	Goleta	27,373	-0.4	6.3	16.2	13.9	25.9	25.4	12.3	35.7	73.4	2.6	12.0	14.4	25.9
06 30693	Granite Bay CDP	21,876	-	5.6	19.4	4.8	21.6	33.6	14.9	44.1	90.8	3.2	5.9	2.1	5.9
06 31596	Hacienda Heights CDP	51,050	-	5.9	17.3	9.5	24.7	27.4	15.2	40.6	38.2	1.1	39.8	22.3	39.1
06 31960	Hanford	49,242	4.6	8.1	19.9	10.4	34.3	17.9	9.3	31.7	74.7	8.7	4.5	13.7	42.2
06 32548	Hawthorne	92,455	-1.0	11.0	19.8	10.7	32.5	19.0	7.0	29.8	47.6	30.8	6.6	16.1	50.6
06 33000	Hayward	132,382	0.6	7.1	17.4	11.3	31.5	23.0	9.8	34.1	37.7	14.8	28.2	23.2	35.8
06 33182	Hemet	77,134	4.3	9.2	17.8	8.5	24.3	16.7	23.6	35.6	74.2	3.4	3.2	22.9	33.2
06 33308	Hercules	24,156	2.9	5.8	17.2	9.6	28.8	29.8	8.7	37.4	26.4	21.7	45.8	8.0	14.0
06 33434	Hesperia	86,738	10.4	9.1	23.3	11.6	27.1	20.0	8.9	28.9	70.6	5.2	2.4	24.8	45.6
06 33588	Highland	54,645	1.5	9.5	24.6	10.3	29.4	19.4	6.8	28.5	60.4	11.5	8.3	23.2	45.8
06 34120	Hollister	32,460	-1.5	8.6	26.1	8.4	29.0	20.9	6.9	29.6	59.9	1.3	7.7	41.6	59.2
06 36000	Huntington Beach	190,487	-0.6	6.0	15.3	8.3	30.8	27.3	12.3	38.6	79.6	1.3	12.3	10.1	17.5
06 36056	Huntington Park	60,719	-1.4	7.9	23.1	12.7	31.4	17.4	7.4	28.6	59.7	0.9	0.5	39.7	
06 36294	Imperial Beach	25,023	-0.4	8.6	18.2	13.2	30.9	21.1	8.1	29.4	75.7	6.3	8.7	14.3	43.9
06 36448	Indio	66,071	18.6	9.3	20.4	12.0	31.2	16.6	10.5	28.8	58.6	2.1	1.0	40.2	61.5
06 36546	Inglewood	117,736	-0.5	9.8	20.4	10.0	29.9	20.9	9.0	31.7	18.8	42.3	2.6	38.6	52.5

STATE City	Percent foreign born	Total households	Household type (percent)						Percent of households with people under 18 years	Percent of households with people 60 years and over
			Family households				Nonfamily households			
			Total family households	Married-couple families	Male householder families	Female householder families	Total nonfamily households	One-person households		
ACS table number:	C05002	B11001	B11001	B11001	B11001	B11001	B11001	B11001	C11005	B11006
	15	16	17	18	19	20	21	22	23	24
California—Cont.										
Citrus Heights	14.0	33,903	64.1	44.2	6.5	13.3	35.9	27.4	32.9	30.4
Claremont	16.2	11,230	68.2	56.6	3.3	8.4	31.8	25.4	32.1	37.2
Clovis	10.9	30,024	71.6	53.8	6.0	11.8	28.4	22.7	42.5	26.0
Coachella	42.3	7,529	92.8	63.9	13.4	15.5	7.2	5.2	70.5	21.1
Colton	26.1	15,842	75.7	48.9	7.9	18.9	24.3	20.8	50.5	21.5
Compton	31.0	23,180	81.5	45.0	10.4	26.2	18.5	15.6	60.5	28.0
Concord	28.6	43,909	67.0	50.4	5.1	11.5	33.0	24.5	33.2	28.8
Corcoran	20.6	3,473	80.3	45.4	11.7	23.2	19.7	16.2	54.2	33.0
Corona	26.3	45,368	80.1	62.4	7.0	10.7	19.9	15.2	51.5	22.0
Coronado	11.5	7,373	62.9	49.9	3.3	9.7	37.1	33.3	27.8	39.6
Costa Mesa	29.8	38,665	59.7	42.5	6.8	10.4	40.3	29.5	31.4	24.2
Covina	21.8	16,395	74.0	48.2	6.9	18.8	26.0	20.0	43.8	29.1
Cudahy	47.6	5,515	92.1	53.7	14.1	24.3	7.9	6.4	70.0	19.3
Culver	26.8	16,802	54.3	40.1	3.8	10.5	45.7	35.7	27.0	32.3
Cupertino	47.8	18,753	81.5	70.1	3.6	7.8	18.5	17.4	49.9	30.4
Cypress	26.4	16,031	78.2	58.0	5.4	14.8	21.8	18.7	43.7	35.4
Daly	53.4	29,843	73.2	54.6	5.9	12.8	26.8	20.3	35.1	37.5
Dana Point	15.3	13,720	64.0	51.3	3.8	8.9	36.0	27.1	25.0	36.8
Danville town	12.7	15,246	79.1	69.1	2.2	7.7	20.9	17.5	39.1	34.3
Davis	18.1	24,333	46.4	38.0	2.4	6.0	53.6	26.5	25.6	19.6
Delano	39.3	9,663	87.4	56.6	10.7	20.0	12.6	7.6	63.2	21.8
Desert Hot Springs	26.6	7,396	63.8	39.5	8.4	15.9	36.2	24.4	47.7	25.0
Diamond Bar	42.6	17,867	82.2	65.0	4.8	12.4	17.8	14.9	43.5	30.5
Dinuba	25.8	5,092	85.1	59.2	9.0	16.9	14.9	14.2	59.0	28.3
Downey	33.5	34,119	76.5	53.6	5.9	17.0	23.5	20.1	46.1	30.6
Duarte	33.4	6,836	71.1	54.0	7.1	10.1	28.9	26.0	37.4	39.4
Dublin	22.7	12,809	70.0	57.7	3.4	8.9	30.0	24.1	39.0	18.9
East Los Angeles CDP	48.0	30,392	82.2	48.1	10.6	23.4	17.8	14.9	56.3	30.5
East Palo Alto	41.9	6,648	76.3	41.7	11.3	23.3	23.7	19.8	55.3	25.7
El Cajon	20.2	32,312	67.8	46.2	6.7	14.9	32.2	25.2	40.1	27.9
El Centro	31.9	13,971	78.7	51.1	7.0	20.6	21.3	20.0	50.6	29.5
El Cerrito	33.3	10,362	58.4	45.5	3.3	9.6	41.6	30.2	26.0	39.0
El Dorado Hills CDP	10.0	10,813	81.0	71.8	4.3	4.9	19.0	13.3	47.7	24.7
Elk Grove	21.6	43,582	80.8	64.7	3.9	12.2	19.2	15.5	52.8	20.8
El Monte	51.8	27,365	84.2	56.0	9.4	18.7	15.8	11.8	55.3	32.0
El Paso de Robles (Paso Robles)	16.5	10,876	72.5	52.6	5.1	14.8	27.5	20.7	39.0	30.8
Encinitas	14.7	22,875	61.6	50.8	2.5	8.3	38.4	27.6	31.2	28.8
Escondido	29.4	44,988	72.0	52.4	7.3	12.4	28.0	21.4	43.4	28.5
Eureka	7.5	11,304	46.3	29.2	3.2	13.9	53.7	41.7	23.3	29.7
Fairfield	22.3	33,330	75.5	52.2	7.6	15.7	24.5	18.5	47.0	26.9
Fair Oaks CDP	11.5	11,044	66.9	52.6	3.4	10.8	33.1	25.0	29.2	39.2
Fallbrook CDP	23.3	10,120	71.8	56.3	3.9	11.5	28.2	22.6	35.8	39.8
Florence-Graham CDP	44.5	14,337	87.5	51.8	12.4	23.3	12.5	10.8	66.0	20.5
Florin CDP	27.1	8,700	66.0	40.6	8.4	17.0	34.0	29.9	36.2	36.5
Folsom	11.6	23,610	69.0	58.4	3.0	7.5	31.0	24.8	40.4	23.1
Fontana	30.8	45,602	86.4	62.6	8.0	15.9	13.6	10.5	61.3	20.1
Foster	37.3	11,967	68.7	60.2	1.9	6.6	31.3	26.6	37.5	25.6
Fountain Valley	30.1	18,685	74.6	61.2	5.2	8.1	25.4	19.6	33.3	40.1
Fremont	43.4	68,264	77.7	63.9	4.9	8.8	22.3	16.5	45.3	25.3
Fresno	21.4	152,113	68.9	43.4	6.4	19.1	31.1	24.5	44.2	26.7
Fullerton	29.7	45,697	68.6	54.2	4.6	9.9	31.4	24.4	36.2	28.3
Galt	16.8	6,739	81.3	64.8	5.0	11.6	18.7	15.8	52.9	28.2
Gardena	33.4	20,263	67.2	40.7	7.0	19.6	32.8	28.6	35.6	37.2
Garden Grove	43.3	46,160	80.4	57.0	8.0	15.4	19.6	15.9	43.9	32.3
Gilroy	26.6	13,740	78.0	56.8	6.2	15.0	22.0	19.0	52.5	25.6
Glendale	54.0	70,771	67.5	50.1	5.5	11.9	32.5	26.6	31.5	36.0
Glendora	16.7	16,744	74.0	58.2	4.7	11.2	26.0	21.5	37.8	34.4
Goleta	24.0	10,576	57.2	48.9	2.5	5.8	42.8	29.3	30.0	29.0
Granite Bay CDP	8.1	7,286	89.1	76.8	3.2	9.1	10.9	9.5	43.5	37.2
Hacienda Heights CDP	40.6	15,334	79.1	59.2	5.3	14.5	20.9	17.8	41.6	45.1
Hanford	16.2	15,916	73.6	51.1	8.4	14.1	26.4	22.3	46.0	26.8
Hawthorne	34.5	29,277	71.9	40.6	6.9	24.4	28.1	23.2	46.4	21.5
Hayward	36.6	41,870	69.9	46.4	7.5	15.9	30.1	22.5	39.8	28.9
Hemet	16.0	29,975	63.4	46.1	4.5	12.8	36.6	31.4	35.8	48.6
Hercules	36.5	7,841	79.9	59.1	5.3	15.4	20.1	17.7	41.8	27.0
Hesperia	17.5	24,573	81.8	61.8	7.5	12.5	18.2	14.2	53.6	26.7
Highland	22.2	15,631	79.4	54.0	7.8	17.5	20.6	14.4	54.9	27.1
Hollister	18.7	10,116	80.4	59.8	7.1	13.5	19.6	16.3	54.9	24.8
Huntington Beach	16.3	73,781	62.9	48.7	4.9	9.3	37.1	27.8	29.2	31.1
Huntington Park	52.1	14,808	81.8	50.8	8.9	22.1	18.2	13.8	55.8	27.9
Imperial Beach	20.9	8,946	68.4	40.3	5.7	22.3	31.6	23.9	35.1	19.8
Indio	30.9	20,574	75.7	52.5	8.6	14.6	24.3	16.9	45.8	29.3
Inglewood	30.1	37,606	68.6	38.0	7.8	22.8	31.4	27.0	44.7	26.0

STATE Place code	STATE City	Total population	Percent change 2005–2007	Population by age (percent)						Median age	Race alone or in combination (percent)		Asian Hawaiian or Pacific Islander	Amer. Indian, Alaska Native, or some other race	Percent Hispanic or Latino
				Under 5 years	5 to 17 years	18 to 24 years	25 to 44 years	45 to 64 years	65 years and over		White	Black			
	ACS table number:	B01003	Population estimates	B01001	B01001	B01001	B01001	B01001	B01001	B01002	B02008	B02009	B02011 + B02012	B02010 + B02013	C03002
		1	2	3	4	5	6	7	8	9	10	11	12	13	14
	California—Cont.														
06 36770	Irvine	186,220	7.7	5.8	16.1	16.6	30.1	24.3	7.2	33.3	59.0	2.5	37.2	4.2	9.0
06 39003	La Canada Flintridge	20,568	-0.7	5.7	25.4	5.0	17.7	32.5	13.8	42.6	73.5	-	25.7	2.6	-
06 39122	Lafayette	24,615	1.3	5.9	20.4	5.8	20.4	32.0	15.6	43.4	88.2	1.9	10.9	3.6	4.9
06 39178	Laguna Beach	23,578	-0.3	3.0	12.1	7.7	23.1	36.1	18.0	47.7	92.4	-	6.1	3.2	-
06 39220	Laguna Hills	30,451	-0.8	4.3	18.6	8.6	26.4	30.3	11.8	41.1	77.0	2.0	11.1	13.4	23.6
06 39248	Laguna Niguel	63,708	-0.2	6.0	18.7	7.7	25.9	30.9	10.8	40.8	83.5	2.0	11.5	6.8	10.8
06 39290	La Habra	60,998	-0.6	8.1	19.7	10.4	30.3	22.0	9.5	33.1	51.7	1.8	9.1	39.7	54.6
06 39486	Lake Elsinore	39,415	25.8	10.5	22.5	10.6	35.2	16.0	5.2	27.8	65.0	5.4	5.0	28.8	45.8
06 39496	Lake Forest	75,572	-0.8	7.5	19.2	7.4	31.0	27.5	7.4	36.9	71.4	2.7	13.7	15.7	22.0
06 39892	Lakewood	84,891	-1.4	7.1	19.1	10.0	27.4	24.7	11.8	36.8	57.4	9.4	19.4	18.4	27.5
06 40004	La Mesa	53,122	1.2	6.4	12.1	14.3	29.4	22.7	15.1	37.2	80.9	7.7	7.8	7.9	16.3
06 40032	La Mirada	48,160	0.8	4.7	20.6	12.4	24.8	22.9	14.6	36.7	59.6	2.1	13.8	28.6	40.8
06 40130	Lancaster	149,624	7.6	8.7	24.5	10.5	26.3	21.3	8.7	30.1	56.9	21.0	5.8	20.4	35.2
06 40326	La Presa CDP	34,312	-	8.5	22.4	10.0	27.3	22.1	9.6	31.5	63.3	17.9	12.9	9.4	45.7
06 40340	La Puente	41,288	-1.5	8.0	22.3	11.8	30.0	18.5	9.4	30.4	59.4	0.3	7.9	33.7	-
06 40354	La Quinta	33,762	13.7	6.0	19.2	6.4	26.6	25.6	16.2	39.6	78.5	1.9	3.5	17.3	31.9
06 40830	La Verne	31,765	0.2	6.4	16.7	8.5	23.9	30.2	14.3	41.2	78.9	3.1	6.9	14.8	27.8
06 40886	Lawndale	31,746	-1.5	10.8	19.9	8.4	34.4	20.8	5.6	31.1	49.5	9.7	11.8	32.0	58.7
06 41124	Lemon Grove	23,508	-0.8	8.2	19.0	10.1	26.4	23.4	12.9	36.2	73.6	11.9	9.7	8.7	38.3
06 41152	Lemoore	24,375	4.5	8.2	23.3	12.9	33.2	15.6	6.9	27.1	72.2	9.3	7.1	17.1	40.6
06 41180	Lennox CDP	24,373	-	8.5	27.6	11.7	30.6	17.9	3.6	26.4	40.8	4.1	0.7	56.0	-
06 41474	Lincoln	32,237	29.2	7.6	12.5	5.6	27.4	21.9	25.0	42.6	84.5	1.8	7.1	10.0	17.1
06 41992	Livermore	77,905	1.6	6.2	21.0	7.5	28.5	28.3	8.5	38.3	79.8	2.6	11.6	12.2	17.3
06 42202	Lodi	64,720	0.0	9.4	18.9	9.8	26.7	21.7	13.5	33.3	79.6	0.9	6.2	15.5	34.6
06 42370	Loma Linda	22,843	2.0	5.9	15.2	9.0	36.2	20.7	13.0	33.7	58.6	7.1	26.9	9.2	19.0
06 42468	Lomita	19,917	-0.8	7.8	18.5	7.2	29.9	27.1	9.5	36.9	65.2	6.6	13.9	21.4	32.2
06 42524	Lompoc	41,087	0.6	8.3	19.8	8.9	31.4	20.7	10.8	33.5	58.0	7.0	5.4	34.1	48.5
06 43000	Long Beach	463,838	-1.2	7.5	19.7	11.4	30.9	21.9	8.6	32.7	45.6	14.5	15.3	28.6	39.9
06 43280	Los Altos	28,727	2.0	5.3	20.7	3.4	20.1	32.8	17.6	45.2	78.2	0.4	24.4	1.4	3.9
06 44000	Los Angeles	3,770,590	0.2	7.2	17.9	11.0	31.9	21.9	10.0	33.6	51.0	10.6	11.7	29.6	48.5
06 44028	Los Banos	33,726	5.3	9.0	26.1	9.2	29.0	18.6	8.1	30.3	74.4	3.9	4.4	21.6	61.1
06 44112	Los Gatos town	29,928	3.9	5.6	17.7	5.8	25.2	29.0	16.6	43.3	84.8	2.5	12.6	2.1	4.7
06 44574	Lynwood	74,020	-0.8	8.9	26.4	11.7	31.4	18.0	3.5	26.8	38.9	12.7	1.6	49.0	82.9
06 45022	Madera	52,215	8.4	10.3	22.2	13.1	29.3	16.6	8.5	26.8	79.0	4.1	3.3	16.8	71.4
06 45400	Manhattan Beach	37,623	0.6	9.7	18.4	6.3	27.4	27.0	11.2	38.0	90.5	0.7	9.8	2.8	5.7
06 45484	Manteca	60,918	2.6	8.3	23.1	10.5	28.1	22.1	8.1	31.8	78.7	5.6	9.2	11.6	33.5
06 46114	Martinez	33,842	-1.1	4.4	15.6	7.0	27.6	33.6	11.7	42.7	83.4	3.7	10.2	7.9	13.4
06 46492	Maywood	28,669	-0.3	10.5	25.7	10.6	29.8	18.4	5.0	26.9	47.9	0.9	-	51.6	-
06 46870	Menlo Park	30,507	1.2	7.0	15.4	6.8	28.6	27.5	14.7	40.7	80.6	6.7	9.5	5.7	16.5
06 46898	Merced	70,460	5.4	9.4	21.8	14.5	27.5	18.0	8.8	27.4	58.6	7.7	12.2	25.7	47.0
06 47486	Millbrae	22,140	1.9	3.6	19.6	7.4	22.7	27.4	19.4	43.3	52.7	3.5	38.3	6.9	12.7
06 47766	Milpitas	65,215	5.4	7.1	15.7	8.7	34.8	26.0	7.8	36.2	26.9	3.6	61.9	10.7	15.0
06 47976	Mira Loma CDP	21,530	-	6.3	25.8	12.6	28.6	20.6	6.2	29.1	59.2	-	1.9	40.8	-
06 48256	Mission Viejo	96,244	-0.8	5.9	19.2	7.1	25.9	28.9	13.2	40.6	81.8	2.1	10.9	9.3	15.7
06 48354	Modesto	203,816	-0.6	8.2	20.5	10.6	26.9	23.0	10.9	33.1	79.1	4.4	8.6	11.6	32.1
06 48648	Monrovia	37,138	-0.5	7.7	14.2	8.7	32.0	24.3	13.1	37.5	63.8	11.3	12.5	16.5	32.6
06 48788	Montclair	35,373	0.6	9.0	20.7	12.4	31.6	18.1	8.2	29.5	44.3	5.6	13.1	44.7	65.9
06 48816	Montebello	63,170	-1.1	8.1	19.8	7.5	31.4	20.6	12.6	33.6	46.2	1.4	11.6	43.1	76.7
06 48872	Monterey	29,421	-2.0	6.2	8.2	19.5	29.3	22.2	14.5	34.3	80.6	2.6	12.1	11.4	13.5
06 48914	Monterey Park	62,584	-0.5	5.5	14.0	8.5	28.6	25.0	18.3	41.1	19.2	0.1	66.1	17.1	-
06 49138	Moorpark	32,627	1.7	7.5	22.5	10.6	26.1	27.8	5.5	34.3	69.4	2.9	9.8	21.8	31.0
06 49270	Moreno Valley	180,835	7.0	9.0	24.8	11.9	30.7	17.5	6.0	27.1	39.0	18.5	7.3	38.2	50.7
06 49278	Morgan Hill	36,036	4.8	6.8	21.5	8.2	27.7	27.1	8.8	36.8	73.0	1.1	13.0	16.0	30.0
06 49670	Mountain View	71,153	1.7	6.3	12.5	7.2	38.4	24.8	10.7	36.9	60.5	2.4	28.4	12.3	21.3
06 50076	Murrieta	91,519	10.5	7.2	23.6	10.1	30.7	19.1	9.3	31.6	75.4	6.7	10.9	13.9	23.3
06 50258	Napa	74,804	1.0	6.9	16.6	9.6	28.6	24.7	13.6	36.7	88.0	1.1	2.6	10.7	34.0
06 50398	National	53,738	-0.8	8.0	20.1	12.6	28.6	18.7	12.0	30.4	58.1	5.5	19.0	19.8	60.8
06 50916	Newark	41,125	-0.5	6.5	18.9	7.7	32.8	24.5	9.6	35.5	50.8	3.5	29.5	21.5	35.6
06 51182	Newport Beach	85,176	-0.1	5.0	14.8	7.1	27.2	27.6	18.3	42.1	89.9	1.2	8.1	2.7	7.1
06 51560	Norco	26,684	0.7	3.4	17.1	11.7	36.3	23.7	7.8	36.1	72.1	8.2	2.6	19.3	33.2
06 51924	North Highlands CDP	42,927	-	9.5	19.4	9.2	27.2	21.4	13.3	32.4	70.3	14.9	7.3	14.1	24.2
06 52379	North Tustin CDP	25,061	-	5.8	19.8	6.1	18.7	32.4	17.2	44.8	91.8	-	6.5	4.2	-
06 52526	Norwalk	108,965	-1.6	6.7	21.9	10.9	29.7	21.5	9.3	32.4	55.4	5.8	14.7	27.3	66.2
06 52582	Novato	51,233	4.3	6.0	15.8	8.6	25.3	31.2	13.0	41.4	78.4	3.5	6.9	13.9	19.8
06 53000	Oakland	372,247	1.7	7.3	16.2	8.6	32.6	24.6	10.8	36.1	37.9	32.6	17.4	16.3	25.3
06 53070	Oakley	29,045	12.5	7.9	25.9	8.8	30.2	20.6	6.5	30.6	70.8	5.7	6.5	22.5	33.8
06 53322	Oceanside	167,443	1.0	8.2	17.9	10.4	28.4	22.1	13.2	34.8	64.5	6.7	9.9	24.0	33.7
06 53448	Oildale CDP	33,368	-	6.7	24.2	11.1	29.3	18.7	10.0	29.6	88.8	0.3	1.3	13.6	14.6
06 53896	Ontario	160,852	-0.3	7.7	21.7	12.4	31.2	20.0	6.9	29.6	49.2	7.6	5.6	42.1	64.6
06 53980	Orange	139,112	-0.4	6.6	19.3	12.0	29.5	22.7	10.0	34.3	68.9	1.8	10.1	21.7	37.4
06 54092	Orangevale CDP	25,888	-	5.2	18.5	9.1	26.9	28.8	11.5	37.9	91.6	0.9	5.0	5.4	7.8
06 54120	Orcutt CDP	28,619	-	6.3	22.0	6.2	21.6	26.3	17.7	41.3	87.7	2.3	4.5	11.3	21.1
06 54652	Oxnard	177,311	1.3	8.2	20.8	12.0	29.8	19.8	9.3	30.4	58.3	5.2	9.6	29.6	70.0
06 54806	Pacifica	37,539	0.7	5.2	15.6	9.1	26.3	33.4	10.4	41.5	69.7	5.1	24.2	7.3	15.1

Table A-4. Cities — Who: Age, Race/Ethnicity, and Household Structure, 2005–2007—*Continued*

STATE City	Percent foreign born	Total households	Household type (percent) — Family households — Total family households	Married-couple families	Male householder families	Female householder families	Nonfamily households — Total nonfamily households	One-person households	Percent of households with people under 18 years	Percent of households with people 60 years and over
ACS table number:	C05002	B11001	B11001	B11001	B11001	B11001	B11001	B11001	C11005	B11006
	15	16	17	18	19	20	21	22	23	24
California—Cont.										
Irvine	33.2	65,999	65.2	51.9	4.0	9.3	34.8	25.0	34.9	21.8
La Canada Flintridge	21.2	6,780	84.5	77.0	2.3	5.3	15.5	13.8	44.5	41.9
Lafayette	10.3	8,998	74.3	64.8	2.1	7.4	25.7	21.3	40.1	39.4
Laguna Beach	13.7	11,012	53.9	43.6	4.2	6.2	46.1	36.9	18.1	40.9
Laguna Hills	24.4	10,319	71.0	59.5	3.0	8.6	29.0	20.7	34.0	28.9
Laguna Niguel	18.6	23,940	71.3	57.7	2.6	11.0	28.7	22.4	37.3	29.2
La Habra	27.0	18,819	74.6	51.4	8.5	14.7	25.4	19.3	44.0	26.6
Lake Elsinore	22.7	11,948	78.9	59.1	6.5	13.3	21.1	18.3	58.4	20.2
Lake Forest	23.6	25,716	72.3	58.0	5.4	9.0	27.7	20.4	39.6	24.1
Lakewood	21.2	26,706	76.6	57.0	6.3	13.2	23.4	18.7	42.2	32.9
La Mesa	13.6	23,612	54.1	36.4	5.9	11.8	45.9	35.6	24.9	30.3
La Mirada	19.9	14,861	78.0	62.8	5.5	9.7	22.0	18.7	38.7	40.9
Lancaster	14.7	43,977	73.1	46.7	5.9	20.5	26.9	21.6	47.0	26.5
La Presa CDP	24.3	10,524	79.7	56.3	7.1	16.3	20.3	17.3	48.3	30.9
La Puente	42.0	9,824	83.0	55.2	12.0	15.8	17.0	11.5	55.4	36.9
La Quinta	13.7	12,484	70.7	55.6	5.1	9.9	29.3	20.4	37.5	37.8
La Verne	15.4	11,143	73.3	58.1	2.9	12.3	26.7	21.3	33.6	40.0
Lawndale	41.7	9,393	75.0	47.9	10.5	16.6	25.0	20.1	51.3	21.4
Lemon Grove	19.8	7,967	70.2	47.2	6.3	16.6	29.8	25.1	39.2	32.5
Lemoore	17.2	7,759	75.6	58.2	4.1	13.4	24.4	20.8	50.8	20.7
Lennox CDP	52.8	5,607	84.8	49.3	11.1	24.3	15.2	13.8	69.0	18.3
Lincoln	14.1	13,717	74.5	62.2	3.6	8.7	25.5	22.1	31.6	48.7
Livermore	15.6	27,601	71.9	57.4	3.8	10.7	20.1	22.8	39.3	23.5
Lodi	21.0	21,887	71.8	51.9	6.0	13.8	28.2	22.8	42.1	32.3
Loma Linda	30.6	8,703	61.2	40.9	5.0	15.3	38.8	29.0	32.3	31.2
Lomita	21.1	7,622	66.5	44.8	8.5	13.3	33.5	29.3	33.7	25.0
Lompoc	25.7	13,343	67.6	51.4	5.0	11.1	32.4	25.4	41.4	30.1
Long Beach	28.9	161,229	60.4	37.9	5.7	16.8	39.6	30.9	36.2	23.7
Los Altos	22.6	10,575	75.7	70.8	1.9	3.0	24.3	21.1	37.4	44.0
Los Angeles	40.0	1,274,791	61.2	39.4	6.8	15.0	38.8	30.3	35.2	27.6
Los Banos	23.4	9,626	78.3	61.0	5.2	12.1	21.7	19.2	54.8	24.0
Los Gatos town	16.6	12,015	66.1	56.7	3.1	6.3	33.9	30.6	32.3	34.5
Lynwood	39.2	14,854	87.8	58.0	10.0	19.8	12.2	8.8	67.6	20.1
Madera	30.9	14,642	80.4	53.6	10.8	16.0	19.6	15.8	56.6	27.2
Manhattan Beach	8.6	13,932	67.8	57.1	2.9	7.8	32.2	24.5	37.8	30.6
Manteca	17.1	19,572	75.3	55.0	6.9	13.4	24.7	19.2	46.7	24.5
Martinez	11.7	13,872	63.9	51.0	3.5	9.3	36.1	31.2	30.4	28.4
Maywood	48.4	6,669	86.7	57.7	8.4	20.7	13.3	8.8	65.2	19.2
Menlo Park	21.9	11,908	61.8	50.3	3.8	7.7	38.2	31.5	29.8	32.2
Merced	21.8	22,993	73.1	45.0	8.4	19.7	26.9	21.1	48.7	24.9
Millbrae	36.6	7,941	74.7	58.1	4.9	11.7	25.3	21.9	34.4	41.5
Milpitas	51.3	18,147	80.5	59.2	7.1	14.2	19.5	15.1	45.1	26.3
Mira Loma CDP	24.6	5,384	83.5	51.0	13.6	18.8	16.5	12.5	57.8	23.1
Mission Viejo	18.6	33,726	74.5	62.3	3.8	8.3	25.5	20.8	37.5	33.8
Modesto	16.7	68,441	69.7	48.5	6.7	14.5	30.3	23.9	39.9	30.5
Monrovia	22.6	13,613	63.5	44.5	5.3	13.8	36.5	28.7	30.5	28.7
Montclair	35.2	9,043	85.8	56.7	9.2	19.9	14.2	11.2	55.3	28.5
Montebello	38.5	19,310	72.8	46.0	7.5	19.3	27.2	21.7	42.0	35.5
Monterey	18.7	12,132	51.1	38.6	4.2	8.3	48.9	41.4	20.5	31.3
Monterey Park	53.6	20,017	75.4	52.8	6.8	15.7	24.6	19.3	34.1	45.2
Moorpark	21.6	9,398	82.6	74.6	3.1	4.9	17.4	13.7	51.6	19.1
Moreno Valley	24.4	47,554	83.8	57.9	6.9	19.0	16.2	12.4	58.8	20.7
Morgan Hill	19.4	11,378	81.3	64.2	4.5	12.6	18.7	12.9	47.1	24.8
Mountain View	40.0	31,508	51.8	40.1	4.6	7.1	48.2	39.1	25.7	22.3
Murrieta	13.2	28,838	76.3	63.3	5.6	7.4	23.7	18.9	49.9	26.7
Napa	23.2	28,109	63.2	48.0	5.9	9.2	36.8	30.5	31.3	35.2
National	40.9	14,474	77.1	47.6	7.8	21.7	22.9	18.9	48.9	32.3
Newark	39.0	12,757	79.5	59.1	8.1	12.2	20.5	16.8	42.3	28.2
Newport Beach	13.4	36,748	55.9	46.1	3.0	6.8	44.1	33.5	23.4	37.6
Norco	13.5	6,797	78.5	65.9	5.0	7.6	21.5	16.1	42.3	32.1
North Highlands CDP	20.4	15,365	71.4	44.1	6.6	20.7	28.6	22.6	43.0	31.3
North Tustin CDP	10.3	8,549	84.5	76.4	2.8	5.3	15.5	13.0	36.5	42.4
Norwalk	37.3	27,720	82.5	60.3	6.6	15.6	17.5	14.6	49.9	31.9
Novato	23.0	19,732	69.9	53.8	4.3	11.7	30.1	25.6	34.7	36.0
Oakland	28.2	145,409	53.6	33.3	4.9	15.4	46.4	37.0	30.1	28.2
Oakley	15.5	8,962	78.6	61.8	5.3	11.5	21.4	16.9	52.4	23.3
Oceanside	22.8	59,615	68.1	51.9	5.2	11.0	31.9	23.9	36.6	32.8
Oildale CDP	5.1	12,199	60.2	38.5	4.9	16.9	39.8	30.0	39.4	28.9
Ontario	30.7	45,269	78.7	54.5	8.0	16.2	21.3	16.0	50.4	24.1
Orange	25.5	42,350	71.9	52.5	6.0	13.4	28.1	21.9	39.9	30.6
Orangevale CDP	6.1	9,644	71.5	54.9	6.0	10.7	28.5	21.2	34.5	29.7
Orcutt CDP	7.7	10,226	76.2	61.8	3.0	11.5	23.8	20.8	38.3	39.1
Oxnard	37.8	47,126	78.7	57.5	6.2	15.0	21.3	15.4	49.0	30.8
Pacifica	20.3	14,004	66.8	53.9	3.7	9.2	33.2	25.6	31.4	32.2

Table A-4. Cities — Who: Age, Race/Ethnicity, and Household Structure, 2005–2007—*Continued*

STATE Place code	STATE City	Total population	Percent change 2005–2007	Population by age (percent) Under 5 years	5 to 17 years	18 to 24 years	25 to 44 years	45 to 64 years	65 years and over	Median age	Race alone or in combination (percent) White	Black	Asian Hawaiian or Pacific Islander	Amer. Indian, Alaska Native, or some other race	Percent Hispanic or Latino
	ACS table number:	B01003	Population estimates	B01001	B01001	B01001	B01001	B01001	B01001	B01002	B02008	B02009	B02011 + B02012	B02010 + B02013	C03002
		1	2	3	4	5	6	7	8	9	10	11	12	13	14
	California—Cont.														
06 55156	Palmdale	144,252	5.2	9.1	26.7	10.0	27.0	21.1	6.2	28.3	51.9	14.7	5.6	32.4	52.0
06 55184	Palm Desert	47,388	2.0	4.4	11.5	7.0	22.2	23.5	31.5	50.0	86.1	3.6	3.9	8.2	20.5
06 55254	Palm Springs	39,931	2.7	4.4	10.0	6.1	25.1	29.9	24.5	48.0	84.4	5.3	6.7	6.0	23.1
06 55282	Palo Alto	63,752	2.2	6.1	17.1	5.8	27.9	28.0	15.1	42.1	71.4	2.4	24.9	3.5	5.9
06 55520	Paradise town	26,691	-0.7	3.5	13.9	5.7	22.0	28.9	26.0	47.7	95.1	-	2.8	5.1	8.1
06 55618	Paramount	55,940	-1.2	9.7	25.3	11.1	31.6	16.6	5.7	27.6	34.2	13.2	2.8	51.0	76.8
06 55837	Parkway-South Sacramento CDP	31,373	-	9.8	20.3	12.2	27.2	21.5	9.0	28.7	50.0	16.6	21.1	19.0	40.4
06 56000	Pasadena	136,294	0.2	6.7	14.1	9.5	32.3	24.7	12.8	36.9	56.5	14.0	13.4	19.3	33.0
06 56700	Perris	56,112	18.6	11.5	24.8	12.0	32.5	14.2	5.0	25.8	46.4	11.3	4.1	41.0	67.2
06 56784	Petaluma	58,335	0.0	6.4	18.5	8.0	29.2	27.0	10.8	38.0	85.0	1.5	6.8	11.0	23.2
06 56924	Pico Rivera	67,111	-1.5	6.9	21.2	10.4	27.2	22.5	11.9	33.9	52.4	1.4	2.1	46.2	91.8
06 57456	Pittsburg	62,670	1.3	8.9	19.4	12.4	27.1	23.9	8.3	30.9	38.9	19.2	19.0	27.4	38.8
06 57526	Placentia	50,516	-0.1	7.5	18.3	9.7	28.6	24.8	11.2	36.3	64.0	1.9	14.6	22.6	35.6
06 57764	Pleasant Hill	33,980	-0.2	6.2	15.3	9.5	27.5	28.3	13.2	39.0	79.1	4.2	17.0	5.6	7.4
06 57792	Pleasanton	70,893	1.0	7.1	22.4	6.3	26.2	28.8	9.3	39.0	72.5	2.8	21.9	7.5	10.4
06 58072	Pomona	155,488	-0.3	9.6	22.4	11.7	30.1	19.2	7.0	28.4	40.6	9.3	7.6	45.8	70.8
06 58240	Porterville	50,095	1.9	8.2	24.6	10.5	28.7	19.5	8.5	28.7	66.2	2.3	4.9	30.1	57.0
06 58296	Port Hueneme	23,201	-2.3	9.4	15.9	17.3	29.3	18.3	9.8	29.9	66.7	6.0	9.7	27.5	45.7
06 58520	Poway	48,676	0.0	5.4	21.9	8.4	24.6	29.2	10.4	39.7	87.0	2.4	10.8	3.8	14.2
06 59444	Rancho Cordova	57,799	8.2	7.2	18.3	10.0	31.8	22.6	10.1	32.7	68.7	11.3	12.1	12.2	19.3
06 59451	Rancho Cucamonga	155,634	1.2	6.7	20.2	10.8	32.2	23.5	6.5	32.6	67.9	9.8	11.0	16.9	30.4
06 59514	Rancho Palos Verdes	45,702	-1.3	5.9	20.6	5.0	21.1	28.1	19.3	43.4	64.3	4.4	30.3	4.9	8.7
06 59550	Rancho San Diego CDP	20,569	-	6.4	19.6	8.7	25.4	29.2	10.8	39.6	90.9	2.1	7.0	2.8	8.1
06 59587	Rancho Santa Margarita	49,046	-0.7	8.8	23.5	6.3	32.1	25.1	4.2	34.2	83.5	3.2	10.3	6.3	15.5
06 59920	Redding	88,954	1.4	5.6	15.7	11.6	27.3	24.1	15.7	37.1	91.3	1.8	3.5	6.3	7.4
06 59962	Redlands	70,127	0.5	5.5	20.7	11.6	26.6	22.9	12.6	34.2	77.5	4.7	6.9	14.7	25.1
06 60018	Redondo Beach	66,968	0.7	7.4	13.3	5.9	37.0	26.8	9.7	38.2	82.9	2.8	14.3	4.4	14.8
06 60102	Redwood	75,508	0.9	8.1	15.2	8.9	31.8	24.6	11.4	37.9	77.8	3.3	11.3	10.2	36.0
06 60242	Reedley	23,624	3.3	9.1	19.6	14.0	28.7	18.4	10.3	30.6	69.6	-	5.1	25.6	-
06 60466	Rialto	102,468	-0.1	9.1	23.4	13.3	29.3	18.2	6.7	27.8	61.6	18.3	3.8	20.1	65.1
06 60620	Richmond	97,867	0.5	6.8	19.0	9.6	29.9	25.2	9.5	34.0	34.7	31.6	15.7	20.8	33.5
06 60704	Ridgecrest	27,684	-1.1	8.6	20.1	9.1	28.9	21.2	12.1	31.8	83.7	5.8	6.4	8.5	17.6
06 61068	Riverbank	19,877	4.5	10.6	21.1	10.3	29.7	20.2	8.0	28.9	83.6	2.1	0.8	15.1	52.4
06 62000	Riverside	305,568	2.3	7.8	19.7	14.6	31.1	18.8	8.0	28.6	60.2	7.7	7.4	29.6	47.4
06 62364	Rocklin	54,226	4.6	6.8	18.6	12.2	31.5	21.9	9.0	33.8	86.5	1.6	8.7	6.3	9.0
06 62546	Rohnert Park	40,113	-0.9	6.8	16.7	14.9	29.1	24.6	8.0	32.9	78.4	2.9	7.6	14.2	20.0
06 62896	Rosemead	53,445	-0.6	6.5	16.6	8.6	27.3	25.8	15.2	39.0	20.6	-	58.3	21.8	-
06 62910	Rosemont CDP	25,490	-	6.0	24.6	10.7	31.1	19.7	7.9	28.7	65.6	16.8	9.4	15.2	19.8
06 62938	Roseville	112,754	3.2	6.5	17.1	9.8	32.8	21.1	12.8	34.9	84.0	2.8	9.3	7.7	12.6
06 63218	Rowland Heights CDP	50,822	-	5.8	17.0	11.9	26.2	28.3	10.7	36.5	25.8	2.2	50.7	23.0	34.6
06 63260	Rubidoux CDP	36,337	-	7.1	20.4	14.8	30.8	19.9	7.0	28.4	44.0	7.7	2.6	47.8	63.7
06 64000	Sacramento	446,721	2.0	7.1	17.7	10.4	31.6	22.1	11.1	33.4	53.0	16.1	20.8	15.1	24.8
06 64224	Salinas	146,578	-1.3	10.1	21.6	11.4	31.5	17.6	7.8	28.8	59.1	2.1	8.2	32.9	70.0
06 65000	San Bernardino	208,770	-0.2	9.8	23.3	11.8	29.9	18.1	7.1	27.9	58.4	16.3	5.2	22.4	57.2
06 65028	San Bruno	42,401	0.9	7.3	14.3	8.9	30.5	28.2	10.9	38.3	57.0	2.9	30.5	13.4	25.7
06 65042	San Buenaventura (Ventura)	103,119	-0.2	6.3	17.3	9.3	27.8	26.6	12.7	37.9	76.6	2.0	4.3	22.9	31.3
06 65070	San Carlos	28,221	0.9	7.2	16.6	4.3	27.6	30.5	13.9	41.8	83.8	1.2	14.8	3.8	10.4
06 65084	San Clemente	60,355	1.9	6.7	17.5	7.8	25.8	28.7	13.6	40.0	85.7	1.2	5.7	11.2	13.5
06 66000	San Diego	1,264,263	0.6	7.1	16.0	13.0	32.0	21.6	10.3	33.0	68.3	7.8	17.3	10.3	27.0
06 66070	San Dimas	35,283	-1.2	5.8	17.5	8.1	23.7	31.7	13.2	41.0	71.8	2.8	11.1	16.5	25.3
06 66140	San Fernando	23,542	-1.2	8.9	20.6	14.2	31.7	17.3	7.3	28.8	72.1	-	-	28.6	-
06 67000	San Francisco	757,604	1.8	5.1	9.1	7.6	38.2	25.5	14.5	39.5	56.3	7.6	33.8	5.4	14.0
06 67042	San Gabriel	40,254	-0.7	5.7	14.5	9.5	30.5	26.3	13.5	38.8	28.6	1.5	57.0	14.5	26.8
06 67056	Sanger	21,999	15.2	7.5	23.8	11.7	30.4	15.7	10.9	30.1	70.2	1.4	2.2	29.2	-
06 67112	San Jacinto	35,921	24.3	9.5	22.2	8.8	29.2	19.0	11.4	30.6	55.9	5.5	4.2	40.5	49.7
06 68000	San Jose	898,901	3.0	7.5	17.2	9.3	32.6	23.8	9.5	35.4	51.9	3.8	33.1	14.7	31.3
06 68028	San Juan Capistrano	34,144	0.1	5.5	19.0	9.4	21.2	29.4	15.5	40.0	75.9	0.4	3.6	20.8	32.5
06 68084	San Leandro	85,888	-0.4	7.1	16.6	7.3	29.4	26.1	13.5	38.9	48.5	13.2	31.8	10.3	21.3
06 68112	San Lorenzo CDP	23,318	-	6.8	18.5	8.5	27.2	26.4	12.6	39.0	53.9	10.0	25.4	15.7	30.2
06 68154	San Luis Obispo	46,347	-1.1	3.1	7.8	39.8	24.3	15.9	9.2	24.8	87.7	2.2	6.9	6.5	14.9
06 68196	San Marcos	72,609	5.8	10.4	18.5	9.4	31.8	19.0	10.8	32.6	73.9	3.3	9.8	16.3	37.6
06 68252	San Mateo	90,954	1.0	6.0	14.4	7.0	31.1	25.8	15.7	40.1	70.4	3.3	23.5	6.6	21.0
06 68294	San Pablo	31,155	0.2	7.3	20.8	10.5	31.7	20.1	9.6	33.0	37.0	16.4	18.6	31.5	53.8
06 68364	San Rafael	54,776	0.6	7.4	12.8	8.0	29.2	27.7	14.9	38.9	78.2	3.3	8.8	12.5	24.6
06 68378	San Ramon	57,104	-0.9	6.8	19.0	7.1	33.1	27.8	6.3	37.0	67.8	2.9	26.0	8.0	11.7
06 69000	Santa Ana	333,236	0.0	10.0	22.6	11.3	33.8	16.5	6.0	28.2	53.1	1.3	10.1	36.7	78.5
06 69070	Santa Barbara	88,978	-0.2	5.9	12.4	13.1	29.5	25.0	14.1	37.5	80.9	2.5	3.8	16.6	33.4
06 69084	Santa Clara	109,363	4.1	9.1	12.4	10.6	36.7	21.1	10.1	34.4	49.8	2.8	39.0	12.3	19.1
06 69088	Santa Clarita	179,230	-0.8	7.4	21.5	9.3	28.6	25.1	8.1	35.1	72.9	3.6	8.9	20.7	27.8
06 69112	Santa Cruz	56,052	0.8	4.2	9.4	27.8	26.8	23.0	8.8	31.2	89.5	2.1	8.0	5.3	16.5
06 69196	Santa Maria	84,368	1.0	10.6	21.6	11.3	29.2	17.8	9.6	28.5	79.5	2.5	5.8	15.0	65.6
06 70000	Santa Monica	86,916	-0.2	4.6	9.5	6.3	37.4	27.4	14.8	40.5	82.2	4.5	10.6	6.7	12.3
06 70042	Santa Paula	28,991	0.7	11.2	20.0	9.5	27.5	22.2	9.5	30.0	54.3	-	0.9	46.9	

Table A-4. Cities — Who: Age, Race/Ethnicity, and Household Structure, 2005–2007—*Continued*

STATE City	Percent foreign born	Total households	Household type (percent)						Percent of households with people under 18 years	Percent of households with people 60 years and over
			Family households				Nonfamily households			
			Total family households	Married-couple families	Male householder families	Female householder families	Total nonfamily households	One-person households		
ACS table number:	C05002	B11001	B11001	B11001	B11001	B11001	B11001	B11001	C11005	B11006
	15	16	17	18	19	20	21	22	23	24
California—Cont.										
Palmdale	25.1	38,914	82.6	57.5	6.2	18.9	17.4	13.6	56.9	23.8
Palm Desert	18.7	22,563	56.7	44.3	4.4	8.0	43.3	35.3	19.1	52.0
Palm Springs	19.8	20,347	38.5	28.1	3.9	6.5	61.5	47.0	16.7	44.8
Palo Alto	30.8	25,486	62.8	53.2	3.0	6.6	37.2	31.2	33.1	35.2
Paradise town	4.9	11,671	55.5	42.5	3.5	9.5	44.5	36.7	22.7	48.7
Paramount	40.0	14,366	80.7	51.2	8.9	20.6	19.3	15.5	58.7	23.1
Parkway-South Sacramento CDP	33.7	10,557	68.7	40.9	7.5	20.3	31.3	24.1	43.8	28.5
Pasadena	26.9	51,973	56.2	40.3	5.2	10.7	43.8	35.2	27.3	29.0
Perris	31.7	14,029	84.1	58.5	7.0	18.6	15.9	11.7	63.6	19.4
Petaluma	19.5	21,081	69.4	54.9	5.8	8.7	30.6	23.0	36.0	32.0
Pico Rivera	31.2	17,270	81.0	56.6	8.6	15.7	19.0	16.7	47.6	40.3
Pittsburg	31.8	19,308	78.0	52.7	8.9	16.4	22.0	17.6	47.3	28.7
Placentia	28.0	16,022	74.4	55.3	5.8	13.3	25.6	18.7	38.8	33.2
Pleasant Hill	22.2	13,673	60.1	47.3	3.9	8.9	39.9	29.3	29.3	32.7
Pleasanton	20.0	24,917	75.0	63.7	3.5	7.9	25.0	20.2	44.6	24.7
Pomona	36.1	38,643	79.4	50.8	8.7	19.9	20.6	15.3	54.7	24.6
Porterville	21.4	15,151	77.5	48.4	9.9	19.1	22.5	18.7	51.3	26.1
Port Hueneme	23.5	7,267	65.0	48.5	4.4	12.1	35.0	26.8	41.1	29.2
Poway	14.9	16,147	79.7	66.0	3.1	10.6	20.3	16.0	40.9	29.3
Rancho Cordova	24.9	21,801	64.2	43.8	5.7	14.7	35.8	26.4	34.8	25.6
Rancho Cucamonga	16.5	50,890	73.9	55.5	5.1	13.3	26.1	20.8	42.8	22.4
Rancho Palos Verdes	30.2	16,061	80.5	68.8	4.3	7.4	19.5	17.7	40.8	42.7
Rancho San Diego CDP	14.9	7,166	77.5	65.2	2.5	9.7	22.5	18.1	37.9	31.6
Rancho Santa Margarita	15.0	16,658	75.6	62.9	4.0	8.7	24.4	20.2	49.0	13.2
Redding	4.0	35,621	63.2	44.2	5.3	13.6	36.8	30.4	32.2	34.4
Redlands	11.5	25,468	66.1	46.0	6.3	13.8	33.9	28.4	36.5	30.6
Redondo Beach	16.7	28,634	55.6	43.2	3.3	9.1	44.4	34.7	27.8	22.4
Redwood	32.1	27,423	65.3	49.1	5.9	10.3	34.7	26.7	35.6	29.5
Reedley	33.9	6,050	76.0	50.0	8.0	18.0	24.0	21.3	49.7	31.6
Rialto	29.7	25,781	82.9	56.1	7.8	19.0	17.1	14.8	57.1	25.9
Richmond	31.1	33,997	68.4	42.9	7.4	18.1	31.6	26.5	39.1	29.2
Ridgecrest	9.2	10,331	66.0	45.4	8.4	12.1	34.0	29.2	40.4	31.5
Riverbank	24.1	5,958	77.8	64.3	3.9	9.6	22.2	19.2	47.9	25.8
Riverside	24.9	91,780	71.2	51.2	6.0	14.0	28.8	20.5	44.4	24.4
Rocklin	10.3	19,851	73.7	59.8	5.1	8.8	26.3	20.6	43.5	22.5
Rohnert Park	16.4	15,665	58.2	43.6	4.2	10.5	41.8	29.7	34.5	22.8
Rosemead	56.2	14,110	80.9	59.7	7.6	13.6	19.1	16.0	45.9	36.8
Rosemont CDP	21.1	8,660	64.9	46.1	8.7	10.1	35.1	27.3	40.3	23.4
Roseville	11.8	43,353	68.4	52.5	4.1	11.9	31.6	24.8	38.7	27.6
Rowland Heights CDP	53.5	14,518	84.6	62.8	6.1	15.7	15.4	10.9	43.4	35.4
Rubidoux CDP	35.1	9,439	83.0	59.4	8.5	15.1	17.0	12.9	51.5	24.6
Sacramento	22.4	169,544	58.7	36.8	6.0	15.9	41.3	31.5	33.1	27.5
Salinas	38.0	40,426	75.4	51.9	8.1	15.5	24.6	20.2	49.9	25.8
San Bernardino	23.9	61,617	72.3	42.3	9.8	20.2	27.7	20.5	50.1	23.3
San Bruno	34.8	15,486	68.2	50.6	3.9	13.7	31.8	25.1	33.1	29.6
San Buenaventura (Ventura)	13.9	39,476	63.3	46.8	5.6	10.9	36.7	29.8	32.4	31.8
San Carlos	17.1	11,607	64.6	56.6	1.7	6.3	35.4	29.4	31.9	34.0
San Clemente	14.5	22,971	68.7	57.4	5.0	6.3	31.3	25.0	33.4	32.5
San Diego	25.9	464,555	58.8	43.2	4.5	11.1	41.2	29.7	31.4	26.5
San Dimas	17.3	12,727	73.9	55.8	5.8	12.4	26.1	22.6	36.3	34.5
San Fernando	37.2	5,838	81.5	54.7	8.6	18.2	18.5	15.7	50.0	27.6
San Francisco	35.7	321,692	44.1	32.2	3.8	8.0	55.9	42.2	18.8	30.3
San Gabriel	53.2	12,430	77.0	55.5	8.2	13.2	23.0	16.2	36.4	33.6
Sanger	24.8	6,369	81.8	48.1	13.1	20.6	18.2	15.2	52.2	31.7
San Jacinto	21.7	11,687	72.9	48.8	6.4	17.7	27.1	22.5	47.8	32.4
San Jose	39.0	286,965	72.0	54.3	5.9	11.8	28.0	22.1	41.1	27.2
San Juan Capistrano	22.7	11,460	73.6	57.1	5.4	11.1	26.4	22.1	36.3	41.3
San Leandro	34.8	30,805	65.7	47.5	5.3	13.0	34.3	27.3	34.2	35.2
San Lorenzo CDP	30.0	7,643	74.1	53.3	6.6	14.1	25.9	22.3	40.9	36.5
San Luis Obispo	9.8	21,510	38.1	27.4	4.4	6.3	61.9	32.8	15.4	19.1
San Marcos	25.4	24,220	69.8	54.2	5.2	10.5	30.2	22.4	41.0	31.0
San Mateo	34.2	36,501	60.7	48.4	3.2	9.1	39.3	32.2	28.7	31.7
San Pablo	42.2	9,277	71.8	41.8	12.3	17.7	28.2	21.4	47.6	30.6
San Rafael	27.1	22,466	55.8	41.8	4.8	9.2	44.2	34.4	27.0	35.8
San Ramon	22.8	21,097	72.6	61.4	5.0	6.2	27.4	21.9	39.7	20.0
Santa Ana	51.0	73,863	80.4	55.2	10.2	15.0	19.6	13.5	56.7	24.1
Santa Barbara	22.5	35,455	53.5	38.2	4.7	10.7	46.5	29.8	25.1	30.9
Santa Clara	37.9	40,665	62.0	48.5	4.5	9.0	38.0	29.9	34.2	25.1
Santa Clarita	19.4	58,144	74.4	59.1	5.7	9.7	25.6	20.3	44.4	25.3
Santa Cruz	12.8	21,222	46.1	32.5	5.2	8.3	53.9	32.3	21.9	26.2
Santa Maria	34.3	25,116	73.6	53.0	5.2	15.5	26.4	20.8	48.2	28.7
Santa Monica	22.9	46,357	35.4	26.4	2.9	6.1	64.6	53.9	15.7	27.7
Santa Paula	30.1	8,408	77.4	57.8	3.6	16.0	22.6	19.3	50.4	33.3

Table A-4. Cities — Who: Age, Race/Ethnicity, and Household Structure, 2005–2007—*Continued*

STATE Place code	STATE City	Total population	Percent change 2005–2007	Population by age (percent)						Median age	Race alone or in combination (percent)				Percent Hispanic or Latino
				Under 5 years	5 to 17 years	18 to 24 years	25 to 44 years	45 to 64 years	65 years and over		White	Black	Asian Hawaiian or Pacific Islander	Amer. Indian, Alaska Native, or some other race	
	ACS table number:	B01003	Population estimates	B01001	B01001	B01001	B01001	B01001	B01001	B01002	B02008	B02009	B02011 + B02012	B02010 + B02013	C03002
		1	2	3	4	5	6	7	8	9	10	11	12	13	14
	California—Cont.														
06 70098	Santa Rosa	148,063	1.0	6.2	16.5	10.2	27.5	26.1	13.4	37.6	77.9	3.2	6.7	16.2	23.5
06 70224	Santee	53,393	1.1	6.2	20.5	9.0	27.7	26.8	9.8	36.6	87.5	3.3	6.1	7.7	14.4
06 70280	Saratoga	30,616	1.5	4.2	21.8	4.5	18.7	33.1	17.7	45.5	61.6	-	37.7	1.2	2.6
06 70686	Seal Beach	24,127	-0.4	2.1	9.7	4.3	16.4	29.8	37.7	58.7	87.1	1.2	8.7	5.3	5.3
06 70742	Seaside	32,866	-1.1	10.6	16.2	14.8	32.1	17.3	8.9	29.0	52.4	12.2	13.2	28.4	43.4
06 70882	Selma	22,373	2.5	11.0	23.1	9.9	28.7	17.9	9.4	28.2	73.0	-	5.5	24.5	-
06 72016	Simi Valley	124,347	2.2	7.0	19.7	8.9	28.9	26.4	9.2	36.4	77.2	1.6	8.7	14.9	20.7
06 72520	Soledad	25,720	2.1	6.8	15.8	10.1	43.0	21.1	3.1	32.8	55.5	12.8	3.4	31.7	69.6
06 72996	South El Monte	19,547	-0.1	10.0	19.0	15.6	28.9	18.7	7.8	28.9	61.7	-	10.2	28.4	-
06 73080	South Gate	102,469	-1.4	9.8	23.1	11.7	29.9	18.6	7.0	28.3	49.9	0.6	0.7	49.7	95.4
06 73108	South Lake Tahoe	22,566	-0.9	5.4	9.8	15.0	37.2	23.7	9.0	32.8	80.2	-	5.7	15.3	-
06 73220	South Pasadena	26,389	-0.8	4.6	18.3	6.9	30.4	29.4	10.3	38.9	61.0	2.9	32.2	8.1	20.0
06 73262	South San Francisco	61,659	2.1	6.9	15.0	8.9	29.2	27.2	12.8	38.4	42.9	3.1	41.1	20.0	32.1
06 73430	South Whittier CDP	58,504	-	6.7	22.5	10.3	30.6	20.4	9.5	32.2	52.4	0.8	4.1	44.7	76.3
06 73696	Spring Valley CDP	26,601	-	9.8	18.8	9.4	27.1	25.8	9.1	34.3	78.1	10.0	7.4	8.4	28.8
06 73962	Stanton	37,235	-0.6	9.7	20.1	10.0	30.8	19.2	10.2	32.1	41.1	3.2	21.5	36.5	51.8
06 75000	Stockton	288,166	1.3	8.4	21.4	11.7	28.8	19.7	10.1	29.8	52.3	13.3	23.8	15.4	37.0
06 75630	Suisun	27,655	1.7	9.1	19.7	9.2	30.2	24.5	7.3	32.5	45.2	20.5	23.0	17.5	24.1
06 75826	Sun CDP	20,936	-	3.5	10.0	2.9	19.3	17.6	46.7	62.7	81.9	4.4	5.6	10.0	19.3
06 77000	Sunnyvale	136,162	1.7	7.9	14.2	6.7	36.6	24.0	10.7	36.3	49.3	3.8	38.5	11.9	17.6
06 78120	Temecula	91,658	6.1	8.5	22.8	9.7	32.6	19.7	6.6	31.2	73.7	3.8	10.6	16.0	22.9
06 78148	Temple	35,710	2.2	5.4	15.8	7.7	25.5	29.7	16.0	42.3	39.1	0.8	52.6	9.0	17.4
06 78582	Thousand Oaks	126,849	-0.2	6.3	19.5	8.6	25.3	28.1	12.0	39.3	83.4	1.5	9.8	7.7	14.1
06 80000	Torrance	141,593	-0.4	5.4	16.9	7.1	28.2	27.8	14.6	41.1	57.4	2.4	34.6	10.3	16.0
06 80238	Tracy	81,464	0.5	9.1	22.7	8.8	34.6	19.7	5.1	30.7	57.6	11.8	17.5	19.7	31.8
06 80644	Tulare	56,591	7.8	10.6	23.2	11.7	28.6	16.9	8.9	27.6	73.9	4.3	3.1	21.1	54.5
06 80812	Turlock	70,412	1.5	6.3	20.6	13.2	29.4	20.4	10.1	30.3	78.2	2.4	7.3	14.6	36.2
06 80854	Tustin	68,934	2.8	8.6	19.5	7.7	34.7	21.3	8.2	33.4	56.9	3.4	20.4	21.2	36.3
06 80994	Twentynine Palms	26,963	-1.6	10.1	13.5	34.8	22.4	12.0	7.2	22.8	79.4	9.0	4.7	10.1	16.2
06 81204	Union	69,748	1.4	6.6	18.7	8.5	29.5	25.3	11.5	36.5	31.2	6.5	52.0	13.3	21.8
06 81344	Upland	76,982	-0.9	7.2	19.1	10.5	28.7	24.1	10.4	33.8	65.5	8.8	10.3	23.2	33.4
06 81554	Vacaville	91,814	-0.4	5.1	19.3	10.0	29.8	25.8	10.1	36.7	73.7	11.8	9.9	11.0	17.1
06 81638	Valinda CDP	21,256	-	6.1	26.0	9.8	30.6	19.8	7.6	30.4	64.2	2.3	9.4	27.6	-
06 81666	Vallejo	113,938	-0.9	7.3	17.5	9.8	27.0	26.5	12.0	36.2	37.5	25.1	28.5	14.0	18.8
06 82590	Victorville	102,760	18.3	10.0	24.3	10.7	29.7	17.6	7.7	28.2	60.9	17.3	6.0	20.0	42.9
06 82852	Vineyard CDP	20,351	-	7.8	23.0	7.4	31.2	24.3	6.4	33.0	50.4	12.3	36.4	6.7	11.8
06 82954	Visalia	114,238	7.0	9.7	20.0	9.9	28.2	21.6	10.6	30.8	82.6	2.8	6.4	10.9	39.7
06 82996	Vista	93,205	0.0	8.1	19.1	12.3	30.8	20.4	9.2	31.4	68.3	3.9	6.4	26.0	42.7
06 83332	Walnut	30,497	-1.1	4.0	19.4	12.9	21.0	32.3	10.3	40.7	25.1	4.3	61.7	11.5	19.4
06 83346	Walnut Creek	65,068	-0.2	3.7	12.3	7.5	22.3	29.1	25.2	48.1	82.7	2.0	13.4	3.9	7.3
06 83542	Wasco	22,851	1.9	7.5	19.5	17.3	33.4	17.3	4.9	27.6	62.2	9.1	1.5	29.3	73.4
06 83668	Watsonville	43,725	3.6	11.3	22.5	10.0	29.5	18.4	8.3	28.1	78.4	1.6	4.6	17.6	77.1
06 84144	West Carson CDP	22,150	-	4.1	16.7	7.9	29.4	26.9	15.0	40.0	36.8	11.0	29.2	23.4	31.9
06 84200	West Covina	111,572	-1.2	6.5	20.5	10.0	28.8	23.5	10.8	34.1	38.9	6.2	25.2	32.8	51.1
06 84410	West Hollywood	34,675	-1.2	2.6	4.4	5.5	44.8	25.8	16.9	40.8	83.4	5.2	6.5	8.0	11.8
06 84550	Westminster	91,734	-0.7	5.2	18.7	8.2	29.9	24.4	13.6	37.2	43.7	3.2	44.0	11.6	22.8
06 84592	Westmont CDP	31,753	-	10.8	26.9	9.8	27.9	17.6	7.1	27.2	11.9	58.7	-	29.6	-
06 84774	West Puente Valley CDP	24,529	-	9.1	20.3	10.5	29.1	18.3	12.8	32.2	49.1	0.8	11.2	41.8	-
06 84816	West Sacramento	43,954	10.1	8.6	18.9	10.7	31.6	21.4	8.8	31.2	72.0	5.5	12.0	15.7	32.2
06 84921	West Whittier-Los Nietos CDP	27,553	-	12.3	22.7	9.7	29.1	15.3	11.0	29.1	47.3	0.6	3.3	52.8	-
06 85292	Whittier	89,173	-1.5	6.8	19.9	11.4	28.1	22.4	11.4	33.7	59.4	1.1	3.8	39.1	64.2
06 85446	Wildomar CDP	23,554	-	9.0	23.4	7.0	30.8	21.1	8.7	30.6	75.4	7.1	3.3	17.4	28.7
06 85614	Willowbrook CDP	35,269	-	9.6	27.1	11.0	28.4	16.4	7.6	26.6	23.1	42.2	0.9	34.5	54.4
06 85922	Windsor town	26,843	1.9	7.4	22.7	8.8	27.4	25.1	8.6	34.5	84.6	1.0	4.9	12.1	26.9
06 86328	Woodland	50,690	4.0	6.6	21.2	9.0	29.1	22.8	11.4	35.3	71.5	2.0	6.5	24.9	40.9
06 86832	Yorba Linda	64,965	1.7	5.0	21.4	8.8	23.8	30.6	10.4	40.1	80.6	2.2	13.2	6.6	13.8
06 86972	Yuba	59,019	4.9	8.4	17.9	11.4	28.9	21.5	11.9	32.1	66.6	4.1	16.4	18.4	25.8
06 87042	Yucaipa	49,667	2.6	6.1	20.4	8.9	26.7	25.8	12.0	36.5	84.8	1.7	4.3	13.2	26.1
06 87056	Yucca Valley town	18,499	4.0	6.7	17.6	7.3	22.4	24.4	21.6	40.8	87.4	-	0.5	10.8	13.2
08 00000	**Colorado**	4,767,161	4.0	7.2	17.5	9.7	30.1	25.5	10.0	35.5	85.5	4.6	3.5	9.3	19.6
08 03455	Arvada	103,459	2.9	6.2	18.4	9.0	24.9	29.4	12.1	40.3	91.8	1.6	2.7	7.2	13.9
08 04000	Aurora	296,999	5.0	8.9	18.1	9.2	31.8	23.4	8.6	33.1	71.8	16.2	5.4	9.8	27.4
08 07850	Boulder	90,507	1.2	3.7	9.5	26.5	30.2	22.1	8.0	29.7	90.1	1.6	5.2	5.5	8.4
08 08675	Brighton	30,654	9.6	9.4	21.9	7.6	34.5	18.1	8.5	31.9	73.8	1.6	0.8	27.2	39.1
08 09280	Broomfield	51,235	10.6	7.1	19.4	9.4	32.2	25.1	6.8	34.2	90.4	1.5	6.2	5.3	10.9
08 12415	Castle Rock town	37,422	20.2	9.6	20.7	8.2	36.0	21.3	4.3	31.5	93.9	1.7	3.8	3.9	9.7
08 12815	Centennial	102,822	1.3	5.8	20.5	7.4	23.7	32.3	10.2	40.3	90.5	3.5	4.9	3.7	5.6
08 15165	Clifton CDP	20,325	-	9.7	19.3	10.4	32.9	18.0	9.7	29.7	90.9	0.8	0.9	10.9	-
08 16000	Colorado Springs	390,397	1.4	7.0	18.0	9.3	30.9	24.8	10.0	34.9	82.3	8.6	4.7	9.3	14.2
08 16110	Columbine CDP	24,358	-	4.8	21.1	5.9	22.6	32.2	13.4	43.0	92.5	1.6	2.1	6.2	8.1
08 16495	Commerce	35,048	19.9	10.8	19.9	6.2	39.2	18.1	5.7	29.7	75.1	5.3	2.5	19.6	51.5
08 20000	Denver	576,842	3.9	8.7	15.3	8.1	34.5	22.8	10.6	35.1	74.5	10.8	3.9	13.5	34.2
08 24785	Englewood	28,657	0.7	5.2	12.5	8.6	33.9	26.3	13.6	37.9	89.0	4.1	3.3	6.9	14.5

STATE City	Percent foreign born	Total households	Household type (percent)						Percent of households with people under 18 years	Percent of households with people 60 years and over
			Family households				Nonfamily households			
			Total family households	Married-couple families	Male householder families	Female householder families	Total nonfamily households	One-person households		
ACS table number:	C05002	B11001	B11001	B11001	B11001	B11001	B11001	B11001	C11005	B11006
	15	16	17	18	19	20	21	22	23	24
California—Cont.										
Santa Rosa	18.9	58,637	60.4	45.0	5.1	10.3	39.6	31.1	32.5	32.1
Santee	10.2	18,827	72.8	54.9	5.4	12.5	27.2	22.3	39.3	29.3
Saratoga	30.1	10,826	83.4	74.4	2.8	6.2	16.6	15.0	40.2	40.6
Seal Beach	11.8	12,747	45.3	38.2	1.3	5.8	54.7	49.6	12.6	64.9
Seaside	35.2	9,962	71.7	49.9	7.5	14.2	28.3	20.0	42.8	28.9
Selma	27.9	6,294	85.0	58.4	6.2	20.4	15.0	12.3	60.1	30.2
Simi Valley	17.1	39,696	78.4	62.1	4.8	11.5	21.6	16.8	43.4	27.3
Soledad	30.6	3,478	90.5	70.5	5.3	14.8	9.5	8.1	67.9	19.2
South El Monte	50.6	4,819	83.8	51.1	13.9	18.7	16.2	11.1	54.9	31.7
South Gate	46.1	24,222	88.2	57.1	9.0	22.2	11.8	10.0	59.0	30.4
South Lake Tahoe	21.3	9,429	50.8	35.8	5.1	9.9	49.2	32.4	23.4	20.8
South Pasadena	31.6	10,441	64.7	43.2	2.2	19.3	35.3	29.3	34.3	26.3
South San Francisco	40.4	20,118	76.7	57.0	5.5	14.3	23.3	20.4	36.6	37.8
South Whittier CDP	30.2	15,312	82.3	63.4	5.5	13.4	17.7	13.2	51.3	29.7
Spring Valley CDP	16.5	9,344	71.4	51.1	4.2	16.0	28.6	23.5	42.3	30.9
Stanton	41.5	10,652	72.9	54.3	3.4	15.3	27.1	22.1	47.4	30.9
Stockton	27.6	89,867	71.8	46.8	8.1	16.9	28.2	22.4	46.5	28.9
Suisun	22.1	8,184	81.6	60.5	6.7	14.4	18.4	14.9	46.3	25.5
Sun CDP	14.9	9,954	58.4	48.2	3.2	7.0	41.6	39.2	15.6	74.3
Sunnyvale	43.0	52,492	63.9	49.5	5.0	9.3	36.1	29.9	33.3	25.4
Temecula	14.9	29,185	81.3	64.9	4.2	12.2	18.7	14.6	53.4	19.5
Temple	45.2	11,277	76.8	57.2	4.0	15.6	23.2	18.9	36.1	37.5
Thousand Oaks	17.0	44,065	74.0	61.8	3.7	8.5	26.0	20.8	37.0	32.8
Torrance	30.4	54,379	66.7	51.1	4.8	10.7	33.3	28.4	34.2	33.8
Tracy	23.8	24,208	80.0	61.0	8.0	11.0	20.0	15.5	53.4	18.9
Tulare	19.5	16,223	77.8	54.8	7.4	15.6	22.2	18.1	52.1	26.9
Turlock	25.7	21,934	73.8	55.8	5.2	12.7	26.2	20.8	44.7	28.3
Tustin	35.9	24,314	68.2	50.9	5.9	11.4	31.8	25.4	38.3	24.6
Twentynine Palms	5.6	7,570	69.1	49.4	6.0	13.8	30.9	22.2	39.9	20.7
Union	47.2	19,152	84.0	64.6	8.0	11.4	16.0	12.4	48.6	30.7
Upland	17.0	26,079	73.3	51.2	8.0	14.1	26.7	20.9	38.4	30.0
Vacaville	9.8	29,669	71.8	53.0	5.1	13.7	28.2	23.1	40.5	29.9
Valinda CDP	40.6	5,105	84.3	62.6	10.2	11.5	15.7	12.6	55.4	31.0
Vallejo	25.1	39,033	69.4	46.2	6.4	16.9	30.6	25.3	40.0	31.7
Victorville	17.8	28,869	78.4	54.2	6.5	17.8	21.6	16.3	53.3	26.2
Vineyard CDP	25.1	6,290	84.5	65.9	4.5	14.0	15.5	12.2	53.0	20.4
Visalia	13.3	37,616	73.3	53.8	7.2	12.3	26.7	22.7	44.3	29.2
Vista	26.0	28,955	73.1	53.8	6.3	13.0	26.9	19.4	40.7	25.0
Walnut	44.8	8,306	90.7	76.6	5.9	8.2	9.3	7.1	48.3	30.9
Walnut Creek	19.9	30,700	53.1	43.6	3.5	6.0	46.9	38.4	20.2	45.5
Wasco	27.8	4,922	84.3	52.0	11.2	21.1	15.7	12.0	58.7	23.6
Watsonville	38.0	12,103	79.0	52.8	8.0	18.2	21.0	16.2	54.7	27.0
West Carson CDP	35.3	6,933	73.1	50.5	7.3	15.2	26.9	20.9	35.9	42.2
West Covina	34.1	32,289	79.9	56.2	7.0	16.7	20.1	15.6	46.3	32.4
West Hollywood	34.4	22,227	20.4	13.8	2.3	4.3	79.6	64.6	6.7	25.8
Westminster	45.5	26,881	74.7	55.8	7.3	11.6	25.3	19.4	39.9	40.3
Westmont CDP	21.1	9,584	69.0	29.7	6.9	32.5	31.0	29.4	53.5	23.5
West Puente Valley CDP	40.4	5,017	85.5	63.3	5.9	16.3	14.5	12.5	57.0	48.9
West Sacramento	26.8	15,339	64.7	45.7	6.1	12.9	35.3	27.0	37.7	26.4
West Whittier-Los Nietos CDP	22.0	6,702	83.5	53.2	10.0	20.3	16.5	13.5	55.5	38.0
Whittier	20.1	28,971	70.6	50.0	6.2	14.4	29.4	24.8	40.1	33.4
Wildomar CDP	11.6	6,842	86.1	73.6	6.6	6.0	13.9	11.4	56.9	27.7
Willowbrook CDP	26.1	8,231	80.1	41.8	12.5	25.7	19.9	16.5	56.8	30.6
Windsor town	14.4	8,364	75.1	60.0	4.8	10.3	24.9	17.9	48.0	28.9
Woodland	21.2	17,907	70.7	52.1	5.5	13.1	29.3	24.8	41.1	29.7
Yorba Linda	16.2	21,047	82.3	72.1	4.3	5.9	17.7	14.2	42.2	32.3
Yuba	23.3	20,293	71.4	52.5	5.6	13.3	28.6	23.5	40.8	32.1
Yucaipa	12.0	17,301	71.0	57.1	4.3	9.6	29.0	24.8	39.7	32.0
Yucca Valley town	7.3	7,747	61.0	40.3	6.5	14.3	39.0	35.1	30.6	48.1
Colorado	10.1	1,838,303	64.5	50.3	4.4	9.7	35.5	28.3	33.9	25.3
Arvada	5.4	40,405	70.0	55.0	4.8	10.3	30.0	24.2	33.9	32.5
Aurora	20.6	112,759	64.3	44.7	5.7	13.8	35.7	29.4	37.6	22.0
Boulder	11.8	37,174	43.5	34.4	2.7	6.3	56.5	36.9	21.0	19.8
Brighton	11.4	9,591	78.3	59.9	5.6	12.8	21.7	17.8	46.9	22.9
Broomfield	7.3	17,507	68.3	53.5	4.3	10.4	31.7	25.7	39.6	19.9
Castle Rock town	5.1	13,234	76.8	66.2	3.6	7.0	23.2	18.6	47.2	13.2
Centennial	7.8	38,127	75.2	62.8	3.5	8.9	24.8	20.2	37.7	28.5
Clifton CDP	5.0	7,398	67.0	42.7	7.9	16.4	33.0	25.5	41.9	23.6
Colorado Springs	8.9	155,741	62.7	47.3	4.3	11.0	37.3	30.8	33.5	24.4
Columbine CDP	4.0	9,011	80.4	67.7	3.0	9.7	19.6	16.7	38.2	34.0
Commerce	21.5	11,306	77.3	56.9	8.4	12.0	22.7	17.0	50.1	18.5
Denver	18.3	244,261	48.9	34.2	4.4	10.2	51.1	42.1	25.8	25.4
Englewood	7.5	14,091	46.4	31.9	4.9	9.6	53.6	44.7	21.6	27.3

STATE Place code	STATE / City	Total population	Percent change 2005–2007	Under 5 years	5 to 17 years	18 to 24 years	25 to 44 years	45 to 64 years	65 years and over	Median age	White	Black	Asian Hawaiian or Pacific Islander	Amer. Indian, Alaska Native, or some other race	Percent Hispanic or Latino
	ACS table number:	B01003	Population estimates	B01001	B01001	B01001	B01001	B01001	B01001	B01002	B02008	B02009	B02011 + B02012	B02010 + B02013	C03002
		1	2	3	4	5	6	7	8	9	10	11	12	13	14
	Colorado—Cont.														
08 27425	Fort Collins	135,397	3.0	5.8	14.1	20.7	31.1	20.4	7.9	29.1	91.9	1.9	3.7	6.0	9.9
08 31660	Grand Junction	51,849	4.7	5.7	14.1	13.0	24.8	24.9	17.5	38.7	90.8	1.4	1.4	8.5	12.8
08 32155	Greeley	90,913	3.5	6.8	17.1	19.8	27.6	19.4	9.4	28.1	85.2	0.5	2.8	13.8	33.5
08 36410	Highlands Ranch CDP	90,843	-	8.9	22.6	7.5	35.9	21.2	3.9	32.0	91.4	2.1	5.5	3.0	6.6
08 40377	Ken Caryl CDP	32,538	-	5.9	21.9	7.8	27.8	29.4	7.1	37.1	92.8	0.3	3.0	6.3	-
08 41835	Lafayette	24,478	3.3	8.7	18.6	7.3	28.6	29.8	6.9	37.7	88.9	1.7	5.0	10.6	19.6
08 43000	Lakewood	143,157	0.4	5.7	15.1	9.8	28.0	27.6	13.7	38.8	84.0	2.6	4.0	12.0	19.6
08 45255	Littleton	43,741	0.8	6.2	14.3	8.5	24.9	29.0	17.1	41.9	92.0	2.0	4.3	3.5	10.0
08 45970	Longmont	84,936	2.8	7.8	18.7	8.0	30.8	25.6	9.1	35.0	84.7	1.5	3.4	12.5	23.8
08 46465	Loveland	62,754	6.3	7.3	17.8	8.6	30.2	24.2	11.9	35.3	94.6	1.4	1.3	5.5	11.9
08 54330	Northglenn	35,046	0.2	6.8	17.4	9.7	34.2	21.5	10.5	33.5	84.1	3.5	4.3	11.3	27.7
08 57630	Parker town	36,975	12.5	10.3	19.7	9.6	36.9	19.2	4.2	30.5	93.5	3.8	3.3	2.5	6.0
08 62000	Pueblo	104,719	1.2	6.7	16.9	11.4	26.2	23.0	15.8	35.8	81.4	3.6	1.2	17.9	45.4
08 62220	Pueblo West CDP	24,534	-	7.1	21.7	5.7	29.6	24.7	11.3	36.1	93.2	1.2	0.9	6.8	23.8
08 68847	Security-Widefield CDP	34,182	-	8.3	23.2	9.5	28.6	21.5	8.9	32.3	82.6	12.6	3.5	7.2	15.2
08 77290	Thornton	109,720	6.0	9.5	19.8	8.6	34.3	22.1	5.8	31.7	81.3	2.1	5.0	15.7	27.7
08 83835	Westminster	105,299	1.3	6.7	19.5	9.7	30.4	25.5	8.1	34.1	87.1	1.5	6.4	7.7	17.1
08 84440	Wheat Ridge	30,160	-0.7	5.5	12.8	7.1	26.9	28.5	19.2	43.3	87.5	1.5	2.2	11.2	18.7
09 00000	**Connecticut**	3,494,851	0.5	6.1	17.6	9.1	27.0	26.7	13.5	38.9	81.6	10.4	3.7	6.3	11.2
09 08000	Bridgeport	130,748	-0.8	7.8	18.7	11.4	28.8	22.7	10.7	33.2	47.4	35.9	3.2	15.2	33.3
09 08420	Bristol	60,806	-0.1	6.0	15.0	9.0	28.5	27.0	14.4	39.9	88.5	6.1	1.7	6.8	7.9
09 13435	Central Manchester CDP	29,324	-	5.5	17.3	10.6	29.4	25.3	11.8	36.3	78.6	11.6	3.4	11.1	12.1
09 18430	Danbury	77,704	1.6	6.1	14.0	9.4	33.4	26.1	11.1	36.9	76.6	7.2	7.1	10.9	20.9
09 18920	Darien CDP	20,750	-	9.2	26.1	4.9	22.5	26.9	10.3	38.6	96.0	-	3.0	-	-
09 22700	East Hartford CDP	49,051	-	6.6	17.4	8.8	28.1	24.9	14.3	37.7	56.0	23.5	4.5	17.8	21.9
09 22980	East Haven CDP	29,115	-	3.7	16.5	8.4	26.4	27.8	17.2	41.9	92.1	2.2	4.1	2.0	6.5
09 37000	Hartford	118,655	0.5	7.5	20.2	12.8	30.1	20.4	9.0	30.4	31.3	40.5	2.5	28.7	41.1
09 46450	Meriden	58,844	0.0	6.2	16.5	8.8	29.4	26.4	12.7	38.3	74.8	10.2	3.0	14.5	24.9
09 47290	Middletown	46,850	1.7	5.0	14.3	14.1	30.4	23.9	12.3	35.7	80.3	14.6	4.3	3.8	5.0
09 47515	Milford (balance)	50,208	2.0	6.1	15.3	6.1	29.8	28.1	14.7	40.5	92.3	2.6	4.1	2.4	5.6
09 49880	Naugatuck borough	31,699	0.8	6.6	19.5	8.4	30.2	25.0	10.3	35.5	91.3	4.0	2.8	5.3	7.7
09 50370	New Britain	67,699	-0.1	7.3	14.5	15.1	26.1	22.7	14.3	34.2	79.5	11.8	2.4	8.4	29.2
09 52000	New Haven	123,507	-0.1	6.6	16.6	17.4	32.6	17.5	9.3	29.5	46.7	37.7	5.4	13.4	24.0
09 52210	Newington CDP	30,434	-	6.6	13.6	7.9	26.5	28.4	17.1	41.7	87.3	4.2	5.6	4.2	5.5
09 52280	New London	27,210	-1.2	4.3	15.8	21.5	30.5	17.3	10.7	29.4	60.2	20.5	6.0	18.4	22.1
09 54940	North Haven CDP	24,967	-	4.6	17.7	6.9	23.6	30.0	17.3	43.3	88.8	3.7	6.1	2.4	3.8
09 55990	Norwalk	81,323	-0.2	7.6	14.3	9.3	30.5	26.4	11.9	37.3	74.3	14.3	3.7	8.9	22.5
09 56200	Norwich	36,919	-0.4	6.2	16.3	8.9	30.9	24.6	13.0	35.3	74.9	13.8	5.9	9.5	7.9
09 68100	Shelton	39,448	2.5	5.3	16.4	6.6	23.4	30.8	17.5	44.0	93.2	2.1	3.4	2.2	4.9
09 73000	Stamford	118,008	-0.4	6.7	15.9	6.9	31.8	25.8	12.9	37.8	65.9	14.0	7.3	14.4	21.6
09 74260	Stratford CDP	52,143	-	6.2	17.2	7.9	25.2	27.1	16.4	41.6	80.3	14.9	2.1	4.2	11.9
09 76500	Torrington	35,960	-0.3	5.4	14.8	7.3	29.0	27.0	16.4	41.4	94.4	2.4	2.8	2.4	6.6
09 77270	Trumbull CDP	36,568	-	6.7	20.1	6.0	22.8	26.5	17.9	41.8	92.1	2.3	4.9	1.0	3.9
09 80000	Waterbury	108,554	0.0	8.5	19.4	8.9	27.4	22.5	13.3	34.2	70.8	22.3	3.1	9.9	27.1
09 82660	West Hartford CDP	63,804	-	5.8	17.5	7.8	23.7	27.3	17.9	41.9	84.7	5.8	7.7	3.6	9.9
09 82800	West Haven	54,217	-0.2	5.7	16.4	10.9	29.1	26.0	11.9	37.2	75.0	18.7	3.3	4.5	13.5
09 83570	Westport CDP	24,906	-	6.6	23.6	3.3	19.2	32.6	14.6	43.4	95.2	0.6	3.2	-	5.2
09 84970	Wethersfield CDP	27,184	-	4.7	15.6	7.6	23.7	27.0	21.3	44.0	93.0	3.4	1.7	4.7	8.1
10 00000	**Delaware**	852,689	2.9	6.8	17.1	9.8	27.2	25.7	13.4	37.6	74.1	21.3	3.3	3.1	6.3
10 21200	Dover	33,796	4.3	7.0	16.8	18.6	25.1	19.5	13.1	29.8	52.6	45.8	3.2	4.3	6.2
10 50670	Newark	29,916	0.1	3.3	8.6	46.3	15.9	15.2	10.7	21.8	86.9	9.1	4.0	1.0	3.5
10 77580	Wilmington	63,619	0.5	6.7	16.7	8.1	30.1	25.6	12.9	36.8	40.5	56.3	0.8	3.9	10.3
11 00000	**District of Columbia**	585,267	1.1	6.1	13.4	12.5	32.7	23.4	11.9	35.0	35.5	56.4	3.7	6.1	8.3
11 50000	Washington	585,267	1.1	6.1	13.4	12.5	32.7	23.4	11.9	35.0	35.5	56.4	3.7	6.1	8.3
12 00000	**Florida**	18,014,927	2.9	6.3	16.0	8.8	26.7	25.4	16.9	39.8	77.8	16.0	2.7	5.4	20.1
12 00950	Altamonte Springs	41,498	-2.2	5.2	14.7	8.7	34.7	23.9	12.8	35.7	73.9	14.8	4.7	10.9	20.6
12 01700	Apopka	38,624	7.6	9.7	19.1	6.6	32.8	23.1	8.6	34.1	74.9	15.4	2.6	8.3	23.9
12 02681	Aventura	28,205	1.2	4.3	7.7	6.2	22.4	25.5	33.8	54.2	93.9	2.3	1.2	3.1	-
12 04162	Bayonet Point CDP	24,564	-	4.9	14.4	5.5	22.8	20.4	32.0	47.3	96.4	-	2.9	0.6	-
12 05462	Bellview CDP	23,293	-	4.6	18.9	7.3	28.3	28.3	12.6	37.3	81.6	11.7	5.9	3.6	2.6
12 06875	Bloomingdale CDP	20,180	-	6.6	23.4	6.6	24.8	31.2	7.5	39.4	89.4	5.6	3.9	3.0	8.9
12 07235	Boca Del Mar CDP	23,707	-	4.4	13.5	6.5	23.7	26.7	25.1	46.2	92.3	2.5	-	5.4	-
12 07300	Boca Raton	82,124	-0.8	3.8	13.8	9.2	23.1	29.9	20.2	45.1	89.5	3.6	3.9	3.7	10.4
12 07525	Bonita Springs	40,746	11.3	4.4	11.6	4.4	20.3	27.4	31.8	53.5	90.1	0.5	1.7	8.4	22.3
12 07875	Boynton Beach	62,389	2.2	6.0	15.4	7.7	24.2	24.8	21.9	42.5	62.4	28.8	1.8	8.3	12.5
12 07950	Bradenton	53,270	-0.7	6.6	13.7	9.7	22.8	22.1	25.1	43.1	79.9	15.0	0.9	5.0	13.6
12 08150	Brandon CDP	90,550	-	7.6	18.1	8.7	30.3	25.1	10.1	35.6	80.8	13.1	3.2	6.1	20.6
12 08300	Brent CDP	25,041	-	7.6	14.9	23.5	24.3	19.5	10.3	28.8	55.6	38.0	5.5	3.3	4.8
12 10275	Cape Coral	144,118	12.5	7.1	17.6	6.1	29.4	24.9	14.5	38.4	91.9	3.3	1.5	4.4	17.7
12 11050	Casselberry	23,927	-0.8	5.5	11.6	9.9	30.1	29.2	13.6	40.4	87.0	4.6	4.1	5.4	18.8
12 12425	Citrus Park CDP	24,398	-	9.2	17.8	7.4	27.5	29.1	9.0	36.6	80.9	10.2	2.4	8.2	29.2
12 12875	Clearwater	106,855	-1.6	5.2	14.0	8.8	25.0	27.4	19.6	42.4	86.1	11.1	1.9	3.3	14.1

STATE City	Percent foreign born	Total households	Household type (percent)						Percent of households with people under 18 years	Percent of households with people 60 years and over
			Family households				Nonfamily households			
			Total family households	Married-couple families	Male householder families	Female householder families	Total nonfamily households	One-person households		
ACS table number:	C05002	B11001	B11001	B11001	B11001	B11001	B11001	B11001	C11005	B11006
	15	16	17	18	19	20	21	22	23	24
Colorado—Cont.										
Fort Collins	6.2	53,122	54.8	42.1	4.0	8.7	45.2	29.5	28.8	17.9
Grand Junction	5.5	22,355	58.0	41.6	5.3	11.2	42.0	33.8	27.5	33.8
Greeley	12.6	31,035	60.9	47.4	3.3	10.1	39.1	29.2	34.3	24.8
Highlands Ranch CDP	6.8	31,013	78.9	69.6	2.8	6.5	21.1	16.8	50.0	12.9
Ken Caryl CDP	4.0	12,661	70.1	55.6	3.2	11.3	29.9	24.9	39.0	21.3
Lafayette	13.9	9,695	67.6	46.1	5.8	15.7	32.4	25.4	41.4	19.7
Lakewood	8.9	62,037	58.5	41.2	5.7	11.6	41.5	33.8	28.3	28.4
Littleton	8.9	18,200	61.6	48.6	4.9	8.2	38.4	32.7	27.6	34.5
Longmont	14.3	32,079	67.5	50.6	6.0	10.9	32.5	26.4	39.5	25.5
Loveland	3.9	25,047	67.1	51.3	4.8	10.9	32.9	27.2	35.2	26.8
Northglenn	11.2	13,574	63.9	48.1	3.5	12.3	36.1	29.2	33.3	24.6
Parker town	5.2	13,350	74.1	62.6	4.2	7.4	25.9	19.4	47.1	11.1
Pueblo	4.0	41,438	62.9	41.4	4.7	16.8	37.1	31.5	32.4	32.8
Pueblo West CDP	1.9	8,632	80.5	68.7	2.9	8.9	19.5	14.8	40.2	30.7
Security-Widefield CDP	6.8	10,976	81.9	64.6	4.4	12.9	18.1	15.5	48.1	25.2
Thornton	11.1	37,790	73.0	57.9	5.4	9.7	27.0	19.9	43.9	16.8
Westminster	9.2	40,362	66.4	51.8	5.2	9.4	33.6	26.3	35.3	21.7
Wheat Ridge	7.6	14,265	52.6	36.5	5.3	10.8	47.4	39.3	23.2	32.5
Connecticut	12.6	1,323,431	67.3	51.2	4.0	12.1	32.7	27.1	34.4	32.8
Bridgeport	25.4	48,037	63.1	31.4	6.2	25.4	36.9	31.7	36.7	31.1
Bristol	8.3	25,120	63.8	47.9	3.7	12.2	36.2	30.0	28.5	32.2
Central Manchester CDP	10.2	12,826	54.1	38.4	3.6	12.1	45.9	39.0	27.7	32.4
Danbury	31.9	29,303	64.3	50.0	4.5	9.8	35.7	26.8	32.9	29.5
Darien CDP	8.9	6,791	81.3	72.0	1.4	7.8	18.7	16.5	52.0	32.1
East Hartford CDP	16.2	19,118	64.3	38.0	6.7	19.6	35.7	29.3	34.0	33.5
East Haven CDP	8.5	11,285	65.9	51.3	4.2	10.5	34.1	28.5	29.7	37.0
Hartford	20.2	43,407	59.0	22.1	5.9	31.0	41.0	34.1	38.2	27.4
Meriden	10.2	23,499	64.6	42.3	5.0	17.3	35.4	27.6	32.5	30.2
Middletown	9.6	19,727	55.8	40.7	4.0	11.1	44.2	34.0	28.6	28.2
Milford (balance)	8.8	20,265	66.2	53.2	2.5	10.6	33.8	28.6	30.0	34.7
Naugatuck borough	10.2	11,518	74.0	54.3	4.4	15.3	26.0	20.9	39.0	22.9
New Britain	22.9	26,528	59.8	36.7	5.2	17.9	40.2	32.5	29.6	31.0
New Haven	16.9	46,302	54.5	29.5	4.2	20.9	45.5	35.5	33.0	24.9
Newington CDP	18.0	11,945	64.4	51.1	5.1	8.1	35.6	30.3	29.9	39.6
New London	13.5	10,387	51.9	33.4	5.0	13.6	48.1	34.3	29.2	24.2
North Haven CDP	9.5	9,091	75.7	65.5	3.0	7.2	24.3	20.2	34.4	42.1
Norwalk	22.8	31,844	63.6	47.4	4.6	11.7	36.4	30.0	31.1	29.8
Norwich	13.7	15,129	60.3	37.6	6.5	16.2	39.7	31.5	28.9	29.5
Shelton	11.5	14,473	72.8	58.8	4.9	9.0	27.2	23.4	34.1	37.3
Stamford	34.0	46,184	63.8	47.6	4.8	11.3	36.2	29.6	32.6	31.1
Stratford CDP	13.2	19,823	67.7	50.4	4.3	13.1	32.3	29.2	33.2	39.1
Torrington	6.8	15,133	60.4	44.8	4.2	11.4	39.6	32.9	29.9	34.4
Trumbull CDP	12.4	12,178	82.5	70.6	4.9	7.0	17.5	15.9	43.0	41.5
Waterbury	13.4	41,939	61.4	36.1	4.9	20.4	38.6	33.2	35.3	31.9
West Hartford CDP	17.1	24,325	66.6	52.9	3.2	10.5	33.4	28.3	34.5	37.7
West Haven	14.9	20,826	65.0	43.3	7.0	14.6	35.0	28.5	33.7	30.1
Westport CDP	10.9	8,998	77.5	68.6	1.5	7.4	22.5	19.0	42.0	38.9
Wethersfield CDP	13.8	11,204	66.0	53.5	2.8	9.7	34.0	31.1	29.1	44.6
Delaware	7.6	321,748	67.7	49.9	4.7	13.2	32.3	26.2	34.0	32.7
Dover	7.7	12,933	59.9	37.8	4.7	17.5	40.1	34.5	35.6	32.1
Newark	7.9	8,489	51.1	41.9	3.7	5.6	48.9	30.3	21.5	28.5
Wilmington	7.3	26,690	53.5	25.5	4.6	23.4	46.5	39.4	29.4	31.5
District of Columbia	12.7	249,805	42.9	21.7	3.8	17.5	57.1	47.9	21.6	28.2
Washington	12.7	249,805	42.9	21.7	3.8	17.5	57.1	47.9	21.6	28.2
Florida	18.7	7,077,123	65.3	48.4	4.6	12.3	34.7	27.9	30.5	37.5
Altamonte Springs	15.5	17,884	57.4	36.9	6.0	14.5	42.6	34.1	26.6	26.8
Apopka	16.3	13,274	74.4	55.7	6.2	12.4	25.6	19.1	39.8	23.3
Aventura	42.0	15,006	52.5	43.4	3.3	5.9	47.5	43.1	13.0	54.7
Bayonet Point CDP	6.3	11,293	54.3	40.7	3.0	10.6	45.7	39.3	21.7	55.6
Bellview CDP	6.1	9,257	68.7	56.5	3.2	8.9	31.3	26.0	32.3	34.8
Bloomingdale CDP	8.8	6,767	88.7	78.0	2.3	8.5	11.3	8.9	47.0	24.0
Boca Del Mar CDP	23.8	10,530	52.6	40.4	3.1	9.1	47.4	39.5	24.4	42.1
Boca Raton	18.7	34,381	58.0	46.9	3.7	7.3	42.0	33.5	23.4	40.5
Bonita Springs	19.3	19,145	65.1	57.9	2.9	4.3	34.9	29.2	17.6	54.8
Boynton Beach	20.4	26,429	55.0	40.1	2.9	11.9	45.0	37.3	24.3	43.6
Bradenton	10.5	23,102	58.1	39.7	3.4	15.0	41.9	32.5	24.4	42.4
Brandon CDP	10.5	34,621	70.9	52.6	5.0	13.2	29.1	22.5	36.3	26.0
Brent CDP	7.6	7,685	64.2	37.5	3.2	23.5	35.8	29.5	38.8	32.2
Cape Coral	13.4	57,429	72.6	57.0	4.7	10.9	27.4	19.7	35.3	33.0
Casselberry	12.0	10,724	51.1	35.7	4.9	10.5	48.9	37.5	21.8	32.0
Citrus Park CDP	17.9	9,302	66.0	46.0	5.9	14.1	34.0	25.0	38.5	25.1
Clearwater	16.6	46,282	56.2	40.0	3.9	12.3	43.8	35.7	23.6	40.5

STATE Place code	STATE / City (ACS table number)	Total population B01003	Percent change 2005–2007 Population estimates	Under 5 years B01001	5 to 17 years B01001	18 to 24 years B01001	25 to 44 years B01001	45 to 64 years B01001	65 years and over B01001	Median age B01002	White B02008	Black B02009	Asian Hawaiian or Pacific Islander B02011+B02012	Amer. Indian, Alaska Native, or some other race B02010+B02013	Percent Hispanic or Latino C03002
		1	2	3	4	5	6	7	8	9	10	11	12	13	14
	Florida—Cont.														
12 13275	Coconut Creek	48,087	0.9	6.5	14.8	5.4	27.6	22.0	23.6	42.8	81.6	13.3	3.8	3.3	16.1
12 14125	Cooper	30,465	-2.2	6.2	23.2	7.9	23.2	31.4	8.2	39.3	87.2	6.5	4.8	4.6	19.2
12 14250	Coral Gables	43,519	-1.1	3.2	14.3	16.3	23.6	26.7	16.0	40.0	93.3	2.9	2.3	2.0	46.1
12 14400	Coral Springs	126,339	-2.0	5.8	22.4	9.0	26.8	28.7	7.3	36.5	78.7	13.2	5.8	4.9	21.7
12 14412	Coral Terrace CDP	22,499	-	3.2	12.3	10.6	25.1	27.4	21.4	44.2	94.3	1.8	1.2	6.1	-
12 14895	Country Club CDP	34,832	-	9.0	18.6	9.2	35.0	20.8	7.3	32.4	76.9	17.1	2.0	5.9	73.7
12 15968	Cutler Bay town	37,011	-1.7	6.6	23.4	9.2	26.7	21.6	12.4	35.4	77.9	12.1	3.9	7.6	41.7
12 16335	Dania Beach	31,047	-1.2	5.5	14.0	6.4	28.2	30.7	15.2	42.2	75.8	20.4	1.4	5.6	21.7
12 16475	Davie town	94,221	0.8	6.1	19.2	9.4	28.7	26.0	10.6	37.3	85.6	5.8	4.5	5.7	29.3
12 16525	Daytona Beach	66,941	0.7	5.0	12.8	18.8	23.3	22.1	17.9	36.0	60.2	36.5	2.5	2.2	4.6
12 16725	Deerfield Beach	76,020	-1.9	5.9	11.7	8.5	26.3	24.6	23.0	43.4	73.7	22.5	1.5	4.3	12.7
12 16875	De Land	27,017	9.9	5.6	14.0	14.3	24.7	22.2	19.2	38.5	79.4	16.5	2.6	3.7	16.0
12 17100	Delray Beach	59,683	-0.6	4.6	12.9	7.5	25.3	26.3	23.4	44.8	64.6	30.8	1.8	3.3	6.7
12 17200	Deltona	85,671	3.5	6.8	18.8	8.4	31.6	22.7	11.8	34.8	80.5	10.2	2.1	9.5	26.4
12 17935	Doral	37,735	11.3	10.5	19.3	8.5	37.7	19.3	4.7	31.6	87.6	2.8	5.3	7.8	76.0
12 18575	Dunedin	37,435	-1.0	5.6	11.6	6.5	21.4	29.1	25.7	47.6	94.8	3.3	1.4	1.4	4.6
12 19206	East Lake CDP	32,683	-	5.0	18.1	6.5	22.6	32.5	15.3	43.8	93.2	0.8	5.7	-	3.6
12 19825	Edgewater	22,671	2.7	4.1	16.5	8.8	27.7	23.4	19.5	40.3	96.6	3.3	0.7	0.4	1.2
12 20108	Egypt Lake-Leto CDP	33,987	-	9.6	17.1	8.4	33.9	20.2	10.8	33.0	79.6	10.3	4.1	8.4	48.7
12 22275	Ferry Pass CDP	29,015	-	6.6	11.7	15.2	25.1	22.2	19.2	36.9	79.9	17.8	3.0	-	2.3
12 24000	Fort Lauderdale	166,751	0.0	6.1	13.8	7.1	28.6	30.3	14.0	41.8	62.7	33.1	1.8	3.7	11.7
12 24125	Fort Myers	58,138	10.2	9.1	15.9	14.0	30.2	20.0	12.8	31.1	52.5	34.8	1.1	13.0	21.8
12 24300	Fort Pierce	40,307	2.6	8.4	18.7	10.7	27.6	19.2	15.4	31.4	48.1	43.4	2.6	6.6	20.0
12 24562	Fountainebleau CDP	60,411	-	5.5	14.1	8.7	30.5	26.4	14.8	40.2	91.6	2.6	1.4	5.3	92.7
12 24581	Four Corners CDP	22,808	-	7.7	15.8	9.9	34.8	19.1	12.7	33.6	76.0	12.9	3.3	11.6	28.5
12 24925	Fruit Cove CDP	28,538	-	5.9	23.1	9.0	28.9	26.2	6.9	36.2	91.9	3.1	5.6	1.7	6.0
12 25175	Gainesville	113,942	2.0	4.6	10.2	33.2	26.5	16.7	8.7	25.6	68.6	24.5	6.3	2.7	8.1
12 26300	Golden Gate CDP	25,312	-	12.3	16.7	10.2	38.7	17.0	5.1	29.0	80.3	12.6	-	7.2	-
12 26375	Golden Glades CDP	36,059	-	8.3	17.9	11.0	27.2	23.4	12.3	34.9	23.4	71.6	2.0	4.1	17.0
12 27313	Greater Carrollwood CDP	31,248	-	4.7	15.4	7.6	28.8	29.3	14.1	41.5	86.7	8.4	2.4	3.9	18.5
12 27317	Greater Northdale CDP	23,585	-	5.9	17.4	8.5	29.3	27.4	11.4	37.6	82.1	11.3	3.4	3.0	-
12 27322	Greenacres	33,383	-0.2	8.0	14.6	7.8	30.4	21.3	17.8	37.3	70.9	12.4	3.7	14.1	31.6
12 28452	Hallandale Beach	34,965	4.7	4.3	11.4	7.8	24.7	25.7	26.1	46.8	76.5	20.3	2.7	4.1	29.2
12 30000	Hialeah	211,955	-2.9	5.5	14.1	8.1	26.8	25.5	20.0	42.3	92.0	3.8	0.6	4.5	94.2
12 31075	Holiday CDP	24,769	-	6.3	10.6	10.2	25.5	24.8	22.6	43.1	92.7	3.6	1.8	2.9	9.9
12 32000	Hollywood	139,132	-1.7	6.4	15.2	7.6	28.9	26.9	15.0	40.2	78.7	15.1	2.9	6.7	27.4
12 32275	Homestead	47,509	28.4	10.1	22.8	10.7	31.6	17.2	7.7	28.8	75.3	17.1	1.9	7.1	61.3
12 35000	Jacksonville	797,966	2.3	7.7	18.5	9.1	29.2	25.2	10.3	35.6	63.7	31.0	4.1	3.0	5.9
12 35050	Jacksonville Beach	20,697	0.0	5.9	14.7	5.4	29.6	30.2	14.1	41.9	86.5	9.9	2.5	2.5	2.9
12 35350	Jasmine Estates CDP	20,508	-	6.6	16.7	9.2	33.1	19.5	14.9	34.8	94.5	1.6	2.6	3.2	11.6
12 35875	Jupiter town	50,922	2.6	5.5	14.5	8.8	26.9	27.7	16.5	41.2	88.3	1.4	2.2	9.1	14.6
12 36062	Kendale Lakes CDP	58,276	-	7.0	16.7	11.3	25.2	25.3	14.4	37.3	93.2	0.9	2.0	4.7	79.0
12 36100	Kendall CDP	84,249	-	5.1	17.6	9.1	25.6	26.4	16.3	40.6	86.6	4.0	3.8	6.8	58.4
12 36121	Kendall West CDP	40,708	-	9.9	17.5	10.5	30.6	23.7	7.8	34.6	85.7	4.2	0.5	12.0	-
12 36462	Keystone CDP	21,816	-	8.0	21.1	4.5	24.8	31.6	10.1	40.1	88.1	5.6	4.5	-	8.4
12 36550	Key West	23,503	-4.8	4.6	11.0	7.2	31.9	33.5	11.8	43.0	83.0	12.5	2.1	2.8	-
12 36950	Kissimmee	59,031	4.0	8.7	17.9	10.8	32.8	20.3	9.4	30.5	71.3	12.8	4.3	15.5	52.5
12 38250	Lakeland	95,266	4.6	7.1	14.6	10.8	25.2	21.4	20.8	37.9	72.7	21.2	1.5	7.3	9.9
12 38350	Lake Magdalene CDP	29,664	-	5.4	12.9	8.6	28.8	30.0	14.4	41.6	86.2	5.0	4.3	6.4	15.6
12 38813	Lakeside CDP	32,946	-	7.2	17.4	9.5	24.5	30.2	11.1	38.4	79.6	13.7	6.1	4.7	8.2
12 39075	Lake Worth	33,835	-1.4	8.2	12.5	10.1	34.4	19.8	15.0	36.0	61.6	12.9	1.4	24.7	44.9
12 39200	Land O' Lakes CDP	31,048	-	6.9	19.9	6.4	30.9	25.8	10.0	36.5	87.7	8.0	2.6	2.5	9.8
12 39425	Largo	75,795	-1.3	4.8	11.1	7.3	23.6	26.4	26.8	47.7	88.5	7.2	2.6	3.3	6.7
12 39525	Lauderdale Lakes	33,310	-1.2	9.8	17.0	10.3	24.8	23.9	14.3	35.7	20.1	78.1	0.6	2.7	-
12 39550	Lauderhill	67,633	-1.7	10.1	17.7	9.1	29.0	22.7	11.4	34.4	20.5	76.5	1.2	3.1	7.1
12 39875	Leesburg	19,337	11.1	4.8	17.6	6.6	28.8	19.1	23.2	38.1	64.7	27.6	1.1	8.3	-
12 39925	Lehigh Acres CDP	61,869	-	8.1	21.8	8.5	30.4	19.5	11.6	32.8	74.2	17.9	1.7	7.7	23.1
12 41775	Lutz CDP	20,041	-	6.2	19.5	9.7	24.4	30.6	9.6	38.6	90.2	5.2	1.7	3.3	13.7
12 43125	Margate	54,494	-2.0	4.7	14.1	7.0	26.6	27.9	19.7	43.3	71.3	20.6	4.0	5.0	18.4
12 43975	Melbourne	74,830	0.7	4.6	13.2	11.6	25.0	25.5	20.1	42.4	85.0	10.2	3.4	3.2	7.1
12 44275	Merritt Island CDP	34,830	-	4.3	15.5	7.6	22.2	30.3	20.2	45.3	89.6	6.3	1.9	3.3	7.4
12 45000	Miami	352,064	7.0	6.7	14.1	9.2	28.5	24.0	17.4	39.5	72.0	22.9	1.0	5.7	68.8
12 45025	Miami Beach	80,250	-2.4	4.7	9.3	7.0	37.7	23.4	17.9	40.4	88.4	3.0	1.5	9.2	52.2
12 45060	Miami Gardens	96,450	-1.2	7.1	18.4	12.1	26.6	24.3	11.6	34.6	17.2	77.9	0.6	5.1	19.8
12 45100	Miami Lakes town	30,179	-1.5	6.9	17.9	9.9	30.8	23.4	11.1	36.5	87.2	4.7	1.8	8.8	-
12 45975	Miramar	114,899	2.0	8.3	22.1	10.1	32.0	21.0	6.6	32.2	43.4	46.1	6.7	8.9	35.5
12 47625	Naples	19,455	-0.3	3.1	10.1	3.8	11.8	27.1	44.1	62.4	94.3	5.2	0.6	-	-
12 48625	New Smyrna Beach	21,306	4.0	4.2	11.1	6.1	17.8	29.9	31.0	52.7	93.0	7.0	-	0.7	-
12 49350	North Fort Myers CDP	42,589	-	3.0	9.8	3.5	15.2	26.6	41.9	59.1	96.3	1.3	0.6	2.6	5.9
12 49425	North Lauderdale	45,035	-0.5	9.9	22.3	10.3	32.5	18.8	6.2	29.8	42.6	48.7	4.6	5.3	28.2

Table A-4. Cities — Who: Age, Race/Ethnicity, and Household Structure, 2005–2007—*Continued*

STATE City	Percent foreign born	Total households	Household type (percent)						Percent of households with people under 18 years	Percent of households with people 60 years and over
			Family households				Nonfamily households			
			Total family households	Married-couple families	Male householder families	Female householder families	Total nonfamily households	One-person households		
ACS table number:	C05002	B11001	B11001	B11001	B11001	B11001	B11001	B11001	C11005	B11006
	15	16	17	18	19	20	21	22	23	24
Florida—Cont.										
Coconut Creek	24.2	20,863	58.2	46.2	2.7	9.2	41.8	35.7	28.2	45.7
Cooper	20.4	9,741	86.2	71.4	3.9	10.9	13.8	10.3	50.9	24.7
Coral Gables	35.9	16,994	59.1	45.3	3.6	10.2	40.9	32.7	24.3	38.2
Coral Springs	26.0	42,242	78.7	58.3	4.6	15.8	21.3	17.1	46.0	24.5
Coral Terrace CDP	65.1	7,929	72.1	44.6	7.7	19.9	27.9	23.0	27.1	50.9
Country Club CDP	44.4	12,373	74.1	49.6	5.4	19.1	25.9	21.5	45.5	21.0
Cutler Bay town	31.2	12,163	68.9	52.6	4.9	11.4	31.1	25.4	39.8	33.8
Dania Beach	25.7	12,691	59.2	36.0	7.3	15.9	40.8	33.4	26.5	35.3
Davie town	23.5	34,893	66.6	48.4	4.1	14.1	33.4	24.4	35.8	28.1
Daytona Beach	10.7	27,243	48.9	27.7	4.8	16.4	51.1	41.2	22.4	37.7
Deerfield Beach	30.9	33,078	51.4	36.3	3.4	11.8	48.6	39.4	20.5	46.9
De Land	10.2	10,215	48.8	34.7	2.1	12.0	51.2	40.3	27.9	35.7
Delray Beach	22.1	26,811	52.2	38.3	3.0	10.9	47.8	38.5	20.4	46.1
Deltona	9.1	30,610	74.3	57.2	5.4	11.6	25.7	20.1	39.1	28.8
Doral	62.2	12,823	73.8	58.0	4.5	11.3	26.2	17.6	47.7	12.6
Dunedin	8.7	17,842	52.8	40.9	3.5	8.4	47.2	39.7	20.5	47.5
East Lake CDP	10.7	13,599	68.7	58.8	1.8	8.1	31.3	25.9	29.8	34.2
Edgewater	3.9	8,835	66.5	49.2	3.4	13.8	33.5	22.7	29.5	41.4
Egypt Lake-Leto CDP	31.5	13,715	58.9	37.7	6.4	14.8	41.1	34.0	35.9	25.8
Ferry Pass CDP	4.9	12,770	56.8	41.6	3.8	11.4	43.2	34.2	24.4	31.4
Fort Lauderdale	21.3	71,357	48.3	32.3	3.8	12.3	51.7	40.6	22.2	32.9
Fort Myers	20.8	24,177	55.9	31.1	6.4	18.4	44.1	33.7	32.7	28.4
Fort Pierce	23.8	14,331	62.1	32.1	9.8	20.2	37.9	29.9	34.5	37.8
Fountainbleau CDP	76.2	22,004	73.9	48.7	6.4	18.8	26.1	22.0	36.1	39.3
Four Corners CDP	19.6	8,576	71.0	54.2	6.3	10.5	29.0	19.6	33.7	30.4
Fruit Cove CDP	6.5	9,254	85.0	74.8	1.3	8.9	15.0	11.3	50.7	21.8
Gainesville	10.7	46,860	39.5	23.8	2.9	12.8	60.5	39.4	19.5	22.4
Golden Gate CDP	44.4	7,002	70.2	49.1	8.4	12.7	29.8	17.2	44.2	17.6
Golden Glades CDP	45.9	10,798	71.1	40.1	8.8	22.2	28.9	24.4	37.7	28.3
Greater Carrollwood CDP	15.0	13,965	61.3	48.0	2.7	10.6	38.7	33.7	27.2	31.3
Greater Northdale CDP	12.6	8,897	68.5	53.1	2.9	12.4	31.5	26.1	35.2	24.8
Greenacres	28.6	13,370	58.7	39.9	5.7	13.1	41.3	33.6	28.9	38.6
Hallandale Beach	41.4	17,177	47.4	32.3	4.0	11.1	52.6	46.0	15.0	46.3
Hialeah	70.8	72,215	77.7	53.7	6.9	17.1	22.3	19.0	37.6	46.7
Holiday CDP	14.9	10,814	58.3	40.2	4.0	14.1	41.7	30.0	24.9	43.5
Hollywood	31.6	57,751	58.3	41.3	4.7	12.3	41.7	33.6	28.3	34.8
Homestead	39.2	15,578	67.0	37.0	9.2	20.8	33.0	25.1	44.9	21.5
Jacksonville	8.2	316,400	64.1	44.4	4.5	15.3	35.9	29.3	33.7	26.6
Jacksonville Beach	3.7	9,565	56.4	45.3	3.5	7.6	43.6	36.0	24.8	30.3
Jasmine Estates CDP	9.6	8,357	60.5	39.2	6.8	14.5	39.5	31.9	30.9	36.1
Jupiter town	16.9	20,264	63.6	49.7	5.5	8.5	36.4	30.5	28.8	37.8
Kendale Lakes CDP	51.6	19,520	79.1	53.7	5.6	19.8	20.9	16.3	40.6	38.6
Kendall CDP	42.7	29,572	67.5	50.9	3.2	13.4	32.5	27.6	34.7	32.6
Kendall West CDP	58.4	12,709	81.6	55.8	5.7	20.1	18.4	15.0	50.4	24.5
Keystone CDP	11.6	7,572	82.8	72.5	2.4	7.9	17.2	11.4	43.3	27.1
Key West	18.7	9,671	52.2	39.6	4.3	8.3	47.8	31.6	21.7	32.1
Kissimmee	29.1	21,922	71.7	44.7	5.6	21.4	28.3	17.8	45.3	25.1
Lakeland	8.4	40,968	63.5	45.1	4.6	13.8	36.5	30.3	28.5	38.7
Lake Magdalene CDP	12.3	12,778	58.9	46.6	3.3	9.1	41.1	31.0	24.1	30.5
Lakeside CDP	6.7	11,954	77.9	59.2	5.0	13.8	22.1	16.7	41.0	30.9
Lake Worth	40.8	12,538	52.2	30.6	8.5	13.1	47.8	36.0	28.0	31.2
Land O' Lakes CDP	10.7	10,887	76.8	67.4	4.6	4.7	23.2	17.6	40.4	24.5
Largo	11.0	36,675	52.2	40.2	3.5	8.6	47.8	39.2	18.3	47.4
Lauderdale Lakes	45.2	11,478	65.0	38.0	5.9	21.1	35.0	28.7	34.8	41.4
Lauderhill	34.1	24,760	66.4	33.9	7.9	24.6	33.6	29.9	36.7	31.1
Leesburg	8.2	8,112	60.8	39.3	4.8	16.7	39.2	34.2	29.8	43.9
Lehigh Acres CDP	19.2	22,043	76.0	56.8	5.8	13.5	24.0	16.7	44.0	29.7
Lutz CDP	7.5	7,056	76.5	64.4	2.5	9.6	23.5	17.6	38.1	24.4
Margate	28.2	22,552	58.6	42.5	3.8	12.3	41.4	33.5	23.6	42.2
Melbourne	7.9	32,907	55.6	38.5	3.8	13.3	44.4	35.9	22.8	40.2
Merritt Island CDP	6.3	14,505	64.4	51.0	2.8	10.6	35.6	29.0	25.4	42.9
Miami	58.4	135,902	59.1	33.7	6.8	18.5	40.9	33.8	28.3	40.3
Miami Beach	53.9	43,319	38.2	27.0	4.1	7.0	61.8	52.3	14.3	29.6
Miami Gardens	29.6	31,509	71.7	35.4	9.4	27.0	28.3	24.8	36.3	38.7
Miami Lakes town	44.5	10,704	76.3	56.4	2.8	17.1	23.7	19.6	40.0	30.7
Miramar	42.4	34,173	81.9	56.4	7.0	18.5	18.1	14.2	54.5	20.7
Naples	10.0	9,525	60.4	54.4	2.2	3.8	39.6	36.4	11.6	69.2
New Smyrna Beach	3.2	10,145	55.1	42.1	3.8	9.1	44.9	36.4	18.9	52.2
North Fort Myers CDP	6.1	21,381	59.1	50.5	2.2	6.4	40.9	32.9	13.8	62.4
North Lauderdale	41.3	13,224	74.5	48.1	6.5	19.9	25.5	18.5	48.5	22.2

Table A-4. Cities — Who: Age, Race/Ethnicity, and Household Structure, 2005–2007—*Continued*

STATE Place code	STATE / City	Total population	Percent change 2005–2007	Population by age (percent)						Median age	Race alone or in combination (percent)				Percent Hispanic or Latino
				Under 5 years	5 to 17 years	18 to 24 years	25 to 44 years	45 to 64 years	65 years and over		White	Black	Asian Hawaiian or Pacific Islander	Amer. Indian, Alaska Native, or some other race	
	ACS table number:	B01003	Population estimates	B01001	B01001	B01001	B01001	B01001	B01001	B01002	B02008	B02009	B02011 + B02012	B02010 + B02013	C03002
		1	2	3	4	5	6	7	8	9	10	11	12	13	14
	Florida—Cont.														
12 49450	North Miami	59,464	-1.7	8.9	18.3	13.7	26.5	25.0	7.7	31.9	32.1	61.4	2.9	6.4	24.1
12 49475	North Miami Beach	44,825	-2.3	6.7	19.9	10.7	26.4	26.4	9.9	35.2	44.0	47.6	4.6	5.3	-
12 49675	North Port	45,229	29.3	6.9	16.3	8.1	29.4	23.6	15.7	37.9	89.3	7.1	0.7	5.0	6.6
12 50575	Oakland Park	41,775	-1.4	6.8	14.2	9.7	32.6	27.8	8.9	37.8	65.4	22.5	1.6	12.9	24.8
12 50638	Oak Ridge CDP	22,378	-	11.4	17.9	11.6	30.7	23.4	5.0	30.7	37.7	37.5	5.3	21.5	40.5
12 50750	Ocala	55,909	7.5	7.6	17.8	11.0	27.1	18.4	18.2	34.7	71.9	25.0	0.9	2.9	9.0
12 51075	Ocoee	29,335	5.9	8.4	18.3	7.3	30.8	25.3	9.8	37.5	76.6	11.5	5.8	8.7	17.3
12 53000	Orlando	218,070	5.9	8.4	15.8	9.1	36.1	21.0	9.6	33.5	58.8	30.3	2.7	10.4	20.7
12 53150	Ormond Beach	38,893	0.2	4.1	13.6	4.6	20.2	29.1	28.2	49.4	94.7	3.2	1.7	0.4	-
12 53575	Oviedo	30,644	2.9	6.8	23.4	8.6	28.4	27.2	5.7	34.7	82.1	11.2	4.6	6.0	13.8
12 54000	Palm Bay	95,009	8.8	6.5	17.7	9.1	26.6	25.3	14.8	38.5	75.4	18.8	2.9	5.8	11.0
12 54075	Palm Beach Gardens	40,834	0.6	5.3	12.9	6.1	24.3	28.7	22.7	45.7	91.4	4.4	1.8	2.7	8.7
12 54175	Palm CDP	22,098	-	5.2	17.5	6.4	21.9	25.0	24.1	44.6	94.2	-	2.4	2.6	-
12 54200	Palm Coast	63,474	17.1	5.4	14.5	8.2	27.0	22.6	22.1	41.1	84.4	11.6	2.6	3.3	8.5
12 54275	Palmetto Bay village	24,914	-2.4	8.0	24.0	6.3	22.4	28.5	10.8	38.5	85.6	4.6	3.3	7.4	37.1
12 54350	Palm Harbor CDP	54,746	-	2.6	13.8	6.9	21.4	31.5	23.8	47.7	96.6	1.1	1.5	1.6	4.0
12 54387	Palm River-Clair Mel CDP	22,150	-	8.8	20.2	9.6	29.1	24.2	8.2	33.5	58.7	32.8	1.6	9.2	33.5
12 54525	Palm Valley CDP	20,265	-	3.4	17.7	11.3	21.6	34.0	11.9	42.6	94.5	-	3.4	1.9	-
12 54700	Panama	37,044	-1.9	6.0	15.9	9.1	27.3	25.0	16.7	40.2	73.3	23.2	2.6	3.0	5.5
12 55125	Parkland	20,918	8.4	7.1	24.8	6.4	21.3	31.7	8.6	39.6	92.1	4.0	3.8	1.4	-
12 55775	Pembroke Pines	156,829	-1.9	5.7	19.2	7.1	28.1	24.4	15.4	38.8	70.8	19.4	5.3	7.2	35.9
12 55925	Pensacola	53,949	-1.6	5.9	16.3	7.4	25.1	28.3	17.2	41.8	71.8	26.7	1.9	2.8	2.0
12 56825	Pine Hills CDP	39,797	-	8.7	23.8	8.9	29.3	20.6	8.8	32.5	26.1	61.7	4.1	9.5	14.9
12 56975	Pinellas Park	49,639	-0.2	4.1	15.5	7.3	26.0	27.6	19.5	43.5	86.1	5.6	7.6	1.7	6.8
12 57425	Plantation	85,031	-1.4	7.1	16.1	7.1	28.7	28.4	12.6	38.8	73.9	18.9	3.8	5.8	17.4
12 57550	Plant	35,079	2.5	9.2	21.7	9.3	26.3	22.2	11.2	31.8	75.9	13.1	2.6	11.1	27.7
12 57900	Poinciana CDP	26,947	-	7.7	25.7	8.4	34.9	16.6	6.8	30.0	56.0	30.5	2.0	14.9	56.2
12 58050	Pompano Beach	104,303	-0.9	5.0	14.0	7.7	26.5	27.7	19.1	43.0	68.4	27.5	1.0	6.0	15.8
12 58350	Port Charlotte CDP	46,247	-	4.1	12.5	7.1	21.7	26.1	28.5	47.9	85.4	9.2	2.6	4.5	9.7
12 58575	Port Orange	53,614	3.0	5.5	13.3	8.4	22.3	28.8	21.7	45.3	94.0	4.6	2.1	0.4	2.2
12 58715	Port St. Lucie	137,903	16.6	6.7	17.7	7.2	28.7	23.7	16.0	38.6	83.7	12.1	2.1	3.9	15.0
12 60230	Richmond West CDP	31,214	-	9.4	21.9	9.5	31.3	20.9	6.9	32.0	78.7	7.3	1.3	14.8	74.6
12 60975	Riviera Beach	35,006	9.1	10.5	20.6	8.6	26.3	20.3	13.8	32.5	31.3	63.0	2.2	4.2	10.6
12 61500	Rockledge	25,240	2.4	7.9	15.2	7.7	24.3	27.7	17.2	42.4	80.0	15.9	3.1	3.0	4.7
12 62100	Royal Palm Beach village	32,180	-0.8	6.4	20.9	7.5	29.5	22.9	12.6	36.7	71.5	20.9	4.7	5.3	17.1
12 62625	St. Cloud	28,383	12.8	8.3	17.5	7.0	27.2	23.0	17.0	37.9	91.8	3.5	1.2	4.6	19.8
12 63000	St. Petersburg	240,507	-0.7	6.1	15.0	7.6	27.4	28.4	15.6	41.2	71.2	25.0	3.7	2.4	5.0
12 63650	Sanford	47,952	6.3	7.8	17.3	11.6	31.1	23.5	8.8	33.7	61.6	31.3	2.3	7.9	19.3
12 64175	Sarasota	50,584	-1.6	5.7	13.5	9.2	28.2	22.9	20.4	39.3	76.1	16.6	1.7	7.0	17.5
12 64825	Sebastian	19,170	5.0	5.6	13.4	6.4	22.8	27.4	24.5	45.8	93.8	3.6	3.2	-	5.0
12 67258	South Bradenton CDP	23,588	-	7.6	13.4	9.1	27.2	20.8	21.9	38.5	84.1	6.2	-	9.7	13.4
12 67575	South Miami Heights CDP	33,839	-	8.2	16.7	12.7	25.9	24.7	12.0	36.6	63.1	24.8	1.7	11.5	-
12 68350	Spring Hill CDP	92,144	-	6.0	15.2	7.5	25.9	23.0	22.5	41.3	92.0	4.8	1.7	3.0	10.8
12 69700	Sunrise	89,431	-0.4	6.8	17.9	8.3	28.6	22.7	15.7	37.2	62.9	27.5	3.9	8.3	23.8
12 70600	Tallahassee	162,907	3.4	6.0	11.6	27.0	28.2	19.2	8.1	27.2	60.1	35.9	3.5	2.3	4.7
12 70675	Tamarac	61,820	0.1	4.9	11.0	5.1	24.1	25.7	29.2	49.1	75.9	17.8	1.8	6.0	22.4
12 70700	Tamiami CDP	55,154	-	6.7	15.5	8.6	25.6	26.3	17.3	40.8	94.4	1.2	0.4	5.3	-
12 71000	Tampa	325,265	3.0	6.8	17.3	11.2	29.0	24.2	11.4	35.6	67.2	26.3	3.9	4.4	22.1
12 71150	Tarpon Springs	23,074	4.2	3.7	15.1	5.4	22.1	29.5	24.1	47.7	91.4	5.9	0.9	0.8	-
12 71400	Temple Terrace	23,870	1.1	6.9	14.7	14.6	26.3	24.7	12.7	36.2	69.7	19.2	5.6	7.8	13.6
12 71567	The Crossings CDP	25,173	-	5.7	19.0	10.9	25.0	29.4	9.9	37.7	82.1	3.1	3.5	11.8	-
12 71569	The Hammocks CDP	52,495	-	6.2	20.3	10.9	29.5	25.2	7.9	34.9	83.2	6.8	3.1	9.3	-
12 71900	Titusville	43,422	0.6	5.4	16.6	7.5	25.0	25.2	20.3	42.2	84.5	11.5	2.3	2.6	3.8
12 72145	Town 'n' Country CDP	73,414	-	6.4	15.6	8.4	32.5	25.2	11.9	36.5	78.6	9.7	4.3	9.5	36.2
12 73163	University CDP	31,726	-	9.6	14.0	18.0	33.4	14.8	10.2	27.4	55.0	32.0	4.2	10.8	32.5
12 73287	University Park CDP	25,835	-	3.6	11.6	13.7	22.7	23.9	24.5	43.6	91.1	4.8	1.7	2.7	-
12 73900	Venice	20,760	0.7	1.8	6.0	2.2	12.8	23.5	53.8	66.5	97.6	-	-	-	-
12 74200	Vero Beach South CDP	25,355	-	6.1	16.2	8.7	25.8	22.8	20.4	40.6	91.2	6.4	2.3	1.3	6.4
12 75725	Wekiwa Springs CDP	23,104	-	3.6	19.5	6.6	21.1	34.3	15.0	44.3	93.2	1.0	4.0	2.2	-
12 75812	Wellington village	55,394	2.6	6.0	25.3	6.9	24.9	27.6	9.2	37.0	80.3	10.4	4.0	7.7	14.6
12 75912	West and East Lealman CDP	26,061	-	4.2	19.7	7.3	24.6	28.1	16.1	41.7	88.9	4.2	5.9	1.9	6.9
12 76062	Westchase CDP	20,396	-	8.4	19.2	7.4	36.5	23.4	5.1	34.9	85.0	7.3	6.1	2.3	10.3
12 76075	Westchester CDP	29,423	-	3.7	12.1	9.0	21.5	24.5	29.1	46.9	96.0	0.8	-	3.8	-
12 76487	West Little River CDP	31,466	-	6.8	23.2	9.1	25.5	22.3	13.1	34.9	38.0	58.6	0.5	3.1	39.0
12 76582	Weston	67,990	-1.8	8.8	25.3	6.8	28.3	23.3	7.1	34.8	86.9	4.3	5.5	5.4	42.3
12 76600	West Palm Beach	89,302	2.7	7.5	14.2	9.0	28.0	24.3	16.9	38.4	54.5	31.8	2.6	12.7	21.1
12 76675	West Pensacola CDP	23,449	-	9.5	20.3	7.8	27.3	20.9	14.1	34.7	53.4	45.4	2.3	5.6	2.9
12 78250	Winter Garden	27,872	11.7	9.4	20.1	6.0	30.7	21.9	11.8	35.3	71.5	17.4	4.8	10.2	18.9

Table A-4. Cities — Who: Age, Race/Ethnicity, and Household Structure, 2005–2007—*Continued*

STATE City	Percent foreign born	Total households	Household type (percent) Family households Total family households	Married-couple families	Male householder families	Female householder families	Nonfamily households Total nonfamily households	One-person households	Percent of households with people under 18 years	Percent of households with people 60 years and over
ACS table number:	C05002	B11001	B11001	B11001	B11001	B11001	B11001	B11001	C11005	B11006
	15	16	17	18	19	20	21	22	23	24
Florida—Cont.										
North Miami	48.8	19,698	67.6	41.2	7.4	19.1	32.4	26.7	40.6	27.3
North Miami Beach	50.0	14,490	69.3	40.2	7.3	21.8	30.7	23.6	40.4	28.7
North Port	12.8	17,891	71.0	56.7	3.7	10.5	29.0	22.0	36.0	33.3
Oakland Park	29.5	16,981	52.5	30.6	7.8	14.1	47.5	35.5	28.0	24.6
Oak Ridge CDP	40.8	7,348	74.4	39.0	12.4	23.1	25.6	16.9	45.4	17.1
Ocala	4.6	21,583	59.5	38.9	3.8	16.7	40.5	35.0	31.7	34.7
Ocoee	15.6	10,690	77.9	54.9	5.9	17.1	22.1	15.2	43.1	23.8
Orlando	18.4	92,509	52.3	30.9	4.6	16.8	47.7	36.0	29.9	23.1
Ormond Beach	7.8	17,064	64.4	51.3	3.3	9.7	35.6	31.4	21.6	52.5
Oviedo	8.2	9,596	84.7	67.9	4.0	12.8	15.3	10.5	51.0	21.5
Palm Bay	13.9	34,995	70.4	51.7	5.1	13.6	29.6	23.5	33.9	34.9
Palm Beach Gardens	13.3	19,020	57.5	47.6	2.8	7.1	42.5	35.0	21.4	43.5
Palm CDP	6.8	9,044	72.5	59.6	6.5	6.4	27.5	24.0	33.6	46.9
Palm Coast	14.4	28,498	69.3	56.2	3.3	9.9	30.7	20.2	28.9	41.6
Palmetto Bay village	27.2	8,026	82.3	72.8	1.7	7.8	17.7	15.1	43.8	31.3
Palm Harbor CDP	8.7	24,848	62.8	53.8	2.0	7.0	37.2	32.0	22.4	42.8
Palm River-Clair Mel CDP	19.4	7,727	76.9	50.6	3.8	22.5	23.1	20.4	44.4	26.1
Palm Valley CDP	6.8	8,002	67.6	57.0	3.2	7.4	32.4	28.0	32.5	28.8
Panama	6.9	16,559	61.4	38.9	5.0	17.5	38.6	30.8	29.5	33.9
Parkland	16.9	6,831	81.6	70.6	2.6	8.4	18.4	14.8	52.4	25.3
Pembroke Pines	35.0	56,240	70.1	53.2	4.3	12.6	29.9	25.1	37.6	38.2
Pensacola	3.1	23,953	60.8	41.6	4.1	15.1	39.2	32.9	25.6	37.1
Pine Hills CDP	26.8	13,466	70.0	34.5	6.4	29.1	30.0	24.1	44.9	28.3
Pinellas Park	12.6	20,620	60.8	42.0	6.2	12.7	39.2	30.2	27.1	41.5
Plantation	23.6	32,670	67.8	51.1	5.1	11.7	32.2	26.9	33.4	30.6
Plant	16.1	12,155	72.0	53.1	5.6	13.3	28.0	22.8	43.1	31.6
Poinciana CDP	19.5	8,393	87.5	58.1	7.5	21.9	12.5	9.5	60.3	21.5
Pompano Beach	27.5	43,411	52.6	36.4	5.6	10.5	47.4	37.3	22.2	41.0
Port Charlotte CDP	16.3	21,248	65.0	52.0	3.2	9.9	35.0	27.8	24.2	49.9
Port Orange	5.7	22,490	65.3	51.2	3.6	10.6	34.7	27.3	25.7	46.3
Port St. Lucie	16.0	52,860	72.7	57.5	4.8	10.4	27.3	21.4	35.8	36.9
Richmond West CDP	48.5	8,656	90.4	70.6	4.5	15.3	9.6	6.8	57.7	23.0
Riviera Beach	16.2	12,039	66.6	35.0	5.7	25.9	33.4	26.9	37.9	33.3
Rockledge	7.7	9,491	72.0	58.5	4.3	9.2	28.0	24.0	32.7	37.3
Royal Palm Beach village	18.6	10,965	75.2	60.3	3.6	11.4	24.8	18.9	40.7	32.6
St. Cloud	7.8	11,360	72.2	51.4	2.2	18.6	27.8	22.1	38.9	35.0
St. Petersburg	10.9	105,116	54.7	37.1	5.1	12.4	45.3	37.7	25.3	34.3
Sanford	10.3	17,975	59.1	35.0	6.6	17.4	40.9	33.2	33.6	23.8
Sarasota	18.3	22,294	48.6	32.0	3.9	12.8	51.4	40.7	22.5	39.6
Sebastian	7.3	8,479	72.5	54.3	5.1	13.1	27.5	24.0	31.9	47.4
South Bradenton CDP	15.9	11,100	56.6	38.6	5.6	12.3	43.4	35.4	23.6	41.8
South Miami Heights CDP	50.9	10,922	78.1	48.6	7.7	21.8	21.9	19.6	43.0	38.2
Spring Hill CDP	7.3	35,639	72.7	59.9	3.9	8.9	27.3	21.9	32.9	45.4
Sunrise	33.7	33,412	63.9	45.6	4.5	13.8	36.1	30.7	33.8	36.0
Tallahassee	6.5	70,467	46.7	29.1	4.1	13.5	53.3	37.8	23.3	18.8
Tamarac	27.5	29,780	52.8	37.3	3.4	12.1	47.2	41.0	19.0	53.4
Tamiami CDP	64.4	17,096	82.9	63.2	4.6	15.1	17.1	13.6	42.2	43.7
Tampa	14.8	131,532	56.6	34.6	5.8	16.2	43.4	34.4	30.2	27.7
Tarpon Springs	10.7	10,014	66.3	55.4	3.1	7.7	33.7	28.6	22.6	47.8
Temple Terrace	10.7	10,058	57.5	38.0	5.9	13.6	42.5	32.5	28.2	26.8
The Crossings CDP	44.2	8,682	72.3	56.3	2.8	13.2	27.7	21.3	37.6	25.0
The Hammocks CDP	53.1	16,966	76.9	50.5	6.8	19.6	23.1	17.0	46.2	24.7
Titusville	6.2	18,607	59.3	44.1	3.8	11.4	40.7	33.8	25.5	40.6
Town 'n' Country CDP	23.2	30,609	60.7	42.0	5.6	13.1	39.3	28.6	31.0	26.8
University CDP	20.7	13,613	44.5	18.7	8.6	17.2	55.5	43.0	29.3	14.0
University Park CDP	67.1	8,862	77.8	54.1	6.0	17.7	22.2	19.4	24.7	55.0
Venice	9.2	11,162	54.8	48.4	2.5	3.8	45.2	39.4	8.4	75.6
Vero Beach South CDP	9.2	10,689	68.3	54.4	5.5	8.4	31.7	25.7	33.2	41.1
Wekiwa Springs CDP	9.6	9,145	70.8	61.3	2.5	7.0	29.2	24.9	32.4	36.9
Wellington village	18.8	17,813	79.8	63.5	6.2	10.1	20.2	13.3	50.5	25.0
West and East Lealman CDP	11.8	10,880	55.9	36.5	7.7	11.7	44.1	35.6	28.2	37.2
Westchase CDP	12.8	7,870	65.7	55.5	3.7	6.4	34.3	26.9	38.2	15.1
Westchester CDP	69.4	9,996	78.4	54.8	5.0	18.6	21.6	18.4	31.1	63.7
West Little River CDP	39.5	9,746	70.6	34.2	8.1	28.2	29.4	25.0	45.2	41.5
Weston	38.4	21,168	83.9	71.2	1.5	11.1	16.1	13.5	55.2	21.5
West Palm Beach	26.8	36,703	52.1	34.1	4.6	13.4	47.9	39.3	26.1	34.4
West Pensacola CDP	3.5	9,584	60.6	29.8	5.2	25.5	39.4	29.2	35.7	33.6
Winter Garden	18.4	9,468	71.8	58.4	2.0	11.4	28.2	22.7	41.7	27.3

Table A-4. Cities — Who: Age, Race/Ethnicity, and Household Structure, 2005–2007—*Continued*

STATE Place code	STATE City ACS table number:	Total population B01003	Percent change 2005–2007 Population estimates	Population by age (percent)							Race alone or in combination (percent)				Percent Hispanic or Latino
				Under 5 years B01001	5 to 17 years B01001	18 to 24 years B01001	25 to 44 years B01001	45 to 64 years B01001	65 years and over B01001	Median age B01002	White B02008	Black B02009	Asian Hawaiian or Pacific Islander B02011 + B02012	Amer. Indian, Alaska Native, or some other race B02010 + B02013	C03002
		1	2	3	4	5	6	7	8	9	10	11	12	13	14
	Florida—Cont.														
12 78275	Winter Haven	29,342	10.3	8.9	12.9	8.5	23.7	22.6	23.4	40.3	66.8	30.1	1.1	3.8	7.1
12 78300	Winter Park	28,146	-1.6	6.3	15.8	7.8	22.4	29.0	18.6	43.5	87.9	8.3	1.3	4.0	8.1
12 78325	Winter Springs	35,094	0.8	5.5	18.3	9.4	24.6	31.0	11.1	39.6	90.1	5.4	2.6	4.8	16.0
12 78800	Wright CDP	22,302	-	8.4	14.3	9.6	28.9	27.6	11.1	36.0	79.4	16.5	5.4	3.7	6.5
12 78975	Yeehaw Junction CDP	24,256	-	6.8	17.0	11.5	30.4	23.4	11.1	32.7	66.7	13.1	4.9	19.0	64.8
13 00000	**Georgia**	9,331,515	4.8	7.7	18.8	9.8	29.9	24.0	9.8	34.6	63.4	30.2	3.1	4.7	7.4
13 01052	Albany	76,574	0.2	8.4	19.5	12.9	26.0	21.4	11.8	31.2	31.2	67.2	0.9	1.5	1.4
13 01696	Alpharetta	65,168	0.2	8.5	21.6	4.1	33.9	26.3	5.7	36.2	76.6	9.8	11.5	3.2	6.3
13 03440	Athens-Clarke County (balance)	110,311	4.3	6.5	12.3	28.6	28.7	15.7	8.2	26.3	66.7	26.6	4.1	3.4	8.6
13 04000	Atlanta	439,275	7.5	6.6	14.5	12.1	33.7	24.1	9.0	35.0	38.6	57.3	2.3	2.9	4.7
13 04204	Augusta-Richmond County (balance)	191,991	0.1	8.0	18.6	11.4	26.9	23.5	11.6	33.6	44.7	53.0	2.5	2.3	2.7
13 12834	Candler-McAfee CDP	30,010	-	6.0	19.2	8.5	23.8	31.3	11.2	38.6	4.7	93.5	-	1.7	-
13 12988	Canton	14,002	21.6	9.8	18.9	12.9	34.2	14.1	10.1	28.4	62.3	11.0	2.6	25.8	26.1
13 13492	Carrollton	22,362	7.8	7.0	16.2	22.0	27.8	15.2	11.8	27.4	67.5	26.9	1.2	5.7	5.2
13 17776	College Park	16,603	-2.2	8.4	22.6	8.2	31.3	24.4	5.1	31.6	11.5	84.0	2.6	2.0	-
13 19000	Columbus	189,173	-0.8	7.8	19.2	12.4	25.4	23.5	11.5	33.4	50.1	46.3	2.9	3.2	4.0
13 21380	Dalton	30,089	4.0	11.0	19.5	8.9	31.7	19.6	9.3	30.7	56.4	6.5	3.1	35.3	-
13 23900	Douglasville	24,174	8.9	8.2	21.5	9.7	34.7	19.2	6.7	30.9	44.3	50.3	3.1	4.1	5.2
13 24600	Duluth	26,041	6.8	6.1	18.3	8.7	34.8	26.5	5.6	35.1	61.9	18.1	16.4	4.4	10.6
13 24768	Dunwoody CDP	39,583	-	8.1	17.2	5.7	29.5	27.2	12.4	38.5	82.5	7.9	8.4	2.4	4.2
13 25720	East Point	37,246	5.5	8.0	17.0	8.0	33.4	26.7	6.9	34.4	16.1	71.6	1.1	10.6	-
13 30536	Forest Park	23,287	-0.9	9.8	17.9	8.9	34.4	20.7	8.2	31.6	36.3	40.6	4.7	18.7	27.2
13 31908	Gainesville	32,576	7.9	10.2	17.1	10.8	34.5	16.8	10.7	28.9	79.3	11.3	2.6	6.8	41.0
13 35324	Griffin	21,480	1.4	8.4	19.6	8.6	29.5	20.3	13.7	33.3	49.9	48.6	-	2.1	-
13 38964	Hinesville	31,271	1.7	11.1	22.1	14.4	32.7	16.2	3.4	25.9	45.3	49.3	4.0	5.8	6.8
13 42425	Johns Creek	83,445	-3.1	8.3	25.3	5.0	28.9	27.7	4.9	37.0	72.7	10.1	16.9	1.9	5.5
13 43192	Kennesaw	27,898	4.1	9.3	20.1	9.4	34.1	18.6	8.4	33.4	68.8	20.2	6.9	4.6	11.5
13 44340	LaGrange	27,863	2.1	9.0	18.5	12.8	25.5	21.1	13.1	30.6	48.1	50.0	1.4	1.7	4.0
13 45488	Lawrenceville	30,270	3.0	11.7	19.2	8.9	30.5	21.1	8.5	31.6	63.1	22.2	3.5	13.1	27.1
13 48288	Mableton CDP	33,481	-	8.2	15.7	7.3	32.1	27.2	9.5	37.4	49.7	36.2	3.2	12.0	14.6
13 49000	Macon	92,094	-1.2	8.5	20.4	10.6	24.7	22.5	13.3	33.8	31.6	66.7	0.7	1.4	1.8
13 49756	Marietta	57,353	3.5	10.8	12.6	13.3	33.3	20.6	9.5	31.6	51.4	30.2	3.3	17.7	21.2
13 50036	Martinez CDP	27,470	-	7.3	22.0	9.4	24.5	28.5	8.3	35.5	83.9	10.7	5.4	1.0	1.4
13 51492	Milledgeville	18,803	2.2	3.0	12.3	29.7	26.2	20.6	8.2	28.7	49.3	50.6	0.9	-	-
13 55020	Newnan	21,963	17.9	9.1	16.0	10.1	36.0	19.8	8.9	33.0	64.4	31.2	1.6	4.0	7.9
13 56000	North Atlanta CDP	39,874	-	10.5	12.1	9.5	42.0	18.2	7.8	33.1	60.5	10.5	5.3	24.5	36.1
13 56168	North Druid Hills CDP	20,099	-	5.8	7.4	11.9	35.9	20.8	18.2	37.1	74.7	11.4	5.7	9.0	-
13 59724	Peachtree	33,336	1.6	5.2	20.9	8.3	21.9	32.9	10.8	40.9	84.8	9.8	4.6	2.8	2.6
13 63952	Redan CDP	38,502	-	8.0	22.6	10.3	31.2	24.2	3.8	31.2	4.6	93.4	2.0	-	1.9
13 66668	Rome	35,176	0.2	7.9	17.1	11.2	26.0	22.7	15.1	34.4	64.5	27.8	3.1	5.5	12.9
13 67284	Roswell	101,851	1.5	8.1	18.1	5.8	31.8	27.9	8.3	36.6	80.1	10.5	3.8	6.6	17.9
13 68516	Sandy Springs	98,043	-3.2	6.3	13.9	9.1	35.2	26.8	8.6	36.3	72.8	16.3	4.2	8.2	11.0
13 69000	Savannah	127,526	0.6	7.4	17.4	13.6	26.2	22.3	13.2	33.1	39.2	58.2	1.9	2.1	2.8
13 71492	Smyrna	46,297	3.9	9.5	11.9	8.4	40.6	21.2	8.4	34.1	55.7	30.2	5.5	10.0	15.7
13 71604	Snellville	17,299	4.6	4.2	20.2	7.8	22.4	30.1	15.3	42.2	80.8	16.1	-	2.3	-
13 73256	Statesboro	25,953	2.7	4.8	9.6	51.6	15.1	11.7	7.2	21.7	55.1	42.3	3.1	2.6	2.4
13 77652	Tucker CDP	30,107	-	6.9	13.3	5.2	28.5	29.8	16.3	42.7	74.6	13.2	8.4	5.2	12.5
13 78800	Valdosta	47,746	2.8	8.4	17.0	19.1	27.0	18.8	9.6	27.6	46.9	51.0	2.1	2.4	2.4
13 80508	Warner Robins	56,916	3.5	8.5	19.8	9.7	28.9	21.9	11.2	32.4	60.5	36.4	3.2	3.3	4.5
13 84176	Woodstock	18,394	16.9	9.4	17.5	11.3	37.6	19.7	4.6	31.4	77.6	8.7	5.0	10.2	12.9
15 00000	**Hawaii**	1,276,534	1.2	6.4	15.9	9.7	28.2	25.7	14.0	37.7	41.7	3.5	78.7	4.7	8.1
15 14650	Hilo CDP	50,289	-	5.2	14.6	13.7	23.0	26.6	17.0	39.3	43.9	2.1	88.4	5.1	9.2
15 17000	Honolulu CDP	359,694	-0.1	5.2	12.2	8.8	27.4	27.4	19.0	42.5	30.9	2.6	82.2	2.7	3.6
15 22700	Kahului CDP	22,669	-	6.2	19.1	6.7	29.6	20.9	17.5	37.6	21.4	-	99.8	4.6	7.7
15 23150	Kailua CDP (Honolulu County)	35,841	-	6.5	15.7	7.1	25.1	29.6	16.0	42.0	66.5	1.8	56.3	4.8	7.4
15 28250	Kaneohe CDP	35,712	-	5.6	16.4	8.8	27.0	25.7	16.5	40.0	46.8	2.4	94.7	5.5	8.3
15 36500	Kihei CDP	20,022	-	6.7	15.2	10.0	31.7	27.7	8.7	35.8	72.2	3.3	44.3	4.3	14.7
15 51050	Mililani Town CDP	28,505	-	5.2	17.9	8.5	27.5	30.4	10.4	38.6	35.0	5.9	85.7	3.2	7.6
15 62600	Pearl CDP	28,340	-	6.6	15.6	8.4	23.9	23.8	21.8	41.5	28.4	8.8	80.8	5.1	5.8
15 77750	Waimalu CDP	29,417	-	4.9	13.5	9.9	28.1	30.6	13.1	41.2	29.7	8.8	83.5	3.1	4.2
15 79700	Waipahu CDP	36,059	-	5.9	17.8	11.4	25.0	24.0	15.9	37.2	15.2	1.2	96.8	4.6	7.2
16 00000	**Idaho**	1,463,059	5.2	7.8	19.4	10.0	26.9	24.2	11.6	34.2	94.1	1.0	1.9	5.3	9.5
16 08830	Boise	204,777	1.2	6.8	17.1	10.8	29.7	25.1	10.4	34.6	94.2	2.0	3.2	3.2	6.7
16 12250	Caldwell	32,119	15.1	8.8	21.8	9.3	31.1	18.6	10.4	29.4	86.4	1.5	1.6	13.8	30.2
16 16750	Coeur d'Alene	40,147	5.9	5.6	17.8	11.3	28.9	22.0	14.4	35.5	97.9	0.4	1.3	2.7	4.2
16 39700	Idaho Falls	52,590	2.8	9.1	18.9	9.8	25.8	24.4	12.0	33.7	94.5	1.1	1.5	4.2	9.7
16 46540	Lewiston	31,489	1.9	5.7	15.9	9.8	25.5	25.1	18.0	40.0	97.4	1.3	1.8	2.9	2.7
16 52120	Meridian	58,254	22.3	9.8	22.4	7.2	34.5	18.4	7.8	31.8	94.4	1.5	2.6	2.9	3.9

Table A-4. Cities — Who: Age, Race/Ethnicity, and Household Structure, 2005–2007—*Continued*

STATE City	Percent foreign born	Total households	Household type (percent) Family households				Nonfamily households		Percent of households with people under 18 years	Percent of households with people 60 years and over
			Total family households	Married-couple families	Male householder families	Female householder families	Total nonfamily households	One-person households		
ACS table number:	C05002	B11001	B11001	B11001	B11001	B11001	B11001	B11001	C11005	B11006
	15	16	17	18	19	20	21	22	23	24
Florida—Cont.										
Winter Haven	7.9	13,309	61.6	41.2	4.1	16.3	38.4	32.7	28.2	41.6
Winter Park	8.3	12,380	54.0	41.2	2.3	10.5	46.0	39.8	24.3	41.3
Winter Springs	12.6	13,078	75.9	59.3	4.4	12.1	24.1	19.8	36.3	29.2
Wright CDP	6.5	10,276	59.2	38.8	4.8	15.7	40.8	34.2	25.6	28.4
Yeehaw Junction CDP	26.4	8,324	80.4	57.0	6.2	17.2	19.6	16.8	45.5	29.6
Georgia	9.0	3,364,749	68.2	49.0	4.6	14.7	31.8	26.4	37.3	26.5
Albany	1.7	29,481	62.5	32.7	3.8	26.0	37.5	32.7	35.6	29.1
Alpharetta	17.0	23,562	68.2	55.2	3.1	9.9	31.8	26.3	42.1	18.1
Athens-Clarke County (balance)	10.0	42,033	49.7	31.2	4.7	13.8	50.3	33.6	26.2	20.1
Atlanta	6.7	168,252	44.2	23.9	4.0	16.3	55.8	46.7	23.6	24.0
Augusta-Richmond County (balance)	3.5	73,453	63.2	37.2	4.4	21.6	36.8	32.5	35.1	30.0
Candler-McAfee CDP	3.4	9,418	63.4	27.6	10.2	25.5	36.6	32.4	34.3	34.9
Canton	21.8	5,210	66.4	44.7	7.1	14.6	33.6	30.4	40.2	21.3
Carrollton	6.5	8,856	50.2	30.7	2.7	16.8	49.8	33.4	27.7	26.5
College Park	7.9	5,924	49.6	18.0	5.1	26.4	50.4	37.9	31.5	17.7
Columbus	3.9	71,365	66.4	40.2	5.1	21.2	33.6	29.5	36.9	29.6
Dalton	31.3	10,316	68.9	47.4	5.9	15.5	31.1	24.4	42.6	24.5
Douglasville	6.7	9,153	67.2	40.3	4.2	22.8	32.8	28.8	38.1	17.8
Duluth	22.9	10,115	62.9	46.7	2.3	13.9	37.1	29.7	39.4	16.9
Dunwoody CDP	14.3	16,174	63.6	54.8	2.2	6.6	36.4	31.0	29.3	27.7
East Point	9.8	12,064	59.5	25.5	8.7	25.4	40.5	34.4	32.6	23.6
Forest Park	24.5	6,087	60.4	32.3	6.7	21.4	39.6	31.5	40.8	31.5
Gainesville	31.8	9,481	64.7	40.7	7.4	16.6	35.3	30.8	39.9	28.6
Griffin	3.9	7,956	61.9	33.0	3.6	25.3	38.1	31.0	37.6	27.8
Hinesville	6.1	11,042	68.0	41.2	3.8	22.9	32.0	26.1	45.5	11.5
Johns Creek	20.6	26,400	81.8	71.1	2.0	8.7	18.2	15.1	55.7	15.7
Kennesaw	17.5	9,993	69.3	51.5	4.5	13.3	30.7	25.7	42.0	19.3
LaGrange	4.3	10,492	63.8	34.5	5.4	23.9	36.2	29.1	36.7	30.5
Lawrenceville	26.8	9,442	68.1	45.5	7.0	15.6	31.9	26.3	45.3	22.9
Mableton CDP	13.7	13,167	64.4	48.3	2.8	13.2	35.6	30.8	32.7	24.9
Macon	1.9	35,960	56.6	28.9	4.4	23.2	43.4	38.4	30.8	32.7
Marietta	22.8	22,111	56.3	37.2	6.6	12.5	43.7	36.5	31.6	22.5
Martinez CDP	5.2	10,116	78.2	62.3	4.5	11.4	21.8	17.7	41.9	22.9
Milledgeville	2.4	4,470	58.4	31.7	5.1	21.6	41.6	31.3	31.5	26.4
Newnan	6.4	8,223	67.8	45.6	2.5	19.7	32.2	25.1	38.8	21.5
North Atlanta CDP	31.4	15,709	44.9	32.0	4.2	8.7	55.1	43.3	22.5	17.3
North Druid Hills CDP	20.6	9,361	36.9	29.5	5.8	1.6	63.1	46.6	13.2	27.2
Peachtree	8.4	12,277	77.7	63.4	1.8	12.4	22.3	20.6	44.5	28.1
Redan CDP	8.8	12,868	68.1	33.2	4.6	30.4	31.9	27.0	46.3	13.2
Rome	11.1	13,167	58.5	37.2	3.9	17.4	41.5	36.7	30.7	36.8
Roswell	22.2	35,228	67.0	55.6	2.5	8.9	33.0	26.6	35.3	23.5
Sandy Springs	20.4	40,279	54.5	41.8	3.3	9.4	45.5	36.0	26.1	22.1
Savannah	3.9	51,732	57.5	32.0	6.8	18.8	42.5	34.5	29.2	31.9
Smyrna	20.7	20,493	51.0	36.5	2.9	11.5	49.0	41.3	26.1	18.0
Snellville	7.1	6,259	73.1	56.8	1.7	14.6	26.9	20.5	36.3	36.8
Statesboro	2.6	8,751	41.9	22.1	4.2	15.7	58.1	39.9	24.8	15.8
Tucker CDP	18.3	11,668	62.1	47.8	4.0	10.2	37.9	29.6	29.2	34.9
Valdosta	4.2	18,760	62.5	36.5	3.5	22.6	37.5	27.9	35.4	23.0
Warner Robins	4.4	22,954	62.5	39.3	4.6	18.6	37.5	34.5	36.6	25.8
Woodstock	12.8	7,624	67.1	51.1	2.2	13.8	32.9	27.6	39.6	13.4
Hawaii	16.9	433,664	70.0	52.1	5.3	12.6	30.0	23.5	35.3	36.8
Hilo CDP	7.6	17,977	70.3	50.9	4.8	14.6	29.7	23.2	31.4	42.8
Honolulu CDP	25.9	141,535	60.0	43.9	4.6	11.4	40.0	33.0	25.2	41.7
Kahului CDP	31.8	6,336	71.1	52.4	6.0	12.7	28.9	23.0	43.5	48.3
Kailua CDP (Honolulu County)	7.9	11,975	75.6	61.9	3.4	10.3	24.4	18.2	35.1	41.0
Kaneohe CDP	5.7	11,406	80.6	57.5	5.5	17.6	19.4	16.4	37.2	43.6
Kihei CDP	17.3	7,604	59.2	46.1	2.9	10.2	40.8	29.1	32.6	23.6
Mililani Town CDP	10.6	9,433	84.3	62.9	7.1	14.3	15.7	11.7	43.7	35.6
Pearl CDP	12.8	9,141	79.3	61.3	4.0	13.9	20.7	17.3	31.1	52.6
Waimalu CDP	18.8	10,460	72.4	56.3	5.4	10.7	27.6	20.7	30.1	36.2
Waipahu CDP	36.5	7,961	85.5	59.5	9.6	16.4	14.5	9.6	48.9	48.5
Idaho	5.6	545,171	70.1	57.0	4.1	9.0	29.9	23.7	36.9	28.8
Boise	6.3	84,734	60.2	46.6	4.0	9.5	39.8	30.9	31.4	23.6
Caldwell	13.0	11,439	69.1	47.3	7.6	14.2	30.9	27.5	42.7	26.7
Coeur d'Alene	2.7	16,984	59.2	42.3	3.9	13.0	40.8	32.9	31.6	29.3
Idaho Falls	5.2	20,178	68.8	54.5	3.9	10.3	31.2	26.1	35.0	31.0
Lewiston	2.1	13,158	64.4	48.1	6.1	10.3	35.6	27.4	32.2	32.9
Meridian	3.7	20,502	76.7	66.3	2.6	7.8	23.3	17.3	46.2	22.2

Table A-4. Cities — Who: Age, Race/Ethnicity, and Household Structure, 2005–2007—*Continued*

STATE Place code	STATE / City	Total population	Percent change 2005–2007	Population by age (percent)						Median age	Race alone or in combination (percent)		Asian Hawaiian or Pacific Islander	Amer. Indian, Alaska Native, or some other race	Percent Hispanic or Latino
				Under 5 years	5 to 17 years	18 to 24 years	25 to 44 years	45 to 64 years	65 years and over		White	Black			
ACS table number:	B01003	Population estimates	B01001	B01001	B01001	B01001	B01001	B01001	B01002	B02008	B02009	B02011 + B02012	B02010 + B02013	C03002	
		1	2	3	4	5	6	7	8	9	10	11	12	13	14
	Idaho—Cont.														
16 54550	Moscow	22,686	2.2	5.6	10.7	35.9	23.8	16.2	7.7	24.2	93.1	1.9	4.6	4.1	3.5
16 56260	Nampa	74,558	9.7	10.2	21.8	10.2	31.6	16.4	9.8	28.9	90.7	1.4	1.9	8.4	21.3
16 64090	Pocatello	52,137	2.3	8.7	17.8	14.7	26.5	21.5	10.6	29.7	95.6	1.1	2.4	3.2	5.9
16 64810	Post Falls	24,765	9.6	8.6	21.3	8.8	30.1	20.8	10.3	32.0	98.0	0.9	0.7	2.3	-
16 67420	Rexburg	23,215	4.1	11.3	12.3	44.3	18.6	8.9	4.6	21.4	96.7	-	2.7	0.8	3.5
16 82810	Twin Falls	40,924	7.3	9.1	18.0	11.3	28.2	19.3	14.1	32.0	94.5	0.6	3.5	3.9	10.8
17 00000	**Illinois**	12,783,049	1.0	7.0	18.1	10.0	28.4	24.5	12.0	35.7	72.5	15.4	4.6	9.2	14.6
17 00243	Addison village	37,655	0.0	9.3	14.4	12.6	30.2	25.5	8.0	33.2	77.6	3.0	6.7	13.5	36.4
17 00685	Algonquin village	29,828	4.3	9.1	21.2	6.3	31.2	25.0	7.2	36.2	91.1	0.4	6.1	3.4	7.6
17 01114	Alton	27,329	-0.3	8.8	16.9	9.5	26.1	23.4	15.2	35.3	70.8	28.3	-	2.4	3.0
17 02154	Arlington Heights village	76,958	-1.2	6.9	17.0	6.0	25.9	27.9	16.1	40.9	90.2	0.9	7.2	3.3	5.1
17 03012	Aurora	176,413	2.3	10.3	21.1	9.1	35.8	17.8	5.9	29.8	67.9	12.5	6.4	15.3	37.8
17 04013	Bartlett village	41,488	7.5	9.8	20.3	7.5	31.9	24.6	5.8	35.0	83.3	2.5	13.6	1.8	7.2
17 04078	Batavia	26,030	1.3	7.6	21.4	7.6	25.2	29.1	9.1	38.1	91.9	4.1	1.6	3.3	5.3
17 04845	Belleville	41,287	0.3	4.8	16.2	11.1	30.1	23.3	14.5	36.4	76.9	23.4	1.8	0.7	1.4
17 05092	Belvidere	25,113	7.9	8.5	19.9	12.5	31.2	17.1	10.8	31.0	87.5	3.4	1.7	8.4	30.0
17 05248	Bensenville village	20,570	-1.1	7.5	17.6	8.7	32.8	21.6	11.9	34.9	77.6	5.1	6.1	15.3	-
17 05573	Berwyn	56,180	-2.0	8.5	18.9	8.4	32.4	21.8	10.0	33.6	61.1	5.8	2.3	32.8	52.7
17 06587	Bloomingdale village	21,732	0.0	4.2	15.4	8.0	27.4	29.8	15.1	41.2	81.8	3.5	13.8	1.0	6.5
17 06613	Bloomington	70,482	3.2	7.2	17.4	12.4	31.5	22.1	9.4	32.6	83.0	11.5	5.2	2.8	3.4
17 06704	Blue Island	24,227	-1.6	7.1	21.4	12.1	26.8	24.4	8.2	33.5	50.2	27.2	-	23.2	-
17 07133	Bolingbrook village	69,661	3.1	8.4	21.7	9.5	35.0	21.0	4.3	30.9	55.6	23.3	9.5	15.0	22.0
17 09447	Buffalo Grove village	44,330	0.8	5.9	20.5	7.0	24.5	30.7	11.3	40.7	86.5	1.2	11.9	1.7	3.9
17 09642	Burbank	29,288	0.1	7.3	18.8	11.3	24.7	25.1	12.9	36.3	86.8	-	2.9	10.2	-
17 10487	Calumet	41,614	-1.8	9.5	21.8	9.4	27.1	20.4	11.8	33.8	25.4	67.8	-	7.7	-
17 11163	Carbondale	25,101	2.2	3.8	8.9	46.0	24.6	10.9	5.8	22.9	66.1	23.9	8.5	2.8	4.3
17 11332	Carol Stream village	39,380	-0.5	6.2	21.9	9.1	29.5	26.2	7.1	35.6	77.2	5.5	13.5	4.7	12.9
17 11358	Carpentersville village	38,331	1.3	10.7	24.1	9.8	35.9	15.1	4.4	28.9	68.6	5.8	5.5	22.0	49.2
17 12385	Champaign	75,872	3.1	5.5	12.6	31.6	26.2	16.4	7.8	25.1	72.5	16.8	10.2	2.8	4.8
17 12567	Charleston	19,626	0.1	3.9	9.0	47.6	17.4	13.3	8.8	22.4	91.1	5.4	3.2	1.0	1.9
17 14000	Chicago	2,740,224	-0.1	7.5	17.2	10.7	32.2	22.0	10.4	33.6	38.9	35.6	5.4	21.8	28.1
17 14026	Chicago Heights	31,681	-1.7	8.3	24.9	9.2	26.5	20.1	10.9	30.0	42.9	45.1	0.7	14.7	30.4
17 14351	Cicero town	83,149	-2.0	11.0	23.9	10.3	33.6	15.6	5.7	27.7	20.9	0.5	1.2	68.2	83.8
17 15599	Collinsville	25,438	1.3	6.7	14.7	10.3	29.4	24.5	14.5	36.8	88.0	10.3	0.6	2.9	4.5
17 17458	Crest Hill	18,753	6.9	5.3	14.5	10.1	32.4	25.7	12.0	36.1	70.2	17.4	1.9	12.3	-
17 17887	Crystal Lake	41,277	2.2	6.4	21.5	10.3	28.6	23.1	10.2	36.0	95.3	1.6	2.3	2.3	10.3
17 18563	Danville	32,494	-0.8	8.1	17.2	9.7	25.9	22.8	16.4	35.9	67.3	28.1	1.5	5.3	5.5
17 18628	Darien	23,653	-1.1	6.8	15.8	7.2	24.4	32.0	13.8	42.6	81.3	5.1	11.7	2.3	-
17 18823	Decatur	75,000	-1.0	6.3	16.3	11.4	23.0	26.0	17.0	38.9	77.4	22.7	1.4	1.7	1.5
17 19161	DeKalb	44,495	2.4	5.7	12.0	39.1	23.9	12.8	6.6	23.3	77.2	11.9	5.8	7.3	11.7
17 19642	Des Plaines	59,518	0.6	6.2	15.6	7.7	25.6	27.6	17.3	42.0	78.3	1.2	11.6	9.5	14.3
17 20292	Dolton village	29,100	-1.8	8.2	26.0	9.9	25.9	20.5	9.5	30.5	6.8	91.9	1.4	1.2	2.1
17 20591	Downers Grove village	45,806	-0.4	5.3	16.2	7.6	23.3	31.8	15.8	43.3	89.4	3.0	6.2	2.7	4.2
17 22073	East Moline	21,994	-0.2	7.9	13.9	11.5	25.9	24.9	15.8	36.6	80.1	8.9	3.5	9.9	18.6
17 22164	East Peoria	24,598	1.1	5.9	16.1	8.8	27.9	24.8	16.6	38.9	98.0	0.8	-	1.5	-
17 22255	East St. Louis	26,441	-2.1	10.4	21.1	10.9	20.5	23.7	13.3	32.6	-	99.3	-	0.5	-
17 22697	Edwardsville	23,977	1.4	5.8	15.7	24.3	25.5	20.6	8.1	28.4	88.8	8.2	3.4	0.6	1.5
17 23074	Elgin	100,014	6.3	8.5	19.4	10.2	32.5	21.1	8.3	31.7	71.8	7.7	4.8	18.3	41.5
17 23256	Elk Grove Village village	35,048	-1.3	5.8	17.5	6.9	28.9	28.3	12.6	39.6	80.8	2.1	12.4	5.5	9.0
17 23620	Elmhurst	43,687	0.9	6.8	20.8	7.5	25.7	25.9	13.4	39.3	92.8	0.5	5.1	1.9	8.0
17 23724	Elmwood Park village	25,191	-1.4	6.6	14.4	10.2	26.2	25.8	16.8	41.1	89.0	1.5	1.7	8.1	-
17 24582	Evanston	68,913	1.0	6.5	13.0	16.0	27.9	24.5	12.1	35.5	69.5	20.9	7.7	5.7	7.5
17 27884	Freeport	24,046	-2.1	5.1	17.3	8.7	25.1	25.4	18.5	41.2	81.2	15.7	1.8	3.9	3.6
17 28326	Galesburg	32,156	-2.0	5.3	15.6	11.2	27.4	23.5	17.0	37.3	83.8	12.2	1.5	3.8	5.6
17 28872	Geneva	24,497	3.6	8.4	21.9	7.4	26.9	26.4	9.0	35.3	96.1	1.8	2.5	1.3	4.9
17 29730	Glendale Heights village	33,588	-1.4	7.6	17.5	11.9	31.9	23.9	7.3	33.3	61.3	7.1	27.4	4.7	24.1
17 29756	Glen Ellyn village	26,654	0.0	6.0	23.6	6.5	23.2	28.6	12.2	40.5	91.7	2.8	4.4	2.3	6.0
17 29938	Glenview village	46,159	0.8	6.5	19.4	5.4	21.5	28.8	18.4	43.5	84.5	1.3	12.3	3.0	4.2
17 30926	Granite	28,495	-0.9	5.2	17.0	9.1	26.3	26.4	16.0	39.5	93.4	5.4	0.8	2.0	2.0
17 31121	Grayslake village	21,694	2.5	8.8	21.1	8.5	33.0	22.4	6.1	33.5	91.6	1.2	5.2	-	-
17 32018	Gurnee village	32,770	1.2	7.7	21.7	9.5	27.2	26.5	7.4	34.8	76.7	8.9	11.9	5.2	9.2
17 32746	Hanover Park village	39,230	-0.7	7.6	21.2	9.2	32.8	24.1	5.0	32.8	61.7	7.9	17.2	13.8	32.3
17 33383	Harvey	31,082	-1.8	9.4	24.9	12.9	26.0	19.8	6.9	26.8	11.4	81.7	2.1	6.8	11.5
17 34722	Highland Park	28,915	1.3	7.0	18.8	6.4	21.1	30.4	16.3	43.0	93.7	0.9	2.8	2.6	6.8
17 35411	Hoffman Estates village	53,052	2.1	7.8	19.1	8.1	28.8	28.2	8.0	37.5	69.0	5.0	19.0	7.7	13.3
17 35835	Homer Glen village	25,607	4.9	6.4	21.0	9.6	25.2	28.9	8.8	37.1	94.9	-	3.2	1.3	-
17 36750	Huntley village	20,893	24.1	6.5	14.9	4.6	27.6	21.7	24.6	43.2	87.1	6.1	6.3	2.4	5.4
17 38570	Joliet	138,057	8.0	9.5	19.9	10.1	33.8	18.3	8.4	30.1	69.2	16.8	1.6	14.3	25.5
17 38934	Kankakee	27,493	-0.1	8.9	22.0	9.9	28.9	19.7	10.5	30.4	54.2	42.1	0.3	5.3	15.8
17 41105	Lake Forest	20,113	1.1	4.2	22.4	11.8	16.0	30.6	15.0	42.6	95.6	-	3.7	1.0	-
17 41183	Lake in the Hills village	29,955	2.8	8.6	23.1	8.9	35.5	20.0	3.8	31.4	86.5	1.0	8.1	6.7	10.7
17 41417	Lake Zurich village	20,738	2.0	5.7	23.3	7.0	29.7	27.1	7.3	35.6	90.5	0.7	5.1	4.7	-
17 42028	Lansing	27,742	-1.6	9.6	18.6	5.0	26.2	25.5	15.2	36.6	73.5	22.4	-	4.7	-
17 43250	Libertyville village	21,285	1.4	5.8	22.5	8.8	21.0	28.6	13.3	39.9	92.0	1.3	5.9	2.8	4.1

Table A-4. Cities — Who: Age, Race/Ethnicity, and Household Structure, 2005–2007—*Continued*

STATE City	Percent foreign born	Total households	Household type (percent)						Percent of households with people under 18 years	Percent of households with people 60 years and over
			Family households				Nonfamily households			
			Total family households	Married-couple families	Male householder families	Female householder families	Total nonfamily households	One-person households		
ACS table number:	C05002	B11001	B11001	B11001	B11001	B11001	B11001	B11001	C11005	B11006
	15	16	17	18	19	20	21	22	23	24
Idaho—Cont.										
Moscow..........................	4.4	8,081	52.6	42.5	3.4	6.6	47.4	31.8	28.1	16.0
Nampa............................	9.0	26,198	71.4	54.4	5.1	11.8	28.6	22.2	44.1	23.6
Pocatello........................	2.9	19,823	64.8	50.2	4.2	10.4	35.2	27.0	34.4	24.7
Post Falls.......................	2.8	9,307	70.7	53.6	6.6	10.6	29.3	21.3	40.7	29.1
Rexburg..........................	2.9	5,784	68.4	57.8	0.5	10.2	31.6	10.9	35.0	14.8
Twin Falls.......................	6.4	15,686	67.2	50.3	3.9	13.0	32.8	26.5	39.0	29.8
Illinois...........................	13.7	4,724,462	66.8	49.9	4.4	12.5	33.2	27.9	35.3	30.1
Addison village	36.6	11,892	78.9	63.2	4.2	11.5	21.1	17.3	40.0	24.7
Algonquin village	11.3	9,786	81.0	70.2	3.1	7.7	19.0	15.8	46.3	21.9
Alton	0.9	11,562	60.7	37.2	4.8	18.7	39.3	33.1	31.2	32.3
Arlington Heights village	16.8	30,865	65.9	56.7	3.3	5.9	34.1	31.5	31.9	35.1
Aurora	25.5	57,614	73.2	54.7	5.8	12.7	26.8	21.0	48.0	17.5
Bartlett village..................	16.6	13,373	82.0	71.9	4.1	6.1	18.0	14.4	50.5	20.1
Batavia...........................	4.3	9,408	73.0	62.4	1.1	9.5	27.0	23.4	39.1	26.1
Belleville.........................	1.1	17,647	58.2	41.5	4.3	12.4	41.8	34.9	29.1	28.4
Belvidere.........................	15.0	8,379	70.4	50.3	5.1	15.1	29.6	25.9	43.5	26.6
Bensenville village	34.0	7,212	71.8	54.2	8.7	9.0	28.2	21.0	39.1	28.2
Berwyn	25.8	18,971	69.6	46.0	7.0	16.6	30.4	25.1	41.7	31.2
Bloomingdale village	18.6	7,985	68.6	55.2	3.4	10.0	31.4	27.3	31.5	31.2
Bloomington.....................	6.6	28,607	61.6	49.8	2.4	9.4	38.4	30.5	33.0	21.8
Blue Island	21.8	8,176	71.9	43.6	9.7	18.6	28.1	23.8	41.9	27.3
Bolingbrook village	20.0	21,241	80.5	67.3	3.6	9.6	19.5	16.7	49.3	16.2
Buffalo Grove village..........	22.0	16,450	72.6	63.4	1.6	7.6	27.4	25.0	39.6	27.6
Burbank..........................	30.0	9,314	78.2	61.3	3.3	13.6	21.8	19.1	41.2	38.9
Calumet..........................	7.1	15,460	64.0	35.0	5.7	23.3	36.0	32.5	41.9	31.1
Carbondale......................	10.3	10,541	28.7	20.1	0.9	7.7	71.3	52.5	15.0	15.9
Carol Stream village	20.0	13,977	74.2	56.4	4.5	13.3	25.8	21.6	45.6	20.1
Carpentersville village	34.8	11,126	77.0	57.5	8.0	11.5	23.0	17.4	52.9	15.3
Champaign.......................	10.2	30,072	45.7	32.2	3.3	10.2	54.3	36.8	23.7	17.7
Charleston	4.1	7,785	42.9	30.2	3.5	9.1	57.1	32.0	23.5	20.1
Chicago	21.7	1,014,120	57.9	33.7	5.7	18.5	42.1	34.9	32.3	28.0
Chicago Heights	13.3	10,235	72.3	41.2	6.0	25.1	27.7	24.8	43.1	33.2
Cicero town......................	45.4	21,533	81.8	57.6	8.8	15.4	18.2	14.3	59.5	23.3
Collinsville.......................	3.8	10,730	65.5	46.9	4.8	13.9	34.5	26.8	31.3	30.5
Crest Hill	10.0	6,840	69.6	49.9	4.0	15.7	30.4	26.3	31.3	31.1
Crystal Lake	9.9	13,976	71.5	55.7	5.4	10.4	28.5	24.8	42.1	26.1
Danville...........................	3.1	13,360	59.4	37.4	5.3	16.7	40.6	34.6	33.3	37.0
Darien.............................	18.4	9,028	74.0	62.5	2.2	9.3	26.0	23.2	34.3	35.1
Decatur...........................	2.4	33,018	59.9	42.0	3.9	14.0	40.1	34.4	28.1	33.8
DeKalb............................	11.0	14,278	52.6	35.3	3.7	13.6	47.4	27.6	30.3	16.7
Des Plaines......................	29.3	22,018	67.2	53.9	4.5	8.8	32.8	29.0	33.0	41.3
Dolton village...................	2.4	8,910	73.7	33.4	9.8	30.6	26.3	21.4	48.7	28.8
Downers Grove village	10.7	18,732	64.0	55.1	2.0	6.9	36.0	31.6	29.5	36.2
East Moline......................	8.9	8,910	60.2	44.1	2.9	13.2	39.8	35.2	29.5	32.4
East Peoria.......................	1.6	10,167	69.5	57.0	3.6	8.8	30.5	26.1	32.8	32.3
East St. Louis....................	-	10,691	64.1	18.4	5.0	40.7	35.9	33.3	38.9	36.2
Edwardsville......................	4.5	8,639	63.2	50.2	2.4	10.6	36.8	25.4	35.8	24.7
Elgin	27.4	33,486	70.8	51.6	6.4	12.8	29.2	24.6	40.9	25.8
Elk Grove Village village	17.1	13,531	69.8	56.8	3.1	9.8	30.2	26.9	33.1	32.2
Elmhurst	11.2	15,531	72.5	62.8	2.0	7.7	27.5	24.5	38.4	34.5
Elmwood Park village.........	24.3	9,438	65.1	43.9	6.3	14.9	34.9	29.9	29.7	39.8
Evanston..........................	16.7	27,419	53.9	41.6	3.1	9.2	46.1	38.4	26.3	28.7
Freeport..........................	2.2	10,568	58.1	40.0	2.1	16.0	41.9	35.7	28.2	35.7
Galesburg........................	1.9	13,171	58.0	41.2	5.3	11.5	42.0	37.7	30.7	36.3
Geneva............................	5.0	8,034	81.7	69.6	2.9	9.1	18.3	15.0	46.1	23.9
Glendale Heights village.....	35.9	11,751	70.9	53.3	4.6	13.0	29.1	23.4	40.2	21.5
Glen Ellyn village...............	10.6	10,009	69.9	59.2	3.0	7.7	30.1	28.2	38.3	32.7
Glenview village................	21.1	16,766	76.0	64.5	3.1	8.3	24.0	23.0	38.5	40.2
Granite	2.1	12,478	65.0	43.9	5.2	15.9	35.0	30.6	32.0	32.4
Grayslake village	10.3	7,448	71.2	58.9	3.1	9.3	28.8	23.3	45.9	18.8
Gurnee village...................	16.8	11,054	74.9	61.6	3.4	10.0	25.1	22.7	44.1	22.8
Hanover Park village..........	37.1	11,880	81.4	64.3	7.7	9.4	18.6	15.7	53.4	18.2
Harvey............................	8.1	9,033	75.2	33.6	9.3	32.3	24.8	23.9	53.4	28.9
Highland Park	12.9	10,542	76.2	67.8	1.8	6.6	23.8	21.2	35.1	41.1
Hoffman Estates village......	26.0	18,541	74.4	61.1	4.4	8.9	25.6	21.8	42.0	24.4
Homer Glen village	10.7	7,487	87.9	79.5	2.8	5.6	12.1	9.1	42.1	28.8
Huntley village	12.6	8,082	74.6	69.3	1.1	4.2	25.4	21.3	29.6	54.8
Joliet..............................	14.8	44,188	72.2	53.9	5.0	13.2	27.8	22.6	46.7	24.2
Kankakee.........................	9.5	9,690	64.3	37.5	5.2	21.7	35.7	30.1	42.3	28.6
Lake Forest	7.2	6,749	77.5	71.7	2.3	3.6	22.5	21.1	35.3	43.7
Lake in the Hills village.......	16.8	9,473	80.9	68.1	4.4	8.4	19.1	15.9	54.0	12.6
Lake Zurich village.............	14.5	6,488	80.0	71.6	2.0	6.4	20.0	16.2	48.1	21.7
Lansing village	6.4	10,948	65.2	47.3	4.1	13.8	34.8	31.6	33.1	32.7
Libertyville village..............	9.5	7,400	72.9	63.0	2.9	7.1	27.1	23.4	40.8	32.1

Table A-4. Cities — Who: Age, Race/Ethnicity, and Household Structure, 2005–2007—*Continued*

STATE Place code	STATE City ACS table number:	Total population B01003	Percent change 2005–2007 Population estimates	Population by age (percent)						Median age B01002	Race alone or in combination (percent)				
				Under 5 years B01001	5 to 17 years B01001	18 to 24 years B01001	25 to 44 years B01001	45 to 64 years B01001	65 years and over B01001		White B02008	Black B02009	Asian Hawaiian or Pacific Islander B02011 + B02012	Amer. Indian, Alaska Native, or some other race B02010 + B02013	Percent Hispanic or Latino C03002
		1	2	3	4	5	6	7	8	9	10	11	12	13	14
	Illinois—Cont.														
17 43939	Lisle village........................	21,961	-0.7	4.2	17.0	12.5	28.5	29.3	8.5	36.2	84.7	3.9	10.7	2.3	4.7
17 44225	Lockport............................	22,401	11.3	7.3	17.6	11.4	32.8	21.7	9.2	32.7	94.9	1.2	1.1	3.5	7.2
17 44407	Lombard village	42,675	0.0	6.7	15.7	8.4	29.0	25.8	14.4	38.6	84.1	5.8	9.2	1.6	6.7
17 45031	Loves Park.........................	25,104	5.7	8.2	15.1	9.2	32.3	24.5	10.8	35.3	89.0	5.9	3.9	1.8	7.5
17 45694	McHenry............................	25,510	6.9	8.3	18.9	8.0	32.2	22.0	10.5	33.6	87.4	-	1.8	10.6	-
17 45726	Machesney Park village	22,248	4.8	7.1	17.8	9.2	29.5	25.1	11.4	36.7	96.2	1.2	2.6	-	2.2
17 47774	Maywood village................	25,006	-1.9	5.8	20.8	9.8	30.0	22.1	11.5	33.8	12.4	77.0	-	10.9	-
17 48242	Melrose Park village	23,746	-2.1	10.2	19.8	12.3	28.1	19.2	10.4	30.0	48.6	5.9	2.0	43.5	-
17 49867	Moline...............................	43,791	0.6	6.1	17.2	9.2	28.2	24.1	15.3	35.9	86.2	4.6	3.3	8.0	12.5
17 50647	Morton Grove village	22,547	1.5	5.0	15.5	7.1	23.2	28.6	20.6	44.5	69.7	-	28.9	3.7	5.3
17 51089	Mount Prospect village.......	55,316	-1.3	6.0	16.0	7.9	27.5	27.4	15.3	40.5	76.7	2.7	10.1	11.2	15.5
17 51349	Mundelein village...............	32,189	0.9	8.3	18.5	8.7	33.0	24.2	7.2	33.2	74.9	2.0	8.6	16.6	29.8
17 51622	Naperville...........................	143,956	1.5	6.6	23.9	8.7	28.1	26.0	6.6	34.8	82.0	4.1	13.0	2.3	5.4
17 52584	New Lenox village..............	24,437	6.3	8.1	23.6	9.1	29.3	22.8	7.1	34.1	96.8	-	-	1.6	-
17 53000	Niles village........................	30,378	-1.6	3.1	13.2	7.2	22.5	30.3	23.8	48.0	79.6	2.0	16.3	2.6	9.1
17 53234	Normal town.......................	50,398	3.1	5.3	11.9	36.8	22.9	15.3	7.7	23.5	88.6	8.9	2.8	1.1	3.2
17 53481	Northbrook village..............	34,080	-0.5	5.8	19.0	6.3	17.6	32.1	19.2	45.9	89.8	0.3	9.6	0.5	1.8
17 53559	North Chicago	28,559	-2.7	8.1	16.2	29.0	28.8	11.7	6.2	23.5	54.5	32.6	4.0	12.0	29.3
17 54638	Oak Forest	28,841	-0.7	7.4	18.8.	8.5	26.8	28.9	9.6	36.8	92.5	1.4	2.2	5.3	10.5
17 54820	Oak Lawn village................	54,526	-1.0	5.2	15.2	9.5	22.5	28.1	19.5	43.6	88.7	3.3	1.9	6.5	-
17 54885	Oak Park village	53,013	-1.6	7.7	17.0	6.3	29.0	30.1	9.8	39.1	69.4	22.9	6.5	3.2	6.1
17 55249	O'Fallon	27,348	5.5	7.4	20.9	8.4	30.7	24.0	8.7	34.8	83.3	15.1	3.8	-	2.1
17 56640	Orland Park village	59,144	0.5	4.3	18.9	7.9	21.0	30.3	17.5	43.8	91.7	0.7	4.3	4.5	7.0
17 56887	Oswego village	23,191	24.6	10.9	22.5	8.5	32.4	20.2	5.5	30.3	88.6	5.3	2.4	5.2	9.3
17 57225	Palatine village...................	68,172	0.0	7.0	18.2	8.3	31.1	25.0	10.5	36.5	81.5	3.8	11.7	5.2	16.2
17 57732	Park Forest village.............	24,450	-1.2	6.3	19.4	7.1	28.0	27.2	12.0	36.6	44.5	53.3	0.9	3.4	4.5
17 57875	Park Ridge	37,293	-0.3	6.1	19.2	6.2	20.0	31.0	17.5	44.2	92.9	-	5.7	2.2	-
17 58447	Pekin	32,268	0.7	6.5	16.0	8.1	29.5	23.7	16.2	37.0	95.2	2.5	1.4	1.7	1.9
17 59000	Peoria	111,351	0.7	7.9	17.6	12.5	25.5	23.2	13.3	33.7	68.4	27.6	4.0	2.3	2.9
17 60287	Plainfield village	31,680	25.1	11.0	22.4	7.2	36.4	18.2	4.8	31.8	85.7	4.1	7.5	4.6	8.0
17 62367	Quincy................................	40,360	0.6	5.9	16.6	11.9	25.0	22.5	18.2	37.3	94.2	5.7	1.1	1.7	1.1
17 65000	Rockford............................	147,794	2.3	7.4	18.4	9.0	28.8	22.4	14.0	35.0	72.7	20.6	2.2	6.5	13.9
17 65078	Rock Island	37,332	-0.4	5.8	17.1	12.6	24.1	24.0	16.4	38.0	75.4	21.7	0.9	4.5	8.5
17 65338	Rolling Meadows	23,303	-1.2	7.6	16.7	9.8	29.8	24.5	11.7	35.3	78.9	-	8.2	11.0	21.3
17 65442	Romeoville village	38,388	2.0	9.9	20.9	10.9	36.2	15.9	6.2	28.9	71.4	9.9	4.7	16.4	27.4
17 65806	Roselle village	24,489	-0.2	6.3	19.2	9.3	29.4	27.9	7.9	37.1	88.9	-	9.2	2.2	-
17 66040	Round Lake Beach village...	28,845	0.1	9.0	23.2	9.4	35.5	18.0	4.8	29.2	77.2	4.3	4.5	14.9	45.0
17 66703	St. Charles	34,961	1.4	7.3	18.9	9.2	26.6	28.3	9.7	36.0	92.0	2.2	2.8	3.5	-
17 68003	Schaumburg village............	74,271	-0.8	5.4	15.7	9.3	32.5	26.6	10.5	37.4	75.4	4.1	17.4	4.7	8.0
17 70122	Skokie village	67,330	3.1	5.6	17.7	9.3	22.4	29.4	15.6	41.7	67.3	7.5	23.4	3.1	6.9
17 70720	South Elgin village..............	22,517	1.9	11.6	21.3	6.9	36.4	17.5	6.3	31.9	88.7	1.9	7.3	4.0	-
17 70850	South Holland village	25,008	-1.4	8.0	21.1	6.6	24.6	25.2	14.4	38.7	22.0	75.0	0.8	2.9	4.5
17 72000	Springfield	110,957	1.2	7.1	16.6	9.7	27.8	25.2	13.7	36.7	80.5	18.4	2.5	1.9	1.7
17 73157	Streamwood village	41,258	0.1	9.9	17.0	7.7	33.6	24.0	7.8	34.0	75.7	2.5	13.0	12.6	30.9
17 75484	Tinley Park village	59,670	2.8	6.3	19.2	7.7	25.9	28.7	12.2	39.6	88.7	4.5	3.7	4.3	6.7
17 77005	Urbana	37,096	1.4	4.2	9.5	37.2	25.8	13.9	9.4	24.7	66.5	15.7	17.5	2.2	4.1
17 77694	Vernon Hills village............	25,499	1.8	9.1	19.3	8.6	29.8	26.0	7.2	35.3	76.0	3.4	16.2	5.2	11.0
17 77993	Villa Park village................	21,339	-1.2	5.4	17.3	9.8	30.3	26.5	10.7	37.9	83.8	4.2	4.4	8.4	13.6
17 79293	Waukegan	85,072	0.7	8.4	20.3	10.2	32.5	20.7	7.9	30.6	60.9	19.3	4.1	17.4	52.7
17 80060	West Chicago	26,654	0.1	10.3	19.9	12.2	31.1	20.2	6.3	30.8	78.3	1.0	8.1	14.9	-
17 80645	Westmont village................	22,919	0.4	5.5	16.6	8.5	26.6	26.9	15.9	39.7	73.5	8.8	14.3	5.8	7.7
17 81048	Wheaton	53,784	-0.4	5.9	17.7	11.7	24.1	28.4	12.2	38.4	91.2	3.6	4.8	1.9	4.5
17 81087	Wheeling village	35,718	-1.3	6.5	16.3	9.2	32.7	24.3	11.1	35.7	74.8	2.7	10.2	14.3	25.4
17 82075	Wilmette village	27,791	-1.2	5.8	23.6	4.9	18.1	31.9	15.6	43.7	90.0	0.8	9.4	-	1.1
17 83245	Woodridge village..............	33,661	0.6	6.9	16.6	10.7	30.3	28.5	7.0	37.0	72.9	11.4	12.9	4.0	11.3
17 83349	Woodstock	21,842	6.0	9.0	17.7	8.8	30.6	23.1	10.8	33.2	86.4	3.0	1.2	10.5	19.6
17 84220	Zion	24,399	4.5	8.4	24.0	10.9	28.4	19.9	8.4	29.4	61.6	28.4	2.9	10.7	27.9
18 00000	**Indiana**	6,301,687	1.4	6.9	18.2	9.7	27.6	25.2	12.4	36.3	87.2	9.4	1.6	3.4	4.7
18 01468	Anderson............................	57,149	-0.1	6.8	15.2	11.1	27.5	22.8	16.6	37.6	81.3	17.4	0.4	2.5	-
18 05860	Bloomington.......................	74,039	1.2	4.2	8.1	41.3	25.1	13.1	8.2	23.3	87.3	5.5	8.0	1.9	3.1
18 10342	Carmel................................	64,490	4.9	6.1	22.3	8.4	24.9	28.0	10.3	37.8	89.4	3.3	7.5	1.5	2.5
18 12934	Clarksville town	22,679	2.7	6.1	17.1	9.2	27.9	24.8	14.9	38.2	87.3	8.4	-	4.4	-
18 14734	Columbus...........................	40,879	1.3	7.0	17.5	7.2	27.2	26.0	15.1	38.6	91.7	3.5	4.9	1.7	3.4
18 16138	Crown Point	21,287	6.5	5.3	16.2	8.3	24.5	29.2	16.5	41.7	91.8	5.0	3.2	1.3	3.5
18 19486	East Chicago	30,475	-1.5	8.2	21.4	9.6	26.2	22.1	12.6	31.6	21.4	41.5	-	39.0	-
18 20728	Elkhart...............................	52,361	1.3	9.6	18.6	9.3	32.7	20.2	9.6	30.4	71.3	16.6	1.4	13.8	23.7
18 22000	Evansville...........................	113,627	0.3	7.0	16.1	11.2	26.6	24.3	14.7	36.6	86.3	12.7	1.4	1.6	1.5
18 23278	Fishers town	63,420	15.5	10.1	23.3	6.8	37.5	18.0	4.2	31.0	87.1	7.8	4.5	1.4	3.1
18 25000	Fort Wayne	249,830	1.4	7.9	18.4	9.5	27.8	24.4	12.0	35.1	78.9	16.7	3.0	4.7	6.8
18 25450	Franklin..............................	21,972	4.7	7.0	18.2	12.0	28.9	21.1	12.8	33.1	98.6	0.8	-	0.8	-
18 27000	Gary...................................	86,723	-1.3	8.5	21.2	8.4	23.4	25.0	13.6	35.2	12.1	86.5	0.4	4.1	4.8
18 28386	Goshen...............................	31,263	3.3	9.7	15.7	9.4	30.9	19.1	15.2	32.6	81.8	2.3	3.4	14.3	23.9
18 28800	Granger CDP.......................	30,539	-	6.9	24.1	5.6	22.8	30.7	9.9	39.4	93.9	2.0	3.9	1.0	1.5
18 29898	Greenwood	46,864	9.9	8.2	18.7	8.9	32.2	20.7	11.4	32.1	95.0	-	2.7	2.7	3.6

STATE City	Percent foreign born	Total households	Household type (percent)							Percent of households with people under 18 years	Percent of households with people 60 years and over
			Family households				Nonfamily households				
			Total family households	Married-couple families	Male householder families	Female householder families	Total nonfamily households	One-person households			
ACS table number:	C05002	B11001	B11001	B11001	B11001	B11001	B11001	B11001		C11005	B11006
	15	16	17	18	19	20	21	22		23	24
Illinois—Cont.											
Lisle village	17.0	9,087	57.2	48.9	2.9	5.4	42.8	32.0		28.6	22.1
Lockport	7.1	7,704	76.3	61.8	2.7	11.8	23.7	20.0		42.9	22.7
Lombard village	12.8	17,204	64.2	52.6	2.4	9.2	35.8	32.0		31.3	31.7
Loves Park	8.6	9,813	67.1	51.8	5.1	10.2	32.9	28.1		34.5	26.6
McHenry	15.1	9,213	68.7	53.3	4.2	11.2	31.3	25.6		40.5	26.3
Machesney Park village	2.8	8,004	77.9	58.7	4.2	15.0	22.1	19.1		37.6	28.5
Maywood village	8.8	7,628	70.1	39.4	7.0	23.7	29.9	25.4		39.2	38.5
Melrose Park village	41.6	7,723	73.9	49.1	7.9	17.0	26.1	23.2		44.5	29.9
Moline	9.0	18,857	62.9	49.1	2.8	11.0	37.1	32.3		30.0	32.0
Morton Grove village	35.1	8,286	73.0	64.3	2.2	6.6	27.0	23.7		32.3	49.6
Mount Prospect village	30.7	20,956	71.3	58.6	4.7	8.0	28.7	23.6		31.5	35.7
Mundelein village	29.7	9,891	76.3	62.2	3.7	10.4	23.7	17.9		45.7	20.1
Naperville	16.0	47,975	75.5	66.7	2.0	6.7	24.5	20.3		46.8	19.8
New Lenox village	5.2	7,345	85.4	72.6	3.6	9.2	14.6	12.8		50.3	23.0
Niles village	40.4	11,927	65.2	53.0	4.0	8.2	34.8	31.4		23.4	50.3
Normal town	3.4	17,352	53.8	40.6	3.0	10.2	46.2	28.5		27.8	18.5
Northbrook village	15.1	12,413	77.4	70.1	0.9	6.5	22.6	19.8		35.5	44.7
North Chicago	19.3	6,881	69.9	41.5	10.2	18.3	30.1	23.9		48.1	20.5
Oak Forest	8.2	10,016	74.8	60.6	2.4	11.8	25.2	22.7		39.2	28.2
Oak Lawn village	16.8	22,199	61.8	46.0	4.6	11.1	38.2	34.7		26.7	41.4
Oak Park village	10.4	22,120	62.0	47.4	2.7	12.0	38.0	34.1		34.1	25.7
O'Fallon	3.7	10,424	69.6	58.1	1.5	10.0	30.4	26.5		38.5	24.5
Orland Park village	12.9	21,939	72.4	62.2	2.7	7.6	27.6	25.8		31.0	43.3
Oswego village	6.6	7,323	81.3	71.5	1.9	7.8	18.7	16.0		55.0	17.2
Palatine village	24.4	26,542	64.1	50.1	5.0	9.0	35.9	31.6		33.7	25.9
Park Forest village	3.5	9,558	61.2	36.1	4.5	20.6	38.8	36.0		34.9	32.5
Park Ridge	15.7	13,884	70.7	61.0	3.0	6.8	29.3	26.2		34.2	41.6
Pekin	2.1	13,436	62.3	45.5	3.7	13.1	37.7	32.1		29.8	31.9
Peoria	5.0	46,255	56.4	37.5	3.3	15.7	43.6	36.9		30.3	29.7
Plainfield village	9.9	9,372	85.0	70.2	1.7	5.1	15.0	12.8		54.1	15.3
Quincy	0.8	17,125	58.2	42.3	3.3	12.6	41.8	35.4		29.7	35.2
Rockford	11.2	57,032	61.1	40.7	4.8	15.7	38.9	33.8		32.9	31.1
Rock Island	3.5	15,077	56.9	41.0	3.3	12.6	43.1	38.5		25.9	35.5
Rolling Meadows	22.3	8,750	66.4	52.0	3.8	10.7	33.6	28.3		32.8	30.3
Romeoville village	16.0	11,904	79.1	62.8	5.2	11.2	20.9	17.5		52.0	20.4
Roselle village	18.8	8,836	73.0	60.7	4.9	7.4	27.0	21.3		38.9	22.1
Round Lake Beach village	25.8	8,160	77.6	57.6	6.9	13.1	22.4	17.6		51.7	18.0
St. Charles	8.1	13,082	70.2	59.1	2.4	8.7	29.8	25.8		36.8	26.6
Schaumburg village	24.4	31,630	59.2	45.6	2.0	11.6	40.8	34.2		27.8	24.7
Skokie village	40.0	23,228	75.6	60.4	4.0	11.3	24.4	22.8		36.5	40.0
South Elgin village	11.8	7,048	79.0	63.8	7.0	8.2	21.0	16.7		54.1	12.7
South Holland village	6.0	7,845	76.1	54.1	4.1	18.0	23.9	21.4		43.8	39.8
Springfield	3.0	49,391	56.4	38.4	4.3	13.8	43.6	36.9		30.3	28.7
Streamwood village	29.7	13,155	76.6	63.3	4.8	8.5	23.4	19.6		41.8	23.4
Tinley Park village	8.8	21,667	70.5	58.7	3.9	7.9	29.5	25.9		35.2	32.2
Urbana	17.4	14,417	42.1	30.7	3.0	8.3	57.9	39.9		18.7	19.8
Vernon Hills village	28.8	8,989	75.1	62.2	3.4	9.5	24.9	21.0		43.2	20.4
Villa Park village	15.1	8,000	68.0	55.6	4.3	8.1	32.0	27.5		35.4	28.3
Waukegan	33.2	27,692	67.5	44.2	6.5	16.8	32.5	27.9		43.3	22.7
West Chicago	35.9	7,281	78.5	68.2	4.5	5.7	21.5	14.1		53.1	20.0
Westmont village	20.2	9,267	57.8	46.2	2.5	9.1	42.2	36.8		29.4	30.6
Wheaton	9.0	18,930	69.8	58.5	4.2	7.1	30.2	26.6		34.8	29.3
Wheeling village	39.4	14,407	60.6	46.9	3.6	10.1	39.4	35.4		30.5	27.8
Wilmette village	13.2	10,056	76.1	68.6	1.8	5.8	23.9	22.7		41.3	40.3
Woodridge village	20.3	12,569	71.3	55.2	4.4	11.7	28.7	23.2		34.3	22.0
Woodstock	15.4	8,136	68.9	53.0	3.5	12.4	31.1	25.2		37.1	25.2
Zion	15.3	7,928	70.2	50.5	6.1	13.6	29.8	25.1		44.4	23.0
Indiana	4.1	2,447,887	67.5	51.6	4.4	11.5	32.5	27.0		34.5	29.5
Anderson	1.4	23,932	57.0	38.5	4.1	14.4	43.0	36.4		28.8	33.2
Bloomington	9.5	26,733	38.2	27.2	2.1	8.9	61.8	42.9		19.5	20.6
Carmel	8.8	22,934	76.3	66.4	3.3	6.6	23.7	19.7		42.0	26.4
Clarksville town	3.5	9,538	60.3	38.8	7.0	14.5	39.7	33.9		33.3	28.6
Columbus	7.2	16,303	66.3	50.9	4.9	10.5	33.7	28.3		33.7	30.1
Crown Point	6.4	8,604	59.9	49.7	2.4	7.8	40.1	34.8		27.6	35.8
East Chicago	14.0	11,148	70.1	29.7	8.9	31.5	29.9	26.7		41.5	32.5
Elkhart	16.6	20,032	60.6	39.1	6.1	15.4	39.4	31.2		37.3	25.5
Evansville	2.2	49,733	56.8	38.2	5.4	13.2	43.2	37.3		29.4	31.1
Fishers town	6.1	22,188	72.1	61.2	3.1	7.8	27.9	20.8		49.1	12.5
Fort Wayne	6.0	101,243	62.3	44.6	4.1	13.6	37.7	31.0		33.8	26.4
Franklin	1.5	8,432	69.0	51.3	5.7	12.0	31.0	26.7		35.5	28.7
Gary	1.1	33,637	62.8	27.5	5.2	30.1	37.2	32.0		35.7	35.4
Goshen	18.0	11,562	67.5	49.0	7.9	10.6	32.5	26.0		37.6	31.9
Granger CDP	4.9	10,285	85.8	77.7	2.0	6.1	14.2	12.4		43.0	27.7
Greenwood	4.7	18,941	66.7	52.0	4.2	10.5	33.3	25.5		38.7	25.3

Table A-4. Cities — Who: Age, Race/Ethnicity, and Household Structure, 2005–2007—Continued

STATE Place code	STATE / City	Total population	Percent change 2005–2007	Population by age (percent)						Median age	Race alone or in combination (percent)				Percent Hispanic or Latino
				Under 5 years	5 to 17 years	18 to 24 years	25 to 44 years	45 to 64 years	65 years and over		White	Black	Asian Hawaiian or Pacific Islander	Amer. Indian, Alaska Native, or some other race	
	ACS table number:	B01003	Population estimates	B01001	B01001	B01001	B01001	B01001	B01001	B01002	B02008	B02009	B02011 + B02012	B02010 + B02013	C03002
		1	2	3	4	5	6	7	8	9	10	11	12	13	14
	Indiana—Cont.														
18 31000	Hammond	77,197	-1.6	8.4	19.2	10.5	27.5	22.8	11.7	33.8	56.4	21.5	1.0	24.0	29.0
18 33466	Highland town	23,954	-1.0	5.1	15.9	8.8	25.6	28.2	16.4	42.2	91.1	-	1.9	7.0	-
18 34114	Hobart	27,929	1.4	6.6	16.5	6.5	26.3	28.7	15.4	40.1	88.7	8.1	0.9	3.3	-
18 36003	Indianapolis (balance)	790,815	0.8	8.3	18.3	8.3	30.6	23.8	10.7	35.1	68.3	27.2	2.1	4.8	6.6
18 38358	Jeffersonville	26,328	3.7	6.0	14.5	7.6	30.4	27.8	13.8	38.9	84.2	13.6	-	2.9	1.8
18 40392	Kokomo	46,235	-0.7	7.1	17.8	8.1	28.0	24.4	14.6	36.8	87.2	11.1	1.8	1.3	2.2
18 40788	Lafayette	63,486	3.3	8.5	15.8	11.9	32.2	20.3	11.2	31.5	89.4	5.9	1.7	4.3	11.6
18 42246	La Porte	21,304	1.1	7.1	15.4	9.8	28.6	22.5	16.6	38.2	93.7	4.7	-	3.4	-
18 42426	Lawrence	42,694	3.6	8.4	21.1	7.1	32.0	22.7	8.8	33.8	71.7	23.2	2.8	4.6	6.9
18 46908	Marion	28,837	-1.7	6.2	16.0	12.3	24.7	24.6	16.2	35.8	81.7	17.5	0.2	2.5	3.7
18 48528	Merrillville town	32,652	3.1	5.7	16.7	7.5	29.1	26.6	14.5	38.7	53.0	42.1	1.1	4.8	9.2
18 48798	Michigan	31,553	-0.8	7.0	16.6	8.9	29.2	24.3	14.0	35.8	70.9	27.7	0.5	3.6	3.7
18 49932	Mishawaka	47,770	2.4	8.9	15.8	11.0	29.5	22.2	12.5	33.4	88.6	9.3	2.0	2.5	2.7
18 51876	Muncie	63,808	-1.2	4.7	12.9	25.6	23.4	20.0	13.5	29.3	85.8	13.1	1.2	2.0	1.6
18 51912	Munster town	24,223	0.0	3.8	21.7	7.6	20.0	29.7	17.3	43.3	86.8	2.0	7.0	5.4	1.6
18 52326	New Albany	34,725	1.0	6.5	15.8	9.5	25.7	27.5	15.1	38.9	90.3	9.8	0.8	0.8	-
18 54180	Noblesville	43,308	7.0	9.2	20.6	6.7	33.3	22.2	8.0	32.0	94.1	2.8	0.8	4.1	3.3
18 60246	Plainfield town	22,130	9.4	5.3	16.2	9.7	35.7	23.0	10.1	34.8	92.3	5.6	0.6	1.8	-
18 61092	Portage	36,118	3.5	6.9	19.0	9.9	27.8	25.8	10.6	34.5	87.9	7.1	1.2	5.1	11.2
18 64260	Richmond	35,359	-1.0	7.0	15.8	10.0	26.1	24.7	16.4	38.2	87.8	10.8	1.3	2.5	2.9
18 68220	Schererville town	29,000	2.4	7.0	16.6	7.4	27.0	30.4	11.6	40.3	90.8	4.7	1.7	3.5	-
18 71000	South Bend	98,516	-0.6	7.8	18.9	10.2	26.4	23.1	13.7	34.6	65.9	27.4	1.6	8.6	10.8
18 75428	Terre Haute	57,585	0.8	6.4	15.1	19.2	25.0	20.8	13.5	32.0	88.2	10.8	1.4	1.2	1.8
18 78326	Valparaiso	29,744	2.4	4.5	15.1	19.6	26.3	22.1	12.4	32.0	95.6	2.4	1.6	1.5	5.4
18 82700	Westfield town	28,773	7.6	9.2	23.3	7.9	33.9	20.5	5.1	32.1	92.4	1.9	4.2	1.6	3.5
18 82862	West Lafayette	27,664	4.5	2.9	8.0	50.8	19.5	10.5	8.4	22.5	81.0	3.3	16.0	0.5	2.2
19 00000	**Iowa**	2,972,066	1.1	6.5	17.4	10.4	25.4	25.6	14.7	37.9	94.1	2.9	1.8	2.5	3.8
19 01855	Ames	54,181	4.0	5.3	8.5	38.6	24.9	14.8	7.8	23.9	86.8	3.4	9.5	1.3	2.0
19 02305	Ankeny	39,490	12.6	10.9	19.8	7.6	35.2	19.2	7.3	31.3	98.0	1.5	0.8	1.1	1.7
19 06355	Bettendorf	32,923	2.3	5.8	20.5	7.4	23.2	29.3	13.7	40.3	96.6	1.8	2.0	1.6	2.7
19 09550	Burlington	25,459	0.2	7.1	17.4	8.7	24.4	25.9	16.5	39.7	93.8	6.6	-	1.8	-
19 11755	Cedar Falls	38,255	2.6	5.4	12.3	31.1	19.1	20.0	12.1	25.7	95.0	3.1	2.4	0.8	0.9
19 12000	Cedar Rapids	124,515	1.9	6.9	17.7	9.9	29.1	23.5	12.9	35.6	91.6	5.8	2.8	1.8	2.7
19 14430	Clinton	27,116	-0.9	5.8	17.3	11.0	23.3	26.2	16.4	39.8	95.6	4.8	1.1	3.1	1.8
19 16860	Council Bluffs	59,232	0.5	7.6	17.7	9.4	27.8	23.9	13.6	35.7	94.7	2.0	1.2	3.7	5.4
19 19000	Davenport	97,090	0.7	7.5	17.5	11.1	27.0	24.8	12.1	35.5	83.2	11.6	2.7	4.7	6.3
19 21000	Des Moines	197,039	0.9	7.9	17.4	8.9	29.8	24.3	11.7	35.4	82.2	9.5	4.2	6.5	10.2
19 22395	Dubuque	56,853	-0.1	6.2	15.4	13.0	24.3	24.4	16.7	38.4	96.0	2.8	1.1	1.3	2.0
19 28515	Fort Dodge	25,351	-0.1	6.5	16.7	10.0	25.8	24.3	16.7	36.8	93.2	6.2	1.4	1.6	3.5
19 38595	Iowa	65,219	1.7	4.9	11.5	32.9	25.7	17.6	7.5	25.3	87.4	4.8	6.4	2.6	3.2
19 49485	Marion	30,073	5.7	7.7	18.3	7.1	28.9	26.0	11.9	37.1	95.5	2.5	1.8	1.5	1.3
19 49755	Marshalltown	26,619	0.2	8.3	16.6	9.7	23.7	23.8	17.9	37.9	88.5	2.8	1.7	8.5	17.7
19 50160	Mason	27,867	-1.1	6.5	15.2	10.2	25.0	25.0	18.1	39.6	95.6	2.9	-	2.4	-
19 55110	Muscatine	22,009	0.2	7.3	19.2	9.3	26.6	25.7	11.9	35.6	94.0	2.1	0.8	4.9	13.9
19 60465	Ottumwa	24,166	-0.7	6.7	16.2	10.7	25.0	24.3	17.1	38.5	90.9	1.8	1.4	6.4	8.7
19 73335	Sioux	82,385	0.4	7.5	19.0	10.6	25.8	24.2	12.9	35.4	86.7	3.9	2.9	8.9	13.3
19 79950	Urbandale	36,032	6.7	7.0	20.3	6.3	28.1	27.4	11.0	38.1	92.5	3.2	5.1	0.3	1.5
19 82425	Waterloo	66,406	-0.6	7.5	17.0	9.3	27.0	25.0	14.2	36.8	83.2	14.9	1.1	2.8	4.0
19 83910	West Des Moines	53,430	3.7	7.2	17.0	10.7	32.4	22.8	10.0	33.4	92.6	2.8	4.4	1.2	4.0
20 00000	**Kansas**	2,757,827	1.3	7.1	18.1	10.5	26.5	24.9	13.0	36.1	87.6	6.7	2.6	5.7	8.5
20 17800	Derby	22,152	7.0	7.6	25.5	6.5	27.0	24.2	9.1	33.8	93.4	4.6	2.9	2.4	5.4
20 18250	Dodge	26,678	0.6	10.2	22.7	10.2	29.1	18.2	9.5	29.3	77.7	1.9	2.3	19.6	53.6
20 21275	Emporia	26,271	0.0	6.7	15.1	22.1	25.3	20.5	10.3	29.4	87.9	4.8	3.2	8.5	24.2
20 25325	Garden	26,766	-0.9	9.8	20.4	13.1	26.6	22.3	7.9	30.7	79.6	1.9	4.1	15.5	42.9
20 31100	Hays	19,801	1.0	6.7	12.0	21.8	24.2	21.3	14.1	30.5	96.6	-	1.7	1.8	-
20 33625	Hutchinson	41,044	-0.4	6.3	15.5	10.8	26.4	24.3	16.6	38.1	92.2	4.8	0.9	6.6	8.0
20 36000	Kansas	141,791	-0.4	8.7	19.9	9.0	28.5	23.4	10.5	33.4	57.7	30.1	2.0	12.6	23.2
20 38900	Lawrence	89,968	1.3	5.1	12.5	27.5	29.0	17.8	8.0	27.1	85.9	6.3	5.2	5.0	4.2
20 39000	Leavenworth	34,702	0.5	6.5	18.6	9.8	32.0	23.6	9.5	35.1	76.8	19.1	2.5	5.5	6.1
20 39075	Leawood	32,559	2.9	5.7	21.7	5.9	18.5	33.4	14.8	43.6	94.5	1.8	3.5	0.7	-
20 39350	Lenexa	45,452	5.2	7.6	17.2	9.6	28.0	27.5	10.1	35.8	89.5	5.3	3.6	2.4	6.1
20 39825	Liberal	20,368	1.7	11.8	20.5	10.5	28.9	19.8	8.5	29.7	68.9	3.8	3.1	28.0	52.9
20 44250	Manhattan	51,497	4.5	5.4	10.1	36.6	25.5	14.6	7.8	24.1	89.5	6.5	4.7	2.9	4.4
20 52575	Olathe	114,931	6.0	8.5	21.4	9.6	32.7	22.0	5.7	32.0	86.9	6.8	4.4	4.2	8.1
20 53775	Overland Park	165,314	2.8	7.0	18.2	8.2	28.8	26.1	11.8	37.5	89.1	4.0	6.0	2.9	4.8
20 57575	Prairie Village	20,972	-0.1	5.5	13.4	7.2	26.8	28.7	18.3	43.3	98.2	1.6	0.5	0.7	1.6
20 62700	Salina	46,437	1.0	7.8	17.0	9.2	26.7	24.8	14.4	37.1	92.1	4.7	2.7	3.7	8.6
20 64500	Shawnee	59,657	4.1	7.8	19.8	8.1	30.0	25.8	8.5	35.7	88.4	7.3	3.4	3.8	6.2
20 71000	Topeka	121,184	0.7	7.9	16.5	9.5	27.3	24.7	14.2	36.1	78.5	13.8	1.6	9.5	11.0
20 79000	Wichita	356,564	1.8	7.8	18.6	9.8	28.0	24.1	11.7	34.5	76.3	12.9	5.1	9.5	11.9

STATE City	Percent foreign born	Total households	Household type (percent)						Percent of households with people under 18 years	Percent of households with people 60 years and over
			Family households				Nonfamily households			
			Total family households	Married-couple families	Male householder families	Female householder families	Total nonfamily households	One-person households		
ACS table number:	C05002	B11001	B11001	B11001	B11001	B11001	B11001	B11001	C11005	B11006
	15	16	17	18	19	20	21	22	23	24
Indiana—Cont.										
Hammond	11.9	28,994	66.4	40.4	6.7	19.3	33.6	29.4	36.9	27.8
Highland town	7.8	10,057	61.5	47.7	5.3	8.5	38.5	35.3	26.2	35.9
Hobart	2.7	11,072	66.6	51.3	5.6	9.6	33.4	27.8	30.3	35.5
Indianapolis (balance)	6.8	323,756	59.3	38.4	5.0	16.0	40.7	33.7	32.6	25.3
Jeffersonville	2.1	12,499	54.8	35.2	5.1	14.5	45.2	37.1	28.0	29.5
Kokomo	2.3	20,256	63.7	42.3	4.3	17.0	36.3	31.6	31.9	29.8
Lafayette	8.8	27,209	59.1	37.5	6.2	15.4	40.9	33.2	33.0	24.6
La Porte	7.9	8,841	62.1	45.9	4.8	11.3	37.9	31.8	31.7	34.2
Lawrence	4.8	16,594	68.1	51.1	3.8	13.2	31.9	26.5	41.7	21.7
Marion	1.7	12,019	59.4	38.3	4.7	16.5	40.6	35.7	28.8	34.1
Merrillville town	5.5	12,931	62.2	44.8	3.7	13.7	37.8	30.7	30.7	32.8
Michigan	2.7	12,182	62.3	35.4	5.3	21.6	37.7	32.5	32.6	32.7
Mishawaka	4.6	20,311	56.9	39.4	6.3	11.2	43.1	38.3	29.8	28.8
Muncie	2.5	26,427	51.5	32.9	4.8	13.8	48.5	35.8	23.8	29.5
Munster town	10.5	9,008	73.0	63.3	3.4	6.4	27.0	25.3	34.0	41.8
New Albany	1.9	15,099	59.9	38.2	4.6	17.1	40.1	34.5	30.5	32.9
Noblesville	4.2	15,765	77.2	63.4	3.5	10.3	22.8	17.5	42.8	21.9
Plainfield town	4.6	8,905	70.3	49.6	6.9	13.8	29.7	26.4	36.0	25.5
Portage	3.3	14,095	67.8	50.6	2.8	14.3	32.2	27.8	35.0	27.4
Richmond	2.9	15,031	59.4	40.3	7.0	12.0	40.6	34.7	30.2	35.3
Schererville town	10.9	11,198	68.3	55.2	4.1	8.9	31.7	25.7	31.4	28.4
South Bend	8.5	39,718	55.4	35.6	3.3	16.5	44.6	37.3	30.9	31.0
Terre Haute	2.0	22,507	54.5	37.0	3.4	14.1	45.5	36.7	28.4	31.3
Valparaiso	3.9	12,243	52.3	40.3	1.9	10.1	47.7	38.2	26.2	26.7
Westfield town	7.1	9,629	79.6	65.5	6.1	8.0	20.4	16.2	51.6	13.4
West Lafayette	19.1	10,928	33.8	27.8	1.4	4.7	66.2	37.0	15.2	18.4
Iowa	3.8	1,206,848	65.5	52.8	3.5	9.2	34.5	28.3	31.7	31.5
Ames	12.1	20,106	48.9	40.4	2.3	6.2	51.1	31.6	21.8	17.9
Ankeny	1.4	15,571	67.4	57.4	1.8	8.1	32.6	25.3	41.2	19.4
Bettendorf	2.3	13,307	68.7	57.2	2.5	9.0	31.3	28.0	32.9	30.5
Burlington	1.3	11,068	66.3	45.8	4.3	16.2	33.7	28.3	32.3	35.7
Cedar Falls	4.1	13,848	58.2	49.2	1.9	7.1	41.8	26.7	24.8	27.2
Cedar Rapids	3.3	53,704	57.9	43.8	3.4	10.7	42.1	32.7	31.0	27.3
Clinton	1.3	11,783	60.3	46.8	3.1	10.5	39.7	32.3	29.3	34.9
Council Bluffs	3.7	24,205	65.8	46.3	5.0	14.5	34.2	27.6	32.8	30.8
Davenport	4.8	39,066	60.2	42.1	4.1	14.1	39.8	32.4	30.2	28.5
Des Moines	9.4	82,567	60.0	42.3	4.8	12.9	40.0	33.7	31.7	27.2
Dubuque	2.2	23,651	61.5	47.8	3.1	10.5	38.5	31.9	29.1	32.1
Fort Dodge	2.2	10,664	62.5	42.5	8.3	11.7	37.5	32.5	32.8	35.4
Iowa	8.5	26,564	44.8	35.7	2.1	6.9	55.2	35.9	23.5	17.9
Marion	2.5	12,732	64.4	50.1	3.4	10.9	35.6	30.4	35.5	26.6
Marshalltown	10.6	10,411	62.4	47.8	3.1	11.5	37.6	29.2	35.0	33.0
Mason	1.3	11,962	59.6	46.8	2.9	9.8	40.4	33.6	28.7	33.3
Muscatine	4.0	8,875	63.6	48.4	4.0	11.2	36.4	29.8	34.5	30.1
Ottumwa	5.9	10,291	61.1	47.8	3.0	10.3	38.9	32.8	28.6	36.7
Sioux	8.8	31,388	64.0	46.4	5.5	12.1	36.0	29.0	31.5	30.4
Urbandale	7.5	14,275	69.7	61.0	1.9	6.8	30.3	26.2	37.1	27.6
Waterloo	6.9	28,072	62.0	44.2	4.4	13.4	38.0	31.6	31.6	31.2
West Des Moines	7.8	23,158	59.2	48.3	2.4	8.5	40.8	30.0	31.5	22.6
Kansas	6.0	1,083,868	66.8	52.8	3.9	10.1	33.2	27.9	34.3	29.5
Derby	1.4	7,490	80.9	67.3	4.6	9.0	19.1	17.2	49.3	23.4
Dodge	29.5	8,390	74.6	52.1	4.9	17.6	25.4	20.2	51.5	21.7
Emporia	14.6	10,672	59.5	40.1	5.1	14.3	40.5	29.9	32.5	23.8
Garden	21.4	8,566	70.3	52.1	5.5	12.7	29.7	23.8	43.4	27.1
Hays	1.3	8,419	57.9	45.9	4.8	7.2	42.1	33.2	26.1	27.8
Hutchinson	1.9	16,852	61.0	46.8	3.6	10.6	39.0	34.2	28.6	33.5
Kansas	13.4	53,730	64.2	41.1	5.8	17.3	35.8	30.5	36.9	27.3
Lawrence	8.3	34,951	50.2	35.8	3.4	11.0	49.8	34.3	26.8	20.1
Leavenworth	4.2	11,849	70.1	51.0	4.7	14.5	29.9	25.7	41.1	26.3
Leawood	6.0	11,718	80.6	74.6	1.5	4.5	19.4	18.2	39.7	34.0
Lenexa	7.3	17,189	70.0	58.4	3.1	8.6	30.0	24.5	33.9	22.5
Liberal	28.9	6,711	70.0	45.7	8.4	15.8	30.0	22.6	44.2	22.5
Manhattan	6.0	17,913	51.4	41.1	2.8	7.4	48.6	33.5	24.0	19.8
Olathe	8.9	40,008	74.5	60.9	3.5	10.1	25.5	20.0	46.0	17.0
Overland Park	8.2	66,420	63.7	52.2	4.1	7.4	36.3	29.5	33.4	26.4
Prairie Village	2.4	9,752	56.6	47.1	3.2	6.2	43.4	38.6	25.2	35.1
Salina	4.1	18,852	61.6	44.8	5.4	11.4	38.4	33.5	31.4	31.6
Shawnee	6.4	22,537	70.1	57.7	4.0	8.3	29.9	23.7	39.8	22.7
Topeka	4.9	53,100	58.3	39.7	4.2	14.4	41.7	36.2	30.8	31.4
Wichita	9.1	145,140	62.3	45.1	4.7	12.4	37.7	32.2	33.4	27.7

Table A-4. Cities — Who: Age, Race/Ethnicity, and Household Structure, 2005–2007—*Continued*

STATE Place code	STATE City	Total population	Percent change 2005–2007	Population by age (percent)						Median age	Race alone or in combination (percent)				Percent Hispanic or Latino
				Under 5 years	5 to 17 years	18 to 24 years	25 to 44 years	45 to 64 years	65 years and over		White	Black	Asian Hawaiian or Pacific Islander	Amer. Indian, Alaska Native, or some other race	
	ACS table number:	B01003	Population estimates	B01001	B01001	B01001	B01001	B01001	B01001	B01002	B02008	B02009	B02011 + B02012	B02010 + B02013	C03002
		1	2	3	4	5	6	7	8	9	10	11	12	13	14
21 00000	**Kentucky**	4,205,648	1.7	6.6	17.2	9.3	28.1	25.9	12.8	37.3	90.4	8.1	1.3	1.5	2.1
21 02368	Ashland	21,419	0.6	6.6	15.2	7.1	24.9	27.7	18.5	42.1	95.0	3.8	-	2.0	-
21 08902	Bowling Green	53,463	3.0	6.9	13.7	21.8	27.5	18.5	11.6	28.6	82.9	13.5	2.7	2.3	4.4
21 17848	Covington	41,880	0.7	7.8	17.5	9.3	30.1	24.8	10.5	34.9	87.5	12.3	0.4	1.7	2.5
21 24274	Elizabethtown	25,369	1.4	7.5	19.6	7.1	28.0	23.4	14.3	37.2	86.5	10.4	2.3	2.1	4.2
21 27982	Florence	28,877	4.2	7.2	16.3	10.9	30.2	22.7	12.8	35.0	92.0	5.6	2.5	2.4	3.4
21 28900	Frankfort	27,203	-0.9	7.6	14.5	11.4	28.0	25.5	12.9	37.4	82.2	16.1	1.5	1.6	2.6
21 30700	Georgetown	24,576	4.5	8.7	18.0	14.0	32.9	18.3	8.0	29.8	91.9	7.4	1.4	1.3	1.7
21 35866	Henderson	27,661	1.0	7.5	16.2	9.0	28.4	25.3	13.7	36.5	86.7	12.3	0.8	1.0	2.1
21 37918	Hopkinsville	35,899	1.0	7.7	21.3	8.9	26.3	22.7	13.0	35.3	64.4	32.6	0.7	3.4	2.2
21 39142	Independence	18,834	11.1	8.5	22.5	6.4	35.6	21.0	6.0	33.1	97.5	-	3.1		-
21 40222	Jeffersontown	26,031	0.1	8.0	15.4	7.2	28.3	29.4	11.7	36.8	86.4	11.6	2.2	2.4	4.2
21 46027	Lexington-Fayette urban county	275,726	2.5	6.8	15.0	12.7	31.0	24.0	10.4	34.7	80.8	14.6	3.4	2.9	5.2
21 48006	Louisville/Jefferson County (balance)	560,454	0.1	7.1	17.5	8.6	27.9	26.3	12.6	37.7	74.8	22.9	2.1	2.0	2.9
21 56136	Nicholasville	24,444	6.0	8.5	16.9	10.5	31.7	23.2	9.2	32.6	93.8	7.0	-	1.5	-
21 58620	Owensboro	53,408	0.4	7.7	16.5	9.1	25.2	24.9	16.6	37.9	90.5	8.6	0.6	2.0	2.0
21 58836	Paducah	24,967	0.2	7.8	13.5	10.9	23.2	26.2	18.4	41.0	74.5	25.9	0.8	1.7	1.2
21 63912	Radcliff	22,001	2.0	7.5	20.8	11.1	28.0	23.4	9.2	31.0	69.7	26.4	5.9	2.7	4.2
21 65226	Richmond	28,435	3.8	6.3	12.1	27.5	29.4	14.9	9.8	26.7	91.8	7.0	1.0	2.9	2.2
22 00000	**Louisiana**	4,344,053	-4.5	7.0	18.4	10.9	26.8	24.9	12.0	35.5	65.0	32.5	1.6	2.1	3.0
22 00975	Alexandria	47,200	0.5	8.0	19.9	9.0	25.0	23.5	14.5	35.3	41.3	57.0	1.6	1.0	1.0
22 05000	Baton Rouge	224,555	2.0	6.7	17.5	17.8	25.1	21.8	11.1	30.1	42.3	54.6	3.2	1.6	1.9
22 08920	Bossier	61,405	2.5	8.4	18.5	11.8	28.9	21.6	10.9	32.2	69.6	26.7	3.0	1.9	5.2
22 33245	Harvey CDP	22,387	-	7.6	19.0	9.8	24.6	29.3	9.7	35.7	50.1	42.6	5.0	4.1	5.1
22 36255	Houma	33,212	1.2	7.5	16.6	10.0	27.7	24.4	13.8	37.1	69.7	22.4	2.8	6.1	3.2
22 39475	Kenner	65,556	-6.1	7.0	16.7	10.3	27.2	26.8	12.0	37.1	66.4	26.6	3.8	5.1	15.0
22 40735	Lafayette	114,109	1.2	6.4	15.9	13.8	26.0	25.3	12.6	34.6	66.7	30.6	2.0	1.7	2.6
22 41155	Lake Charles	69,871	0.3	7.2	17.7	11.5	25.4	23.5	14.6	34.5	50.1	49.2	1.3	2.2	1.7
22 42030	Laplace CDP	31,491	-	7.6	21.6	10.0	26.7	26.0	8.1	34.4	57.0	39.4	1.3	3.4	5.7
22 48785	Marrero CDP	34,664	-	8.4	19.3	8.3	25.4	23.2	15.3	35.9	45.8	49.8	4.0	2.2	2.6
22 50115	Metairie CDP	129,469	-	5.2	14.4	8.8	24.5	29.2	17.9	42.9	85.5	9.6	3.5	3.0	10.4
22 51410	Monroe	47,611	-1.3	8.0	17.8	14.7	24.0	22.2	13.3	31.5	36.2	63.3	0.4	0.9	0.4
22 54035	New Iberia	33,123	2.3	9.0	20.3	9.2	26.5	22.5	12.4	32.6	52.9	42.0	4.3	1.8	2.0
22 55000	New Orleans	301,016	-47.3	6.1	15.2	12.8	26.0	27.6	12.3	38.2	32.3	64.1	3.0	1.8	4.0
22 58045	Opelousas	26,398	2.1	8.4	18.1	10.6	22.8	23.6	16.6	36.5	26.0	73.7	-	-	-
22 66655	Ruston	19,135	-0.4	5.9	13.2	33.5	21.7	14.5	11.2	23.9	56.2	42.2	-	1.6	-
22 70000	Shreveport	200,528	0.6	7.6	18.8	10.9	26.1	23.3	13.4	34.1	44.0	54.2	1.3	1.8	2.4
22 70805	Slidell	27,413	2.8	7.7	18.7	8.0	25.0	26.5	14.2	37.5	80.4	16.8	3.0	3.6	4.2
22 75180	Terrytown CDP	21,565	-	11.9	16.0	10.5	25.7	22.9	13.0	33.1	52.2	40.1	2.0	5.6	-
23 00000	**Maine**	1,314,780	0.4	5.4	16.2	8.7	26.0	29.2	14.7	41.1	97.0	1.3	1.2	2.1	1.1
23 02060	Auburn	22,754	-0.3	6.0	17.4	7.1	28.2	26.7	14.6	40.6	93.2	4.5	2.2	5.7	0.7
23 02795	Bangor	30,165	2.5	4.9	13.5	14.6	27.1	26.5	13.4	38.0	96.3	1.4	2.1	2.1	1.0
23 04860	Biddeford	24,059	-1.6	5.6	15.6	12.5	27.2	25.1	14.0	36.9	95.0	1.4	2.3	1.0	-
23 38740	Lewiston	37,807	-0.7	7.1	14.0	14.6	26.3	22.0	15.9	35.6	91.5	7.8	0.8	9.4	1.5
23 60545	Portland	62,986	-1.0	4.7	12.6	10.5	31.8	26.6	13.8	38.6	88.3	6.6	4.1	2.5	2.3
23 71900	South Portland	23,079	0.4	4.5	14.1	9.8	28.6	28.6	14.4	42.2	96.7	0.8	1.9	1.3	-
24 00000	**Maryland**	5,597,843	0.8	6.7	17.7	9.5	28.3	26.1	11.6	37.2	62.6	29.8	5.5	4.1	6.0
24 01600	Annapolis	35,409	0.7	7.3	12.8	11.4	31.5	24.6	12.3	35.3	66.9	23.5	2.2	8.7	11.5
24 01975	Arbutus CDP	20,079	-	5.8	15.2	12.7	28.8	21.4	16.1	37.0	77.7	13.2	8.0	1.7	1.5
24 02275	Arnold CDP	23,031	-	5.2	21.0	7.0	26.8	31.0	9.0	40.0	90.2	4.9	5.2	0.4	2.4
24 02825	Aspen Hill CDP	51,104	-	7.5	16.6	10.7	28.4	24.4	12.4	36.7	54.8	23.2	11.7	13.1	20.1
24 04000	Baltimore	639,493	-0.4	7.2	17.2	11.1	27.9	24.6	12.0	35.4	32.4	64.6	2.3	2.1	2.4
24 05825	Bel Air North CDP	28,179	-	7.4	20.6	6.7	28.0	27.9	9.5	36.6	93.1	6.2	1.6	0.4	1.2
24 05950	Bel Air South CDP	45,345	-	7.3	19.7	9.8	30.3	24.2	9.9	35.2	91.2	6.7	2.1	0.8	1.9
24 07125	Bethesda CDP	56,842	-	5.8	17.2	7.1	24.2	29.4	16.1	42.1	86.2	3.5	10.4	1.8	4.8
24 08775	Bowie	58,429	-1.4	7.3	19.6	7.0	29.3	26.4	10.4	38.1	50.7	45.4	3.7	3.0	4.3
24 13325	Carney CDP	29,012	-	5.1	15.0	10.3	25.8	24.8	19.0	40.2	83.3	10.0	5.4	2.1	4.0
24 14125	Catonsville CDP	42,649	-	5.6	12.9	13.8	25.2	25.2	17.3	40.1	77.8	17.8	3.3	2.3	2.0
24 16875	Chillum CDP	32,365	-	10.8	13.2	10.4	32.6	22.3	10.8	32.5	14.3	56.6	1.4	30.6	38.0
24 17900	Clinton CDP	28,830	-	6.3	22.4	5.8	28.4	28.2	9.0	38.3	16.7	81.3	2.0	-	4.2
24 18250	Cockeysville CDP	21,212	-	3.6	14.2	15.0	32.4	25.9	8.8	34.2	78.4	10.9	9.2	3.2	3.1
24 18750	College Park	25,901	-2.8	3.5	7.6	54.2	15.8	12.5	6.4	20.7	66.4	16.3	12.8	7.0	10.5
24 19125	Columbia CDP	91,398	-	7.3	16.2	8.9	30.8	27.5	9.3	36.7	65.4	25.0	9.6	4.3	7.0
24 20875	Crofton CDP	20,135	-	9.0	21.9	6.3	32.1	21.7	8.9	34.3	89.2	5.7	5.4	2.7	3.0
24 21325	Cumberland	21,579	-0.8	6.7	15.3	9.3	23.7	24.9	20.1	40.9	94.6	6.0	-	1.1	-
24 23975	Dundalk CDP	62,459	-	6.1	17.2	8.3	26.9	25.1	16.5	39.7	86.2	11.8	1.8	1.8	2.1
24 25150	Edgewood CDP	26,021	-	8.5	18.5	13.5	30.7	21.1	7.8	30.8	58.2	37.6	2.6	5.6	5.6
24 25575	Eldersburg CDP	30,635	-	6.8	20.5	7.7	29.0	26.2	9.8	38.4	93.1	4.8	2.3	1.5	1.7
24 25750	Elkridge CDP	23,473	-	9.1	18.1	6.9	38.2	22.2	5.5	33.7	75.9	10.7	14.0	1.6	2.9
24 26000	Ellicott CDP	64,257	-	5.7	22.1	8.2	23.5	29.2	11.3	39.9	72.3	11.7	16.3	1.7	1.1
24 26600	Essex CDP	39,643	-	8.5	17.8	8.5	29.2	24.2	11.8	35.2	69.9	27.1	1.7	3.3	3.2
24 27250	Fairland CDP	21,312	-	7.1	16.4	8.1	31.8	27.0	9.5	36.8	33.6	44.4	15.4	8.8	14.2

Table A-4. Cities — Who: Age, Race/Ethnicity, and Household Structure, 2005–2007—*Continued*

STATE City	Percent foreign born	Total households	Household type (percent)						Percent of households with people under 18 years	Percent of households with people 60 years and over
			Family households				Nonfamily households			
			Total family households	Married-couple families	Male householder families	Female householder families	Total nonfamily households	One-person households		
ACS table number:	C05002	B11001	B11001	B11001	B11001	B11001	B11001	B11001	C11005	B11006
	15	16	17	18	19	20	21	22	23	24
Kentucky	2.7	1,654,119	67.3	50.8	4.2	12.3	32.7	28.0	33.6	31.0
Ashland	1.1	9,359	62.2	45.1	3.2	13.9	37.8	32.8	27.5	37.8
Bowling Green	8.3	21,579	54.4	35.8	5.0	13.5	45.6	35.2	29.3	25.4
Covington	1.5	17,825	52.6	32.2	3.9	16.6	47.4	40.5	29.8	27.7
Elizabethtown	3.2	10,224	68.2	47.8	5.2	15.2	31.8	29.1	35.6	28.6
Florence	5.1	11,861	60.0	39.3	4.0	16.8	40.0	31.8	32.6	23.6
Frankfort	3.7	12,232	55.9	36.2	2.9	16.8	44.1	39.9	28.9	30.9
Georgetown	2.0	8,896	68.6	50.4	3.8	14.4	31.4	24.9	39.6	22.0
Henderson	1.6	11,901	62.7	43.6	3.1	16.0	37.3	35.2	30.1	30.9
Hopkinsville	1.7	13,036	67.1	40.7	3.7	22.7	32.9	30.8	38.1	34.4
Independence	3.0	6,660	79.4	65.5	4.7	9.2	20.6	17.3	50.4	18.4
Jeffersontown	4.2	11,026	62.4	46.4	4.4	11.6	37.6	34.7	30.5	27.7
Lexington-Fayette urban county	7.8	117,478	57.0	42.2	3.9	10.9	43.0	33.4	29.2	24.0
Louisville/Jefferson County (balance)	4.8	231,425	60.7	40.8	4.6	15.3	39.3	33.4	31.3	29.5
Nicholasville	0.9	9,599	70.8	48.0	7.2	15.6	29.2	23.4	38.7	23.6
Owensboro	1.5	24,541	61.5	40.8	3.8	16.9	38.5	34.3	32.0	34.9
Paducah	1.4	11,489	56.2	36.5	2.4	17.3	43.8	39.9	27.5	37.5
Radcliff	8.1	8,532	68.2	48.7	4.4	15.1	31.8	26.7	37.6	26.0
Richmond	2.9	11,008	51.7	32.8	4.2	14.7	48.3	37.9	26.3	22.9
Louisiana	3.1	1,605,203	67.9	46.8	4.7	16.5	32.1	27.2	35.8	31.0
Alexandria	2.6	18,066	62.0	35.6	4.4	22.0	38.0	34.9	36.5	33.8
Baton Rouge	4.5	89,468	57.2	32.3	5.2	19.7	42.8	34.0	30.1	27.4
Bossier	5.2	24,039	65.6	46.4	4.1	15.1	34.4	28.2	34.5	25.7
Harvey CDP	8.1	7,591	67.3	39.6	12.0	15.8	32.7	27.2	36.3	32.0
Houma	2.4	12,281	70.2	49.5	3.7	17.1	29.8	24.4	36.1	35.2
Kenner	12.8	22,991	67.3	48.1	4.5	14.8	32.7	27.3	36.7	32.1
Lafayette	4.5	47,481	59.5	39.3	4.8	15.5	40.5	31.9	30.9	26.3
Lake Charles	2.1	28,608	59.9	36.8	6.0	17.1	40.1	34.4	30.8	33.8
Laplace CDP	3.7	10,588	76.3	54.9	6.6	14.8	23.7	21.1	40.2	23.3
Marrero CDP	5.1	11,209	72.5	39.8	7.5	25.3	27.5	22.4	41.3	40.2
Metairie CDP	11.5	54,163	61.0	45.4	4.3	11.3	39.0	33.2	26.0	39.7
Monroe	0.9	17,661	59.0	31.0	4.1	23.9	41.0	37.9	31.5	31.7
New Iberia	3.8	11,632	70.6	45.2	4.4	21.0	29.4	25.6	37.4	31.3
New Orleans	5.3	101,221	54.4	29.9	3.9	20.6	45.6	38.8	25.9	32.2
Opelousas	1.5	9,107	67.1	27.4	7.5	32.2	32.9	30.8	33.5	39.5
Ruston	1.7	7,916	50.2	30.9	5.0	14.4	49.8	33.1	25.0	24.9
Shreveport	2.1	77,562	60.9	34.3	4.4	22.2	39.1	34.4	33.9	32.0
Slidell	3.4	9,252	77.5	56.2	5.6	15.7	22.5	18.6	36.2	35.9
Terrytown CDP	11.1	7,547	71.0	43.8	9.4	17.8	29.0	23.6	34.2	33.4
Maine	3.2	542,424	65.3	51.2	4.3	9.8	34.7	27.4	30.4	33.2
Auburn	5.4	9,826	60.6	42.3	4.6	13.7	39.4	34.2	33.4	30.9
Bangor	2.7	13,457	48.5	33.2	3.8	11.5	51.5	42.4	23.7	28.4
Biddeford	4.2	9,518	64.7	45.7	5.7	13.3	35.3	24.5	32.8	28.3
Lewiston	6.0	15,644	59.1	42.3	6.8	10.0	40.9	32.3	27.6	32.0
Portland	10.2	28,515	44.8	31.2	2.9	10.6	55.2	40.1	21.2	26.6
South Portland	5.7	10,377	57.8	42.3	4.8	10.7	42.2	32.8	25.8	29.5
Maryland	12.1	2,082,573	67.0	48.7	4.6	13.8	33.0	27.0	35.5	30.1
Annapolis	14.6	15,039	57.7	38.3	4.6	14.9	42.3	33.4	27.2	32.8
Arbutus CDP	14.0	8,133	62.3	41.6	6.5	14.2	37.7	27.9	29.1	32.5
Arnold CDP	6.6	8,468	70.9	60.0	3.3	7.7	29.1	24.7	38.0	25.2
Aspen Hill CDP	39.4	17,520	73.6	50.8	7.4	15.4	26.4	20.1	36.1	34.2
Baltimore	5.9	235,734	53.0	24.8	5.2	23.0	47.0	39.8	28.6	31.7
Bel Air North CDP	2.2	10,184	78.7	64.3	2.7	11.7	21.3	18.0	44.4	29.4
Bel Air South CDP	4.3	17,693	68.9	59.2	2.6	7.2	31.1	26.3	37.5	26.5
Bethesda CDP	22.8	23,900	61.2	52.6	1.8	6.8	38.8	32.7	31.4	37.9
Bowie	11.0	20,597	71.1	57.0	3.2	10.8	28.9	24.1	36.6	27.1
Carney CDP	10.6	12,351	59.0	43.0	3.1	12.8	41.0	33.5	27.4	37.6
Catonsville CDP	6.2	15,333	57.4	43.9	4.5	9.0	42.6	36.8	28.1	39.0
Chillum CDP	44.0	11,054	61.9	30.9	9.3	21.7	38.1	29.1	35.4	24.9
Clinton CDP	6.7	9,370	70.0	53.5	4.8	11.7	30.0	25.0	40.7	29.0
Cockeysville CDP	15.8	9,388	47.4	35.8	4.6	7.0	52.6	37.8	24.2	22.5
College Park	16.4	5,584	49.8	34.9	5.7	9.1	50.2	26.7	24.5	26.0
Columbia CDP	17.7	35,883	68.3	54.2	3.1	11.0	31.7	25.5	37.8	24.4
Crofton CDP	6.3	7,352	71.2	57.4	5.0	8.8	28.8	23.7	39.8	19.9
Cumberland	1.1	9,613	54.2	35.2	4.5	14.5	45.8	40.4	26.8	39.9
Dundalk CDP	3.0	24,823	63.7	39.9	6.7	17.1	36.3	30.2	32.7	39.3
Edgewood CDP	4.3	8,958	70.5	41.7	6.8	22.1	29.5	24.3	44.1	24.7
Eldersburg CDP	2.8	10,301	80.2	69.7	3.8	6.7	19.8	15.0	44.8	27.6
Elkridge CDP	13.3	8,743	69.3	55.1	2.7	11.5	30.7	24.2	44.9	20.7
Ellicott CDP	16.4	22,658	75.3	62.9	3.4	9.0	24.7	20.9	45.1	27.2
Essex CDP	5.7	15,816	64.6	42.2	4.2	18.2	35.4	29.9	35.0	30.1
Fairland CDP	34.8	8,510	62.1	40.1	4.7	17.4	37.9	32.6	34.0	21.0

STATE Place code	STATE City	Total population	Percent change 2005–2007	Under 5 years	5 to 17 years	18 to 24 years	25 to 44 years	45 to 64 years	65 years and over	Median age	White	Black	Asian Hawaiian or Pacific Islander	Amer. Indian, Alaska Native, or some other race	Percent Hispanic or Latino
	ACS table number:	B01003	Population estimates	B01001	B01001	B01001	B01001	B01001	B01001	B01002	B02008	B02009	B02011 + B02012	B02010 + B02013	C03002
		1	2	3	4	5	6	7	8	9	10	11	12	13	14
	Maryland—Cont.														
24 29525	Fort Washington CDP.........	24,641	-	4.7	21.3	5.5	24.7	30.4	13.5	41.2	22.4	66.1	10.0	6.4	6.2
24 30325	Frederick......................	61,719	2.8	8.7	15.9	11.8	32.5	20.8	10.3	32.3	72.2	19.3	6.1	4.9	7.9
24 31175	Gaithersburg..................	56,255	0.6	8.7	16.0	10.8	32.8	23.7	8.0	34.7	56.6	14.9	19.2	11.2	21.3
24 32025	Germantown CDP.............	58,930	-	8.6	18.0	9.0	35.2	25.0	4.4	33.9	58.3	20.4	16.4	8.6	20.2
24 32650	Glen Burnie CDP..............	37,677	-	6.3	17.3	9.8	27.9	24.7	14.1	37.5	80.8	14.8	3.1	3.2	4.4
24 34711	Greater Landover CDP	22,665	-	10.5	22.6	10.9	29.2	19.9	6.9	28.0	10.1	86.5	1.7	-	-
24 34712	Greater Upper Marlboro CDP..........................	20,930	-	4.4	16.9	8.3	33.0	32.3	5.1	38.9	14.5	82.8	2.4	1.7	2.3
24 34775	Greenbelt	21,425	-1.7	6.3	13.6	14.9	34.3	22.1	8.9	34.8	39.4	48.5	11.6	4.0	4.5
24 36075	Hagerstown....................	37,626	3.6	7.9	15.8	8.8	32.9	20.7	13.8	34.4	79.7	20.2	1.0	1.9	2.0
24 45612	Lanham-Seabrook CDP	22,555	-	8.1	19.4	8.5	30.9	25.9	7.3	34.7	22.0	57.7	9.4	12.8	20.2
24 45900	Laurel	23,094	-1.1	7.3	17.2	9.6	33.9	25.6	6.5	34.7	43.5	46.0	9.0	4.7	9.0
24 47450	Lochearn CDP..................	26,328	-	7.2	16.2	12.1	26.6	26.5	11.4	37.9	14.2	83.5	-	1.0	-
24 52300	Middle River CDP	23,102	-	6.4	16.1	8.2	26.2	26.6	16.4	40.0	79.3	17.9	2.8	2.4	4.2
24 52562	Milford Mill CDP	28,148	-	6.8	22.6	7.9	31.9	22.1	8.7	32.7	14.4	82.5	2.4	2.4	5.4
24 53325	Montgomery Village CDP...	39,204	-	8.7	15.7	8.0	32.8	27.3	7.4	36.0	52.6	27.0	11.6	11.6	15.3
24 56337	North Bethesda CDP	40,114	-	6.1	10.7	9.4	28.6	25.7	19.5	41.8	78.0	6.9	12.4	4.3	11.2
24 56875	North Potomac CDP..........	26,127	-	5.6	25.0	7.5	20.2	34.5	7.2	40.5	60.4	7.5	31.5	2.7	4.7
24 58300	Odenton CDP..................	24,599	-	7.7	18.5	6.6	36.5	21.7	9.0	35.5	76.6	19.4	5.4	1.0	3.0
24 58900	Olney CDP......................	34,712	-	5.3	24.5	6.5	24.1	30.9	8.6	39.7	79.2	11.4	8.4	3.2	7.2
24 59425	Owings Mills CDP	27,495	-	6.0	15.3	8.2	40.3	22.7	7.5	33.3	46.1	49.4	5.5	1.5	2.8
24 59505	Oxon Hill-Glassmanor CDP..........................	33,721	-	4.9	16.7	11.5	30.0	27.6	9.2	36.9	8.0	86.3	3.7	3.6	4.3
24 60275	Parkville CDP..................	30,768	-	6.0	15.6	11.7	26.0	25.6	15.1	38.3	66.9	30.3	3.2	0.6	1.5
24 60975	Perry Hall CDP.................	28,997	-	5.7	15.5	8.0	29.9	27.3	13.5	39.3	84.1	7.7	7.7	1.1	2.2
24 61400	Pikesville CDP.................	29,593	-	5.9	14.9	4.5	21.6	27.8	25.2	47.6	83.7	10.0	5.6	-	-
24 63300	Potomac CDP..................	47,294	-	6.3	20.3	6.8	19.7	30.4	16.5	43.2	77.0	8.7	13.7	1.8	4.7
24 64950	Randallstown CDP............	31,659	-	7.1	21.1	7.1	28.7	25.0	11.0	37.5	16.1	81.1	2.7	1.7	1.3
24 65600	Reisterstown CDP	24,391	-	8.3	20.2	8.3	30.4	22.7	10.0	34.1	68.1	27.3	4.9	3.5	5.3
24 67675	Rockville	53,279	2.9	7.2	14.6	7.2	29.0	28.5	13.5	39.8	66.6	9.4	18.8	7.1	12.9
24 69350	St. Charles CDP...............	36,590	-	6.9	20.4	10.5	35.6	20.9	5.8	32.9	47.2	49.9	2.6	4.4	5.5
24 69925	Salisbury......................	25,794	5.5	5.6	17.1	19.9	26.3	19.0	12.2	29.3	56.3	38.4	2.8	4.2	5.1
24 71150	Severn CDP....................	37,356	-	9.4	20.1	7.6	33.7	24.0	5.3	34.0	56.5	37.0	8.1	2.7	5.1
24 71200	Severna Park CDP	29,505	-	6.2	21.5	7.2	20.9	30.7	13.5	40.7	91.4	4.0	4.8	-	-
24 72450	Silver Spring CDP	74,572	-	7.3	15.0	9.9	33.2	25.2	9.5	35.3	47.6	25.1	10.0	19.8	26.9
24 73550	South Gate CDP...............	30,113	-	6.9	16.7	12.7	34.6	20.9	8.3	31.5	68.6	26.5	5.2	1.5	5.6
24 75762	Suitland-Silver Hill CDP.......	30,773	-	8.0	20.4	10.2	31.6	22.2	7.6	30.9	4.8	94.4	-	-	-
24 78425	Towson CDP...................	53,401	-	4.6	12.5	20.4	21.6	22.7	18.3	37.5	85.2	8.9	5.8	1.4	2.0
24 81175	Waldorf CDP...................	25,849	-	9.0	21.1	8.0	32.5	25.1	4.3	32.3	42.8	48.4	8.3	3.1	4.3
24 83837	Wheaton-Glenmont CDP ...	56,707	-	8.4	15.6	8.8	31.1	24.9	11.2	36.1	49.0	21.5	14.4	18.9	32.2
24 84375	White Oak CDP................	20,665	-	10.2	16.0	9.4	31.1	24.8	8.5	34.2	37.9	42.6	13.7	9.4	15.5
24 86475	Woodlawn CDP (Baltimore County)	35,514	-	6.4	17.2	8.2	27.8	29.1	11.3	39.0	32.4	60.1	5.8	2.5	4.6
25 00000	**Massachusetts**............	6,437,759	0.3	5.9	16.6	9.9	28.2	26.1	13.3	38.3	84.5	6.8	5.2	5.3	8.0
25 00765	Agawam.......................	27,727	-0.3	4.9	15.2	8.4	25.3	29.3	17.0	42.5	97.6	0.5	1.2	1.1	1.9
25 01640	Arlington CDP.................	41,223	-	6.0	13.6	4.8	32.0	27.5	16.1	41.7	89.4	2.9	9.8	0.6	1.5
25 02690	Attleboro	42,693	-0.1	7.2	16.2	7.8	32.5	24.1	12.2	37.5	90.4	2.0	5.4	2.5	5.4
25 03690	Barnstable Town	46,469	-1.7	4.1	15.3	9.0	25.0	26.7	20.0	42.8	92.8	4.2	1.1	3.4	1.7
25 05105	Belmont CDP..................	24,092	-	6.1	17.5	5.6	29.2	26.4	15.3	41.6	89.7	1.2	8.7	0.9	3.2
25 05595	Beverly........................	40,429	-0.7	5.2	14.6	10.9	26.4	26.3	16.6	40.0	94.2	2.8	3.1	0.5	1.3
25 07000	Boston.........................	600,980	0.5	5.8	13.3	14.6	35.6	20.4	10.3	33.2	58.4	25.3	8.8	10.2	15.6
25 07700	Braintree CDP.................	33,367	-	4.5	17.5	8.2	23.4	28.9	17.6	42.8	91.7	2.2	5.8	0.4	1.7
25 09000	Brockton......................	94,994	-0.7	7.4	19.1	9.8	29.5	24.3	9.9	34.5	53.8	33.2	3.4	13.1	9.0
25 09210	Brookline CDP.................	58,529	-	5.5	12.4	10.7	32.7	25.7	13.0	36.5	80.8	3.0	15.6	2.4	4.6
25 09875	Burlington CDP...............	23,253	-	6.3	15.3	6.8	29.8	25.3	16.5	40.1	82.3	3.1	13.6	0.9	2.1
25 11000	Cambridge....................	91,867	1.0	5.0	8.5	14.8	39.8	21.4	10.5	32.6	69.7	13.9	15.5	3.7	6.1
25 13205	Chelsea........................	33,027	1.5	8.4	17.8	9.7	34.0	18.8	11.2	34.0	76.2	18.5	1.9	16.5	58.4
25 13660	Chicopee......................	55,144	-0.9	5.3	16.0	11.5	25.7	26.4	15.1	38.6	89.1	3.4	2.6	6.3	11.5
25 16285	Danvers CDP..................	24,901	-	4.9	16.3	8.3	22.5	30.8	17.2	44.0	95.9	1.9	2.0	-	2.9
25 16530	Dedham CDP..................	23,097	-	6.0	16.8	7.9	24.6	27.7	17.0	42.0	91.6	5.0	3.3	1.1	4.4
25 21990	Everett........................	39,812	0.9	4.4	14.6	12.1	32.1	24.7	12.1	38.2	78.9	11.0	6.5	5.5	13.6
25 23000	Fall River	90,523	-0.5	5.4	15.2	10.1	30.4	23.8	15.1	37.0	91.8	4.1	3.1	3.7	5.3
25 23875	Fitchburg......................	41,147	0.2	5.6	17.5	15.7	27.3	22.0	12.0	32.7	85.6	4.3	5.1	6.3	20.9
25 24960	Framingham CDP.............	63,083	-	6.3	13.7	9.8	30.1	27.1	13.0	38.4	76.2	4.3	6.9	13.5	10.4
25 25100	Franklin.......................	30,484	2.0	7.0	20.9	8.6	28.6	26.4	8.6	36.9	95.2	1.0	4.2	-	0.8
25 25485	Gardner........................	21,169	-0.7	7.1	13.2	8.9	30.7	26.7	13.4	38.5	89.5	5.7	1.6	4.0	4.6
25 26150	Gloucester	27,858	-0.3	3.3	17.4	6.6	23.0	33.9	15.8	44.9	98.2	0.6	1.0	1.1	1.2
25 29405	Haverhill	59,666	0.4	6.8	17.1	8.9	31.4	23.7	12.1	35.5	87.0	4.7	2.2	8.0	10.2
25 30840	Holyoke........................	38,993	-0.9	7.2	20.4	8.3	26.6	22.8	14.8	35.6	89.6	3.2	1.3	7.6	45.8
25 34550	Lawrence......................	71,319	-0.7	9.0	20.8	12.0	29.4	20.8	8.0	30.3	32.2	5.1	2.9	62.9	69.4
25 35075	Leominster	41,216	-0.8	7.3	15.2	8.6	29.0	25.3	14.6	38.8	89.0	4.4	3.1	5.5	10.9
25 35250	Lexington CDP.................	30,168	-	5.3	21.8	5.2	18.2	31.7	17.8	44.7	82.3	0.9	17.6	1.0	-
25 37000	Lowell..........................	100,659	0.1	6.9	17.8	11.2	30.7	23.2	10.2	34.1	64.4	6.1	19.6	11.8	14.8

STATE City	Percent foreign born	Total households	Household type (percent)						Percent of households with people under 18 years	Percent of households with people 60 years and over
			Family households				Nonfamily households			
			Total family households	Married-couple families	Male householder families	Female householder families	Total nonfamily households	One-person households		
ACS table number:	C05002	B11001	B11001	B11001	B11001	B11001	B11001	B11001	C11005	B11006
	15	16	17	18	19	20	21	22	23	24
Maryland—Cont.										
Fort Washington CDP........	15.8	8,339	80.7	65.2	3.9	11.5	19.3	16.8	36.6	38.8
Frederick............................	12.4	24,399	58.5	42.2	4.3	12.0	41.5	31.4	33.7	25.3
Gaithersburg.....................	36.4	21,368	66.8	49.9	6.7	10.3	33.2	27.5	36.4	22.8
Germantown CDP...............	31.9	21,751	66.8	47.7	3.4	15.6	33.2	27.0	41.8	14.7
Glen Burnie CDP................	5.6	15,036	64.1	45.0	4.6	14.5	35.9	26.0	34.4	31.4
Greater Landover CDP	12.3	7,534	71.1	32.4	8.2	30.6	28.9	23.3	48.2	22.8
Greater Upper Marlboro CDP..................................	7.6	7,793	68.3	46.9	4.4	17.0	31.7	28.3	35.3	17.4
Greenbelt	24.1	9,542	52.4	28.6	4.0	19.9	47.6	39.0	28.6	21.5
Hagerstown........................	4.3	16,589	57.7	34.4	4.9	18.5	42.3	35.3	34.1	27.8
Lanham-Seabrook CDP	35.3	7,036	73.6	51.1	8.7	13.7	26.4	19.0	40.1	27.2
Laurel...............................	24.2	9,924	53.1	34.7	5.2	13.1	46.9	39.0	31.1	21.2
Lochearn CDP.....................	9.7	9,720	69.8	41.5	8.1	20.2	30.2	24.2	35.5	31.1
Middle River CDP...............	6.6	9,038	66.6	44.5	4.8	17.3	33.4	26.8	32.1	37.2
Milford Mill CDP................	12.3	10,891	66.3	37.3	6.0	23.0	33.7	25.5	45.3	21.3
Montgomery Village CDP...	28.6	14,457	71.7	53.8	4.6	13.3	28.3	24.0	37.9	24.5
North Bethesda CDP..........	28.8	17,803	52.2	40.6	2.5	9.0	47.8	38.2	22.9	33.5
North Potomac CDP...........	30.7	8,075	88.8	76.4	6.2	6.2	11.2	11.0	55.0	26.6
Odenton CDP	5.8	9,735	66.7	51.1	3.3	12.2	33.3	28.8	36.9	25.3
Olney CDP	14.6	11,292	84.1	70.3	2.3	11.5	15.9	12.9	50.6	27.3
Owings Mills CDP	11.7	11,914	58.7	38.5	4.1	16.1	41.3	31.7	31.1	18.5
Oxon Hill-Glassmanor CDP	8.9	14,346	56.7	26.5	6.2	24.0	43.3	39.3	29.2	24.2
Parkville CDP.....................	6.6	12,860	63.1	39.7	4.9	18.6	36.9	30.6	30.7	31.1
Perry Hall CDP...................	9.3	11,615	66.2	53.6	2.8	9.8	33.8	24.4	31.7	31.5
Pikesville CDP....................	18.4	13,250	61.3	52.3	1.8	7.3	38.7	34.8	25.6	50.1
Potomac CDP......................	25.0	16,286	82.1	71.6	2.4	8.1	17.9	16.1	41.8	41.9
Randallstown CDP	8.3	11,313	73.4	46.4	5.7	21.4	26.6	23.2	42.0	29.3
Reisterstown CDP	14.6	9,345	68.3	49.9	5.2	13.3	31.7	27.0	37.8	23.6
Rockville	34.1	20,328	70.2	56.9	3.2	10.1	29.8	24.7	33.5	31.6
St. Charles CDP.................	5.8	13,149	72.1	45.9	4.7	21.5	27.9	23.7	42.9	19.7
Salisbury	7.2	10,034	51.3	26.2	8.0	17.1	48.7	35.3	28.9	30.3
Severn CDP........................	7.9	13,884	73.5	55.7	4.6	13.2	26.5	22.4	44.0	18.4
Severna Park CDP	5.3	9,980	84.0	71.6	3.2	9.3	16.0	13.9	42.9	36.8
Silver Spring CDP	35.8	29,448	57.4	40.1	4.8	12.5	42.6	33.0	31.6	25.2
South Gate CDP.................	8.6	12,204	61.0	41.1	4.6	15.4	39.0	29.6	33.5	21.1
Suitland-Silver Hill CDP	4.2	12,901	61.6	22.1	10.7	28.8	38.4	33.3	37.4	21.8
Towson CDP.......................	9.4	20,885	51.3	40.9	3.0	7.4	48.7	37.7	23.9	38.6
Waldorf CDP......................	7.1	8,955	74.7	54.9	3.4	16.4	25.3	20.9	46.0	15.6
Wheaton-Glenmont CDP ...	42.3	19,497	70.8	51.9	6.8	12.1	29.2	23.1	36.9	34.5
White Oak CDP..................	35.8	7,473	70.8	47.9	8.5	14.4	29.2	25.4	42.0	22.9
Woodlawn CDP (Baltimore County)	10.9	14,297	64.0	41.6	5.5	17.0	36.0	31.4	32.6	29.1
Massachusetts................	14.2	2,448,608	64.0	47.9	4.1	12.0	36.0	29.0	32.5	32.1
Agawam............................	7.2	11,201	64.6	54.5	4.4	5.7	35.4	29.6	27.5	36.5
Arlington CDP....................	15.0	18,192	57.2	46.0	2.2	9.0	42.8	34.7	26.2	33.4
Attleboro	9.5	16,403	67.2	49.3	5.5	12.4	32.8	26.3	35.5	30.4
Barnstable Town	12.6	20,176	66.4	52.1	4.3	10.0	33.6	25.9	28.6	39.5
Belmont CDP	17.3	9,552	69.3	55.9	2.5	10.9	30.7	25.5	34.7	33.7
Beverly..............................	8.1	15,182	62.3	48.0	2.8	11.5	37.7	31.0	29.5	33.6
Boston...............................	27.7	232,099	47.5	26.1	4.2	17.1	52.5	39.4	24.3	25.6
Braintree CDP	10.9	12,845	67.5	50.0	3.0	14.6	32.5	26.4	30.5	39.6
Brockton............................	23.6	33,324	68.1	40.9	6.3	20.9	31.9	25.3	42.0	29.9
Brookline CDP...................	23.3	25,591	53.8	44.3	2.0	7.5	46.2	32.9	24.3	31.1
Burlington CDP..................	17.6	8,619	77.0	63.5	5.9	7.6	23.0	19.3	38.3	38.5
Cambridge.........................	28.3	41,174	41.2	31.3	2.0	7.9	58.8	43.1	18.8	26.1
Chelsea.............................	37.4	11,564	62.2	32.2	10.1	19.9	37.8	31.5	39.1	26.8
Chicopee...........................	9.8	23,427	57.4	39.4	3.8	14.2	42.6	37.0	26.1	36.0
Danvers CDP	5.3	9,476	71.0	57.1	3.8	10.1	29.0	25.2	31.6	35.9
Dedham CDP	14.3	8,786	72.6	54.8	5.3	12.5	27.4	24.9	33.1	36.6
Everett..............................	33.0	14,958	62.9	43.0	6.4	13.5	37.1	31.0	30.0	30.6
Fall River	19.8	38,538	59.8	38.0	3.6	18.3	40.2	33.5	31.5	32.3
Fitchburg..........................	9.3	14,918	64.4	43.9	6.4	14.1	35.6	26.9	33.4	30.0
Framingham CDP...............	25.6	25,076	63.2	49.0	3.4	10.8	36.8	30.5	29.5	31.1
Franklin............................	7.5	10,768	70.8	61.0	3.6	6.2	29.2	22.7	44.6	25.5
Gardner............................	6.0	8,073	56.3	43.4	2.9	10.0	43.7	31.2	28.1	33.6
Gloucester	5.2	11,865	60.9	51.0	3.2	6.7	39.1	33.1	26.0	35.5
Haverhill	7.7	22,494	64.0	44.8	4.4	14.8	36.0	26.7	35.5	27.0
Holyoke	4.2	14,938	60.7	35.0	5.0	20.7	39.3	31.9	36.5	29.6
Lawrence..........................	35.2	24,358	69.3	32.9	9.9	26.5	30.7	25.1	46.1	24.5
Leominster........................	12.5	16,685	64.6	48.4	5.0	11.3	35.4	31.5	32.0	33.0
Lexington CDP	21.1	10,936	79.8	68.0	3.7	8.1	20.2	18.9	42.2	39.7
Lowell...............................	26.4	36,943	61.1	37.6	6.0	17.5	38.9	31.3	35.2	27.1

STATE Place code	STATE / City	Total population	Percent change 2005–2007	Under 5 years	5 to 17 years	18 to 24 years	25 to 44 years	45 to 64 years	65 years and over	Median age	White	Black	Asian Hawaiian or Pacific Islander	Amer. Indian, Alaska Native, or some other race	Percent Hispanic or Latino
ACS table number:		B01003	Population estimates	B01001	B01001	B01001	B01001	B01001	B01001	B01002	B02008	B02009	B02011 + B02012	B02010 + B02013	C03002
		1	2	3	4	5	6	7	8	9	10	11	12	13	14
	Massachusetts—Cont.														
25 37490	Lynn	86,922	-0.9	6.8	18.2	10.1	30.8	22.6	11.4	34.3	70.6	15.9	6.1	10.3	25.5
25 37875	Malden	56,331	-0.6	5.2	13.2	10.3	33.9	25.8	11.6	36.5	66.9	11.5	17.8	5.0	7.3
25 38435	Marblehead CDP	20,151	-	7.3	17.0	5.4	21.0	33.1	16.2	44.4	98.5	-	1.0	-	-
25 38715	Marlborough	37,078	1.4	7.2	14.1	7.3	33.2	25.7	12.4	38.5	89.9	1.4	5.1	5.9	13.1
25 39835	Medford	55,670	-0.4	5.5	11.2	11.6	33.3	22.3	16.1	37.8	80.9	10.8	5.5	4.0	6.7
25 40115	Melrose	27,655	1.3	6.0	16.9	5.3	27.5	26.8	17.5	42.1	93.1	2.6	2.5	2.5	3.8
25 40710	Methuen	44,262	-0.4	6.3	17.8	8.8	27.9	25.7	13.4	38.2	85.6	1.5	4.4	9.8	15.7
25 41200	Milford CDP	26,407	-	8.0	14.0	8.9	30.5	26.1	12.5	38.0	89.5	2.2	2.6	7.6	6.3
25 41725	Milton CDP	25,709	-	6.7	19.3	7.9	21.8	30.0	14.3	40.9	81.7	13.6	4.3	0.8	3.0
25 44140	Needham CDP	28,588	-	7.3	20.6	5.2	20.6	30.7	15.7	42.5	93.8	0.3	6.3	-	-
25 45000	New Bedford	93,812	-0.8	7.2	17.9	8.6	28.7	23.0	14.6	36.1	78.2	10.4	1.4	13.8	12.3
25 45560	Newton	91,309	-0.1	4.9	15.6	16.5	23.0	26.7	13.4	38.1	86.1	3.8	9.4	2.3	3.7
25 46330	Northampton	28,418	-0.5	4.4	11.7	17.3	29.2	26.3	11.1	36.0	89.4	3.7	3.1	6.3	6.6
25 50285	Norwood CDP	28,599	-	6.8	14.1	8.9	29.5	24.8	15.9	38.9	84.2	4.6	6.3	6.2	4.5
25 52490	Peabody	50,377	1.4	4.9	15.5	8.1	24.4	28.7	18.6	43.2	94.4	1.0	2.7	3.6	5.2
25 53960	Pittsfield	45,953	-1.4	5.7	15.0	9.5	24.8	26.9	18.2	41.3	93.0	5.5	1.4	1.8	2.3
25 55745	Quincy	84,368	1.9	5.0	11.2	8.8	34.4	25.6	15.0	39.2	74.8	4.6	20.6	1.4	2.1
25 55990	Randolph CDP	29,422	-	4.3	14.8	8.8	31.0	28.1	13.1	40.3	54.1	33.0	12.3	2.0	4.6
25 56165	Reading CDP	24,743	-	6.2	19.9	7.1	24.2	28.2	14.3	41.0	96.9	-	3.5	-	-
25 56585	Revere	55,942	4.2	9.0	14.3	4.9	34.0	22.4	15.3	38.4	80.6	6.6	4.8	9.3	17.1
25 59105	Salem	41,667	-1.0	7.2	13.1	10.1	31.2	25.0	13.3	36.9	85.9	5.6	1.8	8.5	13.7
25 60050	Saugus CDP	27,613	-	5.2	15.4	6.6	25.5	30.3	17.0	42.7	96.7	1.8	2.2	1.4	2.6
25 62535	Somerville	70,801	-1.0	3.4	7.8	17.7	41.6	19.2	10.3	32.1	79.5	6.4	6.7	9.2	9.5
25 67000	Springfield	148,136	-0.6	7.4	19.2	12.7	27.7	22.2	10.9	32.3	53.0	23.5	2.5	24.1	33.6
25 67700	Stoneham CDP	22,487	-	6.6	15.0	6.8	24.6	29.1	18.0	43.1	95.2	2.4	3.1	1.7	2.1
25 69170	Taunton	57,229	-0.3	6.4	16.8	8.4	32.1	24.0	12.3	36.6	91.3	5.6	1.4	3.3	4.4
25 72250	Wakefield CDP	24,551	-	4.8	16.7	7.4	27.6	29.4	14.1	41.4	97.3	0.8	3.1	-	-
25 72600	Waltham	58,989	0.1	6.3	9.6	17.5	30.7	23.9	12.1	36.0	77.2	8.3	10.9	4.6	8.5
25 73440	Watertown	30,954	0.4	5.4	8.6	10.5	34.8	24.9	15.8	37.8	89.5	2.8	6.8	-	5.9
25 74210	Wellesley CDP	30,238	-	5.3	20.9	17.3	17.8	24.9	13.7	36.4	86.1	2.6	11.1	1.4	3.4
25 76030	Westfield	41,981	-0.3	5.9	18.4	12.2	25.3	24.8	13.4	37.3	95.4	1.7	1.1	2.4	4.2
25 77850	West Springfield	28,048	-0.8	5.3	16.2	10.9	26.5	26.6	14.3	39.1	94.5	2.7	2.1	1.3	5.4
25 78900	Weymouth CDP	52,279	-	5.1	14.6	7.8	28.7	29.5	14.4	41.4	93.3	2.9	3.1	1.4	1.5
25 80195	Wilmington CDP	22,633	-	5.4	20.5	6.4	30.0	27.2	10.5	39.5	95.9	-	3.0	-	-
25 80545	Winchester CDP	22,604	-	7.2	21.4	5.4	21.7	27.0	17.2	41.7	91.8	-	8.6	0.9	-
25 80695	Winthrop CDP	20,170	-	7.0	16.6	7.3	27.4	26.9	14.9	39.7	95.2	4.3	1.3	3.8	-
25 81035	Woburn	37,477	-0.6	5.6	15.0	7.0	31.7	26.4	14.3	39.5	88.8	3.8	6.2	2.0	1.9
25 82000	Worcester	165,965	-0.4	5.7	16.0	13.2	29.6	22.7	12.9	34.4	79.8	9.4	6.3	6.1	17.7
26 00000	**Michigan**	10,094,027	-0.4	6.4	18.2	9.7	27.0	26.1	12.6	37.3	81.1	14.9	2.7	3.2	3.9
26 00440	Adrian	21,867	-0.9	7.1	16.5	14.1	25.4	21.7	15.2	32.8	87.0	6.9	1.0	8.5	13.0
26 01380	Allen Park	30,043	-4.4	5.5	16.6	8.0	26.1	27.3	16.6	41.1	96.5	0.3	0.8	3.2	-
26 03000	Ann Arbor	113,100	0.4	4.4	11.3	28.5	29.5	18.3	7.9	27.9	75.2	8.6	16.6	2.5	3.6
26 04105	Auburn Hills	19,146	-0.4	6.6	13.0	17.7	33.5	21.7	7.4	31.7	70.8	13.2	13.8	4.0	5.6
26 05920	Battle Creek	51,275	-1.1	7.7	18.4	8.5	28.7	24.1	12.6	34.8	76.7	20.4	2.9	2.8	5.6
26 06020	Bay	34,501	-2.1	6.6	17.5	9.4	28.2	25.5	13.0	36.9	93.9	4.0	-	4.9	7.3
26 09190	Bloomfield Township CDP	41,887	-	4.1	18.3	5.3	17.7	35.7	18.9	47.6	88.2	4.8	6.8	0.7	0.8
26 12060	Burton	30,900	-1.1	8.1	18.7	7.8	29.5	25.0	10.9	36.3	92.8	5.5	0.9	1.7	1.3
26 13110	Canton CDP	91,948	-	7.9	21.0	6.5	31.7	25.5	7.3	35.5	76.5	8.7	14.3	2.1	2.7
26 16510	Clinton CDP	94,408	-	6.3	15.6	8.6	27.4	26.7	15.3	39.8	88.3	9.1	2.4	2.0	2.9
26 21000	Dearborn	102,643	-4.8	9.0	20.3	8.9	26.1	23.2	12.5	35.0	92.2	4.8	2.3	1.9	3.2
26 21020	Dearborn Heights	58,505	-4.3	5.8	17.9	6.8	27.7	24.1	17.7	38.9	93.6	3.4	2.3	2.3	3.3
26 22000	Detroit	837,711	-0.4	7.1	22.2	9.4	27.6	23.1	10.5	33.2	11.2	84.0	1.3	5.2	6.1
26 24120	East Lansing	47,395	-1.1	2.1	6.7	60.6	15.3	9.7	5.6	21.5	82.4	7.8	9.3	2.5	3.3
26 24290	Eastpointe	32,564	-1.2	6.1	17.1	8.4	32.2	23.4	12.8	35.2	77.0	21.1	3.3	0.5	0.9
26 27440	Farmington Hills	83,455	-1.1	5.8	16.6	7.6	25.3	29.2	15.5	41.6	76.2	14.2	10.0	0.9	1.1
26 27880	Ferndale	19,158	-0.9	6.1	14.3	7.9	37.0	26.1	8.7	36.4	91.1	7.6	1.2	1.7	2.5
26 29000	Flint	108,304	-2.3	7.7	20.4	10.3	28.1	23.3	10.2	32.5	42.6	56.1	0.6	3.9	3.1
26 29580	Forest Hills CDP	24,530	-	7.8	22.9	5.6	22.3	32.3	9.1	40.1	96.1	0.7	3.2	-	-
26 31420	Garden	30,698	-4.5	5.7	18.3	8.5	26.6	27.2	13.8	39.7	92.5	5.2	1.4	1.4	4.0
26 34000	Grand Rapids	193,671	-0.2	8.0	18.0	12.6	30.3	20.3	10.8	31.5	68.7	21.8	1.9	10.2	16.4
26 36280	Hamtramck	20,485	-3.6	7.9	21.4	9.0	27.4	24.6	9.7	33.5	59.1	22.2	18.3	0.6	-
26 36810	Harrison CDP	22,965	-	2.5	16.3	9.1	25.4	34.5	12.3	43.3	96.2	2.8	0.8	0.5	-
26 38640	Holland	32,030	-0.7	6.2	17.5	15.1	29.3	18.2	13.8	31.0	80.9	2.5	3.1	15.8	22.7
26 40680	Inkster	29,018	-4.6	7.6	22.6	7.6	29.6	22.0	10.5	31.9	24.8	71.4	4.9	4.5	1.6
26 41420	Jackson	33,364	-1.8	9.6	19.5	10.2	29.0	21.1	10.6	31.3	75.1	23.0	1.4	3.4	3.9
26 42160	Kalamazoo	71,441	-0.8	6.9	13.2	27.0	25.9	17.6	9.5	26.2	73.7	22.5	3.5	2.9	4.8
26 42820	Kentwood	46,417	1.8	7.9	17.9	9.6	32.5	21.1	11.0	34.2	77.7	15.1	7.4	3.7	5.9
26 46000	Lansing	115,366	-1.3	8.1	17.7	13.3	29.2	22.3	9.3	31.3	70.3	24.7	3.9	5.3	10.8
26 47800	Lincoln Park	41,994	-4.5	5.9	18.7	7.8	29.5	27.1	11.0	37.6	90.5	5.3	0.2	5.7	11.1
26 49000	Livonia	101,595	-3.8	4.3	17.3	8.1	23.9	30.7	15.7	42.8	94.8	2.1	2.7	2.0	2.5
26 50560	Madison Heights	30,174	-1.2	6.8	14.0	9.1	31.4	25.6	13.2	37.8	86.3	3.4	10.3	0.9	0.6
26 51900	Marquette	20,640	0.0	3.6	9.3	31.2	21.5	20.9	13.5	30.3	93.6	4.4	0.7	2.6	1.2
26 53780	Midland	41,013	-0.9	5.5	17.4	11.9	25.0	25.2	14.9	37.3	94.1	2.4	4.0	1.5	1.8

STATE City	Percent foreign born	Total households	Household type (percent)						Percent of households with people under 18 years	Percent of households with people 60 years and over
			Family households				Nonfamily households			
			Total family households	Married-couple families	Male householder families	Female householder families	Total nonfamily households	One-person households		
ACS table number:	C05002	B11001	B11001	B11001	B11001	B11001	B11001	B11001	C11005	B11006
	15	16	17	18	19	20	21	22	23	24
Massachusetts—Cont.										
Lynn	29.6	32,339	63.3	36.9	8.1	18.3	36.7	32.6	37.1	30.8
Malden	35.8	22,682	60.1	41.7	5.5	12.9	39.9	32.5	28.4	28.1
Marblehead CDP	5.6	8,209	67.9	60.3	1.5	6.1	32.1	28.5	30.7	38.6
Marlborough	19.0	14,776	59.5	50.8	2.0	6.7	40.5	31.8	30.1	28.8
Medford	21.2	21,354	62.6	47.5	5.9	9.2	37.4	28.6	25.9	34.6
Melrose	11.5	10,864	66.1	53.8	2.9	9.4	33.9	29.7	29.9	39.9
Methuen	12.9	16,567	64.3	48.1	3.7	12.6	35.7	30.3	36.7	30.5
Milford CDP	23.3	9,495	68.4	51.9	4.3	12.2	31.6	24.0	33.6	29.8
Milton CDP	11.4	9,058	75.7	61.2	1.9	12.7	24.3	21.5	41.5	40.2
Needham CDP	10.2	10,424	74.2	66.4	1.3	6.5	25.8	23.4	43.6	38.4
New Bedford	21.5	38,019	62.3	35.1	5.4	21.7	37.7	32.3	34.2	32.6
Newton	18.0	31,873	66.1	55.5	2.7	7.8	33.9	27.4	33.4	35.3
Northampton	7.5	12,108	44.7	32.3	3.1	9.3	55.3	39.6	23.5	28.5
Norwood CDP	21.6	11,569	62.3	45.4	3.7	13.2	37.7	29.1	31.2	33.2
Peabody	13.2	19,286	65.4	47.8	3.2	14.3	34.6	29.2	28.8	42.3
Pittsfield	4.1	19,989	60.0	39.8	7.2	13.0	40.0	34.8	29.8	38.5
Quincy	25.3	37,903	50.2	37.1	4.1	8.9	49.8	39.2	22.4	32.5
Randolph CDP	26.7	11,040	66.4	47.5	5.2	13.8	33.6	28.4	30.6	33.8
Reading CDP	5.3	8,954	73.7	65.2	1.6	6.9	26.3	24.7	35.9	36.5
Revere	25.4	20,176	62.3	45.1	6.1	11.1	37.7	28.5	32.6	36.1
Salem	14.8	17,332	56.7	35.5	5.5	15.6	43.3	34.4	29.2	31.2
Saugus CDP	8.9	9,983	73.7	55.0	4.9	13.8	26.3	23.4	30.3	40.9
Somerville	27.1	29,057	43.5	27.1	4.5	11.9	56.5	34.5	17.6	24.4
Springfield	10.1	55,363	60.8	30.4	5.7	24.7	39.2	32.7	35.3	28.6
Stoneham CDP	7.9	8,809	63.6	45.6	5.1	12.9	36.4	31.3	33.1	37.8
Taunton	11.0	22,187	65.5	47.0	4.9	13.5	34.5	28.8	35.8	27.6
Wakefield CDP	5.6	9,408	67.7	58.7	2.8	6.2	32.3	25.1	31.3	30.9
Waltham	23.5	22,778	50.9	38.7	3.0	9.2	49.1	39.0	24.9	29.2
Watertown	22.8	13,817	50.6	39.7	2.5	8.4	49.4	37.8	20.5	31.7
Wellesley CDP	16.3	9,430	75.8	63.3	2.4	10.1	24.2	20.9	44.0	36.5
Westfield	9.4	15,170	65.3	50.9	4.5	10.0	34.7	27.7	33.1	34.1
West Springfield	13.2	11,798	55.6	38.4	4.8	12.3	44.4	37.3	27.7	28.9
Weymouth CDP	9.0	21,835	61.3	46.7	3.3	11.4	38.7	32.5	27.8	32.3
Wilmington CDP	6.1	7,376	80.7	68.0	2.6	10.1	19.3	14.6	43.7	31.0
Winchester CDP	12.2	7,962	72.2	64.0	0.8	7.4	27.8	25.6	41.4	39.0
Winthrop CDP	9.0	7,874	59.0	42.8	4.4	11.8	41.0	35.2	28.2	35.5
Woburn	14.3	14,834	64.7	48.4	2.9	13.4	35.3	28.5	30.1	34.1
Worcester	18.0	64,535	57.4	37.1	4.9	15.4	42.6	34.6	31.5	29.8
Michigan	6.0	3,864,307	66.8	50.2	4.3	12.3	33.2	27.9	33.6	30.8
Adrian	3.5	8,079	59.3	42.4	5.1	11.8	40.7	35.0	33.5	33.6
Allen Park	6.6	11,615	64.6	51.0	5.1	8.5	35.4	31.2	29.8	36.7
Ann Arbor	18.0	44,559	47.5	37.5	3.1	6.9	52.5	35.6	22.9	20.7
Auburn Hills	16.6	8,186	55.9	40.8	1.9	13.1	44.1	35.6	28.0	19.0
Battle Creek	5.2	20,599	62.4	40.7	4.7	17.0	37.6	33.1	36.2	30.6
Bay	1.3	14,613	61.2	42.4	3.8	15.0	38.8	33.3	31.6	29.2
Bloomfield Township CDP	14.0	16,377	75.3	66.5	2.4	6.5	24.7	23.3	30.2	44.6
Burton	1.1	12,313	65.7	46.9	5.4	13.5	34.3	28.8	35.1	28.4
Canton CDP	15.2	31,992	73.1	61.7	2.0	9.4	26.9	22.8	40.9	20.3
Clinton CDP	8.3	40,991	61.2	44.8	3.2	13.3	38.8	33.7	28.8	32.8
Dearborn	27.0	34,687	65.6	50.5	4.0	11.1	34.4	30.3	36.4	32.8
Dearborn Heights	13.4	22,393	65.1	46.9	6.5	11.7	34.9	32.1	29.4	39.8
Detroit	5.4	285,912	61.0	23.7	6.3	30.9	39.0	34.8	37.9	31.1
East Lansing	12.6	14,040	34.0	25.9	3.1	5.1	66.0	36.5	16.1	16.3
Eastpointe	4.1	13,530	60.2	41.2	3.5	15.6	39.8	35.2	31.4	31.0
Farmington Hills	18.8	33,623	65.7	53.7	2.7	9.2	34.3	29.3	31.0	30.9
Ferndale	4.5	9,350	46.6	29.6	3.0	14.0	53.4	42.8	23.9	19.9
Flint	1.4	43,773	57.3	26.3	6.3	24.7	42.7	37.1	33.6	28.2
Forest Hills CDP	8.5	8,390	82.9	79.2	0.8	3.0	17.1	16.3	46.5	27.3
Garden	3.2	11,280	68.1	50.3	4.7	13.2	31.9	28.2	33.4	35.1
Grand Rapids	12.5	73,360	58.6	37.0	5.1	16.5	41.4	32.0	33.8	25.0
Hamtramck	39.5	6,446	63.1	36.2	10.9	15.9	36.9	33.1	39.0	26.0
Harrison CDP	4.3	10,178	59.5	45.7	3.2	10.7	40.5	34.0	25.6	31.4
Holland	10.9	11,401	68.0	53.2	4.7	10.0	32.0	26.6	35.5	28.3
Inkster	6.3	10,188	65.1	31.5	9.3	24.3	34.9	31.2	37.4	29.8
Jackson	3.1	13,798	62.0	34.1	5.7	22.1	38.0	32.4	39.3	25.7
Kalamazoo	5.8	27,790	45.9	28.3	4.7	13.0	54.1	37.6	25.3	23.5
Kentwood	12.1	19,163	63.0	45.4	4.3	13.2	37.0	31.2	34.1	24.3
Lansing	8.1	47,792	56.3	34.8	4.5	17.1	43.7	34.9	31.1	23.3
Lincoln Park	5.3	15,265	65.8	43.1	6.7	16.0	34.2	29.4	33.0	30.8
Livonia	8.4	37,791	71.2	60.8	3.1	7.3	28.8	26.1	31.5	36.4
Madison Heights	17.0	12,826	57.3	43.6	2.1	11.6	42.7	38.1	27.0	30.9
Marquette	2.3	7,605	49.7	39.0	2.2	8.5	50.3	36.6	20.1	31.1
Midland	4.9	16,908	62.7	50.5	2.3	9.9	37.3	31.0	31.3	31.3

Table A-4. Cities — Who: Age, Race/Ethnicity, and Household Structure, 2005–2007—*Continued*

STATE Place code	STATE City	Total population	Percent change 2005–2007	Under 5 years	5 to 17 years	18 to 24 years	25 to 44 years	45 to 64 years	65 years and over	Median age	White	Black	Asian Hawaiian or Pacific Islander	Amer. Indian, Alaska Native, or some other race	Percent Hispanic or Latino
	ACS table number:	B01003	Population estimates	B01001	B01001	B01001	B01001	B01001	B01001	B01002	B02008	B02009	B02011 + B02012	B02010 + B02013	C03002
		1	2	3	4	5	6	7	8	9	10	11	12	13	14
	Michigan—Cont.														
26 55020	Monroe	22,187	-0.5	6.0	19.4	10.9	30.2	21.7	11.8	33.2	91.4	7.4	-	3.9	6.4
26 56020	Mount Pleasant	24,174	0.4	4.4	7.6	51.2	19.0	10.3	7.6	22.0	87.2	7.1	3.7	5.1	2.9
26 56320	Muskegon	40,738	-0.5	6.3	16.9	11.6	31.7	23.3	10.1	33.6	57.9	36.9	0.7	6.9	9.0
26 59140	Norton Shores	23,752	0.2	5.8	19.3	7.1	24.2	27.2	16.4	40.6	95.8	2.1	1.5	2.4	2.9
26 59440	Novi	52,495	2.3	5.7	19.7	8.0	30.2	27.3	9.1	37.5	81.1	4.6	14.5	1.5	3.6
26 59920	Oak Park	28,427	-1.3	6.6	18.7	10.2	27.2	26.9	10.3	36.1	45.2	52.6	2.1	-	1.0
26 60340	Okemos CDP	22,031	-	5.0	19.3	9.4	23.8	29.3	13.1	38.8	81.3	6.5	12.9	1.3	1.6
26 65085	Plymouth Township CDP	30,066	-	6.9	16.0	8.9	22.9	31.3	14.1	42.5	92.6	2.5	4.1	0.7	1.1
26 65440	Pontiac	62,881	-0.8	8.3	20.9	10.8	31.0	20.6	8.4	31.3	34.4	53.6	3.1	13.0	15.5
26 65560	Portage	46,475	0.6	6.1	18.7	9.6	27.4	26.0	12.1	37.3	90.8	5.5	3.5	2.8	2.9
26 65820	Port Huron	31,870	-1.2	7.8	18.6	9.4	31.2	20.8	12.2	31.3	88.4	10.4	0.8	3.9	6.3
26 67620	Redford CDP	50,734	-	6.6	16.9	8.1	30.2	26.0	12.3	38.8	77.2	20.2	1.3	2.7	4.0
26 69035	Rochester Hills	71,728	-0.6	6.4	17.9	8.5	25.4	30.2	11.6	40.3	85.5	4.2	10.2	1.5	3.4
26 69420	Romulus	26,192	-0.3	11.0	20.3	6.0	29.8	25.8	7.0	34.1	55.9	43.6	-	1.8	
26 69800	Roseville	45,441	-1.2	5.6	17.7	7.4	31.0	24.0	14.3	38.1	90.8	7.1	2.4	1.6	2.5
26 70040	Royal Oak	56,790	-1.1	5.0	10.9	9.2	32.4	29.0	13.5	40.1	94.7	2.6	2.4	1.1	1.6
26 70520	Saginaw	54,190	-2.7	7.8	21.5	11.3	25.7	22.7	11.0	32.2	49.9	47.2	-	4.1	11.5
26 70545	Saginaw Township North CDP	25,581	-	6.0	13.4	11.8	22.6	26.1	20.1	42.0	81.7	10.7	6.2	5.6	6.6
26 70760	St. Clair Shores	59,856	-1.1	4.8	14.5	7.0	26.1	27.3	20.3	43.4	95.9	2.7	1.8	1.5	1.5
26 72818	Shelby CDP	71,984	-	5.2	18.6	8.9	27.6	28.0	11.7	39.2	94.5	2.0	3.0	1.6	3.0
26 74900	Southfield	71,895	-1.5	5.4	16.6	8.1	26.5	27.8	15.5	39.8	32.9	65.4	1.9	2.0	1.2
26 74960	Southgate	31,506	-3.2	5.1	16.2	8.2	27.7	26.3	16.5	40.0	89.7	6.6	1.8	3.4	6.4
26 76460	Sterling Heights	131,113	-0.2	5.6	17.3	8.9	28.8	26.8	12.7	38.0	88.8	3.9	6.9	1.5	1.9
26 79000	Taylor	66,225	-3.7	7.4	17.4	8.5	28.0	26.3	12.4	36.8	82.7	13.9	1.6	3.2	4.3
26 80700	Troy	81,542	-0.3	5.6	18.9	8.0	25.1	30.9	11.5	40.2	78.2	4.4	16.8	1.9	1.0
26 82960	Walker	23,732	1.2	7.4	16.3	13.9	29.5	22.3	10.6	31.7	94.4	2.6	1.2	3.3	3.3
26 84000	Warren	132,464	-0.4	6.7	16.4	8.0	28.7	23.9	16.2	38.3	85.6	10.2	4.7	1.8	1.4
26 84220	Waterford CDP	73,163	-	5.9	16.0	8.9	28.9	28.5	11.7	39.9	92.9	4.0	1.2	3.5	4.8
26 85510	West Bloomfield Township CDP	65,942	-	5.6	18.9	7.4	21.9	30.5	15.6	42.4	82.8	8.3	9.4	0.2	0.9
26 86000	Westland	87,539	-4.0	6.1	16.1	8.6	29.8	25.4	13.9	38.4	81.7	13.8	3.6	2.8	4.0
26 88900	Wyandotte	29,090	-4.5	3.9	19.2	6.3	30.8	27.0	12.9	39.9	97.1	1.5	1.2	2.0	3.8
26 88940	Wyoming	71,119	0.4	7.8	19.0	10.0	32.9	21.7	8.6	31.7	81.2	6.3	3.6	11.4	15.7
26 89140	Ypsilanti	22,546	-0.2	6.5	9.1	31.0	28.2	18.1	7.1	26.3	64.7	33.5	2.3	0.9	1.9
27 00000	**MINNESOTA**	5,155,344	1.6	6.7	17.7	9.9	27.8	25.7	12.2	36.9	89.5	5.0	3.9	3.4	3.8
27 01486	Andover	30,105	2.8	7.5	25.6	6.8	30.1	26.3	3.8	35.1	94.1	1.2	3.5	0.5	1.4
27 01900	Apple Valley	49,624	1.0	6.7	20.2	8.8	28.1	28.0	8.1	36.2	88.5	5.5	5.7	2.3	3.6
27 02908	Austin	22,836	-0.8	7.1	16.1	9.1	24.7	22.4	20.7	39.5	93.4	2.1	1.7	3.2	10.1
27 06382	Blaine	54,995	3.6	7.3	17.8	9.4	33.1	25.3	7.1	34.4	87.9	3.8	8.1	2.6	2.3
27 06616	Bloomington	82,521	-0.1	5.5	14.4	7.2	25.8	29.8	17.3	43.4	84.1	7.5	5.4	4.5	5.0
27 07948	Brooklyn Center	30,678	-0.7	8.5	19.3	8.5	26.7	23.2	13.8	34.3	61.3	24.0	13.1	6.7	9.0
27 07966	Brooklyn Park	73,328	3.6	8.9	21.0	8.4	29.6	24.8	7.3	34.0	64.2	24.2	12.4	2.4	4.0
27 08794	Burnsville	60,049	0.4	6.0	17.6	10.4	30.0	26.2	9.8	36.1	82.6	9.3	6.1	4.2	4.7
27 10846	Champlin	24,250	0.8	7.4	23.6	7.5	29.8	26.7	5.0	35.7	91.0	4.9	4.2	0.5	1.9
27 10918	Chanhassen	24,132	3.1	6.8	23.5	10.0	28.3	26.2	5.1	35.1	93.1	3.0	4.6	-	1.0
27 10972	Chaska	21,967	5.3	7.4	21.9	9.1	33.4	22.2	6.1	32.4	92.1	-	2.1	5.6	
27 13114	Coon Rapids	60,600	0.0	6.6	19.6	9.2	29.8	25.4	9.4	35.2	91.6	4.4	3.3	2.3	2.7
27 13456	Cottage Grove	32,229	3.0	6.0	23.4	9.8	30.8	23.7	6.2	33.2	88.9	5.2	4.8	3.4	4.9
27 14158	Crystal	21,955	-0.6	8.2	13.5	6.4	31.6	27.4	13.0	39.9	86.8	7.4	4.1	4.6	6.5
27 17000	Duluth	84,532	-0.4	5.6	14.0	19.6	23.5	23.6	13.7	33.6	94.1	2.5	1.5	3.6	0.9
27 17288	Eagan	61,949	0.7	6.5	19.7	7.9	32.1	28.2	5.6	35.6	87.4	5.8	6.9	1.9	2.6
27 18116	Eden Prairie	61,262	1.2	7.0	20.7	6.5	30.9	28.3	6.5	36.7	85.8	4.8	7.9	3.4	3.6
27 18188	Edina	48,959	0.3	6.2	18.2	4.0	21.6	29.4	20.7	45.1	93.0	2.4	3.7	1.5	2.5
27 18674	Elk River	21,177	7.4	8.4	20.1	11.2	31.3	21.8	7.1	31.1	96.7	1.6	2.1	-	-
27 20546	Faribault	20,609	0.0	6.6	17.1	9.6	31.3	22.4	13.0	34.7	92.3	4.2	1.2	2.9	12.6
27 22814	Fridley	25,709	-1.2	5.2	17.0	9.0	27.6	27.1	14.1	38.7	85.6	9.3	3.0	5.2	4.1
27 24308	Golden Valley	20,765	-0.5	5.9	13.9	5.4	24.5	31.1	19.2	45.1	89.5	7.0	5.1	1.1	1.5
27 27530	Hastings	20,249	4.1	7.7	18.7	8.7	26.2	26.6	12.1	35.8	97.9	0.5	1.0	1.0	-
27 31076	Inver Grove Heights	32,148	1.5	6.8	18.3	9.8	28.7	27.6	8.8	37.6	90.0	4.0	3.8	3.6	4.5
27 35180	Lakeville	53,789	5.7	8.6	26.2	6.4	31.6	22.9	4.3	33.1	92.7	2.8	4.2	2.1	2.7
27 39878	Mankato	35,586	2.0	5.6	11.5	28.5	26.7	16.4	11.3	26.8	91.4	4.0	3.7	2.8	2.6
27 40166	Maple Grove	59,705	3.0	8.2	20.8	6.4	29.6	29.7	5.4	37.6	89.3	3.5	5.3	3.1	2.5
27 40382	Maplewood	35,919	2.3	6.8	17.8	6.7	25.5	27.4	15.8	41.1	85.4	7.9	6.3	3.3	3.5
27 43000	Minneapolis	362,513	0.7	7.3	13.6	13.3	34.1	23.2	8.4	33.7	70.8	19.5	5.7	7.4	9.5
27 43252	Minnetonka	51,057	0.1	5.5	16.5	5.8	24.3	33.4	14.5	43.9	93.6	3.6	3.4	1.4	1.4
27 43864	Moorhead	33,533	3.9	5.9	13.6	26.0	21.9	19.3	13.2	28.0	94.1	1.4	2.1	4.4	3.5
27 45430	New Brighton	21,654	0.6	6.4	17.0	6.4	25.4	27.6	17.1	41.4	87.1	7.6	5.6	1.2	3.8
27 45628	New Hope	20,344	0.9	6.5	13.8	6.9	27.7	24.9	20.1	42.1	87.2	6.4	5.1	2.8	8.1
27 47680	Oakdale	27,166	0.2	6.3	19.3	12.4	26.9	27.5	7.6	34.8	87.9	6.4	4.8	2.6	2.4
27 49300	Owatonna	24,548	3.1	7.9	18.6	9.1	28.3	24.0	12.1	35.2	93.6	3.3	1.4	1.8	7.1
27 51730	Plymouth	70,488	1.4	6.7	18.8	7.3	27.9	29.8	9.5	38.7	88.6	4.3	7.6	1.1	1.9
27 52594	Prior Lake	19,319	5.5	9.0	20.1	7.3	32.8	25.1	5.7	35.4	94.1	1.5	2.5	2.8	1.1
27 53026	Ramsey	21,392	6.0	7.1	23.3	8.6	31.1	25.2	4.7	34.7	94.8	2.3	2.0	2.5	3.6

Table A-4. Cities — Who: Age, Race/Ethnicity, and Household Structure, 2005–2007—*Continued*

STATE City	Percent foreign born	Total households	Household type (percent)						Percent of households with people under 18 years	Percent of households with people 60 years and over
			Family households				Nonfamily households			
			Total family households	Married-couple families	Male householder families	Female householder families	Total nonfamily households	One-person households		
ACS table number:	C05002	B11001	B11001	B11001	B11001	B11001	B11001	B11001	C11005	B11006
	15	16	17	18	19	20	21	22	23	24
Michigan—Cont.										
Monroe	4.4	8,887	66.4	45.8	4.6	16.0	33.6	28.1	39.0	27.8
Mount Pleasant	4.0	7,958	37.1	23.8	2.7	10.5	62.9	32.5	20.4	20.4
Muskegon	4.3	13,974	57.7	33.1	3.1	21.5	42.3	36.8	33.6	28.4
Norton Shores	2.0	9,935	66.3	52.6	4.5	9.2	33.7	29.5	33.5	35.9
Novi	18.4	21,316	66.0	55.1	2.5	8.4	34.0	29.7	36.4	22.6
Oak Park	13.4	11,322	62.8	39.1	6.7	16.9	37.2	31.5	32.4	31.1
Okemos CDP	17.2	8,724	65.6	55.0	2.2	8.4	34.4	26.9	33.0	26.0
Plymouth Township CDP	7.5	11,252	71.0	64.5	2.4	4.0	29.0	26.5	31.4	36.7
Pontiac	8.3	23,180	59.8	28.8	7.4	23.6	40.2	34.6	37.0	23.9
Portage	5.5	19,378	62.5	49.1	4.2	9.3	37.5	31.2	32.5	29.1
Port Huron	2.8	12,921	62.9	40.2	5.3	17.4	37.1	30.8	36.2	28.3
Redford CDP	3.6	19,360	63.8	44.3	5.8	13.6	36.2	30.5	31.9	29.0
Rochester Hills	16.6	27,252	71.4	61.2	3.4	6.8	28.6	24.6	35.3	30.7
Romulus	1.8	9,144	69.6	44.7	4.8	20.1	30.4	27.5	39.3	23.4
Roseville	4.4	19,218	60.3	42.8	4.8	12.8	39.7	33.8	30.2	31.8
Royal Oak	5.9	27,759	48.6	37.6	3.6	7.4	51.4	42.5	20.0	25.9
Saginaw	1.1	20,067	61.4	28.4	5.1	27.8	38.6	33.3	39.0	27.1
Saginaw Township North CDP	5.6	10,800	62.7	51.9	2.3	8.5	37.3	30.7	26.6	39.0
St. Clair Shores	5.5	26,818	59.5	46.3	4.1	9.0	40.5	36.9	23.9	40.6
Shelby CDP	10.2	27,591	70.6	58.9	3.7	8.1	29.4	24.8	33.8	30.9
Southfield	10.7	31,611	57.2	35.2	4.6	17.4	42.8	39.5	29.4	35.0
Southgate	6.2	13,109	59.3	45.7	3.4	10.3	40.7	36.2	27.0	36.5
Sterling Heights	21.4	49,429	70.1	57.4	4.2	8.6	29.9	25.3	32.7	33.0
Taylor	5.6	24,233	69.7	46.3	5.5	17.9	30.3	25.5	34.5	30.4
Troy	21.9	31,159	72.3	62.5	3.3	6.4	27.7	23.8	36.8	31.9
Walker	3.7	9,387	61.9	50.8	3.2	7.9	38.1	29.0	32.6	22.7
Warren	10.2	54,157	64.1	45.5	5.4	13.2	35.9	32.4	30.6	34.5
Waterford CDP	5.9	30,516	63.1	47.3	4.7	11.1	36.9	32.1	30.0	27.9
West Bloomfield Township CDP	22.7	24,387	74.2	65.8	2.5	6.0	25.8	23.7	35.4	38.5
Westland	8.3	34,331	61.5	43.6	4.2	13.6	38.5	34.2	30.4	30.8
Wyandotte	2.4	11,654	59.3	45.3	3.8	10.3	40.7	34.4	30.1	31.2
Wyoming	11.6	26,717	66.4	47.7	5.8	12.9	33.6	26.7	35.5	22.9
Ypsilanti	4.4	8,541	44.2	31.4	2.4	10.4	55.8	37.8	20.5	18.3
Minnesota	6.5	2,041,466	65.4	52.3	4.0	9.2	34.6	27.9	33.3	28.0
Andover	4.4	9,489	86.2	78.4	4.1	3.7	13.8	10.9	50.4	17.0
Apple Valley	7.7	18,419	74.1	56.7	4.9	12.5	25.9	21.0	40.6	21.8
Austin	6.2	9,820	61.4	43.9	6.0	11.5	38.6	30.8	27.5	40.2
Blaine	8.8	20,448	74.3	59.1	5.4	9.9	25.7	19.0	37.5	20.7
Bloomington	10.1	35,347	61.5	48.1	3.6	9.9	38.5	32.5	26.5	35.6
Brooklyn Center	20.1	10,859	71.7	44.8	8.5	18.4	28.3	21.5	41.7	31.4
Brooklyn Park	19.3	25,695	73.7	53.4	4.4	15.9	26.3	20.4	44.6	20.7
Burnsville	11.8	24,475	64.3	45.1	5.2	14.0	35.7	28.0	33.8	23.5
Champlin	5.7	8,309	81.4	68.6	3.2	9.6	18.6	17.0	49.4	14.9
Chanhassen	6.6	8,488	78.3	69.9	1.9	6.5	21.7	16.2	46.3	16.1
Chaska	9.1	8,281	71.3	58.6	2.8	10.0	28.7	22.9	42.0	18.1
Coon Rapids	6.3	23,451	68.5	52.0	4.1	12.4	31.5	25.5	37.9	23.2
Cottage Grove	5.4	11,220	79.1	65.0	4.0	10.1	20.9	17.6	47.9	19.4
Crystal	10.8	9,468	58.1	45.8	3.8	8.5	41.9	35.0	28.0	30.1
Duluth	2.7	35,619	52.2	38.5	3.0	10.7	47.8	35.8	26.0	30.3
Eagan	9.3	24,997	65.5	53.0	4.3	8.2	34.5	27.9	37.1	16.8
Eden Prairie	12.1	23,106	71.1	59.3	3.8	8.0	28.9	23.7	39.4	17.8
Edina	8.1	21,347	60.3	53.2	2.6	4.5	39.7	35.9	29.8	42.2
Elk River	2.8	7,517	71.4	61.7	4.8	4.8	28.6	21.5	43.5	19.7
Faribault	9.0	7,672	65.0	45.8	3.9	15.3	35.0	27.1	34.0	31.6
Fridley	9.3	10,996	63.8	44.2	6.5	13.1	36.2	29.3	30.9	29.8
Golden Valley	8.0	8,949	62.1	51.3	2.9	7.9	37.9	31.2	25.9	37.7
Hastings	1.7	7,721	73.4	59.2	3.0	11.3	26.6	22.9	40.5	28.9
Inver Grove Heights	4.6	12,894	66.2	53.1	2.5	10.6	33.8	26.2	34.3	23.1
Lakeville	5.5	17,508	84.2	67.8	5.5	10.9	15.8	12.8	54.9	14.8
Mankato	6.5	13,943	47.7	33.4	4.0	10.4	52.3	33.6	26.8	26.0
Maple Grove	7.2	21,558	74.7	63.7	3.1	7.9	25.3	21.9	42.9	19.5
Maplewood	6.7	14,328	67.1	51.6	4.9	10.6	32.9	27.9	31.5	34.9
Minneapolis	15.3	155,155	45.3	29.1	4.8	11.4	54.7	42.7	24.3	19.9
Minnetonka	6.1	22,173	62.0	52.0	3.9	6.1	38.0	31.5	29.2	31.9
Moorhead	3.5	12,827	58.6	45.1	4.3	9.1	41.4	30.4	29.1	27.2
New Brighton	7.7	9,271	61.7	48.7	1.7	11.3	38.3	31.7	27.9	35.3
New Hope	11.3	8,320	58.6	45.0	2.7	10.9	41.4	36.9	26.6	37.7
Oakdale	9.6	11,205	62.8	47.6	4.8	10.4	37.2	30.5	34.8	20.8
Owatonna	4.0	9,325	71.9	59.3	2.9	9.6	28.1	25.4	35.7	27.7
Plymouth	10.3	27,801	67.8	56.3	2.3	9.2	32.2	26.3	36.4	25.5
Prior Lake	4.1	6,955	72.2	62.4	2.2	7.6	27.8	22.0	41.5	19.1
Ramsey	4.3	6,955	85.2	74.5	5.2	5.5	14.8	10.5	48.7	16.1

Table A-4. Cities — Who: Age, Race/Ethnicity, and Household Structure, 2005–2007—*Continued*

STATE Place code	STATE City	Total population	Percent change 2005–2007	Population by age (percent) Under 5 years	5 to 17 years	18 to 24 years	25 to 44 years	45 to 64 years	65 years and over	Median age	Race alone or in combination (percent) White	Black	Asian Hawaiian or Pacific Islander	Amer. Indian, Alaska Native, or some other race	Percent Hispanic or Latino
	ACS table number:	B01003	Population estimates	B01001	B01001	B01001	B01001	B01001	B01001	B01002	B02008	B02009	B02011 + B02012	B02010 + B02013	C03002
		1	2	3	4	5	6	7	8	9	10	11	12	13	14
	Minnesota—Cont.														
27 54214	Richfield	33,749	-0.8	7.4	12.8	8.2	31.8	25.6	14.2	37.9	74.1	9.9	6.0	12.3	14.7
27 54880	Rochester	95,179	3.9	8.0	16.8	8.3	30.9	24.1	12.0	35.7	88.1	5.4	7.1	1.0	3.5
27 55726	Rosemount	19,989	9.3	9.1	22.1	6.6	31.5	24.1	6.6	34.9	89.9	5.3	4.5	0.8	1.7
27 55852	Roseville	33,811	0.6	4.7	14.1	10.9	20.9	25.8	23.5	44.6	86.3	6.1	6.5	2.1	4.0
27 56896	St. Cloud	63,270	1.2	6.2	11.5	24.9	25.5	21.3	10.7	28.9	90.1	5.2	4.0	1.9	1.1
27 57220	St. Louis Park	44,139	1.2	6.9	13.0	8.4	35.6	23.7	12.3	35.8	87.8	8.7	3.6	4.7	5.1
27 58000	St. Paul	271,203	0.1	7.6	18.2	11.4	29.8	23.0	10.0	33.6	69.1	15.6	12.9	6.1	8.7
27 58738	Savage	26,750	5.1	8.3	23.2	9.3	34.6	20.5	4.1	31.4	88.2	3.5	7.6	0.9	-
27 59350	Shakopee	33,942	8.2	9.9	18.6	9.3	37.7	17.4	7.2	31.0	84.4	4.1	9.2	3.4	4.7
27 59998	Shoreview	26,118	0.0	5.5	17.5	7.0	25.3	32.6	12.2	42.1	94.4	-	4.7	0.4	-
27 69970	White Bear Lake	24,576	-0.2	6.0	17.1	6.5	25.2	28.7	16.6	42.0	96.4	2.1	1.7	1.3	2.3
27 71032	Winona	26,008	-0.3	4.9	11.7	28.6	21.6	19.7	13.6	28.1	95.9	1.9	2.7	0.7	0.8
27 71428	Woodbury	56,008	7.0	8.2	20.5	6.9	33.2	24.4	6.8	34.1	86.2	4.4	9.1	2.3	3.8
28 00000	**Mississippi**	2,906,118	0.6	7.4	19.0	10.7	26.3	24.3	12.4	35.1	60.9	37.5	1.0	1.6	1.8
28 06220	Biloxi	42,311	-12.5	5.7	16.6	13.0	26.9	25.0	12.9	36.9	72.7	20.1	5.9	3.7	5.9
28 08300	Brandon	18,577	6.6	6.6	16.9	8.5	28.0	27.8	12.2	36.0	85.6	14.5	-	-	-
28 14420	Clinton	28,234	1.3	6.1	18.2	15.4	25.5	22.5	12.4	33.0	64.3	32.5	2.8	3.4	1.7
28 15380	Columbus	23,955	-1.1	7.4	19.1	9.6	23.3	24.0	16.6	37.7	40.2	59.2	-	-	-
28 29180	Greenville	38,897	-4.0	8.1	21.7	9.8	25.0	23.1	12.3	33.7	25.4	75.2	-	0.5	-
28 29700	Gulfport	69,084	-9.6	7.8	19.1	9.0	27.6	24.5	12.1	35.0	59.0	37.7	2.1	3.5	3.9
28 31020	Hattiesburg	47,420	3.6	7.1	13.4	24.0	26.1	18.6	10.8	27.3	45.1	50.3	2.5	3.1	2.4
28 33700	Horn Lake	21,536	9.7	7.3	22.0	11.8	32.7	19.1	7.0	30.2	76.3	21.9	-	1.1	-
28 36000	Jackson	174,983	-1.1	8.6	20.2	11.9	26.2	23.0	10.2	31.9	22.3	76.5	0.7	1.2	1.4
28 46640	Meridian	36,351	-0.5	9.1	18.8	8.7	25.2	22.5	15.7	35.7	38.1	60.5	-	0.4	-
28 54040	Olive Branch	29,150	10.5	7.2	21.0	6.8	30.8	24.5	9.8	34.6	80.5	18.3	0.6	0.6	-
28 55360	Pascagoula	21,865	-5.8	6.4	19.4	9.1	27.3	24.7	13.1	35.9	65.1	33.7	-	2.7	-
28 55760	Pearl	23,707	1.4	7.3	17.8	11.9	26.1	25.6	11.3	33.4	77.5	20.9	0.8	-	-
28 62520	Ridgeland	23,411	0.6	6.5	15.2	15.5	33.8	19.9	9.1	30.8	71.2	25.4	2.2	1.2	-
28 69280	Southaven	42,469	10.2	8.8	22.4	8.4	31.6	19.6	9.2	30.2	76.5	21.0	2.2	1.7	3.4
28 70240	Starkville	23,577	4.8	7.2	13.2	32.3	23.8	15.0	8.4	24.4	61.9	35.0	4.5	0.4	-
28 74840	Tupelo	35,901	1.7	10.1	19.3	7.4	28.2	23.0	12.1	34.5	66.6	32.9	1.0	1.8	2.2
28 76720	Vicksburg	25,113	-0.2	8.6	20.1	9.4	24.3	24.1	13.5	35.0	31.1	66.0	1.4	1.5	1.2
29 00000	**Missouri**	5,834,644	1.6	6.7	17.7	9.7	27.0	25.6	13.4	37.3	85.6	12.0	1.8	2.5	2.9
29 00280	Affton CDP	20,516	-	4.9	13.1	11.1	27.2	27.7	16.0	40.2	97.7	-	1.3	-	-
29 01972	Arnold	19,744	2.2	5.5	16.5	11.1	28.4	26.6	11.8	38.5	98.7	0.5	-	-	-
29 03160	Ballwin	30,961	-0.8	6.6	18.3	7.5	25.4	29.2	12.9	39.4	93.8	1.6	4.6	0.3	3.2
29 04384	Belton	22,903	2.7	6.6	21.3	9.8	28.1	23.9	10.3	32.6	87.6	8.2	1.5	4.7	8.0
29 06652	Blue Springs	51,881	3.6	8.2	20.8	7.1	27.8	28.5	7.6	35.8	92.5	5.5	1.9	2.0	2.4
29 11242	Cape Girardeau	37,525	2.4	6.5	14.3	18.5	24.5	22.3	13.9	32.5	87.0	11.7	2.1	1.2	1.5
29 13600	Chesterfield	49,055	-1.3	5.1	17.0	7.0	19.2	32.9	18.7	46.0	90.3	2.2	7.0	1.1	1.6
29 15670	Columbia	93,863	5.6	6.3	12.9	25.1	28.2	18.5	8.9	28.0	83.5	11.1	5.0	3.1	3.1
29 23986	Ferguson	20,600	-1.3	7.7	20.8	10.8	26.5	22.9	11.4	33.7	40.8	58.6	-	0.9	-
29 24778	Florissant	52,077	-1.3	7.6	18.9	9.0	25.3	24.0	15.2	37.4	77.4	22.0	1.0	1.5	-
29 27190	Gladstone	26,384	2.8	6.7	16.4	8.2	25.0	27.8	15.8	40.8	89.3	7.8	1.3	3.4	6.5
29 28324	Grandview	23,294	-1.8	7.2	17.0	9.0	28.3	25.9	12.6	38.4	52.8	40.7	1.4	7.3	7.3
29 31276	Hazelwood	25,015	0.1	5.6	17.3	8.9	25.6	30.8	11.7	39.7	69.4	28.9	1.1	1.2	-
29 35000	Independence	116,214	-0.6	7.2	16.4	7.2	26.9	27.0	15.2	39.7	91.2	5.2	1.1	4.9	7.0
29 37000	Jefferson	41,014	1.3	6.4	13.9	11.2	27.2	27.1	14.2	38.9	83.3	13.7	2.5	3.1	2.1
29 37592	Joplin	47,599	3.7	8.3	14.3	11.5	27.9	23.0	15.1	35.2	92.5	3.4	1.2	3.8	3.5
29 38000	Kansas	436,562	1.5	7.5	17.3	9.2	30.2	24.5	11.3	35.4	64.5	30.6	2.7	4.8	8.8
29 39044	Kirkwood	27,025	-0.5	6.3	15.3	8.0	22.8	31.5	16.2	43.5	92.2	6.5	0.7	1.4	-
29 41348	Lee's Summit	89,464	3.4	8.3	21.8	7.0	28.7	24.5	9.7	36.4	89.8	7.6	2.7	1.7	2.5
29 42032	Liberty	28,303	3.7	7.4	18.6	10.2	27.5	26.6	9.7	35.6	94.4	5.1	0.8	3.1	3.2
29 46586	Maryland Heights	26,226	-1.3	5.0	13.5	10.9	33.6	26.5	10.5	36.4	81.1	7.8	9.9	1.7	3.1
29 47180	Mehlville CDP	28,471	-	5.1	15.1	9.8	23.3	28.5	18.2	42.7	94.2	2.3	2.4	1.1	-
29 53876	Oakville CDP	35,771	-	4.2	18.0	10.3	19.7	34.2	13.6	43.3	97.3	0.7	2.2	-	0.3
29 54074	O'Fallon	69,868	8.3	9.0	21.7	7.9	33.6	20.7	7.1	32.3	94.1	3.9	2.2	0.9	1.2
29 60788	Raytown	29,969	-1.8	7.0	15.9	6.5	26.5	26.4	17.6	41.2	77.7	19.7	2.8	2.1	4.8
29 64082	St. Charles	61,813	2.6	5.4	14.8	14.4	26.6	25.2	13.7	37.9	93.6	4.8	2.1	1.2	3.8
29 64550	St. Joseph	73,476	1.3	6.8	16.7	11.0	27.8	23.2	14.6	36.6	93.0	6.1	0.9	2.5	3.3
29 65000	St. Louis	352,389	-0.5	7.4	17.8	9.5	28.9	24.5	11.9	35.8	47.2	50.4	2.4	1.7	2.6
29 65126	St. Peters	52,420	2.2	6.0	19.1	9.6	29.6	26.2	9.4	35.4	92.7	4.5	2.3	1.9	2.0
29 66440	Sedalia	20,039	2.2	6.7	17.9	9.2	27.7	22.5	16.1	36.1	91.7	5.1	0.8	4.1	7.7
29 69266	Spanish Lake CDP	21,594	-	10.6	23.5	9.1	29.4	18.8	8.6	30.3	25.2	73.8	1.7	1.8	-
29 70000	Springfield	153,727	1.4	5.9	13.1	17.2	27.2	21.8	14.8	34.0	92.8	4.7	2.1	2.8	2.8
29 75220	University	32,885	-1.4	5.7	13.7	11.3	27.4	25.3	16.6	38.1	51.9	42.6	4.7	2.0	2.1
29 78154	Webster Groves	21,552	-1.4	4.8	18.7	6.3	24.2	30.0	16.0	42.8	90.5	8.1	1.1	0.5	-
29 78442	Wentzville	18,838	24.4	11.4	22.1	8.5	33.1	17.6	7.2	29.5	88.3	10.7	1.7	1.0	1.5
29 79820	Wildwood	36,786	-1.2	6.2	24.8	8.6	22.9	31.3	6.2	38.2	93.2	3.8	3.2	1.7	2.6

STATE City	Percent foreign born	Total households	Household type (percent)						Percent of households with people under 18 years	Percent of households with people 60 years and over
			Family households				Nonfamily households			
			Total family households	Married-couple families	Male householder families	Female householder families	Total nonfamily households	One-person households		
ACS table number:	C05002	B11001	B11001	B11001	B11001	B11001	B11001	B11001	C11005	B11006
	15	16	17	18	19	20	21	22	23	24
Minnesota—Cont.										
Richfield...........................	17.7	14,435	55.3	38.4	6.5	10.4	44.7	37.0	24.1	33.0
Rochester........................	10.9	39,203	60.8	49.8	2.5	8.5	39.2	32.6	32.7	25.9
Rosemount......................	6.9	7,038	78.7	67.1	3.4	8.3	21.3	18.3	47.0	17.7
Roseville.........................	9.6	14,451	54.2	43.6	2.3	8.3	45.8	40.0	21.2	45.2
St. Cloud	5.3	24,580	52.7	41.5	4.0	7.3	47.3	31.2	25.9	23.2
St. Louis Park	9.9	20,652	49.7	37.5	3.1	9.2	50.3	41.0	23.8	22.8
St. Paul	14.7	107,237	53.0	34.3	5.0	13.8	47.0	37.9	29.7	23.3
Savage............................	10.1	8,561	81.8	71.2	4.1	6.5	18.2	12.1	50.8	14.4
Shakopee.........................	12.9	12,105	70.8	56.0	4.7	10.1	29.2	21.0	42.7	18.6
Shoreview........................	5.4	10,734	67.2	56.5	4.1	6.6	32.8	28.3	30.9	33.1
White Bear Lake................	3.1	10,488	62.3	49.4	2.8	10.1	37.7	34.1	28.2	31.8
Winona	3.5	10,487	49.5	41.8	1.7	5.9	50.5	40.2	22.6	30.6
Woodbury........................	10.3	20,464	73.5	63.5	2.8	7.2	26.5	20.8	41.4	19.0
Mississippi	1.7	1,079,584	69.8	46.9	4.7	18.2	30.2	26.3	37.4	31.9
Biloxi.............................	8.4	17,042	60.0	39.2	6.7	14.0	40.0	32.1	29.3	29.8
Brandon..........................	1.7	7,558	64.8	54.3	2.0	8.5	35.2	32.7	31.8	27.6
Clinton	2.0	10,112	67.5	48.0	2.5	17.0	32.5	29.1	32.4	29.8
Columbus........................	1.1	9,343	66.1	39.3	5.2	21.6	33.9	30.9	37.5	31.3
Greenville	0.4	14,495	67.5	30.4	6.5	30.6	32.5	29.9	39.3	33.5
Gulfport..........................	3.9	26,208	68.0	41.8	5.5	20.7	32.0	27.2	39.0	30.1
Hattiesburg......................	4.2	18,876	51.3	25.6	5.1	20.6	48.7	38.7	26.1	25.6
Horn Lake........................	3.8	7,999	69.8	46.0	5.5	18.4	30.2	22.8	39.1	21.0
Jackson...........................	1.4	63,674	61.9	29.3	5.7	26.9	38.1	33.1	37.4	26.7
Meridian..........................	0.3	15,946	58.9	27.9	4.9	26.0	41.1	37.3	35.7	32.0
Olive Branch	3.7	10,719	79.2	67.4	2.5	9.3	20.8	17.0	45.7	28.4
Pascagoula.......................	3.2	8,388	65.3	40.5	6.2	18.7	34.7	30.8	35.4	28.6
Pearl	2.2	9,368	68.3	43.4	4.8	20.1	31.7	27.5	34.7	29.6
Ridgeland	4.5	11,099	52.0	36.2	5.1	10.6	48.0	38.0	27.3	18.5
Southaven	3.8	15,900	71.0	49.2	4.7	17.0	29.0	22.3	42.4	23.6
Starkville.........................	3.4	9,858	48.9	31.4	2.9	14.6	51.1	34.4	28.9	19.2
Tupelo	1.3	13,258	67.0	44.1	4.4	18.5	33.0	29.5	38.1	28.3
Vicksburg.........................	1.8	10,461	60.7	29.9	5.1	25.8	39.3	35.6	36.4	29.1
Missouri	3.5	2,300,211	66.1	50.0	4.1	11.9	33.9	28.4	33.3	31.2
Affton CDP......................	12.4	9,112	60.4	43.3	4.3	12.8	39.6	33.8	24.9	33.1
Arnold............................	1.3	7,705	71.0	58.5	4.3	8.2	29.0	24.2	31.5	31.6
Ballwin............................	5.9	11,733	73.2	59.1	5.4	8.7	26.8	23.0	34.6	32.4
Belton	3.4	8,511	71.6	54.3	4.3	13.0	28.4	23.9	39.1	25.0
Blue Springs.....................	2.2	19,307	73.3	58.0	4.6	10.7	26.7	22.6	42.1	21.5
Cape Girardeau	2.4	15,325	60.1	40.3	4.5	15.3	39.9	31.7	29.6	27.9
Chesterfield	8.7	19,225	72.2	65.5	2.3	4.4	27.8	25.3	31.9	39.6
Columbia.........................	7.5	40,155	51.1	36.9	4.4	9.9	48.9	33.3	27	19.2
Ferguson..........................	0.7	8,494	66.6	32.0	7.0	27.5	33.4	30.1	38.9	24.4
Florissant	1.9	21,058	66.1	43.6	3.7	18.8	33.9	30.8	34.9	33.9
Gladstone........................	3.7	10,813	61.7	47.2	3.8	10.8	38.3	30.5	29.2	31.4
Grandview........................	5.8	9,703	58.7	38.4	3.9	16.4	41.3	34.5	31.5	26.0
Hazelwood	3.4	11,131	59.7	39.9	5.7	14.0	40.3	35.7	29.9	29.8
Independence...................	4.1	49,133	61.3	44.2	3.7	13.4	38.7	32.3	28.8	33.7
Jefferson.........................	4.1	16,806	55.9	43.3	2.5	10.0	44.1	38.3	27.8	26.3
Joplin.............................	2.7	19,829	59.7	43.5	3.9	12.3	40.3	32.5	31.2	35.6
Kansas............................	7.3	184,172	56.6	36.8	4.0	15.7	43.4	36.0	30.4	27.2
Kirkwood..........................	3.5	11,702	64.9	51.3	1.9	11.6	35.1	29.4	30.8	35.3
Lee's Summit.....................	2.9	33,160	73.4	60.2	3.2	9.9	26.6	22.2	42.8	26.4
Liberty	2.5	10,261	71.3	55.2	2.0	14.1	28.7	23.3	37.8	25.5
Maryland Heights..............	14.1	12,087	57.5	45.5	3.8	8.2	42.5	35.2	24.7	21.7
Mehlville CDP	8.7	12,456	57.6	45.7	2.9	9.1	42.4	36.9	25.4	35.2
Oakville CDP	4.0	13,561	75.0	66.8	2.8	5.5	25.0	22.4	35.5	32.8
O'Fallon	3.1	24,238	76.2	64.9	2.8	8.5	23.8	18.6	45.7	19.8
Raytown	4.5	12,713	66.1	46.1	6.6	13.4	33.9	31.2	31.7	34.7
St. Charles	3.9	25,475	61.5	47.9	3.2	10.4	38.5	30.0	27.6	30.0
St. Joseph	1.9	28,489	63.1	45.5	5.6	12.1	36.9	30.7	34.2	32.1
St. Louis	6.5	140,934	50.0	24.3	5.2	20.5	50.0	43.9	27.1	28.4
St. Peters	3.7	20,171	68.6	55.7	3.2	9.7	31.4	23.7	37.2	25.9
Sedalia............................	3.2	8,411	57.1	40.3	5.0	11.8	42.9	35.8	28.7	37.1
Spanish Lake CDP	1.4	8,387	66.5	36.4	4.8	25.3	33.5	30.4	44.6	24.8
Springfield	2.9	68,354	51.4	37.0	3.6	10.7	48.6	38.2	24.0	30.0
University.........................	8.0	15,366	53.8	34.0	3.5	16.3	46.2	37.4	22.8	33.8
Webster Groves	2.4	9,369	61.5	53.1	2.9	5.6	38.5	34.1	29.3	34.3
Wentzville........................	1.4	6,082	81.6	70.1	2.9	8.7	18.4	13.1	49.8	22.7
Wildwood.........................	6.0	11,973	83.6	73.6	3.3	6.7	16.4	13.2	49.1	24.5

Table A-4. Cities — Who: Age, Race/Ethnicity, and Household Structure, 2005–2007—*Continued*

STATE Place code	STATE City	Total population	Percent change 2005–2007	Population by age (percent)						Median age	Race alone or in combination (percent)				Percent Hispanic or Latino
				Under 5 years	5 to 17 years	18 to 24 years	25 to 44 years	45 to 64 years	65 years and over		White	Black	Asian Hawaiian or Pacific Islander	Amer. Indian, Alaska Native, or some other race	
	ACS table number:	B01003	Population estimates	B01001	B01001	B01001	B01001	B01001	B01001	B01002	B02008	B02009	B02011 + B02012	B02010 + B02013	C03002
		1	2	3	4	5	6	7	8	9	10	11	12	13	14
30 00000	**Montana**	946,815	2.4	6.1	17.1	10.1	24.7	28.2	13.8	39.3	91.6	0.9	1.2	8.5	2.5
30 06550	Billings	97,053	3.1	7.0	16.0	10.1	26.4	25.5	15.0	38.1	91.9	1.9	1.7	6.7	5.1
30 08950	Bozeman	34,836	8.5	6.4	8.2	29.6	30.7	18.0	7.2	27.2	93.9	-	2.5	4.9	3.0
30 11397	Butte-Silver Bow (balance)	32,086	-0.4	5.5	16.6	10.0	23.1	28.1	16.6	41.4	96.4	0.8	0.2	4.0	3.1
30 32800	Great Falls	58,397	1.1	6.6	17.5	8.6	24.9	26.2	16.2	39.6	91.9	1.9	1.7	7.2	3.3
30 35600	Helena	26,939	4.1	5.4	14.2	13.7	23.3	28.9	14.5	39.6	95.3	0.7	1.8	4.0	2.7
30 40075	Kalispell	18,392	9.9	7.9	15.7	7.5	27.8	23.4	17.6	36.1	96.4	1.7	0.5	2.5	-
30 50200	Missoula	62,982	4.2	5.3	12.8	19.4	29.6	22.6	10.3	30.7	94.7	1.3	2.7	3.8	2.6
31 00000	**Nebraska**	1,764,131	1.2	7.3	18.0	10.6	26.1	24.8	13.3	36.0	90.4	4.8	2.1	4.6	7.3
31 03950	Bellevue	43,643	2.3	7.7	19.1	12.0	26.9	22.4	11.9	33.8	87.4	6.4	4.6	4.0	8.9
31 10110	Columbus	21,504	2.6	7.9	18.9	8.8	26.1	22.7	15.5	36.7	92.9	-	1.8	6.3	-
31 17670	Fremont	25,797	0.7	6.8	17.0	11.0	24.8	22.7	17.7	37.6	93.9	-	1.1	5.6	7.1
31 19595	Grand Island	43,793	2.6	8.7	19.1	8.3	27.4	23.5	13.1	34.9	91.2	1.4	1.8	6.7	20.8
31 21415	Hastings	26,251	-0.4	6.7	16.7	13.1	23.2	24.0	16.1	36.1	94.7	1.0	2.9	2.9	7.7
31 25055	Kearney	29,351	2.7	7.8	13.9	23.7	25.6	18.6	10.4	27.7	94.8	1.7	1.3	3.5	4.7
31 28000	Lincoln	247,246	2.5	7.6	15.7	15.0	29.9	21.8	10.0	31.8	90.8	4.3	3.9	2.8	4.6
31 34615	Norfolk	23,461	-3.4	8.2	17.5	13.2	23.8	23.6	13.8	34.6	92.9	2.0	2.0	5.0	10.3
31 35000	North Platte	24,190	0.2	7.4	16.2	9.7	26.7	24.7	15.3	36.3	95.5	-	0.9	4.8	-
31 37000	Omaha	379,851	2.3	7.6	17.7	11.1	27.8	23.9	11.9	34.3	78.7	14.8	2.6	6.7	11.0
31 38295	Papillion	18,487	8.7	7.4	22.5	8.5	25.2	27.3	9.1	36.1	95.6	3.0	1.7	1.2	3.0
32 00000	**Nevada**	2,488,917	6.5	7.5	18.3	8.3	30.0	24.9	11.1	35.6	77.2	8.3	7.8	10.1	24.3
32 09700	Carson	55,244	-1.3	7.3	16.5	8.5	24.9	27.0	15.8	40.8	85.7	2.1	2.5	11.8	18.8
32 23770	Enterprise CDP	65,408	-	8.4	16.6	9.7	39.6	20.4	5.3	31.6	70.3	7.3	17.8	7.5	15.1
32 31900	Henderson	236,506	7.5	6.7	17.4	6.8	29.5	27.5	12.2	38.5	84.4	5.0	8.0	6.4	12.3
32 40000	Las Vegas	558,892	2.6	8.0	18.9	7.3	30.8	23.5	11.4	35.5	73.6	11.9	7.1	11.3	29.2
32 51800	North Las Vegas	189,305	20.2	10.8	22.7	8.9	33.5	18.2	5.8	29.6	67.2	19.6	8.2	8.6	38.6
32 53800	Pahrump CDP	35,011	-	5.2	16.5	8.8	21.2	25.4	23.0	44.3	90.4	2.8	1.9	7.4	11.4
32 54600	Paradise CDP	203,890	-	6.3	16.3	8.9	32.4	25.3	10.8	35.8	73.7	9.0	10.2	10.5	27.1
32 60600	Reno	211,183	4.1	7.4	15.4	12.4	29.6	24.2	11.0	34.6	78.0	3.8	7.8	13.3	22.1
32 68400	Sparks	80,216	5.9	7.1	20.6	6.6	29.0	25.4	11.4	36.5	81.2	2.6	7.1	11.4	23.5
32 68585	Spring Valley CDP	151,169	-	5.9	14.9	8.5	31.5	27.9	11.3	37.8	71.4	8.9	16.7	6.0	17.2
32 71400	Sunrise Manor CDP	192,664	-	8.5	22.5	8.4	30.3	21.7	8.6	32.1	69.1	13.0	9.3	12.4	41.3
32 71600	Sun Valley CDP	21,418	-	10.7	23.1	6.6	28.0	22.8	8.9	31.5	76.0	2.3	2.7	22.4	31.1
32 83800	Whitney CDP	24,527	-	9.0	15.8	10.8	33.7	21.8	9.1	33.1	81.1	7.6	6.9	9.2	40.8
32 84600	Winchester CDP	26,271	-	9.3	13.7	6.0	29.1	29.0	13.0	39.3	61.8	8.3	10.0	21.6	38.4
33 00000	**New Hampshire**	1,310,254	1.0	5.8	17.3	9.1	27.3	28.1	12.4	39.3	96.0	1.4	2.2	1.6	2.4
33 14200	Concord	42,019	0.7	5.0	14.9	9.5	30.4	26.3	14.0	38.1	94.6	2.5	2.8	1.1	2.4
33 17860	Derry CDP	23,526	-	6.7	18.7	10.5	29.6	25.6	8.9	35.8	96.0	1.6	1.7	1.6	2.5
33 18820	Dover	27,932	1.0	6.4	14.0	9.3	33.2	24.5	12.7	37.1	94.2	1.7	3.8	1.3	1.0
33 39300	Keene	24,269	-0.9	3.8	12.9	21.8	26.4	21.2	14.0	32.5	97.0	0.5	1.8	1.9	1.8
33 45140	Manchester	109,777	-0.2	7.3	15.7	9.9	30.9	24.1	12.0	36.4	91.2	4.3	2.6	3.1	7.3
33 50260	Nashua	86,969	-0.1	6.1	17.2	7.5	30.1	26.8	12.3	38.5	88.0	2.4	7.5	3.5	6.8
33 62900	Portsmouth	21,497	-0.4	7.0	12.9	8.3	33.7	26.5	11.7	36.6	93.5	1.6	5.2	1.4	1.5
33 65140	Rochester	30,039	1.7	6.3	17.5	7.1	29.3	25.6	14.1	38.4	98.6	1.0	0.7	1.4	0.9
34 00000	**New Jersey**	8,669,815	0.3	6.5	17.5	8.7	28.3	26.0	13.0	38.2	70.9	14.3	7.8	8.6	15.6
34 02080	Atlantic	35,770	-0.9	9.0	16.0	7.0	30.2	21.6	16.2	37.8	25.0	41.6	15.5	21.1	24.4
34 03580	Bayonne	61,323	-3.3	5.2	17.5	7.8	28.8	26.7	14.0	39.7	69.9	7.8	8.7	14.7	21.7
34 04690	Belleville CDP	35,712	-	5.8	15.8	10.6	31.2	24.8	11.9	36.4	57.9	6.9	11.5	24.7	39.0
34 05170	Bergenfield borough	26,606	0.1	5.1	15.7	9.2	27.5	29.4	13.2	40.5	52.2	10.6	27.2	11.7	19.7
34 06250	Bloomfield CDP	47,066	-	6.3	13.4	10.7	28.3	29.6	11.7	38.3	61.4	17.1	9.0	13.9	18.5
34 07600	Bridgeton	23,522	3.1	10.1	15.5	11.9	36.5	17.4	8.7	30.9	35.8	41.8	0.7	23.7	36.3
34 10000	Camden	70,390	-0.6	9.6	23.4	12.0	28.4	18.8	7.8	27.7	14.2	50.8	2.8	34.1	42.1
34 10750	Carteret borough	21,046	6.6	8.2	18.7	7.6	29.2	23.0	13.4	37.3	53.5	12.2	20.8	15.1	26.9
34 13570	Cliffside Park borough	20,736	0.1	3.5	10.6	8.9	30.2	29.0	17.8	42.9	73.5	3.5	11.8	12.6	-
34 13690	Clifton	78,444	-0.4	5.3	14.8	9.3	28.5	26.3	15.6	39.4	69.8	4.4	8.6	18.8	26.5
34 15670	Cranford CDP	22,944	-	6.3	17.6	7.7	23.8	29.0	15.7	41.2	92.0	3.6	3.3	1.5	3.8
34 18970	East Brunswick CDP	47,495	-	5.8	20.3	7.3	24.5	31.3	10.8	40.8	74.4	3.6	21.4	2.7	4.3
34 19390	East Orange	62,240	-2.3	7.5	20.0	9.8	28.2	22.1	12.3	34.4	5.5	89.6	1.5	4.6	7.7
34 20260	Edison CDP	102,175	-	6.6	14.7	8.6	30.6	25.3	14.2	38.4	51.1	9.4	36.1	5.0	7.8
34 21000	Elizabeth	126,538	0.4	9.0	18.0	10.1	31.9	21.2	9.7	32.9	45.8	21.8	2.9	31.1	56.2
34 21480	Englewood	26,462	7.9	5.4	16.8	11.4	25.8	26.9	13.8	40.1	45.7	39.5	7.5	11.3	27.3
34 22180	Ewing CDP	37,582	-	5.0	12.8	17.7	27.7	22.4	14.4	37.1	67.9	28.0	3.7	2.7	7.6
34 22470	Fair Lawn borough	34,728	-1.0	4.5	17.2	8.2	24.9	27.8	17.4	42.4	87.0	1.8	8.4	3.1	8.2
34 24420	Fort Lee borough	34,776	-0.8	6.0	10.7	5.2	30.6	26.6	20.9	43.2	59.7	2.4	34.8	4.0	9.6
34 25770	Garfield	29,940	-0.9	6.2	16.6	9.3	31.5	24.9	11.4	35.4	75.9	7.3	3.4	15.3	31.6
34 28680	Hackensack	44,998	-0.6	6.4	11.5	8.5	35.5	25.6	12.5	37.5	49.1	27.1	6.8	19.3	36.0
34 32250	Hoboken	40,681	1.8	4.6	6.5	10.6	57.6	13.5	7.3	32.9	80.3	4.6	7.4	11.2	17.6
34 34440	Irvington CDP	59,532	-	8.9	20.5	7.7	32.6	22.4	7.9	32.8	6.3	88.3	1.7	5.3	8.2
34 36000	Jersey	234,914	1.3	6.9	16.3	9.3	35.4	22.2	9.8	35.0	36.2	28.8	19.6	17.6	27.7
34 36510	Kearny town	38,415	-3.6	5.2	15.1	9.8	35.3	24.4	10.1	36.9	77.8	5.1	5.3	12.6	35.9
34 38580	Lakewood CDP	44,449	-	18.9	27.9	13.0	27.7	7.7	4.6	20.4	82.9	8.3	0.5	9.8	17.1
34 40350	Linden	41,552	-0.5	6.0	15.5	7.7	28.0	29.7	13.0	40.3	61.7	27.6	3.4	8.6	20.9
34 40920	Livingston CDP	29,580	-	7.0	19.6	7.8	21.5	28.7	15.3	41.8	79.7	1.1	18.0	1.4	-
34 41100	Lodi borough	25,827	-0.4	5.6	17.0	7.1	30.3	25.2	14.8	39.1	76.3	3.0	9.8	11.6	25.5

STATE City	Percent foreign born	Total households	Household type (percent)						Percent of households with people under 18 years	Percent of households with people 60 years and over
			Family households				Nonfamily households			
			Total family households	Married-couple families	Male householder families	Female householder families	Total nonfamily households	One-person households		
ACS table number:	C05002	B11001	B11001	B11001	B11001	B11001	B11001	B11001	C11005	B11006
	15	16	17	18	19	20	21	22	23	24
Montana	1.9	369,329	64.7	52.6	3.7	8.4	35.3	28.7	29.8	32.4
Billings	1.9	40,056	58.9	46.2	2.5	10.2	41.1	33.3	28.5	32.3
Bozeman	4.1	13,013	47.6	41.8	1.9	3.9	52.4	32.8	22.6	17.3
Butte-Silver Bow (balance)	1.4	13,972	58.7	44.1	3.3	11.3	41.3	32.0	25.9	33.1
Great Falls	2.0	23,810	62.2	47.5	4.8	9.9	37.8	32.2	31.2	34.7
Helena	2.2	11,317	51.4	39.7	3.3	8.4	48.6	43.1	22.3	31.0
Kalispell	0.9	7,122	55.9	42.5	3.0	10.3	44.1	37.9	26.2	34.1
Missoula	2.9	25,638	49.1	36.2	3.9	9.0	50.9	35.1	23.0	24.4
Nebraska	5.6	698,163	65.9	52.8	3.7	9.5	34.1	28.4	33.5	29.5
Bellevue	7.6	17,047	68.5	51.7	3.9	12.9	31.5	24.3	36.9	26.8
Columbus	7.6	8,845	68.7	53.6	2.1	13.0	31.3	28.0	34.3	32.0
Fremont	4.0	10,209	66.5	52.6	3.3	10.7	33.5	28.9	33.6	33.8
Grand Island	12.6	16,938	67.5	49.3	2.4	15.8	32.5	28.1	37.1	28.8
Hastings	6.5	10,128	65.3	50.4	2.3	12.5	34.7	29.0	33.5	34.0
Kearney	3.8	11,411	57.9	48.0	2.0	7.9	42.1	31.0	29.1	22.5
Lincoln	7.4	98,577	60.3	47.4	3.7	9.2	39.7	30.7	32.2	22.9
Norfolk	6.6	9,371	59.3	48.8	3.2	7.2	40.7	35.2	28.9	32.9
North Platte	1.9	10,384	63.0	48.8	5.6	8.6	37.0	28.1	33.1	30.8
Omaha	8.9	152,940	58.8	40.5	4.6	13.6	41.2	34.1	30.8	27.1
Papillion	1.5	6,718	77.6	61.9	5.0	10.7	22.4	19.1	43.0	24.5
Nevada	18.5	932,715	65.5	47.9	6.0	11.6	34.5	26.7	34.4	29.9
Carson	11.5	21,330	64.6	46.8	5.6	12.1	35.4	30.2	31.9	37.5
Enterprise CDP	20.2	24,277	64.7	44.2	7.5	13.0	35.3	22.5	35.7	17.5
Henderson	11.1	92,431	68.2	52.8	5.4	10.1	31.8	24.3	32.0	31.7
Las Vegas	21.5	207,313	66.3	47.1	6.3	12.8	33.7	26.3	36.5	30.6
North Las Vegas	23.9	59,139	74.5	53.9	7.0	13.6	25.5	18.4	48.9	20.4
Pahrump CDP	7.5	11,556	71.3	58.2	4.1	8.9	28.7	22.6	25.2	52.9
Paradise CDP	23.3	84,725	56.1	37.0	7.4	11.7	43.9	33.7	28.3	28.9
Reno	17.8	86,500	53.6	37.9	5.0	10.7	46.4	36.4	28.5	28.7
Sparks	15.5	29,798	67.8	50.6	5.9	11.3	32.2	24.6	37.7	28.3
Spring Valley CDP	25.8	64,497	58.4	41.1	5.3	11.9	41.6	31.9	27.9	29.0
Sunrise Manor CDP	27.1	63,820	73.0	48.5	8.4	16.1	27.0	21.3	44.7	25.8
Sun Valley CDP	15.9	6,678	78.1	57.9	6.9	13.2	21.9	17.3	49.0	32.1
Whitney CDP	27.0	8,783	67.6	41.8	9.2	16.6	32.4	23.4	33.1	26.7
Winchester CDP	31.0	11,427	52.0	30.8	5.9	15.3	48.0	40.8	26.8	34.6
New Hampshire	5.4	500,671	67.7	54.3	4.0	9.3	32.3	24.8	33.6	30.1
Concord	5.3	16,851	58.1	41.5	3.5	13.0	41.9	33.2	30.9	28.7
Derry CDP	5.8	8,927	63.6	46.7	3.5	13.4	36.4	25.8	39.1	22.6
Dover	6.8	11,920	56.7	47.7	3.6	5.4	43.3	31.7	27.0	26.0
Keene	2.8	8,872	59.3	46.7	4.4	8.1	40.7	27.9	27.6	30.6
Manchester	11.9	43,992	57.1	38.4	5.4	13.3	42.9	33.0	29.3	26.7
Nashua	13.3	34,526	64.2	49.1	5.3	9.8	35.8	27.8	32.4	29.2
Portsmouth	6.5	9,960	48.7	38.4	1.8	8.5	51.3	39.2	22.4	27.9
Rochester	1.5	11,849	69.5	50.9	4.5	14.1	30.5	25.1	32.5	30.1
New Jersey	19.7	3,143,408	69.5	52.2	4.6	12.7	30.5	25.7	36.5	33.2
Atlantic	26.1	15,977	53.6	24.2	5.4	24.1	46.4	40.6	32.1	33.3
Bayonne	25.9	24,161	60.9	42.2	4.6	14.2	39.1	35.0	33.4	33.2
Belleville CDP	32.1	13,083	69.2	47.0	9.3	12.9	30.8	26.6	37.2	28.8
Bergenfield borough	45.1	9,057	72.7	58.2	5.9	8.6	27.3	23.1	35.0	35.4
Bloomfield CDP	22.0	18,383	62.9	47.2	5.2	10.6	37.1	31.5	29.2	28.7
Bridgeton	22.5	6,146	64.1	30.8	9.1	24.2	35.9	30.5	42.9	29.6
Camden	12.0	23,700	69.7	21.6	7.8	40.3	30.3	25.1	49.0	25.5
Carteret borough	29.5	7,061	70.8	48.4	4.4	18.0	29.2	26.8	43.7	34.5
Cliffside Park borough	43.8	9,614	55.2	41.1	6.9	7.2	44.8	37.5	20.7	38.7
Clifton	32.2	29,480	65.8	49.4	5.2	11.2	34.2	29.0	28.7	39.0
Cranford CDP	7.4	8,115	74.2	64.0	3.4	6.8	25.8	24.4	33.9	37.3
East Brunswick CDP	25.7	16,063	80.9	68.8	1.6	10.5	19.1	16.0	42.8	30.7
East Orange	23.1	24,279	57.0	21.4	7.6	28.0	43.0	39.0	36.4	32.9
Edison CDP	36.3	34,666	72.8	61.1	3.3	8.5	27.2	22.8	39.2	30.1
Elizabeth	46.4	41,616	69.9	37.8	10.0	22.1	30.1	24.9	43.1	29.4
Englewood	29.5	9,572	72.2	51.6	4.4	16.3	27.8	22.8	32.3	37.3
Ewing CDP	9.5	12,895	62.5	43.2	4.6	14.7	37.5	28.4	31.4	34.9
Fair Lawn borough	31.8	12,582	74.8	66.3	2.0	6.5	25.2	21.6	34.6	36.9
Fort Lee borough	47.8	16,654	56.4	44.6	3.0	8.9	43.6	39.2	25.2	41.4
Garfield	40.0	10,974	68.3	43.9	5.3	19.1	31.7	27.5	37.6	32.3
Hackensack	37.7	18,996	56.9	34.4	7.9	14.6	43.1	37.2	27.2	31.3
Hoboken	17.8	20,755	37.1	28.7	2.0	6.4	62.9	45.6	16.0	15.9
Irvington CDP	25.7	20,695	66.1	30.7	8.1	27.3	33.9	28.4	42.2	27.0
Jersey	36.7	87,919	60.1	34.7	5.9	19.5	39.9	32.3	33.1	26.7
Kearny town	42.8	12,774	71.9	50.6	5.9	15.4	28.1	23.9	37.8	26.4
Lakewood CDP	16.0	10,507	80.7	65.7	3.4	11.6	19.3	16.5	61.7	16.3
Linden	28.6	14,924	69.7	46.2	6.3	17.2	30.3	24.2	32.8	37.9
Livingston CDP	22.9	9,563	83.2	71.1	4.8	7.3	16.8	15.4	45.5	41.4
Lodi borough	34.6	9,321	62.1	44.4	2.3	15.4	37.9	34.6	35.9	33.6

Table A-4. Cities — Who: Age, Race/Ethnicity, and Household Structure, 2005–2007—Continued

STATE Place code	STATE / City — ACS table number:	Total population B01003 (1)	Percent change 2005–2007 Population estimates (2)	Under 5 years B01001 (3)	5 to 17 years B01001 (4)	18 to 24 years B01001 (5)	25 to 44 years B01001 (6)	45 to 64 years B01001 (7)	65 years and over B01001 (8)	Median age B01002 (9)	White B02008 (10)	Black B02009 (11)	Asian Hawaiian or Pacific Islander B02011 + B02012 (12)	Amer. Indian, Alaska Native, or some other race B02010 + B02013 (13)	Percent Hispanic or Latino C03002 (14)
	New Jersey—Cont.														
34 41310	Long Branch	31,868	0.3	7.5	12.3	13.6	32.1	24.0	10.6	35.1	68.4	15.1	3.4	17.3	28.7
34 43830	Maplewood CDP	24,588	-	8.6	19.7	6.8	28.4	27.0	9.6	37.4	57.6	37.4	3.0	3.5	4.8
34 45495	Mercerville-Hamilton Square CDP	27,514	-	4.5	19.4	7.5	21.1	31.6	16.0	42.5	94.9	1.7	2.9	1.1	3.0
34 46680	Millville	27,272	2.7	6.2	19.8	8.2	29.2	24.3	12.3	36.9	75.8	18.7	1.3	5.2	14.3
34 47490	Montclair CDP	37,248	-	7.4	18.8	5.5	27.9	29.4	11.1	39.3	64.8	30.5	4.7	3.7	6.5
34 51000	Newark	265,375	0.8	8.1	18.4	11.3	31.1	21.6	9.4	32.3	22.5	54.4	1.8	23.3	31.7
34 51210	New Brunswick	46,903	1.3	7.8	14.9	30.5	30.0	12.0	4.8	23.5	40.9	15.3	6.4	40.3	48.2
34 52605	North Brunswick Township CDP	38,565	-	6.3	16.5	9.0	33.5	26.3	8.5	36.5	52.0	19.1	19.7	10.6	14.4
34 53280	North Plainfield borough	22,177	-2.2	9.1	17.0	9.5	31.0	25.0	8.4	35.2	57.1	20.4	2.7	20.5	-
34 53670	Nutley CDP	28,387	-	5.4	17.1	8.8	25.6	27.7	15.4	40.3	84.8	3.4	9.2	3.5	7.2
34 54690	Old Bridge CDP	22,609	-	7.3	19.2	8.2	27.3	26.0	12.1	38.8	82.7	4.3	10.7	3.7	9.0
34 55020	Orange CDP	30,851	-	8.2	16.3	10.6	33.2	21.5	10.1	33.2	9.1	76.6	0.4	14.6	17.7
34 55950	Paramus borough	26,991	-0.1	3.5	18.6	7.8	20.2	28.4	21.4	44.9	75.8	1.5	22.7	0.8	6.9
34 56550	Passaic	66,028	-0.5	10.3	20.7	9.8	31.6	19.1	8.3	30.4	35.3	10.5	5.1	52.2	67.0
34 57000	Paterson	142,443	-1.0	9.3	19.8	11.0	30.3	21.0	8.6	31.1	26.4	31.6	2.3	41.2	55.3
34 57690	Pennsauken CDP	33,674	-	5.8	19.7	9.3	26.6	25.7	12.9	36.5	53.8	26.6	7.1	15.0	19.4
34 58200	Perth Amboy	48,729	0.8	8.2	17.8	11.6	33.8	19.5	9.1	32.2	50.4	9.0	0.8	41.2	76.1
34 59190	Plainfield	40,751	-1.3	6.7	20.2	10.2	29.1	25.6	8.1	34.4	18.6	59.8	1.7	20.4	28.8
34 61530	Rahway	27,150	3.4	3.9	17.1	10.4	28.6	26.0	14.1	39.6	56.3	28.1	2.0	16.0	22.5
34 63000	Ridgewood village	26,243	-0.9	8.0	22.4	6.8	21.6	27.5	13.7	40.2	84.4	1.0	15.7	0.7	5.4
34 64620	Roselle borough	21,688	-1.3	8.7	15.7	11.8	27.6	26.9	9.3	36.5	22.9	57.5	6.2	13.8	-
34 65790	Sayreville borough	43,876	-0.9	5.2	14.7	8.4	31.0	26.4	14.2	39.8	72.7	11.0	14.6	2.3	10.4
34 66090	Scotch Plains CDP	21,952	-	5.8	19.8	5.4	25.6	28.6	14.7	41.7	82.8	6.8	8.2	2.4	-
34 68370	Somerset CDP	23,102	-	7.8	17.8	8.7	29.5	25.1	11.2	36.0	42.1	41.0	11.3	7.1	16.6
34 69390	South Plainfield borough	24,525	-1.0	6.9	16.5	7.5	28.2	28.3	12.6	38.5	70.8	10.5	12.8	7.2	15.3
34 71430	Summit	22,041	-1.2	10.2	20.5	5.3	26.0	26.0	11.9	38.0	87.8	6.1	4.6	2.2	11.1
34 72390	Teaneck CDP	43,737	-	6.5	19.5	8.8	25.0	27.0	13.3	37.8	53.9	29.9	11.4	6.1	14.1
34 73110	Toms River CDP	89,441	-	6.1	16.7	7.8	27.7	25.8	15.8	39.4	91.1	3.0	3.8	3.4	7.7
34 74000	Trenton	80,144	-1.3	7.7	18.5	10.2	32.2	21.2	10.1	32.5	34.4	52.3	1.0	14.4	30.8
34 74510	Union CDP	57,700	-	5.2	16.6	10.8	26.7	25.4	15.4	39.6	59.7	26.2	10.7	5.2	11.8
34 74630	Union	65,765	-3.5	8.2	16.4	10.0	32.8	21.8	10.8	34.2	69.9	5.8	1.5	24.7	78.1
34 76070	Vineland	61,593	1.3	7.8	17.8	9.3	28.1	23.3	13.7	36.2	74.4	15.9	1.7	10.2	32.1
34 77870	Wayne CDP	56,147	-	6.4	19.2	7.5	22.1	27.7	17.1	41.8	89.2	2.5	8.2	0.7	7.8
34 79040	Westfield town	29,556	-0.1	6.2	23.0	6.1	22.9	28.8	13.0	40.6	88.4	3.1	6.4	3.4	6.6
34 79430	West Milford CDP	27,251	-	6.3	18.9	8.9	25.6	30.2	10.2	39.3	95.4	1.3	1.9	1.6	-
34 79610	West New York town	46,963	-0.3	7.2	16.6	8.0	33.7	21.9	12.6	35.5	69.9	6.4	3.8	21.7	79.1
34 79790	West Orange CDP	44,656	-	6.4	17.3	5.2	25.6	29.2	16.2	42.2	62.7	22.7	8.3	8.0	14.7
35 00000	**New Mexico**	1,942,847	2.8	7.2	18.4	10.5	26.5	24.9	12.5	35.6	71.4	2.7	1.8	27.2	44.1
35 01780	Alamogordo	35,324	-0.3	6.2	18.5	10.6	29.5	21.5	13.7	35.3	76.5	8.5	3.1	16.0	33.3
35 02000	Albuquerque	505,578	3.9	7.5	16.7	10.7	28.8	24.2	12.0	35.1	70.6	4.1	3.2	25.6	43.7
35 12150	Carlsbad	25,106	1.0	8.6	17.5	11.1	24.2	23.8	14.8	35.9	76.0	4.2	1.1	23.6	43.0
35 16420	Clovis	34,320	-0.9	8.8	21.9	8.7	26.9	21.7	12.0	33.0	60.8	10.5	3.6	28.2	37.4
35 25800	Farmington	45,346	1.7	10.2	18.6	10.7	27.5	22.5	10.5	30.8	70.9	3.1	1.1	29.7	21.2
35 32520	Hobbs	30,273	3.2	8.3	21.7	10.6	27.8	20.4	11.1	30.3	81.5	8.4	-	11.0	47.1
35 39380	Las Cruces	91,294	8.5	7.3	17.8	15.5	27.6	19.1	12.8	30.9	84.0	2.8	2.3	12.8	55.4
35 63460	Rio Rancho	69,080	16.0	7.2	19.8	9.2	30.2	23.1	10.4	34.6	81.1	4.3	2.4	16.5	32.8
35 64930	Roswell	46,280	1.8	8.4	18.7	11.4	24.5	22.4	14.6	33.7	78.9	1.3	1.6	27.1	50.6
35 70500	Santa Fe	65,163	3.4	5.2	12.7	9.0	26.7	29.6	16.8	42.4	78.4	1.3	1.9	20.9	46.4
35 74520	South Valley CDP	36,924	-	7.0	20.6	7.8	28.9	23.4	12.3	34.4	77.4	1.9	0.7	21.7	76.3
36 00000	**New York**	19,280,753	0.2	6.2	16.9	10.1	28.1	25.5	13.1	37.4	67.8	16.5	7.2	10.4	16.2
36 01000	Albany	90,382	-0.2	5.8	13.1	19.4	27.8	20.7	13.2	31.9	63.8	31.6	3.5	4.5	6.1
36 03078	Auburn	23,856	-1.1	5.6	12.7	9.4	30.9	24.4	17.0	39.8	91.0	7.2	-	2.8	2.2
36 04143	Baldwin CDP	22,200	-	6.8	16.5	10.1	29.3	25.6	11.8	37.7	59.0	25.9	5.0	11.6	20.4
36 04935	Bay Shore CDP	28,454	-	7.7	15.3	10.1	29.8	26.7	10.3	40.2	63.9	21.4	5.4	11.5	28.7
36 06607	Binghamton	43,059	-0.8	5.8	14.9	12.6	25.5	24.4	16.8	37.7	83.1	11.7	4.7	3.6	5.0
36 08026	Brentwood CDP	53,776	-	8.5	18.9	10.0	31.2	21.9	9.4	33.4	64.7	18.4	1.5	18.6	61.3
36 08257	Brighton CDP	34,765	-	5.1	13.5	8.9	27.5	26.8	18.2	40.7	86.4	5.0	9.4	1.3	2.9
36 11000	Buffalo	263,030	-2.1	5.9	18.3	12.6	26.5	23.9	12.7	34.7	53.8	41.1	2.0	5.6	8.3
36 13376	Centereach CDP	28,233	-	6.0	21.0	9.4	27.5	26.8	9.3	36.8	92.0	5.0	3.4	1.9	-
36 13552	Central Islip CDP	34,849	-	9.7	17.4	9.4	32.0	22.0	9.5	32.4	50.7	30.5	3.7	19.3	42.6
36 15000	Cheektowaga CDP	77,674	-	4.7	14.5	9.7	25.4	25.6	20.0	42.0	91.6	7.3	0.5	1.3	2.2
36 17530	Commack CDP	36,105	-	4.9	20.9	8.9	23.0	26.5	15.8	40.1	93.5	-	5.7	0.2	-
36 18146	Copiague CDP	21,668	-	10.8	15.3	7.5	28.4	26.4	11.5	36.5	80.3	6.8	5.0	10.0	19.2
36 18157	Coram CDP	38,294	-	7.4	17.9	9.1	29.5	25.3	10.8	36.9	85.1	10.6	3.7	4.7	13.3
36 19972	Deer Park CDP	29,712	-	6.6	19.2	10.2	26.1	24.1	13.9	37.7	82.1	12.3	4.7	1.4	-
36 20687	Dix Hills CDP	24,259	-	4.2	23.4	7.5	21.1	32.1	11.7	41.7	86.4	2.9	10.3	2.0	5.6
36 21809	Eastchester CDP	20,142	-	5.6	19.0	4.7	24.0	28.5	18.2	42.3	89.3	-	9.1	-	-
36 22502	East Meadow CDP	35,791	-	3.2	18.0	10.2	21.3	30.9	16.5	43.7	79.6	5.0	9.2	8.8	11.7
36 22612	East Northport CDP	22,001	-	7.3	23.6	7.2	24.9	25.9	11.0	37.7	95.9	-	2.4	-	-
36 22733	East Patchogue CDP	22,740	-	7.6	15.5	10.2	26.9	26.8	13.0	38.2	88.3	3.1	1.5	8.0	13.1
36 24229	Elmira	29,494	-0.4	6.9	15.7	14.4	27.6	22.1	13.4	32.1	86.4	13.7	1.3	2.8	3.1
36 24273	Elmont CDP	33,929	-	7.1	18.6	11.9	23.6	27.9	11.0	36.5	32.5	43.1	11.3	15.1	21.0

STATE City	Percent foreign born	Total households	Household type (percent)							Percent of households with people under 18 years	Percent of households with people 60 years and over
			Family households				Nonfamily households				
			Total family households	Married-couple families	Male householder families	Female householder families	Total nonfamily households	One-person households		
ACS table number:	C05002	B11001	B11001	B11001	B11001	B11001	B11001	B11001	C11005	B11006
	15	16	17	18	19	20	21	22	23	24
New Jersey—Cont.										
Long Branch	29.5	12,426	60.6	37.6	9.1	13.9	39.4	32.2	30.9	30.8
Maplewood CDP	20.5	8,406	75.0	60.5	3.1	11.4	25.0	21.2	45.1	28.1
Mercerville-Hamilton Square CDP	7.4	9,293	74.6	61.1	3.0	10.5	25.4	21.8	35.6	36.3
Millville	1.9	9,978	65.6	44.0	5.4	16.2	34.4	26.5	37.8	30.2
Montclair CDP	13.2	14,465	63.8	45.8	3.7	14.3	36.2	31.0	39.9	29.2
Newark	27.8	91,491	62.8	26.7	8.3	27.8	37.2	32.3	39	28.5
New Brunswick	35.1	12,483	55.8	29.3	7.6	19.0	44.2	25.3	39.4	20.4
North Brunswick Township CDP	29.8	13,927	68.4	50.1	4.9	13.5	31.6	26.2	38.2	23.8
North Plainfield borough	33.7	6,891	79.0	57.8	6.8	14.3	21.0	16.5	42.4	27.8
Nutley CDP	16.4	10,898	66.8	54.8	2.6	9.5	33.2	30.3	31.7	37.2
Old Bridge CDP	15.3	6,946	85.7	72.3	3.4	9.9	14.3	13.2	45.8	30.0
Orange CDP	37.1	11,468	60.0	29.1	7.4	23.6	40.0	33.6	39.3	29.2
Paramus borough	26.7	8,371	78.7	69.2	3.1	6.4	21.3	17.4	39.4	47.2
Passaic	45.8	19,405	70.4	40.8	7.9	21.7	29.6	24.6	46.3	27.4
Paterson	34.5	44,069	70.3	34.2	9.0	27.1	29.7	25.1	41.9	27.9
Pennsauken CDP	12.7	12,535	69.7	46.9	5.1	17.7	30.3	27.2	39.1	38.7
Perth Amboy	38.3	15,008	76.4	39.1	9.4	27.9	23.6	19.7	45.5	26.5
Plainfield	26.4	15,050	61.8	34.6	7.1	20.0	38.2	34.0	37.9	24.7
Rahway	22.8	9,877	67.1	47.3	4.3	15.5	32.9	29.2	33.5	35.9
Ridgewood village	17.6	8,605	80.9	68.4	3.3	9.2	19.1	17.5	50.6	36.2
Roselle borough	30.0	7,495	67.2	41.2	6.2	19.7	32.8	29.2	40.3	31.0
Sayreville borough	25.7	15,651	70.0	53.7	5.8	10.6	30.0	24.4	34.2	29.2
Scotch Plains CDP	16.8	7,885	77.0	65.6	2.8	8.7	23.0	20.4	39.6	39.2
Somerset CDP	24.9	8,174	69.8	51.9	4.9	13.0	30.2	25.5	37.2	30.2
South Plainfield borough	19.5	7,588	82.9	63.8	7.5	11.7	17.1	14.1	42.8	33.4
Summit	17.3	7,441	79.4	65.5	3.6	10.3	20.6	18.1	43.6	30.0
Teaneck CDP	26.6	14,194	76.3	58.8	3.0	14.4	23.7	19.3	41.3	38.5
Toms River CDP	8.4	33,247	70.9	56.7	4.4	9.8	29.1	23.9	35.3	35.8
Trenton	20.2	26,488	62.3	25.0	9.8	27.5	37.7	31.0	37.9	31.1
Union CDP	31.8	19,403	72.3	54.6	5.0	12.7	27.7	23.9	35.4	37.6
Union	58.4	22,080	68.3	37.9	9.8	20.6	31.7	24.7	37.5	29.3
Vineland	9.4	20,807	69.3	46.0	5.8	17.5	30.7	25.9	37.8	34.4
Wayne CDP	18.6	17,520	80.1	69.1	3.6	7.3	19.9	18.7	40.4	38.2
Westfield town	12.9	9,954	76.6	65.2	4.0	7.4	23.4	20.8	41.7	33.8
West Milford CDP	6.8	8,976	75.9	66.4	1.6	7.8	24.1	20.0	40.6	27.5
West New York town	59.1	17,906	64.0	38.0	9.1	17.0	36.0	29.6	35.0	32.6
West Orange CDP	25.7	16,476	69.6	55.6	3.6	10.3	30.4	25.8	34.3	35.5
New Mexico	9.4	728,508	65.9	47.3	5.4	13.2	34.1	28.0	34.8	31.2
Alamogordo	10.0	14,532	66.5	52.8	3.6	10.1	33.5	28.4	34.5	32.7
Albuquerque	10.9	209,324	58.7	40.9	5.4	12.5	41.3	33.9	31.3	27.6
Carlsbad	3.4	10,239	66.9	44.8	9.5	12.6	33.1	25.7	36.8	33.9
Clovis	6.7	13,731	62.5	43.4	5.3	13.8	37.5	31.2	36.9	29.4
Farmington	3.7	15,290	69.7	53.0	5.6	11.2	30.3	25.2	37.9	25.6
Hobbs	10.5	10,458	74.7	52.2	4.9	17.6	25.3	21.8	41.5	28.7
Las Cruces	13.3	35,208	60.9	41.4	3.6	15.9	39.1	29.0	32.4	28.1
Rio Rancho	5.1	24,767	70.4	54.7	4.9	10.8	29.6	23.1	38.3	25.8
Roswell	10.7	17,477	67.0	44.2	6.5	16.4	33.0	27.5	37.7	35.2
Santa Fe	12.7	26,688	52.4	36.5	3.9	12.0	47.6	37.0	23.5	36.5
South Valley CDP	15.8	13,421	71.1	46.7	7.1	17.4	28.9	24.2	40.6	32.1
New York	21.6	7,096,035	64.7	45.2	4.9	14.6	35.3	29.4	33.4	33.2
Albany	8.3	38,195	44.4	23.3	4.2	16.9	55.6	42.4	23.8	25.8
Auburn	2.5	10,672	51.8	34.1	4.2	13.6	48.2	41.1	25.9	35.0
Baldwin CDP	27.8	7,212	74.1	58.0	2.8	13.3	25.9	22.9	38.5	36.4
Bay Shore CDP	20.7	7,989	68.2	47.5	7.3	13.4	31.8	25.3	42.9	31.8
Binghamton	8.3	20,305	49.7	29.3	4.5	15.9	50.3	42.5	27.3	34.0
Brentwood CDP	39.1	13,043	84.4	56.3	10.9	17.2	15.6	11.1	53.7	34.4
Brighton CDP	15.7	15,460	54.4	45.6	2.9	5.9	45.6	38.2	26.9	34.0
Buffalo	5.2	113,429	53.0	25.2	5.1	22.6	47.0	39.4	30.3	28.0
Centereach CDP	10.9	8,685	83.7	64.8	6.1	12.9	16.3	14.2	47.9	29.7
Central Islip CDP	36.7	9,949	75.7	50.4	6.2	19.2	24.3	17.8	47.3	34.0
Cheektowaga CDP	4.1	33,915	60.7	45.5	3.9	11.4	39.3	32.8	26.1	40.1
Commack CDP	9.8	11,549	84.9	75.4	2.5	7.0	15.1	13.3	42.2	37.9
Copiague CDP	22.0	7,235	74.3	61.6	4.6	8.0	25.7	21.1	39.9	33.4
Coram CDP	11.3	13,381	71.0	57.3	2.4	11.3	29.0	23.4	37.1	29.9
Deer Park CDP	14.4	9,704	75.0	59.8	2.7	12.5	25.0	23.2	39.6	39.4
Dix Hills CDP	15.4	7,460	90.1	81.7	2.0	6.4	9.9	8.0	44.4	36.8
Eastchester CDP	21.9	7,796	69.2	58.0	3.4	7.9	30.8	29.2	34.8	42.6
East Meadow CDP	16.8	11,735	76.5	64.0	3.3	9.3	23.5	22.4	33.8	45.8
East Northport CDP	6.3	6,795	82.7	68.6	2.7	11.4	17.3	13.0	49.4	32.6
East Patchogue CDP	11.3	8,303	67.9	51.6	5.6	10.7	32.1	27.7	35.9	35.1
Elmira	3.2	11,005	59.1	36.7	3.7	18.7	40.9	34.1	36.2	33.3
Elmont CDP	43.8	9,313	83.5	58.5	5.6	19.4	16.5	14.6	48.6	36.8

STATE Place code	STATE / City	Total population	Percent change 2005–2007 / Population estimates	Under 5 years	5 to 17 years	18 to 24 years	25 to 44 years	45 to 64 years	65 years and over	Median age	White	Black	Asian Hawaiian or Pacific Islander	Amer. Indian, Alaska Native, or some other race	Percent Hispanic or Latino
	ACS table number:	B01003	B01001 estimates	B01001	B01001	B01001	B01001	B01001	B01001	B01002	B02008	B02009	B02011 + B02012	B02010 + B02013	C03002
		1	2	3	4	5	6	7	8	9	10	11	12	13	14
	New York—Cont.														
36 27309	Franklin Square CDP	31,942	-	4.8	16.1	7.6	24.9	29.5	17.1	42.7	87.3	-	6.3	7.1	-
36 27485	Freeport village	41,272	-1.6	9.0	16.7	9.9	29.3	23.6	11.6	36.0	46.0	35.8	2.0	18.7	35.9
36 28178	Garden village	21,721	0.1	5.2	21.5	11.4	16.3	30.8	14.8	41.9	95.1	1.2	2.7	1.6	-
36 29113	Glen Cove	24,789	-1.3	5.4	13.4	9.3	25.0	27.3	19.6	43.0	80.9	6.4	5.0	8.5	-
36 32402	Harrison village	28,817	1.9	5.6	17.0	17.7	24.6	21.6	13.6	34.7	82.5	3.4	5.5	9.1	12.0
36 32732	Hauppauge CDP	20,711	-	6.0	19.0	8.1	25.5	29.3	12.2	40.6	90.7	1.2	5.6	2.8	-
36 33139	Hempstead village	49,645	-1.1	9.1	16.7	12.4	30.3	21.2	10.4	32.1	29.6	57.4	1.3	13.6	35.8
36 34374	Hicksville CDP	41,728	-	5.4	15.2	10.1	26.4	27.3	15.7	40.3	71.9	1.5	19.6	7.4	-
36 35056	Holbrook CDP	25,880	-	5.3	16.6	7.2	28.4	32.1	10.4	40.1	90.9	4.0	3.0	2.4	-
36 37044	Huntington Station CDP	28,929	-	8.5	16.9	8.4	31.7	25.8	8.8	35.4	75.5	12.1	5.4	8.4	25.1
36 37737	Irondequoit CDP	52,526	-	5.6	16.3	6.6	23.8	28.2	19.5	43.2	88.2	9.5	1.7	2.1	4.4
36 38077	Ithaca	31,180	0.1	2.0	7.4	53.1	22.4	9.9	5.2	22.2	75.8	8.2	17.4	3.2	6.3
36 38264	Jamestown	31,299	-1.6	7.2	16.2	13.8	25.7	23.1	13.9	34.2	95.6	5.0	-	2.3	4.5
36 39727	Kingston	24,151	-1.2	7.4	15.5	10.8	28.9	24.0	13.4	35.7	79.0	17.4	2.0	4.7	8.1
36 39853	Kiryas Joel village	14,051	15.4	20.5	38.8	12.0	21.1	5.8	1.7	14.4			-	-	-
36 42081	Levittown CDP	53,315	-	5.6	17.7	9.1	26.5	28.0	13.1	39.9	89.4	0.7	4.9	5.6	-
36 42554	Lindenhurst village	27,931	-1.7	4.9	19.2	10.0	24.9	28.4	12.6	39.8	95.5	1.4	1.5	2.1	9.3
36 43082	Lockport	21,891	-1.5	4.8	18.8	11.3	25.5	25.4	14.2	37.9	91.6	7.8	1.5	1.0	1.7
36 43335	Long Beach	33,395	-1.3	4.8	13.7	7.4	25.6	32.8	15.8	43.9	80.4	10.2	4.1	6.3	8.7
36 45986	Massapequa CDP	20,848	-	5.8	19.4	7.6	22.4	31.3	13.5	42.8	96.2	1.0	2.9	-	-
36 46404	Medford CDP	22,430	-	5.6	16.9	11.9	26.5	29.1	9.9	38.4	89.9	6.3	0.6	6.6	-
36 46668	Merrick CDP	21,902	-	4.1	20.7	9.8	19.1	34.0	12.4	43.2	97.1	0.7	2.7	0.6	-
36 47042	Middletown	26,314	-0.2	8.2	20.6	10.9	29.3	22.9	8.1	30.4	54.4	15.4	3.1	29.9	38.8
36 49121	Mount Vernon	65,759	-1.0	6.9	17.7	9.5	27.8	24.8	13.2	36.5	27.5	62.0	2.0	11.0	12.8
36 50034	Newburgh	31,400	-0.6	10.5	21.1	14.0	30.9	16.3	7.2	26.4	41.3	36.1	0.7	25.7	42.3
36 50100	New CDP	33,399	-	5.8	19.3	7.1	20.1	34.2	13.5	43.5	84.8	5.0	9.3	1.4	7.4
36 50617	New Rochelle	72,585	-0.5	7.3	16.1	12.0	25.2	24.2	15.3	37.6	64.7	19.3	4.5	13.3	23.6
36 51000	New York	8,246,310	0.7	6.8	16.3	9.6	31.4	23.7	12.2	36.0	45.3	26.2	12.1	18.4	27.4
36 51055	Niagara Falls	48,388	-1.6	5.5	17.7	10.7	24.1	24.7	17.4	39.2	77.1	20.8	1.1	4.6	2.6
36 53682	North Tonawanda	32,113	-1.3	6.7	14.1	7.8	27.9	28.9	14.7	40.8	98.3	0.5	1.2	-	-
36 54441	Oceanside CDP	33,333	-	4.3	19.3	8.4	21.0	31.3	15.8	43.1	94.2	1.1	1.7	4.5	-
36 55530	Ossining village	21,991	1.1	6.5	14.1	8.0	35.9	24.6	10.8	37.6	63.8	17.8	5.0	15.3	-
36 56979	Peekskill	25,691	1.8	7.9	10.4	10.3	35.9	23.7	11.8	35.7	54.3	21.1	4.0	21.0	38.8
36 58442	Plainview CDP	25,321	-	5.5	18.5	6.3	20.6	31.5	17.7	44.4	91.3	-	6.9	0.5	-
36 59223	Port Chester village	25,874	0.5	6.7	11.5	9.3	33.9	24.4	14.3	37.1	59.7	7.4	2.8	32.4	-
36 59641	Poughkeepsie	30,121	-1.1	5.9	17.2	13.6	28.7	22.2	12.5	33.4	51.8	37.4	2.1	13.6	17.3
36 63000	Rochester	199,697	-1.2	6.7	18.6	13.5	30.1	22.0	9.0	31.5	50.3	43.2	3.4	6.2	13.6
36 63264	Rockville Centre village	24,676	-1.6	6.1	19.2	8.2	20.4	30.2	16.0	41.6	91.7	4.1	2.6	2.2	10.0
36 63418	Rome	34,389	-0.8	4.8	15.9	12.0	28.0	24.6	14.8	37.8	88.9	9.1	0.8	4.5	5.8
36 63473	Ronkonkoma CDP	21,151	-	6.4	20.9	10.0	31.1	25.1	6.5	34.7	92.2	2.3	6.1	3.0	-
36 63924	Rotterdam CDP	21,055	-	3.7	17.6	7.9	23.3	28.0	19.4	43.7	96.3	1.9	2.0	0.4	1.5
36 65255	Saratoga Springs	27,081	2.8	3.2	13.8	17.7	25.7	24.8	14.8	37.3	96.6	2.8	2.0	1.0	2.0
36 65508	Schenectady	62,258	0.5	7.1	16.0	13.3	27.6	23.0	12.9	34.6	69.2	19.9	4.0	8.9	7.4
36 66212	Selden CDP	21,669	-	8.3	18.3	12.6	29.1	21.8	9.9	34.4	86.6	-	4.8	7.4	-
36 67070	Shirley CDP	27,845	-	6.7	21.8	12.7	29.1	23.9	5.6	31.9	88.7	4.7	3.6	5.1	15.0
36 67851	Smithtown CDP	26,389	-	6.9	20.9	6.8	26.3	24.7	14.5	39.4	95.9	0.7	3.0	0.4	-
36 70420	Spring Valley village	25,149	0.4	10.4	22.0	10.6	30.9	19.8	6.3	28.4	44.5	42.2	4.9	7.8	25.9
36 73000	Syracuse	139,896	-1.6	6.6	17.8	17.2	27.2	20.0	11.2	29.7	64.8	30.9	5.2	4.1	6.0
36 74183	Tonawanda CDP	60,378	-	5.5	14.3	10.1	23.4	27.4	19.3	42.0	95.3	2.4	2.0	0.9	1.3
36 75484	Troy	47,763	-0.7	6.5	14.5	18.9	28.3	19.6	12.1	30.6	84.0	15.4	3.7	4.7	5.4
36 76089	Uniondale CDP	25,294	-	5.8	18.0	15.1	26.9	26.0	8.3	32.4	24.4	62.4	3.1	13.4	24.7
36 76540	Utica	60,177	-0.7	6.3	17.2	11.6	28.0	21.7	15.2	34.6	81.8	15.3	3.1	2.5	7.7
36 76705	Valley Stream village	38,233	-1.8	6.8	16.1	10.9	25.4	27.9	12.8	39.0	59.6	15.7	11.2	15.0	20.9
36 78608	Watertown	29,590	0.5	8.5	18.3	10.6	32.5	18.5	11.7	31.2	89.7	8.8	1.3	3.4	3.0
36 79246	West Babylon CDP	41,060	-	6.0	17.2	9.2	29.1	25.6	13.0	38.5	84.1	8.5	3.5	5.0	12.1
36 80302	West Islip CDP	27,120	-	6.6	21.2	8.6	24.9	26.6	12.2	38.7	97.7	0.5	0.7	0.9	-
36 80907	West Seneca CDP	45,475	-	4.6	15.5	7.9	24.5	29.1	18.3	43.4	98.2	0.7	0.7	1.1	0.7
36 81677	White Plains	52,802	0.2	5.9	14.6	8.1	30.7	26.0	14.7	38.9	64.4	14.2	6.1	16.3	28.6
36 84000	Yonkers	195,817	0.4	6.6	16.9	9.0	27.2	25.6	14.7	38.0	57.5	19.3	6.1	18.4	29.7
37 00000	**North Carolina**	8,869,861	4.4	7.0	17.4	9.6	28.5	25.3	12.1	36.6	71.7	22.1	2.2	5.7	6.7
37 01520	Apex town	33,601	9.3	8.5	23.8	4.7	39.7	19.0	4.3	34.2	82.5	8.4	7.7	6.1	5.4
37 02080	Asheboro	23,046	3.5	7.5	18.5	8.4	30.1	21.9	13.6	34.4	71.6	12.0	2.2	15.0	24.5
37 02140	Asheville	74,897	2.5	5.3	13.9	10.4	28.2	25.6	16.7	39.5	83.2	15.2	1.1	1.6	4.2
37 09060	Burlington	49,599	4.6	7.6	17.0	8.4	29.3	22.3	15.4	36.3	59.5	27.2	1.3	13.0	17.4
37 10740	Cary town	116,910	13.0	7.9	20.5	7.2	29.6	27.2	7.7	35.8	79.5	8.1	9.6	5.1	8.2
37 11800	Chapel Hill town	54,091	2.9	5.0	12.6	29.7	25.2	18.6	8.8	26.7	77.7	11.1	9.7	2.9	4.9
37 12000	Charlotte	649,578	6.1	8.2	18.0	9.4	32.3	23.8	8.3	34.3	57.4	34.9	4.5	5.1	10.6
37 14100	Concord	66,283	7.0	8.7	17.8	9.3	30.9	23.1	10.2	34.1	80.1	16.0	1.7	3.7	10.5
37 14420	Cornelius town	21,751	15.1	6.6	16.6	5.5	32.2	31.1	8.1	38.9	87.5	7.0	1.9	-	-
37 19000	Durham	207,933	5.4	8.2	16.0	11.8	33.9	21.4	8.7	32.9	44.9	41.5	4.9	11.2	12.4
37 22920	Fayetteville	176,007	-0.8	7.9	19.2	11.0	27.1	24.0	10.7	34.2	49.3	45.7	3.9	5.8	5.7
37 24260	Fort Bragg CDP	22,339	-	11.8	16.2	32.6	35.2	4.2	0.1	22.7	69.8	20.9	5.2	10.7	12.9
37 25480	Garner town	21,156	12.0	9.6	17.1	9.1	27.4	26.4	10.5	34.5	59.9	31.6	2.9	6.2	6.6
37 25580	Gastonia	68,867	3.6	7.3	16.7	8.6	30.2	24.0	13.3	35.9	65.6	25.8	2.0	7.9	8.7

Table A-4. Cities — Who: Age, Race/Ethnicity, and Household Structure, 2005–2007—*Continued*

STATE City	Percent foreign born	Total households	Family households Total family households	Married-couple families	Male householder families	Female householder families	Nonfamily households Total nonfamily households	One-person households	Percent of households with people under 18 years	Percent of households with people 60 years and over
ACS table number:	C05002	B11001	B11001	B11001	B11001	B11001	B11001	B11001	C11005	B11006
	15	16	17	18	19	20	21	22	23	24
New York—Cont.										
Franklin Square CDP	19.6	10,381	78.6	62.5	5.9	10.2	21.4	17.3	35.9	46.0
Freeport village	30.4	13,373	68.5	42.5	7.2	18.8	31.5	25.9	39.6	33.4
Garden village	8.4	6,760	84.5	77.8	2.6	4.1	15.5	14.9	44.1	39.6
Glen Cove	25.4	9,475	65.6	47.9	5.6	12.1	34.4	30.3	28.5	40.0
Harrison village	18.8	8,726	74.9	61.9	3.4	9.6	25.1	19.4	36.0	35.8
Hauppauge CDP	10.1	7,401	75.7	65.6	3.1	7.1	24.3	19.9	37.8	32.8
Hempstead village	38.1	15,007	69.7	34.3	7.8	27.6	30.3	25.6	44.0	32.4
Hicksville CDP	29.1	13,517	79.0	67.2	2.8	9.0	21.0	17.4	36.3	38.9
Holbrook CDP	9.1	8,746	78.6	61.5	5.7	11.5	21.4	16.6	38.5	35.7
Huntington Station CDP	23.3	9,657	71.0	51.0	6.9	13.1	29.0	23.4	42.5	27.4
Irondequoit CDP	7.4	22,107	64.9	46.7	4.9	13.3	35.1	31.2	28.4	40.6
Ithaca	15.8	10,908	27.3	20.4	1.0	5.9	72.7	40.3	15.0	13.8
Jamestown	1.3	13,264	60.6	40.0	5.9	14.7	39.4	32.6	33.6	28.7
Kingston	10.3	10,112	54.2	34.1	4.1	16.0	45.8	35.9	29.8	31.1
Kiryas Joel village	8.5	2,756	90.9	84.8	4.0	2.2	9.1	9.1	-	-
Levittown CDP	11.7	17,253	80.8	62.1	5.4	13.4	19.2	16.9	39.5	39.1
Lindenhurst village	14.1	8,981	77.6	63.2	3.0	11.4	22.4	18.0	41.0	35.5
Lockport	2.5	9,425	56.2	36.6	2.6	17.0	43.8	33.9	30.5	31.0
Long Beach	11.2	14,200	54.2	41.8	2.8	9.7	45.8	36.5	22.9	35.6
Massapequa CDP	6.4	6,805	85.2	71.3	4.1	9.8	14.8	11.7	40.9	38.3
Medford CDP	9.3	7,094	80.9	61.2	5.9	13.8	19.1	16.5	40.6	36.0
Merrick CDP	6.5	7,282	85.8	75.2	4.6	5.9	14.2	12.3	42.4	37.0
Middletown	21.4	9,124	65.1	39.9	6.6	18.6	34.9	28.7	39.8	29.9
Mount Vernon	29.5	24,073	62.9	35.8	4.1	23.0	37.1	33.5	35.3	31.6
Newburgh	25.8	9,449	68.4	31.6	9.3	27.6	31.6	27.2	50.4	23.3
New CDP	16.0	10,883	86.2	77.4	1.6	7.2	13.8	11.6	41.2	40.5
New Rochelle	30.0	25,049	64.7	48.0	4.6	12.2	35.3	30.9	34.5	37.6
New York	36.7	3,022,151	60.4	36.1	5.6	18.8	39.6	33.4	32.4	31.8
Niagara Falls	4.1	21,426	57.9	33.1	4.6	20.2	42.1	38.0	27.2	34.9
North Tonawanda	4.4	13,827	63.0	48.9	2.9	11.2	37.0	33.1	28.1	33.3
Oceanside CDP	11.1	11,400	80.7	67.6	3.5	9.5	19.3	16.8	39.1	40.9
Ossining village	28.5	8,076	58.0	39.4	6.1	12.5	42.0	33.8	35.2	27.7
Peekskill	36.7	8,938	65.9	45.4	8.2	12.3	34.1	27.7	30.4	26.2
Plainview CDP	13.6	8,712	78.2	69.3	3.2	5.7	21.8	17.2	37.7	47.5
Port Chester village	45.1	9,521	66.1	46.4	8.4	11.4	33.9	25.0	28.0	30.6
Poughkeepsie	19.1	11,821	55.5	32.4	5.3	17.8	44.5	35.2	30.9	28.3
Rochester	7.4	80,803	52.0	23.3	5.3	23.4	48.0	39.1	32.7	21.9
Rockville Centre village	11.2	8,876	70.2	56.3	3.5	10.4	29.8	27.7	35.6	39.8
Rome	3.2	14,338	54.0	34.6	4.2	15.2	46.0	37.8	28.8	34.1
Ronkonkoma CDP	8.8	6,609	79.3	65.1	4.2	10.0	20.7	15.4	48.5	26.2
Rotterdam CDP	5.2	8,621	67.0	50.9	3.3	12.9	33.0	28.4	30.5	41.0
Saratoga Springs	4.2	11,064	59.6	47.1	4.5	8.1	40.4	33.8	27.1	30.4
Schenectady	12.9	24,069	55.4	33.2	6.6	15.7	44.6	38.3	29.2	29.3
Selden CDP	14.9	6,936	79.6	61.1	7.0	11.5	20.4	15.9	45.9	33.7
Shirley CDP	9.5	7,648	87.0	64.2	7.1	15.8	13.0	8.6	51.8	22.0
Smithtown CDP	8.1	8,361	82.2	70.9	3.9	7.4	17.8	14.7	44.4	38.0
Spring Valley village	48.7	6,834	72.5	48.7	5.3	18.5	27.5	22.3	46.8	24.8
Syracuse	8.9	55,317	48.7	23.6	5.0	20.1	51.3	39.4	29.3	26.9
Tonawanda CDP	5.0	26,345	60.6	47.5	3.1	9.9	39.4	34.0	26.4	38.8
Troy	7.4	19,177	53.3	30.2	4.0	19.1	46.7	35.7	28.8	27.9
Uniondale CDP	35.7	6,529	81.9	51.8	9.7	20.4	18.1	11.7	47.9	31.8
Utica	12.8	24,952	58.3	33.7	5.6	18.9	41.7	34.8	30.6	32.5
Valley Stream village	32.1	12,424	77.7	59.6	5.8	12.3	22.3	17.5	41.9	35.5
Watertown	3.5	11,821	61.4	38.9	4.7	17.8	38.6	33.0	39.3	25.6
West Babylon CDP	13.6	13,699	73.0	55.5	5.7	11.9	27.0	21.9	38.9	34.5
West Islip CDP	4.3	8,264	85.2	74.2	3.0	7.9	14.8	12.1	46.0	31.0
West Seneca CDP	2.3	18,803	66.1	51.2	3.8	11.1	33.9	29.5	27.2	40.1
White Plains	31.6	21,410	57.8	41.4	5.4	10.9	42.2	34.8	24.3	34.7
Yonkers	28.2	72,616	64.1	42.9	5.3	16.0	35.9	31.3	32.2	35.7
North Carolina	6.8	3,471,751	66.9	49.5	4.3	13.0	33.1	27.7	34.0	29.8
Apex town	10.8	11,573	77.5	66.4	2.9	8.1	22.5	16.2	52.2	14.9
Asheboro	17.8	9,624	59.1	39.8	3.6	15.8	40.9	37.1	32.1	30.8
Asheville	5.7	33,725	51.0	36.8	2.6	11.6	49.0	38.7	23.5	34.8
Burlington	13.1	19,631	66.1	41.6	6.3	18.2	33.9	26.7	34.5	33.2
Cary town	16.4	42,553	72.5	61.5	2.8	8.1	27.5	22.5	42.5	18.8
Chapel Hill town	15.4	20,961	49.7	39.7	2.5	7.5	50.3	36.1	26.8	23.2
Charlotte	13.3	265,874	60.2	41.0	4.8	14.4	39.8	32.3	33.6	21.7
Concord	8.2	25,483	67.0	48.9	4.7	13.3	33.0	24.4	36.6	25.2
Cornelius town	9.0	8,992	65.8	55.8	2.0	8.0	34.2	26.2	30.3	23.4
Durham	15.5	84,894	56.2	36.7	3.9	15.6	43.8	35.7	31.7	21.2
Fayetteville	5.6	71,704	65.8	42.4	3.9	19.4	34.2	28.3	38.3	25.3
Fort Bragg CDP	6.3	3,573	96.0	77.3	1.8	17.0	4.0	4.0	-	-
Garner town	7.1	8,047	64.8	47.6	4.5	12.7	35.2	32.5	31.8	26.8
Gastonia	7.9	26,573	67.3	46.2	4.5	16.6	32.7	28.0	34.2	30.6

Table A-4. Cities — Who: Age, Race/Ethnicity, and Household Structure, 2005–2007—*Continued*

STATE Place code	STATE / City	Total population	Percent change 2005–2007	Population by age (percent) Under 5 years	5 to 17 years	18 to 24 years	25 to 44 years	45 to 64 years	65 years and over	Median age	Race alone or in combination (percent) White	Black	Asian Hawaiian or Pacific Islander	Amer. Indian, Alaska Native, or some other race	Percent Hispanic or Latino
	ACS table number:	B01003	Population estimates	B01001	B01001	B01001	B01001	B01001	B01001	B01002	B02008	B02009	B02011 + B02012	B02010 + B02013	C03002
		1	2	3	4	5	6	7	8	9	10	11	12	13	14
	North Carolina—Cont.														
37 26880	Goldsboro	35,381	-1.5	8.6	13.8	11.9	25.8	24.3	15.6	36.3	41.2	57.1	1.5	2.0	2.1
37 28000	Greensboro	237,423	4.1	7.1	15.8	14.0	28.7	22.6	11.8	33.8	53.0	40.4	3.4	5.1	6.5
37 28080	Greenville	68,962	8.2	6.8	13.3	26.9	27.9	17.1	8.0	26.1	61.3	36.2	1.9	2.6	2.5
37 30120	Havelock	18,615	-1.1	10.5	14.3	27.8	29.8	13.3	4.4	24.3	74.8	17.5	3.9	7.9	6.4
37 31060	Hickory	40,381	2.4	6.7	16.7	9.9	30.5	22.9	13.3	35.6	73.5	15.0	2.4	11.2	14.2
37 31400	High Point	97,505	5.1	7.2	19.1	7.8	28.3	25.6	11.9	37.1	58.7	33.6	4.6	4.2	6.1
37 33120	Huntersville town	42,901	16.6	10.3	20.0	6.3	35.9	23.1	4.3	34.6	85.5	7.9	3.1	4.5	5.5
37 34200	Jacksonville	70,746	1.9	8.9	15.0	37.2	23.6	10.3	4.9	22.2	68.8	22.5	4.9	7.7	9.3
37 35200	Kannapolis	39,997	6.7	8.2	18.6	8.6	28.7	22.0	13.9	34.9	74.8	18.1	0.7	6.2	11.6
37 35600	Kernersville town	22,407	4.4	7.4	16.2	8.1	32.2	25.5	10.6	36.8	82.0	13.7	1.1	5.2	11.8
37 35920	Kinston	22,649	-1.3	6.8	17.7	8.1	20.5	27.5	19.4	42.7	31.3	66.8	0.5	1.9	
37 38060	Lexington	20,487	0.1	7.2	15.9	10.0	26.5	25.5	14.9	38.8	68.5	25.3	3.8	2.3	17.7
37 39700	Lumberton	24,159	1.8	9.8	19.6	7.4	29.8	21.7	11.6	32.7	42.1	37.9	0.6	20.7	4.7
37 41960	Matthews town	27,135	5.4	6.4	20.5	5.7	27.3	29.2	10.8	39.9	84.3	9.2	4.5	3.1	3.8
37 43920	Monroe	33,248	7.2	9.1	15.9	12.2	33.1	20.0	9.7	31.1	61.6	27.4	0.8	11.2	26.6
37 44220	Mooresville town	30,166	5.5	6.7	20.6	10.6	31.5	19.4	11.2	32.9	84.9	10.4	2.3	3.2	6.9
37 46340	New Bern	25,999	6.4	8.5	16.3	8.8	22.8	26.5	17.1	39.0	59.9	35.9	1.9	2.6	3.8
37 55000	Raleigh	341,891	8.7	7.5	14.9	14.0	34.1	21.7	7.8	32.4	61.4	29.0	4.2	6.9	9.5
37 57500	Rocky Mount	53,692	1.6	7.1	19.1	10.4	24.6	26.0	12.8	36.7	36.1	61.7	0.9	1.8	1.6
37 58860	Salisbury	29,140	1.6	6.4	14.0	11.8	24.6	24.8	18.4	39.1	56.2	37.8	1.1	5.7	9.9
37 59280	Sanford	26,336	7.4	8.7	17.9	8.9	29.2	22.0	13.4	35.7	53.0	26.6	1.5	19.7	26.2
37 61200	Shelby	19,516	1.1	5.6	17.1	9.6	21.4	26.8	19.5	42.9	62.1	37.6	1.0	0.7	0.9
37 64740	Statesville	23,245	5.2	7.7	16.7	9.1	27.6	24.9	14.1	35.5	57.1	34.6	2.1	6.8	10.0
37 67420	Thomasville	25,042	2.3	4.7	19.0	7.0	30.8	22.3	16.1	36.8	74.1	23.1	1.6	1.2	8.0
37 70540	Wake Forest town	22,020	25.8	10.8	21.2	6.6	34.8	18.7	8.0	35.0	83.0	13.9	3.4	-	4.0
37 74440	Wilmington	98,825	2.8	5.8	14.3	15.7	26.7	23.4	14.0	34.9	73.8	22.1	1.2	3.8	3.7
37 74540	Wilson	46,415	2.1	7.3	18.1	9.2	27.0	24.5	13.9	36.4	45.1	47.3	1.0	8.3	9.5
37 75000	Winston-Salem	213,889	3.3	7.8	16.6	11.0	27.7	24.2	12.7	35.3	55.2	34.9	1.9	9.1	12.2
38 00000	**North Dakota**	637,709	0.6	6.1	16.4	13.0	24.6	25.4	14.5	37.0	92.3	1.2	1.3	6.7	1.6
38 07200	Bismarck	58,820	2.9	5.9	14.9	13.2	27.3	24.5	14.1	36.4	93.4	0.8	1.0	5.9	1.0
38 25700	Fargo	94,603	0.8	6.0	13.9	19.3	29.6	20.9	10.2	30.5	94.0	2.5	2.4	2.5	2.1
38 32060	Grand Forks	50,743	1.8	5.8	13.4	26.5	25.0	20.2	9.1	26.9	93.4	2.0	2.2	4.6	2.1
38 53380	Minot	36,682	-0.5	7.1	16.9	14.1	24.4	23.1	14.5	34.7	94.7	1.6	1.9	4.1	3.1
38 84780	West Fargo	20,681	13.8	9.1	19.4	8.6	36.0	20.2	6.7	31.1	94.5	2.8	1.8	3.3	2.1
39 00000	**OHIO**	11,463,403	0.1	6.5	17.7	9.5	26.8	26.1	13.4	37.6	85.4	12.6	1.8	1.9	2.4
39 01000	Akron	200,172	-1.2	6.8	17.5	11.2	28.3	23.9	12.3	34.9	66.2	31.8	2.2	1.5	1.7
39 01420	Alliance	21,503	-0.7	6.5	15.4	14.8	24.4	23.2	15.7	34.2	88.0	10.0	1.5	2.1	2.1
39 02568	Ashland	20,923	1.6	4.3	13.0	17.0	26.4	23.1	16.2	37.6	96.9	1.4	1.7		1.4
39 02736	Athens	23,772	0.3	1.4	6.0	65.3	15.5	7.7	4.1	21.1	91.4	3.0	6.2	1.5	2.5
39 03184	Austintown CDP	31,277	-	6.8	14.3	9.8	25.5	26.9	16.6	40.8	92.8	7.1	1.2	0.8	2.1
39 03464	Avon Lake	21,902	6.2	6.9	21.5	5.4	24.4	28.5	13.4	39.2	96.8	-	0.8	0.3	-
39 03828	Barberton	27,195	-1.4	7.5	16.8	9.1	24.7	25.6	16.3	38.6	93.0	6.9	-	-	-
39 04720	Beavercreek	41,469	-0.4	4.6	17.4	11.5	23.8	30.4	12.3	40.5	93.0	1.8	5.4	2.0	2.4
39 07454	Boardman CDP	36,098	-	4.6	14.5	9.2	24.0	29.2	18.6	43.5	92.7	5.3	1.2	1.9	2.4
39 07972	Bowling Green	29,972	0.1	3.3	7.5	50.4	17.3	13.3	8.1	22.3	90.8	5.7	2.3	1.4	3.7
39 09680	Brunswick	36,224	-0.3	7.0	18.7	9.2	30.2	25.8	9.0	35.1	96.0	2.3	1.9	0.3	-
39 12000	Canton	76,738	-1.2	7.0	17.2	11.9	26.8	23.6	13.5	34.9	75.3	25.4	0.8	2.1	1.1
39 13190	Centerville	23,654	-0.5	5.1	16.1	6.9	22.4	28.4	21.1	44.8	90.4	5.9	3.3	1.3	2.2
39 14184	Chillicothe	20,079	1.1	5.6	14.5	8.4	26.0	25.6	19.9	41.7	92.7	6.1	1.0	3.2	1.0
39 15000	Cincinnati	302,471	0.3	7.3	15.7	12.3	28.5	24.1	12.0	34.8	52.0	46.5	2.0	2.0	1.7
39 16000	Cleveland	405,014	-2.7	6.9	19.2	9.4	27.7	24.5	12.3	36.3	41.0	54.2	1.8	5.4	8.3
39 16014	Cleveland Heights	46,147	-3.0	7.3	16.0	10.3	27.7	26.8	11.9	36.4	54.2	43.4	2.9	1.3	1.7
39 18000	Columbus	724,095	1.2	8.2	16.1	12.6	33.3	21.1	8.8	32.2	67.5	27.8	4.6	2.5	4.0
39 19778	Cuyahoga Falls	48,700	1.0	5.4	15.4	8.9	27.7	26.6	16.0	39.5	96.0	2.6	1.2	0.5	0.9
39 21000	Dayton	146,762	-1.8	7.5	16.9	13.4	26.3	23.3	12.7	34.3	53.8	45.0	0.9	1.9	1.8
39 21434	Delaware	32,145	6.1	7.1	15.1	18.1	30.1	18.9	10.8	29.4	92.4	6.2	2.8	1.8	2.5
39 22694	Dublin	41,127	7.8	7.8	25.5	3.9	30.4	26.8	5.6	35.9	82.9	2.4	14.7	0.2	1.9
39 23380	East Cleveland	19,417	-3.0	7.1	18.5	9.5	23.6	25.4	16.0	36.6	4.9	94.5	-	0.6	-
39 25256	Elyria	53,951	-1.2	6.2	18.6	9.4	28.3	23.5	14.0	36.3	84.6	15.0	0.9	1.9	3.2
39 25704	Euclid	51,357	-2.8	5.6	17.7	7.0	27.2	26.0	16.5	40.0	53.0	45.2	1.5	1.3	1.5
39 25914	Fairborn	35,000	1.1	6.3	14.1	21.1	24.6	19.2	14.7	29.6	87.1	12.1	2.0	1.3	1.6
39 25970	Fairfield	44,794	0.4	5.4	17.4	8.6	28.5	28.3	11.8	37.6	86.6	11.9	1.6	0.5	3.3
39 27048	Findlay	40,463	-4.1	6.0	16.2	13.3	27.8	22.4	14.2	34.8	92.0	2.3	2.8	4.6	5.2
39 29106	Gahanna	34,005	0.8	7.0	18.7	6.6	28.2	28.6	10.9	38.3	86.5	10.9	3.0	0.6	0.8
39 29428	Garfield Heights	29,550	-2.8	6.5	19.0	7.4	27.3	25.3	14.6	38.1	66.9	29.5	1.8	1.8	3.7
39 31860	Green	25,294	0.1	6.2	18.9	6.9	24.6	29.2	14.2	41.3	97.2	0.9	2.0		
39 32592	Grove	32,981	6.1	6.4	22.7	6.0	28.2	25.3	11.3	37.5	95.2	3.2	1.3	1.8	1.9
39 33012	Hamilton	58,186	1.2	7.3	16.0	11.3	28.7	23.2	13.6	35.7	90.7	8.0	0.4	2.0	4.3
39 35476	Hilliard	30,124	2.2	7.2	24.4	5.2	31.7	24.5	7.0	35.5	90.4	2.3	6.6	1.6	2.1
39 36610	Huber Heights	37,239	-1.5	6.9	19.6	9.0	27.5	25.6	11.4	36.8	85.2	13.4	3.3	2.9	2.8
39 36651	Hudson	23,585	0.2	6.7	26.2	5.6	19.5	30.1	11.9	40.1	93.3	2.2	5.1	-	-
39 39872	Kent	27,119	-0.2	3.5	9.6	41.3	23.1	16.2	6.3	23.5	89.7	7.8	3.0	2.4	1.6
39 40040	Kettering	55,834	-2.0	6.0	15.2	8.3	27.1	26.6	16.8	40.2	96.3	2.6	1.2	1.7	1.2

STATE City	Percent foreign born	Total households	Household type (percent)						Percent of households with people under 18 years	Percent of households with people 60 years and over
			Family households				Nonfamily households			
			Total family households	Married-couple families	Male householder families	Female householder families	Total nonfamily households	One-person households		
ACS table number:	C05002	B11001	B11001	B11001	B11001	B11001	B11001	B11001	C11005	B11006
	15	16	17	18	19	20	21	22	23	24
North Carolina—Cont.										
Goldsboro	2.1	14,056	62.1	37.2	3.0	21.9	37.9	33.4	33.9	34.3
Greensboro	9.8	98,318	56.4	36.7	4.8	14.8	43.6	35.7	30.2	26.0
Greenville	4.1	30,393	46.1	27.5	2.7	15.9	53.9	39.7	26.0	18.2
Havelock	5.5	5,834	72.2	57.9	3.7	10.7	27.8	19.2	45.0	14.8
Hickory	11.4	16,174	59.4	39.3	4.7	15.5	40.6	36.5	32.2	29.5
High Point	9.4	38,615	65.9	43.6	4.5	17.7	34.1	29.6	36.4	27.8
Huntersville town	8.6	15,864	74.1	62.1	2.5	9.5	25.9	19.3	44.0	15.0
Jacksonville	5.6	17,597	74.0	54.0	2.6	17.3	26.0	22.1	46.2	18.2
Kannapolis	9.1	15,899	66.5	42.8	7.0	16.7	33.5	29.8	36.7	31.1
Kernersville town	7.7	9,281	68.1	51.1	3.9	13.1	31.9	26.4	34.9	29.0
Kinston	2.5	10,047	56.5	33.2	3.8	19.5	43.5	40.1	27.9	39.0
Lexington	13.5	7,592	67.1	41.8	6.1	19.2	32.9	29.2	33.8	36.0
Lumberton	3.9	8,548	60.6	33.3	2.2	25.2	39.4	35.9	37.8	29.7
Matthews town	7.3	10,495	74.0	62.9	3.7	7.4	26.0	23.5	40.6	24.3
Monroe	19.8	11,731	68.9	47.5	4.5	16.9	31.1	24.0	40.9	25.4
Mooresville town	5.3	10,839	70.8	57.1	3.0	10.7	29.2	21.3	28.0	36.1
New Bern	4.6	12,554	58.8	35.5	4.2	19.1	41.2	37.7	30.1	19.4
Raleigh	13.3	136,993	55.5	39.3	4.0	12.1	44.5	36.5	33.6	31.2
Rocky Mount	2.7	21,928	62.9	37.7	4.3	21.0	37.1	31.9	30.2	35.9
Salisbury	8.2	11,521	63.0	41.7	5.0	16.3	37.0	32.6		
Sanford	18.1	9,594	71.2	44.6	6.6	20.0	28.8	25.7	38.7	31.3
Shelby	1.2	7,992	63.3	40.9	3.4	19.1	36.7	34.6	28.4	35.2
Statesville	8.3	9,850	55.0	36.8	4.6	13.7	45.0	42.5	28.4	29.1
Thomasville	8.0	10,287	62.3	39.6	4.2	18.5	37.7	31.5	30.8	33.6
Wake Forest town	5.0	7,761	71.3	63.1	0.9	7.3	28.7	23.5	43.7	21.1
Wilmington	4.4	45,016	50.2	34.3	2.9	13.0	49.8	38.0	24.1	30.0
Wilson	7.1	18,112	62.3	36.5	3.4	22.3	37.7	32.3	33.4	30.1
Winston-Salem	9.8	87,371	61.6	40.3	4.3	17.0	38.4	33.2	32.5	29.0
North Dakota	2.3	271,131	61.9	51.0	3.5	7.4	38.1	31.0	29.5	29.9
Bismarck	1.7	25,732	57.3	45.2	3.0	9.0	42.7	33.9	27.2	28.4
Fargo	4.7	44,136	49.3	36.8	3.1	9.4	50.7	37.8	25.5	19.3
Grand Forks	2.8	21,356	50.4	39.5	3.0	7.9	49.6	35.1	24.5	22.6
Minot	3.6	16,624	57.4	45.8	4.2	7.4	42.6	35.5	28.8	28.7
West Fargo	2.3	8,293	67.5	55.8	1.4	10.3	32.5	23.6	40.3	18.0
Ohio	3.6	4,500,621	65.9	49.2	4.2	12.5	34.1	28.9	33.1	31.4
Akron	3.4	83,935	56.7	34.0	4.7	18.0	43.3	35.4	29.6	28.7
Alliance	2.0	8,313	66.2	46.5	4.6	15.1	33.8	30.3	30.7	38.2
Ashland	2.7	8,134	58.1	42.7	4.2	11.1	41.9	35.1	27.1	36.2
Athens	8.1	6,045	31.6	24.9	1.1	5.6	68.4	34.9	17.2	14.7
Austintown CDP	2.1	13,895	62.2	43.0	5.9	13.2	37.8	31.9	30.3	36.1
Avon Lake	3.2	8,117	72.4	64.2	3.5	4.6	27.6	25.4	38.7	34.4
Barberton	2.1	11,547	63.7	41.7	2.9	19.1	36.3	31.7	29.5	35.5
Beavercreek	5.5	16,577	72.2	62.6	3.2	6.4	27.8	21.3	32.5	30.2
Boardman CDP	3.8	15,739	63.0	51.2	1.9	9.9	37.0	33.8	28.4	36.5
Bowling Green	3.6	11,155	40.4	29.7	3.9	6.8	59.6	35.0	18.4	18.4
Brunswick	5.3	13,051	75.1	60.9	3.4	10.7	24.9	21.1	37.2	26.6
Canton	1.9	31,390	58.6	32.0	4.8	21.8	41.4	34.5	33.2	29.3
Centerville	5.0	10,208	66.6	54.2	3.2	9.2	33.4	30.9	26.7	44.2
Chillicothe	1.5	8,734	59.1	40.1	3.4	15.6	40.9	35.0	26.5	40.4
Cincinnati	4.5	128,357	47.8	24.8	4.1	18.9	52.2	45.6	26.6	26.6
Cleveland	4.6	168,557	54.9	25.0	5.4	24.5	45.1	39.8	32.0	30.1
Cleveland Heights	8.0	19,419	57.6	40.0	3.5	14.1	42.4	35.1	29.7	30.3
Columbus	9.3	303,031	54.5	34.4	5.1	15.0	45.5	35.8	30.7	21.5
Cuyahoga Falls	2.3	21,237	61.8	49.1	3.4	9.3	38.2	33.4	26.3	32.1
Dayton	2.1	61,271	52.6	27.3	4.5	20.8	47.4	40.0	29.0	30.1
Delaware	2.7	12,571	64.7	47.6	4.9	12.2	35.3	30.2	36.8	24.4
Dublin	14.5	14,472	78.9	72.5	1.7	4.7	21.1	17.6	51.7	15.4
East Cleveland	2.6	8,685	48.0	20.1	4.5	23.3	52.0	47.5	26.7	33.7
Elyria	2.2	21,827	65.3	43.2	3.4	18.6	34.7	28.4	34.2	31.3
Euclid	4.6	23,614	52.0	33.7	2.5	15.8	48.0	41.5	27.8	32.4
Fairborn	4.3	14,548	57.3	37.1	3.7	16.5	42.7	33.6	29.6	22.4
Fairfield	5.2	16,637	66.1	49.1	4.5	12.4	33.9	27.4	31.5	27.2
Findlay	3.5	17,844	59.1	45.3	3.2	10.6	40.9	33.7	27.9	29.1
Gahanna	5.0	12,928	70.3	57.5	5.2	7.6	29.7	24.7	36.2	28.4
Garfield Heights	4.1	11,789	64.2	41.3	5.2	17.7	35.8	32.2	35.7	36.1
Green	3.3	9,679	73.2	61.8	2.3	9.0	26.8	25.0	34.7	33.0
Grove	2.3	12,628	67.9	54.8	3.2	9.9	32.1	27.9	40.5	29.1
Hamilton	3.6	23,564	62.6	41.2	5.9	15.6	37.4	32.9	33.2	28.7
Hilliard	6.3	10,727	75.7	62.3	2.9	10.5	24.3	22.1	46.6	19.4
Huber Heights	3.8	14,188	73.0	55.2	5.6	12.2	27.0	22.4	37.4	29.5
Hudson	4.5	7,861	84.0	74.5	2.5	7.0	16.0	15.3	47.1	31.9
Kent	4.6	9,963	44.0	31.2	2.3	10.4	56.0	35.1	21.7	17.7
Kettering	2.9	25,125	58.4	45.4	3.4	9.7	41.6	35.4	26.0	33.8

STATE Place code	STATE / City	Total population	Percent change 2005–2007	Population by age (percent) Under 5 years	5 to 17 years	18 to 24 years	25 to 44 years	45 to 64 years	65 years and over	Median age	Race alone or in combination (percent) White	Black	Asian Hawaiian or Pacific Islander	Amer. Indian, Alaska Native, or some other race	Percent Hispanic or Latino
	ACS table number:	B01003	Population estimates	B01001	B01001	B01001	B01001	B01001	B01001	B01002	B02008	B02009	B02011 + B02012	B02010 + B02013	C03002
		1	2	3	4	5	6	7	8	9	10	11	12	13	14
	Ohio—Cont.														
39 41664	Lakewood	54,765	-3.0	6.5	15.2	9.8	33.8	23.8	11.0	35.9	92.9	6.0	1.8	1.1	3.5
39 41720	Lancaster	37,549	1.4	7.4	15.7	9.6	29.3	23.4	14.6	35.1	98.1	1.9	0.4	1.3	1.0
39 42364	Lebanon	19,263	3.0	7.7	20.0	9.4	34.2	18.8	9.9	32.8	94.7	4.5	-	-	-
39 43554	Lima	38,494	-1.3	8.7	18.5	11.3	27.6	21.9	12.0	33.3	72.8	25.8	0.9	3.6	3.0
39 44856	Lorain	63,859	0.5	7.5	18.3	8.7	27.9	23.9	13.6	35.3	69.4	22.3	0.5	13.7	22.2
39 47138	Mansfield	49,871	-1.3	5.9	14.9	10.0	29.9	23.9	15.4	37.0	77.0	23.4	0.9	1.8	1.5
39 47306	Maple Heights	24,166	-2.8	7.0	19.2	6.5	27.3	27.2	12.8	38.0	33.7	65.8	1.4	1.0	1.5
39 47754	Marion	35,215	-2.2	6.0	15.9	9.0	32.2	24.2	12.7	36.3	89.9	9.2	-	4.8	2.0
39 48188	Mason	30,328	3.6	7.0	25.5	6.8	31.5	21.4	7.8	34.7	88.4	3.3	6.8	2.7	3.5
39 48244	Massillon	32,289	1.0	7.2	15.7	8.0	27.2	26.5	15.5	38.9	91.6	8.2	0.7	-	-
39 48790	Medina	28,597	-0.7	7.5	19.3	9.0	31.9	22.0	10.3	34.1	96.2	2.9	1.3	1.0	2.8
39 49056	Mentor	48,812	0.5	5.1	16.9	8.0	24.0	31.4	14.5	42.2	97.4	1.1	1.7	0.5	0.7
39 49840	Middletown	48,818	0.1	7.4	17.7	9.5	29.1	23.1	13.1	34.5	86.2	13.1	1.4	1.9	2.0
39 54040	Newark	45,949	0.5	8.1	15.9	11.5	26.9	24.3	13.3	35.0	96.3	3.4	0.8	1.2	0.7
39 56882	North Olmsted	32,878	-2.5	5.4	16.2	7.2	25.3	29.6	16.3	42.5	95.5	1.0	2.5	1.8	2.8
39 56966	North Ridgeville	27,271	6.3	7.4	16.2	7.8	27.8	28.4	12.4	39.6	97.1	1.2	1.4	0.9	2.0
39 57008	North Royalton	30,363	0.1	5.6	16.0	9.8	24.5	31.2	12.9	41.8	94.1	3.0	3.2	0.6	1.5
39 57386	Norwood	19,595	-2.7	8.1	14.9	11.9	28.6	23.3	13.2	34.7	94.0	3.5	0.5	3.7	-
39 59234	Oxford	21,971	2.5	2.4	4.7	66.8	11.6	8.3	6.1	21.1	92.7	3.6	3.0	1.7	1.2
39 61000	Parma	83,161	-2.7	6.1	16.1	7.9	25.2	26.6	18.1	41.1	94.9	2.3	1.8	1.8	2.7
39 62848	Piqua	20,705	-0.3	6.7	17.9	8.3	28.7	24.2	14.3	36.5	95.6	4.6	1.3	0.5	1.0
39 64304	Portsmouth	19,072	0.2	7.0	14.1	14.4	24.2	22.4	17.9	36.5	94.6	6.1	0.8	1.1	1.5
39 66390	Reynoldsburg	36,315	0.8	6.6	23.7	7.6	27.9	24.4	9.8	35.4	77.6	17.8	3.3	3.2	4.1
39 67468	Riverside	25,544	-1.8	5.8	17.9	11.6	29.0	22.1	13.5	35.2	91.4	5.4	3.3	1.1	3.1
39 70380	Sandusky	25,809	-2.0	6.8	17.2	10.2	24.5	24.9	16.4	37.7	75.7	24.4	0.5	2.1	1.9
39 71682	Shaker Heights	28,777	-2.8	4.7	22.7	5.6	23.7	28.3	15.1	40.9	55.3	38.4	5.4	2.5	2.2
39 72424	Sidney	19,862	-0.4	8.9	18.4	8.2	29.3	23.2	12.0	34.4	92.4	5.2	2.0	2.2	1.7
39 72928	Solon	23,728	-0.7	4.6	22.6	6.9	22.5	33.8	9.5	41.6	81.0	9.6	8.9	1.2	1.3
39 73264	South Euclid	23,167	-2.9	8.1	17.7	7.0	26.2	27.8	13.2	38.6	61.6	35.8	2.9	1.4	0.9
39 74118	Springfield	61,763	-1.4	7.5	17.0	11.3	25.4	23.5	15.3	35.1	80.4	20.4	0.6	1.5	1.4
39 74944	Stow	35,048	-0.8	5.7	19.2	7.5	28.2	27.6	11.8	37.5	95.1	3.6	1.3	0.7	1.2
39 75098	Strongsville	47,077	-1.8	5.1	19.6	8.0	23.8	30.5	13.0	42.1	92.8	1.6	5.9	0.5	1.0
39 77000	Toledo	289,103	-2.1	7.4	17.9	11.0	27.9	23.3	12.5	34.1	69.7	26.9	1.6	4.5	6.2
39 77504	Trotwood	24,968	-0.8	7.0	17.0	9.9	20.8	27.2	18.2	42.1	31.8	68.0	-	0.7	-
39 77588	Troy	23,518	-0.2	7.1	18.7	7.8	29.5	24.8	12.2	36.3	92.9	5.5	2.1	1.6	1.3
39 79002	Upper Arlington	35,150	-0.4	5.6	20.9	4.8	24.1	29.5	15.1	42.1	93.7	2.1	4.9	0.5	1.8
39 80304	Wadsworth	19,551	2.7	5.9	20.1	10.0	26.2	23.8	13.9	36.4	99.1	0.8	-	-	-
39 80892	Warren	44,473	-2.3	7.2	18.2	10.2	25.1	24.7	14.7	36.8	71.3	28.7	0.5	1.7	1.0
39 83342	Westerville	36,209	2.2	4.6	20.0	12.7	22.0	29.4	11.2	39.0	92.3	5.7	1.4	2.2	1.2
39 83622	Westlake	32,588	-1.4	4.6	18.0	5.5	23.0	29.3	19.6	44.4	93.0	1.3	5.4	1.7	2.1
39 85484	Willoughby	23,753	0.5	5.5	15.3	9.0	27.0	25.8	17.3	40.6	92.6	1.5	4.2	2.6	3.4
39 86548	Wooster	25,516	0.2	7.7	15.0	13.6	24.4	23.3	16.0	35.2	93.9	4.1	2.3	0.4	1.1
39 86772	Xenia	22,960	-0.5	7.4	16.7	11.2	27.0	23.6	14.2	34.7	85.5	15.0	0.3	1.1	1.2
39 88000	Youngstown	68,592	-2.9	5.7	17.1	11.2	24.2	25.3	16.5	37.8	50.4	48.3	0.3	2.9	6.8
39 88084	Zanesville	25,112	-0.2	6.6	17.4	9.7	26.8	23.1	16.3	37.5	90.7	11.3	-	1.9	-
40 00000	**Oklahoma**	3,576,929	2.3	7.1	17.8	10.5	26.5	24.9	13.2	36.0	80.6	8.6	2.2	14.7	6.9
40 02600	Ardmore	25,613	2.0	7.1	18.4	8.3	25.3	24.3	16.7	38.5	75.4	11.2	0.4	15.0	5.4
40 04450	Bartlesville	34,681	2.8	5.6	16.9	9.6	22.3	26.7	19.0	40.9	87.0	4.4	1.8	13.2	3.8
40 06400	Bixby	17,233	8.3	8.3	18.7	8.1	30.7	23.5	10.7	35.6	93.7	1.7	0.9	6.8	4.5
40 09050	Broken Arrow	90,178	5.8	7.0	20.9	8.1	28.2	26.8	9.1	36.2	87.5	5.4	2.1	9.2	4.8
40 19900	Del	21,976	0.2	6.4	19.4	9.0	27.5	21.7	16.1	35.4	73.1	21.6	1.2	9.4	5.4
40 21900	Duncan	23,782	1.7	8.1	15.3	11.3	23.1	24.6	17.6	38.9	88.9	4.1	0.9	9.2	6.4
40 23200	Edmond	80,663	3.9	8.2	20.3	10.1	26.5	24.9	10.1	33.8	90.6	5.6	3.2	3.4	3.4
40 23950	Enid	47,394	1.2	8.0	17.5	8.8	25.2	24.7	15.8	36.7	87.1	4.9	3.2	8.3	7.0
40 41850	Lawton	90,346	2.1	9.4	19.9	13.7	28.3	19.3	9.4	29.4	64.6	25.5	5.2	12.6	10.3
40 48350	Midwest	54,336	1.5	9.8	17.4	9.2	26.6	23.3	13.7	34.0	73.2	21.7	3.6	7.8	4.6
40 49200	Moore	47,505	6.5	7.0	20.1	10.7	31.6	22.9	7.6	31.6	85.4	5.9	2.3	12.8	8.0
40 50050	Muskogee	39,682	1.2	7.1	16.5	11.2	24.8	24.7	15.7	37.4	68.1	17.6	1.3	19.3	4.8
40 52500	Norman	103,057	4.6	5.5	13.7	22.6	28.0	21.1	9.0	29.4	86.5	6.2	5.2	8.8	3.9
40 55000	Oklahoma	540,321	2.7	8.2	17.7	9.6	28.7	24.4	11.4	34.7	72.7	16.1	4.9	13.0	13.9
40 56650	Owasso	26,650	10.3	9.0	22.8	7.4	31.7	20.9	8.1	34.0	86.1	2.2	7.1	11.0	4.9
40 59850	Ponca	24,754	-1.1	8.1	18.3	8.1	24.4	25.5	15.6	37.7	85.7	4.0	1.6	13.0	6.3
40 65400	Sapulpa	20,827	2.1	6.1	14.8	9.2	25.7	25.6	18.6	40.7	85.1	4.9	0.7	16.4	2.9
40 66800	Shawnee	30,546	2.6	6.6	16.5	14.8	26.7	21.7	13.6	32.9	83.0	6.7	1.0	17.3	4.0
40 70300	Stillwater	45,533	2.9	5.4	9.3	38.6	24.4	14.3	8.0	24.1	83.1	5.9	7.0	7.7	3.1
40 75000	Tulsa	384,040	0.7	7.9	17.0	10.1	27.5	24.6	12.9	35.4	72.6	18.0	2.5	12.7	11.2
40 82950	Yukon	21,395	3.7	6.5	16.0	12.8	23.4	29.7	11.6	37.8	93.5	1.0	3.4	4.6	3.8
41 00000	**Oregon**	3,689,498	3.2	6.3	17.0	9.1	27.8	26.9	12.9	37.6	89.1	2.4	4.8	7.0	10.2
41 01000	Albany	46,931	5.4	7.2	17.6	10.3	29.9	22.8	12.2	34.6	92.5	1.0	1.4	7.1	8.2
41 01650	Aloha CDP	47,901	-	7.9	21.5	6.1	34.1	24.1	6.3	33.6	80.8	4.3	11.1	10.2	18.0
41 01850	Altamont CDP	21,003	-	8.5	18.4	8.6	23.8	24.7	16.0	36.4	94.7	-	-	7.9	-
41 03050	Ashland	20,219	2.4	4.0	14.0	17.1	22.9	25.9	16.1	36.7	96.2	1.0	3.9	3.0	4.3
41 05350	Beaverton	85,696	3.2	7.0	17.3	9.2	33.6	23.8	9.1	34.6	76.1	3.1	13.0	11.4	13.8

Table A-4. Cities — Who: Age, Race/Ethnicity, and Household Structure, 2005–2007—*Continued*

STATE City	Percent foreign born	Total households	Household type (percent)						Percent of households with people under 18 years	Percent of households with people 60 years and over
			Family households				Nonfamily households			
			Total family households	Married-couple families	Male householder families	Female householder families	Total nonfamily households	One-person households		
ACS table number:	C05002	B11001	B11001	B11001	B11001	B11001	B11001	B11001	C11005	B11006
	15	16	17	18	19	20	21	22	23	24
Ohio—Cont.										
Lakewood	10.2	24,898	49.0	34.2	3.6	11.2	51.0	42.4	25.3	24.2
Lancaster	0.9	15,582	63.1	46.4	3.4	13.3	36.9	31.4	34.6	33.2
Lebanon	1.6	6,598	73.3	51.5	4.6	17.2	26.7	21.6	45	21.9
Lima	1.6	14,695	60.8	36.8	3.6	20.4	39.2	32.3	37.3	29.9
Lorain	3.0	24,557	66.5	41.0	5.6	19.9	33.5	29.6	35.8	32.4
Mansfield	1.5	19,521	58.8	40.3	3.2	15.3	41.2	34.1	29.6	34.1
Maple Heights	2.4	10,379	59.5	32.1	5.7	21.7	40.5	35.6	31.0	33.0
Marion	1.2	13,099	62.3	41.6	5.6	15.0	37.7	32.8	33.7	34.2
Mason	9.4	10,216	75.3	64.2	2.3	8.9	24.7	21.8	48.3	19.5
Massillon	0.7	12,664	66.4	46.0	4.8	15.6	33.6	28.9	33.7	33.5
Medina	3.4	10,649	72.1	56.0	1.9	14.2	27.9	23.5	40.9	23
Mentor	5.1	18,969	70.5	57.1	4.0	9.4	29.5	24.7	30.8	34.4
Middletown	2.3	20,172	62.0	40.6	5.1	16.4	38.0	31.4	32.5	31.3
Newark	0.8	19,060	61.0	40.3	5.4	15.3	39.0	30.5	32.6	30.1
North Olmsted	7.4	13,446	65.6	53.4	2.9	9.3	34.4	29.8	26.3	37.2
North Ridgeville	3.0	9,951	73.0	60.1	4.4	8.5	27.0	24.0	35.0	31.7
North Royalton	9.1	12,299	64.8	55.0	2.2	7.6	35.2	31.1	28.4	30.3
Norwood	4.8	8,162	48.8	34.3	2.9	11.6	51.2	44.3	27.2	31.9
Oxford	3.0	5,698	36.0	28.7	0.0	7.3	64.0	35.3	15.3	20.3
Parma	10.2	33,609	64.2	48.9	4.2	11.0	35.8	31.5	29.2	38.2
Piqua	1.0	8,305	66.2	46.5	3.9	15.8	33.8	30.4	35.3	31.4
Portsmouth	1.2	8,707	55.1	30.6	5.2	19.4	44.9	38.2	29.0	38.4
Reynoldsburg	5.5	13,696	71.1	49.0	6.0	16.1	28.9	24.5	42.3	28.8
Riverside	4.9	10,431	64.1	47.2	2.6	14.4	35.9	30.6	30.4	32.2
Sandusky	1.0	11,333	58.5	37.8	5.7	15.0	41.5	35.2	31.1	33.3
Shaker Heights	7.7	11,723	68.0	47.3	2.7	18.0	32.0	29.1	38.6	33.9
Sidney	3.7	8,311	66.1	46.3	4.7	15.1	33.9	31.8	35.4	29.2
Solon	11.4	8,094	83.2	70.2	3.2	9.8	16.8	13.6	45.1	29.5
South Euclid	8.7	9,269	69.5	52.4	2.8	14.3	30.5	27.9	34.9	29.8
Springfield	1.3	24,493	59.1	37.4	4.7	17.0	40.9	35.5	32.8	34.8
Stow	3.1	13,922	68.8	57.4	3.1	8.2	31.2	25.8	36.3	27.8
Strongsville	8.6	17,627	73.8	63.6	3.0	7.2	26.2	23.2	35.4	33.6
Toledo	3.3	119,248	57.7	34.9	4.9	17.9	42.3	35.0	31.7	28.7
Trotwood	1.5	10,674	57.6	30.6	3.7	23.2	42.4	33.3	33.7	33.7
Troy	2.2	9,546	64.8	47.0	4.1	13.7	35.2	29.6	33.8	29.7
Upper Arlington	7.4	13,929	69.8	59.4	2.0	8.4	30.2	26.2	36.9	34.4
Wadsworth	1.2	7,424	71.7	57.2	3.5	11.0	28.3	25.7	37.3	33.2
Warren	1.1	17,980	57.6	33.8	3.7	20.1	42.4	37.6	29.9	32.6
Westerville	4.4	13,510	69.3	58.0	3.8	7.4	30.7	26.5	35.0	28.7
Westlake	10.1	13,317	63.8	55.1	1.1	7.5	36.2	33.0	28.0	38.0
Willoughby	7.2	10,744	57.3	40.7	3.1	13.5	42.7	38.2	29.5	32.8
Wooster	3.8	10,464	59.2	42.7	4.0	12.5	40.8	34.7	28.8	37.6
Xenia	1.3	9,444	66.2	43.4	4.9	17.9	33.8	28.8	35.9	31.4
Youngstown	3.0	27,930	60.0	30.1	5.0	25.0	40.0	34.7	29.5	38.2
Zanesville	0.4	9,978	59.9	37.6	3.9	18.4	40.1	34.5	30.7	35.6
Oklahoma	4.9	1,386,849	67.1	50.6	4.4	12.0	32.9	28.0	33.9	31.7
Ardmore	2.6	10,205	64.2	44.8	4.3	15.1	35.8	31.2	32.4	32.3
Bartlesville	3.6	14,148	65.4	51.3	2.6	11.5	34.6	31.4	29.5	39.6
Bixby	2.5	6,438	75.8	66.3	1.3	8.2	24.2	20.8	36.2	26.9
Broken Arrow	5.3	32,906	77.8	64.8	3.5	9.5	22.2	17.4	40.6	24.2
Del	2.8	8,945	63.0	41.2	5.4	16.4	37.0	31.2	31.5	33.8
Duncan	1.1	9,927	64.9	49.5	5.7	9.7	35.1	29.2	28.4	33.3
Edmond	5.2	30,175	69.9	56.7	3.4	9.8	30.1	24.2	38.4	25.1
Enid	4.8	18,720	65.0	50.5	3.5	10.9	35.0	28.6	32.3	31.4
Lawton	5.3	32,171	69.1	46.6	3.4	19.0	30.9	26.3	39.3	27.5
Midwest	3.9	22,960	60.1	40.0	4.7	15.4	39.9	36.8	30.6	31.8
Moore	3.6	17,752	74.5	58.3	5.6	10.5	25.5	20.8	40.1	20.9
Muskogee	3.5	15,646	60.0	40.7	4.7	14.5	40.0	35.4	33.7	37.2
Norman	7.1	42,147	57.2	42.3	5.5	9.4	42.8	31.0	29.7	21.4
Oklahoma	10.8	217,431	61.8	44.0	4.7	13.1	38.2	32.1	32.5	28.3
Owasso	5.5	9,562	75.5	61.1	1.7	12.7	24.5	22.0	44.8	19.5
Ponca	4.7	10,470	64.2	46.2	4.3	13.6	35.8	32.6	33.7	33.6
Sapulpa	2.7	8,419	65.3	50.4	5.4	9.5	34.7	32.9	27.9	39.0
Shawnee	1.8	11,433	64.5	44.9	5.9	13.7	35.5	29.3	35.4	32.1
Stillwater	9.9	15,222	44.7	34.3	3.6	6.8	55.3	37.2	20.7	21.1
Tulsa	8.6	163,394	57.6	38.3	5.3	14.0	42.4	36.0	30.1	28.9
Yukon	3.2	8,480	72.5	59.5	1.2	11.9	27.5	23.4	35.9	31.5
Oregon	9.7	1,447,409	64.0	49.8	4.1	10.0	36.0	28.1	31.4	30.8
Albany	4.6	18,466	62.8	49.6	4.4	8.8	37.2	29.7	34.7	29.0
Aloha CDP	18.2	16,396	70.3	53.6	5.5	11.1	29.7	23.3	41.2	19.6
Altamont CDP	4.6	7,823	73.9	52.4	5.4	16.1	26.1	22.0	37.3	36.7
Ashland	4.3	9,147	50.2	35.9	1.8	12.5	49.8	38.9	22.4	33.8
Beaverton	22.1	33,306	59.6	47.1	4.5	8.0	40.4	31.3	33.2	22.3

STATE Place code	STATE City	Total population	Percent change 2005–2007	Population by age (percent)						Median age	Race alone or in combination (percent)				Percent Hispanic or Latino
				Under 5 years	5 to 17 years	18 to 24 years	25 to 44 years	45 to 64 years	65 years and over		White	Black	Asian Hawaiian or Pacific Islander	Amer. Indian, Alaska Native, or some other race	
ACS table number:		B01003	Population estimates	B01001	B01001	B01001	B01001	B01001	B01001	B01002	B02008	B02009	B02011 + B02012	B02010 + B02013	C03002
		1	2	3	4	5	6	7	8	9	10	11	12	13	14
	Oregon—Cont.														
41 05800	Bend	69,737	11.3	6.6	15.6	8.7	32.6	24.4	12.1	35.3	94.8	1.1	2.2	4.7	5.7
41 15800	Corvallis	51,388	1.9	4.3	11.7	28.9	24.9	19.8	10.4	27.3	86.1	2.3	9.4	6.0	6.2
41 23850	Eugene	150,430	2.7	4.5	13.5	17.1	28.3	23.3	13.4	34.4	89.0	2.1	6.7	5.9	6.5
41 26200	Forest Grove	19,532	3.0	8.8	19.8	12.7	29.1	18.7	10.9	31.0	87.2	-	4.2	8.5	21.9
41 30550	Grants Pass	33,740	3.2	6.8	17.1	9.2	26.2	22.9	17.8	37.4	95.2	0.5	1.3	6.4	7.1
41 31250	Gresham	101,537	3.1	8.3	19.8	8.1	28.5	24.6	10.7	35.0	83.9	3.7	5.5	9.8	18.3
41 32850	Hayesville CDP	21,852	-	9.5	20.6	9.0	28.3	22.8	9.8	30.4	83.6	4.4	3.3	11.0	30.8
41 34100	Hillsboro	83,264	8.0	9.9	18.5	8.9	35.4	20.8	6.5	30.9	80.6	2.6	9.6	10.9	21.5
41 38500	Keizer	36,225	2.6	8.0	19.4	8.4	28.0	23.3	12.8	34.7	91.0	2.2	3.1	8.5	15.6
41 40550	Lake Oswego	38,355	1.2	4.4	19.7	7.4	21.8	33.6	13.0	42.6	92.0	2.5	6.5	1.1	1.8
41 45000	McMinnville	30,336	5.1	7.1	16.8	14.5	25.9	21.1	14.6	32.1	85.9	1.0	2.6	14.1	19.2
41 47000	Medford	72,429	3.0	7.3	17.0	9.6	27.6	23.2	15.4	35.4	93.8	1.5	2.9	5.3	10.9
41 48650	Milwaukie	20,160	0.2	4.7	14.5	10.7	29.0	27.7	13.3	39.5	95.7	0.6	3.9	3.0	5.6
41 52100	Newberg	19,097	7.9	7.6	17.0	17.2	28.4	20.0	9.8	30.6	87.3	1.3	2.1	11.6	11.1
41 55200	Oregon	29,889	3.4	6.8	16.4	12.8	26.8	26.4	10.8	36.1	95.0	1.8	2.8	5.4	8.9
41 59000	Portland	541,550	2.5	6.5	14.8	8.1	33.2	26.9	10.4	37.1	81.9	7.9	8.5	5.7	8.5
41 61200	Redmond	22,532	13.3	7.0	22.1	10.7	28.9	20.0	11.2	31.6	96.1	-	2.3	2.7	-
41 63650	Roseburg	22,262	1.8	6.2	16.6	9.7	25.8	26.1	15.6	39.0	95.3	0.9	2.4	3.1	2.4
41 64900	Salem	148,233	3.1	7.1	17.6	10.6	30.3	23.1	11.3	34.3	85.7	1.8	4.2	11.6	19.2
41 69600	Springfield	55,536	1.5	8.0	16.8	9.0	30.3	25.3	10.5	33.9	90.1	1.7	2.4	8.4	8.7
41 73650	Tigard	45,849	3.2	6.3	17.6	7.2	30.8	27.5	10.7	37.7	86.3	2.0	10.3	5.8	12.6
41 74950	Tualatin	27,251	1.8	8.7	21.1	6.7	32.8	25.3	5.3	34.0	86.6	2.5	3.5	9.6	18.9
41 80150	West Linn	26,356	0.5	4.8	20.8	5.9	27.1	32.0	9.3	38.7	93.2	0.8	7.1	1.7	-
41 83750	Woodburn	22,284	2.1	8.9	18.6	9.7	30.3	16.1	16.4	32.8	61.4	-	1.6	40.1	-
42 00000	**Pennsylvania**	12,400,959	0.5	5.9	16.7	9.6	25.9	26.7	15.2	39.5	85.0	11.1	2.6	2.7	4.3
42 02000	Allentown	108,900	0.5	8.1	17.5	11.5	29.0	20.9	13.0	32.8	67.4	11.6	1.9	21.9	34.6
42 02184	Altoona	47,271	-0.8	7.4	15.0	10.6	25.3	25.2	16.5	38.6	97.1	2.8	0.3	1.2	1.1
42 03714	Back Mountain CDP	24,131	-	4.2	16.1	6.8	25.8	31.3	15.9	43.5	94.6	4.5	0.6	0.3	-
42 06064	Bethel Park municipality	35,654	-1.7	5.9	16.7	6.8	21.6	29.2	19.8	44.4	96.9	1.7	1.8	-	0.9
42 06088	Bethlehem	70,736	0.1	5.2	15.6	15.6	26.5	22.1	15.0	34.9	80.4	6.6	2.6	13.9	21.3
42 13208	Chester	30,409	-0.3	7.4	21.9	12.9	23.2	22.4	12.2	30.4	17.5	79.9	0.4	3.3	6.0
42 19920	Drexel Hill CDP	30,036	-	7.4	18.6	7.6	30.4	25.3	10.8	36.2	91.2	4.8	4.4	-	1.8
42 21648	Easton	27,333	-0.2	7.5	15.5	17.8	29.6	20.3	9.3	31.3	72.5	18.0	2.6	12.6	15.3
42 24000	Erie	100,393	1.0	7.0	17.7	12.7	26.4	22.1	14.2	34.1	81.1	16.8	1.2	3.4	5.4
42 32800	Harrisburg	45,195	-0.2	6.9	20.4	8.2	29.6	24.3	10.6	34.5	35.6	58.1	2.3	7.1	12.9
42 33408	Hazleton	21,980	-0.8	7.2	15.2	9.4	24.8	24.1	19.4	40.8	88.9	3.5	-	9.1	-
42 38288	Johnstown	20,660	-2.2	6.6	13.6	8.1	25.2	25.5	21.0	43.1	88.3	11.8	0.7	1.4	1.9
42 41216	Lancaster	55,029	-0.2	7.6	18.9	14.3	29.7	19.9	9.6	30.4	68.0	19.6	2.9	12.8	32.4
42 42168	Lebanon	20,953	1.1	6.1	17.8	6.9	29.0	24.7	15.5	37.2	74.5	6.6	1.0	20.3	-
42 42928	Levittown CDP	51,535	-	6.0	17.1	8.1	26.9	27.8	14.2	39.9	94.3	3.7	2.1	0.6	1.1
42 45904	McCandless Township CDP	28,090	-	5.9	16.6	7.7	21.8	30.5	17.5	44.1	94.2	2.5	3.6	-	-
42 46256	McKeesport	20,293	-1.8	6.6	19.1	7.3	22.2	26.6	18.2	40.8	71.6	30.8	-	2.2	-
42 50528	Monroeville municipality	27,659	-1.5	3.7	15.2	7.9	22.8	30.0	20.4	45.2	82.5	10.8	5.8	3.0	3.5
42 51704	Mount Lebanon CDP	32,658	-	6.9	16.6	5.8	23.0	28.6	19.1	43.5	96.1	2.2	2.4	0.4	1.0
42 53368	New Castle	24,300	-1.8	6.9	16.1	8.6	24.5	24.8	19.1	40.2	88.1	13.4	-	1.9	-
42 54656	Norristown borough	33,739	1.8	8.4	16.3	13.1	31.5	20.7	10.1	31.0	53.9	41.4	1.9	6.4	17.5
42 59040	Penn Hills CDP	42,882	-	5.4	16.0	5.0	22.8	31.7	19.2	45.3	66.4	32.9	0.5	2.4	-
42 60000	Philadelphia	1,454,382	-0.7	7.3	17.9	10.8	27.7	23.3	13.0	35.3	43.9	44.9	5.8	7.3	10.3
42 61000	Pittsburgh	296,324	-1.7	5.1	12.7	16.9	25.4	24.5	15.5	36.8	68.3	28.0	4.1	1.9	1.9
42 61536	Plum borough	27,146	-0.8	5.6	17.8	7.3	26.4	28.4	14.5	40.9	95.5	3.6	1.4	-	0.8
42 62416	Pottstown borough	21,685	-0.5	8.2	17.8	9.9	27.3	23.5	13.2	36.5	77.7	21.5	1.8	2.4	4.2
42 63268	Radnor Township CDP	31,098	-	4.2	17.6	23.4	19.4	22.2	13.2	33.6	87.6	4.1	8.4	0.8	1.7
42 63624	Reading	80,951	0.5	9.7	21.8	11.4	29.2	18.3	9.6	29.0	59.4	14.9	2.0	27.0	50.3
42 66356	Ross Township CDP	30,697	-	4.7	13.0	6.4	24.5	30.8	20.6	45.7	96.0	2.1	2.4	-	0.4
42 69000	Scranton	74,566	-0.7	6.6	13.8	14.3	24.0	23.5	17.9	37.6	92.3	4.4	1.6	2.5	5.3
42 69596	Shaler Township CDP	29,282	-	5.2	16.1	5.3	25.4	28.8	19.2	44.3	98.0	-	0.7	-	-
42 73040	Springfield CDP	23,891	-	6.5	17.5	8.0	23.4	27.3	17.3	41.6	96.8	1.0	2.4	-	0.7
42 73808	State College borough	39,603	2.6	1.3	4.3	68.9	13.7	6.1	5.8	21.1	86.6	3.0	9.9	2.2	3.1
42 79277	Upper St. Clair CDP	20,545	-	4.9	22.7	6.4	17.7	31.3	17.0	44.3	92.7	1.9	6.4	-	1.9
42 83512	West Mifflin borough	21,283	-1.8	4.7	16.6	7.0	23.1	28.2	20.5	44.3	90.7	9.6	-	-	-
42 85152	Wilkes-Barre	39,452	-0.5	4.9	15.0	15.7	24.9	21.6	17.8	36.4	87.0	10.1	1.2	4.2	6.2
42 85312	Williamsport	30,211	-1.5	6.8	16.1	19.9	23.8	20.9	12.5	31.4	82.6	17.3	0.8	1.6	1.8
42 87048	York	40,045	0.0	8.6	18.8	13.7	28.4	20.7	9.8	30.2	62.5	30.4	0.8	10.1	23.8
44 00000	**Rhode Island**	1,062,065	-0.8	5.8	16.5	10.7	27.3	25.9	13.9	38.3	84.5	6.4	3.0	8.3	10.9
44 09460	Bristol CDP	22,804	-	4.4	12.1	15.8	23.1	27.0	17.7	40.4	97.8	0.7	1.5	-	-
44 19180	Cranston	82,397	-0.6	5.6	16.2	9.0	27.3	27.0	14.9	39.9	85.0	5.3	4.6	7.1	9.1
44 22960	East Providence	47,168	-1.1	5.0	14.2	6.7	30.0	26.5	17.6	41.4	90.2	6.5	1.1	5.5	2.9
44 49960	Newport	23,368	2.9	4.5	13.0	14.1	29.7	24.9	13.9	36.2	91.0	9.0	1.8	1.3	2.8
44 51904	North Providence CDP	34,022	-	6.1	15.1	7.0	27.7	27.0	17.2	41.2	88.2	6.6	2.0	4.0	6.7
44 54640	Pawtucket	72,335	-1.6	6.5	17.5	9.5	30.4	23.4	12.7	36.6	69.0	15.9	2.8	15.1	15.5
44 59000	Providence	170,220	-1.1	7.3	17.7	18.2	29.7	18.5	8.6	28.7	51.2	17.4	6.4	28.9	36.0
44 74300	Warwick	84,975	-1.9	4.8	15.0	7.6	27.1	29.5	16.0	42.2	95.0	2.2	2.3	1.6	1.8

Table A-4. Cities — Who: Age, Race/Ethnicity, and Household Structure, 2005–2007—*Continued*

STATE City	Percent foreign born	Total households	Household type (percent)						Percent of households with people under 18 years	Percent of households with people 60 years and over
			Family households				Nonfamily households			
			Total family households	Married-couple families	Male householder families	Female householder families	Total nonfamily households	One-person households		
ACS table number:	C05002	B11001	B11001	B11001	B11001	B11001	B11001	B11001	C11005	B11006
	15	16	17	18	19	20	21	22	23	24
Oregon—Cont.										
Bend	5.1	29,290	61.8	51.1	2.4	8.3	38.2	26.0	31.7	25.9
Corvallis	11.4	21,079	48.4	35.5	3.8	9.1	51.6	33.9	24.2	23.3
Eugene	8.4	62,486	51.9	38.9	3.6	9.4	48.1	33.7	24.9	25.4
Forest Grove	14.5	7,048	64.6	51.7	2.8	10.1	35.4	28.9	35.9	29.2
Grants Pass	3.8	14,167	64.6	47.3	5.2	12.0	35.4	31.2	34.4	36.5
Gresham	17.2	36,959	68.8	48.6	5.7	14.5	31.2	25.4	36.8	27.1
Hayesville CDP	22.2	7,570	78.9	54.0	6.9	17.9	21.1	16.9	43.3	29.5
Hillsboro	17.8	29,632	67.0	49.9	4.7	12.4	33.0	24.3	38.5	19.7
Keizer	8.4	13,663	68.1	50.6	4.6	12.9	31.9	22.7	38.4	26.4
Lake Oswego	9.5	15,647	63.4	53.9	2.3	7.2	36.6	30.5	31.5	32.2
McMinnville	10.0	11,060	66.3	47.7	6.5	12.1	33.7	28.7	37.2	31.2
Medford	7.5	29,476	63.0	46.0	4.2	12.8	37.0	30.0	32.9	33.0
Milwaukie	7.1	8,569	57.4	41.4	3.8	12.3	42.6	34.3	28.7	29.0
Newberg	7.6	6,837	69.0	49.5	4.3	15.2	31.0	26.8	35.8	22.9
Oregon	6.4	10,743	67.5	50.5	4.5	12.5	32.5	22.6	33.9	24.0
Portland	13.4	233,398	51.0	37.0	3.8	10.3	49.0	37.6	25.5	24.7
Redmond	8.8	8,548	69.6	54.5	7.3	7.8	30.4	22.7	38.2	27.9
Roseburg	2.4	9,216	60.4	44.6	5.5	10.3	39.6	35.2	31.2	34.3
Salem	14.8	54,946	62.4	44.6	5.1	12.7	37.6	29.6	34.7	29.0
Springfield	6.2	22,353	62.3	44.0	4.5	13.7	37.7	29.7	34.7	26.6
Tigard	17.6	18,435	62.7	50.0	4.1	8.5	37.3	29.6	33.1	25.7
Tualatin	14.8	9,878	67.8	51.4	4.2	12.1	32.2	23.7	43.4	16.6
West Linn	9.5	9,563	74.6	65.4	1.6	7.6	25.4	20.5	42.2	25.5
Woodburn	37.6	7,301	75.9	58.2	9.8	8.0	24.1	19.7	40.8	40.2
Pennsylvania	5.2	4,858,509	65.8	49.9	4.2	11.7	34.2	28.9	31.3	34.6
Allentown	12.7	40,838	60.6	36.7	5.3	18.7	39.4	30.9	35.4	33.0
Altoona	1.1	19,760	60.2	41.5	4.2	14.4	39.8	35.8	29.3	38.4
Back Mountain CDP	1.3	8,856	75.4	65.6	3.0	6.9	24.6	22.1	31.5	39.2
Bethel Park municipality	3.1	14,055	69.7	61.5	1.7	6.5	30.3	28.3	31.8	40.5
Bethlehem	5.9	27,984	60.5	40.7	3.5	16.3	39.5	33.6	30.0	33.9
Chester	2.5	10,710	59.9	17.6	6.8	35.5	40.1	35.1	37.9	33.2
Drexel Hill CDP	8.4	11,610	62.7	47.7	5.5	9.6	37.3	30.9	35.0	30.0
Easton	7.9	8,984	65.1	36.9	6.3	21.9	34.9	30.1	40.3	28.6
Erie	5.6	38,929	56.7	34.7	3.1	18.9	43.3	36.0	31.8	30.2
Harrisburg	6.7	19,121	52.5	23.0	5.0	24.5	47.5	39.9	31.4	25.7
Hazleton	11.8	9,491	58.4	38.8	5.8	13.8	41.6	37.3	31.3	39.9
Johnstown	1.2	10,042	55.2	34.5	4.1	16.6	44.8	39.4	24.0	42.4
Lancaster	8.9	21,031	57.3	32.1	6.7	18.5	42.7	34.1	34.6	24.4
Lebanon	5.0	9,629	50.7	29.2	4.6	16.9	49.3	42.2	28.2	38.7
Levittown CDP	4.2	18,465	74.9	58.1	5.5	11.3	25.1	21.0	36.9	35.5
McCandless Township CDP	4.7	11,394	69.5	58.7	3.4	7.4	30.5	28.3	32.6	34.9
McKeesport	0.9	8,724	51.0	26.0	4.8	20.2	49.0	42.9	29.2	38.1
Monroeville municipality	7.2	11,998	63.7	52.6	1.7	9.4	36.3	32.1	23.9	40.6
Mount Lebanon CDP	5.1	13,620	65.7	57.1	2.4	6.2	34.3	31.3	30.6	40.7
New Castle	1.4	9,646	63.7	43.1	4.6	16.1	36.3	33.6	31.8	38.1
Norristown borough	15.6	12,208	60.3	30.0	6.2	24.1	39.7	32.8	34.1	24.8
Penn Hills CDP	2.6	18,791	66.0	46.3	3.1	16.6	34.0	31.7	27.4	39.1
Philadelphia	10.9	557,985	55.2	28.4	5.6	21.2	44.8	38.7	29.9	32.1
Pittsburgh	7.3	132,054	48.3	29.6	3.7	15.0	51.7	43.2	22.2	32.3
Plum borough	2.6	10,473	75.3	61.9	2.5	10.9	24.7	20.6	36.4	31.6
Pottstown borough	2.4	9,199	56.7	34.0	4.2	18.5	43.3	37.6	32.0	32.1
Radnor Township CDP	12.7	10,040	65.8	56.1	2.5	7.2	34.2	28.1	32.9	34.1
Reading	16.6	29,471	64.1	31.3	8.3	24.5	35.9	30.0	44.1	27.1
Ross Township CDP	3.8	13,193	62.5	52.5	3.6	6.3	37.5	31.0	23.1	40.0
Scranton	5.4	30,069	58.6	38.6	5.6	14.4	41.4	35.4	29.3	39.4
Shaler Township CDP	2.5	11,831	70.4	60.5	0.9	9.0	29.6	26.3	29.8	41.3
Springfield CDP	3.6	8,581	74.9	61.2	4.6	9.2	25.1	21.8	32.8	43.5
State College borough	10.7	11,185	26.0	22.1	1.3	2.6	74.0	40.9	9.4	13.8
Upper St. Clair CDP	7.6	7,102	81.5	74.3	1.6	5.6	18.5	17.4	42.0	40.1
West Mifflin borough	1.4	9,202	63.5	47.3	4.3	12.0	36.5	34.4	27.5	39.3
Wilkes-Barre	3.7	16,462	54.1	32.6	4.7	16.8	45.9	39.7	27.7	37.0
Williamsport	1.2	12,214	54.7	33.3	4.2	17.2	45.3	35.7	29.9	27.7
York	5.6	15,645	56.7	29.1	6.9	20.8	43.3	33.7	35.6	27.2
Rhode Island	12.6	404,549	63.9	47.1	4.1	12.7	36.1	29.5	31.7	32.9
Bristol CDP	14.1	8,306	65.0	51.4	1.6	12.1	35.0	27.9	26.5	39.6
Cranston	11.8	30,436	63.8	48.5	3.3	12.0	36.2	30.9	29.9	35.7
East Providence	14.6	19,676	59.0	43.6	2.7	12.7	41.0	34.2	25.6	35.8
Newport	5.6	9,765	53.2	39.2	3.2	10.8	46.8	40.7	24.7	33.0
North Providence CDP	9.6	14,212	60.9	45.6	4.3	11.0	39.1	35.6	28.1	35.5
Pawtucket	24.1	28,229	59.8	37.1	5.2	17.5	40.2	33.4	32.3	31.3
Providence	28.9	59,064	58.1	31.5	5.8	20.7	41.9	31.9	35.6	23.9
Warwick	5.2	35,757	61.0	46.7	3.7	10.5	39.0	32.1	28.2	36.2

Table A-4. Cities — Who: Age, Race/Ethnicity, and Household Structure, 2005–2007—*Continued*

STATE Place code	STATE / City / ACS table number:	Total population B01003	Percent change 2005–2007 Population estimates	Under 5 years B01001	5 to 17 years B01001	18 to 24 years B01001	25 to 44 years B01001	45 to 64 years B01001	65 years and over B01001	Median age B01002	White B02008	Black B02009	Asian Hawaiian or Pacific Islander B02011 + B02012	Amer. Indian, Alaska Native, or some other race B02010 + B02013	Percent Hispanic or Latino C03002
		1	2	3	4	5	6	7	8	9	10	11	12	13	14
	Rhode Island—Cont.														
44 78260	West Warwick CDP	30,560	-	6.2	15.5	10.4	29.7	25.4	12.7	37.1	93.0	2.4	2.7	2.9	5.3
44 80780	Woonsocket	45,009	-1.3	8.5	15.6	8.3	29.1	22.4	16.2	37.4	83.0	6.9	5.4	7.1	12.3
45 00000	**South Carolina**	4,330,933	3.6	6.7	17.5	9.9	27.2	25.8	12.8	37.0	68.3	29.2	1.5	2.2	3.6
45 00550	Aiken	27,267	3.8	4.7	17.1	8.4	20.3	30.3	19.2	44.7	68.3	29.4	1.9	0.8	1.9
45 01360	Anderson	23,583	2.6	5.5	14.2	11.4	25.9	22.3	20.7	38.8	65.2	33.8	1.2	0.7	0.3
45 13330	Charleston	110,866	1.1	7.0	14.5	15.3	28.2	23.0	11.9	33.3	65.3	32.0	1.9	1.8	2.9
45 16000	Columbia	118,786	0.6	5.2	13.2	25.3	27.7	19.3	9.4	28.7	54.3	41.9	3.7	2.0	3.8
45 21985	Easley	19,706	5.5	6.4	16.7	7.9	30.1	24.3	14.7	39.2	86.7	11.1	-	-	
45 25810	Florence	33,937	0.6	8.3	14.2	9.9	27.5	25.2	14.9	37.9	54.1	44.3	1.8	1.2	1.1
45 29815	Goose Creek	33,582	12.6	7.4	20.8	14.6	28.1	22.8	6.2	30.2	80.2	16.3	4.1	2.9	4.0
45 30850	Greenville	56,458	3.1	6.8	13.2	13.4	29.8	23.0	13.7	34.6	63.7	33.3	1.9	1.8	4.2
45 30895	Greenwood	21,045	0.3	5.6	18.9	14.9	26.9	18.5	15.1	32.4	42.2	50.8	1.3	6.4	9.6
45 30985	Greer	20,838	9.2	8.2	16.1	6.0	35.8	21.9	12.0	34.8	77.8	15.1	1.1	6.3	
45 34045	Hilton Head Island town.....	36,248	-2.5	5.7	14.1	6.1	21.1	25.6	27.4	47.7	87.4	8.8	1.0	3.1	-
45 45115	Mauldin	20,072	4.6	5.7	18.8	7.3	33.4	24.8	10.0	35.8	69.7	22.6	4.8	4.5	4.8
45 48535	Mount Pleasant town........	67,545	9.0	7.6	19.4	5.8	31.0	26.3	9.9	37.1	93.0	5.5	1.5	1.2	1.4
45 49075	Myrtle Beach	24,205	10.8	8.5	12.6	9.4	30.5	20.9	18.1	36.0	76.4	15.7	2.6	7.0	8.3
45 50695	North Augusta	20,732	4.4	7.8	16.4	7.7	28.9	24.4	14.8	36.4	71.2	25.8	1.9	2.3	3.2
45 50875	North Charleston	84,491	3.8	9.1	17.0	12.6	29.8	22.0	9.4	31.6	45.0	49.6	2.6	4.5	7.0
45 61405	Rock Hill	60,329	9.4	6.7	18.5	15.4	29.7	20.0	9.6	30.4	58.1	39.0	2.3	2.3	4.4
45 62395	St. Andrews CDP	22,745		6.5	14.8	16.2	33.0	22.3	7.1	31.6	33.8	65.6	2.0	2.3	1.6
45 68290	Spartanburg	37,123	1.5	8.4	17.1	12.1	23.7	23.3	15.4	34.9	46.3	51.2	2.5	0.3	0.7
45 70270	Summerville town	34,864	14.9	8.0	16.8	9.2	27.9	25.2	13.0	36.7	80.2	18.3	1.3	2.0	3.2
45 70405	Sumter....................	38,776	-2.0	8.6	19.2	10.8	25.2	21.1	15.1	34.9	47.9	49.1	2.4	1.1	3.0
45 71395	Taylors CDP	21,783	-	9.5	17.6	8.2	31.6	23.0	10.2	33.9	82.6	15.0	2.4	0.4	6.0
45 73870	Wade Hampton CDP........	21,459	-	5.3	13.1	9.6	24.9	27.4	19.7	42.0	82.8	8.6	5.9	2.8	9.8
46 00000	**South Dakota**	788,241	2.1	7.0	17.8	10.6	25.1	25.4	14.2	37.1	89.0	1.4	1.2	10.3	2.1
46 00100	Aberdeen	23,459	0.6	6.7	12.9	14.2	24.5	24.3	17.3	37.2	94.0	-	0.9	6.0	-
46 52980	Rapid City	62,500	2.9	8.5	16.9	11.8	25.6	23.9	13.3	34.4	86.5	2.3	1.7	13.7	3.9
46 59020	Sioux Falls	147,085	4.6	7.6	16.9	10.6	29.7	23.7	11.5	34.4	91.0	3.6	1.6	5.4	4.2
46 69300	Watertown	20,589	1.7	7.9	16.6	10.7	26.3	23.4	15.1	35.8	96.7	-	-	3.1	
47 00000	**Tennessee**	6,073,646	2.8	6.7	17.4	9.1	28.3	25.9	12.7	37.2	80.3	17.2	1.5	2.3	3.3
47 03440	Bartlett	49,537	2.5	5.7	21.9	6.1	25.8	29.7	10.9	39.7	87.4	10.5	2.2	-	1.3
47 08280	Brentwood	32,405	9.2	5.7	21.2	8.9	20.5	34.8	9.0	40.9	92.8	2.9	5.1	0.8	1.7
47 08540	Bristol	25,737	1.6	4.9	15.1	8.6	23.6	28.3	19.5	43.2	95.5	2.9	1.0	1.1	1.4
47 14000	Chattanooga	159,111	2.4	6.3	15.1	10.5	25.9	27.1	15.1	38.8	61.4	37.1	1.3	1.8	2.8
47 15160	Clarksville	112,982	5.3	8.9	20.2	11.9	32.1	19.3	7.7	29.9	69.7	25.7	3.7	4.2	6.7
47 15400	Cleveland.................	39,448	2.4	5.9	14.9	14.6	27.8	22.3	14.5	34.2	86.7	8.6	1.6	3.9	3.9
47 16240	Collierville town	42,795	4.7	7.0	22.8	7.3	25.1	30.0	7.8	38.3	84.1	10.2	6.3	1.2	3.2
47 16540	Columbia	34,214	1.5	7.5	18.1	10.3	26.5	24.1	13.6	34.3	74.7	21.2	0.7	3.5	5.5
47 16920	Cookeville	26,953	3.2	6.6	12.1	21.3	26.7	19.2	14.0	30.3	91.7	3.7	2.9	3.2	6.1
47 25760	Farragut town	19,907	3.5	6.1	19.6	5.8	20.7	34.9	12.9	43.6	93.1	3.6	3.5		
47 27740	Franklin..................	55,372	7.6	6.4	19.3	9.3	31.9	24.0	9.0	34.5	87.2	9.2	2.2	2.4	6.2
47 28540	Gallatin	27,085	8.3	8.8	16.7	9.2	31.2	21.8	12.3	32.6	78.7	18.5	-	2.9	-
47 28960	Germantown	40,564	0.0	4.8	20.3	7.0	18.8	37.1	12.0	44.6	90.0	1.9	6.6	1.5	
47 33280	Hendersonville	46,321	5.4	6.1	18.1	8.8	27.7	26.6	12.6	38.5	91.4	6.5	1.4	1.5	1.9
47 37640	Jackson...................	60,461	1.7	8.0	16.9	12.8	26.9	22.5	12.9	33.5	54.5	44.3	1.1	0.9	3.1
47 38320	Johnson..................	58,025	3.3	5.0	14.2	14.3	27.6	23.7	15.2	35.9	91.4	7.2	1.6	1.3	3.5
47 39560	Kingsport.................	45,763	0.7	5.3	15.0	6.6	26.2	26.7	20.1	42.6	93.9	4.9	1.2	1.0	1.3
47 40000	Knoxville.................	177,362	1.9	5.9	14.1	16.6	28.0	22.3	13.0	33.9	81.2	17.1	1.8	1.8	2.3
47 41200	La Vergne	27,401	11.4	10.3	22.5	7.5	37.5	17.3	5.0	29.6	68.1	20.0	6.0	8.5	10.6
47 41520	Lebanon	24,592	4.8	6.2	15.8	12.5	26.9	24.6	14.0	36.1	84.7	13.4	1.3	1.7	5.4
47 46380	Maryville	25,258	4.0	4.4	18.6	9.7	26.7	23.7	16.9	39.9	94.1	3.1	1.9	1.9	2.5
47 48000	Memphis	649,443	-0.4	8.1	19.1	10.8	27.8	24.0	10.2	33.4	32.8	63.1	1.8	3.5	4.6
47 50280	Morristown................	27,739	2.5	8.1	15.2	10.2	26.8	21.0	18.6	36.3	86.3	7.1	1.3	7.5	17.3
47 50780	Mount Juliet	18,152	12.7	9.8	20.5	8.0	33.6	21.1	7.0	32.2	91.2	8.5	-	0.5	-
47 51560	Murfreesboro..............	90,358	11.7	6.6	16.3	19.2	30.6	19.0	8.4	28.8	80.3	14.5	2.7	3.5	4.0
47 52006	Nashville-Davidson (balance).................	586,214	1.9	7.4	16.0	9.6	31.6	24.7	10.7	35.8	65.6	28.9	3.3	3.3	7.3
47 55120	Oak Ridge	27,859	1.6	4.2	15.9	7.3	22.7	29.8	20.1	44.9	86.9	9.0	3.0	2.6	2.1
47 69420	Smyrna town	33,789	8.9	9.9	18.6	7.0	33.9	22.1	8.6	32.5	84.0	10.1	3.6	4.2	7.9
47 70580	Spring Hill	17,158	39.9	11.4	20.4	7.6	36.3	19.2	5.1	29.9	89.8	8.4	1.1	4.2	4.7
48 00000	**Texas**	23,385,340	4.6	8.3	19.4	10.3	29.2	22.7	10.0	33.1	72.1	12.0	3.7	14.0	35.5
48 01000	Abilene	114,477	0.5	7.8	16.9	14.8	27.8	20.5	12.1	31.8	76.9	9.6	2.2	14.0	22.1
48 01924	Allen	74,462	12.1	10.5	22.7	6.9	34.6	21.6	3.7	32.3	77.4	9.6	12.1	5.1	10.2
48 02272	Alvin	21,925	3.7	8.6	19.1	10.4	28.0	23.0	10.7	32.8	86.0	4.8	3.2	6.5	-
48 03000	Amarillo	185,617	1.9	8.6	18.6	10.4	28.0	22.9	11.4	33.3	77.5	7.3	2.2	15.4	26.3
48 04000	Arlington	356,764	2.4	8.8	19.5	10.7	32.3	21.7	7.0	31.4	64.2	18.2	7.0	13.0	25.6
48 04462	Atascocita CDP	61,325	-	9.5	22.6	7.3	35.0	21.6	4.0	31.9	73.8	17.8	4.2	5.7	18.0
48 05000	Austin	725,306	5.6	8.1	15.0	13.6	36.4	20.3	6.6	31.2	65.6	9.1	6.3	21.2	34.2
48 06128	Baytown	71,993	1.2	8.7	20.8	8.9	29.1	22.8	9.7	32.6	61.4	17.9	1.3	20.8	35.6
48 07000	Beaumont.................	112,705	-1.5	8.0	18.6	10.7	27.2	23.7	11.9	33.8	44.7	47.0	3.4	6.2	11.2

Table A-4. Cities — Who: Age, Race/Ethnicity, and Household Structure, 2005–2007—*Continued*

STATE City	Percent foreign born	Total households	Household type (percent)						Percent of households with people under 18 years	Percent of households with people 60 years and over
			Family households				Nonfamily households			
			Total family households	Married-couple families	Male householder families	Female householder families	Total nonfamily households	One-person households		
ACS table number:	C05002	B11001	B11001	B11001	B11001	B11001	B11001	B11001	C11005	B11006
	15	16	17	18	19	20	21	22	23	24
Rhode Island—Cont.										
West Warwick CDP............	10.5	12,775	59.9	40.4	4.5	14.9	40.1	34.8	31.4	27.9
Woonsocket	10.8	17,560	60.5	38.5	4.7	17.3	39.5	31.7	32.8	30.3
South Carolina...............	4.2	1,664,561	67.7	48.5	4.2	15.1	32.3	27.3	33.7	31.9
Aiken.................................	4.4	11,704	63.7	45.4	2.7	15.6	36.3	33.1	28.9	39.6
Anderson..........................	2.2	9,699	60.9	36.7	4.4	19.8	39.1	34.8	28.9	36.0
Charleston........................	4.4	47,049	52.1	35.1	2.5	14.4	47.9	37.8	26.1	28.6
Columbia...........................	5.0	42,576	49.5	32.2	3.2	14.1	50.5	42.5	25.4	25.2
Easley...............................	6.8	7,986	74.5	56.1	2.2	16.2	25.5	21.4	36.6	33.1
Florence............................	2.8	13,127	66.1	39.6	3.2	23.3	33.9	29.1	31.5	31.7
Goose Creek.....................	5.1	10,238	81.6	63.4	5.5	12.6	18.4	13.2	45.2	23.3
Greenville.........................	6.1	24,330	50.8	31.5	2.3	17.0	49.2	43.0	24.1	30.5
Greenwood.......................	8.7	7,975	56.8	31.4	4.4	21.0	43.2	36.4	28.4	30.9
Greer................................	12.9	9,051	58.3	42.5	8.0	7.8	41.7	37.3	29.6	27.5
Hilton Head Island town.....	15.5	15,425	67.0	56.1	4.4	6.5	33.0	25.7	23.3	52.1
Mauldin............................	11.3	8,042	72.2	56.9	2.6	12.6	27.8	24.1	32.2	22.4
Mount Pleasant town........	4.0	26,148	67.2	56.6	1.6	9.0	32.8	25.4	34.0	26.3
Myrtle Beach....................	12.0	11,345	53.3	34.4	4.3	14.6	46.7	34.6	29.2	33.4
North Augusta..................	2.0	8,554	65.2	44.7	3.5	17.0	34.8	31.9	33.0	28.7
North Charleston	7.5	32,438	62.0	35.5	4.8	21.8	38.0	32.1	33.0	24.7
Rock Hill	5.3	22,574	63.5	39.5	4.4	19.6	36.5	28.3	36.5	24.6
St. Andrews CDP	4.4	10,844	49.1	24.8	3.2	21.1	50.9	40.7	26.5	14.5
Spartanburg......................	2.7	15,192	61.1	31.3	3.2	26.6	38.9	35.9	34.5	34.8
Summerville town	3.7	13,007	68.4	51.3	2.8	14.3	31.6	28.5	37.5	29.0
Sumter..............................	3.8	14,810	63.6	36.0	3.4	24.2	36.4	33.3	36.2	33.7
Taylors CDP......................	6.8	8,297	71.0	52.7	7.2	11.1	29.0	25.2	36.5	23.7
Wade Hampton CDP.........	13.4	9,460	59.7	44.9	5.0	9.7	40.3	34.9	21.7	39.1
South Dakota	2.1	311,644	65.7	52.7	3.8	9.3	34.3	28.6	31.7	30.9
Aberdeen..........................	1.4	10,388	56.1	42.2	3.0	10.9	43.9	36.5	25.3	31.2
Rapid................................	2.4	25,352	60.6	44.6	5.1	10.9	39.4	32.8	30.2	29.0
Sioux Falls........................	5.2	57,967	62.0	47.0	3.3	11.7	38.0	31.3	31.7	25.4
Watertown	-	9,016	60.0	48.7	2.9	8.5	40.0	32.3	34.0	32.2
Tennessee	4.0	2,382,975	67.4	49.8	4.5	13.1	32.6	27.7	33.8	30.9
Bartlett	3.5	17,729	81.7	67.5	3.3	10.8	18.3	16.4	41.9	28.6
Brentwood........................	6.3	10,839	87.8	82.3	1.6	4.0	12.2	11.0	45.3	28.8
Bristol...............................	1.7	11,086	64.9	46.0	5.8	13.0	35.1	32.5	28.4	37.0
Chattanooga	3.6	67,082	56.7	37.0	3.5	16.3	43.3	36.3	26.5	34.5
Clarksville	5.2	42,642	71.8	52.0	4.5	15.3	28.2	21.5	43.2	20.0
Cleveland..........................	5.3	16,041	62.7	47.6	4.1	11.0	37.3	30.8	28.9	33.4
Collierville town	6.7	14,477	84.2	71.3	3.0	9.9	15.8	14.3	47.5	22.5
Columbia..........................	4.3	14,489	59.8	39.5	2.6	17.7	40.2	33.4	34.6	28.8
Cookeville.........................	9.2	11,187	55.8	40.9	5.0	9.9	44.2	35.9	26.8	29.4
Farragut town...................	6.5	7,156	82.8	76.7	1.8	4.3	17.2	16.1	39.3	33.7
Franklin.............................	8.1	20,862	71.3	56.7	3.5	11.1	28.7	22.8	39.0	22.6
Gallatin.............................	8.6	10,571	66.5	43.1	3.6	19.8	33.5	26.9	35.3	30.8
Germantown	7.5	14,641	83.7	76.8	1.8	5.0	16.3	14.0	37.5	32.3
Hendersonville	3.1	18,533	70.1	57.7	3.2	9.3	29.9	25.1	34.9	30.0
Jackson.............................	3.7	24,999	62.6	37.9	5.1	19.6	37.4	33.1	35.3	29.0
Johnson............................	4.4	24,266	55.6	39.0	4.3	12.3	44.4	37.5	25.4	33.2
Kingsport..........................	3.3	21,361	58.1	43.3	2.9	11.9	41.9	36.7	27.0	38.2
Knoxville	4.1	79,868	50.5	33.3	4.0	13.2	49.5	40.5	25.7	26.6
La Vergne	12.5	9,673	76.1	52.6	7.1	16.4	23.9	18.9	52.3	18.0
Lebanon	4.8	9,862	64.5	43.3	7.4	13.9	35.5	28.1	33.9	30.8
Maryville	5.1	9,864	70.5	51.6	3.4	15.5	29.5	26.9	36.2	36.9
Memphis	5.4	253,833	59.4	29.3	6.3	23.7	40.6	34.9	33.1	26.8
Morristown........................	14.4	11,249	62.9	42.9	6.7	13.3	37.1	32.2	34.6	36.8
Mount Juliet	2.0	6,310	76.9	63.8	3.2	9.9	23.1	17.8	47.2	19.7
Murfreesboro....................	5.4	36,265	59.5	42.6	3.2	13.7	40.5	25.8	33.6	20.0
Nashville-Davidson (balance).........................	10.4	237,321	56.1	37.0	3.9	15.2	43.9	37.0	28.9	26.0
Oak Ridge.........................	5.1	12,580	60.3	44.7	1.8	13.8	39.7	34.5	24.9	41.2
Smyrna town	7.5	13,096	73.0	52.8	5.0	15.1	27.0	25.1	44.8	22.8
Spring Hill	3.9	5,874	81.3	67.6	3.5	10.2	18.7	13.4	51.3	15.1
Texas	15.8	8,095,025	70.2	51.7	4.9	13.5	29.8	24.8	39.9	27.0
Abilene.............................	4.6	42,510	65.6	48.0	3.7	13.9	34.4	28.7	34.4	29.0
Allen.................................	15.6	23,301	82.4	69.1	3.8	9.5	17.6	14.5	53.3	14.4
Alvin.................................	13.4	8,030	71.4	55.1	6.9	9.4	28.6	23.5	41.8	26.9
Amarillo............................	8.8	68,624	66.0	47.8	4.5	13.7	34.0	28.6	36.3	27.8
Arlington	18.9	128,277	67.5	49.3	5.0	13.2	32.5	26.5	40.0	20.5
Atascocita CDP	10.1	18,180	85.5	68.0	4.6	12.9	14.5	12.6	55.5	18.2
Austin...............................	19.1	294,716	51.7	36.2	4.5	11.0	48.3	36.6	28.9	16.8
Baytown............................	17.5	24,928	69.9	49.1	5.2	15.6	30.1	23.9	42.3	27.5
Beaumont.........................	8.5	43,788	64.5	39.9	4.3	20.2	35.5	29.2	36.1	30.5

Table A-4. Cities — Who: Age, Race/Ethnicity, and Household Structure, 2005–2007—*Continued*

STATE Place code	STATE / City / ACS table number:	Total population B01003	Percent change 2005–2007 Population estimates	Population by age (percent)						Median age B01002	Race alone or in combination (percent)				Percent Hispanic or Latino C03002
				Under 5 years B01001	5 to 17 years B01001	18 to 24 years B01001	25 to 44 years B01001	45 to 64 years B01001	65 years and over B01001		White B02008	Black B02009	Asian Hawaiian or Pacific Islander B02011 + B02012	Amer. Indian, Alaska Native, or some other race B02010 + B02013	
		1	2	3	4	5	6	7	8	9	10	11	12	13	14
	Texas—Cont.														
48 07132	Bedford	48,278	1.4	6.3	16.5	8.5	29.9	27.5	11.3	37.6	81.7	6.4	6.3	7.1	10.3
48 07552	Benbrook	21,810	3.9	6.7	16.0	7.7	25.3	28.8	15.5	41.5	89.0	5.9	2.0	5.4	8.7
48 08236	Big Spring	24,221	0.5	7.4	15.6	9.4	30.6	22.6	14.4	36.3	69.0	6.1	0.6	28.8	47.7
48 10768	Brownsville	172,825	4.6	12.0	24.7	10.8	26.3	17.1	9.1	26.9	86.3	0.8	0.8	13.1	92.0
48 10897	Brushy Creek CDP	20,441	-	9.4	25.4	7.9	31.5	20.8	5.0	31.9	85.4	5.9	9.1	3.8	10.0
48 10912	Bryan	66,501	3.2	9.6	17.3	16.5	28.6	18.1	9.9	28.0	66.5	19.1	1.6	16.7	33.0
48 11428	Burleson	29,955	13.5	9.4	21.5	8.4	30.3	22.1	8.2	31.9	94.5	1.5	1.0	3.9	9.9
48 13024	Carrollton	117,563	4.0	8.2	19.4	8.2	32.9	24.8	6.5	34.2	73.6	6.9	13.6	7.4	28.1
48 13492	Cedar Hill	41,756	6.9	10.0	21.7	8.1	31.3	23.3	5.7	32.7	41.6	47.5	3.2	11.5	18.0
48 13552	Cedar Park	41,933	21.3	9.1	23.6	9.0	31.7	19.7	6.9	31.7	83.2	6.1	4.1	9.4	15.8
48 14236	Channelview CDP	40,209	-	8.3	27.8	10.3	29.2	18.8	5.7	27.6	47.0	14.6	2.3	37.5	56.8
48 15364	Cleburne	31,485	1.9	8.5	19.9	9.3	29.9	20.6	11.7	32.5	87.8	5.8	1.9	7.2	-
48 15628	Cloverleaf CDP	23,402	-	12.4	23.8	9.5	31.5	17.7	5.2	26.8	67.7	10.9	2.1	20.1	-
48 15976	College Station	80,316	5.8	4.8	11.4	45.7	23.8	10.4	3.8	22.3	82.4	5.7	9.5	3.5	12.6
48 15988	Colleyville	23,069	6.9	6.8	23.9	6.2	19.9	35.1	8.0	41.3	91.1	1.2	6.3	1.9	5.1
48 16432	Conroe	48,059	12.4	10.6	16.1	12.5	33.1	18.7	9.0	28.8	74.4	11.4	1.8	13.3	34.7
48 16612	Coppell	41,439	1.4	7.3	27.2	4.8	30.3	26.2	4.3	36.1	81.3	4.6	13.0	2.3	8.1
48 16624	Copperas Cove	30,944	2.1	6.7	23.3	15.8	29.2	18.9	6.1	27.3	67.7	26.0	6.5	7.3	10.7
48 16696	Corinth	19,386	13.0	10.5	18.9	7.1	36.1	21.9	5.6	34.0	90.5	6.1	2.3	5.8	11.3
48 17000	Corpus Christi	284,435	1.2	7.9	19.4	10.8	26.7	24.0	11.2	34.1	78.1	4.9	1.9	17.4	58.0
48 17060	Corsicana	25,996	2.3	9.1	16.9	12.7	30.0	18.0	13.2	32.3	61.0	24.3	-	17.2	30.8
48 19000	Dallas	1,187,603	2.2	9.2	17.4	9.8	34.2	20.8	8.5	32.1	56.9	23.8	2.8	17.8	42.4
48 19624	Deer Park	31,333	4.1	6.5	20.9	10.2	27.6	26.0	8.8	34.2	90.6	2.8	2.1	5.8	19.1
48 19792	Del Rio	37,099	2.5	9.6	21.4	8.8	24.1	20.8	15.4	33.8	84.6	1.3	-	15.1	-
48 19900	Denison	23,427	2.7	7.6	17.7	7.1	27.3	24.2	16.1	38.0	83.6	10.8	-	8.4	8.4
48 19972	Denton	102,056	10.3	6.9	14.0	24.4	29.1	18.2	7.4	27.1	82.2	11.6	3.1	6.9	18.2
48 20092	DeSoto	45,621	5.1	7.9	19.9	5.5	26.2	28.4	12.1	38.8	30.1	61.8	1.8	8.8	9.7
48 21628	Duncanville	36,498	3.1	8.6	21.0	6.0	27.3	25.9	11.1	36.1	56.6	24.3	2.8	18.8	29.0
48 21892	Eagle Pass	25,586	4.5	10.2	21.7	8.2	25.9	21.3	12.7	33.1	52.8	-	0.9	48.7	-
48 22660	Edinburg	63,801	10.9	12.8	21.2	14.3	30.1	14.7	6.8	25.7	61.6	1.3	1.4	37.5	89.4
48 24000	El Paso	592,627	2.7	9.6	21.0	10.9	25.7	21.6	11.3	32.0	78.3	3.5	1.6	18.9	80.2
48 24768	Euless	51,097	2.4	9.0	15.1	9.5	35.3	24.0	7.1	33.6	65.9	11.5	11.8	12.5	18.5
48 25452	Farmers Branch	27,750	0.1	5.5	20.7	8.0	28.5	23.5	13.9	37.1	83.5	3.1	2.9	12.4	46.7
48 26232	Flower Mound town	66,799	6.9	8.1	25.8	6.2	30.4	25.7	3.9	34.5	89.0	3.5	5.5	2.8	7.8
48 26736	Fort Hood CDP	33,524	-	13.6	27.6	25.2	31.5	2.0	0.1	20.6	67.5	27.4	2.7	7.0	22.8
48 27000	Fort Worth	635,612	9.5	9.3	18.9	10.5	31.9	21.1	8.4	31.6	63.0	18.8	3.6	16.4	33.2
48 27648	Friendswood	37,519	1.3	7.6	22.2	7.8	24.2	26.1	12.2	38.0	86.6	2.4	4.9	6.3	12.8
48 27684	Frisco	84,778	25.5	11.6	20.9	5.3	40.6	17.3	4.3	32.7	84.0	6.1	7.5	4.6	13.4
48 28068	Galveston	53,826	-0.7	5.5	12.5	15.0	27.0	27.0	13.0	37.4	68.3	21.1	3.3	9.9	27.9
48 29000	Garland	231,515	1.3	8.1	20.0	8.9	31.2	23.8	8.0	33.2	59.2	13.8	9.6	19.3	36.1
48 29336	Georgetown	39,424	17.9	5.8	16.1	8.8	25.4	22.7	21.1	40.3	87.2	2.9	2.4	9.2	22.3
48 30464	Grand Prairie	155,627	9.9	9.7	22.4	8.3	31.8	21.5	6.3	31.5	61.3	18.2	5.8	17.5	40.2
48 30644	Grapevine	45,696	5.8	7.0	20.4	6.7	30.5	28.8	6.6	36.8	89.2	2.9	3.7	5.7	14.9
48 30920	Greenville	25,971	1.8	8.9	16.6	10.3	30.5	20.7	13.0	33.3	73.4	19.0	0.3	9.0	18.5
48 31928	Haltom	40,716	0.8	7.3	18.7	9.6	33.4	21.7	9.3	33.1	66.1	2.3	12.0	21.1	30.7
48 32312	Harker Heights	21,717	15.0	13.0	24.6	6.4	29.8	19.4	6.7	30.2	81.0	14.6	4.0	6.6	14.7
48 32372	Harlingen	62,661	3.2	10.0	19.2	10.9	24.8	20.2	14.9	31.9	87.2	1.0	1.0	12.6	73.9
48 35000	Houston	2,034,749	6.4	8.8	18.1	10.3	31.6	22.6	8.7	32.5	55.0	24.7	5.7	15.8	41.7
48 35528	Huntsville	37,305	-0.7	4.3	8.1	30.1	30.9	17.8	8.8	28.8	63.8	24.3	2.3	11.1	17.0
48 35576	Hurst	36,634	1.4	6.7	18.0	9.5	27.2	25.5	13.2	36.7	75.6	3.4	3.8	19.0	23.5
48 37000	Irving	212,786	3.1	8.4	18.2	10.5	36.2	20.0	6.6	31.5	66.1	12.4	10.9	12.3	40.6
48 38632	Keller	37,676	6.9	7.8	27.1	4.4	27.7	27.2	6.0	37.3	91.6	3.9	3.0	3.3	6.0
48 39040	Kerrville	22,455	3.6	3.5	16.1	10.4	20.9	21.9	27.2	43.7	88.3	5.2	-	7.4	-
48 39148	Killeen	102,372	8.6	12.2	21.3	9.7	35.6	15.6	5.6	27.6	53.6	38.8	6.8	6.5	18.8
48 39352	Kingsville	24,648	-1.3	8.9	16.6	19.4	24.3	19.2	11.6	28.4	77.6	6.4	1.3	15.5	-
48 39952	Kyle	16,399	31.2	12.9	21.0	7.8	39.7	14.6	4.0	29.3	57.1	9.8	1.0	35.6	-
48 40588	Lake Jackson	27,944	1.6	7.0	21.3	10.0	26.5	25.9	9.3	34.6	89.0	5.1	2.7	5.4	18.9
48 41212	Lancaster	29,866	9.4	8.1	23.8	8.2	32.2	21.1	6.6	31.7	22.5	69.2	0.4	8.8	14.0
48 41440	La Porte	37,141	1.9	9.1	19.3	9.7	26.3	27.1	8.6	34.7	82.7	9.3	2.5	7.8	25.2
48 41464	Laredo	213,616	5.4	13.0	24.0	11.1	26.8	16.9	8.1	26.5	76.1	0.6	0.7	23.8	94.5
48 41980	League	66,930	11.9	9.9	22.0	6.3	32.4	23.6	5.7	33.0	82.9	8.2	5.4	5.4	15.8
48 42016	Leander	20,768	30.2	11.8	19.2	6.9	37.2	20.0	4.8	31.3	82.5	2.3	1.3	16.0	24.0
48 42508	Lewisville	84,626	8.1	8.1	16.9	9.2	40.5	20.0	5.4	31.7	77.5	12.3	6.9	7.4	23.4
48 43012	Little Elm	19,405	31.6	14.3	20.0	6.2	42.5	14.3	2.6	29.6	83.0	11.2	3.2	5.9	26.0
48 43888	Longview	76,332	2.5	8.5	16.9	10.4	27.6	22.9	13.7	34.5	67.2	24.0	1.2	8.9	13.9
48 45000	Lubbock	213,305	2.3	7.6	16.7	17.9	26.6	20.2	10.9	29.5	79.2	8.6	2.1	12.0	29.5
48 45072	Lufkin	33,874	2.0	8.3	17.0	11.2	26.4	21.0	16.0	34.7	64.6	26.7	1.3	7.6	-
48 45384	McAllen	121,171	4.2	10.8	21.4	11.2	28.1	18.7	9.8	29.5	70.6	1.5	2.1	27.8	81.5
48 45744	McKinney	108,356	19.9	10.3	21.3	8.5	35.0	18.7	6.2	31.0	82.4	10.4	2.9	6.8	16.4
48 46452	Mansfield	49,468	16.3	9.1	25.0	6.0	32.5	22.5	4.9	32.6	79.8	12.1	4.3	5.5	15.2
48 46776	Marshall	24,254	1.2	7.8	17.1	14.4	27.5	20.7	12.5	30.6	56.8	37.6	0.9	5.4	12.7
48 47892	Mesquite	135,647	1.5	8.6	22.0	8.5	31.7	21.8	7.5	33.5	72.5	17.9	4.2	7.2	24.5
48 48072	Midland	102,425	5.0	8.1	19.9	11.1	24.1	24.4	12.5	33.7	83.9	8.4	1.4	8.4	34.3
48 48768	Mission	64,670	9.9	10.7	23.1	7.6	27.9	18.1	12.5	30.9	75.1	0.6	1.3	23.8	-

STATE City	Percent foreign born	Total households	Household type (percent)						Percent of households with people under 18 years	Percent of households with people 60 years and over
			Family households				Nonfamily households			
			Total family households	Married-couple families	Male householder families	Female householder families	Total nonfamily households	One-person households		
ACS table number:	C05002	B11001	B11001	B11001	B11001	B11001	B11001	B11001	C11005	B11006
	15	16	17	18	19	20	21	22	23	24
Texas—Cont.										
Bedford	10.4	20,429	61.2	47.7	4.2	9.3	38.8	34.3	29.9	26.6
Benbrook	6.2	9,021	65.5	51.8	2.4	11.3	34.5	31.4	29.8	35.1
Big Spring	19.4	8,059	63.0	41.7	6.7	14.7	37.0	33.7	38.3	36.1
Brownsville	31.0	49,413	83.0	55.1	5.4	22.5	17.0	14.9	57.0	31.1
Brushy Creek CDP	9.7	6,042	85.5	75.3	1.9	8.4	14.5	11.6	58.1	16.7
Bryan	13.7	24,598	59.4	40.5	5.0	13.8	40.6	31.4	36.3	22.7
Burleson	3.0	9,948	77.1	62.4	5.1	9.7	22.9	20.1	44.9	25.2
Carrollton	24.7	40,249	70.7	55.5	4.5	10.7	29.3	24.1	42.1	19.7
Cedar Hill	6.9	13,719	73.5	55.1	3.7	14.7	26.5	23.5	45.4	22.9
Cedar Park	9.0	13,475	74.6	55.1	4.6	15.0	25.4	19.3	50.8	17.1
Channelview CDP	26.4	11,254	80.3	53.7	7.4	19.1	19.7	13.3	58.0	21.1
Cleburne	12.5	9,990	74.7	53.2	4.3	17.2	25.3	21.4	43.2	30.0
Cloverleaf CDP	26.2	6,601	82.5	63.0	3.0	16.6	17.5	13.1	56.2	19.8
College Station	13.7	28,541	44.8	33.5	3.9	7.5	55.2	29.2	24.8	11.9
Colleyville	8.8	7,242	91.3	84.5	1.3	5.5	8.7	8.0	51.2	25.4
Conroe	22.3	15,904	69.8	48.0	5.6	16.2	30.2	24.5	40.8	24.5
Coppell	14.8	13,913	79.8	66.4	3.5	9.9	20.2	17.4	52.5	13.7
Copperas Cove	6.9	9,702	72.8	52.4	2.5	17.9	27.2	23.9	45.0	19.0
Corinth	4.7	5,903	83.5	72.2	3.6	7.7	16.5	10.5	50.0	17.8
Corpus Christi	7.6	103,788	68.7	45.9	6.6	16.2	31.3	25.5	38.1	29.1
Corsicana	14.9	8,606	64.6	45.1	3.1	16.3	35.4	32.0	39.4	37.2
Dallas	26.5	440,633	58.4	37.2	6.1	15.2	41.6	34.6	34.4	22.7
Deer Park	5.1	10,490	78.7	61.1	5.5	12.0	21.3	16.6	41.8	28.2
Del Rio	23.8	11,460	78.1	60.1	2.4	15.6	21.9	20.5	45.8	39.1
Denison	3.0	9,354	65.6	44.9	5.5	15.3	34.4	30.9	35.7	38.2
Denton	12.0	34,146	55.7	40.8	3.5	11.4	44.3	31.2	31.0	20.1
DeSoto	4.2	15,899	70.5	50.0	3.0	17.5	29.5	26.9	41.0	28.9
Duncanville	12.3	13,091	74.0	54.1	4.9	15.0	26.0	23.7	42.5	31.2
Eagle Pass	34.7	7,151	75.5	54.1	5.4	16.0	24.5	22.7	48.5	39.0
Edinburg	18.1	20,059	75.1	50.3	4.4	20.3	24.9	18.3	51.3	24.0
El Paso	26.1	196,788	75.3	49.3	5.4	20.5	24.7	21.2	45.3	30.9
Euless	17.2	21,088	59.6	42.2	5.3	12.0	40.4	33.3	31.5	18.2
Farmers Branch	28.4	10,239	65.4	49.1	6.4	10.0	34.6	28.0	34.5	32.9
Flower Mound town	8.7	19,813	87.1	75.7	4.2	7.1	12.9	9.9	56.1	15.7
Fort Hood CDP	5.7	6,012	98.7	72.9	4.2	21.6	1.3	1.3	-	-
Fort Worth	18.0	222,346	67.0	46.5	5.6	14.9	33.0	27.5	39.5	23.2
Friendswood	8.8	12,477	77.1	63.7	4.3	9.2	22.9	19.8	42.1	32.0
Frisco	13.8	28,494	77.7	66.3	2.9	8.5	22.3	17.5	50.4	11.9
Galveston	13.4	23,710	51.5	32.3	4.1	15.0	48.5	39.8	24.7	31.1
Garland	28.4	75,041	75.4	54.8	6.0	14.6	24.6	20.4	44.4	24.8
Georgetown	12.7	14,093	73.1	62.9	3.0	7.3	26.9	24.9	30.9	47.2
Grand Prairie	19.8	50,273	75.9	54.2	5.7	16.0	24.1	20.9	47.7	19.1
Grapevine	11.5	17,259	68.2	53.7	3.8	10.7	31.8	25.2	39.8	17.4
Greenville	8.7	9,208	65.5	43.1	5.2	17.3	34.5	26.2	36.5	31.4
Haltom	23.0	15,297	61.3	43.5	3.9	13.9	38.7	29.7	37.7	23.5
Harker Heights	6.7	7,076	79.3	58.2	7.2	13.9	20.7	18.7	52.2	21.5
Harlingen	14.0	22,153	74.4	53.3	3.2	18.0	25.6	22.0	41.7	35.7
Houston	28.1	738,807	61.9	40.3	5.8	15.7	38.1	32.2	35.9	24.1
Huntsville	13.5	12,109	53.4	36.7	4.5	12.3	46.6	26.9	26.4	20.5
Hurst	16.0	13,858	68.0	53.9	4.9	9.2	32.0	28.4	35.6	33.1
Irving	32.5	78,209	64.2	44.9	5.7	13.5	35.8	30.6	37.2	18.6
Keller	5.4	12,147	86.7	74.2	4.0	8.5	13.3	11.2	52.7	18.6
Kerrville	6.4	9,081	67.8	48.3	7.4	12.1	32.2	26.3	31.1	46.3
Killeen	8.7	37,738	68.7	47.9	4.4	16.4	31.3	26.6	44.5	14.6
Kingsville	5.1	8,904	64.6	44.4	7.0	13.3	35.4	25.9	38.9	30.0
Kyle	3.9	4,823	79.3	65.4	3.5	10.5	20.7	17.6	52.7	13.9
Lake Jackson	5.3	10,293	73.0	60.0	4.1	8.9	27.0	20.9	38.0	24.3
Lancaster	7.7	10,697	69.2	43.8	4.4	21.0	30.8	28.0	42.0	19.4
La Porte	9.0	11,847	79.4	60.5	6.4	12.5	20.6	17.0	44.6	26.6
Laredo	28.4	57,440	83.2	55.9	5.8	21.5	16.8	14.3	57.3	29.1
League	11.1	23,378	74.9	60.5	4.2	10.2	25.1	19.7	46.0	19.8
Leander	9.6	6,004	81.3	70.2	3.0	8.0	18.7	14.8	49.2	15.7
Lewisville	20.1	32,046	60.9	43.6	4.9	12.3	39.1	33.3	34.8	15.3
Little Elm	17.4	5,850	79.8	66.7	3.3	9.8	20.2	12.9	59.9	9.1
Longview	8.7	29,641	64.5	45.1	4.4	15.0	35.5	30.2	35.3	32.4
Lubbock	4.1	83,759	61.8	44.1	4.8	12.9	38.2	28.4	32.8	25.4
Lufkin	12.4	12,727	65.1	45.5	4.8	14.8	34.9	29.8	31.0	36.7
McAllen	26.3	39,825	77.0	54.8	4.2	18.1	23.0	19.9	48.4	25.9
McKinney	11.1	35,469	75.3	62.0	3.5	9.8	24.7	20.7	47.5	19.1
Mansfield	12.8	14,991	87.0	71.4	5.1	10.6	13.0	10.5	57.1	16.1
Marshall	10.4	8,483	67.9	44.9	2.4	20.6	32.1	29.4	39.5	34.3
Mesquite	15.5	46,276	73.1	50.9	5.8	16.4	26.9	23.6	46.0	23.0
Midland	8.5	38,988	68.3	53.3	3.1	11.9	31.7	27.7	37.6	28.9
Mission	28.5	20,655	83.5	62.0	4.9	16.6	16.5	14.8	51.5	34.7

Table A-4. Cities — Who: Age, Race/Ethnicity, and Household Structure, 2005–2007—*Continued*

STATE Place code	STATE / City	Total population	Percent change 2005–2007	Population by age (percent)						Median age	Race alone or in combination (percent)				Percent Hispanic or Latino
				Under 5 years	5 to 17 years	18 to 24 years	25 to 44 years	45 to 64 years	65 years and over		White	Black	Asian Hawaiian or Pacific Islander	Amer. Indian, Alaska Native, or some other race	
	ACS table number:	B01003	Population estimates	B01001	B01001	B01001	B01001	B01001	B01001	B01002	B02008	B02009	B02011 + B02012	B02010 + B02013	C03002
		1	2	3	4	5	6	7	8	9	10	11	12	13	14
	Texas—Cont.														
48 48772	Mission Bend CDP	35,999	-	6.6	20.7	12.7	31.0	23.5	5.6	31.9	37.8	25.0	23.9	15.4	-
48 48804	Missouri	63,928	6.5	6.5	20.1	9.9	27.2	28.8	7.6	35.7	40.7	38.8	14.7	7.3	14.9
48 50256	Nacogdoches	29,953	2.6	6.9	13.4	30.9	21.9	16.2	10.7	24.5	70.8	25.7	2.0	2.9	15.7
48 50820	New Braunfels	50,680	11.7	7.5	17.8	10.0	29.8	20.6	14.2	32.8	86.3	2.8	1.8	11.1	32.9
48 52356	North Richland Hills	62,916	5.4	6.2	17.4	9.0	27.2	26.5	13.8	38.9	87.2	4.8	2.3	8.5	12.8
48 53388	Odessa	95,485	4.1	9.0	20.5	11.1	26.4	21.7	11.3	31.0	83.5	4.6	1.4	14.5	47.6
48 55080	Paris	25,987	-0.1	7.2	18.2	10.6	26.7	19.8	17.6	35.6	74.2	22.7	0.9	4.6	6.4
48 56000	Pasadena	149,394	0.4	8.3	21.8	9.9	30.7	21.6	7.7	31.1	67.9	2.0	2.7	29.5	57.2
48 56348	Pearland	71,124	21.1	9.8	20.2	7.9	33.8	21.9	6.3	32.7	73.5	12.6	9.3	6.0	16.8
48 57176	Pflugerville	36,755	21.5	8.6	24.6	7.3	35.4	19.3	4.8	31.4	70.9	12.9	8.3	11.7	23.6
48 57200	Pharr	60,391	9.3	13.7	22.6	10.6	27.9	14.7	10.6	27.3	72.6	-	0.4	28.1	-
48 57980	Plainview	21,092	-0.3	9.8	20.1	12.0	24.1	20.7	13.2	32.2	82.2	3.0	-	16.7	57.4
48 58016	Plano	255,591	4.3	6.7	19.6	8.1	31.7	26.5	7.4	35.9	76.7	6.4	14.7	3.5	13.3
48 58820	Port Arthur	52,038	-1.8	7.1	19.4	11.2	23.0	24.0	15.4	36.1	32.4	47.2	4.6	16.7	22.8
48 61796	Richardson	102,341	0.5	6.2	17.6	8.1	29.6	26.3	12.2	38.1	76.5	7.3	14.0	3.6	16.4
48 62828	Rockwall	28,845	16.8	8.0	18.2	9.4	31.0	24.0	9.4	34.7	88.7	4.7	3.7	4.8	8.8
48 63284	Rosenberg	28,433	9.6	9.1	18.6	13.3	30.5	19.7	8.9	30.0	62.4	13.1	-	26.4	-
48 63500	Round Rock	85,152	12.3	9.3	21.1	10.1	35.0	19.9	4.6	30.8	77.6	11.9	5.0	8.9	26.1
48 63572	Rowlett	58,545	3.8	8.5	24.1	7.2	29.0	24.0	7.2	34.6	74.3	12.6	5.4	9.6	14.0
48 64472	San Angelo	89,926	1.3	7.9	17.5	13.8	25.3	21.9	13.6	32.7	79.4	5.4	1.8	15.4	36.3
48 65000	San Antonio	1,267,984	5.2	8.4	19.7	10.7	29.0	22.0	10.3	32.5	66.5	7.1	2.6	26.5	61.0
48 65036	San Benito	25,373	1.5	10.2	18.6	12.3	22.3	18.8	17.9	33.3	80.9	-	-	20.9	-
48 65516	San Juan	33,957	9.2	11.0	26.1	12.3	25.6	16.8	8.2	25.3	66.9	-	-	33.7	-
48 65600	San Marcos	44,851	6.7	4.4	10.4	43.2	24.9	10.8	6.3	23.0	66.0	5.7	1.9	27.6	36.9
48 66128	Schertz	26,184	11.2	5.8	17.7	12.0	28.4	25.2	11.1	37.0	81.2	9.5	2.6	8.4	19.4
48 66644	Seguin	23,925	4.5	7.4	17.5	11.3	27.8	20.2	15.7	32.4	67.4	5.3	1.6	26.9	-
48 67496	Sherman	39,051	3.4	7.4	16.5	13.3	27.9	21.2	13.7	31.8	77.5	11.1	2.4	10.6	16.8
48 68636	Socorro	30,100	8.8	10.3	23.9	12.2	24.7	21.1	7.9	28.6	76.9	1.0	-	24.1	-
48 69032	Southlake	24,870	5.5	5.6	30.5	4.7	23.2	32.4	3.7	39.5	93.5	2.6	3.6	0.6	3.0
48 69596	Spring CDP	49,446	-	9.5	22.3	7.0	31.7	23.5	6.0	33.0	69.9	20.7	3.5	7.8	20.6
48 70808	Sugar Land	72,059	4.3	5.8	19.4	8.2	26.4	31.5	8.7	38.5	62.0	6.4	30.1	2.6	10.4
48 72176	Temple	58,535	2.5	8.0	19.0	7.0	28.1	23.4	14.5	35.4	76.1	15.6	3.1	7.4	22.1
48 72368	Texarkana	35,561	1.6	7.5	15.8	11.2	29.1	22.9	13.5	35.4	61.1	36.4	-	4.3	4.5
48 72392	Texas	43,892	1.2	7.0	16.3	11.6	26.3	25.5	13.2	35.0	64.0	29.9	1.2	6.5	23.4
48 72530	The Colony	37,331	8.7	7.5	20.2	10.1	35.5	23.2	3.5	31.0	82.0	9.3	5.9	5.7	18.2
48 72656	The Woodlands CDP	62,311	-	6.4	22.3	8.9	24.5	27.9	9.9	37.1	89.9	4.4	3.4	3.3	8.4
48 74144	Tyler	90,902	4.9	7.9	17.3	12.7	26.4	21.5	14.2	33.3	62.0	27.0	1.3	11.4	18.3
48 74492	University Park	23,061	2.8	8.0	24.5	12.9	21.4	25.3	7.8	34.4	96.9	1.3	0.8	-	-
48 75428	Victoria	63,670	1.4	7.8	20.4	10.0	26.0	22.9	13.0	33.9	71.4	8.3	1.7	23.7	44.5
48 76000	Waco	116,967	1.7	8.3	17.0	19.8	25.4	18.0	11.5	27.7	69.2	22.6	2.5	7.4	27.4
48 76672	Watauga	22,977	1.5	8.9	22.3	5.0	33.8	24.1	5.8	32.6	82.9	5.2	5.7	11.1	18.5
48 76816	Waxahachie	25,688	8.2	11.0	16.3	14.7	27.6	19.3	11.1	28.4	72.6	14.4	2.1	12.4	22.9
48 76864	Weatherford	21,779	11.1	5.8	15.7	11.5	31.3	21.5	14.1	35.0	88.8	6.0	1.5	4.6	-
48 77272	Weslaco	33,779	4.7	11.7	19.3	8.9	25.1	17.9	17.1	31.8	64.4	-	1.8	34.6	-
48 79000	Wichita Falls	101,393	-1.1	7.5	16.9	14.5	27.3	21.6	12.2	32.4	77.9	13.7	3.4	7.6	16.4
48 80356	Wylie	32,213	20.4	8.4	24.1	8.0	37.2	17.6	4.7	30.9	80.0	9.7	5.7	6.7	18.4
49 00000	**Utah**	2,576,626	5.6	9.7	21.3	12.8	28.2	19.4	8.7	28.3	91.1	1.4	3.5	5.9	11.1
49 01310	American Fork	27,114	5.3	11.5	24.7	8.6	29.2	17.5	8.6	27.6	97.3	-	0.8	2.7	-
49 07690	Bountiful	41,306	1.4	7.2	18.7	11.0	23.5	23.2	16.4	35.4	96.5	0.9	1.8	2.3	3.1
49 11320	Cedar	25,522	12.8	9.1	16.7	25.8	25.0	14.9	8.5	24.6	92.9	-	2.1	6.2	5.7
49 13850	Clearfield	27,916	0.3	12.2	20.3	18.7	30.7	13.8	4.4	24.6	83.9	5.3	4.9	9.0	16.2
49 16270	Cottonwood Heights	34,617	0.8	7.1	17.9	9.6	27.5	26.9	11.0	35.0	92.1	0.5	4.8	3.2	6.3
49 20120	Draper	34,552	11.2	10.5	22.3	6.8	36.6	18.9	5.0	30.7	92.9	1.9	3.1	4.9	7.4
49 36070	Holladay	26,610	0.8	6.3	16.3	8.2	23.5	27.3	18.4	40.9	95.5	1.9	2.0	0.5	2.7
49 40360	Kaysville	25,182	11.3	10.6	29.2	8.2	25.6	19.1	7.3	26.6	98.6	1.5	1.4	0.9	-
49 40470	Kearns CDP	35,200	-	11.6	24.9	10.9	30.6	17.1	4.9	26.2	84.7	2.7	4.1	12.1	26.5
49 43660	Layton	63,519	4.2	9.8	22.0	13.1	28.0	20.8	6.3	27.7	93.9	1.6	3.6	3.5	8.9
49 44320	Lehi	34,984	19.0	16.1	25.4	8.4	34.4	11.0	4.6	25.0	96.3	-	1.1	2.5	-
49 45860	Logan	47,158	1.9	10.0	13.3	31.2	28.7	10.7	6.1	24.1	89.9	1.6	5.5	5.3	10.3
49 47290	Magna CDP	24,979	-	10.8	25.8	11.5	28.9	17.9	5.1	25.9	84.7	0.7	6.0	10.2	18.0
49 49710	Midvale	31,573	2.4	8.1	15.5	12.1	36.2	19.1	8.8	30.2	88.3	2.0	4.2	7.9	27.3
49 50150	Millcreek CDP	30,705	-	10.1	13.7	14.0	31.0	19.5	15.2	32.2	89.6	3.3	6.2	4.4	12.5
49 53230	Murray	46,353	2.5	7.0	16.1	13.9	26.2	24.8	12.0	34.4	95.4	1.0	2.4	2.4	8.6
49 55980	Ogden	79,755	1.3	10.1	19.2	12.5	29.8	18.7	9.7	28.9	90.0	3.2	1.9	6.2	27.8
49 57300	Orem	86,748	0.9	10.0	21.5	15.9	27.6	16.8	8.3	25.8	94.2	0.8	4.2	3.0	11.5
49 60930	Pleasant Grove	31,475	6.0	11.8	27.9	11.1	27.6	16.0	5.6	24.5	98.4	-	1.2	1.1	-
49 62470	Provo	115,163	2.1	9.6	12.0	38.0	25.2	10.0	5.3	23.3	87.3	1.1	5.1	8.9	12.8
49 64340	Riverton	34,551	20.0	11.3	26.7	8.6	28.9	19.6	4.9	27.4	96.9	1.2	2.1	1.9	2.8
49 65110	Roy	37,112	-0.7	10.8	22.6	8.5	32.0	18.3	7.9	28.8	94.2	1.5	3.1	2.7	9.7
49 65330	St. George	69,200	10.5	9.1	18.8	12.9	26.8	14.4	18.0	29.5	91.0	1.4	3.8	5.4	10.1
49 67000	Salt Lake	182,610	1.7	8.6	14.7	12.4	33.3	20.5	10.6	31.6	80.6	4.0	6.2	11.3	21.5
49 67440	Sandy	90,766	2.3	6.8	23.2	11.0	25.6	26.0	7.3	32.1	93.4	0.8	4.5	2.7	4.7
49 70850	South Jordan	40,877	19.5	9.6	27.2	10.1	24.0	22.6	6.4	27.8	96.0	0.6	3.5	1.8	3.8

Table A-4. Cities — Who: Age, Race/Ethnicity, and Household Structure, 2005–2007—*Continued*

STATE City	Percent foreign born	Total households	Household type (percent)						Percent of households with people under 18 years	Percent of households with people 60 years and over
			Family households				Nonfamily households			
			Total family households	Married-couple families	Male householder families	Female householder families	Total nonfamily households	One-person households		
ACS table number:	C05002	B11001	B11001	B11001	B11001	B11001	B11001	B11001	C11005	B11006
	15	16	17	18	19	20	21	22	23	24
Texas—Cont.										
Mission Bend CDP............	38.7	9,067	86.7	67.4	6.0	13.4	13.3	11.9	58.0	22.2
Missouri.......................	21.3	18,170	83.2	62.5	6.7	14.0	16.8	14.5	47.1	26.0
Nacogdoches..................	9.2	11,553	49.7	37.1	2.6	10.0	50.3	37.7	24.0	26.7
New Braunfels	7.1	18,559	70.6	54.4	5.6	10.7	29.4	23.4	38.3	31.7
North Richland Hills..........	7.2	22,585	70.9	55.7	2.7	12.6	29.1	23.6	35.7	26.8
Odessa..........................	10.3	34,671	68.2	50.1	3.6	14.5	31.8	26.4	39.7	28.8
Paris.............................	4.4	10,025	65.6	43.4	3.0	19.2	34.4	31.3	33.5	40.7
Pasadena	26.0	48,080	73.8	52.2	6.7	14.9	26.2	21.1	45.8	23.0
Pearland	11.6	24,753	78.4	64.6	4.5	9.3	21.6	17.3	47.1	19.1
Pflugerville	11.6	11,355	82.0	62.5	5.5	14.0	18.0	12.7	53.6	13.5
Pharr............................	32.8	17,539	85.6	59.4	3.3	22.8	14.4	12.9	56.0	32.5
Plainview	9.5	7,908	70.7	50.7	5.2	14.8	29.3	22.8	40.4	32.9
Plano...........................	21.0	92,356	71.9	59.7	4.2	8.0	28.1	23.5	40.3	20.4
Port Arthur	16.2	19,547	64.3	39.2	6.3	18.8	35.7	33.5	34.5	37.4
Richardson.....................	21.7	38,168	67.0	54.6	4.0	8.4	33.0	26.6	32.6	30.1
Rockwall	6.2	10,159	80.1	68.4	2.0	9.7	19.9	16.6	42.7	27.9
Rosenberg	13.7	7,954	76.8	51.2	7.6	18.1	23.2	19.0	41.6	27.4
Round Rock	13.2	27,407	74.6	59.8	4.4	10.4	25.4	20.0	47.2	12.9
Rowlett.........................	11.6	17,997	84.5	68.0	6.6	9.9	15.5	13.2	50.7	21.2
San Angelo	5.5	35,177	64.0	45.7	4.2	14.0	36.0	30.7	35.5	30.5
San Antonio....................	13.4	438,703	67.0	45.3	5.0	16.6	33.0	27.5	38.3	27.9
San Benito	23.0	7,949	80.6	58.0	2.0	20.6	19.4	16.7	42.2	47.1
San Juan........................	30.9	9,121	88.0	63.2	5.5	19.3	12.0	10.3	62.2	28.8
San Marcos	4.7	14,976	38.5	23.2	5.6	9.7	61.5	39.1	21.9	16.1
Schertz	5.1	9,086	77.7	62.5	4.0	11.2	22.3	21.0	37.2	28.5
Seguin	9.0	8,043	66.2	47.3	5.2	13.7	33.8	28.9	37.2	40.8
Sherman	11.1	14,297	64.8	46.3	3.2	15.2	35.2	27.7	33.3	32.5
Socorro.........................	34.7	8,276	85.4	60.4	5.8	19.2	14.6	12.0	58.4	29.8
Southlake	6.4	7,585	92.9	86.9	2.6	3.4	7.1	6.7	56.4	17.1
Spring CDP	12.0	15,730	80.5	61.7	3.6	15.2	19.5	15.9	48.9	20.2
Sugar Land	30.8	21,593	82.3	71.0	3.0	8.3	17.7	14.8	44.7	26.7
Temple..........................	8.8	22,782	67.3	49.8	4.1	13.4	32.7	29.3	35.7	33.4
Texarkana	3.7	14,102	62.7	37.7	6.6	18.3	37.3	32.1	33.2	28.7
Texas............................	7.9	16,645	64.7	41.3	6.0	17.5	35.3	30.4	33.9	31.9
The Colony	13.9	12,050	73.0	61.0	6.0	6.0	27.0	20.5	46.4	14.5
The Woodlands CDP	10.7	22,326	72.3	62.0	2.9	7.4	27.7	24.7	43.5	24.0
Tyler.............................	11.8	33,236	62.7	43.6	3.4	15.7	37.3	32.4	33.4	32.0
University Park	3.8	7,279	72.6	62.5	3.8	6.4	27.4	22.9	49.1	24.2
Victoria.........................	9.2	23,412	70.3	40.4	5.5	18.3	29.7	25.5	39.0	29.7
Waco............................	11.4	41,484	59.0	37.3	4.2	17.4	41.0	32.3	34.8	26.8
Watauga........................	9.4	7,744	76.3	57.5	5.7	13.0	23.7	18.2	48.8	19.4
Waxahachie	6.3	8,608	73.5	54.6	4.3	14.6	26.5	23.7	39.9	29.5
Weatherford...................	8.5	8,308	67.2	52.9	4.4	9.9	32.8	28.1	33.6	34.2
Weslaco.........................	19.6	11,320	76.7	52.6	4.3	19.8	23.3	19.9	45.6	37.2
Wichita Falls...................	6.7	38,530	64.3	48.0	2.9	13.4	35.7	30.1	35.8	29.5
Wylie............................	12.1	9,977	84.7	65.8	6.8	12.1	15.3	13.1	55.0	14.8
Utah	8.0	812,604	75.5	62.2	4.0	9.2	24.5	19.3	43.2	25.2
American Fork	4.6	7,185	84.5	75.4	1.1	8.0	15.5	13.4	52.7	28.7
Bountiful........................	4.1	13,966	76.3	64.0	2.7	9.7	23.7	21.0	34.9	36.4
Cedar	5.2	8,768	71.0	61.1	4.1	5.8	29.0	17.3	37.5	20.7
Clearfield.......................	8.3	8,605	75.0	57.5	3.7	13.7	25.0	19.9	49.6	14.3
Cottonwood Heights	8.1	12,138	71.8	61.7	3.0	7.1	28.2	20.8	33.4	31.3
Draper...........................	4.3	9,677	77.2	67.5	2.1	7.5	22.8	18.5	49.4	15.3
Holladay	5.7	10,019	68.1	57.0	2.6	8.5	31.9	26.0	29.4	36.6
Kaysville	3.2	6,650	90.3	81.7	1.8	6.8	9.7	9.2	59.4	22.9
Kearns CDP......................	14.7	9,991	82.3	61.7	6.9	13.8	17.7	12.7	56.1	17.9
Layton	4.8	20,487	77.5	64.3	5.3	7.9	22.5	18.5	45.0	17.9
Lehi	2.0	8,997	86.9	76.1	1.8	9.1	13.1	10.3	58.7	17.2
Logan	9.7	14,652	64.9	54.2	2.2	8.5	35.1	20.8	36.2	17.2
Magna CDP	11.3	7,192	81.0	62.8	6.0	12.2	19	15.5	55.5	17.3
Midvale..........................	17.0	11,538	60.1	39.9	8.0	12.3	39.9	30.5	32.7	23.5
Millcreek CDP	12.0	12,543	54.6	40.2	3.0	11.4	45.4	39.9	26.4	26.2
Murray...........................	7.1	17,411	67.6	51.1	6.9	9.5	32.4	27.0	31.0	29.7
Ogden...........................	15.9	28,705	66.1	47.4	5.1	13.7	33.9	29.2	38.3	25.5
Orem............................	7.7	25,846	77.8	66.7	2.3	8.7	22.2	15.7	42.9	25.1
Pleasant Grove.................	3.2	8,436	82.7	71.4	3.3	8.0	17.3	14.5	53.9	20.3
Provo............................	11.6	31,100	67.5	56.4	3.4	7.8	32.5	15.4	33.9	17.2
Riverton.........................	2.2	8,962	91.1	81.1	3.3	6.7	8.9	7.7	58.9	18.2
Roy...............................	3.5	11,962	82.5	66.6	5.9	10.0	17.5	14.6	49.2	23.0
St. George	7.6	24,415	73.4	64.7	3.1	5.5	26.6	21.4	35.8	38.1
Salt Lake	18.5	72,901	54.0	38.2	5.4	10.4	46.0	36.2	29.0	25.2
Sandy	6.3	27,803	80.9	67.6	3.8	9.4	19.1	15.2	45.2	23.2
South Jordan	4.5	10,675	89.1	79.9	2.2	7.0	10.9	9.7	55.0	23.9

Table A-4. Cities — Who: Age, Race/Ethnicity, and Household Structure, 2005–2007—*Continued*

STATE Place code	STATE City	Total population	Percent change 2005–2007	Population by age (percent) Under 5 years	5 to 17 years	18 to 24 years	25 to 44 years	45 to 64 years	65 years and over	Median age	Race alone or in combination (percent) White	Black	Asian Hawaiian or Pacific Islander	Amer. Indian, Alaska Native, or some other race	Percent Hispanic or Latino
ACS table number:		B01003	Population estimates	B01001	B01001	B01001	B01001	B01001	B01001	B01002	B02008	B02009	B02011 + B02012	B02010 + B02013	C03002
		1	2	3	4	5	6	7	8	9	10	11	12	13	14
	Utah—Cont.														
49 71070	South Salt Lake................	22,141	0.8	8.5	14.7	14.2	35.3	20.8	6.6	30.5	75.4	4.1	4.4	17.8	27.2
49 71290	Spanish Fork....................	30,288	8.3	14.3	24.7	10.6	30.9	13.7	5.8	25.2	92.1	-	-	7.4	-
49 72280	Springville......................	25,762	5.1	12.9	25.8	10.4	27.6	16.2	7.2	25.7	92.2	0.8	1.5	6.0	9.7
49 74810	Syracuse........................	19,315	18.3	12.5	27.2	9.5	31.7	15.0	4.1	25.8	94.8	1.7	4.5	1.0	4.8
49 75360	Taylorsville....................	59,625	1.2	8.1	20.3	12.6	29.3	22.4	7.4	30.0	86.9	2.2	6.8	6.0	15.5
49 76680	Tooele..........................	29,749	6.1	10.8	23.9	9.5	32.6	16.1	7.1	27.8	93.0	1.9	1.3	6.9	10.5
49 82950	West Jordan....................	99,348	6.2	11.5	25.1	10.8	30.5	18.3	3.7	26.5	89.7	1.1	4.7	6.1	13.4
49 83470	West Valley.....................	122,409	2.9	10.7	21.8	10.7	31.0	19.7	6.2	28.7	78.5	1.2	9.2	13.5	28.1
50 00000	**Vermont**......................	620,589	0.2	5.2	16.4	9.9	25.7	29.4	13.3	40.4	97.6	1.1	1.4	1.5	1.3
50 10675	Burlington......................	38,600	-0.5	4.8	10.8	26.6	26.6	20.1	11.1	30.4	94.4	3.5	2.0	1.8	2.4
51 00000	**Virginia**......................	7,636,644	2.0	6.7	17.2	10.0	28.8	25.7	11.6	36.8	72.4	20.5	5.4	3.7	6.3
51 01000	Alexandria.....................	138,621	1.8	8.2	11.2	5.9	39.6	24.6	10.5	37.2	68.4	22.4	6.6	5.5	13.3
51 01912	Annandale CDP.................	54,552	-	6.8	15.4	6.8	29.4	28.0	13.6	39.9	68.4	8.2	20.1	5.3	18.3
51 03000	Arlington CDP..................	201,798	2.4	6.4	11.3	7.4	40.6	25.2	9.1	36.9	73.1	8.8	10.0	10.6	16.2
51 04088	Bailey's Crossroads CDP.....	22,284	-	10.8	10.4	13.5	34.6	22.8	7.8	32.0	54.5	15.6	11.4	19.3	40.7
51 07784	Blacksburg town...............	41,492	2.0	2.8	5.7	57.8	19.8	9.0	4.9	21.7	84.0	5.1	11.1	1.4	2.7
51 11464	Burke CDP......................	56,266	-	4.6	18.4	10.4	20.9	37.3	8.4	42.2	76.4	6.3	15.0	6.2	14.3
51 13720	Cave Spring CDP...............	24,645	-	5.2	16.3	8.0	24.1	32.9	13.5	43.2	92.4	3.6	2.9	1.3	2.4
51 14440	Centreville CDP................	53,465	-	8.4	19.3	9.7	33.8	24.3	4.5	33.7	56.8	12.1	28.2	5.9	11.1
51 14744	Chantilly CDP..................	43,540	-	5.9	17.0	10.1	29.3	29.5	8.1	38.0	73.5	6.1	19.4	2.8	9.2
51 14968	Charlottesville................	41,015	1.0	5.6	11.0	25.3	27.5	17.5	13.1	28.9	71.9	22.4	5.3	3.1	3.3
51 16000	Chesapeake....................	218,145	1.2	6.8	19.6	9.9	28.1	26.0	9.5	35.8	66.1	30.7	3.0	2.6	2.8
51 16096	Chester CDP....................	20,950	-	8.5	20.6	8.9	27.9	25.7	8.4	34.9	77.6	19.8	2.7	0.8	6.3
51 21088	Dale CDP........................	63,031	-	9.4	19.7	10.4	33.2	22.1	5.3	31.8	47.5	28.2	10.1	17.6	25.9
51 21344	Danville........................	45,307	-1.6	6.1	15.8	8.1	23.0	26.1	20.8	42.4	52.2	46.1	0.4	2.2	
51 26496	Fairfax.........................	22,743	6.0	5.4	14.2	9.2	29.3	27.6	14.2	40.6	75.1	6.6	16.1	5.4	13.3
51 29552	Franconia CDP..................	34,695	-	6.3	17.9	7.0	30.1	31.4	7.3	38.7	72.1	13.8	10.5	5.3	9.9
51 29744	Fredericksburg................	21,918	5.2	8.4	13.1	20.5	25.6	17.5	14.9	30.7	71.7	21.3	2.7	5.1	7.1
51 33584	Groveton CDP...................	21,814	-	6.3	18.2	10.7	28.4	27.7	8.6	35.6	61.5	21.0	8.0	11.2	24.3
51 35000	Hampton........................	146,672	-0.4	6.5	16.8	12.6	29.3	23.7	11.1	35.1	48.1	48.3	2.7	3.1	3.5
51 35624	Harrisonburg..................	43,430	3.2	5.7	10.6	39.1	20.6	15.0	9.0	22.6	87.7	7.0	4.8	2.1	12.7
51 36648	Herndon town..................	15,524	0.3	5.2	13.5	7.2	36.3	31.8	6.0	37.6	65.2	12.9	13.1	9.9	
51 38424	Hopewell.......................	22,764	2.2	8.9	18.9	8.0	28.5	21.6	14.0	34.3	59.5	38.2	1.0	2.8	3.8
51 40584	Jefferson CDP..................	25,673	-	6.3	12.6	6.2	32.3	31.7	10.9	40.6	62.4	3.8	22.6	13.0	23.1
51 43432	Lake Ridge CDP................	32,150	-	6.9	19.9	8.0	31.7	26.3	7.3	34.6	65.0	22.1	10.8	4.8	9.1
51 44984	Leesburg town.................	36,160	6.8	7.9	20.5	8.6	36.4	20.7	5.9	32.3	80.7	11.1	6.2	5.0	9.9
51 45957	Linton Hall CDP...............	21,118	-	12.6	28.0	3.2	39.2	14.9	2.1	30.7	76.0	8.4	12.9	3.6	11.5
51 47064	Lorton CDP.....................	24,939	-	8.8	19.3	9.8	34.2	23.8	4.1	33.7	47.6	27.6	20.0	8.1	17.5
51 47672	Lynchburg......................	69,784	4.7	6.5	14.4	18.5	23.2	20.9	16.5	33.9	68.3	29.6	2.1	1.8	1.8
51 48376	McLean CDP.....................	40,457	-	4.6	19.8	5.6	19.3	34.5	16.2	45.4	81.1	1.5	15.4	2.6	6.1
51 48952	Manassas.......................	36,133	-4.0	8.8	20.3	8.7	31.5	23.1	7.6	33.2	67.6	13.8	4.3	17.4	25.9
51 50856	Mechanicsville CDP...........	35,309	-	7.1	18.3	8.5	29.2	24.1	12.7	36.3	90.7	8.1	1.4	1.2	1.1
51 54144	Mount Vernon CDP............	33,902	-	8.3	18.8	7.6	31.2	25.8	8.3	36.7	58.4	29.0	7.5	5.9	25.6
51 55752	Newington CDP.................	22,476	-	7.2	20.5	7.5	25.0	30.7	9.1	39.8	67.4	14.8	13.1	8.1	15.8
51 56000	Newport News..................	180,079	-0.9	8.4	20.0	9.8	28.9	22.4	10.4	33.3	53.3	42.8	3.5	3.2	4.7
51 57000	Norfolk.........................	237,309	-0.7	8.2	17.3	16.5	28.5	19.6	9.9	29.4	49.8	45.6	4.0	3.3	4.6
51 58472	Oakton CDP.....................	34,123	-	6.8	18.1	7.7	31.5	28.1	7.9	36.6	67.5	6.8	25.7	1.8	8.3
51 61832	Petersburg....................	32,672	1.4	8.2	16.8	9.0	25.7	24.2	16.1	38.4	20.8	77.4	1.5	0.3	2.6
51 64000	Portsmouth.....................	101,856	1.1	7.9	18.1	11.5	26.7	22.7	13.0	34.4	45.6	52.7	1.9	2.3	2.4
51 66672	Reston CDP.....................	51,042	-	7.0	14.2	5.7	29.4	33.6	10.1	40.9	78.2	8.7	9.7	5.4	8.9
51 67000	Richmond.......................	198,869	1.1	7.4	14.9	12.4	29.1	22.2	14.0	35.3	42.9	54.1	1.9	3.6	4.2
51 68000	Roanoke........................	92,475	0.2	6.1	16.6	6.7	28.5	25.2	17.0	39.9	70.4	27.7	1.5	2.3	2.3
51 70000	Salem..........................	25,048	1.8	4.8	14.7	13.4	24.7	25.7	16.7	40.3	91.9	7.4	1.6	-	1.3
51 74592	Springfield CDP................	34,413	-	7.7	14.6	8.6	28.1	26.7	14.3	38.3	50.8	16.1	19.7	13.9	24.0
51 75216	Staunton.......................	23,525	1.8	5.7	14.6	8.9	24.7	26.0	20.0	41.7	87.0	13.0	0.9	1.1	1.5
51 76432	Suffolk.........................	79,849	4.3	7.7	19.3	9.1	29.7	23.6	10.7	34.9	55.3	41.5	1.8	2.6	2.3
51 79560	Tuckahoe CDP..................	45,649	-	5.2	17.8	6.8	25.9	28.9	15.5	42.5	87.3	10.1	2.9	0.8	4.5
51 82000	Virginia Beach.................	436,903	-0.8	7.0	19.0	9.4	30.7	24.1	9.8	35.2	73.0	21.0	6.8	2.6	5.4
51 83680	Waynesboro....................	21,407	2.5	7.3	17.4	6.1	25.3	25.1	18.8	40.7	85.3	11.8	0.5	3.8	4.6
51 84976	West Springfield CDP.........	29,860	-	6.3	22.2	6.3	25.6	29.1	10.6	39.4	67.2	9.7	14.9	10.5	13.6
51 86720	Winchester.....................	25,744	0.4	7.4	15.1	10.7	28.5	21.9	16.3	35.7	82.3	12.3	2.0	4.0	10.6
51 87312	Woodbridge CDP...............	31,416	-	7.9	19.4	9.7	35.6	20.0	7.4	31.9	52.3	26.3	6.7	17.8	27.2
53 00000	**Washington**..................	6,371,390	3.2	6.5	17.5	9.4	28.7	26.4	11.6	36.8	83.8	4.4	8.5	7.1	9.1
53 03180	Auburn.........................	48,632	4.8	7.9	18.2	8.4	28.2	26.0	11.3	37.4	80.3	5.6	9.5	8.9	11.1
53 03736	Bainbridge Island.............	22,557	0.1	4.7	21.1	4.2	21.4	36.3	12.3	44.4	96.3	-	3.1	1.8	-
53 05210	Bellevue.......................	117,521	3.6	6.0	15.6	7.4	31.8	26.2	13.0	38.6	71.2	2.6	25.2	3.8	5.6
53 05280	Bellingham.....................	75,418	2.6	4.6	11.8	24.5	27.3	20.3	11.4	29.7	89.3	1.6	6.8	5.2	5.5
53 07380	Bothell.........................	33,123	3.4	5.3	17.0	8.2	29.5	29.2	10.8	38.7	88.2	2.0	8.9	3.1	7.8
53 07695	Bremerton......................	34,159	-10.6	7.0	15.3	10.0	32.0	22.9	12.8	35.0	83.4	8.2	9.8	7.0	5.0
53 08850	Burien..........................	31,368	1.4	6.5	15.9	7.9	26.9	30.1	12.6	40.8	79.0	7.3	8.3	10.3	16.0
53 10372	Cascade-Fairwood CDP......	39,493	-	7.5	20.1	8.1	31.0	24.4	8.9	35.6	62.6	13.1	22.9	6.1	8.2
53 14940	Cottage Lake CDP............	25,557	-	5.7	24.2	5.6	24.3	35.8	4.5	40.9	95.5	1.8	4.8	-	1.9

Table A-4. Cities — Who: Age, Race/Ethnicity, and Household Structure, 2005–2007—*Continued*

STATE City	Percent foreign born	Total households	Household type (percent)							Percent of households with people under 18 years	Percent of households with people 60 years and over
			Family households				Nonfamily households				
			Total family households	Married-couple families	Male householder families	Female householder families	Total nonfamily households	One-person households		
ACS table number:	C05002	B11001	B11001	B11001	B11001	B11001	B11001	B11001	C11005	B11006
	15	16	17	18	19	20	21	22	23	24
Utah—Cont.										
South Salt Lake	22.5	7,900	53.9	29.2	5.8	18.9	46.1	36.7	32.2	20.2
Spanish Fork	9.2	7,695	89.7	77.1	5.5	7.1	10.3	9.2	59.5	20.3
Springville	6.6	7,607	83.8	71.3	3.3	9.2	16.2	14.4	54.6	23.3
Syracuse	2.9	5,012	92.8	83.2	3.4	6.3	7.2	6.6	62.3	16.9
Taylorsville......................	12.1	19,590	72.8	54.4	5.8	12.5	27.2	21.2	40.1	22.6
Tooele.............................	2.7	9,755	79.7	61.8	5.0	12.9	20.3	16.3	55.0	20.3
West Jordan.....................	8.5	27,747	83.2	69.5	3.7	10.0	16.8	13.2	56.3	15.5
West Valley	20.0	35,998	77.4	58.1	6.0	13.3	22.6	17.8	49.5	23.1
Vermont.......................	3.7	250,871	64.0	49.5	4.5	10.1	36.0	27.9	31.0	31.6
Burlington.......................	7.0	15,142	44.8	29.7	3.6	11.5	55.2	39.3	23.1	22.4
Virginia	10.1	2,909,223	67.0	50.8	4.1	12.1	33.0	27.3	34.2	29.4
Alexandria	25.3	62,309	44.8	33.5	3.8	7.6	55.2	46.7	19.9	22.4
Annandale CDP	31.7	19,663	70.7	54.7	6.1	9.9	29.3	24.4	32.1	33.6
Arlington CDP..................	25.1	89,525	45.2	35.0	3.4	6.8	54.8	44.2	21.0	21.0
Bailey's Crossroads CDP.....	51.5	8,734	50.4	30.4	10.2	9.8	49.6	40.1	28.5	24.3
Blacksburg town	11.5	12,741	38.8	29.5	3.4	5.9	61.2	27.9	18.7	13.0
Burke CDP	24.3	19,463	79.4	66.4	3.3	9.6	20.6	17.4	36.9	28.1
Cave Spring CDP...............	6.2	11,421	58.0	49.4	1.3	7.3	42	38.6	28.4	33.9
Centreville CDP................	34.5	18,241	68.6	52.5	4.2	11.9	31.4	26.2	42.0	17.0
Chantilly CDP..................	25.9	16,099	66.9	56.4	2.8	7.7	33.1	24.7	34.7	23.2
Charlottesville.................	10.6	16,694	42.2	26.5	2.5	13.3	57.8	43.4	21.5	27.9
Chesapeake.....................	3.8	77,808	75.3	56.2	4.5	14.6	24.7	21.3	42.1	27.8
Chester CDP	5.5	8,005	74.2	49.8	4.4	20.0	25.8	20.0	45.2	22.9
Dale CDP	27.7	21,009	79.9	58.4	6.1	15.4	20.1	16.0	50.2	19.3
Danville..........................	1.8	19,972	59.8	35.0	3.7	21.1	40.2	35.6	29.9	39.9
Fairfax............................	28.9	8,311	61.9	46.7	6.0	9.2	38.1	30.2	26.4	33.3
Franconia CDP	20.9	13,845	62.7	49.8	3.3	9.6	37.3	30.9	32.9	20.8
Fredericksburg	6.2	8,560	48.9	31.1	4.8	13.0	51.1	42.3	26.6	35.1
Groveton CDP	27.9	7,641	64.0	44.8	6.1	13.1	36.0	27.7	36.8	24.8
Hampton	4.7	54,650	62.5	42.7	3.7	16.1	37.5	30.6	33.6	27.8
Harrisonburg....................	13.3	13,920	45.9	33.1	5.5	7.3	54.1	32.7	21.1	24.1
Herndon town	40.2	6,341	57.2	47.2	2.1	7.9	42.8	38.7	26.0	19.1
Hopewell	3.0	8,740	60.4	34.0	6.2	20.2	39.6	33.6	26.9	31.6
Jefferson CDP	37.2	9,565	65.2	49.5	5.1	10.6	34.8	28.4	27.4	34.3
Lake Ridge CDP	16.3	12,128	75.1	57.5	3.6	14.1	24.9	21.6	41.4	20.4
Leesburg town	13.4	12,165	64.4	55.8	2.2	6.4	35.6	30.7	38.5	15.9
Linton Hall CDP...............	17.0	6,194	88.5	79.4	2.5	6.5	11.5	10.9	69.4	10.3
Lorton CDP	30.8	8,306	69.2	48.1	6.0	15.1	30.8	24.6	44.3	13.7
Lynchburg.......................	3.6	25,903	59.5	40.2	3.4	15.9	40.5	33.9	28.8	36.4
McLean CDP	23.5	14,678	73.4	64.3	3.3	5.8	26.6	22.9	34.1	42.6
Manassas......................	23.2	11,703	77.4	56.6	6.2	14.6	22.6	18.1	50.4	24.7
Mechanicsville CDP...........	2.2	13,353	76.7	61.0	4.5	11.2	23.3	18.6	39.9	29.4
Mount Vernon CDP...........	34.1	11,077	70.8	51.6	4.3	14.9	29.2	20.6	39.2	27.5
Newington CDP	26.3	7,292	81.2	69.8	4.1	7.3	18.8	17.0	42.7	27.9
Newport News..................	6.2	73,274	65.5	42.4	5.3	17.8	34.5	29.6	36.2	26.0
Norfolk...........................	5.6	85,129	59.9	36.0	4.7	19.3	40.1	32.3	33.1	26.2
Oakton CDP.....................	31.4	12,488	68.9	56.7	4.6	7.6	31.1	23.7	37.7	23.8
Petersburg	2.3	12,447	58.2	30.3	6.3	21.5	41.8	33.4	28.0	38.3
Portsmouth......................	1.9	38,848	63.6	38.5	5.3	19.7	36.4	31.4	33.4	31.6
Reston CDP......................	19.9	23,348	53.1	44.4	2.6	6.0	46.9	42.0	24.3	26.8
Richmond........................	5.5	81,611	48.7	25.5	4.2	19.1	51.3	42.6	25.9	31.3
Roanoke	4.4	41,822	55.7	36.6	4.4	14.8	44.3	37.4	26.8	34.1
Salem	3.7	9,680	65.1	45.0	6.0	14.2	34.9	29.7	30.5	37.9
Springfield CDP................	35.8	12,000	64.9	47.2	7.0	10.7	35.1	29.2	31.7	37.2
Staunton.........................	2.5	9,712	57.6	41.6	3.7	12.2	42.4	36.0	27.8	35.4
Suffolk............................	3.1	29,858	76.8	56.1	3.5	17.2	23.2	18.8	43.8	27.8
Tuckahoe CDP..................	10.1	18,660	67.3	53.9	2.2	11.3	32.7	26.1	31.5	34.8
Virginia Beach..................	8.4	161,814	69.5	52.2	3.8	13.4	30.5	23.9	38.3	25.3
Waynesboro.....................	2.5	8,595	62.3	46.2	4.0	12.0	37.7	31.1	27.7	35.4
West Springfield CDP........	24.0	10,528	74.1	58.7	3.5	11.8	25.9	22.6	37.8	31.1
Winchester	10.4	10,026	55.8	39.1	3.9	12.8	44.2	35.8	26.3	35.3
Woodbridge CDP..............	27.3	11,371	71.4	46.0	9.3	16.0	28.6	23.0	41.7	20.1
Washington	12.2	2,472,477	64.5	49.9	4.4	10.2	35.5	28.1	33.1	28.7
Auburn...........................	16.0	19,430	61.5	44.1	4.8	12.5	38.5	33.0	36.0	25.7
Bainbridge Island	5.1	8,929	72.7	62.2	2.5	8.0	27.3	22.0	35.2	32.7
Bellevue..........................	29.8	49,391	62.1	51.7	3.6	6.8	37.9	31.1	30.1	28.6
Bellingham......................	10.3	31,830	47.3	35.9	3.1	8.3	52.7	35.4	23.0	24.5
Bothell	12.6	14,040	64.7	54.8	2.9	7.0	35.3	29.2	30.9	28.8
Bremerton	6.7	14,866	53.2	34.6	6.3	12.4	46.8	38.3	28.1	30.7
Burien............................	17.6	13,104	57.5	38.4	4.4	14.7	42.5	35.9	29.9	31.2
Cascade-Fairwood CDP......	22.0	14,351	69.3	53.1	4.9	11.3	30.7	24.0	39.4	23.6
Cottage Lake CDP.............	5.8	8,450	85.4	76.9	2.1	6.4	14.6	9.6	47.6	20.2

Table A-4. Cities — Who: Age, Race/Ethnicity, and Household Structure, 2005–2007—*Continued*

STATE Place code	STATE City	Total population	Percent change 2005–2007	Population by age (percent)						Median age	Race alone or in combination (percent)				Percent Hispanic or Latino
				Under 5 years	5 to 17 years	18 to 24 years	25 to 44 years	45 to 64 years	65 years and over		White	Black	Asian Hawaiian or Pacific Islander	Amer. Indian, Alaska Native, or some other race	
	ACS table number:	B01003	Population estimates	B01001	B01001	B01001	B01001	B01001	B01001	B01002	B02008	B02009	B02011 + B02012	B02010 + B02013	C03002
		1	2	3	4	5	6	7	8	9	10	11	12	13	14
	Washington—Cont.														
53 17635	Des Moines	29,036	0.7	5.0	13.5	7.2	25.4	30.8	18.1	44.3	75.6	10.2	13.9	4.2	6.7
53 19515	East Hill-Meridian CDP	28,788	-	5.0	20.2	8.1	29.1	28.4	9.1	38.6	66.2	8.0	20.0	8.9	4.5
53 20750	Edmonds	39,748	1.2	4.1	15.9	5.4	26.5	30.2	17.9	44.2	89.7	2.0	8.7	2.7	3.8
53 22640	Everett	98,910	1.1	8.0	15.8	11.3	31.3	23.7	9.9	33.0	81.7	4.6	12.0	7.7	10.7
53 23515	Federal Way	85,235	1.3	6.7	19.3	8.3	29.2	26.7	9.8	36.5	68.6	10.8	19.3	5.2	11.3
53 33380	Inglewood-Finn Hill CDP	26,369	-	5.0	16.2	6.5	29.9	34.2	8.2	40.5	88.5	1.7	10.5	3.4	5.5
53 33805	Issaquah	23,974	12.8	7.3	14.1	4.4	33.9	25.1	15.2	38.5	85.0	1.1	13.9	1.5	6.7
53 35170	Kenmore	21,081	3.9	5.3	16.9	8.0	29.5	29.9	10.3	39.7	85.7	4.7	7.7	3.4	5.6
53 35275	Kennewick	63,007	2.0	8.0	19.6	9.2	29.5	23.5	10.3	33.5	82.0	2.4	2.5	15.8	20.0
53 35415	Kent	88,217	2.5	8.2	19.1	9.8	30.4	24.7	7.8	33.9	68.4	12.7	15.7	8.9	11.6
53 35940	Kirkland	45,682	2.6	5.3	12.3	7.8	33.2	30.0	11.3	39.9	84.6	2.5	11.7	5.2	5.4
53 36745	Lacey	34,243	14.3	6.4	16.1	10.9	28.7	23.5	14.4	35.6	81.9	5.9	11.7	5.4	6.8
53 38038	Lakewood	57,221	-0.4	7.1	15.6	10.7	27.3	25.1	14.1	37.2	69.8	13.9	15.0	7.3	11.3
53 40245	Longview	37,585	2.4	7.0	16.3	9.0	26.3	25.4	16.0	38.1	93.4	1.2	3.0	5.8	8.4
53 40840	Lynnwood	33,173	1.2	6.8	17.2	8.4	29.5	25.8	12.2	36.1	77.1	4.5	17.1	6.1	11.3
53 43955	Marysville	33,720	3.5	7.5	21.0	10.3	29.7	21.9	9.6	34.5	85.2	3.4	8.7	5.6	5.2
53 45005	Mercer Island	23,688	3.8	5.8	20.4	4.6	19.4	32.5	17.4	44.9	83.7	2.0	15.1	1.6	1.7
53 47490	Mountlake Terrace	20,226	-0.1	6.4	17.4	8.6	32.0	25.0	10.6	36.3	75.3	4.7	15.5	9.2	7.6
53 47560	Mount Vernon	30,073	4.5	7.1	20.7	11.9	29.7	18.5	12.1	30.2	74.4	1.4	4.2	21.4	32.0
53 47735	Mukilteo	20,437	4.3	4.4	19.0	10.6	25.0	31.6	9.3	39.3	77.1	6.1	16.4	8.5	4.4
53 49665	North Creek CDP	29,964	-	6.9	19.5	8.6	30.6	28.3	6.1	34.8	82.6	3.9	14.6	4.7	5.5
53 49992	North Marysville CDP	21,290	-	5.9	23.4	7.7	29.3	25.4	8.4	35.0	90.3	1.1	4.6	6.2	-
53 50360	Oak Harbor	20,053	1.3	11.1	21.6	8.4	29.8	15.7	13.4	30.9	82.2	4.2	14.2	4.6	5.9
53 51300	Olympia	46,376	1.8	5.0	15.6	11.0	31.2	23.9	13.3	35.5	86.8	4.4	8.1	5.1	5.0
53 52765	Paine Field-Lake Stickney CDP	26,239	-	9.6	14.4	12.5	31.4	23.2	8.8	31.1	73.9	7.5	14.4	10.4	14.8
53 53335	Parkland CDP	27,632	-	6.2	17.3	17.8	27.5	21.0	10.3	30.9	73.7	13.2	12.1	6.7	8.9
53 53545	Pasco	45,862	13.8	11.9	21.4	12.3	29.8	17.4	7.2	26.7	61.9	2.8	1.9	36.4	54.6
53 54215	Picnic Point-North Lynnwood CDP	25,203	-	5.0	11.8	13.9	33.8	27.8	7.6	35.9	80.5	3.0	17.2	3.8	5.7
53 56625	Pullman	26,687	1.7	4.5	8.9	49.8	22.4	10.5	3.9	22.5	82.4	3.8	13.8	3.3	5.2
53 56695	Puyallup	38,217	2.0	6.9	19.7	7.7	30.3	22.5	12.9	34.6	92.4	3.2	7.1	3.3	5.8
53 57535	Redmond	54,340	2.7	7.7	12.6	11.1	36.8	23.4	8.3	33.8	77.2	1.6	20.4	2.6	7.0
53 57745	Renton	61,248	5.6	8.7	15.0	8.9	33.5	24.5	9.4	35.4	61.9	13.0	19.6	9.4	10.7
53 58235	Richland	43,423	2.0	6.0	17.6	9.5	26.0	28.1	12.8	38.1	90.2	1.6	5.6	3.7	6.3
53 61115	Sammamish	45,050	2.2	9.0	23.0	5.0	29.6	27.7	5.7	36.7	81.2	1.5	18.1	1.8	3.5
53 62288	SeaTac	22,011	1.8	8.5	13.6	8.7	32.0	27.7	9.6	36.4	64.7	12.6	18.5	8.6	16.9
53 63000	Seattle	565,809	2.9	5.1	10.5	10.4	35.9	27.1	11.1	37.6	74.1	9.0	16.2	5.4	6.2
53 63052	Seattle Hill-Silver Firs CDP	38,890	-	8.4	22.5	6.6	30.7	26.7	5.1	34.7	86.3	2.1	10.7	4.1	5.2
53 63960	Shoreline	52,547	0.5	3.7	16.0	6.5	26.1	32.0	15.6	43.9	78.3	6.3	16.9	4.0	4.8
53 65922	South Hill CDP	47,770	-	9.4	22.2	7.7	32.5	22.1	6.0	32.4	86.1	4.7	9.0	5.3	7.5
53 66255	Spanaway CDP	26,024	-	6.9	22.0	7.7	33.1	21.6	8.8	32.7	73.6	17.2	11.2	3.8	3.5
53 67000	Spokane	205,559	1.4	6.5	15.8	11.6	29.3	23.7	13.0	34.5	92.1	3.1	4.3	4.7	3.9
53 67167	Spokane Valley	85,210	4.6	6.8	17.9	8.4	26.8	26.2	13.7	36.8	95.5	2.8	2.9	2.3	3.8
53 70000	Tacoma	193,920	0.8	6.6	16.9	9.6	30.7	24.7	11.5	35.7	73.2	14.7	12.0	6.7	8.2
53 73465	University Place	33,835	0.7	7.8	19.0	9.8	25.4	26.0	12.0	36.3	78.0	13.1	11.4	4.2	5.9
53 74060	Vancouver	158,944	2.5	7.1	16.8	8.9	30.6	24.8	11.8	35.2	87.4	4.0	6.6	7.2	9.2
53 75775	Walla Walla	31,524	-0.3	5.0	14.6	16.3	27.9	20.3	15.8	34.0	85.5	2.4	2.8	11.3	19.6
53 77105	Wenatchee	30,756	2.1	7.8	16.5	11.1	26.2	22.9	15.5	36.1	91.0	1.5	1.6	9.4	24.5
53 80010	Yakima	85,226	0.3	9.5	18.4	11.3	25.9	21.2	13.7	32.1	69.8	2.1	2.2	28.0	37.9
54 00000	**West Virginia**	1,808,787	0.4	5.8	15.7	9.0	26.2	27.9	15.4	40.3	95.5	3.9	0.9	1.0	1.0
54 14600	Charleston	51,295	-1.3	6.8	13.6	6.7	28.0	29.9	14.9	41.4	81.3	16.9	2.9	0.5	1.8
54 39460	Huntington	48,988	-0.9	5.5	13.2	17.2	24.0	22.9	17.2	37.0	90.6	9.0	1.4	1.2	1.2
54 55756	Morgantown	27,063	0.9	2.0	7.3	48.4	19.5	15.1	7.6	22.5	88.8	8.1	4.0	0.9	1.4
54 62140	Parkersburg	31,551	-1.6	5.3	15.6	8.7	24.5	27.2	18.6	41.2	96.9	2.2	1.6	1.6	1.3
54 86452	Wheeling	29,307	-1.5	5.3	14.5	9.4	22.7	27.8	20.5	43.8	92.6	6.4	2.0	0.6	0.6
55 00000	**Wisconsin**	5,571,593	1.1	6.4	17.4	9.9	27.1	26.1	13.1	37.7	88.7	6.4	2.3	4.0	4.7
55 02375	Appleton	71,027	0.1	6.8	18.7	10.5	28.9	24.6	10.5	35.0	90.3	1.4	6.3	3.3	4.5
55 06500	Beloit	34,594	2.3	7.5	19.7	10.2	26.6	23.4	12.6	32.3	77.2	15.3	1.8	8.8	13.1
55 10025	Brookfield	38,587	-0.6	5.5	19.0	6.8	19.5	30.1	19.0	44.5	91.7	2.0	5.6	1.5	1.3
55 11950	Caledonia village	27,537	1.1	5.2	18.3	5.2	25.5	29.0	16.9	41.9	94.8	1.7	2.5	1.7	3.1
55 19775	De Pere	24,004	3.1	5.8	19.6	13.5	28.5	21.5	11.1	31.4	95.6	1.4	2.6	1.5	-
55 22300	Eau Claire	64,654	1.9	5.7	14.4	21.8	25.6	21.3	11.2	30.2	94.2	1.4	4.3	1.2	1.2
55 25950	Fitchburg	24,275	2.9	7.4	16.5	8.4	35.2	26.7	5.9	34.1	79.2	7.5	7.6	8.4	12.7
55 26275	Fond du Lac	42,018	-0.1	6.3	16.9	10.8	29.6	22.1	14.3	35.1	92.9	2.4	1.9	4.6	5.1
55 27300	Franklin	34,930	4.4	5.0	16.2	8.3	25.6	32.8	12.0	42.3	86.7	7.4	4.3	3.8	4.1
55 31000	Green Bay	98,476	0.0	7.3	17.1	10.7	29.1	24.7	11.0	35.4	82.8	3.4	3.9	12.0	10.1
55 31175	Greenfield	37,276	-0.6	5.3	13.2	8.2	24.2	28.2	20.8	44.5	91.4	2.6	2.5	4.5	5.8
55 37825	Janesville	62,512	1.5	7.3	18.3	8.0	29.2	24.4	12.9	37.0	93.3	2.6	1.6	3.6	4.8
55 39225	Kenosha	96,653	1.6	7.9	19.0	10.2	29.2	22.0	11.7	34.3	82.0	9.4	2.1	8.9	12.6
55 40775	La Crosse	50,968	-0.1	4.8	12.3	25.2	23.5	20.0	14.2	29.7	93.8	2.5	3.7	0.9	0.9
55 48000	Madison	219,843	2.3	5.7	12.1	20.4	30.8	22.0	9.2	31.2	84.0	7.6	7.4	3.6	5.7

STATE City	Percent foreign born	Total households	Household type (percent)						Percent of households with people under 18 years	Percent of households with people 60 years and over
			Family households				Nonfamily households			
			Total family households	Married-couple families	Male householder families	Female householder families	Total nonfamily households	One-person households		
ACS table number:	C05002	B11001	B11001	B11001	B11001	B11001	B11001	B11001	C11005	B11006
	15	16	17	18	19	20	21	22	23	24
Washington—Cont.										
Des Moines	17.3	10,907	62.4	44.4	5.1	12.9	37.6	32.1	28.3	30.4
East Hill-Meridian CDP	21.9	10,086	74.9	55.9	7.5	11.5	25.1	18.7	40.5	29.2
Edmonds	10.8	17,962	59.4	48.7	2.4	8.3	40.6	34.9	24.7	36.8
Everett	18.3	39,975	54.8	36.7	5.1	13.0	45.2	35.5	31.1	24.5
Federal Way	21.1	33,110	66.9	46.8	6.1	14.0	33.1	26.8	37.1	25.5
Inglewood-Finn Hill CDP	15.8	9,749	71.6	62.2	3.6	5.8	28.4	19.6	32.9	24.6
Issaquah	21.8	10,621	58.6	48.3	3.1	7.2	41.4	32.4	28.1	29.0
Kenmore	19.2	8,084	65.5	53.7	3.4	8.4	34.5	29.2	33.6	29.3
Kennewick	11.2	22,735	64.3	47.0	4.6	12.7	35.7	28.6	36	26.4
Kent	24.6	33,329	63.2	45.1	4.8	13.4	36.8	28.2	36.6	23.5
Kirkland	16.3	22,175	49.0	39.4	4.0	5.6	51.0	41.1	23.1	23.7
Lacey	9.9	14,304	60.4	42.4	3.6	14.4	39.6	33.1	31.8	29.0
Lakewood	15.9	23,989	58.8	40.8	5.2	12.8	41.2	31.9	28.6	31.0
Longview	5.5	15,019	61.2	41.6	5.2	14.4	38.8	32.3	33.8	33.4
Lynnwood	24.6	13,597	60.7	44.2	3.2	13.3	39.3	31.4	31.0	29.9
Marysville	7.8	13,332	65.0	47.4	5.8	11.8	35.0	26.3	39.5	24.0
Mercer Island	16.5	9,292	74.2	65.7	1.6	6.9	25.8	22.6	37.6	41.3
Mountlake Terrace	19.0	8,486	63.1	39.4	7.6	16.1	36.9	29.1	33.9	25.4
Mount Vernon	23.1	10,573	66.5	47.3	5.7	13.6	33.5	27.1	38.4	31.6
Mukilteo	14.3	7,988	67.5	58.1	3.2	6.2	32.5	24.8	31.2	25.0
North Creek CDP	14.3	10,930	74.2	58.3	4.9	10.9	25.8	19.1	43.2	19.5
North Marysville CDP	9.0	7,312	74.7	61.5	3.6	9.5	25.3	20.0	39.0	26.1
Oak Harbor	8.8	7,730	69.0	52.4	2.0	14.7	31.0	25.8	40.6	28.1
Olympia	7.4	19,767	56.1	39.2	3.2	13.7	43.9	31.2	32.2	27.4
Paine Field-Lake Stickney CDP	29.5	10,786	59.9	39.3	6.3	14.4	40.1	32.9	31.1	22.6
Parkland CDP	10.1	10,344	59.8	35.3	10.0	14.6	40.2	29.5	34.2	27.3
Pasco	28.7	13,842	75.8	54.7	8.9	12.3	24.2	20.1	51.5	22.7
Picnic Point-North Lynnwood CDP	17.9	10,716	62.4	50.2	3.2	9.1	37.6	25.8	26.4	20.9
Pullman	15.1	9,598	40.6	35.7	0.7	4.2	59.4	35.7	20.4	11.0
Puyallup	4.7	14,475	66.3	48.5	4.4	13.3	33.7	27.6	36.7	29.3
Redmond	27.3	23,544	55.8	46.2	3.9	5.6	44.2	34.6	28.0	19.6
Renton	24.6	25,524	57.3	39.8	4.2	13.3	42.7	35.1	29.6	24.5
Richland	8.9	16,844	66.2	52.6	3.7	9.8	33.8	29.3	31.6	32.6
Sammamish	17.7	14,875	86.1	78.7	2.9	4.5	13.9	10.9	55.3	17.2
SeaTac	28.8	8,665	57.2	39.7	7.5	10.0	42.8	37.6	30.8	26.7
Seattle	18.4	260,760	43.7	33.2	3.1	7.4	56.3	43.6	20.1	24.8
Seattle Hill-Silver Firs CDP	13.2	12,746	81.8	68.8	3.7	9.3	18.2	12.2	49.0	17.8
Shoreline	18.9	21,348	62.7	46.6	4.7	11.3	37.3	31.6	30.7	30.2
South Hill CDP	7.6	15,837	82.0	66.8	6.6	8.6	18.0	13.5	48.8	20.2
Spanaway CDP	7.4	9,303	70.9	47.0	7.5	16.4	29.1	22.7	40.4	23.1
Spokane	5.5	86,848	55.9	40.4	4.3	11.2	44.1	35.1	29.2	28.5
Spokane Valley	5.0	35,550	64.0	47.3	4.6	12.1	36.0	30.2	33.2	30.5
Tacoma	11.7	77,806	57.4	38.3	4.4	14.8	42.6	34.2	31.6	28.3
University Place	8.8	13,605	63.1	46.3	3.9	12.9	36.9	31.0	35.8	29.9
Vancouver	12.0	62,958	60.4	42.7	4.6	13.2	39.6	32.1	33.6	27.6
Walla Walla	10.4	11,339	56.9	39.7	3.2	14.0	43.1	34.9	30.3	31.7
Wenatchee	12.5	11,899	63.8	47.3	4.0	12.4	36.2	31.7	33.2	37.5
Yakima	17.8	30,703	63.5	44.7	5.0	13.8	36.5	29.1	36.7	32.5
West Virginia	1.3	738,943	67.2	52.1	4.1	10.9	32.8	28.0	30.3	35.4
Charleston	3.3	24,560	52.5	36.8	3.1	12.6	47.5	41.0	23.5	31.9
Huntington	1.9	20,733	54.8	36.1	3.6	15.1	45.2	36.8	25.8	35.5
Morgantown	4.1	8,715	40.5	30.6	4.3	5.6	59.5	42.1	16.7	20.6
Parkersburg	0.7	14,241	60.4	38.6	5.2	16.6	39.6	33.1	25.9	38.8
Wheeling	2.3	13,816	55.5	40.5	2.8	12.1	44.5	39.7	25.4	37.1
Wisconsin	4.3	2,235,246	65.2	51.3	4.2	9.7	34.8	28.3	32.2	29.5
Appleton	6.4	28,606	63.1	50.8	2.8	9.5	36.9	31.6	35.7	24.1
Beloit	8.3	13,632	62.4	39.3	4.4	18.8	37.6	31.6	36.7	29.1
Brookfield	6.7	14,463	78.6	69.5	3.7	5.4	21.4	20.2	34.6	40.5
Caledonia village	4.9	9,702	78.1	66.8	4.4	6.9	21.9	18.4	35.7	28.8
De Pere	2.5	9,219	61.5	47.9	4.1	9.6	38.5	31.0	37.3	27.2
Eau Claire	3.3	26,072	55.8	41.7	4.2	9.9	44.2	32.4	27.8	25.1
Fitchburg	15.6	9,118	62.1	50.2	3.6	8.3	37.9	24.2	34.7	16.6
Fond du Lac	3.8	17,102	59.8	43.6	5.7	10.4	40.2	32.3	30.4	28.2
Franklin	5.6	12,747	68.8	59.8	2.4	6.6	31.2	27.3	29.9	29.5
Green Bay	8.1	40,510	59.7	41.9	5.2	12.6	40.3	33.1	34.0	24.7
Greenfield	7.0	16,475	55.8	43.5	4.7	7.6	44.2	37.8	22.6	39.8
Janesville	4.2	24,942	64.5	49.7	4.5	10.4	35.5	31.0	34.2	31.3
Kenosha	7.7	35,564	64.5	46.0	3.6	14.9	35.5	29.7	38.2	25.7
La Crosse	3.4	21,221	47.1	35.4	2.5	9.2	52.9	39.2	21.9	27.0
Madison	9.9	91,807	48.1	37.6	2.9	7.6	51.9	37.5	23.5	20.7

Table A-4. Cities — Who: Age, Race/Ethnicity, and Household Structure, 2005–2007—*Continued*

STATE Place code	STATE City ACS table number:	Total population B01003	Percent change 2005–2007 Population estimates	Under 5 years B01001	5 to 17 years B01001	18 to 24 years B01001	25 to 44 years B01001	45 to 64 years B01001	65 years and over B01001	Median age B01002	White B02008	Black B02009	Asian Hawaiian or Pacific Islander B02011 + B02012	Amer. Indian, Alaska Native, or some other race B02010 + B02013	Percent Hispanic or Latino C03002
		1	2	3	4	5	6	7	8	9	10	11	12	13	14
	Wisconsin—Cont.														
55 48500	Manitowoc	33,704	-0.6	7.1	17.1	8.8	24.6	25.1	17.3	39.4	94.7	1.4	3.8	1.2	3.6
55 51000	Menomonee Falls village	34,672	2.0	4.4	18.9	8.2	25.7	26.6	16.2	40.0	94.7	2.1	3.1	0.9	2.3
55 51150	Mequon	22,409	-0.1	3.6	18.1	10.0	16.2	36.0	16.1	45.9	93.1	3.5	3.5	0.9	1.7
55 53000	Milwaukee	584,007	0.2	8.4	19.9	11.3	29.2	21.7	9.5	32.0	46.8	40.0	3.6	11.8	15.1
55 54875	Mount Pleasant village	23,732	2.5	5.8	14.0	6.1	21.9	32.3	19.9	46.3	89.3	5.2	2.0	4.6	6.2
55 55275	Muskego	23,414	2.2	6.5	20.6	7.9	26.0	30.0	9.0	39.6	97.6	-	1.7	-	-
55 55750	Neenah	22,898	0.7	5.8	16.1	8.0	31.4	25.9	12.8	37.6	98.2	0.8	-	1.2	1.3
55 56375	New Berlin	37,358	1.1	5.4	16.2	7.0	22.9	34.4	14.2	44.2	95.5	1.0	2.9	0.7	1.7
55 58800	Oak Creek	35,223	1.3	8.8	18.9	6.2	30.5	26.2	9.3	36.9	90.8	3.7	3.1	4.1	4.2
55 60500	Oshkosh	66,356	0.7	5.2	14.1	18.2	28.9	21.7	11.9	33.5	92.6	2.9	3.1	2.1	2.4
55 66000	Racine	77,183	-1.0	8.3	20.1	10.2	28.2	23.4	9.8	32.5	68.4	24.3	0.7	9.6	18.1
55 72975	Sheboygan	48,985	-0.8	6.4	17.5	10.3	28.1	22.6	15.1	35.8	84.0	2.0	8.0	7.7	8.8
55 75125	South Milwaukee	21,571	-0.8	7.4	18.1	5.7	25.7	28.6	14.5	41.7	95.8	1.6	0.8	3.9	6.8
55 77200	Stevens Point	24,374	0.7	3.9	11.2	32.0	23.3	18.9	10.7	25.9	94.2	-	5.1	0.3	-
55 78600	Sun Prairie	27,313	7.1	9.4	17.7	9.0	33.7	21.8	8.4	33.4	90.7	5.4	1.7	4.7	-
55 78650	Superior	26,537	-1.3	5.8	15.5	13.0	26.6	25.2	14.0	36.7	95.2	1.8	2.1	2.5	1.1
55 83975	Watertown	24,271	0.9	8.1	18.1	10.0	29.4	21.9	12.4	34.5	98.4	0.6	0.9	0.8	-
55 84250	Waukesha	66,043	0.3	6.7	15.9	12.6	28.7	24.3	11.8	34.9	90.6	3.0	3.5	5.0	9.9
55 84475	Wausau	36,976	1.0	5.6	16.5	8.7	27.2	25.3	16.7	38.6	89.0	0.9	9.8	1.3	1.2
55 84675	Wauwatosa	50,173	-1.0	8.1	16.4	5.1	28.7	26.7	15.0	40.4	92.6	4.0	3.5	1.6	2.5
55 85300	West Allis	61,854	-0.7	6.2	15.0	8.4	27.2	27.8	15.4	41.0	92.5	3.7	1.7	3.9	7.9
55 85350	West Bend	29,518	1.6	6.2	16.8	9.9	30.3	23.0	13.8	35.6	98.3	-	1.3	0.9	1.1
56 00000	**Wyoming**	514,044	3.2	6.6	17.4	10.5	25.5	27.8	12.2	37.3	93.8	1.3	1.2	6.1	7.2
56 13150	Casper	53,043	2.9	7.5	18.2	10.6	26.1	24.4	13.2	35.1	93.7	1.9	0.8	5.8	6.3
56 13900	Cheyenne	55,199	-0.7	6.3	18.7	8.1	29.0	24.5	13.5	36.2	89.3	4.5	2.1	8.9	12.7
56 31855	Gillette	23,765	11.2	8.7	18.9	10.5	29.3	27.2	5.3	31.3	95.7	0.5	1.0	4.3	4.3
56 45050	Laramie	27,136	-0.8	5.3	11.0	32.6	25.7	17.9	7.5	25.4	91.0	1.7	4.0	6.5	-

STATE City	Percent foreign born	Total households	Household type (percent)						Percent of households with people under 18 years	Percent of households with people 60 years and over
			Family households				Nonfamily households			
			Total family households	Married-couple families	Male householder families	Female householder families	Total nonfamily households	One-person households		
ACS table number:	C05002	B11001	B11001	B11001	B11001	B11001	B11001	B11001	C11005	B11006
	15	16	17	18	19	20	21	22	23	24
Wisconsin—Cont.										
Manitowoc	5.2	14,203	63.2	49.4	3.7	10.2	36.8	33.1	31.2	34.1
Menomonee Falls village	4.7	13,653	70.0	61.8	3.1	5.2	30.0	25.0	32.7	35.3
Mequon	7.9	8,460	76.4	70.4	1.9	4.1	23.6	19.9	33.8	40.5
Milwaukee	9.3	224,817	55.8	29.3	5.3	21.2	44.2	36.3	25.2	24.2
Mount Pleasant village	3.8	10,365	67.9	53.6	5.2	9.2	32.1	28.4	29.6	36.7
Muskego	3.3	8,310	80.5	66.7	4.1	9.7	19.5	15.9	45.5	27.9
Neenah	2.1	10,187	62.0	49.3	4.0	8.6	38.0	28.2	31.2	28.3
New Berlin	4.3	15,189	71.3	64.0	2.4	4.9	28.7	24.6	29.0	32.8
Oak Creek	5.0	13,525	67.4	53.6	4.5	9.4	32.6	28.0	35.9	25.4
Oshkosh	2.6	25,669	52.4	40.7	3.3	8.4	47.6	34.7	27.8	28.1
Racine	7.7	31,163	63.0	37.7	6.9	18.4	37.0	31.3	35.0	24.7
Sheboygan	9.1	20,749	59.5	46.1	4.5	8.8	40.5	33.9	30.8	30.6
South Milwaukee	4.6	8,839	66.4	48.6	4.2	13.7	33.6	29.3	31.0	32.4
Stevens Point	3.9	9,552	47.9	36.3	3.4	8.2	52.1	32.3	20.4	25.8
Sun Prairie	4.0	10,495	65.7	55.2	2.5	8.0	34.3	26.8	38.2	19.6
Superior	1.8	11,480	58.4	40.4	5.1	12.9	41.6	34.5	28.8	33.0
Watertown	3.5	9,029	73.4	56.7	4.1	12.7	26.6	23.6	39.8	29.4
Waukesha	7.2	27,688	58.9	46.5	3.1	9.2	41.1	33.6	30.3	26.8
Wausau	6.4	16,264	55.3	43.7	4.2	7.4	44.7	36.3	28.7	31.5
Wauwatosa	5.4	20,832	61.6	51.0	2.7	8.0	38.4	34.3	29.0	32.1
West Allis	5.8	27,447	53.6	36.7	4.8	12.1	46.4	37.7	25.5	31.6
West Bend	1.1	12,530	61.9	48.0	3.5	10.4	38.1	29.7	29.6	28.5
Wyoming	2.7	205,422	65.6	52.6	4.8	8.2	34.4	27.8	31.1	29.4
Casper	1.9	20,515	63.8	48.0	4.9	11.0	36.2	28.6	33.7	28.9
Cheyenne	3.3	22,929	61.5	45.3	4.4	11.9	38.5	33.8	30.6	29.5
Gillette	0.8	8,441	69.8	51.2	8.4	10.2	30.2	23.5	39.4	17.8
Laramie	5.5	11,787	50.2	37.8	4.9	7.5	49.8	33.1	24.3	16.3

What
Education, Employment, and Income

What: Education, Employment, and Income

What do Americans do? During the years 2005 to 2007, more than 150 million Americans were in the labor force, and almost 80 million were enrolled in school. Many people were in both groups at the same time. Americans' employment and income potential are closely related to their educational attainment. Educational differences among states, cities, and metropolitan areas can influence location decisions of both workers and employers. Employers with low-wage jobs might seek locations with lower education levels, while locations with highly educated work forces might be sought out by other employers.

Education

About 27 percent of Americans (age 25 and over) held bachelor's degrees or advanced degrees, and another 27 percent had attended some college or held associate's degrees. In the District of Columbia, Massachusetts, Colorado, Maryland, Connecticut, and New Jersey, one-third or more of the population held bachelor's or advanced degrees, while less than 20 percent of people in Kentucky, Arkansas, Mississippi, and West Virginia were college-educated. The five metropolitan areas with the highest proportions of college-educated residents—about half of their populations—were Boulder, CO; Ithaca, NY; Ann Arbor, MI; Corvallis, OR; and Ames, IA—all relatively small metropolitan areas with large universities. Among metropolitan areas with more than a million people, there were five where more than 40 percent of the residents had

college degrees: Washington, DC; San Jose and San Francisco, CA; Boston, MA; and Raleigh, NC. There were 18 counties where more than half of the people had bachelor's or advanced degrees, with the top five all suburbs of Washington, DC. There were 13 cities where more than three-quarters of the people were college-educated. Some were university cities; some were suburbs of large metropolitan areas; all had fewer than 100,000 people and most had closer to 20,000 people.

In the United States, 16 percent of adults had not graduated from high school. Another 30 percent had a high school diploma but no further education in regular 2-year or 4-year colleges. Vocational training for specific trades is not measured in the ACS. Thus, 46 percent of the American people were in the group with a high school diploma or less. In eight cities, most of them in California, more than 80 percent of the people had a high school education or less. Most of these cities were separate cities within Los Angeles County. Statewide, 42.9 percent of California's residents were in this group with a high school education or less. In West Virginia, Louisiana, Kentucky, and Arkansas, more than 55 percent of the people had not attended college.

Among 16- to 19-year-olds in the United States, 3 percent were not enrolled in school, not high school graduates, and not in the labor force. This measure provides one way to use ACS data to identify unemployed high school dropouts. Only 19 states exceeded the national level, led by

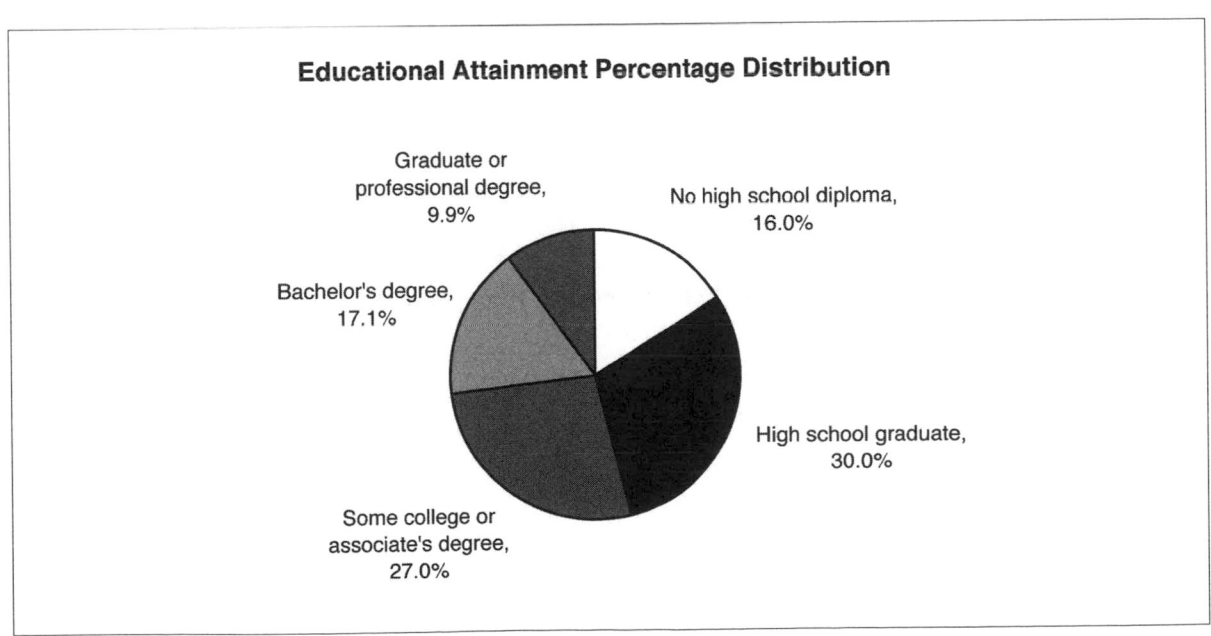

Educational Attainment Percentage Distribution

Graduate or professional degree, 9.9%

No high school diploma, 16.0%

Bachelor's degree, 17.1%

High school graduate, 30.0%

Some college or associate's degree, 27.0%

Louisiana where 5 percent of 16- to 19-year-olds were in this high-risk category. The District of Columbia, Nevada, and New Mexico also had high levels at 4.5 percent or more, while Utah, Minnesota, North Dakota, Vermont, and Iowa had the lowest levels at 1.4 to 1.5 percent.

Of the nearly 80 million people enrolled in school in the United States between 2005 and 2007, 67.7 percent were in kindergarten through 12th grade, 26.1 percent were in college or graduate school, and the remaining 6.2 percent were in preschool. Overall, 16.2 percent of the students were in private schools, but this varied by level of school and by location. Nearly half of preschoolers were in private schools, but the proportion decreased to less than 10 percent of high school students. The proportion of high school students in private schools ranged from below 5 percent in Wyoming, Utah, and Nevada to 15 percent or more in Hawaii, the District of Columbia, Louisiana, and Delaware. Just over 23 percent of undergraduates and 40.3 percent of professional and graduate students attended private schools. In some states with large numbers of private colleges, higher education attracts many students from other states. More than half of the college undergraduates in the District of Columbia were in private schools, as were 48.8 percent in Massachusetts, 41.4 percent in Rhode Island, and 38 percent or more in New York, Connecticut, and Vermont. Private school proportions were even higher for medical, law, and graduate school enrollment in these states.

Employment

About two-thirds of adults (age 16 and over) in the United States were in the labor force—the civilian labor force or the armed forces. Those who were not in the labor force might be retired, in school, disabled, homemakers, or formerly employed individuals who have become discouraged from seeking work. Labor force participation was highest in Alaska, Minnesota, Nebraska, and Wyoming, where over 70 percent of adults were in the labor force. In West Virginia, Mississippi, and Alabama, labor force participation was at 60 percent or lower. But labor force participation does not mean full-time permanent work. Only 39.9 percent of adults worked 35 hours or more per week for 50 to 52 weeks in the past 12 months—full-year, full-time workers. Nevada, Maryland, Nebraska, and Virginia had the highest levels of full-year, full-time workers, over 44 percent. Alaska, with the highest labor force participation rate, ranked in the bottom 10 for full-year, full-time employment, with 37.5 percent. West Virginia had the lowest level of full-year, full-time workers—34 percent.

Half of the adults in the Jacksonville, NC, metropolitan area worked at full-year, full-time jobs, and the rates were above 48 percent in three more metropolitan areas: Sioux Falls, SD; Washington, DC; and Des Moines, IA. Lincoln County, SD, had the highest proportion of full-year, full-time workers—56.4 percent—followed by six counties and independent cities in Virginia and Maryland—most of them suburbs of Washington, DC—and Sarpy County, NE, all at 52 percent or higher. In Apache County, AZ, only 15.2 percent of adults worked at full-year, full-time jobs, while Bee County, TX, and McDowell County, WV, also had low levels of about 20 percent.

During the 2005–2007 period, the national unemployment rate, as measured in the ACS, was 6.6 percent, but many states had higher levels. Michigan and Mississippi were over 9 percent, and the cities of Muskegon and Detroit,

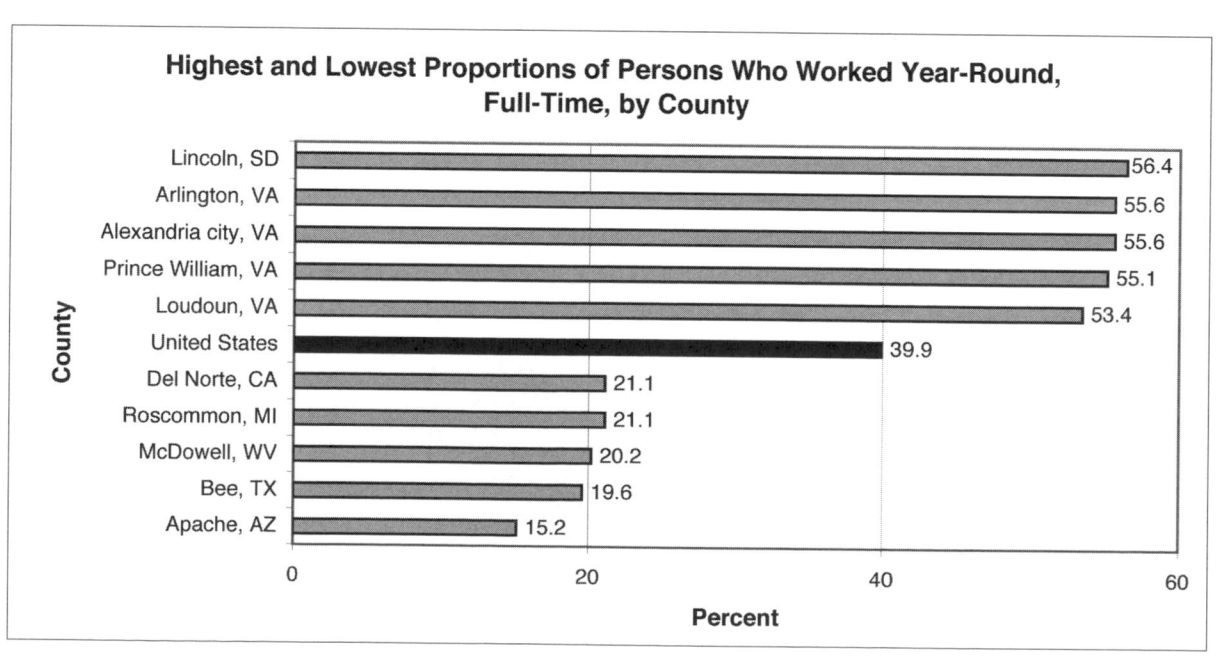

Highest and Lowest Proportions of Persons Who Worked Year-Round, Full-Time, by County

MI, had unemployment rates over 21 percent, along with Harvey, IL, and Greenville, MS. Eighteen metropolitan areas had unemployment rates above 10 percent in 2005–2007. Only one of these had a population of over one million—the Detroit metropolitan area with 4.5 million residents had an unemployment rate of 10.4 percent. Forty-nine metropolitan areas had unemployment rates below 5 percent. Again, most of these were smaller metropolitan areas, with the exceptions of Salt Lake City (1 million) and Washington, DC (5.3 million).

Unemployment was higher among workers aged 16 to 24, whose 14.7 percent national rate compared with 5.1 percent for workers aged 25 to 64. Among workers in that 25- to 64-year-old group, 10 percent of those without a high school diploma were unemployed, while less than 3 percent of college-educated workers were unemployed. Among workers aged 16 to 24, unemployment rates were above the national level (14.7 percent) in 21 states. Mississippi's youth unemployment was 23.1 percent and Michigan's was 19.4 percent.

In the United States, 63.9 percent of children under 18 lived in families with two parents. Around 41 percent of children lived with two parents, where both were in the labor force. Another 22.5 lived with both parents, but only their father was in the labor force. About 25 percent lived with a single parent who was in the labor force. In eight states—all in the Midwest and New England—more than half of the children had two parents in the labor force.

Over 78 percent of employed civilians age 16 and over worked for private employers. In 13 states, more than 80 percent of workers were private employees, led by

Nevada, Indiana, and Michigan with over 82 percent of employees. With the exceptions of Nevada and Florida, these 13 states were all in the Midwest and the Northeast. Alaska, the District of Columbia, and New Mexico had the lowest levels of private sector jobs, below 70 percent. Nationally, 14.5 percent worked for federal, state, or local government agencies, but in 5 states and the District of Columbia, government employment provided 20 percent or more of jobs. The District of Columbia and Alaska had the highest levels of government employment—above 25 percent—followed by New Mexico, Maryland, Hawaii, and Virginia. Government employment was lowest—under 12 percent—in Indiana, Nevada, Michigan, and Pennsylvania. At the national level, 7 percent of workers were self-employed or unpaid family workers. In Montana, Vermont, South Dakota, and Maine, the proportion reached 10 percent or higher. Delaware and Nevada had the lowest levels of self-employment, at just over 5 percent.

Income

The median income for all American households in 2005 through 2007 was $50,007, ranging from a high of $66,873 in Maryland to a low of $35,632 in Mississippi. Two metropolitan areas had median household incomes above $80,000—San Jose, CA, and Washington, DC—while two other metropolitan areas had median household incomes below $30,000—McAllen and Brownsville, TX. Loudoun and Fairfax Counties in Virginia had median household incomes over $100,000, while median incomes in Leflore County, MS, and Clay County, KY, were just over $20,000. Eighty-eight cities had median household incomes over $100,000, topped by Southlake, TX, with a median income of $172,945 and Darien, CT, with a median of $160,274.

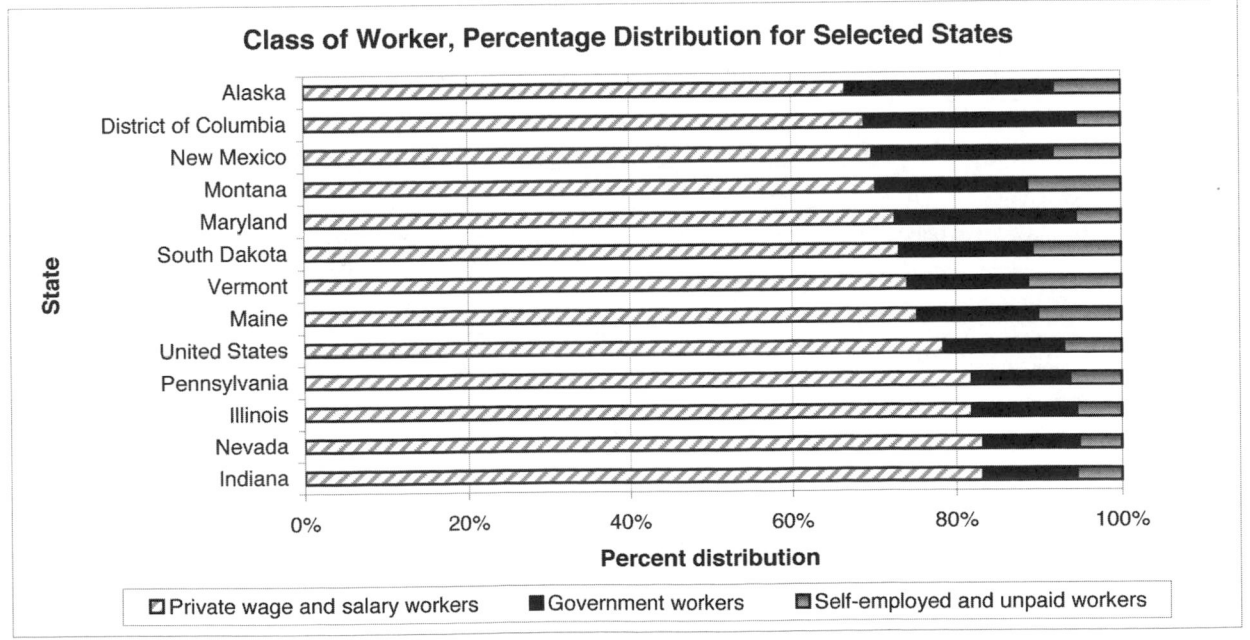

Class of Worker, Percentage Distribution for Selected States

Cities at the lower end of the income spectrum included Carbondale, IL; Kiryas Joel village, NY; and Opelousos, LA, all under $20,000.

In the United States, households headed by 45- to 64-year-olds had higher incomes than other households. Among households of different race and Hispanic origin groups, Asian-headed households had the highest median incomes, followed by non-Hispanic Whites. Among household types, married-couple families had the highest median incomes. Among individuals, the median income for men was about $10,000 higher than the median income for women. Per capita income is the total aggregate income in the geographic area, divided by the population of the area, resulting in a measure of the income for every man, woman, and child. The per capita income for the United States was $26,178. The District of Columbia had the highest per capita income, at $38,009 (partly because it had so many one-person households), followed by Connecticut, New Jersey, Maryland, Massachusetts, and Virginia, all over $30,000. The lowest per capita income—$18,820—was in Mississippi, while West Virginia and Arkansas both had per capita income levels around $20,000.

Nineteen percent of American households had incomes over $100,000. In New Jersey, Maryland, and Connecticut, the proportion in this income bracket was about 30 percent, and in West Virginia, Arkansas, and Mississippi, the proportion was about 10 percent. In eight metropolitan areas, four of them in California, more than 30 percent of households had incomes of $100,000 or more. In the Hinesville-Fort Stewart, GA, metropolitan area, only 6.1 percent of households had incomes in that range. In Loudoun and Fairfax

Counties, VA, more than half of all households had incomes of $100,000 or more. In 17 additional counties, the proportion of $100,000 households was over 40 percent. Most of those counties were in California, Virginia, New York, Maryland, and New Jersey, but they also include Douglas County, CO, and Williamson County, TN. In the city of Southlake, TX, 79.6 percent of households had incomes of $100,000 or more. McLean, VA; Colleyville, TX; and Potomac, MD, also had $100,000 incomes in more than 70 percent of their households. Less than 1 percent of households in the city of San Luis, AZ, had incomes over $100,000, and nine other cities had levels below 3 percent.

Poverty status is determined by a standard national definition that includes a household or family's income and number of household or family members. In the 2005–2007 ACS, an estimated 12.6 percent of households were below the poverty level. The poverty measure does not vary from state to state, despite variations in the cost of living. In Mississippi, 20.6 percent of households had incomes below the poverty level, as did about 18 percent of households in Louisiana and West Virginia and less than 9 percent of households in Maryland, New Hampshire, Connecticut, and New Jersey. In all states, poverty rates were higher for female-headed family households. The national rate for this group was 28.6 percent. In Mississippi and Louisiana, more than 40 percent of female headed family households were below the poverty level, and Maryland's rate of 17.4 percent was the lowest in the nation.

In three metropolitan areas in Texas, more than 25 percent of families were below the poverty level—McAllen, Brownsville, and Laredo. At the other extreme, less than 4 percent of

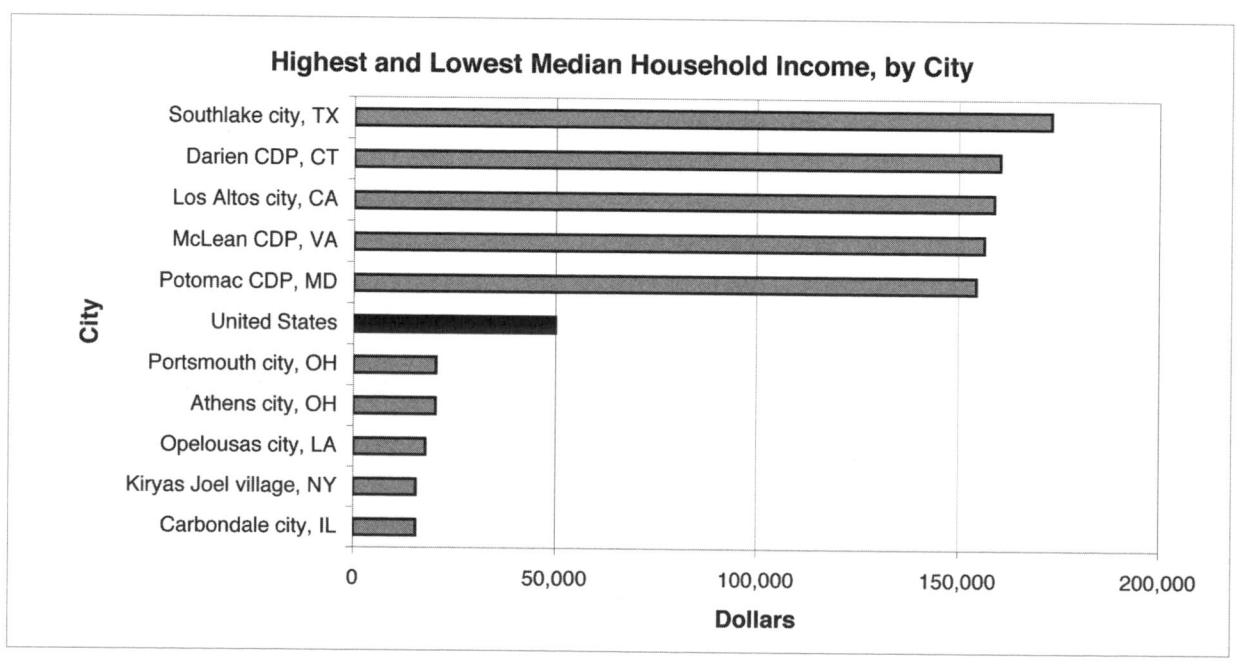

families in the Holland-Grand Haven, MI, and Barnstable, MA, metropolitan areas had incomes below the poverty level. In nine counties, most of them in Texas and Mississippi, more than 30 percent of families had incomes below the poverty level. Loudoun County, VA; Hunterdon County, NJ; and Douglas County, CO; all had poverty rates below 2 percent. Nineteen cities, in 12 states, had family poverty rates over 30 percent. The highest level was in Kiryas Joel village, NY, where families below the poverty level were estimated at 61.5 percent. In 15 cities, less than 1 percent of families had incomes below the poverty level.

Nearly 25 percent of American households had incomes under $25,000, a few thousand dollars higher than the poverty level for a family of four. The proportion was over 35 percent in Mississippi and West Virginia, and less than 18 percent in Maryland, Hawaii, New Hampshire, and Alaska. There were 22 cities where more than half of all households had incomes below $25,000. Kiryas Joel village, NY; Carbondale, IL; and Opelousos, LA, all had levels over 60 percent. In 10 cities, less than 4 percent of households had incomes below $25,000, with Seattle Hill-Silver Firs, WA, at only 3.3 percent.

High school diploma or less rank	State	Percent with a high school diploma or less [B-1, col 2 + 3]	Bachelor's degree or more rank	State	Percent with a bachelor's degree or more [B-1, col 5 + 6]	Labor force participation rate rank	State	Labor force participation rate [B-1, col 20]
	United States	46.0		United States	27.0		United States	64.7
1	West Virginia	60.9	1	District of Columbia	45.4	1	Alaska	71.4
2	Louisiana	55.9	2	Massachusetts	37.1	2	Minnesota	71.0
3	Kentucky	55.5	3	Colorado	34.7	3	Nebraska	70.7
4	Arkansas	55.3	3	Maryland	34.7	4	Wyoming	70.0
5	Mississippi	53.9	5	Connecticut	34.2	5	Colorado	69.8
6	Tennessee	53.4	6	New Jersey	33.6	5	New Hampshire	69.8
7	Alabama	52.3	7	Virginia	32.9	7	South Dakota	69.6
7	Pennsylvania	52.3	8	Vermont	32.7	8	Utah	69.4
9	Indiana	51.9	9	New Hampshire	31.7	9	North Dakota	69.2
10	South Carolina	51.0	10	New York	31.2	10	Vermont	69.0
11	Ohio	50.6	11	Minnesota	30.6	11	Iowa	68.7
12	Oklahoma	48.9	12	Washington	30.0	11	Maryland	68.7
13	Missouri	48.8	13	Rhode Island	29.4	11	Wisconsin	68.7
14	Texas	48.4	14	California	29.1	14	Kansas	68.6
15	Georgia	48.1	15	Illinois	29.0	15	Connecticut	67.4
16	Nevada	47.9	16	Hawaii	28.6	16	Nevada	67.2
17	Delaware	47.6	17	Kansas	28.3	17	Virginia	67.1
17	Maine	47.6	18	Utah	28.2	18	Massachusetts	66.9
19	North Carolina	47.4	19	Oregon	27.6	19	District of Columbia	66.5
20	Florida	46.7	20	Nebraska	27.2	20	Illinois	66.4
21	New Mexico	46.6	21	Montana	26.7	21	Rhode Island	66.0
21	Rhode Island	46.6	22	Delaware	26.6	22	Idaho	65.9
23	Iowa	46.5	22	Georgia	26.6	22	Washington	65.9
24	Wisconsin	46.1	24	Alaska	26.2	24	Georgia	65.8
25	New York	45.7	25	Maine	25.9	24	Indiana	65.8
26	South Dakota	45.3	26	North Dakota	25.6	24	New Jersey	65.8
27	Michigan	45.2	27	Pennsylvania	25.5	27	Hawaii	65.6
28	New Jersey	44.1	28	Arizona	25.3	28	Maine	65.5
29	Illinois	43.6	29	Florida	25.2	29	Montana	65.4
30	Arizona	43.0	30	North Carolina	25.1	30	Texas	65.2
31	California	42.9	30	Wisconsin	25.1	31	Missouri	65.1
32	Vermont	42.7	32	New Mexico	24.9	32	North Carolina	65.0
33	Idaho	42.5	33	Texas	24.8	33	Delaware	64.8
34	Montana	42.2	34	South Dakota	24.5	33	Ohio	64.8
35	Wyoming	42.1	35	Michigan	24.4	35	Oregon	64.6
36	Connecticut	41.8	36	Iowa	24.0	36	California	64.1
36	Kansas	41.8	36	Missouri	24.0	37	Michigan	63.5
36	Virginia	41.8	38	Idaho	23.6	38	Tennessee	62.9
39	Hawaii	41.4	39	Ohio	23.3	39	South Carolina	62.8
39	Nebraska	41.4	40	Wyoming	23.2	40	New York	62.7
41	New Hampshire	41.0	41	South Carolina	22.8	40	Oklahoma	62.7
41	North Dakota	41.0	42	Oklahoma	22.3	42	Arizona	62.6
43	Maryland	40.1	43	Tennessee	21.7	42	Pennsylvania	62.6
44	Massachusetts	40.0	44	Indiana	21.6	44	New Mexico	62.2
45	Alaska	39.4	45	Alabama	21.1	45	Arkansas	61.1
45	Oregon	39.4	46	Nevada	20.9	46	Kentucky	60.9
47	Minnesota	37.8	47	Louisiana	20.1	47	Louisiana	60.8
48	District of Columbia	37.3	48	Kentucky	19.7	48	Florida	60.7
49	Washington	36.7	49	Arkansas	18.7	49	Alabama	60.0
50	Colorado	36.3	50	Mississippi	18.6	49	Mississippi	60.0
50	Utah	36.3	51	West Virginia	16.8	51	West Virginia	55.3

State Rankings, 2005–2007
Selected Rankings

Unemployment rate rank	State	Unemployment rate [B-1, col 23]	Veterans rank	State	Veterans as a percent of population 18 years and over [B-1, col 85]	Families with income below poverty rank	State	Percent of families with income below poverty [B-1, col 140]
	United States	6.6		United States	10.4		United States	9.8
1	Michigan	9.4	1	Alaska	15.5	1	Mississippi	16.6
2	Mississippi	9.2	2	Montana	14.2	2	District of Columbia	15.7
3	District of Columbia	8.8	3	Maine	14.0	3	Louisiana	15.0
4	Alaska	8.6	4	Wyoming	13.9	4	New Mexico	14.2
5	Louisiana	7.9	5	Virginia	13.4	5	Arkansas	13.3
6	Illinois	7.5	6	Washington	13.1	5	Texas	13.3
7	South Carolina	7.3	7	Nevada	12.9	5	West Virginia	13.3
8	Ohio	7.2	8	New Hampshire	12.8	8	Kentucky	13.2
9	Arkansas	7.1	9	Hawaii	12.7	9	Alabama	12.9
9	Georgia	7.1	10	Idaho	12.6	10	Oklahoma	12.5
9	Tennessee	7.1	10	Oklahoma	12.6	11	Tennessee	12.2
12	Alabama	7.0	12	Florida	12.5	12	South Carolina	11.8
12	Kentucky	7.0	12	Oregon	12.5	13	Georgia	11.1
14	Oregon	6.9	12	South Dakota	12.5	14	North Carolina	11.0
14	West Virginia	6.9	15	Arizona	12.4	15	New York	10.7
16	California	6.8	15	New Mexico	12.4	16	Arizona	10.3
16	Indiana	6.8	15	South Carolina	12.4	17	Michigan	9.8
16	North Carolina	6.8	18	Delaware	12.3	17	Missouri	9.8
16	Texas	6.8	18	West Virginia	12.3	19	California	9.7
20	New York	6.7	20	Arkansas	12.2	19	Ohio	9.7
21	Washington	6.5	21	Missouri	12.0	21	Idaho	9.4
22	Missouri	6.4	22	Alabama	11.8	22	Montana	9.3
22	New Mexico	6.4	23	North Dakota	11.7	22	Oregon	9.3
24	Pennsylvania	6.3	24	Colorado	11.6	24	Florida	9.0
25	Connecticut	6.2	24	Nebraska	11.6	25	Illinois	8.9
26	Massachusetts	6.1	26	Kansas	11.5	25	Indiana	8.9
26	New Jersey	6.1	26	Vermont	11.5	27	South Dakota	8.7
26	Rhode Island	6.1	28	Maryland	11.3	28	Maine	8.6
29	Florida	6.0	29	North Carolina	11.2	29	Colorado	8.3
30	Oklahoma	5.9	29	Ohio	11.2	29	Kansas	8.3
31	Colorado	5.8	29	Pennsylvania	11.2	29	Rhode Island	8.3
31	Delaware	5.8	32	Iowa	11.1	32	Pennsylvania	8.2
31	Wisconsin	5.8	32	Tennessee	11.1	33	Washington	8.0
34	Arizona	5.7	34	Georgia	10.7	34	Nebraska	7.9
34	Maine	5.7	34	Indiana	10.7	35	Nevada	7.8
36	Maryland	5.5	34	Kentucky	10.7	36	Alaska	7.6
36	Nevada	5.5	34	Wisconsin	10.7	37	Utah	7.4
38	Idaho	5.4	38	Minnesota	10.6	38	North Dakota	7.3
38	Minnesota	5.4	39	Mississippi	10.3	39	Delaware	7.2
40	Kansas	5.2	40	Rhode Island	10.2	39	Iowa	7.2
40	Vermont	5.2	41	Louisiana	10.1	39	Massachusetts	7.2
42	Montana	5.1	41	Michigan	10.1	42	Virginia	7.1
43	Iowa	4.9	43	Texas	9.8	42	Wisconsin	7.1
44	Nebraska	4.8	44	Connecticut	9.6	44	Vermont	6.9
44	New Hampshire	4.8	45	Massachusetts	9.1	45	Hawaii	6.8
44	Virginia	4.8	46	Illinois	8.7	46	New Jersey	6.5
47	Utah	4.6	47	Utah	8.6	47	Minnesota	6.3
48	South Dakota	4.4	48	California	8.1	48	Connecticut	5.9
49	Hawaii	4.3	49	District of Columbia	8.0	49	Wyoming	5.7
50	Wyoming	4.1	49	New Jersey	8.0	50	Maryland	5.5
51	North Dakota	3.5	51	New York	7.3	51	New Hampshire	4.9

State Rankings, 2005–2007
Selected Rankings

Median household income rank	State	Median household income (dollars) [B-1, col 86]	Households with income less than $25,000 rank	State	Percent of households with income less than $25,000 [B-1, cols 124 + 125 + 126]	Households with income of $100,000 or more rank	State	Percent of households with income of $100,000 or more [B-1, col 134]
	United States	50,007		United States	24.5		United States	19.0
1	Maryland	66,873	1	Mississippi	36.4	1	New Jersey	30.8
2	New Jersey	66,509	2	West Virginia	35.6	2	Maryland	30.0
3	Connecticut	65,496	3	Arkansas	33.5	3	Connecticut	29.4
4	Hawaii	62,543	4	Louisiana	33.0	4	Massachusetts	27.5
5	Massachusetts	61,785	5	Alabama	32.4	5	Hawaii	25.9
6	Alaska	61,766	6	Kentucky	32.3	6	California	25.8
7	New Hampshire	61,459	7	Oklahoma	30.9	7	District of Columbia	25.6
8	Virginia	58,378	8	New Mexico	30.4	8	Alaska	25.2
9	California	58,361	9	Tennessee	29.9	9	Virginia	25.0
10	Minnesota	55,616	10	South Carolina	29.3	10	New Hampshire	23.8
11	Delaware	55,303	11	Montana	28.9	11	New York	22.8
12	Colorado	54,262	12	North Carolina	28.3	12	Delaware	21.6
13	Rhode Island	54,060	12	North Dakota	28.3	13	Colorado	21.5
14	Washington	53,940	14	Missouri	27.2	14	Rhode Island	21.2
15	Nevada	53,753	15	Maine	27.1	15	Illinois	21.1
16	Illinois	53,745	16	South Dakota	27.0	16	Washington	20.7
17	Utah	53,324	17	Texas	26.7	17	Minnesota	20.5
18	New York	52,944	18	District of Columbia	26.4	18	Nevada	19.1
19	District of Columbia	52,187	19	Ohio	26.2	19	Georgia	17.8
20	Wisconsin	50,309	20	Pennsylvania	25.7	20	Texas	17.5
21	Wyoming	50,009	21	Idaho	25.3	21	Arizona	17.4
22	Vermont	49,382	22	Florida	25.1	21	Utah	17.4
23	Michigan	48,642	22	Georgia	25.1	23	Michigan	17.1
24	Arizona	48,609	22	Oregon	25.1	24	Pennsylvania	17.0
25	Georgia	48,540	25	Iowa	25.0	25	Florida	16.4
26	Pennsylvania	47,913	26	Kansas	24.9	25	Vermont	16.4
27	Oregon	47,385	26	Michigan	24.9	27	Oregon	15.7
28	Indiana	47,034	26	Nebraska	24.9	27	Wyoming	15.7
29	Nebraska	46,954	29	Indiana	24.8	29	Wisconsin	15.6
30	Kansas	46,669	30	New York	24.7	30	Kansas	15.3
31	Florida	46,602	31	Rhode Island	23.8	31	Ohio	15.1
32	Iowa	46,399	32	Vermont	23.7	32	North Carolina	14.4
33	Ohio	46,296	33	Arizona	23.5	33	Indiana	14.0
34	Texas	46,248	34	Wisconsin	22.7	34	Missouri	13.9
35	Maine	45,211	35	Illinois	22.5	34	Nebraska	13.9
36	Idaho	44,901	35	Wyoming	22.5	36	Louisiana	13.4
37	Missouri	44,545	37	Colorado	21.3	37	Maine	13.2
38	North Carolina	43,867	38	Washington	21.2	37	New Mexico	13.2
39	South Dakota	43,586	39	Massachusetts	21.0	39	South Carolina	13.1
40	North Dakota	43,442	40	California	20.7	40	Iowa	13.0
41	Montana	42,425	41	Minnesota	19.9	40	Tennessee	13.0
42	South Carolina	42,405	42	Delaware	19.8	42	Alabama	12.9
43	Tennessee	41,821	43	Virginia	19.7	43	Idaho	12.3
44	New Mexico	41,042	44	Nevada	19.6	44	Kentucky	11.8
45	Oklahoma	40,371	45	Utah	18.7	45	Oklahoma	11.7
46	Louisiana	40,160	46	Connecticut	18.0	46	North Dakota	11.5
47	Kentucky	40,138	46	New Jersey	18.0	47	Montana	11.1
48	Alabama	40,052	48	Alaska	17.8	47	South Dakota	11.1
49	Arkansas	37,555	49	New Hampshire	17.3	49	Mississippi	10.4
50	West Virginia	36,088	50	Hawaii	17.2	50	Arkansas	10.2
51	Mississippi	35,632	51	Maryland	16.1	51	West Virginia	9.1

County Rankings, 2005–2007
Selected Rankings

High school diploma or less rank	County	Percent with a high school diploma or less [B-2, col 2]	Bachelor's degree or more rank	County	Percent with a bachelor's degree or more [B-2, col 3]	Unemployment rate rank	County	Unemployment rate [B-2, col 6]
	United States	46.0		United States	27.0		United States	6.6
1	McDowell County, WV	82.0	1	Arlington County, VA	67.0	1	Washington County, MS	23.1
2	Knox County, KY.............	80.4	2	Alexandria city, VA	59.7	2	Holmes County, MS	19.1
3	Holmes County, OH	79.3	3	Fairfax city, VA	58.4	3	Leflore County, MS	18.7
4	Grainger County, TN	79.2	4	Howard County, MD	56.7	4	Bolivar County, MS............	18.1
5	Clay County, KY...............	78.8	5	Montgomery County, MD	56.5	5	Coahoma County, MS...........	16.9
6	Murray County, GA.............	78.6	6	New York County, NY	56.2	6	Cibola County, NM.............	16.0
7	Assumption Parish, LA	78.1	7	Boulder County, CO	55.7	6	St. Francis County, AK	16.0
8	Boone County, WV	78.0	8	Loudoun County, VA.............	55.2	8	Williamsburg County, SC	15.8
9	Starr County, TX.............	77.6	9	Orange County, NC	54.1	9	Yazoo County, MS	15.5
10	Hardee County, FL...............	76.9	10	Marin County, CA	53.5	10	San Jacinto County, TX...........	14.9
11	Wyoming County, WV	76.5	11	Albemarle County, VA............	53.3	11	Roscommon County, MI.........	14.8
12	Hendry County, FL.............	76.2	12	Douglas County, CO	53.2	12	Clare County, MI................	14.7
13	Morgan County, TN..............	75.9	13	Hamilton County, IN.............	53.0	12	Washington County, MO	14.7
13	Yell County, AR..............	75.9	14	Tompkins County, NY.............	52.6	14	Lincoln County, LA................	14.5
15	Washington County, MO	75.7	15	Teton County, WY	52.3	14	Marlboro County, SC	14.5
16	Juniata County, PA	75.2	16	Johnson County, IA.............	51.6	16	Richland County, LA..............	14.3
17	Macon County, TN..............	75.1	17	Washtenaw County, MI...........	51.4	17	Crawford County, MO	14.2
18	Hardeman County, TN............	74.9	18	Johnson County, KS	50.4	18	East Feliciana County, LA.........	14.0
19	Logan County, WV	74.8	19	San Francisco County, CA	49.8	18	Pike County, OH..................	14.0
20	Adams County, OH	74.7	20	Albany County, WY	49.7	20	Petersburg city, VA..............	13.9
21	Tattnall County, GA..............	74.6	21	Somerset County, NJ	49.3	20	Wayne County, MI	13.9
22	LaGrange County, IN.............	74.4	22	Eagle County, CO	49.2	22	Clay County, MS	13.7
23	Campbell County, TN	74.2	22	Williamson County, TN...........	49.2	23	Adams County, MS	13.6
23	Lauderdale County, TN............	74.2	24	Summit County, CO..............	49.0	23	Cheboygan County, MI	13.6
23	Poinsett County, AR..............	74.2	25	Delaware County, OH	48.9	25	Dougherty County, GA...........	13.5
26	Franklin Parish, LA..............	73.8	25	Fairfax city, VA	48.9	26	Jefferson County, AK	13.3
27	Grayson County, KY	73.7	27	Whitman County, WA.............	48.2	26	Mecosta County, MI.............	13.3
27	Hampshire County, WV	73.7	28	Summit County, UT...............	48.1	28	Colusa County, CA.............	13.2
29	Hardin County, TN	73.6	29	Benton County, OR	48.0	28	McCurtain County, OK............	13.2
29	Lincoln County, WV	73.6	30	Morris County, NJ	47.8	28	Montcalm County, MI............	13.2
29	Mingo County, WV	73.6	31	Middlesex County, MA.............	47.6	31	Haralson County, GA	13.1
29	Page County, VA.............	73.6	31	Story County, IA..................	47.6	32	Marion County, SC................	13.0
29	Scott County, TN.............	73.6	33	Hunterdon County, NJ..............	47.3	32	Orleans County, LA	13.0
34	Chattooga County, GA	73.5	34	Collin County, TX..............	47.2	34	Dallas County, AL.................	12.9
35	Dodge County, GA..............	73.4	35	Norfolk County, MA...............	46.8	34	Grenada County, MS.............	12.9
36	Marlboro County, SC	73.3	36	Wake County, NC	46.6	36	Danville city, VA	12.8
37	Mifflin County, PA..............	73.2	37	Boone County, MO	46.5	37	Jackson County, IL.............	12.7
38	Acadia Parish, LA	73.1	38	Routt County, CO	46.2	37	Stevens County, WA	12.7
38	Dillon County, SC..............	73.1	39	Douglas County, KS	46.1	39	Franklin County, LA...............	12.6
38	Wayne County, KY.............	73.1	40	Chester County, PA	46.0	39	Iosco County, MI..................	12.6
41	White County, TN	72.7	41	James City County, VA	45.6	41	Abbeville County, SC..............	12.4
41	Willacy County, TX.............	72.7	42	Gallatin County, MT.............	45.5	41	Graham County, AZ..............	12.4
43	Overton County, TN.............	72.6	43	District of Columbia , DC	45.4	41	Macon County, AL...............	12.4
43	Warren County, TN..............	72.6	44	Fulton County, GA	45.3	41	Muskegon County, MI............	12.4
45	Baker County, FL..............	72.5	45	Chittenden County, VT.............	45.0	41	Panola County, MS...............	12.4
45	DeSoto County, FL..............	72.5	46	Dane County, WI..................	44.7	46	Hendry County, FL................	12.3
47	Avoyelles Parish, LA	72.4	46	Westchester County, NY	44.7	46	Sunflower County, MS	12.3
48	Anson County, NC..............	72.2	48	Santa Clara County, CA	43.9	48	Houston County, TX..............	12.2
49	Tippah County, MS	71.7	49	Charlottesville city, VA............	43.8	48	Kings County, CA.................	12.2
50	Maverick County, TX.............	71.6	50	King County, WA	43.7	50	Logan County, WV................	12.1
50	St. Martin Parish, LA	71.6	51	Bergen County, NJ	43.6	50	Spalding County, GA..............	12.1
52	Burke County, GA..............	71.4	52	DuPage County, IL.................	43.5	52	Chesterfield County, SC	12.0
52	Cocke County, TN.............	71.4	52	Forsyth County, GA.................	43.5	52	Navajo County, AZ	12.0
52	Harlan County, KY	71.4	52	San Mateo County, CA	43.5	52	Scioto County, OH	12.0
52	Scott County, IN..............	71.4	55	Ozaukee County, WI	43.4	52	St. Louis city, MO	12.0
56	Emanuel County, GA..............	71.3	56	Blaine County, ID..................	43.2	56	Apache County, AZ	11.9
56	Hickman County, TN	71.3	57	Montgomery County, PA.........	42.7	56	Carroll County, TN	11.9
58	Carroll County, TN	71.2	58	Champaign County, IL.............	42.6	56	Maverick County, TX.............	11.9
58	Perry County, KY..............	71.2	58	Cobb County, GA	42.6	56	Merced County, CA	11.9
60	Vermilion Parish, LA	71.1	58	Fairfield County, CT...............	42.6	56	Philadelphia County, PA..........	11.9
61	Bibb County, AL..................	71.0	61	Oconee County, GA...............	42.5	61	Henderson County, TN...........	11.8
62	Adair County, OK...................	70.9	62	Hennepin County, MN	42.3	62	Grayson County, KY.............	11.7
62	Williamsburg County, SC	70.9	63	Latah County, ID..................	42.2	62	Scotland County, NC.............	11.7
64	Iberville Parish, LA..............	70.8	63	Travis County, TX.................	42.2	64	Fayette County, TN...............	11.6
65	St. Mary Parish, LA..............	70.7	65	Madison County, MS..............	42.1	64	Giles County, TN.................	11.6
66	McNairy County, TN..............	70.6	66	La Plata County, CO...............	41.9	64	Peach County, GA.................	11.6
67	Lincoln County, KY..............	70.5	67	Clarke County, GA................	41.8	64	Phillips County, AK...............	11.6
68	Elbert County, GA..................	70.4	67	Montgomery County, VA	41.8	68	Burke County, GA.................	11.5
69	Obion County, TN..............	70.3	69	Durham County, NC...............	41.7	68	Isabella County, MI...............	11.5
69	St. Landry Parish, LA..............	70.3	69	Hampshire County, MA...........	41.7	68	Ouachita County, AK..............	11.5
69	Stoddard County, MO	70.3	69	Leon County, FL..................	41.7	71	Barnwell County, SC.............	11.4
72	Bell County, KY..................	70.2	69	Oakland County, MI..............	41.7	71	Lyon County, NV.................	11.4
72	Crisp County, GA..................	70.2	73	Larimer County, CO	41.6	71	Meriwether County, GA...........	11.4
72	Logan County, KY.................	70.2	73	Newport County, RI.................	41.6	71	Nye County, NV.................	11.4
72	Worth County, GA................	70.2	75	York County, VA	41.2	75	Darlington County, SC	11.3
						75	Johnson County, KY..............	11.3

County Rankings, 2005–2007
Selected Rankings

Families with income below poverty rank	County	Percent of families with income below poverty [B-2, col 10]	Households with income less than $25,000 rank	County	Percent of households with income less than $25,000 [B-2, col 11]	Households with income of $100,000 or more	County	Percent of households with income of $100,000 or more [B-2, col 12]
	United States	9.8		United States	24.5		United States	19.0
1	Willacy County, TX	42.2	1	Clay County, KY	60.2	1	Loudoun County, VA	53.1
2	Starr County, TX	37.9	2	McDowell County, WV	59.9	2	Fairfax County, VA	51.5
3	Leflore County, MS	37.1	3	Leflore County, MS	59.0	3	Howard County, MD	48.9
4	Holmes County, MS	34.6	4	Bell County, KY	57.0	4	Hunterdon County, NJ	48.8
5	Sunflower County, MS	33.5	5	Starr County, TX	56.8	5	Somerset County, NJ	47.0
6	Hidalgo County, TX	32.9	6	Willacy County, TX	56.0	6	Douglas County, CO	45.8
7	Cameron County, TX	32.2	7	Holmes County, MS	55.2	7	Morris County, NJ	45.7
8	Knox County, KY	31.7	7	Knox County, KY	55.2	8	Fairfax city, VA	44.8
9	Bolivar County, MS	30.4	9	Sunflower County, MS	53.6	9	Arlington County, VA	44.6
10	McDowell County, WV	29.8	10	Marlboro County, SC	52.5	10	Montgomery County, MD	44.5
11	Maverick County, TX	29.6	11	Bolivar County, MS	52.3	11	Nassau County, NY	43.5
12	Clay County, KY	29.3	11	Luna County, NM	52.3	12	Calvert County, MD	43.0
13	Bell County, KY	29.2	13	Buchanan County, VA	51.5	13	Williamson County, TN	41.7
14	Coahoma County, MS	29.0	14	St. Landry Parish, LA	50.9	14	Marin County, CA	41.5
15	Washington County, MS	28.8	15	Williamsburg County, SC	50.7	14	Santa Clara County, CA	41.5
16	Apache County, AZ	28.7	16	Pike County, AL	50.3	16	Putnam County, NY	40.8
16	Luna County, NM	28.7	17	Coahoma County, MS	49.8	17	Prince William County, VA	40.6
18	McKinley County, NM	28.4	17	Phillips County, AR	49.8	18	San Mateo County, CA	40.3
19	Phillips County, AR	28.3	19	St. Francis County, AR	48.8	19	Stafford County, VA	40.2
20	St. Landry Parish, LA	27.6	20	Emanuel County, GA	48.7	20	Westchester County, NY	39.9
21	Franklin Parish, LA	27.4	21	Floyd County, KY	48.6	21	Rockland County, NY	39.7
22	Webb County, TX	27.1	22	Wayne County, KY	48.3	22	Fairfield County, CT	39.4
23	Dallas County, AL	27.0	23	Lee County, VA	48.2	23	Chester County, PA	39.0
24	Crisp County, GA	26.6	24	Franklin Parish, LA	47.9	24	Monmouth County, NJ	38.9
24	Williamsburg County, SC	26.6	25	Lincoln County, WV	47.6	25	Bergen County, NJ	38.6
26	Robeson County, NC	26.3	26	Dillon County, SC	47.5	26	Forsyth County, GA	38.5
27	Houston County, TX	26.1	27	Dodge County, GA	47.3	27	Suffolk County, NY	38.4
28	Bronx County, NY	25.9	27	Washington County, MS	47.3	27	Summit County, UT	38.4
29	Morehouse Parish, LA	25.1	29	Clarke County, AL	47.2	29	Hamilton County, IN	38.3
30	Pike County, AL	25.0	29	Dallas County, AL	47.2	30	Delaware County, OH	38.1
31	El Paso County, TX	24.9	29	Macon County, AL	47.2	31	Charles County, MD	37.9
32	Adair County, OK	24.4	32	Harlan County, KY	47.1	32	Fauquier County, VA	37.8
33	Scotland County, NC	24.3	33	Jackson County, IL	47.0	33	Alexandria city, VA	37.7
34	Evangeline Parish, LA	24.2	33	Northampton County, NC	47.0	34	Norfolk County, MA	37.2
35	Dillon County, SC	24.1	35	Pike County, MS	46.9	35	Anne Arundel County, MD	36.7
35	Yazoo County, MS	24.1	36	Campbell County, TN	46.7	35	Collin County, TX	36.7
37	Natchitoches Parish, LA	24.0	37	Apache County, AZ	46.2	37	Fort Bend County, TX	36.4
38	Kleberg County, TX	23.9	37	Natchitoches Parish, LA	46.2	37	Goochland County, VA	36.4
39	Floyd County, KY	23.7	37	Toombs County, GA	46.2	37	Sussex County, NJ	36.4
39	Pike County, MS	23.7	40	Robeson County, NC	46.1	40	Lake County, IL	36.3
39	St. Francis County, AR	23.7	41	Avoyelles Parish, LA	45.9	41	Manassas city, VA	36.2
42	Adams County, MS	23.4	42	Marengo County, AL	45.7	42	Contra Costa County, CA	36.1
42	Wayne County, KY	23.4	43	Morehouse Parish, LA	45.6	43	Fayette County, GA	36.0
44	Avoyelles Parish, LA	23.3	44	Winston County, AL	45.5	44	Carroll County, MD	35.7
45	Perry County, KY	23.1	45	Cameron County, TX	45.4	45	Frederick County, MD	35.5
46	Harlan County, KY	22.6	46	McCurtain County, OK	45.2	46	Middlesex County, MA	35.2
46	Mississippi County, AR	22.6	47	Hertford County, NC	45.1	47	Carver County, MN	35.0
48	Crittenden County, AR	22.5	48	Adams County, MS	45.0	48	Scott County, MN	34.7
48	Jim Wells County, TX	22.5	48	Cherokee County, OK	45.0	48	Washington County, MN	34.7
48	Marion County, MS	22.5	48	Oktibbeha County, MS	45.0	50	DuPage County, IL	34.4
51	Hertford County, NC	22.3	48	Whitley County, KY	45.0	50	Montgomery County, PA	34.4
51	Val Verde County, TX	22.3	52	Monroe County, AL	44.9	50	Powhatan County, VA	34.4
53	Dodge County, GA	22.2	53	Hardin County, TN	44.8	53	Orange County, CA	34.2
54	Lee County, VA	22.0	53	Maverick County, TX	44.8	54	Ventura County, CA	33.8
55	McDuffie County, GA	21.9	53	Prentiss County, MS	44.8	55	Middlesex County, NJ	33.6
56	Panola County, MS	21.8	53	Scott County, TN	44.8	56	Oldham County, KY	33.5
56	Whitley County, KY	21.8	57	Wayne County, MS	44.6	57	New York County, NY	33.4
58	Lauderdale County, TN	21.7	58	Bolivar County, MS	44.5	58	Rockwall County, TX	33.2
59	Richmond County, NC	21.6	58	Hidalgo County, TX	44.5	58	Tolland County, CT	33.2
60	Covington County, MS	21.5	58	Johnson County, KY	44.5	60	Juneau City and Borough, AK	33.1
61	McCurtain County, OK	21.4	58	Marion County, MS	44.5	61	San Francisco County, CA	33.0
62	Halifax County, NC	21.3	62	Houston County, TX	44.4	61	York County, VA	33.0
62	Matagorda County, TX	21.3	62	Yazoo County, MS	44.4	63	Hanover County, VA	32.8
64	Waller County, TX	21.2	64	Evangeline Parish, LA	44.3	63	Mercer County, NJ	32.8
65	Marengo County, AL	21.1	64	Texas County, MO	44.3	65	Bucks County, PA	32.5
65	Morgan County, TN	21.1	66	Crisp County, GA	44.2	66	Alameda County, CA	32.0
65	Pike County, OH	21.1	66	Dunklin County, MO	44.2	66	Rockingham County, NH	32.0
68	Abbeville County, SC	21.0	66	Halifax County, NC	44.2	68	McHenry County, IL	31.9
68	Forrest County, MS	21.0	66	Perry County, KY	44.2	69	Elbert County, CO	31.8
68	Lincoln County, WV	21.0	70	Letcher County, KY	44.1	69	Middlesex County, CT	31.8
68	Washington County, GA	21.0	71	Athens County, OH	44.0	71	Queen Anne's County, MD	31.7
72	Monroe County, AL	20.8	71	Marion County, SC	44.0	72	Burlington County, NJ	31.5
72	Wayne County, MS	20.8	73	Adair County, OK	43.7	72	Dakota County, MN	31.5
74	Gallia County, OH	20.7	73	Cocke County, TN	43.7	72	El Dorado County, CA	31.5
74	Marlboro County, SC	20.7	75	Danville city, VA	43.6	72	Johnson County, KS	31.5
74	Okmulgee County, OK	20.7	75	Gallia County, OH	43.6	72	Spotsylvania County, VA	31.5
			75	San Miguel County, NM	43.6			
			75	Scotland County, NC	43.6			

Metropolitan Area Rankings, 2005–2007
Selected Rankings

High school diploma or less rank	Area name	Percent with a high school diploma or less [B-3, col 2]	Bachelor's degree or more rank	Area name	Percent with a bachelor's degree or more [B-3, col 3]
	United States	46.0		United States	27.0
1	Dalton, GA	68.6	1	Boulder, CO	55.7
2	Houma-Bayou Cane-Thibodaux, LA	68.0	2	Ithaca, NY	52.6
3	McAllen-Edinburg-Mission, TX	65.7	3	Ann Arbor, MI	51.4
4	Vineland-Millville-Bridgeton, NJ	65.5	4	Corvallis, OR	48.0
5	Morristown, TN	64.7	5	Ames, IA	47.6
6	Lebanon, PA	64.2	6	Washington-Arlington-Alexandria, DC-VA-MD-WV	46.2
7	El Centro, CA	63.7	7	Lawrence, KS	46.1
8	Laredo, TX	63.5	8	Iowa City, IA	46.0
9	Brownsville-Harlingen, TX	63.1	9	Columbia, MO	44.7
10	Johnstown, PA	62.8	10	San Jose-Sunnyvale-Santa Clara, CA	43.2
11	Pine Bluff, AR	61.9	11	Bridgeport-Stamford-Norwalk, CT	42.6
12	Altoona, PA	61.4	12	San Francisco-Oakland-Fremont, CA	42.5
13	Danville, VA	60.4	13	Fort Collins-Loveland, CO	41.6
13	Hanford-Corcoran, CA	60.4	14	Charlottesville, VA	41.5
15	Weirton-Steubenville, WV-OH	59.8	15	Madison, WI	41.2
16	Mansfield, OH	59.7	16	Durham, NC	41.1
17	Cumberland, MD-WV	59.6	17	Boston-Cambridge-Quincy, MA-NH	40.8
17	Madera, CA	59.6	18	Raleigh-Cary, NC	40.3
17	Visalia-Porterville, CA	59.6	19	State College, PA	40.2
20	Merced, CA	59.5	20	Bloomington-Normal, IL	39.5
20	Odessa, TX	59.5	21	Santa Fe, NM	39.3
22	Elkhart-Goshen, IN	59.3	22	Champaign-Urbana, IL	38.7
23	Rocky Mount, NC	58.5	23	Barnstable Town, MA	38.5
23	Yakima, WA	58.5	24	Burlington-South Burlington, VT	38.4
25	Gainesville, GA	58.3	25	Austin-Round Rock, TX	38.2
25	Harrisonburg, VA	58.3	26	Santa Cruz-Watsonville, CA	37.7
25	Rome, GA	58.3	27	Trenton-Ewing, NJ	37.5
28	Hickory-Lenoir-Morganton, NC	58.2	28	Missoula, MT	36.9
29	Yuma, AZ	58.1	29	Gainesville, FL	36.8
30	Fort Smith, AR-OK	58.0	30	Minneapolis-St. Paul-Bloomington, MN-WI	36.5
31	Bakersfield, CA	57.9	31	Denver-Aurora, CO	36.0
32	Lancaster, PA	57.8	32	Seattle-Tacoma-Bellevue, WA	35.8
32	Youngstown-Warren-Boardman, OH-PA	57.8	33	Lincoln, NE	34.8
34	Wheeling, WV-OH	57.6	34	New York-Northern New Jersey-Long Island, NY-NJ-PA	34.6
35	Jonesboro, AR	57.5	34	Provo-Orem, UT	34.6
36	Anderson, IN	57.4	36	College Station-Bryan, TX	34.4
36	Charleston, WV	57.4	37	Tallahassee, FL	34.1
38	Anniston-Oxford, AL	57.3	38	Huntsville, AL	34.0
38	Danville, IL	57.3	39	Fargo, ND-MN	33.9
40	Florence, SC	57.1	40	Athens-Clarke County, GA	33.7
40	Hagerstown-Martinsburg, MD-WV	57.1	40	Colorado Springs, CO	33.7
40	St. Joseph, MO-KS	57.1	40	Rochester, MN	33.7
40	Williamsport, PA	57.1	43	Atlanta-Sandy Springs-Marietta, GA	33.5
44	Huntington-Ashland, WV-KY-OH	56.8	44	Manchester-Nashua, NH	33.4
44	Reading, PA	56.8	45	San Diego-Carlsbad-San Marcos, CA	33.2
46	Kingsport-Bristol-Bristol, TN-VA	56.7	46	Hartford-West Hartford-East Hartford, CT	33.1
47	Anderson, SC	56.6	46	Lexington-Fayette, KY	33.1
48	Lakeland, FL	56.5	48	Baltimore-Towson, MD	33.0
49	Springfield, OH	56.3	48	Portland-South Portland-Biddeford, ME	33.0
50	Alexandria, LA	56.2	50	Flagstaff, AZ	32.4
50	Lewiston-Auburn, ME	56.2	51	Logan, UT-ID	32.3
52	Owensboro, KY	56.1	52	Portland-Vancouver-Beaverton, OR-WA	31.9
53	Canton-Massillon, OH	55.8	53	Chicago-Naperville-Joliet, IL-IN-WI	31.8
53	Cleveland, TN	55.8	53	Columbus, OH	31.8
53	Johnson City, TN	55.8	55	Omaha-Council Bluffs, NE-IA	31.7
56	Scranton–Wilkes-Barre, PA	55.7	56	Albany-Schenectady-Troy, NY	31.6
56	York-Hanover, PA	55.7	57	Bellingham, WA	31.5
58	Decatur, AL	55.6	57	Des Moines-West Des Moines, IA	31.5
58	Lake Havasu City-Kingman, AZ	55.6	59	Charlotte-Gastonia-Concord, NC-SC	31.2
58	Lima, OH	55.6	59	Kansas City, MO-KS	31.2
58	Parkersburg-Marietta-Vienna, WV-OH	55.6	59	Lafayette, IN	31.2
62	Dothan, AL	55.5	59	Philadelphia-Camden-Wilmington, PA-NJ-DE-MD	31.2
62	El Paso, TX	55.5	59	Worcester, MA	31.2
62	Ocala, FL	55.5	64	Olympia, WA	31.1
65	Erie, PA	55.4	65	New Haven-Milford, CT	30.9
65	Florence-Muscle Shoals, AL	55.4	66	Auburn-Opelika, AL	30.8
67	Michigan City-La Porte, IN	55.3	67	Santa Barbara-Santa Maria-Goleta, CA	30.6
67	Salisbury, MD	55.3	68	Santa Rosa-Petaluma, CA	30.4
67	Sumter, SC	55.3	69	Lansing-East Lansing, MI	30.3
70	Kokomo, IN	55.1	70	Richmond, VA	30.2
70	Texarkana, TX-Texarkana, AR	55.1	70	Rochester, NY	30.2
72	Farmington, NM	54.9	72	Kalamazoo-Portage, MI	30.1
72	Gadsden, AL	54.9	72	Oxnard-Thousand Oaks-Ventura, CA	30.1
72	Modesto, CA	54.9	72	Pittsfield, MA	30.1
75	Lake Charles, LA	54.8	75	Honolulu, HI	30.0
75	Spartanburg, SC	54.8	75	Naples-Marco Island, FL	30.0

Metropolitan Area Rankings, 2005–2007
Selected Rankings

Families with income below poverty rank	Area name	Percent of families with income below poverty [B-3, col 10]	Households with income of $100,000 or more rank	Area name	Percent of households with income of $100,000 or more [B-3, col 12]
	United States	9.8		United States	19.0
1	McAllen-Edinburg-Mission, TX	32.9	1	San Jose-Sunnyvale-Santa Clara, CA	41.2
2	Brownsville-Harlingen, TX	32.2	2	Bridgeport-Stamford-Norwalk, CT	39.4
3	Laredo, TX	27.1	2	Washington-Arlington-Alexandria, DC-VA-MD-WV	39.4
4	El Paso, TX	24.9	4	San Francisco-Oakland-Fremont, CA	35.1
5	Las Cruces, NM	20.5	5	Oxnard-Thousand Oaks-Ventura, CA	33.8
6	Visalia-Porterville, CA	18.8	6	Trenton-Ewing, NJ	32.8
7	El Centro, CA	18.5	7	Boston-Cambridge-Quincy, MA-NH	31.0
8	Monroe, LA	17.1	7	Napa, CA	31.0
9	Bakersfield, CA	16.9	9	Boulder, CO	29.9
10	Pine Bluff, AR	16.5	10	Santa Cruz-Watsonville, CA	29.5
11	Mobile, AL	16.4	11	New York-Northern New Jersey-Long Island, NY-NJ-PA	28.8
12	Fresno, CA	16.3	12	Poughkeepsie-Newburgh-Middletown, NY	28.5
12	Hattiesburg, MS	16.3	13	Manchester-Nashua, NH	28.0
14	Albany, GA	16.2	14	Hartford-West Hartford-East Hartford, CT	27.7
15	Merced, CA	16.1	15	Baltimore-Towson, MD	27.6
16	Columbus, GA-AL	16.0	16	Honolulu, HI	27.5
16	Danville, IL	16.0	17	Anchorage, AK	27.2
18	Jackson, TN	15.8	18	San Diego-Carlsbad-San Marcos, CA	26.8
19	Hinesville-Fort Stewart, GA	15.6	18	Vallejo-Fairfield, CA	26.8
20	College Station-Bryan, TX	15.5	20	Ann Arbor, MI	26.3
20	Shreveport-Bossier City, LA	15.5	20	Santa Rosa-Petaluma, CA	26.3
20	Yakima, WA	15.5	22	Minneapolis-St. Paul-Bloomington, MN-WI	26.2
20	Yuma, AZ	15.5	23	Seattle-Tacoma-Bellevue, WA	26.0
24	Corpus Christi, TX	15.4	24	Worcester, MA	25.7
24	Pueblo, CO	15.4	25	Los Angeles-Long Beach-Santa Ana, CA	25.4
24	Valdosta, GA	15.4	26	Norwich-New London, CT	25.3
27	Greenville, NC	15.3	27	Fairbanks, AK	25.0
28	Alexandria, LA	15.2	27	New Haven-Milford, CT	25.0
28	Rome, GA	15.2	27	Philadelphia-Camden-Wilmington, PA-NJ-DE-MD	25.0
30	Jonesboro, AR	15.1	30	Santa Barbara-Santa Maria-Goleta, CA	24.9
30	Lawton, OK	15.1	31	Raleigh-Cary, NC	24.7
32	Macon, GA	15.0	32	Chicago-Naperville-Joliet, IL-IN-WI	24.6
33	Hanford-Corcoran, CA	14.8	33	Naples-Marco Island, FL	24.1
33	Huntington Ashland, WV KY OH	14.8	34	Denver-Aurora, CO	24.0
33	Sumter, SC	14.8	34	Sacramento–Arden-Arcade–Roseville, CA	24.0
36	Fayetteville, NC	14.6	36	Salinas, CA	23.5
36	Odessa, TX	14.6	37	Atlanta-Sandy Springs-Marietta, GA	23.3
38	Tuscaloosa, AL	14.5	38	Austin-Round Rock, TX	22.7
39	Memphis, TN-MS-AR	14.4	39	Rochester, MN	22.5
40	Danville, VA	14.1	40	Dallas-Fort Worth-Arlington, TX	22.1
41	Florence-Muscle Shoals, AL	14.0	41	Houston-Sugar Land-Baytown, TX	22.0
41	Rocky Mount, NC	14.0	42	Barnstable Town, MA	21.9
43	Fort Smith, AR-OK	13.8	42	Madison, WI	21.9
43	Madera, CA	13.8	44	Richmond, VA	21.6
45	Florence, SC	13.7	45	Santa Fe, NM	21.5
46	Saginaw-Saginaw Township North, MI	13.6	46	Riverside-San Bernardino-Ontario, CA	21.4
47	Augusta-Richmond County, GA-SC	13.5	46	San Luis Obispo-Paso Robles, CA	21.4
47	Texarkana, TX-Texarkana, AR	13.5	48	Detroit-Warren-Livonia, MI	21.3
49	Farmington, NM	13.4	48	Providence-New Bedford-Fall River, RI-MA	21.3
49	Montgomery, AL	13.4	50	Fort Collins-Loveland, CO	21.2
49	Vineland-Millville-Bridgeton, NJ	13.4	51	Bremerton-Silverdale, WA	21.1
52	Anniston-Oxford, AL	13.3	52	Huntsville, AL	20.9
52	Beaumont-Port Arthur, TX	13.3	52	Kingston, NY	20.9
52	Lake Charles, LA	13.3	54	Burlington-South Burlington, VT	20.8
55	Houma-Bayou Cane-Thibodaux, LA	13.2	54	Stockton, CA	20.8
55	San Angelo, TX	13.2	56	Charlottesville, VA	20.4
57	Baton Rouge, LA	13.1	56	Colorado Springs, CO	20.4
57	Gadsden, AL	13.1	58	Albany-Schenectady-Troy, NY	20.3
59	Kingsport-Bristol-Bristol, TN-VA	13.0	58	Bloomington-Normal, IL	20.3
59	Owensboro, KY	13.0	58	Portland-Vancouver-Beaverton, OR-WA	20.3
59	Parkersburg-Marietta-Vienna, WV-OH	13.0	61	Allentown-Bethlehem-Easton, PA-NJ	20.2
59	Pascagoula, MS	13.0	61	Reno-Sparks, NV	20.2
59	Wheeling, WV-OH	13.0	63	Charlotte-Gastonia-Concord, NC-SC	20.0
64	Waco, TX	12.9	63	Phoenix-Mesa-Scottsdale, AZ	20.0
65	Joplin, MO	12.8	65	Atlantic City, NJ	19.8
65	Morristown, TN	12.8	66	Durham, NC	19.7
65	Pocatello, ID	12.8	66	Kansas City, MO-KS	19.7
68	Flint, MI	12.7	66	Olympia, WA	19.7
69	Battle Creek, MI	12.6	66	Salt Lake City, UT	19.7
69	Hot Springs, AR	12.6	70	Corvallis, OR	19.5
69	Lewiston, ID-WA	12.6	70	Kennewick-Richland-Pasco, WA	19.5
72	Goldsboro, NC	12.5	70	Las Vegas-Paradise, NV	19.5
73	Elmira, NY	12.4	73	Fort Walton Beach-Crestview-Destin, FL	19.4
73	Jackson, MS	12.4	74	Midland, TX	19.3
73	Johnson City, TN	12.4	74	Monroe, MI	19.3
73	Lafayette, LA	12.4	74	Ogden-Clearfield, UT	19.3
73	Niles-Benton Harbor, MI	12.4			
73	San Antonio, TX	12.4			

City Rankings, 2005–2007
Selected Rankings

High school diploma or less rank	City	Percent with a high school diploma or less [B-4, col 2]	Bachelor's degree or more rank	City	Percent with a bachelor's degree or more [B-4, col 3]	Unemployment rate rank	City	Unemployment rate [B-4, col 6]
	United States	46.0		United States	27.0		United States	6.6
1	Coachella city, CA	85.6	1	University Park city, TX	83.4	1	Muskegon city, MI	22.1
2	Cudahy city, CA	82.6	2	Mountain Brook city, AL	81.0	2	Detroit city, MI	21.6
2	Florence-Graham CDP, CA	82.6	3	Los Altos city, CA	80.7	3	Harvey city, IL	21.5
4	Lennox CDP, CA	82.0	4	Bethesda CDP, MD	80.5	4	Greenville city, MS	21.0
5	East Los Angeles CDP, CA	81.7	5	McLean CDP, VA	79.3	5	East St. Louis city, IL	20.9
6	Bridgeton city, NJ	81.3	6	Wellesley CDP, MA	79.1	5	San Luis city, AZ	20.9
7	Huntington Park city, CA	80.9	7	Palo Alto city, CA	77.7	7	Dolton village city, IL	19.7
8	Bell Gardens city, CA	80.3	8	West Lafayette city, IN	77.2	7	Portsmouth city, OH	19.7
9	Maywood city, CA	79.7	9	Potomac CDP, MD	77.1	9	Candler-McAfee CDP, GA	19.2
10	South Gate city, CA	79.6	10	Wilmette village, IL	76.9	10	Pontiac city, MI	19.0
11	San Luis city, AZ	79.3	11	Brookline CDP, MA	76.6	11	Lexington city, NC	18.6
12	Lynwood city, CA	78.6	12	Chapel Hill town, NC	75.8	12	Gary city, IN	17.9
13	Wasco city, CA	78.3	13	Lexington CDP, MA	75.6	13	Adelanto city, CA	17.7
14	Delano city, CA	78.0	14	Blacksburg town, VA	74.3	14	Chicago Heights city, IL	17.6
15	Bell city, CA	77.7	14	Mercer Island city, WA	74.3	15	Pine Bluff city, AK	17.3
15	Corcoran city, CA	77.7	16	Westport CDP, CT	74.2	16	Columbus city, MS	17.0
17	South El Monte city, CA	77.5	17	Lake Forest city, IL	74.1	17	Zanesville city, OH	16.9
18	San Juan city, TX	77.1	18	Saratoga city, CA	73.8	18	Carbondale city, IL	16.8
19	Camden city, NJ	76.5	19	Needham CDP, MA	73.6	18	Hartford city, CT	16.8
20	West Little River CDP, FL	75.8	20	Leawood city, KS	73.1	20	Griffin city, GA	16.4
21	Socorro city, TX	75.7	21	Ann Arbor city, MI	73.0	21	Cleveland city, OH	16.3
22	Soledad city, CA	75.2	21	Cupertino city, CA	73.0	21	Greenwood city, SC	16.3
23	Paterson city, NJ	74.2	21	North Potomac CDP, MD	73.0	23	Saginaw city, MI	16.2
24	Hamtramck city, MI	74.0	24	State College borough, PA	72.9	24	Camden city, NJ	16.1
25	Reading city, PA	73.9	25	Hoboken city, NJ	72.0	24	Youngstown city, OH	16.1
26	West Puente Valley CDP, CA	73.7	26	Newton city, MA	71.5	26	Romulus city, MI	16.0
27	La Puente city, CA	73.5	27	Darien CDP, CT	71.1	27	East Cleveland city, OH	15.6
28	Bloomington CDP, CA	72.9	28	Upper Arlington city, OH	70.9	28	Chester city, PA	15.4
28	Golden Gate CDP, FL	72.9	29	Dublin city, OH	70.8	29	Albany city, GA	15.2
30	Cicero town, IL	72.7	30	Radnor Township CDP, PA	70.6	30	Bridgeton city, NJ	14.9
31	Newburgh city, NY	72.6	31	Davis city, CA	70.4	30	Meridian city, MS	14.9
32	Baldwin Park city, CA	72.4	32	Manhattan Beach city, CA	70.2	32	Corsicana city, TX	14.8
33	Chester city, PA	72.3	33	Ridgewood village, NJ	70.1	33	Ruston city, LA	14.6
33	Marrero CDP, LA	72.3	34	Cambridge city, MA	69.8	34	Blue Island city, IL	14.5
35	Blythe city, CA	72.2	35	Belmont CDP, MA	69.7	34	Hamtramck city, MI	14.5
36	El Monte city, CA	71.8	35	Bloomfield Township CDP, MI	69.7	34	Los Banos city, CA	14.5
36	Paramount city, CA	71.8	37	Brentwood city, TN	69.1	34	West Pensacola CDP, FL	14.5
38	Santa Ana city, CA	71.7	37	Dunwoody CDP, GA	69.1	38	York city, PA	14.4
39	Compton city, CA	71.4	39	Lafayette city, CA	69.0	39	East Orange city, NJ	14.3
39	Trenton city, NJ	71.4	40	Hudson city, OH	68.9	39	Kalamazoo city, MI	14.3
41	Cloverleaf CDP, TX	71.2	41	Pullman city, WA	68.7	39	Opelousas city, LA	14.3
41	Pharr city, TX	71.2	41	Southlake city, TX	68.7	39	Wasco city, CA	14.3
41	Willowbrook CDP, CA	71.2	43	Oakton CDP, VA	68.6	43	Taylor city, MI	14.2
44	Lebanon city, PA	71.0	44	Boulder city, CO	68.4	44	Adrian city, MI	14.1
45	Newark city, NJ	70.0	44	Okemos CDP, MI	68.4	44	Lorain city, OH	14.1
46	Watsonville city, CA	69.9	46	Reston CDP, VA	68.3	44	Millville city, NJ	14.1
46	York city, PA	69.9	46	Sammamish city, WA	68.3	44	Parkway-South Sacramento CDP, CA	14.1
48	Valinda CDP, CA	69.8	48	East Lansing city, MI	68.1	48	Calumet city, IL	14.0
48	West Whittier-Los Nietos CDP, CA	69.8	49	Menlo Park city, CA	67.3	48	Trenton city, NJ	14.0
50	Madera city, CA	69.7	49	Winchester CDP, MA	67.3	50	Petersburg city, VA	13.9
50	Opelousas city, LA	69.7	51	Arlington CDP, VA	67.0	51	Flint city, MI	13.8
52	Chelsea city, MA	69.6	52	La Canada Flintridge city, CA	66.9	51	Sumter city, SC	13.8
53	Lawrence city, MA	69.4	53	Upper St. Clair CDP, PA	66.6	53	Atlantic city, NJ	13.6
53	Parkway-South Sacramento CDP, CA	69.4	54	Lake Oswego city, OR	66.4	53	Montclair city, CA	13.6
53	Prichard city, AL	69.4	55	Marblehead CDP, MA	66.0	55	Marion city, IN	13.5
56	Adelanto city, CA	69.3	56	Johns Creek city, GA	65.5	55	Paducah city, KY	13.5
56	Passaic city, NJ	69.3	57	Berkeley city, CA	65.4	55	Port Huron city, MI	13.5
58	San Fernando city, CA	69.2	57	Livingston CDP, NJ	65.4	58	Lima city, OH	13.4
59	Forest Park city, GA	69.1	57	North Bethesda CDP, MD	65.4	58	Muncie city, IN	13.4
60	Perris city, CA	69.0	57	Northbrook village, IL	65.4	58	Prichard city, AL	13.4
61	Johnstown city, PA	68.9	61	Garden City village, NY	65.2	61	Burton city, MI	13.3
62	Elizabeth city, NJ	68.8	62	Bainbridge Island city, WA	64.5	61	Pahrump CDP, NV	13.3
63	East Chicago city, IN	68.7	62	Colleyville city, TX	64.5	61	Riverbank city, CA	13.3
63	Mira Loma CDP, CA	68.7	64	Ithaca city, NY	64.3	61	Turlock city, CA	13.3
65	Dundalk CDP, MD	68.4	65	Westfield town, NJ	64.1	65	Danville city, IL	13.2
66	Woodburn city, OR	68.3	66	Catalina Foothills CDP, AZ	64.0	65	Dayton city, OH	13.2
67	New Bedford city, MA	68.2	67	Coppell city, TX	63.9	67	Hanford city, CA	13.1
67	Rosemead city, CA	68.2	67	Evanston city, IL	63.9	68	Delano city, CA	13.0
69	Perth Amboy city, NJ	68.0	67	Fishers town, IN	63.9	68	East Chicago city, IN	13.0
70	Hialeah city, FL	67.9	67	Naperville city, IL	63.9	68	Kankakee city, IL	13.0
71	Marion city, OH	67.7	71	Summit city, NJ	63.8	68	Lincoln Park city, MI	13.0
71	Melrose Park village, IL	67.7	71	Wildwood city, MO	63.8	68	New Orleans city, LA	13.0
73	Hartford city, CT	67.6	73	Glenview village, IL	63.6	68	Spanish Lake CDP, MO	13.0
74	Del Rio city, TX	67.5	73	Webster Groves city, MO	63.6	74	McMinnville city, OR	12.9
74	Hamilton city, OH	67.5	75	Mequon city, WI	63.4	74	Monroe city, LA	12.9
74	New Iberia city, LA	67.5				74	Porterville city, CA	12.9
						74	Vicksburg city, MS	12.9

City Rankings, 2005–2007
Selected Rankings

Families with income below poverty rank	City	Percent of families with income below poverty [B-4, col 10]	Households with income less than $25,000 rank	City	Percent of households with income less than $25,000 [B-4, col 11]	Households with income of $100,000 or more rank	City	Percent of households with income of $100,000 or more [B-4, col 12]
	United States	9.8		United States	24.5		United States	19.0
1	Kiryas Joel village, NY	61.5	1	Kiryas Joel village, NY	64.9	1	Southlake city, TX	79.6
2	Opelousas city, LA	39.4	2	Carbondale city, IL	62.3	2	McLean CDP, VA	71.5
3	Camden city, NJ	37.9	3	Opelousas city, LA	60.4	3	Colleyville city, TX	70.6
4	Brownsville city, TX	36.6	4	Statesboro city, GA	57.0	4	Potomac CDP, MD	70.3
5	Pharr city, TX	36.1	5	Portsmouth city, OH	56.8	5	North Potomac CDP, MD	69.8
6	Carbondale city, IL	34.5	6	State College borough, PA	56.3	6	Darien CDP, CT	68.5
7	Chester city, PA	33.8	7	Prichard city, AL	55.5	7	Cottage Lake CDP, WA	68.0
7	University CDP, FL	33.8	8	Athens city, OH	54.9	7	Westport CDP, CT	68.0
9	Lakewood CDP, NJ	33.4	9	East St. Louis city, IL	54.8	9	Los Altos city, CA	67.6
10	East St. Louis city, IL	31.8	10	Charleston city, IL	54.3	10	Saratoga city, CA	65.8
10	Hamtramck city, MI	31.8	11	East Cleveland city, OH	53.3	11	Dix Hills CDP, NY	65.5
12	San Juan city, TX	31.6	12	Pullman city, WA	53.2	12	Lake Forest city, IL	65.4
13	Prichard city, AL	31.3	13	Camden city, NJ	52.8	13	Brentwood city, TN	65.1
13	Socorro city, TX	31.3	14	Hamtramck city, MI	52.0	14	Sammamish city, WA	64.9
13	West Memphis city, AR	31.3	15	University CDP, FL	51.9	15	Garden City village, NY	63.9
16	Saginaw city, MI	31.1	16	Oxford city, OH	51.8	16	University Park city, TX	63.4
16	Weslaco city, TX	31.1	17	McKeesport city, PA	51.0	17	Danville town, CA	63.1
18	Homestead city, FL	30.7	18	Meridian city, MS	50.5	18	Mountain Brook city, AL	62.9
19	Edinburg city, TX	30.3	19	Johnstown city, PA	50.4	19	Linton Hall CDP, VA	62.2
20	Westmont CDP, CA	29.9	20	Ruston city, LA	50.3	20	La Canada Flintridge city, CA	62.1
21	Reading city, PA	29.0	21	West Lafayette city, IN	50.2	21	Lexington CDP, MA	61.9
21	Rexburg city, ID	29.0	21	Youngstown city, OH	50.2	22	Manhattan Beach city, CA	61.8
23	Lumberton city, NC	28.9	23	Kinston city, NC	49.7	23	Wellesley CDP, MA	60.9
24	Hartford city, CT	28.8	24	Starkville city, MS	49.5	24	Leawood city, KS	60.8
25	College Park city, GA	28.5	25	Chester city, PA	49.3	24	Newington CDP, VA	60.8
26	Greenville city, MS	28.4	26	Nacogdoches city, TX	48.9	24	Wilmette village, IL	60.8
27	East Cleveland city, OH	28.3	27	Paducah city, KY	48.8	27	Olney CDP, MD	60.5
27	Holyoke city, MA	28.3	28	Saginaw city, MI	48.7	28	El Dorado Hills CDP, CA	60.4
29	San Luis city, AZ	28.2	28	San Luis city, AZ	48.7	29	Burke CDP, VA	59.1
29	York city, PA	28.2	30	West Memphis city, AR	48.2	29	New City CDP, NY	59.1
31	Flint city, MI	28.0	31	Pharr city, TX	48.0	31	Ridgewood village, NJ	58.9
31	San Benito city, TX	28.0	32	Gadsden city, AL	47.8	32	Yorba Linda city, CA	58.6
33	Florence-Graham CDP, CA	27.9	33	Greenville city, MS	47.7	33	Livingston CDP, NJ	58.5
33	Lawrence city, MA	27.9	34	West Pensacola CDP, FL	47.6	34	Bloomfield Township CDP, MI	58.3
35	Meridian city, MS	27.7	34	Brownsville city, TX	47.4	34	Cupertino city, CA	58.3
35	Portsmouth city, OH	27.7	36	Lumberton city, NC	47.3	36	Germantown city, TN	58.2
37	Wasco city, CA	27.3	36	Morgantown city, WV	47.3	37	Lafayette city, CA	58.0
38	Jackson city, MI	27.2	38	Cleveland city, OH	47.0	38	Summit city, NJ	57.8
38	Monroe city, LA	27.2	38	Milledgeville city, GA	47.0	39	Bethesda CDP, MD	57.7
40	Detroit city, MI	27.1	40	Gary city, IN	46.9	39	Northbrook village, IL	57.7
40	Hattiesburg city, MS	27.1	40	San Benito city, TX	46.9	39	Westfield town, NJ	57.7
42	East Chicago city, IN	26.7	42	Reading city, PA	46.7	42	Merrick CDP, NY	57.6
42	Laredo city, TX	26.7	43	Monroe city, LA	46.6	43	Granite Bay CDP, CA	57.5
42	Willowbrook CDP, CA	26.7	44	Macon city, GA	46.3	44	San Ramon city, CA	57.4
45	Kinston city, NC	26.6	45	Bessemer city, AL	46.2	45	Palo Alto city, CA	57.3
46	Corsicana city, TX	26.5	45	College Station city, TX	46.2	46	North Tustin CDP, CA	57.2
46	Gary city, IN	26.5	47	Stillwater city, OK	46.1	46	Wildwood city, MO	57.2
48	Eagle Pass city, TX	26.4	47	Vicksburg city, MS	46.1	48	Needham CDP, MA	57.0
49	Harlingen city, TX	26.0	47	Williamsport city, PA	46.1	49	Pleasanton city, CA	56.9
49	Macon city, GA	26.0	50	San Marcos city, TX	46.0	50	Los Gatos town, CA	56.3
51	Harrisburg city, PA	25.7	51	Hartford city, CT	45.9	51	Highland Park city, IL	56.2
51	Kingsville city, TX	25.7	51	Zanesville city, OH	45.9	52	Hudson city, OH	56.1
53	Rochester city, NY	25.6	53	Mount Pleasant city, MI	45.8	53	Brushy Creek CDP, TX	55.9
53	Syracuse city, NY	25.6	53	Tuscaloosa city, AL	45.8	54	Keller city, TX	55.8
55	Marshall city, TX	25.5	55	Huntsville city, TX	45.7	55	Dublin city, OH	55.6
56	West Pensacola CDP, FL	25.3	55	Syracuse city, NY	45.7	55	Johns Creek city, GA	55.6
57	Cleveland city, OH	25.2	57	Alexandria city, LA	45.6	57	Dublin city, CA	55.5
57	Lennox CDP, CA	25.2	58	Huntington city, WV	45.3	58	Severna Park CDP, MD	55.1
59	Elmira city, NY	25.1	58	West Little River CDP, FL	45.3	59	Rancho Palos Verdes city, CA	54.9
59	Passaic city, NJ	25.1	60	Binghamton city, NY	45.2	60	Coppell city, TX	54.8
61	Parkway-South Sacramento CDP, CA	25.0	60	Kent city, OH	45.2	61	Mercer Island city, WA	54.7
61	Youngstown city, OH	25.0	60	Miami city, FL	45.2	62	Keystone CDP, FL	54.6
63	McKeesport city, PA	24.9	63	Bloomington city, IN	45.1	63	Flower Mound town, TX	54.5
64	Newburgh city, NY	24.8	64	Socorro city, TX	45.0	63	Libertyville village, IL	54.5
65	Dayton city, OH	24.3	65	East Chicago city, IN	44.9	65	Agoura Hills city, CA	54.2
65	Emporia city, KS	24.3	65	Weslaco city, TX	44.9	65	Fort Washington CDP, MD	54.2
65	Paducah city, KY	24.3	65	Westmont CDP, CA	44.9	67	Newport Beach city, CA	54.1
68	Springfield city, MA	24.2	65	Wilkes-Barre city, PA	44.9	68	Plainview CDP, NY	53.9
69	Ruston city, LA	24.1	69	Flint city, MI	44.8	69	Oakton CDP, VA	53.8
70	Corcoran city, CA	24.0	69	Hot Springs city, AR	44.8	70	Chantilly CDP, VA	53.6
70	Danville city, IL	24.0	69	Morristown city, TN	44.8	71	Parkland city, FL	53.5
70	McAllen city, TX	24.0	72	Hattiesburg city, MS	44.7	72	Ellicott City CDP, MD	52.3
73	Bridgeton city, NJ	23.9	73	Buffalo city, NY	44.6	73	Commack CDP, NY	52.2
73	Spartanburg city, SC	23.9	74	Dayton city, OH	44.5	74	Calabasas city, CA	52.1
75	Adelanto city, CA	23.7	75	Muncie city, IN	44.4	74	Newton city, MA	52.1
75	Bessemer city, AL	23.7	75	York city, PA	44.4			
75	Binghamton city, NY	23.7						

Table B-1. States — What: Education, Employment, and Income, 2005–2007

State code	STATE	Educational attainment (percent)						School enrollment by level of school			
		Total population 25 years and over	No high school diploma	High school graduate	Some college or associate's degree	Bachelor's degree	Graduate or professional degree	Total enrolled in school	Percent enrolled in preschool	Percent enrolled in grades K-12	Percent enrolled in college or graduate school
	ACS table number:	C15002	C15002	C15002	C15002	C15002	C15002	C14002	C14002	C14002	C14002
		1	2	3	4	5	6	7	8	9	10

Table B-1. States — What: Education, Employment, and Income, 2005–2007—*Continued*

STATE	Percent enrolled in private schools by level of school									Labor force participation (percent)		
	All levels	Preschool, nursery school	Kinder-garten	Grades 1–8	Grades 9–12	College, under-graduate	Graduate or professional school	Total population 16 years and over	Total labor force	Total	Men	Women
ACS table number:	C14002	C14002	C14002	C14002	C14002	C14002	C14002	C20005	C23001	C23001	C23001	C23001
	11	12	13	14	15	16	17	18	19	20	21	22

Table B-1. States — What: Education, Employment, and Income, 2005–2007—*Continued*

STATE	Unemployment rates by age (percent unemployed)				Total labor force 25 to 64 years	Unemployment rates for the labor force age 25 to 64 by educational attainment				
						Unemployment rate (percent unemployed)				
	Total labor force	16 to 24 years	25 to 64 years	65 years and over		Total 25 to 64 years	No high school diploma	High school graduate	Some college or associate's degree	Bachelor's degree or higher
ACS table number:	C23001	C23001	C23001	C23001	B23006	B23006	B23006	B23006	B23006	B23006
	23	24	25	26	27	28	29	30	31	32

Table B-1. States — What: Education, Employment, and Income, 2005–2007—*Continued*

STATE	Total population 16 to 19 years	16 to 19 years not enrolled in school, not h.s. graduate, not in labor force	Total population 16 years and over	Percent of population 16 years and over who worked full-time, year-round in the past 12 months			Total households	Percent of house-holds with no workers	Children under 18 years in families			
				Total	Male	Female			Number	Percent living with two parents, both in labor force	Percent living with two parents, father only in labor force	Percent living with one parent, who is in labor force
ACS table number:	C14005	C14005	C20005	C20005	C20005	C20005	C08202	C08202	C23008	C23008	C23008	C23008
	33	34	35	36	37	38	39	40	41	42	43	44

Table B-1. States — What: Education, Employment, and Income, 2005–2007—*Continued*

STATE	Family status of children under 18 years, by employment status of parents and age of children								Employment status of family householders				
	Children under 6 years in families				Children 6–17 years in families					Married-couple families		Other families	
	Number	Percent living with two parents, both in labor force	Percent living with two parents, father only in labor force	Percent living with one parent, who is in labor force	Number	Percent living with two parents, both in labor force	Percent living with two parents, father only in labor force	Percent living with one parent, who is in labor force	Total families	Total	Percent with both in the labor force	Total	Percent with house-holder in the labor force
ACS table number:	C23008	C23008	C23008	C23008	C23008	C23008	C23008	C23008	C23007	C23007	C23007	C23007	C23007
	45	46	47	48	49	50	51	52	53	54	55	56	57

Table B-1. States — What: Education, Employment, and Income, 2005–2007—*Continued*

STATE	Women 20 to 64 years in households by presence of children and labor force status			Class of worker for employed civilians 16 years and over				Occupation (percent)			
	Total women 20 to 64 years in house-holds	Percent with children under 18 years	Percent with children under 18 years in labor force	Civilian employed population 16 years and over	Percent private wage and salary workers	Percent government workers	Percent self-employed and unpaid workers	Civilian employed population 16 years and over	Manage-ment, professional, and related	Service	Sales and office
ACS table number:	B23003	B23003	B23003	C24080	C24080	C24080	C24080	C24060	C24060	C24060	C24060
	58	59	60	61	62	63	64	65	66	67	68

Table B-1. States — What: Education, Employment, and Income, 2005–2007—*Continued*

STATE	Occupation (percent)			Industry (percent)							
	Farming, fishing, and forestry	Construction extraction, maintenance, and repair	Production, transportation, and material moving	Agriculture, forestry, fishing and hunting, and mining	Construction	Manufacturing	Wholesale trade	Retail trade	Transportation and warehousing, and utilities	Information	Finance and insurance and real estate and rental and leasing
ACS table number:	C24060	C24060	C24060	C24070	C24070	C24070	C24070	C24070	C24070	C24070	C24070
	69	70	71	72	73	74	75	76	77	78	79

Table B-1. States — What: Education, Employment, and Income, 2005–2007—*Continued*

STATE	Industry (percent)						Median income in the past 12 months (in 2007 inflation-adjusted dollars)				
								Median household income by age of householder			
	Professional, scientific, and management, and administrative and waste management	Educational services, and health care and social assistance	Arts, enter-tainment, and recre-ation, and accommoda-tion and food services	Other services, except public administra-tion	Public administration	Veterans as a percent of the population 18 years and over	All households	House-holder under 25 years	Householder 25 to 44 years	Householder 45 to 64 years	Householder 65 years and over
ACS table number:	C24070	C24070	C24070	C24070	C24070	B21002	B19049	B19049	B19049	B19049	B19049
	80	81	82	83	84	85	86	87	88	89	90

Table B-1. States — What: Education, Employment, and Income, 2005–2007—*Continued*

STATE	Median income in the past 12 months (in 2007 inflation-adjusted dollars)								
	Median household income by race and Hispanic origin of householder								
	White alone	Black alone	Amer. Indian, Alaska Native alone	Asian alone	Native Hawaiian and other Pacific Islander alone	Some other race alone	Two or more races	White alone, not Hispanic or Latino	Hispanic or Latino
ACS table number:	B19013A	B19013B	B19013C	B19013D	B19013E	B19013F	B19013G	B19013H	B19013I
	91	92	93	94	95	96	97	98	99

Table B-1. States — What: Education, Employment, and Income, 2005–2007—*Continued*

STATE	Median income in the past 12 months (in 2007 inflation-adjusted dollars)											
	Median family income by type of family							Median nonfamily household income			Median individual income	
	All families	Married-couple families with children	Married-couple families, no children	Male house-holder with children	Male householder, no children	Female householder with children	Female house-holder, no children	All nonfamily house-holds	Living alone, 65 years and over		Persons 15 years and over who worked full-time, year-round	
									Male	Female	Male	Female
ACS table number:	B19126	B19126	B19126	B19126	B19126	B19126	B19126	B19215	B19215	B19215	B19326	B19326
	100	101	102	103	104	105	106	107	108	109	110	111

Table B-1. States — What: Education, Employment, and Income, 2005–2007—*Continued*

STATE	Per capita income in the past 12 months (in 2007 inflation-adjusted dollars)	Households by type of income (percent)									
		Total number of households	With wage or salary income	With self-employment income	With interest, dividends, or net rental income	With Social Security	With Supple-mental Security Income (SSI)	With public assistance income	With cash public assistance or Food Stamps	With retirement income	With other types of income
ACS table number:	B19301	B19052	B19052	B19053	B19054	B19055	B19056	B19057	B19058	B19059	B19060
	112	113	114	115	116	117	118	119	120	121	122

Table B-1. States — What: Education, Employment, and Income, 2005–2007—*Continued*

STATE	Household income in the past 12 months (in 2007 inflation-adjusted dollars)										
	Households by income group (percent)										
	Total number of households	Less than $10,000	$10,000 to $14,999	$15,000 to $24,999	$25,000 to $34,999	$35,000 to $49,999	$50,000 to $74,999	$75,000 to $99,999	$100,000 to $149,999	$150,000 to $199,999	$200,000 or more
ACS table number:	C19001	C19001	C19001	C19001	C19001	C19001	C19001	C19001	C19001	C19001	C19001
	123	124	125	126	127	128	129	130	131	132	133

Table B-1. States — What: Education, Employment, and Income, 2005–2007—Continued

STATE	Households with income over $100,000 by age of householder (percent)					Total households with income below poverty as a percent of all households in group						
	All households	Householder under 25 years	Householder 25 to 44 years	Householder 45 to 64 years	Householder 65 years and over	All households	Family households	Married-couple family household	Male householder family households	Female householder family households	Male householder nonfamily households	Female householder nonfamily households
ACS table number:	C19001	C19037	C19037	C19037	C19037	C17017	C17017	C17017	C17017	C17017	C17017	C17017
	134	135	136	137	138	139	140	141	142	143	144	145

Table B-1. States — What: Education, Employment, and Income, 2005–2007—Continued

STATE	Population for whom poverty status is determined	Persons with income below poverty by age (percent of persons in group)				Persons with income below poverty by selected race and Hispanic origin groups (percent of persons in group)			
		All persons	Under 18 years	18 to 64 years	65 years and over	White alone, not Hispanic or Latino	Black alone	Asian alone	Hispanic or Latino
ACS table number:	C17001	C17001	C17001	C17001	C17001	C17001H	C17001B	C17001D	C17001I
	146	147	148	149	150	151	152	153	154

Table B-2. Counties — What: Education, Employment, and Income, 2005–2007

STATE County code	STATE County	Educational attainment			Employment status				Percent of households with no workers	Median household income (dollars)	Percent of families with income below poverty	Percent of households with income less than $25,000	Percent of households with income of $100,000 or more
		Total population 25 years and over	Percent with a high school diploma or less	Percent with a bachelor's degree or more	Total population 16 years and over	Percent in the labor force	Unemployment rate	Percent who worked full-time, year-round					
ACS table number:		C15002	C15002	C15002	C20005	C23001	C23001	C20005	C08202	B19013	C17015	C19001	C19001
		1	2	3	4	5	6	7	8	9	10	11	12

Table B-3. Metropolitan Areas — What: Education, Employment, and Income, 2005–2007

Metro area or division code	Area name	Educational attainment			Employment status				Percent of households with no workers	Median household income (dollars)	Percent of families with income below poverty	Percent of households with income less than $25,000	Percent of households with income of $100,000 or more
		Total population 25 years and over	Percent with a high school diploma or less	Percent with a bachelor's degree or more	Total population 16 years and over	Percent in the labor force	Unemployment rate	Percent who worked full-time, year-round					
ACS table number:		C15002	C15002	C15002	C20005	C23001	C23001	C20005	C08202	B19013	C17015	C19001	C19001
		1	2	3	4	5	6	7	8	9	10	11	12

Table B-4. Cities — What: Education, Employment, and Income, 2005–2007

STATE Place code	STATE City	Educational attainment			Employment status				Percent of households with no workers	Median household income (dollars)	Percent of families with income below poverty	Percent of households with income less than $25,000	Percent of households with income of $100,000 or more
		Total population 25 years and over	Percent with a high school diploma or less	Percent with a bachelor's degree or more	Total population 16 years and over	Percent in the labor force	Unemployment rate	Percent who worked full-time, year-round					
ACS table number:		C15002	C15002	C15002	C20005	C23001	C23001	C20005	C08202	B19013	C17015	C19001	C19001
		1	2	3	4	5	6	7	8	9	10	11	12

Table B-1. States — What: Education, Employment, and Income, 2005–2007

State code	STATE	Educational attainment (percent)						School enrollment by level of school			
		Total population 25 years and over	No high school diploma	High school graduate	Some college or associate's degree	Bachelor's degree	Graduate or professional degree	Total enrolled in school	Percent enrolled in preschool	Percent enrolled in grades K-12	Percent enrolled in college or graduate school
	ACS table number:	C15002	C15002	C15002	C15002	C15002	C15002	C14002	C14002	C14002	C14002
		1	2	3	4	5	6	7	8	9	10
00	United States............	195,646,383	16.0	30.0	27.0	17.1	9.9	78,992,572	6.2	67.7	26.1
01	Alabama......................	3,015,910	20.0	32.3	26.6	13.3	7.8	1,165,158	6.0	69.6	24.4
02	Alaska........................	418,136	9.8	29.6	34.4	16.5	9.7	188,536	5.7	70.6	23.7
04	Arizona......................	3,949,023	16.5	26.5	31.7	16.1	9.2	1,613,255	5.3	70.2	24.5
05	Arkansas....................	1,842,453	19.4	35.9	26.1	12.4	6.3	703,521	6.8	70.1	23.1
06	California..................	23,080,916	20.0	22.9	28.0	18.7	10.4	10,341,546	5.6	66.9	27.4
08	Colorado....................	3,130,207	11.7	24.6	29.1	22.4	12.3	1,234,798	6.3	66.6	27.0
09	Connecticut................	2,349,541	12.2	29.6	23.9	19.4	14.8	938,101	6.8	66.4	26.8
10	Delaware	565,305	14.1	33.5	25.8	16.0	10.6	218,735	6.2	66.1	27.7
11	District of Columbia...	397,937	15.9	21.4	17.3	20.4	25.0	148,220	5.7	55.0	39.3
12	Florida......................	12,412,464	15.6	31.1	28.1	16.4	8.8	4,270,716	6.7	67.9	25.4
13	Georgia	5,945,347	17.8	30.3	25.4	17.3	9.3	2,531,690	7.4	69.2	23.4
15	Hawaii.......................	867,609	11.3	30.1	30.0	19.1	9.5	311,839	6.0	66.4	27.7
16	Idaho........................	917,853	12.6	29.9	33.8	16.3	7.3	392,020	5.0	71.5	23.5
17	Illinois......................	8,292,894	14.8	28.8	27.4	18.2	10.8	3,527,163	7.0	66.1	27.0
18	Indiana......................	4,107,829	14.8	37.1	26.5	13.7	7.9	1,656,822	6.1	68.5	25.4
19	Iowa.........................	1,951,982	10.8	35.7	29.5	16.5	7.5	781,872	6.6	66.2	27.3
20	Kansas.......................	1,773,908	11.5	30.3	29.9	18.6	9.7	757,770	6.4	66.0	27.6
21	Kentucky....................	2,808,673	20.7	34.8	24.8	11.7	8.0	1,042,674	5.8	69.6	24.6
22	Louisiana	2,766,825	20.6	35.3	24.0	13.3	6.8	1,159,395	6.9	69.8	23.2
23	Maine.......................	917,697	11.2	36.4	26.5	17.0	8.9	309,492	4.8	68.8	26.4
24	Maryland	3,699,555	13.1	27.0	25.2	19.3	15.4	1,517,786	6.1	65.3	28.6
25	Massachusetts	4,355,378	12.1	27.9	22.9	21.4	15.7	1,706,541	6.7	63.0	30.3
26	Michigan....................	6,634,147	13.0	32.2	30.3	15.1	9.3	2,771,385	5.5	67.2	27.3
27	Minnesota	3,385,006	9.3	28.5	31.7	20.9	9.7	1,352,061	6.3	67.8	25.9
28	Mississippi.................	1,829,680	22.0	31.9	27.5	12.2	6.4	789,041	6.9	70.5	22.6
29	Missouri.....................	3,847,339	15.1	33.7	27.2	15.4	8.6	1,493,074	6.4	69.0	24.7
30	Montana....................	631,746	9.9	32.3	31.0	18.5	8.2	231,491	5.2	69.0	25.7
31	Nebraska	1,131,474	10.6	30.8	31.4	18.7	8.5	476,770	6.0	66.7	27.4
32	Nevada......................	1,640,801	16.6	31.3	31.2	13.9	7.0	595,071	4.2	75.2	20.7
33	New Hampshire	889,007	10.1	30.9	27.2	20.4	11.3	336,090	5.8	67.4	26.8
34	New Jersey................	5,835,145	13.7	30.4	22.2	21.2	12.4	2,264,786	7.9	67.6	24.6
35	New Mexico..............	1,240,342	18.3	28.3	28.5	14.3	10.6	534,002	5.3	67.2	27.5
36	New York...................	12,866,461	16.1	29.6	23.1	17.9	13.3	5,104,805	6.0	65.4	28.6
37	North Carolina...........	5,849,056	17.8	29.6	27.6	16.8	8.3	2,297,020	6.1	67.7	26.2
38	North Dakota.............	411,298	11.9	29.1	33.4	19.0	6.6	167,560	4.4	61.9	33.7
39	Ohio	7,598,399	13.7	36.9	26.1	14.8	8.5	2,992,816	6.0	68.0	26.0
40	Oklahoma..................	2,311,130	15.8	33.1	28.9	15.0	7.3	927,941	6.2	68.6	25.2
41	Oregon......................	2,496,987	12.5	26.9	33.0	17.6	10.0	906,278	5.3	68.4	26.3
42	Pennsylvania	8,404,685	13.7	38.6	22.2	15.8	9.7	3,096,168	5.9	66.8	27.3
44	Rhode Island..............	711,837	17.3	29.3	24.0	17.9	11.5	285,185	5.2	61.2	33.7
45	South Carolina...........	2,851,898	18.6	32.4	26.1	14.9	7.9	1,092,652	5.7	70.5	23.8
46	South Dakota.............	509,779	11.7	33.6	30.1	17.5	7.0	202,347	6.5	68.6	24.9
47	Tennessee	4,061,516	19.1	34.3	24.9	14.1	7.6	1,469,527	5.4	71.4	23.2
48	Texas........................	14,482,842	21.4	27.0	26.9	16.7	8.1	6,524,040	6.6	70.4	23.0
49	Utah.........................	1,449,914	10.0	26.3	35.5	19.2	9.0	825,539	6.0	65.9	28.2
50	Vermont	424,832	10.3	32.4	24.6	20.0	12.7	156,755	5.9	64.6	29.6
51	Virginia.....................	5,053,592	14.7	27.1	25.3	19.6	13.3	1,998,510	6.3	65.6	28.2
53	Washington	4,243,790	11.1	25.6	33.3	19.4	10.6	1,603,163	5.7	69.0	25.3
54	West Virginia	1,257,231	19.0	41.9	22.3	10.2	6.6	409,933	5.4	68.7	25.9
55	Wisconsin	3,692,408	11.5	34.6	28.7	16.8	8.3	1,440,653	5.2	68.2	26.6
56	Wyoming...................	336,599	9.5	32.6	34.7	15.6	7.6	130,259	6.3	68.2	25.5

Table B-1. States — What: Education, Employment, and Income, 2005–2007—*Continued*

STATE	Percent enrolled in private schools by level of school							Total population 16 years and over	Total labor force	Labor force participation (percent)		
	All levels	Preschool, nursery school	Kinder-garten	Grades 1–8	Grades 9–12	College, under-graduate	Graduate or professional school			Total	Men	Women
ACS table number:	C14002	C14002	C14002	C14002	C14002	C14002	C14002	C20005	C23001	C23001	C23001	C23001
	11	12	13	14	15	16	17	18	19	20	21	22
United States	16.9	46.1	13.9	11.0	9.5	23.2	40.3	233,658,279	151,062,383	64.7	71.2	58.4
Alabama	14.9	49.2	17.6	11.0	11.4	14.9	18.9	3,596,728	2,158,683	60.0	67.2	53.4
Alaska........................	11.4	45.9	12.9	7.3	6.3	13.9	20.3	516,556	368,891	71.4	76.4	66.0
Arizona......................	11.1	42.2	9.4	6.3	6.3	14.8	29.4	4,704,044	2,942,422	62.6	69.8	55.3
Arkansas....................	11.2	33.4	9.6	7.8	6.8	15.3	18.4	2,190,608	1,338,876	61.1	67.2	55.4
California...................	14.2	44.9	12.3	9.5	7.9	16.2	42.2	27,949,362	17,924,457	64.1	71.7	56.7
Colorado	13.9	44.6	11.6	8.2	8.1	17.1	34.1	3,722,302	2,599,647	69.8	76.2	63.4
Connecticut...............	21.5	50.8	12.8	9.7	10.7	38.8	54.2	2,768,150	1,866,542	67.4	73.6	61.8
Delaware	21.6	55.4	24.6	18.3	15.2	18.9	44.7	671,869	435,403	64.8	70.9	59.3
District of Columbia...	37.9	44.5	25.1	19.2	18.4	54.2	79.1	483,781	321,698	66.5	70.8	62.8
Florida	18.3	54.2	15.8	12.5	10.3	22.9	39.7	14,471,701	8,784,451	60.7	67.0	54.8
Georgia	15.8	43.8	13.4	9.9	9.1	21.8	36.8	7,131,317	4,694,864	65.8	72.6	59.5
Hawaii	24.0	65.8	20.7	18.2	18.5	26.4	37.5	1,025,421	673,009	65.6	71.8	59.4
Idaho	13.1	53.0	9.7	7.6	6.1	22.4	22.5	1,108,188	730,360	65.9	72.9	58.9
Illinois	19.5	40.4	16.4	12.5	10.4	28.1	48.8	9,946,551	6,599,900	66.4	72.9	60.1
Indiana	17.1	51.1	15.4	12.6	8.9	22.9	26.5	4,900,909	3,222,941	65.8	72.2	59.6
Iowa	16.3	36.6	10.7	10.2	7.1	28.0	32.8	2,346,630	1,611,994	68.7	74.2	63.5
Kansas	14.2	39.8	13.7	11.4	7.9	16.3	22.5	2,143,455	1,469,617	68.6	74.9	62.5
Kentucky	15.3	35.5	14.0	12.5	10.9	18.8	24.6	3,316,988	2,019,501	60.9	67.1	55.1
Louisiana	18.6	37.2	19.0	17.0	16.2	17.1	23.7	3,371,197	2,048,978	60.8	66.9	55.2
Maine	16.2	47.5	9.3	7.5	10.6	29.4	33.0	1,069,271	700,027	65.5	70.9	60.4
Maryland	22.2	58.0	21.4	17.5	14.0	22.8	43.6	4,396,011	3,019,455	68.7	74.2	63.7
Massachusetts	27.8	55.1	15.4	11.3	13.8	48.8	69.9	5,167,254	3,458,626	66.9	72.7	61.7
Michigan	13.6	35.0	12.5	10.7	8.0	17.1	24.2	7,915,981	5,029,931	63.5	69.0	58.4
Minnesota	17.4	39.4	15.0	12.1	8.1	26.1	41.9	4,046,604	2,872,156	71.0	76.0	66.1
Mississippi.................	12.5	32.8	14.6	9.8	10.0	11.9	23.0	2,230,412	1,337,301	60.0	65.7	54.8
Missouri	19.2	42.4	14.9	14.3	11.5	26.4	43.9	4,578,206	2,981,717	65.1	70.8	59.8
Montana....................	11.1	49.7	10.9	7.8	6.4	12.0	18.6	754,965	493,585	65.4	70.3	60.5
Nebraska	17.7	49.2	13.9	14.0	10.4	21.1	29.4	1,370,844	969,211	70.7	76.9	64.7
Nevada	9.4	46.5	9.7	4.6	4.6	15.8	27.0	1,914,702	1,285,865	67.2	74.1	60.0
New Hampshire	21.9	67.4	29.3	9.0	11.0	36.7	52.5	1,040,007	730,431	69.8	75.7	64.2
New Jersey.................	21.3	51.6	18.8	12.5	12.7	30.5	50.2	6,835,521	4,496,262	65.8	72.9	59.2
New Mexico................	10.6	37.7	10.5	7.9	7.1	11.0	18.3	1,505,362	936,724	62.2	68.0	56.7
New York...................	25.0	50.4	17.5	15.1	13.6	38.8	60.9	15,355,670	9,621,146	62.7	68.9	56.9
North Carolina...........	14.5	50.2	10.1	9.0	7.5	19.4	32.2	6,946,929	4,515,041	65.0	71.6	58.8
North Dakota.............	10.3	33.2	10.7	8.8	5.4	11.8	13.0	512,164	354,513	69.2	74.6	63.9
Ohio..........................	18.3	47.3	14.5	13.6	10.9	24.5	33.2	9,019,907	5,844,257	64.8	70.6	59.4
Oklahoma..................	11.3	25.9	9.8	7.2	6.7	17.4	25.2	2,789,374	1,748,680	62.7	69.6	56.1
Oregon......................	15.1	55.7	14.9	9.6	7.8	19.3	33.3	2,934,587	1,897,202	64.6	71.0	58.4
Pennsylvania	24.5	57.5	18.5	15.9	12.6	37.6	54.6	9,947,004	6,224,260	62.6	68.7	56.9
Rhode Island.............	25.9	54.9	20.8	12.8	12.7	41.4	58.9	854,785	563,758	66.0	71.6	60.8
South Carolina...........	15.5	44.9	15.0	11.0	8.7	21.5	30.7	3,406,212	2,139,979	62.8	68.8	57.3
South Dakota.............	13.4	37.6	9.8	10.2	6.2	19.2	22.2	616,374	428,900	69.6	74.0	65.2
Tennessee	16.4	44.2	13.2	10.6	11.6	24.1	35.8	4,779,974	3,007,789	62.9	69.6	56.7
Texas........................	11.5	38.4	9.5	6.9	6.2	16.0	28.6	17,596,586	11,470,560	65.2	73.2	57.4
Utah.........................	13.6	50.3	6.0	4.5	4.1	26.1	32.4	1,862,740	1,293,379	69.4	78.5	60.4
Vermont	20.4	47.0	15.5	8.0	11.1	38.0	42.7	505,187	348,421	69.0	73.4	64.8
Virginia	17.3	59.5	15.4	10.2	9.0	21.6	35.8	6,025,175	4,044,664	67.1	73.5	61.1
Washington	14.3	54.2	12.8	9.4	6.8	17.5	35.4	5,028,054	3,312,856	65.9	72.3	59.6
West Virginia	10.2	30.9	7.3	6.7	6.5	14.7	18.7	1,466,327	810,337	55.3	61.6	49.3
Wisconsin	17.3	43.6	15.7	15.6	8.6	19.3	37.9	4,408,022	3,029,239	68.7	73.5	64.1
Wyoming...................	8.9	36.5	5.0	5.3	3.7	12.8	17.0	405,511	283,877	70.0	75.6	64.3

Table B-1. States — What: Education, Employment, and Income, 2005–2007—*Continued*

STATE	Unemployment rates by age (percent unemployed)				Total labor force 25 to 64 years	Unemployment rates for the labor force age 25 to 64 by educational attainment				
						Unemployment rate (percent unemployed)				
	Total labor force	16 to 24 years	25 to 64 years	65 years and over		Total 25 to 64 years	No high school diploma	High school graduate	Some college or associate's degree	Bachelor's degree or higher
ACS table number:	C23001	C23001	C23001	C23001	B23006	B23006	B23006	B23006	B23006	B23006
	23	24	25	26	27	28	29	30	31	32
United States	6.6	14.7	5.1	3.8	122,246,104	5.1	10.0	6.3	4.8	2.7
Alabama	7.0	17.6	5.0	3.2	1,738,032	5.0	10.4	6.1	4.4	2.1
Alaska	8.6	17.0	6.8	5.7	294,385	6.8	15.3	10.6	6.0	2.2
Arizona	5.7	11.8	4.6	3.8	2,371,356	4.6	8.5	5.3	4.2	2.5
Arkansas	7.1	16.0	5.5	3.6	1,071,122	5.5	10.7	6.5	4.9	2.1
California	6.8	14.3	5.5	4.3	14,533,135	5.5	8.9	6.7	5.2	3.3
Colorado	5.8	12.8	4.6	3.0	2,126,410	4.6	8.2	6.0	4.8	2.8
Connecticut	6.2	14.8	4.8	3.8	1,523,116	4.8	11.6	5.7	5.2	2.8
Delaware	5.8	13.6	4.4	4.6	351,969	4.4	8.3	6.1	3.7	2.0
District of Columbia	8.8	15.9	7.8	3.6	259,359	7.8	16.3	15.2	9.4	3.3
Florida	6.0	13.4	4.7	4.7	7,130,801	4.7	8.2	5.5	4.4	2.9
Georgia	7.1	17.0	5.4	4.1	3,854,490	5.4	10.4	6.4	5.1	2.8
Hawaii	4.3	9.6	3.4	2.1	545,243	3.4	6.0	4.6	3.2	2.1
Idaho	5.4	11.8	4.1	3.4	577,929	4.1	7.7	5.4	3.6	2.3
Illinois	7.5	16.7	5.8	3.9	5,325,517	5.8	11.6	7.7	5.8	3.0
Indiana	6.8	15.2	5.3	3.4	2,608,728	5.3	11.2	6.4	4.8	2.3
Iowa	4.9	10.4	3.8	3.0	1,255,770	3.8	9.4	5.0	3.5	1.7
Kansas	5.2	11.7	4.0	2.6	1,150,877	4.0	9.0	5.3	3.7	1.9
Kentucky	7.0	16.0	5.4	2.9	1,636,100	5.4	11.9	6.1	5.0	2.3
Louisiana	7.9	17.2	6.0	2.8	1,622,559	6.0	13.2	6.8	5.2	2.4
Maine	5.7	13.6	4.4	4.0	570,526	4.4	12.6	5.6	3.6	2.5
Maryland	5.5	14.2	4.1	3.2	2,466,533	4.1	10.2	5.6	3.7	2.1
Massachusetts	6.1	13.3	4.9	4.1	2,823,380	4.9	10.9	6.5	5.2	2.9
Michigan	9.4	19.4	7.6	5.1	4,064,967	7.6	17.5	10.0	6.9	3.4
Minnesota	5.4	12.1	4.1	3.1	2,299,097	4.1	10.6	5.6	4.1	2.2
Mississippi	9.2	23.1	6.4	3.5	1,059,368	6.4	13.0	7.6	5.2	2.7
Missouri	6.4	13.7	5.1	3.5	2,383,579	5.1	11.4	6.2	4.8	2.3
Montana	5.1	11.4	3.9	3.5	393,974	3.9	12.6	4.6	3.7	1.9
Nebraska	4.8	10.5	3.6	2.6	749,737	3.6	9.2	4.5	3.1	2.1
Nevada	5.5	11.6	4.6	4.5	1,062,984	4.6	7.1	5.2	4.4	2.5
New Hampshire	4.8	11.7	3.6	3.1	599,483	3.6	8.1	4.4	3.6	2.3
New Jersey	6.1	14.8	4.9	4.6	3,737,928	4.9	9.7	6.1	4.9	3.1
New Mexico	6.4	13.6	5.1	3.2	742,177	5.1	9.9	5.2	4.8	3.1
New York	6.7	15.8	5.2	4.2	7,912,300	5.2	10.4	6.3	5.2	3.1
North Carolina	6.8	15.2	5.3	3.6	3,670,459	5.3	10.4	6.6	4.8	2.7
North Dakota	3.5	7.9	2.5	1.8	267,676	2.5	5.4	3.3	2.6	1.4
Ohio	7.2	16.0	5.7	3.2	4,702,034	5.7	14.9	6.8	5.0	2.6
Oklahoma	5.9	13.0	4.5	2.6	1,371,371	4.5	9.8	5.0	4.4	2.2
Oregon	6.9	15.2	5.5	4.0	1,559,776	5.5	10.0	6.6	5.5	3.2
Pennsylvania	6.3	14.6	4.9	3.8	5,045,939	4.9	10.8	5.9	4.6	2.6
Rhode Island	6.1	12.5	4.9	3.7	450,417	4.9	11.0	5.8	4.6	2.6
South Carolina	7.3	16.0	5.7	4.7	1,721,396	5.7	12.1	7.1	4.9	2.4
South Dakota	4.4	9.9	3.4	2.3	331,330	3.4	11.5	4.1	3.0	1.3
Tennessee	7.1	16.1	5.6	4.0	2,456,974	5.6	11.6	6.9	4.7	2.5
Texas	6.8	15.5	5.2	3.9	9,252,813	5.2	8.1	6.5	4.9	2.7
Utah	4.6	9.1	3.3	2.9	963,586	3.3	6.7	3.9	3.3	1.9
Vermont	5.2	13.0	3.8	3.2	282,175	3.8	10.0	5.3	3.2	2.2
Virginia	4.8	12.3	3.5	2.6	3,296,025	3.5	7.6	4.6	3.5	1.9
Washington	6.5	14.7	5.1	4.0	2,719,424	5.1	11.2	6.2	4.7	3.2
West Virginia	6.9	16.1	5.5	1.7	666,046	5.5	10.8	6.2	5.3	2.3
Wisconsin	5.8	12.4	4.5	3.4	2,421,908	4.5	10.5	5.8	4.2	2.2
Wyoming	4.1	8.4	3.3	2.8	223,831	3.3	7.6	4.2	3.0	1.6

Table B-1. States — What: Education, Employment, and Income, 2005–2007—*Continued*

STATE	Total population 16 to 19 years	16 to 19 years not enrolled in school, not h.s. graduate, not in labor force	Total population 16 years and over	Percent of population 16 years and over who worked full-time, year-round in the past 12 months			Total households	Percent of house-holds with no workers	Children under 18 years in families			
				Total	Male	Female			Number	Percent living with two parents, both in labor force	Percent living with two parents, father only in labor force	Percent living with one parent, who is in labor force
ACS table number:	C14005	C14005	C20005	C20005	C20005	C20005	C08202	C08202	C23008	C23008	C23008	C23008
	33	34	35	36	37	38	39	40	41	42	43	44
United States	17,144,008	3.0	233,658,279	39.9	48.7	31.6	111,609,629	26.2	69,123,922	41.4	22.5	25.2
Alabama..................	262,905	4.1	3,596,728	38.3	47.4	30.1	1,798,304	30.9	1,031,937	37.8	20.3	28.5
Alaska......................	42,882	2.9	516,556	37.5	43.1	31.4	233,861	20.9	170,875	41.5	23.5	25.1
Arizona...................	334,774	4.1	4,704,044	39.5	48.3	30.8	2,215,761	27.7	1,515,776	35.7	26.7	26.3
Arkansas.................	161,298	3.1	2,190,608	37.7	45.4	30.5	1,096,622	30.8	638,347	41.1	19.3	27.1
California................	2,171,488	2.9	27,949,362	38.6	47.7	29.6	12,140,888	24.0	8,813,978	37.6	26.9	23.3
Colorado	256,055	2.7	3,722,302	42.3	51.4	33.2	1,838,303	21.6	1,110,057	43.8	24.2	22.9
Connecticut..............	199,047	1.9	2,768,150	41.2	50.6	32.6	1,323,431	24.3	787,103	46.4	21.5	23.0
Delaware..................	48,435	2.7	671,869	42.0	50.1	34.5	321,748	25.6	188,997	43.2	19.4	28.2
District of Columbia...	31,707	4.9	483,781	42.4	47.3	38.2	249,805	28.1	102,532	24.2	11.5	44.0
Florida	922,344	3.7	14,471,701	39.2	47.1	31.7	7,077,123	30.6	3,741,855	39.5	20.9	28.9
Georgia	541,688	4.4	7,131,317	42.3	51.3	33.9	3,364,749	23.7	2,292,053	39.4	21.7	28.3
Hawaii	65,350	2.0	1,025,421	42.8	50.6	35.1	433,664	22.9	262,586	46.1	20.3	22.3
Idaho	86,953	2.7	1,108,188	38.1	47.3	28.9	545,171	25.0	375,374	44.0	29.7	18.6
Illinois	747,763	2.7	9,946,551	40.6	49.3	32.3	4,724,462	25.0	3,035,983	42.3	23.3	24.8
Indiana	362,282	3.1	4,900,909	40.6	49.7	31.9	2,447,887	26.0	1,483,856	44.0	20.7	25.4
Iowa	176,562	1.5	2,346,630	42.5	51.2	34.2	1,206,848	25.5	677,033	54.6	15.7	21.6
Kansas	161,288	1.6	2,143,455	43.0	52.6	33.8	1,083,868	23.6	654,462	48.2	20.5	23.4
Kentucky	228,653	3.8	3,316,908	37.4	45.2	30.1	1,654,119	31.2	928,922	41.1	20.7	24.2
Louisiana	269,293	5.0	3,371,197	36.2	43.7	29.2	1,605,203	29.2	1,018,516	35.0	18.4	31.7
Maine	72,172	1.8	1,069,271	38.5	46.7	30.9	542,424	28.8	265,316	46.4	18.5	23.9
Maryland	327,099	2.7	4,396,011	44.9	53.2	37.4	2,082,573	21.7	1,277,742	45.2	18.9	27.6
Massachusetts	365,461	1.9	5,167,254	40.4	49.6	31.9	2,448,608	26.0	1,381,606	47.2	20.3	22.0
Michigan	597,030	3.0	7,915,981	35.9	43.9	28.5	3,864,307	29.4	2,349,952	43.1	20.9	25.0
Minnesota	299,843	1.4	4,046,604	42.4	50.9	34.0	2,041,466	23.1	1,205,536	52.7	18.1	21.4
Mississippi................	183,979	4.0	2,230,412	36.3	43.7	29.5	1,079,584	31.1	696,269	34.5	16.5	34.2
Missouri...................	330,045	3.2	4,578,206	40.6	48.3	33.3	2,300,211	27.2	1,337,791	45.1	18.9	26.0
Montana..................	55,379	3.1	754,965	37.3	44.7	30.1	369,329	27.0	206,783	46.9	21.7	21.8
Nebraska..................	105,230	1.8	1,370,844	44.9	54.7	35.5	698,163	22.8	423,667	52.8	18.4	21.5
Nevada	123,414	4.8	1,914,702	44.9	53.0	36.6	932,715	22.7	594,173	38.7	23.8	27.0
New Hampshire	76,772	1.8	1,046,807	43.2	53.1	33.7	500,671	21.6	288,267	50.2	21.4	20.7
New Jersey................	467,702	2.5	6,835,521	41.9	51.7	32.7	3,143,408	24.1	1,978,975	44.4	24.0	22.4
New Mexico..............	119,563	4.5	1,505,362	37.0	44.5	29.8	728,508	27.8	460,153	35.5	21.0	29.2
New York..................	1,123,300	3.0	15,355,670	39.2	47.3	31.7	7,096,035	27.4	4,202,623	38.6	22.9	25.5
North Carolina..........	492,437	3.4	6,946,929	40.6	49.6	32.2	3,471,751	26.6	2,021,440	41.1	20.8	27.5
North Dakota............	41,377	1.5	512,164	42.3	51.6	33.0	271,131	24.2	135,830	57.4	15.9	19.1
Ohio........................	651,969	2.4	9,019,907	39.0	47.5	31.1	4,500,621	28.3	2,613,326	43.4	19.6	26.2
Oklahoma................	204,987	3.7	2,789,374	39.5	48.2	31.2	1,386,849	28.3	820,953	39.7	22.4	26.3
Oregon	195,808	2.5	2,934,587	36.4	45.2	27.9	1,447,409	27.3	803,569	42.5	24.4	23.7
Pennsylvania	730,270	2.8	9,947,004	38.7	47.5	30.7	4,858,509	29.1	2,647,784	43.6	21.3	23.9
Rhode Island	65,597	2.3	854,785	38.9	48.0	30.6	404,549	27.6	226,569	45.9	16.1	25.6
South Carolina..........	254,942	3.5	3,406,212	39.4	47.8	31.7	1,664,561	28.5	968,495	38.6	18.8	30.9
South Dakota............	47,833	2.3	616,374	43.9	51.6	36.4	311,644	24.0	183,315	54.2	13.0	24.3
Tennessee	325,040	3.0	4,779,974	39.6	48.4	31.5	2,382,975	28.3	1,355,550	39.0	21.1	27.3
Texas.......................	1,376,159	3.5	17,596,586	41.4	51.0	32.1	8,095,025	22.6	6,066,897	37.6	26.1	25.1
Utah	168,477	1.4	1,862,740	39.9	51.9	27.8	812,604	18.8	766,056	43.2	35.9	14.7
Vermont	38,332	1.5	505,187	40.6	48.3	33.3	250,871	25.0	127,449	51.2	15.1	24.8
Virginia	436,698	2.1	6,025,175	44.7	54.0	36.0	2,909,223	23.2	1,711,756	44.6	22.1	24.4
Washington	350,853	3.0	5,028,054	38.1	47.0	29.5	2,472,477	25.6	1,438,423	41.9	24.7	23.2
West Virginia	93,984	3.9	1,466,327	34.0	41.6	26.8	738,943	36.1	359,704	38.5	24.1	20.8
Wisconsin	321,380	2.1	4,408,022	41.5	49.8	33.4	2,235,246	25.0	1,261,576	50.7	16.8	23.7
Wyoming..................	30,109	3.0	405,511	42.5	52.1	32.9	205,422	22.7	116,135	48.3	19.7	24.8

Table B-1. States — What: Education, Employment, and Income, 2005–2007—*Continued*

	Family status of children under 18 years, by employment status of parents and age of children								Employment status of family householders				
	Children under 6 years in families				Children 6–17 years in families					Married-couple families		Other families	
STATE	Number	Percent living with two parents, both in labor force	Percent living with two parents, father only in labor force	Percent living with one parent, who is in labor force	Number	Percent living with two parents, both in labor force	Percent living with two parents, father only in labor force	Percent living with one parent, who is in labor force	Total families	Total	Percent with both in the labor force	Total	Percent with house-holder in the labor force
ACS table number:	C23008	C23008	C23008	C23008	C23008	C23008	C23008	C23008	C23007	C23007	C23007	C23007	C23007
	45	46	47	48	49	50	51	52	53	54	55	56	57
United States	23,292,733	37.1	27.6	24.0	45,831,189	43.6	20.0	25.8	74,625,059	55,603,280	53.1	19,021,779	73.0
Alabama	345,529	34.1	23.6	28.4	686,408	39.7	18.7	28.5	1,230,451	893,237	48.7	337,214	66.5
Alaska	57,642	35.6	29.6	23.7	113,233	44.5	20.3	25.8	159,829	119,465	58.5	40,364	79.1
Arizona	542,028	31.2	32.8	24.6	973,748	38.3	23.3	27.3	1,469,097	1,097,059	46.0	372,038	74.8
Arkansas	221,494	37.2	23.5	26.8	416,853	43.2	17.0	27.3	749,762	563,092	50.4	186,670	70.2
California	2,966,824	34.1	32.1	21.5	5,847,154	39.4	24.2	24.3	8,293,161	6,044,996	50.4	2,248,165	73.4
Colorado	391,729	39.1	30.1	20.8	718,328	46.4	21.0	24.1	1,185,583	925,072	57.2	260,511	78.6
Connecticut	247,176	41.9	28.2	20.5	539,927	48.4	18.4	24.1	890,199	677,138	58.1	213,061	75.7
Delaware	64,854	37.2	24.9	27.9	124,143	46.4	16.5	28.3	217,909	160,625	53.4	57,284	76.6
District of Columbia	38,881	29.3	15.5	32.7	63,651	21.0	9.1	51.0	107,252	54,237	58.7	53,015	64.5
Florida	1,265,759	35.5	25.8	27.6	2,476,096	41.5	18.3	29.5	4,619,809	3,424,330	46.9	1,195,479	74.4
Georgia	804,154	35.2	26.8	26.8	1,487,899	41.7	18.9	29.1	2,296,389	1,648,132	54.0	648,257	74.0
Hawaii	91,709	40.3	26.5	21.4	170,877	49.2	17.0	22.8	303,732	225,902	52.9	77,830	66.4
Idaho	129,983	37.9	37.3	17.4	245,391	47.1	25.6	19.2	382,116	310,762	52.7	71,354	76.4
Illinois	1,019,555	38.1	28.3	23.5	2,016,428	44.5	20.7	25.4	3,155,370	2,357,325	55.1	798,045	73.9
Indiana	498,912	38.8	25.0	25.7	984,944	46.7	18.6	25.3	1,652,168	1,262,601	55.6	389,567	75.2
Iowa	223,127	49.8	19.7	21.4	453,906	56.9	13.7	21.7	790,876	637,768	61.1	153,108	77.5
Kansas	223,057	42.1	25.8	23.1	431,405	51.4	17.7	23.5	723,983	571,810	58.9	152,173	78.4
Kentucky	315,523	37.9	24.4	23.8	613,399	42.8	18.8	24.4	1,113,366	840,501	49.5	272,865	66.8
Louisiana	344,083	32.7	20.4	31.7	674,433	36.2	17.4	31.7	1,090,538	751,034	48.9	339,504	67.8
Maine	81,334	41.1	25.1	21.8	183,982	48.7	15.6	24.8	354,315	277,646	56.2	76,669	72.5
Maryland	425,392	41.2	24.6	25.5	852,350	47.2	16.0	28.7	1,395,276	1,013,474	58.9	381,802	77.3
Massachusetts	442,877	44.1	26.5	19.0	938,729	48.7	17.5	23.4	1,566,639	1,173,091	58.4	393,548	71.4
Michigan	741,016	39.3	25.4	24.0	1,608,934	44.9	18.8	25.5	2,579,798	1,939,163	52.5	640,635	71.7
Minnesota	401,012	49.4	22.1	20.5	804,524	54.3	16.1	21.9	1,335,646	1,066,850	62.5	268,796	80.1
Mississippi	238,328	31.3	18.6	35.3	457,941	36.2	15.4	33.6	753,580	506,173	50.3	247,407	66.9
Missouri	444,405	40.5	23.0	26.0	893,386	47.4	16.9	26.0	1,520,360	1,151,019	54.8	369,341	73.9
Montana	66,060	41.1	29.5	20.6	140,723	49.7	18.0	22.4	238,953	194,172	54.4	44,781	76.0
Nebraska	148,587	48.9	22.2	21.5	275,080	55.0	16.3	21.4	460,061	368,374	62.3	91,687	78.8
Nevada	208,741	33.9	30.8	24.7	385,432	41.3	19.9	28.3	610,886	446,711	51.7	164,175	77.5
New Hampshire	88,084	44.3	28.9	18.7	200,183	52.8	18.1	21.6	338,891	272,100	60.1	66,791	77.6
New Jersey	645,883	39.8	30.0	20.2	1,333,092	46.7	21.1	23.4	2,184,537	1,639,583	54.9	544,954	74.8
New Mexico	156,847	30.0	24.8	29.8	303,306	38.4	19.1	28.9	480,192	344,615	48.0	135,577	70.9
New York	1,373,334	34.7	28.6	23.4	2,829,289	40.5	20.1	26.6	4,589,413	3,208,929	51.7	1,380,484	69.7
North Carolina	702,787	37.1	25.9	26.1	1,318,653	43.2	18.1	28.2	2,322,524	1,719,721	53.5	602,803	73.2
North Dakota	44,702	52.5	20.2	18.5	91,128	59.8	13.7	19.4	167,770	138,154	62.6	29,616	77.0
Ohio	854,518	39.4	23.3	26.2	1,758,808	45.4	17.9	26.2	2,964,250	2,215,565	54.5	748,685	72.4
Oklahoma	285,283	34.1	27.3	26.7	535,670	42.6	19.8	26.1	930,073	702,154	50.7	227,919	71.6
Oregon	265,689	38.1	30.5	21.4	537,880	44.7	21.4	24.9	926,083	721,038	51.8	205,045	74.7
Pennsylvania	841,312	39.2	25.8	22.9	1,806,472	45.6	19.3	24.3	3,195,089	2,424,483	53.5	770,606	69.5
Rhode Island	72,235	41.5	20.9	25.7	154,334	48.0	13.8	25.6	258,434	190,509	57.6	67,925	72.2
South Carolina	326,873	34.6	21.9	31.2	641,622	40.6	17.3	30.7	1,126,306	806,508	51.1	319,798	70.5
South Dakota	63,062	49.0	14.9	26.2	120,253	56.9	12.0	23.4	204,767	164,145	62.9	40,622	79.8
Tennessee	457,226	34.0	25.5	27.4	898,324	41.5	18.9	27.2	1,605,364	1,185,780	51.1	419,584	69.5
Texas	2,181,216	32.5	31.1	24.3	3,885,681	40.5	23.3	25.6	5,679,333	4,186,442	51.3	1,492,891	74.1
Utah	286,095	37.2	43.4	12.6	479,961	46.7	31.4	16.0	613,317	505,530	53.0	107,787	77.1
Vermont	37,702	48.0	19.9	22.8	89,747	52.5	13.1	25.7	160,579	124,135	61.2	36,444	76.8
Virginia	580,776	40.8	26.9	22.7	1,130,980	46.5	19.6	25.2	1,948,885	1,477,226	55.9	471,659	75.0
Washington	472,460	36.8	30.9	21.5	965,963	44.4	21.7	24.0	1,594,289	1,234,960	53.2	359,329	76.5
West Virginia	117,153	34.9	27.9	20.1	242,551	40.3	22.3	21.1	496,360	385,197	43.3	111,163	59.9
Wisconsin	410,365	46.7	21.2	23.4	851,211	52.7	14.7	23.9	1,456,670	1,146,767	60.1	309,903	77.7
Wyoming	39,360	40.7	27.0	24.9	76,775	52.1	16.0	24.8	134,829	107,980	58.6	26,849	82.1

Table B-1. States — What: Education, Employment, and Income, 2005–2007—*Continued*

STATE	Women 20 to 64 years in households by presence of children and labor force status			Class of worker for employed civilians 16 years and over				Civilian employed population 16 years and over	Occupation (percent)		
	Total women 20 to 64 years in households	Percent with children under 18 years	Percent with children under 18 years in labor force	Civilian employed population 16 years and over	Percent private wage and salary workers	Percent government workers	Percent self-employed and unpaid workers	Civilian employed population 16 years and over	Management, professional, and related	Service	Sales and office
ACS table number:	B23003	B23003	B23003	C24080	C24080	C24080	C24080	C24060	C24060	C24060	C24060
	58	59	60	61	62	63	64	65	66	67	68
United States............	88,778,014	38.5	27.3	140,148,744	78.5	14.5	7.0	140,148,744	34.1	16.6	25.8
Alabama..................	1,376,882	38.9	27.4	1,995,943	77.8	15.7	6.6	1,995,943	30.6	15.1	25.4
Alaska......................	200,673	40.2	28.7	322,285	66.7	25.2	8.1	322,285	34.7	17.0	24.0
Arizona...................	1,753,925	38.1	25.3	2,756,363	79.1	14.4	6.5	2,756,363	32.7	17.7	27.0
Arkansas..................	820,178	39.1	28.2	1,237,351	76.3	16.1	7.6	1,237,351	29.1	16.1	25.0
California.................	10,650,901	38.9	25.4	16,564,988	76.9	14.0	9.1	16,564,988	35.0	16.8	25.9
Colorado	1,446,731	38.0	27.1	2,424,534	78.3	13.9	7.8	2,424,534	37.3	16.0	25.7
Connecticut..............	1,044,012	39.5	29.1	1,742,282	79.9	12.9	7.2	1,742,282	39.0	16.0	25.9
Delaware	256,342	37.2	28.3	407,918	80.8	13.9	5.2	407,918	35.9	15.8	26.7
District of Columbia...	192,360	24.6	18.1	286,354	69.0	25.6	5.4	286,354	54.8	16.4	20.1
Florida	5,244,786	35.8	25.8	8,204,726	80.7	12.9	6.3	8,204,726	31.8	18.1	28.4
Georgia	2,842,370	39.4	28.2	4,309,992	78.5	15.0	6.4	4,309,992	33.5	15.2	26.2
Hawaii	372,868	36.5	26.7	605,769	71.3	20.5	8.1	605,769	32.8	21.4	26.5
Idaho	415,574	42.5	29.1	685,821	74.9	15.5	9.5	685,821	31.9	15.7	25.0
Illinois	3,785,302	39.4	28.2	6,087,756	81.9	12.6	5.5	6,087,756	34.3	16.1	26.4
Indiana	1,853,304	39.4	29.1	3,000,711	83.2	11.3	5.5	3,000,711	30.0	15.7	24.7
Iowa	846,899	40.0	32.3	1,530,424	78.3	13.7	8.0	1,530,424	32.5	15.7	25.1
Kansas	793,858	40.8	30.9	1,380,019	75.9	16.4	7.6	1,380,019	34.5	15.9	24.9
Kentucky	1,272,970	38.3	27.1	1,863,500	78.0	15.1	6.9	1,863,500	30.5	15.7	25.1
Louisiana	1,299,025	38.8	27.4	1,872,077	77.2	16.3	6.5	1,872,077	29.8	17.7	26.1
Maine	401,794	35.3	26.6	656,374	75.4	14.6	10.1	656,374	32.9	17.2	25.1
Maryland	1,740,683	37.6	28.8	2,827,380	72.7	21.8	5.5	2,827,380	42.1	15.4	25.1
Massachusetts	1,973,479	36.7	27.0	3,241,335	80.5	12.7	6.9	3,241,335	41.4	16.1	24.8
Michigan	3,007,674	38.4	28.0	4,552,649	82.3	11.8	5.9	4,552,649	32.6	17.1	25.2
Minnesota	1,521,887	39.6	31.2	2,713,719	80.9	12.1	7.0	2,713,719	36.8	15.5	25.3
Mississippi................	851,868	41.0	29.9	1,201,649	74.5	18.3	7.2	1,201,649	28.2	16.8	24.6
Missouri...................	1,734,945	39.0	29.4	2,774,004	79.7	13.2	7.1	2,774,004	32.1	16.4	26.7
Montana	277,977	35.5	26.1	464,894	70.3	18.4	11.3	464,894	32.4	18.1	25.0
Nebraska	504,192	41.4	32.4	916,556	77.2	14.3	8.4	916,556	34.0	15.9	25.4
Nevada	732,760	36.9	25.5	1,206,844	83.2	11.6	5.2	1,206,844	26.2	24.7	26.0
New Hampshire	399,236	37.7	28.4	694,200	78.5	13.2	8.3	694,200	36.5	14.9	26.2
New Jersey................	2,615,683	39.4	28.0	4,212,168	80.2	14.4	5.4	4,212,168	38.4	15.5	27.4
New Mexico..............	571,581	38.4	26.4	868,087	69.9	21.9	8.2	868,087	33.8	18.6	24.8
New York..................	5,860,404	36.2	25.2	8,954,596	76.8	16.6	6.6	8,954,596	37.0	18.8	25.9
North Carolina	2,687,508	38.4	28.0	4,132,955	78.4	14.8	6.8	4,132,955	32.9	15.8	24.4
North Dakota............	179,590	38.8	31.1	336,940	72.7	17.4	9.9	336,940	33.7	17.1	24.4
Ohio........................	3,417,279	38.3	28.4	5,412,125	81.4	12.7	5.9	5,412,125	32.3	16.5	25.7
Oklahoma.................	1,042,314	39.2	27.4	1,626,851	75.0	16.9	8.2	1,626,851	31.1	17.0	25.8
Oregon	1,111,230	35.8	25.2	1,764,359	77.4	13.6	9.0	1,764,359	33.3	16.6	25.7
Pennsylvania	3,639,866	36.9	26.8	5,825,366	81.8	11.8	6.3	5,825,366	34.2	16.1	26.2
Rhode Island.............	320,590	36.5	27.8	526,547	80.5	13.4	6.1	526,547	35.2	17.8	25.6
South Carolina..........	1,308,643	37.5	27.7	1,950,817	77.8	15.7	6.5	1,950,817	30.8	16.2	25.3
South Dakota............	220,906	39.3	32.6	407,566	73.2	16.1	10.7	407,566	33.5	16.4	25.4
Tennessee	1,846,797	38.0	26.9	2,778,510	78.2	13.7	8.1	2,778,510	30.4	15.7	26.0
Texas.......................	6,816,943	42.0	28.2	10,602,396	78.0	14.3	7.7	10,602,396	32.6	16.6	25.9
Utah	714,187	45.3	28.5	1,228,935	78.8	15.6	5.7	1,228,935	32.3	14.7	28.6
Vermont	190,607	35.8	28.6	329,732	74.2	14.5	11.3	329,732	38.0	16.7	23.1
Virginia	2,341,794	37.9	27.7	3,739,725	74.0	20.3	5.7	3,739,725	39.8	15.0	24.3
Washington	1,938,960	37.3	25.9	3,051,540	76.8	16.0	7.1	3,051,540	36.6	16.0	24.9
West Virginia	544,268	35.4	22.9	753,192	75.8	18.2	6.0	753,192	29.2	17.5	25.1
Wisconsin	1,642,645	38.4	30.3	2,849,104	81.4	12.2	6.4	2,849,104	32.2	15.7	24.8
Wyoming..................	150,764	37.2	28.4	268,816	72.1	19.3	8.6	268,816	31.0	16.8	22.4

Table B-1. States — What: Education, Employment, and Income, 2005–2007—*Continued*

STATE	Occupation (percent)			Industry (percent)							
	Farming, fishing, and forestry	Construction extraction, maintenance, and repair	Production, transportation, and material moving	Agriculture, forestry, fishing and hunting, and mining	Construction	Manufacturing	Wholesale trade	Retail trade	Transportation and warehousing, and utilities	Information	Finance and insurance and real estate and rental and leasing
ACS table number:	C24060	C24060	C24060	C24070	C24070	C24070	C24070	C24070	C24070	C24070	C24070
	69	70	71	72	73	74	75	76	77	78	79
United States	0.7	9.8	12.9	1.8	7.8	11.5	3.4	11.5	5.1	2.5	7.2
Alabama.................	0.7	11.3	16.9	1.9	8.1	15.4	3.5	12.3	5.3	1.9	6.0
Alaska.....................	1.4	12.2	10.7	4.5	9.0	3.8	2.2	11.4	8.3	2.3	4.6
Arizona...................	0.6	12.1	10.0	1.3	10.8	8.0	3.0	12.1	4.8	1.9	8.4
Arkansas.................	1.4	10.5	18.0	3.4	7.7	15.7	3.2	13.0	5.7	1.9	5.1
California................	1.4	9.5	11.5	2.0	7.9	10.7	3.7	11.2	4.6	3.0	7.5
Colorado................	0.6	10.9	9.5	2.1	9.7	7.4	3.2	11.4	4.8	3.5	8.0
Connecticut............	0.2	8.5	10.5	0.4	6.8	12.3	3.1	11.3	3.9	2.8	9.7
Delaware	0.5	10.1	10.9	1.1	8.2	10.1	2.7	12.1	4.8	1.7	10.5
District of Columbia...	0.2	4.0	4.5	0.3	3.2	1.4	0.7	5.1	3.2	4.9	6.7
Florida...................	0.7	11.5	9.4	1.0	10.3	5.9	3.6	12.8	5.1	2.4	8.5
Georgia	0.6	10.9	13.6	1.2	8.9	11.6	3.7	11.9	6.1	2.8	6.9
Hawaii	0.8	10.3	8.1	1.6	8.3	3.2	2.8	11.8	5.7	2.1	6.9
Idaho.....................	2.6	12.1	12.7	5.4	10.1	10.7	3.1	12.1	4.7	2.1	5.9
Illinois...................	0.3	8.3	14.6	1.0	6.5	13.5	3.8	10.9	5.9	2.4	8.0
Indiana	0.5	9.8	19.4	1.3	6.8	20.3	3.3	11.2	5.3	1.9	5.7
Iowa	1.0	8.9	16.9	4.0	6.5	15.6	3.6	11.8	4.9	2.2	7.5
Kansas	1.0	9.7	14.1	3.7	6.4	13.9	3.3	11.1	5.2	2.9	6.3
Kentucky	0.8	10.5	17.3	3.2	7.3	14.9	3.2	11.6	6.0	1.9	5.8
Louisiana	0.6	12.6	13.2	4.2	8.8	8.7	3.3	12.1	5.3	1.7	5.7
Maine.....................	1.6	10.8	12.4	2.5	8.3	10.5	2.9	13.5	3.9	2.1	6.2
Maryland	0.2	9.0	8.1	0.6	7.8	5.5	2.5	10.2	4.5	2.8	7.2
Massachusetts	0.2	7.9	9.5	0.4	6.6	10.3	3.1	10.8	3.8	2.9	8.4
Michigan	0.5	8.6	16.0	1.1	6.0	19.0	3.1	11.5	4.1	2.0	5.8
Minnesota	0.7	8.5	13.3	2.3	6.7	14.4	3.5	11.5	4.5	2.3	7.5
Mississippi..............	1.1	11.3	17.9	2.9	7.8	15.0	3.2	11.7	5.5	1.7	5.0
Missouri.................	0.6	9.9	14.2	1.8	7.6	12.5	3.4	12.1	5.4	2.5	7.1
Montana.................	1.7	12.3	10.4	7.4	9.5	5.0	2.8	12.9	4.8	1.9	5.8
Nebraska	1.6	9.0	14.0	5.1	6.8	11.1	3.5	11.5	6.1	2.1	7.8
Nevada	0.2	13.0	10.0	1.4	11.4	4.6	2.9	10.7	5.0	1.7	7.0
New Hampshire	0.4	10.1	11.9	0.8	8.1	13.5	3.7	13.5	4.0	2.5	6.5
New Jersey...............	0.2	8.2	10.3	0.4	6.4	9.7	4.0	11.3	5.9	3.3	9.3
New Mexico..............	1.0	12.0	9.9	3.9	9.1	5.4	2.4	11.9	4.4	2.0	5.3
New York.................	0.3	7.9	10.2	0.6	6.1	7.6	3.1	10.6	5.3	3.4	8.8
North Carolina..........	0.8	11.2	14.8	1.5	9.1	14.2	3.3	11.5	4.5	2.1	6.6
North Dakota............	1.7	10.4	12.7	8.5	6.8	8.1	3.5	12.0	5.3	2.0	5.8
Ohio......................	0.3	8.3	16.8	1.1	6.0	17.0	3.4	11.6	5.0	2.0	6.8
Oklahoma................	0.8	11.2	14.1	4.3	7.2	10.7	3.5	11.4	5.3	2.5	6.2
Oregon	2.0	9.4	13.0	3.5	7.8	12.7	3.6	12.3	4.3	2.1	6.5
Pennsylvania	0.4	8.8	14.2	1.3	6.4	13.4	3.4	11.8	5.3	2.1	6.7
Rhode Island.............	0.2	8.2	13.0	0.4	6.6	12.4	2.9	12.1	3.7	2.0	7.6
South Carolina..........	0.5	11.2	16.1	1.0	8.9	15.1	3.1	12.0	5.0	1.8	6.0
South Dakota............	1.9	9.2	13.4	7.4	6.7	10.0	3.0	11.6	4.4	2.0	8.1
Tennessee	0.5	10.2	17.2	1.1	7.7	15.5	3.5	12.0	6.3	2.1	6.0
Texas.....................	0.6	11.7	12.6	2.8	9.2	10.1	3.6	11.6	5.7	2.3	7.0
Utah	0.4	11.0	12.9	1.8	8.7	11.0	3.3	12.6	5.0	2.5	7.3
Vermont	1.0	10.0	11.1	2.4	8.3	11.7	2.8	11.7	3.6	2.2	4.9
Virginia..................	0.4	9.9	10.5	1.2	8.2	8.6	2.4	11.1	4.3	2.8	6.8
Washington	1.6	9.3	11.6	2.5	7.8	11.0	3.6	11.5	5.1	2.9	6.5
West Virginia	0.6	13.0	14.7	4.7	7.7	9.5	2.8	12.7	6.1	1.8	4.6
Wisconsin	0.9	8.7	17.6	2.5	6.5	19.4	3.3	11.5	4.5	2.0	6.4
Wyoming.................	1.3	15.1	13.4	11.3	9.0	4.7	2.3	11.9	6.3	1.5	4.4

Table B-1. States — What: Education, Employment, and Income, 2005–2007—*Continued*

STATE	Professional, scientific, and management, and administrative and waste management	Educational services, and health care and social assistance	Arts, entertainment, and recreation, and accommodation and food services	Other services, except public administration	Public administration	Veterans as a percent of the population 18 years and over	All households	Householder under 25 years	Householder 25 to 44 years	Householder 45 to 64 years	Householder 65 years and over
ACS table number:	C24070	C24070	C24070	C24070	C24070	B21002	B19049	B19049	B19049	B19049	B19049
	80	81	82	83	84	85	86	87	88	89	90
United States	10.1	21.0	8.7	4.8	4.7	10.4	50,007	26,207	54,830	61,527	31,185
Alabama	8.1	20.1	7.2	5.0	5.1	11.8	40,052	19,805	45,412	49,663	26,380
Alaska	8.0	21.7	8.4	5.1	10.7	15.5	61,766	38,139	62,368	72,751	39,983
Arizona	11.0	18.5	10.2	4.7	5.2	12.4	48,609	30,002	52,591	59,080	34,398
Arkansas	6.3	21.8	7.2	4.8	4.3	12.2	37,555	20,854	42,629	45,891	25,511
California	11.9	18.8	9.1	5.2	4.4	8.1	58,361	32,414	61,778	71,581	36,769
Colorado	12.5	17.9	9.9	5.1	4.5	11.6	54,262	27,375	57,646	66,770	34,511
Connecticut	10.6	23.4	7.6	4.3	3.7	9.6	65,496	33,269	71,570	81,583	36,156
Delaware	9.6	21.4	8.1	4.6	5.0	12.3	55,303	31,248	61,139	68,388	35,450
District of Columbia	22.2	19.6	9.2	8.2	15.5	8.0	52,187	29,045	60,261	56,070	35,533
Florida	11.5	18.5	10.4	5.1	4.8	12.5	46,602	28,599	52,304	56,009	32,438
Georgia	10.4	18.6	7.9	4.8	5.2	10.7	48,540	25,613	52,286	58,521	29,526
Hawaii	9.8	19.4	15.1	4.7	8.6	12.7	62,543	37,046	63,205	74,265	49,098
Idaho	9.2	19.3	8.2	4.1	5.2	12.6	44,901	27,134	49,482	54,271	30,432
Illinois	10.4	20.6	8.4	4.7	3.8	8.7	53,745	25,643	59,737	66,432	31,929
Indiana	7.1	20.8	8.2	4.7	3.4	10.7	47,034	24,595	52,008	58,711	29,906
Iowa	6.3	23.2	7.1	4.3	3.1	11.1	46,399	25,151	53,663	58,406	29,159
Kansas	8.0	22.7	7.6	4.4	4.5	11.5	46,669	24,378	51,254	60,489	30,712
Kentucky	7.2	21.9	7.8	4.6	4.5	10.7	40,138	22,208	46,160	48,070	24,836
Louisiana	8.2	22.1	9.2	5.2	5.6	10.1	40,160	20,604	45,614	49,203	25,356
Maine	7.8	25.7	8.0	4.4	4.2	14.0	45,211	26,943	50,837	54,797	27,716
Maryland	14.3	21.2	7.3	5.3	10.8	11.3	66,873	35,246	71,092	82,090	40,174
Massachusetts	12.3	25.3	7.9	4.4	3.9	9.1	61,785	31,158	70,381	76,399	31,976
Michigan	8.5	21.8	8.8	4.5	3.5	10.1	48,642	22,931	54,310	60,877	30,787
Minnesota	9.2	22.5	8.0	4.4	3.2	10.6	55,616	29,581	63,057	68,037	31,798
Mississippi	6.3	22.3	8.5	4.8	5.3	10.3	35,632	19,509	40,350	43,143	23,520
Missouri	8.2	21.5	8.6	4.9	4.5	12.0	44,545	24,251	50,189	54,737	28,759
Montana	7.5	21.2	10.2	5.0	6.1	14.2	42,425	23,995	45,714	51,821	28,690
Nebraska	7.8	22.3	7.8	4.4	3.9	11.6	46,954	27,452	52,644	58,895	29,388
Nevada	10.1	13.4	23.7	3.9	4.2	12.9	53,753	38,522	57,823	61,440	36,877
New Hampshire	9.4	21.9	7.7	4.4	3.9	12.8	61,459	34,371	68,288	70,879	34,048
New Jersey	11.8	21.4	7.5	4.5	4.6	8.0	66,509	32,259	73,775	81,950	36,276
New Mexico	10.9	22.5	10.4	4.6	7.2	12.4	41,042	21,808	42,869	52,401	29,809
New York	10.7	25.6	8.5	4.9	4.8	7.3	52,944	26,789	59,297	64,547	30,918
North Carolina	8.9	21.6	8.1	4.6	4.2	11.2	43,867	23,123	48,482	52,852	28,178
North Dakota	6.3	24.1	8.2	4.2	5.1	11.7	43,442	22,215	51,050	56,941	25,817
Ohio	8.5	22.1	8.4	4.4	3.8	11.2	46,296	22,873	52,087	57,762	29,247
Oklahoma	7.8	21.4	8.6	5.2	5.8	12.6	40,371	23,037	43,704	50,588	28,475
Oregon	9.8	19.5	9.0	4.5	4.4	12.5	47,385	24,412	51,442	57,320	32,431
Pennsylvania	9.3	23.9	7.7	4.7	4.1	11.2	47,913	23,764	54,957	60,456	28,195
Rhode Island	8.7	24.9	10.0	4.4	4.3	10.2	54,060	27,383	61,322	67,837	29,028
South Carolina	8.4	19.8	9.1	4.9	4.8	12.4	42,405	22,735	47,098	50,718	28,606
South Dakota	5.8	22.6	8.9	4.6	5.0	12.5	43,586	24,099	50,292	54,104	27,739
Tennessee	8.3	20.1	8.3	5.0	4.1	11.1	41,821	22,587	46,233	51,096	26,981
Texas	10.2	19.8	8.2	5.3	4.2	9.8	46,248	23,735	48,992	57,660	30,777
Utah	10.3	19.6	8.3	4.4	5.4	8.6	53,324	30,754	54,608	69,384	37,150
Vermont	8.2	25.8	9.1	4.6	4.8	11.5	49,382	28,147	52,587	59,978	30,167
Virginia	13.4	19.3	7.7	5.1	9.0	13.4	58,378	31,008	63,100	70,963	35,256
Washington	10.9	20.0	8.5	4.6	5.2	13.1	53,940	29,262	58,151	66,011	35,130
West Virginia	7.3	23.8	8.6	4.5	6.1	12.3	36,088	17,064	41,840	44,886	24,889
Wisconsin	7.2	21.1	8.1	3.9	3.4	10.7	50,309	27,607	56,319	62,296	29,579
Wyoming	6.5	21.6	10.1	4.5	5.9	13.9	50,009	30,561	54,381	61,893	31,382

Table B-1. States — What: Education, Employment, and Income, 2005–2007—*Continued*

STATE	Median income in the past 12 months (in 2007 inflation-adjusted dollars)								
	Median household income by race and Hispanic origin of householder								
	White alone	Black alone	Amer. Indian, Alaska Native alone	Asian alone	Native Hawaiian and other Pacific Islander alone	Some other race alone	Two or more races	White alone, not Hispanic or Latino	Hispanic or Latino
ACS table number:	B19013A	B19013B	B19013C	B19013D	B19013E	B19013F	B19013G	B19013H	B19013I
	91	92	93	94	95	96	97	98	99
United States	53,000	33,407	35,200	65,429	51,096	39,613	43,673	54,189	39,852
Alabama..................	46,095	25,739	31,843	51,203	30,536	35,924	30,625	46,243	35,453
Alaska....................	67,919	50,440	38,399	58,349	41,513	49,967	49,031	68,178	54,857
Arizona...................	50,958	38,475	30,375	58,275	47,479	39,250	42,760	53,693	38,175
Arkansas.................	40,863	24,056	35,286	48,781	34,812	30,213	28,960	41,037	31,494
California................	61,842	41,748	46,254	70,867	61,673	45,217	55,246	67,229	45,068
Colorado	56,471	38,658	41,889	57,814	46,121	39,405	46,386	59,782	36,819
Connecticut.............	70,314	42,688	39,955	78,587	78,088	38,203	52,792	72,040	39,513
Delaware	59,144	42,190	46,953	78,555	39,107	44,717	50,565	59,949	41,366
District of Columbia...	88,925	35,112	71,932	63,867	-	41,630	49,780	91,594	44,699
Florida...................	49,224	34,011	41,661	56,190	46,536	41,996	42,058	50,887	41,137
Georgia	55,568	34,951	38,133	61,937	40,568	37,935	42,876	56,274	39,003
Hawaii	63,870	52,244	44,167	65,327	54,836	51,643	59,526	64,702	55,036
Idaho	45,601	36,367	30,258	51,797	62,396	36,843	34,416	46,414	33,096
Illinois	58,156	34,015	42,176	70,419	45,238	43,268	46,525	58,879	45,808
Indiana	49,224	30,649	43,172	54,054	35,625	36,825	36,425	49,482	36,719
Iowa	47,078	24,564	29,683	52,439	32,708	35,484	32,638	47,272	35,936
Kansas...................	48,381	31,569	35,371	56,170	58,355	35,042	35,666	48,972	35,351
Kentucky	41,263	27,518	26,325	52,334	34,233	38,114	30,455	41,313	36,823
Louisiana	47,980	24,840	36,389	50,529	36,276	37,981	34,320	48,215	39,215
Maine	45,670	26,968	23,933	40,145	46,950	34,800	34,439	45,758	33,706
Maryland	73,597	52,098	51,724	82,332	53,165	57,582	61,948	73,977	60,728
Massachusetts	64,818	39,917	37,075	69,552	-	31,569	45,811	65,939	31,075
Michigan	51,608	31,534	36,087	68,611	31,297	36,686	37,349	51,794	38,187
Minnesota	57,314	28,667	34,365	59,909	24,280	36,939	40,367	57,608	39,081
Mississippi..............	44,659	23,164	35,869	40,849	72,396	37,917	34,698	44,714	36,881
Missouri..................	46,896	29,704	33,043	50,219	33,977	35,530	34,215	46,981	39,359
Montana.................	43,461	24,213	25,842	35,789	54,434	34,250	37,522	43,613	33,809
Nebraska	48,319	26,637	27,625	58,827	42,500	38,864	31,972	48,922	36,374
Nevada	55,966	39,594	39,922	57,164	50,063	46,168	47,123	58,620	45,323
New Hampshire	61,500	45,139	38,125	69,037	46,107	73,601	53,698	61,604	55,611
New Jersey...............	72,244	44,858	42,241	93,111	59,301	42,480	57,011	74,658	46,408
New Mexico.............	43,829	35,515	28,471	53,584	32,933	36,159	32,910	49,966	34,481
New York................	58,907	38,682	36,453	56,532	32,640	33,338	43,893	60,242	37,019
North Carolina..........	49,333	30,099	31,014	55,371	36,350	32,658	34,366	49,701	34,711
North Dakota...........	44,539	25,088	25,044	32,344	26,085	29,653	22,948	44,550	34,479
Ohio.....................	49,271	28,077	35,022	59,130	65,345	34,045	36,853	49,422	35,733
Oklahoma................	43,055	26,760	33,338	42,954	27,264	30,885	33,224	43,480	31,652
Oregon	48,288	30,569	32,947	55,353	50,310	38,980	38,230	49,007	35,447
Pennsylvania	50,545	30,167	30,931	57,585	34,044	29,983	35,767	50,824	31,391
Rhode Island............	57,279	35,697	37,051	55,765	-	31,092	34,229	58,237	31,620
South Carolina..........	49,745	27,553	32,114	52,089	50,938	34,356	39,988	50,148	35,527
South Dakota............	45,164	34,763	24,970	43,308	-	33,793	26,601	45,242	33,642
Tennessee	44,642	29,584	29,288	55,715	47,809	33,393	33,463	44,807	34,935
Texas.....................	50,497	33,325	40,319	61,180	49,516	34,761	42,367	57,321	34,306
Utah	54,323	42,924	32,271	50,262	55,227	41,438	42,102	55,372	39,621
Vermont	49,624	38,022	36,483	60,272	90,131	-	29,688	49,626	46,567
Virginia	63,147	40,903	46,901	78,396	49,458	53,918	51,733	63,374	56,284
Washington	55,520	39,718	35,092	60,371	48,883	35,472	46,199	56,281	36,998
West Virginia	36,495	22,474	32,692	52,039	26,466	40,254	29,661	36,526	30,779
Wisconsin	52,231	27,104	36,927	52,663	32,056	33,489	39,178	52,459	36,165
Wyoming.................	50,845	41,171	37,973	38,750	31,397	45,017	32,796	51,055	44,840

Table B-1. States — What: Education, Employment, and Income, 2005–2007—*Continued*

	Median income in the past 12 months (in 2007 inflation-adjusted dollars)											
	Median family income by type of family							Median nonfamily household income			Median individual income	
STATE	All families	Married-couple families with children	Married-couple families, no children	Male householder with children	Male householder, no children	Female householder with children	Female householder, no children	All nonfamily households	Living alone, 65 years and over		Persons 15 years and over who worked full-time, year-round	
									Male	Female	Male	Female
ACS table number:	B19126	B19126	B19126	B19126	B19126	B19126	B19126	B19215	B19215	B19215	B19326	B19326
	100	101	102	103	104	105	106	107	108	109	110	111
United States	60,374	75,344	67,830	37,070	50,231	23,673	41,130	30,350	21,989	16,959	45,255	35,044
Alabama	50,210	66,197	58,597	32,673	38,397	17,310	30,070	21,579	18,119	14,141	41,391	29,860
Alaska......................	72,008	84,187	85,884	44,227	55,982	29,334	43,637	39,956	23,010	21,510	52,513	40,542
Arizona...................	57,004	69,760	65,448	37,377	48,758	26,116	42,348	32,367	23,265	18,795	41,703	34,851
Arkansas..................	46,340	58,900	52,722	28,661	37,229	17,831	30,409	20,939	18,405	14,007	36,909	28,029
California..................	66,420	77,807	80,704	41,059	57,548	27,348	48,833	39,212	25,482	19,370	47,162	39,833
Colorado..................	67,069	78,719	76,284	41,424	50,683	25,701	44,244	34,458	25,447	18,110	47,728	37,776
Connecticut..............	80,906	100,623	87,584	50,210	63,255	30,067	53,123	36,831	25,224	19,051	56,725	43,722
Delaware	66,828	83,754	74,539	42,115	54,372	28,071	50,639	33,863	22,747	18,509	49,591	38,607
District of Columbia ...	60,970	112,765	113,181	32,479	52,624	24,170	43,887	46,251	26,154	20,542	52,508	50,057
Florida......................	55,534	70,707	61,845	35,657	47,337	25,427	39,831	30,308	23,090	17,379	40,619	32,687
Georgia	57,724	73,684	67,577	35,419	47,061	23,350	36,090	30,666	19,967	15,197	42,776	33,785
Hawaii.....................	71,784	80,829	81,809	46,936	61,311	27,520	57,542	37,591	29,723	18,339	44,318	35,843
Idaho.......................	53,186	60,706	58,118	31,858	45,404	21,171	37,388	26,836	20,905	15,861	40,316	29,676
Illinois.....................	65,504	80,675	73,538	39,205	54,509	25,185	44,189	32,104	23,227	18,248	49,799	36,860
Indiana....................	57,602	71,123	63,323	34,030	46,461	22,250	38,936	27,117	22,088	17,096	44,707	32,019
Iowa	58,513	71,534	61,392	34,183	45,277	23,147	39,167	26,568	21,268	17,188	42,041	31,687
Kansas.....................	58,791	70,616	64,744	35,249	47,823	23,668	38,203	26,609	23,226	17,171	42,765	32,067
Kentucky..................	49,832	64,789	54,776	30,654	38,268	18,384	32,626	22,523	16,766	14,361	41,262	30,867
Louisiana..................	49,649	68,698	59,192	34,100	42,581	16,999	30,484	22,152	17,098	13,606	42,298	28,902
Maine......................	55,346	68,499	59,449	32,640	45,601	21,055	37,444	25,787	19,530	15,012	42,637	31,934
Maryland	80,669	101,769	90,570	47,556	63,636	35,048	56,130	41,808	27,806	19,819	54,717	44,383
Massachusetts	77,409	98,998	83,529	46,984	60,786	26,744	52,523	36,165	21,359	17,201	55,025	42,642
Michigan	60,269	76,765	66,186	36,190	48,422	22,460	39,936	33,054	22,845	17,897	49,109	37,251
Minnesota	68,849	83,829	71,700	40,572	55,968	27,280	47,816	33,054	22,845	17,897	49,109	37,251
Mississippi................	44,169	60,922	54,190	29,771	33,892	16,884	27,360	19,371	15,674	12,732	37,289	27,202
Missouri...................	55,014	69,500	60,441	33,200	46,152	21,575	37,999	24,525	19,837	16,218	42,499	31,499
Montana...................	52,357	61,096	55,866	34,564	42,753	18,902	34,729	24,525	19,837	16,218	39,113	27,299
Nebraska	58,523	69,927	62,085	32,978	47,798	21,895	40,806	26,876	21,293	16,586	40,453	31,078
Nevada	62,222	71,549	71,901	43,811	54,341	28,600	47,755	36,423	24,655	18,789	43,463	33,979
New Hampshire	73,246	87,768	75,520	42,217	61,635	29,377	53,098	34,998	21,473	17,582	51,681	36,688
New Jersey................	80,780	100,830	89,173	44,796	64,219	31,237	55,407	37,659	24,655	18,674	56,599	43,312
New Mexico..............	48,798	59,488	60,129	31,697	41,435	19,432	33,057	26,526	20,356	16,402	39,529	30,426
New York..................	64,107	82,885	74,345	38,276	56,673	24,752	46,198	32,751	21,766	16,706	48,725	39,485
North Carolina	53,770	68,859	61,450	33,738	42,187	21,243	34,303	26,298	18,332	15,300	40,400	32,117
North Dakota............	57,299	68,182	59,202	37,413	48,139	21,259	35,983	24,048	19,939	15,433	40,539	28,482
Ohio........................	57,999	74,713	63,805	35,273	47,046	21,738	38,677	26,775	21,704	16,979	45,506	33,916
Oklahoma................	50,119	60,735	57,705	31,734	40,457	18,516	33,395	23,589	19,719	16,235	39,250	29,881
Oregon	57,716	69,574	64,606	35,075	46,800	22,240	40,020	29,254	23,242	17,847	44,009	34,091
Pennsylvania	60,243	77,122	64,628	36,364	50,900	23,707	41,116	26,385	20,883	16,156	46,151	34,438
Rhode Island............	68,740	84,320	77,063	40,899	59,453	24,448	49,106	30,626	19,865	16,120	49,360	38,346
South Carolina..........	51,954	67,949	60,757	34,252	41,897	20,124	31,819	25,448	18,910	14,792	40,315	30,461
South Dakota............	54,306	67,266	57,476	31,383	41,166	21,936	33,769	24,862	20,401	15,906	37,875	28,718
Tennessee	51,438	65,452	58,281	31,109	41,105	19,717	34,198	24,896	18,285	14,629	40,503	30,829
Texas.......................	54,165	65,309	66,127	34,146	43,831	21,639	35,892	29,980	19,905	16,183	40,842	32,458
Utah........................	60,564	66,816	64,691	38,556	55,122	26,655	45,186	31,362	23,766	18,694	43,994	31,223
Vermont	61,143	74,884	66,054	39,243	50,747	24,839	44,676	29,621	21,742	16,329	42,434	34,520
Virginia....................	69,609	86,577	77,738	41,300	55,416	27,140	45,003	36,755	25,245	17,639	49,911	38,103
Washington	65,428	78,669	73,033	41,375	54,451	25,190	44,507	34,538	26,377	19,699	40,513	38,600
West Virginia	45,705	57,431	49,852	27,244	38,934	15,488	29,749	19,740	19,742	14,670	45,216	27,155
Wisconsin	62,607	76,225	66,627	38,855	50,529	23,625	42,347	29,647	21,512	17,027	46,346	33,505
Wyoming..................	60,344	71,626	65,498	41,239	50,129	22,339	39,034	30,373	22,697	18,370		29,973

Table B-1. States — What: Education, Employment, and Income, 2005–2007—*Continued*

STATE	Per capita income in the past 12 months (in 2007 inflation-adjusted dollars)	Total number of households	Households by type of income (percent)								
			With wage or salary income	With self-employment income	With interest, dividends, or net rental income	With Social Security	With Supplemental Security Income (SSI)	With public assistance income	With cash public assistance or Food Stamps	With retirement income	With other types of income
ACS table number:	B19301	B19052	B19052	B19053	B19054	B19055	B19056	B19057	B19058	B19059	B19060
	112	113	114	115	116	117	118	119	120	121	122
United States	26,178	111,609,629	77.0	12.1	25.1	26.8	4.0	2.3	8.6	17.4	13.1
Alabama	22,011	1,798,304	73.0	10.3	19.4	31.3	5.6	1.4	10.7	19.6	14.2
Alaska	27,988	233,861	84.6	17.3	46.8	17.0	2.9	6.4	10.9	16.7	46.4
Arizona	24,587	2,215,761	75.4	10.8	23.3	28.2	3.1	2.0	7.6	18.8	11.9
Arkansas	20,309	1,096,622	72.8	11.7	20.0	32.3	5.2	1.7	12.2	17.3	14.4
California	28,049	12,140,888	77.9	14.9	25.2	23.3	4.9	3.2	5.5	15.3	12.6
Colorado	28,642	1,838,303	81.0	14.9	27.5	20.6	2.7	1.9	5.7	15.3	11.9
Connecticut	35,295	1,323,431	78.4	12.6	32.6	27.6	3.1	2.3	6.4	17.7	11.9
Delaware	27,879	321,748	78.1	9.6	26.7	29.0	2.9	2.0	7.4	23.1	12.8
District of Columbia	38,009	249,805	77.6	9.9	26.2	19.7	3.6	4.3	10.7	15.9	9.3
Florida	26,125	7,077,123	72.6	10.3	24.5	32.5	3.4	1.3	7.5	19.2	12.2
Georgia	24,558	3,364,749	79.8	11.1	19.3	23.6	3.7	1.4	8.7	15.4	12.2
Hawaii	27,814	433,664	78.9	14.9	31.0	29.7	3.4	3.3	7.5	22.0	12.0
Idaho	21,844	545,171	77.5	16.4	23.9	25.9	3.4	2.4	7.6	16.2	15.7
Illinois	27,511	4,724,462	79.0	10.5	27.0	25.2	3.2	1.9	8.5	16.3	11.6
Indiana	23,620	2,447,887	78.5	10.6	24.1	26.9	3.3	2.4	9.1	18.1	13.7
Iowa	24,078	1,206,848	77.7	15.2	29.7	28.6	3.1	2.5	8.4	15.8	14.9
Kansas	24,579	1,083,868	79.0	14.3	27.2	26.3	3.0	2.2	7.0	15.6	13.2
Kentucky	21,618	1,654,119	72.6	11.5	20.3	30.6	6.5	2.2	13.2	19.3	14.6
Louisiana	21,176	1,605,203	75.0	10.5	19.2	28.1	5.7	2.0	18.2	16.4	13.8
Maine	24,344	542,424	73.2	16.6	28.1	30.7	4.8	4.5	13.2	18.4	15.7
Maryland	32,933	2,082,573	81.7	11.4	28.4	23.8	3.0	1.8	5.5	19.7	12.1
Massachusetts	32,113	2,448,608	77.1	12.3	30.3	26.8	4.7	2.5	7.0	16.8	12.7
Michigan	24,966	3,864,307	75.7	10.4	26.0	28.0	4.0	3.2	10.5	21.1	14.9
Minnesota	28,536	2,041,466	80.1	14.4	29.5	24.5	2.7	3.0	5.9	15.0	13.5
Mississippi	18,820	1,079,584	73.0	10.5	15.7	31.2	6.8	2.3	15.6	16.5	14.6
Missouri	23,667	2,300,211	76.3	12.1	24.8	28.8	4.1	2.3	10.8	18.2	13.3
Montana	22,152	369,329	74.4	18.9	28.7	28.9	3.4	2.0	8.4	17.7	14.9
Nebraska	23,900	698,163	79.3	16.2	28.7	26.6	2.6	2.4	7.3	13.3	14.7
Nevada	26,980	932,715	81.0	9.4	19.2	24.1	2.9	1.8	4.8	16.4	11.3
New Hampshire	29,672	500,671	80.0	14.7	29.5	26.3	3.2	2.6	5.8	17.0	12.5
New Jersey	33,219	3,143,408	79.3	9.9	29.9	27.2	3.0	2.0	4.8	17.4	12.1
New Mexico	21,586	728,508	75.1	12.9	21.0	27.7	4.5	2.6	10.0	18.9	12.3
New York	29,230	7,096,035	75.6	11.0	26.1	27.5	5.1	3.1	10.2	17.9	11.7
North Carolina	23,767	3,471,751	77.2	11.5	22.1	27.3	3.6	1.6	9.3	17.7	13.5
North Dakota	23,594	271,131	78.0	17.8	30.3	26.8	2.4	2.0	7.2	11.3	13.7
Ohio	24,296	4,500,621	76.0	10.5	24.9	27.7	4.0	2.6	9.8	20.0	13.8
Oklahoma	21,700	1,386,849	74.6	12.8	22.2	28.8	4.2	3.6	11.5	17.5	13.7
Oregon	25,097	1,447,409	75.3	14.8	27.6	27.0	3.3	2.6	11.6	17.7	15.0
Pennsylvania	25,692	4,858,509	74.4	10.4	28.6	31.1	4.5	3.0	8.5	20.2	13.6
Rhode Island	27,515	404,549	75.8	10.9	27.9	28.1	5.6	2.9	7.2	17.9	14.7
South Carolina	22,560	1,664,561	75.3	10.4	19.4	29.3	3.9	1.4	10.3	19.3	13.3
South Dakota	22,561	311,644	77.7	18.9	28.0	27.6	2.8	2.4	8.2	13.7	14.6
Tennessee	22,937	2,382,975	74.8	12.5	20.4	28.7	4.6	2.7	12.6	17.4	13.2
Texas	23,294	8,095,025	80.0	13.1	20.1	22.9	3.6	1.6	10.0	13.8	12.7
Utah	21,845	812,604	83.7	13.7	25.0	21.2	2.4	1.8	6.0	15.9	13.6
Vermont	26,223	250,871	76.3	19.7	34.1	27.8	4.3	3.3	9.2	16.7	15.3
Virginia	30,651	2,909,223	80.3	11.0	27.7	25.0	3.2	1.7	6.7	20.0	12.7
Washington	28,290	2,472,477	77.9	12.8	29.1	24.3	3.8	3.4	9.1	17.8	15.0
West Virginia	20,111	738,943	68.0	8.6	19.6	35.7	6.9	2.2	13.0	23.7	14.2
Wisconsin	25,742	2,235,246	78.7	11.9	31.3	26.7	3.2	1.6	6.5	16.8	15.1
Wyoming	25,885	205,422	79.5	15.5	26.8	26.2	2.6	1.8	5.7	16.1	14.0

STATE	Total number of households	Household income in the past 12 months (in 2007 inflation-adjusted dollars)									
		Households by income group (percent)									
		Less than $10,000	$10,000 to $14,999	$15,000 to $24,999	$25,000 to $34,999	$35,000 to $49,999	$50,000 to $74,999	$75,000 to $99,999	$100,000 to $149,999	$150,000 to $199,999	$200,000 or more
ACS table number:	C19001	C19001	C19001	C19001	C19001	C19001	C19001	C19001	C19001	C19001	C19001
	123	124	125	126	127	128	129	130	131	132	133
United States	111,609,629	7.6	5.8	11.1	11.0	14.6	18.8	12.1	11.4	3.9	3.7
Alabama	1,798,304	11.0	7.7	13.7	12.2	14.9	17.5	10.2	8.4	2.4	2.1
Alaska	233,861	4.8	4.6	8.4	8.6	13.3	20.2	14.9	16.2	5.6	3.4
Arizona	2,215,761	6.9	5.2	11.4	11.9	15.8	19.2	12.1	10.8	3.4	3.2
Arkansas	1,096,622	10.8	8.0	14.7	13.5	16.0	17.5	9.3	6.8	1.8	1.6
California	12,140,888	5.6	5.3	9.8	9.6	13.1	18.0	12.8	14.3	5.7	5.8
Colorado	1,838,303	6.7	4.8	9.8	10.3	14.6	19.3	13.1	13.0	4.5	3.9
Connecticut	1,323,431	5.6	4.3	8.1	8.2	12.2	17.9	14.4	15.9	6.1	7.3
Delaware	321,748	5.9	4.2	9.7	10.0	14.9	19.8	13.9	13.7	4.4	3.4
District of Columbia	249,805	11.9	5.3	9.2	9.3	12.5	15.8	10.4	11.6	5.9	8.2
Florida	7,077,123	7.3	5.8	12.0	12.3	15.9	19.1	11.3	10.0	3.1	3.3
Georgia	3,364,749	8.4	5.7	11.0	11.2	15.1	19.0	12.0	10.8	3.6	3.4
Hawaii	433,664	6.0	3.8	7.4	8.6	13.4	20.2	14.7	15.8	5.7	4.3
Idaho	545,171	6.8	6.0	12.5	13.3	16.7	20.9	11.5	8.1	2.2	2.0
Illinois	4,724,462	7.2	5.1	10.2	10.1	13.9	19.4	13.0	12.6	4.4	4.1
Indiana	2,447,887	7.4	5.7	11.7	12.1	16.0	20.7	12.5	9.5	2.5	2.0
Iowa	1,206,848	6.7	6.1	12.2	12.2	16.4	21.0	12.3	8.8	2.2	2.0
Kansas	1,083,868	7.1	5.7	12.1	12.2	16.0	19.6	12.0	9.9	2.9	2.5
Kentucky	1,654,119	11.1	7.7	13.5	12.1	15.4	18.0	10.4	8.0	2.1	1.7
Louisiana	1,605,203	11.7	8.0	13.3	11.7	14.5	16.9	10.5	8.8	2.4	2.2
Maine	542,424	8.0	6.7	12.4	12.0	15.6	20.5	11.6	8.8	2.4	2.1
Maryland	2,082,573	5.0	3.8	7.3	8.3	12.4	18.8	14.4	17.1	6.8	6.2
Massachusetts	2,448,608	7.2	5.2	8.6	8.3	11.8	17.8	13.8	15.7	6.0	5.8
Michigan	3,864,307	7.9	5.7	11.3	11.4	14.9	19.3	12.4	11.1	3.4	2.7
Minnesota	2,041,466	5.8	4.8	9.3	10.0	14.7	20.7	14.2	13.0	4.0	3.5
Mississippi	1,079,584	13.0	8.6	14.8	12.9	14.8	16.7	8.9	7.0	1.8	1.6
Missouri	2,300,211	8.3	6.5	12.4	12.3	15.8	19.5	11.3	9.1	2.6	2.2
Montana	369,329	8.3	6.8	13.8	12.5	16.9	19.8	10.9	7.5	2.0	1.6
Nebraska	698,163	7.0	6.0	11.9	12.3	15.8	21.0	12.2	9.5	2.3	2.0
Nevada	932,715	5.7	4.2	9.7	11.0	15.5	21.1	13.7	12.2	3.6	3.3
New Hampshire	500,671	4.9	4.2	8.2	9.3	13.5	20.7	15.4	14.9	5.1	3.8
New Jersey	3,143,408	5.6	4.2	8.2	8.0	11.8	17.7	13.9	16.6	7.1	7.2
New Mexico	728,508	10.1	7.1	13.2	12.6	15.7	17.8	10.3	8.5	2.6	2.1
New York	7,096,035	8.7	5.7	10.3	9.7	13.0	17.7	12.0	12.7	4.8	5.3
North Carolina	3,471,751	9.0	6.7	12.6	12.2	15.6	18.7	10.9	9.0	2.8	2.6
North Dakota	271,131	8.4	6.8	13.1	12.2	16.4	20.6	11.1	7.9	1.9	1.7
Ohio	4,500,621	8.3	6.1	11.8	11.8	15.5	19.6	11.9	9.9	2.8	2.3
Oklahoma	1,386,849	9.8	7.3	13.8	13.0	16.0	18.4	10.0	7.8	2.0	2.0
Oregon	1,447,409	7.5	6.0	11.6	11.7	15.6	19.8	12.1	10.1	3.0	2.6
Pennsylvania	4,858,509	7.6	6.2	11.9	11.3	14.7	19.2	12.0	10.7	3.3	3.0
Rhode Island	404,549	7.6	6.3	9.9	9.9	12.9	18.2	14.0	13.3	4.5	3.4
South Carolina	1,664,561	9.7	6.7	12.9	12.4	15.6	18.6	11.0	8.5	2.4	2.2
South Dakota	311,644	7.9	6.4	12.7	13.1	16.8	20.8	11.0	7.6	1.7	1.8
Tennessee	2,382,975	10.0	7.0	12.9	12.5	15.7	18.6	10.3	8.1	2.4	2.4
Texas	8,095,025	8.5	6.1	12.1	11.7	14.9	17.9	11.3	10.5	3.5	3.5
Utah	812,604	5.0	4.2	9.5	11.3	16.4	22.4	13.8	11.7	3.2	2.6
Vermont	250,871	6.4	5.9	11.4	10.7	16.1	20.3	12.7	11.0	3.0	2.4
Virginia	2,909,223	6.3	4.6	8.8	9.6	13.7	19.0	13.1	14.0	5.6	5.4
Washington	2,472,477	6.6	4.8	9.8	10.2	14.7	19.9	13.2	13.0	4.1	3.6
West Virginia	738,943	11.4	8.7	15.5	13.2	15.5	17.4	9.3	6.3	1.5	1.4
Wisconsin	2,235,246	6.2	5.6	10.9	11.4	15.6	21.3	13.5	10.6	2.6	2.4
Wyoming	205,422	5.4	5.1	12.0	11.4	16.1	21.0	13.4	10.8	2.7	2.2

STATE	Households with income over $100,000 by age of householder (percent)					Total households with income below poverty as a percent of all households in group						
	All households	Householder under 25 years	Householder 25 to 44 years	Householder 45 to 64 years	Householder 65 years and over	All house-holds	Family house-holds	Married-couple family household	Male householder family households	Female householder family households	Male householder nonfamily households	Female householder nonfamily households
ACS table number:	C19001	C19037	C19037	C19037	C19037	C17017	C17017	C17017	C17017	C17017	C17017	C17017
	134	135	136	137	138	139	140	141	142	143	144	145
United States	19.0	2.7	19.3	26.1	9.2	12.6	9.8	4.8	13.2	28.6	15.7	20.8
Alabama	12.9	1.1	12.4	18.9	6.3	16.9	12.9	5.4	17.2	37.3	21.0	29.1
Alaska	25.2	5.5	23.8	32.0	14.3	9.2	7.6	3.3	12.9	23.9	13.2	11.9
Arizona	17.4	3.6	17.5	24.4	8.9	12.2	10.3	5.8	13.9	27.6	14.1	17.8
Arkansas	10.2	0.8	10.5	14.9	4.7	17.3	13.3	6.7	19.4	38.0	23.1	28.6
California	25.8	5.8	26.1	33.6	14.1	11.4	9.7	5.8	11.6	24.2	13.2	16.7
Colorado	21.5	2.6	20.7	29.6	10.3	11.1	8.3	4.3	11.5	27.2	14.4	18.1
Connecticut	29.4	4.8	30.7	38.7	13.3	8.5	5.9	2.2	7.8	21.1	11.9	15.6
Delaware	21.6	3.2	21.7	30.0	10.4	9.7	7.2	2.7	10.6	23.1	13.2	16.5
District of Columbia	25.6	5.9	28.7	29.0	18.7	16.3	15.7	4.8	11.7	30.2	15.2	18.0
Florida	16.4	2.6	16.7	22.8	9.6	11.9	9.0	4.7	11.7	25.0	14.0	20.3
Georgia	17.8	2.3	17.3	24.5	8.3	13.8	11.1	4.8	14.9	30.8	15.5	23.1
Hawaii	25.9	6.4	22.3	34.4	20.0	9.8	6.8	3.6	7.8	19.5	13.5	20.4
Idaho	12.3	1.4	11.4	18.5	6.2	12.5	9.4	5.7	12.7	31.6	16.3	23.1
Illinois	21.1	2.8	22.0	28.8	9.2	11.6	8.9	4.0	12.2	27.4	14.7	18.8
Indiana	14.0	1.2	13.4	20.8	5.7	11.8	8.9	3.7	13.7	30.0	15.0	20.7
Iowa	13.0	0.9	13.3	20.0	5.2	10.9	7.2	3.2	13.1	28.4	15.8	19.9
Kansas	15.3	0.9	14.6	23.1	7.3	11.7	8.3	3.9	13.0	29.2	16.1	20.6
Kentucky	11.8	1.0	11.7	17.0	5.0	17.3	13.2	7.3	18.3	35.6	22.4	28.4
Louisiana	13.4	1.6	13.4	18.8	6.9	18.7	15.0	6.0	16.5	40.1	21.7	30.7
Maine	13.2	2.0	12.4	19.2	5.3	12.9	8.6	4.0	14.7	30.1	18.5	22.8
Maryland	30.0	6.1	29.9	39.6	15.2	7.9	5.5	2.1	6.8	17.4	11.0	14.0
Massachusetts	27.5	5.9	30.1	35.7	11.0	10.7	7.2	2.8	9.1	24.1	15.0	18.6
Michigan	17.1	1.6	17.4	24.2	6.8	12.8	9.8	4.2	15.7	30.6	16.1	21.1
Minnesota	20.5	2.4	22.1	28.3	7.5	9.5	6.3	2.7	12.4	24.4	13.3	17.6
Mississippi	10.4	1.5	9.8	14.8	5.7	20.6	16.6	6.7	20.2	41.2	25.1	34.1
Missouri	13.9	1.4	13.8	20.3	6.1	13.3	9.8	4.5	14.7	30.4	17.6	22.3
Montana	11.1	1.3	9.7	16.3	5.8	13.4	9.3	5.2	15.3	32.0	17.4	24.4
Nebraska	13.9	1.1	13.7	21.1	5.9	11.4	7.9	3.5	12.3	30.8	15.3	20.6
Nevada	19.1	5.4	19.1	24.7	11.1	9.8	7.8	4.3	8.7	21.9	11.6	16.0
New Hampshire	23.8	4.2	25.4	30.3	10.0	7.9	4.9	2.0	9.9	19.6	11.6	16.6
New Jersey	30.8	6.2	33.1	39.6	13.3	8.8	6.5	3.0	8.4	19.8	11.4	16.0
New Mexico	13.2	1.3	11.1	19.7	8.2	17.2	14.2	7.5	18.6	36.2	21.9	24.2
New York	22.8	4.6	24.5	29.3	11.3	13.6	10.7	5.2	12.8	27.2	16.0	21.0
North Carolina	14.4	1.5	14.3	20.3	7.0	14.4	11.0	5.0	15.8	32.2	18.7	23.4
North Dakota	11.5	0.5	11.8	18.4	5.2	13.2	7.3	3.3	11.0	32.9	18.1	27.4
Ohio	15.1	1.1	15.2	21.6	6.3	13.0	9.7	3.9	15.1	31.0	17.0	21.0
Oklahoma	11.7	1.0	10.8	17.6	6.7	15.9	12.5	6.3	18.0	36.3	19.9	25.5
Oregon	15.7	1.8	15.3	21.9	8.0	13.0	9.3	4.6	14.3	30.8	18.3	20.5
Pennsylvania	17.0	2.0	17.8	24.1	6.6	11.8	8.2	3.5	13.0	26.8	15.7	21.0
Rhode Island	21.2	3.7	21.8	28.7	9.7	11.9	8.3	2.8	11.2	27.6	16.3	20.0
South Carolina	13.1	2.0	12.3	18.1	7.6	15.2	11.8	4.9	14.4	33.4	18.3	25.5
South Dakota	11.1	0.6	10.7	16.9	5.8	13.0	8.7	4.1	18.0	30.9	17.6	24.6
Tennessee	13.0	1.1	11.9	19.1	6.6	15.6	12.2	5.9	17.6	34.4	18.9	25.9
Texas	17.5	2.0	16.5	24.9	9.4	15.3	13.3	7.8	15.7	33.6	16.2	23.6
Utah	17.4	2.2	14.6	28.5	9.0	9.8	7.4	4.6	10.3	25.3	13.4	20.8
Vermont	16.4	1.7	14.2	23.4	8.5	10.9	6.9	2.8	10.8	25.0	14.8	20.7
Virginia	25.0	4.9	24.7	33.6	13.0	9.9	7.1	3.1	9.5	23.2	12.2	18.5
Washington	20.7	3.3	20.9	28.1	9.4	11.2	8.0	4.0	11.9	26.3	15.4	18.6
West Virginia	9.1	1.0	9.4	13.1	4.1	17.6	13.3	7.8	19.9	37.2	23.1	28.9
Wisconsin	15.6	2.1	15.6	22.8	6.3	10.4	7.1	2.8	11.6	28.1	14.1	18.5
Wyoming	15.7	3.7	14.7	22.6	7.2	9.2	5.7	2.6	7.0	24.5	12.0	20.0

Table B-1. States — What: Education, Employment, and Income, 2005–2007—*Continued*

STATE	Population for whom poverty status is determined	Persons with income below poverty by age (percent of persons in group)				Persons with income below poverty by selected race and Hispanic origin groups (percent of persons in group)			
		All persons	Under 18 years	18 to 64 years	65 years and over	White alone, not Hispanic or Latino	Black alone	Asian alone	Hispanic or Latino
ACS table number:	C17001	C17001	C17001	C17001	C17001	C17001H	C17001B	C17001D	C17001I
	146	147	148	149	150	151	152	153	154
United States	290,858,668	13.3	18.3	11.9	9.9	9.2	25.3	11.0	21.5
Alabama	4,466,259	16.8	24.0	14.9	12.6	11.2	30.7	14.7	28.1
Alaska......................	659,004	10.4	13.9	9.4	5.6	6.5	19.5	8.3	14.6
Arizona....................	6,038,283	14.2	20.0	12.9	8.4	8.5	21.3	12.1	22.3
Arkansas..................	2,723,361	17.5	25.0	15.6	12.6	13.5	34.0	11.0	27.5
California.................	35,482,447	13.0	18.0	11.7	8.3	7.9	20.6	10.3	18.9
Colorado	4,662,879	11.8	15.6	10.9	8.7	8.1	22.0	12.7	23.1
Connecticut..............	3,380,853	8.2	11.2	7.4	6.7	4.9	17.2	8.4	22.7
Delaware	827,220	10.6	14.9	9.7	7.3	7.1	18.6	6.7	25.5
District of Columbia...	555,366	18.8	29.3	16.3	15.6	8.4	25.4	11.5	16.4
Florida	17,607,556	12.6	17.6	11.5	9.9	8.6	23.3	10.2	16.7
Georgia	9,065,898	14.5	20.0	12.5	12.7	9.0	23.9	9.0	22.8
Hawaii	1,245,609	9.1	11.3	8.5	8.4	8.8	5.9	6.9	12.5
Idaho.......................	1,427,587	13.0	16.5	12.3	8.5	11.2	26.0	13.5	26.2
Illinois	12,467,824	12.1	16.7	10.9	8.8	7.7	27.9	9.2	16.8
Indiana	6,103,829	12.5	17.3	11.4	8.0	10.2	27.1	13.9	22.6
Iowa	2,868,031	11.0	13.7	10.6	8.0	9.5	34.4	14.9	24.1
Kansas.....................	2,672,003	11.9	15.1	11.3	8.1	9.5	25.5	11.8	24.1
Kentucky	4,086,505	17.1	23.0	15.5	13.4	15.6	29.9	15.0	27.0
Louisiana	4,216,250	19.3	27.7	16.8	14.0	11.5	34.3	17.4	18.3
Maine......................	1,277,940	12.8	17.1	11.9	10.1	12.0	45.6	19.5	17.8
Maryland	5,456,359	8.2	10.4	7.4	8.1	5.5	13.6	5.8	10.8
Massachusetts	6,234,062	10.1	13.0	9.3	9.4	7.0	21.9	14.8	29.1
Michigan	9,852,614	13.7	18.9	12.7	8.4	10.0	30.6	12.3	23.3
Minnesota	5,023,673	9.6	12.0	8.9	8.3	7.2	33.5	16.4	22.1
Mississippi...............	2,808,952	21.1	29.7	18.4	15.6	12.0	35.7	18.4	23.4
Missouri...................	5,664,799	13.4	18.5	12.2	9.8	10.8	28.5	14.6	21.6
Montana...................	922,391	14.0	18.1	13.5	9.5	12.0	28.3	14.0	25.2
Nebraska	1,710,521	11.3	14.7	10.3	9.1	8.8	35.3	10.0	21.9
Nevada	2,450,606	10.8	14.8	9.6	7.6	7.9	18.8	7.2	15.9
New Hampshire	1,270,007	7.7	9.6	7.0	7.6	7.2	25.5	8.8	16.3
New Jersey...............	8,489,015	8.7	11.7	7.6	8.5	5.1	17.7	6.2	16.7
New Mexico..............	1,898,977	18.4	25.5	16.5	13.2	10.6	24.0	10.0	23.2
New York..................	18,748,563	14.0	19.6	12.3	12.2	9.0	21.9	15.6	24.8
North Carolina	8,601,522	14.8	20.5	13.2	11.4	9.9	26.0	12.7	27.4
North Dakota............	610,774	11.9	13.4	11.4	11.9	10.2	22.7	16.5	20.0
Ohio	11,148,353	13.2	18.5	12.1	8.4	10.3	30.5	11.9	24.2
Oklahoma.................	3,459,056	16.6	23.3	15.1	10.5	13.1	30.9	13.0	28.6
Oregon	3,611,297	13.5	17.4	13.2	8.3	11.3	29.5	14.8	25.9
Pennsylvania	11,968,623	11.9	16.6	10.9	8.9	8.8	28.6	13.8	30.6
Rhode Island.............	1,023,538	11.7	17.1	10.4	8.7	7.9	27.3	15.2	29.5
South Carolina..........	4,193,756	15.6	22.2	13.7	12.0	9.7	27.8	10.3	25.2
South Dakota............	759,263	13.3	16.8	12.3	11.7	9.6	32.7	14.9	28.0
Tennessee	5,913,533	15.9	22.4	14.0	12.9	12.7	28.3	10.3	27.6
Texas.......................	22,765,577	16.9	23.9	14.5	12.4	8.9	24.5	11.8	26.0
Utah........................	2,534,619	10.3	11.4	10.2	6.7	8.2	18.9	14.3	21.6
Vermont	599,979	10.7	13.7	10.1	9.0	10.2	33.9	13.5	25.4
Virginia	7,390,120	9.9	13.0	8.9	9.4	7.4	18.2	7.5	13.3
Washington	6,237,571	11.8	15.3	11.1	8.6	9.5	24.0	10.5	24.0
West Virginia	1,760,344	17.7	24.9	16.9	10.7	17.0	30.6	12.6	26.6
Wisconsin	5,415,795	10.8	14.6	9.9	8.3	8.1	34.8	17.0	23.9
Wyoming..................	499,705	8.9	11.2	8.5	6.3	8.0	NA	13.7	13.8

Table B-2. Counties — What: Education, Employment, and Income, 2005–2007

STATE County code	STATE County	Educational attainment			Employment status				Percent of households with no workers	Median household income (dollars)	Percent of families with income below poverty	Percent of households with income less than $25,000	Percent of households with income of $100,000 or more
		Total population 25 years and over	Percent with a high school diploma or less	Percent with a bachelor's degree or more	Total population 16 years and over	Percent in the labor force	Unemployment rate	Percent who worked full-time, year-round					
	ACS table number:	C15002	C15002	C15002	C20005	C23001	C23001	C20005	C08202	B19013	C17015	C19001	C19001
		1	2	3	4	5	6	7	8	9	10	11	12
00 000	United States	195,646,383	46.0	27.0	233,658,279	64.7	6.6	39.9	26.2	50,007	9.8	24.5	19.0
01 000	**Alabama**	3,015,910	52.3	21.1	3,596,728	60.0	7.0	38.3	30.9	40,052	12.9	32.4	12.9
01 001	Autauga	31,540	51.1	20.6	37,336	65.7	5.7	44.7	23.6	48,052	8.4	24.2	14.3
01 003	Baldwin	114,231	43.7	26.3	132,445	60.3	4.4	38.6	30.1	46,251	9.3	23.4	16.5
01 005	Barbour	19,058	68.2	11.2	22,368	50.3	8.6	32.0	37.3	32,071	19.4	41.3	5.9
01 007	Bibb	14,208	71.0	11.0	16,843	-	-	38.9	34.4	38,302	9.0	29.5	9.6
01 009	Blount	37,562	63.1	11.6	43,473	59.5	3.9	41.4	28.9	44,665	8.2	28.5	10.9
01 013	Butler	13,332	62.3	12.3	15,930	56.0	5.7	36.9	35.0	31,829	13.8	40.4	7.3
01 015	Calhoun	74,731	57.3	17.0	89,576	58.9	9.3	37.2	33.6	37,736	13.3	34.3	10.2
01 017	Chambers	23,974	63.6	10.2	27,627	59.1	7.8	36.5	35.7	33,570	8.5	35.9	4.9
01 019	Cherokee	17,526	69.5	8.5	19,765	58.8	10.7	35.6	37.6	37,549	11.4	35.8	7.0
01 021	Chilton	28,030	66.0	10.2	32,484	60.1	5.3	39.5	30.7	37,023	13.7	33.0	10.1
01 025	Clarke	17,010	68.1	13.4	20,784	-	-	27.8	41.7	26,273	20.6	47.2	10.3
01 031	Coffee	31,007	50.5	20.2	36,129	60.6	6.4	39.1	30.2	40,040	12.2	30.6	13.2
01 033	Colbert	37,625	57.5	15.7	43,962	55.3	5.4	37.6	36.4	37,090	13.8	35.2	9.3
01 039	Covington	25,429	62.9	13.6	29,514	57.2	8.1	35.9	38.0	32,367	13.6	38.9	6.3
01 043	Cullman	54,596	59.5	13.7	63,254	59.8	5.5	37.0	30.7	37,189	10.7	34.7	9.9
01 045	Dale	30,954	49.3	14.8	36,402	60.8	4.9	40.4	28.0	40,865	11.1	29.7	8.3
01 047	Dallas	27,223	62.2	14.2	32,967	52.0	12.9	31.5	45.5	26,486	27.0	47.2	6.2
01 049	DeKalb	45,326	65.5	11.3	52,166	58.5	8.4	36.4	34.0	31,717	16.2	39.8	7.1
01 051	Elmore	49,147	55.7	18.2	58,866	56.6	8.3	39.2	27.0	50,675	9.3	22.6	14.7
01 053	Escambia	25,434	65.4	10.6	29,924	52.8	8.0	33.5	37.7	33,990	18.0	37.2	7.4
01 055	Etowah	70,437	54.9	14.8	82,017	55.9	7.2	35.6	35.6	34,207	13.1	36.5	8.3
01 059	Franklin	20,442	67.2	9.9	23,953	59.2	7.6	37.8	32.6	30,149	11.7	40.7	4.4
01 061	Geneva	17,912	65.2	8.7	20,695	54.0	7.2	35.9	37.8	32,304	13.2	39.9	5.3
01 069	Houston	63,514	50.6	19.8	74,117	60.5	5.4	41.2	30.5	39,837	11.7	32.7	13.4
01 071	Jackson	36,976	67.2	10.5	42,484	55.3	8.1	35.6	35.8	34,907	15.2	37.9	6.6
01 073	Jefferson	437,623	43.5	27.9	517,890	63.0	7.8	40.6	28.4	44,283	11.5	29.2	16.3
01 077	Lauderdale	59,430	54.0	19.5	71,578	55.3	7.7	33.1	37.8	36,515	14.1	36.6	11.8
01 079	Lawrence	23,510	68.6	9.2	27,289	59.4	4.8	38.1	27.8	43,017	9.3	29.8	8.5
01 081	Lee	71,089	41.6	30.8	102,395	63.1	6.0	36.8	28.9	38,849	11.9	35.4	12.4
01 083	Limestone	48,276	56.3	17.0	56,659	58.4	4.7	37.7	27.8	43,979	9.4	26.0	14.4
01 087	Macon	13,312	48.7	22.7	18,213	52.4	12.4	28.4	36.9	26,670	17.0	47.2	6.7
01 089	Madison	200.356	35.3	38.1	239,571	65.8	6.6	42.0	24.2	53,001	7.9	22.7	22.4
01 091	Marengo	13,766	64.4	14.0	16,315	55.0	10.4	30.0	38.9	29,852	21.1	45.7	10.0
01 093	Marion	21,115	65.7	9.6	24,057	56.1	6.8	37.1	37.1	32,149	13.3	42.5	6.4
01 095	Marshall	57,883	57.4	14.8	66,543	58.7	5.0	37.9	33.6	35,754	16.6	35.3	10.1
01 097	Mobile	256,937	54.1	19.4	307,881	60.1	7.1	37.6	30.7	38,596	16.4	33.5	11.3
01 099	Monroe	14,768	61.6	14.7	17,549	-	-	37.7	39.4	28,802	20.8	44.9	6.8
01 101	Montgomery	140,048	44.5	30.4	172,757	63.7	8.1	40.4	28.0	41,973	15.0	30.8	15.0
01 103	Morgan	77,215	51.6	19.2	89,156	62.8	5.6	40.7	29.0	41,990	11.3	30.3	13.3
01 109	Pike	18,034	60.3	20.4	23,725	61.2	7.3	35.0	31.4	24,849	25.0	50.3	9.3
01 111	Randolph	14,988	66.7	11.6	17,548	56.7	11.1	31.9	32.4	34,908	16.1	33.4	8.4
01 113	Russell	32,960	61.7	10.5	38,600	57.7	10.2	36.6	35.1	31,256	17.8	40.9	5.6
01 115	St. Clair	50,473	60.2	13.9	58,828	58.6	4.8	41.9	28.7	50,453	7.6	24.7	12.6
01 117	Shelby	113,909	31.4	39.0	134,654	71.1	4.0	48.6	17.1	66,966	4.8	15.0	28.8
01 121	Talladega	54,153	63.7	11.8	63,571	55.4	9.1	35.4	37.2	35,751	14.9	38.7	8.9
01 123	Tallapoosa	28,269	58.8	16.0	32,615	56.9	7.1	36.6	37.1	35,256	14.2	37.7	10.4
01 125	Tuscaloosa	106,962	46.9	26.4	139,084	60.8	5.9	36.7	29.7	38,740	12.7	35.6	12.4
01 127	Walker	47,974	61.1	8.8	55,265	53.3	7.7	33.4	37.6	35,751	13.5	36.1	8.5
01 133	Winston	16,879	68.4	9.4	19,769	52.0	8.1	29.9	36.9	29,182	18.5	45.5	4.6
02 000	**Alaska**	418,136	39.4	26.2	516,556	71.4	8.6	37.5	20.9	61,766	7.6	17.8	25.2
02 020	Anchorage	174,249	33.2	31.8	212,318	73.1	7.2	42.3	18.9	66,244	6.6	15.5	28.1
02 090	Fairbanks North Star	55,615	33.7	26.9	72,065	73.3	7.0	42.2	19.4	63,044	6.3	17.1	25.0
02 110	Juneau	20,259	31.1	36.1	24,876	75.4	6.7	41.5	16.0	76,185	5.1	14.0	33.1
02 122	Kenai Peninsula	34,020	46.6	20.3	41,007	64.3	9.2	29.9	28.3	54,406	6.5	23.1	21.3
02 170	Matanuska-Susitna	47,828	44.2	19.6	60,695	66.4	10.2	31.8	23.0	62,841	8.0	16.7	23.0
04 000	**Arizona**	3,949,023	43.1	25.2	4,704,044	62.6	5.7	39.5	27.7	48,609	10.3	23.5	17.4
04 001	Apache	38,715	61.5	11.1	50,178	44.1	11.9	15.2	40.3	28,015	28.7	46.2	5.1
04 003	Cochise	83,152	42.6	20.5	99,473	56.1	6.5	34.3	34.1	40,656	12.9	31.3	12.3
04 005	Coconino	74,989	37.8	32.4	97,978	68.2	5.2	37.1	20.1	48,171	11.1	24.4	17.1
04 007	Gila	35,433	54.3	14.5	40,947	47.1	7.2	25.8	45.7	34,989	12.5	32.3	6.7
04 009	Graham	20,198	53.8	14.4	25,754	52.6	12.4	28.6	33.3	38,525	15.0	33.3	6.5
04 012	La Paz	15,101	63.3	7.7	16,840	41.3	6.7	23.6	52.5	28,973	12.5	41.4	6.0
04 013	Maricopa	2,396,555	41.4	27.2	2,841,949	66.0	5.1	43.5	24.2	53,549	9.0	20.4	20.6
04 015	Mohave	134,772	55.6	11.4	152,778	53.3	7.5	30.8	39.6	37,941	11.4	29.0	10.3
04 017	Navajo	63,684	53.0	13.6	79,986	55.6	12.0	28.1	32.2	37,660	18.8	32.9	8.9
04 019	Pima	621,398	38.5	29.6	747,314	60.9	6.4	36.1	29.6	44,386	10.3	26.8	15.1
04 021	Pinal	174,355	49.6	17.2	207,588	53.9	5.4	35.7	32.4	45,034	11.9	24.6	12.0
04 023	Santa Cruz	24,534	62.1	15.1	30,007	52.2	6.2	34.6	26.8	37,683	17.6	31.3	9.6
04 025	Yavapai	147,413	42.4	22.8	169,838	55.1	4.2	31.4	38.9	43,170	8.8	26.0	12.0
04 027	Yuma	113,924	58.1	12.5	137,791	54.8	9.4	31.6	36.5	38,502	15.5	31.1	9.6

STATE County code	STATE County	Educational attainment			Employment status				Percent of house-holds with no workers	Median house-hold income (dollars)	Percent of families with income below poverty	Percent of house-holds with income less than $25,000	Percent of house-holds with income of $100,000 or more
		Total population 25 years and over	Percent with a high school diploma or less	Percent with a bachelor's degree or more	Total population 16 years and over	Percent in the labor force	Unemployment rate	Percent who worked full-time, year-round					
ACS table number:		C15002	C15002	C15002	C20005	C23001	C23001	C20005	C08202	B19013	C17015	C19001	C19001
		1	2	3	4	5	6	7	8	9	10	11	12
05 000	**Arkansas**	1,842,453	55.3	18.7	2,190,608	61.1	7.1	37.7	30.8	37,555	13.3	33.5	10.2
05 003	Ashley	15,133	66.7	12.8	17,736	57.5	11.1	35.0	35.6	31,708	16.4	40.2	8.5
05 005	Baxter	30,509	59.2	11.6	34,211	51.3	8.1	30.2	45.6	34,321	9.9	34.8	6.2
05 007	Benton	125,265	47.7	24.6	147,587	66.0	5.2	43.4	22.6	48,986	8.3	21.1	15.9
05 009	Boone	25,202	59.4	13.2	28,882	60.8	7.5	38.5	34.6	36,849	9.9	34.7	7.8
05 015	Carroll	18,937	61.0	14.1	21,548	61.7	4.1	39.1	30.3	30,940	16.6	37.6	8.2
05 019	Clark	13,841	54.0	23.8	19,061	57.1	9.6	28.6	31.3	32,264	10.9	39.6	7.7
05 023	Cleburne	18,246	59.6	11.6	20,726	54.6	5.5	31.9	43.2	36,152	13.1	35.1	7.4
05 027	Columbia	15,711	56.2	19.4	19,663	59.5	8.0	35.8	35.8	32,582	14.5	39.6	9.8
05 029	Conway	13,874	60.9	15.4	16,312	56.7	6.1	36.2	38.7	35,164	9.3	39.5	9.7
05 031	Craighead	56,563	52.6	23.0	70,361	66.0	7.9	38.2	28.5	37,907	13.9	32.3	11.5
05 033	Crawford	38,018	59.1	11.1	44,506	58.9	5.8	38.7	29.9	36,557	14.1	34.1	8.4
05 035	Crittenden	31,306	60.0	14.5	37,830	62.5	9.7	37.7	29.4	32,347	22.5	40.9	9.9
05 045	Faulkner	60,491	45.6	26.7	79,356	67.0	6.9	39.2	21.6	43,322	10.1	27.5	14.4
05 051	Garland	67,072	48.4	19.0	77,382	56.4	7.8	33.8	39.8	34,451	12.6	35.8	8.4
05 055	Greene	26,853	68.4	11.5	30,859	60.4	7.1	36.5	33.5	36,689	16.1	36.2	4.4
05 057	Hempstead	15,004	62.9	13.8	18,060	62.2	6.5	41.5	26.9	35,616	19.2	35.5	8.0
05 059	Hot Spring	21,958	59.9	12.4	25,117	59.5	10.1	34.0	33.9	35,739	12.6	33.6	7.2
05 063	Independence	23,400	60.3	13.6	27,387	58.3	5.5	37.9	34.1	33,845	12.2	34.8	5.7
05 069	Jefferson	51,671	59.7	15.3	62,748	59.4	13.3	35.7	33.6	34,330	17.7	37.5	7.9
05 071	Johnson	15,881	68.9	13.3	18,734	57.9	5.7	36.2	32.4	29,049	14.4	43.4	4.3
05 083	Logan	15,463	68.9	9.3	17,813	56.5	5.9	34.5	38.0	32,147	12.3	39.6	7.0
05 085	Lonoke	39,718	52.8	16.8	47,004	66.3	5.9	42.6	23.5	49,215	9.0	23.8	13.3
05 091	Miller	28,365	60.1	14.9	32,929	59.8	7.3	36.3	30.6	38,186	12.9	34.4	7.9
05 093	Mississippi	29,516	62.8	9.6	34,896	57.4	8.7	34.6	34.2	30,627	22.6	40.4	6.6
05 103	Ouachita	17,624	63.2	11.1	21,063	54.0	11.5	32.5	38.6	30,624	16.6	43.3	7.6
05 107	Phillips	13,759	62.6	10.4	16,462	56.7	11.6	33.4	35.3	25,099	28.3	49.8	4.7
05 111	Poinsett	16,687	74.2	7.4	19,458	57.1	10.3	32.7	36.3	31,898	18.8	42.1	4.3
05 113	Polk	13,770	59.6	10.1	15,904	55.7	6.0	32.5	36.2	34,229	15.2	35.4	5.6
05 115	Pope	36,701	53.0	20.1	40,060	61.7	6.9	37.4	30.0	37,230	12.0	33.5	11.4
05 119	Pulaski	244,742	39.7	31.3	285,925	67.0	6.4	43.5	25.4	44,153	10.6	26.8	15.9
05 123	St. Francis	17,551	65.6	11.9	20,819	51.2	16.0	28.3	36.2	26,357	23.7	48.8	6.2
05 125	Saline	63,355	50.9	20.3	73,875	64.8	4.0	40.7	27.7	49,914	8.3	20.8	13.0
05 131	Sebastian	79,112	53.8	17.2	92,248	62.9	6.2	40.6	28.3	37,249	12.1	34.0	11.0
05 139	Union	29,525	58.1	17.2	34,169	56.2	8.1	36.7	36.9	35,233	15.6	37.7	10.1
05 143	Washington	115,301	46.2	27.6	144,985	67.4	4.7	43.1	21.6	42,784	10.3	28.5	11.4
05 145	White	46,059	60.2	15.7	57,236	60.3	7.0	33.0	31.5	37,022	12.4	33.3	8.0
05 149	Yell	13,714	75.9	8.8	16,609	59.3	6.6	42.5	29.0	34,647	13.2	34.9	3.3
06 000	**California**	23,080,916	43.0	29.1	27,949,362	64.1	6.8	38.6	24.0	58,361	9.7	20.6	25.8
06 001	Alameda	974,141	36.1	39.1	1,149,328	65.9	7.2	39.8	23.4	66,430	8.2	19.1	32.0
06 005	Amador	28,472	48.3	19.0	32,604	53.4	8.6	30.5	34.4	57,522	6.9	19.1	19.7
06 007	Butte	136,278	39.4	24.4	177,150	58.4	9.7	27.3	35.0	40,011	11.3	32.4	12.6
06 009	Calaveras	33,258	45.1	19.8	39,178	54.9	6.5	33.4	37.6	54,356	8.2	21.1	19.1
06 011	Colusa	12,656	58.5	11.8	15,496	63.1	13.2	29.3	25.1	42,398	12.9	26.0	14.6
06 013	Contra Costa	667,520	32.8	37.2	789,786	65.1	6.1	38.9	23.6	75,483	6.2	14.6	36.1
06 015	Del Norte	19,584	54.5	13.5	23,707	48.8	10.8	21.1	42.9	33,173	15.8	40.0	10.9
06 017	El Dorado	118,842	31.0	31.2	141,220	67.0	5.9	37.1	25.0	68,640	5.3	15.4	31.5
06 019	Fresno	515,516	52.1	18.8	650,245	62.2	9.1	35.2	27.1	44,979	16.3	28.3	16.0
06 021	Glenn	17,123	55.5	12.6	21,092	59.1	7.5	33.0	30.2	39,834	12.2	27.0	11.6
06 023	Humboldt	85,245	38.5	26.2	106,273	60.6	7.1	28.8	33.0	38,987	9.7	33.0	12.3
06 025	Imperial	91,414	63.7	10.4	117,003	51.4	9.5	28.1	30.0	35,933	18.5	34.8	11.2
06 029	Kern	451,672	57.9	14.4	564,731	59.8	9.6	33.6	25.9	44,620	16.9	27.6	15.7
06 031	Kings	87,345	60.4	11.6	110,425	57.9	12.2	33.2	23.6	45,796	14.8	25.2	13.3
06 033	Lake	44,436	49.3	14.8	51,773	54.8	8.8	27.1	35.6	40,710	11.9	31.6	10.1
06 035	Lassen	24,499	51.8	11.3	29,604	40.8	7.9	26.2	26.5	46,581	8.7	23.8	14.5
06 037	Los Angeles	6,239,833	48.0	27.6	7,564,003	64.1	6.8	39.7	22.7	52,628	12.4	23.8	22.7
06 039	Madera	87,967	59.6	11.7	107,444	55.9	10.2	32.6	28.7	44,534	13.8	24.6	15.4
06 041	Marin	180,462	21.8	53.5	203,750	64.9	4.3	35.7	24.9	83,732	4.1	13.5	41.5
06 045	Mendocino	59,126	44.1	24.3	69,768	60.5	7.3	29.0	31.2	42,663	10.8	28.6	12.6
06 047	Merced	136,896	59.5	12.7	173,695	61.8	11.9	32.7	26.9	44,141	16.1	29.3	14.3
06 053	Monterey	249,937	50.9	23.6	308,558	65.3	8.8	34.6	23.6	58,197	9.1	18.1	23.5
06 055	Napa	88,198	40.3	28.3	105,183	64.9	5.7	35.5	25.8	66,663	5.4	16.7	31.0
06 057	Nevada	70,069	30.4	31.7	81,633	61.3	6.7	29.9	32.1	56,344	4.6	18.0	21.7
06 059	Orange	1,924,417	37.3	34.6	2,300,880	66.8	5.1	42.2	20.6	71,601	6.4	14.4	34.2
06 061	Placer	220,695	30.8	32.9	260,591	64.5	4.6	38.3	27.8	68,463	3.7	14.6	30.0
06 063	Plumas	15,381	37.2	23.0	17,676	59.0	5.9	32.7	38.5	44,281	-	26.2	11.2
06 065	Riverside	1,223,118	49.6	19.6	1,498,859	62.4	7.4	37.3	26.4	55,881	9.3	20.3	22.5
06 067	Sacramento	879,835	39.4	27.5	1,054,630	64.6	7.3	38.4	25.3	55,822	9.3	20.4	21.5
06 069	San Benito	33,136	51.6	18.4	40,235	70.6	7.0	41.0	19.8	69,740	6.2	16.6	30.2
06 071	San Bernardino	1,160,801	51.4	17.7	1,457,343	62.9	7.6	38.5	22.1	54,093	10.9	20.8	20.2
06 073	San Diego	1,875,222	36.1	33.2	2,298,030	65.7	5.4	41.4	23.1	60,970	7.9	18.5	26.8
06 075	San Francisco	592,536	30.5	49.8	660,649	67.2	5.8	41.5	25.9	65,519	7.4	22.1	33.0
06 077	San Joaquin	399,430	52.8	16.8	492,655	61.9	9.4	35.7	25.4	52,872	11.0	22.2	20.8
06 079	San Luis Obispo	170,006	35.5	29.5	217,150	60.1	6.2	30.3	27.4	53,589	6.6	23.3	21.4
06 081	San Mateo	487,977	30.4	43.5	562,064	66.6	5.5	42.2	22.4	81,573	4.4	12.5	40.3

Table B-2. Counties — What: Education, Employment, and Income, 2005–2007—*Continued*

STATE County code	STATE County	Educational attainment			Employment status				Percent of households with no workers	Median household income (dollars)	Percent of families with income below poverty	Percent of households with income less than $25,000	Percent of households with income of $100,000 or more
		Total population 25 years and over	Percent with a high school diploma or less	Percent with a bachelor's degree or more	Total population 16 years and over	Percent in the labor force	Unemployment rate	Percent who worked full-time, year-round					
	ACS table number:	C15002	C15002	C15002	C20005	C23001	C23001	C20005	C08202	B19013	C17015	C19001	C19001
		1	2	3	4	5	6	7	8	9	10	11	12
	California—Cont.												
06 083	Santa Barbara	248,680	39.2	30.6	318,190	62.8	5.6	34.0	26.4	57,059	8.3	19.7	24.9
06 085	Santa Clara	1,153,689	32.1	43.9	1,351,925	66.0	6.2	41.5	20.3	83,074	5.9	14.3	41.5
06 087	Santa Cruz	163,501	32.3	37.7	203,068	68.8	6.8	33.4	23.4	63,333	6.7	17.9	29.5
06 089	Shasta	120,022	43.0	17.8	143,783	57.8	8.9	30.3	35.1	43,988	11.6	27.9	14.1
06 093	Siskiyou	31,205	42.9	19.7	36,808	53.6	10.5	24.3	42.5	35,567	12.8	36.6	9.6
06 095	Solano	261,613	40.9	22.3	315,259	63.8	7.4	36.9	23.4	65,533	7.4	16.0	26.8
06 097	Sonoma	312,174	37.6	30.4	372,452	65.6	5.6	37.0	25.3	62,311	5.8	18.2	26.3
06 099	Stanislaus	304,893	54.9	15.3	376,839	61.5	10.4	34.6	26.9	50,375	10.6	23.4	17.7
06 101	Sutter	56,769	47.3	17.9	68,853	63.8	10.4	33.2	28.1	52,486	7.4	20.7	19.3
06 103	Tehama	39,938	54.6	11.5	47,581	54.2	10.0	29.2	37.7	35,382	17.0	34.0	8.9
06 107	Tulare	234,743	59.6	12.3	295,436	59.9	10.0	35.1	26.9	41,837	18.8	29.0	13.5
06 109	Tuolumne	41,368	45.3	17.6	47,641	48.0	7.8	24.5	40.1	43,661	8.9	26.3	15.4
06 111	Ventura	503,006	39.0	30.1	609,864	66.8	5.3	40.6	21.5	72,984	6.4	14.5	33.8
06 113	Yolo	110,254	37.8	38.0	152,239	64.2	7.8	33.8	24.8	54,307	7.8	22.3	24.7
06 115	Yuba	41,362	56.3	11.6	51,670	62.4	10.0	33.5	30.1	41,620	12.7	28.4	12.6
08 000	**Colorado**	3,130,207	36.3	34.6	3,722,302	69.8	5.8	42.3	21.6	54,262	8.3	21.3	21.5
08 001	Adams	257,799	50.9	19.2	305,457	72.1	7.0	46.8	17.9	52,923	10.5	20.9	16.5
08 005	Arapahoe	352,767	33.1	37.2	414,318	71.7	5.6	45.3	19.2	58,302	8.1	17.8	23.8
08 013	Boulder	186,982	22.0	55.7	232,799	70.2	5.9	38.1	20.2	63,064	6.2	19.9	29.9
08 014	Broomfield	32,849	27.5	40.0	39,343	76.7	7.3	45.8	16.0	69,419	5.6	13.3	31.1
08 029	Delta	21,204	52.9	19.0	24,202	57.6	2.9	34.2	33.0	37,910	9.5	29.3	8.1
08 031	Denver	391,711	40.0	37.7	450,092	69.1	6.5	41.9	25.1	43,748	13.6	28.7	17.3
08 035	Douglas	163,509	17.0	53.2	190,187	76.8	4.0	50.7	10.1	93,819	1.7	5.4	45.8
08 037	Eagle	33,941	31.4	49.2	39,240	-	-	48.1	15.5	67,565	-	13.1	29.2
08 039	Elbert	14,972	37.5	26.2	18,032	74.1	6.0	45.3	15.3	71,473	3.4	13.6	31.8
08 041	El Paso	368,977	31.8	33.8	443,283	70.5	6.1	43.4	20.9	54,839	7.4	20.3	20.4
08 043	Fremont	35,147	56.6	16.1	39,971	40.6	6.0	28.7	36.9	35,879	14.0	35.3	9.7
08 045	Garfield	33,612	46.0	25.5	39,235	74.4	2.5	44.3	14.8	63,617	4.0	13.2	23.3
08 059	Jefferson	358,137	31.8	37.5	420,554	71.0	5.6	43.8	20.8	63,857	5.4	15.9	26.8
08 067	La Plata	32,280	28.6	41.9	40,486	69.5	3.0	35.9	21.7	51,254	5.7	23.5	19.7
08 069	Larimer	181,296	28.3	41.6	227,710	70.4	6.3	38.7	22.3	53,502	7.1	21.5	21.2
08 075	Logan	13,880	48.9	15.7	16,874	59.8	4.9	38.5	26.3	40,269	4.3	27.7	9.6
08 077	Mesa	90,196	44.8	23.4	107,268	66.0	4.9	37.1	27.2	46,490	9.2	25.4	13.5
08 083	Montezuma	17,006	49.4	20.8	19,593	64.7	8.2	35.5	29.8	38,855	13.7	32.9	8.2
08 085	Montrose	25,878	51.0	19.1	30,048	61.1	4.0	36.8	32.9	42,618	7.9	30.8	12.2
08 087	Morgan	17,333	60.6	14.0	20,821	68.5	6.7	41.3	24.6	41,557	10.8	25.9	9.1
08 101	Pueblo	100,081	46.0	20.5	119,658	60.8	7.8	34.3	32.6	39,570	15.4	32.7	11.1
08 107	Routt	15,564	26.0	46.2	18,029	-	-	45.8	16.4	62,753	-	15.0	22.0
08 117	Summit	19,078	29.1	49.0	21,627	-	-	47.8	12.2	65,281	-	7.9	28.2
08 119	Teller	15,482	34.1	30.3	17,746	70.4	7.0	39.7	17.9	60,401	5.9	17.3	19.8
08 123	Weld	142,163	46.2	24.3	177,518	71.0	5.2	44.4	20.3	52,457	9.1	22.3	17.0
09 000	**Connecticut**	2,349,541	41.8	34.3	2,768,150	67.4	6.2	41.2	24.3	65,496	5.9	18.0	29.4
09 001	Fairfield	596,501	37.0	42.6	694,008	66.6	5.8	41.2	21.7	78,353	5.0	15.4	39.4
09 003	Hartford	591,402	43.2	32.1	694,037	66.9	7.1	41.5	26.6	61,437	7.1	19.9	26.1
09 005	Litchfield	132,111	40.9	32.5	151,546	69.8	4.9	41.6	23.7	67,591	3.1	15.7	27.9
09 007	Middlesex	113,018	38.4	35.4	131,005	69.1	4.0	44.4	21.7	73,307	3.3	13.3	31.8
09 009	New Haven	564,716	45.0	30.9	670,086	66.9	6.9	40.2	26.5	58,528	7.8	21.2	25.0
09 011	New London	181,247	43.8	29.4	212,806	68.4	4.9	42.6	22.5	61,842	4.1	15.2	25.3
09 013	Tolland	93,096	36.0	36.3	121,285	69.4	5.2	38.9	20.3	74,949	3.5	13.9	33.2
09 015	Windham	77,450	53.1	21.5	93,377	69.9	7.7	41.0	24.1	55,786	6.0	20.6	16.5
10 000	**Delaware**	565,305	47.6	26.6	671,869	64.8	5.8	42.0	25.6	55,303	7.2	19.9	21.6
10 001	Kent	94,750	52.8	18.5	114,317	64.5	6.8	42.1	27.6	50,112	8.8	23.4	16.6
10 003	New Castle	343,125	43.4	31.2	412,413	66.8	5.6	43.2	22.1	61,045	6.4	17.6	25.5
10 005	Sussex	127,430	55.0	20.3	145,139	59.4	5.7	38.3	33.6	48,615	8.0	23.2	15.0
11 000	**District of Columbia**	397,937	37.3	45.4	483,781	66.5	8.8	42.4	28.1	52,187	15.7	26.4	25.6
11 001	District of Columbia	397,937	37.3	45.4	483,781	66.5	8.8	42.4	28.1	52,187	15.7	26.4	25.6
12 000	**Florida**	12,412,464	46.7	25.2	14,471,701	60.7	6.0	39.2	30.6	46,602	9.0	25.0	16.4
12 001	Alachua	137,345	33.2	39.0	196,397	61.9	6.2	35.2	26.7	38,243	11.3	35.0	15.1
12 003	Baker	15,727	72.5	5.9	19,319	55.8	8.6	37.0	30.3	43,458	11.9	25.2	7.7
12 005	Bay	112,441	45.9	21.1	129,895	65.0	5.2	41.6	26.0	46,106	10.5	25.2	13.4
12 007	Bradford	18,666	60.7	9.4	23,284	-	-	31.4	32.0	41,061	11.5	29.2	8.6
12 009	Brevard	379,268	41.0	26.2	437,283	58.1	5.4	36.1	34.2	47,973	6.6	23.5	16.4
12 011	Broward	1,207,122	43.8	28.5	1,396,587	65.9	6.0	42.8	26.1	51,221	8.3	23.2	20.4
12 015	Charlotte	119,443	50.5	19.5	131,959	47.8	5.3	29.0	45.8	44,576	6.7	23.6	11.8
12 017	Citrus	105,430	55.0	16.1	117,058	44.2	7.2	26.6	49.3	36,100	8.1	31.9	8.3
12 019	Clay	114,947	42.8	23.4	136,986	67.8	6.1	42.2	21.5	59,792	6.5	14.8	20.3
12 021	Collier	226,350	44.7	30.0	253,925	55.4	4.5	35.4	39.5	57,166	6.5	18.1	24.1
12 023	Columbia	44,143	58.4	13.5	52,818	55.3	6.7	35.1	31.1	39,740	13.8	31.0	9.0
12 027	DeSoto	23,020	72.5	10.2	27,628	52.8	6.6	36.1	39.2	36,825	19.0	33.5	8.8
12 031	Duval	547,571	45.1	24.8	647,205	67.8	6.2	44.5	23.3	48,034	9.3	23.2	15.6
12 033	Escambia	199,530	44.4	23.2	245,215	60.8	6.8	36.2	30.8	42,866	11.3	28.8	12.2
12 035	Flagler	60,455	44.2	20.5	68,354	52.4	4.1	34.2	39.2	45,486	9.0	25.1	11.8
12 039	Gadsden	30,619	64.4	11.4	36,390	54.1	6.6	37.0	32.3	35,235	17.6	35.5	6.9

Table B-2. Counties — What: Education, Employment, and Income, 2005–2007—*Continued*

STATE County code	STATE County	Educational attainment			Employment status				Percent of house-holds with no workers	Median house-hold income (dollars)	Percent of families with income below poverty	Percent of house-holds with income less than $25,000	Percent of house-holds with income of $100,000 or more
		Total population 25 years and over	Percent with a high school diploma or less	Percent with a bachelor's degree or more	Total population 16 years and over	Percent in the labor force	Unem-ployment rate	Percent who worked full-time, year-round					
ACS table number:		C15002	C15002	C15002	C20005	C23001	C23001	C20005	C08202	B19013	C17015	C19001	C19001
		1	2	3	4	5	6	7	8	9	10	11	12
	Florida—Cont.												
12 049	Hardee	18,112	76.9	6.9	21,482	52.4	8.8	34.9	28.3	39,497	16.9	29.9	6.4
12 051	Hendry	23,030	76.2	7.4	29,235	58.9	12.3	38.0	28.0	38,116	20.6	37.0	9.7
12 053	Hernando	119,558	54.4	15.0	135,085	49.0	8.1	29.0	45.8	41,991	7.5	27.9	11.1
12 055	Highlands	72,448	62.0	13.9	81,146	45.3	7.5	28.3	51.5	32,903	10.3	35.2	5.6
12 057	Hillsborough	760,798	44.0	28.1	901,145	67.0	6.0	44.0	23.4	48,647	9.6	23.4	18.0
12 061	Indian River	95,171	44.7	25.3	107,774	54.5	6.5	32.7	39.4	46,397	9.2	23.4	16.6
12 063	Jackson	34,078	61.0	12.0	40,223	45.9	8.8	29.1	34.5	35,015	11.4	36.2	9.3
12 069	Lake	211,027	50.7	19.9	237,390	51.9	6.2	32.5	42.5	43,443	7.7	24.1	11.9
12 071	Lee	409,807	47.2	24.1	462,849	57.4	5.3	36.9	35.7	49,742	6.7	20.0	17.4
12 073	Leon	153,342	30.3	41.7	210,415	68.9	6.4	41.6	20.8	45,438	9.9	27.7	16.8
12 075	Levy	26,521	64.4	11.2	31,107	53.6	6.6	33.5	37.4	33,889	16.5	36.9	7.3
12 081	Manatee	222,173	46.6	25.7	251,527	57.8	4.8	38.0	34.7	47,761	7.3	22.4	16.5
12 083	Marion	225,461	55.5	15.6	257,840	51.7	6.3	32.4	41.3	39,295	9.6	29.6	9.3
12 085	Martin	104,002	42.4	28.7	117,213	55.1	5.9	33.9	39.1	52,952	5.7	20.3	21.9
12 086	Miami-Dade	1,591,512	51.4	25.7	1,888,725	61.3	6.3	41.4	25.1	41,943	13.2	30.6	16.0
12 087	Monroe	58,397	36.0	31.1	63,803	64.4	2.8	41.8	30.1	55,550	6.1	20.3	23.7
12 089	Nassau	46,533	52.7	21.2	53,787	60.4	6.8	40.8	30.0	55,604	6.2	17.3	18.3
12 091	Okaloosa	123,195	37.0	28.1	143,567	65.8	4.2	42.9	26.2	54,999	7.2	18.8	19.4
12 093	Okeechobee	26,170	67.0	9.4	31,147	54.9	8.6	36.3	35.3	38,139	14.0	30.6	6.9
12 095	Orange	678,617	41.7	29.4	814,127	69.9	6.0	45.6	19.5	49,768	8.5	21.7	17.9
12 097	Osceola	158,409	51.8	19.0	187,502	65.7	6.6	43.5	22.8	46,058	10.8	23.3	12.4
12 099	Palm Beach	900,135	41.9	30.4	1,025,913	58.7	6.1	37.1	36.4	52,351	7.2	22.5	21.8
12 101	Pasco	318,285	52.7	18.4	362,398	55.6	6.9	34.6	38.2	42,912	8.3	27.4	13.0
12 103	Pinellas	682,279	43.2	26.6	767,775	59.1	5.0	38.7	35.2	43,591	8.2	27.0	14.9
12 105	Polk	374,804	56.5	17.2	438,083	58.6	5.6	40.4	32.3	42,534	10.1	26.4	10.8
12 107	Putnam	49,551	67.3	11.5	58,204	50.8	8.5	32.2	41.2	31,493	15.3	39.4	7.3
12 109	St. Johns	117,641	33.7	36.0	136,901	63.0	4.1	39.8	27.8	61,281	4.7	17.8	28.5
12 111	St. Lucie	173,293	52.5	17.4	200,780	56.9	6.6	35.8	35.5	46,288	7.8	22.8	13.5
12 113	Santa Rosa	98,253	45.1	23.7	114,941	61.6	6.7	36.6	27.1	51,780	7.3	20.2	15.2
12 115	Sarasota	285,434	41.9	28.8	314,823	52.7	5.5	32.7	42.7	49,030	5.4	22.4	17.9
12 117	Seminole	275,613	35.9	33.0	323,560	67.9	4.8	45.8	20.3	57,318	6.0	17.3	23.2
12 119	Sumter	53,176	60.1	12.6	58,013	44.9	7.0	30.6	38.9	39,387	10.8	30.1	9.4
12 121	Suwannee	26,594	68.6	9.2	30,643	51.2	9.3	30.9	39.8	36,254	12.8	36.8	8.6
12 127	Volusia	351,677	48.5	20.0	408,854	56.8	5.6	35.3	35.8	41,772	8.3	28.0	11.7
12 129	Wakulla	20,204	54.9	16.9	23,479	63.0	5.6	39.8	24.5	52,366	9.0	26.6	11.0
12 131	Walton	30,920	47.3	24.6	41,837	57.5	5.3	38.6	31.6	47,906	6.9	26.4	16.1
12 133	Washington	15,489	65.2	10.1	17,959	56.4	10.0	36.5	35.2	34,814	16.0	36.0	6.5
13 000	**Georgia**	5,945,347	48.0	26.6	7,131,317	65.8	7.1	42.3	23.7	48,540	11.1	25.0	17.8
13 009	Baldwin	27,947	61.3	16.8	37,631	49.8	5.1	31.0	34.6	37,500	14.0	36.4	8.8
13 013	Barrow	39,677	61.0	11.3	46,487	66.3	9.2	43.9	20.9	49,763	11.2	22.8	11.7
13 015	Bartow	57,779	59.9	16.3	66,980	66.3	5.6	44.9	22.7	48,118	10.3	23.7	14.5
13 021	Bibb	97,524	51.9	22.3	117,188	58.4	10.2	34.5	34.2	36,567	17.4	36.4	12.3
13 029	Bryan	17,926	45.6	26.5	21,522	71.1	5.0	46.6	14.8	67,294	-	16.3	25.6
13 031	Bulloch	33,703	49.9	23.4	52,486	61.5	7.2	33.0	24.6	35,329	13.0	36.5	8.6
13 033	Burke	13,370	71.4	9.1	16,559	61.4	11.5	35.3	34.1	33,245	16.7	38.2	6.5
13 035	Butts	15,598	69.9	10.2	18,242	57.6	8.7	35.5	25.4	53,477	6.5	21.4	13.8
13 039	Camden	27,509	46.0	18.4	34,379	69.2	4.9	48.6	20.0	44,593	9.2	24.0	12.5
13 045	Carroll	67,379	57.7	18.0	82,840	66.3	8.1	39.6	25.4	44,160	11.2	27.4	10.7
13 047	Catoosa	40,763	50.2	15.4	47,260	65.3	5.8	43.8	25.0	46,729	8.9	23.8	11.3
13 051	Chatham	155,323	44.2	28.7	189,297	62.5	5.3	40.8	26.8	43,443	11.1	29.0	15.3
13 055	Chattooga	18,039	73.5	7.1	21,103	53.6	6.1	39.9	35.3	31,846	16.6	39.8	3.3
13 057	Cherokee	121,849	38.2	31.7	143,394	73.0	5.1	49.3	14.8	64,362	4.9	13.2	27.3
13 059	Clarke	59,015	37.7	41.8	92,410	61.9	6.7	32.5	25.6	34,938	14.3	38.9	11.4
13 063	Clayton	163,693	53.4	17.3	197,330	70.0	9.7	44.9	18.0	43,077	11.8	23.6	10.3
13 067	Cobb	440,526	31.9	42.6	519,546	71.4	5.6	46.2	16.8	65,123	6.3	15.0	28.8
13 069	Coffee	24,541	61.2	13.7	29,877	55.9	5.2	39.5	29.2	32,863	17.4	38.8	7.2
13 071	Colquitt	27,878	68.2	8.8	33,638	62.3	8.9	40.9	28.1	30,941	20.5	41.6	7.0
13 073	Columbia	66,392	38.2	33.8	80,172	67.2	4.6	44.7	19.0	66,040	4.4	14.0	25.2
13 077	Coweta	72,999	48.4	23.2	84,951	70.1	6.5	46.2	18.8	61,384	7.9	16.8	23.3
13 081	Crisp	13,526	70.2	10.8	16,548	60.4	9.1	37.6	32.7	28,674	26.6	44.2	8.0
13 085	Dawson	13,831	59.4	14.6	15,885	-	-	40.1	20.4	56,201	-	20.6	14.1
13 087	Decatur	18,109	62.9	12.4	21,568	57.2	4.9	39.8	33.0	31,289	19.1	40.1	7.6
13 089	DeKalb	483,594	37.7	37.1	571,163	71.2	9.7	44.2	20.7	51,330	10.8	22.3	20.3
13 091	Dodge	12,595	73.4	11.6	16,330	-	-	28.4	42.0	28,201	22.2	47.3	6.9
13 095	Dougherty	57,990	47.9	21.2	72,496	59.6	13.5	34.8	33.7	35,208	18.4	36.9	10.8
13 097	Douglas	73,688	47.4	23.2	88,143	70.8	8.1	46.7	18.7	55,939	8.1	17.5	17.7
13 103	Effingham	30,324	63.0	13.3	36,316	68.7	6.7	44.9	18.0	51,422	8.5	18.5	14.6
13 105	Elbert	13,921	70.4	10.0	16,207	57.3	8.2	37.0	35.3	31,225	17.8	40.7	8.3
13 107	Emanuel	14,133	71.3	8.0	17,261	52.5	8.1	37.0	35.9	25,866	18.0	48.7	5.4
13 111	Fannin	16,116	62.9	16.4	18,283	-	-	35.8	35.6	37,958	11.0	30.4	10.4
13 113	Fayette	68,477	33.7	39.1	82,377	67.1	4.4	41.9	20.4	79,498	3.5	10.4	36.0
13 115	Floyd	61,926	58.3	16.4	74,114	59.1	5.6	35.4	31.4	39,987	15.2	33.7	11.4
13 117	Forsyth	94,547	30.8	43.5	108,790	70.8	3.5	50.0	14.6	84,815	4.9	8.7	38.5
13 119	Franklin	14,634	69.0	10.1	17,185	59.6	5.9	38.2	33.3	35,335	8.2	33.4	7.8
13 121	Fulton	634,771	33.3	45.3	748,085	68.8	7.5	44.4	21.5	57,286	10.7	21.4	29.0

Table B-2. Counties — What: Education, Employment, and Income, 2005–2007—*Continued*

STATE County code	STATE County	Educational attainment			Employment status				Percent of house-holds with no workers	Median house-hold income (dollars)	Percent of families with income below poverty	Percent of house-holds with income less than $25,000	Percent of house-holds with income of $100,000 or more
		Total population 25 years and over	Percent with a high school diploma or less	Percent with a bachelor's degree or more	Total population 16 years and over	Percent in the labor force	Unem-ployment rate	Percent who worked full-time, year-round					
ACS table number:		C15002	C15002	C15002	C20005	C23001	C23001	C20005	C08202	B19013	C17015	C19001	C19001
		1	2	3	4	5	6	7	8	9	10	11	12
	Florida—Cont.												
13 123	Gilmer	18,968	66.1	11.8	21,879	59.9	6.4	38.6	32.7	33,833	13.9	35.5	8.4
13 127	Glynn	48,328	47.6	26.5	56,935	62.9	4.0	39.8	30.2	46,743	9.5	26.7	16.7
13 129	Gordon	32,893	65.9	11.4	38,486	64.7	5.6	43.0	24.8	40,153	13.3	29.4	9.1
13 131	Grady	15,811	63.7	13.2	18,865	61.5	9.7	37.8	35.8	32,549	17.7	40.1	6.9
13 135	Gwinnett	469,241	37.5	34.6	553,978	72.8	5.8	48.8	14.4	65,033	6.4	13.5	25.9
13 137	Habersham	26,581	61.6	16.8	31,776	57.4	4.1	39.6	29.0	40,043	13.2	31.7	11.4
13 139	Hall	108,576	58.3	18.6	128,465	65.9	5.2	44.6	20.7	49,474	8.7	21.7	15.5
13 143	Haralson	18,823	67.5	9.8	21,837	61.7	13.1	37.3	31.8	39,628	11.4	34.5	11.5
13 145	Harris	18,880	44.9	25.6	22,194	63.8	6.2	42.5	25.7	57,045	12.1	27.0	19.5
13 147	Hart	16,775	67.2	13.1	19,227	55.7	8.0	32.8	34.8	36,087	16.8	37.1	8.7
13 151	Henry	108,537	44.7	23.3	129,131	71.7	6.6	47.1	16.8	62,223	6.0	12.1	21.8
13 153	Houston	80,588	43.3	23.2	97,362	67.3	6.9	42.8	24.4	51,713	9.8	23.0	17.1
13 157	Jackson	35,963	65.9	12.1	42,301	65.9	5.0	41.5	23.8	41,590	12.3	29.7	12.7
13 169	Jones	17,670	56.3	18.3	20,649	66.0	7.6	37.5	26.0	47,553	10.0	25.5	11.7
13 175	Laurens	30,774	63.5	14.7	35,883	59.0	6.1	44.5	30.1	36,950	15.5	37.3	11.2
13 177	Lee	19,822	48.5	19.2	24,455	71.6	5.2	43.7	15.6	60,242	-	14.4	22.3
13 179	Liberty	32,398	46.6	14.6	42,594	71.2	8.8	43.9	20.2	40,941	15.8	28.3	6.9
13 185	Lowndes	59,267	48.0	23.7	76,949	66.7	6.1	40.5	23.5	39,585	14.8	30.5	11.9
13 187	Lumpkin	15,721	53.6	21.6	20,653	63.6	5.7	37.0	24.3	42,539	10.2	30.3	10.9
13 189	McDuffie	14,070	69.2	9.2	16,452	58.7	6.3	37.2	30.3	33,473	21.9	39.2	6.9
13 195	Madison	18,374	69.6	11.8	21,374	61.6	8.8	40.9	30.1	37,752	14.2	36.5	6.8
13 199	Meriwether	15,049	68.1	11.0	17,530	60.0	11.4	35.4	32.9	35,560	15.4	36.2	6.4
13 205	Mitchell	15,107	69.8	7.5	18,491	58.7	5.5	42.0	31.6	31,611	15.2	43.1	5.7
13 207	Monroe	15,553	53.5	21.8	19,058	61.6	4.5	43.3	26.0	50,655	6.0	21.6	21.5
13 213	Murray	25,959	78.6	6.0	30,165	61.9	7.6	44.2	22.3	36,610	11.9	29.1	6.0
13 215	Muscogee	114,407	47.4	22.6	143,742	62.0	7.3	38.0	31.8	40,347	16.0	32.3	12.3
13 217	Newton	55,833	52.9	18.7	67,052	68.1	9.4	44.6	23.0	50,913	9.0	19.7	11.2
13 219	Oconee	19,312	35.0	42.5	23,382	68.4	3.1	42.3	18.4	63,713	4.5	17.8	27.6
13 223	Paulding	74,480	55.5	19.0	86,116	72.4	5.3	49.3	14.8	57,854	7.8	14.6	12.9
13 225	Peach	14,662	54.3	17.3	19,605	60.3	11.6	37.8	26.5	40,789	15.9	31.4	12.6
13 227	Pickens	20,554	52.6	24.6	23,220	60.8	5.9	39.7	30.0	47,963	8.6	23.8	15.4
13 233	Polk	26,176	67.2	9.1	31,141	62.0	8.8	42.4	29.2	38,720	11.3	28.1	7.1
13 237	Putnam	13,676	54.1	17.9	15,811	-	-	38.4	29.7	44,099	12.8	28.6	14.5
13 245	Richmond	122,200	51.2	19.6	151,098	61.0	8.4	37.3	32.4	36,992	18.9	33.7	9.5
13 247	Rockdale	50,303	48.5	21.7	61,199	66.0	8.3	41.8	20.5	53,455	7.7	18.6	19.1
13 255	Spalding	39,950	65.7	11.5	47,036	65.2	12.1	39.2	27.2	40,178	15.5	30.5	10.0
13 257	Stephens	16,953	61.6	15.6	20,031	58.7	9.0	33.7	32.6	34,884	11.1	36.0	9.0
13 261	Sumter	19,694	58.4	19.1	25,058	60.9	9.2	36.9	31.3	32,354	19.4	37.2	9.4
13 267	Tattnall	14,771	74.6	10.7	18,469	54.4	8.1	34.3	27.0	36,039	16.1	33.8	7.7
13 275	Thomas	29,448	56.5	21.0	34,969	53.9	6.0	36.6	33.1	40,498	13.1	33.5	12.1
13 277	Tift	25,194	54.7	16.9	31,067	65.8	9.2	40.7	23.9	36,445	18.3	35.2	12.2
13 279	Toombs	16,436	63.6	12.8	20,579	55.4	5.1	30.6	34.8	28,750	20.0	46.2	7.8
13 285	Troup	39,856	56.7	19.0	47,444	64.1	6.5	38.5	27.6	39,313	13.2	33.5	9.7
13 291	Union	15,096	53.2	18.4	16,832	-	-	34.6	37.6	38,110	8.0	28.7	12.2
13 293	Upson	18,446	68.1	11.0	21,584	59.3	8.7	36.3	35.4	34,041	16.4	35.3	7.1
13 295	Walker	43,609	61.1	11.2	50,430	60.2	8.1	36.8	29.8	37,685	11.9	29.0	7.7
13 297	Walton	51,376	61.9	15.3	60,069	68.5	5.4	43.9	20.9	52,133	9.1	21.7	15.9
13 299	Ware	23,186	61.3	12.9	27,862	52.0	7.6	33.9	40.0	33,431	14.9	40.2	6.8
13 303	Washington	13,399	63.5	12.0	16,167	52.8	7.8	37.5	37.0	30,371	21.0	42.5	7.7
13 305	Wayne	18,985	66.0	11.9	22,409	52.4	5.2	35.0	30.5	39,334	10.6	33.5	8.9
13 311	White	16,164	57.7	18.2	19,327	61.5	5.7	34.5	31.7	40,140	15.7	32.2	11.3
13 313	Whitfield	57,255	64.0	14.2	67,251	66.5	7.4	45.8	22.5	41,862	12.1	29.3	12.9
13 321	Worth	13,924	70.2	8.1	16,772	59.4	9.8	38.3	28.3	36,256	13.7	32.5	7.6
15 000	**Hawaii**	867,609	41.4	28.6	1,025,421	65.6	4.3	42.8	22.9	62,543	6.8	17.3	25.9
15 001	Hawaii	114,933	44.0	26.0	135,821	64.4	5.1	40.3	27.0	55,431	10.6	22.1	19.2
15 003	Honolulu	611,172	40.2	30.0	727,183	64.9	4.2	43.2	22.5	64,355	6.2	16.4	27.5
15 007	Kauai	43,350	45.0	23.4	50,001	68.2	3.5	43.3	22.4	61,440	7.6	18.8	25.2
15 009	Maui	98,062	44.2	25.4	112,324	70.6	3.9	43.6	21.0	61,704	5.0	16.1	24.7
16 000	**Idaho**	917,853	42.6	23.6	1,108,188	65.9	5.4	38.1	25.0	44,901	9.4	25.3	12.3
16 001	Ada	233,227	32.4	34.1	274,476	70.3	4.8	43.2	20.8	54,610	5.6	18.4	19.4
16 005	Bannock	46,658	35.9	27.9	58,850	66.7	5.5	35.4	24.6	40,897	12.4	30.1	11.2
16 011	Bingham	25,095	47.6	16.7	30,692	65.5	5.4	37.2	25.1	43,099	10.8	25.3	10.7
16 013	Blaine	14,840	28.6	43.2	17,173	-	-	39.1	25.0	57,398	-	20.6	23.1
16 017	Bonner	28,571	43.0	19.4	32,804	61.2	3.8	32.6	31.5	42,928	8.8	25.7	12.6
16 019	Bonneville	56,452	40.0	25.0	67,864	68.2	4.5	40.7	22.8	47,373	7.5	23.9	14.7
16 027	Canyon	102,630	52.2	16.4	123,541	65.7	6.9	38.4	23.0	43,329	11.6	25.7	8.0
16 031	Cassia	12,237	45.0	15.5	14,884	60.7	5.4	35.5	25.8	36,815	13.7	31.6	5.7
16 039	Elmore	17,532	42.3	17.1	21,062	73.3	3.9	50.9	15.5	45,023	9.3	22.2	8.4
16 051	Jefferson	12,452	50.0	15.1	15,620	65.4	5.2	38.6	19.4	45,303	10.0	20.2	10.5
16 053	Jerome	11,537	59.0	9.7	14,251	-	-	44.4	25.4	39,803	9.2	27.5	5.8
16 055	Kootenai	86,483	41.7	20.5	102,247	65.2	5.9	35.4	28.5	41,576	9.7	27.1	10.3
16 057	Latah	20,233	30.8	42.2	29,924	64.0	7.8	27.1	24.4	38,814	6.0	34.2	9.6
16 065	Madison	14,359	28.5	27.6	26,642	62.2	6.6	24.6	16.4	39,673	20.1	33.1	9.0
16 069	Nez Perce	26,458	48.3	16.7	31,139	62.2	7.8	35.1	33.1	41,445	12.1	29.7	10.9

Table B-2. Counties — What: Education, Employment, and Income, 2005–2007—*Continued*

STATE County code	STATE County	Educational attainment			Employment status				Percent of house-holds with no workers	Median house-hold income (dollars)	Percent of families with income below poverty	Percent of house-holds with income less than $25,000	Percent of house-holds with income of $100,000 or more
		Total population 25 years and over	Percent with a high school diploma or less	Percent with a bachelor's degree or more	Total population 16 years and over	Percent in the labor force	Unem-ployment rate	Percent who worked full-time, year-round					
ACS table number:		C15002	C15002	C15002	C20005	C23001	C23001	C20005	C08202	B19013	C17015	C19001	C19001
		1	2	3	4	5	6	7	8	9	10	11	12
	Idaho—Cont.												
16 075	Payette	13,968	55.9	13.1	16,575	62.2	8.0	36.9	30.6	42,102	8.7	26.2	7.5
16 083	Twin Falls	45,153	47.2	17.6	54,305	64.9	4.4	41.5	25.9	40,336	12.8	26.7	9.4
17 000	**Illinois**	8,292,894	43.6	29.0	9,946,551	66.4	7.5	40.6	25.0	53,745	8.9	22.5	21.1
17 001	Adams	44,890	50.9	20.4	53,728	66.7	6.0	40.4	28.5	41,506	8.1	29.7	9.3
17 007	Boone	31,994	54.6	19.2	39,140	67.5	7.9	40.2	23.6	56,703	9.3	21.3	19.2
17 011	Bureau	24,031	53.0	16.5	28,044	65.0	6.2	39.7	30.2	44,204	7.7	27.3	10.4
17 019	Champaign	106,034	32.3	42.6	154,507	66.8	6.1	34.8	23.9	43,434	9.3	31.1	15.0
17 021	Christian	24,051	58.7	13.6	27,691	58.0	6.5	36.4	33.8	39,100	11.0	31.9	9.2
17 027	Clinton	24,560	49.3	17.1	29,218	62.3	4.9	38.7	28.2	52,104	6.7	21.2	13.8
17 029	Coles	29,844	49.2	20.9	42,682	59.4	9.5	31.0	28.7	34,266	10.5	37.4	10.1
17 031	Cook	3,450,859	44.0	31.2	4,109,740	65.5	8.8	40.5	25.4	52,358	11.5	24.1	21.6
17 037	DeKalb	56,704	39.9	28.4	81,499	71.2	7.8	38.4	19.6	53,758	6.7	21.8	18.7
17 043	DuPage	609,228	29.9	43.5	721,508	70.3	5.2	44.8	18.6	75,128	3.5	11.3	34.4
17 049	Effingham	22,265	47.8	20.4	26,606	68.8	3.1	45.5	24.8	46,583	7.7	27.5	12.4
17 051	Fayette	14,716	63.0	11.0	17,310	59.6	6.6	37.3	31.8	35,060	12.3	34.5	8.0
17 055	Franklin	27,302	54.5	13.5	31,621	54.4	9.6	30.4	40.3	32,735	13.5	37.6	5.5
17 057	Fulton	26,254	54.6	13.6	30,297	56.5	7.9	33.1	33.1	40,361	10.4	30.4	8.5
17 063	Grundy	29,745	47.1	16.8	35,310	69.4	6.6	41.8	22.0	64,249	3.2	12.6	21.9
17 073	Henry	34,027	49.4	18.7	39,771	64.5	5.9	38.2	30.0	45,445	8.1	26.6	11.3
17 075	Iroquois	20,824	59.8	14.4	24,189	61.3	5.6	39.7	23.3	44,511	7.8	24.7	10.9
17 077	Jackson	32,430	37.6	34.9	49,682	60.8	12.7	26.0	36.5	27,832	19.6	47.0	7.9
17 081	Jefferson	27,807	55.0	15.3	32,355	59.2	5.4	37.2	30.6	40,800	9.8	28.9	9.0
17 083	Jersey	14,731	50.6	18.0	17,873	66.0	4.7	42.5	30.5	52,029	3.3	21.8	11.1
17 085	Jo Daviess	16,176	49.1	21.4	18,484	68.1	4.4	43.2	26.2	49,800	6.7	20.8	13.6
17 089	Kane	299,246	42.4	31.1	358,811	71.9	6.1	45.3	17.6	67,219	6.6	14.4	29.1
17 091	Kankakee	70,286	50.7	17.4	84,318	63.9	9.3	35.6	27.5	49,931	9.3	23.3	13.4
17 093	Kendall	54,140	38.4	29.3	64,980	74.6	5.1	46.2	15.9	74,539	2.7	8.4	28.9
17 095	Knox	36,423	53.2	15.0	42,617	57.3	7.9	33.5	34.4	36,017	12.9	35.1	8.2
17 097	Lake	438,454	33.6	41.0	527,957	70.9	6.2	44.0	17.8	76,940	4.4	12.4	36.3
17 099	LaSalle	75,245	53.4	14.7	88,813	65.5	7.0	38.9	28.3	46,741	8.8	25.6	13.1
17 103	Lee	24,490	53.0	16.2	28,470	65.3	7.1	40.3	24.9	49,518	6.7	21.9	15.1
17 105	Livingston	26,292	59.2	13.3	31,128	59.6	5.4	38.5	28.1	49,213	8.1	24.1	14.9
17 107	Logan	20,458	55.4	16.2	25,018	56.0	4.3	33.6	27.2	48,164	7.8	23.2	10.0
17 109	McDonough	17,366	38.6	35.8	27,647	58.1	10.1	25.5	32.8	32,371	11.3	41.3	10.0
17 111	McHenry	196,797	38.1	30.2	233,512	72.6	6.1	43.9	18.7	75,095	3.9	11.5	31.9
17 113	McLean	95,265	33.6	39.5	129,068	69.8	5.9	40.0	19.9	54,252	7.2	22.7	20.3
17 115	Macon	72,755	51.1	20.0	86,913	61.6	6.4	38.6	30.2	43,316	11.3	29.4	14.0
17 117	Macoupin	32,814	54.7	14.3	38,875	63.3	7.7	37.3	31.9	44,791	8.7	26.0	11.7
17 119	Madison	176,298	45.6	22.9	211,368	64.4	6.6	39.5	28.6	50,356	7.8	23.5	16.4
17 121	Marion	27,002	53.9	13.9	31,631	62.5	8.0	33.7	32.6	34,937	12.7	35.5	7.6
17 133	Monroe	21,214	40.7	24.2	25,195	71.4	4.7	44.6	21.8	62,627	2.7	15.6	22.7
17 135	Montgomery	20,923	62.0	12.6	24,398	56.2	8.2	33.1	34.5	38,844	11.2	31.9	8.3
17 137	Morgan	23,708	55.0	21.2	28,752	62.0	9.8	32.7	32.1	41,196	10.9	31.7	10.6
17 141	Ogle	36,060	52.1	18.3	43,126	67.5	7.1	39.1	26.6	52,309	4.4	20.3	15.1
17 143	Peoria	117,611	41.8	27.5	141,916	63.9	6.9	39.1	28.7	46,332	9.9	25.4	15.5
17 145	Perry	15,462	58.5	11.6	18,708	51.4	7.7	31.5	31.2	38,972	11.3	31.7	6.6
17 157	Randolph	22,894	61.7	12.3	26,930	53.4	7.6	31.7	32.6	42,275	9.7	28.2	8.9
17 161	Rock Island	98,320	47.5	19.9	117,385	63.3	7.2	36.7	31.7	44,028	10.4	27.9	12.4
17 163	St. Clair	166,801	43.0	23.0	200,428	66.8	8.3	40.9	26.8	46,462	10.1	25.9	15.6
17 165	Saline	17,872	49.9	15.1	21,021	55.9	6.1	32.7	38.4	31,898	17.5	39.8	6.6
17 167	Sangamon	130,976	41.3	29.3	152,356	67.9	6.6	42.5	27.0	48,803	9.7	24.6	16.8
17 173	Shelby	15,082	55.0	15.2	17,773	63.9	6.0	41.8	31.4	44,192	8.2	27.6	8.0
17 177	Stephenson	32,018	50.8	16.6	37,424	66.0	7.9	39.2	30.5	42,449	12.0	28.3	9.6
17 179	Tazewell	89,298	44.4	21.8	103,829	64.5	5.8	41.1	27.6	52,151	6.9	20.8	15.1
17 183	Vermilion	54,624	57.3	12.5	64,123	59.6	10.1	35.7	36.2	37,784	16.0	33.4	7.7
17 195	Whiteside	40,305	54.6	14.2	47,241	64.9	7.1	35.6	29.9	41,865	9.1	27.0	10.6
17 197	Will	404,328	40.2	29.5	486,466	71.0	5.9	44.3	17.8	73,159	4.2	11.7	30.8
17 199	Williamson	44,237	47.7	20.1	51,520	61.0	9.8	36.9	34.6	38,424	11.6	32.3	10.3
17 201	Winnebago	193,962	51.4	19.9	227,613	66.0	8.4	38.9	27.6	46,732	10.1	26.4	14.4
17 203	Woodford	24,431	43.6	24.7	29,459	67.9	4.5	38.3	22.5	60,901	4.3	15.7	20.9
18 000	**Indiana**	4,107,829	51.9	21.6	4,900,909	65.8	6.8	40.6	26.0	47,034	8.9	24.8	14.0
18 001	Adams	20,496	62.1	11.9	24,523	69.0	6.5	40.5	27.9	43,976	10.7	26.1	9.2
18 003	Allen	221,398	44.5	24.9	262,670	68.6	6.7	43.7	23.0	47,692	8.7	23.0	14.3
18 005	Bartholomew	49,658	50.4	25.7	56,856	66.5	5.7	42.8	24.0	52,172	8.4	20.7	16.2
18 011	Boone	34,516	39.5	35.3	39,789	66.1	4.3	44.1	24.0	64,589	4.2	15.2	29.8
18 017	Cass	26,861	64.4	12.3	30,895	61.4	6.9	41.1	27.3	41,467	7.5	26.7	9.4
18 019	Clark	70,709	52.9	17.4	81,256	68.6	6.3	44.1	25.1	44,551	8.4	24.9	11.3
18 021	Clay	17,975	57.6	16.1	20,983	64.8	5.3	40.6	26.9	42,464	9.4	27.0	9.3
18 023	Clinton	22,027	64.6	13.7	25,905	64.8	6.3	42.0	25.8	46,062	7.6	23.1	12.0
18 027	Daviess	19,149	68.1	9.5	22,518	66.3	6.4	40.0	27.5	39,240	12.5	29.9	8.0
18 029	Dearborn	32,753	60.7	15.2	38,266	69.8	5.9	44.6	24.6	56,124	4.0	16.5	16.2
18 031	Decatur	16,634	63.4	12.5	19,232	68.5	5.2	41.4	25.6	43,878	7.1	22.0	8.3
18 033	DeKalb	27,257	58.8	15.6	32,066	69.1	7.4	41.9	22.8	44,939	4.9	21.8	10.8
18 035	Delaware	71,881	53.5	21.7	94,898	59.7	9.7	30.7	31.6	36,853	12.3	32.5	9.7

Table B-2. Counties — What: Education, Employment, and Income, 2005–2007—*Continued*

STATE County code	STATE County	Educational attainment			Employment status				Percent of households with no workers	Median household income (dollars)	Percent of families with income below poverty	Percent of households with income less than $25,000	Percent of households with income of $100,000 or more
		Total population 25 years and over	Percent with a high school diploma or less	Percent with a bachelor's degree or more	Total population 16 years and over	Percent in the labor force	Unemployment rate	Percent who worked full-time, year-round					
	ACS table number:	C15002	C15002	C15002	C20005	C23001	C23001	C20005	C08202	B19013	C17015	C19001	C19001
		1	2	3	4	5	6	7	8	9	10	11	12
	Indiana—Cont.												
18 037	Dubois	27,388	61.6	17.9	31,790	68.5	3.3	46.8	24.9	52,489	5.8	20.6	14.6
18 039	Elkhart	124,184	59.3	16.8	145,992	71.3	6.8	45.6	19.8	47,999	8.1	22.2	12.8
18 041	Fayette	17,104	67.1	9.0	19,389	59.3	9.2	33.1	36.3	38,603	13.7	33.8	7.6
18 043	Floyd	48,496	49.8	20.9	56,984	66.9	6.6	43.0	25.6	51,662	7.9	21.9	16.3
18 047	Franklin	15,328	59.5	17.4	17,936	64.2	5.1	40.3	27.3	51,486	7.1	21.4	13.0
18 049	Fulton	14,011	66.0	10.5	16,057	63.3	8.0	37.9	28.5	42,484	8.5	27.4	6.8
18 051	Gibson	22,322	56.0	14.3	26,042	65.1	4.8	44.0	26.2	45,732	5.4	25.0	7.7
18 053	Grant	45,858	60.1	15.4	56,251	60.4	9.9	34.2	34.5	37,264	12.7	32.3	8.2
18 055	Greene	22,558	64.6	11.4	26,027	61.4	9.1	36.5	33.2	38,129	13.9	33.4	7.9
18 057	Hamilton	157,273	22.5	53.0	183,772	74.4	3.2	49.2	13.7	81,297	2.7	10.0	38.3
18 059	Hancock	42,781	44.9	24.9	50,254	69.9	4.1	46.1	20.1	61,418	3.5	14.7	22.9
18 061	Harrison	24,783	57.2	13.7	29,044	68.7	5.2	42.7	22.1	50,116	8.0	20.7	12.0
18 063	Hendricks	85,031	38.9	30.0	99,662	71.2	3.8	47.8	17.6	64,566	3.9	12.6	23.5
18 065	Henry	33,402	61.6	13.8	38,294	56.9	6.8	36.9	33.0	42,167	8.9	27.7	9.1
18 067	Howard	57,440	54.3	18.0	65,642	58.6	7.3	34.8	31.4	45,772	13.5	25.6	14.6
18 069	Huntington	25,231	58.7	16.3	29,994	67.7	5.8	41.3	26.0	46,243	6.7	20.9	11.1
18 071	Jackson	28,364	61.3	13.1	32,685	65.3	6.9	42.1	25.3	40,903	8.2	26.1	9.0
18 073	Jasper	20,411	59.1	16.1	24,788	67.6	6.1	37.8	28.2	49,727	6.4	20.0	11.3
18 075	Jay	14,347	65.6	11.0	16,356	65.3	4.7	37.8	27.7	35,147	10.1	32.4	5.7
18 077	Jefferson	21,371	61.3	18.0	25,878	62.9	6.1	37.2	30.6	39,912	12.5	33.3	9.3
18 079	Jennings	18,675	68.7	8.4	21,408	67.1	9.2	42.7	28.5	43,550	8.8	23.5	5.7
18 081	Johnson	86,134	46.9	24.8	103,015	67.3	4.8	45.5	20.7	59,031	4.4	16.8	20.0
18 083	Knox	24,822	52.9	14.5	30,891	62.1	5.6	38.5	31.3	40,105	14.3	34.2	10.1
18 085	Kosciusko	49,959	58.4	18.5	58,395	68.8	6.6	42.6	21.9	49,599	6.4	20.4	13.3
18 087	LaGrange	21,825	74.4	8.0	26,187	66.8	4.6	38.6	22.9	50,812	9.9	21.3	10.0
18 089	Lake	317,946	53.0	18.2	377,310	63.4	8.7	37.0	29.3	47,650	12.2	26.3	14.5
18 091	LaPorte	75,000	55.3	16.4	86,933	62.1	6.8	38.1	26.9	46,546	9.2	24.4	12.1
18 093	Lawrence	32,186	66.5	11.7	36,364	60.5	8.4	36.8	33.2	40,763	11.2	29.5	8.1
18 095	Madison	89,741	57.4	16.2	104,775	59.1	8.6	36.2	32.3	42,616	9.6	27.3	10.1
18 097	Marion	568,558	47.0	26.7	664,699	69.2	8.2	43.4	24.6	44,339	11.8	26.9	13.6
18 099	Marshall	30,280	60.7	17.1	35,650	68.0	6.4	42.8	23.2	51,615	7.0	20.1	12.3
18 103	Miami	25,159	60.4	11.6	29,280	60.5	8.1	37.2	32.5	41,904	9.8	29.2	9.3
18 105	Monroe	70,757	36.3	39.7	107,202	57.7	5.6	30.3	29.4	38,834	10.0	34.7	12.6
18 107	Montgomery	25,235	60.0	17.2	29,856	66.4	7.0	41.1	25.8	47,110	6.8	22.1	8.7
18 109	Morgan	46,488	57.1	14.5	54,125	66.2	6.2	43.7	23.8	54,379	4.9	18.5	16.0
18 113	Noble	30,618	62.7	13.4	36,031	66.8	6.1	41.0	22.5	47,800	7.2	20.2	9.6
18 119	Owen	15,337	66.8	9.5	17,859	64.9	6.5	42.3	28.4	44,001	9.3	28.8	8.7
18 127	Porter	103,806	46.3	24.7	124,645	66.9	6.4	38.8	24.6	59,245	6.7	19.6	20.6
18 129	Posey	17,858	56.3	16.8	21,048	65.8	4.0	43.7	27.6	58,602	5.4	20.0	16.8
18 133	Putnam	23,920	60.2	14.8	29,848	61.8	5.2	37.0	25.1	46,655	7.9	24.0	11.3
18 135	Randolph	18,166	66.6	9.8	20,605	63.5	8.6	38.0	31.2	40,213	8.3	26.9	5.9
18 137	Ripley	18,079	64.0	13.7	20,859	65.9	4.2	42.8	27.9	46,824	7.8	25.6	11.2
18 141	St. Joseph	166,970	48.5	25.8	205,697	64.9	6.2	38.6	26.9	44,533	8.3	25.7	13.2
18 143	Scott	16,081	71.4	10.1	18,587	61.1	5.4	40.7	26.7	36,111	12.8	30.4	4.7
18 145	Shelby	29,468	59.5	14.0	34,050	66.7	6.2	43.2	23.9	50,097	5.7	21.4	13.2
18 147	Spencer	13,920	53.4	17.8	16,243	66.9	3.5	44.0	25.5	50,057	6.5	21.5	13.2
18 149	Starke	15,769	67.8	9.8	18,518	57.2	8.8	32.1	34.0	37,227	10.0	32.5	6.6
18 151	Steuben	22,119	55.9	18.2	26,476	69.6	5.0	41.3	23.7	45,254	11.4	25.8	11.4
18 153	Sullivan	14,918	58.6	12.5	17,447	59.2	5.8	35.3	28.6	40,676	8.0	28.7	7.4
18 157	Tippecanoe	88,163	40.2	35.0	130,371	63.5	8.0	33.9	25.8	41,472	10.0	31.5	13.3
18 163	Vanderburgh	114,281	47.7	21.2	137,900	64.4	6.4	40.0	29.9	41,898	9.4	30.6	12.7
18 167	Vigo	65,938	50.3	22.9	84,424	60.4	7.1	33.8	31.7	36,249	12.0	34.2	10.3
18 169	Wabash	22,262	60.7	17.7	26,810	61.2	8.7	35.9	30.4	44,129	8.6	23.5	8.8
18 173	Warrick	37,803	44.7	24.7	44,353	67.6	4.8	44.2	22.4	60,748	4.1	15.9	18.7
18 175	Washington	18,671	68.6	9.5	21,653	62.6	8.6	36.9	32.4	36,299	13.6	32.6	7.8
18 177	Wayne	46,531	58.9	14.5	54,643	63.6	8.3	38.8	30.7	39,462	9.4	30.4	8.8
18 179	Wells	18,778	57.3	13.5	21,951	68.9	6.6	41.4	25.8	45,312	3.9	23.1	8.2
18 181	White	16,415	62.0	11.3	19,009	65.9	5.3	41.0	26.4	42,676	8.5	23.5	9.2
18 183	Whitley	21,666	50.8	17.4	25,367	70.4	5.6	44.5	23.6	54,268	5.9	21.2	14.4
19 000	**Iowa**	1,951,982	46.5	24.0	2,346,630	68.7	4.9	42.5	25.5	46,399	7.2	25.0	13.0
19 011	Benton	17,797	53.5	15.5	20,922	70.1	5.2	44.7	25.1	51,538	5.3	21.7	14.8
19 013	Black Hawk	79,290	46.8	24.9	101,922	66.2	7.0	36.4	28.6	42,274	9.3	29.6	11.4
19 015	Boone	18,024	47.5	19.0	21,010	68.3	4.0	45.3	26.2	47,281	6.4	20.9	13.3
19 017	Bremer	15,161	44.9	25.4	19,172	67.1	3.1	41.5	27.1	50,432	4.8	21.8	10.7
19 019	Buchanan	13,542	51.3	19.5	16,154	66.6	4.3	43.8	23.9	46,661	9.0	23.1	10.5
19 027	Carroll	14,078	55.8	16.4	16,464	70.3	4.5	45.6	27.4	47,096	5.3	27.7	12.1
19 033	Cerro Gordo	30,722	42.2	22.5	35,736	66.8	4.2	40.6	29.9	42,098	8.1	28.2	10.9
19 045	Clinton	33,091	53.5	16.6	38,952	66.6	5.8	40.0	30.2	41,722	7.5	27.6	9.1
19 049	Dallas	35,188	34.5	36.7	41,599	73.7	3.4	50.6	17.9	62,318	2.9	15.1	25.3
19 057	Des Moines	27,763	47.7	18.1	32,162	64.6	5.9	40.0	30.8	41,025	7.8	29.6	9.0
19 061	Dubuque	59,605	49.3	25.3	72,051	70.1	4.0	42.5	25.1	46,633	7.0	24.4	12.0
19 065	Fayette	14,105	58.5	15.2	16,677	63.9	4.0	37.4	31.6	37,003	7.3	33.7	8.0
19 087	Henry	13,565	48.3	20.8	15,942	68.7	4.0	43.0	24.8	42,119	10.2	27.5	7.9
19 097	Jackson	13,865	59.2	12.5	16,098	66.8	3.8	40.5	25.6	41,373	12.7	29.2	8.5
19 099	Jasper	25,707	55.7	16.2	29,592	64.4	4.8	40.9	26.2	45,882	7.6	25.2	12.0
19 103	Johnson	71,507	23.0	51.6	101,132	72.1	3.5	40.5	18.6	49,295	8.3	27.6	18.7

STATE County code	STATE County	Educational attainment			Employment status					Percent of house-holds with no workers	Median house-hold income (dollars)	Percent of families with income below poverty	Percent of house-holds with income less than $25,000	Percent of house-holds with income of $100,000 or more
		Total population 25 years and over	Percent with a high school diploma or less	Percent with a bachelor's degree or more	Total population 16 years and over	Percent in the labor force	Unem-ployment rate	Percent who worked full-time, year-round						
ACS table number:		C15002	C15002	C15002	C20005	C23001	C23001	C20005	C08202	B19013	C17015	C19001	C19001
		1	2	3	4	5	6	7	8	9	10	11	12
	Iowa—Cont.												
19 105	Jones	14,124	58.5	13.0	16,632	62.6	4.5	41.0	25.2	43,852	7.5	23.6	8.1
19 111	Lee	24,924	57.4	14.6	28,975	58.3	7.4	37.3	34.7	40,098	11.4	32.8	9.2
19 113	Linn	133,377	38.3	28.8	157,561	71.2	5.3	44.5	23.3	50,358	6.7	22.4	16.4
19 123	Mahaska	14,723	57.2	15.1	17,496	68.4	5.3	41.4	27.5	43,879	5.0	25.0	8.8
19 125	Marion	21,211	51.8	22.7	25,881	70.4	4.1	41.1	25.7	51,193	7.9	24.6	14.0
19 127	Marshall	26,268	51.2	18.5	30,525	63.7	6.3	40.3	26.8	45,923	7.9	22.5	11.5
19 139	Muscatine	27,299	49.0	21.9	32,686	68.9	7.7	45.0	25.4	49,614	9.1	24.7	13.8
19 149	Plymouth	16,075	47.6	22.1	19,073	72.6	2.8	49.4	24.7	50,422	3.8	19.6	14.9
19 153	Polk	268,455	38.5	32.5	313,817	73.6	4.9	48.3	21.0	54,268	5.9	19.4	18.4
19 155	Pottawattamie	59,329	51.9	17.0	69,656	69.6	6.3	45.5	24.1	48,084	8.5	22.4	13.0
19 163	Scott	104,614	41.2	30.0	124,639	68.6	5.7	41.5	25.5	48,346	8.3	24.0	17.4
19 167	Sioux	18,858	48.5	22.3	25,053	73.2	1.6	40.0	22.9	47,429	3.3	21.4	9.7
19 169	Story	45,348	24.8	47.6	70,280	69.9	4.8	34.0	21.1	45,991	6.2	26.7	16.2
19 179	Wapello	24,074	58.5	12.9	28,458	63.4	8.0	36.1	34.7	36,789	9.6	31.3	7.3
19 181	Warren	28,305	44.7	24.1	34,452	73.6	3.4	46.6	19.8	58,811	5.4	16.3	17.4
19 183	Washington	14,273	53.9	18.1	16,592	68.6	5.6	43.0	27.5	47,900	9.5	24.6	12.7
19 187	Webster	25,862	50.0	16.9	30,854	66.9	6.8	39.9	31.4	41,155	8.6	27.9	8.3
19 191	Winneshiek	12,921	45.7	29.1	17,314	70.1	3.5	38.6	28.3	46,529	5.7	23.6	10.9
19 193	Woodbury	64,173	50.2	21.1	76,938	67.9	6.6	40.2	26.1	43,844	10.4	28.7	11.1
20 000	**Kansas**	1,773,908	41.8	28.3	2,143,455	68.6	5.2	43.0	23.6	46,669	8.3	25.0	15.3
20 009	Barton	18,393	46.8	20.4	22,089	65.5	4.4	39.2	28.7	40,826	8.8	27.5	7.3
20 015	Butler	40,048	39.0	23.7	48,586	68.3	6.3	42.6	20.3	53,433	6.9	19.5	18.6
20 021	Cherokee	14,435	57.1	14.0	17,029	64.1	6.4	37.7	28.8	34,453	11.6	36.2	5.3
20 035	Cowley	22,520	45.3	19.1	27,067	63.8	6.2	37.7	28.1	37,855	10.0	33.1	9.1
20 037	Crawford	23,562	39.9	28.7	30,933	62.5	4.8	35.8	29.9	32,927	9.2	38.4	7.8
20 045	Douglas	63,816	25.0	46.1	93,497	72.3	6.1	38.1	19.5	44,547	8.0	28.6	15.1
20 051	Ellis	16,782	34.4	34.0	22,386	73.2	4.4	42.0	24.1	43,121	5.7	29.9	9.9
20 055	Finney	21,572	55.1	17.3	27,191	73.2	5.3	51.2	15.7	47,806	10.1	21.1	13.8
20 057	Ford	19,615	59.3	13.9	23,670	73.2	4.4	47.2	17.4	42,546	16.3	25.7	7.6
20 059	Franklin	17,198	52.4	18.5	20,461	69.8	5.4	41.9	25.5	46,560	8.1	24.8	10.6
20 061	Geary	15,013	41.3	20.8	18,405	69.8	4.0	51.0	20.5	41,791	8.6	27.8	5.9
20 079	Harvey	21,977	44.7	24.0	26,432	66.7	5.8	40.9	27.3	44,550	4.0	24.9	11.6
20 091	Johnson	336,975	21.9	50.4	395,185	74.0	3.8	48.4	16.7	71,540	2.8	11.9	31.5
20 099	Labette	14,646	48.2	16.4	17,405	64.1	3.8	38.8	27.0	35,629	10.4	36.2	5.3
20 103	Leavenworth	47,559	46.9	25.9	56,470	64.6	5.1	42.0	20.9	57,746	6.7	19.8	21.4
20 111	Lyon	21,214	48.9	25.3	28,249	68.4	7.0	38.9	24.4	36,298	19.8	35.3	4.7
20 113	McPherson	19,386	44.5	25.4	23,550	68.5	1.6	41.6	24.7	50,035	6.7	22.1	12.0
20 121	Miami	19,840	44.4	21.2	23,662	70.6	4.7	44.6	21.6	60,573	4.7	17.5	20.4
20 125	Montgomery	23,444	46.4	16.4	27,518	62.1	7.0	38.4	32.8	34,098	12.4	34.7	6.3
20 155	Reno	42,845	47.9	17.3	50,328	63.2	4.0	39.2	25.4	40,693	8.0	27.9	8.1
20 161	Riley	33,857	26.2	41.0	56,483	65.2	3.5	35.5	19.9	38,747	9.4	31.0	11.3
20 169	Saline	35,868	47.9	21.2	42,106	70.8	4.0	43.8	24.8	42,037	8.9	28.3	9.7
20 173	Sedgwick	297,301	44.0	26.2	353,851	69.6	6.6	44.3	23.9	46,294	10.0	25.1	15.5
20 175	Seward	13,103	64.2	13.6	16,126	70.7	6.6	45.8	15.7	38,356	-	31.4	7.4
20 177	Shawnee	114,810	43.2	28.8	134,759	67.4	6.5	42.7	27.1	45,274	9.9	25.6	15.3
20 191	Sumner	15,774	49.7	15.5	18,719	65.6	5.5	40.5	27.6	48,766	8.8	24.4	13.9
20 209	Wyandotte	96,108	60.7	13.8	114,627	66.1	10.7	40.4	28.5	37,278	15.5	31.6	8.6
21 000	**Kentucky**	2,808,673	55.5	19.7	3,316,988	60.9	7.0	37.4	31.2	40,138	13.2	32.3	11.8
21 005	Anderson	14,070	61.0	14.7	16,201	68.7	4.8	47.2	23.3	49,778	5.0	18.8	11.5
21 009	Barren	28,270	66.1	14.8	32,279	62.0	8.1	37.8	32.5	38,352	12.5	34.0	10.4
21 013	Bell	19,997	70.2	11.6	23,330	43.6	5.4	26.2	47.4	20,817	29.2	57.0	3.8
21 015	Boone	69,497	43.6	25.8	82,069	75.8	4.5	48.4	16.6	62,334	5.7	15.7	21.8
21 019	Boyd	34,349	54.8	16.6	39,300	51.6	5.6	31.9	38.5	40,053	11.1	31.8	12.4
21 021	Boyle	19,094	56.5	21.5	22,974	58.9	8.7	34.9	35.4	38,228	12.5	30.5	10.2
21 029	Bullitt	48,433	61.4	10.9	56,373	68.5	6.0	43.5	21.3	51,451	6.3	21.2	12.6
21 035	Calloway	21,893	46.6	27.6	30,142	61.8	9.8	30.2	30.5	36,934	8.3	38.0	8.0
21 037	Campbell	57,221	47.8	25.6	68,300	67.6	5.5	43.3	25.5	50,084	8.1	24.5	17.9
21 043	Carter	18,410	66.0	13.8	21,765	52.9	7.7	29.1	33.9	31,702	16.8	40.6	7.1
21 047	Christian	44,584	52.4	14.9	56,291	63.5	7.2	39.5	28.8	37,615	14.4	30.6	8.3
21 049	Clark	24,379	56.8	16.4	27,855	63.5	7.2	41.8	33.2	44,540	11.4	29.6	12.2
21 051	Clay	16,213	78.8	10.0	18,986	-	-	22.4	51.6	20,202	29.3	60.2	1.3
21 059	Daviess	61,845	54.1	16.7	72,617	61.3	6.7	39.2	32.0	40,608	12.9	32.3	10.9
21 067	Fayette	180,369	34.4	38.9	221,572	68.8	4.4	42.6	21.8	45,622	9.8	27.2	17.6
21 071	Floyd	29,089	66.4	12.5	33,979	45.3	10.5	27.1	48.2	26,289	23.7	48.6	8.8
21 073	Franklin	33,253	51.2	25.1	39,238	64.6	6.2	43.0	27.1	47,360	10.2	26.7	14.2
21 081	Grant	16,202	69.1	9.6	18,948	66.3	7.1	38.4	24.9	42,354	14.1	26.6	9.4
21 083	Graves	25,336	60.6	13.5	29,632	57.6	7.5	30.7	37.0	35,514	13.6	34.7	7.2
21 085	Grayson	17,459	73.7	7.3	20,003	54.9	11.7	31.8	41.6	32,185	19.0	40.3	5.0
21 089	Greenup	26,284	58.8	12.3	30,161	53.7	7.7	33.8	38.6	39,688	13.0	32.0	10.3
21 093	Hardin	62,075	48.6	19.1	74,817	64.4	5.6	43.3	24.5	45,435	9.6	24.0	13.6
21 095	Harlan	21,449	71.4	11.1	24,868	44.1	10.0	27.7	45.6	27,588	22.6	47.1	5.2
21 101	Henderson	31,023	58.0	15.1	35,881	62.5	4.9	38.9	28.3	38,096	10.3	30.7	10.8
21 107	Hopkins	32,126	61.2	12.8	36,932	57.8	7.1	36.6	34.5	38,628	11.8	34.1	8.7
21 111	Jefferson	475,858	44.3	27.3	553,828	64.9	7.2	40.3	29.1	43,791	10.7	28.2	14.9
21 113	Jessamine	28,681	47.3	27.1	34,342	68.7	6.4	39.9	21.6	44,299	11.6	28.0	13.8

Table B-2. Counties — What: Education, Employment, and Income, 2005–2007—*Continued*

STATE County code	STATE County	Educational attainment			Employment status				Percent of house-holds with no workers	Median house-hold income (dollars)	Percent of families with income below poverty	Percent of house-holds with income less than $25,000	Percent of house-holds with income of $100,000 or more
		Total population 25 years and over	Percent with a high school diploma or less	Percent with a bachelor's degree or more	Total population 16 years and over	Percent in the labor force	Unem-ployment rate	Percent who worked full-time, year-round					
	ACS table number:	C15002	C15002	C15002	C20005	C23001	C23001	C20005	C08202	B19013	C17015	C19001	C19001
		1	2	3	4	5	6	7	8	9	10	11	12
	Kentucky—Cont.												
21 115	Johnson	16,378	68.7	11.7	19,074	46.7	11.3	29.6	46.0	32,218	19.8	44.5	9.7
21 117	Kenton	101,854	45.2	26.9	119,786	69.0	5.4	45.0	22.7	52,600	7.8	21.5	17.8
21 121	Knox	21,288	80.4	10.0	25,179	41.1	6.4	26.0	49.8	20,586	31.7	55.2	5.4
21 125	Laurel	38,222	65.1	14.1	44,067	57.9	7.4	36.0	34.2	33,325	15.7	37.5	8.4
21 133	Letcher	17,048	63.4	11.4	19,500	48.1	7.3	30.1	42.2	30,146	19.1	44.1	5.9
21 137	Lincoln	17,001	70.5	10.9	19,556	58.0	7.1	36.8	33.9	32,680	12.9	38.4	5.9
21 141	Logan	18,580	70.2	10.1	21,432	61.6	7.6	36.2	33.3	37,458	9.5	33.9	7.5
21 145	McCracken	44,856	46.8	21.2	51,658	59.3	8.6	34.5	35.4	39,006	12.7	33.2	11.3
21 151	Madison	48,861	46.8	28.3	63,802	65.7	7.1	35.6	27.2	39,260	14.1	32.4	11.1
21 157	Marshall	22,217	60.5	14.2	25,578	59.6	8.5	33.1	35.3	38,313	12.4	30.3	8.4
21 163	Meade	18,107	55.4	13.2	21,313	62.3	10.4	37.1	31.8	42,772	14.8	31.0	11.7
21 167	Mercer	15,096	57.9	17.6	17,178	66.3	6.6	40.6	27.3	42,120	8.9	23.7	12.0
21 173	Montgomery	16,922	64.2	13.7	19,220	58.8	4.1	39.4	31.9	35,035	13.5	38.8	7.1
21 177	Muhlenberg	22,084	68.8	8.9	25,456	52.6	8.8	28.9	37.1	35,117	16.6	37.4	5.2
21 179	Nelson	27,377	57.5	15.5	31,886	67.0	6.6	41.5	25.8	47,160	6.9	23.6	9.7
21 183	Ohio	16,093	67.9	8.7	18,523	55.3	8.5	34.9	33.0	35,952	13.3	34.4	6.0
21 185	Oldham	36,213	36.9	33.7	42,778	65.8	4.4	40.1	18.7	70,615	3.1	11.9	33.5
21 193	Perry	19,668	71.2	11.2	23,116	46.9	11.0	31.4	41.9	30,841	23.1	44.2	7.7
21 195	Pike	45,956	69.0	12.5	52,978	48.6	9.1	31.0	44.8	32,033	16.4	41.5	7.6
21 199	Pulaski	41,438	61.7	14.2	47,562	54.0	6.5	33.3	37.5	32,557	15.9	38.8	6.6
21 205	Rowan	12,729	57.9	22.9	17,988	57.1	8.5	27.6	33.5	34,106	18.6	40.9	7.3
21 209	Scott	25,734	48.5	23.7	31,444	68.2	6.6	42.6	22.1	56,270	9.1	20.4	19.6
21 211	Shelby	25,493	55.7	21.6	30,374	67.6	3.5	45.0	21.6	53,252	7.6	21.9	18.7
21 217	Taylor	15,993	65.4	15.5	19,270	58.8	7.8	35.2	35.7	34,811	16.0	36.6	3.7
21 227	Warren	63,473	45.2	28.4	81,120	67.5	5.1	39.7	22.3	43,254	12.2	29.3	13.7
21 231	Wayne	13,936	73.1	10.8	16,075	52.8	7.7	35.5	42.8	25,967	23.4	48.3	5.7
21 235	Whitley	25,015	68.5	13.8	29,950	47.3	7.6	27.0	40.4	27,481	21.8	45.0	4.8
21 239	Woodford	16,346	42.7	34.1	19,143	70.2	5.0	45.7	21.4	58,168	-	20.7	21.0
22 000	**Louisiana**	2,766,825	55.9	20.1	3,371,197	60.8	7.9	36.2	29.2	40,160	15.0	33.0	13.4
22 001	Acadia	36,652	73.1	10.1	44,833	56.9	7.0	31.2	33.4	29,974	20.2	42.4	6.8
22 003	Allen	16,512	68.6	9.8	19,942	48.0	6.3	33.6	33.8	34,038	18.1	38.2	8.2
22 005	Ascension	57,569	57.3	18.8	70,424	67.7	5.6	44.8	22.6	53,866	9.9	22.4	19.9
22 007	Assumption	14,685	78.1	8.3	18,166	52.7	7.4	32.4	33.9	37,458	20.0	37.3	9.2
22 009	Avoyelles	27,177	72.4	9.1	32,477	53.3	9.8	30.0	35.2	28,072	23.3	45.9	4.7
22 011	Beauregard	22,477	61.6	13.0	26,577	59.1	7.6	33.8	30.0	41,539	11.7	28.2	10.1
22 015	Bossier	67,362	46.3	20.6	81,234	68.0	7.6	44.5	23.9	48,223	10.2	24.7	14.5
22 017	Caddo	162,026	53.1	22.1	194,925	60.4	9.7	33.9	33.1	34,518	17.5	37.4	11.6
22 019	Calcasieu	117,945	54.9	18.4	142,204	62.6	8.3	35.3	29.7	39,713	13.5	33.2	14.1
22 031	De Soto	16,869	65.5	13.7	20,197	56.2	7.9	36.9	34.3	35,484	20.5	37.6	10.9
22 033	East Baton Rouge	257,254	40.9	31.9	330,690	66.6	7.7	39.0	24.3	43,323	14.2	30.6	17.1
22 037	East Feliciana	14,130	61.1	12.4	16,599	54.0	14.0	32.8	28.7	37,629	15.2	32.3	10.2
22 039	Evangeline	22,271	69.6	11.1	26,919	49.7	6.2	30.3	37.3	30,997	24.2	44.3	8.3
22 041	Franklin	13,292	73.8	10.0	15,604	53.6	12.6	26.0	36.6	26,382	27.4	47.9	6.4
22 045	Iberia	46,701	70.0	13.2	56,385	61.4	7.4	34.2	27.5	38,862	19.0	33.8	11.7
22 047	Iberville	21,266	70.8	12.4	25,697	57.1	10.4	39.2	30.8	37,808	15.2	37.3	12.1
22 051	Jefferson	288,678	51.2	22.7	340,261	63.5	7.4	37.6	26.5	46,498	10.3	26.7	16.1
22 053	Jefferson Davis	19,643	68.4	11.7	23,451	58.9	6.6	32.9	32.2	35,331	14.9	34.1	8.2
22 055	Lafayette	126,120	46.0	27.7	155,659	67.8	5.2	40.0	21.7	43,726	12.0	28.6	16.8
22 057	Lafourche	60,037	68.7	13.7	72,477	57.0	4.3	35.0	29.2	41,442	12.3	30.4	13.7
22 061	Lincoln	22,222	42.3	30.6	34,510	60.2	14.5	29.0	32.1	32,669	18.1	42.2	10.5
22 063	Livingston	70,656	59.7	14.3	84,671	63.8	4.2	42.6	25.2	50,348	9.9	22.5	13.6
22 067	Morehouse	19,315	66.7	12.3	22,648	51.2	9.5	32.3	40.0	29,027	25.1	45.6	5.4
22 069	Natchitochesv	22,848	58.3	19.8	30,619	55.8	10.9	30.4	35.1	27,478	24.0	46.2	8.3
22 071	Orleans	198,423	47.7	29.0	245,235	60.2	13.0	32.1	33.4	35,409	18.6	38.2	14.6
22 073	Ouachita	92,174	51.8	22.5	114,247	61.3	8.2	37.3	30.1	36,738	16.9	36.0	11.5
22 075	Plaquemines	14,976	58.2	11.6	18,164	50.0	7.3	34.3	29.1	45,099	7.3	24.5	13.6
22 077	Pointe Coupee	14,604	67.6	12.8	17,476	58.4	7.0	35.9	32.7	32,025	19.9	42.7	12.4
22 079	Rapides	83,320	55.0	18.7	99,473	60.3	7.0	36.5	29.3	36,464	15.8	35.9	11.7
22 083	Richland	13,288	65.1	12.1	15,825	56.3	14.3	35.3	32.9	36,414	19.7	38.1	9.6
22 085	Sabine	15,722	67.6	11.3	18,446	54.0	5.2	31.1	37.3	34,995	15.0	39.2	9.3
22 089	St. Charles	32,282	52.6	18.8	39,332	65.3	6.8	40.8	22.2	58,120	8.8	20.6	18.9
22 093	St. James	13,520	65.4	14.1	16,410	60.9	5.5	41.7	28.7	48,254	11.1	25.0	14.8
22 095	St. John the Baptist	28,108	60.9	15.1	34,969	63.2	8.5	42.3	24.0	46,273	13.5	24.5	14.1
22 097	St. Landry	56,521	70.3	11.7	68,309	51.9	8.6	31.8	40.2	24,243	27.6	50.9	7.0
22 099	St. Martin	32,563	71.6	9.8	38,911	63.3	7.1	39.8	27.2	37,509	13.7	33.9	12.5
22 101	St. Mary	33,057	70.7	10.1	39,232	62.3	7.2	36.3	27.2	37,608	18.5	34.9	10.9
22 103	St. Tammany	142,830	40.6	30.2	171,029	62.4	4.7	38.2	24.6	58,653	8.0	19.9	23.7
22 105	Tangipahoa	67,966	60.3	17.9	85,655	55.5	9.3	28.9	35.0	34,071	18.8	39.6	10.5
22 109	Terrebonne	68,164	67.3	13.6	82,459	60.1	5.3	38.1	26.5	44,258	14.0	29.7	14.0
22 111	Union	15,172	63.3	15.6	17,668	56.2	5.8	37.3	31.3	34,040	18.4	38.5	9.0
22 113	Vermilion	35,613	71.1	10.0	42,933	57.1	3.7	33.6	31.0	37,609	14.9	34.5	11.7
22 115	Vernon	27,607	56.3	16.1	35,074	65.3	5.1	43.7	25.4	38,495	13.7	30.4	8.8
22 117	Washington	28,530	66.8	12.0	34,170	54.1	9.5	30.3	37.6	31,532	18.6	41.9	7.5
22 119	Webster	27,400	65.1	12.8	32,635	55.7	7.3	31.7	36.0	32,436	18.5	41.6	7.3
22 121	West Baton Rouge	14,154	62.7	17.5	17,126	65.9	6.7	42.7	25.1	42,776	15.9	30.9	9.5

Table B-2. Counties — What: Education, Employment, and Income, 2005–2007—*Continued*

STATE County code	STATE County	Educational attainment			Employment status				Percent of house-holds with no workers	Median house-hold income (dollars)	Percent of families with income below poverty	Percent of house-holds with income less than $25,000	Percent of house-holds with income of $100,000 or more
		Total population 25 years and over	Percent with a high school diploma or less	Percent with a bachelor's degree or more	Total population 16 years and over	Percent in the labor force	Unem-ployment rate	Percent who worked full-time, year-round					
ACS table number:		C15002	C15002	C15002	C20005	C23001	C23001	C20005	C08202	B19013	C17015	C19001	C19001
		1	2	3	4	5	6	7	8	9	10	11	12
23 000	**Maine**	917,697	47.5	25.9	1,069,271	65.5	5.7	38.5	28.8	45,211	8.6	27.1	13.2
23 001	Androscoggin	72,782	56.2	17.2	85,504	65.4	7.5	40.8	27.4	42,725	10.6	28.4	9.5
23 003	Aroostook	51,376	57.6	16.1	59,772	57.4	5.6	33.7	37.0	34,225	11.5	38.3	6.8
23 005	Cumberland	190,501	34.7	38.9	222,219	69.7	4.5	41.4	24.6	53,768	7.0	21.8	20.3
23 007	Franklin	20,237	48.4	26.7	24,641	65.2	8.4	33.3	30.7	38,975	9.1	30.1	7.7
23 009	Hancock	38,165	45.6	28.7	44,079	66.9	5.6	36.9	26.4	45,822	5.3	24.5	13.0
23 011	Kennebec	84,176	48.3	25.3	98,320	65.0	5.3	39.8	28.9	45,248	9.1	26.3	13.3
23 013	Knox	29,793	48.7	25.4	33,801	66.1	5.0	36.3	30.8	42,495	7.9	29.4	12.8
23 015	Lincoln	25,623	43.2	30.1	28,811	64.2	5.8	36.5	33.5	45,620	6.7	27.6	12.4
23 017	Oxford	40,273	57.5	16.2	46,057	61.5	7.6	35.2	32.9	37,175	11.5	31.1	9.0
23 019	Penobscot	99,907	49.1	22.9	121,213	62.4	6.0	36.0	30.7	41,336	8.9	30.8	11.1
23 023	Sagadahoc	25,360	47.3	26.2	29,042	69.3	4.1	43.0	24.5	52,569	6.4	20.4	14.6
23 025	Somerset	36,227	60.2	15.1	41,716	60.0	8.2	35.1	34.4	36,154	12.7	34.0	7.5
23 027	Waldo	26,930	53.5	20.2	31,085	66.3	7.6	37.3	27.7	40,470	11.6	29.0	9.0
23 029	Washington	23,478	56.3	18.6	26,912	58.8	9.4	29.5	37.5	33,171	15.5	39.2	5.4
23 031	York	140,422	46.6	26.2	161,752	68.5	4.8	41.7	25.9	52,726	5.6	21.1	15.5
24 000	**Maryland**	3,699,555	40.2	34.7	4,396,011	68.7	5.5	44.9	21.7	66,873	5.5	16.1	30.0
24 001	Allegany	49,702	58.3	15.1	60,654	54.7	8.1	30.5	37.8	35,453	9.2	35.0	8.5
24 003	Anne Arundel	340,313	38.0	34.2	401,064	69.0	4.2	46.6	19.3	79,294	3.0	10.9	36.7
24 005	Baltimore	532.284	40.5	33.8	630,782	67.1	5.1	43.2	24.3	60,701	4.9	17.4	24.5
24 009	Calvert	57,092	43.5	28.5	67,771	71.7	3.2	48.9	18.5	88,989	3.2	9.9	43.0
24 011	Caroline	21,252	60.8	15.5	25,367	67.5	3.8	43.1	24.5	51,191	8.6	21.0	15.4
24 013	Carroll	111,168	43.2	29.6	131,675	69.6	3.3	47.0	19.2	78,912	2.5	12.9	35.7
24 015	Cecil	65,416	52.9	20.1	76,595	69.7	6.7	45.2	24.0	62,608	6.6	18.1	23.7
24 017	Charles	88,816	43.8	23.7	105,611	73.7	4.2	52.4	16.4	80,573	3.9	11.2	37.9
24 019	Dorchester	22,176	62.0	15.8	25,444	66.6	8.0	42.2	26.4	42,322	11.8	28.8	13.0
24 021	Frederick	144,296	38.5	33.6	170,967	72.5	3.4	49.0	16.4	76,920	2.9	10.3	35.5
24 023	Garrett	20,677	59.8	15.5	23,834	65.9	5.5	41.7	27.0	42,460	9.9	26.3	10.4
24 025	Harford	157,353	38.0	30.1	185,278	70.5	3.4	40.0	20.2	72,005	3.9	11.8	31.5
24 027	Howard	178,005	21.3	56.7	208,224	72.9	3.3	48.9	14.0	97,837	3.1	7.6	48.9
24 031	Montgomery	623,443	23.5	56.5	725,173	71.2	4.2	46.3	18.0	89,284	2.9	9.0	44.5
24 033	Prince George's	530,984	42.1	30.1	646,251	72.8	7.1	48.6	17.9	68,410	5.5	12.7	29.0
24 035	Queen Anne's	31,184	43.0	28.6	36,529	68.3	4.1	46.4	21.7	73,964	4.6	13.0	31.7
24 037	St. Mary's	62,551	47.7	25.8	75,556	70.2	4.2	49.6	17.3	71,559	5.4	13.9	30.5
24 039	Somerset	17,018	65.3	14.8	21,787	44.5	7.5	28.2	31.3	38,086	12.7	32.2	13.1
24 041	Talbot	26,249	39.8	32.6	29,788	63.3	3.4	40.4	27.7	57,966	5.5	16.0	23.3
24 043	Washington	98,605	56.1	18.1	114,365	65.8	5.2	42.8	24.1	51,034	6.8	22.1	16.3
24 045	Wicomico	58,980	52.4	24.2	73,060	67.3	7.1	41.5	25.4	49,194	8.7	23.9	16.2
24 047	Worcester	36,341	47.9	26.2	41,048	62.2	6.1	39.8	31.3	50,181	6.5	20.8	18.7
24 510	Baltimore city	412,404	55.2	23.3	502,258	60.7	11.1	36.0	32.4	36,304	16.7	35.2	11.5
25 000	**Massachusetts**	4,355,378	40.0	37.1	5,167,254	66.9	6.1	40.4	26.0	61,785	7.2	20.9	27.5
25 001	Barnstable	166,732	33.2	38.5	188,587	61.0	5.5	34.1	33.9	58,422	3.8	18.3	21.9
25 003	Berkshire	91,051	43.3	30.1	108,306	62.5	6.4	35.9	31.9	48,836	7.8	26.3	16.4
25 005	Bristol	369,036	52.7	23.5	432,678	66.8	7.0	40.0	28.2	54,070	8.3	24.3	21.4
25 009	Essex	491,691	40.4	35.3	577,669	66.3	5.4	40.6	26.4	61,505	8.0	21.8	28.4
25 011	Franklin	50,510	42.5	32.0	59,471	67.9	5.8	39.2	25.8	51,231	6.8	22.2	14.9
25 013	Hampden	299,443	51.1	23.8	361,123	62.7	8.3	36.4	32.5	45,935	13.1	29.9	15.5
25 015	Hampshire	95,209	33.7	41.7	130,530	66.9	6.2	32.5	25.5	53,170	5.6	23.4	19.5
25 017	Middlesex	1,008,311	32.9	47.6	1,184,506	68.8	5.1	42.6	22.3	74,010	4.8	15.9	35.2
25 021	Norfolk	448,597	30.9	46.8	521,645	67.7	5.0	42.5	23.3	77,294	4.1	15.1	37.2
25 023	Plymouth	324,131	40.7	31.2	381,932	69.0	6.3	41.7	21.9	70,335	4.2	15.6	31.1
25 025	Suffolk	474,143	44.9	37.1	585,728	66.2	8.0	38.8	28.7	48,735	15.6	30.0	20.8
25 027	Worcester	517,984	43.4	31.2	613,758	67.6	6.1	41.8	25.6	60,709	6.8	20.7	25.7
26 000	**Michigan**	6,634,147	45.2	24.5	7,915,981	63.5	9.4	35.9	29.4	48,642	9.8	24.9	17.1
26 005	Allegan	73,589	51.7	19.5	86,897	66.5	6.8	39.6	25.2	51,285	7.5	21.7	12.8
26 007	Alpena	21,054	49.8	15.9	24,597	59.0	7.6	33.0	36.6	35,329	10.3	35.2	8.3
26 009	Antrim	17,167	50.3	21.3	19,721	57.0	8.1	30.2	37.4	43,849	10.7	26.6	10.8
26 015	Barry	39,739	51.4	17.1	46,480	66.4	6.7	38.7	26.2	50,835	5.6	20.7	14.4
26 017	Bay	74,209	50.0	16.9	86,768	63.0	8.8	36.0	33.1	43,353	8.4	26.6	11.9
26 021	Berrien	106,707	48.7	23.0	125,226	62.9	8.3	36.3	29.2	42,188	12.4	29.8	13.5
26 023	Branch	31,760	55.4	13.9	36,987	55.8	8.5	35.0	31.9	42,331	10.8	29.1	10.5
26 025	Calhoun	90,876	49.1	18.4	107,160	61.5	8.5	37.3	31.0	42,181	12.6	30.2	12.2
26 027	Cass	34,945	54.7	15.0	40,665	65.3	7.9	39.0	26.7	42,601	10.5	24.8	12.7
26 029	Charlevoix	18,260	46.9	23.5	21,059	65.0	7.5	38.1	29.1	48,741	6.1	20.7	13.8
26 031	Cheboygan	19,304	55.3	17.2	22,043	58.3	13.6	26.7	38.6	38,064	12.5	32.2	9.1
26 033	Chippewa	26,514	51.8	19.3	32,208	54.5	9.7	27.8	34.3	37,735	11.5	32.8	8.8
26 035	Clare	21,642	61.6	9.4	24,914	51.0	14.7	25.0	44.3	34,602	13.2	37.0	4.3
26 037	Clinton	45,616	37.8	26.3	54,127	68.8	6.0	43.8	23.9	59,991	4.6	17.3	20.9
26 041	Delta	26,214	51.4	17.6	30,842	60.2	7.1	31.8	33.9	37,884	8.3	31.2	7.7
26 043	Dickinson	18,932	55.2	17.6	21,808	57.5	5.8	35.0	36.6	39,240	8.7	33.8	12.5
26 045	Eaton	71,479	41.6	22.8	85,614	67.9	7.5	39.5	27.0	52,592	6.5	20.8	16.2
26 047	Emmet	23,006	38.6	28.7	26,869	67.4	9.2	36.8	29.8	46,402	5.3	23.3	13.0
26 049	Genesee	286,221	47.7	18.8	337,100	60.4	10.3	33.7	33.1	44,277	12.7	27.3	13.6

Table B-2. Counties — What: Education, Employment, and Income, 2005–2007—Continued

STATE County code	STATE County	Educational attainment			Employment status				Percent of house-holds with no workers	Median house-hold income (dollars)	Percent of families with income below poverty	Percent of house-holds with income less than $25,000	Percent of house-holds with income of $100,000 or more
		Total population 25 years and over	Percent with a high school diploma or less	Percent with a bachelor's degree or more	Total population 16 years and over	Percent in the labor force	Unemployment rate	Percent who worked full-time, year-round					
ACS table number:		C15002	C15002	C15002	C20005	C23001	C23001	C20005	C08202	B19013	C17015	C19001	C19001
		1	2	3	4	5	6	7	8	9	10	11	12
	Michigan—Cont.												
26 051	Gladwin	19,135	59.4	9.9	21,843	50.3	9.5	26.4	45.4	35,535	15.5	32.8	5.9
26 055	Grand Traverse	58,332	37.2	29.6	67,662	67.4	5.9	39.4	25.3	49,066	6.2	21.2	14.5
26 057	Gratiot	27,332	57.3	13.0	33,176	59.3	8.5	31.6	29.6	42,193	12.5	29.7	8.8
26 059	Hillsdale	31,054	56.7	14.6	37,122	61.5	7.6	33.1	30.4	42,075	9.9	28.3	10.1
26 061	Houghton	20,911	51.6	23.1	29,272	58.5	6.1	25.8	34.3	31,076	10.8	41.8	6.5
26 063	Huron	24,094	59.6	12.3	27,647	60.6	7.2	34.7	36.1	38,222	8.6	31.3	7.4
26 065	Ingham	164,929	35.4	34.7	224,721	63.8	7.7	35.5	27.1	45,313	12.4	29.2	15.5
26 067	Ionia	41,559	55.9	12.1	50,081	60.0	9.7	33.1	28.5	46,354	9.8	24.8	9.1
26 069	Iosco	19,439	56.0	13.7	22,042	50.9	12.6	25.1	48.7	35,753	10.7	33.1	4.8
26 073	Isabella	34,053	45.1	27.6	55,731	64.2	11.5	27.7	27.1	38,830	11.1	33.9	10.6
26 075	Jackson	109,152	49.0	17.5	128,393	59.1	8.1	36.0	29.5	45,946	11.5	27.1	13.2
26 077	Kalamazoo	150,793	34.1	34.0	193,769	67.3	8.9	36.5	27.8	45,681	9.3	27.1	16.7
26 081	Kent	377,836	40.4	29.1	454,944	70.4	7.8	40.8	22.7	49,432	9.0	22.1	16.4
26 087	Lapeer	61,274	50.1	15.8	72,017	65.6	9.1	36.5	25.6	56,208	7.3	17.7	18.4
26 089	Leelanau	15,717	32.5	39.6	17,907	63.7	5.4	34.4	30.2	54,502	4.2	16.2	21.0
26 091	Lenawee	67,018	50.4	18.5	79,944	65.4	8.8	36.9	29.7	50,074	7.2	21.6	14.0
26 093	Livingston	119,722	33.5	31.8	141,775	70.8	7.0	41.9	20.8	73,237	3.5	11.6	31.4
26 099	Macomb	566,522	45.9	21.1	657,486	65.6	8.9	38.4	27.9	55,724	6.5	19.9	19.9
26 101	Manistee	18,038	55.4	15.7	20,563	54.3	10.3	29.2	39.3	38,092	10.3	30.1	6.9
26 103	Marquette	43,293	42.5	29.7	54,694	59.5	7.5	30.6	32.6	43,939	7.4	30.5	11.8
26 105	Mason	20,191	49.4	19.4	23,495	59.7	9.4	33.9	36.2	37,914	11.4	33.6	9.0
26 107	Mecosta	25,166	50.9	19.6	34,520	56.7	13.3	25.3	38.5	36,085	12.5	33.5	8.2
26 109	Menominee	17,237	57.0	12.4	19,822	63.6	6.6	38.1	30.7	41,808	8.3	29.5	6.9
26 111	Midland	54,703	39.8	31.9	65,883	62.5	8.7	34.5	31.6	48,911	8.5	26.8	18.6
26 115	Monroe	101,699	50.9	16.3	120,734	66.1	7.4	38.6	26.6	55,922	5.6	18.2	19.3
26 117	Montcalm	41,978	56.3	12.8	49,402	62.6	13.2	33.4	34.5	39,766	12.8	28.4	9.1
26 121	Muskegon	113,623	48.2	17.3	135,380	61.9	12.4	34.1	31.4	41,984	11.6	28.2	9.9
26 123	Newaygo	32,176	57.0	13.6	37,943	62.4	10.9	34.2	31.7	42,818	12.6	29.0	8.7
26 125	Oakland	818,077	30.7	41.7	951,138	67.9	7.1	40.9	23.7	67,619	5.0	16.1	31.1
26 127	Oceana	18,225	57.2	13.3	21,674	59.8	9.7	31.4	33.1	38,295	14.5	31.6	6.4
26 129	Ogemaw	15,233	61.8	10.7	17,545	51.6	9.0	26.7	45.0	33,980	15.6	36.4	6.6
26 133	Osceola	15,639	60.8	11.7	18,335	54.8	9.8	29.2	36.4	36,731	12.8	34.1	5.3
26 137	Otsego	16,597	51.6	19.6	19,166	61.8	8.9	33.1	31.2	43,486	11.3	25.8	8.7
26 139	Ottawa	157,163	42.5	27.9	196,862	70.2	5.4	39.3	21.1	57,536	3.2	15.9	18.7
26 143	Roscommon	19,031	56.5	12.4	21,723	45.6	14.8	21.1	53.2	30,947	18.6	39.7	5.7
26 145	Saginaw	133,918	50.6	17.9	160,033	57.5	10.2	32.1	35.7	42,074	13.6	30.0	13.2
26 147	St. Clair	114,403	51.4	14.9	133,805	64.1	10.9	34.6	30.1	50,419	8.2	22.6	15.7
26 149	St. Joseph	40,731	59.1	12.8	47,998	63.9	8.6	39.7	28.6	41,839	11.5	28.9	9.6
26 151	Sanilac	29,552	62.6	10.2	34,583	61.2	9.9	33.7	33.5	40,639	10.3	30.2	7.5
26 155	Shiawassee	48,393	50.1	15.4	56,613	63.9	9.7	34.9	28.4	45,330	10.7	25.4	12.8
26 157	Tuscola	38,327	57.9	11.9	45,576	59.6	9.3	32.5	32.5	42,344	10.5	26.8	9.1
26 159	Van Buren	51,236	51.7	18.8	60,022	65.3	10.4	35.4	28.8	43,067	13.7	29.1	12.9
26 161	Washtenaw	214,503	24.7	51.4	280,832	66.3	6.6	35.8	22.5	59,887	7.3	22.4	26.3
26 163	Wayne	1,297,844	51.2	19.4	1,533,809	60.1	13.9	33.3	34.0	43,232	15.3	30.1	15.0
26 165	Wexford	21,428	53.7	16.2	24,870	61.8	9.3	34.2	31.2	38,687	12.3	31.2	7.4
27 000	**Minnesota**	3,385,006	37.8	30.6	4,046,604	71.0	5.4	42.4	23.1	55,616	6.3	19.9	20.5
27 003	Anoka	209,783	38.9	25.5	247,481	75.2	5.5	47.6	17.2	67,275	4.2	11.8	24.3
27 005	Becker	21,541	45.8	20.8	25,327	66.9	5.3	38.1	27.0	44,005	7.1	26.5	11.6
27 007	Beltrami	25,893	40.5	26.7	33,632	65.0	10.3	31.7	29.4	42,337	10.6	31.9	11.4
27 009	Benton	24,983	45.0	18.8	30,193	75.9	5.8	44.2	18.7	51,533	3.7	18.6	13.4
27 013	Blue Earth	35,467	37.4	29.4	48,878	72.1	4.5	37.3	22.9	47,744	6.3	24.4	12.5
27 015	Brown	17,657	53.1	17.8	21,324	71.2	3.3	40.8	23.0	48,697	5.8	21.9	9.7
27 017	Carlton	22,673	44.6	20.1	27,082	64.3	6.8	35.8	31.1	49,792	8.5	23.0	10.8
27 019	Carver	53,577	30.1	39.1	64,030	76.6	3.7	50.0	13.4	78,035	3.1	10.7	35.0
27 021	Cass	20,081	48.6	20.2	23,366	60.3	8.3	32.2	34.6	40,107	9.2	29.7	9.8
27 025	Chisago	31,982	46.2	17.6	38,037	67.6	5.5	38.7	21.2	64,172	5.7	13.0	20.0
27 027	Clay	31,870	34.5	31.7	43,360	70.1	4.0	39.3	24.2	47,461	7.6	27.0	13.3
27 035	Crow Wing	41,737	42.4	21.1	48,643	64.7	5.4	35.4	32.0	42,763	5.4	25.1	11.2
27 037	Dakota	248,122	29.0	37.7	293,365	77.1	5.0	48.9	16.6	72,393	3.8	11.5	31.5
27 041	Douglas	24,521	42.5	19.3	29,085	67.7	4.5	38.1	30.3	43,002	9.8	29.2	10.7
27 045	Fillmore	14,275	52.5	18.2	16,696	68.0	3.8	42.8	27.4	43,405	7.2	26.6	9.5
27 047	Freeborn	22,064	53.1	14.9	25,430	62.4	5.5	38.7	32.3	41,917	3.4	26.2	8.8
27 049	Goodhue	30,713	43.2	22.9	36,480	70.5	5.6	41.8	25.5	55,098	5.7	20.7	16.8
27 053	Hennepin	763,161	29.4	42.3	893,579	72.7	5.8	44.0	21.3	60,115	7.0	18.9	26.3
27 059	Isanti	25,266	46.8	16.2	29,867	74.3	6.8	41.1	20.6	57,199	5.5	15.2	17.2
27 061	Itasca	30,661	43.8	19.1	36,204	60.3	6.2	33.3	33.1	42,413	7.9	27.3	9.3
27 067	Kandiyohi	27,041	43.8	21.1	32,236	69.7	4.4	40.0	23.1	47,888	6.3	23.8	12.9
27 079	Le Sueur	18,429	48.2	20.4	21,801	73.2	7.4	44.6	23.5	55,587	4.6	16.2	14.9
27 083	Lyon	15,395	44.1	26.8	19,518	71.3	3.7	41.3	22.2	45,043	7.4	26.9	13.2
27 085	McLeod	24,275	48.0	17.9	28,404	72.0	2.6	44.8	21.7	55,480	4.3	18.1	17.1
27 091	Martin	14,395	49.4	17.7	16,651	63.0	1.8	40.3	32.8	42,654	6.3	26.1	11.6
27 093	Meeker	15,467	52.5	14.6	18,185	68.2	5.7	40.7	26.2	49,918	6.2	23.3	11.8
27 095	Mille Lacs	17,445	54.1	12.8	20,511	66.8	9.6	36.6	28.5	45,163	7.4	27.4	8.3
27 097	Morrison	21,630	55.8	13.6	25,550	69.1	5.9	39.4	26.5	48,329	7.0	25.6	10.1
27 099	Mower	25,457	47.9	16.8	29,767	65.9	4.7	40.0	31.9	43,979	8.8	27.2	13.3

STATE County code	STATE County	Educational attainment			Employment status				Percent of house-holds with no workers	Median house-hold income (dollars)	Percent of families with income below poverty	Percent of house-holds with income less than $25,000	Percent of house-holds with income of $100,000 or more
		Total population 25 years and over	Percent with a high school diploma or less	Percent with a bachelor's degree or more	Total population 16 years and over	Percent in the labor force	Unem-ployment rate	Percent who worked full-time, year-round					
	ACS table number:	C15002	C15002	C15002	C20005	C23001	C23001	C20005	C08202	B19013	C17015	C19001	C19001
		1	2	3	4	5	6	7	8	9	10	11	12
	Minnesota—Cont.												
27 103	Nicollet	18,930	34.2	34.2	25,171	73.5	3.4	41.0	23.1	54,689	4.8	20.4	16.3
27 105	Nobles	13,132	55.4	17.4	15,499	66.4	6.9	40.2	29.5	37,129	14.6	34.7	11.6
27 109	Olmsted	90,767	31.6	37.8	106,483	72.5	3.0	46.8	20.2	61,863	4.9	15.7	24.5
27 111	Otter Tail	39,539	47.7	18.8	46,508	62.7	4.3	36.4	32.3	40,864	8.1	29.7	9.5
27 115	Pine	19,293	57.0	12.7	22,613	64.9	7.5	32.7	29.2	44,178	7.8	26.7	9.1
27 119	Polk	20,213	48.3	17.8	24,881	69.3	7.5	34.2	27.3	43,610	7.9	29.7	9.5
27 123	Ramsey	325,857	35.0	38.0	390,848	68.8	6.7	39.5	25.6	51,862	9.3	22.5	20.2
27 131	Rice	36,983	44.0	25.4	49,152	69.8	5.1	40.0	22.3	55,747	6.4	17.2	16.9
27 137	St. Louis	131,412	40.4	24.7	162,796	62.4	7.0	33.3	33.5	43,110	8.0	29.0	11.5
27 139	Scott	75,675	32.2	35.0	89,599	78.0	4.2	50.5	13.8	80,968	2.3	8.7	34.7
27 141	Sherburne	51,233	37.6	25.1	62,669	75.0	5.3	44.3	16.5	67,428	4.1	12.2	24.4
27 145	Stearns	87,879	43.6	23.2	115,111	71.5	5.1	39.5	21.4	50,800	6.7	22.6	14.5
27 147	Steele	23,365	48.7	20.9	27,832	72.7	2.9	47.2	21.7	52,785	3.1	18.6	12.5
27 153	Todd	15,843	53.6	12.7	19,193	64.9	5.1	38.5	27.4	40,938	8.8	29.3	9.4
27 157	Wabasha	14,793	49.3	18.6	17,452	69.8	4.0	43.9	25.9	53,351	5.2	25.1	15.2
27 163	Washington	143,155	28.8	39.4	169,495	73.8	4.4	46.4	18.0	78,067	3.0	10.1	34.7
27 169	Winona	29,857	41.5	25.3	40,819	71.8	6.1	37.4	23.4	42,827	6.5	27.7	11.5
27 171	Wright	71,151	41.6	22.0	84,159	76.8	4.4	49.0	17.6	65,419	3.7	12.9	21.0
28 000	**Mississippi**	1,829,680	53.9	18.6	2,230,412	60.0	9.2	36.3	31.1	35,632	16.6	36.4	10.4
28 001	Adams	20,946	54.8	19.8	25,206	53.9	13.6	29.5	38.8	27,986	23.4	45.0	8.6
28 003	Alcorn	24,143	64.6	13.0	27,765	55.7	6.5	38.9	37.0	32,782	11.5	40.3	7.5
28 011	Bolivar	21,685	59.0	23.6	28,923	57.6	18.1	26.5	30.4	23,711	30.4	52.3	7.8
28 025	Clay	13,603	58.7	14.6	16,242	60.6	13.7	36.9	32.4	30,034	18.4	44.5	4.1
28 027	Coahoma	16,326	57.3	14.1	20,229	56.6	16.9	32.8	37.4	25,165	29.0	49.8	4.9
28 029	Copiah	18,186	58.3	14.3	22,611	55.5	8.6	34.2	37.4	33,410	13.7	40.3	8.3
28 031	Covington	12,990	58.9	14.4	15,293	.	.	38.2	31.2	33,230	21.5	39.0	9.1
28 033	DeSoto	89,260	48.7	19.6	106,123	71.6	6.3	47.9	18.5	55,597	7.0	17.3	17.1
28 035	Forrest	44,810	44.9	26.0	60,007	63.6	9.2	34.2	27.8	32,393	21.0	40.3	7.5
28 039	George	13,427	63.5	14.2	15,671	56.0	8.4	31.3	32.8	47,106	10.6	31.2	11.2
28 043	Grenada	15,186	61.8	15.5	17,817	58.0	12.9	34.6	34.8	31,255	18.2	41.6	8.6
28 045	Hancock	28,369	51.3	21.1	33,115	54.9	8.3	33.7	37.0	41,182	10.8	30.4	13.2
28 047	Harrison	117,037	48.6	19.0	139,486	62.8	9.1	37.3	29.4	43,654	11.3	28.4	13.7
28 049	Hinds	151,325	40.5	27.1	189,420	63.1	8.5	39.1	27.8	37,728	17.1	33.7	11.8
28 051	Holmes	11,765	69.5	12.1	15,205	50.8	19.1	25.2	46.4	22,067	34.6	55.2	3.0
28 057	Itawamba	15,146	67.8	9.9	18,390	64.0	8.3	38.8	27.9	37,651	14.2	31.0	6.3
28 059	Jackson	84,649	50.5	18.0	100,554	61.5	9.3	35.5	28.4	44,185	13.3	26.7	13.0
28 067	Jones	42,886	60.6	13.7	51,360	54.8	4.7	37.9	33.4	33,290	17.4	37.9	7.1
28 071	Lafayette	22,869	38.7	37.0	34,553	56.8	7.0	29.6	27.6	38,688	11.6	33.8	14.3
28 073	Lamar	28,210	39.7	29.2	34,701	65.3	4.6	39.4	24.7	46,528	8.4	24.0	18.9
28 075	Lauderdale	48,988	52.5	17.5	59,287	62.7	9.2	36.7	34.1	31,378	18.7	41.5	10.2
28 079	Leake	13,636	65.8	9.1	16,892	56.3	6.9	35.9	31.0	32,225	14.6	38.4	4.7
28 081	Lee	50,987	50.7	21.2	59,993	63.4	7.6	40.0	28.1	37,804	14.7	34.1	11.5
28 083	Leflore	20,756	60.0	16.4	26,606	54.6	18.7	31.6	37.9	20,103	37.1	59.0	5.4
28 085	Lincoln	22,765	55.1	14.8	26,448	58.5	7.7	35.2	32.9	39,381	14.7	35.5	8.9
28 087	Lowndes	37,264	50.9	20.3	45,415	64.3	10.3	40.3	28.7	37,459	15.1	36.6	9.6
28 089	Madison	53,928	33.6	42.1	64,996	67.1	5.9	45.7	21.8	56,617	7.8	20.8	25.8
28 091	Marion	16,222	67.8	10.9	19,431	50.7	6.4	29.1	37.5	28,326	22.5	44.5	10.5
28 093	Marshall	23,216	68.8	9.3	28,133	51.1	11.1	31.5	36.0	32,648	19.2	40.2	5.9
28 095	Monroe	24,610	65.1	12.0	29,066	57.9	8.5	35.0	32.9	31,850	19.0	42.5	8.2
28 099	Neshoba	18,586	61.8	11.8	22,493	53.4	9.4	33.4	35.8	29,835	19.0	40.5	6.7
28 101	Newton	13,662	56.6	13.4	16,952	57.3	8.5	35.4	31.4	33,787	14.4	36.5	6.8
28 105	Oktibbeha	21,842	40.3	35.5	35,178	60.5	10.6	30.0	29.2	30,493	19.5	45.0	11.7
28 107	Panola	21,971	62.9	11.2	26,611	62.4	12.4	35.1	30.7	33,593	21.8	38.2	5.3
28 109	Pearl River	36,020	55.3	14.7	43,078	54.9	9.7	29.1	35.6	35,817	15.3	37.1	10.4
28 113	Pike	25,028	56.6	13.1	29,695	52.8	8.2	29.7	36.3	26,652	23.7	46.9	5.9
28 115	Pontotoc	18,321	66.2	11.0	21,883	62.5	7.0	39.1	26.1	36,782	14.3	32.6	7.6
28 117	Prentiss	16,441	61.1	12.3	20,090	53.7	7.2	33.5	38.2	27,533	15.9	44.8	6.0
28 121	Rankin	87,310	40.5	28.1	104,228	67.5	4.9	45.4	19.8	51,550	6.7	21.6	18.6
28 123	Scott	17,909	68.1	8.4	21,888	57.5	4.2	34.2	30.5	33,907	17.6	37.5	7.0
28 127	Simpson	17,920	59.8	14.4	21,329	60.2	6.8	39.3	34.3	30,241	15.4	42.9	9.2
28 133	Sunflower	18,778	64.0	12.7	24,255	42.0	12.3	22.2	36.6	22,569	33.5	53.6	4.4
28 137	Tate	16,450	57.1	13.9	20,431	65.3	7.5	38.0	26.2	37,526	14.1	33.3	8.8
28 139	Tippah	14,060	71.7	6.1	16,302	55.9	10.6	33.7	30.6	28,233	20.3	41.6	3.9
28 145	Union	17,410	64.2	11.1	20,751	58.8	8.7	35.3	33.5	34,381	12.3	34.1	4.5
28 149	Warren	30,984	47.7	22.6	37,010	64.1	9.1	43.6	29.0	37,063	14.5	35.8	12.9
28 151	Washington	34,352	59.0	18.1	41,834	58.2	23.1	28.8	38.4	26,697	28.8	47.3	8.0
28 153	Wayne	13,297	69.8	8.5	16,035	53.3	4.7	33.0	34.2	27,427	20.8	44.6	5.7
28 163	Yazoo	17,320	58.0	10.3	20,707	55.1	15.5	30.7	35.6	30,162	24.1	44.4	11.4
29 000	**Missouri**	3,847,339	48.8	24.0	4,578,206	65.1	6.4	40.6	27.2	44,545	9.8	27.2	13.9
29 001	Adair	12,949	50.3	24.9	20,656	60.4	5.2	32.4	29.7	31,076	11.9	41.9	4.4
29 007	Audrain	17,849	65.8	12.5	20,357	57.5	3.1	40.9	28.4	38,316	12.7	31.2	7.9
29 009	Barry	23,929	64.6	11.4	27,408	59.8	6.7	37.4	31.4	34,817	15.4	34.1	7.6
29 019	Boone	88,148	30.5	46.5	119,885	70.8	5.5	39.5	20.0	43,171	9.7	28.9	15.3
29 021	Buchanan	56,800	56.7	16.3	68,118	62.5	8.0	38.8	28.9	38,737	11.0	32.4	10.0
29 023	Butler	28,215	62.4	13.2	32,615	59.9	5.5	40.6	35.3	33,660	17.0	39.3	5.6

Table B-2. Counties — What: Education, Employment, and Income, 2005–2007—*Continued*

STATE County code	STATE County	Educational attainment			Employment status				Percent of house-holds with no workers	Median house-hold income (dollars)	Percent of families with income below poverty	Percent of house-holds with income less than $25,000	Percent of house-holds with income of $100,000 or more
		Total population 25 years and over	Percent with a high school diploma or less	Percent with a bachelor's degree or more	Total population 16 years and over	Percent in the labor force	Unem-ployment rate	Percent who worked full-time, year-round					
ACS table number:		C15002	C15002	C15002	C20005	C23001	C23001	C20005	C08202	B19013	C17015	C19001	C19001
		1	2	3	4	5	6	7	8	9	10	11	12
	Missouri—Cont.												
29 027	Callaway	27,806	56.2	19.8	33,980	65.2	6.1	43.4	23.7	46,557	10.5	24.3	9.0
29 029	Camden	28,769	51.7	18.0	32,849	56.9	3.9	35.1	35.2	39,996	7.8	25.2	13.2
29 031	Cape Girardeau	46,193	52.2	25.6	57,829	65.8	6.3	37.8	27.8	41,669	11.3	30.8	10.8
29 037	Cass	61,409	47.6	20.5	72,493	69.9	5.4	44.9	21.8	58,376	6.6	16.6	17.7
29 043	Christian	45,302	44.5	23.2	53,361	70.5	4.2	44.8	19.5	46,542	7.5	21.9	11.0
29 047	Clay	135,549	40.1	28.9	158,987	71.5	4.9	46.9	19.3	56,574	4.9	16.6	19.7
29 049	Clinton	13,582	52.9	17.0	16,205	67.7	5.8	43.6	25.0	47,707	4.8	23.1	12.0
29 051	Cole	48,573	47.5	28.1	57,889	67.0	3.8	46.2	22.6	48,539	7.1	22.8	13.6
29 055	Crawford	15,916	66.4	10.3	18,605	59.1	14.2	32.8	35.1	35,611	12.0	34.6	3.2
29 069	Dunklin	21,231	68.4	10.9	24,690	52.9	9.6	33.2	39.9	28,225	18.9	44.2	6.4
29 071	Franklin	65,799	53.2	16.1	76,963	66.5	6.3	41.2	25.5	48,567	7.7	22.3	12.8
29 077	Greene	168,752	42.4	26.7	208,706	64.9	4.9	40.0	26.5	40,370	8.6	30.4	10.3
29 083	Henry	15,815	62.6	14.2	17,947	59.3	9.8	37.2	36.5	34,708	12.5	37.2	8.2
29 091	Howell	25,859	63.0	11.0	30,256	54.7	5.0	37.7	37.9	30,311	15.6	41.7	3.9
29 095	Jackson	439,907	44.4	26.5	513,281	67.7	7.5	43.4	26.4	44,859	11.4	27.0	14.5
29 097	Jasper	73,119	54.9	17.7	86,686	65.3	7.0	39.9	29.0	35,783	12.5	33.4	7.6
29 099	Jefferson	140,312	52.2	15.5	165,347	69.6	6.1	43.6	23.0	55,295	7.4	19.5	16.0
29 101	Johnson	29,930	45.8	22.2	40,626	65.6	5.8	39.3	25.0	43,610	8.0	28.7	10.7
29 105	Laclede	23,280	61.4	11.0	27,097	60.6	5.5	37.4	30.2	34,253	9.8	33.3	7.0
29 107	Lafayette	22,248	60.6	14.7	25,982	62.8	5.6	36.8	28.6	44,895	8.2	28.0	10.7
29 109	Lawrence	24,687	64.3	13.2	28,766	59.9	5.3	39.4	31.0	36,992	12.7	35.2	6.6
29 113	Lincoln	31,456	63.4	10.2	37,403	68.6	8.6	41.1	25.0	52,945	7.0	19.4	12.5
29 119	McDonald	14,699	64.1	9.0	17,215	64.5	7.2	42.2	30.0	35,208	12.7	33.2	6.5
29 127	Marion	18,596	60.7	15.2	21,974	63.4	8.5	37.4	32.0	34,825	12.8	34.6	5.9
29 131	Miller	16,735	66.6	11.7	19,445	63.6	6.8	39.2	30.6	37,620	11.4	32.5	4.9
29 141	Morgan	14,371	63.0	14.0	16,407	53.5	5.7	32.2	36.3	35,237	11.8	31.5	8.3
29 145	Newton	36,623	51.6	18.2	43,009	64.2	6.3	38.7	26.9	40,753	13.3	30.6	9.6
29 147	Nodaway	12,416	49.8	24.9	18,742	65.2	6.4	36.4	28.5	37,418	9.7	36.5	7.6
29 159	Pettis	26,548	54.4	15.5	31,288	62.6	7.2	37.3	31.4	35,483	9.7	32.3	6.3
29 161	Phelps	26,558	47.9	24.7	34,033	60.3	7.8	32.0	29.3	37,160	12.1	35.0	9.2
29 165	Platte	56,082	31.5	35.7	65,190	73.4	4.4	48.3	17.1	64,065	4.6	13.1	28.1
29 167	Polk	18,623	60.6	13.0	23,203	57.4	7.4	31.6	35.3	34,329	15.1	36.7	7.9
29 169	Pulaski	24,010	52.7	15.8	33,839	73.2	5.2	41.6	23.7	40,638	9.9	28.4	7.2
29 175	Randolph	17,295	64.0	11.1	20,108	52.2	3.8	35.5	28.5	34,393	13.6	34.5	5.9
29 177	Ray	15,558	59.7	12.5	18,378	66.5	5.1	44.5	24.5	49,797	8.6	23.7	12.4
29 183	St. Charles	214,790	37.5	31.3	256,551	73.6	3.8	47.1	18.7	66,370	3.0	12.6	26.0
29 187	St. Francois	42,506	59.7	11.8	50,177	56.5	10.1	33.6	31.6	37,180	12.1	32.0	7.1
29 189	St. Louis	670,333	34.5	38.1	791,223	66.3	6.0	41.7	25.3	56,280	6.1	19.9	23.6
29 195	Saline	14,712	60.4	19.4	18,054	61.2	5.0	41.1	27.3	40,138	11.8	30.2	6.0
29 201	Scott	26,929	67.9	13.0	31,446	63.5	7.8	38.4	31.4	34,601	15.1	39.3	8.3
29 207	Stoddard	20,760	70.3	11.3	24,011	58.7	9.2	34.4	37.9	33,431	14.0	39.0	6.8
29 209	Stone	22,617	55.6	16.1	25,616	58.1	8.5	29.3	38.4	40,121	6.9	27.2	9.0
29 213	Taney	30,102	51.0	19.7	35,490	66.3	5.7	37.0	28.6	35,684	10.2	32.8	5.8
29 215	Texas	16,041	66.0	10.4	18,563	49.0	7.8	31.4	40.5	28,282	17.3	44.3	4.1
29 217	Vernon	13,302	64.5	16.4	15,666	63.7	7.7	37.1	33.1	33,649	18.2	37.2	7.0
29 219	Warren	19,570	56.8	15.1	23,006	63.3	7.0	38.4	27.1	49,510	8.9	21.8	14.6
29 221	Washington	15,907	75.7	5.5	18,673	54.9	14.7	29.4	37.1	35,661	12.9	36.2	4.3
29 225	Webster	22,674	60.6	14.4	26,681	62.1	6.6	37.7	30.0	38,186	15.2	30.3	7.4
29 510	St. Louis city	230,050	51.3	24.0	274,240	62.4	12.0	36.6	32.6	33,221	20.5	39.3	8.5
30 000	**Montana**	631,746	42.3	26.7	754,965	65.4	5.1	37.3	27.0	42,425	9.3	28.8	11.1
30 013	Cascade	54,589	41.7	23.5	63,885	62.7	5.0	38.9	30.3	41,802	9.6	29.4	9.7
30 029	Flathead	57,826	42.7	25.1	67,326	64.8	5.4	38.4	26.2	45,021	7.1	24.8	11.6
30 031	Gallatin	52,267	26.2	45.5	68,041	73.5	3.3	39.9	16.9	49,870	6.2	21.4	15.2
30 047	Lake	18,829	47.3	19.2	22,068	61.9	10.2	30.2	30.2	38,443	14.1	32.8	9.0
30 049	Lewis and Clark	39,818	34.8	32.6	47,082	68.8	3.9	41.0	24.9	47,459	6.5	26.3	13.6
30 063	Missoula	67,250	34.8	36.9	84,696	68.1	4.7	36.6	25.0	42,687	8.9	30.0	13.2
30 081	Ravalli	27,493	45.2	22.5	31,830	60.3	5.7	30.6	32.0	42,139	7.5	29.6	11.4
30 093	Silver Bow	22,191	50.8	23.1	26,317	63.4	5.4	36.3	30.9	36,273	9.9	33.3	7.1
30 111	Yellowstone	92,202	40.5	27.1	108,135	67.7	3.5	40.9	23.9	44,910	8.1	26.4	12.7
31 000	**Nebraska**	1,131,474	41.4	27.2	1,370,844	70.7	4.8	44.9	22.8	46,954	7.9	24.9	13.9
31 001	Adams	21,096	42.9	21.4	25,927	67.9	4.4	41.5	26.0	41,101	10.9	29.3	8.6
31 019	Buffalo	26,088	35.4	33.6	35,209	74.1	5.1	44.4	20.7	44,817	8.2	25.6	11.8
31 025	Cass	16,883	39.7	22.3	19,775	71.4	4.5	49.3	18.1	59,599	3.0	15.5	17.4
31 043	Dakota	12,172	60.7	13.1	14,964	71.6	7.1	48.1	20.3	43,408	11.5	24.2	10.2
31 047	Dawson	15,253	61.4	15.2	18,285	70.9	4.6	46.3	22.8	41,342	10.6	30.9	6.7
31 053	Dodge	23,886	56.7	18.9	28,365	66.5	7.3	39.8	28.8	40,661	12.9	28.9	8.2
31 055	Douglas	311,009	35.4	35.4	375,478	71.6	6.2	44.4	22.5	50,372	9.4	23.5	18.5
31 067	Gage	16,043	52.8	18.0	18,649	66.9	4.2	45.7	29.5	42,081	8.4	31.0	8.6
31 079	Hall	35,606	54.9	16.0	41,601	70.9	5.0	45.9	22.0	43,632	8.0	24.7	8.6
31 109	Lancaster	169,428	31.5	35.3	214,249	74.2	4.7	45.2	19.1	49,898	6.8	23.9	15.4
31 111	Lincoln	23,701	44.5	18.5	27,746	68.2	5.3	43.4	25.2	42,424	8.8	27.5	12.4
31 119	Madison	21,838	47.9	18.0	26,817	70.8	3.5	45.8	25.0	40,928	7.0	28.6	9.8
31 141	Platte	20,413	46.7	20.1	24,122	72.1	4.3	48.7	26.0	47,937	7.6	24.1	11.8

STATE County code	STATE County	Educational attainment			Employment status				Percent of households with no workers	Median household income (dollars)	Percent of families with income below poverty	Percent of households with income less than $25,000	Percent of households with income of $100,000 or more
		Total population 25 years and over	Percent with a high school diploma or less	Percent with a bachelor's degree or more	Total population 16 years and over	Percent in the labor force	Unemployment rate	Percent who worked full-time, year-round					
	ACS table number:	C15002	C15002	C15002	C20005	C23001	C23001	C20005	C08202	B19013	C17015	C19001	C19001
		1	2	3	4	5	6	7	8	9	10	11	12
	Nebraska—Cont.												
31 153	Sarpy	86,221	28.8	35.8	105,602	75.7	3.9	52.0	14.9	63,661	4.4	12.3	22.8
31 155	Saunders	13,476	45.8	21.4	15,807	73.2	3.5	48.5	18.1	56,445	4.9	16.4	15.7
31 157	Scotts Bluff	24,195	49.4	18.5	28,175	65.7	3.9	42.0	28.8	35,417	13.2	37.1	8.4
32 000	**Nevada**	1,640,801	47.9	20.9	1,914,702	67.2	5.5	44.9	22.7	53,753	7.8	19.6	19.1
32 001	Churchill	16,004	47.9	15.5	18,486	61.3	8.0	37.9	28.7	48,103	8.6	26.6	13.8
32 003	Clark	1,166,163	49.0	20.4	1,355,085	67.9	5.6	46.3	21.6	54,299	8.0	18.9	19.5
32 005	Douglas	33,280	33.4	27.4	38,137	62.1	4.8	37.2	30.5	63,363	4.3	16.1	25.4
32 007	Elko	28,315	52.2	15.2	34,398	69.6	3.9	47.1	17.1	59,756	9.1	18.7	19.2
32 019	Lyon	30,653	54.6	14.1	37,064	57.0	11.4	35.4	31.5	45,104	7.2	21.5	10.8
32 023	Nye	29,551	59.8	9.5	34,138	53.2	11.4	28.6	43.3	42,601	10.8	28.7	9.7
32 031	Washoe	263,757	41.5	26.8	311,540	68.9	4.3	44.4	22.4	53,535	7.0	20.3	20.3
32 510	Carson City	37,425	44.6	20.6	43,480	62.7	7.0	39.3	31.7	50,140	8.4	23.4	14.7
33 000	**New Hampshire**	889,007	41.0	31.8	1,046,807	69.8	4.8	43.2	21.6	61,459	4.9	17.3	23.8
33 001	Belknap	43,725	48.3	25.6	49,910	65.6	3.7	43.4	23.4	53,776	4.9	20.0	17.6
33 003	Carroll	34,476	43.0	28.5	38,827	65.0	3.7	37.8	30.2	50,992	6.2	21.8	15.7
33 005	Cheshire	51,645	46.2	29.2	63,877	67.8	4.6	40.3	22.4	54,761	4.9	18.8	17.4
33 007	Coos	24,037	56.1	16.6	27,408	62.3	6.0	35.8	33.0	42,306	6.8	30.2	8.8
33 009	Grafton	56,380	42.2	34.1	70,871	65.0	3.6	37.8	26.3	51,470	4.6	20.9	17.3
33 011	Hillsborough	269,021	38.7	33.4	312,750	72.1	5.0	45.6	19.1	67,276	5.0	15.7	28.0
33 013	Merrimack	100,239	40.0	31.5	118,663	69.0	4.6	43.7	22.0	58,508	5.4	17.8	21.1
33 015	Rockingham	201,955	36.1	35.7	233,223	72.4	4.8	45.0	18.9	72,600	3.0	12.2	32.0
33 017	Strafford	77,320	44.7	28.4	96,928	68.8	5.7	41.0	23.0	56,455	7.3	21.4	17.8
33 019	Sullivan	30,209	53.1	25.5	34,350	67.2	4.1	40.9	25.5	48,177	6.5	23.2	12.7
34 000	**New Jersey**	5,835,145	44.2	33.7	6,835,521	65.8	6.1	41.9	24.1	66,509	6.5	17.9	30.8
34 001	Atlantic	181,380	51.9	22.8	211,866	65.8	7.6	41.7	26.2	53,473	7.8	22.0	19.8
34 003	Bergen	624,828	35.5	43.6	719,380	65.4	5.0	43.1	22.9	78,314	3.9	14.1	38.6
34 005	Burlington	303,878	40.5	32.8	353,876	67.8	5.8	43.3	21.3	72,466	3.6	13.0	31.5
34 007	Camden	336,728	49.3	27.0	398,971	67.0	7.1	41.6	24.6	58,841	8.8	20.7	23.5
34 009	Cape May	70,429	49.2	26.9	80,428	61.7	7.0	35.5	33.3	52,771	6.7	21.5	19.2
34 011	Cumberland	102,771	65.5	12.7	120,731	59.6	10.4	35.8	29.3	48,464	13.4	26.8	15.5
34 013	Essex	506,447	49.3	30.8	601,641	64.5	8.9	39.0	26.2	53,351	11.1	25.1	24.7
34 015	Gloucester	185,431	48.4	25.6	222,179	68.5	5.9	42.2	22.1	69,990	5.4	15.7	29.9
34 017	Hudson	412,810	49.7	31.6	482,626	67.8	7.4	44.9	23.6	49,878	13.1	26.4	21.5
34 019	Hunterdon	88,772	31.4	47.3	102,439	67.0	3.5	43.9	19.2	97,793	1.5	8.6	48.8
34 021	Mercer	240,395	41.4	37.5	290,469	65.9	6.7	41.3	25.0	68,582	6.5	17.6	32.8
34 023	Middlesex	526,940	41.7	37.3	625,351	65.9	5.3	43.8	20.7	74,732	4.9	14.0	33.6
34 025	Monmouth	430,957	37.6	38.4	503,748	66.7	5.5	40.8	22.7	79,633	4.2	14.7	38.9
34 027	Morris	331,431	31.7	47.8	382,907	68.6	4.6	44.5	19.7	92,018	2.1	10.0	45.7
34 029	Ocean	390,204	50.4	23.9	445,820	57.5	6.0	34.5	36.8	56,373	6.1	20.9	23.1
34 031	Passaic	317,721	56.5	23.2	379,664	64.1	5.7	40.5	23.6	53,471	11.9	24.8	23.9
34 033	Salem	44,435	53.7	18.0	52,227	65.9	6.9	39.8	27.7	57,345	6.3	20.9	20.7
34 035	Somerset	216,871	30.5	49.3	248,176	69.2	4.2	46.9	18.5	94,036	2.3	9.6	47.0
34 037	Sussex	100,439	42.1	31.0	118,611	71.1	5.1	43.8	18.0	79,434	3.5	11.5	36.4
34 039	Union	348,080	48.3	31.0	408,592	66.1	6.0	43.8	24.0	64,236	6.2	17.8	29.5
34 041	Warren	74,198	46.2	27.4	85,819	67.6	5.5	42.5	24.0	64,817	3.6	17.0	26.6
35 000	**New Mexico**	1,240,342	46.6	24.9	1,505,362	62.2	6.4	37.0	27.8	41,042	14.2	30.4	13.2
35 001	Bernalillo	402,494	39.2	31.5	482,295	66.3	5.7	40.4	24.9	45,022	11.1	26.3	15.8
35 005	Chaves	38,734	56.2	15.1	47,630	57.2	8.0	32.7	32.1	36,021	18.2	34.0	8.5
35 006	Cibola	17,105	64.0	10.0	20,868	52.3	16.0	29.2	34.8	38,010	18.8	38.6	6.6
35 009	Curry	27,202	47.8	18.4	33,168	64.8	5.1	40.6	27.9	35,568	16.0	36.9	10.0
35 013	Dona Ana	114,132	48.6	24.6	146,968	61.3	8.3	34.7	27.4	34,118	20.5	38.3	9.3
35 015	Eddy	32,747	55.4	16.0	39,071	61.5	5.9	36.9	29.1	41,693	13.7	28.2	10.6
35 017	Grant	19,749	48.4	21.2	23,961	56.5	6.6	31.5	36.8	31,988	10.4	36.5	6.2
35 025	Lea	34,429	62.5	10.9	42,747	58.7	4.3	40.0	26.1	40,343	13.9	27.4	9.6
35 027	Lincoln	14,453	43.5	24.5	17,005	57.6	3.3	30.4	38.6	41,220	9.9	31.8	12.3
35 029	Luna	17,094	66.6	11.5	20,036	51.7	10.7	23.4	46.0	23,308	28.7	52.3	4.1
35 031	McKinley	39,126	67.0	11.2	50,586	52.3	7.7	25.9	29.3	32,117	28.4	39.6	8.5
35 035	Otero	39,992	46.3	16.4	49,010	60.3	6.2	37.8	29.6	37,354	15.9	32.6	6.5
35 039	Rio Arriba	25,996	58.6	15.0	31,338	59.7	8.2	37.3	28.6	40,626	18.6	32.3	12.2
35 043	Sandoval	71,978	41.5	27.3	86,050	66.6	6.5	41.0	23.6	53,848	8.1	20.0	17.1
35 045	San Juan	74,080	54.9	13.4	92,100	60.4	4.4	38.6	25.3	42,331	13.4	29.7	12.5
35 047	San Miguel	18,492	50.3	23.4	22,953	49.7	10.5	30.8	42.5	29,797	17.9	43.6	7.9
35 049	Santa Fe	98,490	38.3	39.3	114,662	68.0	5.1	37.5	24.2	51,341	8.7	23.5	21.5
35 055	Taos	21,723	40.4	27.9	25,573	62.7	8.0	35.3	33.2	34,930	14.6	34.6	9.3
35 061	Valencia	44,175	53.9	15.0	53,767	58.6	9.9	34.4	28.6	40,565	15.5	28.1	11.5
36 000	**New York**	12,866,461	45.7	31.2	15,355,670	62.7	6.7	39.2	27.4	52,944	10.7	24.6	22.8
36 001	Albany	197,816	37.2	36.5	245,015	65.5	5.3	41.3	26.8	52,871	7.2	22.1	20.4
36 003	Allegany	30,389	53.5	18.6	40,751	61.6	10.4	31.3	32.8	39,620	11.0	31.0	7.3
36 005	Bronx	834,699	62.0	16.4	1,026,258	57.4	11.0	35.8	34.4	32,409	25.9	40.9	9.4
36 007	Broome	130,997	46.7	24.9	161,255	60.8	6.4	35.5	33.2	41,520	11.1	30.2	12.8
36 009	Cattaraugus	53,299	55.7	18.3	64,568	63.2	7.0	35.4	31.0	39,985	10.5	30.7	8.3
36 011	Cayuga	55,267	52.5	17.7	65,301	61.4	6.0	37.1	29.0	46,151	8.4	25.0	12.4
36 013	Chautauqua	89,053	53.8	18.9	109,029	60.9	7.7	33.5	32.2	38,234	12.3	32.4	9.0
36 015	Chemung	59,678	51.2	21.0	70,982	59.1	8.3	34.5	33.2	39,989	12.4	30.8	13.3

Table B-2. Counties — What: Education, Employment, and Income, 2005–2007—*Continued*

STATE County code	STATE County	Educational attainment			Employment status				Percent of house-holds with no workers	Median house-hold income (dollars)	Percent of families with income below poverty	Percent of house-holds with income less than $25,000	Percent of house-holds with income of $100,000 or more
		Total population 25 years and over	Percent with a high school diploma or less	Percent with a bachelor's degree or more	Total population 16 years and over	Percent in the labor force	Unem-ployment rate	Percent who worked full-time, year-round					
	ACS table number:	C15002	C15002	C15002	C20005	C23001	C23001	C20005	C08202	B19013	C17015	C19001	C19001
		1	2	3	4	5	6	7	8	9	10	11	12
	New York—Cont.												
36 017	Chenango	35,100	55.2	17.4	41,349	62.3	6.7	38.5	29.7	42,150	8.0	28.2	10.4
36 019	Clinton	54,936	51.1	22.1	68,340	58.5	6.2	36.3	30.5	45,758	8.9	27.2	14.0
36 021	Columbia	44,166	46.3	28.8	51,607	65.0	4.6	37.7	21.8	54,207	6.4	22.5	20.6
36 023	Cortland	29,786	49.4	24.4	39,209	62.7	6.4	38.7	27.5	44,307	9.2	26.9	10.7
36 025	Delaware	32,396	53.7	20.0	38,621	59.7	7.2	34.1	35.5	41,094	8.5	29.7	10.8
36 027	Dutchess	192,068	42.2	30.6	233,652	65.2	5.5	39.8	23.5	66,296	5.4	15.7	28.5
36 029	Erie	617,963	43.8	27.7	740,051	62.0	6.9	36.0	32.8	44,650	10.1	28.5	15.3
36 031	Essex	27,439	48.5	23.7	32,013	57.2	6.8	35.7	30.8	42,759	8.8	27.3	10.8
36 033	Franklin	34,939	56.7	15.7	41,827	53.0	5.7	31.5	32.5	37,891	12.2	32.4	9.2
36 035	Fulton	38,329	58.7	15.1	44,575	59.5	8.4	37.4	32.8	38,677	13.3	31.5	9.6
36 037	Genesee	39,583	50.3	16.9	46,923	65.7	7.0	38.2	27.2	44,966	8.6	25.7	10.2
36 039	Greene	33,354	50.7	20.0	39,870	58.9	7.7	33.6	31.5	45,177	8.9	23.8	11.6
36 043	Herkimer	43,094	51.6	17.5	51,012	63.2	6.8	40.3	30.2	40,726	7.7	28.0	9.1
36 045	Jefferson	74,015	50.7	18.4	90,694	63.7	8.3	38.3	28.1	40,702	13.0	29.8	10.1
36 047	Kings	1,624,325	53.2	27.4	1,953,771	59.1	7.8	38.3	29.6	40,942	19.2	33.5	15.4
36 049	Lewis	17,684	63.3	14.5	20,911	63.3	7.1	39.1	28.5	40,012	11.1	27.1	9.7
36 051	Livingston	40,347	47.3	22.5	52,330	60.1	5.0	33.9	25.4	48,880	9.1	24.1	13.3
36 053	Madison	44,194	46.8	24.0	56,806	63.6	5.8	38.2	27.2	50,126	7.2	21.4	14.7
36 055	Monroe	475,892	39.6	33.2	582,037	62.8	6.6	36.8	29.8	49,374	9.4	25.1	18.0
36 057	Montgomery	33,417	57.9	14.1	38,970	63.3	6.6	39.4	30.9	43,157	9.7	28.2	10.5
36 059	Nassau	881,970	37.3	40.0	1,043,446	63.5	4.4	41.1	22.7	87,658	3.3	11.8	43.5
36 061	New York	1,199,596	30.0	56.2	1,369,272	67.0	7.1	42.4	26.8	62,268	15.1	25.6	33.4
36 063	Niagara	145,856	50.6	19.0	173,839	61.8	7.3	36.0	32.8	45,161	8.9	27.2	13.2
36 065	Oneida	157,498	50.1	20.4	188,076	59.2	6.5	35.6	31.5	42,559	11.3	29.1	12.5
36 067	Onondaga	297,638	41.1	30.5	360,844	64.6	6.1	38.4	29.1	48,174	9.5	26.2	17.0
36 069	Ontario	69,581	39.9	28.8	83,283	67.3	5.4	39.6	25.7	51,746	5.3	20.3	17.5
36 071	Orange	233,179	47.1	26.1	285,001	67.2	6.1	41.5	21.2	66,445	7.7	17.3	28.5
36 073	Orleans	28,626	59.3	13.4	34,252	58.0	9.4	34.9	31.2	44,623	9.3	27.3	9.2
36 075	Oswego	77,708	57.3	15.1	97,302	62.7	8.9	35.4	29.6	43,137	11.4	28.7	11.8
36 077	Otsego	39,664	49.5	25.9	52,795	62.6	7.5	33.5	31.2	44,423	7.5	27.4	9.6
36 079	Putnam	67,101	36.7	36.7	78,305	65.8	4.4	40.7	17.7	84,306	2.1	10.1	40.8
36 081	Queens	1,569,460	51.1	28.0	1,830,997	63.1	7.4	41.3	24.4	52,299	9.8	22.9	19.5
36 083	Rensselaer	102,688	46.2	25.6	124,984	67.9	6.4	40.7	27.0	52,257	8.2	22.1	17.8
36 085	Richmond	318,506	47.7	27.1	377,333	59.9	5.6	40.2	25.1	68,135	7.7	18.7	30.3
36 087	Rockland	187,193	36.7	39.0	225,008	63.4	3.9	41.2	20.5	81,471	6.2	13.9	39.7
36 089	St. Lawrence	69,749	54.7	18.3	90,095	53.6	6.5	30.9	34.2	39,815	13.0	30.8	8.7
36 091	Saratoga	146,570	39.7	32.7	172,162	67.8	4.1	43.5	23.0	61,825	4.3	16.8	23.9
36 093	Schenectady	100,802	42.7	29.6	119,524	61.9	6.0	39.3	31.5	52,185	7.0	23.1	19.0
36 095	Schoharie	21,526	59.1	17.6	26,436	60.2	7.6	35.1	31.8	50,516	9.3	23.8	14.2
36 099	Seneca	23,640	52.9	20.1	28,125	58.6	5.6	37.2	25.2	44,210	10.8	24.1	11.4
36 101	Steuben	66,338	51.6	19.5	77,827	61.7	7.4	35.4	31.8	41,192	9.2	30.0	11.1
36 103	Suffolk	961,715	42.5	31.1	1,135,438	65.5	4.7	41.8	22.4	81,130	3.7	12.2	38.4
36 105	Sullivan	51,812	53.3	19.9	61,045	60.6	6.3	36.4	27.1	47,325	8.9	26.0	15.9
36 107	Tioga	34,292	53.4	20.3	40,302	64.2	6.3	39.5	28.1	48,282	8.3	24.3	12.2
36 109	Tompkins	56,331	27.8	52.6	87,040	61.5	4.3	31.0	27.2	46,225	6.0	28.6	18.1
36 111	Ulster	124,028	44.7	28.6	149,016	64.0	5.0	36.7	26.2	54,871	7.5	21.3	20.9
36 113	Warren	46,314	46.8	25.3	54,234	63.3	6.3	37.3	29.9	48,402	7.5	24.5	16.6
36 115	Washington	43,209	54.9	17.8	51,279	60.7	6.7	36.1	29.0	43,821	8.1	24.6	9.7
36 117	Wayne	61,638	49.6	21.3	72,129	65.7	6.2	40.5	28.2	51,260	8.4	23.4	14.7
36 119	Westchester	635,291	36.6	44.7	744,706	64.3	5.8	40.9	23.1	77,856	5.0	15.3	39.9
36 121	Wyoming	29,654	58.2	14.6	34,749	57.9	5.4	35.2	27.2	48,312	8.0	22.9	9.7
36 123	Yates	15,756	54.3	21.0	19,367	62.3	5.4	35.7	28.0	42,590	10.1	27.5	12.9
37 000	**North Carolina**	5,849,056	47.4	25.0	6,946,929	65.0	6.8	40.6	26.6	43,867	11.0	28.2	14.4
37 001	Alamance	94,326	51.8	19.8	112,226	66.3	6.4	41.2	24.1	42,370	12.1	29.1	10.7
37 003	Alexander	24,562	66.0	12.9	28,100	66.5	6.0	41.6	29.0	40,589	9.9	33.3	9.4
37 007	Anson	17,333	72.2	7.0	20,216	51.8	10.5	34.0	36.6	31,938	16.9	39.4	3.9
37 009	Ashe	18,732	60.8	13.7	21,154	59.3	5.3	35.8	34.0	32,512	13.3	38.9	6.6
37 013	Beaufort	31,617	56.3	17.7	36,448	60.0	7.8	34.9	32.5	38,570	11.1	31.7	10.2
37 017	Bladen	21,418	57.5	12.0	25,417	56.9	7.1	34.7	36.4	31,117	17.4	42.2	6.2
37 019	Brunswick	66,373	50.5	20.1	76,155	59.4	7.0	33.6	33.3	41,385	10.1	28.5	11.4
37 021	Buncombe	155,936	41.2	30.9	180,634	64.5	4.8	38.2	29.0	43,208	8.0	27.7	13.3
37 023	Burke	61,164	59.9	15.0	71,328	59.4	7.5	36.8	34.1	35,222	11.5	35.5	5.8
37 025	Cabarrus	101,582	46.2	22.4	118,676	70.1	7.4	45.5	21.6	52,174	8.0	21.2	17.2
37 027	Caldwell	55,244	62.2	12.1	63,186	60.3	8.9	36.7	33.2	36,866	11.8	32.5	7.9
37 031	Carteret	45,906	44.2	24.1	52,164	60.7	6.8	38.8	32.5	46,803	8.4	24.5	14.9
37 033	Caswell	16,523	62.2	11.6	18,811	57.3	10.1	33.7	35.5	36,644	13.1	34.4	4.2
37 035	Catawba	104,429	53.2	19.4	120,824	65.6	7.0	43.1	26.8	42,718	8.5	27.5	11.9
37 037	Chatham	41,425	45.1	32.4	47,395	67.8	6.3	43.3	26.9	51,794	10.9	25.1	19.4
37 039	Cherokee	19,100	52.6	14.3	21,403	57.7	5.3	34.4	34.7	36,411	12.8	34.5	6.3
37 045	Cleveland	66,207	55.7	16.3	77,260	60.0	9.1	36.2	32.0	37,304	15.6	33.6	8.2
37 047	Columbus	35,863	59.4	10.9	42,309	57.5	6.8	32.7	37.7	30,032	19.5	42.7	7.1
37 049	Craven	61,347	43.2	20.7	74,037	62.0	5.7	41.9	30.2	43,480	12.0	29.1	12.3
37 051	Cumberland	184,077	42.6	21.1	229,091	65.6	8.0	41.3	26.2	42,036	15.0	29.9	11.0
37 053	Currituck	16,070	53.0	16.2	18,658	68.7	4.5	44.7	21.4	53,844	8.2	18.1	17.4

Table B-2. Counties — What: Education, Employment, and Income, 2005–2007—*Continued*

STATE County code	STATE County	Educational attainment			Employment status				Percent of house-holds with no workers	Median house-hold income (dollars)	Percent of families with income below poverty	Percent of house-holds with income less than $25,000	Percent of house-holds with income of $100,000 or more
		Total population 25 years and over	Percent with a high school diploma or less	Percent with a bachelor's degree or more	Total population 16 years and over	Percent in the labor force	Unem-ployment rate	Percent who worked full-time, year-round					
	ACS table number:	C15002	C15002	C15002	C20005	C23001	C23001	C20005	C08202	B19013	C17015	C19001	C19001
		1	2	3	4	5	6	7	8	9	10	11	12
	North Carolina—Cont.												
37 055	Dare	24,249	35.6	32.1	27,246	71.1	3.4	43.2	24.1	52,063	6.8	19.8	17.6
37 057	Davidson	106,154	58.4	14.4	122,594	65.9	8.4	42.0	27.1	42,666	9.6	27.8	10.4
37 059	Davie	26,963	50.5	20.7	31,382	62.8	6.3	41.5	29.2	48,492	7.6	20.7	16.5
37 061	Duplin	34,533	67.0	8.8	40,316	64.0	6.7	39.3	31.2	33,279	16.6	39.2	8.0
37 063	Durham	162,342	35.4	41.7	195,504	69.4	7.2	42.5	22.3	47,599	10.4	25.0	18.4
37 065	Edgecombe	34,858	66.6	10.3	41,030	59.4	10.3	35.6	32.2	30,263	18.3	41.5	6.0
37 067	Forsyth	219,489	42.5	30.4	259,275	66.0	5.6	42.3	25.0	46,610	10.5	25.6	15.9
37 069	Franklin	36,956	58.7	15.3	43,739	62.3	9.2	40.8	26.5	40,875	12.8	31.2	9.9
37 071	Gaston	134,996	54.2	17.1	156,212	63.9	8.8	41.0	28.0	40,834	10.7	29.0	11.2
37 077	Granville	35,870	57.2	12.4	42,942	61.9	6.7	42.4	24.1	45,746	7.0	26.3	10.4
37 079	Greene	13,404	63.2	7.7	15,919	58.3	9.2	37.5	24.6	34,390	15.5	38.8	8.4
37 081	Guilford	299,171	41.2	31.9	360,129	67.5	7.3	41.0	23.6	45,366	11.0	27.2	16.3
37 083	Halifax	37,168	63.9	11.9	43,606	55.1	9.2	34.3	37.1	29,141	21.3	44.2	8.5
37 085	Harnett	66,777	54.0	14.8	80,671	64.5	8.6	39.4	25.7	39,953	13.3	31.0	8.8
37 087	Haywood	41,238	48.8	18.6	46,159	58.4	5.3	35.4	34.8	37,565	9.4	33.6	10.6
37 089	Henderson	70,984	42.5	25.1	80,368	57.7	5.1	34.9	35.2	43,013	9.7	26.2	11.4
37 091	Hertford	15,284	59.4	15.6	18,826	53.9	9.8	30.3	39.6	28,080	22.3	45.1	5.5
37 093	Hoke	24,165	52.1	15.3	29,563	61.6	6.7	40.8	25.7	42,290	11.2	31.3	9.3
37 097	Iredell	97,378	50.8	20.2	113,261	66.4	5.8	43.5	25.7	47,123	8.9	26.0	14.9
37 099	Jackson	23,064	46.4	24.9	30,659	60.3	4.7	34.9	27.7	39,157	12.9	33.9	9.3
37 101	Johnston	98,701	51.5	17.5	114,480	70.0	4.8	47.6	22.0	48,104	9.2	23.9	13.2
37 105	Lee	37,176	54.3	15.5	43,719	62.9	6.5	40.1	28.7	40,785	11.9	30.4	12.6
37 107	Lenoir	38,605	56.9	13.3	44,690	60.4	7.1	36.0	33.2	31,304	17.7	41.1	6.6
37 109	Lincoln	48,368	56.7	16.5	55,833	63.5	5.8	41.1	25.4	45,975	8.9	27.9	11.9
37 111	McDowell	30,435	60.8	11.7	34,680	61.4	7.4	38.6	32.0	35,615	11.1	33.0	4.5
37 113	Macon	23,479	51.8	21.3	26,615	53.7	4.9	32.1	36.8	38,242	11.9	30.5	8.7
37 115	Madison	13,849	59.1	21.2	16,572	58.4	5.9	31.3	32.3	37,489	11.7	35.3	8.1
37 117	Martin	16,362	62.7	12.0	18,918	55.4	5.9	34.7	35.2	30,862	18.5	41.6	5.5
37 119	Mecklenburg	540,515	32.9	39.7	637,770	73.6	7.0	45.9	18.3	54,152	8.0	20.4	23.1
37 123	Montgomery	17,648	62.6	12.7	21,202	55.7	5.0	34.7	31.6	30,350	19.6	43.0	7.7
37 125	Moore	58,170	46.3	25.7	66,531	56.0	8.6	32.8	38.0	44,988	6.9	26.5	13.7
37 127	Nash	60,962	53.9	18.7	71,663	63.6	6.5	41.3	30.1	43,589	11.4	28.8	13.3
37 129	New Hanover	125,337	34.5	35.0	150,949	65.8	5.6	38.0	28.3	46,556	8.4	26.7	16.6
37 131	Northampton	14,455	67.9	12.7	17,070	51.3	10.1	29.8	45.7	28,389	15.2	47.0	3.9
37 133	Onslow	82,512	45.4	15.7	121,530	72.0	5.2	50.8	22.8	42,173	11.9	26.4	10.1
37 135	Orange	75,540	29.0	54.1	101,628	65.2	5.4	35.4	23.7	48,926	7.7	26.3	24.9
37 139	Pasquotank	24,800	50.8	16.3	31,094	62.8	9.5	37.2	30.6	41,970	14.5	31.2	10.7
37 141	Pender	33,355	56.0	15.7	38,642	59.3	8.2	36.1	31.5	41,845	9.3	27.8	9.8
37 145	Person	25,625	62.4	12.8	29,569	62.0	10.6	39.6	29.8	41,930	13.1	29.3	11.7
37 147	Pitt	88,214	43.0	29.1	116,667	64.9	8.3	36.6	26.9	36,881	15.2	37.1	12.3
37 151	Randolph	94,274	62.3	12.4	108,221	66.4	7.7	41.8	27.8	38,304	13.6	32.4	8.7
37 153	Richmond	30,159	62.5	11.1	35,723	54.7	9.7	33.9	37.2	29,321	21.6	42.6	6.9
37 155	Robeson	79,320	66.9	12.4	96,288	56.3	8.3	35.6	33.1	27,948	26.3	46.1	5.7
37 157	Rockingham	64,844	63.4	10.8	73,675	61.8	8.8	37.6	32.5	38,965	12.4	31.5	8.0
37 159	Rowan	91,636	56.0	16.0	107,493	61.9	8.0	39.3	29.7	43,976	11.4	29.0	11.5
37 161	Rutherford	43,487	55.8	14.7	49,845	59.3	9.5	34.2	35.9	34,322	13.1	36.2	6.9
37 163	Sampson	41,394	64.4	11.4	48,755	62.1	7.4	38.4	29.7	33,331	15.6	38.1	8.4
37 165	Scotland	23,532	61.0	15.9	28,015	49.9	11.7	29.2	41.9	30,483	24.3	43.6	7.7
37 167	Stanly	39,740	60.9	13.7	46,738	59.1	8.2	38.5	30.9	40,418	10.1	30.9	8.6
37 169	Stokes	32,135	65.8	10.5	36,399	61.7	8.5	39.9	29.0	38,130	5.9	29.3	8.5
37 171	Surry	50,205	62.1	13.2	57,139	62.1	5.6	38.4	30.4	36,886	12.7	36.3	8.6
37 175	Transylvania	21,140	44.5	28.6	24,966	51.2	5.4	27.5	41.6	38,171	10.1	32.5	10.1
37 179	Union	108,577	45.3	25.5	129,299	69.6	4.5	45.3	19.1	57,485	7.0	17.2	21.3
37 181	Vance	27,884	62.1	12.1	32,760	57.6	10.1	35.9	32.4	33,924	19.1	37.7	8.1
37 183	Wake	508,678	28.3	46.6	609,528	71.3	4.7	46.4	17.0	61,984	5.7	17.2	27.8
37 189	Watauga	24,839	38.5	32.3	38,460	64.6	6.9	27.6	25.6	33,024	11.0	41.3	10.6
37 191	Wayne	73,825	53.6	15.6	87,651	61.4	6.2	40.1	28.3	39,316	12.5	31.7	9.1
37 193	Wilkes	47,077	65.2	11.1	53,308	61.5	5.4	39.9	32.3	35,649	11.7	34.6	6.9
37 195	Wilson	50,440	58.8	16.8	59,226	62.8	8.6	38.3	30.8	36,740	15.1	35.2	10.4
37 197	Yadkin	25,976	65.6	10.2	29,661	61.8	4.2	42.1	30.9	37,553	12.3	33.6	7.4
38 000	**North Dakota**	411,298	41.0	25.6	512,164	69.2	3.5	42.3	24.2	43,442	7.3	28.3	11.5
38 015	Burleigh	49,546	34.0	31.2	61,048	72.2	2.7	46.7	20.8	50,017	5.4	24.2	15.4
38 017	Cass	83,338	30.6	34.8	107,745	76.6	3.9	45.8	18.8	44,853	7.4	27.1	15.0
38 035	Grand Forks	37,571	33.7	32.7	54,011	70.9	3.1	39.9	21.4	41,989	8.3	30.1	11.3
38 059	Morton	16,901	47.8	21.5	20,218	72.1	3.1	44.4	23.0	43,159	5.8	28.8	9.2
38 089	Stark	14,107	44.3	24.9	18,194	68.4	3.5	39.9	26.1	42,218	5.9	31.6	8.9
38 093	Stutsman	14,035	49.2	21.9	17,155	65.2	2.7	42.5	29.1	40,678	5.1	32.3	9.7
38 101	Ward	34,375	40.4	24.5	43,261	70.2	2.1	46.4	23.2	45,467	5.3	25.4	10.0
39 000	**Ohio**	7,598,399	50.6	23.3	9,019,907	64.8	7.2	39.0	28.3	46,296	9.7	26.3	15.1
39 001	Adams	18,745	74.7	10.0	21,797	56.5	7.5	31.4	33.7	33,520	17.8	37.5	9.0
39 003	Allen	68,465	55.6	16.0	82,415	63.9	8.4	35.5	31.9	43,466	10.7	26.9	11.5
39 005	Ashland	35,188	59.8	16.9	43,200	61.9	5.6	37.5	28.1	46,592	7.9	26.1	8.8
39 007	Ashtabula	69,644	61.8	12.5	80,149	60.0	7.4	35.8	31.2	39,041	12.5	30.9	8.7
39 009	Athens	31,903	50.1	26.3	53,689	55.5	9.9	23.9	33.2	30,886	16.0	44.0	7.7
39 011	Auglaize	30,719	59.8	14.8	36,370	69.7	4.9	43.8	25.7	51,558	5.9	20.7	14.3

STATE County code	STATE County	Educational attainment			Employment status				Percent of house-holds with no workers	Median house-hold income (dollars)	Percent of families with income below poverty	Percent of house-holds with income less than $25,000	Percent of house-holds with income of $100,000 or more
		Total population 25 years and over	Percent with a high school diploma or less	Percent with a bachelor's degree or more	Total population 16 years and over	Percent in the labor force	Unem-ployment rate	Percent who worked full-time, year-round					
	ACS table number:	C15002	C15002	C15002	C20005	C23001	C23001	C20005	C08202	B19013	C17015	C19001	C19001
		1	2	3	4	5	6	7	8	9	10	11	12
	Ohio—Cont.												
39 013	Belmont..............	48,791	60.1	14.1	56,248	55.6	7.8	33.3	35.4	36,019	12.8	34.5	6.8
39 015	Brown................	29,153	69.5	9.1	33,957	61.2	9.1	36.9	29.3	43,494	12.0	26.3	9.0
39 017	Butler................	223,448	50.5	24.7	274,689	65.8	6.0	40.0	24.5	53,133	7.8	22.1	19.2
39 019	Carroll...............	20,062	69.0	11.3	22,969	64.5	6.3	37.8	25.8	40,778	10.0	25.2	9.0
39 021	Champaign............	26,603	63.8	14.0	30,899	68.3	6.9	41.8	23.7	47,625	10.1	23.3	10.8
39 023	Clark.................	94,948	56.3	16.2	111,735	61.9	8.8	36.1	33.4	43,109	11.1	28.9	10.9
39 025	Clermont.............	124,951	50.5	23.8	146,376	67.6	6.2	43.3	23.0	54,547	6.5	18.9	20.7
39 027	Clinton...............	27,945	61.1	14.2	33,143	66.8	7.6	41.7	28.1	46,103	12.8	26.7	10.2
39 029	Columbiana...........	75,951	63.4	11.3	88,118	60.6	8.4	34.6	30.5	39,161	13.7	31.5	8.3
39 031	Coshocton............	24,686	69.0	10.1	28,917	61.0	9.2	33.7	34.2	37,355	11.2	31.3	7.3
39 033	Crawford.............	31,010	66.7	10.9	35,812	63.9	8.3	40.1	31.3	41,669	8.6	29.4	7.9
39 035	Cuyahoga.............	888,281	46.0	27.4	1,035,587	63.9	9.2	37.5	31.5	43,162	12.2	30.3	15.2
39 037	Darke.................	35,399	63.9	11.0	41,290	66.4	7.5	41.7	27.0	45,072	7.0	25.5	9.2
39 039	Defiance..............	25,866	62.9	12.5	30,340	65.3	7.0	39.0	28.9	45,645	8.1	23.3	8.9
39 041	Delaware.............	98,061	25.5	48.9	116,544	73.1	3.9	49.0	15.8	80,526	3.1	12.1	38.1
39 043	Erie...................	53,925	53.3	19.1	62,271	62.8	7.1	36.6	32.2	46,476	8.4	25.3	14.6
39 045	Fairfield..............	91,901	48.1	22.6	108,447	67.8	5.6	43.5	23.7	56,730	6.1	19.7	20.1
39 047	Fayette...............	19,194	65.4	11.9	22,111	66.6	6.6	41.8	29.0	41,289	10.7	28.4	10.6
39 049	Franklin..............	710,643	40.1	34.5	856,766	69.1	6.9	42.3	23.9	47,770	11.0	24.8	17.2
39 051	Fulton................	28,124	58.5	11.4	33,019	67.7	5.8	41.1	25.9	47,949	6.7	20.7	11.1
39 053	Gallia.................	20,677	68.1	11.4	24,450	54.1	8.5	28.0	38.1	33,113	20.7	43.6	8.5
39 055	Geauga................	63,004	40.1	33.9	74,216	67.3	4.7	40.0	21.2	68,393	4.0	13.5	28.8
39 057	Greene................	96,655	38.1	33.4	124,143	66.1	5.4	40.7	22.7	56,859	7.1	20.1	21.8
39 059	Guernsey..............	27,313	62.8	11.1	31,687	59.1	6.8	38.0	35.6	34,966	14.1	34.9	5.6
39 061	Hamilton..............	554,729	44.3	30.8	664,254	65.2	7.1	39.2	28.6	47,232	9.8	27.3	17.9
39 063	Hancock..............	48,328	48.6	23.1	58,090	69.3	5.1	42.3	25.2	47,374	8.2	25.1	12.0
39 065	Hardin................	19,424	67.5	12.7	25,268	59.8	6.7	33.1	33.6	40,541	9.9	32.6	8.0
39 069	Henry.................	19,899	64.2	11.1	22,836	61.2	6.6	38.6	26.2	49,149	6.2	21.8	9.8
39 071	Highland..............	28,092	66.1	9.8	32,895	60.3	9.1	36.3	32.3	39,106	12.7	31.7	7.9
39 073	Hocking...............	19,585	64.0	10.8	22,625	59.5	5.9	38.7	30.1	40,855	11.8	28.1	7.7
39 075	Holmes................	24,097	79.3	7.8	28,735	68.0	2.4	44.5	17.3	46,264	7.2	19.9	13.1
39 077	Huron.................	39,141	66.8	11.2	45,657	67.0	6.9	39.8	29.3	46,393	9.7	24.2	9.7
39 079	Jackson...............	22,537	67.3	12.8	26,088	58.2	9.0	36.2	39.6	34,446	13.2	38.3	8.9
39 081	Jefferson..............	48,885	59.3	14.1	57,614	53.1	5.5	30.3	38.0	36,064	12.0	35.1	8.7
39 083	Knox..................	37,818	59.2	16.5	46,702	64.6	5.2	38.1	28.2	44,014	7.1	25.3	9.7
39 085	Lake..................	161,546	47.3	24.1	186,971	67.5	5.4	42.7	25.1	53,242	5.7	19.0	17.0
39 087	Lawrence.............	43,012	60.7	12.0	49,740	53.0	7.1	32.9	38.2	31,366	18.6	39.6	6.3
39 089	Licking...............	102,341	52.1	21.6	121,433	68.9	7.0	41.6	24.7	53,239	7.3	21.1	18.0
39 091	Logan.................	30,992	63.8	12.7	35,923	68.4	7.2	42.5	26.7	47,016	11.3	24.6	12.5
39 093	Lorain................	199,308	50.0	19.8	235,343	65.1	8.0	38.7	27.7	50,993	9.7	23.9	16.7
39 095	Lucas.................	286,963	47.6	22.8	345,458	65.2	9.9	36.4	31.0	43,527	12.9	29.8	14.3
39 097	Madison...............	27,709	62.6	14.5	33,047	59.2	6.0	39.6	26.3	53,479	7.8	19.6	17.9
39 099	Mahoning.............	167,240	54.4	19.8	196,208	60.3	8.1	32.8	34.6	38,906	11.8	32.8	11.2
39 101	Marion................	45,215	64.4	11.3	52,585	58.4	7.3	38.9	30.5	41,192	11.2	29.5	8.4
39 103	Medina................	111,446	43.5	28.0	130,681	70.7	5.4	43.0	20.5	65,111	4.7	15.0	24.2
39 105	Meigs.................	15,932	69.5	9.3	18,448	54.6	9.5	30.9	36.9	32,003	16.3	40.4	6.0
39 107	Mercer................	26,293	62.1	12.3	31,195	71.4	4.0	43.5	22.6	48,292	6.1	22.2	11.5
39 109	Miami.................	68,507	53.8	19.7	79,823	65.7	5.4	42.7	27.0	49,870	6.7	21.7	14.9
39 113	Montgomery...........	360,277	45.4	24.0	427,856	63.0	7.8	37.4	30.8	43,237	11.3	27.6	14.1
39 117	Morrow...............	22,944	61.2	13.8	26,758	68.6	5.2	42.2	21.0	48,777	4.4	17.6	9.9
39 119	Muskingum............	56,780	61.5	12.8	67,047	63.0	11.0	34.5	33.4	38,748	12.2	32.0	9.2
39 123	Ottawa................	29,293	47.0	19.6	33,650	64.9	5.4	37.5	31.0	53,186	6.1	22.3	16.8
39 127	Perry..................	22,861	66.9	8.9	26,735	60.2	9.4	35.2	33.3	39,843	13.2	31.6	6.2
39 129	Pickaway..............	35,790	63.9	13.7	42,462	56.7	6.8	36.5	28.3	50,833	8.4	20.1	14.7
39 131	Pike...................	18,656	69.3	12.6	21,597	55.0	14.0	29.2	41.2	31,380	21.1	41.3	6.1
39 133	Portage...............	98,763	50.9	24.3	126,086	69.2	6.8	38.8	22.8	48,339	7.4	23.6	15.4
39 135	Preble................	28,627	64.0	10.5	33,131	65.2	5.8	40.7	27.3	47,543	7.3	23.5	11.1
39 137	Putnam................	21,872	57.5	16.2	26,391	69.8	4.9	44.0	26.6	53,637	4.9	19.6	15.4
39 139	Richland..............	86,311	59.7	14.1	100,804	59.0	7.3	36.5	30.9	41,563	7.8	28.3	10.9
39 141	Ross...................	52,202	65.7	11.8	60,337	58.0	10.4	33.6	30.7	40,558	9.6	27.5	8.7
39 143	Sandusky..............	41,029	58.9	12.7	48,261	66.1	6.5	39.1	28.3	46,366	7.0	24.2	10.0
39 145	Scioto.................	51,410	61.0	11.4	60,751	51.8	12.0	28.4	43.8	30,354	17.8	42.9	6.8
39 147	Seneca................	37,529	57.7	15.3	44,891	68.2	5.9	42.3	25.0	43,467	8.1	26.0	10.5
39 149	Shelby................	31,658	59.8	15.9	36,852	69.9	3.3	49.2	22.1	49,394	9.6	23.0	11.8
39 151	Stark..................	257,796	54.8	19.9	302,183	64.5	7.1	37.2	29.6	44,894	9.0	27.2	12.7
39 153	Summit................	366,795	44.5	28.7	428,933	66.0	6.9	40.9	28.0	46,997	9.0	25.0	16.4
39 155	Trumbull..............	149,484	60.5	15.5	172,993	59.4	7.0	36.4	33.6	42,378	9.6	28.5	10.3
39 157	Tuscarawas............	62,704	65.1	13.4	72,028	63.6	5.8	39.6	29.8	41,114	8.7	29.4	8.5
39 159	Union.................	30,217	50.8	23.9	35,025	67.5	3.7	49.1	18.8	67,455	3.9	15.0	22.9
39 161	Van Wert..............	19,559	62.4	14.0	22,828	69.8	6.9	43.6	26.5	43,034	5.8	22.1	7.7
39 165	Warren................	129,921	40.4	33.9	151,795	69.8	4.8	45.4	18.8	69,046	4.1	12.7	29.4
39 167	Washington............	42,528	56.3	16.9	50,109	59.4	6.2	35.8	31.6	39,425	10.0	30.9	9.6
39 169	Wayne.................	73,367	59.9	18.3	87,887	66.4	6.3	39.9	24.7	47,233	7.6	23.7	12.7
39 171	Williams..............	26,410	59.0	11.4	30,654	64.9	5.8	41.6	26.0	44,051	8.2	22.9	8.7
39 173	Wood..................	74,726	42.6	29.6	101,463	69.6	7.2	38.3	23.9	51,001	6.3	23.2	17.9
39 175	Wyandot...............	15,544	63.2	12.3	17,909	69.8	6.1	44.1	24.3	47,526	4.4	19.9	10.0

STATE County code	STATE County	Educational attainment			Employment status				Percent of households with no workers	Median household income (dollars)	Percent of families with income below poverty	Percent of households with income less than $25,000	Percent of households with income of $100,000 or more
		Total population 25 years and over	Percent with a high school diploma or less	Percent with a bachelor's degree or more	Total population 16 years and over	Percent in the labor force	Unemployment rate	Percent who worked full-time, year-round					
	ACS table number:	C15002	C15002	C15002	C20005	C23001	C23001	C20005	C08202	B19013	C17015	C19001	C19001
		1	2	3	4	5	6	7	8	9	10	11	12
40 000	**Oklahoma**	2,311,130	48.9	22.2	2,789,374	62.7	5.9	39.5	28.3	40,371	12.5	30.9	11.7
40 001	Adair	13,590	70.9	10.5	16,417	47.9	4.6	34.3	37.4	29,640	24.4	43.7	2.1
40 013	Bryan	24,949	53.5	20.5	30,446	58.7	8.9	39.3	34.7	33,427	17.4	36.8	7.8
40 015	Caddo	18,435	60.1	13.9	22,992	57.4	8.2	35.9	31.9	38,123	15.4	32.1	6.2
40 017	Canadian	64,741	38.7	24.8	77,713	66.3	3.6	45.1	21.9	54,482	5.7	18.0	18.2
40 019	Carter	31,435	60.9	16.9	36,681	61.1	3.8	44.9	29.3	36,565	12.7	34.0	7.8
40 021	Cherokee	26,544	51.6	23.2	36,073	50.2	8.2	30.4	37.9	28,916	19.2	45.0	6.9
40 027	Cleveland	143,656	36.8	29.6	185,296	67.3	5.4	41.4	22.6	49,125	6.8	22.8	15.9
40 031	Comanche	66,486	49.5	18.8	83,659	63.9	6.1	38.5	26.0	41,902	15.1	29.3	9.2
40 037	Creek	45,971	61.1	13.3	53,944	61.2	6.9	37.7	30.5	39,757	12.4	30.7	10.0
40 039	Custer	15,400	47.5	23.1	20,743	61.8	5.0	36.1	28.7	36,215	17.2	33.6	6.7
40 041	Delaware	27,512	61.3	15.1	32,033	55.1	9.2	31.3	38.3	34,129	16.2	35.8	8.8
40 047	Garfield	38,227	51.7	20.4	44,568	64.5	4.5	41.7	25.1	38,674	13.7	30.7	9.5
40 049	Garvin	18,596	66.1	14.4	21,464	59.4	4.8	38.6	32.2	35,091	14.2	33.6	9.1
40 051	Grady	32,133	53.4	18.0	38,828	64.6	5.5	42.1	24.9	42,311	12.9	29.3	13.7
40 065	Jackson	15,783	49.0	18.0	19,280	64.2	6.3	44.5	26.4	38,513	15.8	33.1	9.3
40 071	Kay	30,222	52.7	18.7	35,708	60.2	7.5	36.0	33.8	37,294	13.8	35.6	10.0
40 079	Le Flore	32,688	62.1	10.6	38,401	52.9	4.9	32.1	34.8	34,621	16.4	39.6	5.0
40 081	Lincoln	21,207	61.2	13.0	25,215	58.9	6.1	39.1	32.0	38,306	12.1	31.9	7.5
40 083	Logan	23,451	50.3	22.0	28,421	63.7	5.5	40.9	26.9	43,746	7.3	28.9	16.6
40 087	McClain	19,819	52.9	18.6	24,066	66.5	3.3	44.5	23.1	49,387	7.4	25.2	13.8
40 089	McCurtain	22,267	63.6	13.3	25,867	57.0	13.2	32.1	39.0	30,754	21.4	45.2	8.2
40 097	Mayes	26,465	61.4	11.3	30,945	62.0	8.0	39.8	32.4	38,526	11.7	31.3	8.7
40 101	Muskogee	46,662	55.0	17.1	55,743	56.3	6.6	34.9	35.3	35,167	14.5	37.7	8.6
40 109	Oklahoma	444,851	41.8	28.2	530,967	66.0	6.3	41.1	26.5	40,513	12.7	29.8	13.5
40 111	Okmulgee	25,345	58.7	12.7	30,740	59.1	8.1	34.2	34.4	31,960	20.7	41.0	7.5
40 113	Osage	30,543	52.7	18.1	36,388	57.7	7.0	39.5	30.7	39,365	11.5	32.3	12.6
40 115	Ottawa	21,506	54.8	13.4	25,903	57.3	8.7	33.2	35.9	32,423	13.4	39.5	5.7
40 119	Payne	43,287	39.6	33.4	65,329	63.0	6.0	31.1	25.8	33,541	12.5	38.9	9.1
40 121	Pittsburg	30,828	58.0	16.3	35,784	53.2	5.3	36.4	36.1	36,915	11.8	34.8	8.4
40 123	Pontotoc	22,820	48.6	24.5	28,435	66.4	6.3	38.7	27.9	34,271	13.7	38.2	9.6
40 125	Pottawatomie	44,005	53.6	17.0	53,741	57.8	6.8	34.7	33.3	35,510	15.7	34.7	8.3
40 131	Rogers	53,011	49.3	19.6	63,376	66.0	5.7	42.5	23.2	52,608	5.8	21.0	15.5
40 133	Seminole	15,897	61.5	13.1	18,824	55.2	8.9	32.4	35.7	32,024	19.7	41.6	6.0
40 135	Sequoyah	26,295	60.0	13.7	31,863	53.5	5.5	34.0	33.2	34,673	14.9	36.6	4.1
40 137	Stephens	28,789	58.1	16.5	33,886	58.9	4.7	37.8	28.7	40,641	12.1	30.6	10.8
40 139	Texas	11,841	58.9	17.9	14,692	68.1	5.6	45.2	20.8	39,194	-	28.0	10.8
40 143	Tulsa	373,657	40.2	29.0	442,164	67.1	5.7	43.1	25.2	43,706	11.9	27.4	15.6
40 145	Wagoner	42,266	48.7	19.0	50,877	67.0	4.3	43.6	21.5	50,196	9.8	23.2	14.0
40 147	Washington	33,420	45.1	26.2	39,651	61.2	4.2	37.9	34.3	42,919	9.6	30.6	13.8
41 000	**Oregon**	2,490,987	39.4	27.0	2,934,587	64.0	6.9	36.4	27.3	47,385	9.3	25.2	15.7
41 003	Benton	48,862	23.0	48.0	67,565	64.1	4.8	31.1	24.9	47,117	6.9	27.4	19.5
41 005	Clackamas	253,492	34.6	30.9	295,737	67.1	6.1	38.7	23.8	59,709	5.8	18.5	24.7
41 007	Clatsop	25,703	42.0	19.7	30,337	61.4	5.3	33.1	32.7	39,479	10.2	31.2	9.8
41 009	Columbia	32,701	47.3	15.4	38,429	64.8	8.1	38.5	26.7	55,153	4.8	17.1	14.2
41 011	Coos	46,632	49.2	17.5	53,084	52.9	6.7	28.4	41.0	36,271	11.6	35.7	9.1
41 013	Crook	15,483	54.3	14.1	17,968	61.3	5.0	35.9	28.4	44,951	12.4	22.7	8.2
41 015	Curry	16,935	47.6	17.2	18,873	49.9	7.4	26.7	44.7	36,316	8.7	35.4	8.8
41 017	Deschutes	102,618	34.7	28.2	118,804	66.0	4.9	38.6	26.6	53,436	5.2	18.9	16.0
41 019	Douglas	74,010	52.0	14.7	85,084	56.4	9.0	30.4	37.2	38,722	9.2	30.8	9.1
41 027	Hood River	13,992	43.3	29.7	16,042	68.9	5.6	32.0	28.1	46,415	12.0	25.4	11.4
41 029	Jackson	136,019	41.7	23.5	159,457	62.0	6.6	34.3	32.4	43,446	8.9	27.5	11.7
41 031	Jefferson	12,724	56.9	16.7	15,141	64.2	11.2	34.5	30.7	40,154	10.9	26.8	7.4
41 033	Josephine	58,218	46.9	16.6	66,269	52.5	7.5	27.6	39.7	37,647	12.5	31.6	9.5
41 035	Klamath	43,992	51.9	16.7	51,975	60.4	7.8	32.5	31.3	39,437	14.0	33.6	10.6
41 039	Lane	230,576	37.2	27.6	279,000	62.0	6.8	32.2	29.8	42,079	9.6	28.7	11.6
41 041	Lincoln	33,557	41.3	21.6	38,143	54.8	6.3	31.1	40.4	36,671	11.9	36.3	8.8
41 043	Linn	74,995	47.9	15.5	87,850	61.1	7.1	35.3	30.7	42,853	11.7	28.0	10.8
41 045	Malheur	19,697	57.4	13.7	23,967	56.3	7.7	30.2	31.7	38,560	11.3	30.8	7.3
41 047	Marion	196,374	46.9	20.8	234,333	64.7	8.4	36.7	26.9	45,490	11.1	25.3	12.6
41 051	Multnomah	476,534	34.8	35.1	549,090	68.5	7.0	39.4	24.6	46,811	11.0	26.2	17.0
41 053	Polk	47,241	39.1	27.5	58,572	60.6	9.7	30.4	32.3	46,953	8.9	24.9	15.5
41 057	Tillamook	18,173	46.1	18.7	20,630	56.9	3.6	34.7	35.7	37,744	10.9	34.7	10.2
41 059	Umatilla	46,998	51.7	15.2	56,102	62.6	9.6	34.9	25.2	41,827	10.2	27.6	9.6
41 061	Union	15,837	47.5	20.7	19,668	62.0	5.9	29.4	32.1	40,413	10.9	29.8	10.0
41 065	Wasco	16,098	46.2	19.4	18,769	60.6	9.4	31.3	32.9	40,220	9.7	25.7	10.5
41 067	Washington	337,190	30.6	37.4	391,285	71.6	5.8	43.7	18.0	60,254	6.8	17.0	23.9
41 071	Yamhill	59,926	47.1	22.0	74,038	64.8	8.2	35.3	25.8	48,485	11.5	23.5	14.5
42 000	**Pennsylvania**	8,404,685	52.3	25.6	9,947,004	62.6	6.3	38.7	29.1	47,913	8.2	25.8	17.0
42 001	Adams	66,852	60.9	18.6	80,280	67.5	4.3	44.6	23.4	52,616	5.9	18.9	14.1
42 003	Allegheny	851,128	42.4	32.8	1,001,521	62.2	6.3	37.8	31.4	45,266	8.4	28.4	16.7
42 005	Armstrong	50,036	65.4	13.8	57,090	58.1	6.4	36.5	36.5	38,693	8.9	31.9	8.4
42 007	Beaver	123,741	55.1	18.8	142,495	61.4	5.8	37.8	31.1	44,262	6.2	26.7	11.3
42 009	Bedford	35,297	68.1	12.7	40,350	59.8	6.2	36.1	31.1	38,187	10.7	31.2	7.2
42 011	Berks	264,853	56.8	21.5	314,487	66.1	5.5	41.4	25.7	52,241	7.7	22.2	16.5
42 013	Blair	87,737	61.4	16.7	101,828	60.1	6.6	36.8	34.3	40,196	9.1	30.6	9.2

Table B-2. Counties — What: Education, Employment, and Income, 2005–2007—*Continued*

STATE County code	STATE County	Educational attainment			Employment status						Percent of families with income below poverty	Percent of households with income less than $25,000	Percent of households with income of $100,000 or more
		Total population 25 years and over	Percent with a high school diploma or less	Percent with a bachelor's degree or more	Total population 16 years and over	Percent in the labor force	Unemployment rate	Percent who worked full-time, year-round	Percent of households with no workers	Median household income (dollars)			
	ACS table number:	C15002	C15002	C15002	C20005	C23001	C23001	C20005	C08202	B19013	C17015	C19001	C19001
		1	2	3	4	5	6	7	8	9	10	11	12
	Pennsylvania—Cont.												
42 015	Bradford	42,673	63.9	15.5	49,087	59.1	6.5	36.8	32.7	37,663	11.6	30.7	8.6
42 017	Bucks	421,864	40.7	34.4	492,683	67.3	4.2	42.4	22.5	71,161	3.5	15.0	32.5
42 019	Butler	122,118	46.9	27.8	144,538	64.7	4.9	38.9	26.7	53,323	5.2	22.0	18.9
42 021	Cambria	103,014	62.8	17.2	121,167	55.2	7.2	33.6	37.5	37,030	10.7	32.9	8.6
42 025	Carbon	44,722	63.2	12.7	50,912	62.2	8.0	36.4	33.6	45,359	8.1	26.1	11.3
42 027	Centre	79,318	41.0	40.2	122,821	59.1	5.9	30.4	28.0	42,976	5.9	29.6	13.7
42 029	Chester	315,321	33.4	46.0	374,475	68.6	4.3	44.0	19.7	80,818	3.6	12.7	39.0
42 031	Clarion	26,327	65.1	15.6	33,149	57.5	5.3	33.4	34.2	37,666	10.7	34.6	6.8
42 033	Clearfield	58,398	67.4	12.6	67,633	55.5	8.3	36.1	34.1	34,995	11.4	36.1	7.3
42 035	Clinton	24,665	64.0	15.4	30,599	58.1	5.5	33.6	31.6	38,089	8.5	32.9	5.8
42 037	Columbia	42,684	64.3	17.2	54,178	60.1	7.7	34.0	33.8	39,214	7.2	31.4	9.5
42 039	Crawford	60,200	65.3	16.3	71,442	59.0	6.8	34.1	33.1	36,928	10.4	31.6	8.7
42 041	Cumberland	153,465	45.6	31.9	184,222	65.4	4.7	42.6	24.9	58,268	3.8	17.7	20.3
42 043	Dauphin	174,954	51.1	25.9	201,552	67.5	5.0	45.7	26.1	50,954	7.7	22.9	17.1
42 045	Delaware	361,185	43.7	33.7	437,475	63.9	6.3	39.3	26.0	58,644	6.7	19.4	25.6
42 047	Elk	23,457	64.1	14.4	26,875	63.4	5.4	41.6	31.9	42,802	4.9	25.2	10.1
42 049	Erie	182,698	55.4	23.0	222,012	61.7	6.8	37.0	30.1	42,073	10.1	29.5	11.6
42 051	Fayette	103,214	66.7	12.8	118,576	52.2	8.4	30.1	39.9	32,077	15.3	40.3	6.8
42 055	Franklin	96,692	61.9	16.9	110,788	65.2	3.8	42.9	26.3	50,048	5.1	21.1	12.7
42 059	Greene	27,759	62.1	16.5	32,739	52.8	8.1	33.0	38.2	36,647	13.7	35.3	9.7
42 061	Huntingdon	32,237	67.3	13.6	37,877	54.2	8.1	34.1	34.3	39,044	7.3	30.1	8.2
42 063	Indiana	55,818	62.4	19.1	73,839	57.9	7.2	32.3	33.4	36,520	10.3	35.9	7.7
42 065	Jefferson	31,844	69.9	12.5	36,699	57.8	5.8	33.9	34.0	35,448	11.3	34.9	6.9
42 067	Juniata	16,004	75.2	8.2	18,322	63.6	4.6	41.4	29.3	42,445	4.5	25.2	9.5
42 069	Lackawanna	144,661	53.9	22.3	171,488	60.5	5.2	36.4	31.5	40,382	9.7	32.0	11.7
42 071	Lancaster	324,515	57.8	23.2	382,874	66.5	4.1	42.8	22.7	52,933	6.1	19.3	16.6
42 073	Lawrence	63,565	59.8	18.4	74,381	58.8	7.7	35.3	33.9	41,491	10.0	30.0	10.8
42 075	Lebanon	87,314	64.2	18.0	101,061	66.8	4.9	43.6	25.0	49,805	5.7	20.9	12.6
42 077	Lehigh	226,181	50.2	26.7	263,984	65.0	6.2	40.4	26.8	51,857	7.2	22.2	18.7
42 079	Luzerne	220,606	56.6	19.6	257,350	59.6	6.1	37.2	33.8	40,643	9.1	31.2	10.8
42 081	Lycoming	79,620	57.1	17.6	95,269	62.3	7.8	36.8	32.0	40,430	9.1	30.7	9.4
42 083	McKean	30,737	64.3	15.7	35,692	58.0	6.3	36.7	32.5	38,629	8.2	30.0	8.3
42 085	Mercer	80,912	59.8	18.2	95,486	56.2	5.4	35.5	32.7	40,353	8.3	29.8	9.9
42 087	Mifflin	32,582	73.2	10.4	37,175	57.2	7.5	34.6	35.1	33,869	11.2	35.7	5.4
42 089	Monroe	105,155	52.0	22.3	127,709	65.1	8.5	38.5	23.5	54,632	6.6	19.4	18.9
42 091	Montgomery	530,104	35.9	42.7	615,282	68.7	4.2	44.4	21.5	73,701	3.2	13.8	34.4
42 095	Northampton	195,583	50.0	25.2	233,382	64.5	5.1	41.1	25.3	57,135	5.1	19.7	21.3
42 097	Northumberland	65,945	66.8	14.3	75,515	59.1	6.4	36.1	34.8	37,219	9.4	34.1	7.3
42 099	Perry	30,903	68.5	13.0	35,673	67.6	5.5	44.6	25.4	49,614	6.1	18.9	10.5
42 101	Philadelphia	931,064	58.6	21.0	1,131,973	57.8	11.9	33.6	36.1	34,767	19.3	38.0	10.4
42 103	Pike	39,431	51.5	22.5	45,569	61.2	7.3	35.9	31.7	52,168	7.4	21.9	16.6
42 107	Schuylkill	106,822	66.4	13.4	121,714	57.1	6.7	36.0	34.2	38,865	9.3	30.0	8.6
42 109	Snyder	24,845	66.1	16.4	30,675	64.1	5.1	36.6	27.6	44,084	6.1	25.0	10.7
42 111	Somerset	56,665	68.7	13.8	64,607	57.2	5.1	35.8	34.9	36,355	8.1	34.2	7.2
42 115	Susquehanna	28,775	61.0	15.1	33,280	61.6	7.0	36.4	30.3	39,722	11.1	28.7	8.9
42 117	Tioga	27,587	59.3	17.5	33,428	58.4	8.0	34.5	33.6	38,084	10.7	31.9	7.9
42 119	Union	29,441	58.9	22.2	36,858	49.4	4.3	29.4	28.2	43,989	6.9	25.5	14.3
42 121	Venango	38,891	63.9	14.5	44,564	60.7	7.4	36.1	34.9	37,053	10.3	31.6	7.9
42 123	Warren	29,499	61.1	16.8	33,815	60.2	5.1	37.9	31.1	39,602	9.0	29.1	7.6
42 125	Washington	144,106	53.7	23.7	167,962	60.3	5.7	36.6	31.0	47,336	6.8	25.8	15.4
42 127	Wayne	36,743	57.4	18.9	41,606	55.5	5.2	35.9	33.0	40,890	8.5	27.0	10.4
42 129	Westmoreland	260,992	52.0	23.0	300,242	60.1	5.0	37.4	31.3	45,289	6.5	27.3	14.2
42 131	Wyoming	19,039	59.2	16.7	22,387	62.4	5.9	39.6	27.3	44,769	6.4	23.8	10.3
42 133	York	284,102	55.7	21.3	328,553	68.6	5.0	45.3	23.5	53,641	5.4	19.5	16.8
44 000	**Rhode Island**	711,837	46.6	29.4	854,785	66.0	6.1	38.9	27.6	54,060	8.3	23.7	21.2
44 001	Bristol	34,445	37.3	40.3	41,719	64.3	4.8	37.5	25.0	65,730	3.5	18.0	30.0
44 003	Kent	119,527	42.9	28.8	137,915	68.4	5.0	43.6	25.6	59,833	4.0	18.3	22.2
44 005	Newport	58,834	35.7	41.6	68,079	66.6	4.8	38.2	27.7	61,894	3.9	19.7	27.9
44 007	Providence	414,799	52.5	24.6	503,011	64.7	7.0	37.8	29.2	47,976	11.8	28.1	17.4
44 009	Washington	84,232	34.8	40.7	104,061	69.2	4.6	38.6	24.1	68,504	3.0	15.5	29.9
45 000	**South Carolina**	2,851,898	51.0	22.8	3,406,212	62.8	7.3	39.4	28.5	42,405	11.8	29.3	13.1
45 001	Abbeville	17,066	60.9	16.2	20,392	59.9	12.4	31.9	37.4	33,190	21.0	42.5	5.9
45 003	Aiken	100,726	50.4	22.4	118,439	61.1	6.7	36.6	31.4	43,958	12.1	29.8	14.6
45 007	Anderson	120,194	56.6	17.3	139,436	61.4	8.3	37.0	31.4	41,078	11.7	31.1	10.3
45 011	Barnwell	14,699	62.1	11.8	17,770	59.5	11.4	37.5	36.8	35,828	14.6	38.2	7.3
45 013	Beaufort	94,602	36.2	36.2	112,450	61.3	4.7	39.3	32.1	52,595	8.7	20.9	21.3
45 015	Berkeley	99,885	53.9	16.0	121,556	67.1	6.0	43.9	22.1	48,608	8.3	21.5	11.5
45 019	Charleston	223,165	38.0	36.5	269,111	65.4	5.5	41.7	26.1	46,653	11.1	26.2	18.6
45 021	Cherokee	36,535	67.4	11.0	41,908	61.3	10.6	34.7	34.1	35,159	14.3	36.3	7.4
45 023	Chester	21,962	69.3	9.5	25,652	55.9	8.0	39.7	31.7	31,335	19.1	41.2	6.3
45 025	Chesterfield	28,703	64.6	10.9	33,532	59.0	12.0	36.1	36.8	33,075	16.0	40.3	7.1
45 027	Clarendon	21,300	69.8	11.3	26,086	54.2	11.1	33.4	33.2	30,379	18.4	41.5	5.9
45 029	Colleton	25,251	67.0	12.4	29,739	59.4	9.6	36.0	32.4	34,072	18.5	37.2	5.1
45 031	Darlington	44,667	62.8	16.6	52,533	59.7	11.3	38.8	31.7	38,416	14.4	33.3	9.4

STATE County code	STATE County	Educational attainment			Employment status				Percent of house-holds with no workers	Median house-hold income (dollars)	Percent of families with income below poverty	Percent of house-holds with income less than $25,000	Percent of house-holds with income of $100,000 or more
		Total population 25 years and over	Percent with a high school diploma or less	Percent with a bachelor's degree or more	Total population 16 years and over	Percent in the labor force	Unem-ployment rate	Percent who worked full-time, year-round					
ACS table number:		C15002	C15002	C15002	C20005	C23001	C23001	C20005	C08202	B19013	C17015	C19001	C19001
		1	2	3	4	5	6	7	8	9	10	11	12
	South Carolina—Cont.												
45 033	Dillon	19,605	73.1	9.0	23,204	56.5	8.0	36.2	34.0	26,891	24.1	47.5	4.7
45 035	Dorchester	75,085	45.1	21.7	90,676	66.1	5.9	44.7	21.6	52,339	7.8	20.4	15.1
45 037	Edgefield	17,265	58.0	14.0	20,554	55.7	7.2	36.1	27.9	46,316	13.7	31.3	14.6
45 039	Fairfield	15,699	69.1	13.1	18,525	57.7	5.4	39.9	35.2	33,129	13.8	38.4	7.2
45 041	Florence	85,227	54.2	20.8	101,836	62.3	8.6	40.2	28.0	39,796	13.4	31.2	11.9
45 043	Georgetown	41,039	49.5	21.9	47,842	55.6	5.7	33.9	36.7	40,947	13.6	32.6	13.7
45 045	Greenville	277,623	46.1	28.3	326,246	65.8	6.6	41.3	25.3	45,616	9.7	26.9	15.9
45 047	Greenwood	44,301	51.8	23.0	53,348	63.4	10.0	37.8	30.9	38,771	10.3	31.9	11.0
45 049	Hampton	13,265	67.9	10.7	16,147	52.4	7.0	40.5	34.0	34,302	13.9	38.2	6.2
45 051	Horry	168,232	49.3	20.6	193,532	63.7	5.5	39.0	29.6	41,975	11.8	27.7	11.0
45 053	Jasper	13,814	67.3	9.2	16,685	59.4	8.6	40.4	27.8	33,959	14.9	35.6	7.0
45 055	Kershaw	37,880	57.3	19.1	44,729	61.6	5.9	40.5	28.2	42,943	11.6	29.4	13.1
45 057	Lancaster	48,443	66.5	12.3	56,784	54.8	8.6	36.6	34.2	36,589	13.3	34.0	8.5
45 059	Laurens	46,643	63.9	14.5	55,250	57.3	9.7	35.7	31.3	35,232	15.8	34.3	7.0
45 063	Lexington	158,308	43.9	26.6	185,492	68.7	4.8	46.9	22.1	50,628	9.1	22.3	16.8
45 067	Marion	22,495	70.0	14.5	26,820	57.1	13.0	35.5	34.4	29,542	20.5	44.0	7.7
45 069	Marlboro	19,180	73.3	7.0	22,514	50.8	14.5	29.0	39.7	23,788	20.7	52.5	3.9
45 071	Newberry	25,037	58.7	18.5	29,447	63.3	7.6	39.0	32.5	40,641	11.2	31.7	10.3
45 073	Oconee	49,329	53.3	19.5	56,436	58.4	6.6	37.3	34.8	40,933	9.5	29.0	12.2
45 075	Orangeburg	56,881	60.8	16.1	71,002	56.8	10.7	33.5	35.0	31,374	19.2	40.8	6.6
45 077	Pickens	71,895	52.5	22.3	93,370	59.8	7.2	34.1	28.5	42,027	8.6	29.7	10.8
45 079	Richland	216,777	36.9	35.8	278,233	68.3	6.3	41.5	22.3	46,818	9.7	25.1	16.0
45 083	Spartanburg	181,168	54.8	18.6	213,069	62.2	7.9	39.4	29.7	40,743	11.3	30.5	12.1
45 085	Sumter	65,871	55.3	16.9	79,522	58.1	10.3	38.8	32.8	36,194	14.8	35.5	8.2
45 087	Union	19,563	63.8	11.6	22,460	56.0	9.8	32.6	35.0	34,368	15.3	39.4	5.3
45 089	Williamsburg	22,782	70.9	11.3	27,466	51.6	15.8	31.3	38.9	24,687	26.6	50.7	4.7
45 091	York	129,224	45.5	25.2	154,126	69.2	7.6	42.7	23.1	50,407	8.8	22.7	17.9
46 000	**South Dakota**	509,779	45.3	24.5	616,374	69.6	4.4	43.9	24.0	43,586	8.7	27.1	11.1
46 011	Brookings	15,799	37.2	35.1	24,091	69.8	2.8	37.8	20.3	39,897	5.8	30.1	11.1
46 013	Brown	23,126	47.7	22.4	28,231	70.1	2.9	46.3	23.2	43,039	6.5	28.1	9.8
46 029	Codington	17,307	53.8	19.7	20,398	72.7	4.1	45.3	25.4	40,350	12.3	30.2	10.1
46 081	Lawrence	14,790	37.7	32.3	19,037	66.6	4.2	37.7	29.5	38,385	11.0	33.5	10.9
46 083	Lincoln	21,919	36.7	32.2	26,526	80.5	3.3	56.4	15.2	64,784	2.1	11.2	23.2
46 093	Meade	15,539	44.1	21.8	18,715	72.5	4.6	47.9	19.7	44,539	8.2	20.6	8.1
46 099	Minnehaha	111,361	41.0	28.1	132,000	74.7	3.6	49.0	20.2	48,915	6.7	22.7	13.6
46 103	Pennington	61,341	37.5	27.3	73,752	69.4	4.5	41.6	24.9	44,994	9.5	25.3	12.6
46 135	Yankton	14,654	44.2	28.5	17,459	64.6	4.7	41.2	28.5	41,586	8.6	30.4	9.9
47 000	**Tennessee**	4,061,516	53.5	21.7	4,779,974	62.9	7.1	39.6	28.3	41,821	12.2	29.9	13.0
47 001	Anderson	51,341	54.0	20.9	58,537	57.0	6.0	38.6	35.8	41,346	12.0	31.1	12.3
47 003	Bedford	28,304	68.6	13.8	33,179	64.5	8.5	41.4	28.5	37,583	13.6	30.7	7.5
47 009	Blount	81,664	51.1	20.5	94,936	62.5	7.2	38.3	30.5	46,009	10.6	26.3	12.6
47 011	Bradley	63,320	52.9	20.0	74,390	62.4	8.1	38.6	28.3	39,761	10.6	29.4	10.4
47 013	Campbell	28,706	74.2	8.7	32,747	47.3	7.3	29.8	43.9	27,274	19.9	46.7	4.7
47 017	Carroll	20,114	71.2	11.5	23,301	56.4	11.9	34.8	38.4	35,765	19.9	35.5	8.0
47 019	Carter	41,900	64.2	14.5	48,651	58.2	6.4	37.0	36.0	32,819	15.5	39.2	4.5
47 021	Cheatham	25,851	59.2	14.5	30,076	69.8	7.2	43.8	22.8	48,058	11.2	23.0	14.3
47 025	Claiborne	21,506	68.6	11.0	24,899	54.3	8.8	37.3	40.6	30,691	15.9	40.1	5.0
47 029	Cocke	25,051	71.4	8.0	28,281	55.4	7.4	31.0	37.3	29,825	17.9	43.7	4.7
47 031	Coffee	34,740	60.2	18.1	40,312	59.2	7.7	36.7	34.0	37,076	14.9	32.8	9.9
47 035	Cumberland	37,628	62.8	15.6	42,410	51.4	8.6	30.8	43.1	35,471	12.9	35.1	6.1
47 037	Davidson	412,033	42.4	32.3	484,874	67.4	5.9	44.2	23.6	44,486	11.2	26.2	15.5
47 043	Dickson	31,092	63.1	14.5	36,172	66.1	5.4	42.8	24.5	45,528	8.2	26.7	10.0
47 045	Dyer	25,385	68.4	10.7	29,407	58.9	4.4	40.9	31.4	36,473	16.1	36.9	7.1
47 047	Fayette	23,937	57.6	16.8	27,935	64.6	11.6	40.3	28.9	49,566	12.0	24.5	16.7
47 051	Franklin	27,510	59.5	17.2	32,858	58.3	8.1	35.4	32.2	41,953	8.2	29.8	10.3
47 053	Gibson	32,893	62.8	13.6	38,068	58.1	8.8	37.6	36.9	32,840	14.6	40.5	7.4
47 055	Giles	20,065	65.7	14.9	23,321	60.2	11.6	39.7	34.3	37,926	10.9	34.3	8.7
47 057	Grainger	15,837	79.2	5.7	18,160	58.8	6.4	34.7	36.6	33,626	10.9	37.7	5.3
47 059	Greene	45,840	69.9	11.6	52,589	56.9	7.3	36.7	32.5	34,438	15.8	36.6	5.2
47 063	Hamblen	41,340	62.0	13.8	48,234	61.3	5.8	41.0	29.1	37,661	13.6	33.8	7.8
47 065	Hamilton	222,165	46.2	25.7	262,950	64.2	7.2	39.6	27.6	44,384	9.0	28.0	15.6
47 069	Hardeman	19,081	74.9	7.1	22,489	50.2	9.6	31.2	33.4	30,734	17.9	38.3	5.6
47 071	Hardin	18,293	73.6	8.9	21,045	55.0	7.3	33.3	38.5	29,123	18.3	44.8	4.6
47 073	Hawkins	39,944	63.1	11.7	45,177	56.4	8.7	34.2	36.8	34,376	13.9	36.6	5.1
47 077	Henderson	18,078	66.6	10.8	20,773	60.7	11.8	37.3	34.3	37,647	13.8	36.1	9.0
47 079	Henry	22,561	64.0	12.3	25,550	55.8	8.8	36.5	36.6	35,081	13.6	33.8	7.5
47 081	Hickman	16,054	71.3	8.0	18,520	56.6	5.1	36.2	33.0	35,839	15.8	34.2	6.2
47 089	Jefferson	33,205	61.3	13.7	39,535	62.9	6.7	37.7	29.7	38,436	12.7	34.1	9.6
47 093	Knox	277,663	42.7	31.8	333,967	64.7	5.3	40.8	26.7	45,309	9.5	27.5	15.7
47 097	Lauderdale	17,590	74.2	7.0	20,867	51.5	8.0	36.9	33.9	29,891	21.7	41.9	5.9
47 099	Lawrence	27,271	67.8	10.1	31,647	58.2	9.0	30.6	36.3	35,445	13.5	35.2	7.6
47 103	Lincoln	22,281	62.6	15.3	25,892	62.9	6.2	40.4	32.5	41,170	7.9	27.6	12.3
47 105	Loudon	31,420	54.0	20.5	35,799	58.9	5.7	35.8	35.5	46,548	8.6	25.7	12.6
47 107	McMinn	36,330	64.1	13.8	41,119	58.3	6.9	36.5	34.3	33,437	14.5	37.3	8.4
47 109	McNairy	17,514	70.6	10.1	20,008	56.2	9.7	33.0	38.1	33,298	16.2	39.7	5.0

Table B-2. Counties — What: Education, Employment, and Income, 2005–2007—*Continued*

STATE County code	STATE County	Educational attainment			Employment status				Percent of house-holds with no workers	Median house-hold income (dollars)	Percent of families with income below poverty	Percent of house-holds with income less than $25,000	Percent of house-holds with income of $100,000 or more
		Total population 25 years and over	Percent with a high school diploma or less	Percent with a bachelor's degree or more	Total population 16 years and over	Percent in the labor force	Unem-ployment rate	Percent who worked full-time, year-round					
ACS table number:		C15002	C15002	C15002	C20005	C23001	C23001	C20005	C08202	B19013	C17015	C19001	C19001
		1	2	3	4	5	6	7	8	9	10	11	12
	Tennessee—Cont.												
47 111	Macon	14,635	75.1	10.5	16,802	60.1	6.9	37.7	32.1	30,776	15.1	43.3	6.2
47 113	Madison	61,583	48.1	23.8	74,301	64.5	7.3	40.9	28.2	39,721	15.8	32.6	12.7
47 115	Marion	19,565	68.7	8.9	22,473	61.6	7.3	38.5	32.6	37,185	13.4	34.1	8.3
47 117	Marshall	19,562	67.0	10.2	22,368	65.4	8.6	43.7	26.2	37,359	15.7	31.6	9.7
47 119	Maury	51,823	57.2	15.4	60,751	65.1	8.0	40.5	25.2	44,990	8.9	26.4	11.5
47 123	Monroe	29,730	69.3	12.0	34,402	60.0	8.4	37.1	32.9	36,614	11.9	34.4	7.1
47 125	Montgomery	91,505	41.4	22.7	111,167	66.8	5.8	44.9	20.5	49,248	9.7	23.2	12.9
47 129	Morgan	14,165	75.9	5.0	16,234	49.6	9.0	32.3	37.7	31,448	21.1	40.5	4.4
47 131	Obion	22,072	70.3	10.6	25,229	60.1	5.2	40.4	32.1	35,391	9.9	33.9	6.4
47 133	Overton	14,550	72.6	10.1	16,677	53.3	7.0	36.0	34.6	31,523	17.1	40.0	6.4
47 141	Putnam	43,660	55.8	22.7	55,036	58.0	5.8	33.0	31.6	34,923	14.8	36.9	8.5
47 143	Rhea	20,299	66.6	11.0	23,732	55.7	8.7	31.7	34.8	35,563	14.8	36.8	4.7
47 145	Roane	38,002	58.1	16.9	43,436	55.3	6.6	35.3	36.4	41,496	10.1	30.4	12.1
47 147	Robertson	40,473	62.0	12.7	47,490	68.9	5.2	45.9	20.8	50,242	8.3	21.3	10.0
47 149	Rutherford	142,111	47.1	25.6	176,146	70.6	6.6	45.7	18.8	50,623	8.5	21.2	14.4
47 151	Scott	14,449	73.6	7.8	16,687	57.6	10.8	33.0	36.0	27,243	20.2	44.8	3.4
47 155	Sevier	57,415	59.4	14.8	65,551	66.7	4.5	39.4	24.9	39,534	10.2	28.8	9.5
47 157	Shelby	571,072	44.6	27.1	686,853	66.5	9.1	41.0	24.7	43,512	15.0	29.0	17.1
47 163	Sullivan	109,952	54.4	19.3	124,888	58.5	7.1	36.6	34.9	37,559	12.4	32.8	10.9
47 165	Sumner	99,188	50.3	22.2	115,600	68.5	7.4	43.6	23.7	52,970	7.2	21.2	16.7
47 167	Tipton	36,624	55.2	14.0	43,647	67.7	7.3	41.8	22.7	51,105	13.8	23.8	15.1
47 177	Warren	27,237	72.6	10.2	31,229	56.9	6.5	34.1	31.9	32,969	16.4	40.7	7.4
47 179	Washington	78,128	49.8	26.5	92,987	60.6	5.8	38.3	30.1	39,238	10.7	30.0	11.7
47 183	Weakley	21,395	60.9	16.4	27,040	56.9	6.4	35.0	33.9	32,926	15.8	37.4	5.2
47 185	White	16,940	72.7	9.3	19,494	60.6	6.7	37.2	31.7	32,253	15.1	37.2	5.5
47 187	Williamson	103,305	26.3	49.2	121,713	70.2	4.1	44.6	17.0	84,205	3.2	10.5	41.7
47 189	Wilson	68,268	49.1	22.1	80,207	69.0	4.2	46.0	19.2	60,503	4.9	17.4	21.1
48 000	**Texas**	14,482,842	48.4	24.7	17,596,586	65.2	6.8	41.4	22.6	46,248	13.3	26.7	17.5
48 001	Anderson	39,180	62.4	11.8	46,482	42.7	8.9	27.2	32.3	37,924	12.5	33.8	9.4
48 005	Angelina	52,208	56.5	15.7	62,498	60.7	7.7	37.9	27.4	38,753	13.2	30.6	10.1
48 007	Aransas	17,224	48.5	21.6	19,714	-	-	30.1	44.1	38,824	12.0	34.4	15.4
48 013	Atascosa	26,159	64.3	9.8	31,876	63.0	8.5	38.2	27.8	42,800	16.6	31.6	11.6
48 015	Austin	17,042	54.2	16.4	20,425	65.7	4.5	40.8	24.2	51,141	7.1	24.6	21.3
48 019	Bandera	13,427	47.0	21.0	16,066	-	-	35.4	34.1	38,848	15.0	30.7	12.3
48 021	Bastrop	45,132	55.6	17.1	53,486	65.5	7.2	43.3	24.4	49,799	7.1	20.8	14.9
48 025	Bee	21,327	64.6	10.3	26,816	34.0	5.2	19.6	35.6	30,685	17.0	40.0	8.4
48 027	Bell	158,685	41.1	21.6	192,727	66.3	6.2	45.8	22.7	45,953	10.2	23.0	12.5
48 029	Bexar	951,892	47.1	24.1	1,162,285	64.2	6.3	40.9	24.5	44,664	13.3	27.2	15.5
48 037	Bowie	60,503	52.8	16.7	71,705	59.1	7.8	37.0	30.6	38,932	13.8	33.4	11.4
48 039	Brazoria	178,632	43.6	24.4	213,758	64.6	5.6	42.6	20.1	58,583	8.6	19.0	24.4
48 041	Brazos	81,392	39.3	39.5	135,450	61.8	6.3	31.9	23.3	36,125	16.4	39.5	13.0
48 049	Brown	25,087	61.6	13.9	30,524	52.7	4.9	37.5	34.9	36,967	13.9	34.5	8.5
48 053	Burnet	29,222	50.0	20.1	33,808	59.4	5.5	36.5	34.1	47,355	8.1	24.0	13.4
48 055	Caldwell	23,042	64.4	14.5	27,770	55.1	7.3	33.9	24.6	39,885	16.7	29.3	8.5
48 057	Calhoun	13,134	60.2	13.2	15,456	61.0	4.5	35.0	28.9	42,104	12.9	29.9	10.6
48 061	Cameron	209,078	63.1	14.5	262,381	53.4	7.5	31.8	30.9	28,026	32.2	45.4	7.9
48 067	Cass	20,317	58.2	13.9	23,805	54.7	6.9	32.9	38.2	35,933	14.2	37.7	9.5
48 071	Chambers	18,782	49.7	13.7	22,085	67.7	5.0	47.1	20.9	56,080	8.8	21.5	19.2
48 073	Cherokee	30,587	62.1	12.8	36,613	57.7	7.1	38.1	31.3	35,934	15.2	34.2	10.0
48 085	Collin	442,864	24.1	47.2	519,618	73.5	4.5	50.2	12.7	77,671	4.0	11.3	36.7
48 089	Colorado	13,739	61.1	16.5	16,278	58.8	4.7	36.7	33.0	38,167	10.7	32.8	11.6
48 091	Comal	66,602	39.5	29.9	78,272	63.3	5.1	40.0	25.5	59,450	6.6	19.0	25.2
48 097	Cooke	24,827	51.5	18.9	29,629	67.1	5.4	43.3	23.0	48,041	12.4	24.4	12.3
48 099	Coryell	39,239	43.0	17.3	52,467	64.1	6.0	42.8	24.2	44,817	13.9	23.9	11.1
48 113	Dallas	1,466,802	49.3	26.6	1,745,152	69.2	7.3	45.3	19.5	46,330	13.6	24.9	17.9
48 121	Denton	360,583	30.4	38.1	440,452	74.8	5.7	48.7	13.1	68,624	4.9	14.3	30.2
48 135	Ector	75,694	59.5	12.2	93,603	63.3	4.5	41.2	23.7	41,322	14.6	30.8	11.4
48 139	Ellis	84,616	52.3	18.7	103,369	68.4	7.3	44.4	21.7	54,900	10.0	20.9	19.3
48 141	El Paso	415,887	55.5	18.0	522,820	58.9	8.8	34.6	25.9	33,684	24.9	38.6	9.4
48 143	Erath	19,997	50.5	24.4	27,980	64.6	6.0	36.5	25.7	38,777	9.8	32.1	11.2
48 147	Fannin	22,614	59.9	13.1	26,444	56.1	9.0	33.9	31.3	42,526	11.4	29.4	7.7
48 149	Fayette	15,761	63.3	15.6	18,221	57.0	2.9	40.8	32.3	40,882	9.2	32.9	12.4
48 157	Fort Bend	296,976	36.4	37.9	363,648	68.5	6.3	45.5	13.2	76,635	6.0	11.9	36.4
48 167	Galveston	180,668	42.9	25.4	215,767	65.1	7.3	41.3	24.0	51,885	10.2	24.5	20.7
48 171	Gillespie	17,320	44.4	27.0	18,918	-	-	34.5	32.8	50,400	4.4	20.9	14.6
48 179	Gray	14,980	61.1	8.7	17,233	51.7	6.4	30.0	32.5	37,243	14.2	33.6	9.9
48 181	Grayson	77,979	49.8	18.9	91,979	63.0	6.3	39.1	29.1	44,045	10.5	27.2	12.4
48 183	Gregg	73,882	46.0	22.1	88,737	64.9	7.5	40.5	27.0	39,707	12.5	29.9	14.2
48 185	Grimes	16,963	64.8	13.9	20,100	54.3	6.9	35.0	28.1	42,729	-	31.9	10.5
48 187	Guadalupe	68,159	49.7	22.2	82,974	66.1	5.6	41.6	24.2	53,009	8.6	21.7	18.1
48 189	Hale	21,269	64.3	14.9	26,892	54.4	5.1	35.0	24.8	32,749	14.5	36.8	7.0
48 199	Hardin	33,660	58.6	13.2	39,881	61.4	5.7	38.1	28.1	50,980	10.6	22.2	14.6
48 201	Harris	2,379,423	48.5	27.0	2,862,855	68.6	7.4	44.7	18.5	48,604	13.6	24.9	20.3
48 203	Harrison	40,397	53.6	15.8	49,321	59.9	9.0	36.2	31.3	39,890	17.2	32.0	12.5
48 209	Hays	74,582	38.4	32.6	104,916	69.0	7.0	39.4	18.6	52,396	5.2	23.7	21.0

Table B-2. Counties — What: Education, Employment, and Income, 2005–2007—*Continued*

STATE County code	STATE County	Educational attainment			Employment status				Percent of house-holds with no workers	Median house-hold income (dollars)	Percent of families with income below poverty	Percent of house-holds with income less than $25,000	Percent of house-holds with income of $100,000 or more
		Total population 25 years and over	Percent with a high school diploma or less	Percent with a bachelor's degree or more	Total population 16 years and over	Percent in the labor force	Unem-ployment rate	Percent who worked full-time, year-round					
	ACS table number:	C15002	C15002	C15002	C20005	C23001	C23001	C20005	C08202	B19013	C17015	C19001	C19001
		1	2	3	4	5	6	7	8	9	10	11	12
	Texas—Cont.												
48 213	Henderson	53,694	58.2	13.1	62,500	55.7	8.2	35.6	33.4	36,187	14.1	32.9	9.3
48 215	Hidalgo..................	366,829	65.7	15.0	466,814	57.6	10.5	30.9	29.3	28,328	32.9	44.5	7.5
48 217	Hill........................	23,034	56.6	14.3	27,085	58.6	6.4	34.2	32.4	37,924	12.0	32.4	9.4
48 219	Hockley..................	13,328	54.5	16.3	17,406	60.0	7.3	37.2	26.9	43,263	11.4	30.1	11.4
48 221	Hood	33,386	45.0	22.8	38,689	59.5	6.7	35.3	33.4	51,526	9.3	22.8	18.7
48 223	Hopkins..................	22,130	56.3	16.6	25,987	62.8	6.4	41.0	24.2	39,142	12.3	30.8	9.1
48 225	Houston..................	15,866	69.0	11.2	18,512	57.9	12.2	34.7	38.2	29,893	26.1	44.4	5.8
48 227	Howard	21,530	59.9	10.6	25,556	47.9	9.2	29.2	33.5	34,549	18.9	37.9	8.9
48 231	Hunt......................	53,060	56.7	16.1	64,231	63.3	8.3	41.0	25.9	41,254	11.7	30.4	12.8
48 233	Hutchinson	14,106	57.7	12.5	16,793	59.1	5.0	36.1	34.5	39,368	14.3	31.9	6.2
48 241	Jasper	23,111	64.0	14.2	26,950	50.7	6.5	33.6	37.4	34,392	17.0	38.0	9.2
48 245	Jefferson.................	158,571	52.7	17.9	190,614	57.8	8.3	34.4	32.3	39,327	14.3	32.9	13.2
48 249	Jim Wells	24,389	64.7	9.2	30,163	56.1	7.1	32.2	27.6	31,616	22.5	40.0	8.1
48 251	Johnson..................	93,367	54.7	15.8	112,339	64.9	8.2	40.6	22.2	50,188	10.5	21.7	15.2
48 257	Kaufman.................	58,020	54.7	15.0	69,782	69.2	7.6	43.8	20.7	55,238	8.6	18.7	17.7
48 259	Kendall	19,818	36.2	36.3	23,446	64.0	3.7	40.2	25.7	56,882	-	21.2	26.9
48 265	Kerr.......................	32,869	47.3	23.8	38,000	54.8	5.6	32.6	34.9	41,041	10.6	28.1	13.8
48 273	Kleberg	17,425	56.0	17.8	23,374	58.3	9.2	32.7	31.6	32,472	23.9	39.6	8.2
48 277	Lamar	32,263	55.2	16.4	38,242	59.3	8.2	36.4	35.1	36,804	13.1	33.1	9.7
48 281	Lampasas	13,336	52.4	17.4	15,896	57.3	7.8	32.3	26.4	43,718	12.5	24.6	11.0
48 291	Liberty	48,230	65.2	7.5	57,644	53.9	8.2	32.7	29.2	41,369	10.1	28.7	11.1
48 293	Limestone...............	14,994	63.4	10.6	17,574	52.6	2.5	34.6	29.8	36,840	18.4	33.0	8.6
48 303	Lubbock..................	152,203	46.3	27.2	200,080	65.2	6.3	39.1	23.5	40,221	11.6	31.0	12.0
48 309	McLennan................	134,247	51.1	19.6	174,281	62.7	7.8	38.0	27.6	39,088	12.9	33.5	11.0
48 321	Matagorda...............	23,318	59.8	13.7	28,233	61.2	8.9	39.6	28.0	39,123	21.3	34.7	11.7
48 323	Maverick	27,755	71.6	11.7	35,360	55.9	11.9	28.5	30.3	27,953	29.6	44.8	6.0
48 325	Medina	27,307	54.8	17.4	33,051	56.3	6.9	31.2	33.6	43,977	9.7	28.5	11.4
48 329	Midland	75,489	46.5	25.1	92,434	67.2	3.2	41.5	20.7	47,163	11.4	27.1	19.3
48 331	Milam	16,684	63.0	11.8	19,221	59.4	7.1	39.5	34.2	35,977	13.7	34.6	10.6
48 339	Montgomery.............	248,975	42.8	27.9	297,385	65.9	6.4	41.0	20.0	62,376	8.4	17.7	27.5
48 341	Moore	11,580	63.5	10.4	14,161	63.2	6.7	42.2	24.3	42,150	11.6	29.2	9.8
48 347	Nacogdoches............	34,313	53.0	24.1	48,536	61.7	8.3	32.8	31.0	32,813	12.2	39.6	10.0
48 349	Navarro	30,994	59.1	13.1	37,862	60.6	10.4	36.3	32.6	36,893	17.0	34.4	8.2
48 355	Nueces	198,993	50.6	19.6	242,713	63.1	6.8	37.9	25.2	39,917	16.5	32.2	13.8
48 361	Orange	54,787	57.4	12.0	64,968	59.2	9.1	35.3	30.9	43,682	12.2	29.3	13.1
48 363	Palo Pinto	18,261	60.3	13.3	21,288	58.2	6.4	39.2	31.3	35,292	12.5	32.5	8.4
48 365	Panola	15,199	54.4	13.3	18,427	53.2	6.4	33.2	34.5	39,708	10.8	30.4	7.5
48 367	Parker....................	68,755	49.5	18.5	82,633	62.3	6.7	39.9	21.7	57,985	5.1	20.1	19.6
48 373	Polk	31,839	65.9	10.4	37,254	44.3	7.3	26.7	42.8	30,147	18.3	42.7	6.7
48 375	Potter	74,410	56.1	13.6	89,477	63.5	7.1	41.1	27.6	33,015	18.3	37.0	7.9
48 381	Randall	69,859	33.4	30.5	86,806	72.3	4.0	46.3	20.3	52,161	6.6	22.1	18.7
48 397	Rockwall.................	42,731	34.1	34.9	51,019	72.1	5.0	47.6	13.5	75,915	2.9	8.1	33.2
48 401	Rusk	32,676	59.1	13.8	38,369	53.1	4.9	34.3	29.7	42,855	8.5	31.9	11.6
48 407	San Jacinto	16,563	64.1	10.4	19,567	52.3	14.9	28.9	41.9	37,034	17.7	37.2	7.8
48 409	San Patricio.............	41,218	58.3	14.0	51,064	60.5	7.0	37.8	28.7	39,132	12.1	31.8	10.7
48 419	Shelby....................	17,054	66.4	12.9	20,153	56.0	7.2	34.0	31.5	30,383	15.2	39.5	9.0
48 423	Smith.....................	124,332	44.9	22.7	149,804	62.7	6.7	36.8	28.0	42,934	11.8	29.0	14.5
48 427	Starr	31,612	77.6	8.2	40,625	52.3	8.1	24.6	31.0	20,963	37.9	56.8	5.2
48 439	Tarrant...................	1,042,718	42.4	27.8	1,248,305	70.1	6.5	46.0	18.8	52,755	10.3	21.1	20.7
48 441	Taylor	76,432	46.5	22.9	96,825	63.6	4.9	41.0	24.9	39,107	12.6	30.5	10.2
48 449	Titus	17,313	64.2	11.9	20,929	60.7	5.9	42.1	25.4	38,883	13.0	27.4	9.7
48 451	Tom Green..............	65,501	49.7	21.2	82,307	64.6	4.6	39.7	26.8	38,830	13.3	32.2	10.4
48 453	Travis	595,038	33.5	42.2	730,150	72.8	5.9	46.9	17.6	52,073	10.5	22.3	22.7
48 457	Tyler......................	14,641	59.2	13.1	16,760	45.5	8.5	26.9	39.6	34,707	15.3	35.1	8.1
48 459	Upshur...................	25,329	56.8	13.9	29,490	59.6	7.7	35.6	28.5	38,468	11.3	31.1	10.0
48 463	Uvalde	15,702	59.6	13.3	19,522	55.3	7.2	31.3	34.0	32,424	20.1	35.8	10.2
48 465	Val Verde	28,374	66.2	15.2	34,498	57.6	7.3	35.0	30.8	33,440	22.3	40.5	7.4
48 467	Van Zandt	35,126	58.7	12.8	41,193	60.8	6.5	36.5	28.6	42,223	12.2	29.7	10.1
48 469	Victoria..................	53,721	52.2	16.5	64,775	66.1	7.7	40.4	25.2	43,294	11.4	26.4	13.5
48 471	Walker....................	39,965	59.2	15.8	54,478	42.6	11.1	21.2	31.9	29,817	16.6	38.1	7.4
48 473	Waller....................	20,250	59.1	17.3	27,357	65.4	6.7	41.4	20.1	40,187	21.2	34.0	15.1
48 477	Washington	20,809	52.4	20.8	25,555	60.5	5.1	37.1	28.0	43,591	9.8	33.6	16.7
48 479	Webb	117,257	63.5	16.5	150,284	62.8	8.6	36.2	21.8	34,236	27.1	38.8	9.0
48 481	Wharton..................	25,830	57.7	14.1	31,221	65.4	5.0	41.7	24.0	39,966	10.0	31.7	13.2
48 485	Wichita...................	79,695	50.7	20.7	100,381	63.8	5.4	39.2	26.1	40,263	11.8	29.3	11.0
48 489	Willacy...................	11,932	72.7	11.2	15,064	-	-	25.3	43.3	22,238	42.2	56.0	4.6
48 491	Williamson..............	219,571	32.9	36.3	260,933	71.8	6.1	47.2	16.8	66,468	4.5	11.9	26.3
48 493	Wilson	24,364	57.9	16.5	29,438	65.8	5.4	42.4	21.5	58,005	6.4	19.0	19.6
48 497	Wise......................	36,707	57.4	14.0	43,617	66.0	4.9	43.6	21.9	53,968	6.5	18.0	17.8
48 499	Wood	28,805	55.8	15.3	33,707	54.4	9.0	32.2	35.9	38,394	10.9	28.4	8.9
49 000	**Utah**	1,449,914	36.3	28.2	1,862,740	69.4	4.6	39.9	18.8	53,324	7.4	18.6	17.4
49 003	Box Elder	26,698	43.8	20.3	33,630	67.3	4.0	39.8	21.9	52,305	6.2	16.5	12.2
49 005	Cache....................	52,416	31.5	34.7	76,835	72.2	4.8	34.3	16.4	45,029	9.4	24.2	12.7
49 011	Davis.....................	153,809	30.5	31.9	197,992	70.5	4.1	42.7	15.2	63,184	4.4	12.0	23.3
49 021	Iron.......................	21,162	37.6	25.4	30,335	65.6	5.6	34.2	20.3	39,697	15.2	27.6	8.6

Table B-2. Counties — What: Education, Employment, and Income, 2005–2007—*Continued*

STATE County code	STATE County	Educational attainment			Employment status				Percent of households with no workers	Median household income (dollars)	Percent of families with income below poverty	Percent of households with income less than $25,000	Percent of households with income of $100,000 or more
		Total population 25 years and over	Percent with a high school diploma or less	Percent with a bachelor's degree or more	Total population 16 years and over	Percent in the labor force	Unemployment rate	Percent who worked full-time, year-round					
	ACS table number:	C15002	C15002	C15002	C20005	C23001	C23001	C20005	C08202	B19013	C17015	C19001	C19001
		1	2	3	4	5	6	7	8	9	10	11	12
	Utah—Cont.												
49 035	Salt Lake	589,516	37.1	28.8	727,296	71.9	4.6	43.1	17.8	54,214	7.1	18.4	19.3
49 039	Sanpete	12,879	46.6	20.3	17,718	60.6	4.5	31.8	25.1	41,003	12.4	28.4	8.0
49 043	Summit	22,213	26.3	48.1	27,241	75.2	3.5	46.4	12.8	83,167	-	11.1	38.4
49 045	Tooele	29,818	43.2	18.6	36,494	71.3	5.0	46.1	15.5	59,023	5.6	12.9	14.0
49 047	Uintah	16,424	54.2	12.5	20,206	69.1	3.7	38.2	22.4	57,414	9.6	20.7	21.2
49 049	Utah	225,309	26.7	35.1	323,358	67.5	4.3	33.8	15.1	53,692	8.2	18.0	17.1
49 051	Wasatch	11,606	34.7	31.1	14,287	-	-	41.2	16.4	57,542	-	15.2	17.0
49 053	Washington	75,586	40.9	20.5	93,929	60.0	4.3	34.0	32.8	46,993	5.9	18.8	12.7
49 057	Weber	128,941	41.9	22.0	159,517	69.0	5.5	42.3	21.8	52,160	8.5	20.2	14.5
50 000	**Vermont**	424,832	42.7	32.7	505,187	69.0	5.2	40.6	25.0	49,382	6.9	23.8	16.4
50 001	Addison	23,785	46.9	29.7	29,727	70.3	3.5	41.4	22.1	53,475	5.3	19.6	17.1
50 003	Bennington	25,857	45.1	31.5	30,167	63.8	4.7	38.2	28.6	45,579	5.7	22.9	17.7
50 005	Caledonia	20,901	48.1	27.8	24,945	63.6	6.1	35.0	30.3	38,707	10.4	31.6	10.7
50 007	Chittenden	98,612	30.3	45.0	122,529	72.3	4.8	41.7	20.2	58,376	6.1	19.3	23.2
50 011	Franklin	31,959	52.2	19.1	36,935	69.8	5.7	45.4	25.1	51,145	7.4	23.1	13.6
50 015	Lamoille	16,579	36.9	31.7	19,849	72.2	5.9	39.5	24.9	48,084	8.8	26.3	12.9
50 017	Orange	20,122	46.1	30.0	23,666	70.6	5.5	41.8	23.8	49,298	4.7	20.6	13.3
50 019	Orleans	19,225	57.3	20.2	22,200	63.1	5.6	40.3	32.5	38,610	11.6	33.1	8.1
50 021	Rutland	44,386	50.6	24.8	52,267	66.2	6.4	38.9	27.1	42,916	7.4	26.8	11.9
50 023	Washington	40,835	40.7	35.4	48,240	71.7	4.4	44.3	21.4	51,333	5.8	22.3	17.6
50 025	Windham	30,972	42.4	33.8	35,979	69.3	5.2	37.3	28.0	44,372	6.8	26.6	14.2
50 027	Windsor	41,537	43.7	33.6	47,221	66.4	5.2	39.4	28.0	49,532	6.4	25.5	16.6
51 000	**Virginia**	5,053,592	41.8	32.9	6,025,175	67.1	4.8	44.7	23.2	58,378	7.1	19.7	25.0
51 001	Accomack	26,912	62.4	16.6	30,823	63.5	9.4	41.3	31.4	38,801	9.6	33.2	10.5
51 003	Albemarle	58,797	27.7	53.3	74,102	63.8	3.5	39.5	23.2	62,335	4.8	17.0	27.5
51 009	Amherst	21,543	58.7	16.3	26,215	61.7	3.8	40.5	29.0	44,104	9.0	27.3	10.0
51 013	Arlington	151,102	20.2	67.0	169,317	76.5	2.5	55.6	16.5	90,047	4.5	10.8	44.6
51 015	Augusta	49,562	60.1	17.3	56,631	61.5	3.1	42.9	26.0	47,745	6.4	22.7	13.6
51 019	Bedford	45,989	49.3	23.0	53,030	66.7	2.8	46.0	24.2	52,878	7.0	20.2	16.7
51 023	Botetourt	22,697	51.0	24.0	26,042	64.7	3.8	44.4	24.9	58,187	5.4	18.6	20.4
51 027	Buchanan	17,522	70.0	8.1	20,267	-	-	24.8	54.4	23,975	20.0	51.5	2.4
51 031	Campbell	36,587	58.1	16.2	42,282	64.9	4.8	44.3	27.3	42,122	7.9	26.1	9.6
51 033	Caroline	17,629	62.2	13.5	20,800	64.9	4.4	42.2	23.3	51,454	6.2	20.5	15.6
51 035	Carroll	21,301	65.7	13.3	24,012	-	-	37.6	34.3	34,892	11.7	34.7	3.9
51 041	Chesterfield	187,741	35.9	35.8	227,774	72.3	4.2	49.0	16.2	70,350	4.7	11.0	28.4
51 047	Culpeper	29,338	55.9	19.4	34,185	66.9	4.4	42.6	22.0	59,138	6.6	19.8	22.8
51 053	Dinwiddie	17,386	60.7	14.7	20,330	63.7	4.6	46.0	20.7	52,473	6.1	16.5	14.4
51 059	Fairfax	675,523	21.9	58.4	787,726	72.4	3.3	49.3	14.9	102,460	3.5	7.5	51.5
51 061	Fauquier	43,426	42.6	28.7	51,117	72.0	3.1	48.0	18.0	80,549	-	11.7	37.8
51 065	Fluvanna	17,339	42.9	28.0	19,591	-	-	51.8	26.8	57,721	8.0	18.1	15.3
51 067	Franklin	35,334	58.3	14.5	41,098	60.7	6.5	40.3	31.7	43,956	6.6	24.3	11.2
51 069	Frederick	46,981	48.7	22.8	54,990	70.3	4.5	47.5	18.6	61,114	5.4	16.0	23.4
51 073	Gloucester	26,003	52.8	15.6	30,321	63.9	2.6	47.1	19.6	54,947	7.5	17.7	16.2
51 075	Goochland	14,320	49.6	30.9	16,318	-	-	37.7	20.4	85,639	-	10.8	36.4
51 083	Halifax	24,744	64.9	12.0	28,546	55.7	9.5	34.6	40.2	32,901	15.5	40.1	7.4
51 085	Hanover	64,686	38.5	32.7	77,309	69.8	3.7	47.3	19.3	74,273	3.6	12.1	32.8
51 087	Henrico	193,031	35.4	38.1	223,848	70.8	5.0	46.8	20.5	58,743	6.4	16.1	23.2
51 089	Henry	39,753	64.6	9.8	45,882	59.4	6.6	36.4	33.8	33,448	12.0	35.7	4.9
51 093	Isle of Wight	23,165	48.9	24.0	27,071	67.6	3.0	44.6	23.7	56,955	5.0	22.2	24.2
51 095	James City	41,556	27.6	45.6	48,370	63.7	3.1	41.7	26.6	67,984	3.1	13.2	28.8
51 099	King George	13,769	45.7	28.5	16,586	71.5	4.2	52.2	14.8	74,375	-	13.3	30.8
51 105	Lee	16,460	63.9	12.7	19,052	54.2	7.4	34.1	38.5	26,204	22.0	48.2	2.2
51 107	Loudoun	166,291	21.8	55.2	192,110	77.1	2.9	53.4	11.2	104,612	1.0	6.0	53.1
51 109	Louisa	21,656	62.0	14.9	24,545	64.4	5.1	46.4	28.4	50,559	9.1	25.0	16.6
51 117	Mecklenburg	22,884	65.0	11.6	26,081	54.9	7.2	36.6	37.7	32,459	12.1	38.3	7.4
51 121	Montgomery	46,137	36.6	41.8	75,838	59.9	5.5	32.4	25.2	41,000	7.4	31.3	12.9
51 137	Orange	21,689	55.6	18.6	25,138	62.9	3.9	42.0	28.5	53,650	6.7	18.6	19.0
51 139	Page	17,081	73.6	9.3	19,403	59.7	6.0	39.3	29.9	39,752	10.8	30.0	9.9
51 143	Pittsylvania	42,804	62.3	12.7	49,401	61.6	8.4	38.0	31.8	37,866	10.4	31.7	8.6
51 145	Powhatan	20,065	57.1	19.5	22,063	-	-	30.7	16.9	78,309	-	9.7	34.4
51 147	Prince Edward	11,733	59.2	21.8	17,709	52.2	6.3	27.9	29.5	37,750	8.5	34.4	8.5
51 149	Prince George	21,804	51.5	16.4	29,456	65.4	5.2	48.8	19.6	63,211	3.3	12.2	22.5
51 153	Prince William	216,534	35.6	36.5	258,259	77.0	4.0	55.1	12.1	85,538	3.6	7.7	40.6
51 155	Pulaski	25,470	57.7	12.8	28,886	58.6	7.4	36.9	32.1	36,397	12.4	34.3	7.2
51 161	Roanoke	62,280	38.9	31.5	72,362	66.8	3.0	45.8	25.6	55,856	3.6	17.5	21.5
51 163	Rockbridge	15,195	55.8	24.6	17,336	62.8	4.2	41.1	29.4	41,298	-	28.5	10.5
51 165	Rockingham	48,978	61.0	20.1	57,981	66.8	2.6	46.2	23.8	50,181	4.6	21.3	13.1
51 167	Russell	20,511	67.6	11.3	23,416	52.3	7.9	32.4	42.7	31,357	14.6	38.4	5.2
51 169	Scott	16,699	66.5	8.0	18,942	54.6	5.8	33.9	35.8	29,243	16.7	41.3	4.2
51 171	Shenandoah	28,261	59.7	17.4	31,848	65.0	4.1	46.7	26.4	47,364	5.5	20.9	12.2
51 173	Smyth	23,234	61.3	10.4	26,232	57.2	5.7	38.3	35.7	37,184	11.5	34.7	6.1
51 177	Spotsylvania	74,654	44.1	29.2	88,595	70.8	5.8	48.6	18.3	73,948	4.6	12.5	31.5
51 179	Stafford	72,883	38.1	33.6	88,970	71.4	4.1	49.0	13.0	85,793	3.6	7.4	40.2
51 185	Tazewell	31,562	60.5	14.0	36,013	51.5	7.0	30.9	41.6	32,390	14.5	40.9	8.3
51 187	Warren	23,734	55.8	20.0	27,795	69.3	4.8	45.5	22.7	56,443	10.6	19.9	21.4

Table B-2. Counties — What: Education, Employment, and Income, 2005–2007—*Continued*

STATE County code	STATE County	Educational attainment			Employment status				Percent of house-holds with no workers	Median house-hold income (dollars)	Percent of families with income below poverty	Percent of house-holds with income less than $25,000	Percent of house-holds with income of $100,000 or more
		Total population 25 years and over	Percent with a high school diploma or less	Percent with a bachelor's degree or more	Total population 16 years and over	Percent in the labor force	Unem-ployment rate	Percent who worked full-time, year-round					
	ACS table number:	C15002	C15002	C15002	C20005	C23001	C23001	C20005	C08202	B19013	C17015	C19001	C19001
		1	2	3	4	5	6	7	8	9	10	11	12
	Virginia—Cont.												
51 191	Washington	37,414	55.2	18.1	43,560	58.7	5.3	35.4	32.6	37,730	10.5	33.8	9.3
51 195	Wise	28,369	67.9	11.0	34,097	48.3	8.0	30.0	43.2	30,341	16.0	40.7	5.6
51 197	Wythe	20,380	61.1	12.2	23,050	63.9	5.8	38.0	30.1	35,945	10.1	31.7	7.3
51 199	York	39,943	25.6	41.2	48,520	69.8	2.3	47.4	18.8	77,335	2.9	9.3	33.0
51 510	Alexandria city	103,579	22.7	59.7	113,557	75.3	3.6	55.6	18.6	77,797	4.7	11.7	37.7
51 540	Charlottesville city	23,828	37.5	43.8	34,792	59.5	4.8	32.1	32.1	36,013	10.8	37.9	12.4
51 550	Chesapeake city	138,804	41.1	26.6	167,814	69.4	4.9	46.1	19.7	63,113	4.9	15.3	24.4
51 590	Danville city	31,681	57.9	14.3	36,642	54.9	12.8	30.4	41.4	29,528	19.8	43.6	6.9
51 600	Fairfax city	16,180	28.4	48.9	18,808	69.1	4.4	46.1	18.9	93,441	-	7.0	44.8
51 630	Fredericksburg city	12,701	47.0	29.8	17,641	57.6	5.0	34.6	29.4	42,909	-	29.9	16.4
51 650	Hampton city	94,048	46.0	20.7	116,707	66.8	6.9	44.9	24.9	47,408	9.9	22.9	11.9
51 660	Harrisonburg city	19,360	51.3	33.1	37,101	52.7	5.8	23.8	27.4	34,905	-	37.1	10.6
51 670	Hopewell city	14,600	60.6	11.1	16,841	61.5	5.6	42.9	31.8	39,931	10.2	29.5	5.4
51 680	Lynchburg city	42,299	48.0	27.8	56,786	57.9	7.3	30.7	32.5	36,385	15.1	33.8	11.2
51 683	Manassas city	22,455	47.3	26.4	26,699	71.0	4.8	51.4	15.4	74,221	-	10.5	36.2
51 700	Newport News city	111,233	42.2	21.7	134,565	69.1	6.1	44.1	23.5	46,082	11.2	25.9	12.0
51 710	Norfolk city	137,679	48.2	22.9	182,896	68.5	6.8	44.5	26.2	40,361	14.0	29.1	11.3
51 730	Petersburg city	21,546	64.4	15.3	25,235	61.0	13.9	40.0	33.7	34,573	10.2	31.5	5.8
51 740	Portsmouth city	63,660	50.6	18.5	78,305	65.1	6.7	42.1	28.9	43,473	11.7	26.7	11.8
51 760	Richmond city	129,899	46.7	32.0	159,089	63.4	10.6	37.1	31.3	37,442	16.2	33.8	12.9
51 770	Roanoke city	65,332	51.7	20.6	73,831	61.1	6.9	38.0	34.9	35,530	13.7	32.9	8.5
51 775	Salem city	16,003	48.6	23.1	20,815	64.5	4.3	39.3	27.0	46,997	3.6	21.3	12.1
51 790	Staunton city	16,649	52.8	23.4	19,175	58.6	3.6	36.5	30.1	39,756	10.3	32.1	7.2
51 800	Suffolk city	51,035	46.0	23.4	60,748	68.0	5.7	45.8	22.8	61,464	9.0	19.8	22.1
51 810	Virginia Beach city	282,498	34.0	31.1	337,218	72.3	3.7	48.8	18.5	62,477	5.2	13.0	23.3
51 820	Waynesboro city	14,821	59.6	21.4	16,813	-	-	38.2	34.8	44,039	11.0	29.0	9.0
51 840	Winchester city	17,182	50.3	26.9	20,780	66.9	5.8	41.0	28.0	43,760	6.1	22.6	14.8
53 000	**Washington**	4,743,790	36.7	30.0	5,028,054	65.9	6.5	38.1	25.6	53,940	8.0	21.3	20.7
53 003	Asotin	14,372	46.0	18.8	16,661	59.5	6.9	31.3	37.6	40,049	13.6	31.3	8.1
53 005	Benton	101,367	40.6	25.5	120,359	65.4	7.6	38.4	24.5	53,050	8.9	21.7	21.6
53 007	Chelan	45,775	47.1	22.1	54,703	61.9	6.6	33.2	31.5	44,633	10.0	26.2	12.7
53 009	Clallam	50,438	40.9	21.7	58,032	52.1	5.7	28.0	42.4	41,797	10.4	26.9	11.1
53 011	Clark	266,533	37.6	24.8	313,237	67.4	7.6	39.3	23.6	56,098	7.5	18.3	20.3
53 015	Cowlitz	65,636	46.7	13.4	77,015	60.7	8.8	31.4	31.3	44,227	11.6	25.9	11.4
53 017	Douglas	22,397	49.4	17.8	27,009	66.1	7.4	35.5	25.1	41,862	15.0	25.2	12.1
53 021	Franklin	36,770	59.0	13.8	46,142	65.9	7.7	37.7	22.4	43,102	16.3	26.7	13.6
53 025	Grant	48,525	57.0	13.5	59,509	63.4	10.8	33.4	29.0	39,604	14.8	29.6	9.2
53 027	Grays Harbor	48,322	54.0	12.7	57,037	56.9	10.1	29.2	36.9	40,896	12.2	29.3	9.4
53 029	Island	54,115	32.6	27.2	64,504	60.5	4.2	34.8	34.6	53,606	6.1	20.0	17.4
53 031	Jefferson	22,088	31.7	34.8	24,906	55.5	8.3	23.5	42.9	43,409	6.8	25.7	11.4
53 033	King	1,280,963	27.5	43.7	1,480,514	69.7	5.3	42.0	21.8	64,915	6.0	17.4	29.3
53 035	Kitsap	159,845	33.2	27.6	188,574	64.5	7.0	36.9	26.2	57,139	5.6	18.3	21.1
53 037	Kittitas	21,794	39.1	30.4	31,783	59.6	6.0	25.9	30.9	39,390	12.3	37.2	11.6
53 039	Klickitat	13,894	52.7	17.2	15,784	55.1	7.9	27.9	39.7	41,137	14.1	33.5	8.8
53 041	Lewis	48,915	49.9	15.3	58,107	56.9	7.7	30.6	34.7	43,424	10.6	27.5	10.4
53 045	Mason	38,371	48.9	16.5	44,725	51.4	7.9	30.6	38.2	45,671	8.5	25.6	10.1
53 047	Okanogan	26,257	52.5	17.5	31,248	57.5	7.5	27.8	33.8	35,182	16.6	38.9	7.9
53 049	Pacific	15,761	45.5	16.4	17,880	53.0	8.0	29.0	39.3	37,092	11.4	31.8	6.7
53 053	Pierce	495,529	41.5	23.0	590,714	66.0	6.7	40.1	25.1	54,440	8.2	19.7	19.2
53 057	Skagit	76,072	42.5	22.2	90,518	61.1	4.6	33.7	31.4	50,107	9.2	22.5	15.9
53 061	Snohomish	438,089	36.8	27.0	515,828	69.9	5.5	42.5	21.6	61,881	5.4	16.0	23.9
53 063	Spokane	293,788	34.7	26.8	354,256	63.9	6.8	35.4	28.1	44,694	8.8	27.0	13.0
53 065	Stevens	27,688	50.0	15.8	32,898	57.4	12.7	26.5	38.5	39,474	11.9	30.7	9.5
53 067	Thurston	157,968	34.2	31.1	186,997	65.7	6.2	38.9	25.6	55,129	7.7	20.2	19.7
53 071	Walla Walla	36,308	42.1	23.1	46,017	58.1	7.8	29.2	28.8	42,269	13.8	30.6	10.9
53 073	Whatcom	120,650	36.1	31.5	152,873	64.6	6.2	32.7	27.6	46,766	8.1	27.2	14.8
53 075	Whitman	20,561	23.2	48.2	35,358	58.0	6.5	23.9	31.1	32,083	10.8	42.4	11.4
53 077	Yakima	138,305	58.5	15.7	168,613	63.8	10.6	33.8	27.9	40,321	15.5	31.5	10.4
54 000	**West Virginia**	1,257,231	60.9	16.9	1,466,327	55.3	6.9	34.0	36.1	36,088	13.3	35.6	9.1
54 003	Berkeley	64,072	56.3	19.4	74,053	68.0	5.6	45.8	24.0	52,795	7.0	20.9	14.7
54 005	Boone	17,829	78.0	7.4	20,152	-	-	31.1	41.2	37,815	12.6	35.6	8.5
54 009	Brooke	17,108	62.7	13.4	19,886	59.3	7.6	31.8	32.2	38,711	8.1	28.9	8.9
54 011	Cabell	62,932	51.1	20.9	77,017	56.4	6.6	32.4	37.4	33,971	13.4	37.9	10.4
54 019	Fayette	32,233	70.0	11.7	37,594	51.3	6.4	30.9	39.2	29,229	17.4	42.9	4.8
54 025	Greenbrier	24,677	59.6	18.0	28,530	53.6	5.3	30.2	38.3	32,608	13.5	37.6	5.6
54 027	Hampshire	15,425	73.7	10.0	17,760	56.8	8.1	36.7	33.6	36,071	14.4	36.0	7.6
54 029	Hancock	22,481	58.6	14.1	25,381	58.4	7.2	33.7	33.8	39,700	9.4	30.8	10.6
54 033	Harrison	47,751	55.7	19.8	54,876	58.0	7.0	35.1	34.2	38,386	15.5	34.0	11.5
54 035	Jackson	19,753	57.4	16.1	22,719	52.9	7.9	31.6	38.3	40,924	14.7	33.0	9.7
54 037	Jefferson	33,073	50.6	26.6	38,935	65.5	4.5	47.8	22.8	63,462	4.7	16.1	25.8
54 039	Kanawha	137,139	53.4	22.5	155,733	59.5	6.8	38.2	33.2	40,041	10.2	31.0	11.1
54 043	Lincoln	15,618	73.6	7.6	17,812	45.0	9.9	27.0	45.5	27,850	21.0	47.6	6.0
54 045	Logan	25,411	74.8	8.7	28,927	42.6	12.1	26.6	46.2	30,977	20.4	39.3	6.3
54 047	McDowell	16,717	82.0	5.0	19,034	33.2	6.5	20.2	59.9	20,634	29.8	59.9	3.0
54 049	Marion	39,214	55.6	19.5	46,581	57.4	5.4	36.2	34.8	34,079	11.2	36.4	8.4

Table B-2. Counties — What: Education, Employment, and Income, 2005–2007—Continued

STATE County code	STATE County	Educational attainment			Employment status				Percent of households with no workers	Median household income (dollars)	Percent of families with income below poverty	Percent of households with income less than $25,000	Percent of households with income of $100,000 or more
		Total population 25 years and over	Percent with a high school diploma or less	Percent with a bachelor's degree or more	Total population 16 years and over	Percent in the labor force	Unemployment rate	Percent who worked full-time, year-round					
	ACS table number:	C15002	C15002	C15002	C20005	C23001	C23001	C20005	C08202	B19013	C17015	C19001	C19001
		1	2	3	4	5	6	7	8	9	10	11	12
	West Virginia—Cont.												
54 051	Marshall	23,927	60.9	11.7	27,332	54.5	8.6	32.3	37.2	32,034	12.8	37.9	5.1
54 053	Mason	18,247	65.9	13.1	20,740	54.5	8.9	30.0	37.1	33,506	14.6	38.3	6.5
54 055	Mercer	43,278	62.6	16.8	49,610	47.6	5.9	30.3	45.0	30,447	17.2	42.5	5.7
54 057	Mineral	18,489	63.1	12.3	21,705	59.1	5.9	35.3	28.7	36,551	12.8	34.2	8.0
54 059	Mingo	18,625	73.6	9.0	21,500	38.9	7.2	24.2	52.6	30,061	17.2	43.5	6.2
54 061	Monongalia	50,079	46.9	34.3	73,183	58.0	5.2	32.7	27.2	38,119	9.7	34.5	13.0
54 067	Nicholas	18,687	64.9	13.3	21,429	54.0	7.8	33.4	39.7	36,445	14.8	37.7	7.0
54 069	Ohio	30,983	51.1	24.7	36,764	59.2	7.8	34.9	36.5	35,609	13.6	36.7	10.3
54 077	Preston	21,361	67.5	12.1	24,635	52.6	6.7	32.9	36.3	32,788	14.1	36.8	5.4
54 079	Putnam	37,461	52.0	21.9	42,971	60.1	3.8	41.1	29.2	46,407	10.5	27.4	16.4
54 081	Raleigh	56,244	61.0	15.2	64,146	52.5	6.6	32.9	38.8	37,001	11.6	37.7	8.0
54 083	Randolph	19,985	67.3	16.9	23,014	53.0	5.7	33.2	36.5	33,606	12.9	38.1	6.2
54 097	Upshur	15,628	65.8	16.4	18,968	53.6	7.9	31.3	36.0	31,822	18.2	39.2	6.9
54 099	Wayne	29,151	64.0	12.5	33,314	51.0	6.9	30.1	41.4	32,157	18.3	39.7	7.3
54 107	Wood	60,920	54.0	17.4	69,722	57.9	8.4	33.4	34.9	36,956	14.9	35.4	9.7
54 109	Wyoming	17,249	76.5	8.0	19,592	43.6	4.9	29.2	46.0	29,461	17.0	43.3	3.9
55 000	**Wisconsin**	3,692,408	46.2	25.1	4,408,022	68.7	5.8	41.5	25.0	50,309	7.1	22.6	15.6
55 001	Adams	15,665	60.3	11.2	17,466	54.2	8.5	31.9	35.6	37,607	11.8	29.6	7.8
55 005	Barron	31,607	56.2	16.8	37,047	66.4	6.0	39.9	27.8	42,163	8.6	29.2	9.9
55 009	Brown	157,603	45.2	25.7	187,881	70.9	6.2	43.0	23.2	51,624	7.6	21.9	16.2
55 015	Calumet	29,056	48.3	24.5	34,134	74.5	3.9	45.9	17.1	58,729	5.2	16.6	16.4
55 017	Chippewa	40,454	51.8	16.0	47,664	69.6	6.0	41.8	26.9	47,887	6.9	24.2	10.8
55 019	Clark	21,471	65.3	10.8	25,410	67.2	5.4	43.4	26.2	42,526	7.1	26.3	8.1
55 021	Columbia	37,973	48.4	20.8	43,965	68.5	4.1	44.7	24.8	54,095	4.0	19.9	16.4
55 025	Dane	304,001	27.0	44.7	377,743	73.9	4.3	44.1	19.1	59,103	4.6	17.8	23.1
55 027	Dodge	60,981	57.5	14.6	71,355	65.4	4.9	41.2	23.7	51,571	5.5	20.0	13.3
55 029	Door	20,809	46.3	24.3	23,410	66.6	5.1	38.9	29.1	43,711	4.8	25.3	11.6
55 031	Douglas	29,748	47.0	19.9	35,176	64.1	5.5	35.5	30.4	40,944	9.2	29.9	11.2
55 033	Dunn	24,856	49.5	23.8	34,324	68.2	6.6	36.9	20.3	47,993	5.7	23.3	10.1
55 035	Eau Claire	59,432	38.1	29.6	77,937	70.1	5.2	37.7	24.0	45,415	7.1	26.9	13.1
55 039	Fond du Lac	66,391	54.2	17.5	78,779	69.7	5.2	43.2	25.2	50,647	5.4	21.0	11.9
55 043	Grant	31,096	53.2	18.4	39,979	65.7	4.6	39.8	27.8	42,219	4.9	27.6	9.3
55 045	Green	23,983	50.4	18.5	27,897	71.9	4.8	49.1	22.1	50,327	4.5	20.2	14.1
55 049	Iowa	15,856	47.9	23.6	18,343	74.8	4.9	49.9	19.7	51,518	3.9	20.2	11.9
55 055	Jefferson	52,778	50.6	20.5	63,231	72.4	5.7	43.8	23.5	53,256	5.0	19.8	14.8
55 057	Juneau	18,280	61.6	12.4	21,273	66.5	6.2	40.5	27.5	43,663	9.0	24.5	8.5
55 059	Kenosha	103,865	47.3	20.8	123,964	67.5	7.4	40.5	23.4	54,012	7.6	21.4	18.0
55 061	Kewaunee	14,003	60.2	13.2	16,414	70.8	4.5	47.7	26.5	51,734	4.6	22.6	10.8
55 063	La Crosse	69,634	38.2	29.2	89,231	70.2	5.0	40.6	23.5	46,604	7.3	26.2	13.5
55 067	Langlade	14,388	60.7	12.6	16,539	63.9	7.1	34.2	31.8	38,546	8.6	29.4	8.5
55 069	Lincoln	20,763	56.2	14.5	24,121	65.5	4.7	41.0	28.0	45,953	7.1	23.0	11.1
55 071	Manitowoc	55,678	54.0	17.7	65,282	69.4	5.5	42.5	27.5	47,075	5.5	23.6	10.9
55 073	Marathon	86,676	50.5	20.5	101,948	72.7	5.2	46.0	22.9	52,241	4.7	20.2	14.4
55 075	Marinette	29,921	59.4	14.1	35,173	63.2	6.2	34.9	31.9	40,488	9.5	29.8	8.5
55 079	Milwaukee	610,116	47.7	25.5	729,055	65.3	8.9	39.0	28.4	42,205	13.5	29.0	12.8
55 081	Monroe	28,023	56.1	14.2	32,823	69.0	4.5	43.7	25.1	43,845	9.3	25.1	8.9
55 083	Oconto	26,032	57.7	13.4	30,177	68.5	6.1	39.7	26.3	45,944	7.8	25.5	10.7
55 085	Oneida	26,619	42.5	22.3	30,542	62.9	4.1	36.4	31.6	44,526	6.9	25.0	12.5
55 087	Outagamie	112,619	45.7	24.7	133,532	72.8	5.4	44.0	21.6	55,856	5.0	19.6	16.1
55 089	Ozaukee	57,522	29.0	43.4	68,315	69.6	3.1	42.1	22.6	73,197	2.4	13.3	31.0
55 093	Pierce	24,088	41.9	25.0	31,808	76.9	5.4	42.5	18.6	58,011	2.3	17.9	17.8
55 095	Polk	30,286	50.4	17.8	35,214	67.7	5.6	40.7	27.6	50,206	5.2	21.9	11.4
55 097	Portage	42,271	46.0	26.1	55,269	69.7	5.7	38.2	24.0	50,465	5.7	23.8	14.2
55 101	Racine	127,791	47.5	22.9	150,504	66.9	5.6	41.5	23.1	53,250	7.3	20.9	16.8
55 105	Rock	105,153	52.8	18.4	123,091	67.8	6.8	41.2	28.1	48,698	8.2	22.1	12.8
55 109	St. Croix	51,541	35.5	32.1	60,631	76.5	4.1	48.9	18.2	67,347	3.9	14.0	24.7
55 111	Sauk	39,610	51.0	20.1	46,012	72.5	5.1	45.1	21.5	47,691	6.4	20.9	12.6
55 115	Shawano	28,325	63.0	11.9	32,907	65.9	6.3	41.4	28.5	44,141	10.0	26.0	8.0
55 117	Sheboygan	77,528	50.7	20.8	90,692	70.3	5.3	44.0	23.7	51,464	5.1	19.0	14.1
55 121	Trempealeau	19,060	55.0	16.9	22,004	68.8	3.5	44.9	27.2	44,381	6.0	26.7	10.3
55 123	Vernon	19,112	53.7	18.0	22,423	64.1	4.2	41.4	28.3	39,800	9.5	29.7	8.2
55 125	Vilas	16,624	41.8	26.4	18,724	58.9	5.9	31.9	34.0	42,188	5.9	25.2	14.4
55 127	Walworth	64,572	47.0	24.8	79,944	71.0	5.7	38.1	23.8	53,099	5.7	21.5	17.3
55 131	Washington	85,334	43.1	25.1	99,450	73.6	4.2	47.7	20.4	62,776	4.6	14.9	22.2
55 133	Waukesha	254,915	33.5	38.3	299,629	70.6	3.9	44.2	22.1	71,907	2.4	12.7	30.7
55 135	Waupaca	36,124	58.7	16.0	41,737	65.7	6.0	39.1	28.4	46,755	7.6	25.0	10.4
55 137	Waushara	17,351	61.5	12.3	20,316	58.4	6.9	35.2	33.9	41,951	7.6	26.2	6.5
55 139	Winnebago	107,246	47.6	24.2	130,491	67.2	5.3	40.6	25.0	49,395	6.3	22.7	13.7
55 141	Wood	51,208	50.7	19.0	59,315	66.8	5.6	38.8	28.6	47,879	5.4	24.6	11.2

Table B-2. Counties — What: Education, Employment, and Income, 2005–2007—*Continued*

STATE County code	STATE County	Educational attainment			Employment status				Percent of house-holds with no workers	Median house-hold income (dollars)	Percent of families with income below poverty	Percent of house-holds with income less than $25,000	Percent of house-holds with income of $100,000 or more
		Total population 25 years and over	Percent with a high school diploma or less	Percent with a bachelor's degree or more	Total population 16 years and over	Percent in the labor force	Unem-ployment rate	Percent who worked full-time, year-round					
	ACS table number:	C15002	C15002	C15002	C20005	C23001	C23001	C20005	C08202	B19013	C17015	C19001	C19001
		1	2	3	4	5	6	7	8	9	10	11	12
56 000	**Wyoming**	336,599	42.1	23.1	405,511	70.0	4.1	42.5	22.7	50,009	5.7	22.5	15.7
56 001	Albany	17,466	25.2	49.7	27,347	69.5	3.7	33.9	19.9	40,768	8.1	31.0	14.1
56 005	Campbell	24,094	47.0	16.8	29,284	79.8	4.4	50.2	14.4	71,335	-	13.7	28.7
56 013	Fremont	24,205	46.2	21.6	28,560	65.1	4.0	37.7	26.4	43,349	7.9	26.0	12.3
56 021	Laramie	56,321	38.8	22.6	66,317	70.7	4.7	45.5	23.2	49,748	5.1	20.7	15.0
56 025	Natrona	45,986	42.0	19.7	55,413	67.8	4.6	43.6	23.9	47,648	6.8	25.3	15.5
56 029	Park	18,199	37.8	25.8	21,995	68.8	4.0	39.1	24.8	41,361	5.3	27.0	10.2
56 033	Sheridan	19,080	41.0	21.5	22,051	67.6	3.7	42.8	27.1	45,040	3.1	25.1	13.4
56 037	Sweetwater	24,312	47.4	16.9	29,371	73.6	3.7	46.0	16.9	64,050	6.3	14.4	22.7
56 039	Teton	14,509	25.9	52.3	16,182	-	-	44.2	20.9	63,968	-	12.0	25.5
56 041	Uinta	12,354	46.1	16.0	14,848	73.7	5.6	46.2	15.8	53,698	6.6	17.2	17.6

Table B-3. Metropolitan Areas — What: Education, Employment, and Income, 2005–2007

Metro area or division code	Area name	Educational attainment			Employment status				Percent of households with no workers	Median household income (dollars)	Percent of families with income below poverty	Percent of households with income less than $25,000	Percent of households with income of $100,000 or more
		Total population 25 years and over	Percent with a high school diploma or less	Percent with a bachelor's degree or more	Total population 16 years and over	Percent in the labor force	Unemployment rate	Percent who worked full-time, year-round					
	ACS table number:	C15002	C15002	C15002	C20005	C23001	C23001	C20005	C08202	B19013	C17015	C19001	C19001
		1	2	3	4	5	6	7	8	9	10	11	12
10180	Abilene, TX	99,021	49.9	20.2	123,814	60.1	4.8	38.7	26.1	39,371	11.7	30.3	9.7
10420	Akron, OH	465,558	45.9	27.7	555,019	66.7	6.9	40.4	26.9	47,336	8.7	24.7	16.2
10500	Albany, GA	101,269	53.0	17.9	125,562	61.5	11.2	37.0	29.9	39,166	16.2	33.4	11.9
10580	Albany-Schenectady-Troy, NY	569,402	41.3	31.6	688,121	65.7	5.4	41.2	26.9	54,755	6.7	21.0	20.3
10740	Albuquerque, NM	530,414	41.0	29.2	637,100	65.4	6.2	39.7	25.1	45,634	11.1	25.8	15.4
10780	Alexandria, LA	97,383	56.2	17.7	115,762	59.1	6.6	36.6	29.8	36,753	15.2	35.0	11.1
10900	Allentown-Bethlehem-Easton, PA-NJ	540,684	50.7	25.1	634,097	64.9	5.9	40.6	26.4	54,420	6.0	20.9	20.2
11020	Altoona, PA	87,737	61.4	16.7	101,828	60.1	6.6	36.8	34.3	40,196	9.1	30.6	9.2
11100	Amarillo, TX	150,037	45.3	21.6	183,130	67.5	5.4	43.7	24.1	41,944	12.1	29.3	13.5
11180	Ames, IA	45,348	24.8	47.6	70,280	69.9	4.8	34.0	21.1	45,991	6.2	26.7	16.2
11260	Anchorage, AK	222,077	35.6	29.1	273,013	71.6	7.8	39.9	19.6	65,534	6.8	15.7	27.2
11300	Anderson, IN	89,741	57.4	16.2	104,775	59.1	8.6	36.2	32.3	42,616	9.6	27.3	10.1
11340	Anderson, SC	120,194	56.6	17.3	139,436	61.4	8.3	37.0	31.4	41,078	11.7	31.1	10.3
11460	Ann Arbor, MI	214,503	24.7	51.4	280,832	66.3	6.6	35.8	22.5	59,887	7.3	22.4	26.3
11500	Anniston-Oxford, AL	74,731	57.3	17.0	89,576	58.9	9.3	37.2	33.6	37,736	13.3	34.3	10.2
11540	Appleton, WI	141,675	46.3	24.7	167,666	73.1	5.1	44.4	20.7	56,436	5.0	19.0	16.2
11700	Asheville, NC	282,007	43.5	27.2	323,733	61.6	5.0	36.6	31.5	42,153	8.9	28.5	12.2
12020	Athens-Clarke County, GA	105,849	45.2	33.7	147,641	62.8	6.6	35.8	25.6	40,115	12.2	34.9	13.2
12060	Atlanta-Sandy Springs-Marietta, GA	3,290,191	40.9	33.5	3,887,346	70.0	7.2	45.3	19.1	57,307	8.5	18.6	23.3
12100	Atlantic City, NJ	181,380	51.9	22.8	211,866	65.8	7.6	41.7	26.2	53,473	7.8	22.0	19.8
12220	Auburn-Opelika, AL	71,089	41.6	30.8	102,395	63.1	6.0	36.8	28.9	38,849	11.9	35.4	12.4
12260	Augusta-Richmond County, GA-SC	334,023	50.3	22.1	403,274	61.9	7.1	38.4	29.3	43,190	13.5	29.0	14.1
12420	Austin-Round Rock, TX	957,365	35.5	38.2	1,177,255	71.5	6.1	45.9	17.9	54,827	8.6	20.3	22.7
12540	Bakersfield, CA	451,672	57.9	14.4	564,731	59.8	9.6	33.6	25.9	44,620	16.9	27.6	15.7
12580	Baltimore-Towson, MD	1,762,711	41.5	33.0	2,095,810	67.0	5.7	43.4	23.6	62,524	6.3	18.6	27.6
12620	Bangor, ME	99,907	49.1	22.9	121,213	62.4	6.0	36.0	30.7	41,336	8.9	30.8	11.1
12700	Barnstable Town, MA	166,732	33.2	38.5	188,587	61.0	5.5	34.1	33.9	58,422	3.8	18.3	21.9
12940	Baton Rouge, LA	467,034	50.3	24.4	582,983	64.6	7.2	40.0	25.2	44,303	13.1	29.3	16.0
12980	Battle Creek, MI	90,876	49.1	18.4	107,160	61.5	8.5	37.3	31.0	42,181	12.6	30.2	12.2
13020	Bay City, MI	74,209	50.0	16.9	86,768	63.0	8.8	36.0	33.1	43,353	8.4	26.6	11.9
13140	Beaumont-Port Arthur, TX	247,018	54.5	16.0	295,463	58.6	8.1	35.1	31.4	42,056	13.3	30.7	13.4
13380	Bellingham, WA	120,650	36.1	31.5	152,873	64.6	6.2	32.7	27.6	46,766	8.1	27.2	14.8
13460	Bend, OR	102,618	34.7	28.2	118,804	66.0	4.9	38.6	26.6	53,436	5.2	18.9	16.0
13740	Billings, MT	99,143	40.5	27.3	116,091	67.4	3.5	40.5	24.4	44,925	7.9	26.4	12.9
13780	Binghamton, NY	165,289	48.1	23.9	201,557	61.5	6.4	36.3	32.2	42,930	10.4	29.1	12.7
13820	Birmingham-Hoover, AL	729,779	46.3	25.6	859,437	62.9	6.6	41.4	27.4	46,667	10.2	27.2	17.0
13900	Bismarck, ND	66,447	37.5	28.7	81,266	72.2	2.8	46.1	21.3	48,261	5.5	25.3	13.9
13980	Blacksburg-Christiansburg-Radford, VA	90,349	45.3	29.0	132,947	58.4	6.8	32.4	29.5	37,827	9.6	33.8	10.3
14020	Bloomington, IN	108,652	46.5	29.6	151,088	59.2	6.4	32.8	30.0	39,395	10.8	33.7	11.2
14060	Bloomington-Normal, IL	95,265	33.6	39.5	129,068	69.8	5.9	40.0	19.9	54,252	7.2	22.7	20.3
14260	Boise City-Nampa, ID	358,541	39.3	27.8	424,415	68.4	5.6	41.3	22.0	50,297	7.7	21.3	15.5
14460	Boston-Cambridge-Quincy, MA-NH	3,026,148	37.1	40.8	3,581,631	68.1	5.7	41.6	23.9	66,870	6.4	18.9	31.0
14460 14484	•Boston-Quincy, MA Division	1,246,871	38.8	39.0	1,489,305	67.5	6.5	40.8	25.1	63,620	7.7	21.0	29.3
14460 15764	•Cambridge-Newton-Framingham, MA Division	1,008,311	32.9	47.6	1,184,506	68.8	5.1	42.6	22.3	74,010	4.8	15.9	35.2
14460 37764	•Peabody, MA Division	491,691	40.4	35.3	577,669	66.3	5.4	40.6	26.4	61,505	8.0	21.8	28.4
14460 40484	•Rockingham County-Strafford County, NH Division	279,275	38.5	33.7	330,151	71.3	5.0	43.8	20.1	67,353	4.2	14.8	27.9
14500	Boulder, CO	186,982	22.0	55.7	232,799	70.2	5.9	38.1	20.2	63,064	6.2	19.9	29.9
14540	Bowling Green, KY	71,862	47.9	26.2	90,686	66.7	5.4	39.4	23.3	42,383	11.9	29.7	12.7
14740	Bremerton-Silverdale, WA	159,845	33.2	27.6	188,574	64.5	7.0	36.9	26.2	57,139	5.6	18.3	21.1
14860	Bridgeport-Stamford-Norwalk, CT	596,501	37.0	42.6	694,008	66.6	5.8	41.2	21.7	78,353	5.0	15.4	39.4
15180	Brownsville-Harlingen, TX	209,078	63.1	14.5	262,381	53.4	7.5	31.8	30.9	28,026	32.2	45.4	7.9
15260	Brunswick, GA	65,912	53.5	22.0	77,586	63.0	5.0	40.9	29.7	44,613	10.0	27.3	14.7
15380	Buffalo-Niagara Falls, NY	763,819	45.1	26.1	913,890	62.0	7.0	36.0	32.8	44,747	9.9	28.2	14.9
15500	Burlington, NC	94,326	51.8	19.8	112,226	66.3	6.4	41.2	24.1	42,370	12.1	29.1	10.7
15540	Burlington-South Burlington, VT	135,964	36.0	38.4	165,602	71.6	5.1	42.4	21.5	56,284	6.5	20.2	20.8
15940	Canton-Massillon, OH	277,858	55.8	19.3	325,152	64.5	7.0	37.3	29.3	44,530	9.1	27.1	12.5
15980	Cape Coral-Fort Myers, FL	409,807	47.2	24.1	462,849	57.4	5.3	36.9	35.7	49,742	6.7	20.0	17.4
16180	Carson City, NV	37,425	44.6	20.6	43,480	62.7	7.0	39.3	31.7	50,140	8.4	23.4	14.7
16220	Casper, WY	45,986	42.0	19.7	55,413	67.8	4.6	43.6	23.9	47,648	6.8	25.3	15.5
16300	Cedar Rapids, IA	165,298	41.7	26.1	195,115	70.4	5.2	44.2	23.6	49,948	6.7	22.5	15.6
16580	Champaign-Urbana, IL	127,001	35.9	38.7	179,032	66.6	6.0	35.5	24.1	44,115	9.1	30.1	14.7
16620	Charleston, WV	214,968	57.4	19.7	244,678	57.1	6.4	36.9	34.4	39,526	11.6	32.3	11.2
16700	Charleston-North Charleston, SC	398,135	43.3	28.6	481,343	66.0	5.7	42.8	24.3	48,315	9.7	24.1	16.3
16740	Charlotte-Gastonia-Concord, NC-SC	1,032,227	40.5	31.2	1,216,299	70.6	7.1	44.6	20.7	51,702	8.5	21.8	20.0
16820	Charlottesville, VA	123,096	37.5	41.5	154,745	62.6	3.9	39.9	26.2	53,076	6.6	22.8	20.4
16860	Chattanooga, TN-GA	344,824	50.8	21.1	405,197	63.4	7.0	39.4	28.1	42,801	9.9	28.4	13.4

Table B-3. Metropolitan Areas — What: Education, Employment, and Income, 2005–2007—*Continued*

Metro area or division code	Area name	Educational attainment			Employment status				Percent of households with no workers	Median household income (dollars)	Percent of families with income below poverty	Percent of households with income less than $25,000	Percent of households with income of $100,000 or more
		Total population 25 years and over	Percent with a high school diploma or less	Percent with a bachelor's degree or more	Total population 16 years and over	Percent in the labor force	Unemployment rate	Percent who worked full-time, year-round					
	ACS table number:	C15002	C15002	C15002	C20005	C23001	C23001	C20005	C08202	B19013	C17015	C19001	C19001
		1	2	3	4	5	6	7	8	9	10	11	12
16940	Cheyenne, WY	56,321	38.8	22.6	66,317	70.7	4.7	45.5	23.2	49,748	5.1	20.7	15.0
16980	Chicago-Naperville-Joliet, IL-IN-WI	6,095,362	41.9	31.8	7,281,818	67.4	7.6	41.6	23.2	58,946	8.7	20.2	24.6
16980 16974	•Chicago-Naperville-Joliet, IL Division	5,101,047	41.6	32.4	6,091,826	67.3	7.7	41.7	23.1	58,624	9.0	20.4	24.6
16980 23844	•Gary, IN Division	451,996	51.9	19.4	538,071	64.4	8.0	37.5	28.1	50,440	10.5	24.3	15.7
16980 29404	•Lake County-Kenosha County, IL-WI Division	542,319	36.2	37.1	651,921	70.3	6.4	43.3	18.9	71,683	5.0	14.2	32.5
17020	Chico, CA	136,278	39.4	24.4	177,150	58.4	9.7	27.3	35.0	40,011	11.3	32.4	12.6
17140	Cincinnati-Middletown, OH-KY-IN	1,379,095	47.6	27.1	1,644,606	66.8	6.3	41.4	25.3	51,926	8.1	23.0	19.0
17300	Clarksville, TN-KY	154,314	47.0	19.5	188,219	64.6	6.5	41.8	24.9	44,531	11.4	26.5	11.2
17420	Cleveland, TN	74,697	55.8	18.1	87,126	61.7	8.1	38.2	29.7	38,605	11.2	31.1	10.0
17460	Cleveland-Elyria-Mentor, OH	1,423,585	46.3	26.3	1,662,798	65.1	8.1	38.8	29.1	47,600	10.0	26.4	16.8
17660	Coeur d'Alene, ID	86,483	41.7	20.5	102,247	65.2	5.9	35.4	28.5	41,576	9.7	27.1	10.3
17780	College Station-Bryan, TX	102,954	44.2	34.4	160,735	61.7	6.5	33.6	24.5	36,599	15.5	38.4	12.6
17820	Colorado Springs, CO	384,459	31.9	33.7	461,029	70.5	6.1	43.3	20.8	55,064	7.3	20.2	20.4
17860	Columbia, MO	94,468	32.2	44.7	127,930	70.4	5.6	39.5	20.4	43,063	9.8	28.9	14.8
17900	Columbia, SC	451,729	43.3	29.4	553,591	67.3	5.8	43.0	23.6	46,973	9.9	25.3	15.5
17980	Columbus, GA-AL	177,572	50.0	20.5	219,750	61.9	7.5	38.8	31.9	38,924	16.0	33.5	11.5
18020	Columbus, IN	49,658	50.4	25.7	56,856	66.5	5.7	42.8	24.0	52,172	8.4	20.7	16.2
18140	Columbus, OH	1,119,606	42.6	31.8	1,340,482	68.6	6.4	47.8	23.3	51,687	8.9	22.5	19.2
18580	Corpus Christi, TX	257,435	51.7	18.8	313,941	62.0	6.8	37.4	27.0	39,723	15.4	32.3	13.4
18700	Corvallis, OR	48,862	23.0	48.0	67,565	64.1	4.8	31.1	24.9	47,117	6.9	27.4	19.5
19060	Cumberland, MD-WV	68,191	59.6	14.3	82,359	55.8	7.5	31.8	35.3	35,787	10.3	34.8	8.4
19100	Dallas-Fort Worth-Arlington, TX	3,754,317	42.9	29.5	4,485,023	70.2	6.5	46.1	18.1	53,748	10.0	20.7	22.1
19100 19124	•Dallas-Plano-Irving, TX Division	2,512,770	42.3	31.2	2,998,129	70.7	6.5	46.5	17.5	54,180	10.1	20.6	23.1
19100 23104	•Fort Worth-Arlington, TX Division	1,241,547	44.2	26.0	1,486,894	69.2	6.6	45.2	19.3	52,888	9.9	21.0	20.2
19140	Dalton, GA	83,214	68.6	11.6	97,416	65.1	7.5	45.3	22.4	40,011	12.1	29.2	10.8
19180	Danville, IL	54,624	57.3	12.5	64,123	59.6	10.1	35.7	36.2	37,784	16.0	33.4	7.7
19260	Danville, VA	74,485	60.4	13.4	86,043	58.8	10.2	34.8	36.0	34,570	14.1	36.9	7.9
19340	Davenport-Moline-Rock Island, IA-IL	248,445	45.5	23.7	295,124	65.9	6.4	39.1	28.7	46,028	8.9	25.7	14.4
19380	Dayton, OH	554,066	46.1	24.4	664,953	64.0	7.0	38.8	28.8	46,249	9.7	25.4	15.4
19460	Decatur, AL	100,725	55.6	16.9	116,445	62.0	5.4	40.1	28.7	42,204	10.8	30.2	12.2
19500	Decatur, IL	72,755	51.1	20.0	86,913	61.6	6.4	38.6	30.2	43,316	11.3	29.4	14.0
19660	Deltona-Daytona Beach-Ormond Beach, FL	351,677	48.5	20.0	408,854	56.8	5.6	35.3	35.8	41,772	8.3	28.0	11.7
19740	Denver-Aurora, CO	1,594,298	35.6	36.0	1,863,293	71.6	5.9	44.9	19.9	58,039	8.0	19.3	24.0
19780	Des Moines-West Des Moines, IA	349,779	39.2	31.5	410,521	73.3	4.5	48.2	20.7	55,342	5.5	18.8	18.8
19820	Detroit-Warren-Livonia, MI	2,977,842	43.8	26.1	3,490,030	64.0	10.4	36.8	29.1	53,593	9.7	22.9	21.3
19820 19804	•Detroit-Livonia-Dearborn, MI Division	1,297,844	51.2	19.4	1,533,809	60.1	13.9	33.3	34.0	43,232	15.3	30.1	15.0
19820 47644	•Warren-Troy-Farmington Hills, MI Division	1,679,998	38.1	31.2	1,956,221	67.0	8.0	39.5	25.4	61,987	5.7	17.6	25.9
20020	Dothan, AL	92,270	55.5	17.1	108,030	59.1	6.0	39.8	32.5	37,137	12.1	34.4	11.0
20100	Dover, DE	94,750	52.8	18.5	114,317	64.5	6.8	42.1	27.6	50,112	8.8	23.4	16.6
20220	Dubuque, IA	59,605	49.3	25.3	72,051	70.1	4.0	42.5	25.1	46,633	7.0	24.4	12.0
20260	Duluth, MN-WI	183,833	42.0	23.4	225,054	62.9	6.8	33.9	32.8	43,582	8.3	28.5	11.3
20500	Durham, NC	304,932	37.4	41.1	374,096	67.4	6.9	40.5	23.8	47,808	10.0	25.7	19.7
20740	Eau Claire, WI	99,886	43.6	24.1	125,601	69.9	5.5	39.3	25.1	46,360	7.0	25.9	12.2
20940	El Centro, CA	91,414	63.7	10.4	117,003	51.4	9.5	28.1	30.0	35,933	18.5	34.8	11.2
21060	Elizabethtown, KY	71,455	50.1	18.3	85,660	64.1	5.7	42.2	25.7	44,912	9.3	24.7	13.3
21140	Elkhart-Goshen, IN	124,184	59.3	16.8	145,992	71.3	6.8	45.6	19.8	47,999	8.1	22.2	12.8
21300	Elmira, NY	59,678	51.2	21.0	70,982	59.1	8.3	34.5	33.2	39,989	12.4	30.8	13.3
21340	El Paso, TX	415,887	55.5	18.0	522,820	58.9	8.8	34.6	25.9	33,684	24.9	38.6	9.4
21500	Erie, PA	182,698	55.4	23.0	222,012	61.7	6.8	37.0	30.1	42,073	10.1	29.5	11.6
21660	Eugene-Springfield, OR	230,576	37.2	27.6	279,000	62.0	6.8	32.2	29.8	42,079	9.6	28.7	11.6
21780	Evansville, IN-KY	232,714	51.0	19.4	276,334	64.6	5.6	41.0	28.2	45,162	8.0	27.4	13.1
21820	Fairbanks, AK	55,615	33.7	26.9	72,065	73.3	7.0	42.2	19.4	63,044	6.3	17.1	25.0
22020	Fargo, ND-MN	115,208	31.7	33.9	151,105	74.7	3.9	43.9	20.2	45,513	7.5	27.1	14.6
22140	Farmington, NM	74,080	54.9	13.4	92,100	60.4	4.4	38.6	25.3	42,331	13.4	29.7	12.5
22180	Fayetteville, NC	208,242	43.7	20.4	258,654	65.1	7.8	41.2	26.1	42,051	14.6	30.1	10.9
22220	Fayetteville-Springdale-Rogers, AR-MO	265,402	48.6	24.7	321,599	66.4	5.0	43.0	22.6	44,732	9.6	25.5	13.1
22380	Flagstaff, AZ	74,989	37.8	32.4	97,978	68.2	5.2	37.1	20.1	48,171	11.1	24.4	17.1
22420	Flint, MI	286,221	47.7	18.8	337,100	60.4	10.3	33.7	33.1	44,277	12.7	27.3	13.6
22500	Florence, SC	129,894	57.1	19.4	154,369	61.4	9.5	39.7	29.3	39,414	13.7	31.9	11.1
22520	Florence-Muscle Shoals, AL	97,055	55.4	18.1	115,540	55.3	6.9	34.8	37.2	36,755	14.0	36.0	10.8
22540	Fond du Lac, WI	66,391	54.2	17.5	78,779	69.7	5.2	43.2	25.2	50,647	5.4	21.0	11.9
22660	Fort Collins-Loveland, CO	181,296	28.3	41.6	227,710	70.4	6.3	38.7	22.3	53,502	7.1	21.5	21.2
22900	Fort Smith, AR-OK	188,271	58.0	14.0	221,320	58.5	5.9	37.2	31.1	35,726	13.8	35.9	8.3

Table B-3. Metropolitan Areas — What: Education, Employment, and Income, 2005–2007—*Continued*

Metro area or division code	Area name	Educational attainment			Employment status				Percent of households with no workers	Median household income (dollars)	Percent of families with income below poverty	Percent of households with income less than $25,000	Percent of households with income of $100,000 or more
		Total population 25 years and over	Percent with a high school diploma or less	Percent with a bachelor's degree or more	Total population 16 years and over	Percent in the labor force	Unemployment rate	Percent who worked full-time, year-round					
	ACS table number:	C15002	C15002	C15002	C20005	C23001	C23001	C20005	C08202	B19013	C17015	C19001	C19001
		1	2	3	4	5	6	7	8	9	10	11	12
23020	Fort Walton Beach-Crestview-Destin, FL............	123,195	37.0	28.1	143,567	65.8	4.2	42.9	26.2	54,999	7.2	18.8	19.4
23060	Fort Wayne, IN.........................	261,842	45.9	23.4	309,988	68.7	6.6	43.6	23.3	48,006	8.2	22.8	13.9
23420	Fresno, CA..............................	515,516	52.1	18.8	650,245	62.2	9.1	35.2	27.1	44,979	16.3	28.3	16.0
23460	Gadsden, AL............................	70,437	54.9	14.8	82,017	55.9	7.2	35.6	35.6	34,207	13.1	36.5	8.3
23540	Gainesville, FL.........................	147,840	35.4	36.8	209,907	61.9	6.1	35.3	26.8	38,561	11.3	34.5	14.7
23580	Gainesville, GA........................	108,576	58.3	18.6	128,465	65.9	5.2	44.6	20.7	49,474	8.7	21.7	15.5
24020	Glens Falls, NY........................	89,523	50.7	21.7	105,513	62.0	6.5	36.7	29.5	46,168	7.8	24.5	13.4
24140	Goldsboro, NC.........................	73,825	53.6	15.6	87,651	61.4	6.2	40.1	28.3	39,316	12.5	31.7	9.1
24220	Grand Forks, ND-MN	57,784	38.8	27.5	78,892	70.4	4.5	38.1	23.2	42,516	8.1	30.0	10.7
24300	Grand Junction, CO	90,196	44.8	23.4	107,268	66.0	4.9	37.1	27.2	46,490	9.2	25.4	13.5
24340	Grand Rapids-Wyoming, MI......	491,310	43.7	25.7	589,448	68.7	8.1	39.5	24.0	48,889	9.0	22.7	15.2
24500	Great Falls, MT........................	54,589	41.7	23.5	63,885	62.7	5.0	38.9	30.3	41,802	9.6	29.4	9.7
24540	Greeley, CO............................	142,163	46.2	24.3	177,518	71.0	5.2	44.4	20.3	52,457	9.1	22.3	17.0
24580	Green Bay, WI.........................	197,638	47.9	23.2	234,472	70.6	6.1	42.9	23.9	50,910	7.5	22.4	15.1
24660	Greensboro-High Point, NC	458,289	48.7	24.9	542,025	66.5	7.6	40.7	25.6	42,789	11.7	28.8	13.7
24780	Greenville, NC.........................	101,618	45.7	26.3	132,586	64.1	8.4	36.7	26.7	36,498	15.3	37.3	11.9
24860	Greenville-Mauldin-Easley, SC ...	396,161	49.4	25.6	474,866	63.7	7.0	39.2	26.6	43,711	10.2	28.2	14.0
25060	Gulfport-Biloxi, MS	155,087	49.5	18.8	184,443	61.4	8.8	36.7	30.5	43,241	11.3	29.0	13.5
25180	Hagerstown-Martinsburg, MD-WV.............................	174,330	57.1	18.1	201,406	66.3	5.6	43.8	24.7	50,783	7.3	22.1	15.0
25260	Hanford-Corcoran, CA..............	87,345	60.4	11.6	110,425	57.9	12.2	33.2	23.6	45,796	14.8	25.2	13.3
25420	Harrisburg-Carlisle, PA	359,322	50.2	27.4	421,447	66.6	4.9	44.2	25.6	53,496	5.9	20.4	17.9
25500	Harrisonburg, VA	68,338	58.3	23.8	95,082	61.3	3.7	37.4	25.0	44,860	5.5	26.5	12.3
25540	Hartford-West Hartford-East Hartford, CT............................	797,516	41.7	33.1	946,327	67.6	6.4	41.6	25.1	64,989	6.1	18.3	27.7
25620	Hattiesburg, MS.......................	81,216	45.1	25.6	103,892	63.4	7.4	36.3	27.5	36,285	16.3	35.0	10.6
25860	Hickory-Lenoir-Morganton, NC ...	245,399	58.2	16.0	283,438	63.0	7.4	39.9	30.2	39,793	10.1	31.2	9.3
25980	Hinesville-Fort Stewart, GA	38,203	49.0	13.9	50,364	70.7	9.0	43.4	21.1	40,970	15.6	28.7	6.1
26100	Holland-Grand Haven, MI	157,163	42.5	27.9	196,862	70.2	5.4	39.3	21.1	57,536	3.2	15.9	18.7
26180	Honolulu, HI	611,172	40.2	30.0	727,183	64.9	4.2	43.2	22.5	64,355	6.2	16.4	27.5
26300	Hot Springs, AR	67,072	48.4	19.0	77,382	56.4	7.8	33.8	39.8	34,451	12.6	35.8	8.4
26380	Houma-Bayou Cane-Thibodaux, LA..	128,201	68.0	13.6	154,936	58.7	4.9	36.6	27.8	42,856	13.2	30.0	13.9
26420	Houston-Sugar Land-Baytown, TX..	3,405,541	46.8	27.3	4,100,491	67.7	7.1	43.9	18.9	51,685	12.1	23.3	22.0
26580	Huntington-Ashland, WV-KY-OH..............................	195,728	56.8	15.8	229,532	53.7	6.7	32.3	38.5	34,606	14.8	36.7	9.4
26620	Huntsville, AL..........................	248,632	39.4	34.0	296,230	64.4	6.3	41.2	24.8	51,275	8.2	23.3	20.9
26820	Idaho Falls, ID	68,904	41.8	23.2	83,484	67.7	4.7	40.3	22.2	47,099	8.0	23.3	14.0
26900	Indianapolis-Carmel, IN	1,084,900	43.6	29.6	1,271,322	69.4	6.3	44.7	22.0	52,607	7.9	21.3	19.1
26980	Iowa City, IA	85,780	28.1	46.0	117,724	71.6	3.8	40.8	19.9	49,075	8.5	27.2	17.8
27060	Ithaca, NY..............................	56,331	27.8	52.6	87,040	61.5	4.3	31.0	27.2	46,225	6.0	28.6	18.1
27100	Jackson, MI.............................	109,152	49.0	17.5	128,393	59.1	8.1	36.0	29.5	45,946	11.5	27.1	13.2
27140	Jackson, MS............................	328,669	41.4	28.4	402,584	64.3	7.0	41.6	25.6	42,921	12.4	29.3	15.6
27180	Jackson, TN............................	71,925	50.3	22.3	87,016	63.6	7.7	39.7	28.9	38,352	15.8	33.2	11.9
27260	Jacksonville, FL.......................	842,419	44.1	25.6	994,198	66.5	5.9	43.2	24.1	51,269	8.1	21.1	17.9
27340	Jacksonville, NC	82,512	45.4	15.7	121,530	72.0	5.2	50.8	22.8	42,173	11.9	26.4	10.1
27500	Janesville, WI	105,153	52.8	18.4	123,091	67.8	6.8	41.2	28.1	48,698	8.2	22.1	12.8
27620	Jefferson City, MO	95,209	53.4	22.7	114,076	65.8	4.3	45.0	23.9	46,672	8.4	24.1	11.5
27740	Johnson City, TN	132,891	55.8	21.5	156,343	59.1	6.2	37.4	32.9	36,853	12.4	33.7	8.9
27780	Johnstown, PA.........................	103,014	62.8	17.2	121,167	55.2	7.2	33.6	37.5	37,030	10.7	32.9	8.6
27860	Jonesboro, AR.........................	73,250	57.5	19.5	89,819	64.1	8.4	37.0	30.3	36,527	15.1	34.5	9.9
27900	Joplin, MO..............................	109,742	53.8	17.8	129,695	64.9	6.8	39.5	28.3	37,158	12.8	32.5	8.2
28020	Kalamazoo-Portage, MI............	202,029	38.6	30.1	253,791	66.9	9.3	36.2	28.1	45,011	10.5	27.5	15.8
28100	Kankakee-Bradley, IL	70,286	50.7	17.4	84,318	63.9	9.3	35.6	27.5	49,931	9.3	23.3	13.4
28140	Kansas City, MO-KS	1,286,531	40.0	31.2	1,509,454	69.7	5.9	44.8	22.5	53,564	7.7	20.9	19.7
28420	Kennewick-Richland-Pasco, WA..	138,137	45.5	22.4	166,501	65.6	7.7	38.2	24.0	50,907	11.0	23.0	19.5
28660	Killeen-Temple-Fort Hood, TX....	211,260	42.2	20.5	261,090	65.3	6.2	44.4	23.1	45,577	11.0	23.2	12.2
28700	Kingsport-Bristol-Bristol, TN-VA......................................	216,454	56.7	16.7	246,708	58.0	7.1	35.8	35.0	36,017	13.0	35.0	8.8
28740	Kingston, NY	124,028	44.7	28.6	149,016	64.0	5.0	36.7	26.2	54,871	7.5	21.3	20.9
28940	Knoxville, TN..........................	454,910	47.2	27.1	538,164	62.9	5.7	39.7	29.0	44,511	10.1	28.0	14.3
29020	Kokomo, IN............................	68,516	55.1	17.2	78,516	59.1	6.5	36.3	31.3	47,040	12.1	24.8	14.1
29100	La Crosse, WI-MN	83,005	39.6	27.7	104,878	70.3	5.1	40.7	23.7	47,259	7.1	25.7	13.1
29140	Lafayette, IN...........................	107,862	43.9	31.2	153,053	63.9	7.5	35.2	26.2	42,250	9.0	30.0	12.9
29180	Lafayette, LA...........................	158,683	51.2	24.0	194,570	66.9	5.6	40.0	22.8	42,596	12.4	29.6	16.0
29340	Lake Charles, LA	122,776	54.8	18.1	147,872	62.8	8.1	35.4	29.4	40,312	13.3	32.9	14.0
29420	Lake Havasu City-Kingman, AZ .	134,772	55.6	11.4	152,778	53.3	7.5	30.8	39.6	37,941	11.4	29.0	10.3
29460	Lakeland, FL............................	374,804	56.5	17.2	438,083	58.6	5.6	40.4	32.3	42,534	10.1	26.4	10.8
29540	Lancaster, PA...........................	324,515	57.8	23.2	382,874	66.5	4.1	42.8	22.7	52,933	6.1	19.3	16.6
29620	Lansing-East Lansing, MI..........	282,024	37.4	30.3	364,462	65.5	7.3	37.7	26.6	49,169	9.5	23.3	16.5
29700	Laredo, TX..............................	117,257	63.5	16.5	150,284	62.8	8.6	36.2	21.8	34,236	27.1	38.8	9.0
29740	Las Cruces, NM	114,132	48.6	24.6	146,968	61.3	8.3	34.7	27.4	34,118	20.5	38.3	9.3
29820	Las Vegas-Paradise, NV	1,166,163	49.0	20.4	1,355,085	67.9	5.6	46.3	21.6	54,299	8.0	18.9	19.5

Metro area or division code	Area name	Educational attainment			Employment status								
		Total population 25 years and over	Percent with a high school diploma or less	Percent with a bachelor's degree or more	Total population 16 years and over	Percent in the labor force	Unemployment rate	Percent who worked full-time, year-round	Percent of households with no workers	Median household income (dollars)	Percent of families with income below poverty	Percent of households with income less than $25,000	Percent of households with income of $100,000 or more
ACS table number:		C15002	C15002	C15002	C20005	C23001	C23001	C20005	C08202	B19013	C17015	C19001	C19001
		1	2	3	4	5	6	7	8	9	10	11	12
29940	Lawrence, KS	63,816	25.0	46.1	93,497	72.3	6.1	38.1	19.5	44,547	8.0	28.6	15.1
30020	Lawton, OK	66,486	49.5	18.8	83,659	63.9	6.1	38.5	26.0	41,902	15.1	29.3	9.2
30140	Lebanon, PA	87,314	64.2	18.0	101,061	66.8	4.9	43.6	25.0	49,805	5.7	20.9	12.6
30300	Lewiston, ID-WA	40,830	47.5	17.4	47,800	61.3	7.5	33.8	34.7	41,009	12.6	30.3	10.0
30340	Lewiston-Auburn, ME	72,782	56.2	17.2	85,504	65.4	7.5	40.8	27.4	42,725	10.6	28.4	9.5
30460	Lexington-Fayette, KY	289,034	40.4	33.1	349,987	68.1	5.1	42.4	23.0	46,311	10.5	27.0	16.7
30620	Lima, OH	68,465	55.6	16.0	82,415	63.9	8.4	35.5	31.9	43,466	10.7	26.9	11.5
30700	Lincoln, NE	179,554	32.0	34.8	227,684	74.1	4.6	45.0	19.4	49,920	6.6	23.7	15.1
30780	Little Rock-North Little Rock-Conway, AR	427,032	44.5	26.9	508,466	66.4	5.9	42.3	25.1	45,554	9.9	25.7	14.8
30860	Logan, UT-ID	59,372	34.1	32.3	85,266	71.9	4.8	34.4	16.6	44,389	9.7	24.5	12.1
30980	Longview, TX	131,887	51.3	18.5	156,596	61.0	7.0	38.1	27.9	40,170	11.3	30.6	12.8
31020	Longview, WA	65,636	46.7	13.4	77,015	60.7	8.8	31.4	31.3	44,227	11.6	25.9	11.4
31100	Los Angeles-Long Beach-Santa Ana, CA	8,164,250	45.5	29.3	9,864,883	64.7	6.4	40.3	22.2	56,680	10.9	21.6	25.4
31100 31084	•Los Angeles-Long Beach-Glendale, CA Division	6,239,833	48.0	27.6	7,564,003	64.1	6.8	39.7	22.7	52,628	12.4	23.8	22.7
31100 42044	•Santa Ana-Anaheim-Irvine, CA Division	1,924,417	37.3	34.6	2,300,880	66.8	5.1	42.2	20.6	71,601	6.4	14.4	34.2
31140	Louisville-Jefferson County, KY-IN	820,804	48.6	23.3	956,918	65.8	6.8	41.1	27.3	46,095	9.5	26.0	14.9
31180	Lubbock, TX	156,236	46.7	26.9	204,831	65.0	6.2	39.0	23.5	39,955	11.8	31.1	11.8
31340	Lynchburg, VA	159,781	53.2	21.2	193,992	62.6	5.0	39.6	28.5	43,161	9.8	27.3	11.9
31420	Macon, GA	144,646	54.4	20.5	172,931	59.7	8.9	36.4	31.8	39,652	15.0	33.7	13.0
31460	Madera, CA	87,967	59.6	11.7	107,444	55.9	10.2	32.6	28.7	44,534	13.8	24.6	15.4
31540	Madison, WI	357,830	30.2	41.2	440,051	73.4	4.3	44.4	19.7	58,090	4.5	18.1	21.9
31700	Manchester-Nashua, NH	269,021	38.7	33.4	312,750	72.1	5.0	45.6	19.1	67,276	5.0	15.7	28.0
31900	Mansfield, OH	86,311	59.7	14.1	100,804	59.0	7.3	36.5	30.9	41,563	7.8	28.3	10.9
32580	McAllen-Edinburg-Mission, TX	366,029	65.7	15.0	466,814	57.6	10.5	30.9	29.3	28,328	32.9	44.5	7.5
32780	Medford, OR	136,019	41.7	23.5	159,457	62.0	6.6	34.3	32.4	43,446	8.9	27.5	11.7
32820	Memphis, TN-MS-AR	798,626	47.7	23.9	959,134	66.4	8.9	41.3	24.5	44,495	14.4	28.4	16.1
32900	Merced, CA	136,896	59.5	12.7	173,695	61.8	11.9	32.7	26.9	44,141	16.1	29.3	14.3
33100	Miami-Fort Lauderdale-Pompano Beach, FL	3,698,769	46.6	27.8	4,311,225	62.2	6.2	40.8	28.3	47,527	10.2	26.1	19.0
33100 22744	•Fort Lauderdale-Pompano Beach-Deerfield Beach, FL Division	1,207,122	43.8	28.5	1,396,587	65.9	6.0	42.8	26.1	51,221	8.3	23.2	20.4
33100 33124	•Miami-Miami Beach-Kendall, FL Division	1,591,512	51.4	25.7	1,888,725	61.3	6.3	41.4	25.1	41,943	13.2	30.6	16.0
33100 48424	•West Palm Beach-Boca Raton-Boynton Beach, FL Division	900,135	41.9	30.4	1,025,913	58.7	6.1	37.1	36.4	52,351	7.2	22.5	21.8
33140	Michigan City-La Porte, IN	75,000	55.3	16.4	86,933	62.1	6.8	38.1	26.9	46,546	9.2	24.4	12.1
33260	Midland, TX	75,480	46.5	25.1	92,434	67.2	3.2	41.5	20.7	47,163	11.4	27.1	19.3
33340	Milwaukee-Waukesha-West Allis, WI	1,007,887	42.6	29.7	1,196,449	67.6	6.8	41.2	25.9	51,669	8.9	23.0	18.9
33460	Minneapolis-St. Paul-Bloomington, MN-WI	2,074,591	32.7	36.5	2,455,568	73.5	5.5	44.9	20.0	63,866	5.6	16.2	26.2
33540	Missoula, MT	67,250	34.8	36.9	84,696	68.1	4.7	36.6	25.0	42,687	8.9	30.0	13.2
33660	Mobile, AL	256,937	54.1	19.4	307,881	60.1	7.1	37.6	30.7	38,596	16.4	33.5	11.3
33700	Modesto, CA	304,893	54.9	15.3	376,839	61.5	10.4	34.6	26.9	50,375	10.6	23.4	17.7
33740	Monroe, LA	107,346	53.4	21.5	131,915	60.6	7.9	37.3	30.3	36,364	17.1	36.4	11.1
33780	Monroe, MI	101,699	50.9	16.3	120,734	66.1	7.4	38.6	26.6	55,922	5.6	18.2	19.3
33860	Montgomery, AL	228,869	48.6	25.8	278,751	62.3	7.9	40.5	27.6	43,654	13.4	29.0	14.6
34060	Morgantown, WV	71,440	53.0	27.7	97,818	56.6	5.5	32.7	29.6	36,283	11.1	35.1	10.9
34100	Morristown, TN	90,382	64.7	12.3	105,929	61.5	6.2	38.7	30.5	37,368	12.8	34.5	8.0
34580	Mount Vernon-Anacortes, WA	76,072	42.5	22.2	90,518	61.1	4.6	33.7	31.4	50,107	9.2	22.5	15.9
34620	Muncie, IN	71,881	53.5	21.7	94,898	59.7	9.7	30.7	31.6	36,853	12.3	32.5	9.7
34740	Muskegon-Norton Shores, MI	113,623	48.2	17.3	135,380	61.9	12.4	34.1	31.4	41,984	11.6	28.2	9.9
34820	Myrtle Beach-Conway-North Myrtle Beach, SC	168,232	49.3	20.6	193,532	63.7	5.5	39.0	29.6	41,975	11.8	27.7	11.0
34900	Napa, CA	88,198	40.3	28.3	105,183	64.9	5.7	35.5	25.8	66,663	5.4	16.7	31.0
34940	Naples-Marco Island, FL	226,350	44.7	30.0	253,925	55.4	4.5	35.4	39.5	57,166	6.5	18.1	24.1
34980	Nashville-Davidson-Murfreesboro-Franklin, TN	979,887	46.3	28.2	1,158,784	68.0	5.9	44.2	22.2	49,979	8.8	23.1	17.6
35300	New Haven-Milford, CT	564,716	45.0	30.9	670,086	66.9	6.9	40.2	26.5	58,528	7.8	21.2	25.0
35380	New Orleans-Metairie-Kenner, LA	727,265	49.2	24.8	875,761	61.9	8.4	36.5	27.8	45,802	11.7	28.1	17.1
35620	New York-Northern New Jersey-Long Island, NY-NJ-PA	12,614,787	44.6	34.6	14,849,058	63.6	6.5	40.8	25.5	60,964	9.8	21.9	28.8
35620 20764	•Edison, NJ Division	1,564,972	41.2	35.9	1,823,095	64.6	5.4	41.1	25.2	73,063	4.7	15.4	34.1
35620 35004	•Nassau-Suffolk, NY Division	1,843,685	40.0	35.4	2,178,884	64.6	4.6	41.4	22.6	84,099	3.5	12.0	40.8
35620 35084	•Newark-Union, NJ-PA Division	1,414,600	43.3	35.6	1,659,759	66.4	6.5	42.0	23.3	68,264	6.4	17.8	32.7
35620 35644	•New York-White Plains-Wayne, NY-NJ Division	7,791,530	46.6	33.9	9,187,320	62.6	7.2	40.4	26.6	52,633	13.3	26.1	24.4
35660	Niles-Benton Harbor, MI	106,707	48.7	23.0	125,226	62.9	8.3	36.3	29.2	42,188	12.4	29.8	13.5
35980	Norwich-New London, CT	181,247	43.8	29.4	212,806	68.4	4.9	42.6	22.5	61,842	4.1	15.2	25.3

Table B-3. Metropolitan Areas — What: Education, Employment, and Income, 2005–2007—*Continued*

Metro area or division code	Area name	Educational attainment			Employment status				Percent of households with no workers	Median household income (dollars)	Percent of families with income below poverty	Percent of households with income less than $25,000	Percent of households with income of $100,000 or more
		Total population 25 years and over	Percent with a high school diploma or less	Percent with a bachelor's degree or more	Total population 16 years and over	Percent in the labor force	Unemployment rate	Percent who worked full-time, year-round					
	ACS table number:	C15002	C15002	C15002	C20005	C23001	C23001	C20005	C08202	B19013	C17015	C19001	C19001
		1	2	3	4	5	6	7	8	9	10	11	12
36100	Ocala, FL	225,461	55.5	15.6	257,840	51.7	6.3	32.4	41.3	39,295	9.6	29.6	9.3
36140	Ocean City, NJ	70,429	49.2	26.9	80,428	61.7	7.0	35.5	33.3	52,771	6.7	21.5	19.2
36220	Odessa, TX	75,694	59.5	12.2	93,603	63.3	4.5	41.2	23.7	41,322	14.6	30.8	11.4
36260	Ogden-Clearfield, UT	287,309	35.7	27.3	363,478	69.9	4.7	42.5	18.2	57,743	6.2	15.7	19.3
36420	Oklahoma City, OK	749,858	42.2	26.9	910,506	66.0	5.8	41.6	25.4	43,652	10.6	27.4	14.3
36500	Olympia, WA	157,968	34.2	31.1	186,997	65.7	6.2	38.9	25.6	55,129	7.7	20.2	19.7
36540	Omaha-Council Bluffs, NE-IA	520,304	37.4	31.7	626,030	72.0	5.5	46.0	21.1	52,914	7.7	21.0	18.5
36740	Orlando-Kissimmee, FL	1,323,666	43.1	27.4	1,562,579	66.3	5.8	43.4	23.6	49,789	8.2	21.4	17.4
36780	Oshkosh-Neenah, WI	107,246	47.6	24.2	130,491	67.2	5.3	40.6	25.0	49,395	6.3	22.7	13.7
36980	Owensboro, KY	74,310	56.1	15.4	87,051	61.2	6.2	38.8	31.7	40,819	13.0	32.4	10.7
37100	Oxnard-Thousand Oaks-Ventura, CA	503,006	39.0	30.1	609,864	66.8	5.3	40.6	21.5	72,984	6.4	14.5	33.8
37340	Palm Bay-Melbourne-Titusville, FL	379,268	41.0	26.2	437,283	58.1	5.4	36.1	34.2	47,973	6.6	23.5	16.4
37380	Palm Coast, FL	60,455	44.2	20.5	68,354	52.4	4.1	34.2	39.2	45,486	9.0	25.1	11.8
37460	Panama City-Lynn Haven, FL	112,441	45.9	21.1	129,895	65.0	5.2	41.6	26.0	46,106	10.5	25.2	13.4
37620	Parkersburg-Marietta-Vienna, WV-OH	112,532	55.6	17.0	130,567	58.3	7.7	34.3	34.1	37,685	13.0	34.0	9.3
37700	Pascagoula, MS	98,076	52.2	17.4	116,225	60.7	9.2	35.0	29.0	44,580	13.0	27.2	12.8
37860	Pensacola-Ferry Pass-Brent, FL	297,783	44.7	23.3	360,156	61.0	6.8	36.3	29.7	45,288	10.0	26.2	13.1
37900	Peoria, IL	244,566	43.4	24.4	290,532	64.4	6.2	39.6	27.9	49,795	8.1	22.9	15.7
37980	Philadelphia-Camden-Wilmington, PA-NJ-DE-MD	3,838,551	45.8	31.2	4,568,149	65.0	6.8	40.4	26.1	57,831	8.1	21.7	25.0
37980 15804	•Camden, NJ Division	826,037	45.9	28.8	975,026	67.6	6.4	42.4	22.9	65,494	6.1	16.8	27.8
37980 37964	•Philadelphia, PA Division	2,559,538	45.7	32.6	3,051,888	63.7	7.1	39.3	27.7	54,566	9.1	23.9	24.2
37980 48864	•Wilmington, DE-MD-NJ Division	452,976	45.8	28.3	541,235	67.1	5.9	43.2	22.9	61,031	6.5	18.0	24.8
38060	Phoenix-Mesa-Scottsdale, AZ	2,570,910	42.0	26.5	3,049,537	65.2	5.1	42.9	24.8	52,857	9.3	20.7	20.0
38220	Pine Bluff, AR	67,112	61.9	14.5	81,226	57.8	12.4	35.1	33.7	34,348	16.5	37.4	8.2
38300	Pittsburgh, PA	1,655,335	48.4	27.2	1,932,424	61.1	6.0	37.2	31.6	44,814	8.0	28.2	15.1
38340	Pittsfield, MA	91,051	43.3	30.1	108,306	62.5	6.4	35.9	31.9	48,836	7.8	26.3	16.4
38540	Pocatello, ID	51,351	37.5	27.7	64,598	66.6	6.0	35.7	25.1	39,755	12.8	30.0	10.8
38860	Portland-South Portland-Biddeford, ME	356,283	40.3	33.0	413,013	69.2	4.6	41.6	25.1	53,270	6.4	21.4	18.1
38900	Portland-Vancouver-Beaverton, OR-WA	1,433,533	35.2	31.9	1,670,351	68.5	6.7	40.0	22.8	53,935	8.2	21.0	20.3
38940	Port St. Lucie, FL	277,295	48.7	21.7	317,993	56.3	6.3	35.1	36.8	48,391	7.0	21.9	16.6
39100	Poughkeepsie-Newburgh-Middletown, NY	425,247	44.9	28.1	518,653	66.3	5.8	40.7	22.3	66,376	6.7	16.6	28.5
39140	Prescott, AZ	147,413	42.4	22.8	169,838	55.1	4.2	31.4	38.9	43,170	8.8	26.0	12.0
39300	Providence-New Bedford-Fall River, RI-MA	1,080,873	48.7	27.4	1,287,463	66.2	6.4	39.2	27.8	54,064	8.3	23.9	21.3
39340	Provo-Orem, UT	230,478	27.2	34.6	329,738	67.4	4.4	33.9	15.3	53,590	8.2	18.1	16.9
39380	Pueblo, CO	100,081	46.0	20.5	119,658	60.8	7.8	34.3	32.6	39,570	15.4	32.7	11.1
39460	Punta Gorda, FL	119,443	50.5	19.5	131,959	47.8	5.3	29.0	45.8	44,576	6.7	23.6	11.8
39540	Racine, WI	127,791	47.5	22.9	150,504	66.9	5.6	41.5	23.1	53,250	7.3	20.9	16.8
39580	Raleigh-Cary, NC	644,335	33.6	40.3	767,747	70.6	5.0	46.2	18.3	57,974	6.6	19.0	24.7
39660	Rapid City, SD	76,880	38.8	26.2	92,467	70.0	4.5	42.9	23.8	44,865	9.2	24.3	11.6
39740	Reading, PA	264,853	56.8	21.5	314,487	66.1	5.5	41.4	25.7	52,241	7.7	22.2	16.5
39820	Redding, CA	120,022	43.0	17.8	143,783	57.8	8.9	30.3	35.1	43,988	11.6	27.9	14.1
39900	Reno-Sparks, NV	266,050	41.7	26.7	314,235	68.9	4.3	44.4	22.3	53,584	7.0	20.2	20.2
40060	Richmond, VA	791,101	44.0	30.2	941,100	67.1	5.7	44.6	22.8	56,277	7.1	19.1	21.6
40140	Riverside-San Bernardino-Ontario, CA	2,383,919	50.5	18.7	2,956,202	62.6	7.5	37.9	24.4	54,991	10.1	20.6	21.4
40220	Roanoke, VA	206,296	48.9	23.3	238,367	63.5	4.9	41.8	29.9	46,103	7.4	24.3	14.3
40340	Rochester, MN	118,012	35.1	33.7	138,705	72.5	3.2	46.8	20.7	60,342	4.8	16.8	22.5
40380	Rochester, NY	676,084	41.8	30.2	824,031	63.2	6.4	37.2	29.1	49,508	8.9	24.5	17.0
40420	Rockford, IL	225,956	51.8	19.8	266,753	66.2	8.3	39.1	27.1	48,282	10.0	25.7	15.1
40580	Rocky Mount, NC	95,820	58.5	15.6	112,693	62.1	7.8	39.2	30.9	38,195	14.0	33.5	10.6
40660	Rome, GA	61,926	58.3	16.4	74,114	59.1	5.6	35.4	31.4	39,987	15.2	33.7	11.4
40900	Sacramento–Arden-Arcade–Roseville, CA	1,329,626	37.1	29.6	1,608,680	64.8	6.8	37.8	25.6	58,480	7.8	19.2	24.0
40980	Saginaw-Saginaw Township North, MI	133,918	50.6	17.9	160,033	57.5	10.2	32.1	35.7	42,074	13.6	30.0	13.2
41060	St. Cloud, MN	112,862	43.9	22.2	145,304	72.4	5.3	40.5	20.8	50,972	6.1	21.7	14.3
41100	St. George, UT	75,586	40.9	20.5	93,929	60.0	4.3	34.0	32.8	46,993	5.9	18.8	12.7
41140	St. Joseph, MO-KS	81,880	57.1	16.6	97,689	62.6	7.3	39.8	27.7	40,820	9.7	30.5	9.9
41180	St. Louis, MO-IL	1,839,338	42.8	28.0	2,184,767	66.6	6.8	41.3	26.1	51,713	7.9	22.9	18.6
41420	Salem, OR	243,615	45.4	22.1	292,905	63.9	8.6	35.4	27.9	45,814	10.7	25.2	13.1
41500	Salinas, CA	249,937	50.9	23.6	308,558	65.3	8.8	34.6	23.6	58,197	9.1	18.1	23.5
41540	Salisbury, MD	75,998	55.3	22.1	94,847	62.1	7.2	38.5	26.5	46,657	9.4	25.4	15.6
41620	Salt Lake City, UT	641,547	37.0	29.0	791,031	72.0	4.6	43.4	17.5	55,064	6.9	17.9	19.7

Metro area or division code	Area name	Educational attainment			Employment status								
		Total population 25 years and over	Percent with a high school diploma or less	Percent with a bachelor's degree or more	Total population 16 years and over	Percent in the labor force	Unemployment rate	Percent who worked full-time, year-round	Percent of households with no workers	Median household income (dollars)	Percent of families with income below poverty	Percent of households with income less than $25,000	Percent of households with income of $100,000 or more
ACS table number:		C15002	C15002	C15002	C20005	C23001	C23001	C20005	C08202	B19013	C17015	C19001	C19001
		1	2	3	4	5	6	7	8	9	10	11	12
41660	San Angelo, TX........................	66,564	49.9	21.1	83,453	64.7	4.5	39.9	26.6	39,047	13.2	32.0	10.5
41700	San Antonio, TX......................	1,197,728	47.4	23.9	1,457,408	64.1	6.2	40.6	24.8	46,203	12.4	26.4	16.3
41740	San Diego-Carlsbad-San Marcos, CA	1,875,222	36.1	33.2	2,298,030	65.7	5.4	41.4	23.1	60,970	7.9	18.5	26.8
41780	Sandusky, OH...........................	53,925	53.3	19.1	62,271	62.8	7.1	36.6	32.2	46,476	8.4	25.3	14.6
41860	San Francisco-Oakland-Fremont, CA	2,902,636	32.3	42.5	3,365,577	66.0	6.2	40.1	23.9	72,059	6.6	17.2	35.1
41860 36084	•Oakland-Fremont-Hayward, CA Division	1,641,661	34.8	38.3	1,939,114	65.5	6.8	39.4	23.5	70,506	7.3	17.2	33.6
41860 41884	•San Francisco-San Mateo-Redwood City, CA Division........	1,260,975	29.2	47.9	1,426,463	66.7	5.5	40.9	24.5	74,560	5.5	17.2	37.0
41940	San Jose-Sunnyvale-Santa Clara, CA	1,186,825	32.6	43.2	1,392,160	66.1	6.2	41.5	20.3	82,664	5.9	14.4	41.2
42020	San Luis Obispo-Paso Robles, CA	170,006	35.5	29.5	217,150	60.1	6.2	30.3	27.4	53,589	6.6	23.3	21.4
42060	Santa Barbara-Santa Maria-Goleta, CA	248,680	39.2	30.6	318,190	62.8	5.6	34.0	26.4	57,059	8.3	19.7	24.9
42100	Santa Cruz-Watsonville, CA	163,501	32.3	37.7	203,068	68.8	6.8	33.4	23.4	63,333	6.7	17.9	29.5
42140	Santa Fe, NM	98,490	38.3	39.3	114,662	68.0	5.1	37.5	24.2	51,341	8.7	23.5	21.5
42220	Santa Rosa-Petaluma, CA..........	312,174	37.6	30.4	372,452	65.6	5.6	37.0	25.3	62,311	5.8	18.2	26.3
42260	Sarasota-Bradenton-Venice, FL..	507,607	44.0	27.5	566,350	54.9	5.2	35.0	39.2	48,445	6.2	22.4	17.3
42340	Savannah, GA...........................	203,573	47.1	26.2	247,135	64.2	5.5	41.9	24.6	46,084	10.3	26.5	16.0
42540	Scranton–Wilkes-Barre, PA........	384,306	55.7	20.5	451,225	60.1	5.8	37.0	32.6	40,737	9.2	31.2	11.1
42660	Seattle-Tacoma-Bellevue, WA	2,214,581	32.5	35.8	2,587,056	68.9	5.7	41.7	22.5	61,740	6.4	17.6	26.0
42660 42644	•Seattle-Bellevue-Everett, WA Division	1,719,052	29.9	39.4	1,996,342	69.8	5.4	42.2	21.7	64,060	5.8	17.0	27.9
42660 45104	•Tacoma, WA Division...............	495,529	41.5	23.0	590,714	66.0	6.7	40.1	25.1	54,440	8.2	19.7	19.2
42680	Sebastian-Vero Beach, FL	95,171	44.7	25.3	107,774	54.5	6.5	32.7	39.4	46,397	9.2	23.4	16.6
43100	Sheboygan, WI	77,528	50.7	20.8	90,692	70.3	5.3	44.0	23.7	51,464	5.1	19.0	14.1
43300	Sherman-Denison, TX	77,979	49.8	18.9	91,979	63.0	6.3	39.1	29.1	44,045	10.5	27.2	12.4
43340	Shreveport-Bossier City, LA.......	246,257	52.1	21.2	296,356	62.2	8.9	37.0	30.6	38,219	15.5	33.9	12.3
43580	Sioux City, IA-NE-SD.................	89,528	51.7	20.2	107,462	68.9	6.3	42.9	24.6	44,787	9.7	26.6	11.4
43620	Sioux Falls, SD........................	142,894	41.0	28.3	169,843	75.1	3.5	49.9	20.1	50,162	5.9	21.5	14.5
43780	South Bend-Mishawaka, IN-MI	201,915	49.6	23.9	246,362	65.0	6.5	38.7	26.8	44,181	8.8	25.6	13.2
43900	Spartanburg, SC	181,168	54.8	18.6	213,069	62.2	7.9	39.4	29.7	40,743	11.3	30.5	12.1
44060	Spokane, WA...........................	293,788	34.7	26.8	354,256	63.9	6.8	35.4	28.1	44,694	8.8	27.0	13.0
44100	Springfield, IL	139,535	41.6	29.1	162,428	67.9	6.6	42.7	26.9	49,116	9.5	24.3	16.9
44140	Springfield, MA.......................	445,162	46.4	28.5	551,124	64.2	7.5	35.8	30.2	48,265	10.8	27.6	16.3
44180	Springfield, MO......................	266,019	46.7	23.4	324,658	64.8	5.1	40.0	26.5	40,455	9.4	29.8	9.9
44220	Springfield, OH	94,948	56.3	16.2	111,735	61.9	8.8	36.1	33.4	43,109	11.1	28.9	10.9
44300	State College, PA.....................	79,318	41.0	40.2	122,821	59.1	5.9	30.4	28.0	42,976	5.9	29.6	13.7
44700	Stockton, CA...........................	399,430	52.8	16.8	492,655	61.9	9.4	35.7	25.4	52,872	11.0	22.2	20.8
44940	Sumter, SC..............................	65,871	55.3	16.9	79,522	58.1	10.3	38.8	32.8	36,194	14.8	35.5	8.2
45060	Syracuse, NY...........................	419,540	44.7	26.9	514,952	64.1	6.6	37.8	29.0	47,315	9.6	26.1	15.8
45220	Tallahassee, FL........................	215,077	38.7	34.1	284,239	66.3	6.4	40.8	22.6	44,495	11.0	28.6	15.1
45300	Tampa-St. Petersburg-Clearwater, FL	1,880,920	45.8	25.1	2,166,403	61.2	5.9	39.6	31.5	45,243	8.8	25.6	15.6
45460	Terre Haute, IN.......................	110,349	53.9	18.9	136,135	61.0	6.4	35.6	30.0	38,401	10.6	31.4	9.9
45500	Texarkana, TX-Texarkana, AR.....	88,868	55.1	16.1	104,634	59.4	7.6	36.8	30.6	38,650	13.5	33.8	10.3
45780	Toledo, OH.............................	419,106	47.4	23.0	513,590	66.2	8.8	37.2	29.4	45,865	10.7	27.5	14.9
45820	Topeka, KS..............................	152,083	46.1	26.0	179,262	67.5	6.2	42.4	26.6	45,781	9.2	25.2	14.0
45940	Trenton-Ewing, NJ...................	240,395	41.4	37.5	290,469	65.9	6.7	41.3	25.0	68,582	6.5	17.6	32.8
46060	Tucson, AZ..............................	621,398	38.5	29.6	747,314	60.9	6.4	36.1	29.6	44,386	10.3	26.8	15.1
46140	Tulsa, OK	581,907	45.1	24.6	690,245	65.5	5.9	42.0	25.9	43,749	11.7	27.8	14.5
46220	Tuscaloosa, AL	124,156	49.4	24.2	160,278	60.1	7.1	35.9	31.3	37,083	14.5	37.2	11.3
46340	Tyler, TX	124,332	44.9	22.7	149,804	62.7	6.7	36.8	28.0	42,934	11.8	29.0	14.5
46540	Utica-Rome, NY	200,592	50.5	19.8	239,088	60.0	6.5	36.6	31.2	42,105	10.5	28.9	11.7
46660	Valdosta, GA...........................	77,109	51.3	21.3	98,439	66.0	5.9	40.7	23.8	38,696	15.4	31.8	10.7
46700	Vallejo-Fairfield, CA..................	261,613	40.9	22.3	315,259	63.8	7.4	36.9	23.4	65,533	7.4	16.0	26.8
47020	Victoria, TX.............................	71,731	54.3	15.7	86,076	64.9	6.8	39.4	26.2	43,375	11.4	27.1	13.0
47220	Vineland-Millville-Bridgeton, NJ	102,771	65.5	12.7	120,731	59.6	10.4	35.8	29.3	48,464	13.4	26.8	15.5
47260	Virginia Beach-Norfolk-Newport News, VA-NC	1,049,050	41.1	26.6	1,283,860	68.7	5.0	45.6	22.5	54,442	7.8	19.6	18.9
47300	Visalia-Porterville, CA...............	234,743	59.6	12.3	295,436	59.9	10.0	35.1	26.9	41,837	18.8	29.0	13.5
47380	Waco, TX................................	134,247	51.1	19.6	174,281	62.7	7.8	38.0	27.6	39,088	12.9	33.5	11.0
47580	Warner Robins, GA	80,588	43.3	23.2	97,362	67.3	6.9	42.8	24.4	51,713	9.8	23.0	17.1
47900	Washington-Arlington-Alexandria, DC-VA-MD-WV	3,479,121	31.4	46.2	4,107,522	72.1	4.8	48.7	17.9	81,163	4.8	11.9	39.4
47900 13644	•Bethesda-Gaithersburg-Frederick, MD Division	767,739	26.3	52.2	896,140	71.4	4.0	46.8	17.7	86,522	2.9	9.2	42.8
47900 47894	•Washington-Arlington-Alexandria, DC-VA-MD-WV Division	2,711,382	32.9	44.5	3,211,382	72.3	5.0	49.3	18.0	79,720	5.4	12.7	38.4
47940	Waterloo-Cedar Falls, IA...........	102,877	46.5	24.5	130,967	66.3	6.0	37.7	28.3	44,061	8.1	28.0	11.4

Table B-3. Metropolitan Areas — What: Education, Employment, and Income, 2005–2007—*Continued*

Metro area or division code	Area name	Educational attainment			Employment status				Percent of households with no workers	Median household income (dollars)	Percent of families with income below poverty	Percent of households with income less than $25,000	Percent of households with income of $100,000 or more
		Total population 25 years and over	Percent with a high school diploma or less	Percent with a bachelor's degree or more	Total population 16 years and over	Percent in the labor force	Unemployment rate	Percent who worked full-time, year-round					
	ACS table number:	C15002	C15002	C15002	C20005	C23001	C23001	C20005	C08202	B19013	C17015	C19001	C19001
		1	2	3	4	5	6	7	8	9	10	11	12
48140	Wausau, WI............................	86,676	50.5	20.5	101,948	72.7	5.2	46.0	22.9	52,241	4.7	20.2	14.4
48260	Weirton-Steubenville, WV-OH ...	88,474	59.8	14.0	102,881	55.6	6.4	31.4	35.8	37,412	10.6	32.8	9.0
48300	Wenatchee, WA......................	68,172	47.8	20.7	81,712	63.3	6.9	34.0	29.3	43,977	11.7	25.9	12.5
48540	Wheeling, WV-OH	103,701	57.6	16.7	120,344	56.4	8.0	33.6	36.2	34,783	13.0	36.0	7.5
48620	Wichita, KS.............................	375,100	43.7	25.4	447,588	69.1	6.4	43.8	23.9	46,797	9.2	24.5	15.5
48660	Wichita Falls, TX	93,358	51.4	20.4	116,662	64.0	5.4	39.9	26.2	41,541	11.2	28.4	11.3
48700	Williamsport, PA	79,620	57.1	17.6	95,269	62.3	7.8	36.8	32.0	40,430	9.1	30.7	9.4
48900	Wilmington, NC	225,065	42.4	27.7	265,747	63.0	6.3	36.5	30.2	43,940	9.1	27.4	14.2
49020	Winchester, VA-WV	79,588	53.9	21.2	93,530	67.0	5.4	44.0	23.5	51,970	7.2	21.2	18.6
49180	Winston-Salem, NC	304,563	47.6	25.7	356,717	64.9	5.8	42.0	26.2	45,112	9.9	26.2	14.6
49340	Worcester, MA........................	517,984	43.4	31.2	613,758	67.6	6.1	41.8	25.6	60,709	6.8	20.7	25.7
49420	Yakima, WA............................	138,305	58.5	15.7	168,613	63.8	10.6	33.8	27.9	40,321	15.5	31.5	10.4
49620	York-Hanover, PA	284,102	55.7	21.3	328,553	68.6	5.0	45.3	23.5	53,641	5.4	19.5	16.8
49660	Youngstown-Warren-Boardman, OH-PA	397,636	57.8	17.8	464,687	59.1	7.2	34.7	33.8	40,503	10.3	30.6	10.6
49700	Yuba City, CA	98,131	51.1	15.2	120,523	63.2	10.2	33.3	29.0	47,253	9.7	24.1	16.3
49740	Yuma, AZ................................	113,924	58.1	12.5	137,791	54.8	9.4	31.6	36.5	38,502	15.5	31.1	9.6

Table B-4. Cities — What: Education, Employment, and Income, 2005–2007

STATE Place code	STATE City	Educational attainment			Employment status				Percent of households with no workers	Median household income (dollars)	Percent of families with income below poverty	Percent of households with income less than $25,000	Percent of households with income of $100,000 or more
		Total population 25 years and over	Percent with a high school diploma or less	Percent with a bachelor's degree or more	Total population 16 years and over	Percent in the labor force	Unemployment rate	Percent who worked full-time, year-round					
	ACS table number:	C15002	C15002	C15002	C20005	C23001	C23001	C20005	C08202	B19013	C17015	C19001	C19001
		1	2	3	4	5	6	7	8	9	10	11	12
00 00000	**United States**..................	195,646,383	46.0	27.0	233,658,279	64.7	6.6	39.9	26.2	50,007	9.8	24.5	19.0
01 00000	**Alabama**.........................	3,015,910	52.3	21.1	3,596,728	60.0	7.0	38.3	30.9	40,052	12.9	32.4	12.9
01 00820	Alabaster............................	18,232	33.6	32.0	21,654	71.9	3.9	50.1	14.8	68,417	5.9	13.3	22.4
01 01852	Anniston.............................	15,360	57.1	20.4	17,816	54.7	9.5	37.3	39.8	32,638	17.9	41.6	10.1
01 02956	Athens................................	14,155	52.9	19.5	16,649	56.9	7.3	36.4	36.0	35,193	15.0	36.2	12.6
01 03076	Auburn...............................	22,524	20.7	56.5	42,978	55.9	5.4	27.2	33.3	31,012	11.8	44.3	15.5
01 05980	Bessemer	18,365	58.0	10.4	21,716	58.3	11.5	37.5	37.8	28,110	23.7	46.2	8.3
01 07000	Birmingham......................	142,164	50.4	20.9	171,606	60.6	12.7	35.7	34.1	30,014	22.4	42.9	7.4
01 20104	Decatur..............................	36,217	45.0	25.8	41,812	63.2	5.1	41.9	30.6	41,563	12.0	32.3	14.6
01 21184	Dothan...............................	41,550	44.3	24.2	48,424	60.8	5.5	39.9	30.1	40,363	12.8	33.2	14.8
01 24184	Enterprise..........................	14,610	37.6	27.3	16,915	63.6	5.2	40.7	28.1	45,908	10.9	27.0	17.1
01 26896	Florence.............................	23,670	45.8	25.7	30,098	53.8	8.6	30.2	42.0	29,067	18.9	44.0	9.8
01 28696	Gadsden.............................	25,639	62.3	14.0	30,420	52.1	10.7	31.8	40.6	26,499	20.2	47.8	5.3
01 35800	Homewood.........................	16,107	21.4	56.3	21,870	68.2	6.2	39.6	25.4	55,685	4.8	22.3	22.6
01 35896	Hoover...............................	49,475	18.4	55.5	56,215	71.1	3.2	48.2	19.2	75,060	2.1	11.2	36.7
01 37000	Huntsville..........................	109,456	34.5	39.0	134,405	63.7	8.7	37.6	28.3	45,851	10.1	27.8	20.0
01 45784	Madison	23,212	18.4	54.8	27,405	70.7	3.9	50.1	14.1	78,560	5.0	13.7	35.8
01 50000	Mobile...............................	122,966	47.0	25.2	150,029	59.4	7.6	36.2	32.0	35,239	18.7	36.2	11.1
01 51000	Montgomery......................	123,667	43.5	30.7	153,350	64.6	8.4	40.8	28.3	41,285	16.0	31.5	14.2
01 51696	Mountain Brook.................	14,291	6.1	81.0	16,075	-	-	39.5	21.9	126,586	1.8	8.2	62.9
01 55200	Northport	14,320	42.8	31.0	17,537	63.2	5.2	38.6	31.4	43,092	15.7	34.1	14.0
01 57048	Opelika..............................	16,271	46.1	25.1	19,342	66.2	7.4	41.4	30.8	30,308	17.2	37.4	8.8
01 57576	Oxford...............................	14,818	54.7	18.9	16,718	65.4	6.2	43.6	26.1	47,269	8.8	26.2	14.5
01 58848	Pelham...............................	11,970	28.7	36.8	14,223	-	-	52.3	18.5	64,531	5.3	17.3	23.8
01 59472	Phenix...............................	20,079	58.1	13.2	23,453	61.2	9.3	39.2	32.3	31,794	18.1	40.8	6.6
01 62328	Prattville............................	17,992	46.1	25.9	21,196	67.6	4.7	46.2	21.6	50,623	8.0	20.7	16.9
01 62496	Prichard.............................	15,470	69.4	10.2	19,657	48.3	13.4	28.7	44.0	21,409	31.3	55.5	2.8
01 77256	Tuscaloosa.........................	44,922	42.2	33.6	65,879	56.8	7.7	30.0	32.6	28,574	16.8	45.8	10.2
01 78552	Vestavia Hills.....................	23,198	16.0	50.9	26,370	61.8	3.0	42.0	25.4	76,793	2.4	15.6	39.7
02 00000	**Alaska**	418,136	39.4	26.2	516,556	71.4	8.6	37.5	20.9	61,766	7.6	17.8	25.2
02 03000	Anchorage municipality	174,249	33.2	31.8	212,318	73.1	7.7	42.3	18.9	66,244	6.6	15.5	28.1
02 24230	Fairbanks...........................	17,500	39.8	20.7	25,118	76.8	6.0	49.4	24.2	48,364	10.9	25.8	18.7
02 36400	Juneau city and borough....	20,259	31.1	36.1	24,876	75.4	6.7	41.5	16.0	76,185	5.1	14.0	33.1
04 00000	**Arizona**	3,949,023	43.1	25.2	4,704,044	62.6	5.7	39.5	27.7	48,609	10.3	23.5	17.4
04 02830	Apache Junction	30,059	52.2	11.3	34,779	53.3	4.8	34.7	41.6	39,439	10.2	29.2	6.5
04 04720	Avondale	38,167	49.0	19.7	47,129	71.6	7.8	46.3	15.8	58,638	11.3	17.8	18.9
04 07940	Buckeye town....................	16,007	53.0	15.7	19,283	58.8	8.0	36.9	15.3	54,858	7.1	18.7	19.0
04 08220	Bullhead	28,638	57.6	11.9	31,949	57.4	10.2	32.5	37.9	35,952	12.2	28.8	7.7
04 10530	Casa Grande......................	24,744	52.9	17.7	30,384	62.8	6.5	38.8	30.2	41,508	16.5	25.1	10.9
04 10670	Casas Adobes CDP.............	39,544	28.0	35.0	46,009	64.2	5.8	40.0	28.3	53,989	4.7	19.3	19.7
04 11230	Catalina Foothills CDP........	41,630	14.0	64.0	47,249	56.6	2.8	34.6	30.4	82,708	1.8	14.0	43.5
04 12000	Chandler............................	148,166	30.2	36.6	176,178	75.3	4.7	49.9	14.6	68,951	4.9	11.8	29.5
04 20540	Drexel Heights CDP............	16,009	53.3	11.5	19,189	66.3	10.4	42.9	22.4	47,835	10.1	21.4	8.8
04 22220	El Mirage	16,982	56.9	10.8	21,058	70.0	5.4	47.2	13.6	52,789	13.4	15.7	8.7
04 23620	Flagstaff.............................	35,274	31.1	39.2	50,518	72.4	4.0	37.2	17.3	47,289	9.5	25.1	16.4
04 25030	Fortuna Foothills CDP.........	22,113	55.2	11.7	23,049	34.0	7.3	18.9	61.3	42,832	7.1	27.5	9.3
04 25300	Fountain Hills town	18,454	26.4	38.9	19,866	-	-	37.0	35.4	70,096	4.4	12.9	34.0
04 27400	Gilbert town	107,430	24.1	39.0	126,356	74.9	3.4	49.2	12.8	78,992	3.3	7.5	34.0
04 27820	Glendale............................	145,665	47.3	19.3	176,877	67.6	6.0	44.6	20.8	50,229	12.5	23.2	18.4
04 28380	Goodyear...........................	33,196	35.4	28.0	38,150	64.9	4.4	41.7	19.4	74,151	5.3	9.8	30.9
04 29710	Green Valley CDP...............	20,580	31.0	34.7	20,727	-	-	8.4	80.8	43,567	2.1	26.3	12.0
04 37620	Kingman............................	19,219	49.3	16.5	23,186	57.1	7.0	31.1	36.2	43,723	12.5	24.2	9.2
04 39370	Lake Havasu.......................	37,678	50.9	13.2	42,639	53.9	4.6	31.8	40.1	40,916	7.7	25.5	13.1
04 44270	Marana town......................	18,009	30.3	35.1	20,139	58.3	3.9	39.4	29.3	64,332	5.2	12.1	21.2
04 44410	Maricopa...........................	11,954	27.0	34.8	13,949	-	-	59.8	8.7	68,064	2.9	5.6	22.4
04 46000	Mesa.................................	302,945	44.6	22.2	363,664	64.9	5.1	42.5	28.1	49,116	8.1	21.6	15.6
04 49360	New River CDP...................	16,963	26.1	34.6	18,786	72.7	2.8	46.9	17.2	91,676	3.5	8.5	43.6
04 51600	Oro Valley town	29,016	20.5	49.2	32,359	52.5	4.0	31.2	38.7	74,015	3.7	12.9	31.7
04 54050	Peoria	95,082	38.4	26.6	110,407	64.9	4.4	44.7	25.4	64,685	3.6	14.7	24.7
04 55000	Phoenix..............................	885,878	48.3	23.6	1,062,354	68.5	5.3	46.2	19.4	47,223	13.2	24.3	17.4
04 57380	Prescott	32,347	34.3	33.1	37,424	50.3	4.2	28.0	41.5	44,951	5.2	25.2	14.7
04 57450	Prescott Valley town...........	23,864	45.3	15.2	28,790	58.0	4.4	33.5	36.6	41,443	13.2	24.1	7.5
04 58150	Queen Creek town	21,767	36.4	21.1	24,359	74.0	3.8	52.5	12.8	70,814	4.9	10.9	21.6
04 63470	San Luis	8,004	79.3	4.4	10,654	48.0	20.9	21.7	23.0	26,526	28.2	48.7	0.9
04 65000	Scottsdale..........................	161,323	21.9	49.5	180,004	64.2	3.8	41.1	28.2	68,671	4.0	15.5	34.0
04 66820	Sierra Vista........................	24,806	30.9	25.6	30,650	64.0	5.2	40.7	29.6	48,576	7.5	22.8	15.1
04 66845	Sierra Vista Southeast CDP...	12,635	35.8	27.1	15,331	60.1	6.6	37.4	27.8	56,700	7.4	20.1	22.1
04 70320	Sun CDP............................	40,841	44.4	21.6	40,917	-	-	12.7	74.1	34,782	2.8	33.0	6.2
04 70355	Sun West CDP	27,045	38.1	30.0	27,136	-	-	5.8	84.9	43,658	3.4	24.9	10.4
04 71510	Surprise	69,708	38.5	24.8	77,220	55.4	5.1	35.5	37.7	59,679	5.5	16.3	17.0
04 73000	Tempe...............................	96,722	30.9	37.7	137,015	72.1	5.4	42.4	19.3	47,694	9.5	23.8	18.3
04 77000	Tucson...............................	325,548	42.9	25.4	409,108	64.1	7.1	36.9	26.5	36,752	14.0	32.5	9.1
04 85540	Yuma.................................	55,472	52.0	15.8	69,735	62.4	7.5	37.6	30.7	40,352	13.1	28.2	10.4

Table B-4. Cities — What: Education, Employment, and Income, 2005–2007—*Continued*

STATE Place code	STATE City	Educational attainment			Employment status				Percent of households with no workers	Median household income (dollars)	Percent of families with income below poverty	Percent of households with income less than $25,000	Percent of households with income of $100,000 or more
		Total population 25 years and over	Percent with a high school diploma or less	Percent with a bachelor's degree or more	Total population 16 years and over	Percent in the labor force	Unemployment rate	Percent who worked full-time, year-round					
	ACS table number:	C15002	C15002	C15002	C20005	C23001	C23001	C20005	C08202	B19013	C17015	C19001	C19001
		1	2	3	4	5	6	7	8	9	10	11	12
05 00000	**Arkansas**	1,842,453	55.3	18.7	2,190,608	61.1	7.1	37.7	30.8	37,555	13.3	33.5	10.2
05 05290	Benton	15,517	48.4	21.7	18,831	66.3	3.3	42.0	26.5	43,680	10.0	27.1	11.4
05 05320	Bentonville	17,995	40.8	33.2	21,912	70.5	3.3	47.5	14.6	50,698	7.9	19.4	21.9
05 10300	Cabot	13,065	38.5	23.8	15,358	69.4	3.4	46.8	21.5	54,557	8.9	17.8	15.6
05 15190	Conway	29,293	37.0	35.0	43,163	66.9	6.8	35.8	20.3	41,375	12.2	31.4	15.9
05 23290	Fayetteville	39,437	28.5	43.5	56,704	65.9	3.4	39.2	20.1	38,983	12.1	33.6	12.9
05 24550	Fort Smith	54,357	51.9	18.9	63,996	64.0	6.0	40.6	28.3	34,980	13.4	36.8	10.5
05 33400	Hot Springs	26,571	52.4	16.1	31,386	57.7	10.3	33.0	40.2	27,596	18.3	44.8	5.6
05 34750	Jacksonville	16,759	49.0	14.3	21,085	69.0	8.1	45.7	24.7	38,825	11.8	29.2	9.4
05 35710	Jonesboro	37,785	46.0	28.4	48,421	66.3	8.6	37.0	27.7	38,793	15.7	33.3	13.3
05 41000	Little Rock	124,909	33.4	38.9	145,930	68.1	5.8	43.9	23.9	43,524	11.2	26.4	17.7
05 50450	North Little Rock	39,175	50.0	23.6	45,488	63.0	8.8	39.9	32.1	37,340	14.7	35.9	10.6
05 53390	Paragould	15,586	66.9	13.2	18,325	59.5	7.0	35.2	33.6	35,351	17.1	37.5	5.4
05 55310	Pine Bluff	30,965	56.3	17.7	38,700	58.8	17.3	31.8	35.9	30,809	21.9	43.1	6.0
05 60410	Rogers	28,905	49.7	24.6	34,089	71.4	7.1	45.9	18.8	45,826	10.5	24.2	17.1
05 61670	Russellville	16,151	43.0	27.0	21,415	61.1	8.2	35.3	30.2	36,390	12.6	34.9	12.7
05 63020	Searcy	11,314	48.7	26.9	17,117	60.5	7.4	29.4	27.2	32,686	14.1	36.8	9.9
05 63800	Sherwood	16,226	34.6	26.8	18,647	69.6	5.1	46.9	22.4	53,190	6.0	17.9	15.9
05 66080	Springdale	37,785	57.4	18.7	45,378	70.0	6.9	46.1	21.0	44,326	11.5	26.0	9.4
05 68810	Texarkana	19,815	56.3	17.3	23,150	57.7	7.6	33.0	31.5	35,625	15.0	37.0	9.2
05 71480	Van Buren	12,748	51.5	16.2	15,614	61.7	7.0	41.3	27.1	39,884	13.3	30.8	10.5
05 74540	West Memphis	16,387	64.3	10.8	20,263	59.8	11.6	36.0	32.2	26,870	31.3	48.2	7.0
06 00000	**California**	23,080,916	43.0	29.1	27,949,362	64.1	6.8	38.6	24.0	58,361	9.7	20.6	25.8
06 00296	Adelanto	13,620	69.3	7.8	17,573	54.4	17.7	30.0	28.1	42,210	23.7	32.1	4.1
06 00394	Agoura Hills	13,348	14.1	59.1	15,942	72.4	4.7	44.6	16.1	108,862	0.9	6.7	54.2
06 00562	Alameda	53,198	26.0	45.4	60,155	65.7	6.4	40.9	22.9	70,144	7.7	15.8	33.4
06 00884	Alhambra	59,748	42.1	33.4	69,636	61.7	5.6	40.2	22.4	52,090	10.3	21.8	19.1
06 00947	Aliso Viejo	31,116	17.3	53.7	34,962	79.3	3.4	58.0	10.4	92,280	2.4	4.9	44.9
06 01290	Altadena CDP	28,353	31.2	41.4	33,210	65.2	5.5	44.1	22.3	77,020	6.4	14.7	37.0
06 02000	Anaheim	203,208	52.6	22.1	248,540	69.2	6.5	43.2	18.4	56,315	9.7	18.6	22.3
06 02252	Antioch	58,855	42.2	20.9	73,956	66.2	7.9	39.3	22.7	69,165	7.7	15.3	27.6
06 02364	Apple Valley town	41,984	46.9	15.8	50,933	56.5	8.1	34.3	32.8	48,946	13.0	23.8	17.6
06 02462	Arcadia	40,222	24.8	49.1	47,066	61.8	2.9	41.0	21.7	76,823	7.0	16.3	36.5
06 02553	Arden-Arcade CDP	64,242	33.0	35.1	74,735	63.6	6.8	36.0	30.3	48,848	11.2	25.2	20.0
06 02980	Ashland CDP	12,911	51.7	15.9	16,030	63.4	7.5	42.0	22.6	45,613	19.2	24.7	13.5
06 03064	Atascadero	18,493	37.6	23.8	21,746	64.9	5.6	38.2	23.1	54,827	6.2	18.5	21.1
06 03162	Atwater	17,805	54.0	12.2	21,793	60.2	11.4	33.1	27.0	47,638	17.1	25.8	14.8
06 03386	Azusa	27,116	58.8	16.2	35,646	68.1	6.5	41.1	19.8	54,616	8.8	20.9	16.7
06 03526	Bakersfield	181,455	50.3	19.7	225,684	64.7	8.2	37.6	22.5	50,918	14.1	22.5	18.9
06 03666	Baldwin Park	45,332	72.4	9.9	57,278	59.7	6.6	39.3	16.4	47,977	13.0	21.5	12.1
06 03820	Banning	18,974	54.6	14.5	22,467	45.7	6.0	29.8	45.1	40,073	7.6	30.0	9.9
06 04030	Barstow	13,947	56.2	10.7	17,277	61.0	8.6	36.1	27.6	39,564	20.7	34.8	10.2
06 04415	Bay Point CDP	12,088	55.5	15.4	14,771	62.6	7.4	35.8	23.3	52,594	11.9	19.5	18.8
06 04758	Beaumont	12,247	52.7	15.3	14,897	63.6	5.1	39.6	22.9	46,703	14.7	24.2	15.2
06 04870	Bell	21,518	77.7	3.4	26,586	59.8	6.1	39.4	21.4	37,130	17.8	34.8	8.2
06 04982	Bellflower	44,564	57.0	16.3	56,065	66.2	8.2	41.5	22.7	45,678	11.7	23.1	15.4
06 04996	Bell Gardens	23,619	80.3	3.6	30,187	59.7	5.1	40.4	14.1	38,049	20.1	28.5	7.0
06 05108	Belmont	17,581	13.4	59.4	20,113	71.1	3.5	46.5	20.2	99,739	1.5	7.7	49.9
06 05290	Benicia	17,117	19.8	47.0	20,240	68.0	3.2	37.4	24.3	84,025	4.9	13.4	40.8
06 06000	Berkeley	67,416	17.7	65.4	95,675	59.8	6.2	26.1	29.4	52,900	7.8	27.9	26.4
06 06308	Beverly Hills	25,049	19.0	60.3	28,865	56.7	3.0	35.4	28.9	82,669	6.8	17.6	42.9
06 07064	Bloomington CDP	12,485	72.9	6.8	16,198	56.5	9.3	31.5	19.7	45,179	12.6	22.3	12.1
06 07218	Blythe	14,247	72.2	6.2	17,380	-	-	16.5	26.8	36,883	20.3	39.1	10.5
06 08058	Brawley	13,436	66.5	8.1	16,864	62.1	9.7	32.8	27.6	35,414	21.5	37.7	15.2
06 08100	Brea	26,245	29.8	38.8	30,494	67.2	5.7	43.4	19.9	78,156	3.2	11.9	34.4
06 08142	Brentwood	26,434	37.1	26.9	30,437	62.9	4.8	38.1	24.8	87,068	3.9	9.8	40.4
06 08786	Buena Park	51,305	46.4	24.8	62,115	66.5	7.3	43.2	18.5	61,783	7.6	14.1	23.7
06 08954	Burbank	72,160	38.0	31.5	83,156	66.9	5.5	44.1	23.7	55,968	7.2	19.6	22.2
06 09066	Burlingame	21,811	21.4	56.1	24,022	64.3	6.1	41.9	21.9	82,596	1.9	13.7	39.4
06 09598	Calabasas	13,411	13.2	56.3	16,151	66.5	8.5	36.2	20.7	104,935	2.7	11.4	52.1
06 09710	Calexico	17,908	65.5	9.6	24,048	49.7	9.8	23.5	29.4	31,489	21.7	34.3	6.1
06 10046	Camarillo	42,274	27.8	38.7	49,197	66.0	6.9	38.0	28.4	78,677	3.7	11.6	36.8
06 10345	Campbell	26,086	28.2	44.8	29,873	71.4	5.1	44.6	19.8	70,928	4.9	16.0	34.1
06 11194	Carlsbad	65,035	18.9	51.9	73,574	67.4	3.5	43.1	22.9	82,000	4.1	11.6	40.8
06 11390	Carmichael CDP	35,285	31.6	34.0	42,779	61.0	6.0	33.6	32.5	55,991	5.4	19.8	24.9
06 11530	Carson	60,367	45.7	23.9	73,904	62.0	8.1	39.5	21.8	65,017	6.0	14.7	26.4
06 11964	Castro Valley CDP	38,079	32.2	35.7	43,871	66.1	5.4	39.5	25.0	73,756	4.3	15.2	35.4
06 12048	Cathedral	29,212	57.2	16.8	34,567	61.6	7.2	37.5	30.4	43,792	11.1	28.0	13.3
06 12524	Ceres	24,894	63.5	8.4	31,871	59.2	12.5	32.9	24.7	48,336	12.6	21.6	13.5
06 12552	Cerritos	35,909	24.0	51.1	42,715	61.7	3.4	40.3	22.3	91,476	3.0	10.1	44.7
06 13014	Chico	44,836	28.5	35.2	70,798	64.5	10.2	27.2	28.7	36,128	14.0	35.7	11.6
06 13210	Chino	48,114	54.6	15.3	60,643	57.4	7.2	37.1	16.2	70,283	3.4	11.6	27.6

STATE Place code	STATE City	Educational attainment			Employment status				Percent of households with no workers	Median household income (dollars)	Percent of families with income below poverty	Percent of households with income less than $25,000	Percent of households with income of $100,000 or more
		Total population 25 years and over	Percent with a high school diploma or less	Percent with a bachelor's degree or more	Total population 16 years and over	Percent in the labor force	Unemployment rate	Percent who worked full-time, year-round					
	ACS table number:	C15002	C15002	C15002	C20005	C23001	C23001	C20005	C08202	B19013	C17015	C19001	C19001
		1	2	3	4	5	6	7	8	9	10	11	12
	California—Cont.												
06 13214	Chino Hills	48,448	27.8	41.2	58,393	71.6	5.7	45.3	11.1	100,371	2.7	5.9	50.3
06 13392	Chula Vista	134,335	43.0	24.5	162,228	64.4	5.8	41.6	22.2	60,188	8.0	19.2	24.0
06 13588	Citrus Heights	55,825	40.2	17.9	67,746	66.8	6.7	41.5	26.8	52,473	6.1	19.2	15.0
06 13756	Claremont	21,493	19.7	51.8	28,767	59.9	3.7	29.6	25.0	90,256	1.8	14.4	44.0
06 14218	Clovis	52,521	35.7	28.0	65,979	66.9	7.0	40.7	23.5	60,610	7.5	20.0	25.1
06 14260	Coachella	15,503	85.6	4.3	20,723	66.5	7.9	41.6	16.6	35,797	21.4	31.1	5.9
06 14890	Colton	29,907	57.2	13.4	37,653	65.1	9.0	39.9	21.8	42,665	9.9	24.4	11.9
06 15044	Compton	50,412	71.4	7.2	66,671	59.5	10.1	38.2	25.9	40,784	22.8	30.7	9.4
06 16000	Concord	81,247	39.6	29.0	96,609	68.2	6.0	41.1	21.6	62,831	6.7	16.5	26.0
06 16224	Corcoran	17,837	77.7	5.2	20,811	-	-	11.8	32.1	33,367	24.0	40.9	4.1
06 16350	Corona	92,439	41.6	24.3	113,305	73.1	6.7	45.7	14.7	75,497	6.0	11.8	34.0
06 16378	Coronado	14,067	20.3	50.6	19,041	64.5	2.2	46.6	33.9	80,132	3.8	17.4	42.1
06 16532	Costa Mesa	71,064	38.6	31.4	85,821	69.8	4.5	44.2	18.1	61,075	8.0	15.9	25.8
06 16742	Covina	32,449	46.9	20.2	39,557	68.7	9.2	41.0	19.9	57,001	9.1	19.3	24.5
06 17498	Cudahy	12,384	82.6	2.5	16,443	63.1	6.0	40.8	14.8	40,608	20.7	22.3	6.1
06 17568	Culver	29,562	28.4	46.8	33,057	67.1	5.7	42.5	25.4	65,525	4.6	17.5	30.4
06 17610	Cupertino	37,724	11.1	73.0	42,808	61.9	4.9	40.5	20.4	118,635	3.6	9.2	58.3
06 17750	Cypress	32,267	32.1	35.4	38,228	66.0	6.6	39.8	21.0	80,331	5.4	11.1	36.7
06 17918	Daly	68,914	37.3	34.2	81,652	65.7	6.7	40.6	21.3	68,623	3.2	13.8	28.0
06 17946	Dana Point	24,312	25.6	45.1	27,305	63.5	3.6	40.7	28.0	81,665	4.9	14.2	41.7
06 17988	Danville town	28,687	9.5	62.8	32,543	63.8	4.1	40.4	21.7	126,797	2.2	6.3	63.1
06 18100	Davis	33,213	12.4	70.4	56,498	61.9	7.3	26.9	24.5	56,512	5.0	24.9	27.5
06 18394	Delano	27,796	78.0	4.7	34,585	48.6	13.0	22.8	19.6	37,248	21.3	32.4	6.1
06 18996	Desert Hot Springs	13,210	61.5	9.7	16,160	58.8	10.5	36.6	32.3	36,379	16.1	31.6	11.7
06 19192	Diamond Bar	37,767	23.1	46.3	44,510	66.0	5.8	41.8	16.0	87,224	2.5	9.2	41.6
06 19318	Dinuba	10,184	60.7	9.1	13,216	58.3	7.7	32.9	26.6	41,267	22.0	27.6	11.6
06 19766	Downey	67,959	51.5	20.0	81,654	64.1	7.8	41.1	22.8	56,448	7.5	18.3	19.5
06 19990	Duarte	15,499	49.8	22.6	18,348	56.2	6.9	34.1	24.4	57,037	9.1	21.3	23.7
06 20010	Dublin	27,665	30.3	41.4	33,418	65.5	5.9	44.2	10.2	106,195	3.5	6.6	55.5
06 20802	East Los Angeles CDP	71,142	81.7	4.4	89,758	59.9	6.9	40.1	20.9	35,373	23.3	35.2	8.1
06 20956	East Palo Alto	13,985	64.6	15.8	18,120	69.6	11.4	44.8	19.7	49,267	14.1	22.1	16.1
06 21712	El Cajon	58,208	49.4	16.3	70,847	63.3	8.3	37.8	25.1	49,298	11.7	24.5	15.1
06 21782	El Centro	23,858	59.6	13.3	30,307	57.9	10.1	34.5	30.4	36,574	18.3	35.9	10.3
06 21796	El Cerrito	19,968	20.0	56.3	21,980	62.2	5.9	33.3	25.9	77,650	4.8	15.3	37.6
06 21880	El Dorado Hills CDP	20,494	13.5	53.4	24,169	70.0	3.5	41.8	13.7	113,927	2.4	4.8	60.4
06 22020	Elk Grove	84,393	28.4	35.1	99,949	71.0	5.8	46.5	15.3	81,893	3.9	9.3	36.5
06 22230	El Monte	66,759	71.8	10.5	82,148	61.4	9.8	38.2	20.6	39,534	18.1	28.9	11.2
06 22300	El Paso de Robles (Paso Robles)	17,098	42.8	20.6	20,782	65.5	6.4	38.9	24.7	51,172	11.4	21.3	14.9
06 22678	Encinitas	41,315	22.0	52.9	46,531	71.2	4.0	43.0	20.1	79,714	3.1	14.5	42.2
06 22804	Escondido	85,635	49.7	21.0	104,197	67.7	5.5	42.4	21.3	53,191	8.4	21.6	20.3
06 23042	Eureka	17,670	41.8	22.6	22,109	59.6	6.8	27.4	35.5	31,119	14.8	38.6	9.2
06 23182	Fairfield	63,579	42.1	20.1	78,462	66.5	7.5	39.9	20.9	64,682	7.9	15.7	23.8
06 23294	Fair Oaks CDP	19,008	23.3	42.5	22,180	63.3	4.0	36.9	26.1	72,636	5.8	14.6	33.7
06 23462	Fallbrook CDP	19,260	43.4	21.4	22,173	60.8	5.0	37.5	27.0	52,549	7.9	16.6	22.7
06 24477	Florence-Graham CDP	34,117	82.6	3.5	44,464	61.5	6.7	40.4	20.0	33,364	27.9	37.8	6.9
06 24498	Florin CDP	15,325	62.6	9.6	18,612	57.0	10.3	31.8	34.4	38,836	14.1	30.2	6.7
06 24638	Folsom	47,914	31.7	38.7	55,018	61.4	4.9	39.0	17.7	89,865	1.7	9.3	44.6
06 24680	Fontana	101,055	58.7	13.2	129,293	67.3	5.6	42.8	12.7	60,693	9.5	13.2	22.9
06 25338	Foster	21,446	15.5	57.7	24,051	70.8	3.6	50.3	15.9	102,363	2.2	7.5	51.6
06 25380	Fountain Valley	39,481	32.4	34.9	45,882	62.5	3.7	40.0	22.0	78,729	4.0	13.7	37.4
06 26000	Fremont	141,813	29.4	48.0	161,490	67.9	5.7	44.8	16.0	88,645	3.8	9.7	43.9
06 27000	Fresno	269,255	50.8	19.5	343,183	62.6	10.1	35.4	28.4	41,546	18.9	31.1	13.3
06 28000	Fullerton	84,416	32.8	37.5	103,745	65.4	5.2	39.6	21.5	62,872	5.6	17.0	28.2
06 28112	Galt	13,107	53.3	12.1	15,422	66.0	9.8	35.5	24.1	55,465	8.1	17.1	16.1
06 28168	Gardena	39,794	48.0	20.7	46,360	60.5	6.5	37.8	25.9	44,087	13.0	28.3	13.1
06 29000	Garden Grove	106,931	54.0	19.4	128,224	62.6	6.4	38.1	21.7	59,248	11.1	19.3	22.9
06 29504	Gilroy	27,556	51.0	24.4	34,110	66.1	6.2	37.3	22.0	66,401	7.8	20.2	35.4
06 30000	Glendale	138,132	41.4	35.8	160,863	60.6	5.4	38.2	24.4	52,443	9.7	25.4	23.9
06 30014	Glendora	33,149	35.9	28.4	40,115	61.4	5.5	36.5	22.0	72,414	1.1	12.5	32.7
06 30378	Goleta	17,431	27.3	39.1	21,888	67.2	3.4	37.5	23.9	69,242	3.9	15.3	27.5
06 30693	Granite Bay CDP	15,340	23.1	45.7	17,009	59.7	4.5	31.0	25.9	115,980	1.4	7.3	57.5
06 31596	Hacienda Heights CDP	34,380	40.3	32.0	40,896	58.9	3.8	37.8	24.9	68,558	5.4	15.3	30.6
06 31960	Hanford	30,286	51.2	15.8	36,702	64.9	13.1	35.7	27.0	48,962	12.2	24.9	16.5
06 32548	Hawthorne	54,060	53.2	16.9	66,696	64.0	5.3	42.4	20.1	42,082	17.7	27.8	9.1
06 33000	Hayward	85,066	52.4	22.8	103,698	66.7	7.3	41.4	22.4	58,357	7.7	19.3	23.0
06 33182	Hemet	49,800	58.0	11.0	57,921	47.7	12.5	25.4	51.2	33,924	14.2	38.0	7.2
06 33308	Hercules	16,275	25.4	42.5	19,693	69.8	6.6	44.0	14.9	88,966	2.6	8.6	41.8
06 33434	Hesperia	48,606	59.0	7.7	62,244	60.0	10.8	35.0	24.5	48,244	13.4	21.9	16.3
06 33588	Highland	30,418	51.5	18.2	38,079	64.8	9.1	35.3	22.6	54,153	12.7	23.6	21.8
06 34120	Hollister	18,467	53.2	15.8	22,470	70.8	9.8	39.2	16.7	66,038	7.6	18.5	25.5
06 36000	Huntington Beach	134,149	26.4	39.3	154,352	69.4	4.8	42.8	22.1	77,679	3.9	12.1	38.3
06 36056	Huntington Park	34,162	80.9	6.3	43,857	62.8	4.9	42.4	14.1	33,800	20.1	32.0	6.2
06 36294	Imperial Beach	15,027	48.6	18.0	19,177	67.8	6.0	41.7	22.3	46,214	12.2	21.0	12.2

STATE Place code	STATE City	Educational attainment			Employment status				Percent of households with no workers	Median household income (dollars)	Percent of families with income below poverty	Percent of households with income less than $25,000	Percent of households with income of $100,000 or more
		Total population 25 years and over	Percent with a high school diploma or less	Percent with a bachelor's degree or more	Total population 16 years and over	Percent in the labor force	Unemployment rate	Percent who worked full-time, year-round					
	ACS table number:	C15002	C15002	C15002	C20005	C23001	C23001	C20005	C08202	B19013	C17015	C19001	C19001
		1	2	3	4	5	6	7	8	9	10	11	12
	California—Cont.												
06 36448	Indio	38,491	61.7	14.3	48,077	65.3	6.3	41.1	23.2	47,708	14.0	27.0	16.8
06 36546	Inglewood	70,441	56.1	16.3	85,435	64.8	6.7	44.0	22.7	40,110	18.1	30.5	10.0
06 36770	Irvine	114,565	14.2	62.8	150,824	64.8	3.8	41.2	17.7	91,101	4.4	13.3	45.1
06 39003	La Canada Flintridge	13,159	13.0	66.9	15,175	60.8	4.2	39.1	21.7	128,113	2.5	7.3	62.1
06 39122	Lafayette	16,717	11.3	69.0	18,916	63.4	4.4	36.5	23.8	118,974	1.9	7.8	58.0
06 39178	Laguna Beach	18,205	12.1	59.6	20,613	65.4	3.3	37.4	26.3	90,017	3.6	13.9	45.1
06 39220	Laguna Hills	20,871	25.6	43.2	24,774	67.4	2.7	42.3	16.7	89,781	7.7	12.8	45.7
06 39248	Laguna Niguel	43,093	17.4	53.7	49,990	67.3	4.0	41.9	17.6	95,925	2.7	8.3	48.2
06 39290	La Habra	37,692	45.7	21.1	45,970	68.3	5.8	42.4	20.0	59,691	6.7	14.8	24.0
06 39486	Lake Elsinore	22,236	54.6	19.6	27,458	70.0	6.4	41.8	19.2	55,179	11.2	20.1	21.0
06 39496	Lake Forest	49,793	28.3	41.6	57,592	74.0	4.1	50.8	15.8	90,084	4.0	8.6	44.7
06 39892	Lakewood	54,211	39.7	26.0	65,285	68.2	5.2	43.5	22.0	70,820	2.7	12.8	28.3
06 40004	La Mesa	35,676	30.3	31.8	44,185	65.6	5.6	38.1	28.2	47,590	7.9	22.5	14.4
06 40032	La Mirada	29,993	40.3	26.1	37,298	60.9	5.4	38.6	27.5	77,952	3.0	15.0	35.4
06 40130	Lancaster	84,227	52.3	14.8	105,533	57.5	9.7	34.8	29.6	46,666	17.4	27.8	16.4
06 40326	La Presa CDP	20,248	51.0	14.6	25,153	64.9	9.3	42.8	22.2	56,777	7.9	20.9	17.8
06 40340	La Puente	23,905	73.5	9.3	30,026	64.1	5.3	44.2	21.5	46,527	11.2	22.4	10.8
06 40354	La Quinta	23,081	34.3	32.8	25,874	61.2	4.7	36.2	32.5	72,452	3.9	12.6	36.1
06 40830	La Verne	21,726	32.0	32.2	25,440	63.8	7.5	36.6	22.3	75,444	5.9	16.4	34.5
06 40886	Lawndale	19,335	58.8	17.6	22,869	63.5	6.2	43.4	18.2	42,660	12.8	27.7	15.2
06 41124	Lemon Grove	14,739	51.6	14.8	17,770	56.8	7.5	39.1	25.9	50,521	11.9	25.3	13.9
06 41152	Lemoore	13,580	49.1	13.3	17,719	68.5	12.6	39.7	21.0	53,779	7.9	18.6	11.8
06 41180	Lennox CDP	12,718	82.0	3.0	16,565	64.5	6.6	43.8	17.9	35,625	25.2	33.1	3.5
06 41474	Lincoln	23,954	30.0	27.1	26,237	50.7	3.0	30.8	41.8	59,906	5.8	16.2	24.4
06 41992	Livermore	50,884	29.6	37.1	59,355	72.4	5.4	47.4	18.4	94,813	5.0	11.1	47.2
06 42202	Lodi	40,089	51.8	18.8	48,103	62.0	7.8	36.6	28.0	48,074	10.2	24.2	17.5
06 42370	Loma Linda	15,973	27.2	45.8	18,700	65.0	7.4	39.4	24.2	52,272	7.4	19.7	18.9
06 42468	Lomita	13,243	42.7	27.4	15,131	70.2	4.1	43.2	23.1	59,013	5.0	19.7	22.6
06 42524	Lompoc	25,856	54.4	12.3	31,018	57.5	7.0	34.8	25.1	47,867	12.7	24.2	12.3
06 43000	Long Beach	284,770	44.3	26.7	352,122	65.9	8.0	38.5	23.5	47,274	16.1	26.4	19.3
06 43280	Los Altos	20,259	8.0	80.7	22,169	57.8	4.3	36.5	27.0	158,745	2.1	6.6	67.6
06 44000	Los Angeles	2,407,555	49.2	28.8	2,926,676	65.2	7.3	39.2	23.5	46,292	15.8	28.1	20.0
06 44028	Los Banos	18,793	63.0	10.4	23,722	60.5	14.5	34.7	26.0	49,673	14.3	26.1	16.1
06 44112	Los Gatos town	21,204	13.4	61.5	23,829	61.2	4.8	36.5	23.6	116,568	2.5	11.9	56.3
06 44574	Lynwood	39,185	78.6	4.7	50,670	56.7	7.9	37.4	14.8	41,843	18.2	24.4	9.4
06 45022	Madera	28,383	69.7	7.4	36,663	62.0	11.0	36.1	26.4	40,477	18.2	28.6	8.8
06 45400	Manhattan Beach	24,679	10.3	70.2	28,293	67.8	4.9	43.6	22.4	124,048	2.1	8.7	61.8
06 45484	Manteca	35,458	52.2	14.2	44,306	64.0	7.2	38.5	23.7	59,585	9.4	16.8	22.7
06 46114	Martinez	24,699	27.9	35.9	28,194	67.2	5.6	39.1	21.6	73,668	5.9	13.7	35.1
06 46492	Maywood	15,244	79.7	4.3	19,389	62.8	8.7	43.5	16.9	37,678	17.6	31.9	6.5
06 46870	Menlo Park	21,618	15.8	67.3	24,316	66.6	5.9	39.7	23.5	103,702	2.9	7.1	51.8
06 46898	Merced	38,278	51.8	16.0	50,591	62.4	12.0	30.3	31.7	35,042	22.6	38.7	11.1
06 47486	Millbrae	15,363	32.3	39.9	17,841	59.2	3.4	34.6	32.7	70,712	3.8	15.3	36.4
06 47766	Milpitas	44,744	35.0	36.9	52,123	64.3	7.7	44.0	18.1	85,668	5.1	13.3	41.9
06 47976	Mira Loma CDP	11,918	68.7	5.1	15,904	69.4	12.2	37.6	14.5	64,154	12.2	15.9	24.7
06 48256	Mission Viejo	65,312	24.4	41.1	75,253	67.7	4.0	43.2	20.4	92,676	2.5	10.0	44.9
06 48354	Modesto	123,882	48.7	18.5	152,247	60.8	9.8	33.9	29.0	49,047	11.1	24.0	18.6
06 48648	Monrovia	25,775	33.7	36.5	29,996	67.4	5.9	41.5	22.1	63,383	7.7	19.3	28.0
06 48788	Montclair	20,472	62.2	12.6	26,237	64.2	13.6	37.5	20.3	56,147	11.4	19.9	13.2
06 48816	Montebello	40,780	54.5	16.5	47,512	61.2	7.1	39.8	25.8	50,049	12.0	24.6	15.4
06 48872	Monterey	19,441	19.8	50.7	25,656	71.3	4.6	40.8	26.5	56,580	9.9	20.0	25.7
06 48914	Monterey Park	45,007	50.6	26.8	51,791	56.1	5.6	37.4	25.2	49,967	7.7	24.1	18.9
06 49138	Moorpark	19,387	35.1	34.3	24,491	73.9	4.0	47.5	11.3	90,109	5.0	10.3	44.8
06 49270	Moreno Valley	98,202	56.8	13.7	125,935	65.0	7.7	39.6	17.3	55,604	13.1	18.7	17.2
06 49278	Morgan Hill	22,921	32.2	34.3	26,891	67.9	3.9	45.3	18.3	99,243	5.3	11.7	49.7
06 49670	Mountain View	52,589	22.5	57.3	59,298	72.1	4.4	48.0	16.9	82,904	3.9	13.2	40.8
06 50076	Murrieta	54,115	36.4	26.5	67,017	67.1	6.0	38.6	21.4	74,775	4.2	11.3	33.1
06 50258	Napa	50,027	45.5	24.6	59,133	67.0	6.4	36.5	26.2	61,955	6.7	19.0	27.0
06 50398	National	31,882	64.6	9.1	40,399	60.1	8.6	39.8	26.7	35,484	19.7	34.8	7.9
06 50916	Newark	27,528	44.2	28.2	31,599	67.9	6.8	45.1	18.8	78,367	7.3	11.3	34.8
06 51182	Newport Beach	62,273	13.7	60.9	70,085	62.8	2.6	42.3	25.7	107,493	2.4	10.4	54.1
06 51560	Norco	18,095	55.2	13.3	22,020	55.1	5.0	34.3	16.3	81,182	2.2	10.2	37.4
06 51924	North Highlands CDP	26,572	54.8	8.9	31,821	60.6	8.4	34.3	27.4	40,710	15.3	27.1	5.9
06 52379	North Tustin CDP	17,117	15.2	61.2	19,475	62.4	5.0	38.3	22.5	114,149	2.9	10.3	57.2
06 52526	Norwalk	65,875	60.5	13.1	81,591	63.3	9.2	38.9	20.2	55,667	8.6	18.4	14.7
06 52582	Novato	35,666	27.5	41.3	41,666	67.0	3.9	39.4	24.1	78,895	5.7	13.2	36.3
06 53000	Oakland	252,943	42.9	33.7	294,139	65.1	9.9	36.4	28.5	47,179	15.7	28.5	21.2
06 53070	Oakley	16,648	48.6	13.5	20,190	67.6	4.0	41.2	18.7	72,756	4.4	13.9	29.5
06 53322	Oceanside	106,535	41.6	25.5	129,712	64.6	5.2	43.2	26.8	61,813	5.9	16.9	24.0
06 53448	Oildale CDP	19,354	61.8	7.0	24,164	60.7	10.8	37.5	32.2	40,243	15.5	32.0	9.4
06 53896	Ontario	93,502	60.2	14.3	117,840	68.8	7.9	44.9	16.6	55,781	9.8	17.6	18.3
06 53980	Orange	86,476	40.5	29.1	106,927	68.2	5.6	41.7	19.5	72,905	5.2	12.5	34.1
06 54092	Orangevale CDP	17,404	34.5	25.7	20,620	65.8	5.6	40.2	24.9	67,517	5.3	14.4	25.0
06 54120	Orcutt CDP	18,758	32.2	26.6	21,552	61.5	4.1	33.9	29.6	64,269	4.1	11.0	22.9

Table B-4. Cities — What: Education, Employment, and Income, 2005–2007—Continued

STATE Place code	STATE City	Educational attainment			Employment status				Percent of households with no workers	Median household income (dollars)	Percent of families with income below poverty	Percent of households with income less than $25,000	Percent of households with income of $100,000 or more
		Total population 25 years and over	Percent with a high school diploma or less	Percent with a bachelor's degree or more	Total population 16 years and over	Percent in the labor force	Unemployment rate	Percent who worked full-time, year-round					
	ACS table number:	C15002	C15002	C15002	C20005	C23001	C23001	C20005	C08202	B19013	C17015	C19001	C19001
		1	2	3	4	5	6	7	8	9	10	11	12
	California—Cont.												
06 54652	Oxnard	104,459	59.2	15.8	131,380	66.6	6.6	40.3	19.6	55,716	11.6	19.2	21.2
06 54806	Pacifica	26,326	26.2	36.8	30,641	72.1	5.2	43.6	21.4	82,000	4.0	12.0	41.0
06 55156	Palmdale	78,275	55.8	14.8	98,331	63.2	10.5	37.5	22.3	55,240	14.9	21.9	19.7
06 55184	Palm Desert	36,567	32.2	34.0	40,634	53.3	4.7	29.3	42.5	51,999	5.6	20.9	25.8
06 55254	Palm Springs	31,746	37.1	30.5	35,087	55.9	6.0	31.4	38.9	43,615	8.6	27.7	16.7
06 55282	Palo Alto	45,299	9.5	77.7	50,789	64.4	3.8	41.5	23.2	119,046	3.3	11.2	57.3
06 55520	Paradise town	20,530	40.0	18.9	22,737	49.4	4.9	27.0	46.8	40,206	8.7	32.8	14.7
06 55618	Paramount	30,149	71.8	10.2	38,613	64.0	9.9	40.0	18.5	41,824	17.0	26.4	7.5
06 55837	Parkway-South Sacramento CDP	18,116	69.4	7.6	22,784	57.9	14.1	31.0	34.5	33,877	25.0	40.0	3.4
06 56000	Pasadena	95,063	32.5	45.6	111,146	63.6	4.3	42.1	23.9	61,269	9.7	22.2	30.1
06 56700	Perris	29,008	69.0	8.1	37,836	64.6	9.9	38.2	19.5	49,675	13.9	21.4	11.3
06 56784	Petaluma	39,146	37.1	32.2	45,417	70.3	6.1	41.2	20.5	68,949	3.5	14.0	31.8
06 56924	Pico Rivera	41,321	65.8	9.7	50,815	62.2	6.0	41.3	22.5	57,722	8.2	19.7	17.2
06 57456	Pittsburg	37,174	53.2	15.5	47,029	61.1	7.8	37.0	22.5	56,333	12.1	20.8	21.2
06 57526	Placentia	32,602	35.3	31.6	38,812	68.2	5.2	44.0	20.0	77,496	5.7	12.6	33.8
06 57764	Pleasant Hill	23,454	22.6	43.9	27,481	69.2	5.2	39.9	20.9	80,737	2.5	15.5	40.7
06 57792	Pleasanton	45,504	19.3	56.0	52,590	68.6	4.5	43.3	17.5	109,470	1.9	6.9	56.9
06 58072	Pomona	87,583	65.3	13.0	110,726	65.6	9.1	39.5	18.8	47,992	12.2	21.9	14.3
06 58240	Porterville	28,375	60.7	9.8	35,179	59.3	12.9	28.8	30.8	35,633	19.3	32.9	7.5
06 58296	Port Hueneme	13,308	43.3	15.4	17,812	67.3	6.1	40.2	29.6	51,609	9.8	21.2	14.2
06 58520	Poway	31,251	24.3	43.5	37,185	65.9	4.2	43.9	22.3	92,083	4.2	10.0	46.7
06 59444	Rancho Cordova	37,293	42.7	20.8	44,975	66.3	8.9	39.4	24.1	45,472	13.4	24.4	16.3
06 59451	Rancho Cucamonga	96,833	33.0	29.4	119,386	71.1	5.4	43.7	14.2	78,452	4.5	11.4	35.3
06 59514	Rancho Palos Verdes	31,296	16.2	60.3	35,297	54.9	2.7	34.1	27.9	108,640	2.3	8.7	54.9
06 59550	Rancho San Diego CDP	13,437	23.5	44.4	15,742	65.7	5.9	41.3	18.3	91,821	1.0	6.4	45.6
06 59587	Rancho Santa Margarita	30,102	16.7	49.4	34,780	73.5	2.4	48.7	10.5	95,061	1.2	7.5	47.2
06 59920	Redding	59,710	38.8	21.5	72,460	59.8	9.1	31.2	34.4	42,120	13.1	28.8	13.6
06 59962	Redlands	43,559	30.4	36.0	54,379	65.6	7.1	37.0	23.4	61,641	6.6	17.0	26.8
06 60018	Redondo Beach	49,181	19.4	54.4	54,509	74.5	3.2	48.8	17.4	89,460	2.7	11.1	44.2
06 60102	Redwood	51,179	37.8	36.7	59,778	66.1	6.3	42.9	20.7	72,679	6.3	15.0	35.7
06 60242	Reedley	13,539	60.3	14.7	17,541	61.6	8.0	29.6	26.7	42,198	19.0	31.2	14.3
06 60466	Rialto	55,520	65.3	8.1	73,263	62.3	6.2	38.9	19.1	49,255	10.8	21.2	15.5
06 60620	Richmond	63,235	47.2	24.8	75,321	64.6	11.0	36.9	26.0	50,346	14.0	25.5	18.9
06 60704	Ridgecrest	17,218	37.1	26.2	21,111	63.1	9.7	38.1	32.8	50,920	14.4	28.7	20.8
06 61068	Riverbank	11,509	58.7	11.5	14,065	66.1	13.3	36.5	21.6	53,968	9.3	17.0	14.8
06 62000	Riverside	176,970	50.3	20.8	231,934	65.9	8.0	38.7	20.3	54,099	9.7	20.1	19.7
06 62364	Rocklin	33,846	26.5	37.6	42,020	72.4	5.4	43.0	21.3	74,874	1.9	13.1	34.1
06 62546	Rohnert Park	24,756	40.3	24.2	31,607	68.1	6.7	39.6	24.6	58,791	5.1	20.3	18.5
06 62896	Rosemead	36,490	68.2	14.1	42,447	53.9	7.3	34.9	20.8	44,115	11.6	24.2	13.4
06 62910	Rosemont CDP	14,970	42.9	20.5	18,583	69.4	9.0	40.4	17.1	54,297	10.9	17.4	13.8
06 62938	Roseville	75,165	29.2	34.9	89,932	66.1	4.6	42.3	25.7	68,488	4.2	13.9	28.1
06 63218	Rowland Heights CDP	33,180	41.4	34.8	40,846	61.8	4.2	41.4	17.9	67,459	9.5	18.6	33.6
06 63260	Rubidoux CDP	20,945	66.1	8.6	27,518	67.1	11.1	39.7	20.0	51,152	9.4	18.9	19.9
06 64000	Sacramento	289,434	41.8	28.7	348,493	63.3	8.5	36.5	28.0	48,584	12.2	24.6	17.9
06 64224	Salinas	83,435	64.9	12.7	104,919	67.4	10.7	34.1	22.0	51,777	13.0	21.9	17.4
06 65000	San Bernardino	115,051	61.2	12.0	147,361	58.9	9.5	34.6	25.4	38,987	19.6	31.6	8.3
06 65028	San Bruno	29,479	38.4	30.8	34,075	69.2	5.4	42.6	21.3	72,869	6.1	12.4	33.3
06 65042	San Buenaventura (Ventura)	69,198	34.5	29.5	81,613	67.3	5.3	38.9	25.6	63,147	6.9	17.9	27.4
06 65070	San Carlos	20,310	15.5	60.1	22,197	65.5	2.8	41.8	27.4	99,110	2.9	11.4	49.7
06 65084	San Clemente	41,055	22.8	44.7	47,457	66.5	3.4	38.8	24.9	82,842	6.2	13.4	42.9
06 66000	San Diego	807,816	31.9	39.9	1,002,737	66.7	5.1	41.3	22.2	60,185	9.1	19.6	26.9
06 66070	San Dimas	24,198	32.0	30.5	28,328	67.8	4.7	40.2	21.5	70,841	2.8	14.3	32.4
06 66140	San Fernando	13,256	69.2	10.5	17,067	69.3	7.8	40.1	17.2	51,872	12.0	23.4	7.9
06 67000	San Francisco	592,536	30.5	49.8	660,649	67.2	5.8	41.5	25.9	65,519	7.4	22.1	33.0
06 67042	San Gabriel	28,319	47.9	30.2	33,267	61.9	6.1	40.1	20.3	54,663	12.8	23.2	22.3
06 67056	Sanger	12,537	61.7	6.3	15,997	65.2	7.2	38.0	23.3	44,028	13.8	28.4	13.3
06 67112	San Jacinto	21,379	57.1	11.9	25,587	59.3	10.3	33.9	30.0	42,772	18.3	30.7	10.6
06 68000	San Jose	592,871	39.0	35.3	699,686	66.9	6.8	41.8	19.4	76,354	7.4	15.7	37.2
06 68028	San Juan Capistrano	22,555	35.7	35.1	27,076	60.4	6.1	36.7	27.4	67,432	10.1	16.6	34.6
06 68084	San Leandro	59,317	44.2	27.7	68,075	65.5	6.9	42.4	25.8	62,412	6.1	18.2	24.9
06 68112	San Lorenzo CDP	15,457	44.7	21.5	18,020	62.5	7.5	41.8	27.6	67,929	5.4	15.0	26.8
06 68154	San Luis Obispo	22,856	25.5	44.7	42,084	65.9	8.3	25.6	26.1	39,337	7.0	36.6	15.0
06 68196	San Marcos	44,773	41.9	29.3	53,459	69.8	6.5	42.9	21.3	67,719	7.7	17.4	27.3
06 68252	San Mateo	66,045	30.1	42.2	74,221	67.4	4.8	43.9	24.9	79,548	3.8	12.4	39.1
06 68294	San Pablo	19,123	64.9	15.1	23,080	62.8	9.5	33.9	29.2	46,326	16.2	25.0	14.6
06 68364	San Rafael	39,325	30.2	46.6	44,642	68.7	3.7	37.1	24.6	67,789	5.1	17.7	30.9
06 68378	San Ramon	38,323	16.8	53.9	44,068	74.5	3.8	50.3	12.6	111,604	1.6	5.6	57.4
06 69000	Santa Ana	187,251	71.7	11.0	235,885	68.5	6.5	42.9	13.8	53,371	14.1	17.8	17.6
06 69070	Santa Barbara	60,979	30.7	41.2	74,338	66.4	4.0	37.2	24.1	58,073	8.0	19.9	28.7
06 69084	Santa Clara	74,247	28.2	45.8	88,392	66.5	7.5	41.5	22.7	76,850	5.8	16.5	36.1
06 69088	Santa Clarita	110,788	37.1	30.9	133,142	70.8	5.2	42.5	17.1	80,200	4.6	11.4	37.1
06 69112	Santa Cruz	32,828	23.4	51.0	49,685	68.3	8.1	29.8	24.3	59,172	6.2	20.7	26.2
06 69196	Santa Maria	47,678	60.5	12.2	60,176	62.6	6.4	36.9	29.1	45,832	15.5	26.4	12.0

Table B-4. Cities — What: Education, Employment, and Income, 2005–2007—*Continued*

STATE Place code	STATE City	Educational attainment			Employment status				Percent of households with no workers	Median household income (dollars)	Percent of families with income below poverty	Percent of households with income less than $25,000	Percent of households with income of $100,000 or more
		Total population 25 years and over	Percent with a high school diploma or less	Percent with a bachelor's degree or more	Total population 16 years and over	Percent in the labor force	Unemployment rate	Percent who worked full-time, year-round					
	ACS table number:	C15002	C15002	C15002	C20005	C23001	C23001	C20005	C08202	B19013	C17015	C19001	C19001
		1	2	3	4	5	6	7	8	9	10	11	12
	California—Cont.												
06 70000	Santa Monica	69,179	17.3	60.8	76,179	67.1	5.0	40.4	27.1	63,224	5.9	21.5	32.0
06 70042	Santa Paula	17,188	62.3	10.5	21,048	60.6	8.9	35.2	29.1	44,564	13.3	26.4	16.7
06 70098	Santa Rosa	99,366	37.5	28.8	119,104	64.0	6.4	36.4	26.7	56,777	7.9	20.0	22.5
06 70224	Santee	34,341	39.0	20.1	41,256	66.3	4.8	43.0	22.3	67,376	4.1	14.6	27.4
06 70280	Saratoga	21,270	9.5	73.8	23,957	54.1	5.7	36.1	30.2	137,270	3.0	9.0	65.8
06 70686	Seal Beach	20,252	28.8	38.7	21,797	45.9	4.6	26.6	54.2	48,405	1.7	27.5	24.9
06 70742	Seaside	19,166	51.7	18.6	25,171	74.7	6.8	38.4	16.4	54,069	7.8	17.2	14.4
06 70882	Selma	12,530	60.8	10.8	15,583	65.6	7.4	37.1	22.2	41,216	20.1	28.2	11.6
06 72016	Simi Valley	80,172	36.2	30.4	95,461	71.0	3.2	48.3	16.4	85,464	3.2	9.2	40.1
06 72520	Soledad	17,310	75.2	6.2	20,426	32.8	7.6	19.1	16.8	56,453	9.5	17.7	14.6
06 72996	South El Monte	10,837	77.5	8.6	14,419	61.9	8.2	37.5	22.4	39,066	17.8	28.3	7.3
06 73080	South Gate	56,790	79.6	4.9	72,398	60.9	7.3	40.9	18.9	41,834	14.0	26.3	9.3
06 73108	South Lake Tahoe	15,758	41.2	23.3	19,530	73.6	4.2	39.2	24.2	40,411	16.3	32.5	10.6
06 73220	South Pasadena	18,516	20.1	57.7	21,171	69.1	3.4	46.0	20.1	76,438	5.3	15.6	37.5
06 73262	South San Francisco	42,675	40.8	31.5	49,561	65.3	6.2	41.6	24.5	69,203	5.6	15.2	32.4
06 73430	South Whittier CDP	35,358	63.1	11.2	43,396	67.3	5.9	43.0	15.5	63,250	8.8	15.4	21.8
06 73696	Spring Valley CDP	16,483	39.0	22.7	19,920	64.5	7.5	41.6	22.5	61,796	7.6	17.9	19.6
06 73962	Stanton	22,425	57.8	16.2	26,992	67.0	6.1	41.7	21.1	53,303	12.5	21.6	15.2
06 75000	Stockton	168,759	52.8	17.1	212,492	61.1	11.0	33.2	28.2	46,298	14.0	25.7	15.9
06 75630	Suisun	17,144	43.2	16.1	20,617	68.6	9.5	39.3	15.8	72,791	6.2	10.5	26.0
06 75826	Sun CDP	17,505	50.5	13.6	18,295	37.0	7.5	21.8	62.2	37,890	3.3	30.7	8.4
06 77000	Sunnyvale	96,989	25.0	54.2	108,896	69.0	6.0	44.1	19.1	82,622	4.8	12.2	40.8
06 78120	Temecula	54,009	32.7	30.7	65,979	70.5	5.5	43.4	17.0	75,335	5.1	10.7	31.8
06 78148	Temple	25,394	37.7	31.9	29,182	63.0	5.7	41.1	20.0	65,742	7.1	14.5	27.1
06 78582	Thousand Oaks	83,116	23.0	47.8	98,127	66.1	4.4	38.9	19.6	93,695	3.6	10.4	46.9
06 80000	Torrance	99,973	28.4	41.8	114,152	65.0	4.3	41.9	23.2	71,519	3.6	15.0	32.4
06 80238	Tracy	48,458	46.2	19.9	58,462	69.2	7.9	43.3	16.8	77,911	5.6	12.5	36.1
06 80644	Tulare	30,810	59.7	9.1	39,242	61.8	10.0	38.4	24.4	44,330	16.2	24.9	11.8
06 80812	Turlock	42,198	52.2	19.6	53,785	68.6	13.3	37.2	24.8	50,767	7.5	23.9	19.0
06 80854	Tustin	44,288	34.4	39.7	51,209	72.6	6.0	48.7	17.7	66,343	4.4	12.2	30.9
06 80994	Twentynine Palms	11,201	44.7	15.1	20,927	73.3	4.4	54.4	25.4	38,614	10.0	28.1	11.5
06 81204	Union	46,191	42.4	34.4	54,032	65.5	8.0	41.5	17.6	84,384	7.6	12.1	38.9
06 81344	Upland	48,653	34.8	29.6	58,794	67.5	5.5	41.3	19.9	65,531	6.4	14.7	28.0
06 81554	Vacaville	60,245	43.1	18.4	72,464	59.1	4.4	36.1	21.8	68,352	4.9	12.2	29.9
06 81638	Valinda CDP	12,338	69.8	8.7	15,098	67.6	7.1	47.7	17.1	49,297	5.3	10.3	15.4
06 81666	Vallejo	74,568	42.4	22.8	89,079	63.5	10.0	34.7	26.2	58,962	10.5	20.6	22.2
06 82590	Victorville	56,550	55.6	12.4	70,892	55.1	10.8	31.4	27.6	48,462	14.6	26.4	12.2
06 82852	Vineyard CDP	12,589	29.8	38.9	15,025	-	-	47.1	14.1	86,152	5.1	10.2	39.3
06 82954	Visalia	68,979	46.4	20.1	83,525	60.1	6.0	40.8	26.9	50,316	12.6	23.9	19.6
06 82996	Vista	56,415	50.6	19.3	70,822	66.6	6.4	42.4	19.6	52,847	10.6	16.5	19.9
06 83332	Walnut	19,420	23.1	45.8	24,672	61.0	5.2	39.2	17.3	100,360	2.7	5.6	50.3
06 83346	Walnut Creek	49,787	18.5	55.6	56,230	58.8	3.7	35.3	34.7	76,522	1.9	13.0	38.0
06 83542	Wasco	12,725	78.3	4.3	17,199	47.0	14.3	24.3	24.6	32,440	27.3	37.6	6.3
06 83668	Watsonville	24,582	69.9	10.4	30,773	67.8	10.3	32.0	25.1	46,531	15.9	25.8	13.6
06 84144	West Carson CDP	15,791	46.3	26.9	18,407	61.7	5.3	41.4	22.3	65,650	4.0	13.2	23.9
06 84200	West Covina	70,350	45.4	23.9	84,804	65.1	5.2	41.7	20.3	64,336	7.3	16.6	26.3
06 84410	West Hollywood	30,345	17.6	55.7	32,321	71.0	10.2	41.8	30.5	49,082	7.5	28.9	19.5
06 84550	Westminster	62,242	52.0	20.1	72,017	63.8	5.5	42.3	22.4	56,536	8.9	20.7	21.4
06 84592	Westmont CDP	16,695	65.5	6.9	20,765	57.7	11.0	34.3	32.2	29,646	29.9	44.9	5.4
06 84774	West Puente Valley CDP	14,750	73.7	8.5	18,074	59.9	7.1	41.8	19.0	57,907	4.7	18.6	15.8
06 84816	West Sacramento	27,189	49.6	19.4	33,107	66.4	10.1	41.1	28.4	47,683	12.0	24.4	21.2
06 84921	West Whittier-Los Nietos CDP	15,256	69.8	7.1	18,401	61.0	6.7	39.9	27.9	54,234	12.5	20.0	20.4
06 85292	Whittier	55,239	45.9	21.1	68,298	65.8	5.6	41.6	21.3	60,970	6.1	17.3	26.4
06 85446	Wildomar CDP	14,288	47.0	14.7	17,192	64.0	6.1	40.1	19.1	67,587	3.2	11.3	26.9
06 85614	Willowbrook CDP	18,484	71.2	7.8	23,589	54.4	11.8	37.1	34.1	32,423	26.7	40.0	6.6
06 85922	Windsor town	16,394	48.2	23.6	19,796	69.2	5.1	40.1	21.7	76,718	6.4	15.1	33.1
06 86328	Woodland	32,055	50.6	22.6	38,551	67.1	6.3	39.2	23.3	54,496	7.0	18.9	20.3
06 86832	Yorba Linda	42,110	21.8	45.7	50,347	69.5	3.6	43.3	16.6	113,488	1.4	6.7	58.6
06 86972	Yuba	36,800	46.7	17.4	45,142	63.7	11.8	33.2	30.1	49,726	9.2	23.3	17.0
06 87042	Yucaipa	32,035	43.9	19.1	38,065	62.6	6.9	35.1	26.9	55,693	8.1	22.7	24.5
06 87056	Yucca Valley town	12,656	55.2	13.6	14,537	-	-	27.5	40.3	38,204	12.6	33.6	12.3
08 00000	**Colorado**	3,130,207	36.3	34.6	3,722,302	69.8	5.8	42.3	21.6	54,262	8.3	21.3	21.5
08 03455	Arvada	68,683	34.9	32.2	81,421	70.7	6.8	42.9	23.3	64,255	5.5	15.7	25.4
08 04000	Aurora	189,359	44.3	24.6	225,105	71.9	6.7	45.9	19.4	49,464	12.4	22.4	14.8
08 07850	Boulder	54,590	14.7	68.4	80,034	67.2	6.2	30.9	24.5	50,209	7.2	28.3	25.5
08 08675	Brighton	18,717	51.5	17.6	21,750	72.2	7.2	44.5	17.3	63,464	8.6	18.1	17.6
08 09280	Broomfield	32,849	27.5	40.0	39,343	76.7	7.3	45.8	16.0	69,419	5.6	13.3	31.1
08 12415	Castle Rock town	23,040	24.2	42.8	26,827	76.6	4.6	52.0	11.0	81,386	4.3	9.9	32.6
08 12815	Centennial	68,169	18.8	52.5	79,567	72.9	4.1	44.6	15.5	82,485	2.8	8.4	38.5
08 15165	Clifton CDP	12,312	55.9	10.1	15,027	70.8	5.9	40.8	20.7	40,269	12.4	26.7	4.7
08 16000	Colorado Springs	256,423	31.8	34.7	303,470	70.0	6.4	42.4	22.5	51,227	8.2	22.2	18.3

Table B-4. Cities — What: Education, Employment, and Income, 2005–2007—*Continued*

STATE Place code	STATE City	Educational attainment			Employment status				Percent of households with no workers	Median household income (dollars)	Percent of families with income below poverty	Percent of households with income less than $25,000	Percent of households with income of $100,000 or more
		Total population 25 years and over	Percent with a high school diploma or less	Percent with a bachelor's degree or more	Total population 16 years and over	Percent in the labor force	Unemployment rate	Percent who worked full-time, year-round					
	ACS table number:	C15002	C15002	C15002	C20005	C23001	C23001	C20005	C08202	B19013	C17015	C19001	C19001
		1	2	3	4	5	6	7	8	9	10	11	12
	Colorado—Cont.												
08 16110	Columbine CDP	16,625	27.2	40.3	19,080	69.9	4.8	42.3	20.6	78,203	3.5	8.5	34.6
08 16495	Commerce	22,090	61.1	16.1	25,040	70.7	4.6	47.3	16.4	51,034	10.2	22.4	14.2
08 20000	Denver	391,711	40.0	37.7	450,092	69.1	6.5	41.9	25.1	43,748	13.6	28.7	17.3
08 24785	Englewood	21,137	46.5	26.3	24,351	69.2	7.2	42.0	26.6	40,685	9.4	28.4	9.7
08 27425	Fort Collins	80,393	23.5	49.2	111,400	71.7	7.0	35.5	20.9	48,648	7.9	26.0	19.3
08 31660	Grand Junction	34,837	42.9	26.4	42,777	64.8	6.5	34.6	32.0	40,795	11.9	30.8	12.2
08 32155	Greeley	51,217	48.4	26.0	71,510	66.2	6.4	37.9	26.1	39,438	11.7	31.3	12.3
08 36410	Highlands Ranch CDP	55,443	12.2	61.0	64,611	78.3	4.6	52.8	8.5	99,744	1.5	4.6	49.8
08 40377	Ken Caryl CDP	20,933	27.2	38.5	24,534	76.0	4.7	51.2	13.3	74,925	1.6	8.0	32.9
08 41835	Lafayette	16,004	22.9	49.4	18,539	73.3	4.9	42.8	16.2	58,348	10.0	17.2	26.5
08 43000	Lakewood	99,325	38.2	31.3	117,296	68.0	6.5	40.6	23.9	51,333	8.5	22.5	18.5
08 45255	Littleton	31,081	30.1	41.8	35,758	62.5	6.0	37.6	28.4	55,742	6.8	18.4	23.9
08 45970	Longmont	55,658	37.4	36.5	64,957	71.2	6.8	42.9	20.9	56,255	9.1	20.1	23.0
08 46465	Loveland	41,594	35.7	30.0	48,742	70.5	5.7	42.4	23.0	52,281	7.1	18.7	16.6
08 54330	Northglenn	23,188	49.9	17.9	27,259	74.2	7.8	48.7	19.8	53,747	6.7	18.1	11.3
08 57630	Parker town	22,299	20.4	43.8	26,869	80.4	2.4	53.6	7.4	80,769	1.1	5.8	35.0
08 62000	Pueblo	68,065	48.9	18.6	82,777	58.8	9.1	32.0	35.9	32,525	19.8	38.8	7.8
08 62220	Pueblo West CDP	16,081	36.4	24.8	18,218	67.9	5.1	42.8	23.0	61,502	4.5	13.5	21.5
08 68847	Security-Widefield CDP	20,194	37.7	17.4	24,514	69.0	8.5	44.3	19.1	59,517	4.3	12.6	15.6
08 77290	Thornton	68,214	44.2	24.5	80,738	76.3	6.0	52.4	12.6	64,777	6.3	13.7	22.7
08 83835	Westminster	67,451	33.9	31.7	81,275	75.0	5.0	40.3	16.8	59,738	6.2	16.1	22.9
08 84440	Wheat Ridge	22,506	44.6	27.4	25,321	63.7	6.1	38.7	30.0	45,088	9.2	24.3	11.0
09 00000	**Connecticut**	2,349,541	41.8	34.3	2,768,150	67.4	6.2	41.2	24.3	65,496	5.9	18.0	29.4
09 08000	Bridgeport	81,165	64.7	13.6	100,197	67.1	9.7	41.0	26.8	39,684	17.1	32.6	11.4
09 08420	Bristol	42,540	54.5	17.5	49,532	68.8	7.8	43.5	26.9	55,746	5.2	18.4	18.4
09 13435	Central Manchester CDP....	19,526	45.9	26.4	23,348	71.4	5.8	45.8	26.1	48,563	6.5	22.8	14.5
09 18430	Danbury	54,789	50.4	31.0	63,792	69.9	5.7	44.2	21.4	63,118	5.4	17.8	25.3
09 18920	Darien CDP	12,400	13.7	71.1	14,066	59.6	4.8	36.4	21.9	160,274	2.4	8.3	68.5
09 22700	East Hartford CDP	32,976	58.1	14.9	38,767	67.5	9.2	43.5	27.2	47,363	9.5	25.1	12.6
09 22980	East Haven CDP	20,790	58.0	20.1	24,212	66.6	5.2	42.6	26.3	62,167	4.4	18.7	21.6
09 37000	Hartford	70,599	67.6	12.8	89,456	62.3	16.8	30.9	36.0	28,572	28.8	45.9	8.5
09 46450	Meriden	40,306	54.8	18.8	47,484	67.5	8.2	42.6	28.1	52,818	12.7	23.5	18.3
09 47290	Middletown	31,195	44.3	31.6	38,786	67.4	4.9	42.3	23.4	57,042	7.9	21.3	21.5
09 47515	Milford (balance)	36,424	38.0	35.6	40,725	69.0	5.2	42.9	24.5	71,818	2.4	13.6	30.8
09 49880	Naugatuck borough	20,764	50.5	21.4	24,309	72.3	6.6	44.2	21.7	57,763	6.4	17.5	20.9
09 50370	New Britain	42,723	61.0	16.8	54,517	64.5	8.6	38.7	30.9	39,165	13.3	32.7	9.6
09 52000	New Haven	73,363	49.7	30.9	98,028	63.2	9.5	32.9	31.9	36,095	20.2	37.0	12.4
09 52210	Newington CDP	21,881	40.5	31.1	25,170	64.3	4.1	40.6	28.2	66,052	2.4	13.6	25.9
09 52280	New London	15,904	52.8	22.6	22,396	68.0	8.5	37.5	24.0	42,927	11.8	25.3	12.0
09 54040	North Haven CDP.............	17,689	39.6	35.4	20,142	69.9	6.6	42.9	24.9	80,450	1.6	13.1	34.7
09 55990	Norwalk	56,004	41.8	36.8	65,397	70.8	5.1	43.8	18.6	70,672	4.0	14.5	32.7
09 56200	Norwich	25,316	54.5	17.5	29,610	68.7	7.5	39.9	25.5	45,273	10.5	24.9	16.6
09 68100	Shelton	28,283	42.5	31.6	32,063	67.0	4.1	43.1	21.4	80,694	1.8	10.0	37.9
09 73000	Stamford	83,124	36.1	43.1	93,912	71.6	7.0	44.1	20.9	72,315	5.0	16.3	36.3
09 74260	Stratford CDP	35,826	44.4	28.9	41,552	67.6	5.8	42.4	25.3	65,076	2.2	16.2	25.9
09 76500	Torrington	26,032	52.0	19.7	29,595	65.4	7.8	35.7	31.7	47,334	8.0	25.0	14.6
09 77270	Trumbull CDP	24,574	28.5	47.9	27,846	60.4	4.2	36.4	22.1	96,944	2.5	11.1	48.1
09 80000	Waterbury	68,606	61.0	14.5	81,429	63.6	9.9	35.7	31.9	39,115	16.7	32.0	11.4
09 82660	West Hartford CDP	43,945	24.8	56.9	50,894	63.0	5.2	38.8	26.8	79,443	3.8	14.1	38.4
09 82800	West Haven	36,354	52.3	22.0	43,687	67.5	7.1	42.3	24.8	52,465	7.9	20.5	15.0
09 83570	Westport CDP	16,534	12.4	74.2	18,173	60.7	4.8	36.3	21.6	147,391	1.5	5.3	68.0
09 84970	Wethersfield CDP..............	19,597	41.4	36.8	22,653	64.7	4.5	39.8	31.1	66,044	1.4	15.3	28.7
10 00000	**Delaware**	565,305	47.6	26.6	671,869	64.8	5.8	42.0	25.6	55,303	7.2	19.9	21.6
10 21200	Dover	19,473	44.7	24.4	26,934	63.8	9.0	37.3	28.6	42,256	13.0	28.4	13.2
10 50670	Newark	12,504	22.7	47.9	27,164	54.0	5.5	21.9	25.7	49,769	4.3	29.4	24.7
10 77580	Wilmington	43,604	51.1	24.9	50,508	62.3	8.1	40.0	29.7	36,284	19.2	36.2	13.3
11 00000	**District of Columbia**	397,937	37.3	45.4	483,781	66.5	8.8	42.4	28.1	52,187	15.7	26.4	25.6
11 50000	Washington	397,937	37.3	45.4	483,781	66.5	8.8	42.4	28.1	52,187	15.7	26.4	25.6
12 00000	**Florida**	12,412,464	46.7	25.2	14,471,701	60.7	6.0	39.2	30.6	46,602	9.0	25.0	16.4
12 00950	Altamonte Springs	29,660	33.5	31.6	34,435	72.6	4.5	48.3	19.1	49,638	6.2	18.9	12.9
12 01700	Apopka	24,934	42.8	25.8	28,346	73.5	4.9	49.1	13.9	60,656	6.1	15.4	18.6
12 02681	Aventura	23,059	29.8	46.0	25,047	48.3	3.9	29.0	45.8	52,632	5.8	28.5	26.1
12 04162	Bayonet Point CDP............	18,470	64.5	10.0	20,525	-	-	26.9	53.2	32,779	8.1	37.2	3.0
12 05462	Bellview CDP	16,123	43.8	22.4	18,681	64.1	6.7	42.2	25.6	48,215	7.7	23.1	12.5
12 06875	Bloomingdale CDP	12,805	21.1	42.5	15,050	72.9	4.6	48.4	12.8	87,366	2.3	5.4	42.6
12 07235	Boca Del Mar CDP	17,911	31.4	44.4	19,899	57.6	5.2	37.6	35.8	54,034	2.7	19.0	23.4
12 07300	Boca Raton	60,094	27.2	46.6	69,250	59.2	4.3	36.8	31.9	67,531	4.9	16.9	35.3
12 07525	Bonita Springs	32,409	44.1	29.9	34,765	47.0	5.8	30.4	46.8	52,108	6.6	15.9	23.5
12 07875	Boynton Beach	44,223	45.4	23.3	50,661	61.5	7.3	38.4	36.8	44,515	9.2	25.3	15.4
12 07950	Bradenton	37,295	51.1	21.0	43,780	55.7	5.9	36.7	34.7	41,019	10.4	26.1	9.6
12 08150	Brandon CDP	59,329	39.0	27.8	69,603	70.2	4.5	48.6	19.0	55,721	6.2	16.2	16.1
12 08300	Brent CDP	13,543	58.0	13.8	20,093	53.2	7.9	25.0	29.1	31,785	19.7	36.6	5.8

STATE Place code	STATE City	Educational attainment			Employment status				Percent of households with no workers	Median household income (dollars)	Percent of families with income below poverty	Percent of households with income less than $25,000	Percent of households with income of $100,000 or more
		Total population 25 years and over	Percent with a high school diploma or less	Percent with a bachelor's degree or more	Total population 16 years and over	Percent in the labor force	Unemployment rate	Percent who worked full-time, year-round					
	ACS table number:	C15002	C15002	C15002	C20005	C23001	C23001	C20005	C08202	B19013	C17015	C19001	C19001
		1	2	3	4	5	6	7	8	9	10	11	12
	Florida—Cont.												
12 10275	Cape Coral	99,736	45.2	19.9	112,282	66.0	4.8	44.7	25.5	53,516	5.0	16.4	16.0
12 11050	Casselberry	17,459	42.5	24.7	20,495	69.4	4.9	44.1	23.2	44,472	8.5	23.3	9.5
12 12425	Citrus Park CDP	16,008	39.2	30.2	18,562	71.2	5.2	49.3	16.5	58,701	4.5	16.0	20.4
12 12875	Clearwater	76,969	44.6	26.6	88,459	59.9	3.7	41.2	34.4	40,818	11.0	30.6	12.9
12 13275	Coconut Creek	35,257	45.4	29.2	39,030	60.5	4.4	40.2	35.6	45,255	5.0	25.4	16.6
12 14125	Cooper	19,119	29.7	36.8	22,944	71.1	2.5	46.7	12.7	90,878	2.4	5.1	42.9
12 14250	Coral Gables	28,840	19.8	61.7	37,035	59.6	2.9	39.9	23.2	78,157	4.5	15.5	43.6
12 14400	Coral Springs	79,384	35.8	35.7	95,642	73.2	4.8	47.5	13.3	71,283	5.2	12.9	31.6
12 14412	Coral Terrace CDP	16,637	55.6	22.5	19,566	57.6	6.8	40.5	28.3	42,152	12.1	30.1	12.3
12 14895	Country Club CDP	22,008	44.4	26.7	26,632	73.2	5.4	52.7	12.4	47,776	9.3	23.5	13.5
12 15968	Cutler Bay town	22,482	38.3	30.6	27,981	61.9	6.5	41.3	24.3	55,705	5.0	20.6	21.9
12 16335	Dania Beach	23,001	51.5	20.5	25,530	64.0	5.5	43.1	27.6	45,004	13.9	29.1	9.3
12 16475	Davie town	61,517	39.2	29.7	73,343	66.7	3.9	45.0	22.1	57,400	6.8	20.9	25.0
12 16525	Daytona Beach	42,432	47.2	20.7	56,516	53.7	8.2	28.1	38.2	30,532	16.6	40.4	6.4
12 16725	Deerfield Beach	56,204	50.7	23.8	64,040	59.3	6.9	37.8	38.1	40,730	11.3	32.6	11.6
12 16875	De Land	17,861	50.5	21.8	22,279	56.6	5.6	34.2	34.8	35,038	12.0	36.0	9.5
12 17100	Delray Beach	44,751	41.0	30.7	50,311	60.3	7.8	37.3	40.9	45,828	9.6	26.0	18.4
12 17200	Deltona	56,545	53.8	12.4	66,559	64.8	5.8	42.8	23.4	46,385	7.2	19.7	8.5
12 17935	Doral	23,270	20.5	55.5	27,461	67.9	3.1	53.7	11.4	66,698	8.1	12.3	26.8
12 18575	Dunedin	28,542	37.9	28.8	31,993	55.0	6.3	34.4	42.0	40,913	6.5	28.4	12.6
12 19206	East Lake CDP	23,006	20.9	47.0	26,293	60.8	4.7	37.8	32.1	76,490	4.0	11.2	37.5
12 19825	Edgewater	16,002	51.2	13.4	18,710	64.3	7.3	36.8	29.4	42,401	5.0	23.7	7.9
12 20108	Egypt Lake-Leto CDP	22,074	53.5	20.3	25,885	69.1	7.9	43.5	24.7	36,224	17.2	31.2	8.4
12 22275	Ferry Pass CDP	19,300	31.4	34.0	24,087	62.6	5.8	36.9	30.2	43,833	11.2	26.2	12.2
12 24000	Fort Lauderdale	121,555	44.5	30.4	137,417	64.2	7.0	40.1	28.0	50,349	11.5	24.8	22.0
12 24125	Fort Myers	36,625	56.9	20.9	44,816	67.5	6.5	43.1	26.2	35,878	16.8	30.4	10.0
12 24300	Fort Pierce	25,083	66.3	12.9	30,503	59.0	11.9	35.7	34.0	34,083	21.1	35.0	7.1
12 24562	Fountainbleau CDP	43,351	47.4	29.8	50,202	65.1	5.4	47.1	22.1	38,533	12.2	31.9	7.4
12 24581	Four Corners CDP	15,184	44.1	22.2	17,922	69.1	4.0	45.8	19.1	46,475	8.0	18.7	12.5
12 24925	Fruit Cove CDP	17,687	19.2	44.7	21,200	69.2	2.9	45.9	16.1	97,028	2.6	8.2	48.0
12 25175	Gainesville	59,179	31.4	42.0	98,782	56.5	8.1	27.2	31.3	28,923	16.9	44.3	9.4
12 26300	Golden Gate CDP	15,400	72.9	10.4	18,657	-	-	53.5	12.1	46,786	13.0	25.9	7.1
12 26375	Golden Glades CDP	22,676	61.2	14.0	27,258	63.4	9.3	42.0	21.6	38,894	21.2	33.8	9.7
12 27313	Greater Carrollwood CDP	22,584	29.8	40.9	25,482	71.3	5.5	47.6	21.7	56,441	4.3	16.1	25.1
12 27317	Greater Northdale CDP	16,057	29.0	36.4	18,882	74.8	4.3	51.3	12.5	63,668	1.9	5.8	24.1
12 27322	Greenacres	23,204	48.3	20.6	26,696	62.9	5.1	41.3	33.6	44,209	7.7	25.1	11.3
12 28452	Hallandale Beach	26,761	52.9	25.1	30,131	55.8	8.7	35.2	41.2	34,739	14.1	36.7	8.3
12 30000	Hialeah	153,198	67.9	13.8	175,273	56.5	6.9	40.1	29.7	31,689	16.3	39.7	5.0
12 31075	Holiday CDP	18,067	62.4	9.4	20,971	57.8	8.8	36.1	38.3	36,063	13.0	32.2	5.7
12 32000	Hollywood	98,555	47.4	26.4	112,659	65.6	6.4	41.9	27.0	44,870	8.4	26.4	16.2
12 32275	Homestead	26,820	62.0	14.2	33,713	63.9	8.1	43.2	25.3	30,859	30.7	40.7	9.6
12 35000	Jacksonville	516,512	45.8	24.0	612,582	67.7	6.1	44.5	23.1	47,381	9.5	23.5	15.1
12 35050	Jacksonville Beach	15,303	33.7	37.5	16,919	70.2	5.4	45.5	25.6	62,897	3.7	18.8	25.9
12 35350	Jasmine Estates CDP	13,888	65.9	8.1	16,089	-	-	36.9	37.8	30,430	23.6	39.8	2.9
12 35875	Jupiter town	36,236	32.7	39.3	42,605	64.7	4.7	39.3	30.9	70,280	4.4	14.9	30.9
12 36062	Kendale Lakes CDP	37,854	46.9	24.8	45,949	63.9	4.8	43.1	19.2	49,739	7.9	26.0	16.3
12 36100	Kendall CDP	57,505	32.3	40.6	67,328	62.0	3.7	41.4	21.2	59,342	7.5	19.6	26.6
12 36121	Kendall West CDP	25,247	46.6	25.5	30,504	71.0	3.6	51.4	14.1	49,095	6.1	19.3	11.4
12 36462	Keystone CDP	14,482	18.4	51.3	16,054	-	-	46.1	19.8	106,549	2.2	5.4	54.6
12 36550	Key West	18,163	37.4	29.7	20,168	69.7	2.2	47.5	24.1	51,722	7.2	20.9	16.4
12 36950	Kissimmee	36,911	59.0	16.7	44,741	67.6	7.5	43.6	21.9	37,596	15.1	29.3	7.6
12 38250	Lakeland	64,237	51.3	20.7	76,407	57.6	6.6	36.3	34.5	39,757	10.3	29.7	10.1
12 38350	Lake Magdalene CDP	21,706	40.9	31.4	25,116	67.4	7.0	42.0	24.8	49,693	6.6	23.3	22.8
12 38813	Lakeside CDP	21,693	40.4	20.5	25,912	70.3	4.8	44.0	20.8	61,397	6.2	11.9	19.7
12 39075	Lake Worth	23,408	58.5	17.2	27,582	66.5	6.8	43.1	28.6	37,470	15.0	29.0	7.6
12 39200	Land O' Lakes CDP	20,718	33.9	33.9	23,562	71.2	3.9	47.3	17.7	74,957	1.4	10.0	29.7
12 39425	Largo	58,171	48.8	19.9	65,084	54.9	6.5	36.1	40.7	38,042	9.2	31.2	7.2
12 39525	Lauderdale Lakes	20,974	59.2	12.3	25,046	66.8	11.2	37.5	29.3	34,010	15.3	33.2	5.6
12 39550	Lauderhill	42,689	53.8	18.8	50,685	66.5	8.0	40.3	27.2	37,790	17.9	33.8	9.0
12 39875	Leesburg	13,737	53.8	18.3	15,605	53.1	6.8	34.1	42.7	35,757	15.2	31.4	7.7
12 39925	Lehigh Acres CDP	38,114	57.7	14.2	45,823	67.9	5.3	42.8	21.8	47,194	9.2	18.9	10.9
12 41775	Lutz CDP	12,959	33.0	37.0	15,683	67.4	4.7	43.8	17.8	67,119	3.6	10.6	33.2
12 43125	Margate	40,441	50.4	21.5	45,453	63.2	6.8	41.5	33.2	43,413	7.2	25.4	13.5
12 43975	Melbourne	52,845	42.1	23.9	63,143	59.7	5.1	35.2	35.5	40,969	7.8	29.1	11.0
12 44275	Merritt Island CDP	25,310	37.1	29.5	29,129	62.2	4.9	36.8	32.5	52,601	5.8	23.0	23.0
12 45000	Miami	246,405	62.7	20.9	286,759	57.4	6.4	38.2	32.2	28,009	22.5	45.2	9.9
12 45025	Miami Beach	63,410	38.1	40.5	70,004	65.3	4.4	43.2	29.7	38,881	12.1	33.4	18.5
12 45060	Miami Gardens	60,195	61.3	14.7	75,296	63.2	11.1	40.8	25.3	37,691	13.0	31.7	7.9
12 45100	Miami Lakes town	19,694	32.9	33.7	23,458	69.9	3.4	46.8	16.0	67,384	4.6	15.2	29.1
12 45975	Miramar	68,380	38.4	30.4	84,018	74.0	7.2	49.3	10.2	65,179	6.1	13.6	26.1
12 47625	Naples	16,140	27.9	49.4	17,158	-	-	19.1	55.8	71,553	4.6	18.9	39.1
12 48625	New Smyrna Beach	16,764	42.7	24.9	18,532	49.9	7.2	29.4	48.6	39,909	11.3	29.9	14.5
12 49350	North Fort Myers CDP	35,615	61.0	14.1	37,888	39.3	5.9	25.2	55.5	37,648	6.5	30.7	8.1
12 49425	North Lauderdale	25,895	58.1	13.1	32,012	71.3	6.1	46.8	15.0	44,607	15.6	27.9	6.6

Table B-4. Cities — What: Education, Employment, and Income, 2005–2007—*Continued*

STATE Place code	STATE City	Educational attainment			Employment status				Percent of households with no workers	Median household income (dollars)	Percent of families with income below poverty	Percent of households with income less than $25,000	Percent of households with income of $100,000 or more
		Total population 25 years and over	Percent with a high school diploma or less	Percent with a bachelor's degree or more	Total population 16 years and over	Percent in the labor force	Unemployment rate	Percent who worked full-time, year-round					
	ACS table number:	C15002	C15002	C15002	C20005	C23001	C23001	C20005	C08202	B19013	C17015	C19001	C19001
		1	2	3	4	5	6	7	8	9	10	11	12
	Florida—Cont.												
12 49450	North Miami	35,198	60.0	16.3	45,725	67.3	7.7	42.8	18.1	36,311	14.4	29.9	10.9
12 49475	North Miami Beach	28,100	56.3	19.4	34,383	68.0	9.2	43.3	19.3	38,687	17.7	31.4	9.3
12 49675	North Port	31,075	48.7	16.2	35,749	67.3	8.0	45.0	29.3	50,583	4.7	17.9	10.2
12 50575	Oakland Park	28,974	51.1	23.4	34,364	72.8	4.9	44.9	20.2	46,385	9.5	20.6	14.3
12 50638	Oak Ridge CDP	13,231	59.2	11.9	16,662	-	-	51.9	13.2	37,174	15.9	22.6	4.9
12 50750	Ocala	35,595	50.1	19.2	43,213	55.2	5.0	34.1	34.9	35,600	15.9	34.7	9.5
12 51075	Ocoee	19,348	46.7	26.0	22,142	70.9	4.6	49.6	14.4	59,900	7.4	14.7	21.4
12 53000	Orlando	145,393	41.7	30.1	170,175	71.9	6.4	47.4	21.2	41,859	12.5	26.8	14.0
12 53150	Ormond Beach	30,178	38.0	30.9	32,871	52.6	2.1	33.5	41.8	48,468	4.8	26.1	18.7
12 53575	Oviedo	18,777	26.8	40.3	22,412	69.1	5.5	42.4	15.1	77,489	4.7	10.5	32.3
12 54000	Palm Bay	63,284	47.8	18.1	75,824	61.8	7.3	39.0	28.0	43,992	7.4	24.1	8.9
12 54075	Palm Beach Gardens	30,920	24.7	46.9	34,436	58.0	2.7	38.9	34.9	69,630	4.0	14.2	32.2
12 54175	Palm CDP	15,680	29.6	38.5	17,624	-	-	36.8	36.0	67,546	1.2	9.0	34.8
12 54200	Palm Coast	45,559	43.3	19.4	52,083	55.2	4.1	35.5	36.3	46,817	8.8	23.4	11.2
12 54275	Palmetto Bay village	15,382	22.8	52.6	17,846	67.6	3.2	46.4	14.1	95,584	1.8	9.5	46.6
12 54350	Palm Harbor CDP	41,974	36.9	29.4	47,574	61.6	5.4	37.6	34.0	52,000	2.9	20.3	20.1
12 54387	Palm River-Clair Mel CDP	13,609	61.3	14.4	16,586	66.9	8.1	44.4	21.5	41,544	14.9	26.6	6.7
12 54525	Palm Valley CDP	13,693	15.9	56.0	16,699	-	-	40.8	25.4	84,276	2.1	8.8	43.1
12 54700	Panama	25,544	45.4	22.5	30,042	61.1	5.4	36.1	29.9	40,519	13.2	30.6	10.8
12 55125	Parkland	12,898	22.8	50.4	14,887	-	-	46.6	15.6	103,895	2.7	9.9	53.5
12 55775	Pembroke Pines	106,640	39.8	30.3	122,526	65.2	5.2	44.7	25.6	60,789	5.1	19.3	25.8
12 55925	Pensacola	38,025	35.3	35.2	43,321	62.8	6.5	37.7	30.1	44,547	10.1	28.4	15.9
12 56825	Pine Hills CDP	23,348	61.4	14.3	28,374	73.4	6.5	45.4	19.6	37,060	12.3	30.1	6.1
12 56975	Pinellas Park	36,252	54.0	16.4	41,587	61.1	5.1	40.4	30.5	41,463	10.6	29.7	10.3
12 57425	Plantation	59,267	31.5	39.9	67,866	69.9	4.1	46.6	19.1	66,135	6.0	15.8	30.4
12 57550	Plant	20,967	53.4	19.5	25,151	65.3	4.8	43.2	23.9	45,793	8.8	25.1	15.4
12 57900	Poinciana CDP	15,680	51.1	15.2	18,931	70.7	5.9	44.8	17.8	49,589	10.8	17.5	11.6
12 58050	Pompano Beach	76,496	53.2	22.4	86,672	61.0	7.0	39.2	32.9	43,808	11.7	28.0	13.3
12 58350	Port Charlotte CDP	35,264	53.9	15.8	39,611	53.1	7.8	32.5	43.1	40,661	7.4	26.4	7.5
12 58575	Port Orange	39,021	48.5	21.2	44,828	58.4	5.3	35.9	35.0	42,776	4.4	25.3	12.1
12 58715	Port St. Lucie	94,228	49.9	16.8	108,382	61.8	5.6	40.5	29.2	50,851	6.1	18.2	14.5
12 60230	Richmond West CDP	18,471	41.9	23.1	22,292	70.1	6.0	46.6	12.4	67,784	8.1	10.8	24.6
12 60975	Riviera Beach	21,109	50.9	20.9	25,070	64.0	7.9	35.7	30.2	37,215	17.7	32.3	11.4
12 61500	Rockledge	17,466	36.5	29.5	20,050	63.1	7.0	37.3	27.7	57,597	5.9	16.4	21.0
12 62100	Royal Palm Beach village	20,938	42.3	24.5	24,509	66.8	6.0	43.9	24.1	64,470	4.1	14.5	22.8
12 62625	St. Cloud	19,067	49.1	21.0	21,978	62.3	7.3	43.5	30.1	47,907	9.8	26.4	9.6
12 63000	St. Petersburg	171,534	44.4	26.9	196,044	64.0	5.1	42.6	29.3	41,917	9.7	28.3	13.9
12 63650	Sanford	30,385	54.3	16.8	37,043	67.3	7.7	45.2	24.3	38,659	14.1	29.5	9.0
12 64175	Sarasota	36,204	46.0	29.3	41,769	57.1	6.0	35.3	35.7	39,177	12.4	30.1	15.6
12 64825	Sebastian	14,310	51.3	18.1	16,168	54.3	6.4	34.0	35.5	46,471	7.2	21.5	7.3
12 67258	South Bradenton CDP	16,494	60.3	13.7	19,077	60.5	4.6	38.9	35.9	33,482	17.2	37.1	3.4
12 67575	South Miami Heights CDP	21,142	64.5	13.5	26,693	64.1	7.9	43.5	27.9	41,420	15.2	34.0	10.9
12 68350	Spring Hill CDP	65,756	54.0	14.3	74,642	52.7	8.5	30.9	40.6	44,274	7.3	24.9	11.2
12 69700	Sunrise	59,915	45.4	23.1	70,050	68.2	6.4	45.4	26.6	49,713	6.9	25.8	15.9
12 70600	Tallahassee	90,366	27.4	45.9	137,428	67.3	7.9	37.5	22.5	37,762	11.7	33.3	13.3
12 70675	Tamarac	48,830	49.4	23.2	52,899	54.7	6.5	36.2	43.2	39,494	8.3	30.9	9.4
12 70700	Tamiami CDP	38,200	49.4	23.3	44,508	60.6	3.6	44.5	19.6	49,795	4.2	19.1	20.9
12 71000	Tampa	210,239	46.3	29.7	255,491	64.9	7.6	40.8	25.5	42,004	14.3	30.3	17.1
12 71150	Tarpon Springs	17,482	42.1	27.2	19,330	54.1	6.2	29.5	40.4	50,646	9.5	27.3	14.4
12 71400	Temple Terrace	15,212	30.1	39.5	19,282	69.0	4.2	44.6	22.4	44,921	7.8	22.5	16.5
12 71567	The Crossings CDP	16,202	26.4	41.6	19,616	72.4	3.8	50.0	13.2	66,713	2.3	12.4	27.0
12 71569	The Hammocks CDP	32,848	35.4	35.3	41,236	69.5	5.8	48.1	12.4	62,461	6.0	15.1	25.0
12 71900	Titusville	30,608	43.6	20.4	34,920	56.4	3.6	36.0	36.0	41,348	9.2	30.2	9.6
12 72145	Town 'n' Country CDP	51,076	46.2	25.2	59,246	71.8	5.5	47.9	19.0	46,368	9.9	22.0	11.4
12 73163	University CDP	18,527	58.9	19.3	24,820	67.6	10.4	35.5	26.5	23,697	33.8	51.9	2.5
12 73287	University Park CDP	18,388	57.2	24.0	22,160	54.8	2.7	35.6	29.4	41,566	6.5	29.3	16.7
12 73900	Venice	18,691	44.4	32.2	19,250	-	-	18.2	65.6	39,419	3.6	29.5	12.9
12 74200	Vero Beach South CDP	17,476	42.8	24.6	20,199	65.0	4.7	38.0	31.7	46,753	7.0	21.1	16.7
12 75725	Wekiwa Springs CDP	16,252	20.6	51.8	18,672	61.9	2.5	43.9	25.4	76,369	4.0	12.4	35.5
12 75812	Wellington village	34,175	31.9	38.8	40,767	68.2	4.5	46.8	18.8	79,260	4.4	8.5	40.1
12 75912	West and East Lealman CDP	17,947	65.6	9.0	20,840	57.9	5.9	40.3	36.7	30,791	14.7	40.9	5.5
12 76062	Westchase CDP	13,269	15.6	53.7	15,402	76.6	3.9	53.1	12.1	88,993	1.6	6.7	44.8
12 76075	Westchester CDP	22,100	55.9	23.3	25,627	52.6	3.7	37.0	29.8	39,955	7.2	30.8	16.7
12 76487	West Little River CDP	19,152	75.8	6.1	23,472	57.4	11.2	32.3	30.7	27,695	22.2	45.3	2.3
12 76582	Weston	40,239	15.1	59.5	47,208	68.8	4.4	44.5	14.6	91,668	2.7	8.1	46.4
12 76600	West Palm Beach	61,857	44.3	28.9	71,800	63.1	8.9	39.1	31.1	43,601	14.4	27.4	14.9
12 76675	West Pensacola CDP	14,620	64.2	8.9	17,317	56.2	14.5	32.4	38.1	26,329	25.3	47.6	3.4
12 78250	Winter Garden	17,963	41.8	28.1	20,325	69.3	7.6	44.7	17.8	59,025	5.0	18.8	24.7
12 78275	Winter Haven	20,454	57.5	18.6	23,314	55.2	5.3	40.1	39.8	35,452	16.4	36.3	7.9
12 78300	Winter Park	19,714	22.5	54.3	22,605	58.2	5.5	34.4	33.5	59,545	7.5	24.9	30.2
12 78375	Winter Springs	23,425	32.1	38.5	27,821	67.7	5.5	49.1	20.5	62,060	4.0	11.2	29.1
12 78800	Wright CDP	15,099	41.3	22.2	17,591	70.6	6.4	44.9	26.9	48,009	12.2	24.7	12.9
12 78975	Yeehaw Junction CDP	15,718	59.1	15.6	19,344	65.1	10.9	45.0	22.5	43,750	9.5	26.7	9.3

STATE Place code	STATE City	Educational attainment			Employment status				Percent of households with no workers	Median household income (dollars)	Percent of families with income below poverty	Percent of households with income less than $25,000	Percent of households with income of $100,000 or more
		Total population 25 years and over	Percent with a high school diploma or less	Percent with a bachelor's degree or more	Total population 16 years and over	Percent in the labor force	Unemployment rate	Percent who worked full-time, year-round					
	ACS table number:	C15002	C15002	C15002	C20005	C23001	C23001	C20005	C08202	B19013	C17015	C19001	C19001
		1	2	3	4	5	6	7	8	9	10	11	12
13 00000	**Georgia**	5,945,347	48.0	26.6	7,131,317	65.8	7.1	42.3	23.7	48,540	11.1	25.0	17.8
13 01052	Albany	45,308	47.7	21.6	57,799	59.2	15.2	33.7	34.8	32,114	20.8	40.1	8.9
13 01696	Alpharetta	42,938	17.6	61.9	47,588	72.6	3.8	51.5	12.0	91,056	2.8	7.3	46.8
13 03440	Athens-Clarke County (balance)	58,056	37.6	42.0	91,380	61.8	6.7	32.3	25.7	34,723	14.5	39.1	11.3
13 04000	Atlanta	293,450	39.7	41.2	355,869	65.7	9.7	39.3	27.3	44,163	20.2	30.8	22.4
13 04204	Augusta-Richmond County (balance)	118,932	50.9	19.9	147,274	60.8	8.4	37.2	32.8	36,580	19.2	34.1	9.4
13 12834	Candler-McAfee CDP	19,879	62.2	10.4	23,443	59.4	19.2	32.6	30.5	35,310	22.4	37.8	5.4
13 12988	Canton	8,182	60.5	16.2	10,349	-	-	44.9	17.8	35,617	21.5	33.6	11.4
13 13492	Carrollton	12,245	49.6	27.2	18,085	61.4	11.4	31.8	31.1	33,322	14.0	39.2	11.5
13 17776	College Park	10,091	53.6	18.2	12,119	-	-	43.3	27.0	31,004	28.5	38.5	7.4
13 19000	Columbus	114,407	47.4	22.6	143,742	62.0	7.3	38.0	31.8	40,347	16.0	32.3	12.3
13 21380	Dalton	18,232	60.7	20.2	21,886	66.7	8.1	45.4	21.9	37,475	19.6	33.7	13.4
13 23900	Douglasville	14,658	43.0	26.0	17,797	69.7	8.9	47.1	24.2	44,103	13.5	26.1	15.8
13 24600	Duluth	17,428	27.1	49.1	20,329	75.8	2.5	56.0	13.0	62,305	2.5	10.0	23.9
13 24768	Dunwoody CDP	27,301	11.3	69.1	30,358	68.7	3.2	49.4	18.6	89,865	2.3	11.1	45.7
13 25720	East Point	24,972	58.1	18.7	28,911	68.7	10.7	44.2	22.5	40,201	13.4	25.6	7.5
13 30536	Forest Park	14,760	69.1	7.6	17,186	48.6	8.1	34.7	23.8	34,402	18.3	34.4	3.6
13 31908	Gainesville	20,199	61.3	20.2	24,669	59.0	5.2	38.8	21.5	38,908	15.1	30.0	15.3
13 35324	Griffin	13,633	66.6	12.0	16,020	64.6	16.4	35.0	33.6	32,310	23.4	39.3	8.5
13 38964	Hinesville	16,372	40.1	14.8	21,850	74.3	8.9	44.9	18.2	41,871	15.8	27.7	7.7
13 42425	Johns Creek	51,282	11.9	65.5	58,595	73.1	4.4	49.5	8.4	108,416	3.1	5.4	55.6
13 43192	Kennesaw	17,055	28.7	40.7	20,348	72.1	7.1	47.4	17.3	60,523	8.5	16.6	22.8
13 44340	LaGrange	16,638	58.1	19.4	20,887	62.0	6.6	35.5	30.6	30,221	19.8	41.2	8.1
13 45488	Lawrenceville	18,205	57.7	17.0	21,746	62.3	6.6	42.6	20.7	47,091	13.9	28.0	12.5
13 48288	Mableton CDP	23,040	42.6	33.9	26,501	68.7	7.0	44.9	21.4	52,381	5.9	18.7	20.6
13 49000	Macon	56,231	59.3	18.1	68,669	56.3	11.8	31.8	38.4	28,088	26.0	46.3	7.4
13 49756	Marietta	36,344	43.3	33.4	44,940	72.0	7.3	44.2	20.7	43,508	10.4	27.0	15.8
13 50036	Martinez CDP	16,822	33.2	37.4	20,316	68.4	5.0	42.7	16.2	64,355	4.4	12.2	24.6
13 51492	Milledgeville	10,350	67.3	13.3	16,464	-	-	19.5	33.6	26,448	18.4	47.0	7.1
13 55020	Newnan	14,217	46.7	28.2	16,860	67.2	9.0	41.6	20.1	47,506	16.1	23.5	18.5
13 56000	North Atlanta CDP	27,098	37.8	45.5	31,205	73.4	8.5	46.3	20.7	47,032	10.3	23.1	25.1
13 56168	North Druid Hills CDP	15,052	20.8	59.6	17,642	-	-	40.9	24.9	49,790	4.2	20.7	23.2
13 59724	Peachtree	21,868	21.7	51.9	26,077	66.3	3.7	39.8	19.3	84,339	4.4	10.1	39.4
13 63952	Redan CDP	22,794	40.1	25.4	28,120	76.4	9.0	49.1	16.0	51,389	9.8	20.0	10.3
13 66668	Rome	22,441	56.5	20.4	27,337	57.0	7.5	31.9	37.4	31,545	18.6	43.2	11.8
13 67284	Roswell	69,255	25.9	51.0	77,581	71.1	3.3	48.1	16.3	73,568	2.7	9.9	37.0
13 68516	Sandy Springs	69,272	20.4	61.5	80,310	74.5	3.0	53.5	15.4	72,682	3.3	12.3	36.7
13 69000	Savannah	78,650	50.6	23.1	99,586	59.1	6.4	36.8	31.6	32,616	16.5	39.2	8.5
13 71492	Smyrna	32,487	30.7	45.8	37,175	74.5	4.8	49.8	16.5	51,391	7.8	20.1	21.4
13 71604	Snellville	11,727	44.8	28.9	13,733	-	-	44.1	24.4	66,079	5.7	15.1	28.7
13 73256	Statesboro	8,811	46.6	25.7	22,632	54.0	11.1	20.8	27.9	20,824	23.0	57.0	4.3
13 77652	Tucker CDP	22,467	29.5	48.2	24,557	67.9	5.7	46.1	21.9	69,891	2.3	13.5	26.7
13 78800	Valdosta	26,482	47.1	27.1	36,930	65.2	8.6	36.0	26.7	33,800	21.4	36.3	10.1
13 80508	Warner Robins	35,293	45.0	19.2	42,484	65.1	8.7	39.2	28.5	42,847	15.2	28.7	11.7
13 84176	Woodstock	11,377	25.6	37.8	13,799	-	-	54.6	13.7	57,709	4.8	13.8	20.9
15 00000	**Hawaii**	867,609	41.4	28.6	1,025,421	65.6	4.3	42.8	22.9	62,543	6.8	17.3	25.9
15 14650	Hilo CDP	33,470	43.1	26.1	41,753	58.5	7.5	33.8	32.4	53,994	10.0	23.8	19.5
15 17000	Honolulu CDP	265,508	39.3	34.8	304,790	61.2	3.7	40.0	27.8	54,742	7.3	22.1	23.1
15 22700	Kahului CDP	15,416	60.7	15.2	17,630	60.2	2.8	40.6	28.6	56,826	4.9	20.7	18.3
15 23150	Kailua CDP (Honolulu County)	25,333	30.3	41.9	29,092	65.3	4.0	41.7	21.1	87,218	5.0	10.3	42.8
15 28250	Kaneohe CDP	24,724	41.2	27.4	29,040	66.3	4.4	45.0	19.8	77,688	5.1	13.3	33.0
15 36500	Kihei CDP	13,632	38.5	26.5	16,116	-	-	48.0	18.3	62,133	4.9	14.2	19.3
15 51050	Mililani Town CDP	19,501	29.5	34.4	22,918	70.7	3.7	48.6	14.4	87,014	3.3	6.1	39.1
15 62600	Pearl City	19,694	44.9	21.2	22,748	57.8	4.1	39.3	29.4	67,591	4.2	12.4	28.2
15 77750	Waimalu CDP	21,086	31.4	34.8	24,903	73.3	3.8	51.4	14.1	78,695	1.8	7.9	33.4
15 79700	Waipahu CDP	23,404	54.7	15.6	28,437	59.3	5.6	38.2	21.8	59,743	11.2	17.6	27.2
16 00000	**IDAHO**	917,853	42.6	23.6	1,108,188	65.9	5.4	38.1	25.0	44,901	9.4	25.3	12.3
16 08830	Boise	133,688	31.3	36.1	161,260	71.3	5.5	42.8	21.7	50,016	6.7	21.3	16.5
16 12250	Caldwell	19,286	59.7	12.4	23,520	65.0	7.8	36.3	25.2	35,821	13.0	32.1	3.5
16 16750	Coeur d'Alene	26,214	42.0	20.1	32,290	66.2	6.6	35.9	28.4	33,840	11.3	33.2	8.0
16 39700	Idaho Falls	32,715	40.6	26.1	39,226	66.2	5.1	40.4	25.5	42,805	8.3	27.5	14.7
16 46540	Lewiston	21,598	48.4	16.9	25,621	63.1	7.3	36.0	32.3	40,181	12.7	31.5	10.2
16 52120	Meridian	35,336	30.4	32.6	41,081	72.1	3.8	46.7	18.1	62,042	3.2	12.7	22.3
16 54550	Moscow	10,837	20.1	55.6	19,310	62.0	8.8	22.2	24.8	33,888	7.4	40.3	8.1
16 56260	Nampa	43,094	50.8	16.3	53,132	66.1	7.7	38.3	22.3	41,337	12.2	26.9	5.3
16 64090	Pocatello	30,601	32.6	31.5	39,459	67.9	5.4	34.6	25.8	38,551	14.5	31.3	11.0
16 64810	Post Falls	15,174	39.8	15.8	18,046	71.2	5.3	37.3	26.1	43,729	10.3	27.0	5.7
16 67420	Rexburg	7,445	23.3	31.5	18,148	58.5	9.1	17.7	17.2	31,294	29.0	41.0	8.4
16 82810	Twin Falls	25,210	45.3	18.0	30,913	65.1	4.7	41.8	25.5	39,047	13.9	28.1	9.2

Table B-4. Cities — What: Education, Employment, and Income, 2005–2007—*Continued*

STATE Place code	STATE City	Educational attainment			Employment status				Percent of households with no workers	Median household income (dollars)	Percent of families with income below poverty	Percent of households with income less than $25,000	Percent of households with income of $100,000 or more
		Total population 25 years and over	Percent with a high school diploma or less	Percent with a bachelor's degree or more	Total population 16 years and over	Percent in the labor force	Unemployment rate	Percent who worked full-time, year-round					
	ACS table number:	C15002	C15002	C15002	C20005	C23001	C23001	C20005	C08202	B19013	C17015	C19001	C19001
		1	2	3	4	5	6	7	8	9	10	11	12
17 00000	**Illinois**	8,292,894	43.6	29.0	9,946,551	66.4	7.5	40.6	25.0	53,745	8.9	22.5	21.1
17 00243	Addison village	23,964	56.9	17.8	29,662	69.9	7.2	43.9	19.6	62,533	8.8	17.2	21.0
17 00685	Algonquin village	18,919	29.2	38.6	21,832	73.7	3.9	50.2	11.2	90,073	3.3	6.4	45.0
17 01114	Alton	17,701	48.5	16.2	21,167	59.6	10.5	33.6	33.8	34,475	14.7	34.0	7.1
17 02154	Arlington Heights village	53,857	24.4	52.1	60,591	65.7	4.2	43.2	25.4	77,938	2.8	11.9	36.1
17 03012	Aurora	105,031	44.9	32.2	125,499	75.1	7.2	47.4	15.7	59,895	10.0	15.2	23.1
17 04013	Bartlett village	25,891	32.3	37.3	30,282	76.8	3.9	50.0	11.1	86,629	2.4	7.4	42.2
17 04078	Batavia	16,496	22.7	50.7	19,259	74.4	4.4	46.4	19.0	92,772	3.1	10.1	44.2
17 04845	Belleville	28,036	41.3	20.1	33,607	67.4	6.4	41.9	26.5	42,203	5.9	30.0	10.2
17 05092	Belvidere	14,855	61.8	14.5	18,836	66.5	9.5	34.5	29.3	42,581	15.5	31.4	9.4
17 05248	Bensenville village	13,635	61.0	13.3	15,912	70.6	7.3	45.9	21.4	49,080	10.5	20.5	14.4
17 05573	Berwyn	36,120	53.1	17.3	42,686	67.0	9.1	40.6	24.8	49,614	7.3	21.9	15.3
17 06587	Bloomingdale village	15,727	36.6	33.7	18,034	66.8	5.6	46.0	16.9	73,324	5.1	12.1	33.5
17 06613	Bloomington	44,408	30.5	44.0	54,892	73.4	5.3	44.8	18.8	54,213	8.7	22.2	21.6
17 06704	Blue Island	14,396	62.6	12.4	18,155	66.8	14.5	42.0	24.3	47,652	13.9	26.6	11.2
17 07133	Bolingbrook village	42,010	34.3	34.2	50,771	77.9	7.0	50.7	10.6	76,392	3.8	10.5	31.5
17 09447	Buffalo Grove village	29,506	19.2	57.9	34,321	71.8	4.0	45.0	17.4	83,545	1.7	11.4	40.8
17 09642	Burbank	18,345	65.7	10.6	22,629	63.1	8.7	38.7	28.9	53,102	8.1	20.0	16.5
17 10487	Calumet	24,657	49.4	15.2	29,753	65.3	14.0	38.3	31.3	44,703	11.8	26.5	6.9
17 11163	Carbondale	10,363	18.8	54.6	22,449	59.9	16.8	17.0	38.0	15,799	34.5	62.3	6.1
17 11332	Carol Stream village	24,757	39.5	31.5	30,183	74.0	4.8	46.9	18.3	68,893	5.2	13.9	29.7
17 11358	Carpentersville village	21,260	62.2	19.4	25,764	73.6	8.0	49.0	13.5	57,138	4.7	12.4	16.4
17 12385	Champaign	38,210	27.7	49.5	63,616	62.9	6.5	29.1	25.6	35,819	13.0	37.6	13.5
17 12567	Charleston	7,756	37.9	35.7	17,488	54.9	12.7	20.4	32.0	20,811	16.1	54.3	9.5
17 14000	Chicago	1,770,798	47.9	29.4	2,136,493	64.7	10.1	39.9	26.7	44,473	17.2	30.2	17.6
17 14026	Chicago Heights	18,238	55.9	14.3	22,420	59.5	17.6	33.1	32.2	37,932	19.2	35.1	10.6
17 14351	Cicero town	45,626	72.7	7.9	56,852	68.5	10.6	39.1	18.3	41,101	15.7	26.7	7.2
17 15599	Collinsville	17,379	40.8	23.5	20,802	67.6	7.4	41.6	26.0	49,962	8.5	23.0	14.9
17 17458	Crest Hill	13,150	53.3	16.2	15,457	-	-	40.2	23.9	56,177	3.5	15.6	11.3
17 17887	Crystal Lake	25,531	33.3	34.5	31,019	71.6	6.5	41.3	21.7	69,816	3.5	14.1	32.0
17 18563	Danville	21,140	55.4	14.0	25,181	56.1	13.2	30.5	40.2	30,274	24.0	43.4	7.1
17 18628	Darien	16,593	27.3	45.1	18,982	70.3	3.2	44.4	23.1	78,122	1.9	9.0	38.7
17 18823	Decatur	49,470	53.8	18.8	60,276	58.4	7.6	36.1	33.0	37,218	15.8	35.7	10.1
17 19161	DeKalb	19,220	32.8	36.6	37,496	68.4	10.6	28.9	19.6	38,523	11.2	31.3	13.5
17 19642	Des Plaines	41,949	44.5	28.0	48,102	64.4	5.9	41.4	27.4	56,871	4.3	17.3	24.6
17 20292	Dolton village	16,251	42.9	17.1	20,612	64.6	19.7	37.6	29.9	49,017	14.9	23.1	12.9
17 20591	Downers Grove village	32,501	24.2	47.8	37,436	66.6	4.5	41.3	26.6	72,521	1.8	15.9	34.0
17 22073	East Moline	14,661	49.6	16.7	17,696	57.6	10.1	32.8	38.3	37,628	14.6	33.3	9.2
17 22164	East Peoria	17,023	42.9	21.6	19,985	64.7	7.2	41.5	29.1	53,097	4.4	17.9	13.8
17 22255	East St. Louis	15,212	60.4	10.8	19,233	56.0	20.9	27.8	44.7	22,139	31.8	54.8	3.5
17 22697	Edwardsville	12,998	20.4	49.8	19,420	68.8	5.2	35.1	22.4	56,559	7.3	19.2	23.9
17 23074	Elgin	61,845	54.4	20.8	74,593	71.1	6.0	46.6	18.9	53,868	8.6	19.8	17.3
17 23256	Elk Grove Village village	24,452	35.4	34.7	27,712	74.0	4.5	48.4	18.7	71,581	3.2	12.0	29.3
17 23620	Elmhurst	28,380	24.9	49.0	32,847	68.7	4.9	39.9	21.7	81,925	2.5	13.0	39.1
17 23724	Elmwood Park village	17,323	48.1	21.4	20,537	64.4	6.0	38.3	27.2	50,326	10.3	25.1	15.1
17 24582	Evanston	44,433	18.8	63.9	56,713	63.8	5.8	37.1	26.1	63,407	5.8	19.6	33.0
17 27884	Freeport	16,576	50.7	16.2	19,417	63.2	10.3	37.0	36.2	35,306	17.2	34.7	6.2
17 28326	Galesburg	21,825	55.3	15.9	26,048	54.0	9.3	30.8	35.8	30,928	17.6	40.8	7.1
17 28872	Geneva	15,265	19.7	49.7	17,925	69.6	3.1	45.4	15.3	89,850	1.2	5.4	45.3
17 29730	Glendale Heights village	21,179	41.3	28.7	26,029	74.4	6.4	49.1	13.4	57,853	4.1	11.4	18.6
17 29756	Glen Ellyn village	17,044	16.1	60.4	19,788	67.6	5.4	42.6	23.4	88,332	1.8	11.0	44.9
17 29938	Glenview village	31,696	17.5	63.6	35,365	63.8	3.0	41.3	22.0	101,789	2.5	9.9	51.1
17 30926	Granite	19,583	56.3	13.6	23,077	62.4	9.5	37.8	34.4	38,812	9.9	29.4	9.5
17 31121	Grayslake village	13,352	22.3	55.8	15,816	74.9	4.1	49.7	13.2	87,901	4.1	9.4	43.4
17 32018	Gurnee village	20,031	23.6	48.9	24,130	72.4	4.9	48.4	14.9	84,455	3.8	9.9	39.5
17 32746	Hanover Park village	24,276	49.4	25.2	28,898	74.8	6.0	49.8	13.0	62,158	6.7	12.8	19.2
17 33383	Harvey	16,391	58.7	8.9	22,152	58.6	21.5	32.6	32.6	39,378	23.0	36.6	6.3
17 34722	Highland Park	19,611	17.6	62.4	22,445	64.3	4.2	39.0	23.0	113,350	2.2	8.2	56.2
17 35411	Hoffman Estates village	34,485	31.4	40.8	40,573	72.5	6.3	50.2	14.0	74,425	4.2	9.3	33.1
17 35835	Homer Glen village	16,115	35.2	35.6	19,694	71.6	3.6	42.8	16.3	94,586	2.3	6.1	46.0
17 36750	Huntley village	15,450	33.0	36.2	16,743			34.3	39.4	70,180	1.4	10.9	30.4
17 38570	Joliet	83,557	51.4	19.9	101,595	69.8	7.7	43.1	22.4	58,804	8.3	17.9	19.9
17 38934	Kankakee	16,264	57.5	14.2	19,866	59.1	13.0	34.1	35.6	32,524	21.4	38.1	5.3
17 41105	Lake Forest	12,389	8.4	74.1	15,601	55.1	4.2	32.6	24.5	150,670	1.4	6.9	65.4
17 41183	Lake in the Hills village	17,773	34.9	33.1	21,394	75.8	4.9	50.0	11.7	80,992	3.0	6.4	33.6
17 41742	Lake Zurich village	13,274	22.7	52.1	15,394	72.3	3.6	47.4	11.0	101,872	1.5	4.6	51.8
17 42028	Lansing village	18,540	48.8	20.6	20,795	63.4	5.8	38.4	31.0	48,835	9.1	21.1	15.0
17 43250	Libertyville village	13,391	17.4	61.2	16,003	67.2	4.0	39.3	19.3	106,337	2.8	9.6	54.5
17 43939	Lisle village	14,574	18.4	56.4	18,302	74.9	4.7	50.1	16.0	71,570	-	10.1	30.2
17 44225	Lockport	14,259	40.3	25.0	17,376	73.5	6.7	44.1	16.4	72,231	4.8	14.0	31.5
17 44407	Lombard village	29,524	32.2	39.7	34,258	71.1	4.2	46.0	21.7	69,752	1.7	11.2	28.0
17 45031	Loves Park	16,948	46.9	22.1	19,822	75.3	8.2	42.6	22.5	50,483	8.4	22.8	14.9
17 45694	McHenry	16,501	46.2	24.7	19,233	74.7	7.0	44.2	23.3	63,446	7.7	15.0	25.4
17 45726	Machesney Park village	14,675	56.2	11.2	17,354	71.8	6.8	41.9	19.3	53,645	7.1	17.8	14.6
17 47774	Maywood village	15,881	58.0	10.3	19,102	61.5	10.6	37.7	29.2	48,162	11.5	30.1	14.7
17 48242	Melrose Park village	13,692	67.7	10.6	17,101	64.4	9.3	42.2	23.2	38,166	18.6	28.1	9.7

STATE Place code	STATE City	Educational attainment			Employment status				Percent of households with no workers	Median household income (dollars)	Percent of families with income below poverty	Percent of households with income less than $25,000	Percent of households with income of $100,000 or more
		Total population 25 years and over	Percent with a high school diploma or less	Percent with a bachelor's degree or more	Total population 16 years and over	Percent in the labor force	Unemployment rate	Percent who worked full-time, year-round					
	ACS table number:	C15002	C15002	C15002	C20005	C23001	C23001	C20005	C08202	B19013	C17015	C19001	C19001
		1	2	3	4	5	6	7	8	9	10	11	12
	Illinois—Cont.												
17 49867	Moline	29,573	45.4	25.3	34,879	66.1	5.2	38.3	29.5	45,831	8.0	24.0	12.0
17 50647	Morton Grove village	16,324	32.7	40.5	18,751	61.1	3.5	36.3	27.2	67,500	3.6	13.7	31.0
17 51089	Mount Prospect village	38,783	36.8	37.2	44,360	68.3	4.8	43.2	21.5	65,120	3.1	14.0	28.0
17 51349	Mundelein village	20,759	34.4	39.6	24,432	74.8	5.6	47.2	12.5	80,556	3.4	9.1	35.4
17 51622	Naperville	87,481	14.3	63.9	105,310	70.4	4.2	45.5	12.7	97,790	2.0	7.1	48.8
17 52584	New Lenox village	14,472	32.2	33.1	17,493	70.2	4.5	41.6	14.3	86,375	2.7	5.8	38.2
17 53000	Niles village	23,249	45.5	27.6	26,021	57.1	8.6	34.9	36.6	51,882	3.3	21.1	20.3
17 53234	Normal town	23,130	24.1	44.8	42,600	65.5	7.8	30.7	19.9	43,492	8.0	30.7	17.1
17 53481	Northbrook village	23,492	14.1	65.4	26,961	59.6	3.0	34.2	22.9	115,842	1.5	6.5	57.7
17 53559	North Chicago	13,349	53.1	15.5	22,320	78.9	7.0	34.3	22.9	42,401	10.0	25.1	7.7
17 54638	Oak Forest	18,824	47.5	20.2	21,939	71.1	6.4	42.8	20.9	70,203	5.0	15.9	25.2
17 54820	Oak Lawn village	38,206	48.7	24.4	44,641	60.3	7.7	37.5	32.6	52,309	5.0	22.7	19.7
17 54885	Oak Park village	36,579	16.1	62.7	41,353	74.2	5.1	47.1	17.4	74,614	3.0	15.2	37.5
17 55249	O'Fallon	17,333	22.3	43.9	20,619	73.6	5.3	48.0	16.4	68,534	3.7	11.0	28.7
17 56640	Orland Park village	40,739	35.0	37.0	47,653	64.3	5.4	37.9	26.9	76,760	2.4	12.3	36.0
17 56887	Oswego village	13,475	29.2	36.6	16,145	75.2	6.6	45.1	12.6	79,981	4.1	7.3	34.4
17 57225	Palatine village	45,355	30.2	44.4	52,948	71.3	4.5	47.4	16.7	69,336	5.1	13.4	29.1
17 57732	Park Forest village	16,422	36.5	27.0	19,055	67.4	8.4	40.3	25.0	48,101	6.2	22.5	11.0
17 57875	Park Ridge	25,548	25.4	48.1	29,066	65.1	4.5	40.9	26.0	87,013	1.0	10.3	45.0
17 58447	Pekin	22,398	54.3	13.9	25,561	60.4	7.4	39.0	31.2	39,382	11.7	31.4	9.9
17 59000	Peoria	69,051	38.5	32.1	85,694	63.2	8.2	37.2	30.1	42,260	14.2	30.0	14.6
17 60287	Plainfield village	18,838	25.6	48.2	21,917	76.0	5.1	48.4	11.9	101,958	1.4	3.9	52.0
17 62367	Quincy	26,490	50.0	21.6	32,431	64.3	7.2	36.5	32.2	35,173	12.6	36.3	7.3
17 65000	Rockford	96,362	55.3	18.8	113,257	61.6	9.3	36.4	32.5	37,455	15.6	34.2	10.9
17 65078	Rock Island	24,058	48.6	19.6	29,945	60.9	9.7	32.6	35.4	37,186	14.7	35.5	10.8
17 65338	Rolling Meadows	15,368	38.8	30.7	18,383	74.1	6.5	47.8	20.9	61,144	1.9	17.1	24.7
17 65442	Romeoville village	22,359	45.9	21.6	27,410	73.3	7.0	46.2	17.6	62,652	5.7	11.5	16.0
17 65806	Roselle village	15,971	28.5	43.4	19,068	74.7	3.9	46.5	14.1	76,544	1.3	8.9	28.5
17 66040	Round Lake Beach village	16,822	56.3	18.5	20,483	74.2	8.8	45.2	12.4	62,500	9.0	13.1	21.1
17 66703	St. Charles	22,568	23.1	48.5	27,307	70.5	4.3	44.4	17.5	75,181	4.9	11.9	36.8
17 68003	Schaumburg village	51,726	28.8	41.8	60,594	73.7	4.1	49.7	19.0	65,267	3.4	14.1	27.0
17 70122	Skokie village	45,387	30.2	45.7	54,173	65.3	7.1	36.9	23.8	64,312	5.3	16.6	28.3
17 70720	South Elgin village	13,544	36.9	32.4	15,820	-	-	48.9	12.5	79,192	2.9	9.7	34.1
17 70850	South Holland village	16,059	40.0	29.0	18,936	64.0	11.2	37.7	29.9	60,674	5.6	16.1	21.9
17 72000	Springfield	74,007	38.1	31.6	87,599	67.7	7.9	40.9	29.7	44,403	12.9	28.3	16.2
17 73157	Streamwood village	27,008	47.8	26.6	31,016	74.4	6.9	48.1	12.8	68,568	3.9	12.4	23.7
17 75484	Tinley Park village	39,855	42.5	26.8	46,321	66.9	5.7	42.1	25.4	70,480	3.4	11.9	28.4
17 77005	Urbana	18,207	22.7	61.6	32,585	61.9	8.3	23.8	27.1	33,531	12.7	41.2	11.4
17 77694	Vernon Hills village	16,065	25.7	52.6	19,263	74.2	5.9	49.7	16.5	83,358	4.2	11.3	41.0
17 77993	Villa Park village	14,397	42.6	25.8	17,089	74.7	6.2	44.7	22.0	64,394	6.2	16.8	24.6
17 79293	Waukegan	51,990	61.2	16.2	62,883	69.5	11.5	43.6	22.1	46,343	9.1	23.0	11.6
17 80060	West Chicago	15,348	51.7	26.9	19,208	71.9	5.8	44.2	13.3	72,642	9.1	12.8	30.8
17 80645	Westmont village	15,908	31.1	39.6	18,589	63.7	6.5	39.0	24.2	57,595	5.6	18.8	21.5
17 81048	Wheaton	34,839	19.3	57.4	42,545	65.5	4.1	39.9	18.7	85,249	3.1	11.4	41.6
17 81087	Wheeling village	24,295	36.8	37.1	28,341	71.8	6.0	47.0	19.0	54,609	6.4	16.5	15.9
17 82075	Wilmette village	18,250	8.9	76.9	20,655	61.5	3.6	38.4	23.7	120,469	1.3	5.8	60.8
17 83245	Woodridge village	22,148	29.1	40.5	26,572	76.5	6.3	50.3	12.0	68,014	4.7	11.4	31.0
17 83349	Woodstock	14,100	44.0	27.3	16,615	71.7	7.9	43.0	22.6	53,687	6.9	22.5	18.3
17 84220	Zion	13,844	52.7	14.2	17,476	71.0	12.4	43.6	21.0	44,038	9.8	23.3	13.1
18 00000	**Indiana**	4,107,829	51.9	21.6	4,900,909	65.8	6.8	40.6	26.0	47,034	8.9	24.8	14.0
18 01468	Anderson	38,218	61.7	14.6	46,097	57.5	10.7	32.3	37.0	35,326	14.9	35.6	4.4
18 05860	Bloomington	34,342	24.4	53.7	65,715	52.6	6.9	21.9	32.8	28,540	13.7	45.1	11.1
18 10342	Carmel	40,769	14.8	62.4	48,500	71.1	3.7	46.1	15.0	94,128	1.5	8.2	47.4
18 12934	Clarksville town	15,340	58.5	14.7	18,231	65.9	6.4	39.9	26.3	36,257	12.1	32.5	8.5
18 14734	Columbus	27,923	46.1	30.1	31,623	64.5	6.0	41.3	26.0	47,483	10.3	24.7	16.8
18 16138	Crown Point	14,959	45.4	28.7	17,240	64.8	4.0	41.8	27.0	53,818	2.4	17.6	20.6
18 19486	East Chicago	18,559	68.7	10.5	22,400	56.3	13.0	31.4	35.5	27,612	26.7	44.9	6.4
18 20728	Elkhart	32,705	64.0	12.6	38,969	71.3	11.0	44.9	24.0	37,308	13.7	31.2	5.4
18 22000	Evansville	74,636	52.6	16.7	90,053	62.6	8.1	38.0	33.2	34,186	12.6	37.1	7.4
18 23278	Fishers town	37,896	13.3	63.9	44,059	78.7	2.9	54.2	9.9	87,942	2.4	6.2	41.2
18 25000	Fort Wayne	160,515	44.8	24.7	191,136	67.6	7.4	42.5	24.6	42,734	11.2	26.1	11.7
18 25450	Franklin	13,799	50.2	19.9	16,875	66.0	6.5	39.9	24.9	49,920	6.9	22.9	10.5
18 27000	Gary	53,714	57.7	11.7	63,701	54.8	17.9	28.3	44.2	26,911	26.5	46.9	4.9
18 28386	Goshen	20,373	63.5	18.5	24,305	63.9	7.7	39.5	23.8	39,973	10.9	27.2	8.2
18 28800	Granger CDP	19,356	24.8	51.1	22,049	68.7	3.3	43.3	15.4	89,839	1.3	5.1	40.7
18 29898	Greenwood	30,107	42.7	26.1	35,779	70.8	5.2	47.9	20.8	56,681	4.0	18.8	16.4
18 31000	Hammond	47,790	61.4	10.5	58,540	62.5	10.0	36.2	31.0	36,652	19.6	33.2	6.4
18 33466	Highland town	16,817	44.2	22.4	19,660	69.2	7.8	41.0	26.9	59,826	3.0	15.8	16.8
18 34114	Hobart	19,653	53.4	14.1	22,130	65.8	6.2	36.5	21.8	54,302	3.6	16.4	12.3
18 36003	Indianapolis (balance)	514,823	47.2	26.7	602,692	69.0	8.4	43.1	24.8	43,687	12.2	27.4	13.3
18 38358	Jeffersonville	18,943	53.1	16.0	21,347	67.4	7.1	43.9	27.4	39,176	10.2	29.4	9.4
18 40392	Kokomo	30,981	58.3	14.0	35,848	59.1	8.6	34.3	33.7	35,434	19.5	32.9	11.3
18 40788	Lafayette	40,495	49.3	23.5	49,654	69.7	9.8	40.9	27.9	37,696	14.0	32.4	7.8
18 42246	La Porte	14,422	59.3	11.7	16,921	64.8	8.2	39.6	28.2	40,601	10.0	30.1	6.5
18 42426	Lawrence	27,098	39.5	32.2	31,541	75.3	4.7	50.2	17.3	59,340	7.0	17.4	20.4

STATE Place code	STATE City	Educational attainment			Employment status				Percent of households with no workers	Median household income (dollars)	Percent of families with income below poverty	Percent of households with income less than $25,000	Percent of households with income of $100,000 or more
		Total population 25 years and over	Percent with a high school diploma or less	Percent with a bachelor's degree or more	Total population 16 years and over	Percent in the labor force	Unemployment rate	Percent who worked full-time, year-round					
	ACS table number:	C15002	C15002	C15002	C20005	C23001	C23001	C20005	C08202	B19013	C17015	C19001	C19001
		1	2	3	4	5	6	7	8	9	10	11	12
	Indiana—Cont.												
18 46908	Marion......	18,873	62.7	14.5	23,285	56.3	13.5	29.5	40.8	29,056	20.1	40.4	3.9
18 48528	Merrillville town..........	22,917	52.2	17.7	26,266	65.0	7.9	39.4	27.6	45,776	7.6	25.6	9.4
18 48798	Michigan	21,301	60.4	14.2	24,926	57.5	8.9	32.9	29.9	35,345	15.1	34.5	7.5
18 49932	Mishawaka	30,674	52.0	21.7	37,497	67.1	6.1	40.4	27.6	38,597	8.5	31.6	7.5
18 51876	Muncie	36,289	58.1	19.0	54,208	55.9	13.4	25.0	36.9	28,662	20.6	44.4	4.1
18 51912	Munster town..........	16,214	40.0	37.3	18,929	59.9	5.1	35.8	28.5	68,185	3.0	11.3	30.9
18 52326	New Albany	23,707	55.6	16.5	27,780	63.1	8.2	40.3	32.8	39,190	14.4	31.5	7.2
18 54180	Noblesville	27,535	29.1	42.1	31,592	74.5	2.6	49.0	13.4	65,292	4.6	13.2	27.9
18 60246	Plainfield town..........	15,215	46.4	22.9	17,697	62.2	3.0	43.3	22.1	50,601	7.6	18.0	15.8
18 61092	Portage..........	23,179	58.0	12.0	27,832	65.1	8.9	41.1	27.3	47,137	10.1	24.9	11.4
18 64260	Richmond	23,762	59.7	15.0	28,158	61.8	9.8	36.6	34.0	32,560	13.8	38.1	6.1
18 68220	Schererville town	20,011	38.8	31.9	23,125	72.6	4.3	46.9	17.9	68,779	2.8	9.4	28.6
18 71000	South Bend	62,254	53.3	22.4	75,313	62.9	8.5	36.1	31.9	35,204	15.5	34.6	6.6
18 75428	Terre Haute	34,145	53.5	20.6	46,793	57.8	9.7	29.3	35.7	29,297	16.5	42.8	6.9
18 78326	Valparaiso	18,070	34.8	37.1	24,360	67.4	6.1	34.5	27.8	47,191	7.5	26.3	15.2
18 82700	Westfield town	17,141	23.8	50.3	20,187	78.3	3.4	52.9	8.6	84,845	2.3	7.7	35.9
18 82862	West Lafayette	10,627	9.5	77.2	25,031	52.4	7.6	17.3	35.9	24,830	10.3	50.2	14.1
19 00000	**Iowa**	1,951,982	46.5	24.0	2,346,630	68.7	4.9	42.5	25.5	46,399	7.2	25.0	13.0
19 01855	Ames..........	25,749	15.6	60.8	47,479	69.8	5.5	28.0	19.7	40,220	7.1	32.0	15.0
19 02305	Ankeny..........	24,378	21.8	46.5	28,429	79.9	3.0	56.2	16.4	67,459	2.3	14.5	25.1
19 06355	Bettendorf	21,806	25.9	44.0	25,282	69.6	3.9	45.2	22.7	67,057	2.3	15.2	28.7
19 09550	Burlington..........	17,010	48.0	17.1	19,802	63.4	7.4	39.1	34.1	38,484	9.7	33.5	6.9
19 11755	Cedar Falls	19,596	28.9	46.3	32,146	67.5	7.1	30.6	24.6	47,959	6.0	26.5	16.7
19 12000	Cedar Rapids	81,485	38.6	27.9	96,943	70.8	5.7	44.2	24.8	46,480	9.3	24.7	14.3
19 14430	Clinton	17,880	56.5	14.7	21,516	64.3	7.1	36.7	30.7	35,316	9.8	33.4	7.1
19 16860	Council Bluffs	38,659	54.9	14.6	45,947	68.0	7.8	43.3	25.7	42,537	11.6	26.6	8.8
19 19000	Davenport..........	62,091	46.0	26.2	75,365	67.1	7.1	38.4	27.7	41,382	12.1	29.3	11.9
19 21000	Des Moines..........	129,714	49.1	23.2	152,560	70.9	6.9	44.6	24.2	43,215	9.6	26.6	10.1
19 22395	Dubuque	37,212	49.3	26.7	46,136	67.9	4.7	38.8	27.5	40,341	9.6	29.0	9.9
19 28515	Fort Dodge	16,939	48.7	19.1	20,123	65.9	5.8	39.8	33.3	39,543	9.8	30.3	6.5
19 38595	Iowa	33,101	17.2	61.1	55,918	68.9	4.5	31.8	21.3	40,378	10.3	36.7	15.7
19 49485	Marion	20,116	35.8	33.9	23,214	74.1	6.0	46.5	22.4	53,240	2.9	22.7	17.8
19 49755	Marshalltown..........	17,410	52.5	19.0	20,573	60.5	7.2	37.2	29.3	41,145	10.7	25.7	10.2
19 50160	Mason	18,992	43.1	21.1	22,550	65.2	4.8	39.5	31.2	40,383	10.7	31.4	10.5
19 55110	Muscatine	14,130	47.7	22.8	16,855	69.2	9.2	43.7	27.3	45,028	12.7	28.3	10.8
19 60465	Ottumwa	16,057	58.3	13.2	19,358	63.6	9.4	34.9	36.1	33,400	12.5	34.8	5.9
19 73335	Sioux	51,774	51.7	20.7	62,814	66.7	7.2	38.5	26.9	41,825	11.0	30.4	9.8
19 79950	Urbandale..........	23,965	24.8	46.1	27,313	75.6	2.9	49.9	18.0	69,269	1.8	8.8	29.9
19 82425	Waterloo..........	43,978	50.9	18.8	52,030	65.5	7.0	38.0	30.4	37,843	12.2	33.0	8.2
19 83910	West Des Moines	34,799	21.5	50.4	41,622	77.4	4.2	52.3	18.2	61,256	3.5	14.1	25.7
20 00000	**Kansas**..........	1,773,908	41.8	28.3	2,143,455	68.6	5.2	43.0	23.6	46,669	8.3	25.0	15.3
20 17800	Derby..........	13,364	33.6	33.4	15,723	74.3	4.2	48.7	17.7	69,676	2.5	11.3	25.2
20 18250	Dodge	15,172	61.6	13.5	18,702	71.7	5.1	44.5	17.4	38,498	19.0	27.9	7.4
20 21275	Emporia	14,738	48.9	26.6	20,949	68.1	7.6	36.1	25.8	31,442	24.3	39.4	3.7
20 25325	Garden	15,196	53.7	17.0	19,648	70.8	6.3	48.6	19.1	47,333	6.4	20.2	11.7
20 31100	Hays	11,794	28.0	39.1	16,404	72.9	5.2	38.7	25.6	42,918	5.5	30.6	10.1
20 33625	Hutchinson	27,655	46.3	17.2	33,069	61.4	4.6	38.1	27.0	38,811	10.0	31.0	7.9
20 36000	Kansas..........	88,483	61.4	13.4	105,663	65.8	11.1	40.2	29.0	36,609	16.3	32.2	8.3
20 38900	Lawrence	49,337	22.2	49.7	75,715	71.5	6.4	36.0	19.8	40,366	10.0	32.4	14.2
20 39000	Leavenworth	22,604	45.5	28.7	26,685	60.1	5.3	38.1	22.3	49,615	12.2	27.0	14.8
20 39075	Leawood..........	21,721	8.5	73.1	24,733	65.4	2.1	39.9	20.5	117,896	1.0	7.7	60.8
20 39350	Lenexa	29,822	21.9	50.9	35,286	74.0	4.0	47.3	13.4	70,246	3.8	11.1	31.0
20 39825	Liberal..........	11,654	64.5	12.9	14,443	70.6	7.3	45.9	16.1	37,096	17.2	32.6	6.9
20 44250	Manhattan	24,648	23.7	45.2	44,524	62.6	4.1	30.3	20.3	37,337	8.6	33.6	10.8
20 52575	Olathe	69,476	25.3	44.2	83,979	77.9	3.9	51.9	12.9	72,634	2.9	11.8	28.7
20 53775	Overland Park	110,146	18.3	54.7	128,318	73.0	4.5	47.8	18.3	70,405	2.7	11.5	33.2
20 57575	Prairie Village	15,477	14.1	61.9	17,544	71.1	1.6	45.1	24.5	71,646	2.0	12.2	29.7
20 62700	Salina..........	30,611	48.8	20.4	35,984	70.3	4.3	43.0	25.5	39,143	10.0	30.7	9.0
20 64500	Shawnee..........	38,354	27.3	42.6	44,966	75.8	3.8	50.5	16.2	71,512	3.3	12.6	28.1
20 71000	Topeka..........	80,142	45.7	27.0	94,648	66.3	7.1	41.2	29.5	38,186	13.0	30.5	11.5
20 79000	Wichita..........	227,481	44.7	26.4	272,172	68.9	7.4	42.8	25.2	42,536	11.5	27.9	13.9
21 00000	**Kentucky**..........	2,808,673	55.5	19.7	3,316,988	60.9	7.0	37.4	31.2	40,138	13.2	32.3	11.8
21 02368	Ashland..........	15,230	50.4	20.5	17,162	51.7	4.9	33.2	41.2	37,495	13.2	34.3	13.6
21 08902	Bowling Green..........	30,780	42.7	30.2	43,667	65.6	6.3	33.7	26.0	33,076	17.9	38.2	11.5
21 17848	Covington..........	27,399	56.7	17.4	32,582	63.3	7.6	39.6	31.0	37,167	17.3	35.2	9.2
21 24274	Elizabethtown..........	16,668	45.8	23.7	18,961	62.6	5.0	42.2	25.1	41,913	8.8	24.2	14.6
21 27982	Florence..........	18,970	48.9	18.6	22,841	73.5	4.1	47.0	21.6	50,208	8.5	21.8	12.6
21 28900	Frankfort..........	18,070	49.9	26.6	21,946	63.3	7.1	40.6	29.3	39,885	13.7	32.0	11.4
21 30700	Georgetown..........	14,572	49.7	21.6	18,663	67.5	8.3	40.7	24.8	48,966	10.5	24.3	13.9
21 35866	Henderson..........	18,623	59.6	15.1	21,702	61.1	5.7	36.9	29.7	33,523	14.5	35.5	8.1
21 37918	Hopkinsville	22,260	51.6	18.3	26,649	59.3	7.8	37.1	30.7	37,517	15.6	31.8	7.7
21 39142	Independence	11,795	45.3	20.8	13,510	74.3	4.3	51.2	15.2	65,605	5.1	13.1	18.3
21 40222	Jeffersontown..........	18,046	37.1	30.0	20,201	72.4	3.0	49.6	19.8	54,773	3.5	19.1	16.3
21 46027	Lexington-Fayette urban county	180,369	34.4	38.9	221,572	68.8	4.4	42.6	21.8	45,622	9.8	27.2	17.6

Table B-4. Cities — What: Education, Employment, and Income, 2005–2007—*Continued*

STATE Place code	STATE City	Educational attainment			Employment status				Percent of households with no workers	Median household income (dollars)	Percent of families with income below poverty	Percent of households with income less than $25,000	Percent of households with income of $100,000 or more
		Total population 25 years and over	Percent with a high school diploma or less	Percent with a bachelor's degree or more	Total population 16 years and over	Percent in the labor force	Unemployment rate	Percent who worked full-time, year-round					
	ACS table number:	C15002	C15002	C15002	C20005	C23001	C23001	C20005	C08202	B19013	C17015	C19001	C19001
		1	2	3	4	5	6	7	8	9	10	11	12
	Kentucky—Cont.												
21 48006	Louisville/Jefferson County (balance)	374,565	48.0	23.6	438,617	64.6	8.0	39.7	30.1	41,486	12.5	30.5	13.3
21 56136	Nicholasville	15,673	55.7	18.2	18,812	71.4	7.4	43.6	20.2	41,019	13.3	31.8	8.2
21 58620	Owensboro	35,603	51.5	17.4	41,718	59.5	7.9	37.0	38.0	33,596	17.7	39.9	7.8
21 58836	Paducah	16,929	50.8	16.5	20,057	53.8	13.5	25.8	43.7	25,705	24.3	48.8	7.4
21 63912	Radcliff	13,322	47.1	15.4	16,785	62.0	5.8	42.2	21.4	44,804	11.2	24.4	11.2
21 65226	Richmond	15,374	44.6	29.7	23,609	65.6	11.3	30.9	31.1	30,326	23.6	44.2	6.8
22 00000	**Louisiana**	2,766,825	55.9	20.1	3,371,197	60.8	7.9	36.2	29.2	40,160	15.0	33.0	13.4
22 00975	Alexandria	29,740	52.7	20.0	35,575	56.7	8.2	34.6	33.5	29,124	22.0	45.6	11.1
22 05000	Baton Rouge	130,173	42.4	32.4	176,309	64.2	9.6	34.6	28.2	34,506	21.0	38.8	13.0
22 08920	Bossier	37,690	44.0	21.0	46,532	69.8	8.8	46.0	24.8	44,307	10.9	26.4	13.0
22 33245	Harvey CDP	14,231	63.1	10.9	16,968	62.9	11.8	34.3	27.4	42,124	15.3	31.8	9.4
22 36255	Houma	21,906	62.1	16.7	26,201	57.8	4.6	36.1	29.7	42,047	13.5	32.4	14.6
22 39475	Kenner	43,257	48.8	22.7	51,899	64.5	8.3	36.6	24.2	46,009	9.9	25.6	17.5
22 40735	Lafayette	72,885	40.1	34.0	91,964	66.3	5.8	37.6	22.8	42,159	11.7	30.1	16.7
22 41155	Lake Charles	44,367	51.5	22.7	54,647	62.0	9.4	30.3	33.1	33,422	19.4	40.0	13.6
22 42030	Laplace CDP	19,155	55.2	17.7	23,354	65.3	5.6	46.0	20.4	50,848	6.7	19.2	16.7
22 48785	Marrero CDP	22,153	72.3	8.1	26,109	55.7	10.5	28.5	36.0	31,267	22.2	42.1	6.9
22 50115	Metairie CDP	92,699	40.3	32.9	106,550	63.6	5.5	38.7	28.2	49,465	6.6	24.1	19.6
22 51410	Monroe	28,336	47.9	27.0	36,953	56.8	12.9	30.0	37.1	27,786	27.2	46.6	13.2
22 54035	New Iberia	20,363	67.5	15.8	24,649	61.2	9.3	32.6	31.2	35,463	23.6	38.5	9.3
22 55000	New Orleans	198,423	47.7	29.0	245,235	60.2	13.0	32.1	33.4	35,409	18.6	38.2	14.6
22 58045	Opelousas	16,620	69.7	12.8	20,222	46.2	14.3	27.1	46.5	18,142	39.4	60.4	4.1
22 66655	Ruston	9,065	34.6	36.4	15,697	62.3	14.6	27.2	33.9	24,751	24.1	50.3	8.9
22 70000	Shreveport	125,736	51.0	24.4	153,373	60.7	10.2	33.5	33.5	33,112	19.1	38.9	11.0
22 70805	Slidell	17,994	45.6	21.7	20,897	54.3	5.4	32.4	27.3	49,554	9.3	23.4	17.9
22 75180	Terrytown CDP	13,282	54.9	17.7	15,796	-	-	40.7	25.3	42,788	14.0	28.7	11.0
23 00000	**Maine**	917,697	47.5	25.9	1,069,271	65.5	5.7	38.5	28.8	45,211	8.6	27.1	13.2
23 02060	Auburn	15,817	49.8	23.7	18,191	61.6	6.6	40.6	30.9	36,507	12.8	33.5	10.4
23 02795	Bangor	20,191	40.8	27.9	25,315	60.9	3.4	36.7	31.1	37,195	5.9	35.2	12.2
23 04860	Biddeford	15,945	58.6	18.7	19,445	67.3	7.5	40.5	25.7	42,169	6.7	27.3	10.0
23 38740	Lewiston	24,278	62.2	14.3	30,484	62.3	9.2	35.5	31.3	36,964	15.8	36.2	6.4
23 60545	Portland	45,470	34.8	40.7	53,450	69.5	5.7	39.5	26.5	42,830	12.3	30.1	13.5
23 71990	South Portland	16,534	33.4	38.6	19,427	73.2	4.7	43.9	21.3	49,743	7.3	23.5	15.3
24 00000	**Maryland**	3,699,555	40.2	34.7	4,396,011	68.7	5.5	44.9	21.7	66,873	5.5	16.1	30.0
24 01600	Annapolis	24,245	35.9	40.6	28,904	72.2	4.4	45.6	24.1	70,140	7.5	18.1	35.5
24 01975	Arbutus CDP	13,314	51.7	26.1	16,285	68.0	5.0	42.4	24.9	53,096	10.0	23.1	13.4
24 02275	Arnold CDP	15,378	25.6	48.2	17,710	72.6	3.3	48.4	16.0	93,480	2.2	9.0	46.0
24 02825	Aspen Hill CDP	33,318	36.2	41.6	40,012	71.4	7.2	44.1	20.8	75,014	5.4	13.0	33.7
24 04000	Baltimore	412,404	55.2	23.3	502,258	60.7	11.1	36.0	32.4	36,304	16.7	35.2	11.5
24 05265	Bel Air North CDP	18,419	29.4	40.4	21,263	71.4	3.0	47.5	17.3	86,881	3.3	8.3	41.1
24 05950	Bel Air South CDP	29,154	29.0	39.7	34,620	73.4	2.8	50.3	18.9	79,623	0.8	9.4	35.5
24 07125	Bethesda CDP	39,662	6.2	80.5	45,353	68.8	2.8	45.3	21.9	117,723	1.9	7.7	57.7
24 08775	Bowie	38,647	25.7	46.6	44,416	72.9	4.0	50.8	17.1	99,105	0.5	4.8	49.5
24 13325	Carney CDP	20,193	41.4	29.2	23,689	66.6	3.3	43.7	27.9	58,264	3.2	15.2	21.3
24 14125	Catonsville CDP	28,862	39.4	36.8	35,647	56.3	4.4	34.1	30.2	64,918	4.8	18.2	25.0
24 16875	Chillum CDP	21,247	58.0	17.8	25,180	71.9	6.8	47.2	21.9	49,271	6.2	19.7	16.6
24 17900	Clinton CDP	18,910	44.3	21.6	21,311	74.0	4.4	53.0	15.3	90,285	1.4	7.0	41.0
24 18250	Cockeysville CDP	14,237	24.4	47.8	18,302	79.2	4.7	49.3	13.4	60,088	5.2	13.2	26.8
24 18750	College Park	8,971	35.2	43.1	23,410	54.1	8.9	22.8	26.9	66,953	5.2	26.1	25.4
24 19125	Columbia CDP	61,795	16.5	60.7	72,423	74.8	3.9	48.5	14.8	89,448	3.7	8.1	44.7
24 20875	Crofton CDP	12,629	24.3	48.9	14,411	-	-	51.0	12.1	93,198	1.3	3.6	44.5
24 21325	Cumberland	14,842	58.0	14.1	17,361	54.8	9.8	31.1	44.0	28,488	12.8	44.3	7.5
24 23975	Dundalk CDP	42,763	68.4	8.3	49,864	63.8	9.5	42.0	33.3	43,002	9.2	28.6	10.9
24 25150	Edgewood CDP	15,492	48.4	15.4	19,424	72.2	5.0	49.8	20.5	52,974	11.5	18.8	16.1
24 25575	Eldersburg CDP	19,932	34.1	39.0	23,248	69.2	2.3	47.0	19.0	92,541	2.5	10.8	44.2
24 25750	Elkridge CDP	15,466	29.6	44.8	17,629	77.9	2.2	53.8	10.1	88,215	3.2	7.7	42.6
24 26000	Ellicott CDP	41,126	19.3	58.9	48,575	69.2	2.6	47.2	16.0	103,464	2.0	9.0	52.3
24 26600	Essex CDP	25,830	63.1	11.8	29,972	69.8	10.2	45.5	25.3	46,823	8.0	24.5	12.5
24 27250	Fairland CDP	14,574	24.6	50.8	16,708	-	-	53.7	14.7	70,059	3.6	12.4	31.5
24 29525	Fort Washington CDP	16,892	31.4	34.6	19,224	67.6	4.9	48.5	18.7	105,475	2.6	6.0	54.2
24 30325	Frederick	39,253	37.2	34.8	47,983	72.7	4.4	50.2	18.5	60,932	5.4	13.9	22.2
24 31175	Gaithersburg	36,271	26.6	52.5	43,772	73.5	4.6	49.2	17.2	74,883	4.9	11.1	33.9
24 32025	Germantown CDP	37,993	30.5	43.6	45,361	78.4	5.8	50.6	8.7	71,226	3.6	6.9	31.2
24 32650	Glen Burnie CDP	25,113	55.8	15.6	29,755	69.6	6.6	44.8	24.1	55,786	4.4	19.6	17.4
24 34711	Greater Landover CDP	12,688	61.6	12.9	15,739	70.2	10.0	46.6	20.8	49,905	9.2	20.2	11.8
24 34712	Greater Upper Marlboro CDP	14,720	34.4	34.7	16,882	74.8	4.2	60.2	10.1	90,762	1.4	5.5	40.4
24 34775	Greenbelt	13,990	28.4	45.0	17,958	76.4	6.6	48.5	15.4	59,261	4.1	14.9	19.1
24 36075	Hagerstown	25,380	58.0	13.2	29,746	68.2	8.4	41.9	29.4	35,568	16.1	34.4	9.0
24 45612	Lanham-Seabrook CDP	14,431	43.2	34.7	17,017	76.3	3.7	48.4	13.9	79,087	2.9	8.1	38.1
24 45900	Laurel	15,241	35.2	36.2	18,104	76.6	4.2	54.2	16.1	60,795	4.9	11.3	20.3
24 47450	Lochearn CDP	16,998	42.6	24.4	21,253	65.9	8.2	40.1	23.5	53,720	7.7	18.9	14.0
24 52300	Middle River CDP	16,016	62.4	12.3	18,775	64.2	5.7	39.2	27.5	48,806	8.4	22.6	11.9

Table B-4. Cities — What: Education, Employment, and Income, 2005–2007—*Continued*

STATE Place code	STATE City	Educational attainment			Employment status				Percent of households with no workers	Median household income (dollars)	Percent of families with income below poverty	Percent of households with income less than $25,000	Percent of households with income of $100,000 or more
		Total population 25 years and over	Percent with a high school diploma or less	Percent with a bachelor's degree or more	Total population 16 years and over	Percent in the labor force	Unemployment rate	Percent who worked full-time, year-round					
	ACS table number:	C15002	C15002	C15002	C20005	C23001	C23001	C20005	C08202	B19013	C17015	C19001	C19001
		1	2	3	4	5	6	7	8	9	10	11	12
	Maryland—Cont.												
24 52562	Milford Mill CDP	17,666	44.6	22.7	20,582	74.9	5.5	51.9	17.0	52,397	5.4	19.8	13.4
24 53325	Montgomery Village CDP	26,480	23.8	49.9	30,614	77.6	3.9	51.5	14.1	82,129	2.3	5.6	38.4
24 56337	North Bethesda CDP	29,608	16.7	65.4	34,063	66.5	5.1	41.6	25.0	85,136	1.5	9.8	40.6
24 56875	North Potomac CDP	16,158	12.5	73.0	19,437	72.2	3.4	47.2	8.0	134,275	0.5	4.6	69.8
24 58300	Odenton CDP	16,523	28.8	40.4	18,883	75.6	3.9	53.7	15.7	85,137	2.3	8.1	38.8
24 58900	Olney CDP	22,099	20.5	57.1	26,029	71.1	4.2	45.3	11.6	116,319	1.1	5.6	60.5
24 59425	Owings Mills CDP	19,386	27.0	44.2	22,402	76.8	4.8	54.1	12.2	64,648	4.4	10.4	24.2
24 59505	Oxon Hill-Glassmanor CDP	22,560	49.2	19.5	27,273	72.4	10.8	43.7	21.5	53,960	10.5	17.4	16.5
24 60275	Parkville CDP	20,525	49.5	22.0	25,241	67.2	4.6	41.7	24.1	48,072	7.2	21.4	13.4
24 60975	Perry Hall CDP	20,515	35.8	36.8	23,617	72.7	1.9	48.9	20.0	74,450	2.7	10.1	29.7
24 61400	Pikesville CDP	22,082	22.5	56.9	24,170	61.0	4.2	38.2	33.4	73,846	7.1	20.1	36.5
24 63300	Potomac CDP	31,479	9.6	77.1	36,284	63.5	2.9	41.1	19.2	154,370	2.0	5.8	70.3
24 64950	Randallstown CDP	20,481	34.2	33.0	23,783	71.2	4.9	45.8	19.1	59,158	4.0	10.7	23.7
24 65600	Reisterstown CDP	15,402	34.5	36.1	18,310	74.9	4.9	49.2	17.7	57,495	3.2	18.4	22.5
24 67675	Rockville	37,850	23.1	57.6	42,942	69.0	3.5	42.6	17.7	86,085	1.8	9.2	42.2
24 69350	St. Charles CDP	22,780	42.6	24.0	27,539	77.4	4.0	52.8	15.1	71,003	3.0	13.1	31.8
24 69925	Salisbury	14,813	55.8	21.3	20,504	68.2	10.8	38.0	24.6	38,878	10.3	30.8	9.6
24 71150	Severn CDP	23,526	31.1	38.3	27,262	78.2	4.7	56.7	12.2	84,864	3.6	9.5	40.5
24 71200	Severna Park CDP	19,209	23.9	50.1	22,480	66.0	2.5	42.6	20.1	106,983	1.0	5.7	55.1
24 72450	Silver Spring CDP	50,564	31.9	51.4	59,585	76.8	4.6	50.1	16.1	67,255	4.9	12.3	29.1
24 73550	South Gate CDP	19,189	41.1	22.9	24,168	76.6	4.4	51.5	16.0	58,934	2.6	12.7	21.7
24 75762	Suitland-Silver Hill CDP	18,885	52.2	16.8	22,904	74.3	7.7	48.7	20.9	51,130	9.0	19.1	12.2
24 78425	Towson CDP	33,392	23.3	57.1	45,394	57.6	5.2	33.0	31.3	64,313	2.5	20.3	32.0
24 81175	Waldorf CDP	15,989	34.3	26.2	18,790	80.4	4.7	57.4	9.5	86,901	4.9	7.9	40.6
24 83837	Wheaton-Glenmont CDP	38,120	41.6	35.2	44,393	73.5	5.0	45.5	17.6	71,146	4.8	12.0	30.5
24 84375	White Oak CDP	13,302	31.5	47.8	15,567	75.0	7.0	47.2	14.9	67,959	6.9	12.3	28.7
24 86475	Woodlawn CDP (Baltimore County)	24,208	39.1	29.0	28,374	69.6	5.4	47.4	19.6	57,497	5.5	16.3	16.2
25 00000	**Massachusetts**	4,355,378	40.0	37.1	5,167,254	66.9	6.1	40.4	26.0	61,785	7.2	20.9	27.5
25 00765	Agawam	19,821	45.1	27.5	23,011	67.3	4.2	43.6	27.3	61,912	2.6	17.8	20.0
25 01640	Arlington CDP	31,150	23.8	60.6	33,802	71.6	3.6	45.4	22.6	77,279	3.1	14.5	36.4
25 02690	Attleboro	29,399	45.1	28.1	33,727	70.9	5.5	44.6	22.7	61,718	6.6	17.7	26.8
25 03690	Barnstable Town	33,279	35.3	33.9	38,951	64.9	5.9	37.2	28.8	62,060	5.5	16.6	21.7
25 05105	Belmont CDP	17,088	17.8	69.7	19,067	68.5	3.4	44.2	20.9	85,981	1.7	10.2	42.8
25 05595	Beverly	28,009	34.5	40.9	33,461	64.3	4.6	40.3	27.6	66,105	5.5	20.3	29.4
25 07000	Boston	398,929	42.2	40.3	500,460	66.7	8.1	38.7	28.5	48,729	16.7	30.6	21.7
25 07700	Braintree CDP	23,299	38.0	35.8	27,245	65.7	7.2	42.1	25.3	74,360	5.3	14.0	34.7
25 09000	Brockton	60,471	55.5	16.1	72,492	70.2	9.3	42.5	24.2	50,572	9.2	24.2	14.5
25 09210	Brookline CDP	41,780	11.2	76.6	49,178	69.1	3.1	43.1	22.2	82,496	7.5	16.3	42.7
25 09875	Burlington CDP	16,644	27.7	45.2	18,697	71.3	5.4	45.5	20.3	86,052	1.6	9.9	42.3
25 11000	Cambridge	65,851	18.6	69.8	80,770	67.6	4.5	37.7	26.6	58,457	10.3	24.6	28.7
25 13205	Chelsea	21,149	69.6	14.0	25,155	62.9	10.0	39.1	32.0	39,439	18.2	33.1	9.8
25 13660	Chicopee	37,085	58.7	14.5	45,201	63.9	7.4	38.2	33.0	41,039	10.3	32.8	9.7
25 16285	Danvers CDP	17,564	35.9	39.1	20,482	67.1	4.4	43.0	25.7	71,341	5.3	17.8	35.8
25 16530	Dedham CDP	15,997	34.2	39.7	18,334	67.5	6.0	43.7	23.4	78,645	4.6	13.0	36.5
25 21990	Everett	27,444	60.7	16.3	33,349	69.6	8.7	40.9	23.3	51,333	7.5	21.3	12.0
25 23000	Fall River	62,765	66.0	13.6	74,176	61.9	10.0	35.7	34.8	36,291	15.5	36.5	8.4
25 23875	Fitchburg	25,189	55.4	16.6	32,752	65.0	9.5	33.5	31.5	43,828	14.8	30.0	12.6
25 24960	Framingham CDP	44,293	36.5	43.6	51,663	71.3	5.4	42.5	21.5	62,794	5.6	18.6	27.7
25 25100	Franklin	19,377	31.0	46.6	22,746	70.5	5.1	45.4	19.9	85,407	3.2	11.1	43.9
25 25485	Gardner	14,991	56.5	18.5	17,294	64.9	7.9	36.9	30.5	44,697	8.0	28.9	12.6
25 26150	Gloucester	20,242	40.8	32.4	22,656	67.5	5.0	42.2	26.8	58,568	5.5	20.8	25.0
25 29405	Haverhill	40,078	44.0	29.3	46,694	70.5	6.4	45.9	23.9	61,730	7.8	20.0	24.8
25 30840	Holyoke	25,015	52.3	22.5	29,415	57.0	11.7	29.7	41.8	32,650	28.3	40.7	10.1
25 34550	Lawrence	41,509	69.4	10.7	52,718	59.9	7.4	34.3	35.2	31,718	27.9	43.1	7.4
25 35075	Leominster	28,386	49.6	24.3	32,595	66.2	6.9	43.5	30.2	52,368	7.5	25.9	19.4
25 35250	Lexington CDP	20,446	13.8	75.6	23,270	64.2	4.3	38.5	21.0	122,656	1.8	7.3	61.9
25 37000	Lowell	64,552	55.6	21.1	79,312	64.5	6.3	40.7	28.8	47,377	15.6	28.7	14.6
25 37490	Lynn	56,373	59.9	18.3	67,921	65.3	7.9	39.0	29.8	40,928	16.8	34.1	12.3
25 37875	Malden	40,130	51.6	27.3	47,014	72.2	8.3	41.8	26.1	50,229	9.0	22.7	16.5
25 38435	Marblehead CDP	14,176	14.3	66.0	15,804	-	-	42.3	24.2	84,473	2.2	12.7	41.6
25 38715	Marlborough	26,465	42.2	37.7	30,069	71.7	4.3	48.5	22.4	67,935	5.4	17.1	34.3
25 39835	Medford	39,940	41.5	38.0	47,251	65.6	6.3	40.7	26.7	67,100	6.4	18.1	30.0
25 40115	Melrose	19,875	31.5	47.1	21,899	67.4	3.5	43.8	28.0	74,765	2.4	18.6	34.4
25 40710	Methuen	29,657	48.0	23.5	34,611	68.0	6.6	41.3	27.3	59,515	4.1	22.0	27.1
25 41200	Milford CDP	18,263	47.1	26.8	21,157	73.9	6.7	45.9	22.6	58,048	7.3	19.8	26.8
25 41725	Milton CDP	16,992	23.1	54.0	19,764	67.7	5.0	40.1	27.2	88,205	2.3	13.7	43.0
25 44140	Needham CDP	19,143	12.1	73.6	21,743	64.0	1.9	40.4	23.5	116,867	2.2	9.6	57.0
25 45000	New Bedford	62,234	68.2	12.7	73,421	60.1	9.4	35.7	36.9	34,626	19.5	40.1	8.8
25 45560	Newton	57,611	16.7	71.5	74,826	62.2	3.3	38.3	21.1	104,014	2.3	11.5	52.1
25 46330	Northampton	18,924	24.6	50.1	24,572	70.7	4.3	32.7	26.2	45,760	8.0	25.8	17.0
25 50285	Norwood CDP	20,075	33.7	40.4	23,520	70.4	5.6	46.6	23.4	66,743	4.0	15.7	28.4
25 52490	Peabody	36,067	46.2	26.9	41,574	64.6	4.0	40.8	29.6	64,143	5.2	20.3	27.4
25 53960	Pittsfield	32,098	46.9	25.1	37,732	61.9	7.3	37.3	35.9	42,930	13.4	30.4	14.7

Table B-4. Cities — What: Education, Employment, and Income, 2005–2007—*Continued*

STATE Place code	STATE City	Educational attainment			Employment status				Percent of households with no workers	Median household income (dollars)	Percent of families with income below poverty	Percent of households with income less than $25,000	Percent of households with income of $100,000 or more
		Total population 25 years and over	Percent with a high school diploma or less	Percent with a bachelor's degree or more	Total population 16 years and over	Percent in the labor force	Unemployment rate	Percent who worked full-time, year-round					
	ACS table number:	C15002	C15002	C15002	C20005	C23001	C23001	C20005	C08202	B19013	C17015	C19001	C19001
		1	2	3	4	5	6	7	8	9	10	11	12
	Massachusetts—Cont.												
25 55745	Quincy....................	63,281	42.2	35.6	72,177	69.3	6.5	44.3	27.4	58,088	7.3	22.2	23.0
25 55990	Randolph CDP..........	21,221	43.1	29.7	24,378	72.2	5.5	46.7	23.5	70,506	0.7	15.7	27.6
25 56165	Reading CDP.............	16,504	24.7	52.6	19,157	69.2	3.8	42.8	22.1	96,524	1.1	12.4	48.1
25 56585	Revere.....................	40,117	58.8	19.9	44,009	62.8	6.3	39.7	30.6	48,604	7.2	24.2	14.0
25 59105	Salem......................	28,983	37.2	35.3	33,911	69.9	6.0	45.3	26.0	58,981	7.6	23.0	22.6
25 60050	Saugus CDP..............	20,089	51.3	22.9	22,549	64.0	4.8	42.1	26.7	61,340	3.5	18.4	26.1
25 62535	Somerville...............	50,334	36.7	48.7	63,862	72.8	5.8	45.3	22.9	59,146	11.7	24.3	22.6
25 67000	Springfield..............	89,975	59.7	17.5	113,333	58.6	12.2	32.2	36.7	32,319	24.2	40.9	7.7
25 67700	Stoneham CDP..........	16,109	41.3	37.2	18,152	68.3	7.2	41.8	26.6	73,700	6.1	15.5	29.2
25 69170	Taunton...................	39,138	55.7	19.6	45,238	72.0	6.1	44.0	24.8	53,881	7.4	22.9	18.2
25 72250	Wakefield CDP..........	17,445	31.6	44.0	19,875	70.5	4.9	42.2	21.0	82,412	2.1	10.6	38.4
25 72600	Waltham..................	39,329	39.5	41.4	50,607	68.5	6.1	42.3	23.3	60,434	5.7	20.1	25.6
25 73440	Watertown...............	23,382	25.1	54.5	26,994	66.6	4.9	45.7	23.5	66,571	2.8	11.9	26.1
25 74210	Wellesley CDP...........	17,088	9.2	79.1	23,278	60.3	5.9	31.1	22.8	125,814	5.2	13.3	60.9
25 76030	Westfield.................	26,679	50.0	25.0	33,159	62.1	6.9	36.5	30.3	51,398	9.0	26.1	18.6
25 77850	West Springfield........	18,933	44.5	26.7	22,814	68.6	8.1	40.2	28.2	48,189	6.7	23.6	13.1
25 78900	Weymouth CDP.........	37,904	42.2	28.5	43,647	70.6	5.4	44.9	21.9	66,342	4.5	14.4	27.8
25 80195	Wilmington CDP........	15,318	44.2	28.2	17,342	73.1	6.8	43.2	14.2	83,769	1.1	8.4	39.4
25 80545	Winchester CDP.........	14,910	16.2	67.3	16,781	64.5	5.5	38.8	24.1	106,466	1.4	12.0	52.0
25 80965	Winthrop CDP...........	13,948	45.8	28.8	16,104	66.2	4.8	39.8	26.9	64,227	6.5	20.0	25.9
25 81035	Woburn....................	27,135	44.7	29.2	30,622	72.3	5.7	43.3	21.0	66,984	4.0	14.1	25.6
25 82000	Worcester.................	108,138	48.5	28.2	134,879	62.5	6.6	38.1	32.8	43,631	13.9	32.2	15.8
26 00000	**Michigan**..............	6,634,147	45.2	24.5	7,915,981	63.5	9.4	35.9	29.4	48,642	9.8	24.9	17.1
26 00440	Adrian.....................	13,626	55.9	17.7	17,283	63.2	14.1	30.6	35.1	37,679	10.3	33.5	7.4
26 01380	Allen Park................	21,018	45.6	20.4	24,353	60.8	7.6	35.4	35.2	53,518	4.5	16.7	16.2
26 03000	Ann Arbor................	63,033	10.5	73.0	97,681	62.0	6.1	30.1	24.9	51,232	7.9	27.8	24.7
26 04105	Auburn Hills.............	11,980	34.8	37.4	15,763	69.9	5.4	37.9	21.3	46,080	6.0	21.9	13.1
26 05920	Battle Creek..............	33,518	47.1	18.6	39,206	61.6	8.7	35.7	31.9	38,944	16.9	35.2	10.7
26 06020	Bay.........................	22,979	51.2	15.4	27,104	63.3	11.6	35.6	33.9	34,998	13.3	34.2	6.8
26 09190	Bloomfield Township CDP...	30,283	13.4	69.7	33,830	61.1	4.9	37.2	24.3	119,233	1.7	5.7	58.3
26 12060	Burton....................	20,209	54.1	12.8	23,721	63.8	13.3	35.3	36.2	43,271	12.1	24.3	9.3
26 13110	Canton CDP..............	59,300	27.2	45.3	68,069	70.7	7.3	45.9	18.0	82,669	4.0	11.9	37.2
26 16510	Clinton CDP..............	65,518	45.5	18.9	76,264	65.7	9.5	37.2	29.2	48,501	9.2	24.0	16.3
26 21000	Dearborn.................	63,410	45.7	29.0	75,317	57.7	9.9	31.9	32.8	47,946	16.4	27.2	18.2
26 21020	Dearborn Heights.........	40,640	53.6	16.3	46,289	57.7	9.2	33.9	32.9	48,198	8.5	21.9	12.4
26 22000	Detroit....................	512,782	60.1	11.3	624,248	54.9	21.6	27.0	41.7	29,109	27.1	44.0	6.1
26 24120	East Lansing.............	14,490	12.1	68.1	44,077	56.7	8.7	15.9	28.0	29,885	11.1	44.3	15.3
26 24290	Eastpointe...............	22,260	52.5	13.4	25,787	66.7	11.3	42.0	28.0	48,821	7.8	23.1	12.0
26 27440	Farmington Hills.........	58,454	25.0	50.3	67,311	65.6	5.6	39.9	24.3	73,274	3.1	15.6	33.6
26 27880	Ferndale..................	13,739	40.0	32.3	15,851	75.3	9.0	44.2	21.8	46,922	6.8	24.4	12.8
26 29000	Flint.......................	66,696	58.7	12.0	81,377	53.6	13.8	28.8	40.5	27,560	28.0	44.8	4.4
26 29580	Forest Hills CDP.........	15,632	14.8	58.3	17,850	68.9	4.1	41.6	19.5	96,150	2.3	9.4	47.5
26 31420	Garden....................	20,761	55.6	12.1	24,340	63.2	11.1	34.2	33.0	51,880	7.1	20.2	11.3
26 34000	Grand Rapids............	118,982	45.1	26.9	149,168	68.7	10.7	36.9	26.5	38,792	16.8	31.3	9.6
26 36280	Hamtramck..............	12,632	74.0	9.5	15,075	48.5	14.5	24.6	37.4	23,689	31.8	52.0	3.2
26 36810	Harrison CDP............	16,570	41.7	22.2	19,197	70.0	10.4	40.1	26.4	62,591	7.0	18.6	24.0
26 38640	Holland....................	19,633	44.4	32.6	25,167	64.8	5.3	36.0	26.3	44,620	5.2	22.4	11.6
26 40680	Inkster....................	18,034	53.7	13.2	21,480	58.3	12.0	35.9	34.4	37,453	16.8	34.6	8.2
26 41420	Jackson...................	20,251	51.0	14.4	24,427	64.2	11.7	35.2	32.7	31,946	27.2	42.9	5.4
26 42160	Kalamazoo...............	37,840	35.8	34.7	58,522	64.9	14.3	28.4	30.3	31,864	18.6	39.4	9.2
26 42820	Kentwood................	29,960	36.7	31.5	35,687	72.8	7.3	42.0	23.7	49,287	8.5	22.8	13.2
26 46000	Lansing....................	70,238	44.8	22.5	88,495	65.2	9.3	37.8	29.7	35,990	19.5	36.6	7.0
26 47800	Lincoln Park..............	28,400	63.6	9.4	32,657	61.9	13.0	36.5	35.0	45,288	11.8	24.5	8.4
26 49000	Livonia....................	71,387	36.6	31.9	82,788	66.1	5.8	39.8	26.5	70,844	1.6	13.4	28.2
26 50560	Madison Heights...........	21,165	49.1	19.9	24,435	68.3	9.5	41.5	26.9	49,062	7.5	24.7	10.0
26 51900	Marquette................	11,535	40.8	37.3	18,326	53.5	7.2	22.3	34.7	32,786	6.8	43.6	10.1
26 53780	Midland...................	26,725	29.3	42.9	32,859	60.4	7.9	33.9	32.7	51,132	7.4	28.6	21.6
26 55020	Monroe...................	14,122	46.0	18.2	17,306	64.6	7.0	37.9	28.6	46,701	14.2	27.4	14.1
26 56020	Mount Pleasant..........	8,899	32.2	44.1	21,680	60.8	10.1	18.0	25.6	28,874	15.4	45.8	8.4
26 56320	Muskegon................	26,519	55.9	11.2	32,256	51.6	22.1	24.3	37.5	28,986	23.1	43.8	3.7
26 59140	Norton Shores...........	16,109	36.8	31.5	18,470	64.6	9.8	38.0	30.3	52,140	4.4	19.2	13.9
26 59440	Novi.......................	34,944	19.7	56.3	40,856	70.6	4.6	45.5	18.4	78,151	2.7	11.7	38.7
26 59920	Oak Park..................	18,327	36.9	26.2	22,028	67.9	9.7	40.8	27.1	54,706	10.6	24.0	14.8
26 60340	Okemos CDP.............	14,594	15.7	68.4	17,153	64.9	3.7	41.2	23.4	75,736	6.7	17.0	36.1
26 65085	Plymouth Township CDP....	20,511	24.2	47.9	24,047	64.9	5.2	40.2	25.5	90,780	0.8	11.5	45.4
26 65440	Pontiac...................	37,720	60.6	9.9	46,732	61.2	19.0	30.0	37.4	31,107	23.2	42.3	6.2
26 65560	Portage...................	30,437	29.5	37.7	36,378	70.3	7.0	42.5	25.8	51,362	6.7	22.8	18.7
26 65820	Port Huron...............	20,441	57.4	15.7	24,421	65.8	13.5	35.0	35.0	34,859	20.9	36.1	7.8
26 67620	Redford CDP.............	34,737	48.8	19.8	40,026	69.8	10.0	40.6	26.5	53,669	5.6	18.0	13.9
26 69035	Rochester Hills..........	48,152	23.2	51.5	56,113	68.0	6.2	40.0	22.5	82,623	4.0	13.2	39.4
26 69420	Romulus..................	16,404	54.4	12.3	18,691	65.6	16.0	34.9	27.5	45,218	13.9	30.6	13.4
26 69800	Roseville..................	31,472	60.5	9.5	35,968	63.4	9.7	36.6	30.7	42,396	10.4	26.7	7.5
26 70040	Royal Oak................	42,548	28.2	44.2	48,859	71.9	5.9	45.1	23.2	58,484	3.7	17.8	24.6
26 70520	Saginaw...................	32,185	63.3	9.5	40,328	50.6	16.2	25.6	44.5	25,710	31.1	48.7	3.7
26 70545	Saginaw Township North CDP..................	17,595	37.5	30.2	20,992	57.6	6.4	31.7	37.3	46,790	11.4	26.0	16.8

Table B-4. Cities — What: Education, Employment, and Income, 2005–2007—*Continued*

STATE Place code	STATE City	Educational attainment			Employment status				Percent of households with no workers	Median household income (dollars)	Percent of families with income below poverty	Percent of households with income less than $25,000	Percent of households with income of $100,000 or more
		Total population 25 years and over	Percent with a high school diploma or less	Percent with a bachelor's degree or more	Total population 16 years and over	Percent in the labor force	Unemployment rate	Percent who worked full-time, year-round					
	ACS table number:	C15002	C15002	C15002	C20005	C23001	C23001	C20005	C08202	B19013	C17015	C19001	C19001
		1	2	3	4	5	6	7	8	9	10	11	12
	Michigan—Cont.												
26 70760	St. Clair Shores	44,122	45.7	19.5	49,584	62.7	7.8	35.6	35.0	50,729	4.6	21.6	14.3
26 72818	Shelby CDP	48,481	38.8	28.7	57,345	67.2	8.7	37.8	25.6	66,700	4.4	15.9	28.7
26 74900	Southfield	50,193	31.1	38.6	58,170	66.3	9.5	37.3	29.6	50,731	7.8	19.9	18.9
26 74960	Southgate	22,212	51.7	16.3	25,775	63.9	9.8	39.8	34.9	47,709	4.4	22.6	14.0
26 76460	Sterling Heights	89,570	41.5	26.1	105,084	66.5	7.5	38.5	26.2	60,868	5.2	16.7	22.3
26 79000	Taylor	44,200	61.4	9.0	51,882	63.0	14.2	33.5	31.2	46,692	11.5	24.7	11.4
26 80700	Troy	55,035	22.0	55.4	64,670	68.3	5.6	42.3	21.7	85,934	2.5	10.5	41.2
26 82960	Walker	14,798	40.3	22.8	18,726	75.2	7.1	40.2	17.4	48,960	6.3	22.7	15.4
26 84000	Warren	91,153	54.4	17.0	105,358	62.9	10.4	37.4	32.3	46,303	9.1	23.4	12.3
26 84220	Waterford CDP	50,617	42.7	23.9	58,989	66.5	8.0	39.7	27.5	54,951	6.1	18.7	18.7
26 85510	West Bloomfield Township CDP	44,869	19.8	56.6	51,581	63.0	4.7	38.9	23.2	96,233	3.2	10.5	48.3
26 86000	Westland	60,519	50.5	16.8	70,263	64.4	8.3	40.9	28.4	47,864	7.3	23.2	12.1
26 88900	Wyandotte	20,551	53.4	13.9	23,598	66.2	6.8	39.2	32.0	50,718	7.8	25.0	12.5
26 88940	Wyoming	44,945	50.7	18.4	53,843	73.5	8.1	44.3	21.2	45,741	9.0	22.5	9.4
26 89140	Ypsilanti	12,040	32.6	41.8	19,348	66.3	8.7	29.2	25.1	34,959	13.0	39.8	13.0
27 00000	**Minnesota**	3,385,006	37.8	30.6	4,046,604	71.0	5.4	42.4	23.1	55,616	6.3	19.9	20.5
27 01486	Andover	18,104	30.8	33.7	20,983	79.9	4.5	49.0	12.2	88,170	2.1	3.8	39.4
27 01900	Apple Valley	31,904	24.1	42.9	37,853	76.6	4.8	49.0	15.3	76,789	2.7	8.0	33.7
27 02908	Austin	15,483	47.5	19.0	18,035	62.3	5.6	39.1	36.3	40,404	11.0	30.1	14.1
27 06382	Blaine	36,014	34.7	28.9	42,640	79.2	4.9	52.4	14.4	73,074	2.0	8.2	26.6
27 06616	Bloomington	60,160	31.9	36.7	67,941	70.9	4.6	44.2	24.2	59,262	3.3	15.0	23.7
27 07948	Brooklyn Center	19,547	52.4	16.5	23,101	65.8	7.2	41.9	25.8	46,775	8.3	20.6	10.8
27 07966	Brooklyn Park	45,230	38.3	26.3	53,864	76.5	7.3	48.0	16.7	61,766	8.4	16.2	24.8
27 08794	Burnsville	39,665	29.3	38.5	47,724	75.5	7.0	46.6	20.4	61,136	6.9	16.2	26.4
27 10846	Champlin	14,909	31.4	33.6	17,693	81.8	3.8	51.5	12.2	79,229	2.4	9.6	34.1
27 10918	Chanhassen	14,393	16.5	54.0	17,527	-	-	52.2	7.9	92,869	1.8	4.1	46.2
27 10972	Chaska	13,550	30.8	38.1	16,273	75.5	3.8	50.1	13.6	65,081	7.1	11.8	30.2
27 13114	Coon Rapids	39,156	40.3	23.1	46,998	77.0	4.7	47.6	17.0	60,193	5.6	14.4	19.6
27 13456	Cottage Grove	19,579	32.9	31.5	24,236	77.4	4.5	49.6	15.5	79,342	1.6	7.6	31.9
27 14158	Crystal	15,807	36.9	28.7	17,586	77.0	5.6	49.6	22.2	58,282	5.5	15.6	16.4
27 17000	Duluth	51,375	37.7	31.9	69,868	64.0	7.1	32.7	31.2	41,049	10.1	30.9	11.9
27 17288	Eagan	40,823	20.4	49.7	47,933	81.0	4.5	53.5	13.3	77,700	2.3	9.6	36.5
27 18116	Eden Prairie	40,318	15.7	59.0	46,299	77.8	3.8	50.5	12.7	92,461	2.8	7.1	46.5
27 18188	Edina	35,083	14.5	62.0	38,468	63.8	4.3	39.0	29.9	76,805	1.4	12.8	39.7
27 18674	Elk River	12,769	32.1	31.5	16,044	77.8	7.7	43.6	14.9	71,068	3.9	10.8	27.6
27 20546	Faribault	13,741	53.4	15.5	16,492	64.3	4.3	38.5	24.8	46,821	10.4	24.1	10.0
27 22814	Fridley	17,680	45.8	24.2	20,960	70.4	10.1	42.2	25.1	50,309	5.5	18.3	12.2
27 24308	Golden Valley	15,536	19.5	57.4	17,060	69.8	3.7	44.0	23.7	77,976	2.2	12.5	31.6
27 27530	Hastings	13,146	37.8	23.9	15,608	73.3	5.3	43.3	21.6	63,289	5.2	16.6	22.5
27 31076	Inver Grove Heights	20,934	33.7	32.5	25,306	78.9	4.6	49.2	15.6	66,390	5.5	10.0	28.6
27 35180	Lakeville	31,643	23.6	40.5	36,862	80.4	3.8	51.8	11.1	90,014	2.5	6.0	42.7
27 39878	Mankato	19,384	34.7	33.2	30,165	70.3	5.3	31.1	25.5	39,298	8.5	31.1	10.3
27 40166	Maple Grove	38,568	21.7	47.1	44,617	79.3	4.4	52.0	12.3	89,866	2.0	5.4	42.3
27 40382	Maplewood	24,695	38.6	30.4	28,115	65.8	4.8	40.5	28.6	60,654	4.2	17.5	24.3
27 43000	Minneapolis	238,484	34.4	41.2	294,729	72.6	8.2	39.8	23.1	44,478	15.8	29.6	17.3
27 43252	Minnetonka	36,860	16.5	52.3	41,398	70.2	3.8	46.0	21.3	78,840	2.6	11.3	38.7
27 43864	Moorhead	18,256	29.2	38.6	27,746	68.0	4.7	33.0	26.6	41,034	10.1	31.3	11.3
27 45430	New Brighton	15,178	30.9	41.8	17,114	67.0	4.2	40.7	25.7	57,509	4.9	16.8	24.9
27 45628	New Hope	14,803	38.0	27.7	16,648	62.8	4.3	39.6	29.7	46,842	4.1	22.6	16.3
27 47680	Oakdale	16,843	35.9	29.3	21,214	76.7	4.5	47.3	17.9	65,848	4.4	15.5	20.1
27 49300	Owatonna	15,818	47.9	23.3	18,889	72.3	3.0	45.7	21.6	51,085	2.9	19.4	12.9
27 51730	Plymouth	47,329	18.2	53.3	54,822	73.9	4.0	45.3	17.3	80,756	4.0	11.1	38.6
27 52594	Prior Lake	12,291	27.1	39.7	14,292	-	-	49.4	16.3	90,916	1.4	9.0	42.0
27 53026	Ramsey	13,040	33.6	23.5	15,868	79.2	4.8	50.6	13.2	77,356	1.6	4.9	31.1
27 54214	Richfield	24,164	39.9	30.7	27,395	71.0	5.4	43.4	25.1	50,651	6.9	22.8	17.2
27 54880	Rochester	63,759	29.9	40.4	74,240	71.7	3.2	46.3	21.6	57,957	5.9	17.1	22.6
27 55726	Rosemount	12,433	28.8	38.5	14,291	-	-	50.6	11.8	83,826	2.1	7.5	34.3
27 55852	Roseville	23,742	30.7	43.9	28,200	59.6	5.2	35.4	33.8	49,097	3.7	20.1	20.8
27 56896	St. Cloud	36,345	38.6	28.4	53,257	68.8	7.0	33.3	22.2	41,082	9.0	28.9	11.0
27 57220	St. Louis Park	31,625	25.6	44.8	36,391	77.1	3.7	49.9	19.1	54,922	4.8	16.4	21.4
27 58000	St. Paul	170,283	37.2	37.2	208,980	69.7	8.0	38.4	25.1	45,560	14.5	27.9	15.5
27 58738	Savage	15,823	24.9	41.9	19,335	81.8	4.8	50.7	8.4	92,571	2.4	5.3	43.3
27 59350	Shakopee	21,136	32.7	37.0	25,077	77.2	4.5	51.7	14.7	72,523	2.7	11.4	28.2
27 59998	Shoreview	18,289	21.6	48.9	20,990	73.8	4.7	43.7	22.5	77,433	1.7	10.9	33.3
27 69970	White Bear Lake	17,312	35.7	27.9	19,478	69.2	6.5	43.0	26.6	59,104	2.6	16.0	17.9
27 71032	Winona	14,274	37.8	31.1	22,098	69.5	7.4	30.1	27.3	35,311	8.0	35.8	8.8
27 71428	Woodbury	36,052	18.3	52.9	41,084	77.0	3.9	51.5	13.8	92,492	2.0	5.0	44.9
28 00000	**Mississippi**	1,829,680	53.9	18.6	2,230,412	60.0	9.2	36.3	31.1	35,632	16.6	36.4	10.4
28 06220	Biloxi	27,390	44.3	24.4	34,149	65.8	8.0	38.4	28.4	44,528	7.2	25.7	15.6
28 08300	Brandon	12,640	29.7	36.7	14,639	-	-	45.5	21.1	61,446	3.8	17.9	24.6
28 14420	Clinton	17,041	27.7	40.1	21,967	66.0	3.8	43.4	22.4	51,097	7.3	20.7	15.6
28 15380	Columbus	15,304	53.8	22.4	18,427	57.6	17.0	33.4	35.2	29,684	20.9	44.3	9.4
28 29180	Greenville	23,525	59.1	19.0	28,804	58.9	21.0	29.2	36.0	26,410	28.4	47.7	7.1

Table B-4. Cities — What: Education, Employment, and Income, 2005–2007—*Continued*

STATE Place code	STATE City	Educational attainment			Employment status				Percent of households with no workers	Median household income (dollars)	Percent of families with income below poverty	Percent of households with income less than $25,000	Percent of households with income of $100,000 or more
		Total population 25 years and over	Percent with a high school diploma or less	Percent with a bachelor's degree or more	Total population 16 years and over	Percent in the labor force	Unemployment rate	Percent who worked full-time, year-round					
	ACS table number:	C15002	C15002	C15002	C20005	C23001	C23001	C20005	C08202	B19013	C17015	C19001	C19001
		1	2	3	4	5	6	7	8	9	10	11	12
	Mississippi—Cont.												
28 29700	Gulfport................	44,315	51.5	17.8	52,360	60.3	10.4	35.4	32.0	37,963	14.1	33.5	11.6
28 31020	Hattiesburg.............	26,309	38.9	32.4	38,523	64.1	10.4	32.6	29.6	28,987	27.1	44.7	6.7
28 33700	Horn Lake.............	12,671	56.6	9.2	15,904	75.3	6.4	50.9	16.5	44,694	4.8	20.3	8.6
28 36000	Jackson................	103,787	42.9	26.2	130,254	62.7	10.0	37.5	28.7	33,132	21.7	38.7	9.7
28 46640	Meridian...............	23,026	51.8	18.0	27,300	58.1	14.9	32.5	40.2	24,733	27.7	50.5	7.2
28 54040	Olive Branch...........	18,942	41.2	24.3	21,711	71.3	2.8	50.3	18.0	62,816	3.1	13.9	21.6
28 55360	Pascagoula.............	14,233	55.1	14.4	16,846	57.7	9.8	32.2	30.4	35,894	23.4	35.3	10.1
28 55760	Pearl..................	14,932	47.8	18.2	18,545	68.5	4.4	44.6	21.8	36,921	14.2	32.4	9.4
28 62520	Ridgeland..............	14,723	19.1	53.1	18,889	74.6	6.0	49.4	18.4	52,639	3.8	17.0	20.5
28 69280	Southaven..............	25,653	49.8	17.9	30,487	74.0	7.3	47.7	19.0	50,097	12.6	21.4	12.0
28 70240	Starkville.............	11,154	32.8	41.8	19,140	63.2	11.0	29.0	28.7	25,295	22.7	49.5	11.2
28 74840	Tupelo................	22,710	42.8	29.8	26,101	63.1	9.2	39.5	28.6	39,264	15.3	35.3	15.4
28 76720	Vicksburg..............	15,536	49.6	21.0	18,959	61.1	12.9	39.8	34.3	28,150	19.1	46.1	7.3
29 00000	**Missouri**	3,847,339	48.8	24.0	4,578,206	65.1	6.4	40.6	27.2	44,545	9.8	27.2	13.9
29 00280	Affton CDP.............	14,550	50.8	22.8	17,092	69.5	10.3	45.4	29.5	50,895	5.2	21.1	14.7
29 01972	Arnold................	13,201	49.7	18.1	16,026	72.5	5.7	46.2	22.8	60,297	1.9	15.8	16.1
29 03160	Ballwin...............	20,920	19.3	52.4	24,015	69.4	3.9	44.2	21.9	76,831	3.5	9.7	36.9
29 04384	Belton................	14,253	49.9	18.9	17,239	70.3	4.1	45.0	20.0	50,988	9.3	17.9	9.4
29 06652	Blue Springs...........	33,161	34.0	30.8	38,519	76.8	3.7	49.3	15.4	67,498	4.6	13.0	23.8
29 11242	Cape Girardeau	22,774	46.8	31.0	30,557	63.7	7.7	31.8	28.2	36,502	15.6	37.7	10.3
29 13600	Chesterfield...........	34,774	17.3	61.6	39,830	62.3	2.5	39.7	24.3	92,977	0.9	11.8	45.8
29 15670	Columbia...............	52,291	24.3	54.1	77,933	69.6	5.9	35.6	20.0	40,178	10.9	34.1	15.7
29 23986	Ferguson...............	12,521	45.6	18.8	15,468	67.5	12.1	43.9	34.5	36,259	15.1	36.3	8.0
29 24778	Florissant.............	33,581	45.1	20.8	39,750	67.8	5.9	41.7	28.0	49,779	3.8	19.6	10.8
29 27190	Gladstone..............	18,109	41.3	27.5	20,975	67.6	5.9	41.1	22.3	48,754	4.5	19.4	13.8
29 28324	Grandview..............	15,563	49.3	16.0	18,169	68.9	7.1	44.2	24.7	42,212	13.0	26.2	6.8
29 31276	Hazelwood..............	17,055	41.8	24.8	20,200	70.4	7.1	43.2	23.7	49,134	9.9	22.2	14.4
29 35000	Independence...........	80,327	51.1	18.2	91,508	64.5	7.9	41.8	29.6	41,695	9.9	26.2	9.6
29 37000	Jefferson..............	28,111	44.4	30.2	33,720	61.8	4.3	42.7	26.0	44,501	9.0	24.8	13.2
29 37592	Joplin................	31,397	48.8	19.1	37,895	63.6	7.8	36.4	32.5	33,131	14.8	38.7	7.2
29 38000	Kansas................	288,410	43.0	28.8	339,754	68.8	8.1	44.0	26.2	42,548	13.8	29.5	14.3
29 39044	Kirkwood...............	19,038	19.4	56.4	21,941	68.7	3.1	42.3	25.0	70,261	3.9	17.2	31.1
29 41348	Lee's Summit...........	56,264	27.3	42.5	65,558	73.6	3.2	49.5	19.7	71,821	3.7	13.9	29.5
29 42032	Liberty................	18,036	33.5	37.5	21,669	69.4	5.2	42.2	18.3	56,118	4.2	17.4	23.2
29 46586	Maryland Heights........	18,526	30.8	40.4	22,061	77.1	4.7	54.2	15.7	56,199	3.8	15.9	15.6
29 47180	Mehlville CDP...........	19,928	47.5	25.3	23,302	63.1	3.0	39.3	28.5	51,181	4.7	21.2	12.2
29 53876	Oakville CDP...........	24,159	34.7	35.2	29,023	69.3	4.4	42.7	22.0	73,027	1.4	10.1	32.0
29 54074	O'Fallon...............	42,925	34.5	33.5	50,446	75.9	4.0	50.9	13.6	74,426	2.1	9.0	27.9
29 60788	Raytown................	21,139	46.9	22.2	24,147	64.6	8.5	41.6	28.4	48,306	6.4	19.5	10.0
29 64082	St. Charles............	40,470	43.9	28.6	51,189	69.8	4.4	41.7	25.4	51,254	5.1	20.7	18.0
29 64550	St. Joseph.............	48,202	56.3	16.4	58,402	61.8	9.1	37.3	29.7	36,101	12.7	34.9	8.9
29 65000	St. Louis..............	230,050	51.3	24.0	274,240	62.4	12.0	36.6	32.6	33,221	20.5	39.3	8.5
29 65126	St. Peters.............	34,210	38.0	30.1	40,864	77.0	3.7	51.1	18.5	65,054	2.0	12.3	22.6
29 66440	Sedalia................	13,287	53.5	14.5	15,759	62.4	8.9	36.5	35.6	30,773	12.0	38.7	4.1
29 69266	Spanish Lake CDP	12,258	48.3	14.7	14,948	68.4	13.0	42.9	27.4	34,721	18.3	36.9	9.1
29 70000	Springfield............	98,096	44.5	24.8	127,780	63.1	5.9	36.4	29.6	32,325	12.3	38.2	6.6
29 75220	University.............	22,791	28.6	48.1	27,248	63.1	6.5	39.6	31.8	45,256	10.1	25.8	22.3
29 78154	Webster Groves.........	15,146	15.0	63.6	17,150	69.7	3.9	43.3	22.5	70,449	1.4	13.8	32.3
29 78442	Wentzville.............	10,921	34.9	26.3	13,030	-	-	47.1	17.6	70,338	6.5	14.9	25.1
29 79820	Wildwood...............	22,220	14.0	63.8	26,554	70.2	2.9	45.5	12.6	113,270	2.5	6.8	57.2
30 00000	**Montana**	631,746	42.3	26.7	754,965	65.4	5.1	37.3	27.0	42,425	9.3	28.8	11.1
30 06550	Billings...............	64,947	38.4	29.4	76,892	67.1	3.7	39.2	26.0	42,875	8.9	29.0	13.1
30 08950	Bozeman	19,458	18.4	53.7	30,060	71.6	3.6	34.8	15.6	42,972	9.0	28.5	12.5
30 11397	Butte-Silver Bow (balance) ..	21,771	50.6	23.3	25,825	63.5	5.0	36.3	30.7	36,427	9.7	33.1	7.1
30 32800	Great Falls............	39,301	41.8	23.3	46,178	60.7	5.4	37.4	33.0	40,486	10.7	31.7	9.1
30 35600	Helena................	17,977	27.8	42.3	22,317	69.4	4.2	37.2	24.8	44,610	6.0	29.4	13.5
30 40075	Kalispell..............	12,660	39.0	25.3	14,269	-	-	36.5	27.9	40,110	12.5	33.5	7.8
30 50200	Missoula...............	39,381	31.0	41.7	53,112	66.5	5.1	34.1	28.0	35,420	10.9	36.1	10.4
31 00000	**Nebraska**	1,131,474	41.4	27.2	1,370,844	70.7	4.8	44.9	22.8	46,954	7.9	24.9	13.9
31 03950	Bellevue...............	26,695	37.7	27.4	33,151	70.9	5.3	46.2	20.3	53,108	7.8	18.2	14.6
31 10110	Columbus...............	13,839	45.7	22.6	16,325	71.8	4.5	47.7	27.6	44,880	8.9	26.6	11.1
31 17670	Fremont................	16,811	56.0	20.2	20,195	66.4	8.7	38.5	29.8	39,689	14.1	30.3	7.3
31 19595	Grand Island...........	28,020	55.3	15.3	32,861	70.9	5.0	45.3	23.3	40,767	9.1	27.0	8.2
31 21415	Hastings...............	16,639	42.2	21.4	20,700	66.6	4.8	39.8	27.6	39,989	12.7	32.3	8.0
31 25055	Kearney................	16,014	32.9	37.3	23,644	75.0	6.3	40.1	19.3	41,382	10.1	28.2	11.2
31 28000	Lincoln................	152,761	31.4	35.5	195,422	73.9	4.9	44.3	19.7	48,111	7.4	25.3	14.1
31 34615	Norfolk	14,350	47.2	19.4	17,996	72.4	3.7	45.2	25.4	39,064	6.0	30.0	8.8
31 35000	North Platte...........	16,127	47.0	16.3	19,233	67.4	6.7	41.1	26.4	38,623	11.1	31.2	9.6
31 37000	Omaha..................	241,457	39.5	31.5	294,487	70.0	7.2	42.1	24.9	44,143	11.8	27.4	13.7
31 38295	Papillion..............	11,386	24.1	38.9	13,781	72.7	4.2	49.0	17.5	72,136	2.5	11.6	27.9
32 00000	**Nevada**	1,640,801	47.9	20.9	1,914,702	67.2	5.5	44.9	22.7	53,753	7.8	19.6	19.1
32 09700	Carson................	37,425	44.6	20.6	43,480	62.7	7.0	39.3	31.7	50,140	8.4	23.4	14.7
32 23770	Enterprise CDP.........	42,696	37.6	28.3	50,300	76.2	4.7	52.6	12.4	72,205	5.0	9.7	28.8

STATE Place code	STATE City	Educational attainment			Employment status				Percent of households with no workers	Median household income (dollars)	Percent of families with income below poverty	Percent of households with income less than $25,000	Percent of households with income of $100,000 or more
		Total population 25 years and over	Percent with a high school diploma or less	Percent with a bachelor's degree or more	Total population 16 years and over	Percent in the labor force	Unemployment rate	Percent who worked full-time, year-round					
ACS table number:		C15002	C15002	C15002	C20005	C23001	C23001	C20005	C08202	B19013	C17015	C19001	C19001
		1	2	3	4	5	6	7	8	9	10	11	12
	Nevada—Cont.												
32 31900	Henderson	163,470	38.7	26.3	186,242	68.0	4.3	45.7	21.3	66,429	4.1	12.9	28.2
32 40000	Las Vegas	367,590	49.6	20.7	422,680	66.1	5.9	45.6	23.7	53,551	8.7	20.7	19.9
32 51800	North Las Vegas	109,054	55.6	14.4	131,968	70.6	5.3	49.3	16.3	56,716	8.8	16.4	17.4
32 53800	Pahrump CDP	24,342	60.4	8.1	28,345	51.9	13.3	26.1	46.7	40,768	12.3	30.0	8.7
32 54600	Paradise CDP	139,701	50.5	19.0	162,829	70.8	6.8	46.0	21.8	46,465	9.2	24.3	14.6
32 60600	Reno	136,904	41.4	28.6	167,906	69.1	4.6	42.7	23.8	47,042	9.6	25.0	16.6
32 68400	Sparks	52,746	45.3	20.5	60,642	69.5	5.0	47.5	21.6	56,728	6.0	17.2	17.4
32 68585	Spring Valley CDP	106,925	43.6	23.9	123,520	70.5	5.6	49.0	21.5	54,309	6.1	16.7	18.7
32 71400	Sunrise Manor CDP	116,606	64.1	10.2	138,877	66.3	6.9	44.4	20.4	46,042	12.2	22.3	10.1
32 71600	Sun Valley CDP	12,778	65.0	6.3	14,745	69.6	6.6	41.7	16.7	47,743	6.8	17.3	7.9
32 83800	Whitney CDP	15,819	63.3	11.9	18,962	71.3	6.8	47.8	21.4	46,353	6.0	17.0	9.4
32 84600	Winchester CDP	18,654	57.7	17.3	20,731	65.0	5.3	45.8	27.8	37,203	12.9	29.4	8.9
33 00000	**New Hampshire**	889,007	41.0	31.8	1,046,807	69.8	4.8	43.2	21.6	61,459	4.9	17.3	23.8
33 14200	Concord	29,705	36.7	37.1	34,935	64.7	6.1	39.5	24.8	50,642	8.2	23.1	16.2
33 17860	Derry CDP	15,074	45.5	23.8	18,236	76.1	6.0	48.5	17.4	58,095	6.4	15.8	21.2
33 18820	Dover	19,630	34.0	37.8	22,924	73.2	4.8	47.3	21.9	57,708	4.9	16.4	19.0
33 39300	Keene	14,936	43.2	31.9	20,725	66.8	3.4	36.5	25.4	51,192	4.2	21.6	18.2
33 45140	Manchester	73,627	47.9	24.3	87,096	70.8	6.0	45.2	23.0	53,326	10.4	23.2	16.3
33 50260	Nashua	60,149	37.2	35.0	69,150	72.3	5.3	45.5	20.9	63,208	4.6	15.9	24.9
33 62900	Portsmouth	15,447	24.7	51.7	17,753	74.1	4.0	47.1	21.4	59,727	7.3	16.6	22.4
33 65140	Rochester	20,745	54.3	15.9	23,804	66.6	7.4	41.1	27.5	48,037	9.9	25.4	10.7
34 00000	**New Jersey**	5,835,145	44.2	33.7	6,835,521	65.8	6.1	41.9	24.1	66,509	6.5	17.9	30.8
34 02080	Atlantic	24,324	63.3	16.2	27,759	64.1	13.6	38.3	35.4	30,791	18.9	41.9	6.6
34 03580	Bayonne	42,645	52.9	24.7	49,196	63.8	8.3	43.2	29.5	47,138	10.0	25.2	18.5
34 04690	Belleville CDP	24,240	50.7	24.5	29,210	66.0	9.2	39.2	20.4	55,318	6.3	19.0	16.6
34 05170	Bergenfield borough	18,651	38.9	37.7	21,679	68.1	3.6	47.0	18.4	73,803	3.7	13.9	34.1
34 06250	Bloomfield CDP	32,769	44.2	33.6	38,805	69.7	6.2	45.6	20.0	65,373	4.7	18.5	26.3
34 07600	Bridgeton	14,710	81.3	6.5	18,033	47.9	14.9	27.2	39.2	29,019	23.9	43.9	7.0
34 10000	Camden	38,727	76.5	6.1	50,316	56.4	16.1	30.3	39.0	23,154	37.9	52.8	3.1
34 10750	Carteret borough	13,795	59.2	19.0	15,947	63.2	7.3	40.6	32.1	51,281	15.0	26.5	22.8
34 13570	Cliffside Park borough	15,964	38.7	44.6	18,227	66.7	6.9	44.8	29.4	62,443	7.4	24.1	27.1
34 13690	Clifton	55,275	51.4	28.0	64,716	62.1	5.2	41.3	28.6	53,782	7.7	21.5	22.8
34 15670	Cranford CDP	15,701	27.1	52.1	17,953	65.8	5.3	43.4	23.4	99,281	1.5	10.8	49.6
34 18970	East Brunswick CDP	31,593	26.3	54.8	36,846	70.2	5.5	43.1	17.4	97,556	3.5	8.5	48.5
34 19390	East Orange	38,947	60.8	15.5	46,937	71.2	14.3	35.2	38.1	35,476	23.2	39.5	7.6
34 20260	Edison CDP	71,587	35.6	45.8	83,167	63.5	4.2	43.5	17.5	80,581	2.7	9.5	37.1
34 21000	Elizabeth	79,543	68.8	12.5	95,634	66.3	7.9	48.4	23.9	42,822	15.4	27.1	12.3
34 21480	Englewood	17,585	37.2	43.3	21,533	66.6	6.0	44.3	22.3	75,731	5.4	18.0	39.3
34 22180	Ewing CDP	24,262	38.3	33.0	32,056	63.1	6.8	37.0	25.4	68,399	4.9	14.3	26.4
34 22470	Fair Lawn borough	24,333	32.5	49.7	28,188	65.4	4.7	42.0	24.5	90,124	1.1	12.6	44.3
34 24420	Fort Lee borough	27,175	27.1	54.8	29,630	60.0	4.4	42.2	30.7	67,500	5.2	17.1	32.0
34 25770	Garfield	20,309	60.3	16.6	23,736	68.9	8.8	47.3	26.1	45,436	9.5	26.2	13.1
34 28680	Hackensack	33,132	44.8	32.2	37,811	68.8	6.4	48.3	22.3	55,893	8.5	19.4	20.9
34 32250	Hoboken	31,884	18.9	72.0	36,744	78.3	3.4	59.1	15.6	96,786	6.0	15.9	48.3
34 34440	Irvington CDP	37,457	61.3	13.1	43,781	71.4	12.3	46.2	20.7	46,262	12.4	25.4	12.0
34 36000	Jersey	158,376	46.4	34.4	185,954	66.9	9.1	41.5	24.5	46,167	16.2	29.0	20.0
34 36510	Kearny town	26,830	62.1	17.1	31,645	65.8	5.6	44.2	18.5	56,609	4.8	15.9	23.5
34 38580	Lakewood CDP	17,825	51.9	22.8	25,127	55.6	6.8	22.8	22.6	31,925	33.4	41.3	11.9
34 40350	Linden	29,394	57.4	18.9	33,976	66.3	7.3	42.6	25.7	54,574	4.8	19.2	18.9
34 40920	Livingston CDP	19,387	18.9	65.4	22,857	60.3	2.7	38.9	21.2	119,877	1.7	6.0	58.5
34 41100	Lodi borough	18,169	55.0	20.9	20,798	-	-	44.5	26.4	51,313	10.5	21.4	20.0
34 41310	Long Branch	21,267	53.6	26.2	26,313	71.2	6.1	39.5	26.2	49,675	11.6	27.1	20.1
34 43830	Maplewood CDP	15,986	25.6	59.1	18,330	73.9	6.2	47.0	15.0	94,253	1.7	8.7	46.3
34 45495	Mercerville-Hamilton Square CDP	18,871	40.7	33.4	21,495	66.9	3.5	44.9	22.4	86,169	2.7	9.0	39.8
34 46680	Millville	17,945	61.0	12.8	21,052	62.6	14.1	37.3	30.3	47,943	18.0	28.8	14.4
34 47490	Montclair CDP	25,440	19.6	62.6	28,595	71.7	6.0	43.1	17.8	92,988	4.7	12.3	47.7
34 51000	Newark	164,871	70.0	11.8	202,832	60.4	11.5	35.3	32.8	33,991	20.5	38.7	8.8
34 51210	New Brunswick	21,942	63.5	21.9	37,130	61.8	4.9	38.3	16.9	46,766	18.8	27.0	14.4
34 52605	North Brunswick Township CDP	26,318	35.1	43.4	30,883	68.8	6.9	43.9	19.5	77,658	4.2	13.6	38.0
34 53280	North Plainfield borough	14,287	53.9	21.5	17,076	71.4	3.8	51.1	16.2	63,420	5.7	16.6	28.6
34 53670	Nutley CDP	19,504	39.6	40.1	23,093	68.3	4.7	41.8	21.4	76,729	1.9	14.3	37.8
34 54690	Old Bridge CDP	14,773	42.1	31.6	17,195	69.5	3.5	47.1	16.3	93,088	1.0	8.0	44.9
34 55020	Orange CDP	19,995	58.6	17.7	23,877	69.7	10.6	41.0	26.5	41,032	13.9	30.5	10.5
34 55950	Paramus borough	18,909	36.5	42.2	21,971	59.3	4.8	36.2	23.7	97,209	2.8	9.4	48.5
34 56550	Passaic	39,012	69.3	16.6	47,806	61.5	5.8	36.4	23.1	29,697	25.1	43.9	9.9
34 57000	Paterson	85,318	74.2	8.5	106,135	60.4	7.2	39.2	26.7	34,129	23.1	39.1	8.5
34 57690	Pennsauken CDP	21,957	53.7	19.6	26,450	69.2	7.4	41.5	25.6	58,829	5.8	18.3	15.8
34 58200	Perth Amboy	30,425	68.0	11.8	37,532	65.9	6.7	48.3	22.4	47,184	14.9	25.0	14.1
34 59190	Plainfield	25,603	55.3	21.6	30,861	68.6	7.1	45.7	26.1	44,441	12.9	31.9	19.3
34 61530	Rahway	18,636	60.7	18.6	22,400	64.1	6.3	42.1	26.7	58,813	3.1	17.8	20.6
34 63000	Ridgewood village	16,476	14.5	70.1	19,301	62.2	3.8	37.7	19.1	121,662	2.5	10.4	58.9

Table B-4. Cities — What: Education, Employment, and Income, 2005–2007—*Continued*

STATE Place code	STATE City	Educational attainment			Employment status				Percent of households with no workers	Median household income (dollars)	Percent of families with income below poverty	Percent of households with income less than $25,000	Percent of households with income of $100,000 or more
		Total population 25 years and over	Percent with a high school diploma or less	Percent with a bachelor's degree or more	Total population 16 years and over	Percent in the labor force	Unemployment rate	Percent who worked full-time, year-round					
	ACS table number:	C15002	C15002	C15002	C20005	C23001	C23001	C20005	C08202	B19013	C17015	C19001	C19001
		1	2	3	4	5	6	7	8	9	10	11	12
	New Jersey—Cont.												
34 64620	Roselle borough	13,834	49.1	21.4	16,854	72.8	9.1	47.9	19.2	57,166	4.4	18.6	21.5
34 65790	Sayreville borough	31,419	49.6	29.3	35,867	64.9	6.6	41.4	21.4	68,762	5.0	16.0	31.2
34 66090	Scotch Plains CDP	15,147	29.7	50.7	16,846	-	-	40.1	20.9	99,214	2.2	10.3	49.5
34 68370	Somerset CDP	15,192	37.1	38.5	17,821	69.3	5.6	49.4	18.9	76,053	2.3	12.5	30.9
34 69390	South Plainfield borough	16,953	47.1	26.9	19,476	69.7	5.5	45.2	16.2	88,425	3.6	7.2	41.0
34 71430	Summit	14,105	19.7	63.8	15,795	65.1	3.8	41.0	19.2	117,986	1.3	9.2	57.8
34 72390	Teaneck CDP	28,534	28.6	52.7	33,986	64.4	6.7	42.6	21.6	89,475	4.5	11.4	46.5
34 73110	Toms River CDP	61,989	46.9	28.0	71,312	63.9	5.3	38.8	27.3	69,141	3.6	16.0	30.1
34 74000	Trenton	50,934	71.4	9.6	61,854	62.9	14.0	36.4	34.8	34,321	20.6	38.1	8.3
34 74510	Union CDP	38,912	48.6	29.3	46,515	66.4	5.2	41.3	24.7	68,979	3.6	13.9	29.3
34 74630	Union	43,014	65.3	18.3	51,778	68.7	7.1	46.9	22.2	37,707	17.6	33.0	10.1
34 76070	Vineland	40,137	62.4	15.2	47,522	64.9	8.7	39.6	26.9	50,757	11.9	23.6	18.0
34 77870	Wayne CDP	37,538	37.3	40.6	43,311	61.8	7.1	36.7	23.1	93,398	3.0	12.4	47.6
34 79040	Westfield town	19,125	19.3	64.1	22,029	65.3	2.7	41.4	22.6	120,978	0.6	7.8	57.7
34 79430	West Milford CDP	17,977	43.9	28.8	21,362	73.7	6.2	44.2	16.3	87,502	1.3	10.0	41.0
34 79610	West New York town	32,058	57.5	22.9	36,834	66.4	7.1	44.9	26.8	41,459	15.1	31.9	13.1
34 79790	West Orange CDP	31,714	31.1	48.6	35,207	66.2	5.9	40.0	20.7	90,334	4.5	13.6	43.1
35 00000	**New Mexico**	1,240,342	46.6	24.9	1,505,362	62.2	6.4	37.0	27.8	41,042	14.2	30.4	13.2
35 01780	Alamogordo	22,857	44.3	16.6	27,920	62.9	4.5	40.5	27.3	37,106	12.7	32.1	5.6
35 02000	Albuquerque	328,732	38.4	32.1	396,641	67.0	5.7	40.9	24.8	44,113	10.9	26.9	14.9
35 12150	Carlsbad	15,785	52.8	17.6	19,122	60.4	4.8	35.1	30.9	38,229	12.3	31.0	8.6
35 16420	Clovis	20,801	48.6	18.2	24,972	65.0	5.3	37.5	28.9	36,021	16.9	37.4	10.4
35 25800	Farmington	27,449	45.5	20.3	33,590	66.9	3.9	41.3	22.2	45,845	10.7	24.7	15.0
35 32520	Hobbs	17,967	62.9	12.6	22,269	57.3	5.1	39.1	25.7	40,479	13.1	28.2	10.1
35 39380	Las Cruces	54,316	39.8	29.8	71,164	63.0	8.8	34.0	28.4	35,625	16.8	36.9	8.9
35 63460	Rio Rancho	44,032	37.1	27.8	52,532	69.5	5.2	44.0	21.9	54,498	5.7	15.5	15.0
35 64930	Roswell	28,459	53.8	15.5	35,570	58.8	8.7	33.9	32.6	35,102	19.6	34.8	8.2
35 70500	Santa Fe	47,654	34.1	44.1	54,928	66.2	4.7	35.3	26.0	48,156	8.8	25.6	20.9
35 74520	South Valley CDP	23,831	63.9	13.1	27,670	58.6	8.3	32.8	32.6	35,374	19.5	34.3	7.6
36 00000	**New York**	12,866,461	45.7	31.2	15,355,670	62.7	6.7	39.2	27.4	52,944	10.7	24.6	22.8
36 01000	Albany	55,732	39.5	35.1	75,246	62.5	7.5	36.9	31.3	38,290	19.1	34.6	11.2
36 03078	Auburn	17,245	52.2	17.1	19,969	55.9	7.3	33.3	36.2	35,164	13.7	35.2	6.8
36 04143	Baldwin CDP	14,808	40.6	40.6	17,496			46.5	20.0	88,774	0.7	8.7	41.3
36 04935	Bay Shore CDP	19,017	49.8	18.5	22,713	56.9	5.1	39.3	25.4	70,140	4.8	15.2	28.1
36 06607	Binghamton	28,727	49.2	22.4	35,342	59.2	10.2	30.8	39.4	27,483	23.7	45.2	8.6
36 08026	Brentwood CDP	33,644	64.0	13.6	40,379	68.4	6.2	45.9	15.1	70,113	6.1	14.5	25.1
36 08257	Brighton CDP	25,192	18.4	60.2	29,352	61.7	3.8	37.7	27.1	58,439	3.1	18.7	23.2
36 11000	Buffalo	166,168	52.2	20.5	207,193	58.4	11.8	30.9	37.7	29,127	23.6	44.6	6.7
36 13376	Centereach CDP	17,939	47.5	25.9	21,665	70.5	3.9	46.4	17.3	86,445	1.8	7.1	38.9
36 13552	Central Islip CDP	22,118	55.7	16.2	26,366	68.5	4.2	46.7	23.1	67,602	5.2	14.6	25.4
36 15000	Cheektowaga CDP	55,214	51.1	17.6	64,363	62.6	6.0	38.5	33.2	44,352	6.0	25.3	8.4
36 17530	Commack CDP	23,553	29.7	43.2	27,710	62.5	2.8	41.5	20.2	102,658	1.4	8.3	52.2
36 18146	Copiague CDP	14,385	56.3	18.5	16,446	67.3	5.1	47.9	20.4	66,660	6.2	11.8	28.6
36 18157	Coram CDP	25,120	37.4	28.6	29,508	72.5	4.8	47.2	18.4	77,804	5.0	13.2	34.3
36 19972	Deer Park CDP	19,031	53.9	19.9	22,777	65.4	3.9	41.9	24.3	72,173	3.9	16.9	32.8
36 20687	Dix Hills CDP	15,742	23.1	57.5	18,951	62.0	2.6	38.4	15.1	127,632	1.3	4.7	65.5
36 21809	Eastchester CDP	14,251	27.3	58.1	15,980	-	-	38.8	22.1	100,643	0.9	8.4	50.3
36 22502	East Meadow CDP	24,566	42.3	34.3	29,019	59.3	2.6	39.6	27.1	86,582	2.5	14.1	41.0
36 22612	East Northport CDP	13,600	33.5	38.1	15,964	65.3	5.0	40.6	21.1	92,892	3.3	8.0	45.3
36 22733	East Patchogue CDP	15,155	51.2	22.6	18,018	67.0	4.1	45.1	26.3	68,089	5.0	19.6	26.1
36 24229	Elmira	18,608	60.4	13.5	23,519	56.0	11.8	29.4	38.5	28,326	25.1	43.4	5.9
36 24273	Elmont CDP	21,181	47.4	27.6	26,511	65.0	5.5	44.9	18.8	73,666	5.0	11.6	31.2
36 27309	Franklin Square CDP	22,825	51.9	25.0	26,165	59.7	3.6	41.7	25.8	80,164	3.8	11.9	36.8
36 27485	Freeport village	26,586	49.6	27.6	31,831	68.9	5.8	45.0	20.8	69,187	10.4	20.1	29.4
36 28178	Garden village	13,435	14.4	65.2	16,635	58.6	2.1	35.9	27.5	142,788	1.5	4.9	63.9
36 29113	Glen Cove	17,813	38.5	38.2	20,806	63.9	5.2	39.1	27.1	64,185	10.8	18.8	29.2
36 32402	Harrison village	17,225	34.2	48.9	23,010	61.6	4.2	35.5	15.0	100,681	0.6	7.7	50.3
36 32732	Hauppauge CDP	13,873	36.0	37.1	16,167	68.5	4.6	41.3	18.3	90,136	1.9	6.6	45.1
36 33139	Hempstead village	30,734	60.8	19.7	38,269	69.6	9.8	46.7	23.2	50,347	10.6	22.8	19.5
36 34374	Hicksville CDP	28,934	44.5	33.2	34,108	61.7	4.8	42.2	23.3	76,110	3.6	11.3	36.9
36 35056	Holbrook CDP	18,349	44.0	28.3	20,959	71.8	5.4	47.6	14.3	96,530	3.2	8.5	47.8
36 37044	Huntington Station CDP	19,160	46.0	31.8	22,379	70.2	7.9	41.3	20.9	73,875	8.5	14.5	34.5
36 37737	Irondequoit CDP	37,595	41.6	30.5	42,382	62.3	5.8	38.1	31.2	50,264	4.2	20.7	14.4
36 38077	Ithaca	11,708	22.1	64.3	28,825	52.4	5.9	17.3	33.8	30,061	8.9	43.4	10.4
36 38264	Jamestown	19,634	56.0	18.3	24,753	63.1	12.3	31.5	35.5	32,133	18.2	39.4	6.1
36 39727	Kingston	16,012	53.7	18.9	19,256	68.3	8.6	38.4	29.2	43,035	15.9	29.2	10.1
36 39853	Kiryas Joel village	-	-	-	-	-	-	-	18.3	15,848	61.5	64.9	2.4
36 42081	Levittown CDP	36,035	46.9	24.4	42,275	65.8	4.3	42.9	21.3	85,479	1.4	10.7	37.3
36 42554	Lindenhurst village	18,408	50.1	20.9	21,926	66.0	4.3	40.8	19.1	79,684	2.9	13.3	36.4
36 43082	Lockport	14,245	53.3	15.9	17,438	62.0	12.4	31.8	34.1	34,888	15.5	37.4	9.1
36 43335	Long Beach	24,783	32.2	42.8	27,852	65.6	3.2	44.7	21.3	75,842	5.0	11.7	37.5
36 45986	Massapequa CDP	14,005	33.2	42.5	16,116	62.8	3.5	37.3	19.5	99,859	3.2	6.1	49.9
36 46404	Medford CDP	14,711	50.6	22.8	17,861	73.1	6.2	44.0	17.6	81,400	2.3	11.1	35.0
36 46668	Merrick CDP	14,325	25.1	52.2	17,154	66.9	3.0	37.8	15.8	111,536	1.4	6.3	57.6

STATE Place code	STATE City	Educational attainment			Employment status				Percent of households with no workers	Median household income (dollars)	Percent of families with income below poverty	Percent of households with income less than $25,000	Percent of households with income of $100,000 or more
		Total population 25 years and over	Percent with a high school diploma or less	Percent with a bachelor's degree or more	Total population 16 years and over	Percent in the labor force	Unemployment rate	Percent who worked full-time, year-round					
ACS table number:		C15002	C15002	C15002	C20005	C23001	C23001	C20005	C08202	B19013	C17015	C19001	C19001
		1	2	3	4	5	6	7	8	9	10	11	12
	New York—Cont.												
36 47042	Middletown	15,854	56.0	20.6	19,755	70.8	11.3	44.2	24.2	50,380	14.8	29.4	19.6
36 49121	Mount Vernon	43,301	48.2	25.2	51,507	63.0	9.4	42.6	24.5	49,705	9.5	22.4	19.9
36 50034	Newburgh	17,084	72.6	10.4	22,567	68.3	11.5	38.7	28.9	35,635	24.8	35.7	7.2
36 50100	New CDP	22,618	26.9	51.3	26,083	64.2	3.3	42.4	16.6	117,734	2.2	5.5	59.1
36 50617	New Rochelle	46,932	43.8	39.1	57,890	61.2	6.0	38.1	26.1	64,756	6.3	20.4	32.4
36 51000	New York	5,546,586	48.6	32.1	6,557,631	61.6	7.9	39.7	28.1	47,581	16.2	29.2	20.7
36 51055	Niagara Falls	32,029	60.6	12.0	38,679	58.0	10.8	32.2	41.2	30,324	17.4	42.7	5.2
36 53682	North Tonawanda	22,955	44.2	21.9	26,416	64.1	5.6	38.3	29.6	44,692	5.1	22.7	10.8
36 54441	Oceanside CDP	22,695	35.1	41.9	26,949	64.3	4.0	41.7	24.6	100,167	2.0	12.8	50.1
36 55530	Ossining village	15,697	45.0	32.6	17,863	66.9	6.6	43.0	22.9	65,420	4.0	17.3	26.6
36 56979	Peekskill	18,347	60.4	19.1	21,469	72.7	9.1	44.3	26.2	55,953	8.8	22.4	22.8
36 58442	Plainview CDP	17,667	25.1	55.5	20,001	62.8	3.6	39.9	25.3	106,045	0.5	9.2	53.9
36 59223	Port Chester village	18,764	56.4	22.9	21,859	71.8	6.4	41.3	22.7	49,856	3.5	23.4	20.6
36 59641	Poughkeepsie	19,091	50.1	22.8	24,093	66.0	8.6	38.7	31.2	36,648	19.7	35.3	13.4
36 63000	Rochester	122,101	52.5	21.6	154,929	58.8	10.6	34.2	35.5	29,329	25.6	43.1	5.8
36 63264	Rockville Centre village	16,417	25.1	55.2	19,275	63.8	3.7	41.0	24.6	99,299	3.6	14.3	49.8
36 63418	Rome	23,181	54.3	16.4	28,164	56.4	6.9	34.8	32.2	35,120	14.8	34.2	8.4
36 63473	Ronkonkoma CDP	13,271	46.6	23.5	16,330	68.3	3.2	47.0	16.4	87,896	4.6	11.2	39.7
36 63924	Rotterdam CDP	14,894	48.8	19.0	17,163	64.1	4.3	42.4	35.0	53,239	3.7	21.4	15.6
36 65255	Saratoga Springs	17,700	32.4	46.3	23,126	59.3	3.6	35.0	27.0	58,113	4.0	20.3	21.7
36 65508	Schenectady	39,556	56.5	18.3	49,679	59.0	9.9	37.0	34.0	34,982	14.4	33.8	7.3
36 66212	Selden CDP	13,191	54.5	20.1	16,641	66.1	3.3	44.7	18.7	75,671	2.4	12.1	27.0
36 67070	Shirley CDP	16,346	54.5	15.2	20,873	74.9	6.2	49.3	12.3	80,594	4.0	7.8	31.7
36 67851	Smithtown CDP	17,279	31.0	39.8	19,944	65.6	3.6	38.6	22.1	99,826	0.8	10.4	49.9
36 70420	Spring Valley village	14,311	56.0	21.2	17,723	70.7	6.6	42.2	16.4	49,136	15.4	24.0	13.6
36 73000	Syracuse	81,667	51.7	24.0	109,610	57.8	9.9	29.4	36.7	27,844	25.6	45.7	6.5
36 74183	Tonawanda CDP	42,307	40.1	28.7	49,752	62.1	5.3	33.6	36.0	45,361	6.8	25.4	11.9
36 75484	Troy	28,660	51.2	21.0	38,711	63.0	10.5	33.4	35.1	34,981	20.8	36.2	9.2
36 76089	Uniondale CDP	15,481	53.1	22.0	20,032	64.9	5.7	44.1	20.0	71,941	6.2	15.1	27.4
36 76540	Utica	39,060	55.8	16.4	47,701	58.2	9.7	32.4	37.9	29,990	23.5	42.7	7.9
36 76705	Valley Stream village	25,288	42.5	33.3	30,461	66.5	5.2	43.1	19.3	77,905	4.2	15.4	32.5
36 78608	Watertown	18,531	54.2	17.7	22,359	62.3	9.2	34.8	31.9	33,021	20.8	38.7	6.6
36 79246	West Babylon CDP	27,782	52.1	23.5	32,953	63.1	6.1	43.3	24.6	75,580	2.2	14.2	32.0
36 80302	West Islip CDP	17,274	41.1	30.0	20,392	67.1	4.6	38.7	18.0	96,270	1.6	7.1	48.5
36 80907	West Seneca CDP	32,739	45.2	23.0	37,407	64.3	5.1	41.1	30.9	50,927	5.2	20.5	16.2
36 81677	White Plains	37,715	32.4	51.0	43,561	68.7	7.4	44.4	25.5	73,744	7.3	17.4	36.7
36 84000	Yonkers	132,250	51.1	28.4	154,396	60.8	7.6	39.9	28.7	53,320	10.5	23.8	23.1
37 00000	**North Carolina**	5,849,056	47.4	25.0	6,946,929	65.0	6.8	40.6	26.6	43,867	11.0	28.2	14.4
37 01520	Apex town	21,159	19.7	55.4	23,700	74.5	3.0	49.0	10.1	81,545	1.2	8.3	34.6
37 02080	Asheboro	15,115	56.3	17.0	17,551	64.9	10.3	35.5	33.7	28,927	22.1	43.0	6.6
37 02140	Asheville	52,796	34.8	38.3	62,551	64.4	5.6	35.0	31.9	37,996	11.5	31.9	12.7
37 09060	Burlington	33,211	51.0	19.9	38,829	65.3	7.6	37.5	24.6	41,048	15.9	28.5	9.4
37 10740	Cary town	75,339	16.6	61.1	87,323	72.7	3.5	48.8	13.1	85,597	3.1	10.1	41.3
37 11800	Chapel Hill town	28,491	13.2	75.8	46,089	59.4	4.8	28.4	27.0	47,424	8.7	32.6	28.6
37 12000	Charlotte	418,512	34.0	39.2	497,005	73.3	7.7	45.1	19.0	51,050	9.3	22.6	21.2
37 14100	Concord	42,575	46.3	24.2	50,679	71.1	7.3	45.8	21.1	50,967	7.0	19.8	16.1
37 14700	Cornelius town	15,515	23.8	48.5	17,197	-	-	50.1	17.1	76,520	2.9	10.3	38.6
37 19000	Durham	133,167	34.8	43.0	162,276	70.5	7.5	41.9	22.0	45,361	12.1	27.0	16.8
37 22920	Fayetteville	108,805	39.4	23.4	133,764	63.7	8.9	38.4	27.2	42,450	15.3	30.2	11.3
37 24260	Fort Bragg CDP	8,819	28.6	25.5	16,507	-	-	64.9	19.5	39,655	13.2	23.5	6.4
37 25480	Garner town	13,591	39.8	29.6	15,777	-	-	47.1	20.6	51,884	5.9	19.8	18.6
37 25580	Gastonia	46,410	50.6	21.2	54,044	64.3	9.1	40.6	28.4	37,893	12.6	31.9	12.2
37 26880	Goldsboro	23,235	53.4	18.1	28,259	54.0	9.3	32.4	35.9	31,053	20.9	41.4	7.8
37 28000	Greensboro	149,749	38.7	35.2	188,448	66.5	7.8	38.8	24.8	39,824	14.0	31.2	13.1
37 28080	Greenville	36,526	33.9	37.3	56,573	64.6	10.4	32.0	27.4	31,586	17.9	41.8	10.4
37 30120	Havelock	8,833	40.0	12.3	14,369	80.6	3.5	64.8	14.2	44,517	6.7	24.3	8.1
37 31060	Hickory	26,916	47.6	28.8	32,006	67.8	8.3	42.7	26.1	37,614	13.3	30.8	14.9
37 31400	High Point	64,191	44.2	28.4	75,321	67.2	9.8	40.2	25.6	42,945	13.1	29.4	15.5
37 33120	Huntersville town	27,204	23.9	48.8	30,819	77.4	3.9	52.6	12.0	80,328	2.5	9.8	38.2
37 34200	Jacksonville	27,511	35.1	22.0	55,429	77.4	3.7	59.7	20.7	42,149	12.1	24.3	10.0
37 35200	Kannapolis	25,841	57.5	15.8	30,487	64.9	12.4	40.7	28.2	35,693	17.0	35.0	6.7
37 35600	Kernersville town	15,304	40.1	26.3	17,412	72.0	4.3	47.9	17.6	47,236	7.4	23.2	15.8
37 35920	Kinston	15,278	58.5	15.8	17,751	50.4	10.1	28.0	43.7	25,502	26.6	49.7	6.1
37 38060	Lexington	13,695	62.6	11.9	16,276	56.8	18.6	32.4	36.5	28,731	21.7	43.0	7.3
37 39700	Lumberton	15,258	58.4	20.0	17,817	54.1	6.4	35.0	35.8	27,082	28.9	47.3	9.9
37 41960	Matthews town	18,287	21.4	47.7	20,990	72.6	2.4	46.0	16.3	80,635	2.6	11.9	33.9
37 43920	Monroe	20,878	61.0	14.9	25,638	70.3	5.7	41.8	19.1	41,541	16.5	26.5	8.4
37 44220	Mooresville town	18,720	40.5	26.6	22,831	66.3	7.0	42.4	21.8	53,230	8.4	24.4	21.3
37 46340	New Bern	17,271	40.4	25.4	20,163	57.1	8.6	32.1	38.5	32,598	22.9	39.3	7.9
37 55000	Raleigh	217,388	29.6	46.5	273,453	69.8	5.6	43.5	19.2	51,647	8.2	22.7	21.7
37 57500	Rocky Mount	34,041	53.2	22.1	41,166	63.4	9.1	38.2	31.7	36,007	16.8	35.0	11.7
37 58860	Salisbury	19,752	53.6	25.7	23,853	56.8	12.3	33.2	36.3	37,276	15.5	36.9	11.5
37 59280	Sanford	16,992	59.3	16.3	20,030	62.5	5.9	39.2	26.5	36,852	20.3	35.7	10.5
37 61200	Shelby	13,205	48.0	23.8	15,895	55.8	12.1	32.3	35.5	35,290	19.5	36.9	9.7
37 64740	Statesville	15,461	50.4	21.5	18,016	64.9	8.1	42.6	32.7	35,029	13.3	38.2	8.2

Table B-4. Cities — What: Education, Employment, and Income, 2005–2007—*Continued*

STATE Place code	STATE City	Educational attainment			Employment status				Percent of households with no workers	Median household income (dollars)	Percent of families with income below poverty	Percent of households with income less than $25,000	Percent of households with income of $100,000 or more
		Total population 25 years and over	Percent with a high school diploma or less	Percent with a bachelor's degree or more	Total population 16 years and over	Percent in the labor force	Unemployment rate	Percent who worked full-time, year-round					
	ACS table number:	C15002	C15002	C15002	C20005	C23001	C23001	C20005	C08202	B19013	C17015	C19001	C19001
		1	2	3	4	5	6	7	8	9	10	11	12
	North Carolina—Cont.												
37 67420	Thomasville......................	17,344	62.7	12.4	19,795	64.6	10.3	38.0	31.6	36,236	15.2	38.6	4.8
37 70540	Wake Forest town.............	13,526	23.4	50.3	15,341	-	-	45.5	16.9	58,948	5.3	15.5	29.3
37 74440	Wilmington	63,391	35.4	35.0	81,203	63.4	6.9	34.1	32.0	37,011	12.5	35.3	13.9
37 74540	Wilson	30,363	54.8	20.5	35,874	61.1	9.0	37.0	32.9	33,265	19.9	39.0	12.4
37 75000	Winston-Salem	138,097	43.8	30.4	166,634	64.4	6.1	40.9	26.7	41,202	14.4	30.2	13.9
38 00000	**North Dakota**................	411,298	41.0	25.6	512,164	69.2	3.5	42.3	24.2	43,442	7.3	28.3	11.5
38 07200	Bismarck	38,771	34.7	31.1	48,063	71.8	3.0	45.4	22.7	44,732	5.9	27.3	13.8
38 25700	Fargo	57,496	30.1	36.4	78,024	75.1	4.5	42.5	20.7	39,406	9.7	31.6	13.2
38 32060	Grand Forks	27,550	32.0	35.9	41,997	71.5	3.2	37.7	22.0	39,276	9.8	33.2	10.5
38 53380	Minot	22,719	39.0	27.3	28,743	69.6	2.3	44.8	26.3	42,861	6.7	28.2	9.5
38 84780	West Fargo	13,006	34.2	29.7	15,273	80.6	3.4	54.7	13.0	57,722	3.8	17.6	15.1
39 00000	**Ohio**.............................	7,598,399	50.6	23.3	9,019,907	64.8	7.2	39.0	28.3	46,296	9.7	26.3	15.1
39 01000	Akron...............................	129,163	53.0	19.3	156,807	64.2	10.2	37.6	32.5	33,672	16.1	36.1	7.7
39 01420	Alliance............................	13,622	65.7	12.0	17,368	62.1	8.3	31.5	32.2	33,872	12.1	35.8	5.7
39 02568	Ashland............................	13,745	56.5	21.6	17,726	58.6	5.9	34.0	32.5	36,175	7.3	35.2	6.9
39 02736	Athens..............................	6,489	19.3	59.9	22,225	47.6	9.9	9.7	28.3	20,665	13.6	54.9	7.4
39 03184	Austintown CDP................	21,600	55.7	16.3	25,246	65.1	5.3	36.2	30.9	39,445	11.2	31.5	8.2
39 03464	Avon Lake........................	14,517	24.3	50.6	16,419	68.8	4.4	42.2	26.0	78,703	0.3	10.4	39.2
39 03828	Barberton.........................	18,120	62.8	11.3	21,331	62.8	8.3	37.0	34.5	34,090	20.2	38.4	5.2
39 04720	Beavercreek......................	27,574	26.7	46.3	33,590	69.4	4.5	45.6	17.9	76,243	1.5	9.5	32.1
39 07454	Boardman CDP..................	25,917	43.3	29.2	30,426	64.9	4.3	38.3	32.4	42,068	5.7	28.6	14.6
39 07972	Bowling Green...................	11,626	28.5	48.5	27,237	66.4	11.4	22.6	24.3	35,769	6.2	38.7	13.2
39 09680	Brunswick.........................	23,579	49.0	20.4	28,205	74.7	6.0	44.3	16.8	62,593	3.6	13.2	20.6
39 12000	Canton.............................	48,997	62.2	13.0	60,308	61.6	12.7	31.9	34.9	28,333	22.0	44.2	4.7
39 13190	Centerville........................	17,010	23.1	47.1	19,327	60.5	4.8	37.2	31.5	63,372	6.4	21.0	29.6
39 14184	Chillicothe........................	14,350	60.2	16.2	16,510	58.0	10.0	31.0	36.4	35,988	13.5	34.1	9.7
39 15000	Cincinnati.........................	195,567	49.0	27.7	240,927	62.1	10.4	34.9	33.3	31,916	20.6	40.7	10.9
39 16000	Cleveland..........................	261,326	63.1	12.5	312,237	59.8	16.3	32.0	37.9	27,007	25.2	47.0	4.8
39 16014	Cleveland Heights..............	30,678	28.5	45.9	36,654	65.9	7.9	38.1	30.3	47,974	12.9	27.3	19.6
39 18000	Columbus..........................	457,157	43.0	31.0	565,708	69.0	7.8	41.7	25.0	42,031	14.6	29.1	11.3
39 19778	Cuyahoga Falls..................	34,240	43.1	28.0	39,692	67.4	6.2	43.9	27.6	47,510	5.4	22.6	10.9
39 21000	Dayton.............................	91,374	56.2	14.7	115,219	58.2	13.2	31.1	38.8	28,381	24.3	44.5	5.1
39 21434	Delaware	19,214	40.0	29.8	25,777	68.1	6.5	44.6	22.0	47,713	7.9	24.6	14.9
39 22694	Dublin..............................	25,829	11.1	70.8	28,732	73.9	3.4	49.1	12.5	110,310	2.9	7.6	55.6
39 23380	East Cleveland	12,614	59.4	10.9	14,826	54.8	15.6	30.6	44.3	22,440	28.3	53.3	3.8
39 25256	Elyria...............................	35,498	53.5	14.6	41,875	66.3	7.5	41.5	28.5	41,318	13.9	29.9	7.6
39 25704	Euclid...............................	35,779	48.8	19.0	41,271	65.9	9.3	38.4	32.5	37,736	11.0	33.4	7.1
39 25914	Fairborn............................	20,478	48.1	20.6	28,430	63.6	6.7	37.8	27.2	37,039	15.5	32.0	9.3
39 25970	Fairfield............................	30,717	54.1	22.5	35,487	66.5	4.8	43.8	20.6	54,476	3.9	16.6	14.0
39 27048	Findlay.............................	26,080	46.8	25.0	32,409	69.4	6.4	39.7	26.9	41,471	10.0	29.2	11.5
39 29106	Gahanna...........................	23,022	28.9	45.4	26,187	72.5	4.1	45.3	16.8	72,813	3.3	11.4	31.5
39 29428	Garfield Heights................	19,858	61.4	12.7	23,020	65.9	11.0	38.6	32.2	42,057	10.9	30.9	7.6
39 31860	Green...............................	17,198	39.9	31.6	19,668	66.4	4.5	42.6	24.3	62,631	4.9	16.7	22.8
39 32592	Grove...............................	21,397	47.8	22.0	24,414	70.8	5.3	46.0	22.1	60,857	5.5	18.6	20.3
39 33012	Hamilton...........................	38,108	67.5	11.8	46,058	62.1	7.7	38.5	28.2	37,732	14.4	32.3	6.4
39 35476	Hilliard.............................	19,036	26.0	48.4	21,589	76.4	3.6	47.5	15.7	78,172	3.6	11.0	37.5
39 36610	Huber Heights....................	24,022	45.4	20.0	28,606	67.1	6.1	41.1	24.1	53,376	6.9	17.8	14.7
39 36651	Hudson.............................	14,518	11.9	68.9	16,943	62.7	2.6	39.5	23.6	112,740	3.2	8.0	56.1
39 39872	Kent..................................	12,372	35.3	42.1	24,066	67.9	7.9	25.6	24.5	31,063	21.7	45.2	10.1
39 40040	Kettering...........................	39,351	34.7	32.0	45,584	66.1	4.6	39.9	29.0	48,002	6.3	20.9	15.3
39 41664	Lakewood..........................	37,570	35.1	39.5	44,325	72.7	5.4	43.6	23.0	42,602	10.9	28.9	14.1
39 41720	Lancaster..........................	25,283	57.8	15.7	29,736	64.3	7.8	38.0	32.1	39,363	12.0	31.8	9.5
39 42364	Lebanon............................	12,116	43.7	25.3	14,511	70.0	5.9	48.5	17.3	58,611	9.1	20.1	23.6
39 43554	Lima.................................	23,706	65.3	9.8	29,254	59.4	13.4	31.3	37.1	30,860	22.4	39.0	4.2
39 44856	Lorain...............................	41,847	60.0	10.6	48,907	63.1	14.1	34.3	35.0	35,908	17.8	37.1	9.0
39 47138	Mansfield..........................	34,519	60.6	13.0	40,507	50.8	10.0	29.5	37.6	31,468	13.0	40.2	6.0
39 47306	Maple Heights...................	16,264	50.6	16.7	18,459	68.1	9.1	45.4	29.5	43,089	14.0	29.8	10.5
39 47754	Marion..............................	24,337	67.7	8.2	28,363	51.5	10.1	33.1	35.7	33,564	17.6	38.6	5.0
39 48188	Mason	18,425	27.8	49.0	21,334	76.2	4.4	47.1	15.5	83,082	1.8	8.2	41.6
39 48244	Massillon..........................	22,329	62.8	13.2	25,817	65.6	9.9	37.3	31.1	38,048	12.2	31.7	7.9
39 48790	Medina..............................	18,366	36.1	34.3	21,929	68.2	5.3	41.8	24.5	61,644	9.8	22.5	21.3
39 49056	Mentor..............................	34,148	41.7	28.6	39,408	68.5	3.4	43.4	23.9	60,146	3.1	13.2	21.7
39 49840	Middletown.......................	31,930	62.0	12.2	37,562	63.3	9.9	37.7	35.2	37,001	16.8	33.9	9.6
39 54040	Newark.............................	29,635	58.2	16.0	36,011	66.5	9.7	37.7	29.7	38,143	15.3	32.5	10.1
39 56882	North Olmsted..................	23,419	41.2	28.7	26,803	69.0	5.9	42.2	24.9	55,259	4.3	18.5	17.8
39 56966	North Ridgeville................	18,712	48.5	22.8	21,746	70.6	4.7	48.4	21.2	61,567	2.6	14.6	19.4
39 57008	North Royalton	20,834	36.0	33.9	24,550	72.9	6.6	44.8	20.3	63,033	4.4	15.6	24.4
39 57386	Norwood...........................	12,753	57.4	27.1	15,683	-	-	39.5	27.6	35,201	12.3	36.2	10.1
39 59234	Oxford..............................	5,734	27.6	53.4	20,610	49.7	7.3	11.0	30.5	21,930	12.8	51.8	11.6
39 61000	Parma..............................	58,141	50.9	19.4	66,958	64.6	6.8	40.1	30.6	48,164	5.1	24.3	11.6
39 62848	Piqua	13,895	63.1	12.3	16,223	64.9	8.2	39.9	31.3	40,912	8.3	30.8	6.7
39 64304	Portsmouth.......................	12,289	54.1	18.3	15,488	50.3	19.7	24.7	52.0	20,740	27.7	56.8	6.6
39 66390	Reynoldsburg....................	22,541	42.3	25.7	26,685	71.7	6.1	45.5	22.3	53,258	7.9	18.5	17.6
39 67468	Riverside...........................	16,518	55.2	13.1	19,843	62.6	6.9	39.0	28.9	38,248	7.7	27.1	5.5

Table B-4. Cities — What: Education, Employment, and Income, 2005–2007—*Continued*

STATE Place code	STATE City	Educational attainment			Employment status				Percent of households with no workers	Median household income (dollars)	Percent of families with income below poverty	Percent of households with income less than $25,000	Percent of households with income of $100,000 or more
		Total population 25 years and over	Percent with a high school diploma or less	Percent with a bachelor's degree or more	Total population 16 years and over	Percent in the labor force	Unemployment rate	Percent who worked full-time, year-round					
	ACS table number:	C15002	C15002	C15002	C20005	C23001	C23001	C20005	C08202	B19013	C17015	C19001	C19001
		1	2	3	4	5	6	7	8	9	10	11	12
	Ohio—Cont.												
39 70380	Sandusky	16,987	61.7	14.4	20,314	62.5	8.6	34.5	34.1	32,594	16.3	38.9	6.9
39 71682	Shaker Heights	19,279	15.4	61.9	22,330	67.3	5.5	41.3	23.4	68,793	6.1	18.0	35.9
39 72424	Sidney	12,821	60.4	14.3	14,893	69.0	4.7	47.2	25.1	36,517	18.0	33.6	6.3
39 72928	Solon	15,620	20.7	56.5	18,315	71.0	4.3	43.8	16.2	94,369	1.6	7.2	47.2
39 73264	South Euclid	15,576	30.3	38.2	17,953	69.6	6.6	40.4	22.7	53,263	5.3	19.0	14.6
39 74118	Springfield	39,611	61.4	14.2	48,164	56.5	11.8	30.7	40.5	31,436	19.2	40.8	5.3
39 74944	Stow	23,718	30.1	43.1	27,462	71.5	3.8	46.1	22.4	63,868	4.0	14.2	24.1
39 75098	Strongsville	31,702	30.8	40.6	36,780	69.3	4.3	42.7	22.7	79,715	1.2	12.0	33.3
39 77000	Toledo	184,071	52.9	17.3	224,599	64.0	12.5	34.4	34.2	34,839	18.0	36.7	7.6
39 77504	Trotwood	16,522	54.1	16.5	19,494	56.7	7.7	34.9	34.2	36,895	15.2	31.5	7.5
39 77588	Troy	15,634	51.9	21.7	17,980	67.6	7.4	46.8	26.9	41,624	12.8	26.2	13.2
39 79002	Upper Arlington	24,154	11.5	70.9	27,140	66.1	4.1	42.5	23.9	88,365	3.9	10.4	44.6
39 80304	Wadsworth	12,495	41.3	30.2	14,887	72.2	6.2	40.7	23.7	55,695	3.6	18.8	20.5
39 80892	Warren	28,662	65.1	11.6	34,201	53.4	12.6	30.6	40.3	33,122	22.1	40.6	5.4
39 83342	Westerville	22,683	21.6	52.8	28,585	70.6	4.3	40.5	19.8	73,540	3.0	14.9	33.7
39 83622	Westlake	23,435	29.4	44.4	26,205	63.5	2.9	40.5	27.9	63,252	3.3	16.5	31.7
39 85484	Willoughby	16,670	44.1	28.8	19,460	66.8	3.7	41.7	26.8	47,466	5.9	23.2	13.8
39 86548	Wooster	16,256	49.7	26.5	20,609	61.6	5.6	32.9	30.6	37,438	12.7	35.0	8.5
39 86772	Xenia	14,871	55.1	19.1	17,879	63.7	7.6	38.5	29.7	39,531	12.2	30.2	7.6
39 88000	Youngstown	45,272	66.0	10.4	55,063	52.4	16.1	25.1	44.0	24,924	25.0	50.2	3.1
39 88084	Zanesville	16,630	66.3	11.1	19,863	58.6	16.9	28.1	40.4	27,458	23.3	45.9	5.3
40 00000	**Oklahoma**	2,311,130	48.9	22.2	2,789,374	62.7	5.9	39.5	28.3	40,371	12.5	30.9	11.7
40 02600	Ardmore	16,964	58.2	18.7	19,761	60.9	6.0	42.2	33.4	33,598	16.6	37.0	7.5
40 04450	Bartlesville	23,574	41.2	29.5	28,120	59.8	3.8	36.7	35.8	41,721	8.7	30.6	13.8
40 06400	Bixby	11,201	33.1	37.1	13,024	68.1	3.4	47.4	19.9	59,714	3.8	13.4	25.1
40 09050	Broken Arrow	57,787	32.7	31.5	67,728	71.2	3.6	48.6	17.3	61,668	5.3	14.9	21.3
40 19900	Del	14,332	51.3	10.2	16,600	65.4	9.2	40.5	32.9	36,090	6.7	32.8	4.7
40 21900	Duncan	15,529	56.1	19.2	18,641	59.5	5.5	38.7	30.6	36,560	12.9	30.5	11.3
40 23200	Edmond	49,607	21.6	51.3	60,142	69.8	3.3	43.1	19.6	63,028	5.3	18.9	28.7
40 23950	Enid	31,144	52.3	20.1	36,612	63.6	5.0	40.2	25.9	36,027	15.1	32.4	9.2
40 41850	Lawton	51,508	49.5	18.1	66,528	64.2	7.0	37.1	26.2	40,011	17.6	31.5	6.9
40 48350	Midwest	34,549	40.2	20.8	40,874	66.0	4.0	43.5	27.7	40,865	12.0	26.1	7.3
40 49200	Moore	29,527	42.8	17.1	36,114	72.0	5.4	48.1	19.2	52,852	4.8	16.3	12.0
40 50050	Muskogee	25,871	53.2	17.2	31,332	57.2	7.7	34.1	37.0	31,157	19.2	41.5	7.1
40 52500	Norman	59,920	27.1	43.6	85,771	66.7	6.9	35.5	24.9	42,003	10.0	30.7	15.1
40 55000	Oklahoma	348,396	43.7	26.1	416,033	66.2	6.3	41.0	26.1	40,751	13.1	30.0	13.5
40 56650	Owasso	16,188	34.2	32.0	19,051	70.8	2.9	47.4	19.7	59,480	8.9	18.8	19.3
40 59850	Ponca	16,205	50.9	20.3	19,097	61.8	6.7	38.4	32.8	37,889	15.1	36.8	11.7
40 65400	Sapulpa	14,553	54.8	18.1	17,077	61.8	6.9	35.1	29.3	40,171	10.0	28.5	10.2
40 66800	Shawnee	18,962	50.6	19.6	24,166	59.7	8.0	33.9	32.7	32,133	21.3	39.5	7.8
40 70300	Stillwater	21,295	27.2	46.4	39,473	64.1	6.0	26.7	24.8	28,390	14.8	46.1	8.2
40 75000	Tulsa	249,681	41.1	29.3	298,186	66.1	6.8	41.3	27.5	38,054	15.5	32.1	13.5
40 82950	Yukon	13,834	37.7	25.5	17,006	66.2	4.7	43.2	25.5	52,449	5.8	21.9	17.7
41 00000	**Oregon**	2,496,987	39.4	27.6	2,934,587	64.6	6.9	36.4	27.3	47,385	9.3	25.2	15.7
41 01000	Albany	30,438	40.2	20.6	36,389	67.5	7.1	39.3	26.8	43,777	10.1	26.9	12.8
41 01650	Aloha CDP	30,897	38.6	25.3	35,349	72.9	7.6	46.3	16.8	56,174	10.7	16.1	14.9
41 01850	Altamont CDP	13,546	55.4	12.6	15,826	63.2	5.7	36.3	28.2	43,676	11.7	29.0	10.0
41 03050	Ashland	13,114	17.9	52.0	17,317	63.5	10.0	24.1	36.5	35,642	9.9	34.1	11.7
41 05350	Beaverton	56,995	28.8	40.7	67,115	71.7	6.4	45.0	17.6	53,659	6.2	18.9	20.7
41 05800	Bend	48,228	29.6	34.5	56,199	69.7	5.0	40.4	23.7	53,365	5.3	19.1	17.0
41 15800	Corvallis	28,319	18.5	53.9	44,384	62.0	5.1	26.1	27.9	39,756	8.8	34.4	16.7
41 23850	Eugene	97,734	27.7	39.2	127,025	61.6	6.7	30.1	29.9	40,207	10.1	32.9	13.0
41 26200	Forest Grove	11,460	45.1	22.6	14,554	68.1	6.8	34.8	27.4	41,651	15.5	30.4	10.3
41 30550	Grants Pass	22,590	44.0	17.1	26,873	57.2	7.4	30.1	35.4	35,616	17.0	33.9	8.2
41 31250	Gresham	64,695	46.4	18.7	75,866	66.5	6.5	39.9	24.5	46,584	13.0	25.2	13.2
41 32850	Hayesville CDP	13,297	58.1	13.6	15,836	69.4	9.7	37.4	22.4	36,855	16.5	32.9	7.9
41 34100	Hillsboro	52,285	37.6	30.9	61,578	73.9	6.0	43.3	14.5	54,191	10.1	17.8	18.6
41 38500	Keizer	23,235	38.4	23.0	27,356	66.9	8.2	39.2	25.0	51,617	11.9	21.4	13.5
41 40550	Lake Oswego	26,253	8.7	66.4	30,488	63.5	3.7	32.9	23.5	76,883	4.0	14.7	38.3
41 45000	McMinnville	18,664	51.1	21.0	23,732	61.7	12.9	32.5	32.1	38,821	16.6	32.5	10.9
41 47000	Medford	47,866	41.8	22.6	56,627	63.9	6.1	37.4	30.3	42,519	10.5	26.4	11.8
41 48650	Milwaukie	14,121	40.8	19.1	16,829	66.5	6.7	40.5	26.0	47,189	6.9	26.9	8.7
41 52100	Newberg	11,109	39.3	24.3	15,102	70.4	5.6	33.5	22.4	46,066	9.2	22.6	7.1
41 55200	Oregon	19,122	37.9	23.0	23,798	68.5	8.1	36.2	23.9	56,321	6.5	20.4	18.1
41 59000	Portland	382,060	32.8	38.2	438,275	68.7	7.0	39.2	25.0	45,512	11.2	27.2	17.0
41 61200	Redmond	13,553	48.4	13.6	16,776	66.4	8.4	38.5	28.4	44,236	5.8	23.4	5.4
41 63650	Roseburg	15,018	40.8	21.3	17,919	60.1	9.6	29.7	35.8	41,255	9.2	31.4	12.0
41 64900	Salem	95,860	41.6	25.6	115,604	64.4	9.5	35.6	27.8	42,050	11.3	27.2	12.9
41 69600	Springfield	36,724	50.1	15.8	43,131	65.8	8.4	37.4	26.9	37,395	14.9	31.6	6.0
41 73650	Tigard	31,608	27.3	37.9	36,083	70.9	5.7	44.0	21.2	61,331	6.8	18.8	25.0
41 74950	Tualatin	17,300	28.8	38.9	20,045	74.9	5.8	44.9	14.0	59,821	5.7	17.8	24.5
41 80150	West Linn	18,042	16.8	56.0	20,463	-	-	41.2	17.1	94,844	3.2	9.4	47.0
41 83750	Woodburn	14,010	68.3	12.2	16,595	61.9	12.1	31.0	38.9	40,750	8.2	24.8	4.8

Table B-4. Cities — What: Education, Employment, and Income, 2005–2007—*Continued*

STATE Place code	STATE City	Educational attainment			Employment status				Percent of households with no workers	Median household income (dollars)	Percent of families with income below poverty	Percent of households with income less than $25,000	Percent of households with income of $100,000 or more
		Total population 25 years and over	Percent with a high school diploma or less	Percent with a bachelor's degree or more	Total population 16 years and over	Percent in the labor force	Unemployment rate	Percent who worked full-time, year-round					
	ACS table number:	C15002	C15002	C15002	C20005	C23001	C23001	C20005	C08202	B19013	C17015	C19001	C19001
		1	2	3	4	5	6	7	8	9	10	11	12
42 00000	**Pennsylvania**	8,404,685	52.3	25.6	9,947,004	62.6	6.3	38.7	29.1	47,913	8.2	25.8	17.0
42 02000	Allentown	68,600	60.0	16.7	83,906	62.4	9.0	36.5	30.0	36,630	17.5	32.3	7.1
42 02184	Altoona	31,646	63.9	14.8	37,864	56.6	7.5	33.0	39.3	33,833	14.1	36.8	4.9
42 03714	Back Mountain CDP	17,599	49.7	26.4	19,853	58.3	3.8	39.9	27.7	54,488	3.5	17.8	19.8
42 06064	Bethel Park municipality	25,188	38.6	36.1	28,925	61.1	2.7	39.3	28.6	59,125	4.1	18.7	23.5
42 06088	Bethlehem	44,968	48.0	27.8	57,650	60.5	6.8	35.5	30.5	43,524	10.1	30.3	13.7
42 13208	Chester	17,572	72.3	10.4	22,660	51.3	15.4	29.1	41.0	25,448	33.8	49.3	3.2
42 19920	Drexel Hill CDP	19,950	41.1	36.2	23,067	70.7	3.7	44.6	18.3	63,337	3.4	15.4	25.5
42 21648	Easton	16,178	60.8	13.8	21,729	55.7	7.8	33.6	24.7	41,136	13.2	29.7	7.8
42 24000	Erie	62,921	61.6	18.2	78,332	59.8	8.6	34.4	33.5	31,687	17.7	40.2	6.2
42 32800	Harrisburg	29,109	63.9	16.6	34,460	66.6	10.2	41.3	31.0	31,121	25.7	41.0	5.4
42 33408	Hazleton	14,997	65.2	13.7	17,452	59.6	7.2	34.2	37.4	30,678	15.7	41.1	4.7
42 38288	Johnstown	14,810	68.9	11.9	16,708	52.8	8.5	31.7	46.1	24,758	23.1	50.4	2.7
42 41216	Lancaster	32,557	65.8	17.3	42,074	60.1	9.7	34.9	29.4	31,599	22.5	39.1	5.9
42 42168	Lebanon	14,501	71.0	11.3	16,608	64.1	11.8	37.3	35.8	31,368	18.0	39.4	3.5
42 42928	Levittown CDP	35,468	53.6	14.4	41,086	66.7	4.3	41.1	24.7	60,623	4.1	16.7	17.2
42 45904	McCandless Township CDP	19,597	29.2	49.6	22,517	64.6	5.8	39.0	25.6	69,273	2.2	15.5	32.9
42 46256	McKeesport	13,592	62.4	10.8	15,657	52.1	10.5	30.2	44.2	24,461	24.9	51.0	4.0
42 50528	Monroeville municipality	20,235	32.9	41.1	23,241	64.6	4.3	41.5	27.5	55,825	4.0	18.0	19.5
42 51704	Mount Lebanon CDP	23,106	17.1	61.2	25,951	62.1	4.7	40.4	28.5	73,765	0.8	14.3	35.9
42 53368	New Castle	16,624	62.3	15.1	19,344	55.7	12.7	30.5	37.9	31,443	19.7	41.4	5.9
42 54656	Norristown borough	21,025	65.8	16.8	26,526	65.8	6.8	39.1	26.3	40,725	17.3	31.2	9.4
42 59040	Penn Hills CDP	31,584	44.3	24.0	34,963	64.4	8.3	40.0	30.9	43,291	8.1	27.5	9.0
42 60000	Philadelphia	931,064	58.6	21.0	1,131,973	57.8	11.9	33.6	36.1	34,767	19.3	38.0	10.4
42 61000	Pittsburgh	193,676	45.6	31.9	250,049	58.9	8.5	32.5	35.7	32,344	15.7	40.2	10.5
42 61536	Plum borough	18,795	40.4	29.8	21,575	70.0	5.7	43.7	20.0	61,644	3.4	12.6	19.4
42 62416	Pottstown borough	13,883	61.1	16.9	16,775	68.1	8.5	39.2	29.2	39,581	12.4	33.7	8.7
42 63268	Radnor Township CDP	17,052	16.1	70.6	25,254	55.3	3.8	29.4	25.8	86,812	2.7	16.1	41.7
42 63624	Reading	46,232	73.9	10.2	58,180	61.9	11.3	33.2	33.7	27,047	29.0	46.7	2.9
42 66356	Ross Township CDP	23,297	36.8	39.1	25,883	62.8	2.7	41.6	29.8	57,001	3.0	20.7	19.6
42 69000	Scranton	48,721	58.1	18.3	61,134	55.9	5.5	31.0	35.3	32,484	15.3	38.6	5.7
42 69596	Shaler Township CDP	21,488	47.1	29.4	23,800	63.6	3.1	41.9	30.1	60,421	2.8	18.5	18.6
42 73040	Springfield CDP	16,237	37.4	36.2	19,056	61.1	3.2	38.3	29.2	81,101	2.9	12.4	35.6
42 73808	State College borough	10,125	16.1	72.9	38,083	47.1	8.5	10.5	33.9	20,847	12.1	56.3	9.0
42 79277	Upper St. Clair CDP	13,570	17.3	66.6	15,752	58.3	3.8	34.9	26.8	102,307	3.5	11.8	51.4
42 83512	West Mifflin borough	15,271	52.1	16.2	17,160	60.8	5.7	37.7	34.3	43,212	7.8	28.5	10.8
42 85152	Wilkes-Barre	25,374	63.2	14.3	32,728	55.1	7.9	33.0	40.2	28,777	16.6	44.9	5.3
42 85312	Williamsport	17,279	57.4	17.4	23,964	59.5	12.1	31.5	38.8	26,920	18.6	46.1	5.2
42 87048	York	23,594	69.9	11.2	30,406	65.8	14.4	35.8	31.3	28,716	28.2	44.4	3.1
44 00000	**Rhode Island**	711,837	46.6	29.4	854,785	66.0	6.1	38.9	27.6	54,060	8.3	23.7	21.2
44 09460	Bristol CDP	15,446	47.3	30.1	19,807	63.5	5.4	37.2	24.6	60,876	4.2	22.1	25.5
44 19180	Cranston	57,026	47.6	28.3	66,795	62.6	6.3	37.9	27.2	56,707	4.4	20.3	20.6
44 22960	East Providence	34,953	56.1	21.1	39,191	65.9	6.5	40.1	29.0	48,726	6.7	24.5	13.3
44 49960	Newport	16,004	34.3	43.5	19,963	67.3	3.8	36.3	26.7	52,145	5.7	24.7	21.9
44 51940	North Providence CDP	24,448	48.7	24.9	27,763	65.5	7.1	38.9	29.2	51,222	7.1	25.0	17.2
44 54640	Pawtucket	48,126	57.5	17.9	56,869	67.7	7.5	38.9	30.2	40,299	14.6	33.4	10.5
44 59000	Providence	96,683	52.8	29.4	132,709	63.4	9.8	34.0	30.9	35,264	23.1	38.0	13.0
44 74300	Warwick	61,717	41.8	30.2	70,262	67.8	5.4	43.6	26.4	59,445	3.9	17.4	19.0
44 78260	West Warwick CDP	20,725	51.1	21.6	24,850	69.2	4.8	44.0	25.6	43,903	7.8	25.9	14.9
44 80780	Woonsocket	30,451	66.4	11.5	35,353	61.3	5.4	39.5	33.7	39,553	16.9	33.6	11.9
45 00000	**South Carolina**	2,851,898	51.0	22.8	3,406,212	62.8	7.3	39.4	28.5	42,405	11.8	29.3	13.1
45 00550	Aiken	19,054	34.8	43.5	22,144	58.9	7.0	33.2	35.4	48,005	10.1	28.2	24.4
45 01360	Anderson	16,250	57.5	20.1	19,417	57.1	12.4	30.4	38.9	30,173	18.9	43.4	10.4
45 13330	Charleston	70,005	32.4	44.2	89,335	64.5	5.0	40.4	28.2	44,765	11.5	30.1	18.2
45 16000	Columbia	67,004	37.0	39.1	100,825	63.2	7.3	32.8	28.2	36,930	13.0	34.7	14.1
45 21985	Easley	13,619	50.6	22.9	15,689	66.0	5.0	40.2	28.6	47,936	8.9	25.3	14.6
45 25810	Florence	22,955	47.1	28.2	27,007	62.2	9.2	38.7	26.1	42,884	10.9	32.3	14.2
45 29815	Goose Creek	19,179	42.5	22.6	25,043	73.7	4.6	47.0	13.7	56,042	4.3	8.9	15.4
45 30850	Greenville	37,567	41.0	37.1	46,193	62.2	6.8	36.0	29.6	34,482	15.5	37.1	15.3
45 30895	Greenwood	12,759	60.1	16.9	16,807	64.8	16.3	33.6	32.4	29,189	14.5	43.3	4.9
45 30985	Greer	14,529	54.0	20.1	16,120	-	-	46.0	27.7	36,983	12.0	32.8	9.0
45 34045	Hilton Head Island town	26,853	26.4	49.3	30,112	53.2	3.2	31.7	40.8	65,214	6.2	15.8	29.3
45 45115	Mauldin	13,700	36.0	32.2	15,564	-	-	47.1	17.9	56,181	3.2	20.1	17.7
45 48535	Mount Pleasant town	45,442	17.1	56.9	51,113	72.0	3.2	47.6	17.2	77,066	3.3	10.4	35.3
45 49075	Myrtle Beach	16,811	46.7	26.1	19,568	65.1	4.7	36.7	29.3	35,141	22.1	34.0	11.4
45 50695	North Augusta	14,109	38.5	28.0	16,111	66.1	6.7	42.6	28.7	46,238	10.4	29.3	14.1
45 50875	North Charleston	51,758	54.7	15.8	64,234	65.4	7.6	41.6	26.1	34,296	18.9	34.6	6.9
45 61405	Rock Hill	35,809	46.9	25.3	46,690	69.2	8.3	39.9	23.4	42,136	13.2	29.0	13.4
45 62395	St. Andrews CDP	14,214	36.6	32.9	18,545	81.3	6.8	53.0	17.9	36,510	10.5	26.8	3.3
45 68290	Spartanburg	23,162	51.2	26.1	28,714	55.8	9.9	30.5	37.5	32,235	23.9	41.6	10.2
45 70270	Summerville town	23,039	38.1	26.9	27,316	64.8	3.7	43.4	22.8	52,806	2.2	15.5	14.9
45 70405	Sumter	23,814	50.6	23.2	29,265	53.5	13.8	34.0	38.6	29,474	17.6	43.1	9.5
45 71395	Taylors CDP	14,107	34.7	32.7	16,430	75.6	8.0	48.5	20.9	47,906	7.4	16.9	14.3
45 73870	Wade Hampton CDP	15,442	37.1	36.3	18,220	63.9	8.0	40.5	29.2	45,951	7.9	27.0	12.4

Table B-4. Cities — What: Education, Employment, and Income, 2005–2007—*Continued*

STATE Place code	STATE City	Educational attainment			Employment status				Percent of households with no workers	Median household income (dollars)	Percent of families with income below poverty	Percent of households with income less than $25,000	Percent of households with income of $100,000 or more
		Total population 25 years and over	Percent with a high school diploma or less	Percent with a bachelor's degree or more	Total population 16 years and over	Percent in the labor force	Unemployment rate	Percent who worked full-time, year-round					
ACS table number:		C15002	C15002	C15002	C20005	C23001	C23001	C20005	C08202	B19013	C17015	C19001	C19001
		1	2	3	4	5	6	7	8	9	10	11	12
46 00000	**South Dakota**	509,779	45.3	24.5	616,374	69.6	4.4	43.9	24.0	43,586	8.7	27.1	11.1
46 00100	Aberdeen	15,526	48.1	22.3	19,499	69.9	3.1	45.1	24.5	41,138	6.9	31.3	8.0
46 52980	Rapid	39,236	37.6	29.7	48,064	68.6	5.1	39.8	27.5	41,514	10.8	27.5	11.3
46 59020	Sioux Falls	95,453	39.4	30.2	114,396	74.1	4.0	48.0	21.0	47,551	7.6	23.8	14.1
46 69300	Watertown	13,344	53.9	20.2	16,038	72.1	4.5	42.4	27.5	37,318	14.1	33.0	9.2
47 00000	**Tennessee**	4,061,516	53.5	21.7	4,779,974	62.9	7.1	39.6	28.3	41,821	12.2	29.9	13.0
47 03440	Bartlett	32,879	33.0	33.8	37,744	70.5	3.3	48.3	17.3	74,091	3.2	8.6	30.0
47 08280	Brentwood	20,819	11.6	69.1	24,832	66.3	4.9	41.9	15.7	126,579	1.9	5.6	65.1
47 08540	Bristol	18,362	54.4	20.5	21,155	56.5	7.8	35.3	33.2	36,454	10.9	33.1	9.9
47 14000	Chattanooga	108,343	51.0	22.5	129,254	61.1	9.9	35.5	32.0	35,913	13.2	35.5	11.3
47 15160	Clarksville	66,680	40.4	22.4	83,090	67.7	6.3	45.0	20.0	47,810	9.6	23.4	12.1
47 15400	Cleveland	25,496	46.1	25.2	31,908	60.7	9.0	32.8	31.6	35,439	15.1	34.3	10.3
47 16420	Collierville town	26,958	24.2	47.1	31,843	70.3	4.3	45.4	13.4	99,239	5.0	9.2	49.7
47 16540	Columbia	21,953	58.9	15.4	26,446	63.6	9.3	39.8	29.4	38,451	12.5	33.0	8.8
47 16920	Cookeville	16,150	42.9	31.7	22,545	58.1	5.8	31.5	30.4	31,678	12.5	41.4	7.4
47 25760	Farragut town	13,621	20.3	56.5	15,509	-	-	41.7	19.6	94,420	1.4	6.9	47.2
47 27740	Franklin	35,954	29.0	47.3	42,679	73.3	3.7	45.7	16.9	71,914	3.3	13.3	34.0
47 28540	Gallatin	17,686	55.2	17.4	20,739	64.3	9.8	37.6	31.9	43,053	16.5	30.8	9.3
47 28960	Germantown	27,541	13.5	63.0	31,620	65.7	2.3	43.8	15.0	113.733	1.5	5.7	58.2
47 33280	Hendersonville	31,009	38.3	32.0	36,424	70.5	7.1	44.3	23.4	56,902	4.7	18.4	20.3
47 37640	Jackson	37,673	47.7	24.6	47,228	63.7	9.0	38.6	30.5	34,944	20.3	36.7	10.5
47 38320	Johnson	38,584	41.7	33.2	48,087	60.0	6.2	35.3	31.1	35,746	12.5	34.2	12.8
47 39560	Kingsport	33,415	52.9	24.1	37,600	55.4	8.0	34.5	41.4	34,391	14.9	37.8	11.7
47 40000	Knoxville	112,391	48.1	27.3	145,830	61.0	7.3	35.0	32.7	32,538	16.8	39.1	7.5
47 41200	La Vergne	16,366	54.2	18.5	19,378	75.8	7.4	52.9	12.2	54,271	9.0	13.6	7.8
47 41520	Lebanon	16,102	57.9	17.9	19,761	63.2	3.8	40.0	24.0	41,781	7.4	27.4	12.4
47 46380	Maryville	16,987	40.3	31.2	20,214	59.9	8.3	36.1	32.2	48,467	11.2	26.6	17.1
47 48000	Memphis	402,418	50.8	21.8	492.919	64.9	11.2	38.3	27.7	35,181	20.2	35.6	10.5
47 50280	Morristown	18,446	65.4	12.0	22,045	56.5	6.2	35.8	34.3	29,917	18.4	44.8	6.4
47 50780	Mount Juliet	11,206	39.0	28.2	13,341	-	-	54.0	15.6	71,466	5.2	11.7	26.9
47 51560	Murfreesboro	52,388	38.3	34.3	71,608	69.4	7.4	41.3	20.4	44,528	10.6	26.5	16.4
47 52006	Nashville-Davidson (balance)	392,648	43.0	31.5	462,982	67.6	6.0	44.3	23.6	43,887	11.6	26.8	14.6
47 55120	Oak Ridge	20,235	35.5	36.2	22,987	57.1	7.3	36.9	37.8	45,474	8.1	26.3	17.4
47 69420	Smyrna town	21,805	50.8	19.1	25,181	70.4	5.9	50.3	21.6	49,906	11.4	24.5	12.9
47 70580	Spring Hill	10,398	27.6	38.0	12,049	-	-	53.9	11.8	69,382	2.6	5.8	27.5
48 00000	**Texas**	14,482,842	48.4	24.7	17,596,586	65.2	6.8	41.4	22.6	46,248	13.3	26.7	17.5
48 01000	Abilene	69,237	49.2	22.1	89,314	60.0	5.3	38.0	24.7	37,805	13.8	31.8	9.6
48 01924	Allen	44,624	18.9	49.4	51,676	76.5	4.3	52.2	9.2	90,710	2.0	5.4	45.2
48 02272	Alvin	13,553	54.2	15.8	16,437	65.7	7.8	40.4	21.3	40,697	8.0	28.9	11.2
48 03000	Amarillo	115,761	46.5	20.5	139,895	67.8	5.8	44.0	24.4	40,171	12.8	30.4	12.2
48 04000	Arlington	217,738	40.7	27.7	266,165	73.6	7.4	47.0	17.0	51,531	10.3	20.3	17.7
48 04462	Atascocita CDP	37,141	33.8	31.0	43,173	71.9	4.4	48.4	8.9	80,366	2.6	7.5	37.9
48 05000	Austin	458,787	34.0	42.9	573,418	73.5	6.2	46.7	17.9	48,227	12.6	24.6	19.8
48 06128	Baytown	44,331	54.9	13.4	52,594	65.9	11.4	38.6	25.6	42,548	12.0	28.0	13.4
48 07000	Beaumont	70,719	49.3	23.4	86,421	63.6	8.5	36.7	30.0	37,787	17.0	35.3	14.6
48 07132	Bedford	33,156	29.9	35.1	38,376	74.0	4.7	51.5	18.7	56,051	3.0	15.5	24.3
48 07552	Benbrook	15,189	29.6	34.9	17,269	66.9	8.4	44.5	24.2	54,695	5.2	17.1	21.2
48 08236	Big Spring	16,360	61.3	10.7	19,297	43.6	9.6	26.2	35.2	29,053	22.7	42.1	6.2
48 10768	Brownsville	90,733	63.4	15.2	115,210	56.6	8.4	31.6	27.2	26,878	36.6	47.4	7.0
48 10897	Brushy Creek CDP	11,711	10.1	61.2	13,863	-	-	49.2	12.1	107,465	-	3.8	55.9
48 10912	Bryan	37,622	51.6	27.3	50,573	65.3	6.8	37.0	24.1	35,827	21.8	38.8	9.6
48 11428	Burleson	18,151	44.9	25.3	21,748	69.9	7.6	44.2	20.2	59,855	4.8	14.3	17.4
48 13024	Carrollton	75,530	34.9	36.0	89,249	74.8	4.4	50.8	11.5	66,313	6.3	12.1	28.0
48 13492	Cedar Hill	25,171	39.8	28.8	29,799	73.9	9.4	49.8	17.1	60,737	3.5	12.9	24.3
48 13552	Cedar Park	24,418	28.1	37.7	29,648	73.6	6.8	46.5	15.0	64,797	5.7	12.6	26.4
48 14236	Channelview CDP	21,591	67.1	8.1	27,040	65.7	8.5	41.1	18.4	45,046	19.5	23.8	11.2
48 15364	Cleburne	19,608	60.3	15.1	23,056	62.6	8.2	39.5	25.8	40,767	19.1	30.8	9.8
48 15628	Cloverleaf CDP	12,722	71.2	9.2	15,969	-	-	41.0	16.5	37,433	21.2	33.3	12.4
48 15976	College Station	30,567	21.4	57.4	68,458	57.3	6.9	25.0	24.6	29,565	15.5	46.2	13.5
48 15988	Colleyville	14,548	12.6	64.5	17,032	-	-	45.0	14.2	148,789	2.1	3.8	70.6
48 16432	Conroe	29,219	58.4	16.1	36,358	66.7	7.8	37.1	19.5	43,196	17.4	26.6	12.7
48 16612	Coppell	25,185	13.3	63.9	28,854	76.4	3.7	51.6	8.7	106,783	2.1	7.8	54.8
48 16624	Copperas Cove	16,776	36.5	19.2	22,861	65.3	8.4	43.5	23.1	44,918	12.8	23.8	10.2
48 16696	Corinth	12,315	26.2	45.2	14,243	-	-	55.6	10.6	95,967	1.3	3.7	46.3
48 17000	Corpus Christi	176,150	49.3	20.3	215,253	63.7	6.8	38.5	24.7	39,975	16.0	32.2	13.7
48 17060	Corsicana	15,914	60.4	10.6	19,968	61.2	14.8	32.3	36.6	31,346	26.5	41.1	5.8
48 19000	Dallas	755,773	51.5	27.3	901,320	68.2	7.9	44.1	21.5	40,147	18.7	30.0	16.1
48 19624	Deer Park	19,564	44.4	18.2	23,696	72.4	6.2	49.7	17.2	72,980	3.1	11.4	28.0
48 19792	Del Rio	22,367	67.5	14.2	26,849	55.8	7.9	32.9	32.4	31,994	23.4	42.4	7.2
48 19900	Denison	15,833	54.9	16.1	18,014	62.6	7.7	34.5	32.5	34,988	19.2	37.8	7.5
48 19972	Denton	55,843	34.4	34.9	82,736	68.0	6.9	34.8	19.6	43,647	10.7	30.9	15.4
48 20092	DeSoto	30,434	36.1	30.5	34,379	66.5	7.0	45.5	19.0	61,052	3.9	17.5	24.1
48 21628	Duncanville	23,471	45.2	22.7	26,802	68.2	6.4	46.4	23.3	48,369	8.9	22.0	17.1
48 21892	Eagle Pass	15,325	65.1	16.7	18,560	53.9	8.1	29.2	33.6	31,470	26.4	42.1	8.4

Table B-4. Cities — What: Education, Employment, and Income, 2005–2007—*Continued*

STATE Place code	STATE City	Educational attainment			Employment status						Percent of families with income below poverty	Percent of households with income less than $25,000	Percent of households with income of $100,000 or more
		Total population 25 years and over	Percent with a high school diploma or less	Percent with a bachelor's degree or more	Total population 16 years and over	Percent in the labor force	Unemployment rate	Percent who worked full-time, year-round	Percent of households with no workers	Median household income (dollars)			
	ACS table number:	C15002	C15002	C15002	C20005	C23001	C23001	C20005	C08202	B19013	C17015	C19001	C19001
		1	2	3	4	5	6	7	8	9	10	11	12
	Texas—Cont.												
48 22660	Edinburg	32,963	54.1	21.2	43,855	63.3	9.4	32.4	25.4	29,754	30.3	43.1	9.1
48 24000	El Paso	347,193	52.4	20.1	431,247	59.3	8.4	35.2	26.6	34,626	23.4	37.9	10.2
48 24768	Euless	33,941	35.5	30.6	39,790	77.1	5.1	52.3	12.5	51,102	10.7	19.1	14.1
48 25452	Farmers Branch	18,279	52.5	25.5	21,509	69.8	6.5	48.3	21.5	50,745	6.9	18.2	18.3
48 26232	Flower Mound town	40,061	19.8	49.1	46,413	75.1	5.6	50.7	8.5	105,823	2.3	4.4	54.5
48 26736	Fort Hood CDP	11,279	27.6	21.6	20,341	-	-	56.1	14.7	35,158	17.8	21.7	3.8
48 27000	Fort Worth	389,821	49.5	24.4	473,840	67.5	7.2	43.3	21.7	44,804	14.3	26.9	15.6
48 27648	Friendswood	23,445	24.1	41.8	27,693	66.9	4.2	44.1	17.8	86,432	2.8	9.6	41.3
48 27684	Frisco	52,712	16.6	56.8	58,793	76.3	3.6	56.1	8.4	96,676	2.3	6.4	47.7
48 28068	Galveston	36,067	46.6	27.5	45,183	60.7	9.4	35.8	31.6	34,153	16.9	37.7	9.4
48 29000	Garland	145,793	52.3	19.2	172,727	71.8	7.2	45.9	16.3	50,174	10.9	19.9	15.7
48 29336	Georgetown	27,297	35.8	37.2	31,529	55.6	4.7	36.1	35.6	59,593	4.8	13.3	22.6
48 30464	Grand Prairie	92,744	50.4	21.4	110,931	70.9	8.3	47.3	18.5	50,163	12.4	21.1	14.9
48 30644	Grapevine	30,107	24.5	45.4	34,870	75.1	4.3	51.8	11.6	75,995	4.6	9.6	34.9
48 30920	Greenville	16,682	58.3	16.6	20,101	62.3	7.6	39.3	24.2	38,829	13.4	34.2	10.8
48 31928	Haltom	26,180	58.6	14.3	30,971	72.6	7.5	47.6	18.6	40,826	13.6	27.8	11.4
48 32312	Harker Heights	12,138	30.9	32.8	14,279	70.3	5.8	46.5	16.8	59,150	8.1	13.1	18.8
48 32372	Harlingen	37,522	57.0	16.9	45,850	49.9	5.7	34.6	37.3	31,011	26.0	41.3	10.5
48 35000	Houston	1,278,180	51.6	27.1	1,544,747	67.2	8.3	43.0	21.3	40,285	18.1	31.1	15.8
48 35528	Huntsville	21,451	54.4	20.6	33,139	41.7	10.9	17.9	30.2	27,054	21.7	45.7	6.7
48 35576	Hurst	24,140	39.7	26.1	28,821	67.6	7.6	43.0	25.5	50,441	7.9	19.7	20.2
48 37000	Irving	133,799	46.9	28.3	161,843	74.3	7.3	48.7	15.5	46,574	12.2	23.4	15.8
48 38632	Keller	22,911	20.6	47.7	25,951	73.1	2.8	50.6	12.1	107,518	2.5	6.7	55.8
48 39040	Kerrville	15,710	48.4	23.2	18,536	50.8	4.2	30.5	38.4	39,243	7.3	26.6	12.3
48 39148	Killeen	58,213	39.2	16.1	70,871	72.4	8.3	49.5	18.4	44,786	13.2	23.5	8.5
48 39352	Kingsville	13,572	55.9	17.1	18,867	59.1	9.8	32.4	31.1	31,228	25.7	41.2	7.0
48 39952	Kyle	9,562	39.6	25.4	11,140	-	-	54.6	10.8	67,636	4.8	9.9	18.7
48 40588	Lake Jackson	17,230	28.1	32.7	20,896	66.3	3.3	45.3	21.1	68,051	4.2	11.3	32.3
48 41212	Lancaster	17,882	44.6	21.1	21,508	70.8	6.8	49.7	17.1	47,258	10.8	21.1	10.0
48 41440	La Porte	23,019	51.1	14.5	27,732	68.2	5.8	46.3	17.7	63,913	7.1	16.6	22.2
48 41464	Laredo	110,790	62.6	17.1	141,301	63.1	8.5	36.6	21.7	34,958	26.7	38.5	9.2
48 41980	League	41,331	26.5	39.5	47,297	73.8	4.5	50.8	13.9	78,250	5.2	10.6	32.8
48 42016	Leander	12,890	40.1	26.9	14,818	-	-	46.1	12.3	68,729	5.3	12.6	21.9
48 42508	Lewisville	55,777	37.3	31.8	65,863	81.1	7.0	52.7	11.5	51,184	5.6	15.4	18.4
48 43012	Little Elm	11,537	34.7	29.6	12,937	-	-	57.2	6.9	73,870	1.2	4.9	20.8
48 43888	Longview	48,973	45.9	24.0	59,021	64.4	7.7	39.6	27.7	38,339	12.5	29.4	13.7
48 45000	Lubbock	123,040	43.3	29.1	166,634	65.2	6.8	38.0	24.0	38,777	12.3	32.2	11.3
48 45072	Lufkin	21,500	52.1	21.9	26,139	60.5	9.2	38.5	27.8	38,890	12.9	30.3	12.6
48 45384	McAllen	68,557	49.0	26.2	85,921	61.1	7.0	36.4	23.9	38,871	24.0	35.2	12.6
48 45744	McKinney	64,931	25.5	42.0	76,531	72.4	4.3	48.1	14.7	74,790	6.1	13.7	35.0
48 46452	Mansfield	29,628	35.3	34.8	34,695	72.0	3.5	50.1	11.8	83,296	4.9	12.0	38.1
48 46776	Marshall	14,726	53.7	20.5	18,835	59.2	12.0	30.7	32.6	32,400	25.5	39.3	11.9
48 47892	Mesquite	82,739	50.5	20.0	99,262	71.5	5.9	48.4	16.5	51,453	7.6	19.0	14.8
48 48072	Midland	62,431	44.8	27.4	76,859	66.6	3.4	40.0	21.8	46,976	10.8	27.8	19.5
48 48768	Mission	37,879	57.4	18.5	45,193	55.1	7.8	34.1	33.4	36,265	22.4	35.8	11.6
48 48772	Mission Bend CDP	21,616	46.3	24.7	27,365	68.7	6.1	47.0	10.0	57,386	8.2	12.7	22.6
48 48804	Missouri	40,596	30.6	42.4	49,375	70.9	6.1	44.8	13.8	79,471	7.7	10.8	36.0
48 50256	Nacogdoches	14,618	47.1	32.5	24,309	62.7	8.8	28.7	32.5	25,956	14.7	48.9	9.5
48 50820	New Braunfels	32,721	43.2	27.9	38,962	64.2	5.0	40.5	24.9	53,471	7.7	23.6	20.3
48 52356	North Richland Hills	42,443	36.3	28.5	50,074	68.1	4.6	46.2	17.3	63,006	6.8	15.3	23.0
48 53388	Odessa	56,725	55.6	15.2	70,482	64.4	4.3	41.4	23.4	41,924	14.1	30.2	13.0
48 55080	Paris	16,647	56.1	14.9	20,002	56.9	11.1	32.3	40.8	29,067	19.6	40.9	7.0
48 56000	Pasadena	89,591	63.0	14.0	109,436	67.1	9.6	42.2	20.9	45,127	15.2	26.7	14.4
48 56348	Pearland	44,161	27.1	41.3	51,470	75.0	3.5	51.3	13.2	83,706	3.6	9.3	37.6
48 57176	Pflugerville	21,887	33.6	34.0	25,426	79.5	3.5	54.6	12.4	82,338	4.3	9.6	34.1
48 57200	Pharr	32,110	71.2	13.0	40,302	58.7	10.1	31.2	29.3	27,031	36.1	48.0	4.4
48 57980	Plainview	12,233	62.4	18.3	15,334	64.4	5.8	38.9	24.1	32,546	16.5	37.3	7.0
48 58016	Plano	167,652	21.7	52.2	196,828	72.8	4.7	49.5	13.0	79,687	3.7	10.6	40.1
48 58820	Port Arthur	32,453	60.9	11.4	39,758	53.5	12.8	29.9	38.2	27,386	20.0	43.7	6.9
48 61796	Richardson	69,707	25.8	49.2	81,225	68.0	4.1	45.1	18.2	68,436	4.3	15.6	28.4
48 62828	Rockwall	18,588	28.1	39.6	22,014	72.6	4.7	49.7	13.3	79,152	1.7	7.5	38.5
48 63284	Rosenberg	16,790	64.0	8.5	20,996	69.1	9.6	46.5	22.8	44,004	14.7	28.6	12.0
48 63500	Round Rock	50,690	32.4	35.6	62,253	77.0	6.7	51.7	10.7	67,492	4.5	10.1	27.1
48 63572	Rowlett	35,251	36.3	30.3	41,408	71.7	3.8	49.8	13.0	78,043	3.1	7.2	33.5
48 64472	San Angelo	54,673	49.0	21.8	69,659	65.1	4.7	39.5	27.6	36,917	14.7	33.4	9.4
48 65000	San Antonio	775,924	48.8	23.1	948,693	63.9	6.6	40.5	25.1	42,217	14.7	29.2	13.8
48 65036	San Benito	14,958	67.1	8.5	18,851	49.8	10.6	26.2	37.1	26,702	28.0	46.9	3.7
48 65516	San Juan	17,155	77.1	8.8	22,968	58.2	12.3	28.5	24.0	27,371	31.6	42.8	2.2
48 65600	San Marcos	18,825	48.9	26.0	38,785	66.6	10.3	27.4	22.2	26,641	10.3	46.0	6.9
48 66128	Schertz	16,920	33.9	31.3	20,942	67.3	7.4	43.1	21.6	69,213	2.4	10.7	26.4
48 66644	Seguin	15,249	65.8	13.5	18,692	61.0	5.0	38.1	30.6	37,919	15.9	35.8	8.4
48 67496	Sherman	24,510	49.7	21.0	30,883	61.0	8.8	35.4	31.9	38,679	12.9	30.5	7.8
48 68636	Socorro	16,148	75.7	5.0	21,043	54.8	10.9	29.3	26.4	28,017	31.3	45.0	2.6
48 69032	Southlake	14,739	8.9	68.7	17,320	69.0	2.6	45.7	7.7	172,945	1.6	5.0	79.6

Table B-4. Cities — What: Education, Employment, and Income, 2005–2007—*Continued*

STATE Place code	STATE City	Educational attainment			Employment status				Percent of households with no workers	Median household income (dollars)	Percent of families with income below poverty	Percent of households with income less than $25,000	Percent of households with income of $100,000 or more
		Total population 25 years and over	Percent with a high school diploma or less	Percent with a bachelor's degree or more	Total population 16 years and over	Percent in the labor force	Unemployment rate	Percent who worked full-time, year-round					
	ACS table number:	C15002	C15002	C15002	C20005	C23001	C23001	C20005	C08202	B19013	C17015	C19001	C19001
		1	2	3	4	5	6	7	8	9	10	11	12
	Texas—Cont.												
48 69596	Spring CDP	30,279	39.4	21.9	35,434	72.2	5.4	50.4	13.4	64,968	7.2	11.7	23.6
48 70808	Sugar Land	47,983	23.8	53.7	56,471	66.7	6.1	42.9	15.6	94,895	4.6	9.1	47.7
48 72176	Temple	38,621	44.8	25.6	44,594	61.2	4.1	42.5	28.7	41,719	9.9	28.2	12.4
48 72368	Texarkana	23,286	48.8	21.1	27,839	61.5	9.9	36.4	32.4	36,852	16.1	37.4	11.8
48 72392	Texas	28,563	55.5	10.0	34,843	59.3	10.2	36.7	28.8	36,660	14.3	32.8	9.6
48 72530	The Colony	23,232	30.4	33.2	28,328	78.5	5.5	57.1	9.1	74,580	3.0	6.7	28.0
48 72656	The Woodlands CDP	38,835	16.4	56.4	46,750	64.5	4.1	42.3	19.2	89,597	5.4	12.8	44.6
48 74144	Tyler	56,418	42.6	26.5	70,398	62.8	8.8	34.6	29.7	38,904	15.8	33.3	14.6
48 74492	University Park	12,580	4.6	83.4	16,434	60.4	4.6	36.1	15.2	151,418	2.5	9.0	63.4
48 75428	Victoria	39,381	51.9	17.0	47,768	65.0	8.3	40.1	27.6	40,171	12.9	28.5	12.3
48 76000	Waco	64,253	53.5	19.6	90,495	59.3	10.8	32.2	32.0	30,354	19.0	44.0	8.5
48 76672	Watauga	14,639	44.1	19.6	16,702	76.9	5.1	53.8	11.6	64,197	6.5	11.8	15.3
48 76816	Waxahachie	14,890	56.0	15.3	19,270	63.8	8.1	40.0	27.1	40,589	14.1	30.0	10.4
48 76864	Weatherford	14,573	45.9	21.2	17,654	-	-	42.1	26.2	50,833	5.4	24.2	12.4
48 77272	Weslaco	20,296	61.7	16.5	24,359	53.1	9.5	29.3	39.8	27,615	31.1	44.9	8.3
48 79000	Wichita Falls	61,926	49.0	21.9	79,469	63.3	5.0	37.6	25.9	37,603	12.8	31.7	10.9
48 80356	Wylie	19,182	37.5	26.5	22,764	-	-	48.7	11.7	69,189	6.5	12.6	20.5
49 00000	**Utah**	1,449,914	36.3	28.2	1,862,740	69.4	4.6	39.9	18.8	53,324	7.4	18.6	17.4
49 01310	American Fork	14,972	28.9	31.2	18,148	65.6	2.0	39.5	16.7	64,634	3.3	11.0	19.5
49 07690	Bountiful	26,048	24.7	37.9	31,869	64.6	3.3	38.5	21.6	61,237	4.0	12.7	25.8
49 11320	Cedar	12,359	32.9	29.8	19,514	66.6	6.7	32.3	18.0	38,339	15.3	29.7	9.2
49 13850	Clearfield	13,645	48.6	14.7	20,097	68.2	6.7	38.7	19.1	42,642	13.9	26.1	7.2
49 16270	Cottonwood Heights	22,629	21.3	42.6	27,112	71.6	3.4	39.9	19.1	65,463	3.8	15.1	28.6
49 20120	Draper	20,887	22.6	38.8	24,274	62.9	5.0	41.0	10.6	80,524	4.5	7.4	37.7
49 36070	Holladay	18,418	18.2	46.3	21,496	66.1	3.6	37.0	23.8	63,222	4.4	13.9	31.2
49 40360	Kaysville	13,094	23.2	38.1	16,491	68.5	4.3	37.6	14.8	73,049	4.2	9.1	32.0
49 40470	Kearns CDP	18,520	55.5	11.4	23,823	75.8	3.3	51.4	12.0	51,732	5.9	12.6	9.1
49 43060	Layton	34,977	34.4	30.5	45,449	73.7	3.6	44.9	14.0	61,596	4.1	12.8	19.4
49 44320	Lehi	17,463	26.6	30.8	21,152	72.2	2.6	43.1	12.1	63,430	2.8	9.5	17.6
49 45860	Logan	21,449	28.3	37.0	37,332	73.3	5.3	28.9	15.5	33,007	14.7	36.4	10.6
49 47290	Magna CDP	12,960	55.5	9.8	16,732	75.1	7.5	46.8	16.7	50,531	10.0	17.8	9.7
49 49710	Midvale	20,277	49.5	17.2	24,784	72.2	6.3	44.5	20.8	44,440	11.3	20.0	8.7
49 50150	Millcreek CDP	20,194	34.6	32.4	23,970	67.8	4.4	41.7	24.9	42,790	12.3	25.3	9.4
49 53230	Murray	29,221	36.4	28.1	36,775	70.1	4.4	42.4	21.0	51,173	6.3	18.8	15.3
49 55980	Ogden	46,432	49.0	18.3	58,300	67.2	8.1	40.3	24.8	39,711	16.6	31.5	8.4
49 57300	Orem	45,658	24.7	38.0	62,194	68.7	3.4	36.4	17.0	49,558	8.8	17.7	16.5
49 60930	Pleasant Grove	15,479	23.0	38.3	20,096	71.9	4.3	39.8	12.8	62,415	5.1	9.5	23.1
49 62470	Provo	46,566	23.0	41.4	92,610	64.4	5.6	23.1	16.8	36,258	17.5	34.2	11.0
49 64340	Riverton	18,451	32.8	28.6	22,758	74.3	3.8	44.5	8.9	78,411	2.4	6.0	33.1
49 65110	Roy	21,596	42.2	17.8	25,957	73.9	4.3	47.6	15.4	56,092	3.7	10.5	14.2
49 65330	St. George	40,970	39.3	22.0	51,863	59.9	4.4	34.7	34.0	44,782	4.8	19.4	11.9
49 67000	Salt Lake	117,555	33.6	37.0	143,706	69.4	4.9	39.5	23.6	41,864	12.8	29.5	15.3
49 67440	Sandy	53,522	26.6	35.8	67,572	73.8	3.8	43.5	13.1	73,322	3.1	10.7	33.5
49 70850	South Jordan	21,694	26.7	35.8	27,472	74.3	3.5	42.2	12.6	85,311	1.0	4.6	38.2
49 71070	South Salt Lake	13,861	56.7	14.9	17,523	64.4	9.0	37.1	22.4	31,868	17.2	36.8	5.7
49 71290	Spanish Fork	15,264	38.8	24.6	19,560	71.2	6.6	38.7	13.1	57,252	4.9	13.7	10.7
49 72280	Springville	13,110	32.0	28.9	16,562	69.4	4.9	40.4	14.7	50,902	9.9	17.4	12.8
49 74810	Syracuse	9,824	28.0	32.7	12,443	77.0	3.5	49.7	9.8	75,165	1.9	3.7	26.0
49 75360	Taylorsville	35,235	41.9	19.6	44,470	75.5	5.2	46.2	15.2	53,573	5.9	16.4	13.0
49 76680	Tooele	16,597	44.2	16.0	20,350	70.2	7.0	45.6	17.4	53,175	7.5	16.1	10.1
49 82950	West Jordan	52,228	39.3	22.1	66,529	77.3	3.1	47.1	10.1	62,374	3.5	9.5	17.5
49 83470	West Valley	69,668	57.9	11.3	86,441	74.0	5.1	47.3	14.1	49,022	9.3	20.0	10.0
50 00000	**Vermont**	424,832	42.7	32.7	505,187	69.0	5.2	40.6	25.0	49,382	6.9	23.8	16.4
50 10675	Burlington	22,314	33.4	43.4	33,390	67.1	7.5	30.7	25.3	38,288	13.5	32.0	12.3
51 00000	**Virginia**	5,053,592	41.8	32.9	6,025,175	67.1	4.8	44.7	23.2	58,378	7.1	19.7	25.0
51 01000	Alexandria	103,579	22.7	59.7	113,557	75.3	3.6	55.6	18.6	77,797	4.7	11.7	37.7
51 01912	Annandale CDP	38,767	26.2	51.0	43,673	70.3	2.5	47.3	18.1	90,711	2.5	7.5	46.1
51 03000	Arlington CDP	151,102	20.2	67.0	169,317	76.5	2.5	55.6	16.5	90,047	4.5	10.8	44.6
51 04088	Bailey's Crossroads CDP	14,527	40.9	41.6	17,918	76.9	5.3	50.8	22.1	68,929	19.1	20.6	31.2
51 07784	Blacksburg town	13,974	12.4	74.3	38,519	51.2	8.2	19.6	23.5	31,605	11.8	43.8	14.2
51 11464	Burke CDP	37,455	17.9	59.5	45,249	73.1	3.8	49.2	12.1	113,034	1.0	4.3	59.1
51 13720	Cave Spring CDP	17,376	23.8	45.1	20,224	69.7	2.2	49.1	27.7	57,100	2.5	16.1	26.1
51 14440	Centreville CDP	33,462	25.9	50.6	40,219	78.1	5.0	52.7	9.3	87,932	4.4	8.1	42.2
51 14744	Chantilly CDP	29,165	19.3	59.7	34,840	76.1	2.3	53.0	12.0	105,838	2.3	4.7	53.6
51 14968	Charlottesville	23,828	37.5	43.8	34,792	59.5	4.8	32.1	32.1	36,013	10.8	37.9	12.4
51 16000	Chesapeake	138,804	41.1	26.6	167,814	69.4	4.9	46.1	19.7	63,113	4.9	15.3	24.4
51 16096	Chester CDP	12,994	47.3	27.3	15,612	72.4	6.5	47.4	23.3	56,104	16.7	21.1	19.7
51 21088	Dale CDP	38,180	42.4	26.5	46,698	77.6	4.5	54.0	11.3	79,075	2.8	7.1	33.1
51 21344	Danville	31,681	57.9	14.3	36,642	54.9	12.8	30.4	41.4	29,528	19.8	43.6	6.9
51 26496	Fairfax	16,180	28.4	48.9	18,808	69.1	4.4	46.1	18.9	93,441	1.2	7.0	44.8
51 29552	Franconia CDP	23,868	20.1	61.2	27,412	74.8	1.3	56.4	11.6	100,161	2.4	5.2	50.1
51 29744	Fredericksburg	12,701	47.0	29.8	17,641	57.6	5.0	34.6	29.4	42,909	5.2	29.9	16.4
51 33584	Groveton CDP	14,132	39.5	39.9	16,947	74.0	3.3	52.8	16.0	71,582	4.7	9.1	33.7
51 35000	Hampton	94,048	46.0	20.7	116,707	66.8	6.9	44.9	24.9	47,408	9.9	22.9	11.9

STATE Place code	STATE City	Educational attainment			Employment status					Percent of households with no workers	Median household income (dollars)	Percent of families with income below poverty	Percent of households with income less than $25,000	Percent of households with income of $100,000 or more
		Total population 25 years and over	Percent with a high school diploma or less	Percent with a bachelor's degree or more	Total population 16 years and over	Percent in the labor force	Unemployment rate	Percent who worked full-time, year-round						
	ACS table number:	C15002	C15002	C15002	C20005	C23001	C23001	C20005	C08202	B19013	C17015	C19001	C19001
		1	2	3	4	5	6	7	8	9	10	11	12
	Virginia—Cont.												
51 35624	Harrisonburg	19,360	51.3	33.1	37,101	52.7	5.8	23.8	27.4	34,905	8.4	37.1	10.6
51 36648	Herndon town	11,501	35.7	42.9	13,010	-	-	50.5	12.6	92,947	-	10.8	43.8
51 38424	Hopewell	14,600	60.6	11.1	16,841	61.5	5.6	42.9	31.8	39,931	10.2	29.5	5.4
51 40584	Jefferson CDP	19,244	37.0	40.1	21,407	69.5	2.3	50.3	18.7	80,924	4.7	10.3	36.2
51 43432	Lake Ridge CDP	20,965	22.3	48.2	24,523	77.6	5.0	54.5	11.9	93,430	1.9	5.2	45.5
51 44984	Leesburg town	22,797	24.2	51.7	26,748	76.3	1.9	51.8	10.4	87,346	-	7.0	40.9
51 45957	Linton Hall CDP	11,856	22.9	50.3	13,029	-	-	58.1	5.4	115,581	-	3.6	62.2
51 47064	Lorton CDP	15,489	30.1	45.9	18,942	79.7	3.1	55.4	7.2	83,911	-	6.3	37.9
51 47672	Lynchburg	42,299	48.0	27.8	56,786	57.9	7.3	30.7	32.5	36,385	15.1	33.8	11.2
51 48376	McLean CDP	28,306	9.0	79.3	31,616	64.5	1.9	42.9	20.1	156,292	1.4	5.5	71.5
51 48952	Manassas	22,455	47.3	26.4	26,699	71.0	4.8	51.4	15.4	74,221	6.8	10.5	36.2
51 50856	Mechanicsville CDP	23,323	36.9	30.8	27,267	70.7	3.1	50.1	20.6	69,438	2.0	9.6	27.8
51 54144	Mount Vernon CDP	22,139	43.2	34.1	26,008	71.5	6.1	51.2	16.2	76,524	6.0	9.8	40.0
51 55752	Newington CDP	14,558	22.9	56.7	16,925	72.5	2.5	49.8	13.2	112,675	2.1	4.6	60.8
51 56000	Newport News	111,233	42.2	21.7	134,565	69.1	6.1	44.1	23.5	46,082	11.2	25.9	12.0
51 57000	Norfolk	137,679	48.2	22.9	182,896	68.5	6.8	44.5	26.2	40,361	14.0	29.1	11.3
51 58472	Oakton CDP	23,005	17.1	68.6	26,652	70.6	4.3	50.9	13.8	107,537	4.5	8.5	53.8
51 61832	Petersburg	21,546	64.4	15.3	25,235	61.0	13.9	40.0	33.7	34,573	10.2	31.5	5.8
51 64000	Portsmouth	63,660	50.6	18.5	78,305	65.1	6.7	42.1	28.9	43,473	11.7	26.7	11.8
51 66672	Reston CDP	37,297	14.5	68.3	41,582	73.8	3.2	51.2	16.3	93,417	3.4	9.0	46.1
51 67000	Richmond	129,899	46.7	32.0	159,089	63.4	10.6	37.1	31.3	37,442	16.2	33.8	12.9
51 68000	Roanoke	65,332	51.7	20.6	73,831	61.1	6.9	38.0	34.9	35,530	13.7	32.9	8.5
51 70000	Salem	16,803	48.6	23.1	20,815	64.5	4.3	39.3	27.0	46,997	3.6	21.3	12.1
51 74592	Springfield CDP	23,770	32.1	40.6	27,439	67.9	5.8	45.5	28.3	77,188	7.6	12.0	35.6
51 75216	Staunton	16,649	52.8	23.4	19,175	58.6	3.6	36.5	30.1	39,756	10.3	32.1	7.2
51 76432	Suffolk	51,035	46.0	23.4	60,748	68.0	5.7	45.8	22.8	61,464	9.0	19.8	22.1
51 79560	Tuckahoe CDP	32,068	24.1	50.8	36,608	67.4	2.7	46.2	23.7	66,203	5.6	11.3	30.9
51 82000	Virginia Beach	282,498	34.0	31.1	337,218	72.3	3.7	48.8	18.5	62,477	5.2	13.0	23.3
51 83680	Waynesboro	14,821	59.6	21.4	16,813	-	-	38.2	34.8	44,039	11.0	29.0	9.0
51 84976	West Springfield CDP	19,478	18.0	60.0	22,350	70.1	4.4	43.9	14.6	97,203	1.6	3.6	48.3
51 86720	Winchester	17,182	50.3	26.9	20,780	66.9	5.8	41.0	28.0	43,760	6.1	22.6	14.8
51 87312	Woodbridge CDP	19,809	46.4	25.8	23,747	78.0	5.1	56.0	10.5	67,360	4.0	10.1	25.7
53 00000	**Washington**	4,243,790	36.7	30.0	5,028,054	65.9	6.5	38.1	25.6	53,940	8.0	21.3	20.7
53 03180	Auburn	31,890	46.8	19.2	37,762	63.6	6.3	39.7	29.4	47,104	10.8	26.3	15.7
53 03736	Bainbridge Island	15,799	11.4	64.5	17,712	62.9	4.3	30.5	28.9	88,243	4.9	14.8	45.5
53 05210	Bellevue	83,451	16.7	58.9	94,842	67.6	5.3	40.0	23.5	76,641	5.3	13.7	35.9
53 05280	Bellingham	44,529	30.8	37.1	64,592	64.9	6.4	27.9	29.5	37,405	9.3	35.1	11.3
53 07380	Bothell	23,028	26.3	40.8	26,620	71.6	4.2	41.5	21.7	63,445	4.9	16.7	31.0
53 07695	Bremerton	23,103	39.1	19.3	27,448	62.0	11.2	33.2	35.1	37,947	12.0	31.4	9.4
53 08850	Burien	21,846	43.3	25.2	25,565	67.6	5.0	39.3	26.7	49,700	8.7	23.0	17.1
53 10372	Cascade-Fairwood CDP	25,392	32.4	35.5	29,798	73.7	6.4	46.1	19.1	67,097	7.3	11.7	27.3
53 14940	Cottage Lake CDP	16,504	12.7	60.4	18,937	73.4	6.2	44.9	10.8	131,565	1.2	4.4	68.0
53 17635	Des Moines	21,571	36.6	21.7	24,448	59.7	5.1	37.3	23.6	54,698	3.4	16.2	21.2
53 19515	East Hill-Meridian CDP	19,178	40.0	28.8	22,533	70.3	6.2	43.4	18.7	66,143	6.1	12.8	26.7
53 20750	Edmonds	29,647	24.9	40.8	32,898	65.9	5.6	39.7	27.1	61,105	3.6	16.8	25.6
53 22640	Everett	64,185	44.0	20.4	77,467	69.3	8.1	41.9	25.9	45,069	11.8	26.1	11.4
53 23515	Federal Way	56,004	37.3	27.3	65,428	69.0	5.4	43.7	21.7	56,400	10.4	19.3	21.0
53 33380	Inglewood-Finn Hill CDP	19,073	23.6	45.9	21,585	71.1	5.3	45.2	16.0	90,301	2.9	9.0	40.5
53 33805	Issaquah	17,792	20.3	54.0	19,350	67.4	3.4	43.6	22.3	75,280	1.6	13.7	34.7
53 35170	Kenmore	14,718	23.8	45.8	16,824	-	-	42.9	16.1	79,847	3.8	10.2	38.6
53 35275	Kennewick	39,898	47.2	18.8	47,617	65.2	7.8	37.9	26.4	44,110	11.8	24.7	16.0
53 35415	Kent	55,467	41.1	24.4	66,665	71.2	6.0	43.5	19.9	52,641	9.7	19.9	19.5
53 35940	Kirkland	34,045	20.5	51.3	38,655	70.9	4.0	44.3	21.6	74,022	2.6	14.5	34.3
53 36745	Lacey	22,790	34.5	28.5	27,154	63.8	6.2	40.7	29.9	47,451	9.3	22.3	15.0
53 38038	Lakewood	38,085	40.8	24.8	45,468	60.9	7.0	36.8	29.8	45,096	13.2	24.9	13.7
53 40245	Longview	25,449	48.0	14.1	29,821	57.3	11.0	26.5	36.2	34,798	18.1	34.3	9.0
53 40840	Lynnwood	22,415	36.8	27.2	26,135	64.3	7.2	38.3	31.1	44,324	10.4	24.7	16.8
53 43955	Marysville	20,616	44.4	19.9	25,080	70.2	4.4	44.2	25.3	52,617	6.0	19.5	18.8
53 45005	Mercer Island	16,404	10.7	74.3	18,229	57.2	4.5	35.1	29.8	115,864	1.5	8.5	54.7
53 47490	Mountlake Terrace	13,671	32.2	27.4	16,035	69.0	3.4	43.1	24.0	52,128	7.7	15.5	13.5
53 47560	Mount Vernon	18,112	50.6	19.5	22,665	61.2	4.7	32.8	30.4	42,855	12.9	28.1	12.5
53 47735	Mukilteo	13,483	17.4	49.2	16,424	72.9	4.1	43.7	14.5	86,043	2.7	10.8	41.9
53 49665	North Creek CDP	19,481	25.0	36.4	23,015	75.4	3.9	49.2	12.7	78,228	3.5	8.5	36.3
53 49992	North Marysville CDP	13,421	46.9	14.0	15,894	70.3	6.8	43.1	19.8	65,694	3.5	10.4	15.7
53 50360	Oak Harbor	11,815	37.6	22.7	14,192	60.2	5.6	36.8	31.6	43,298	10.1	23.6	9.3
53 51300	Olympia	31,736	26.4	42.5	38,071	66.6	5.3	36.0	28.4	47,413	10.1	26.2	16.6
53 52765	Paine Field-Lake Stickney CDP	16,660	45.4	21.0	20,733	70.7	5.7	40.5	24.7	44,082	9.1	29.3	10.0
53 53335	Parkland CDP	16,249	52.3	13.5	21,975	66.4	8.9	37.6	25.6	43,264	14.5	27.2	8.5
53 53545	Pasco	24,973	60.9	12.7	32,058	67.4	8.7	38.8	23.5	40,687	16.9	27.9	12.1
53 54215	Picnic Point-North Lynnwood CDP	17,457	30.8	35.4	21,504	75.7	5.6	45.7	17.4	62,061	5.8	14.8	25.5
53 56625	Pullman	9,830	11.6	68.7	23,467	55.4	7.8	17.0	31.0	22,087	16.8	53.2	11.3
53 56695	Puyallup	25,096	38.2	22.6	29,172	65.5	5.9	37.8	24.8	52,418	7.2	17.7	19.3

Table B-4. Cities — What: Education, Employment, and Income, 2005–2007—*Continued*

STATE Place code	STATE City	Educational attainment			Employment status				Percent of households with no workers	Median household income (dollars)	Percent of families with income below poverty	Percent of households with income less than $25,000	Percent of households with income of $100,000 or more
		Total population 25 years and over	Percent with a high school diploma or less	Percent with a bachelor's degree or more	Total population 16 years and over	Percent in the labor force	Unemployment rate	Percent who worked full-time, year-round					
	ACS table number:	C15002	C15002	C15002	C20005	C23001	C23001	C20005	C08202	B19013	C17015	C19001	C19001
		1	2	3	4	5	6	7	8	9	10	11	12
	Washington—Cont.												
53 57535	Redmond..................	37,283	16.8	56.8	44,531	72.3	3.5	47.2	17.1	82,349	3.6	12.4	35.3
53 57745	Renton....................	41,288	36.0	29.3	47,861	71.8	6.5	47.4	22.0	53,654	8.6	18.5	15.9
53 58235	Richland..................	29,044	27.1	37.5	34,371	64.7	8.0	38.3	24.3	60,100	6.5	18.3	28.2
53 61115	Sammamish	28,379	11.3	68.3	32,200	70.3	3.2	46.3	11.4	122,750	1.4	4.6	64.9
53 62288	SeaTac....................	15,244	52.9	14.6	17,579	65.8	5.3	43.4	23.7	44,226	11.6	26.6	11.6
53 63000	Seattle...................	419,208	22.9	52.5	486,432	70.7	5.9	40.4	23.9	56,319	7.3	22.3	26.0
53 63052	Seattle Hill-Silver Firs CDP....	24,344	29.5	31.4	28,159	75.6	4.2	48.1	9.9	93,262	1.5	3.3	45.4
53 63960	Shoreline	38,743	29.2	41.3	43,516	66.6	4.4	40.1	23.9	61,238	4.1	18.5	23.7
53 65922	South Hill CDP	28,993	32.7	30.0	34,397	74.2	6.2	47.8	14.9	74,639	2.9	8.8	31.2
53 66255	Spanaway CDP	16,520	50.8	11.3	19,364	67.8	8.1	42.1	20.3	56,083	7.4	16.4	16.9
53 67000	Spokane	135,665	35.1	26.5	164,930	63.1	7.1	33.6	29.9	37,899	11.4	32.1	9.3
53 67167	Spokane Valley..........	56,919	41.0	20.5	66,286	66.5	7.2	39.5	29.0	42,524	9.0	28.2	9.9
53 70000	Tacoma..................	129,617	43.8	23.2	152,789	63.1	7.6	38.2	29.9	44,533	12.1	27.2	14.2
53 73465	University Place	21,445	32.5	34.2	26,110	68.3	6.2	40.0	27.2	49,825	9.0	21.8	18.3
53 74060	Vancouver...............	106,906	38.8	23.6	125,277	66.3	8.1	38.8	27.5	46,574	11.0	24.2	14.7
53 75775	Walla Walla	20,190	46.1	21.1	26,075	52.7	9.4	26.2	32.9	36,906	16.9	36.5	7.3
53 77105	Wenatchee	19,884	49.2	22.1	24,049	61.4	7.8	34.0	33.1	40,945	12.9	30.4	10.6
53 80010	Yakima...................	51,836	54.4	18.5	64,066	63.0	10.6	34.4	30.4	35,820	15.3	35.3	10.4
54 00000	**West Virginia**.........	1,257,231	60.9	16.9	1,466,327	55.3	6.9	34.0	36.1	36,088	13.3	35.6	9.1
54 14600	Charleston	37,355	40.4	35.6	41,704	61.5	6.6	37.8	33.3	37,955	13.4	35.8	14.9
54 39460	Huntington	31,433	50.1	21.0	40,669	54.0	8.0	28.8	41.3	27,382	21.0	45.3	7.1
54 55756	Morgantown	11,435	37.3	43.2	25,082	49.5	6.4	21.0	30.1	26,937	12.3	47.3	11.1
54 62140	Parkersburg	22,202	57.7	14.0	25,588	54.3	10.3	29.2	38.9	30,817	20.4	43.1	6.6
54 86452	Wheeling	20,784	51.0	24.7	24,237	58.1	8.2	33.0	40.4	30,355	15.8	42.2	7.5
55 00000	**Wisconsin**...............	3,692,408	46.2	25.1	4,408,022	68.7	5.8	41.5	25.0	50,309	7.1	22.6	15.6
55 02375	Appleton	45,458	40.4	31.3	55,256	72.3	6.1	41.8	21.6	51,190	8.9	24.1	14.0
55 06500	Beloit	21,634	64.4	13.5	26,120	65.7	10.9	37.4	32.4	35,300	17.4	32.8	5.0
55 10025	Brookfield	26,476	22.4	55.0	30,277	61.3	4.8	37.5	29.9	82,091	1.5	9.7	40.9
55 11950	Caledonia village...........	19,638	37.6	37.6	21,598	65.2	4.1	42.9	18.9	66,410	2.1	13.1	23.8
55 19775	De Pere	14,673	33.3	34.5	18,649	71.2	5.7	42.2	24.0	49,852	4.1	21.2	17.7
55 22300	Eau Claire	37,567	35.4	31.5	52,958	70.0	5.3	35.4	23.9	39,900	8.6	30.1	10.9
55 25950	Fitchburg	16,455	25.1	48.6	19,197	74.1	6.0	47.9	15.1	69,415	5.9	14.3	26.8
55 26275	Fond du Lac	27,740	53.5	17.6	33,360	68.3	6.5	41.2	27.0	44,610	7.1	26.3	8.5
55 27300	Franklin	24,601	37.8	33.2	28,474	64.3	2.5	40.8	22.4	70,421	2.9	10.8	29.0
55 31000	Green Bay	63,894	51.6	20.8	77,523	69.3	7.2	41.1	26.9	42,088	12.3	29.8	10.4
55 31175	Greenfield...............	27,321	44.0	24.6	31,305	65.1	4.7	42.1	31.7	51,297	2.2	17.5	16.8
55 37825	Janesville................	41,519	49.1	21.2	48,494	66.1	5.9	39.4	29.5	48,502	7.5	21.6	12.9
55 39225	Kenosha	60,802	50.2	18.8	73,305	64.8	8.6	37.6	26.4	46,440	11.2	25.0	12.8
55 40775	La Crosse	29,439	40.0	28.6	43,222	65.5	6.8	33.6	28.9	35,929	10.3	35.7	7.1
55 48000	Madison	136,101	24.2	50.9	184,881	71.3	4.4	38.5	20.7	50,852	7.3	23.0	17.9
55 48500	Manitowoc	22,591	52.2	17.9	26,434	65.0	7.7	39.1	32.3	40,433	7.4	28.2	9.2
55 51000	Menomonee Falls village	23,737	38.2	36.2	27,750	69.3	3.1	43.7	24.7	68,366	1.6	13.3	28.0
55 51150	Mequon	15,316	16.4	63.4	18,380	63.5	4.0	36.7	23.6	97,797	1.5	8.2	48.4
55 53000	Milwaukee	352,774	54.0	19.7	437,227	64.8	11.4	36.9	29.1	35,233	20.5	35.8	7.4
55 54875	Mount Pleasant village	17,580	41.0	24.1	19,534	64.9	4.6	40.7	27.8	55,577	3.0	16.9	21.9
55 55275	Muskego	15,211	36.5	33.6	17,972	73.8	3.3	46.2	17.1	80,924	2.1	11.5	34.9
55 55750	Neenah...................	16,048	44.7	23.4	18,628	73.4	5.8	46.1	24.2	54,251	5.7	19.0	13.8
55 56375	New Berlin	26,703	33.0	39.0	30,196	71.6	3.8	46.4	22.0	75,972	1.4	10.9	33.0
55 58800	Oak Creek	23,271	45.5	22.3	26,505	71.7	5.1	48.7	20.8	65,016	5.3	16.4	22.6
55 60500	Oshkosh	41,507	49.4	23.7	55,350	62.7	5.5	33.5	26.5	42,298	7.3	28.9	8.8
55 66000	Racine	47,401	55.2	16.6	57,821	67.1	7.9	39.4	26.2	40,325	13.5	30.8	8.4
55 72975	Sheboygan...............	32,240	55.8	18.0	38,646	68.7	6.7	42.0	26.7	41,302	8.5	25.2	7.9
55 75125	South Milwaukee..............	14,844	53.3	18.0	16,643	64.9	3.4	41.0	29.7	50,046	6.0	22.7	12.4
55 77200	Stevens Point	12,883	42.1	32.6	21,186	65.5	7.5	29.8	25.9	39,529	10.0	31.4	9.9
55 78600	Sun Prairie	17,463	25.3	39.5	20,480	77.2	5.6	49.9	15.5	64,681	3.4	13.3	27.1
55 78650	Superior..................	17,440	46.1	19.3	21,528	65.8	5.0	34.8	30.9	37,655	10.5	33.8	10.6
55 83975	Watertown...............	15,476	54.3	17.2	18,490	72.7	8.8	43.6	23.2	48,822	7.7	23.3	11.0
55 84250	Waukesha	42,797	38.3	32.7	52,888	72.8	4.1	44.5	23.2	52,994	5.6	20.7	16.9
55 84475	Wausau	25,568	47.5	22.6	30,001	66.5	7.3	40.2	29.1	41,296	6.9	28.4	11.9
55 84675	Wauwatosa..............	35,333	23.9	51.2	39,484	67.6	3.5	42.4	23.6	65,827	2.3	14.6	28.3
55 85300	West Allis................	43,542	52.7	17.8	50,143	66.8	7.1	43.8	30.0	43,475	7.2	25.7	7.6
55 85350	West Bend...............	19,804	47.1	21.4	23,424	72.7	5.0	45.9	24.8	51,259	5.5	22.9	12.6
56 00000	**Wyoming**	336,599	42.1	23.1	405,511	70.0	4.1	42.5	22.7	50,009	5.7	22.5	15.7
56 13150	Casper....................	33,814	39.5	21.3	40,961	67.6	4.4	42.4	24.0	46,669	7.3	25.9	15.9
56 13900	Cheyenne	36,944	37.5	22.5	42,952	69.1	4.3	44.5	24.6	46,544	4.2	22.4	12.4
56 31855	Gillette...................	14,696	47.1	17.5	18,031	82.2	4.8	51.2	13.8	65,275	4.2	15.5	30.4
56 45050	Laramie..................	13,859	23.4	52.1	23,414	68.9	4.1	32.3	20.0	38,439	9.1	34.0	13.2

Where
Migration, Housing, and Transportation

Where: Migration, Housing, and Transportation

Migration

An important question that the ACS can help to answer is how many people have moved recently, and from where to where. Nationally, 83.4 percent of Americans lived in the same home as they did one year earlier. However, there was much variation among the smaller geographic areas. About one-third of those people who moved stayed in the same city or town, and just one in five moved to a new state.

Among the states, Nevada had the highest proportion of movers (21.7 percent) and New Jersey had the lowest proportion (11.7 percent). The District of Columbia and Hawaii had the highest percentages of residents who moved from abroad. The District of Columbia (8.9 percent), Alaska (5.6 percent), and Nevada (5.6 percent) had the highest proportions of movers from other states. California, Michigan, and New York had the lowest proportion of movers from out of state—each with 1.4 percent.

In five metropolitan areas, about 90 percent of the residents had not moved in the past year. Most of these were smaller metropolitan areas, but among them was New York—the metropolitan area with the largest population. There were four metropolitan areas where less than 70 percent of the population had lived in the same house—all of them with large student or military populations: Ames, IA; Hinesville-Fort Stewart, GA; Ithaca, NY; and Jacksonville, NC. These same large college and military populations were areas where 15 to 20 percent of the population had moved into the metropolitan area within one year. In seven metropolitan areas, less than 3 percent of the population was new to the area. The New York metropolitan area had the lowest level of in-migration (2.1 percent). The other metropolitan areas with few new residents proportional to the total population were Detroit, MI; Chicago, IL; Houma, LA; Cleveland, OH; and Pittsburgh, PA.

In eight counties, more than 20 percent of the population had moved into the county within the past year. These were all small counties with universities or military bases. Among larger counties, 15.3 percent of the residents of Pinal County, AZ, (near Phoenix) had moved into the county within the past year, and 14 percent of the population of Richland County, SC, (near Columbia) were new residents in that county. Harlan County, KY, had the lowest level of in-migration with new residents comprising only 1.1 percent of its population. Most of the counties with low proportions of new residents had small populations, with the exception of New York City. Only 1.7 percent of the residents of Richmond County (Staten Island) had moved there within the year, and Kings (Brooklyn), Bronx, and Queens Counties were all in the bottom 20 rates of in-migration. However, despite their low proportions, these four counties had nearly 150,000 new residents in a year, and New York City's fifth borough—New York County—had almost 100,000 new residents, more than 6 percent of its population.

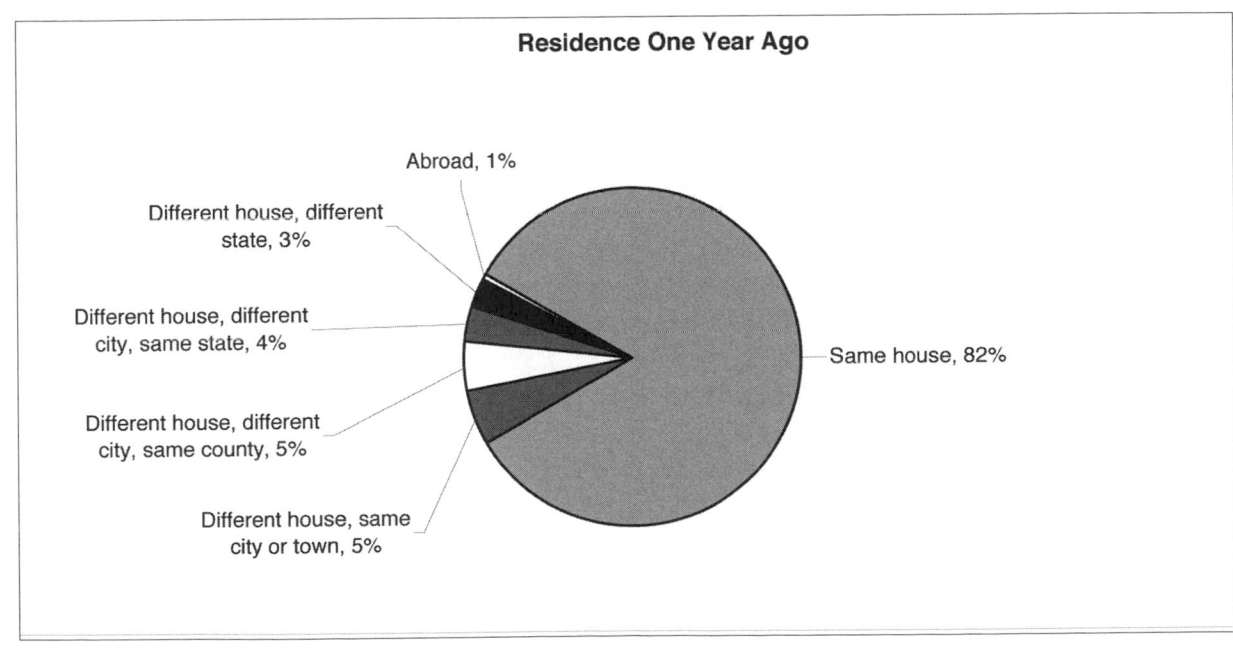

In nine cities, more than 95 percent of the residents lived in the same house they had lived in one year earlier. All were relatively small cities. Walnut, CA, (95.1 percent) was the only one of these cities not in the New York metropolitan area. The other eight were suburban cities in New York, New Jersey, and Connecticut. At the other extreme, less than half of the population in 10 cities lived in the same house a year earlier. These were also small cities, all with universities or military bases. Among larger cities, in-migrants within the past year included 13.5 percent of the residents of Raleigh, NC, and 13 percent of the residents of Minneapolis, MN. New Orleans and Atlanta had rates of about 12 percent. Only 3 percent of New York's residents were new to the city.

Owning and Renting

Homeownership in the United States continued at record high levels into the 21st century: owners occupied fully two-thirds of American housing units. Two states—Michigan and Minnesota—had rates exceeding 75 percent. The state with the smallest proportion of owner-occupied units was New York (55.6 percent). The District of Columbia (44.1 percent) had a lower rate than any of the states. However, the District of Columbia's homeownership rates were higher than cities like Boston, Los Angeles, New York, and Miami. New York City's relatively low homeownership rate of 33.9 percent brought down the state's overall rate.

Homeownership rates vary considerably by race of householder. Nationally, close to three in four non-Hispanic White households lived in a home they owned, while fewer than half of Black and Hispanic householders were homeowners. Eleven states—led by Mississippi with 56.1 percent—had 50 percent or more of Black householders

residing in owner-occupied units. More than 50 percent of Hispanic households were homeowners in 24 states—including Texas and Florida, both with large Hispanic populations. About 60 percent of Asian-headed households were homeowners.

Homeownership varied even more by age of householder. For all householders age 25 to 44, 57.6 percent owned their own homes, compared with 76.7 percent of 45- to 64-year-olds and 78.8 percent of householders 65 years old and over. Minnesota had the highest proportion of younger homeowners, with 77.2 percent of 25- to 44-year-olds. Michigan and Iowa also had high proportions of homeowners in this age group. Utah had the highest homeownership rate among householders 65 and older, with 86.8 percent. In West Virginia, Idaho, and Mississippi, more than 85 percent of these older householders owned their homes.

Nearly 83 percent of married-couple family households were homeowners, while only 48.9 percent of female-headed family households owned their homes. The homeownership rate of nonfamily households was slightly higher, at 52.1 percent. More than 60 percent of nonfamily households in Delaware, West Virginia, and Florida owned their homes. Over 90 percent of married-couple families in Minnesota and Michigan owned their homes.

In four metropolitan areas, more than 80 percent of housing units were owner-occupied. The highest level was in Punta Gorda, FL, with a homeownership rate of 83.4 percent. The other three metropolitan areas were in Michigan. The metropolitan area with the lowest homeownership rate (51.3 percent) was Hinesville-Fort Stewart, GA, a small metropolitan area with a military base. But the homeown-

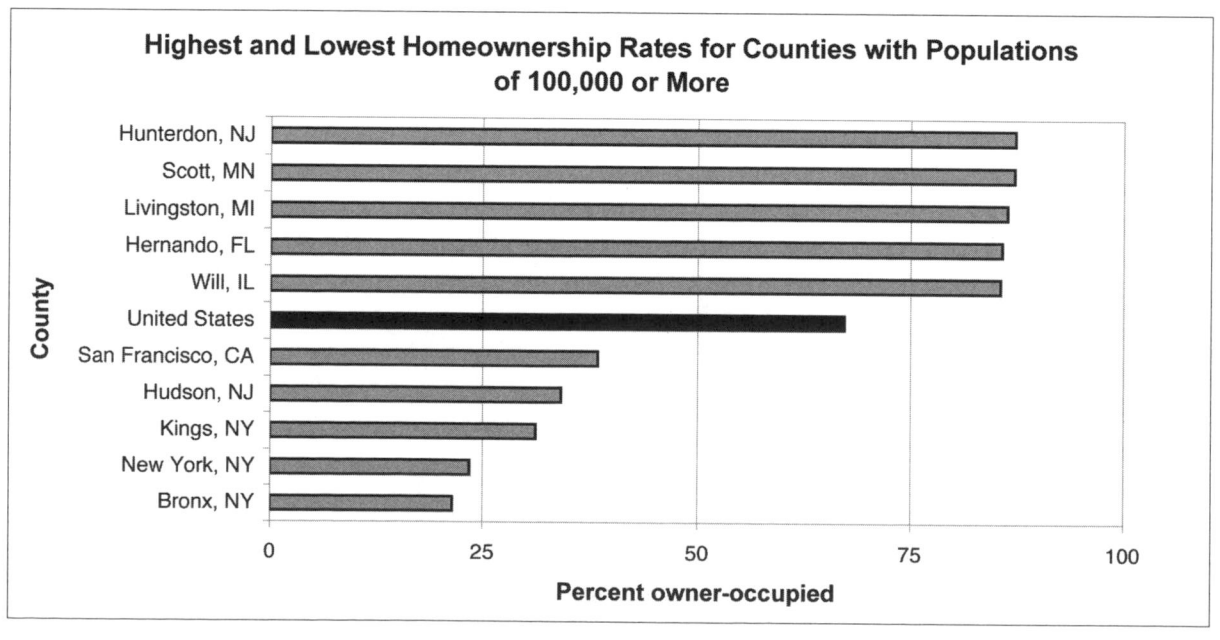

ership rates for the Los Angeles (52.3 percent) and New York (53.7 percent) areas were not significantly higher.

About 200 counties had homeownership rates over 80 percent, most of them counties with populations between 20,000 and 100,000. Bronx County had the lowest home-ownership rate (21.5 percent) in the country and New York County (Manhattan) was only slightly higher at 23.5 percent. Kings County (Brooklyn) and Hudson County, NJ, (Jersey City) were also below 35 percent.

Dozens of cities had homeownership rates over 90 percent, and dozens more were below 30 percent. New York City's overall homeownership rate was one-third, and Los Angeles, Chicago, Houston, Dallas, and San Francisco were all below one-half. None of the largest cities exceeded home-ownership rates of 60 to 65 percent.

American households had an average size of 2.6 persons per household. Owner-occupied households tended to be slightly larger than renter-occupied households. Only Utah exceeded three persons per household, but owner-occupied households in California and Hawaii averaged over three persons per household. Housing quality is sometimes mea-sured by crowding (more than one person per room is con-sidered crowded) and lack of complete plumbing (which consists of hot and cold piped water, a flush toilet, and a bathtub or shower). Nationally, 3.4 percent of housing units were considered substandard by this definition, but between 8 and 10 percent of housing units in Alaska, Hawaii, and California did not meet these standards.

Housing Value and Costs

The median income for renter-occupied households ($30,473) was less than half of that for owner-occupied households

($62,257). Among owner-occupied households, those with a mortgage had a median income of $72,728, compared with $39,994 for households without a mortgage.

The median value of owner-occupied housing units in the United States was $181,800. California and Hawaii had the most expensive houses, with median values over $500,000. The median value was under $100,000 in five states: North Dakota, Oklahoma, Arkansas, West Virginia, and Mississippi. In 12 metropolitan areas—all in California and Hawaii—the median value was over $500,000, with the San Jose and Santa Cruz metropolitan areas topping the list at over $700,000. Sixty metropolitan areas had median housing values below $100,000, the lowest being the Odessa, TX, metropolitan area with a median value estimated at $58,800. Housing values topped $700,000 in five California counties and New York County (Manhattan), while McDowell County, WV, and Wil-lacy County, TX, had estimated values below $40,000. The disparities become more pronounced at the city level, with 16 California cities and 2 Connecticut cities having median values above the million dollar level. Three cities in Texas and two in Pennsylvania had median values below $50,000.

Two-thirds of owner-occupants held mortgages on their homes. More than 76 percent of homeowners in Nevada, Maryland, Colorado, California, and the District of Columbia held mortgages, while barely 50 percent of West Virginia's homeowners did. Nearly 18 percent of all owner-occupants held a second mortgage and/or a home equity loan. More than 23 percent of homeowners in Colorado, California, Maryland, and Utah held second mortgages or home equity loans, while less than 8 percent had them in Texas, Arkansas, and Mississippi.

For all Americans, the median monthly housing cost was $920. For owners, this included mortgages, real estate

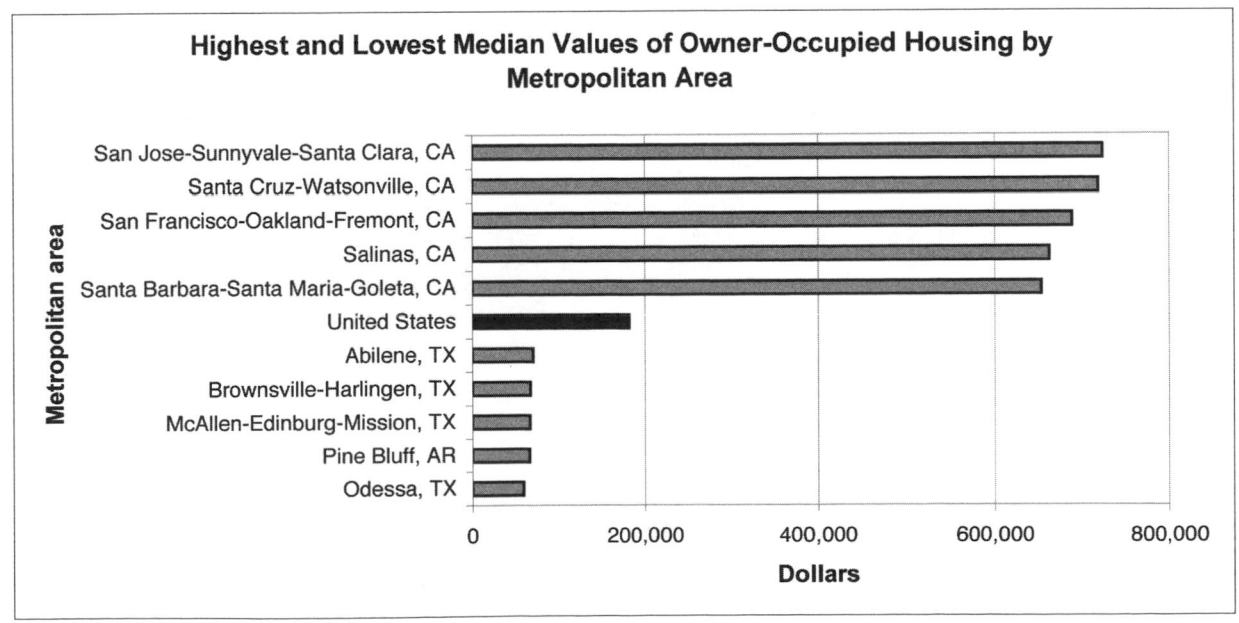

taxes, insurance, utilities, fuel, and condominium fees, where appropriate. For renters, this included the contract rent, utilities, and fuels if paid by the renter. Median housing costs were highest in New Jersey and California (over $1,300) and lowest in West Virginia and North Dakota (under $600).

On average, renters devoted a relatively high share of their monthly income to rent: a median of nearly 30 percent. Even owners with a mortgage spent relatively less on their housing—24.7 percent of monthly household income. (Those with no mortgage spent 12.7 percent.) In part, this difference reflects the age profile of renters. More than half of householders under 25 and over 65 spent at least 30 percent of their incomes on housing costs.

Among the states, renters in Florida paid the highest proportion of their incomes for their rental costs—32.9 percent—while renters in Wyoming paid only 23.3 percent of their incomes. Median gross rents were highest in Hawaii,

California, and New Jersey—all over $1,000. The lowest median gross rents were in North Dakota ($513) and West Virginia ($516). Ten counties in California, Virginia, New York, and Maryland had median gross rents over $1,400. Sixteen counties had median gross rents under $400.

California homeowners with mortgages paid 30.5 percent of their incomes for owner costs, while those in West Virginia paid only 20.1 percent. In 23 metropolitan areas—almost all of them in California—homeowners with a mortgage paid more than 30 percent of their incomes for monthly owner costs. In twelve cities, the median monthly owner costs for mortgaged housing units were more than 40 percent of income. These include Beverly Hills, CA where the median housing value was over a million dollars and Hamtramck, MI where the median housing value was under $100,000. Median owner costs for mortgaged properties in California were $2,180. New Jersey's median owner costs were about the same ($2,177), but they amounted to a median of 27.7 percent of household income in New Jersey. Fourteen

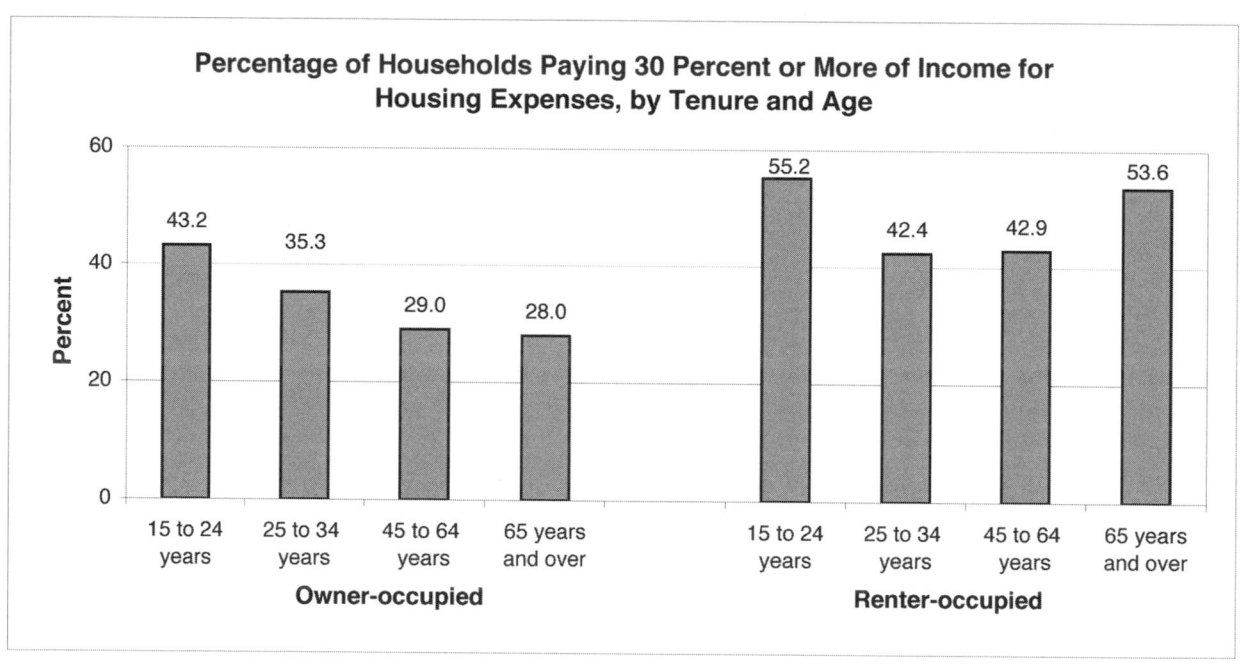

Percentage of Households Paying 30 Percent or More of Income for Housing Expenses, by Tenure and Age

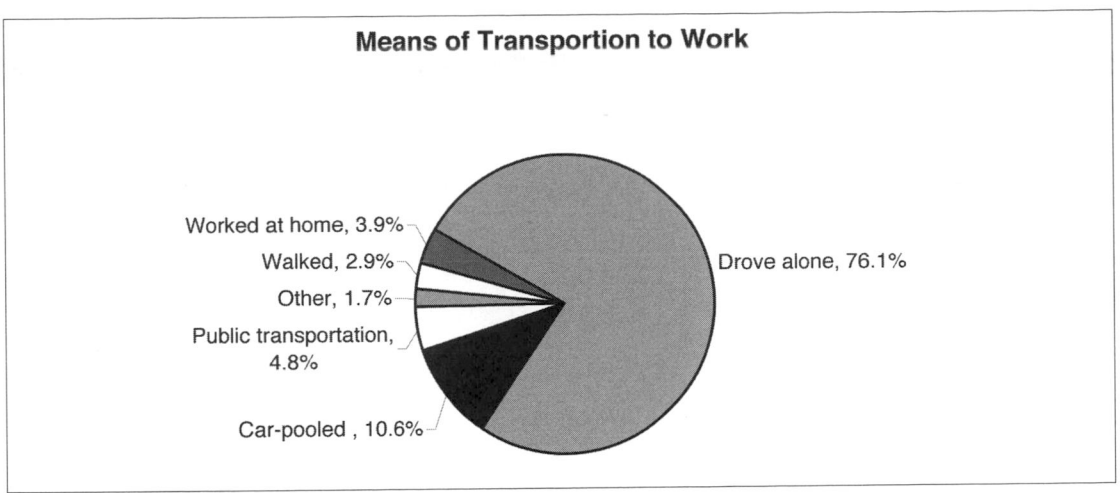

Means of Transportion to Work

Worked at home, 3.9%

Walked, 2.9%

Other, 1.7%

Public transportation, 4.8%

Car-pooled , 10.6%

Drove alone, 76.1%

other states had median monthly owner costs over $1,500 for mortgaged housing units. In West Virginia, median monthly owner costs for households with a mortgage were $870. Only three other states (Oklahoma, Mississippi, and Arkansas) had median monthly owner costs under $1,000 for mortgaged housing units.

Transportation

Ninety-three percent of housing units had at least one vehicle. More than half had two or more vehicles, and the share of housing units with three or more vehicles was more than double the share without any at all. In the New York metropolitan area, 30.3 percent of households had no vehicle, more than double the proportion of any other metropolitan area. In New York County (Manhattan), 77.5 percent of households had no vehicle, while well over half of the residents of Bronx and Kings (Brooklyn) Counties also had no cars. About one-third or more of residents of the District of Columbia; Queens County, NY; Hudson County, NJ; Philadelphia County, PA; and Suffolk County, MA, (Boston) had no vehicles. The level was 32 percent in Holmes County, OH, with a large Amish population, and about 30 percent in Baltimore and San Francisco.

Three out of four Americans drove their cars to work alone, and one-tenth car pooled. Less than 5 percent took public transportation, and about the same number walked, bicycled, or used "other means." Americans' average commute (excluding those who worked at home) was 25 minutes.

This ranged from 31.2 minutes in New York to 16 minutes in North Dakota. Nationally, commuting by public transportation averaged about twice as long as commuting by car, but car trips ranged from an average of 29.2 minutes in Maryland to 16.3 minutes in North Dakota. Public transportation ranged from 55 minutes in Connecticut to 23.6 minutes in North Dakota.

Commuting patterns are influenced by local conditions, so broad national averages are not very revealing. Walking or biking are generally more popular in a climate with good weather, and the presence or absence of public transport obviously determines how many people use it. For instance, 37.8 percent of people who lived in the District of Columbia took public transportation to work, as did 26.3 percent in New York state, 10.3 percent in New Jersey, and more than 8 percent in Massachusetts, Maryland, and Illinois—not many other Americans have this option.

State Rankings, 2005–2007
Selected Rankings

Lived in the same house one year ago rank	State	Percent who lived in the same house one year ago [C-1, col 2]	Did not live in the state one year ago rank	State	Percent who did not live in the state one year ago [C-1, cols 6 + 7]	Owner-occupied housing unit rank	State	Percent owner-occupied housing unit [C-1, col 9]
	United States	83.4		United States	3.2		United States	67.3
1	New Jersey	88.3	1	District of Columbia	10.3	1	Minnesota	75.8
2	New York	87.8	2	Alaska	6.5	2	Michigan	75.1
3	Connecticut	86.9	3	Nevada	6.4	3	West Virginia	74.9
3	Pennsylvania	86.9	4	Hawaii	6.1	4	Delaware	73.6
3	West Virginia	86.9	5	Wyoming	6.0	5	Iowa	73.3
6	Rhode Island	86.6	6	Idaho	5.8	6	New Hampshire	73.2
7	Massachusetts	85.9	7	Arizona	5.7	7	Maine	72.9
8	New Hampshire	85.7	8	Delaware	4.9	8	Vermont	72.2
9	Michigan	85.4	9	Colorado	4.8	9	Indiana	72.1
10	Maine	85.2	9	Utah	4.8	10	Utah	71.9
10	Minnesota	85.2	11	New Mexico	4.6	11	Pennsylvania	71.7
12	Vermont	85.0	12	Georgia	4.5	12	Idaho	71.6
13	Illinois	84.9	12	North Dakota	4.5	13	Alabama	71.3
13	Maryland	84.9	12	Oregon	4.5	14	Mississippi	70.9
15	Delaware	84.5	12	Vermont	4.5	15	Kentucky	70.8
16	Wisconsin	84.3	12	Virginia	4.5	16	Missouri	70.7
17	Ohio	84.2	17	Montana	4.4	17	Florida	70.3
18	Hawaii	83.8	17	North Carolina	4.4	17	South Carolina	70.3
19	California	83.5	17	South Carolina	4.4	17	Wisconsin	70.3
20	South Carolina	83.4	17	Washington	4.4	20	Illinois	70.1
21	Alabama	83.3	21	Florida	4.2	20	Montana	70.1
21	Kentucky	83.3	21	New Hampshire	4.2	20	Tennessee	70.1
23	Indiana	83.2	23	Arkansas	4.0	23	Kansas	70.0
24	Iowa	83.1	23	Kansas	4.0	23	Ohio	70.0
24	Virginia	83.1	25	Maryland	3.9	23	Wyoming	70.0
26	Mississippi	82.9	25	Oklahoma	3.9	26	Connecticut	69.7
26	South Dakota	82.9	25	South Dakota	3.9	26	Virginia	69.7
26	Tennessee	82.9	28	Rhode Island	3.7	28	New Mexico	69.6
29	Louisiana	82.6	29	Tennessee	3.6	29	Maryland	69.4
29	Missouri	82.6	30	Nebraska	3.5	30	South Dakota	69.1
31	North Dakota	82.5	31	Alabama	3.4	31	Colorado	68.7
32	Nebraska	82.3	32	Kentucky	3.3	32	Arizona	68.6
32	New Mexico	82.3	32	Texas	3.3	33	Nebraska	68.5
34	North Carolina	82.0	34	Iowa	3.2	34	North Carolina	68.4
35	Florida	81.9	34	Maine	3.2	35	Oklahoma	68.3
36	Montana	81.7	34	Mississippi	3.2	36	Louisiana	68.1
37	Kansas	81.1	34	Missouri	3.2	37	Arkansas	68.0
38	Georgia	81.0	34	West Virginia	3.2	38	Georgia	67.9
39	Arkansas	80.7	39	Connecticut	3.1	39	New Jersey	67.4
40	Wyoming	80.3	40	Massachusetts	3.0	40	North Dakota	66.5
41	Texas	80.2	41	Indiana	2.8	41	Washington	65.6
42	Oklahoma	80.0	41	Louisiana	2.8	42	Texas	65.2
42	Washington	80.0	43	Minnesota	2.6	43	Massachusetts	65.0
44	Oregon	79.7	43	New Jersey	2.6	44	Oregon	64.7
45	Colorado	79.6	45	Illinois	2.5	45	Alaska	63.7
46	Utah	79.5	45	Pennsylvania	2.5	46	Rhode Island	63.3
47	District of Columbia	79.4	47	California	2.3	47	Nevada	61.0
48	Idaho	79.1	48	New York	2.2	48	Hawaii	58.9
49	Arizona	78.7	48	Wisconsin	2.2	49	California	58.4
50	Alaska	78.6	50	Ohio	2.0	50	New York	55.6
51	Nevada	78.3	51	Michigan	1.8	51	District of Columbia	44.1

State Rankings, 2005–2007
Selected Rankings

Median value of owner-occupied housing units rank	State	Median value of owner-occupied housing units (dollars) [C-1, col 45]	Mean travel time to work rank	State	Mean travel time to work (minutes) [C-1, col 77]	Median selected monthly owner (with a mortgage) costs as a percentage of household income rank	State	Median selected monthly owner (with a mortgage) costs as a percentage of household income [C-1, col 58]
	United States	181,800		United States	25.1		United States	24.7
1	California	513,200	1	New York	31.2	1	California	30.5
2	Hawaii	510,500	2	Maryland	30.8	2	Nevada	28.3
3	District of Columbia	424,200	3	District of Columbia	29.4	3	Florida	28.0
4	Massachusetts	366,200	3	New Jersey	29.4	4	Hawaii	27.7
5	New Jersey	358,400	5	Illinois	28.0	4	New Jersey	27.7
6	Maryland	323,400	6	Georgia	27.1	6	Rhode Island	26.7
7	Nevada	302,600	7	California	27.0	7	Massachusetts	26.5
8	Connecticut	294,100	7	Massachusetts	27.0	8	New Hampshire	26.3
9	New York	293,400	9	Virginia	26.8	9	Washington	26.1
10	Rhode Island	289,400	10	Florida	25.9	10	New York	26.0
11	Washington	261,200	11	Hawaii	25.7	11	Oregon	25.9
12	New Hampshire	250,700	12	Washington	25.3	12	Connecticut	25.8
13	Virginia	238,600	12	West Virginia	25.3	13	Colorado	25.6
14	Oregon	232,000	14	Pennsylvania	25.1	14	Illinois	25.5
15	Colorado	230,400	15	Arizona	25.0	15	Vermont	25.0
16	Delaware	225,200	15	New Hampshire	25.0	16	Arizona	24.9
17	Arizona	221,800	17	Louisiana	24.9	17	District of Columbia	24.6
18	Florida	217,800	18	Texas	24.7	18	Maryland	24.4
19	Alaska	213,400	19	Connecticut	24.5	18	Wisconsin	24.4
20	Minnesota	207,200	20	Colorado	23.8	20	Michigan	24.3
21	Illinois	198,100	20	Delaware	23.8	21	Minnesota	24.2
22	Vermont	191,500	22	Mississippi	23.7	21	Utah	24.2
23	Utah	189,700	23	Alabama	23.6	23	Virginia	24.0
24	Maine	167,700	23	Michigan	23.6	24	Alaska	23.9
25	Wisconsin	162,000	23	Nevada	23.6	25	Montana	23.8
26	Idaho	158,600	23	Tennessee	23.6	26	Georgia	23.7
27	Georgia	156,300	27	South Carolina	23.3	26	Idaho	23.7
28	Montana	152,300	28	North Carolina	23.2	26	Maine	23.7
29	Michigan	152,200	29	Missouri	23.1	29	Texas	23.6
30	Wyoming	150,500	30	Rhode Island	22.7	30	Pennsylvania	23.5
31	Pennsylvania	144,100	31	Maine	22.6	31	Delaware	23.4
32	New Mexico	140,100	32	Indiana	22.4	32	Ohio	23.3
33	North Carolina	136,800	32	Ohio	22.4	33	North Carolina	23.0
34	Ohio	134,400	34	Kentucky	22.3	34	Mississippi	22.9
35	Missouri	131,100	35	Minnesota	22.1	34	New Mexico	22.9
36	South Carolina	122,600	36	Oregon	22.0	36	Tennessee	22.8
37	Tennessee	122,500	37	New Mexico	21.2	37	South Carolina	22.7
38	Indiana	119,400	37	Vermont	21.2	38	Nebraska	22.3
39	Nebraska	118,200	39	Utah	20.9	39	Missouri	22.2
40	Kansas	114,400	39	Wisconsin	20.9	40	South Dakota	22.0
41	Texas	113,800	41	Arkansas	20.8	41	Indiana	21.8
42	Louisiana	113,500	42	Oklahoma	20.2	42	Kansas	21.6
43	Iowa	112,600	43	Idaho	20.1	43	Alabama	21.5
44	South Dakota	110,900	44	Kansas	18.5	43	Iowa	21.5
45	Kentucky	109,700	45	Iowa	18.2	43	Kentucky	21.5
46	Alabama	106,800	46	Alaska	18.0	46	Louisiana	21.4
47	North Dakota	97,400	47	Wyoming	17.9	47	Oklahoma	21.2
48	Oklahoma	95,200	48	Nebraska	17.7	48	Wyoming	21.1
49	Arkansas	93,700	49	Montana	17.4	49	North Dakota	20.9
50	West Virginia	89,500	50	South Dakota	16.2	50	Arkansas	20.6
51	Mississippi	88,100	51	North Dakota	16.0	51	West Virginia	20.1

Lived in the same house one year ago rank	County	Percent who lived in the same house one year ago [C-2, col 1]	Did not live in the county one year ago rank	County	Percent who did not live in the county one year ago [C-2, col 2]	Mean travel time to work rank	County	Mean travel time to work (minutes) [C-2, col 11]
	United States	83.4		United States	6.8		United States	25.1
1	Fairfield County, SC	96.5	1	Harrisonburg city, VA	36.2	1	Richmond County, NY	42.6
2	Washington County, GA	96.3	2	Pulaski County, MO	27.9	2	Kings County, NY	42.1
3	Adair County, OK	95.2	3	Charlottesville city, VA	26.2	2	Pike County, PA	42.1
4	Buchanan County, VA	94.6	4	Whitman County, WA	22.6	4	Queens County, NY	41.7
5	McKinley County, NM	93.8	5	Walker County, TX	21.8	5	Bronx County, NY	41.2
6	Elk County, PA	93.2	6	Riley County, KS	21.3	6	Elbert County, CO	40.7
7	Covington County, MS	93.0	7	Liberty County, GA	20.9	7	Stafford County, VA	40.3
7	Santa Cruz County, AZ	93.0	8	Madison County, ID	20.8	8	Calvert County, MD	39.4
7	Willacy County, TX	93.0	9	Coryell County, TX	19.7	9	Spotsylvania County, VA	39.1
10	Copiah County, MS	92.9	10	Staunton city, VA	19.3	10	Prince William County, VA	39.0
10	McDowell County, WV	92.9	11	Powhatan County, VA	19.0	11	Monroe County, PA	38.7
12	Assumption Parish, LA	92.8	12	Onslow County, NC	18.9	11	Paulding County, GA	38.7
13	Williamsburg County, SC	92.7	13	Lassen County, CA	18.8	13	Charles County, MD	38.5
14	Dodge County, GA	92.4	14	Fredericksburg city, VA	18.7	14	San Jacinto County, TX	38.3
14	Nassau County, NY	92.4	15	Winchester city, VA	18.6	15	Fauquier County, VA	38.2
16	Garrett County, MD	92.3	16	Athens County, OH	18.5	15	Sussex County, NJ	38.2
17	Nicholas County, WV	92.2	17	Latah County, ID	18.3	17	Warren County, VA	38.1
18	Clarke County, AL	92.0	18	Bee County, TX	17.7	18	Hampshire County, WV	37.6
18	Franklin County, IN	92.0	19	Manassas city, VA	17.6	19	Culpeper County, VA	37.4
18	Northampton County, NC	92.0	20	Douglas County, GA	17.5	20	Page County, VA	37.1
21	Geauga County, OH	91.9	21	Vernon Parish, LA	17.4	21	Barnwell County, SC	36.7
21	Holmes County, OH	91.9	22	Bulloch County, GA	17.3	22	Hickman County, TN	36.6
21	Putnam County, OH	91.9	23	Clark County, AR	17.1	23	Jefferson County, WV	36.5
21	Richmond County, NY	91.9	23	Hays County, TX	17.1	23	Pearl River County, MS	36.5
25	Ashe County, NC	91.8	25	Iron County, UT	17.0	25	Lincoln County, WV	36.2
25	Chester County, SC	91.8	26	McDonough County, IL	16.8	26	Putnam County, NY	35.9
25	St. James Parish, LA	91.8	27	Brazos County, TX	16.7	27	Perry County, OH	35.7
28	Barnwell County, SC	91.7	27	Caldwell County, TX	16.7	28	Prince George's County, MD	35.6
28	Cocke County, TN	91.7	27	Lincoln Parish, LA	16.7	29	Carter County, KY	35.4
28	Dubois County, IN	91.7	30	Centre County, PA	16.6	29	Louisa County, VA	35.4
28	Rockland County, NY	91.7	31	Prince George County, VA	16.4	31	Orange County, VA	35.3
32	Carroll County, MD	91.6	32	King George County, VA	16.3	31	Warren County, NJ	35.3
32	Clarendon County, SC	91.6	33	Albany County, WY	16.2	33	Assumption Parish, LA	35.2
32	Montgomery County, NC	91.6	33	Albemarle County, VA	16.2	33	Caroline County, VA	35.2
32	Spencer County, IN	91.6	33	Lumpkin County, GA	16.2	33	King George County, VA	35.2
36	Bureau County, IL	91.4	36	Adair County, MO	16.1	33	Marion County, MS	35.2
36	Butler County, AL	91.4	37	Logan County, CO	15.9	33	Simpson County, MS	35.2
36	Coffee County, GA	91.4	38	Leavenworth County, KS	15.8	38	Van Zandt County, TX	34.7
39	Putnam County, WV	91.3	39	Dawson County, GA	15.6	39	Hampton County, SC	34.5
40	Augusta County, VA	91.2	39	Montgomery County, VA	15.6	39	Liberty County, TX	34.5
40	Bucks County, PA	91.2	41	Story County, IA	15.4	39	Washington County, MO	34.5
40	Flathead County, MT	91.2	42	Alexandria city, VA	15.3	42	Cherokee County, GA	34.3
40	Kewaunee County, WI	91.2	42	Broomfield County, CO	15.3	43	Matanuska-Susitna Borough, AK	34.1
40	Sumter County, SC	91.2	42	Pinal County, AZ	15.3	44	Frederick County, MD	33.9
40	Trempealeau County, WI	91.2	45	Monroe County, IN	15.2	45	Brown County, OH	33.8
46	Botetourt County, VA	91.1	46	Jackson County, IL	15.1	45	Queen Anne's County, MD	33.8
46	Langlade County, WI	91.1	47	Clarke County, GA	14.8	45	Will County, IL	33.8
46	Putnam County, NY	91.1	48	DeKalb County, IL	14.7	48	Carroll County, MD	33.7
46	Wyoming County, WV	91.1	48	Phelps County, MO	14.7	49	McHenry County, IL	33.6
50	Mecklenburg County, VA	91.0	50	Salem city, VA	14.6	50	Adams County, OH	33.5
51	Jackson County, WV	90.9	51	Lafayette County, MS	14.5	50	East Feliciana Parish, LA	33.5
51	Orange County, VT	90.9	51	Oktibbeha County, MS	14.5	52	Hunterdon County, NJ	33.4
53	Rio Arriba County, NM	90.8	51	Payne County, OK	14.5	52	Teller County, CO	33.4
53	Tate County, MS	90.8	51	Taney County, MO	14.5	54	Isanti County, MN	33.3
55	Clark County, WI	90.7	55	Lynchburg city, VA	14.4	55	Clay County, FL	33.2
55	Huron County, MI	90.7	55	Mecosta County, MI	14.4	55	Currituck County, NC	33.2
55	Kings County, NY	90.7	57	Benton County, OR	14.2	55	Livingston Parish, LA	33.2
55	Suffolk County, NY	90.7	57	Isabella County, MI	14.2	58	Mason County, WA	33.1
55	Susquehanna County, PA	90.7	57	Johnson County, MO	14.2	58	Waller County, TX	33.1
60	Bedford County, PA	90.6	60	Kittitas County, WA	14.1	60	Fayette County, TN	33.0
60	Holmes County, MS	90.6	61	Grimes County, TX	14.0	60	Lapeer County, MI	33.0
60	Hunterdon County, NJ	90.6	61	Richland County, SC	14.0	60	Montgomery County, MD	33.0
60	Richmond County, NC	90.6	61	Rockwall County, TX	14.0	63	Loudoun County, VA	32.9
64	Brooke County, WV	90.5	64	Elmore County, ID	13.9	63	Monmouth County, NJ	32.9
64	Effingham County, IL	90.5	65	Bell County, TX	13.8	63	Sabine Parish, LA	32.9
64	Kandiyohi County, MN	90.5	65	Comanche County, OK	13.8	63	San Benito County, CA	32.9
64	Westmoreland County, PA	90.5	65	Somerset County, MD	13.8	67	Colleton County, SC	32.8
68	Alexander County, NC	90.4	65	Waynesboro city, VA	13.8	67	Nassau County, NY	32.8
68	Cherokee County, NC	90.4	69	Howard County, TX	13.7	69	Atascosa County, TX	32.7
68	Morgan County, TN	90.4	69	Newport News city, VA	13.7	69	Calaveras County, CA	32.7
68	Morris County, NJ	90.4	69	Stafford County, VA	13.7	69	Douglas County, GA	32.7
68	Trumbull County, OH	90.4	72	Fremont County, CO	13.6	69	Franklin County, NC	32.7
73	Jefferson County, PA	90.3	72	Walton County, FL	13.6	69	Gwinnett County, GA	32.7
73	Lawrence County, PA	90.3	74	Tippecanoe County, IN	13.5	69	Lincoln County, MS	32.7
73	Passaic County, NJ	90.3	75	Elmore County, AL	13.4	69	Pickens County, SC	32.7
73	Shawano County, WI	90.3				69	Rockwall County, TX	32.7
73	Somerset County, NJ	90.3						
73	St. Martin Parish, LA	90.3						

Median value of owner-occupied housing units rank	County	Median value of owner-occupied housing units (dollars) [C-2, col 5]	Median selected monthly owner (with a mortgage) costs as a percentage of household income rank	County	Median selected monthly owner (with a mortgage) costs as a percentage of household income [C-2, col 6]	Median gross rent as a percentage of household income rank	County	Median gross rent as a percentage of household income [C-2, col 9]
	United States	181,800		United States	24.7		United States	29.8
1	Marin County, CA.................	895,100	1	Holmes County, MS	39.2	1	Adair County, MO..............	50.1[1]
2	San Mateo County, CA	807,400	2	Monroe County, FL	38.3	1	Athens County, OH.............	50.1[1]
3	San Francisco County, CA	789,400	3	Miami-Dade County, FL......	34.2	1	Watauga County, NC	50.1[1]
4	New York County, NY	767,200	4	Monterey County, CA	33.9	4	Roscommon County, MI......	49.0
5	Santa Clara County, CA	725,800	5	San Benito County, CA.......	33.7	4	Waller County, TX	49.0
6	Santa Cruz County, CA	718,700	6	Kings County, NY...............	33.4	6	Kittitas County, WA	48.6
7	Monroe County, FL	671,800	7	Mendocino County, CA.....	33.3	7	Oktibbeha County, MS........	45.9
8	San Benito County, CA..........	669,000	7	Queens County, NY.............	33.3	8	Teller County, CO.............	45.3
9	Monterey County, CA	662,300	9	Santa Cruz County, CA	32.6	9	Lincoln Parish, LA..............	45.2
10	Orange County, CA...............	656,600	10	Bronx County, NY	32.4	10	Jackson County, IL..............	42.4
11	Teton County, WY................	655,500	11	Lake County, CA...............	32.2	11	Whitman County, WA.........	42.2
12	Santa Barbara County, CA.....	653,400	11	Riverside County, CA..........	32.2	12	Covington County, MS........	41.8
13	Napa County, CA.................	638,600	11	Sonoma County, CA	32.2	13	Coles County, IL................	41.5
14	Alameda County, CA	633,000	14	Blaine County, ID	32.0	14	Hendry County, FL.............	41.2
15	Ventura County, CA..............	631,000	15	Santa Barbara County, CA ...	31.9	15	Abbeville County, SC	40.6
16	Contra Costa County, CA......	618,800	16	Sunflower County, MS	31.8	16	Clark County, AR	40.4
17	Maui County, HI...................	613,600	17	Los Angeles County, CA......	31.7	17	McDonough County, IL	39.6
18	Sonoma County, CA	611,300	17	Tuolumne County, CA........	31.7	18	Morehouse Parish, LA	39.5
19	Arlington County, VA............	585,000	19	Hudson County, NJ	31.6	18	Natchitoches Parish, LA.......	39.5
20	Kauai County, HI	577,400	20	Nevada County, CA............	31.5	20	Brazos County, TX..............	39.2
21	Westchester County, NY	571,700	20	San Joaquin County, CA.....	31.5	21	Washington County, TX	39.1
22	Blaine County, ID	566,500	20	San Luis Obispo County, CA..	31.5	22	Monroe County, IN	38.6
23	San Luis Obispo County, CA....	562,400	23	Broward County, FL............	31.4	23	Pike County, AL.................	38.4
24	San Diego County, CA	559,400	23	Napa County, CA...............	31.4	24	Macon County, AL..............	37.7
25	Fairfax County, VA	554,900	25	Merced County, CA	31.3	24	Mineral County, WV...........	37.7
26	Los Angeles County, CA........	550,000	26	Contra Costa County, CA...	31.2	26	Bolivar County, MS.............	37.6
27	Loudoun County, VA.............	541,700	26	St. Lucie County, FL............	31.2	27	Centre County, PA..............	37.2
28	Kings County, NY.................	533,900	28	Marin County, CA.............	31.1	27	Miami-Dade County, FL.......	37.2
29	Alexandria city, VA...............	527,300	28	Osceola County, FL............	31.1	29	Chester County, SC	37.1
30	Fairfax city, VA	523,100	30	San Diego County, CA	31.0	29	Indiana County, PA.............	37.1
31	Honolulu County, HI..............	521,500	31	Glenn County, CA..............	30.9	29	Otsego County, MI.............	37.1
32	El Dorado County, CA...........	510,500	31	San Mateo County, CA	30.9	29	Walker County, TX.............	37.1
33	Montgomery County, MD	500,500	31	Solano County, CA	30.9	33	Tyler County, TX................	37.0
34	Fairfield County, CT.............	495,200	31	Stanislaus County, CA........	30.9	34	Douglas County, NV............	36.9
35	Nassau County, NY	493,400	35	Alameda County, CA	30.7	35	Edgecombe County, NC	36.8
36	Rockland County, NY	491,100	35	Maui County, HI................	30.7	36	Douglas County, MN...........	36.7
37	Placer County, CA................	490,600	35	Suffolk County, NY	30.7	36	Gallia County, OH..............	36.7
38	Bergen County, NJ	486,000	38	Passaic County, NJ..............	30.6	36	Passaic County, NJ..............	36.7
39	Morris County, NJ	485,600	38	San Francisco County, CA ..	30.6	39	Lake County, CA................	36.5
40	Solano County, CA...............	472,500	40	Palm Beach County, FL.......	30.5	40	Nobles County, MN............	36.4
41	Nevada County, CA..............	466,700	41	Collier County, FL..............	30.4	40	Tippecanoe County, IN........	36.4
42	Queens County, NY...............	465,200	42	Charlotte County, FL	29.9	42	Marengo County, AL...........	36.2
43	Eagle County, CO.................	461,600	42	Essex County, NJ	29.9	43	Marion County, MS.............	36.1
44	Richmond County, NY...........	461,400	42	Jefferson County, OR..........	29.9	44	Cooke County, TX..............	36.0
45	Hunterdon County, NJ...........	459,200	42	Nassau County, NY	29.9	44	Nacogdoches County, TX	36.0
46	Howard County, MD	456,400	46	Orange County, CA............	29.8	44	Ocean County, NJ	36.0
47	Summit County, UT...............	448,900	47	Barnstable County, MA	29.7	47	Butte County, CA...............	35.9
48	Summit County, CO	445,100	47	El Dorado County, CA........	29.7	47	Hampshire County, WV.......	35.9
49	Yolo County, CA	444,700	47	San Bernardino County, CA ..	29.7	49	Fayette County, IN..............	35.8
50	Somerset County, NJ.............	443,700	47	Santa Clara County, CA......	29.7	49	Santa Barbara County, CA...	35.8
51	Middlesex County, MA..........	440,600	51	Ventura County, CA...........	29.6	49	Wakulla County, FL	35.8
52	Monmouth County, NJ..........	438,200	52	Flagler County, FL..............	29.5	52	Indian River County, FL........	35.6
53	Suffolk County, NY	436,200	52	Suffolk County, MA	29.5	52	Leon County, FL.................	35.6
54	Mendocino County, CA.........	434,400	54	Imperial County, CA...........	29.4	52	Pearl River County, MS........	35.6
55	Norfolk County, MA..............	428,700	55	Sacramento County, CA......	29.3	52	Pike County, MS.................	35.6
56	Douglas County, NV..............	424,800	56	Placer County, CA..............	29.2	56	San Luis Obispo County, CA...	35.5
57	Putnam County, NY	424,400	56	Routt County, CO	29.2	57	Alachua County, FL.............	35.4
58	District of Columbia , DC	424,200	56	Union County, NJ	29.2	57	Champaign County, IL.........	35.4
59	Prince William County, VA.....	421,300	56	Willacy County, TX............	29.2	57	Grimes County, TX..............	35.4
60	Barnstable County, MA	412,900	60	Clark County, NV	29.1	57	Johnson County, IA.............	35.4
61	Suffolk County, MA	411,700	60	Dare County, NC................	29.1	57	Phillips County, AR.............	35.4
62	Collier County, FL.................	409,000	60	Putnam County, NY............	29.1	62	Bulloch County, GA............	35.3
63	Fauquier County, VA	407,800	63	Lee County, FL...................	29.0	63	Humboldt County, CA..........	35.2
64	Union County, NJ.................	403,800	63	Pike County, PA.................	29.0	63	Prentiss County, MS	35.2
65	Newport County, RI...............	403,600	63	Sarasota County, FL............	29.0	63	Volusia County, FL..............	35.2
66	Essex County, NJ	401,700	66	Bergen County, NJ	28.9	63	Williamsburg County, SC	35.2
67	San Joaquin County, CA........	401,100	66	Douglas County, NV...........	28.9	67	Bandera County, TX	35.1
68	Routt County, CO	398,100	66	Summit County, CO	28.9	68	Pitt County, NC..................	35.0
69	Riverside County, CA............	395,100	69	Atlantic County, NJ	28.8	68	Washington County, FL	35.0
70	Calaveras County, CA	390,900	69	Ocean County, NJ	28.8	70	Halifax County, NC.............	34.9
71	Passaic County, NJ...............	389,900	69	Yuba County, CA	28.8	71	Fredericksburg city, VA........	34.8
72	King County, WA	389,200	72	Cook County, IL	28.7	71	Greenup County, KY	34.8
73	Essex County, MA	387,700	72	Currituck County, NC.........	28.7	71	Montgomery County, VA	34.8
74	Calvert County, MD	387,600	72	Richmond County, NY........	28.7	74	Boulder County, CO...........	34.7
75	Stafford County, VA	386,900	75	Madera County, CA	28.6	74	Manassas city, VA...............	34.7

1. 50.1 is the top code symbolizing a median gross rent as a percentage of household income of 50.1 percent or more.

Lived in the same house one year ago rank	Area name	Percent who lived in the same house one year ago [C-3, col 1]	Did not live in the MSA one year ago rank	Area name	Percent who did not live in the MSA one year ago [C-3, col 2]
	United States	83.4		United States	11.4
1	Sumter, SC	91.2	1	Hinesville-Fort Stewart, GA	20.6
2	Barnstable Town, MA	89.6	2	Jacksonville, NC	18.9
3	Monroe, MI	89.4	3	State College, PA	16.6
4	New York-Northern New Jersey-Long Island, NY-NJ-PA	89.1	4	Ames, IA	15.4
5	Weirton-Steubenville, WV-OH	89.0	5	Corvallis, OR	14.8
6	Youngstown-Warren-Boardman, OH-PA	88.6	6	College Station-Bryan, TX	14.6
7	Wheeling, WV-OH	88.2	7	Killeen-Temple-Fort Hood, TX	14.0
8	Worcester, MA	88.0	8	Lawton, OK	13.8
9	Pittsfield, MA	87.9	9	Auburn-Opelika, AL	13.1
9	Vineland-Millville-Bridgeton, NJ	87.9	9	Ithaca, NY	13.1
11	Johnstown, PA	87.8	11	Fairbanks, AK	13.0
11	Wausau, WI	87.8	12	Hanford-Corcoran, CA	12.8
13	Houma-Bayou Cane-Thibodaux, LA	87.7	13	Lawrence, KS	12.5
13	Pittsburgh, PA	87.7	13	Palm Coast, FL	12.5
15	Bridgeport-Stamford-Norwalk, CT	87.6	15	Blacksburg-Christiansburg-Radford, VA	12.1
15	Brownsville-Harlingen, TX	87.6	16	Lafayette, IN	11.9
15	Charleston, WV	87.6	16	St. George, UT	11.9
15	Philadelphia-Camden-Wilmington, PA-NJ-DE-MD	87.6	18	Bloomington, IN	11.8
19	Bay City, MI	87.4	18	Columbus, GA-AL	11.8
19	Ocean City, NJ	87.4	20	Gainesville, FL	11.6
21	Danville, IL	87.3	20	Iowa City, IA	11.6
21	Racine, WI	87.3	22	Boulder, CO	11.3
23	Akron, OH	87.2	22	Harrisonburg, VA	11.3
23	Altoona, PA	87.2	24	Ann Arbor, MI	11.2
23	Sandusky, OH	87.2	24	Champaign-Urbana, IL	11.2
26	Dubuque, IA	87.0	26	Grand Forks, ND-MN	11.1
26	Lancaster, PA	87.0	27	Charlottesville, VA	10.9
26	Lebanon, PA	87.0	27	Clarksville, TN-KY	10.9
26	Rochester, MN	87.0	29	Fayetteville, NC	10.8
26	Scranton–Wilkes-Barre, PA	87.0	29	Fort Walton Beach-Crestview-Destin, FL	10.8
26	York-Hanover, PA	87.0	29	Lake Havasu City-Kingman, AZ	10.8
32	Hartford-West Hartford-East Hartford, CT	86.9	32	Logan, UT-ID	10.7
32	New Haven-Milford, CT	86.9	32	Morgantown, WV	10.7
34	Detroit-Warren-Livonia, MI	86.8	34	Colorado Springs, CO	10.5
34	Providence-New Bedford-Fall River, RI-MA	86.8	35	Bloomington-Normal, IL	10.2
36	Holland-Grand Haven, MI	86.6	36	Wichita Falls, TX	10.1
36	Visalia-Porterville, CA	86.6	37	Abilene, TX	10.0
38	Buffalo-Niagara Falls, NY	86.5	38	Athens-Clarke County, GA	9.9
39	Janesville, WI	86.3	38	Columbia, MO	9.9
39	Los Angeles-Long Beach-Santa Ana, CA	86.3	40	Bowling Green, KY	9.8
41	Hagerstown-Martinsburg, MD-WV	86.2	40	Greenville, NC	9.8
41	Hickory-Lenoir-Morganton, NC	86.2	40	San Luis Obispo-Paso Robles, CA	9.8
43	Cleveland-Elyria-Mentor, OH	86.1	43	Elizabethtown, KY	9.7
43	Danville, VA	86.1	43	Flagstaff, AZ	9.7
43	Fort Wayne, IN	86.1	43	San Angelo, TX	9.7
43	Oxnard-Thousand Oaks-Ventura, CA	86.1	46	Myrtle Beach-Conway-North Myrtle Beach, SC	9.6
43	Saginaw-Saginaw Township North, MI	86.1	46	Panama City-Lynn Haven, FL	9.6
48	Appleton, WI	86.0	48	Fort Collins-Loveland, CO	9.4
48	Trenton-Ewing, NJ	86.0	49	Valdosta, GA	9.3
50	Canton-Massillon, OH	85.9	50	Provo-Orem, UT	9.2
50	Dalton, GA	85.9	50	Yuma, AZ	9.2
50	Parkersburg-Marietta-Vienna, WV-OH	85.9	52	Ocala, FL	9.1
50	Poughkeepsie-Newburgh-Middletown, NY	85.9	52	Pensacola-Ferry Pass-Brent, FL	9.1
54	Allentown-Bethlehem-Easton, PA-NJ	85.7	52	Sebastian-Vero Beach, FL	9.1
54	Farmington, NM	85.7	52	Warner Robins, GA	9.1
54	Kingston, NY	85.7	56	Oshkosh-Neenah, WI	9.0
54	Reading, PA	85.7	56	Pocatello, ID	9.0
58	Binghamton, NY	85.5	56	Santa Fe, NM	9.0
58	Dothan, AL	85.5	59	Bremerton-Silverdale, WA	8.9
58	Rochester, NY	85.5	59	Durham, NC	8.9
61	Boston-Cambridge-Quincy, MA-NH	85.4	61	Punta Gorda, FL	8.8
61	Chicago-Naperville-Joliet, IL-IN-WI	85.4	61	Rapid City, SD	8.8
61	Niles-Benton Harbor, MI	85.4	63	Chico, CA	8.7
61	Portland-South Portland-Biddeford, ME	85.4	63	Greeley, CO	8.7
61	South Bend-Mishawaka, IN-MI	85.4	65	Cape Coral-Fort Myers, FL	8.6
66	Glens Falls, NY	85.3	65	Hattiesburg, MS	8.6
66	Green Bay, WI	85.3	65	Missoula, MT	8.6
66	Sheboygan, WI	85.3	65	Tuscaloosa, AL	8.6
69	Baltimore-Towson, MD	85.2	69	Idaho Falls, ID	8.5
69	El Paso, TX	85.2	69	Madera, CA	8.5
69	Manchester-Nashua, NH	85.2	69	Muncie, IN	8.5
69	Springfield, OH	85.2	72	Gulfport-Biloxi, MS	8.4
69	St. Louis, MO-IL	85.2	72	Medford, OR	8.4
74	Albany-Schenectady-Troy, NY	85.1	72	Yuba City, CA	8.4
74	Flint, MI	85.1	75	Austin-Round Rock, TX	8.3
74	Peoria, IL	85.1	75	Carson City, NV	8.3
74	Rocky Mount, NC	85.1	75	Grand Junction, CO	8.3
74	Utica-Rome, NY	85.1			
74	Williamsport, PA	85.1			

Metropolitan Area Rankings, 2005–2007
Selected Rankings

Mean travel time to work rank	Area name	Mean travel time to work (minutes) [C-3, col 11]	Median value of owner-occupied housing units rank	Area name	Median value of owner-occupied housing units (dollars) [C-3, col 5]
	United States	25.1		United States	181,800
1	New York-Northern New Jersey-Long Island, NY-NJ-PA	34.3	1	San Jose-Sunnyvale-Santa Clara, CA	723,600
2	Washington-Arlington-Alexandria, DC-VA-MD-WV	33.3	2	Santa Cruz-Watsonville, CA	718,700
3	Poughkeepsie-Newburgh-Middletown, NY	31.0	3	San Francisco-Oakland-Fremont, CA	687,900
4	Chicago-Naperville-Joliet, IL-IN-WI	30.9	4	Salinas, CA	662,300
5	Atlanta-Sandy Springs-Marietta, GA	30.8	5	Santa Barbara-Santa Maria-Goleta, CA	653,400
6	Riverside-San Bernardino-Ontario, CA	30.7	6	Napa, CA	638,600
7	Stockton, CA	29.6	7	Oxnard-Thousand Oaks-Ventura, CA	631,000
8	Vallejo-Fairfield, CA	29.5	8	Santa Rosa-Petaluma, CA	611,300
9	Bremerton-Silverdale, WA	29.2	9	Los Angeles-Long Beach-Santa Ana, CA	583,300
10	Winchester, VA-WV	29.0	10	San Luis Obispo-Paso Robles, CA	562,400
11	Baltimore-Towson, MD	28.9	11	San Diego-Carlsbad-San Marcos, CA	559,400
12	San Francisco-Oakland-Fremont, CA	28.5	12	Honolulu, HI	521,500
13	Boston-Cambridge-Quincy, MA-NH	28.4	13	Bridgeport-Stamford-Norwalk, CT	495,200
14	Los Angeles-Long Beach-Santa Ana, CA	28.3	14	Vallejo-Fairfield, CA	472,500
15	Houston-Sugar Land-Baytown, TX	28.2	15	New York-Northern New Jersey-Long Island, NY-NJ-PA	450,200
15	Miami-Fort Lauderdale-Pompano Beach, FL	28.2	16	Washington-Arlington-Alexandria, DC-VA-MD-WV	439,800
17	Bridgeport-Stamford-Norwalk, CT	28.1	17	Barnstable Town, MA	412,900
18	Philadelphia-Camden-Wilmington, PA-NJ-DE-MD	28.0	18	Naples-Marco Island, FL	409,000
19	Hagerstown-Martinsburg, MD-WV	27.8	19	Sacramento–Arden-Arcade–Roseville, CA	407,800
20	Seattle-Tacoma-Bellevue, WA	27.7	20	Stockton, CA	401,100
21	Yuba City, CA	27.6	21	Boston-Cambridge-Quincy, MA-NH	398,400
22	Madera, CA	27.4	22	Riverside-San Bernardino-Ontario, CA	379,700
23	Allentown-Bethlehem-Easton, PA-NJ	26.9	23	Modesto, CA	359,100
24	Honolulu, HI	26.8	24	Reno-Sparks, NV	345,900
24	Orlando-Kissimmee, FL	26.8	25	Boulder, CO	342,400
24	Trenton-Ewing, NJ	26.8	26	Seattle-Tacoma-Bellevue, WA	341,700
24	Worcester, MA	26.8	27	Merced, CA	333,300
28	Dallas-Fort Worth-Arlington, TX	26.6	28	Ocean City, NJ	328,600
28	Phoenix-Mesa-Scottsdale, AZ	26.6	29	Madera, CA	328,100
30	Modesto, CA	26.5	30	Poughkeepsie-Newburgh-Middletown, NY	319,500
31	Baton Rouge, LA	26.4	31	Bend, OR	313,800
32	Gainesville, GA	26.3	32	Las Vegas-Paradise, NV	307,300
33	Denver-Aurora, CO	26.2	33	Trenton-Ewing, NJ	304,600
34	Oxnard-Thousand Oaks-Ventura, CA	26.1	34	Providence-New Bedford-Fall River, RI-MA	301,600
35	Birmingham-Hoover, AL	25.9	35	Carson City, NV	298,700
35	Detroit-Warren-Livonia, MI	25.9	36	Yuba City, CA	292,600
35	Port St. Lucie, FL	25.9	37	Miami-Fort Lauderdale-Pompano Beach, FL	292,100
38	Kingston, NY	25.8	38	Worcester, MA	289,600
38	New Orleans-Metairie-Kenner, LA	25.8	39	Baltimore-Towson, MD	286,900
40	Nashville-Davidson–Murfreesboro–Franklin, TN	25.7	40	Fresno, CA	284,800
40	Sacramento–Arden-Arcade–Roseville, CA	25.7	41	Santa Fe, NM	281,500
42	Tampa-St. Petersburg-Clearwater, FL	25.6	42	Bellingham, WA	277,700
43	Cape Coral-Fort Myers, FL	25.4	43	Manchester-Nashua, NH	276,300
43	Jacksonville, FL	25.4	44	Medford, OR	275,800
43	Raleigh-Cary, NC	25.4	45	Chico, CA	273,500
43	Santa Cruz-Watsonville, CA	25.4	46	New Haven-Milford, CT	264,800
47	Austin-Round Rock, TX	25.3	47	Redding, CA	263,000
48	Charlotte-Gastonia-Concord, NC-SC	25.2	48	Portland-Vancouver-Beaverton, OR-WA	262,600
48	San Diego-Carlsbad-San Marcos, CA	25.2	49	Bremerton-Silverdale, WA	260,700
50	Manchester-Nashua, NH	25.1	50	Flagstaff, AZ	258,200
50	Naples-Marco Island, FL	25.1	51	Norwich-New London, CT	252,400
50	York-Hanover, PA	25.1	52	Charlottesville, VA	251,300
53	Flint, MI	25.0	53	Chicago-Naperville-Joliet, IL-IN-WI	247,500
53	Lakeland, FL	25.0	54	Atlantic City, NJ	247,000
53	Vineland-Millville-Bridgeton, NJ	25.0	55	Sarasota-Bradenton-Venice, FL	243,700
56	Pascagoula, MS	24.9	56	Phoenix-Mesa-Scottsdale, AZ	243,500
57	Pittsburgh, PA	24.8	57	Hartford-West Hartford-East Hartford, CT	243,000
58	Santa Rosa-Petaluma, CA	24.7	58	Cape Coral-Fort Myers, FL	242,700
58	St. Louis, MO-IL	24.7	58	Denver-Aurora, CO	242,700
60	Mount Vernon-Anacortes, WA	24.6	60	Mount Vernon-Anacortes, WA	241,900
60	Portland-Vancouver-Beaverton, OR-WA	24.6	61	Bakersfield, CA	241,100
60	San Antonio, TX	24.6	62	Minneapolis-St. Paul-Bloomington, MN-WI	241,000
63	Houma-Bayou Cane-Thibodaux, LA	24.5	63	Fort Collins-Loveland, CO	239,700
63	San Jose-Sunnyvale-Santa Clara, CA	24.5	64	Kingston, NY	237,400
65	Las Vegas-Paradise, NV	24.4	65	Anchorage, AK	237,100
66	Monroe, MI	24.3	66	Olympia, WA	236,100
67	Anderson, IN	24.2	67	Palm Coast, FL	235,000
67	Merced, CA	24.2	68	Portland-South Portland-Biddeford, ME	234,500
69	Minneapolis-St. Paul-Bloomington, MN-WI	24.1	69	St. George, UT	233,900
69	Ocala, FL	24.1	70	Corvallis, OR	233,200
69	Pensacola-Ferry Pass-Brent, FL	24.1	71	Ann Arbor, MI	231,600
69	Richmond, VA	24.1	72	Port St. Lucie, FL	230,000
73	Mobile, AL	24.0	73	Prescott, AZ	229,800
73	Morristown, TN	24.0	74	Orlando-Kissimmee, FL	229,400
73	Napa, CA	24.0	75	Philadelphia-Camden-Wilmington, PA-NJ-DE-MD	228,200

Metropolitan Area Rankings, 2005–2007
Selected Rankings

Median selected monthly owner (with a mortgage) costs as a percentage of household income rank	Area name	Median selected monthly owner (with a mortgage) costs as a percentage of household income [C-3, col 6]	Median gross rent as a percentage of household income rank	Area name	Median gross rent as a percentage of household income [C-3, col 9]
	United States	24.7		United States	29.8
1	Salinas, CA	33.9	1	College Station-Bryan, TX	37.3
2	Santa Cruz-Watsonville, CA	32.6	2	State College, PA	37.2
3	Miami-Fort Lauderdale-Pompano Beach, FL	32.3	3	Bloomington, IN	36.7
4	Santa Rosa-Petaluma, CA	32.2	4	Chico, CA	35.9
5	Santa Barbara-Santa Maria-Goleta, CA	31.9	5	Santa Barbara-Santa Maria-Goleta, CA	35.8
6	San Luis Obispo-Paso Robles, CA	31.5	6	Miami-Fort Lauderdale-Pompano Beach, FL	35.7
6	Stockton, CA	31.5	7	Sebastian-Vero Beach, FL	35.6
8	Napa, CA	31.4	8	San Luis Obispo-Paso Robles, CA	35.5
9	Merced, CA	31.3	9	Deltona-Daytona Beach-Ormond Beach, FL	35.2
10	Los Angeles-Long Beach-Santa Ana, CA	31.1	10	Gainesville, FL	35.1
11	Riverside-San Bernardino-Ontario, CA	31.0	10	Lafayette, IN	35.1
11	San Diego-Carlsbad-San Marcos, CA	31.0	12	Iowa City, IA	34.9
13	Modesto, CA	30.9	13	Greenville, NC	34.8
13	San Francisco-Oakland-Fremont, CA	30.9	14	Boulder, CO	34.7
13	Vallejo-Fairfield, CA	30.9	14	Tallahassee, FL	34.7
16	Naples-Marco Island, FL	30.4	16	Laredo, TX	34.5
17	Punta Gorda, FL	29.9	17	Ann Arbor, MI	34.4
18	San Jose-Sunnyvale-Santa Clara, CA	29.8	17	Saginaw-Saginaw Township North, MI	34.4
19	Barnstable Town, MA	29.7	19	Jackson, MI	34.3
20	Oxnard-Thousand Oaks-Ventura, CA	29.6	20	Jackson, TN	34.2
20	Port St. Lucie, FL	29.6	20	McAllen-Edinburg-Mission, TX	34.2
22	Palm Coast, FL	29.5	20	Palm Coast, FL	34.2
23	El Centro, CA	29.4	23	Modesto, CA	34.0
24	Sacramento–Arden-Arcade–Roseville, CA	29.2	23	Santa Cruz-Watsonville, CA	34.0
25	Las Vegas-Paradise, NV	29.1	23	Vallejo-Fairfield, CA	34.0
26	Cape Coral-Fort Myers, FL	29.0	26	Las Cruces, NM	33.9
26	New York-Northern New Jersey-Long Island, NY-NJ-PA	29.0	27	Champaign-Urbana, IL	33.8
28	Atlantic City, NJ	28.8	27	Riverside-San Bernardino-Ontario, CA	33.8
28	Sarasota-Bradenton-Venice, FL	28.8	29	Athens-Clarke County, GA	33.7
30	Madera, CA	28.6	29	Muncie, IN	33.7
31	Yuba City, CA	28.5	31	Battle Creek, MI	33.6
32	Ocean City, NJ	28.4	31	Stockton, CA	33.6
33	Brownsville-Harlingen, TX	28.0	33	Blacksburg-Christiansburg-Radford, VA	33.5
34	Chico, CA	27.9	33	Lawrence, KS	33.5
34	Medford, OR	27.9	35	Corvallis, OR	33.4
34	Reno-Sparks, NV	27.9	35	Merced, CA	33.4
37	Redding, CA	27.8	37	Muskegon-Norton Shores, MI	33.3
37	Sebastian-Vero Beach, FL	27.8	37	Pueblo, CO	33.3
39	Laredo, TX	27.6	39	Pine Bluff, AR	33.1
40	Bakersfield, CA	27.5	39	Tyler, TX	33.1
40	Carson City, NV	27.5	39	Waco, TX	33.1
40	Honolulu, HI	27.5	42	Bellingham, WA	33.0
40	McAllen-Edinburg-Mission, TX	27.5	43	Los Angeles-Long Beach-Santa Ana, CA	32.9
44	Bridgeport-Stamford-Norwalk, CT	27.4	43	Orlando-Kissimmee, FL	32.9
44	Chicago-Naperville-Joliet, IL-IN-WI	27.4	43	Parkersburg-Marietta-Vienna, WV-OH	32.9
44	Deltona-Daytona Beach-Ormond Beach, FL	27.4	43	San Diego-Carlsbad-San Marcos, CA	32.9
44	Mount Vernon-Anacortes, WA	27.4	43	Tuscaloosa, AL	32.9
48	Bend, OR	27.2	48	Auburn-Opelika, AL	32.8
48	Coeur d'Alene, ID	27.2	48	Brownsville-Harlingen, TX	32.8
48	Poughkeepsie-Newburgh-Middletown, NY	27.2	48	Fort Collins-Loveland, CO	32.8
48	Visalia-Porterville, CA	27.2	48	Ithaca, NY	32.8
52	Fresno, CA	27.1	48	Sarasota-Bradenton-Venice, FL	32.8
52	Orlando-Kissimmee, FL	27.1	48	Vineland-Millville-Bridgeton, NJ	32.8
52	Tampa-St. Petersburg-Clearwater, FL	27.1	54	Alexandria, LA	32.7
55	Boston-Cambridge-Quincy, MA-NH	26.9	54	Rochester, NY	32.7
55	Seattle-Tacoma-Bellevue, WA	26.9	54	Savannah, GA	32.7
57	Bellingham, WA	26.7	57	Elmira, NY	32.6
57	Hanford-Corcoran, CA	26.7	57	Santa Rosa-Petaluma, CA	32.6
59	Greeley, CO	26.6	59	Barnstable Town, MA	32.5
59	Prescott, AZ	26.6	59	Palm Bay-Melbourne-Titusville, FL	32.5
59	Providence-New Bedford-Fall River, RI-MA	26.6	61	Lubbock, TX	32.4
62	Manchester-Nashua, NH	26.5	61	Monroe, LA	32.4
63	New Haven-Milford, CT	26.4	61	Redding, CA	32.4
63	Palm Bay-Melbourne-Titusville, FL	26.4	64	Naples-Marco Island, FL	32.3
65	Portland-Vancouver-Beaverton, OR-WA	26.2	64	Sacramento–Arden-Arcade–Roseville, CA	32.3
66	Denver-Aurora, CO	26.1	66	Fresno, CA	32.2
66	Eugene-Springfield, OR	26.1	66	Morgantown, WV	32.2
68	Salem, OR	26.0	66	Port St. Lucie, FL	32.2
69	Lake Havasu City-Kingman, AZ	25.9	69	Anderson, IN	32.1
69	Pueblo, CO	25.9	69	Honolulu, HI	32.1
71	Bremerton-Silverdale, WA	25.8	69	Kalamazoo-Portage, MI	32.1
71	Kingston, NY	25.8	69	Oxnard-Thousand Oaks-Ventura, CA	32.1
71	Lakeland, FL	25.8	73	Ames, IA	32.0
71	St. George, UT	25.8	73	Burlington-South Burlington, VT	32.0
71	Trenton-Ewing, NJ	25.8	73	Hot Springs, AR	32.0
			73	Memphis, TN-MS-AR	32.0
			73	Missoula, MT	32.0

City Rankings, 2005–2007
Selected Rankings

Lived in the same house one year ago rank	City	Percent who lived in the same house one year ago [C-4, col 1]	Did not live in the city one year ago rank	City	Percent who did not live in the city one year ago [C-4, col 2]	Mean travel time to work rank	City	Mean travel time to work (minutes) [C-4, col 11]
	United States	83.4		United States	11.4		United States	25.1
1	Plainview CDP, NY	97.3	1	Fort Bragg CDP, NC	56.1	1	Linton Hall CDP, VA	46.3
2	Westfield town, NJ	96.1	2	Fort Hood CDP, TX	50.4	2	Poinciana CDP, FL	44.0
3	Deer Park CDP, NY	95.8	3	South Salt Lake city, UT	43.0	3	Tracy city, CA	43.8
3	West Islip CDP, NY	95.8	4	Athens city, OH	40.1	4	Brentwood city, CA	43.2
5	Massapequa CDP, NY	95.6	5	State College borough, PA	38.6	5	Fort Washington CDP, MD	42.5
5	New CDP, NY	95.6	6	Maricopa city, AZ	38.3	6	Los Banos city, CA	41.8
7	Trumbull CDP, CT	95.5	7	Statesboro city, GA	38.2	7	Clinton CDP, MD	41.7
8	Commack CDP, NY	95.4	8	Jacksonville city, NC	36.9	8	Dale CDP, VA	41.3
9	Walnut, CA	95.1	8	University CDP, FL	36.9	9	Bainbridge Island city, WA	41.2
10	Danvers CDP, MA	94.8	10	Harrisonburg city, VA	36.2	9	Queen Creek town city, AZ	41.2
11	Springfield CDP, PA	94.7	11	Enterprise CDP, NV	36.0	11	Antioch city, CA	40.7
12	Cranford CDP, NJ	94.6	12	St. Andrews CDP, SC	35.2	12	Hesperia city, CA	40.3
13	Champlin, MN	94.5	13	North Chicago city, IL	33.9	12	Long Beach city, NY	40.3
14	Centereach CDP, NY	94.4	14	Pullman city, WA	33.1	14	Palmdale city, CA	40.2
14	Garden village, NY	94.4	15	Oildale CDP, CA	32.9	15	Sun CDP, CA	40.0
14	Wilmette village, IL	94.4	16	Twentynine Palms city, CA	32.8	16	Plainfield village city, IL	39.8
14	Wilmington CDP, MA	94.4	17	Oxford city, OH	31.7	17	Wildomar CDP, CA	39.4
18	Levittown CDP, NY	94.2	18	Havelock city, NC	31.6	18	New York city, NY	39.3
18	North Haven CDP, CT	94.2	18	Huntsville city, TX	31.6	19	Greater Upper Marlboro CDP, MD	39.1
18	Shirley CDP, NY	94.2	20	North Druid Hills CDP, GA	31.5	19	The Hammocks CDP, FL	39.1
21	Rockville Centre village, NY	94.1	21	Buckeye town, AZ	31.3	21	Oakley city, CA	39.0
22	Bloomfield Township CDP, MI	94.0	22	Carbondale city, IL	30.9	22	Richmond West CDP, FL	38.9
23	Moorpark, CA	93.9	22	Rexburg city, ID	30.9	23	Lake Elsinore city, CA	38.8
24	Morton Grove village, IL	93.8	24	Paine Field-Lake Stickney CDP, WA	30.5	23	Lake Ridge CDP, VA	38.8
24	Nutley CDP, NJ	93.8	25	North Atlanta CDP, GA	30.0	23	Oxon Hill-Glassmanor CDP, MD	38.8
26	Summit, NJ	93.7	26	College Park city, MD	29.9	26	Lake in the Hills village city, IL	38.7
27	Reading CDP, MA	93.6	26	Morgantown city, WV	29.9	27	Fairland CDP, MD	38.1
27	Rosemead, CA	93.6	26	Urbana city, IL	29.9	27	Kendall West CDP, FL	38.1
29	Maplewood CDP, NJ	93.5	29	Clearfield city, UT	29.8	29	Elmont CDP, NY	38.0
29	North Tustin CDP, CA	93.5	30	Chillum CDP, MD	29.7	29	St. Charles CDP, MD	38.0
29	Smithtown CDP, NY	93.5	31	East Lansing city, MI	29.4	31	Candler-McAfee CDP, GA	37.9
32	Clinton CDP, MD	93.4	32	Adelanto city, CA	29.1	32	Algonquin village city, IL	37.8
32	Franklin Square CDP, NY	93.4	32	Bowling Green city, OH	29.1	32	White Oak CDP, MD	37.8
32	Hudson, OH	93.4	32	Four Corners CDP, FL	29.1	34	Dix Hills CDP, NY	37.6
32	Monterey Park, CA	93.4	35	Charleston city, IL	28.9	34	Round Lake Beach village city, IL	37.6
36	Huntington Station CDP, NY	93.3	36	Queen Creek town, AZ	28.8	36	Little Elm city, TX	37.3
37	Levittown CDP, PA	93.2	37	Blacksburg town, VA	28.6	37	Darien CDP, CT	37.2
37	Medford CDP, NY	93.2	38	Columbia city, SC	27.7	37	Huntley village city, IL	37.2
37	Shaler Township CDP, PA	93.2	39	Egypt Lake-Leto CDP, FL	27.6	39	Romeoville village city, IL	36.9
40	East Los Angeles CDP, CA	93.1	39	Parkland CDP, WA	27.6	40	Bowie city, MD	36.8
40	Oakville CDP, MO	93.1	41	Mount Pleasant city, MI	27.5	41	Adelanto city, CA	36.7
40	Valley Stream village, NY	93.1	42	Hayesville CDP, OR	27.3	41	Dolton village city, IL	36.7
43	Allen Park, MI	93.0	43	Millcreek CDP, UT	27.2	41	Hoboken city, NJ	36.7
43	Diamond Bar, CA	93.0	43	Provo city, UT	27.2	41	Westport CDP, FL	36.7
43	Upper St. Clair CDP, PA	93.0	45	Forest Park city, GA	27.1	41	Woodbridge CDP, VA	36.7
43	West Mifflin borough, PA	93.0	45	San Marcos city, TX	27.1	46	Chino Hills city, CA	36.6
47	Andover, MN	92.9	47	Moscow city, ID	26.8	46	Hercules city, CA	36.6
47	Newington CDP, VA	92.9	48	Sandy Springs city, GA	26.7	48	Waldorf CDP, MD	36.5
49	Bethel Park municipality, PA	92.8	49	Kent city, OH	26.5	48	Walnut city, CA	36.5
49	Hicksville CDP, NY	92.8	50	Charlottesville city, VA	26.2	50	Garden village, NY	36.4
49	Livonia, MI	92.8	50	West Pensacola CDP, FL	26.2	50	Palmetto Bay village city, FL	36.4
49	Saugus CDP, MA	92.8	52	Oak Ridge CDP, FL	26.0	52	Perris city, CA	36.2
49	Wethersfield CDP, CT	92.8	53	Ferry Pass CDP, FL	25.8	52	Redan CDP, GA	36.2
54	Elmont CDP, NY	92.7	54	Leavenworth city, KS	25.5	54	Calumet city, IL	36.0
54	Mercerville-Hamilton Square CDP, NJ	92.7	55	Corcoran city, CA	25.4	54	South Miami Heights CDP, FL	36.0
56	Cuyahoga Falls, OH	92.5	56	Picnic Point-North Lynnwood CDP, WA	25.3	56	East Brunswick CDP, NJ	35.9
56	Huntington Park, CA	92.5	57	Clifton city, CO	25.1	56	Moreno Valley city, CA	35.9
56	Park Ridge, IL	92.5	57	College Park city, GA	25.1	58	Grayslake village city, IL	35.8
56	Ramsey, MN	92.5	59	Bentonville city, AR	24.8	59	Diamond Bar city, CA	35.7
56	Stoneham CDP, MA	92.5	59	Monterey city, CA	24.8	59	Kendale Lakes CDP, FL	35.7
61	Glen Cove, NY	92.4	61	Wade Hampton CDP, SC	24.7	61	Coram CDP, NY	35.6
61	Scotch Plains CDP, NJ	92.4	61	Bloomington city, IN	24.6	61	South Holland village city, IL	35.6
61	West Seneca CDP, NY	92.4	62	College Station city, TX	24.6	63	The Crossings CDP, FL	35.4
64	Irondequoit CDP, NY	92.3	62	Wasco city, CA	24.6	64	Old Bridge CDP, NJ	35.3
64	Olney CDP, MD	92.3	65	Sierra Vista city, AZ	24.5	64	Olney CDP, MD	35.3
66	Des Plaines, IL	92.2	66	Bozeman city, MT	24.3	64	Pittsburg city, CA	35.3
66	Gloucester, MA	92.2	67	Kyle city, TX	24.2	67	Edison CDP, NJ	35.2
66	Munster town, IN	92.2	67	Rosemont city, IL	24.2	67	Murrieta city, CA	35.2
66	Severna Park CDP, MD	92.2	69	Cedar City city, UT	24.1	67	West Milford CDP, NJ	35.2
70	Algonquin village, IL	92.1	69	South Bradenton CDP, FL	24.1	70	Chillum CDP, MD	35.1
70	Chesterfield, MO	92.1	71	Ridgeland city, MS	23.9	70	Silver Spring CDP, MD	35.1
70	Union, NJ	92.1	72	Newark city, DE	23.8	72	Centreville CDP, VA	35.0
73	Cooper, FL	92.0	72	Ruston city, LA	23.8	73	Newington CDP, VA	34.9
73	Danville town, CA	92.0	72	Wake Forest town, NC	23.8	73	Rockville Centre village, NY	34.9
73	East Northport CDP, NY	92.0	72	Ypsilanti city, MI	23.8	75	New Lenox village city, IL	34.8
73	Maple Grove, MN	92.0				75	Wheaton-Glenmont CDP, MD	34.8
73	Saratoga, CA	92.0						

City Rankings, 2005–2007
Selected Rankings

Median value of owner-occupied housing units rank	City	Median value of owner-occupied housing units (dollars) [C-4, col 5]	Median selected monthly owner (with a mortgage) costs as a percentage of household income rank	City	Median selected monthly owner (with a mortgage) costs as a percentage of household income [C-4, col 6]	Median gross rent as a percentage of household income rank	City	Median gross rent as a percentage of household income [C-4, col 9]
	United States	181,800		United States	24.7		United States	29.8
1	Beverly Hills city, CA	1,000,00[1]	1	Kiryas Joel village, NY	49.4	1	Athens city, OH	50.1[2]
1	Burlingame city, CA	1,000,00[1]	2	Key West city, FL	47.2	1	Charleston city, IL	50.1[2]
1	Calabasas city, CA	1,000,00[1]	3	East Palo Alto city, CA	47.1	1	College Park city, MD	50.1[2]
1	Coronado city, CA	1,000,00[1]	4	Beverly Hills city, CA	44.2	1	East Lansing city, MI	50.1[2]
1	Darien CDP, CT	1,000,00[1]	5	Hamtramck city, MI	43.7	1	Hudson city, OH	50.1[2]
1	La Canada Flintridge city, CA	1,000,00[1]	6	West Little River CDP, FL	43.2	1	Kiryas Joel village, NY	50.1[2]
1	Lafayette city, CA	1,000,00[1]	7	Union City city, NJ	42.2	1	Oxford city, OH	50.1[2]
1	Laguna Beach city, CA	1,000,00[1]	8	Lodi borough, NJ	41.3	1	Pullman city, WA	50.1[2]
1	Los Altos city, CA	1,000,00[1]	9	Willowbrook CDP, CA	40.6	1	Richmond West CDP, FL	50.1[2]
1	Los Gatos town, CA	1,000,00[1]	10	National City city, CA	40.5	1	San Luis Obispo city, CA	50.1[2]
1	Manhattan Beach city, CA	1,000,00[1]	11	Lennox CDP, CA	40.2	1	Shirley CDP, NY	50.1
1	Menlo Park city, CA	1,000,00[1]	12	Lawrence city, MA	40.0	1	State College borough, PA	50.1
1	Newport Beach city, CA	1,000,00[1]	13	East Orange city, NJ	39.4	1	Streamwood village, IL	50.1
1	Palo Alto city, CA	1,000,00[1]	13	Huntington Park city, CA	39.4	1	West Lafayette city, IN	50.1
1	Rancho Palos Verdes city, CA	1,000,00[1]	15	Copiague CDP, NY	39.2	15	Ruston city, LA	50.0
1	Santa Barbara city, CA	1,000,00[1]	16	Cicero town, IL	39.1	16	South Holland village, IL	49.4
1	Saratoga city, CA	1,000,00[1]	16	Newark city, NJ	39.1	16	Sun City West CDP, AZ	49.4
1	Westport CDP, CT	1,000,00[1]	16	Passaic city, NJ	39.1	18	Starkville city, MS	48.8
19	Danville town, CA	973,100	16	Westmont CDP, CA	39.1	19	Carbondale city, IL	48.2
20	Santa Monica city, CA	950,900	20	Spring Valley village, NY	38.9	20	South Euclid city, OH	47.9
21	Cupertino city, CA	948,200	21	Paterson city, NJ	38.7	21	Morgantown city, WV	47.6
22	Millbrae city, CA	935,500	22	Florence-Graham CDP, CA	38.5	22	Westmont CDP, CA	47.3
23	North Tustin CDP, CA	933,700	23	Soledad city, CA	38.4	23	Lakewood CDP, NJ	46.5
24	San Carlos city, CA	927,200	24	Elizabeth city, NJ	38.3	24	Plainfield city, NJ	46.2
25	Naples city, FL	916,300	24	Hawthorne city, CA	38.3	25	Westchester CDP, FL	45.4
26	Harrison village, NY	915,700	24	North Miami city, FL	38.3	26	Blacksburg town, VA	45.1
27	Wellesley CDP, MA	910,900	27	Bell Gardens city, CA	38.2	27	Newark city, DE	44.9
28	Belmont city, CA	904,600	27	Lakewood CDP, NJ	38.2	28	Chicago Heights city, IL	44.6
29	San Clemente city, CA	883,100	27	Melrose Park village, IL	38.2	29	Passaic city, NJ	44.2
30	Dana Point city, CA	880,400	30	Hialeah city, FL	38.1	30	Webster Groves city, MO	43.9
31	Mercer Island city, WA	878,600	31	North Miami Beach city, FL	38.0	31	Ferguson city, MO	43.7
32	Potomac CDP, MD	874,900	31	Watsonville city, CA	38.0	32	Baldwin CDP, NY	43.6
33	Lake Forest city, IL	869,200	33	Chelsea city, MA	37.8	32	Los Banos city, CA	43.6
34	McLean CDP, VA	863,700	33	Garfield city, NJ	37.8	34	Laguna Hills city, CA	43.4
35	Garden City village, NY	856,200	35	Aventura city, FL	37.7	35	Livingston CDP, NJ	43.2
36	San Rafael city, CA	847,600	35	Paramount city, CA	37.7	35	Saginaw city, MI	43.2
37	University Park city, TX	838,300	37	Fountainbleau CDP, FL	37.6	37	Statesboro city, GA	43.1
38	Yorba Linda city, CA	837,100	37	Golden Gate CDP, FL	37.6	38	Bloomington city, IN	42.8
39	Laguna Niguel city, CA	825,200	37	Yeehaw Junction CDP, FL	37.6	38	Sun City CDP, AZ	42.8
40	Redwood City city, CA	820,900	40	Kihei CDP, HI	37.4	40	East Northport CDP, NY	42.7
41	Pleasanton city, CA	820,000	40	Miami Gardens city, FL	37.4	41	Hacienda Heights CDP, CA	42.5
42	Goleta city, CA	815,800	42	Inglewood city, CA	37.3	41	Huntsville city, TX	42.5
43	Monterey city, CA	810,200	42	Miami city, FL	37.3	43	De Land city, FL	42.3
44	Granite Bay CDP, CA	807,400	42	San Fernando city, CA	37.3	43	West Little River CDP, FL	42.3
45	San Ramon city, CA	806,900	45	North Lauderdale city, FL	36.9	45	College Station city, TX	42.2
46	Agoura Hills city, CA	793,700	46	Maywood city, CA	36.8	45	Highland city, CA	42.2
47	Foster City city, CA	790,500	47	Elmont CDP, NY	36.6	45	Iowa City city, IA	42.2
48	San Francisco city, CA	789,400	47	Roselle borough, NJ	36.6	45	Marrero CDP, LA	42.2
49	Redondo Beach city, CA	788,000	49	Hempstead village, NY	36.5	45	Tamiami CDP, FL	42.2
50	South Pasadena city, CA	785,200	49	Lauderdale Lakes city, FL	36.5	45	Vineyard CDP, CA	42.2
51	San Mateo city, CA	783,900	49	Salinas city, CA	36.5	51	Alexandria city, LA	41.9
52	Santa Cruz city, CA	777,800	52	Long Branch city, NJ	36.4	51	Freeport village, NY	41.9
53	Arcadia city, CA	773,000	52	Richmond city, CA	36.4	53	Bridgeton city, NJ	41.6
54	Kailua CDP (Honolulu County), HI	771,200	52	South Miami Heights CDP, FL	36.4	53	Gilroy city, CA	41.6
55	Dix Hills CDP, NY	763,700	55	El Monte city, CA	36.3	53	Parkland city, FL	41.6
56	Encinitas city, CA	762,400	56	East Cleveland city, OH	36.2	56	Algonquin village, IL	41.4
57	Morgan Hill city, CA	762,300	56	Perris city, CA	36.2	56	San Marcos city, TX	41.4
58	Bethesda CDP, MD	761,500	58	Belleville city, NJ	36.1	56	West Babylon CDP, NY	41.4
59	Coral Gables city, FL	748,000	58	Bridgeport city, CT	36.1	59	Keystone CDP, FL	41.3
60	Key West city, FL	744,700	60	Uniondale CDP, NY	36.0	59	Palmdale city, CA	41.3
61	Huntington Beach city, CA	739,800	61	Everett city, MA	35.9	61	Boulder city, CO	41.2
62	Berkeley city, CA	736,200	62	Brentwood CDP, NY	35.8	61	Hanover Park village, IL	41.2
63	Novato city, CA	729,700	63	Cathedral City city, CA	35.6	61	Homestead city, FL	41.2
64	Mountain View city, CA	727,600	63	South Gate city, CA	35.6	64	La Presa CDP, CA	41.0
65	Summit city, NJ	726,400	65	Lake Elsinore city, CA	35.5	64	Norco city, CA	41.0
66	Thousand Oaks city, CA	724,600	65	South Bradenton CDP, FL	35.5	66	Apple Valley town, CA	40.9
67	Dublin city, CA	723,600	65	Wildomar CDP, CA	35.5	67	Victorville city, CA	40.8
68	Irvine city, CA	716,300	68	Fallbrook CDP, CA	35.4	68	Hialeah city, FL	40.7
69	Laguna Hills city, CA	716,200	69	Valinda CDP, CA	35.3	68	Kendale Lakes CDP, FL	40.7
70	Pacifica city, CA	708,900	70	Los Banos city, CA	35.2	68	Oakley city, CA	40.7
71	Ridgewood village, NJ	708,000	70	Westchester CDP, FL	35.2	68	Tamarac city, FL	40.7
72	Campbell city, CA	705,800	72	Chula Vista city, CA	35.1	72	Adelanto city, CA	40.6
73	Sunnyvale city, CA	705,200	72	La Puente city, CA	35.1	72	Yeehaw Junction CDP, FL	40.6
74	Carlsbad city, CA	699,100	74	Hercules city, CA	35.0	74	San Jacinto city, CA	40.5
75	Winchester city, MA	696,300	74	Richmond West CDP, FL	35.0			

1. $1,000,001 is the top code symbolizing a median value over one million dollars.
2. 50.1 is the top code symbolizing a median gross rent as a percentage of household income of 50.1 percent or more.

Table C-1. States — Where: Migration, Housing, and Transportation, 2005–2007

State code	STATE	Total population 1 year and over	Residence 1 year ago						Total occupied housing units (house-holds)	Percent owner occupied	Homeownership by race and Hispanic origin of households	
			Same house	Different house; same city or town	Different house; different city; same county	Different house; different county; same state	Different house; different state	Abroad			Non-Hispanic White	
											Number of house-holders	Percent owners
	ACS table number:	C07204	C07204	C07204	C07204	C07204	C07204	C07204	B25003	B25003	B25003H	B25003H
		1	2	3	4	5	6	7	8	9	10	11

Table C-1. States — Where: Migration, Housing, and Transportation, 2005–2007—*Continued*

STATE	Homeownership by race and Hispanic origin of householder								Homeownership by age of householder			
	Black		Amer. Indian and Alaska Native		Asian, Hawaiian and Pacific Islander		Hispanic or Latino		15 to 24 years		25 to 44 years	
	Number of house-holders	Percent owners	Number of house-holders	Percent owners	Number of house-holders	Percent owners	Number of householders	Percent owners	Number of house-holders	Percent owners	Number of house-holders	Percent owners
ACS table number:	B25003B	B25003B	B25003C	B25003C	B25003D + B25003E	B25003D + B25003E	B25003I	B25003I	B25007	B25007	B25007	B25007
	12	13	14	15	16	17	18	19	20	21	22	23

Table C-1. States — Where: Migration, Housing, and Transportation, 2005–2007—*Continued*

STATE	Homeownership by age of householder				Homeownership by household type					
	45 to 64 years		65 years and over		Married-couple family households		Male householder families, no wife present		Female householder families, no husband present	
	Number of householders	Percent owners	Number of householders	Percent owners	Number of householders	Percent owners	Number of householders	Percent owners	Number of householders	Percent owners
ACS table number:	B25007	B25007	B25007	B25007	C25115	C25115	C25115	C25115	C25115	C25115
	24	25	26	27	28	29	30	31	32	33

Table C-1. States — Where: Migration, Housing, and Transportation, 2005–2007—*Continued*

STATE	Homeownership by household type		Average household size			Percent of housing units that are crowded or lacking complete plumbing	Median household income in the past 12 months (in 2007 inflation-adjusted dollars)				
	Nonfamily households		All households	Owner-occupied households	Renter-occupied households		All households	Owner-occupied households			Renter-occupied households
	Number of house-holders	Percent owners						All owner-occupied households	Households with a mortgage	House-holds without a mortgage	
ACS table number:	C25115	C25115	B25010	B25010	B25010	C25016	B25119	B25099	B25099	B25099	B25119
	34	35	36	37	38	39	40	41	42	43	44

Table C-1. States — Where: Migration, Housing, and Transportation, 2005–2007—*Continued*

STATE	Median housing value (owner-estimated) (dollars)			Number of owner-occupied housing units	Percent with a mortgage	Percent with a second mortgage and/or a home equity loan	Median monthly housing costs for all housing units with costs (dollars)	Gross rent for renter-occupied housing units		Median selected monthly owner costs for owner-occupied housing units (dollars)		
	All owner-occupied house-holds	House-holds with a mortgage	Households without a mortgage					Median gross rent (dollars)	As a per-centage of house-hold income	All owner-occupied house-holds	House-holds with a mortgage	House-holds without a mortgage
ACS table number:	B25097	B25097	B25097	B25081	B25081	B25081	B25105	B25064	B25071	B25088	B25088	B25088
	45	46	47	48	49	50	51	52	53	54	55	56

Table C-1. States — Where: Migration, Housing, and Transportation, 2005–2007—*Continued*

STATE	Median selected monthly owner costs as a percentage of household income			Households who pay 30 percent or more of income for housing expenses by tenure and age of householder (percent)							
	All owner-occupied households	Households with a mortgage	Households without a mortgage	Owner-occupied households				Renter-occupied households			
				15 to 24 years	25 to 34 years	45 to 64 years	65 years and over	15 to 24 years	25 to 34 years	45 to 64 years	65 years and over
ACS table number:	B25092	B25092	B25092	C25093	C25093	C25093	C25093	C25072	C25072	C25072	C25072
	57	58	59	60	61	62	63	64	65	66	67

Table C-1. States — Where: Migration, Housing, and Transportation, 2005–2007—*Continued*

STATE	Total number of workers 16 years and over	Means of transportation to work (percent)							Number of workers who did not work at home
		Car, truck, or van		Public transportation (excluding taxicab)	Bicycle	Walked	Taxicab, motorcycle, or other means	Worked at home	
		Drove alone	Car-pooled						
ACS table number:	C08301	C08301	C08301	C08301	C08301	C08301	C08301	C08301	C08301
	68	69	70	71	72	73	74	75	76

Table C-1. States — Where: Migration, Housing, and Transportation, 2005–2007—*Continued*

STATE	Mean travel time to work (minutes)					Number of house-holds	Vehicles available (percent of households)				Average vehicles per household
	All workers who did not work at home	By car, truck, or van	Public transportation	Walking	All other means		No vehicles	One vehicle	Two vehicles	Three or more vehicles	
ACS table number:	B08136/C08301	B08136/C08301	B08136/C08301	B08136/C08301	B08136/C08301	B08201	B08201	B08201	B08201	B08201	B25046
	77	78	79	80	81	82	83	84	85	86	87

Table C-2. Counties — Where: Migration, Housing, and Transportation, 2005–2007

STATE County code	STATE County	Percent who lived in the same house one year ago	Percent who did not live in county one year ago	Total occupied housing units	Percent owner-occupied housing units	Median value of owner-occupied housing units (dollars)	Median selected monthly owner costs as a percentage of household income		Median gross rent (dollars)	Median gross rent as a percent-age of house-hold income	Percent of workers who drove alone to work	Mean travel time to work (minutes)	Percent of occupied housing units with no vehicle available
							With a mortgage	Without a mortgage					
ACS table number:		C07204	C07204	B25003	B25003	B25077	B25092	B25092	B25064	B25071	C08301	B08013/ C08012	C25045
		1	2	3	4	5	6	7	8	9	10	11	12

Table C-3. Metropolitan Areas — Where: Migration, Housing, and Transportation, 2005–2007

Metro area or division code	Area name	Percent who lived in the same house one year ago	Percent who did not live in MSA one year ago	Total occupied housing units	Percent owner-occupied housing units	Median value of owner-occupied housing units (dollars)	Median selected monthly owner costs as a percentage of house-hold income		Median gross rent (dollars)	Median gross rent as a percent-age of house-hold income	Percent of workers who drove alone to work	Mean travel time to work (minutes)	Percent of occupied housing units with no vehicle available
							With a mortgage	Without a mortgage					
ACS table number:		C07204	C07201	B25003	B25003	B25077	B25092	B25092	B25064	B25071	C08301	B08013/ C08012	C25045
		1	2	3	4	5	6	7	8	9	10	11	12

Table C-4. Cities — Where: Migration, Housing, and Transportation, 2005–2007

STATE Place code	STATE City	Percent who lived in the same house one year ago	Percent who did not live in city one year ago	Total occupied housing units	Percent owner-occupied housing units	Median value of owner-occupied housing units (dollars)[1]	Median selected monthly owner costs as a percentage of household income		Median gross rent (dollars)	Median gross rent as a percent-age of house-hold income[2]	Percent of workers who drove alone to work	Mean travel time to work (minutes)	Percent of occupied housing units with no vehicle available
							With a mortgage	Without a mortgage					
ACS table number:		C07204	C07204	B25003	B25003	B25077	B25092	B25092	B25064	B25071	C08301	B08013/ C08012	C25045
		1	2	3	4	5	6	7	8	9	10	11	12

State code	STATE	Total population 1 year and over	Residence 1 year ago						Total occupied housing units (households)	Percent owner occu-pied	Homeownership by race and Hispanic origin of households Non-Hispanic White	
			Same house	Different house; same city or town	Different house; different city; same	Different house; different county; same state	Different house; different state	Abroad			Number of house-holders	Percent owners
	ACS table number:	C07204	C07204	C07204	C07204	C07204	C07204	C07204	B25003	B25003	B25003H	B25003H
		1	2	3	4	5	6	7	8	9	10	11
00	United States	294,699,072	83.4	5.3	4.6	3.5	2.6	0.6	111,609,629	67.3	80,633,248	73.9
01	Alabama.................	4,526,092	83.3	4.8	5.2	3.3	3.0	0.4	1,798,304	71.3	1,281,678	77.9
02	Alaska....................	666,867	78.6	8.7	2.9	3.2	5.6	0.9	233,861	63.7	171,669	77.7
04	Arizona..................	6,056,968	78.7	8.0	5.7	1.8	4.7	1.0	2,215,761	68.6	1,544,880	74.2
05	Arkansas...............	2,765,990	80.7	6.3	5.0	4.0	3.7	0.3	1,096,622	68.0	869,166	73.0
06	California...............	35,740,204	83.5	5.9	5.0	3.3	1.4	0.9	12,140,888	58.4	6,539,760	66.1
08	Colorado	4,696,694	79.6	6.8	3.8	5.0	4.1	0.7	1,838,303	68.7	1,426,150	73.4
09	Connecticut	3,454,701	86.9	3.7	4.4	1.9	2.5	0.6	1,323,431	69.7	1,040,590	77.2
10	Delaware	842,750	84.5	2.1	7.5	1.0	4.4	0.5	321,748	73.6	237,594	80.7
11	District of Columbia..	576,545	79.4	10.3	0.0	0.0	8.9	1.4	249,805	44.1	92,243	55.0
12	Florida	17,786,885	81.9	3.8	6.7	3.4	3.3	0.9	7,077,123	70.3	4,800,649	77.2
13	Georgia	9,190,262	81.0	3.4	5.9	5.2	3.9	0.6	3,364,749	67.9	2,137,297	77.3
15	Hawaii	1,259,935	83.8	3.7	5.8	0.6	4.7	1.4	433,664	58.9	136,904	54.1
16	Idaho....................	1,440,013	79.1	6.7	4.5	3.9	5.1	0.7	545,171	71.6	488,202	73.4
17	Illinois...................	12,610,129	84.9	5.8	3.8	3.0	1.9	0.6	4,724,462	70.1	3,387,983	77.4
18	Indiana	6,217,409	83.2	6.4	3.9	3.7	2.4	0.4	2,447,887	72.1	2,102,573	76.1
19	Iowa	2,933,193	83.1	6.5	3.3	3.8	2.9	0.3	1,206,848	73.3	1,126,122	75.1
20	Kansas...................	2,718,061	81.1	7.9	2.9	4.0	3.4	0.6	1,083,868	70.0	919,285	73.3
21	Kentucky	4,150,060	83.3	5.0	4.7	3.7	2.9	0.4	1,654,119	70.8	1,479,887	74.0
22	Louisiana	4,285,054	82.6	5.2	4.7	4.7	2.5	0.3	1,605,203	68.1	1,062,964	76.4
23	Maine.....................	1,299,842	85.2	3.1	5.5	3.0	2.9	0.3	542,424	72.9	522,465	74.0
24	Maryland	5,520,672	84.9	2.9	4.8	3.5	3.1	0.8	2,082,573	69.4	1,306,631	77.9
25	Massachusetts	6,362,615	85.9	4.7	3.6	2.8	2.1	0.9	2,448,608	65.0	2,033,727	70.6
26	Michigan	9,967,484	85.4	4.1	5.1	3.6	1.4	0.4	3,864,307	75.1	3,123,728	80.2
27	Minnesota	5,084,988	85.2	4.4	3.3	4.5	2.1	0.5	2,041,466	75.8	1,830,348	79.1
28	Mississippi.............	2,863,227	82.9	4.6	5.1	4.1	3.0	0.2	1,079,584	70.9	676,387	78.7
29	Missouri.................	5,758,986	82.6	5.1	4.7	4.5	2.9	0.3	2,300,211	70.7	1,944,812	74.7
30	Montana.................	935,008	81.7	6.0	4.4	3.5	4.1	0.3	369,329	70.1	337,493	72.0
31	Nebraska	1,737,312	82.3	8.0	2.5	3.8	3.0	0.5	698,163	68.5	616,507	71.5
32	Nevada	2,450,752	78.3	5.9	8.3	1.1	5.6	0.8	932,715	61.0	626,001	66.5
33	New Hampshire	1,296,529	85.7	3.5	4.1	2.4	3.8	0.4	500,671	73.2	475,437	74.3
34	New Jersey.............	8,559,122	88.3	3.0	3.5	2.6	1.9	0.7	3,143,408	67.4	2,114,661	78.2
35	New Mexico............	1,915,814	82.3	7.3	3.1	2.8	3.9	0.7	728,508	69.6	370,853	73.0
36	New York................	19,044,665	87.8	5.3	2.7	2.0	1.4	0.8	7,096,035	55.6	4,697,740	67.4
37	North Carolina.........	8,749,416	82.0	4.9	5.0	3.7	3.8	0.6	3,471,751	68.4	2,492,387	75.8
38	North Dakota...........	629,762	82.5	7.2	2.3	3.5	3.9	0.6	271,131	66.5	252,146	68.6
39	Ohio	11,317,113	84.2	5.3	5.1	3.4	1.7	0.3	4,500,621	70.0	3,794,810	74.9
40	Oklahoma...............	3,528,291	80.0	7.9	3.9	4.3	3.4	0.5	1,386,849	68.3	1,059,080	73.0
41	Oregon	3,643,171	79.7	6.6	5.4	3.9	3.9	0.6	1,447,409	64.7	1,249,877	67.4
42	Pennsylvania	12,257,517	86.9	3.3	4.5	2.8	2.1	0.4	4,858,509	71.7	4,124,894	75.8
44	Rhode Island...........	1,049,949	86.6	4.2	3.8	1.6	3.1	0.6	404,549	63.3	338,539	68.7
45	South Carolina.........	4,274,946	83.4	2.3	6.6	3.3	3.9	0.5	1,664,561	70.3	1,145,518	77.8
46	South Dakota...........	776,632	82.9	7.0	2.5	3.6	3.6	0.3	311,644	69.1	284,448	72.1
47	Tennessee	5,990,475	82.9	6.0	4.4	3.1	3.2	0.4	2,382,975	70.1	1,909,382	75.1
48	Texas.....................	23,001,298	80.2	7.8	4.1	4.5	2.5	0.8	8,095,025	65.2	4,520,917	72.8
49	Utah......................	2,525,875	79.5	5.5	6.7	3.5	4.0	0.8	812,604	71.9	704,448	74.8
50	Vermont	614,524	85.0	2.6	5.5	2.4	4.1	0.4	250,871	72.2	242,076	72.9
51	Virginia....................	7,535,550	83.1	3.3	3.5	5.6	3.7	0.8	2,909,223	69.7	2,088,573	75.6
53	Washington	6,288,449	80.0	5.4	6.6	3.5	3.5	0.9	2,472,477	65.6	2,025,334	69.2
54	West Virginia	1,790,278	86.9	2.2	5.2	2.5	3.0	0.2	738,943	74.9	699,525	76.0
55	Wisconsin	5,503,499	84.3	6.0	3.8	3.6	1.9	0.3	2,235,246	70.3	1,992,841	73.8
56	Wyoming.................	507,499	80.3	7.1	4.0	2.6	5.5	0.5	205,422	70.0	186,067	71.2

Table C-1. States — Where: Migration, Housing, and Transportation, 2005–2007—*Continued*

	Homeownership by race and Hispanic origin of householder								Homeownership by age of householder			
	Black		Amer. Indian and Alaska Native		Asian, Hawaiian and Pacific Islander		Hispanic or Latino		15 to 24 years		25 to 44 years	
STATE	Number of householders	Percent owners	Number of householders	Percent owners	Number of house-holders	Percent owners	Number of householders	Percent owners	Number of house-holders	Percent owners	Number of house-holders	Percent owners
ACS table number:	B25003B	B25003B	B25003C	B25003C	B25003D+ B25003E	B25003D + B25003E	B25003I	B25003I	B25007	B25007	B25007	B25007
	12	13	14	15	16	17	18	19	20	21	22	23
United States	13,040,866	46.3	793,771	56.0	4,217,014	59.7	11,954,408	49.5	5,368,337	17.8	41,073,201	57.6
Alabama	449,794	54.7	9,161	70.6	14,981	55.2	28,661	43.7	97,175	22.2	627,548	61.2
Alaska....................	8,168	36.3	26,126	57.1	9,064	57.9	10,189	50.7	13,684	15.8	93,198	53.8
Arizona..................	70,383	42.7	72,643	56.7	50,474	63.8	463,833	56.7	115,412	20.3	828,956	57.4
Arkansas................	165,855	47.4	7,276	62.5	9,855	60.4	34,053	47.2	65,071	20.5	382,105	56.6
California...............	796,210	39.7	92,265	50.0	1,406,373	58.5	3,161,315	47.7	523,439	11.2	4,773,212	46.2
Colorado	66,901	44.1	16,688	49.4	44,236	63.3	269,649	52.3	103,811	17.2	731,001	60.4
Connecticut............	112,866	41.0	3,278	52.9	37,376	57.9	118,617	36.7	40,698	15.9	470,310	61.3
Delaware	60,129	52.8	977	68.1	7,875	68.0	13,147	45.6	13,999	25.1	116,434	63.5
District of Columbia ..	129,585	38.5	790	33.5	8,482	37.8	15,963	29.4	13,779	5.4	103,263	35.7
Florida	916,301	50.3	22,893	62.0	130,078	68.6	1,169,021	57.9	311,139	18.1	2,365,856	57.8
Georgia	952,283	51.6	8,615	58.0	77,110	68.1	166,648	43.0	166,837	18.9	1,384,471	59.1
Hawaii	11,102	23.4	1,652	36.1	208,721	66.8	26,842	42.4	18,341	10.0	145,900	40.8
Idaho	2,516	35.5	5,594	60.4	6,122	61.5	36,823	56.0	38,966	21.5	201,046	63.8
Illinois	647,155	43.1	8,027	60.4	177,190	66.0	473,701	57.3	211,807	20.2	1,795,916	62.6
Indiana	207,583	43.5	5,711	64.5	27,921	56.2	84,755	52.4	131,514	22.6	907,585	64.7
Iowa	25,185	36.6	2,788	47.6	15,499	54.6	31,033	52.6	84,745	23.9	406,726	67.6
Kansas..................	59,111	43.9	8,723	57.5	19,044	61.7	66,283	54.3	76,535	20.8	385,495	62.2
Kentucky	122,986	43.2	3,110	58.0	14,592	49.4	22,879	37.9	82,352	21.8	598,629	61.8
Louisiana	463,404	50.8	8,600	69.4	10,675	63.3	40,477	53.7	94,278	21.8	570,546	59.5
Maine	3,631	23.3	2,700	52.4	3,418	48.4	4,163	43.4	21,997	16.7	177,726	64.2
Maryland	573,633	52.5	5,449	63.3	88,045	67.6	88,225	57.1	77,896	17.0	781,545	61.1
Massachusetts	128,040	35.6	5,149	44.1	99,234	51.6	156,362	28.0	78,140	10.3	886,269	55.5
Michigan	497,033	50.1	20,696	63.5	77,696	60.5	109,641	58.5	177,590	23.5	1,375,053	68.0
Minnesota	74,555	29.2	18,647	50.8	50,497	62.2	52,040	51.0	118,482	27.0	759,760	72.2
Mississippi	373,001	57.9	3,797	66.0	7,422	62.4	13,707	43.9	56,825	24.9	383,455	60.8
Missouri.................	246,608	45.9	9,356	55.6	29,046	57.8	46,825	52.3	129,596	21.9	820,948	63.0
Montana................	1,178	40.8	17,332	47.3	2,041	44.7	6,769	56.2	20,603	16.3	115,571	59.8
Nebraska...............	27,263	33.8	4,292	40.6	9,306	56.1	34,992	52.0	50,390	16.1	247,663	61.1
Nevada	68,483	37.3	11,489	53.7	52,859	65.1	162,907	49.7	44,574	18.3	370,528	51.7
New Hampshire	3,742	40.5	1,724	38.0	8,073	61.4	8,784	47.4	17,261	14.0	178,277	66.4
New Jersey..............	413,033	42.0	6,239	53.2	198,787	63.4	394,542	38.6	76,893	16.0	1,148,507	57.4
New Mexico............	14,143	48.0	48,939	62.8	9,690	58.0	281,393	67.8	44,794	21.7	250,899	58.6
New York...............	1,005,183	32.6	25,813	43.0	405,812	46.1	933,226	24.5	232,915	12.1	2,553,403	44.9
North Carolina	709,427	49.7	36,576	66.3	52,056	61.3	156,158	39.5	186,272	16.9	1,311,208	58.6
North Dakota..........	2,120	15.1	9,682	44.3	2,039	27.4	3,127	42.7	28,450	15.3	88,189	61.7
Ohio	519,296	41.4	9,085	53.1	62,295	54.8	79,776	46.4	216,003	17.6	1,589,854	62.0
Oklahoma..............	98,360	42.2	83,262	63.3	19,462	58.7	69,612	50.1	94,645	20.9	481,540	57.5
Oregon	22,693	34.5	19,834	45.5	45,015	63.1	93,190	41.3	76,434	12.4	511,263	53.5
Pennsylvania	458,294	47.6	7,112	54.3	94,936	58.9	151,658	44.0	185,472	16.9	1,613,117	63.6
Rhode Island...........	18,765	35.6	1,398	49.0	8,476	50.0	32,672	29.3	15,354	10.9	143,113	54.6
South Carolina........	445,606	54.7	4,868	64.6	16,687	60.2	41,735	40.0	83,820	19.5	589,653	59.6
South Dakota..........	2,019	25.0	16,886	37.2	1,676	54.8	4,699	35.2	23,387	19.5	103,040	64.6
Tennessee	371,422	50.1	7,547	58.1	25,268	59.5	51,983	37.9	119,014	19.8	878,205	60.3
Texas....................	934,168	46.2	42,649	61.9	245,395	63.8	2,300,451	58.2	470,602	15.6	3,275,362	55.2
Utah	6,639	45.5	8,586	49.9	18,518	57.4	70,112	51.8	62,508	23.3	338,292	65.7
Vermont	1,025	26.2	731	75.6	1,843	64.4	2,633	55.0	9,621	14.3	83,503	61.7
Virginia	543,502	51.4	8,053	64.9	114,763	69.5	126,322	53.4	135,892	17.8	1,102,308	60.2
Washington	76,257	36.5	29,028	46.2	145,163	62.3	155,026	43.3	125,948	13.5	927,763	55.7
West Virginia	23,109	48.5	1,284	74.1	4,202	62.9	5,380	62.0	34,840	22.0	235,217	65.1
Wisconsin	109,746	34.5	17,318	51.6	31,471	51.9	71,353	42.8	132,807	18.7	796,168	64.1
Wyoming...............	1,375	29.5	3,333	54.3	1,163	68.6	11,116	61.9	15,730	22.4	67,605	60.9

Table C-1. States — Where: Migration, Housing, and Transportation, 2005–2007—*Continued*

STATE	Homeownership by age of householder				Homeownership by household type					
	45 to 64 years		65 years and over		Married-couple family households		Male householder families, no wife present		Female householder families, no husband present	
	Number of householders	Percent owners	Number of householders	Percent owners	Number of householders	Percent owners	Number of householders	Percent owners	Number of householders	Percent owners
ACS table number:	B25007	B25007	B25007	B25007	C25115	C25115	C25115	C25115	C25115	C25115
	24	25	26	27	28	29	30	31	32	33
United States	42,350,942	76.7	22,817,149	78.8	55,603,280	82.9	5,103,598	56.8	13,918,181	48.9
Alabama......................	677,472	80.4	396,109	83.5	893,237	86.2	75,719	61.5	261,495	51.7
Alaska........................	100,848	75.7	26,131	77.8	119,465	76.6	13,335	55.8	27,029	52.6
Arizona.......................	793,362	78.0	478,031	83.9	1,097,059	82.4	110,635	56.7	261,403	51.5
Arkansas.....................	402,029	77.9	247,417	82.1	563,092	82.8	46,874	56.7	139,796	45.6
California....................	4,590,482	68.5	2,253,755	74.6	6,044,996	72.5	698,545	47.5	1,549,620	42.6
Colorado	707,994	79.9	295,497	80.3	925,072	84.1	81,723	57.7	178,788	51.1
Connecticut................	528,270	78.6	284,153	75.1	677,138	86.4	52,793	59.8	160,268	48.9
Delaware	121,440	82.9	69,875	83.8	160,625	87.2	14,963	61.9	42,321	53.5
District of Columbia.....	85,165	51.4	47,598	60.6	54,237	69.4	9,401	47.9	43,614	34.7
Florida	2,569,620	78.1	1,830,508	84.3	3,424,330	83.4	322,157	55.8	873,322	53.4
Georgia	1,261,334	78.0	552,107	81.9	1,648,132	83.4	154,974	55.9	493,283	49.4
Hawaii........................	170,869	68.9	98,554	77.2	225,902	68.8	23,145	59.0	54,685	50.4
Idaho.........................	200,334	82.0	104,825	85.1	310,762	83.5	22,340	60.4	49,014	51.4
Illinois.......................	1,763,744	78.6	952,995	79.5	2,357,325	86.4	207,846	61.7	590,199	50.0
Indiana......................	915,869	81.2	492,919	82.0	1,262,601	87.7	107,491	60.9	282,076	51.3
Iowa..........................	439,525	83.1	275,852	81.4	637,768	89.0	42,243	62.8	110,865	53.9
Kansas.......................	398,684	81.5	223,154	80.1	571,810	85.4	42,513	60.3	109,660	50.6
Kentucky....................	630,786	79.5	342,352	82.4	840,501	85.2	68,805	63.6	204,060	50.4
Louisiana....................	612,719	76.0	327,660	81.7	751,034	84.9	74,642	63.8	264,862	49.3
Maine........................	221,782	82.8	120,919	77.5	277,646	87.8	23,509	66.1	53,160	56.2
Maryland	826,153	78.5	396,979	77.1	1,013,474	85.1	95,232	60.0	286,570	53.4
Massachusetts	963,166	75.1	521,033	70.6	1,173,091	83.8	99,176	58.7	294,372	47.8
Michigan	1,508,401	83.5	803,263	82.9	1,939,163	90.4	164,525	69.0	476,110	56.0
Minnesota	771,344	85.5	391,880	78.3	1,066,850	91.5	81,730	70.5	187,066	57.4
Mississippi..................	408,114	78.7	231,190	85.1	506,173	85.8	51,020	62.7	196,387	53.5
Missouri.....................	858,783	79.8	490,884	80.5	1,151,019	87.0	95,262	61.8	274,079	51.9
Montana.....................	151,927	80.1	81,228	79.4	194,172	83.9	13,730	63.0	31,051	53.1
Nebraska	252,634	79.5	147,476	79.7	368,374	84.9	25,538	56.0	66,149	47.9
Nevada	351,524	69.3	166,089	75.8	446,711	75.4	56,026	49.0	108,149	45.7
New Hampshire	209,869	82.4	95,264	76.3	272,100	88.0	20,198	64.8	46,593	57.2
New Jersey..................	1,249,525	75.6	668,483	75.3	1,639,583	82.7	145,973	54.8	398,981	49.1
New Mexico.................	279,405	79.3	153,410	84.0	344,615	83.3	39,393	62.7	96,184	56.6
New York....................	2,774,775	64.4	1,534,942	64.3	3,208,929	74.8	344,321	48.1	1,036,163	37.6
North Carolina.............	1,298,654	78.1	675,617	82.6	1,719,721	84.0	150,063	57.6	452,740	47.8
North Dakota...............	95,314	81.2	59,178	74.4	138,154	85.6	9,467	65.2	20,149	50.5
Ohio	1,726,937	78.6	967,827	79.8	2,215,565	87.6	186,870	60.7	561,815	48.1
Oklahoma...................	508,963	78.5	301,701	83.3	702,154	83.4	61,668	55.4	166,251	48.0
Oregon	563,651	75.5	296,061	76.9	721,038	81.2	59,856	48.9	145,189	45.6
Pennsylvania	1,891,033	80.5	1,168,887	77.5	2,424,483	88.2	203,158	66.1	567,448	54.9
Rhode Island...............	159,498	73.5	86,584	68.5	190,509	83.0	16,579	54.7	51,346	45.5
South Carolina.............	643,831	79.1	347,257	84.6	806,508	85.6	69,173	59.7	250,625	50.9
South Dakota...............	115,013	80.9	70,204	73.0	164,145	85.9	11,793	59.1	28,829	49.6
Tennessee	900,267	79.2	485,489	83.2	1,185,780	85.4	106,961	58.9	312,623	50.5
Texas.........................	2,958,835	76.4	1,390,226	81.8	4,186,442	80.3	396,677	53.9	1,096,214	49.1
Utah..........................	276,807	83.4	134,997	86.8	505,530	81.7	32,722	58.7	75,065	57.3
Vermont.....................	105,954	82.3	51,793	79.4	124,135	88.4	11,208	66.5	25,236	54.8
Virginia......................	1,126,072	79.5	544,951	81.4	1,477,226	84.3	119,895	58.5	351,764	50.7
Washington.................	963,535	76.6	455,231	76.9	1,234,960	82.3	108,320	53.6	251,009	46.8
West Virginia	288,235	82.3	180,651	85.9	385,197	87.5	30,536	65.9	80,627	58.0
Wisconsin	847,012	81.1	459,259	76.2	1,146,767	88.2	92,943	61.7	216,960	47.8
Wyoming....................	83,383	80.2	38,704	83.2	107,980	83.6	9,932	59.6	16,917	52.7

STATE	Homeownership by household type — Nonfamily households		Average household size			Percent of housing units that are crowded or lacking complete plumbing	Median household income in the past 12 months (in 2007 inflation-adjusted dollars)				
								Owner-occupied households			
	Number of householders	Percent owners	All households	Owner-occupied households	Renter-occupied households		All households	All owner-occupied households	Households with a mortgage	Households without a mortgage	Renter-occupied households
ACS table number:	C25115	C25115	B25010	B25010	B25010	C25016	B25119	B25099	B25099	B25099	B25119
	34	35	36	37	38	39	40	41	42	43	44
United States	36,984,570	52.1	2.60	2.70	2.41	3.4	50,007	62,257	72,728	39,994	30,473
Alabama	567,853	58.1	2.48	2.55	2.33	2.1	40,052	49,770	61,226	32,938	22,200
Alaska...................	74,032	48.3	2.80	2.95	2.53	9.8	61,766	76,792	86,335	53,178	41,729
Arizona..................	746,664	56.1	2.73	2.76	2.67	5.1	48,609	59,159	69,117	37,291	31,716
Arkansas.................	346,860	54.6	2.49	2.54	2.38	3.0	37,555	46,904	57,242	32,759	22,997
California................	3,847,727	44.5	2.92	3.01	2.79	8.1	58,361	77,603	87,351	45,265	38,518
Colorado.................	652,720	53.1	2.53	2.63	2.33	2.5	54,262	68,555	75,997	43,235	31,168
Connecticut..............	433,232	52.6	2.55	2.70	2.21	2.2	65,496	82,426	92,189	52,727	34,429
Delaware	103,839	62.3	2.57	2.62	2.45	1.8	55,303	65,961	77,081	41,597	35,175
District of Columbia..	142,553	37.1	2.20	2.32	2.11	3.6	52,187	86,938	96,444	54,984	34,857
Florida	2,457,314	60.0	2.49	2.51	2.44	2.8	46,602	55,072	64,694	37,766	31,752
Georgia	1,068,360	54.3	2.69	2.75	2.59	2.4	48,540	61,244	70,170	37,857	29,170
Hawaii	129,932	45.0	2.86	3.03	2.62	9.3	62,543	78,480	88,783	56,293	44,260
Idaho....................	163,055	56.4	2.62	2.68	2.46	3.0	44,901	53,484	60,340	36,226	27,519
Illinois	1,569,092	54.2	2.64	2.76	2.35	2.8	53,745	66,718	76,195	44,287	29,618
Indiana	795,719	56.2	2.50	2.60	2.23	1.8	47,034	57,354	65,164	37,865	26,217
Iowa	415,972	55.6	2.38	2.49	2.06	1.6	46,399	55,853	65,105	39,175	25,933
Kansas...................	359,885	52.7	2.47	2.58	2.20	1.9	46,669	57,988	68,269	39,017	27,435
Kentucky	540,753	57.2	2.47	2.55	2.28	2.0	40,138	49,748	60,999	31,604	22,779
Louisiana	514,665	53.9	2.63	2.71	2.45	3.5	40,160	50,810	63,362	34,985	22,780
Maine....................	188,109	56.4	2.35	2.46	2.06	1.9	45,211	54,220	64,366	35,536	24,972
Maryland	687,297	54.3	2.62	2.74	2.35	2.0	66,873	82,994	91,906	51,207	39,770
Massachusetts	881,969	46.3	2.54	2.74	2.18	1.8	61,785	80,615	91,018	49,419	33,483
Michigan	1,284,509	59.8	2.55	2.64	2.25	1.9	48,642	58,787	68,499	37,921	25,024
Minnesota	705,820	57.5	2.46	2.59	2.04	2.0	55,616	66,527	75,232	43,493	28,133
Mississippi...............	326,004	59.3	2.60	2.63	2.53	3.4	35,632	43,899	54,129	30,879	21,521
Missouri	779,851	54.3	2.46	2.58	2.19	1.9	44,545	54,913	64,204	37,116	25,263
Montana..................	130,376	54.2	2.49	2.56	2.33	2.0	42,425	50,988	60,427	37,129	25,450
Nebraska	238,102	50.0	2.45	2.59	2.16	1.9	46,954	58,298	67,541	39,673	28,107
Nevada	321,829	48.3	2.63	2.69	2.55	3.9	53,753	66,800	73,577	44,137	37,971
New Hampshire	161,780	53.8	2.54	2.68	2.15	1.7	61,459	77,788	82,016	46,915	35,048
New Jersey...............	958,871	50.9	2.70	2.83	2.41	2.9	66,509	84,936	95,924	53,411	38,457
New Mexico.............	248,316	56.9	2.61	2.69	2.43	4.2	41,042	50,226	61,249	34,637	25,857
New York................	2,506,622	39.6	2.63	2.80	2.42	4.7	52,944	72,125	83,872	48,733	33,663
North Carolina	1,149,227	54.5	2.48	2.54	2.35	2.3	43,867	54,404	64,232	34,618	26,814
North Dakota...........	103,361	44.1	2.25	2.45	1.86	1.3	43,442	55,016	66,544	39,893	25,649
Ohio	1,536,371	53.9	2.48	2.60	2.19	1.4	46,296	58,331	67,201	38,004	25,096
Oklahoma...............	456,776	54.3	2.50	2.56	2.37	2.6	40,371	50,219	60,394	34,975	24,787
Oregon	521,326	49.0	2.49	2.59	2.32	3.1	47,385	60,521	69,150	39,107	29,072
Pennsylvania	1,663,420	54.1	2.46	2.59	2.11	1.4	47,913	58,503	70,426	38,480	26,847
Rhode Island............	146,115	45.0	2.53	2.72	2.20	1.8	54,060	72,984	81,313	45,126	29,661
South Carolina.........	538,255	57.9	2.52	2.56	2.41	2.0	42,405	51,820	61,816	34,306	26,224
South Dakota...........	106,877	49.7	2.43	2.55	2.17	2.3	43,586	53,818	63,095	39,400	24,692
Tennessee	777,611	56.1	2.48	2.55	2.33	2.0	41,821	51,677	60,561	35,863	24,730
Texas....................	2,415,692	48.2	2.82	2.94	2.59	5.2	46,248	59,551	71,344	40,027	29,255
Utah	199,287	54.8	3.12	3.24	2.79	3.6	53,324	63,425	68,759	45,752	31,895
Vermont	90,292	55.6	2.39	2.52	2.06	1.6	49,382	59,813	68,260	41,516	28,016
Virginia	960,338	55.5	2.54	2.62	2.37	1.8	58,378	71,197	82,055	41,831	36,460
Washington..............	878,188	48.9	2.52	2.64	2.28	2.7	53,940	68,772	77,069	44,355	32,565
West Virginia	242,583	61.5	2.39	2.46	2.18	1.5	36,088	43,152	56,319	31,726	19,416
Wisconsin	778,576	51.2	2.42	2.56	2.10	1.8	50,309	61,977	70,274	42,248	28,354
Wyoming.................	70,593	54.8	2.43	2.52	2.24	2.0	50,009	58,640	67,472	42,889	32,708

Table C-1. States — Where: Migration, Housing, and Transportation, 2005–2007—*Continued*

STATE	Median housing value (owner-estimated) (dollars)			Number of owner-occupied housing units	Percent with a mortgage	Percent with a second mortgage and/or a home equity loan	Median monthly housing costs for all housing units with costs (dollars)	Gross rent for renter-occupied housing units		Median selected monthly owner costs for owner-occupied housing units (dollars)		
	All owner-occupied households	Households with a mortgage	Households without a mortgage					Median gross rent (dollars)	As a percentage of household income	All owner-occupied households	Households with a mortgage	Households without a mortgage
ACS table number:	B25097	B25097	B25097	B25081	B25081	B25081	B25105	B25064	B25071	B25088	B25088	B25088
	45	46	47	48	49	50	51	52	53	54	55	56
United States	181,800	203,900	138,700	75,072,666	68.2	17.8	920	781	29.8	1,058	1,427	402
Alabama	106,800	120,400	87,500	1,281,364	60.8	12.9	643	586	28.7	693	1,014	297
Alaska	213,400	226,200	168,100	149,008	70.8	13.6	1,081	898	27.2	1,308	1,654	474
Arizona	221,800	241,000	157,400	1,520,037	70.9	19.1	931	786	29.6	1,067	1,371	327
Arkansas	93,700	103,600	80,900	745,814	58.8	7.5	602	578	28.8	626	916	294
California	513,200	534,800	440,000	7,085,134	76.2	24.3	1,315	1,058	32.2	1,760	2,180	423
Colorado	230,400	236,700	203,600	1,262,790	76.8	25.6	1,087	797	30.0	1,329	1,564	374
Connecticut	294,100	306,200	257,400	922,957	72.1	22.4	1,256	910	29.8	1,567	1,909	680
Delaware	225,200	237,400	191,200	236,646	69.4	20.0	987	868	29.3	1,092	1,414	364
District of Columbia	424,200	440,500	373,100	110,234	76.0	22.6	1,097	906	29.4	1,558	1,941	484
Florida	217,800	236,700	172,100	4,975,273	65.7	16.9	975	892	32.9	1,061	1,450	436
Georgia	156,300	165,700	120,800	2,285,884	72.6	18.4	901	756	29.5	1,056	1,316	334
Hawaii	510,500	521,500	486,200	255,238	68.1	18.4	1,264	1,144	31.0	1,447	1,992	386
Idaho	158,600	166,900	134,500	390,109	69.8	19.8	779	644	27.3	883	1,117	306
Illinois	198,100	215,000	157,400	3,311,632	69.6	17.8	985	780	29.8	1,213	1,598	499
Indiana	119,400	126,300	100,900	1,764,680	70.4	18.3	779	646	28.6	888	1,106	353
Iowa	112,600	122,200	96,700	884,928	62.8	14.9	695	587	26.9	790	1,092	375
Kansas	114,400	129,700	87,400	759,218	65.2	14.0	735	626	27.3	840	1,157	379
Kentucky	109,700	122,400	87,000	1,171,597	62.5	15.9	628	560	27.8	702	1,012	277
Louisiana	113,500	130,600	89,200	1,093,882	57.1	9.6	647	629	30.3	668	1,041	294
Maine	167,700	177,800	142,200	395,213	65.0	17.5	771	650	28.8	873	1,209	393
Maryland	323,400	338,600	246,200	1,445,426	76.8	23.6	1,233	977	29.2	1,475	1,769	473
Massachusetts	366,200	373,900	344,200	1,590,657	72.0	22.3	1,247	952	30.1	1,571	1,958	619
Michigan	152,200	161,200	129,900	2,902,094	69.2	19.9	882	689	31.0	1,024	1,321	423
Minnesota	207,200	219,000	171,300	1,547,161	71.6	22.5	974	719	29.0	1,163	1,470	407
Mississippi	88,100	99,600	75,500	765,111	57.0	7.9	612	591	30.6	627	950	310
Missouri	131,100	140,900	108,600	1,625,909	66.8	14.4	730	623	28.4	834	1,123	334
Montana	152,300	164,000	127,400	258,717	59.2	12.7	667	582	27.4	755	1,127	350
Nebraska	118,200	129,200	96,000	477,911	64.3	16.0	739	610	26.4	874	1,188	402
Nevada	302,600	316,800	234,600	569,150	77.5	22.1	1,141	944	29.8	1,402	1,652	410
New Hampshire	250,700	267,600	220,100	366,320	71.0	20.3	1,175	892	28.7	1,396	1,745	627
New Jersey	358,400	371,200	321,400	2,119,602	71.3	20.6	1,349	1,002	30.2	1,732	2,177	804
New Mexico	140,100	155,800	108,200	507,301	61.2	11.3	684	630	29.2	742	1,102	285
New York	293,400	322,100	223,500	3,948,154	65.2	15.9	1,046	898	30.4	1,266	1,820	622
North Carolina	136,800	147,000	110,400	2,373,264	67.8	19.5	777	674	28.9	892	1,174	324
North Dakota	97,400	116,900	74,900	180,238	54.6	10.6	574	513	25.1	662	1,073	359
Ohio	134,400	141,700	116,900	3,152,182	69.0	20.9	810	645	29.3	970	1,234	409
Oklahoma	95,200	105,000	80,800	947,869	60.5	9.7	636	587	28.1	689	991	314
Oregon	232,000	241,800	201,000	936,407	70.7	21.7	899	735	29.9	1,141	1,447	390
Pennsylvania	144,100	161,200	115,100	3,484,072	62.9	17.4	808	682	28.7	914	1,302	436
Rhode Island	289,400	297,200	262,400	256,248	71.9	22.1	1,069	833	29.3	1,433	1,738	577
South Carolina	122,600	135,500	97,100	1,170,477	64.5	14.8	721	648	28.6	786	1,089	307
South Dakota	110,900	126,700	86,900	215,457	58.4	12.7	629	533	25.3	723	1,090	369
Tennessee	122,500	130,900	106,700	1,669,630	63.6	13.3	702	626	28.4	782	1,088	300
Texas	113,800	128,600	85,900	5,278,915	63.4	7.3	831	725	29.3	967	1,329	418
Utah	189,700	194,000	174,900	584,608	74.3	23.4	945	719	27.6	1,111	1,324	337
Vermont	191,500	200,800	169,600	181,246	67.0	17.0	931	733	29.9	1,074	1,369	533
Virginia	238,600	277,200	161,500	2,026,953	73.1	22.7	1,054	875	28.2	1,206	1,578	355
Washington	261,200	276,600	222,500	1,621,460	73.2	22.4	1,027	799	29.1	1,301	1,611	442
West Virginia	89,500	101,900	77,600	553,122	50.2	9.0	494	516	28.6	481	870	253
Wisconsin	162,000	169,000	145,300	1,571,557	68.6	21.4	866	675	27.9	1,064	1,364	477
Wyoming	150,500	158,900	132,300	143,804	61.2	13.7	685	607	23.3	769	1,104	321

Table C-1. States — Where: Migration, Housing, and Transportation, 2005–2007—*Continued*

STATE	Median selected monthly owner costs as a percentage of household income			Households who pay 30 percent or more of income for housing expenses by tenure and age of householder (percent)							
	All owner-occupied households	Households with a mortgage	Households without a mortgage	Owner-occupied households				Renter-occupied households			
				15 to 24 years	25 to 34 years	45 to 64 years	65 years and over	15 to 24 years	25 to 34 years	45 to 64 years	65 years and over
ACS table number:	B25092	B25092	B25092	C25093	C25093	C25093	C25093	C25072	C25072	C25072	C25072
	57	58	59	60	61	62	63	64	65	66	67
United States	21.3	24.7	12.7	43.2	35.3	29.0	28.0	55.2	42.4	42.9	53.6
Alabama......................	17.9	21.5	11.2	34.2	23.7	21.3	23.2	51.3	37.9	37.6	40.7
Alaska........................	20.6	23.9	10.5	43.1	34.4	26.3	23.9	47.0	36.3	34.3	51.5
Arizona......................	21.2	24.9	10.6	45.4	39.3	29.6	24.0	54.8	42.5	42.2	56.9
Arkansas.....................	17.2	20.6	11.3	32.9	20.4	19.7	20.8	54.7	39.5	37.6	41.4
California....................	26.4	30.5	11.5	64.0	58.2	43.5	31.5	61.9	48.7	48.8	61.9
Colorado	22.9	25.6	10.8	51.2	40.7	31.2	27.0	58.4	43.0	43.9	52.9
Connecticut.................	23.6	25.8	16.3	61.7	40.4	31.9	36.0	55.1	42.5	45.2	51.8
Delaware	20.0	23.4	11.0	38.7	32.5	25.8	23.5	57.3	43.1	40.7	50.1
District of Columbia......	22.1	24.6	11.1	75.5	36.9	30.7	30.1	67.6	41.8	42.4	53.2
Florida	23.4	28.0	14.0	55.4	44.7	36.2	31.1	58.5	49.0	49.4	60.1
Georgia	20.7	23.7	11.3	39.2	31.5	27.1	27.1	54.4	41.9	42.4	51.6
Hawaii	22.0	27.7	8.9	62.4	50.1	35.5	23.3	59.4	48.5	42.3	47.2
Idaho	20.1	23.7	10.5	34.0	33.9	25.2	22.2	47.9	33.7	38.3	45.9
Illinois	22.3	25.5	13.8	46.5	38.2	30.7	29.6	57.1	42.2	42.8	56.1
Indiana	19.2	21.8	11.8	34.6	24.1	21.1	23.6	54.4	39.9	39.4	50.4
Iowa	18.5	21.5	12.4	33.0	23.1	19.0	20.7	51.4	34.6	34.2	44.2
Kansas	18.7	21.6	12.1	35.2	25.1	19.4	22.1	53.0	37.3	33.2	46.9
Kentucky	18.0	21.5	10.7	36.3	22.8	21.0	21.1	49.1	37.0	36.8	45.8
Louisiana	17.1	21.4	10.5	31.0	24.0	20.7	22.0	53.9	42.1	38.9	45.3
Maine	20.6	23.7	13.8	39.6	31.2	26.7	27.1	53.5	38.5	42.5	41.5
Maryland	22.0	24.4	11.7	49.5	39.8	28.7	27.9	54.7	40.2	42.7	55.0
Massachusetts..............	23.9	26.5	15.3	61.8	45.1	33.0	36.2	57.3	42.6	46.2	53.0
Michigan	21.5	24.3	13.6	45.8	34.1	28.0	28.2	57.8	44.8	44.1	53.7
Minnesota	21.3	24.2	11.9	43.0	34.5	26.4	24.7	52.9	39.0	39.9	54.4
Mississippi..................	18.8	22.9	12.4	31.2	24.7	24.7	25.6	55.6	41.2	38.9	41.0
Missouri.....................	18.9	22.2	11.4	33.6	25.0	22.1	22.2	51.6	38.7	38.7	49.2
Montana.....................	19.3	23.8	12.1	38.6	32.9	25.2	23.4	47.4	37.3	33.2	47.9
Nebraska	19.4	22.3	13.0	35.8	23.8	20.8	24.8	45.0	33.1	32.9	48.6
Nevada	24.9	28.3	11.7	57.0	48.7	37.8	33.6	52.1	44.4	45.2	59.4
New Hampshire	23.9	26.3	16.0	57.3	41.7	32.5	35.0	55.5	38.6	42.9	47.7
New Jersey...................	25.4	27.7	18.3	58.7	46.5	37.2	41.3	56.8	43.7	45.3	58.8
New Mexico.................	18.4	22.9	10.2	43.5	29.8	23.8	21.8	52.8	39.1	39.8	50.6
New York....................	22.7	26.0	15.4	45.6	38.4	32.8	35.4	58.8	44.1	45.4	56.9
North Carolina.............	19.8	23.0	11.9	37.2	27.4	24.6	26.5	55.4	39.9	39.7	45.1
North Dakota...............	17.2	20.9	11.6	29.7	18.9	15.9	21.0	44.3	25.4	27.6	50.8
Ohio	20.6	23.3	13.5	40.9	28.6	24.4	27.9	54.3	41.7	41.5	51.3
Oklahoma...................	17.7	21.2	11.4	30.6	23.7	19.8	20.3	48.4	38.6	36.6	46.2
Oregon	22.5	25.9	12.3	54.0	40.4	31.4	27.5	58.8	42.8	42.0	58.7
Pennsylvania	20.4	23.5	14.0	39.3	29.3	25.0	28.8	54.6	37.1	39.9	51.1
Rhode Island	24.2	26.7	16.0	53.6	48.7	33.1	37.6	59.7	40.3	45.2	46.5
South Carolina.............	19.1	22.7	11.4	38.1	25.6	24.3	25.2	53.4	37.8	36.9	43.9
South Dakota...............	18.3	22.0	11.9	39.1	20.7	19.2	20.5	41.6	28.5	29.2	43.6
Tennessee	18.9	22.8	10.7	35.4	26.9	23.4	22.6	52.4	38.4	38.7	43.9
Texas.........................	20.0	23.6	13.1	40.3	31.8	25.2	25.1	55.0	42.4	40.6	53.3
Utah	21.0	24.2	9.3	41.7	37.3	25.4	20.5	46.1	37.8	39.6	46.9
Vermont	22.6	25.0	16.2	35.2	38.8	29.7	34.9	60.3	42.8	42.5	48.4
Virginia	21.0	24.0	10.9	43.2	35.4	27.1	24.9	53.0	37.9	39.6	51.0
Washington	22.8	26.1	12.1	51.0	42.3	31.5	26.9	54.7	40.7	41.9	57.1
West Virginia	15.3	20.1	9.8	31.8	20.3	16.8	17.4	52.1	37.4	36.5	32.0
Wisconsin	21.8	24.4	14.1	43.0	32.5	26.1	29.9	50.3	37.0	37.5	54.3
Wyoming....................	17.0	21.1	9.2	28.3	23.2	17.9	18.0	36.8	26.9	23.9	37.9

STATE	Total number of workers 16 years and over	Car, truck, or van		Public transportation (excluding taxicab)	Bicycle	Walked	Taxicab, motorcycle, or other means	Worked at home	Number of workers who did not work at home
		Drove alone	Car-pooled						
ACS table number:	C08301	C08301	C08301	C08301	C08301	C08301	C08301	C08301	C08301
	68	69	70	71	72	73	74	75	76
United States	136,926,294	76.1	10.6	4.8	0.5	2.9	1.2	3.9	131,558,218
Alabama	1,950,650	83.6	11.1	0.4	0.1	1.3	1.0	2.5	1,902,782
Alaska	320,690	66.6	13.6	1.2	0.9	8.6	3.6	5.5	303,053
Arizona	2,696,991	74.8	13.9	2.1	0.8	2.3	1.6	4.5	2,575,893
Arkansas	1,207,690	80.7	12.4	0.4	0.2	1.8	1.3	3.3	1,167,707
California	16,146,536	73.1	12.3	5.0	0.8	2.8	1.3	4.7	15,394,229
Colorado	2,381,850	75.0	10.5	3.1	1.1	3.2	1.2	5.9	2,240,422
Connecticut	1,695,858	79.7	8.2	4.3	0.3	2.9	1.0	3.6	1,634,159
Delaware	399,007	80.1	10.1	2.6	0.4	2.6	1.1	3.2	386,388
District of Columbia	283,255	36.3	6.8	37.8	1.7	11.5	1.1	4.7	269,844
Florida	8,009,264	79.5	10.8	1.9	0.5	1.7	1.6	4.0	7,691,985
Georgia	4,232,043	78.7	11.3	2.3	0.2	1.7	1.6	4.2	4,055,549
Hawaii	624,884	67.4	15.6	5.5	0.7	4.5	1.8	4.4	597,400
Idaho	670,554	76.6	11.8	0.8	0.9	3.4	1.4	5.1	636,622
Illinois	5,924,170	74.1	9.3	8.6	0.5	3.0	1.0	3.6	5,711,612
Indiana	2,918,625	82.6	9.6	1.0	0.4	2.2	1.0	3.2	2,825,378
Iowa	1,490,814	78.8	10.3	1.0	0.5	3.8	0.9	4.8	1,419,998
Kansas	1,356,521	81.6	9.4	0.5	0.3	2.7	1.1	4.3	1,298,391
Kentucky	1,819,918	81.7	11.0	1.0	0.2	2.1	0.9	3.1	1,762,937
Louisiana	1,825,002	80.9	11.4	1.4	0.3	1.9	1.6	2.4	1,780,461
Maine	639,718	78.5	10.4	0.7	0.4	4.2	1.1	4.8	609,037
Maryland	2,766,335	73.3	10.6	8.6	0.2	2.6	1.0	3.6	2,665,431
Massachusetts	3,147,400	73.6	8.4	8.7	0.5	4.3	0.9	3.7	3,031,089
Michigan	4,412,408	83.2	8.9	1.2	0.3	2.2	0.8	3.3	4,265,327
Minnesota	2,646,371	78.1	9.4	3.0	0.6	3.1	0.8	5.0	2,514,952
Mississippi	1,175,669	82.0	12.0	0.4	0.2	1.8	1.3	2.3	1,148,978
Missouri	2,714,722	80.8	10.4	1.4	0.2	2.1	1.1	4.0	2,605,520
Montana	456,042	73.9	10.9	1.0	1.4	5.1	1.1	6.7	425,638
Nebraska	900,115	79.8	9.9	0.6	0.5	3.3	0.9	5.1	854,329
Nevada	1,183,857	77.5	11.8	3.4	0.5	2.3	1.5	3.0	1,147,838
New Hampshire	674,871	81.6	8.7	0.7	0.3	3.4	0.9	4.5	644,292
New Jersey	4,081,395	72.1	9.3	10.3	0.3	3.3	1.5	3.2	3,950,562
New Mexico	849,465	77.2	12.9	1.0	0.5	2.4	1.2	4.9	807,812
New York	8,686,199	54.3	7.6	26.3	0.4	6.2	1.5	3.7	8,361,731
North Carolina	4,078,167	79.9	12.2	1.0	0.2	1.8	1.2	3.7	3,927,819
North Dakota	333,631	78.5	9.9	0.5	0.5	4.2	0.8	5.5	315,210
Ohio	5,262,290	83.1	8.3	1.9	0.2	2.4	0.8	3.2	5,092,205
Oklahoma	1,598,952	80.6	11.5	0.5	0.2	2.1	1.4	3.7	1,540,373
Oregon	1,715,992	72.5	11.4	4.1	1.7	3.7	1.0	5.6	1,619,714
Pennsylvania	5,665,561	76.6	9.7	5.2	0.3	4.1	0.9	3.3	5,475,788
Rhode Island	508,327	80.8	8.9	2.7	0.2	3.2	1.2	2.9	493,445
South Carolina	1,924,170	81.2	11.3	0.7	0.2	1.8	1.3	3.5	1,856,790
South Dakota	400,491	77.3	10.2	0.4	0.5	4.4	0.8	6.4	375,051
Tennessee	2,710,078	83.3	10.2	0.8	0.1	1.5	1.0	3.2	2,624,642
Texas	10,391,858	78.7	12.5	1.7	0.2	1.8	1.6	3.5	10,027,376
Utah	1,203,101	75.4	12.9	2.5	0.7	2.6	1.0	4.9	1,144,251
Vermont	320,054	75.0	10.7	0.9	0.5	6.1	1.0	5.8	301,475
Virginia	3,741,233	77.2	11.2	3.9	0.2	2.3	1.1	4.2	3,584,734
Washington	3,005,600	73.1	11.6	5.2	0.7	3.4	1.1	4.9	2,857,778
West Virginia	731,398	80.8	11.4	1.0	0.1	2.8	1.1	2.8	711,244
Wisconsin	2,783,421	80.1	9.2	1.7	0.7	3.4	0.9	3.9	2,673,623
Wyoming	263,081	75.1	12.5	1.4	1.0	3.9	0.8	5.2	249,354

STATE	Mean travel time to work (minutes)					Number of households	Vehicles available (percent of households)				Average vehicles per household
	All workers who did not work at home	By car, truck, or van	Public transportation	Walking	All other means		No vehicles	One vehicle	Two vehicles	Three or more vehicles	
ACS table number:	B08136/C08301	B08136/C08301	B08136/C08301	B08136/C08301	B08136/C08301	B08201	B08201	B08201	B08201	B08201	B25046
	77	78	79	80	81	82	83	84	85	86	87
United States	25.1	24.3	47.7	10.4	27.5	111,609,629	8.8	33.1	38.1	20.0	1.8
Alabama......................	23.6	23.7	40.5	9.4	30.0	1,798,304	6.7	31.7	37.8	23.8	1.9
Alaska........................	18.0	17.6	36.4	8.4	37.9	233,861	10.1	31.8	37.9	20.2	1.8
Arizona......................	25.0	24.8	44.7	11.0	29.7	2,215,761	6.4	37.3	38.6	17.7	1.7
Arkansas....................	20.8	21.0	32.5	8.6	22.9	1,096,622	6.6	33.6	40.2	19.6	1.8
California...................	27.0	26.4	46.4	11.5	26.1	12,140,888	7.5	31.8	37.8	23.0	1.9
Colorado....................	23.8	23.5	42.4	9.5	30.7	1,838,303	5.5	31.4	40.2	22.9	1.9
Connecticut................	24.5	23.4	55.0	10.6	26.4	1,323,431	8.2	31.4	39.6	20.8	1.8
Delaware	23.8	23.6	44.4	9.5	22.8	321,748	6.5	33.3	40.9	19.3	1.8
District of Columbia......	29.4	26.6	37.5	15.5	20.4	249,805	36.5	43.1	16.4	4.0	0.9
Florida.......................	25.9	25.7	44.9	10.4	30.8	7,077,123	6.4	39.7	39.0	14.9	1.7
Georgia	27.1	26.6	49.6	11.0	35.3	3,364,749	6.7	32.6	39.0	21.6	1.8
Hawaii	25.7	25.4	43.3	10.1	25.8	433,664	8.6	34.2	36.0	21.2	1.8
Idaho.........................	20.1	20.1	51.0	8.1	26.6	545,171	3.9	26.1	40.9	29.1	2.1
Illinois.......................	28.0	26.5	48.9	10.9	27.8	4,724,462	10.1	34.4	37.9	17.6	1.7
Indiana......................	22.4	22.5	45.6	9.2	23.5	2,447,887	6.2	31.6	40.0	22.1	1.9
Iowa..........................	18.2	18.5	28.1	7.7	18.2	1,206,848	5.3	29.8	39.9	24.9	2.0
Kansas.......................	18.5	18.7	32.7	7.4	24.5	1,083,868	5.0	30.1	39.8	25.1	2.0
Kentucky....................	22.3	22.5	34.0	8.6	26.0	1,654,119	7.8	32.6	38.7	20.9	1.8
Louisiana...................	24.9	24.8	42.5	9.9	31.6	1,605,203	9.0	35.9	38.7	16.5	1.7
Maine.........................	22.6	23.1	35.9	7.4	30.7	542,424	6.3	32.6	41.2	19.9	1.8
Maryland	30.8	29.2	52.5	11.5	28.8	2,082,573	9.2	32.1	37.1	21.6	1.8
Massachusetts	27.0	25.9	44.7	11.9	25.8	2,448,608	11.5	35.7	37.3	15.5	1.6
Michigan	23.6	23.6	43.2	9.2	26.6	3,864,307	6.6	33.3	40.2	19.9	1.8
Minnesota	22.1	22.0	36.4	8.4	27.5	2,041,466	6.5	29.8	41.5	22.2	1.9
Mississippi..................	23.7	23.8	37.0	7.6	32.7	1,079,584	7.1	33.6	37.6	21.8	1.8
Missouri.....................	23.1	23.0	42.2	9.0	28.3	2,300,211	6.9	33.2	39.0	20.9	1.8
Montana.....................	17.4	17.8	41.3	8.1	15.0	369,329	4.9	27.5	38.2	29.4	2.1
Nebraska....................	17.7	17.9	34.4	7.8	21.2	698,163	5.2	29.8	40.1	24.9	2.0
Nevada	23.6	22.8	49.0	12.1	29.7	932,715	7.0	35.8	38.7	18.5	1.8
New Hampshire	25.0	25.3	52.1	8.3	33.7	500,071	5.0	28.3	43.0	23.6	2.0
New Jersey..................	29.4	27.0	54.9	11.2	25.3	3,143,408	11.4	33.6	37.4	17.5	1.7
New Mexico................	21.2	21.1	39.2	10.5	29.0	728,508	5.6	33.6	37.9	22.9	1.9
New York....................	31.2	25.2	50.2	12.8	24.1	7,096,035	28.3	32.4	27.5	11.8	1.3
North Carolina.............	23.2	23.3	38.3	8.9	29.7	3,471,751	6.5	31.8	38.7	23.0	1.9
North Dakota..............	16.0	16.3	23.6	7.2	23.4	271,131	5.5	28.9	37.9	27.8	2.0
Ohio..........................	22.4	22.3	39.3	9.2	27.4	4,500,621	7.8	32.9	38.7	20.6	1.8
Oklahoma...................	20.2	20.4	33.4	8.5	22.3	1,386,849	5.7	33.5	39.9	20.8	1.8
Oregon......................	22.0	21.5	40.1	10.7	25.3	1,447,409	7.4	31.9	38.7	22.0	1.8
Pennsylvania	25.1	24.6	45.4	10.2	28.1	4,858,509	11.2	33.6	37.3	17.9	1.7
Rhode Island...............	22.7	22.4	49.4	9.8	19.4	404,549	8.4	35.1	37.8	18.6	1.7
South Carolina.............	23.3	23.3	45.6	10.1	26.5	1,664,561	7.3	32.9	38.7	21.1	1.8
South Dakota..............	16.2	16.6	36.9	6.2	15.7	311,644	5.1	27.6	39.0	28.3	2.1
Tennessee	23.6	23.7	39.0	9.1	29.5	2,382,975	6.3	32.2	38.8	22.7	1.9
Texas.........................	24.7	24.5	46.1	9.1	28.2	8,095,025	6.2	35.1	40.8	17.9	1.8
Utah..........................	20.9	20.5	41.5	11.5	26.0	812,604	4.2	25.6	42.1	28.1	2.1
Vermont	21.2	22.0	37.6	7.6	21.7	250,871	6.1	32.5	41.5	19.8	1.8
Virginia......................	26.8	26.3	46.4	9.1	33.6	2,909,223	6.2	30.3	38.1	25.4	1.9
Washington	25.3	24.5	45.6	10.5	32.1	2,472,477	6.5	30.8	38.1	24.6	1.9
West Virginia	25.3	25.7	39.2	8.1	21.8	738,943	9.1	33.9	38.4	18.6	1.7
Wisconsin	20.9	21.1	36.1	8.5	21.7	2,235,246	6.5	31.4	41.1	21.0	1.9
Wyoming....................	17.9	17.8	54.3	8.3	16.8	205,422	3.5	27.1	37.2	32.2	2.1

Table C-2. Counties — Where: Migration, Housing, and Transportation, 2005–2007

STATE County code	STATE County	Percent who lived in the same house one year ago	Percent who did not live in county one year ago	Total occupied housing units	Percent owner-occupied housing units	Median value of owner-occupied housing units (dollars)	Median selected monthly owner costs as a percentage of household income — With a mortgage	Without a mortgage	Median gross rent (dollars)	Median gross rent as a percentage of household income	Percent of workers who drove alone to work	Mean travel time to work (minutes)	Percent of occupied housing units with no vehicle available
ACS table number:		C07204	C07204	B25003	B25003	B25077	B25092	B25092	B25064	B25071	C08301	B08013/ C08012	C25045
		1	2	3	4	5	6	7	8	9	10	11	12
00 000	**United States**	83.4	6.8	111,609,629	67.3	181,800	24.7	12.7	781	29.8	76.1	25.1	8.8
01 000	**Alabama**	83.3	6.7	1,798,304	71.3	106,800	21.5	11.2	586	28.7	83.6	23.6	6.7
01 001	Autauga	84.8	7.8	18,275	77.2	121,000	20.9	10.2	702	27.6	85.6	25.3	4.9
01 003	Baldwin	82.2	8.4	68,495	76.4	166,700	23.5	10.4	746	29.8	81.8	24.8	4.4
01 005	Barbour	83.0	9.0	10,491	65.6	81,500	22.0	11.4	493	31.9	82.7	21.0	10.7
01 007	Bibb	87.1	8.7	7,394	74.7	83,800	17.3	10.3	465	20.6	84.9	31.1	5.1
01 009	Blount	87.2	5.4	18,931	81.4	105,100	20.9	9.6	522	25.5	80.5	32.0	3.9
01 013	Butler	91.4	2.2	7,830	68.6	67,400	21.7	12.1	435	25.6	84.9	24.8	10.3
01 015	Calhoun	82.6	6.5	46,849	71.6	90,100	20.5	11.3	554	27.7	88.2	23.3	6.7
01 017	Chambers	87.7	5.6	13,612	74.5	82,200	23.0	12.6	521	29.0	82.6	22.6	7.7
01 019	Cherokee	89.1	4.7	10,038	79.7	90,400	20.9	11.3	466	28.0	76.8	27.4	4.4
01 021	Chilton	87.7	3.9	16,069	77.6	99,200	21.7	12.1	514	30.9	77.7	29.7	5.3
01 025	Clarke	92.0	4.5	9,605	76.2	70,000	18.9	12.2	430	28.7	90.0	22.7	10.2
01 031	Coffee	76.7	12.3	18,673	68.6	105,300	20.1	10.0	508	24.5	82.3	20.1	5.8
01 033	Colbert	82.8	6.4	22,666	72.8	85,800	20.3	11.5	523	29.2	86.7	22.2	5.2
01 039	Covington	86.7	5.8	14,461	75.1	76,700	19.1	12.1	450	25.0	80.9	21.3	6.9
01 043	Cullman	82.7	6.2	30,793	72.8	104,000	22.1	11.1	526	25.4	78.8	28.0	4.3
01 045	Dale	78.2	13.3	18,856	63.6	87,200	18.8	9.6	558	24.1	81.3	18.9	6.4
01 047	Dallas	85.8	3.9	17,022	59.9	66,700	22.7	13.9	515	33.7	84.7	28.7	16.4
01 049	DeKalb	85.0	5.1	24,971	74.5	77,700	20.5	13.3	478	23.7	81.1	24.2	5.1
01 051	Elmore	80.6	13.4	25,229	79.1	122,500	20.6	9.9	641	26.5	83.4	27.2	4.7
01 053	Escambia	85.8	6.0	14,151	76.9	76,800	21.1	10.8	481	30.6	87.4	26.0	4.9
01 055	Etowah	82.4	6.7	43,059	72.9	88,900	20.7	12.8	518	28.8	83.4	23.4	5.9
01 059	Franklin	85.1	5.2	12,192	67.7	75,200	23.3	11.7	447	25.7	74.5	23.1	5.6
01 061	Geneva	83.9	6.4	10,308	75.7	69,300	22.0	9.9	456	25.7	84.6	23.8	4.4
01 069	Houston	84.9	6.3	36,562	69.9	103,200	19.7	9.6	551	27.6	86.1	19.4	6.8
01 071	Jackson	88.0	4.3	21,129	79.3	79,600	20.8	10.6	455	30.0	85.1	25.0	6.2
01 073	Jefferson	81.9	5.1	266,554	67.9	129,200	23.0	12.1	696	29.9	83.8	23.5	7.9
01 077	Lauderdale	83.7	7.3	36,002	73.3	96,400	22.1	10.6	500	29.6	84.7	24.3	7.4
01 079	Lawrence	88.5	4.8	13,246	81.1	87,600	21.1	10.9	484	21.2	86.9	26.4	4.6
01 081	Lee	74.8	13.0	52,996	61.7	125,300	21.3	11.7	586	32.8	81.4	19.9	6.0
01 083	Limestone	83.7	9.2	26,097	75.7	102,800	21.4	9.5	527	23.4	86.4	25.1	4.6
01 087	Macon	78.5	10.3	7,883	66.4	75,200	23.0	14.4	521	37.7	76.6	21.9	11.4
01 089	Madison	80.9	7.5	121,186	70.8	140,600	19.3	8.4	624	26.4	84.9	20.5	4.2
01 091	Marengo	87.5	6.1	8,319	76.4	75,500	22.8	14.4	474	36.2	79.3	20.5	9.9
01 093	Marion	87.7	7.4	12,929	74.1	67,400	19.6	10.8	322	24.6	85.8	21.9	6.4
01 095	Marshall	84.6	5.8	32,853	73.6	96,100	21.4	10.3	466	29.2	81.2	23.3	6.5
01 097	Mobile	84.7	4.1	150,853	68.6	105,700	22.5	12.1	628	30.6	83.9	24.0	7.0
01 099	Monroe	87.7	4.4	9,474	74.7	84,700	20.2	11.3	416	25.1	91.0	22.9	8.9
01 101	Montgomery	80.5	7.8	88,590	63.0	109,700	21.6	9.7	670	30.4	83.7	19.0	8.6
01 103	Morgan	83.5	5.8	45,632	75.0	105,600	20.5	10.1	523	26.0	84.2	22.3	5.6
01 109	Pike	78.5	10.3	12,708	58.7	82,000	20.3	12.1	452	38.4	80.8	19.3	8.3
01 111	Randolph	84.2	8.0	7,870	78.7	82,900	21.3	11.7	453	19.3	74.5	25.3	5.0
01 113	Russell	81.1	7.5	20,729	60.0	88,100	23.4	11.0	532	31.4	78.0	22.3	11.7
01 115	St. Clair	87.5	6.4	25,338	83.9	115,200	19.9	10.3	585	19.3	83.6	30.6	3.3
01 117	Shelby	82.4	8.2	68,254	80.5	183,500	21.5	9.4	769	26.3	85.2	28.1	2.1
01 121	Talladega	86.6	5.3	29,931	72.9	85,600	21.9	12.7	471	28.9	82.4	23.4	9.4
01 123	Tallapoosa	82.9	6.1	16,048	73.2	83,900	21.6	11.8	409	26.7	85.5	23.1	8.7
01 125	Tuscaloosa	78.4	9.8	70,196	62.0	138,700	21.8	10.1	628	33.3	84.4	19.6	8.2
01 127	Walker	85.6	5.1	27,054	77.9	77,400	20.0	11.2	509	30.0	84.5	30.1	5.8
01 133	Winston	83.3	6.7	9,559	72.0	79,300	21.0	11.6	383	27.6	82.0	22.1	5.7
02 000	**Alaska**	78.6	9.7	233,861	63.7	213,400	23.9	10.5	898	27.2	66.6	18.0	10.1
02 020	Anchorage	77.5	8.7	102,476	61.0	248,800	24.6	11.6	949	28.5	76.0	17.9	6.4
02 090	Fairbanks North Star	75.4	13.0	32,550	59.8	188,200	23.7	9.9	859	26.5	70.4	17.8	6.6
02 110	Juneau	77.9	10.7	11,618	66.3	276,100	24.4	11.5	912	28.4	60.2	14.9	8.0
02 122	Kenai Peninsula	82.1	8.1	19,339	72.1	173,500	22.4	9.1	748	27.0	71.1	18.8	5.4
02 170	Matanuska-Susitna	82.4	10.5	21,724	81.0	195,000	24.5	9.5	876	30.5	70.2	34.1	3.2
04 000	**Arizona**	78.7	7.5	2,215,761	68.6	221,800	24.9	10.6	786	29.6	74.8	25.0	6.4
04 001	Apache	90.1	5.6	18,678	78.0	73,100	20.3	8.3	476	18.0	80.3	27.4	12.8
04 003	Cochise	78.3	12.7	48,308	70.6	132,400	23.1	9.9	649	30.4	75.9	18.7	5.2
04 005	Coconino	78.9	9.7	43,286	61.9	258,200	24.1	8.7	839	30.1	68.3	17.6	5.7
04 007	Gila	85.8	6.8	18,685	77.1	135,500	27.7	12.2	617	25.7	77.9	19.9	8.6
04 009	Graham	83.6	8.6	10,447	69.7	98,500	21.5	11.4	566	23.6	71.8	18.2	4.6
04 012	La Paz	-	-	8,932	79.5	85,500	25.2	8.8	465	27.9	72.9	15.3	9.6
04 013	Maricopa	78.3	6.6	1,318,623	68.3	248,800	25.0	10.8	845	29.7	74.7	26.4	6.1
04 015	Mohave	78.0	10.8	75,033	70.2	185,500	25.9	11.3	772	31.0	76.0	19.0	3.3
04 017	Navajo	83.3	8.8	34,143	72.3	100,800	23.0	8.6	564	21.5	71.7	20.7	9.4
04 019	Pima	77.8	7.2	370,126	65.3	194,500	24.4	10.7	686	30.7	75.2	23.7	8.3
04 021	Pinal	75.5	15.3	102,648	75.4	177,600	25.8	10.7	697	27.6	75.1	30.1	7.7
04 023	Santa Cruz	93.0	3.2	10,877	76.8	131,100	28.3	12.1	623	30.3	80.3	18.8	3.9
04 025	Yavapai	82.3	8.1	84,352	72.1	229,800	26.6	11.7	791	30.5	76.3	20.8	4.2
04 027	Yuma	79.1	9.2	68,857	70.3	124,700	24.5	9.9	647	28.6	74.4	19.1	6.1

STATE County code	STATE County	Percent who lived in the same house one year ago	Percent who did not live in county one year ago	Total occupied housing units	Percent owner-occupied housing units	Median value of owner-occupied housing units (dollars)	Median selected monthly owner costs as a percentage of household income — With a mortgage	Without a mortgage	Median gross rent (dollars)	Median gross rent as a percentage of household income	Percent of workers who drove alone to work	Mean travel time to work (minutes)	Percent of occupied housing units with no vehicle available
ACS table number:		C07204	C07204	B25003	B25003	B25077	B25092	B25092	B25064	B25071	C08301	B08013/C08012	C25045
		1	2	3	4	5	6	7	8	9	10	11	12
05 000	**Arkansas**	80.7	8.0	1,096,622	68.0	93,700	20.6	11.3	578	28.8	80.7	20.8	6.6
05 003	Ashley	83.7	6.3	9,279	69.4	62,200	21.1	12.2	477	28.6	86.3	18.4	9.5
05 005	Baxter	80.7	9.3	18,139	77.3	103,200	22.4	10.5	577	28.2	82.1	17.2	4.8
05 007	Benton	79.6	9.1	71,918	71.8	151,200	21.5	9.9	689	27.0	79.9	20.2	3.1
05 009	Boone	80.2	8.0	13,946	73.0	103,500	20.0	12.2	495	25.6	78.0	19.9	4.7
05 015	Carroll	84.2	7.0	10,845	67.4	106,600	26.8	11.0	551	29.7	72.4	19.7	4.4
05 019	Clark	78.1	17.1	8,818	64.1	78,400	19.7	10.7	536	40.4	75.5	22.5	10.1
05 023	Cleburne	83.2	8.7	9,802	79.0	101,500	21.8	11.1	555	30.5	74.7	26.5	4.2
05 027	Columbia	83.5	6.0	10,639	67.1	80,200	18.8	12.6	481	26.7	80.2	17.7	11.0
05 029	Conway	86.9	7.0	8,371	79.7	81,400	20.9	10.6	429	33.5	81.4	23.4	7.3
05 031	Craighead	78.9	8.7	34,095	64.2	100,900	20.4	10.4	560	31.0	82.1	17.4	5.7
05 033	Crawford	80.1	8.3	21,041	73.9	92,000	20.8	11.1	582	29.5	82.1	23.2	5.8
05 035	Crittenden	75.1	6.6	19,899	61.1	94,200	22.9	14.6	601	32.8	82.1	20.6	8.8
05 045	Faulkner	77.4	11.5	37,487	67.1	118,300	19.7	10.1	620	28.3	80.1	24.3	3.6
05 051	Garland	80.4	7.8	38,796	68.1	118,300	22.9	11.3	599	32.0	76.9	21.9	8.1
05 055	Greene	80.9	6.8	16,192	67.2	78,400	19.7	11.3	536	27.7	85.2	20.1	7.4
05 057	Hempstead	83.8	7.0	8,839	70.4	66,300	17.1	9.1	474	29.7	79.7	18.8	9.2
05 059	Hot Spring	83.7	10.0	11,476	78.0	73,600	19.5	10.9	474	23.9	82.0	24.3	5.4
05 063	Independence	80.2	8.3	14,064	73.3	75,800	20.6	9.5	532	24.9	78.7	20.5	5.0
05 069	Jefferson	81.1	7.1	30,446	63.7	66,400	19.4	12.1	599	33.8	85.4	19.3	10.2
05 071	Johnson	84.1	7.7	8,814	73.1	68,900	20.8	11.4	509	31.6	78.7	20.4	5.1
05 083	Logan	84.1	7.6	9,087	76.2	71,200	18.0	13.2	472	30.6	76.8	24.2	3.3
05 085	Lonoke	80.9	10.4	22,120	74.7	107,300	19.5	11.6	611	26.8	84.0	27.6	4.8
05 091	Miller	78.2	10.9	16,533	65.0	78,400	18.1	11.0	556	28.1	82.7	19.2	7.6
05 093	Mississippi	81.9	5.3	18,081	61.0	60,700	19.1	12.1	550	31.8	80.2	18.0	11.8
05 103	Ouachita	85.7	5.9	10,648	70.6	56,600	20.1	12.1	448	29.5	80.8	18.9	8.9
05 107	Phillips	78.6	6.0	8,861	48.6	58,200	19.7	12.8	511	35.4	80.6	17.6	18.0
05 111	Poinsett	79.6	5.7	10,019	64.6	59,500	20.6	11.3	462	29.6	80.0	21.7	6.7
05 113	Polk	85.2	7.2	7,957	78.5	76,000	22.0	10.3	491	28.6	76.9	21.2	4.8
05 115	Pope	79.0	9.4	21,852	69.9	91,300	20.0	10.1	520	25.4	86.5	18.4	3.2
05 119	Pulaski	79.4	6.8	153,273	63.0	123,700	20.9	11.1	688	29.3	83.0	18.9	7.1
05 121	St. Francis	83.1	7.8	10,026	62.1	62,800	21.4	14.8	475	33.7	85.7	19.7	15.0
05 125	Saline	83.7	8.0	35,766	76.0	114,100	19.9	10.2	713	26.0	78.0	23.8	3.7
05 131	Sebastian	79.0	7.3	46,730	61.9	96,500	20.2	11.2	541	27.8	83.2	17.6	7.2
05 139	Union	84.4	5.5	18,325	68.8	64,500	18.4	11.9	520	26.9	83.6	16.8	8.9
05 143	Washington	72.9	10.5	73,409	57.4	148,500	21.4	10.9	647	27.3	78.8	20.2	5.3
05 145	White	78.9	8.5	27,075	69.0	86,600	18.7	12.3	516	24.1	77.4	21.0	5.6
05 149	Yell	81.2	5.2	7,757	69.5	68,400	19.9	9.4	469	25.6	72.5	23.7	4.4
06 000	**California**	83.5	5.6	12,140,888	58.4	513,200	30.5	11.5	1,058	32.2	73.1	27.0	7.5
06 001	Alameda	82.8	6.7	519,056	57.3	633,000	30.7	10.8	1,120	30.6	67.5	27.5	9.3
06 005	Amador	82.2	10.1	14,563	75.4	365,600	26.8	13.5	1,063	30.3	79.7	28.4	3.3
06 007	Butte	76.4	8.7	84,607	59.1	273,500	27.9	12.8	807	35.9	75.9	20.8	7.1
06 009	Calaveras	88.6	4.9	18,393	79.1	390,900	27.6	14.0	834	27.7	77.6	32.7	2.6
06 011	Colusa	82.5	6.8	6,700	63.0	300,100	27.2	10.8	682	27.8	74.7	23.2	7.3
06 013	Contra Costa	84.5	5.6	362,362	71.4	618,800	31.2	11.5	1,194	32.9	70.3	31.9	5.5
06 015	Del Norte	82.8	9.4	9,662	64.5	228,900	25.3	11.7	669	30.6	69.9	14.6	9.0
06 017	El Dorado	84.2	7.7	65,310	74.9	510,500	29.7	12.9	1,029	31.7	75.9	29.1	3.3
06 019	Fresno	82.5	4.3	276,929	56.0	284,800	27.1	11.6	761	32.2	75.5	21.1	8.8
06 021	Glenn	89.9	5.0	9,450	68.0	241,300	30.9	11.8	670	30.2	74.2	20.8	5.6
06 023	Humboldt	79.6	7.6	52,112	57.8	321,800	27.5	10.3	741	35.2	71.7	18.5	6.0
06 025	Imperial	84.2	7.4	45,561	55.3	224,600	29.4	12.3	643	31.8	78.7	18.0	10.3
06 029	Kern	78.4	8.2	235,842	62.0	241,100	27.5	12.5	733	30.1	74.4	22.5	7.5
06 031	Kings	78.1	12.8	38,808	57.2	220,500	26.7	10.0	719	30.0	71.8	20.3	6.8
06 033	Lake	83.3	8.3	24,896	69.7	302,300	32.2	14.5	813	36.5	77.5	27.9	6.2
06 035	Lassen	71.0	18.8	10,324	68.1	217,400	25.8	11.0	811	29.7	75.1	26.2	4.3
06 037	Los Angeles	86.9	3.1	3,176,441	49.3	550,000	31.7	11.3	1,002	33.0	72.3	29.1	9.5
06 039	Madera	81.1	8.5	41,849	63.6	328,900	28.6	12.5	752	30.7	73.3	27.4	6.1
06 041	Marin	84.0	8.5	100,489	65.3	895,100	31.1	11.4	1,442	33.0	66.5	28.2	5.2
06 045	Mendocino	85.6	5.1	33,749	64.7	434,400	33.3	13.3	842	32.3	70.2	19.2	6.8
06 047	Merced	80.6	5.3	72,599	57.5	333,300	31.3	11.6	799	33.4	72.9	24.2	8.2
06 053	Monterey	81.3	7.3	124,146	54.4	662,300	33.9	10.1	1,069	30.5	69.3	21.8	6.8
06 055	Napa	83.0	7.5	48,312	66.3	638,600	31.4	13.5	1,121	29.4	73.4	24.0	5.4
06 057	Nevada	84.2	7.0	39,376	74.7	466,700	31.5	13.4	1,128	32.0	71.7	25.0	3.2
06 059	Orange	84.5	4.9	972,040	62.3	656,600	29.8	10.1	1,343	32.5	77.4	26.1	4.6
06 061	Placer	82.8	8.2	123,247	71.1	490,600	29.2	12.5	1,091	31.0	77.9	26.7	3.3
06 063	Plumas	79.3	10.9	10,012	61.5	284,600	27.1	12.4	749	27.9	75.6	20.6	4.6
06 065	Riverside	81.1	8.3	636,755	69.5	395,100	32.2	12.9	1,025	34.1	75.2	31.5	4.5
06 067	Sacramento	80.0	6.3	500,777	61.0	375,600	29.3	10.7	931	32.4	75.2	25.6	6.9
06 069	San Benito	83.5	8.3	16,647	67.3	669,000	33.7	11.3	1,089	30.7	66.0	32.9	4.1
06 071	San Bernardino	82.2	7.4	591,141	65.5	363,700	29.7	12.3	992	33.5	76.9	29.7	4.9
06 073	San Diego	80.6	6.4	1,041,790	57.3	559,400	31.0	11.3	1,155	32.9	75.2	25.2	6.1
06 075	San Francisco	84.3	7.0	321,692	38.4	789,400	30.6	11.3	1,197	27.3	39.6	29.1	29.7
06 077	San Joaquin	80.5	6.0	207,792	63.0	401,100	31.5	12.1	908	33.6	75.9	29.6	6.1
06 079	San Luis Obispo	76.2	9.8	103,026	59.2	562,400	31.5	11.5	1,077	35.5	73.3	19.7	4.0
06 081	San Mateo	85.9	6.1	252,648	62.9	807,400	30.9	10.5	1,380	28.7	70.7	25.0	5.7

STATE County code	STATE County	Percent who lived in the same house one year ago	Percent who did not live in county one year ago	Total occupied housing units	Percent owner-occupied housing units	Median value of owner-occupied housing units (dollars)	Median selected monthly owner costs as a percentage of household income		Median gross rent (dollars)	Median gross rent as a percentage of household income	Percent of workers who drove alone to work	Mean travel time to work (minutes)	Percent of occupied housing units with no vehicle available
							With a mortgage	Without a mortgage					
	ACS table number:	C07204	C07204	B25003	B25003	B25077	B25092	B25092	B25064	B25071	C08301	B08013/C08012	C25045
		1	2	3	4	5	6	7	8	9	10	11	12
	California—Cont.												
06 083	Santa Barbara	77.9	7.9	140,137	54.5	653,400	31.9	11.1	1,194	35.8	66.8	19.6	5.9
06 085	Santa Clara	82.7	5.3	582,108	60.6	725,800	29.7	9.6	1,287	28.4	77.4	24.2	5.1
06 087	Santa Cruz	80.4	7.4	93,518	60.0	718,700	32.6	12.2	1,197	34.0	70.7	25.4	5.6
06 089	Shasta	83.6	5.4	68,762	64.7	263,000	27.8	11.9	786	32.4	80.1	18.9	6.6
06 093	Siskiyou	83.7	8.3	19,766	65.5	220,000	27.5	11.9	550	31.5	72.8	20.2	6.9
06 095	Solano	82.3	6.9	135,704	66.8	472,500	30.9	11.3	1,127	34.0	76.0	29.5	5.4
06 097	Sonoma	84.1	4.5	177,331	63.1	611,300	32.2	12.3	1,162	32.6	73.8	24.7	5.4
06 099	Stanislaus	81.0	5.2	158,836	63.9	359,100	30.9	12.7	883	34.0	79.2	26.5	7.0
06 101	Sutter	83.6	9.2	30,431	66.3	303,900	28.3	12.0	808	29.8	74.5	26.9	6.9
06 103	Tehama	82.9	7.5	22,817	62.7	225,500	27.8	13.6	663	32.0	78.4	21.9	7.1
06 107	Tulare	86.6	4.3	121,457	59.7	223,600	27.2	11.3	668	28.9	73.9	21.3	7.5
06 109	Tuolumne	80.4	13.0	22,161	68.5	356,200	31.7	14.4	850	32.7	76.1	23.4	4.8
06 111	Ventura	86.1	5.2	255,527	68.5	631,000	29.6	11.4	1,299	32.1	78.9	26.1	3.9
06 113	Yolo	75.6	12.2	66,828	55.3	444,700	28.1	9.5	953	33.3	71.5	21.0	7.0
06 115	Yuba	76.2	12.7	23,801	56.4	272,400	28.8	10.8	706	32.6	75.4	28.4	4.5
08 000	**Colorado**	79.6	9.9	1,838,303	68.7	230,400	25.6	10.8	797	30.0	75.0	23.8	5.5
08 001	Adams	81.7	8.9	144,492	70.0	201,700	28.2	13.3	851	31.3	77.1	27.7	4.9
08 005	Arapahoe	81.9	9.5	208,881	68.0	233,500	25.6	9.7	826	30.2	78.5	26.0	5.2
08 013	Boulder	76.2	11.2	113,419	66.0	342,400	24.6	10.4	946	34.7	67.8	21.3	4.8
08 014	Broomfield	80.6	15.3	17,507	75.1	245,600	24.1	13.9	972	27.4	76.1	26.8	1.9
08 029	Delta	83.4	8.2	11,583	74.7	168,900	25.3	13.2	702	32.3	68.4	20.1	3.8
08 031	Denver	78.7	10.0	244,261	55.6	234,200	27.5	11.6	734	30.0	70.2	23.7	12.5
08 035	Douglas	80.8	12.2	91,557	83.0	334,500	24.2	9.0	1,063	26.3	79.1	27.0	1.1
08 037	Eagle	83.7	9.2	15,207	69.1	461,600	28.2	11.9	1,252	31.4	72.2	19.6	3.2
08 039	Elbert	88.6	9.9	8,035	88.4	332,100	27.0	17.3	808	24.3	77.9	40.7	1.1
08 041	El Paso	76.0	10.7	217,217	67.8	205,200	24.7	9.2	771	29.1	77.5	21.8	4.9
08 043	Fremont	76.9	13.6	16,401	74.3	146,500	26.0	12.5	616	34.5	69.6	27.5	5.4
08 045	Garfield	79.6	9.7	18,765	67.1	309,000	25.1	9.3	923	27.1	66.6	28.5	3.0
08 059	Jefferson	82.6	9.1	213,324	73.5	255,900	25.2	10.2	851	29.8	78.0	26.1	4.2
08 067	La Plata	77.1	10.9	20,639	67.0	319,700	24.1	9.3	874	30.7	73.1	21.1	3.4
08 069	Larimer	75.6	9.4	111,524	68.5	239,700	25.3	10.8	791	32.8	76.4	21.8	3.7
08 075	Logan	73.1	15.9	8,065	65.0	109,600	21.0	11.4	521	22.3	74.6	15.1	4.5
08 077	Mesa	75.3	8.3	53,533	71.3	188,700	24.2	10.0	745	28.5	75.3	20.3	4.6
08 083	Montezuma	82.9	7.1	10,132	73.2	165,100	25.6	12.2	631	27.4	71.5	22.2	5.9
08 085	Montrose	80.0	10.1	15,540	71.8	179,000	25.0	12.1	713	29.5	76.6	17.8	5.0
08 087	Morgan	83.4	6.1	10,014	69.1	132,300	28.2	13.1	645	24.4	75.9	16.7	4.9
08 101	Pueblo	82.1	6.0	58,819	69.8	131,400	25.9	12.1	610	33.3	79.1	20.6	7.3
08 107	Routt	80.6	11.1	10,001	79.2	398,100	29.2	11.8	778	31.0	68.5	18.2	1.9
08 117	Summit	80.8	9.9	9,880	66.8	445,100	28.9	9.7	1,037	28.0	62.6	15.3	3.0
08 119	Teller	79.2	11.5	9,143	82.5	225,000	25.8	7.7	834	45.3	70.9	33.4	1.9
08 123	Weld	80.9	8.7	81,024	71.1	197,200	26.6	12.9	717	30.4	79.3	23.6	4.3
09 000	**Connecticut**	86.9	4.9	1,323,431	69.7	294,100	25.8	16.3	910	29.8	79.7	24.5	8.2
09 001	Fairfield	87.6	4.7	324,360	71.7	495,200	27.4	17.3	1,150	30.9	73.9	28.1	7.9
09 003	Hartford	87.2	3.9	337,494	67.2	237,100	24.6	16.0	836	29.1	82.0	21.7	9.5
09 005	Litchfield	90.1	4.6	74,026	77.8	286,700	26.4	15.1	818	28.3	83.1	26.1	5.0
09 007	Middlesex	89.0	5.8	65,162	75.0	296,600	24.6	14.6	908	26.4	84.1	24.0	4.3
09 009	New Haven	86.9	4.4	322,561	66.3	264,800	26.4	18.2	908	31.9	80.9	23.8	10.7
09 011	New London	83.5	7.2	104,132	69.5	252,400	24.8	14.2	910	28.5	79.6	21.7	5.8
09 013	Tolland	82.9	9.5	52,777	76.5	243,100	23.3	12.8	874	27.2	83.1	25.5	2.9
09 015	Windham	85.4	6.4	42,919	71.1	221,700	26.2	14.3	720	27.3	81.6	25.7	6.1
10 000	**Delaware**	84.5	5.9	321,748	73.6	225,200	23.4	11.0	868	29.3	80.1	23.8	6.5
10 001	Kent	84.1	6.4	55,685	72.8	189,500	24.4	12.4	840	29.8	81.3	23.1	6.5
10 003	New Castle	83.4	6.1	193,434	71.7	237,400	22.9	9.8	893	29.6	79.4	24.1	7.2
10 005	Sussex	88.3	4.9	72,629	79.0	220,100	24.1	12.2	776	27.7	81.5	23.2	4.4
11 000	**District of Columbia**	79.4	10.3	249,805	44.1	424,200	24.6	11.1	906	29.4	36.3	29.4	36.5
11 001	District of Columbia	79.4	10.3	249,805	44.1	424,200	24.6	11.1	906	29.4	36.3	29.4	36.5
12 000	**Florida**	81.9	7.6	7,077,123	70.3	217,800	28.0	14.0	892	32.9	79.5	25.9	6.4
12 001	Alachua	73.3	11.9	95,850	53.9	174,600	24.0	11.1	763	35.4	75.3	20.9	7.0
12 003	Baker	85.2	9.9	7,560	73.8	114,700	20.8	8.7	608	29.5	-	29.7	3.2
12 005	Bay	77.0	9.6	71,417	64.8	176,500	24.3	11.2	781	28.2	80.1	21.0	5.0
12 007	Bradford	82.5	12.2	8,217	80.0	105,500	22.1	11.9	660	27.0	86.1	25.3	4.0
12 009	Brevard	84.8	6.4	217,708	76.7	206,300	26.4	13.0	841	32.5	83.5	23.3	4.3
12 011	Broward	82.7	6.6	676,384	71.2	283,700	31.4	18.6	1,057	34.5	79.9	27.0	7.1
12 015	Charlotte	83.4	8.8	70,376	83.4	202,600	29.9	14.8	935	31.4	82.8	21.7	4.1
12 017	Citrus	84.1	8.3	58,905	82.2	141,100	26.0	12.4	697	29.3	81.4	24.0	3.7
12 019	Clay	81.2	11.2	63,858	78.4	182,700	24.1	9.2	916	26.3	83.4	33.2	2.2
12 021	Collier	85.0	6.4	119,883	75.7	409,000	30.4	14.9	1,061	32.3	75.0	25.1	3.8
12 023	Columbia	78.2	10.5	22,161	71.8	118,600	21.7	11.0	600	28.3	81.7	21.3	4.8
12 027	DeSoto	82.2	8.5	10,906	79.6	106,700	25.7	12.0	679	22.6	60.5	27.6	9.3
12 031	Duval	79.9	6.7	335,842	64.4	170,200	24.2	10.2	805	30.1	80.2	23.7	7.6
12 033	Escambia	77.3	10.6	117,990	68.2	138,000	24.1	11.4	744	32.1	75.1	22.0	7.2
12 035	Flagler	83.1	12.5	37,601	75.9	235,000	29.5	13.2	992	34.2	82.4	22.4	3.1
12 039	Gadsden	87.2	7.5	15,656	74.0	85,200	24.0	12.4	568	23.5	75.0	28.9	9.8

STATE County code	STATE County	Percent who lived in the same house one year ago	Percent who did not live in county one year ago	Total occupied housing units	Percent owner-occupied housing units	Median value of owner-occupied housing units (dollars)	Median selected monthly owner costs as a percentage of household income		Median gross rent (dollars)	Median gross rent as a percentage of household income	Percent of workers who drove alone to work	Mean travel time to work (minutes)	Percent of occupied housing units with no vehicle available
							With a mortgage	Without a mortgage					
ACS table number:		C07204	C07204	B25003	B25003	B25077	B25092	B25092	B25064	B25071	C08301	B08013/C08012	C25045
		1	2	3	4	5	6	7	8	9	10	11	12
	Florida—Cont.												
12 049	Hardee	82.3	9.0	8,644	76.9	95,100	25.9	11.3	679	21.5	67.4	25.5	3.8
12 051	Hendry	74.9	9.0	10,964	68.1	111,500	23.7	13.2	732	41.2	63.9	28.4	10.8
12 053	Hernando	83.2	10.3	66,252	85.8	164,700	27.8	13.4	784	26.4	81.8	28.6	3.6
12 055	Highlands	82.1	8.2	40,152	78.7	117,200	25.4	12.7	676	30.6	75.7	21.3	5.3
12 057	Hillsborough	79.3	7.4	453,926	65.2	203,400	26.4	13.4	851	31.4	80.0	26.0	6.6
12 061	Indian River	82.7	9.1	58,175	75.5	211,400	27.8	15.1	927	35.6	83.6	21.9	5.2
12 063	Jackson	83.3	11.7	16,916	71.4	87,000	21.4	12.2	480	23.8	82.6	21.8	8.2
12 069	Lake	82.3	10.5	114,906	80.1	179,500	26.7	12.6	806	31.9	80.0	27.9	4.2
12 071	Lee	81.0	8.6	243,673	73.9	242,700	29.0	14.3	970	31.7	78.8	25.4	4.5
12 073	Leon	73.2	9.9	107,535	57.5	182,500	24.1	10.0	809	35.6	81.3	20.6	5.8
12 075	Levy	83.4	10.1	14,341	74.1	106,400	26.6	12.0	547	28.4	77.4	29.6	4.4
12 081	Manatee	82.2	8.1	131,981	73.5	231,000	28.5	14.0	912	32.4	79.9	23.3	4.2
12 083	Marion	82.0	9.1	127,764	78.2	142,900	25.7	12.3	732	29.4	81.2	24.1	4.3
12 085	Martin	84.6	8.7	58,784	78.6	293,500	27.2	13.8	978	30.8	79.2	23.4	4.0
12 086	Miami-Dade	84.7	3.9	830,844	59.7	291,900	34.2	18.1	915	37.2	77.3	30.6	11.1
12 087	Monroe	84.6	7.2	31,925	69.3	671,800	38.3	14.7	1,200	34.5	69.7	17.0	8.6
12 089	Nassau	83.9	6.4	25,521	78.9	209,200	22.9	9.7	821	24.4	83.1	27.2	5.4
12 091	Okaloosa	79.0	10.8	74,771	67.6	212,800	23.4	10.6	867	28.0	82.1	21.6	4.1
12 093	Okeechobee	81.5	9.1	12,732	76.9	137,600	26.7	12.8	775	33.8	71.4	26.4	6.8
12 095	Orange	78.5	8.7	393,502	61.1	239,800	27.0	12.2	930	33.3	79.2	26.1	5.7
12 097	Osceola	78.7	12.5	89,369	68.8	220,000	31.1	13.9	981	34.2	81.3	30.8	4.9
12 099	Palm Beach	83.8	6.1	507,904	74.8	304,100	30.5	16.8	1,067	33.8	78.7	25.3	6.4
12 101	Pasco	81.5	10.9	179,419	79.0	162,700	26.8	13.1	786	30.6	81.1	29.4	4.7
12 103	Pinellas	83.7	5.8	410,560	71.2	190,800	27.9	15.8	826	31.9	80.1	23.0	8.0
12 105	Polk	79.0	8.2	222,196	71.6	132,400	25.8	12.7	770	28.9	80.8	25.0	5.5
12 107	Putnam	86.8	6.4	27,661	76.0	96,800	23.3	12.2	550	31.7	77.0	30.3	6.6
12 109	St. Johns	81.6	10.1	65,874	76.7	305,100	25.3	12.1	969	33.5	82.7	24.6	3.9
12 111	St. Lucie	84.0	8.3	98,889	76.3	212,400	31.2	14.7	986	33.2	83.4	27.3	4.2
12 113	Santa Rosa	81.4	10.3	50,026	78.6	183,600	24.6	11.4	766	28.1	79.8	28.4	3.0
12 115	Sarasota	82.3	7.9	168,014	77.5	253,200	29.0	14.5	975	33.3	78.4	21.4	5.4
12 117	Seminole	82.1	10.1	154,503	70.3	248,300	25.5	11.6	986	31.2	82.0	25.8	3.6
12 119	Sumter	82.9	10.0	32,090	79.5	130,400	24.5	9.8	560	24.3	77.0	27.4	3.3
12 121	Suwannee	76.5	9.8	12,527	77.4	100,100	23.5	11.4	592	23.8	70.3	26.9	5.3
12 127	Volusia	83.7	7.5	201,368	75.1	189,900	27.4	14.7	844	35.2	80.6	23.9	5.8
12 129	Wakulla	83.8	9.0	10,605	82.5	133,800	21.8	11.1	781	35.8	74.8	29.7	3.2
12 131	Walton	79.5	13.6	21,458	75.1	234,100	22.7	11.1	826	31.3	75.5	27.6	4.6
12 133	Washington	83.9	6.8	8,709	78.0	102,100	21.3	11.6	544	35.0	80.8	29.1	4.6
13 000	**Georgia**	81.0	9.7	3,364,749	67.9	156,300	23.7	11.3	756	29.5	78.7	27.1	6.7
13 009	Baldwin	81.2	9.8	14,374	66.2	96,700	22.5	14.4	592	32.3	81.4	18.5	10.5
13 013	Barrow	84.2	9.2	21,730	72.4	139,700	23.7	10.8	782	30.2	83.7	29.7	4.3
13 015	Bartow	80.2	7.5	32,966	73.3	143,600	22.6	10.5	764	32.8	87.9	26.9	4.5
13 021	Bibb	78.9	8.3	58,801	60.0	110,600	22.9	12.7	632	32.7	81.2	19.7	11.7
13 029	Bryan	83.0	11.9	10,068	78.4	172,400	21.2	9.2	908	30.9	79.6	30.0	1.9
13 031	Bulloch	71.5	17.3	23,229	58.3	115,300	21.7	8.7	558	35.3	77.7	21.6	5.7
13 033	Burke	-	-	7,814	72.1	65,900	24.1	9.5	410	27.7	79.9	28.3	10.0
13 035	Butts	82.5	13.3	7,538	81.2	127,300	23.3	8.4	788	29.1	81.6	29.8	6.5
13 039	Camden	78.7	12.2	17,498	64.9	144,400	22.0	10.8	691	25.2	84.1	21.8	4.7
13 045	Carroll	76.5	9.6	39,697	68.2	136,400	24.1	12.4	703	30.0	80.7	29.5	4.7
13 047	Catoosa	83.4	10.0	23,550	75.0	123,700	22.1	9.7	586	24.5	86.6	23.5	4.4
13 051	Chatham	82.5	7.5	96,627	59.5	157,600	24.7	12.9	816	33.4	80.6	21.3	9.8
13 055	Chattooga	86.4	5.3	9,107	73.3	83,000	21.2	11.7	459	26.5	89.2	21.2	6.4
13 057	Cherokee	82.7	9.8	70,142	80.6	196,500	25.4	11.0	893	28.7	80.9	34.3	2.2
13 059	Clarke	68.9	14.8	42,540	45.6	158,300	24.7	10.6	685	34.5	74.2	19.1	8.2
13 063	Clayton	77.2	12.4	88,190	63.4	131,000	26.8	11.7	836	33.8	77.7	30.9	6.1
13 067	Cobb	81.0	10.0	248,741	72.1	206,700	23.1	9.3	900	29.0	80.9	30.1	3.0
13 069	Coffee	91.4	3.5	14,270	69.1	73,000	21.9	11.9	481	23.0	82.6	18.8	7.0
13 071	Colquitt	80.6	5.9	15,902	59.6	78,700	19.5	11.6	530	32.4	71.0	22.8	7.2
13 073	Columbia	85.1	8.9	38,232	83.1	155,700	22.0	8.5	784	28.1	83.3	22.8	2.2
13 077	Coweta	83.4	8.6	39,864	75.5	175,600	23.0	9.4	844	27.7	81.9	31.1	3.3
13 081	Crisp	73.6	8.2	8,257	55.9	91,800	19.9	13.0	539	34.1	77.9	19.2	16.9
13 085	Dawson	81.4	15.6	7,343	76.1	205,900	28.2	9.4	841	26.8	78.7	29.5	1.6
13 087	Decatur	84.3	8.3	11,269	67.5	88,100	21.3	14.1	435	30.5	83.5	20.9	11.6
13 089	DeKalb	78.1	11.3	267,301	60.5	192,700	25.9	12.4	869	31.1	72.9	31.4	9.3
13 091	Dodge	92.4	5.3	6,681	68.7	78,400	18.8	12.8	368	25.8	-	21.7	7.9
13 095	Dougherty	75.6	10.6	36,920	48.2	97,800	19.9	12.2	581	28.6	79.4	17.6	13.8
13 097	Douglas	75.6	17.5	41,939	71.1	153,300	24.3	8.8	847	27.7	84.6	32.7	3.2
13 103	Effingham	83.2	7.4	16,568	77.5	128,300	22.8	10.5	736	28.0	81.8	29.8	3.4
13 105	Elbert	84.4	5.4	7,930	70.3	79,600	21.2	10.2	467	33.1	78.6	18.6	15.4
13 107	Emanuel	87.6	4.2	8,161	65.5	69,000	21.1	14.5	453	29.6	74.0	22.4	8.4
13 111	Fannin	88.8	4.7	10,861	76.0	172,900	22.4	11.7	550	25.3	82.3	22.6	4.9
13 113	Fayette	85.1	9.7	36,591	84.4	244,600	23.6	10.1	965	32.1	82.5	29.1	1.7
13 115	Floyd	82.9	6.5	34,506	69.4	113,700	23.4	11.2	614	31.9	80.1	21.3	8.8
13 117	Forsyth	86.5	9.3	51,314	85.2	265,800	24.6	9.3	973	26.6	78.6	31.5	1.9
13 119	Franklin	85.2	4.6	7,965	71.9	92,400	23.3	11.4	566	25.8	83.3	25.9	6.8
13 121	Fulton	78.7	10.2	348,215	58.9	258,900	24.8	12.9	880	29.8	72.2	27.6	11.8
13 123	Gilmer	83.8	8.6	11,553	69.1	123,600	22.4	11.0	592	31.8	76.9	27.2	4.9

STATE County code	STATE County	Percent who lived in the same house one year ago	Percent who did not live in county one year ago	Total occupied housing units	Percent owner-occu-pied housing units	Median value of owner-occupied housing units (dollars)	Median selected monthly owner costs as a percentage of household income		Median gross rent (dollars)	Median gross rent as a percentage of house-hold income	Percent of workers who drove alone to work	Mean travel time to work (minutes)	Percent of occupied housing units with no vehicle available
							With a mortgage	Without a mortgage					
	ACS table number:	C07204	C07204	B25003	B25003	B25077	B25092	B25092	B25064	B25071	C08301	B08013/C08012	C25045
		1	2	3	4	5	6	7	8	9	10	11	12
	Georgia—Cont.												
13 127	Glynn	80.8	8.7	28,652	63.9	165,500	22.4	10.6	723	27.2	81.7	18.6	6.0
13 129	Gordon	82.1	5.8	18,663	69.4	119,500	23.2	11.0	586	28.2	80.7	21.9	6.1
13 131	Grady	86.7	6.7	9,141	66.0	89,000	25.5	14.1	540	27.4	73.8	25.2	5.7
13 135	Gwinnett	80.9	9.7	252,872	73.4	192,300	24.4	10.8	914	28.4	79.2	32.7	2.7
13 137	Habersham	87.1	7.8	14,549	75.4	131,700	22.7	10.5	538	26.0	81.3	24.1	4.2
13 139	Hall	82.9	7.2	54,184	70.8	168,000	24.3	11.6	784	28.6	78.5	26.3	6.1
13 143	Haralson	86.2	7.1	10,531	72.5	108,500	23.5	14.4	615	28.5	77.6	28.2	5.1
13 145	Harris	85.5	10.3	10,676	86.2	169,500	22.5	13.7	499	32.2	87.9	25.2	4.0
13 147	Hart	89.2	5.4	8,884	73.9	111,900	21.8	9.7	559	34.0	81.6	23.1	5.9
13 151	Henry	80.4	12.9	61,139	81.4	168,500	24.8	10.2	944	29.5	82.2	32.3	2.4
13 153	Houston	78.2	9.1	48,519	67.7	120,900	20.6	9.2	687	28.0	85.6	20.5	6.3
13 157	Jackson	82.9	8.7	20,080	73.1	136,900	23.6	12.2	652	31.3	77.7	25.8	4.4
13 169	Jones	88.2	8.2	9,493	84.1	113,400	24.3	10.6	721	27.2	87.3	24.9	2.3
13 175	Laurens	88.6	3.8	17,048	67.2	84,700	20.8	11.3	518	25.7	85.7	21.0	7.8
13 177	Lee	82.0	9.8	10,605	75.0	124,100	19.6	9.5	694	19.5	84.5	20.3	3.5
13 179	Liberty	68.3	20.9	20,465	49.4	98,500	21.7	11.5	724	27.3	78.0	20.8	5.8
13 185	Lowndes	74.6	11.3	38,206	58.6	119,400	21.9	10.8	638	28.4	84.0	17.2	6.5
13 187	Lumpkin	79.2	16.2	9,514	66.3	161,200	27.5	13.6	716	29.3	81.5	30.7	2.1
13 189	McDuffie	82.6	8.1	8,403	68.5	83,800	25.9	10.0	498	26.8	81.4	22.7	11.6
13 195	Madison	83.6	7.5	10,070	73.1	115,000	22.4	12.3	641	34.6	82.7	23.6	4.9
13 199	Meriwether	88.2	6.0	8,783	70.8	101,700	23.0	13.6	595	28.8	78.2	30.0	12.0
13 205	Mitchell	88.0	6.9	8,277	69.1	72,900	25.1	13.1	526	27.8	81.0	19.3	12.3
13 207	Monroe	85.2	10.1	9,028	76.2	141,600	20.9	11.7	632	22.1	84.4	26.5	5.8
13 213	Murray	89.7	4.2	13,604	75.1	90,000	21.7	8.8	518	28.4	87.9	23.1	4.6
13 215	Muscogee	75.6	13.0	71,365	57.3	119,600	22.8	9.7	679	29.4	72.6	18.4	10.5
13 217	Newton	82.5	10.5	32,095	76.1	147,600	25.3	13.1	814	33.6	82.4	31.2	3.3
13 219	Oconee	87.4	11.1	11,097	81.6	203,300	21.7	9.9	797	28.0	84.0	22.2	2.7
13 223	Paulding	84.9	10.6	43,715	79.9	145,200	23.1	11.5	841	25.9	84.8	38.7	2.1
13 225	Peach	84.2	11.4	8,385	67.0	108,100	19.9	10.9	618	30.0	78.9	22.0	6.3
13 227	Pickens	85.4	6.1	11,501	82.6	160,000	24.7	13.1	640	31.1	84.4	32.7	4.7
13 233	Polk	82.8	5.4	15,110	69.6	97,800	22.4	11.9	600	26.1	80.3	27.2	6.9
13 237	Putnam	87.0	6.1	8,014	76.5	133,000	22.3	9.2	637	32.7	75.4	26.6	7.4
13 245	Richmond	75.3	11.2	75,266	57.3	93,800	23.3	12.3	662	28.7	74.7	18.9	9.6
13 247	Rockdale	82.2	11.7	27,104	72.4	166,700	24.0	9.0	848	32.5	79.3	31.8	6.2
13 255	Spalding	79.3	6.7	22,197	63.8	122,100	23.8	12.6	769	33.3	74.3	28.9	7.5
13 257	Stephens	83.5	5.7	8,825	71.6	97,800	21.7	11.1	547	34.0	76.6	20.9	7.7
13 261	Sumter	83.6	5.0	11,917	64.6	82,700	22.4	12.2	547	29.7	73.1	17.1	12.6
13 267	Tattnall	80.5	12.6	7,073	64.4	73,200	18.8	10.4	442	16.2	60.6	26.8	9.1
13 275	Thomas	78.9	7.6	17,350	67.0	118,900	21.1	11.0	574	28.2	78.8	19.5	8.6
13 277	Tift	78.7	10.7	14,997	63.4	102,100	20.4	11.6	553	25.0	78.0	15.2	6.8
13 279	Toombs	84.6	7.4	9,768	63.5	77,000	23.2	10.9	465	26.9	81.6	21.2	9.4
13 285	Troup	77.7	8.3	22,907	65.7	118,500	23.1	12.3	623	29.2	79.4	20.3	9.9
13 291	Union	87.0	7.7	9,154	81.3	164,500	24.3	11.7	607	29.9	-	19.2	5.2
13 293	Upson	80.1	7.1	10,485	68.6	90,900	22.2	12.1	506	27.4	77.7	25.6	11.3
13 295	Walker	81.1	10.0	25,181	73.0	97,900	22.2	10.5	594	25.4	77.4	25.5	5.7
13 297	Walton	82.2	8.5	27,098	73.2	155,500	24.1	9.8	739	29.0	81.2	30.9	4.8
13 299	Ware	85.7	8.1	13,245	64.4	65,800	18.6	11.6	512	29.8	80.6	22.0	9.1
13 303	Washington	96.3	1.9	7,211	69.9	73,500	19.8	15.8	469	28.4	88.0	20.8	6.9
13 305	Wayne	82.7	8.8	9,544	70.2	85,900	20.0	9.1	464	29.1	81.3	23.5	8.9
13 311	White	90.0	2.8	9,369	76.6	163,200	25.0	12.4	672	33.8	86.4	25.7	4.9
13 313	Whitfield	84.2	5.0	31,274	68.5	125,000	22.3	9.4	602	28.8	81.9	18.7	4.9
13 321	Worth	85.9	7.3	7,750	69.9	74,400	21.5	12.0	554	33.1	80.3	24.6	6.2
15 000	**Hawaii**	83.8	6.7	433,664	58.9	510,500	27.7	8.9	1,144	31.0	67.4	25.7	8.6
15 001	Hawaii	85.2	6.2	62,069	66.0	365,300	26.0	8.7	983	27.7	69.5	26.5	4.9
15 003	Honolulu	83.5	6.9	301,189	56.9	521,500	27.5	8.7	1,161	32.1	65.3	26.8	10.3
15 007	Kauai	85.1	5.2	21,739	66.6	577,400	28.5	11.1	1,179	29.0	78.6	19.7	3.5
15 009	Maui	83.4	6.2	48,586	58.6	613,600	30.7	9.5	1,198	29.4	72.6	20.8	5.7
16 000	**Idaho**	79.1	9.7	545,171	71.6	158,600	23.7	10.5	644	27.3	76.6	20.1	3.9
16 001	Ada	76.6	9.5	139,341	70.2	205,200	23.5	10.2	719	27.2	80.2	19.6	4.2
16 005	Bannock	77.0	9.6	28,927	70.4	116,100	20.8	11.9	551	30.0	80.3	17.1	4.3
16 011	Bingham	83.9	7.0	14,025	80.5	110,400	21.6	9.8	544	22.4	75.7	19.6	3.6
16 013	Blaine	79.8	11.4	8,508	70.3	566,500	32.0	10.1	791	30.0	71.3	17.5	1.8
16 017	Bonner	85.4	7.1	15,318	78.2	218,100	27.2	9.6	625	26.6	75.5	23.7	3.4
16 019	Bonneville	79.9	8.9	33,864	73.1	131,300	22.0	9.4	617	27.5	74.5	20.1	4.3
16 027	Canyon	77.7	10.5	59,557	73.4	145,900	24.8	11.5	664	28.4	77.5	24.7	4.6
16 031	Cassia	86.1	6.9	7,321	71.3	95,900	23.1	11.3	490	22.3	78.3	15.0	2.8
16 039	Elmore	75.1	13.9	9,978	68.2	134,200	23.1	9.4	675	23.6	73.0	18.7	2.5
16 051	Jefferson	83.4	11.9	7,046	78.7	127,200	23.2	8.8	526	19.8	75.2	24.3	2.9
16 053	Jerome	86.9	7.7	6,553	66.5	125,500	22.7	11.9	564	24.8	80.8	17.2	3.9
16 055	Kootenai	82.1	7.0	50,628	71.4	214,600	27.2	12.3	734	30.0	78.6	22.2	3.3
16 057	Latah	63.7	18.3	13,625	55.6	164,400	23.0	9.8	616	32.7	61.7	17.9	6.8
16 065	Madison	60.7	20.8	9,582	59.8	148,700	22.8	8.0	589	34.0	62.8	15.1	2.4
16 069	Nez Perce	78.0	10.8	15,844	68.3	136,600	23.1	10.6	538	27.1	81.0	15.3	3.9

STATE County code	STATE County	Percent who lived in the same house one year ago	Percent who did not live in county one year ago	Total occupied housing units	Percent owner-occupied housing units	Median value of owner-occupied housing units (dollars)	Median selected monthly owner costs as a percentage of household income		Median gross rent (dollars)	Median gross rent as a percentage of household income	Percent of workers who drove alone to work	Mean travel time to work (minutes)	Percent of occupied housing units with no vehicle available
							With a mortgage	Without a mortgage					
ACS table number:		C07204	C07204	B25003	B25003	B25077	B25092	B25092	B25064	B25071	C08301	B08013/ C08012	C25045
		1	2	3	4	5	6	7	8	9	10	11	12
	Idaho—Cont.												
16 075	Payette	84.7	8.6	7,966	73.3	116,000	22.3	8.4	500	26.9	76.1	20.5	6.5
16 083	Twin Falls	80.1	8.2	26,912	67.8	130,500	23.7	10.4	609	23.3	79.8	15.3	3.0
17 000	**Illinois**	84.9	5.4	4,724,462	70.1	198,100	25.5	13.8	780	29.8	74.1	28.0	10.1
17 001	Adams	85.2	4.9	27,362	71.2	91,900	19.4	11.6	515	26.3	82.8	16.0	6.6
17 007	Boone	87.4	7.8	16,632	80.9	164,400	26.0	14.2	638	30.3	81.9	30.7	5.7
17 011	Bureau	91.4	4.1	14,750	75.4	101,600	21.7	13.5	519	24.7	82.5	18.6	6.0
17 019	Champaign	72.0	12.6	75,038	56.5	136,500	21.8	10.9	680	35.4	69.6	16.5	8.9
17 021	Christian	85.9	5.8	14,011	77.6	79,400	20.8	13.2	522	29.4	84.5	24.6	5.6
17 027	Clinton	87.7	7.6	13,546	77.7	113,700	20.9	12.0	558	22.4	83.1	25.2	4.5
17 029	Coles	72.2	12.8	20,639	59.6	84,100	20.8	11.2	606	41.5	78.8	16.0	7.7
17 031	Cook	85.0	3.5	1,935,764	62.0	264,800	28.7	15.2	850	31.2	63.9	31.8	16.7
17 037	DeKalb	72.6	14.7	35,451	64.6	189,700	26.0	14.8	749	31.8	80.6	24.4	4.0
17 043	DuPage	87.2	6.2	335,292	78.2	312,900	26.3	14.1	960	27.3	79.3	28.9	3.3
17 049	Effingham	90.5	3.6	13,237	78.1	103,900	20.7	12.6	551	26.7	84.6	17.3	6.9
17 051	Fayette	85.9	4.7	8,005	80.0	65,600	21.4	12.6	522	28.4	79.7	22.8	5.0
17 055	Franklin	85.7	4.6	16,141	78.0	55,700	21.8	13.6	516	27.9	84.5	22.3	7.5
17 057	Fulton	86.1	6.4	14,772	78.3	75,700	21.0	13.4	483	26.0	81.3	27.3	6.3
17 063	Grundy	85.7	9.1	16,696	77.2	187,300	24.2	13.7	809	23.3	84.9	29.3	2.9
17 073	Henry	89.1	6.3	19,825	76.2	96,700	20.8	12.8	566	25.8	84.9	20.5	5.3
17 075	Iroquois	82.0	8.8	11,645	75.1	99,800	21.8	12.0	585	28.5	79.3	23.4	4.0
17 077	Jackson	71.9	15.1	24,471	50.8	90,200	20.9	12.7	527	42.4	80.6	17.3	10.2
17 081	Jefferson	84.8	5.9	15,841	74.6	81,800	21.0	12.4	514	26.2	79.5	21.3	8.6
17 083	Jersey	88.7	5.2	8,633	81.9	105,300	19.8	12.2	493	25.6	82.8	27.2	3.9
17 085	Jo Daviess	88.3	5.6	10,240	77.7	125,000	24.0	13.7	610	23.3	67.2	21.0	5.1
17 089	Kane	85.3	6.7	160,402	78.1	242,400	27.9	14.8	875	30.9	79.1	28.7	4.8
17 091	Kankakee	82.3	7.6	40,249	70.5	132,700	24.1	14.6	682	27.4	81.4	22.5	7.2
17 093	Kendall	84.0	11.6	28,793	86.9	242,500	27.9	16.0	921	26.4	84.1	32.4	2.7
17 095	Knox	87.3	7.0	21,637	70.0	73,800	21.5	12.9	485	27.9	82.6	19.0	9.1
17 097	Lake	85.8	6.4	233,617	79.6	290,200	27.0	15.0	913	29.1	78.7	30.6	3.9
17 099	LaSalle	87.4	4.8	45,375	73.3	118,800	23.3	14.0	623	28.1	82.9	22.6	6.3
17 103	Lee	86.5	6.8	13,490	74.9	110,700	22.2	12.8	555	22.3	80.8	22.2	4.5
17 105	Livingston	80.7	9.3	14,730	76.3	97,100	21.4	13.6	519	21.9	79.1	19.1	4.3
17 107	Logan	79.7	12.4	10,927	75.5	90,000	20.1	12.8	569	26.8	79.3	21.2	4.3
17 109	McDonough	72.5	16.8	12,883	60.3	81,600	19.6	11.9	534	39.6	73.7	15.7	8.3
17 111	McHenry	88.5	4.9	105,901	84.8	250,500	26.5	15.5	948	30.8	81.6	33.6	3.2
17 113	McLean	77.2	10.2	61,177	68.4	143,200	21.8	12.0	674	30.7	77.7	17.4	4.7
17 115	Macon	82.0	5.3	46,343	71.9	86,900	19.4	11.5	555	28.2	86.8	17.6	9.5
17 117	Macoupin	88.8	4.5	19,569	81.1	88,200	20.0	12.7	511	24.7	84.3	27.1	4.7
17 119	Madison	84.8	5.3	107,271	74.4	115,100	21.1	12.6	653	29.4	85.1	24.1	5.4
17 121	Marion	84.8	4.4	16,373	72.1	66,000	21.0	13.5	514	28.3	82.1	20.4	8.0
17 133	Monroe	87.3	6.9	11,741	83.0	179,600	23.3	14.5	725	21.2	83.5	29.7	1.5
17 135	Montgomery	89.7	6.1	11,285	79.1	72,400	20.9	13.0	474	30.3	82.3	23.8	5.6
17 137	Morgan	78.6	8.9	13,700	68.4	86,800	19.7	12.0	505	29.3	80.0	19.2	8.7
17 141	Ogle	86.2	7.4	20,282	76.6	137,000	22.8	14.2	603	23.9	78.9	23.6	4.5
17 143	Peoria	83.8	5.9	74,136	68.8	110,800	21.5	12.3	638	26.7	83.8	18.6	9.3
17 145	Perry	81.2	10.2	8,603	77.1	73,600	20.7	12.6	423	24.4	82.8	23.5	8.8
17 157	Randolph	85.2	9.6	12,252	78.3	85,100	20.9	10.5	477	26.9	85.4	24.2	4.4
17 161	Rock Island	83.9	5.7	60,173	71.7	99,700	21.8	11.8	557	27.4	82.2	18.2	7.6
17 163	St. Clair	83.8	6.5	101,362	69.4	109,200	22.7	13.0	676	28.7	82.1	23.4	8.1
17 165	Saline	89.5	3.8	11,310	73.4	60,200	20.0	13.0	459	31.6	78.3	22.5	10.9
17 167	Sangamon	83.8	5.0	81,172	70.4	112,200	21.8	11.5	615	28.3	83.9	18.7	6.8
17 173	Shelby	89.6	4.2	9,084	81.9	83,300	20.7	11.1	473	27.0	78.7	22.6	4.9
17 177	Stephenson	84.4	4.0	19,336	75.1	99,900	23.5	13.8	519	27.6	79.4	20.3	8.7
17 179	Tazewell	85.4	6.5	52,692	77.5	119,500	21.0	12.4	588	25.2	88.1	20.4	5.2
17 183	Vermilion	87.3	4.4	32,857	71.0	71,700	20.0	12.4	573	29.9	82.1	20.4	9.9
17 195	Whiteside	85.5	5.7	23,855	75.5	90,500	21.5	12.5	580	29.3	81.7	18.6	6.3
17 197	Will	86.6	7.2	210,889	85.6	237,400	27.1	14.1	844	30.6	81.3	33.8	3.1
17 199	Williamson	80.9	10.1	25,852	72.5	85,500	21.1	12.7	554	25.4	85.0	20.5	4.9
17 201	Winnebago	84.5	5.1	110,162	72.5	119,500	23.9	14.2	645	29.6	84.5	21.6	7.5
17 203	Woodford	86.8	8.4	13,896	81.4	139,200	22.1	13.0	633	19.8	83.9	23.5	3.0
18 000	**Indiana**	83.2	6.5	2,447,887	72.1	119,400	21.8	11.8	646	28.6	82.6	22.4	6.2
18 001	Adams	85.5	3.8	12,088	76.4	110,200	22.1	9.4	523	24.9	76.1	21.4	13.2
18 003	Allen	85.8	3.9	135,553	70.9	109,900	20.4	10.3	609	26.5	86.0	20.3	5.6
18 005	Bartholomew	83.9	4.7	27,992	73.8	123,600	20.0	10.1	718	29.2	85.5	19.5	4.1
18 011	Boone	88.6	5.5	19,743	79.8	156,800	22.3	10.8	714	27.9	86.7	22.8	4.2
18 017	Cass	84.8	6.0	15,853	72.0	83,100	20.8	13.5	543	23.4	83.1	19.8	7.1
18 019	Clark	83.6	8.5	43,463	70.4	120,900	22.1	11.2	634	29.3	84.3	22.4	6.4
18 021	Clay	89.2	4.2	10,429	75.7	91,100	19.7	12.2	594	27.4	79.5	24.9	2.9
18 023	Clinton	85.3	5.4	12,203	73.4	101,500	21.7	11.3	602	26.7	79.5	22.1	5.1
18 027	Daviess	88.2	3.9	10,949	77.1	85,900	20.5	11.1	574	27.3	75.7	22.8	9.0
18 029	Dearborn	87.0	5.6	18,143	79.3	152,800	21.8	12.0	650	23.2	80.8	27.6	4.9
18 031	Decatur	84.0	4.5	9,838	73.7	110,000	23.6	11.9	556	23.2	84.3	19.4	3.2
18 033	DeKalb	86.9	4.9	15,613	80.7	111,900	21.9	12.6	574	27.1	84.5	20.8	3.9
18 035	Delaware	75.5	8.5	46,513	66.2	91,200	21.8	12.3	605	33.7	77.5	18.6	7.7

STATE County code	STATE County	Percent who lived in the same house one year ago	Percent who did not live in county one year ago	Total occupied housing units	Percent owner-occu-pied housing units	Median value of owner-occupied housing units (dollars)	Median selected monthly owner costs as a percentage of household income		Median gross rent (dollars)	Median gross rent as a percentage of house-hold income	Percent of workers who drove alone to work	Mean travel time to work (minutes)	Percent of occupied housing units with no vehicle available
							With a mortgage	Without a mortgage					
ACS table number:		C07204	C07204	B25003	B25003	B25077	B25092	B25092	B25064	B25071	C08301	B08013/ C08012	C25045
		1	2	3	4	5	6	7	8	9	10	11	12
	Indiana—Cont.												
18 037	Dubois	91.7	3.1	15,590	79.2	120,300	20.6	9.5	550	22.8	85.8	17.0	4.4
18 039	Elkhart	81.9	5.2	70,835	70.8	123,000	22.0	11.3	678	27.4	79.4	17.8	6.8
18 041	Fayette	87.0	3.4	10,071	73.0	90,700	22.6	12.9	512	35.8	81.8	23.9	11.6
18 043	Floyd	87.6	7.4	28,236	74.7	140,300	22.0	10.4	655	27.0	85.3	20.9	6.6
18 047	Franklin	92.0	4.9	7,967	84.1	125,600	22.0	11.3	578	26.0	84.5	27.1	3.7
18 049	Fulton	87.8	4.8	8,363	77.3	91,400	20.2	12.1	544	26.1	83.6	23.6	5.3
18 051	Gibson	89.6	3.9	12,986	79.3	94,000	19.4	12.8	530	23.9	85.5	22.6	3.7
18 053	Grant	83.5	6.1	27,649	72.5	82,500	21.3	11.2	511	28.5	82.2	18.7	6.8
18 055	Greene	86.0	5.8	13,881	77.9	84,300	19.5	11.3	473	32.6	81.8	29.0	4.7
18 057	Hamilton	84.3	9.1	88,941	80.7	201,300	20.8	10.1	861	24.8	85.7	25.0	1.2
18 059	Hancock	85.8	6.3	24,834	80.8	153,100	21.8	9.6	725	26.2	86.8	27.0	2.3
18 061	Harrison	89.7	3.4	13,505	84.7	121,500	21.1	8.7	607	23.8	84.8	28.4	2.3
18 063	Hendricks	84.6	9.1	49,755	81.3	155,700	22.4	11.1	804	29.2	87.7	25.1	2.4
18 065	Henry	84.9	7.1	18,981	77.0	95,400	21.8	12.7	531	26.5	85.6	28.9	5.4
18 067	Howard	81.9	4.3	34,683	70.3	108,900	20.7	10.6	619	28.0	85.8	17.7	7.6
18 069	Huntington	89.7	3.0	14,435	83.4	97,200	21.5	12.1	557	25.9	80.7	19.9	4.1
18 071	Jackson	83.7	4.7	17,005	72.5	102,500	22.2	11.4	620	26.5	82.5	19.5	4.9
18 073	Jasper	82.7	7.3	11,984	75.3	137,000	21.8	12.1	603	26.1	77.9	25.7	4.0
18 075	Jay	87.8	4.5	8,437	77.9	79,500	21.4	12.0	433	28.8	78.9	25.6	5.0
18 077	Jefferson	84.9	4.7	12,502	74.3	99,900	22.4	14.0	541	28.2	79.5	17.8	7.4
18 079	Jennings	80.1	7.6	11,654	78.1	86,800	21.1	10.5	578	27.6	86.0	25.1	3.3
18 081	Johnson	80.2	11.8	50,241	75.7	139,500	21.7	10.8	734	28.4	85.4	24.8	3.8
18 083	Knox	80.0	6.5	15,077	71.4	84,300	18.9	11.0	484	32.0	81.9	17.9	8.1
18 085	Kosciusko	85.0	5.8	29,822	75.9	127,900	22.0	10.3	629	22.4	78.4	19.4	4.9
18 087	LaGrange	88.9	5.9	12,117	84.8	148,700	24.6	10.6	613	24.5	55.5	21.3	26.0
18 089	Lake	85.8	5.3	184,254	70.7	129,100	23.7	14.4	712	29.8	83.3	26.8	9.1
18 091	LaPorte	84.6	6.1	41,694	75.5	117,500	22.3	12.0	604	27.2	82.9	20.6	5.5
18 093	Lawrence	86.8	2.4	18,719	76.8	97,500	21.6	11.8	543	28.4	85.8	24.7	6.1
18 095	Madison	82.3	6.3	51,392	73.4	97,600	22.0	11.5	606	32.1	84.3	24.2	6.6
18 097	Marion	79.1	6.2	357,445	61.2	121,600	22.7	11.9	676	29.6	81.9	21.9	8.1
18 099	Marshall	83.8	6.2	16,839	80.9	119,400	21.3	11.6	623	21.7	79.1	21.3	5.5
18 103	Miami	84.2	8.6	13,448	77.3	86,500	21.1	12.5	590	27.2	83.0	19.9	5.2
18 105	Monroe	66.9	15.2	46,657	56.9	140,800	21.9	11.8	685	38.6	76.1	17.8	6.3
18 107	Montgomery	82.2	5.8	14,712	74.3	104,800	21.4	13.2	559	26.6	82.6	20.7	3.9
18 109	Morgan	87.7	4.2	24,933	82.3	137,300	23.3	11.4	709	29.0	84.4	28.0	3.1
18 113	Noble	84.7	5.8	17,378	79.7	109,700	22.0	11.6	578	24.0	77.4	21.0	5.1
18 119	Owen	87.2	5.9	8,363	82.4	99,400	21.3	10.7	519	26.5	80.2	29.9	5.5
18 127	Porter	86.0	6.3	61,024	77.1	152,300	21.5	13.2	769	29.4	84.4	26.2	2.9
18 129	Posey	88.3	5.6	10,435	83.2	119,600	18.8	9.8	599	22.8	88.1	22.8	3.0
18 133	Putnam	86.7	7.3	12,674	75.6	114,200	23.0	12.4	642	26.9	80.0	26.1	2.6
18 135	Randolph	86.1	6.5	10,779	80.9	79,100	21.8	11.1	481	25.4	81.2	23.7	5.9
18 137	Ripley	85.6	5.7	10,588	79.6	130,500	23.2	12.4	620	27.7	83.4	25.4	4.5
18 141	St. Joseph	85.0	5.7	100,719	71.8	112,800	21.5	12.1	679	28.4	81.9	19.6	7.1
18 143	Scott	81.4	6.0	9,711	74.4	94,000	23.6	12.6	590	30.8	82.5	23.0	5.9
18 145	Shelby	84.4	5.2	17,008	75.5	116,100	21.8	12.4	640	23.0	82.9	24.3	4.4
18 147	Spencer	91.6	3.9	8,306	82.2	112,800	21.0	11.7	515	23.1	83.0	26.3	3.2
18 149	Starke	85.6	8.1	9,015	82.4	99,700	24.6	15.6	565	30.7	82.1	29.4	3.9
18 151	Steuben	79.1	9.2	14,455	76.4	126,200	22.5	12.3	613	29.2	83.9	21.3	6.1
18 153	Sullivan	85.4	9.0	8,221	78.4	72,400	21.2	11.3	462	25.0	87.1	26.8	3.9
18 157	Tippecanoe	69.6	13.5	60,326	56.5	128,500	22.0	9.4	692	36.4	76.1	17.7	8.1
18 163	Vanderburgh	82.1	5.9	72,465	66.8	107,100	21.0	12.1	613	30.9	84.3	18.3	8.8
18 167	Vigo	80.2	6.9	41,443	66.3	86,400	19.9	13.1	560	31.1	83.6	19.4	8.0
18 169	Wabash	83.6	7.1	13,312	79.0	96,100	20.7	10.5	562	28.3	82.1	18.9	5.4
18 173	Warrick	88.4	5.5	21,648	84.8	135,500	20.5	10.2	662	24.0	88.2	22.4	3.2
18 175	Washington	84.6	7.7	10,657	78.7	96,300	23.6	15.2	490	26.5	77.4	28.3	5.1
18 177	Wayne	81.6	4.2	27,410	71.9	97,500	22.2	13.1	561	27.3	81.0	20.1	8.7
18 179	Wells	86.4	6.5	10,959	78.4	102,000	21.6	11.1	539	23.8	82.5	20.6	4.0
18 181	White	87.0	5.9	9,945	75.9	102,700	23.2	11.2	592	27.4	82.6	24.4	3.9
18 183	Whitley	89.1	5.4	12,836	86.2	122,600	21.0	12.3	570	29.6	84.0	24.2	2.5
19 000	**Iowa**	83.1	7.1	1,206,848	73.3	112,600	21.5	12.4	587	26.9	78.8	18.2	5.3
19 011	Benton	87.0	7.0	10,110	81.2	122,200	22.5	12.0	514	25.4	77.6	23.9	3.5
19 013	Black Hawk	78.4	8.0	50,964	70.0	110,100	21.3	12.4	594	33.3	82.4	15.6	6.8
19 015	Boone	87.3	4.6	10,759	74.5	110,300	21.7	14.7	593	24.4	79.6	19.1	5.1
19 017	Bremer	84.7	8.5	9,651	81.3	123,200	21.4	11.5	529	24.4	77.6	18.2	3.3
19 019	Buchanan	85.3	7.6	8,591	76.9	105,500	21.6	10.9	465	22.4	75.3	21.8	7.7
19 027	Carroll	85.7	5.9	8,570	74.7	105,000	19.1	10.5	456	25.0	77.5	15.3	5.2
19 033	Cerro Gordo	85.6	5.1	19,113	73.8	107,800	20.5	11.9	550	28.6	78.9	15.5	5.2
19 045	Clinton	85.5	4.3	20,708	75.3	95,400	21.1	13.7	509	28.2	82.3	19.0	6.6
19 049	Dallas	80.8	12.8	20,115	77.3	168,800	22.1	13.4	695	24.5	83.4	21.2	3.0
19 057	Des Moines	84.5	4.6	17,223	74.9	84,500	20.7	13.4	550	29.0	84.3	16.1	5.7
19 061	Dubuque	87.0	4.9	36,520	75.8	125,300	22.2	12.2	538	26.6	82.2	15.5	6.0
19 065	Fayette	83.3	11.0	8,653	77.5	79,900	21.8	14.0	426	25.3	70.3	20.4	6.1
19 087	Henry	86.7	7.2	8,093	74.1	92,900	21.6	14.1	513	24.7	77.8	16.9	7.6
19 097	Jackson	86.2	4.0	8,374	74.4	97,000	22.4	13.7	485	24.7	78.6	20.9	7.1
19 099	Jasper	84.3	7.4	15,256	72.2	110,100	21.4	11.9	550	29.5	77.5	20.9	4.6

Table C-2. Counties — Where: Migration, Housing, and Transportation, 2005–2007—*Continued*

STATE County code	STATE County	Percent who lived in the same house one year ago	Percent who did not live in county one year ago	Total occupied housing units	Percent owner-occupied housing units	Median value of owner-occupied housing units (dollars)	Median selected monthly owner costs as a percentage of household income		Median gross rent (dollars)	Median gross rent as a percentage of household income	Percent of workers who drove alone to work	Mean travel time to work (minutes)	Percent of occupied housing units with no vehicle available
							With a mortgage	Without a mortgage					
ACS table number:		C07204	C07204	B25003	B25003	B25077	B25092	B25092	B25064	B25071	C08301	B08013/C08012	C25045
		1	2	3	4	5	6	7	8	9	10	11	12
	Iowa—Cont.												
19 103	Johnson	71.7	13.2	50,082	60.9	170,200	22.8	10.5	699	35.4	68.4	17.3	6.1
19 105	Jones	83.5	5.8	7,759	74.1	99,300	22.6	11.9	513	26.0	76.9	23.4	4.7
19 111	Lee	85.5	6.2	14,802	75.0	76,400	20.5	12.6	463	27.0	83.1	17.0	6.5
19 113	Linn	81.9	6.2	84,535	72.4	127,700	21.9	12.8	588	25.9	82.9	17.4	6.3
19 123	Mahaska	86.5	6.4	9,053	75.5	89,700	19.4	12.8	503	24.5	71.8	17.5	4.4
19 125	Marion	84.9	7.4	12,563	75.8	129,400	20.7	11.9	598	30.9	75.9	19.7	6.8
19 127	Marshall	86.0	5.4	15,723	76.6	96,500	21.9	13.4	563	26.7	76.9	17.1	5.0
19 139	Muscatine	85.2	6.0	16,302	77.2	120,500	22.1	11.7	586	30.4	83.0	17.4	5.2
19 149	Plymouth	88.5	3.8	9,740	82.0	110,000	20.4	10.0	516	20.9	82.0	18.1	4.3
19 153	Polk	81.2	6.4	167,421	71.9	143,800	22.3	13.0	695	27.6	83.3	18.4	5.6
19 155	Pottawattamie	80.3	7.5	36,094	71.9	121,200	22.5	13.1	682	27.3	82.3	19.8	5.1
19 163	Scott	83.2	6.7	64,373	72.1	127,000	21.3	12.1	623	28.3	84.3	18.4	5.7
19 167	Sioux	87.4	6.4	11,132	81.2	110,600	21.3	9.5	447	22.9	68.8	12.4	3.5
19 169	Story	67.7	15.4	31,467	57.3	150,200	21.4	10.7	690	32.0	73.2	16.3	4.8
19 179	Wapello	81.9	9.2	14,987	76.7	71,600	20.6	13.9	539	26.7	77.0	16.5	6.0
19 181	Warren	81.0	10.4	16,362	75.7	144,500	21.5	13.6	657	23.8	78.8	23.2	3.5
19 183	Washington	86.1	5.2	8,447	74.2	116,100	21.3	10.8	592	28.4	72.5	21.4	5.4
19 187	Webster	85.4	3.8	15,776	70.9	87,500	19.1	12.8	510	25.2	82.3	15.5	4.3
19 191	Winneshiek	82.6	7.8	7,952	76.2	136,100	22.5	14.1	495	21.7	69.3	15.0	4.6
19 193	Woodbury	81.6	6.0	38,702	69.0	90,200	21.0	12.3	590	28.7	79.0	16.7	7.1
20 000	**Kansas**	81.1	8.0	1,083,868	70.0	114,400	21.6	12.1	626	27.3	81.6	18.5	5.0
20 009	Barton	82.0	7.7	11,640	73.5	62,900	19.8	11.2	517	22.4	78.9	14.3	6.5
20 015	Butler	81.1	8.3	23,111	77.1	112,900	20.8	13.1	618	27.3	84.1	21.9	4.4
20 021	Cherokee	80.6	6.5	9,007	75.2	62,400	20.0	12.1	466	30.9	81.9	21.0	6.1
20 035	Cowley	79.8	11.1	13,632	68.8	70,900	20.7	13.2	540	28.1	78.6	18.6	6.1
20 037	Crawford	81.0	7.4	16,058	64.3	79,200	22.0	13.1	576	31.4	81.2	15.2	6.1
20 045	Douglas	70.7	12.5	42,996	57.0	168,300	23.5	12.2	729	33.5	77.0	19.6	5.4
20 051	Ellis	78.5	9.1	11,468	66.8	113,000	20.2	11.4	608	30.2	85.1	13.4	6.7
20 055	Finney	84.0	4.3	12,146	71.7	94,100	21.5	11.6	568	26.5	78.6	13.8	5.6
20 057	Ford	80.3	9.2	10,846	65.7	80,800	23.0	11.1	576	28.6	80.6	13.2	5.7
20 059	Franklin	83.0	6.8	10,225	71.4	113,300	23.3	14.4	670	26.9	76.1	24.1	3.6
20 061	Geary	80.8	13.0	10,816	55.6	91,300	21.0	13.7	623	27.8	85.8	16.4	6.4
20 079	Harvey	83.8	8.4	13,170	75.6	94,400	20.2	10.0	544	27.6	81.5	18.2	3.6
20 091	Johnson	82.8	7.8	198,333	72.8	203,000	22.0	10.5	824	25.6	86.3	20.2	2.7
20 099	Labette	81.6	7.5	8,897	70.4	58,800	19.6	12.6	458	24.6	76.5	14.9	5.7
20 103	Leavenworth	74.8	15.8	25,023	69.2	161,300	21.0	12.9	718	26.6	83.7	21.9	4.4
20 111	Lyon	72.9	13.1	14,226	59.0	91,200	22.8	11.5	540	32.1	78.1	15.5	7.9
20 113	McPherson	84.7	6.2	11,838	73.6	110,600	20.1	9.8	543	21.5	79.4	14.2	4.5
20 121	Miami	85.5	8.3	11,480	80.8	170,500	24.7	13.8	664	30.1	83.4	31.1	2.6
20 125	Montgomery	82.2	7.0	14,799	72.5	57,800	19.5	12.8	505	26.7	80.9	15.7	7.5
20 155	Reno	81.5	7.0	25,627	73.8	83,900	21.6	12.5	543	24.9	82.3	16.7	4.5
20 161	Riley	66.1	21.3	23,362	50.5	141,200	22.4	10.4	677	30.7	71.7	15.0	4.2
20 169	Saline	81.2	7.2	21,754	67.6	103,000	21.4	11.3	524	28.3	82.0	14.1	7.0
20 173	Sedgwick	79.5	5.5	184,433	67.5	109,500	20.9	11.5	607	28.4	84.1	17.7	6.0
20 175	Seward	77.0	11.5	7,511	64.1	76,100	20.8	12.0	548	22.0	74.3	14.0	4.7
20 177	Shawnee	81.0	5.7	72,004	67.7	109,000	21.5	11.8	599	28.4	83.5	17.7	6.2
20 191	Sumner	86.4	5.6	9,445	75.3	79,400	19.6	10.2	485	24.1	84.9	23.1	5.0
20 209	Wyandotte	82.5	7.9	58,112	64.5	92,500	26.1	15.3	674	31.5	80.5	20.3	8.8
21 000	**Kentucky**	83.3	7.0	1,654,119	70.8	109,700	21.5	10.7	560	27.8	81.7	22.3	7.8
21 005	Anderson	87.8	3.0	7,917	76.9	132,000	22.5	9.8	610	22.0	84.4	27.3	3.1
21 009	Barren	83.4	6.3	16,226	71.6	93,500	20.1	10.7	514	29.5	83.9	19.0	5.7
21 013	Bell	87.3	3.2	11,275	68.6	51,400	21.1	10.9	384	34.5	82.7	21.4	15.8
21 015	Boone	82.5	9.4	39,646	72.7	171,900	21.8	10.1	736	26.4	85.9	23.2	4.0
21 019	Boyd	83.6	8.6	19,831	72.6	86,400	19.0	10.4	525	26.2	87.7	19.0	9.1
21 021	Boyle	78.6	11.8	10,875	69.3	110,300	20.8	9.8	543	26.4	79.9	22.1	8.2
21 029	Bullitt	88.6	5.1	27,038	81.6	135,900	22.8	10.4	626	26.1	88.6	27.9	3.2
21 035	Calloway	78.0	10.1	14,537	68.3	93,100	21.7	10.1	495	32.1	84.2	17.4	6.6
21 037	Campbell	85.4	5.9	35,156	73.2	137,300	21.0	11.2	631	27.7	81.2	21.4	8.2
21 043	Carter	86.4	4.9	10,534	76.9	69,300	20.2	9.7	499	27.9	76.3	35.4	7.3
21 047	Christian	77.2	13.3	25,079	59.4	87,900	20.2	11.0	657	27.0	77.1	17.4	8.2
21 049	Clark	81.0	6.8	14,518	66.4	130,000	22.6	12.2	566	27.6	83.2	22.1	6.4
21 051	Clay	88.1	2.9	7,283	78.7	47,400	24.3	12.6	432	26.7	-	27.6	11.2
21 059	Daviess	82.3	6.3	38,862	70.0	103,300	19.9	9.9	523	28.3	87.0	18.3	6.0
21 067	Fayette	75.5	9.8	117,478	59.1	152,400	21.5	9.7	639	28.8	80.6	19.6	7.5
21 071	Floyd	87.1	4.7	16,004	73.4	58,100	19.7	9.7	404	28.2	76.9	23.4	12.9
21 073	Franklin	79.2	6.2	21,146	67.0	128,000	19.9	9.6	562	26.8	78.0	17.5	7.0
21 081	Grant	80.3	11.2	8,735	68.4	115,300	23.9	8.8	669	28.1	76.2	29.3	5.0
21 083	Graves	86.8	5.7	14,528	78.5	78,900	20.9	10.2	498	28.9	79.3	24.4	5.2
21 085	Grayson	87.7	3.9	9,404	81.5	81,000	25.1	11.6	456	27.9	80.4	27.5	5.8
21 089	Greenup	86.8	5.2	14,560	82.7	84,500	20.2	10.5	531	34.8	87.1	21.9	5.9
21 093	Hardin	80.4	10.7	37,133	67.4	120,700	21.0	9.1	559	24.2	81.9	20.2	3.7
21 095	Harlan	83.3	1.1	12,101	74.8	51,300	19.0	10.1	418	24.2	-	22.0	7.8
21 101	Henderson	84.2	6.4	18,528	67.8	94,700	19.4	8.7	508	26.3	85.3	19.7	9.7
21 107	Hopkins	80.9	4.5	18,403	71.5	68,700	19.7	9.9	515	24.9	83.9	21.2	6.8
21 111	Jefferson	83.3	5.3	293,129	66.5	140,400	22.7	11.8	629	29.0	82.3	20.8	9.7

STATE County code	STATE County	Percent who lived in the same house one year ago	Percent who did not live in county one year ago	Total occupied housing units	Percent owner-occupied housing units	Median value of owner-occupied housing units (dollars)	Median selected monthly owner costs as a percentage of household income		Median gross rent (dollars)	Median gross rent as a percentage of household income	Percent of workers who drove alone to work	Mean travel time to work (minutes)	Percent of occupied housing units with no vehicle available
							With a mortgage	Without a mortgage					
	ACS table number:	C07204	C07204	B25003	B25003	B25077	B25092	B25092	B25064	B25071	C08301	B08013/C08012	C25045
		1	2	3	4	5	6	7	8	9	10	11	12
	Kentucky—Cont.												
21 113	Jessamine	81.4	10.0	16,645	67.4	138,200	22.4	11.5	668	29.6	79.0	22.0	4.2
21 115	Johnson	87.1	5.4	8,772	76.7	68,500	18.8	12.7	449	30.2	84.5	27.6	10.8
21 117	Kenton	84.2	7.2	61,452	70.3	139,800	21.8	11.4	624	25.8	83.9	21.3	8.2
21 121	Knox	86.7	5.3	12,754	68.6	65,300	22.5	13.2	429	31.0	84.2	21.5	13.7
21 125	Laurel	83.5	7.6	20,047	77.0	93,100	22.7	11.9	489	27.7	85.1	22.5	7.2
21 133	Letcher	86.8	6.1	9,996	74.8	44,800	17.1	8.2	378	22.6	81.5	26.2	13.1
21 137	Lincoln	89.9	4.3	10,305	73.3	77,900	18.8	11.2	507	23.1	76.4	30.0	7.3
21 141	Logan	84.4	7.1	10,468	75.4	84,700	20.0	12.1	526	28.8	77.9	23.2	6.4
21 145	McCracken	82.3	8.9	27,927	68.7	98,100	19.3	10.4	517	28.2	83.0	17.8	7.0
21 151	Madison	77.0	10.1	29,164	62.5	136,000	22.0	10.5	508	28.0	76.8	21.6	6.6
21 157	Marshall	83.8	7.7	13,003	82.7	87,000	21.4	9.8	547	29.4	84.2	21.6	3.6
21 163	Meade	83.1	13.1	9,543	69.3	104,100	20.6	10.7	511	26.7	81.9	28.6	2.3
21 167	Mercer	86.1	8.0	8,815	78.7	122,900	21.5	9.6	497	22.8	78.1	23.4	6.8
21 173	Montgomery	88.1	3.4	9,664	68.3	99,900	20.9	11.5	541	27.9	78.7	23.6	12.9
21 177	Muhlenberg	86.7	5.8	13,061	76.4	66,600	20.4	10.3	454	25.6	81.5	26.5	6.4
21 179	Nelson	88.8	4.7	15,636	79.8	112,500	21.2	10.0	543	24.9	82.6	26.6	3.5
21 183	Ohio	88.7	4.6	8,816	78.2	75,300	20.4	10.2	454	25.2	89.0	24.3	6.9
21 185	Oldham	85.1	11.2	18,889	85.3	217,100	22.2	9.5	675	26.3	85.6	25.1	2.3
21 193	Perry	87.2	3.6	10,926	72.5	53,700	17.9	9.1	408	26.4	83.0	20.4	13.2
21 195	Pike	86.8	4.4	28,102	75.3	65,100	19.9	9.4	456	27.4	83.7	22.8	11.2
21 199	Pulaski	83.3	3.5	23,521	74.8	91,700	21.1	10.4	478	30.8	82.2	22.0	7.8
21 205	Rowan	81.9	10.5	7,885	71.1	86,900	20.5	10.8	479	29.5	75.2	25.2	5.0
21 209	Scott	80.0	8.1	14,875	71.1	147,800	19.0	8.4	612	26.2	79.8	21.0	5.7
21 211	Shelby	79.0	10.9	14,565	72.3	169,700	22.6	11.4	626	28.0	75.2	23.7	4.3
21 217	Taylor	87.4	5.1	9,728	67.7	86,900	22.9	9.8	502	25.7	81.5	17.5	6.9
21 227	Warren	76.5	10.3	39,948	63.4	130,100	21.6	9.5	592	27.7	81.2	19.5	6.9
21 231	Wayne	89.3	4.3	8,117	76.0	64,600	22.1	8.6	373	27.9	80.9	20.4	9.8
21 235	Whitley	82.7	8.7	13,196	71.4	66,500	21.5	10.9	484	27.7	81.3	22.8	8.5
21 239	Woodford	79.9	9.5	9,679	72.8	166,500	20.7	10.8	716	28.1	77.0	20.6	5.4
22 000	**Louisiana**	82.6	7.5	1,605,203	68.1	113,500	21.4	10.5	629	30.3	80.9	24.9	9.0
22 001	Acadia	86.1	4.5	21,908	68.1	80,700	18.7	11.5	440	28.1	82.5	28.6	9.5
22 003	Allen	82.6	10.2	8,428	70.5	65,900	19.4	8.8	475	28.6	82.5	28.5	7.7
22 005	Ascension	84.4	7.3	33,532	79.2	142,300	20.0	9.5	620	26.8	84.1	27.3	6.5
22 007	Assumption	92.8	2.3	8,499	78.9	81,100	20.7	10.5	574	29.0	71.1	35.2	10.9
22 009	Avoyelles	82.0	10.0	15,673	67.4	75,700	23.5	11.4	470	30.9	75.0	31.0	11.7
22 011	Beauregard	80.2	11.7	13,051	77.0	78,700	17.5	9.2	499	24.6	81.2	30.0	3.9
22 015	Bossier	78.9	10.8	41,472	66.5	114,900	20.2	7.9	659	24.8	85.7	20.0	6.2
22 017	Caddo	82.3	6.2	97,241	64.5	97,400	22.4	11.2	597	31.6	81.3	19.3	11.0
22 019	Calcasieu	79.3	6.0	72,001	69.5	93,800	19.4	10.3	607	29.6	82.3	20.2	7.5
22 031	De Soto	83.3	8.3	9,693	71.4	76,700	19.0	9.3	390	27.9	83.6	29.6	9.8
22 033	East Baton Rouge	80.3	7.8	164,450	61.7	138,000	21.6	10.2	710	33.1	81.9	24.2	7.5
22 037	East Feliciana	87.8	7.8	6,933	80.5	95,400	22.7	12.2	473	27.1	80.7	33.5	7.6
22 039	Evangeline	81.5	8.3	12,823	67.3	70,600	18.5	10.4	449	33.5	82.1	32.4	10.7
22 041	Franklin	81.7	8.9	7,716	69.1	58,400	21.2	12.4	465	33.2	71.7	32.5	13.8
22 045	Iberia	88.2	3.4	25,892	69.9	86,300	21.3	10.6	591	27.7	82.0	21.7	8.6
22 047	Iberville	85.3	8.9	11,615	72.9	89,700	21.8	11.5	439	29.1	82.7	24.4	11.8
22 051	Jefferson	82.0	8.7	159,117	65.5	161,800	23.5	10.8	776	30.7	79.8	23.8	7.0
22 053	Jefferson Davis	85.5	5.1	11,790	74.7	77,000	19.8	11.3	522	28.3	83.1	28.4	8.1
22 055	Lafayette	82.5	7.5	80,141	64.9	136,000	20.0	9.5	617	28.0	83.8	23.0	7.3
22 057	Lafourche	89.3	4.8	32,872	76.1	98,800	19.3	9.5	514	25.0	80.5	26.3	8.5
22 061	Lincoln	71.9	16.7	16,005	61.7	97,400	19.3	9.8	572	45.2	76.8	18.0	10.0
22 063	Livingston	88.1	6.6	38,099	82.8	118,400	20.3	9.4	626	24.4	86.7	33.2	3.4
22 067	Morehouse	89.9	1.9	10,852	74.6	65,100	22.4	12.8	531	39.5	88.8	22.2	13.2
22 069	Natchitoches	82.9	6.5	14,590	62.1	82,000	20.4	10.6	496	39.5	77.5	24.6	13.6
22 071	Orleans	71.9	12.3	101,221	50.1	166,500	27.6	12.4	753	34.7	64.9	23.8	21.8
22 073	Ouachita	84.7	5.0	54,511	64.0	98,900	21.3	11.6	589	32.1	84.2	20.2	9.2
22 075	Plaquemines	82.5	10.0	7,501	68.8	167,000	25.0	10.0	1,069	30.6	89.4	28.3	4.5
22 077	Pointe Coupee	86.4	5.8	8,756	76.9	95,300	21.6	12.2	430	30.5	85.2	27.1	9.3
22 079	Rapides	82.8	5.8	49,046	67.8	94,000	21.7	11.1	625	34.1	82.7	21.2	8.7
22 083	Richland	83.2	9.8	7,671	70.8	66,400	18.2	11.9	489	23.4	80.3	23.9	10.3
22 085	Sabine	88.0	5.7	10,023	78.5	69,000	17.9	10.6	404	29.2	78.1	32.9	7.8
22 089	St. Charles	89.2	6.5	17,658	81.1	150,500	20.9	10.9	790	19.8	86.7	28.4	6.0
22 093	St. James	91.8	3.6	7,528	80.1	104,200	20.5	9.7	553	22.9	80.8	23.3	9.2
22 095	St. John the Baptist	87.1	8.0	15,609	79.4	133,200	22.5	9.1	571	28.3	85.1	26.7	6.9
22 097	St. Landry	86.1	5.2	32,007	69.1	82,200	21.5	13.3	434	30.2	83.7	26.6	13.5
22 099	St. Martin	90.3	5.4	19,295	78.3	78,800	20.9	8.7	527	28.6	86.4	28.0	8.2
22 101	St. Mary	84.6	5.1	19,362	71.8	77,100	20.3	11.3	569	28.0	77.9	20.6	11.6
22 103	St. Tammany	84.4	7.9	79,727	80.5	182,000	22.7	10.1	841	30.4	80.9	30.7	3.8
22 105	Tangipahoa	85.4	6.0	40,510	68.3	115,500	22.6	11.2	623	30.8	81.7	31.5	7.6
22 109	Terrebonne	86.4	3.7	38,060	72.1	105,600	19.1	10.7	626	26.7	82.4	23.1	8.7
22 111	Union	86.9	4.5	8,614	78.6	71,400	20.4	9.9	494	34.5	84.6	28.4	8.2
22 113	Vermilion	85.1	4.9	20,445	75.1	82,700	17.8	8.8	468	26.3	85.8	27.0	7.1
22 115	Vernon	73.0	17.4	18,503	56.6	76,700	19.0	8.2	678	24.5	76.9	19.4	5.9
22 117	Washington	80.8	7.0	17,177	75.2	81,400	22.4	9.5	508	31.0	75.5	30.9	8.2
22 119	Webster	82.6	5.1	16,691	65.9	66,500	18.9	10.6	489	31.5	81.5	26.1	12.3
22 121	West Baton Rouge	86.1	8.2	8,639	70.4	130,100	22.2	10.1	540	31.8	84.9	21.9	9.1

STATE County code	STATE County	Percent who lived in the same house one year ago	Percent who did not live in county one year ago	Total occupied housing units	Percent owner-occu-pied housing units	Median value of owner-occupied housing units (dollars)	Median selected monthly owner costs as a percentage of household income		Median gross rent (dollars)	Median gross rent as a percentage of house-hold income	Percent of workers who drove alone to work	Mean travel time to work (minutes)	Percent of occupied housing units with no vehicle available
							With a mortgage	Without a mortgage					
ACS table number:		C07204	C07204	B25003	B25003	B25077	B25092	B25092	B25064	B25071	C08301	B08013/C08012	C25045
		1	2	3	4	5	6	7	8	9	10	11	12
23 000	**Maine**	85.2	6.2	542,424	72.9	167,700	23.7	13.8	650	28.8	78.5	22.6	6.3
23 001	Androscoggin	79.1	7.3	43,450	66.5	144,800	23.5	15.8	602	28.1	79.0	23.2	8.6
23 003	Aroostook	87.8	4.6	31,114	72.1	79,600	19.6	12.1	452	29.1	80.1	16.3	7.8
23 005	Cumberland	84.2	6.4	112,705	69.7	243,300	25.0	15.3	822	30.2	77.9	21.0	7.4
23 007	Franklin	86.2	7.9	12,477	76.1	117,900	22.5	11.6	489	26.3	76.4	22.6	6.0
23 009	Hancock	88.6	5.0	22,229	75.0	194,400	23.9	12.5	661	27.2	74.3	22.2	3.7
23 011	Kennebec	84.9	5.5	50,657	72.7	136,100	21.6	12.4	569	28.2	82.9	22.3	7.4
23 013	Knox	88.3	5.5	17,289	74.0	196,000	25.9	15.7	691	31.3	75.4	19.1	6.2
23 015	Lincoln	87.6	6.9	14,639	82.6	195,600	24.3	14.0	715	26.8	78.4	22.2	4.2
23 017	Oxford	89.2	5.2	23,189	75.9	131,100	23.5	15.2	553	26.0	78.7	26.4	4.8
23 019	Penobscot	82.5	6.8	60,477	71.5	118,200	22.4	13.4	616	30.3	78.7	21.8	7.0
23 023	Sagadahoc	85.3	7.9	14,510	76.7	187,100	24.6	13.7	698	27.3	80.4	21.6	3.5
23 025	Somerset	85.2	5.9	21,689	75.2	99,000	20.6	12.5	517	28.5	81.7	26.5	7.1
23 027	Waldo	88.0	6.6	15,629	78.9	139,200	24.3	13.4	636	26.5	75.6	25.0	3.6
23 029	Washington	86.7	5.2	14,322	74.6	95,900	21.9	12.4	451	27.2	71.0	19.0	7.2
23 031	York	87.0	5.8	80,437	74.9	231,000	25.8	14.5	768	28.0	78.4	26.4	4.3
24 000	**Maryland**	84.9	7.4	2,082,573	69.4	323,400	24.4	11.7	977	29.2	73.3	30.8	9.2
24 001	Allegany	83.9	7.5	29,305	69.9	92,100	20.2	12.5	480	24.9	81.5	20.4	11.6
24 003	Anne Arundel	84.8	8.5	189,828	76.7	367,300	23.9	11.6	1,176	28.4	79.9	28.1	4.4
24 005	Baltimore	84.9	8.8	309,808	67.8	245,200	23.6	11.5	938	29.1	79.8	27.6	7.6
24 009	Calvert	89.8	6.2	29,383	85.3	387,600	23.8	11.6	1,097	26.7	78.1	39.4	2.0
24 011	Caroline	87.6	6.7	12,059	77.1	212,200	27.5	13.3	676	27.1	78.5	30.1	4.6
24 013	Carroll	91.6	4.2	58,795	83.8	351,200	24.0	11.4	829	29.0	80.9	33.7	3.2
24 015	Cecil	84.4	7.6	35,920	73.3	235,900	23.5	12.9	873	27.4	83.0	28.8	4.4
24 017	Charles	88.2	6.4	48,669	80.3	349,700	25.5	11.2	1,117	30.4	78.3	38.5	3.4
24 019	Dorchester	84.4	5.3	13,020	69.6	189,500	26.0	14.7	646	30.8	79.5	22.8	10.1
24 021	Frederick	85.1	7.6	80,360	76.2	362,500	23.9	10.4	1,032	27.7	79.5	33.9	4.7
24 023	Garrett	92.3	2.6	12,741	77.2	151,200	21.7	10.7	482	24.0	73.9	23.3	7.1
24 025	Harford	87.1	6.4	88,958	80.7	283,500	23.3	11.5	881	26.8	82.7	30.8	4.2
24 027	Howard	86.0	9.0	98,093	76.3	456,400	23.4	9.4	1,249	27.6	80.4	29.8	3.4
24 031	Montgomery	84.7	7.3	342,617	70.2	500,500	24.5	10.4	1,304	29.8	66.3	33.0	7.2
24 033	Prince George's	83.6	7.4	298,271	64.8	324,200	27.1	11.5	1,052	28.6	64.1	35.6	9.2
24 035	Queen Anne's	89.6	7.1	17,166	83.0	362,200	25.3	12.4	783	29.8	80.0	33.8	5.4
24 037	St. Mary's	81.6	10.1	36,258	72.3	312,300	24.8	9.2	978	29.1	81.9	28.7	5.5
24 039	Somerset	79.3	13.8	7,991	68.5	132,000	25.8	14.8	603	27.9	77.0	24.1	11.5
24 041	Talbot	85.0	6.3	16,206	73.7	331,000	26.1	10.6	854	27.8	79.3	23.2	4.9
24 043	Washington	85.7	6.1	55,310	64.9	227,800	24.2	10.7	699	26.7	81.6	26.4	7.6
24 045	Wicomico	81.0	7.6	35,678	65.0	176,500	23.4	12.8	832	27.8	78.9	21.0	8.0
24 047	Worcester	85.6	8.4	22,290	75.8	284,000	25.9	13.1	802	28.0	85.0	23.4	5.8
24 510	Baltimore city	83.0	5.7	235,734	51.1	130,900	24.8	15.3	745	32.0	58.6	28.5	30.4
25 000	**Massachusetts**	85.9	5.8	2,448,608	65.0	366,200	26.5	15.3	952	30.1	73.6	27.0	11.5
25 001	Barnstable	89.6	4.1	98,989	79.3	412,900	29.7	15.0	1,067	32.5	81.8	22.9	4.3
25 003	Berkshire	87.9	3.8	55,127	68.0	184,900	23.4	14.2	642	27.8	78.7	18.6	8.9
25 005	Bristol	87.0	4.8	208,881	63.8	323,900	26.3	15.0	748	29.1	81.4	25.5	9.5
25 009	Essex	87.9	4.1	273,755	66.4	387,700	27.4	16.3	957	32.0	78.1	27.0	10.0
25 011	Franklin	85.0	7.0	29,774	69.3	207,200	24.9	13.7	742	29.3	80.1	23.5	5.7
25 013	Hampden	85.3	4.1	175,132	62.6	190,800	24.3	15.2	689	30.8	84.1	21.8	12.4
25 015	Hampshire	82.4	10.5	56,913	67.6	240,900	24.4	14.3	814	32.9	74.3	22.2	7.2
25 017	Middlesex	85.8	6.2	556,748	65.3	440,600	26.2	15.4	1,147	28.9	71.4	27.4	10.2
25 021	Norfolk	87.2	6.9	250,997	71.5	428,700	26.2	15.0	1,172	29.5	72.1	29.8	8.5
25 023	Plymouth	88.8	5.0	173,356	77.9	375,100	27.5	15.9	978	30.4	80.8	32.1	5.2
25 025	Suffolk	77.2	10.0	271,713	39.7	411,700	29.5	17.4	1,092	31.7	43.6	28.9	32.8
25 027	Worcester	88.0	4.2	287,535	68.7	289,600	25.0	15.0	811	29.1	82.7	26.8	7.7
26 000	**Michigan**	85.4	5.4	3,864,307	75.1	152,200	24.3	13.6	689	31.0	83.2	23.6	6.6
26 005	Allegan	89.6	5.5	41,815	83.5	150,500	24.3	12.6	626	28.0	84.2	23.5	3.6
26 007	Alpena	87.6	5.2	12,996	83.3	107,700	24.1	13.9	435	29.6	84.1	16.6	5.7
26 009	Antrim	88.4	6.6	9,878	82.0	150,900	26.3	13.8	608	28.2	77.1	20.3	3.8
26 015	Barry	87.5	5.7	22,525	82.8	149,700	23.9	12.6	594	26.1	83.2	28.6	3.3
26 017	Bay	87.4	3.0	44,733	80.4	109,300	22.4	13.5	530	27.9	85.0	20.9	6.3
26 021	Berrien	85.4	4.5	63,400	73.1	132,600	22.4	12.4	550	29.9	83.7	18.6	7.0
26 023	Branch	86.2	6.9	16,578	81.5	110,800	23.7	13.3	595	29.4	78.3	22.2	5.0
26 025	Calhoun	84.0	4.7	54,257	73.6	111,500	23.4	13.4	611	33.6	82.6	19.2	7.1
26 027	Cass	87.6	5.7	20,897	81.5	122,800	23.2	12.5	598	26.4	84.5	24.7	4.0
26 029	Charlevoix	87.5	6.3	11,707	80.9	164,100	24.3	12.4	613	27.3	82.6	18.7	4.5
26 031	Cheboygan	85.3	4.7	11,744	79.0	127,200	26.6	11.8	498	30.5	73.0	22.8	4.4
26 033	Chippewa	81.0	10.7	14,663	72.7	102,500	21.0	12.8	569	33.1	74.8	15.5	6.3
26 035	Clare	85.5	6.4	12,766	77.9	99,800	25.7	12.9	534	33.2	77.0	27.7	9.4
26 037	Clinton	89.8	4.6	27,361	83.3	169,000	23.8	11.8	708	27.0	85.8	23.4	3.1
26 041	Delta	88.6	3.8	16,571	76.9	99,700	22.5	13.5	466	29.7	80.7	19.6	6.5
26 043	Dickinson	84.7	4.1	11,415	79.4	83,700	22.8	13.1	524	28.1	82.2	15.4	5.9
26 045	Eaton	85.2	8.3	42,291	74.8	157,400	23.2	12.0	672	27.6	84.8	23.0	4.2
26 047	Emmet	85.9	7.2	13,790	76.9	171,700	26.6	13.2	702	28.5	76.5	19.0	4.4
26 049	Genesee	85.1	3.7	173,622	73.2	129,600	24.0	13.7	620	31.4	85.0	25.0	7.2

STATE County code	STATE County	Percent who lived in the same house one year ago	Percent who did not live in county one year ago	Total occupied housing units	Percent owner-occu-pied housing units	Median value of owner-occupied housing units (dollars)	Median selected monthly owner costs as a percentage of household income With a mortgage	Median selected monthly owner costs as a percentage of household income Without a mortgage	Median gross rent (dollars)	Median gross rent as a percentage of house-hold income	Percent of workers who drove alone to work	Mean travel time to work (minutes)	Percent of occupied housing units with no vehicle available
ACS table number:		C07204	C07204	B25003	B25003	B25077	B25092	B25092	B25064	B25071	C08301	B08013/C08012	C25045
		1	2	3	4	5	6	7	8	9	10	11	12
	Michigan—Cont.												
26 051	Gladwin	89.6	5.0	11,537	85.7	120,900	26.0	13.7	423	29.6	75.2	27.6	7.1
26 055	Grand Traverse	85.5	6.4	34,386	76.4	175,000	25.2	13.5	766	29.6	80.6	19.3	5.1
26 057	Gratiot	85.5	7.5	14,317	79.3	97,300	22.9	12.7	562	28.2	79.4	23.3	5.8
26 059	Hillsdale	85.6	6.3	18,206	78.2	120,000	24.5	13.2	603	30.7	77.1	24.4	6.2
26 061	Houghton	79.3	10.7	14,086	70.2	77,800	23.7	14.0	460	31.6	69.8	16.5	7.3
26 063	Huron	90.7	4.0	15,062	82.8	105,200	24.8	13.9	464	31.5	79.1	19.9	5.6
26 065	Ingham	79.8	9.5	107,929	63.5	145,300	23.8	13.3	681	33.3	79.3	19.8	7.3
26 067	Ionia	83.7	9.1	21,847	79.6	126,400	24.6	13.2	635	31.5	79.0	25.7	4.5
26 069	Iosco	85.4	7.5	12,216	82.4	97,700	24.5	13.1	556	30.8	80.9	22.4	6.2
26 073	Isabella	69.1	14.2	24,078	62.5	127,700	24.2	11.1	616	34.4	76.8	17.4	5.3
26 075	Jackson	83.5	6.5	60,667	76.8	138,800	24.0	13.1	665	34.3	84.9	22.9	6.5
26 077	Kalamazoo	77.6	7.6	97,600	66.3	145,000	22.6	12.4	645	32.1	82.6	18.8	6.5
26 081	Kent	82.7	5.7	225,252	72.7	148,800	23.8	13.0	661	29.2	82.6	20.2	5.6
26 087	Lapeer	90.1	5.0	33,228	84.1	173,700	25.1	12.3	714	29.5	82.6	33.0	3.3
26 089	Leelanau	88.9	5.7	9,559	82.8	238,900	26.3	11.1	618	26.5	76.2	20.1	2.8
26 091	Lenawee	86.0	5.6	37,726	81.8	144,400	24.8	13.0	613	27.9	81.7	25.7	4.0
26 093	Livingston	89.6	5.5	66,492	86.4	235,600	24.0	12.4	834	30.3	86.5	31.3	2.3
26 099	Macomb	88.5	4.4	327,282	80.1	171,000	24.6	14.7	713	28.5	87.9	26.2	5.1
26 101	Manistee	84.3	9.4	10,373	80.8	128,100	25.4	13.3	564	29.3	76.0	21.8	7.4
26 103	Marquette	83.8	7.9	25,423	73.5	115,400	19.3	12.2	511	31.4	79.7	17.8	5.9
26 105	Mason	86.1	4.4	12,328	80.1	121,000	25.6	12.6	559	33.8	78.6	19.4	7.2
26 107	Mecosta	75.2	14.4	16,360	72.1	119,400	23.6	12.0	587	33.5	75.5	25.1	7.3
26 109	Menominee	89.4	4.3	10,692	80.8	91,100	22.3	11.5	455	23.3	79.6	18.9	5.0
26 111	Midland	85.5	7.4	32,842	76.5	134,800	20.3	11.8	589	33.7	85.3	20.5	5.0
26 115	Monroe	89.4	4.7	57,946	80.9	168,500	24.0	14.2	696	27.1	87.9	24.3	4.8
26 117	Montcalm	84.0	7.3	22,779	78.6	116,000	24.6	13.0	577	28.9	80.1	28.3	5.4
26 121	Muskegon	84.6	5.4	65,259	79.4	116,700	24.2	12.8	555	33.3	84.2	19.5	7.3
26 123	Newaygo	85.8	7.2	18,950	82.4	115,500	25.7	13.2	579	29.4	79.6	28.5	4.5
26 125	Oakland	87.1	5.2	480,435	76.8	227,400	24.3	14.1	847	28.1	86.6	25.9	4.5
26 127	Oceana	90.1	4.0	10,364	80.7	115,000	26.2	12.3	543	33.1	75.0	22.0	5.2
26 129	Ogemaw	88.1	7.7	8,479	83.3	105,800	26.5	13.6	541	32.7	83.9	22.6	6.3
26 133	Osceola	87.8	5.2	8,665	80.9	100,800	24.6	13.3	514	29.8	74.1	23.3	5.4
26 137	Utsego	87.2	5.6	9,508	84.2	123,300	24.4	13.1	660	37.1	81.3	21.2	3.8
26 139	Ottawa	86.6	6.7	90,396	81.9	164,200	23.2	12.5	708	26.2	84.5	19.8	2.4
26 143	Roscommon	86.7	7.7	11,987	82.5	107,600	27.5	13.1	493	49.0	73.6	25.1	5.7
26 145	Saginaw	86.1	3.8	77,707	75.8	114,400	23.0	13.5	618	34.4	86.2	21.1	8.0
26 147	St. Clair	86.5	4.3	66,121	78.5	158,500	24.3	14.5	664	31.6	84.1	27.3	4.8
26 149	St. Joseph	88.8	4.4	22,810	77.4	115,800	23.0	12.9	550	28.1	82.2	20.6	6.5
26 151	Sanilac	88.6	4.3	17,173	81.5	125,100	27.1	14.3	549	32.1	78.5	30.2	4.5
26 155	Shiawassee	85.6	5.7	27,942	79.2	136,000	23.9	12.4	605	32.1	84.7	27.6	3.9
26 157	Tuscola	88.8	5.2	21,716	84.9	119,200	25.2	12.8	549	27.2	82.3	28.8	3.1
26 159	Van Buren	87.7	5.2	29,437	79.6	124,400	24.0	14.0	543	32.4	80.7	23.0	5.4
26 161	Washtenaw	77.1	11.1	132,861	64.8	231,600	24.4	13.1	840	34.4	75.9	22.0	6.2
26 163	Wayne	85.5	3.0	716,137	68.4	138,200	26.2	15.0	729	34.4	82.7	24.6	12.1
26 165	Wexford	86.7	6.1	12,877	78.3	110,300	25.3	13.3	511	26.8	81.4	21.4	6.4
27 000	**Minnesota**	85.2	7.1	2,041,466	75.8	207,200	24.2	11.9	719	29.0	78.1	22.1	6.5
27 003	Anoka	87.5	6.7	118,098	84.3	227,800	24.7	11.7	814	29.2	83.7	26.6	3.8
27 005	Becker	84.7	7.5	13,180	79.3	153,100	24.4	12.3	551	25.0	75.2	21.8	5.6
27 007	Beltrami	81.9	7.3	15,527	73.8	126,500	23.2	12.5	528	26.5	77.4	19.3	6.0
27 009	Benton	85.2	8.3	14,834	70.1	175,600	25.4	12.4	609	25.5	79.4	22.9	6.4
27 013	Blue Earth	75.2	12.7	23,233	70.4	157,000	23.8	11.9	596	29.8	77.7	16.7	7.2
27 015	Brown	88.2	4.4	10,818	80.2	116,900	21.0	11.5	494	23.9	75.0	14.2	5.2
27 017	Carlton	87.7	6.2	13,565	80.8	157,200	24.1	10.6	633	27.6	81.7	21.1	5.5
27 019	Carver	88.3	8.0	31,431	82.5	282,100	24.6	10.2	822	26.1	81.9	25.5	2.4
27 021	Cass	89.5	5.3	13,025	83.5	177,200	26.1	12.1	470	23.8	72.8	21.5	6.0
27 025	Chisago	87.4	9.7	17,840	86.0	233,500	27.9	13.5	695	31.7	82.1	31.7	4.1
27 027	Clay	81.1	9.7	20,615	72.8	131,900	21.9	11.7	581	33.6	79.0	17.3	5.3
27 035	Crow Wing	85.0	6.8	26,180	77.4	182,400	25.7	11.6	557	28.4	81.1	20.3	6.1
27 037	Dakota	86.9	6.7	146,728	79.8	246,800	24.0	10.6	870	29.3	82.6	23.5	3.8
27 041	Douglas	84.5	6.3	15,902	76.2	167,700	25.2	12.9	554	36.7	80.8	17.2	5.1
27 045	Fillmore	86.6	4.7	8,474	78.7	124,700	23.3	12.7	536	26.3	68.5	24.9	5.2
27 047	Freeborn	86.0	4.6	12,961	81.5	108,100	22.9	12.3	490	24.8	83.4	18.3	5.7
27 049	Goodhue	87.9	5.6	18,438	79.0	192,100	24.7	12.8	628	29.5	78.2	22.1	6.2
27 053	Hennepin	82.3	7.0	463,097	68.2	249,300	24.7	12.9	808	29.6	74.7	21.9	9.6
27 059	Isanti	87.2	9.3	14,579	85.7	211,500	28.3	12.1	755	30.6	81.9	33.3	3.2
27 061	Itasca	85.9	5.3	19,221	78.8	138,200	24.0	11.3	558	25.3	79.9	21.4	5.3
27 067	Kandiyohi	90.5	4.3	16,115	76.0	143,900	22.9	10.9	514	28.1	77.0	17.0	5.6
27 079	Le Sueur	86.5	6.9	10,516	82.7	176,100	24.8	11.1	627	23.3	77.8	24.1	2.7
27 083	Lyon	81.1	9.6	10,195	68.8	130,400	20.2	10.5	510	27.4	77.5	12.9	6.7
27 085	McLeod	88.7	6.9	14,178	82.7	167,000	24.4	13.3	604	24.1	78.6	20.8	4.2
27 091	Martin	85.4	3.3	9,225	76.6	90,700	19.7	11.3	495	26.8	75.3	14.6	4.3
27 093	Meeker	89.3	6.5	9,230	81.8	162,200	24.7	12.6	642	30.9	81.1	23.2	4.8
27 095	Mille Lacs	85.3	10.2	9,998	79.0	173,300	27.9	14.5	548	30.2	77.0	26.9	6.0
27 097	Morrison	89.9	4.3	13,411	82.6	155,000	24.9	12.5	510	26.7	75.3	25.0	4.1
27 099	Mower	88.1	4.2	15,651	78.5	104,400	21.2	11.9	533	28.4	77.8	18.2	6.3

STATE County code	STATE County	Percent who lived in the same house one year ago	Percent who did not live in county one year ago	Total occupied housing units	Percent owner-occu-pied housing units	Median value of owner-occupied housing units (dollars)	Median selected monthly owner costs as a percentage of household income		Median gross rent (dollars)	Median gross rent as a percentage of house-hold income	Percent of workers who drove alone to work	Mean travel time to work (minutes)	Percent of occupied housing units with no vehicle available
							With a mortgage	Without a mortgage					
	ACS table number:	C07204	C07204	B25003	B25003	B25077	B25092	B25092	B25064	B25071	C08301	B08013/C08012	C25045
		1	2	3	4	5	6	7	8	9	10	11	12
	Minnesota—Cont.												
27 103	Nicollet	83.3	10.1	12,009	73.6	164,500	22.8	9.8	609	31.6	79.4	16.0	7.0
27 105	Nobles	85.6	5.9	8,080	71.3	87,700	19.6	10.9	510	36.4	68.7	16.0	9.4
27 109	Olmsted	86.2	5.8	54,279	77.2	168,800	22.3	9.8	682	24.8	78.4	16.1	5.5
27 111	Otter Tail	86.9	5.6	24,584	77.6	145,300	23.6	11.9	493	27.7	75.7	18.5	6.1
27 115	Pine	87.1	6.2	10,795	82.2	163,000	25.0	12.2	561	27.7	76.5	26.7	4.0
27 119	Polk	80.9	11.7	12,399	75.5	100,600	19.9	12.7	472	31.5	75.2	16.1	8.0
27 123	Ramsey	82.8	8.1	199,541	66.0	224,500	25.0	11.9	773	30.4	75.3	21.7	10.2
27 131	Rice	83.4	8.3	21,180	79.3	211,600	26.7	10.8	668	25.1	73.1	20.6	4.9
27 137	St. Louis	83.1	7.1	84,582	74.2	132,200	22.6	11.5	593	31.2	79.4	19.3	9.1
27 139	Scott	88.2	7.6	42,063	87.2	279,500	24.6	11.7	841	26.1	82.4	26.3	2.3
27 141	Sherburne	87.3	7.6	28,316	87.3	235,300	26.4	10.5	742	29.8	81.4	31.5	2.3
27 145	Stearns	81.5	9.3	54,438	74.5	175,600	23.7	12.0	649	30.0	77.7	20.1	5.3
27 147	Steele	85.3	8.2	13,709	79.4	152,200	25.0	12.7	652	27.1	80.9	16.8	4.6
27 153	Todd	87.7	4.7	9,975	81.6	137,500	25.1	12.5	483	25.6	74.1	23.6	5.7
27 157	Wabasha	89.4	5.0	8,958	81.6	155,200	22.5	12.9	538	28.8	72.7	22.9	6.5
27 163	Washington	89.5	6.7	82,901	85.5	271,900	24.5	11.2	924	28.7	83.8	25.4	2.9
27 169	Winona	81.0	9.8	19,237	70.8	150,700	23.0	11.1	540	31.3	73.4	16.3	8.6
27 171	Wright	86.9	7.7	42,939	84.5	227,300	26.7	11.8	732	29.1	81.7	30.0	3.3
28 000	**Mississippi**	82.9	7.3	1,079,584	70.9	88,100	22.9	12.4	591	30.6	82.0	23.7	7.1
28 001	Adams	85.6	6.7	12,768	70.2	69,900	22.0	12.8	496	32.8	80.8	21.1	10.8
28 003	Alcorn	84.9	5.4	13,758	75.6	77,100	19.8	12.3	399	26.9	92.1	19.8	7.3
28 011	Bolivar	82.9	5.7	13,425	56.7	72,400	24.0	17.1	540	37.6	76.1	15.5	14.0
28 025	Clay	84.3	4.5	8,100	69.4	64,700	23.2	15.6	506	29.1	79.4	18.1	6.5
28 027	Coahoma	86.3	5.4	10,263	59.8	51,600	27.4	17.3	551	34.4	69.0	22.0	17.1
28 029	Copiah	92.9	3.0	10,204	73.8	70,700	21.0	12.7	543	28.9	77.1	26.3	10.7
28 031	Covington	93.0	2.4	7,865	83.6	76,900	22.6	11.7	520	41.8	-	28.7	4.0
28 033	DeSoto	82.3	9.5	52,195	78.0	143,600	23.2	10.5	826	27.7	84.5	25.2	3.0
28 035	Forrest	76.9	10.9	29,243	57.5	89,400	23.1	13.5	591	31.3	85.0	20.1	6.5
28 039	George	90.2	4.2	6,785	88.5	82,300	19.6	9.6	545	22.6	79.1	31.3	3.9
28 043	Grenada	77.3	8.4	8,887	64.7	84,000	21.2	14.5	520	25.4	81.2	19.9	9.8
28 045	Hancock	72.5	7.1	17,398	70.3	146,400	24.4	11.7	658	21.8	81.2	29.6	1.7
28 047	Harrison	75.6	10.1	68,755	66.5	123,300	23.6	11.2	760	30.2	79.8	22.5	4.9
28 049	Hinds	80.6	6.0	91,219	62.8	96,800	23.4	12.3	712	33.4	83.5	21.9	7.9
28 051	Holmes	90.6	4.4	7,128	69.7	49,100	39.2	16.8	455	31.4	72.2	31.7	16.4
28 057	Itawamba	83.6	10.2	9,179	79.4	69,200	20.9	11.5	499	19.8	80.7	24.9	4.7
28 059	Jackson	81.6	7.5	48,286	72.1	112,100	22.1	11.5	733	29.9	85.4	24.0	4.8
28 067	Jones	85.7	4.0	25,758	72.3	68,600	21.7	12.6	568	40.5	87.9	21.4	5.6
28 071	Lafayette	72.8	14.5	14,932	63.1	133,100	21.6	10.6	649	29.3	81.4	16.9	3.1
28 073	Lamar	79.5	11.3	14,991	76.7	135,200	20.4	11.2	706	28.7	83.8	23.5	3.4
28 075	Lauderdale	79.1	9.0	30,884	65.9	77,300	22.7	12.4	551	30.7	79.2	19.0	10.1
28 079	Leake	-	-	7,254	79.8	68,100	24.0	10.4	602	26.7	72.4	26.8	4.6
28 081	Lee	80.5	8.2	29,086	69.8	101,400	20.6	12.1	522	30.3	85.7	18.8	7.0
28 083	Leflore	84.8	4.3	13,057	53.9	59,100	25.4	16.2	423	32.4	74.8	17.8	15.3
28 085	Lincoln	89.9	3.1	13,250	75.9	77,400	20.8	12.2	523	25.9	81.0	32.7	5.8
28 087	Lowndes	80.9	7.4	23,161	67.4	90,200	21.3	12.1	526	30.3	83.0	19.9	5.5
28 089	Madison	82.4	10.3	33,106	70.8	162,700	21.3	12.1	756	26.4	85.6	22.7	6.2
28 091	Marion	83.5	4.8	8,830	75.3	73,400	22.9	12.9	440	28.8	78.0	35.2	8.6
28 093	Marshall	90.1	5.1	12,214	77.8	81,300	23.6	15.1	525	36.1	80.6	29.2	9.0
28 095	Monroe	87.5	4.1	15,104	77.2	74,100	21.7	12.3	483	32.4	79.4	23.6	9.2
28 099	Neshoba	83.6	6.5	10,346	72.9	70,700	23.8	12.7	453	27.6	78.2	21.7	12.4
28 101	Newton	85.8	6.5	8,081	80.9	68,800	22.4	12.6	464	24.6	83.4	27.1	7.8
28 105	Oktibbeha	71.0	14.5	16,619	51.2	105,800	22.0	10.9	594	45.9	76.0	15.8	7.2
28 107	Panola	84.5	5.9	11,934	75.7	71,700	21.7	14.6	576	27.6	81.5	23.5	6.6
28 109	Pearl River	82.1	8.2	20,942	75.8	114,600	25.3	12.4	625	35.6	78.2	36.5	5.0
28 113	Pike	86.7	7.0	14,287	74.9	77,700	24.6	13.9	487	35.6	81.5	24.9	9.7
28 115	Pontotoc	85.2	6.0	9,869	76.9	78,400	23.5	9.0	557	26.6	84.5	23.7	5.6
28 117	Prentiss	87.7	6.6	9,816	78.8	62,400	24.2	11.9	511	35.2	85.3	20.2	6.9
28 121	Rankin	83.6	9.0	48,951	77.1	133,700	21.1	9.4	753	31.9	87.0	23.8	2.5
28 123	Scott	82.1	4.8	9,806	76.4	61,400	23.8	12.5	503	29.7	72.9	24.4	7.2
28 127	Simpson	86.2	7.2	10,181	77.9	64,300	22.8	14.4	530	23.8	82.1	35.2	5.4
28 133	Sunflower	80.9	10.3	9,592	54.0	63,000	31.8	13.8	483	34.4	76.9	14.6	9.7
28 137	Tate	90.8	4.6	9,738	78.1	89,900	22.8	13.5	577	24.7	74.5	25.7	5.6
28 139	Tippah	86.7	2.8	7,971	72.0	58,700	26.0	11.3	452	29.2	-	25.6	5.9
28 145	Union	85.3	7.4	9,781	77.3	73,500	22.7	12.3	515	27.8	82.9	23.2	5.7
28 149	Warren	82.7	5.2	19,461	67.1	94,400	20.7	12.5	611	34.7	83.9	20.6	7.3
28 151	Washington	82.1	4.4	21,118	57.6	66,700	26.8	13.2	561	33.5	82.3	18.3	12.6
28 153	Wayne	89.2	4.4	8,630	79.9	53,800	27.1	14.0	449	24.4	85.0	27.2	4.2
28 163	Yazoo	83.3	6.8	9,066	61.9	76,800	23.0	16.2	545	32.7	-	28.6	14.8
29 000	**Missouri**	82.6	7.7	2,300,211	70.7	131,100	22.2	11.4	623	28.4	80.8	23.1	6.9
29 001	Adair	69.1	16.1	9,565	57.3	94,300	19.8	12.5	488	50.1	73.6	12.5	7.9
29 007	Audrain	85.0	7.8	10,058	74.2	81,900	19.2	11.0	468	24.0	83.7	17.3	6.1
29 009	Barry	83.6	8.6	14,411	72.7	102,000	21.4	10.8	483	26.3	76.1	22.8	4.5
29 019	Boone	73.3	10.3	62,559	59.0	143,000	21.2	9.9	677	30.9	77.6	17.3	5.9
29 021	Buchanan	78.6	7.3	33,242	68.1	100,800	21.3	10.5	549	29.3	82.7	17.3	8.9

Table C-2. Counties — Where: Migration, Housing, and Transportation, 2005–2007—*Continued*

STATE County code	STATE County	Percent who lived in the same house one year ago	Percent who did not live in county one year ago	Total occupied housing units	Percent owner-occupied housing units	Median value of owner-occupied housing units (dollars)	Median selected monthly owner costs as a percentage of household income		Median gross rent (dollars)	Median gross rent as a percentage of household income	Percent of workers who drove alone to work	Mean travel time to work (minutes)	Percent of occupied housing units with no vehicle available
ACS table number:		C07204	C07204	B25003	B25003	B25077	With a mortgage B25092	Without a mortgage B25092	B25064	B25071	C08301	B08013/ C08012	C25045
		1	2	3	4	5	6	7	8	9	10	11	12
	Missouri—Cont.												
29 023	Butler	84.9	4.4	16,938	67.6	81,400	20.2	10.9	474	29.1	85.7	16.7	12.2
29 027	Callaway	78.8	10.9	15,559	74.8	109,100	20.7	8.5	539	23.8	78.9	20.9	3.4
29 029	Camden	81.5	8.7	16,206	81.1	169,300	22.7	9.9	571	28.5	73.8	20.5	4.0
29 031	Cape Girardeau	78.6	9.7	29,178	67.8	122,800	20.7	9.9	557	30.4	82.9	18.4	6.0
29 037	Cass	83.7	8.0	35,443	78.8	150,800	23.4	11.2	814	29.1	82.2	28.5	3.0
29 043	Christian	77.3	12.8	26,380	74.2	135,300	22.2	12.0	641	27.3	84.1	23.8	3.3
29 047	Clay	81.2	8.0	77,965	74.5	149,500	22.8	11.3	697	25.5	85.6	22.4	3.7
29 049	Clinton	85.9	9.5	8,126	76.3	137,100	22.4	13.8	617	26.4	75.6	29.6	5.0
29 051	Cole	82.5	8.5	28,671	66.1	123,800	20.1	7.8	536	23.1	83.3	17.8	5.2
29 055	Crawford	79.6	7.7	8,598	74.4	95,700	22.4	11.6	489	29.2	74.7	25.2	8.1
29 069	Dunklin	80.7	7.4	13,208	64.6	65,200	21.8	11.6	402	29.0	80.4	20.0	9.0
29 071	Franklin	85.6	5.9	37,778	75.7	138,100	21.4	11.2	589	25.2	81.4	28.1	4.5
29 077	Greene	77.2	10.1	109,183	64.0	119,100	22.1	10.2	599	28.5	81.6	19.9	6.4
29 083	Henry	82.0	6.6	9,397	72.5	92,500	20.8	12.6	461	30.2	80.0	25.3	4.8
29 091	Howell	88.9	4.7	15,105	70.9	89,400	21.2	11.2	453	27.0	81.4	20.3	6.9
29 095	Jackson	82.0	5.3	272,761	64.7	127,100	23.0	13.4	691	29.9	82.2	22.8	9.0
29 097	Jasper	80.7	6.0	43,507	67.2	86,000	21.5	11.0	580	29.6	80.1	17.7	7.1
29 099	Jefferson	86.8	5.5	78,867	84.5	147,300	22.1	11.0	653	28.1	83.8	30.0	4.1
29 101	Johnson	73.7	14.2	18,299	65.6	126,700	21.6	12.5	580	25.7	74.6	26.9	5.2
29 105	Laclede	80.8	6.7	14,061	70.2	93,900	19.9	10.6	479	24.9	76.6	20.4	6.2
29 107	Lafayette	86.3	6.0	13,151	74.1	118,000	22.0	12.3	515	23.4	79.4	28.3	4.9
29 109	Lawrence	85.8	8.3	13,789	75.5	89,700	22.1	11.3	527	27.0	81.7	23.1	4.6
29 113	Lincoln	84.1	8.0	15,309	79.6	150,300	22.5	9.6	651	25.2	79.6	31.3	4.5
29 119	McDonald	82.1	10.9	8,046	70.5	81,700	21.1	12.4	472	25.4	75.2	30.1	4.1
29 127	Marion	82.5	7.5	11,615	63.0	82,900	19.0	12.4	457	26.5	78.1	16.4	9.4
29 131	Miller	80.3	7.3	9,887	74.2	99,400	21.7	10.3	524	25.5	73.1	24.3	8.5
29 141	Morgan	84.8	9.1	7,975	79.7	109,000	23.9	9.5	505	25.6	69.3	24.9	7.7
29 145	Newton	83.6	8.9	20,779	73.4	95,700	20.2	9.7	527	28.7	80.8	20.1	4.5
29 147	Nodaway	71.5	13.3	7,978	63.2	95,100	19.0	8.3	468	31.7	77.5	14.8	5.7
29 159	Pettis	83.4	5.7	15,512	73.8	88,600	23.0	11.7	560	26.7	80.2	21.9	5.1
29 161	Phelps	71.1	14.7	16,927	62.6	103,300	21.9	8.9	557	28.2	74.2	17.7	6.9
29 165	Platte	81.1	9.3	33,131	68.9	184,700	20.8	10.4	752	24.3	86.1	22.1	3.3
29 167	Polk	80.7	10.2	10,756	73.1	108,300	21.9	10.4	487	28.9	77.6	24.7	6.4
29 169	Pulaski	59.8	27.9	14,127	57.5	112,300	21.6	10.6	649	28.7	57.4	20.1	9.3
29 175	Randolph	82.6	10.5	9,535	71.5	76,500	20.4	12.7	516	27.7	86.5	18.3	5.5
29 177	Ray	87.4	6.8	9,246	78.7	123,200	22.5	10.7	612	32.2	79.4	31.1	3.8
29 183	St. Charles	86.1	7.1	124,517	82.6	186,600	22.3	11.7	792	26.9	86.9	25.0	2.8
29 187	St. Francois	81.1	9.2	22,679	71.2	98,000	20.4	9.9	519	26.2	81.3	25.2	5.5
29 189	St. Louis	86.4	6.7	403,291	75.0	172,500	22.5	11.9	748	29.3	84.3	22.8	5.7
29 195	Saline	78.8	8.6	8,992	72.4	78,400	19.1	12.7	486	24.0	80.8	22.9	6.5
29 201	Scott	85.1	5.8	16,084	68.0	89,600	19.6	11.8	471	29.9	81.5	17.9	9.3
29 207	Stoddard	81.3	5.6	12,162	70.8	78,800	20.2	9.6	478	30.8	79.4	21.4	7.4
29 209	Stone	78.4	11.7	11,787	75.3	140,800	23.5	9.6	592	25.7	78.3	28.2	3.3
29 213	Taney	74.3	14.5	19,241	64.2	120,000	24.1	12.3	607	25.3	79.2	20.6	3.2
29 215	Texas	88.0	5.3	9,327	74.0	83,900	21.7	11.0	427	28.1	79.7	22.7	5.9
29 217	Vernon	81.8	6.2	8,069	69.8	84,200	22.7	11.4	432	28.3	73.3	17.1	8.7
29 219	Warren	83.6	9.6	11,058	75.8	156,000	23.2	11.5	609	22.6	80.1	27.9	2.9
29 221	Washington	86.1	7.9	8,346	78.3	90,900	21.3	8.9	500	28.0	75.9	34.5	6.0
29 225	Webster	79.1	11.4	12,068	74.3	118,800	23.2	9.7	530	28.0	80.7	29.9	7.3
29 510	St. Louis city	80.1	7.3	140,934	50.7	115,700	24.9	13.9	609	31.3	71.1	23.7	21.7
30 000	**Montana**	81.7	8.0	369,329	70.1	152,300	23.8	12.1	582	27.4	73.9	17.4	4.9
30 013	Cascade	81.5	7.2	32,190	67.9	128,100	22.8	12.1	531	24.9	83.2	15.0	6.9
30 029	Flathead	91.2	3.4	30,521	73.2	210,800	26.5	12.4	663	26.3	76.5	18.3	3.2
30 031	Gallatin	73.5	13.0	31,890	65.6	255,900	25.5	12.0	766	29.4	70.1	18.1	3.5
30 047	Lake	84.3	5.8	10,632	70.7	176,900	27.6	10.8	506	23.5	75.8	17.7	3.4
30 049	Lewis and Clark	78.4	9.7	23,068	71.8	159,800	24.1	12.4	598	27.6	74.2	15.7	3.6
30 063	Missoula	77.0	8.6	40,636	62.4	214,200	25.3	12.6	673	32.0	73.1	17.9	5.8
30 081	Ravalli	79.4	9.2	14,896	75.6	211,700	27.6	12.4	682	27.5	71.8	23.7	2.1
30 093	Silver Bow	78.8	7.8	14,280	67.3	93,800	23.4	13.6	509	28.3	77.8	16.2	7.5
30 111	Yellowstone	80.3	7.8	55,196	70.4	150,700	23.2	12.2	588	28.5	79.9	17.1	5.7
31 000	**Nebraska**	82.3	7.2	698,163	68.5	118,200	22.3	13.0	610	26.4	79.8	17.7	5.2
31 001	Adams	82.7	7.3	12,556	70.8	90,200	22.0	13.0	542	25.1	77.7	14.9	5.3
31 019	Buffalo	76.2	10.1	17,278	65.9	120,900	22.2	12.9	596	25.3	81.7	13.7	5.2
31 025	Cass	87.2	7.0	9,451	81.1	135,300	22.5	13.2	591	22.6	84.9	24.8	3.6
31 043	Dakota	78.2	11.3	7,464	71.6	98,000	24.2	13.6	584	26.6	79.2	15.5	3.6
31 047	Dawson	81.4	6.1	8,842	72.8	79,100	19.4	13.5	483	28.1	70.2	14.8	6.2
31 053	Dodge	83.8	6.0	14,223	67.1	111,000	20.3	12.5	596	31.0	83.3	17.4	4.9
31 055	Douglas	81.1	5.8	192,075	64.5	138,900	23.0	13.2	686	28.1	82.1	18.5	7.2
31 067	Gage	83.0	7.7	9,596	70.9	89,800	21.6	13.7	551	24.4	80.2	19.0	6.5
31 079	Hall	78.9	7.8	20,985	66.7	98,700	22.6	12.4	546	24.4	81.5	15.1	4.8
31 109	Lancaster	77.4	7.6	107,799	63.0	141,400	22.6	11.4	637	28.2	80.6	17.9	5.6
31 111	Lincoln	79.7	8.0	14,820	67.6	95,700	21.8	13.3	581	23.2	81.2	15.8	2.7
31 119	Madison	83.5	9.1	13,364	71.1	94,300	21.5	14.0	499	24.8	77.9	15.7	6.5
31 141	Platte	87.8	5.4	12,639	75.2	101,900	20.5	10.3	483	23.5	84.0	14.5	4.6
31 153	Sarpy	83.0	10.7	53,313	70.2	150,200	23.2	12.0	768	24.7	86.8	18.7	1.9

STATE County code	STATE County	Percent who lived in the same house one year ago	Percent who did not live in county one year ago	Total occupied housing units	Percent owner-occupied housing units	Median value of owner-occupied housing units (dollars)	Median selected monthly owner costs as a percentage of household income		Median gross rent (dollars)	Median gross rent as a percentage of household income	Percent of workers who drove alone to work	Mean travel time to work (minutes)	Percent of occupied housing units with no vehicle available
							With a mortgage	Without a mortgage					
ACS table number:		C07204	C07204	B25003	B25003	B25077	B25092	B25092	B25064	B25071	C08301	B08013/ C08012	C25045
		1	2	3	4	5	6	7	8	9	10	11	12
	Nebraska—Cont.												
31 155	Saunders	89.1	7.4	7,773	79.7	133,400	21.1	12.8	629	23.5	78.0	23.6	3.6
31 157	Scotts Bluff	79.7	6.0	15,183	66.0	88,400	23.3	16.0	523	28.1	79.5	15.3	6.5
32 000	**Nevada**	78.3	7.5	932,715	61.0	302,600	28.3	11.7	944	29.8	77.5	23.6	7.0
32 001	Churchill	86.1	8.0	8,888	66.0	193,000	22.8	13.6	743	31.9	84.7	18.5	3.2
32 003	Clark	77.2	7.3	662,025	59.4	307,300	29.1	11.7	973	30.4	78.2	24.4	7.6
32 005	Douglas	85.2	7.7	18,673	79.0	424,800	28.9	10.1	1,090	36.9	75.1	22.2	2.2
32 007	Elko	84.5	9.2	17,003	67.7	145,200	19.6	8.7	652	21.3	68.5	23.8	4.3
32 019	Lyon	87.4	9.5	14,974	71.2	206,600	26.5	12.1	831	29.4	85.1	25.0	2.2
32 023	Nye	80.8	9.8	14,187	74.3	172,900	27.1	12.0	673	25.4	70.1	27.3	2.1
32 031	Washoe	79.0	7.3	155,567	60.1	346,900	27.9	12.7	879	29.2	75.6	21.3	7.0
32 510	Carson City	79.5	8.3	21,330	63.6	298,700	27.5	11.5	842	29.7	79.1	16.5	6.1
33 000	**New Hampshire**	85.7	6.7	500,671	73.2	250,700	26.3	16.0	892	28.7	81.6	25.0	5.0
33 001	Belknap	88.2	4.5	23,909	76.5	226,600	27.2	14.7	836	26.9	83.8	23.5	4.0
33 003	Carroll	89.7	5.6	19,269	79.8	234,600	25.2	14.2	773	27.9	81.0	23.9	4.4
33 005	Cheshire	83.5	7.8	29,687	72.8	188,700	24.8	16.1	829	27.5	78.6	20.6	5.2
33 007	Coos	85.9	5.1	14,267	71.9	117,900	23.2	15.8	547	26.3	78.0	21.0	6.4
33 009	Grafton	81.9	9.8	32,536	71.1	203,200	24.0	14.7	775	27.9	72.3	20.2	5.1
33 011	Hillsborough	85.2	5.7	149,761	70.2	276,300	26.5	15.8	979	29.1	82.8	25.1	5.1
33 013	Merrimack	84.4	8.0	55,379	72.8	239,700	27.1	17.9	861	27.8	80.5	24.4	5.7
33 015	Rockingham	89.1	5.7	113,033	78.9	321,500	26.7	17.0	1,005	29.4	85.1	28.8	3.0
33 017	Strafford	81.7	9.4	45,177	67.0	225,200	26.4	16.1	850	30.2	79.4	24.9	8.1
33 019	Sullivan	86.5	6.3	17,653	72.2	167,600	25.2	14.1	697	27.9	79.2	23.8	8.5
34 000	**New Jersey**	88.3	5.2	3,143,408	67.4	358,400	27.7	18.3	1,002	30.2	72.1	29.4	11.4
34 001	Atlantic	85.0	6.3	102,672	68.3	247,000	28.8	18.9	902	31.0	73.9	23.0	14.1
34 003	Bergen	89.7	4.7	332,065	68.7	486,000	28.9	18.8	1,163	29.3	71.2	28.8	7.9
34 005	Burlington	88.4	5.7	164,400	78.4	256,700	25.9	17.0	996	30.5	82.4	27.6	4.5
34 007	Camden	88.4	4.7	191,148	70.1	207,300	26.2	18.3	830	30.8	74.5	26.9	11.1
34 009	Cape May	87.4	6.3	47,229	74.0	328,600	28.4	18.5	944	31.3	79.0	20.6	8.8
34 011	Cumberland	87.9	5.0	50,165	68.4	156,500	25.6	16.2	788	32.8	81.2	25.0	10.7
34 013	Essex	84.9	5.1	278,402	47.7	401,700	29.9	19.7	909	30.0	60.4	30.4	23.2
34 015	Gloucester	88.5	5.9	99,708	81.5	220,400	25.7	18.0	875	29.5	84.0	27.4	4.4
34 017	Hudson	86.4	5.6	226,987	34.1	381,600	31.6	21.3	973	28.9	41.1	31.7	34.1
34 019	Hunterdon	90.6	6.9	46,256	87.3	459,200	26.7	16.8	1,074	31.9	80.6	33.4	3.0
34 021	Mercer	86.0	6.7	127,253	69.5	304,600	25.8	16.5	971	30.6	72.9	26.8	10.6
34 023	Middlesex	87.7	5.3	269,888	67.5	356,800	27.4	16.8	1,123	27.7	73.0	31.0	8.4
34 025	Monmouth	89.8	4.3	231,344	76.6	438,200	27.7	17.6	1,048	32.0	74.7	32.9	7.1
34 027	Morris	90.4	5.3	173,978	76.8	485,600	26.6	16.6	1,156	27.5	79.8	29.2	4.8
34 029	Ocean	89.1	4.6	221,305	82.7	303,600	28.8	19.9	1,146	36.0	81.9	31.3	6.6
34 031	Passaic	90.3	4.2	160,505	55.7	389,900	30.6	21.7	1,016	36.7	71.1	26.1	15.3
34 033	Salem	89.7	5.1	25,073	75.1	173,600	25.3	15.8	829	31.6	85.3	32.1	8.1
34 035	Somerset	90.3	5.6	113,495	80.8	443,700	26.7	16.5	1,205	29.2	79.5	30.2	4.9
34 037	Sussex	89.8	5.8	54,830	84.1	324,400	27.2	17.6	1,091	32.7	82.0	38.2	3.7
34 039	Union	88.9	4.2	183,634	62.5	403,800	29.2	19.1	1,019	30.6	69.2	27.4	11.9
34 041	Warren	88.9	7.2	42,531	74.6	306,100	27.7	18.4	876	28.9	79.9	35.3	5.1
35 000	**New Mexico**	82.3	7.3	728,508	69.6	140,100	22.9	10.2	630	29.2	77.2	21.2	5.6
35 001	Bernalillo	79.8	6.5	251,101	64.8	169,500	23.7	10.4	664	29.6	78.2	21.7	6.0
35 005	Chaves	79.7	7.6	22,742	70.0	74,200	19.6	10.1	519	26.6	70.4	15.5	4.0
35 006	Cibola	82.2	11.7	8,121	68.6	64,100	16.1	8.9	481	24.7	77.0	22.5	10.5
35 009	Curry	77.5	11.2	17,542	61.3	89,100	22.0	10.7	518	26.5	81.9	14.5	5.7
35 013	Dona Ana	78.4	8.1	68,164	64.9	118,200	23.1	11.9	597	33.9	76.1	18.5	6.2
35 015	Eddy	80.5	6.1	19,789	73.6	78,000	19.7	8.7	543	25.2	75.7	16.5	3.8
35 017	Grant	83.3	6.6	12,083	71.7	115,700	22.6	12.1	501	26.2	72.1	16.6	4.4
35 025	Lea	85.4	6.5	21,101	70.6	72,600	18.5	9.0	539	22.3	79.7	17.7	5.6
35 027	Lincoln	81.5	8.9	7,989	78.5	144,200	22.5	11.5	579	25.8	66.3	15.2	2.5
35 029	Luna	84.0	6.6	9,842	73.7	79,300	25.5	10.4	444	28.9	76.1	13.3	8.5
35 031	McKinley	93.8	4.2	19,029	74.6	63,500	18.7	9.1	477	21.6	78.2	22.2	11.9
35 035	Otero	81.6	8.5	24,552	66.8	89,200	22.4	9.1	570	27.7	79.1	18.7	4.1
35 039	Rio Arriba	90.8	4.1	13,995	79.8	151,400	21.9	9.5	538	24.0	73.4	29.2	4.3
35 043	Sandoval	83.5	10.5	38,606	81.8	167,100	23.7	9.0	901	31.5	77.5	28.4	4.1
35 045	San Juan	85.7	5.5	38,466	75.3	125,800	20.6	8.8	638	25.4	84.7	23.0	5.8
35 047	San Miguel	84.2	5.7	10,727	69.2	102,400	24.2	15.2	520	31.3	73.2	19.1	5.8
35 049	Santa Fe	81.6	8.9	52,956	72.2	281,500	25.3	10.3	889	31.4	71.6	21.6	3.8
35 055	Taos	88.7	5.1	12,775	71.7	210,400	27.0	10.6	683	33.3	71.0	17.2	5.1
35 061	Valencia	81.7	10.3	24,193	79.4	118,600	23.3	11.8	659	29.0	77.8	30.4	4.4
36 000	**New York**	87.8	4.2	7,096,035	55.6	293,400	26.0	15.4	898	30.4	54.3	31.2	28.3
36 001	Albany	84.5	7.7	122,538	59.6	178,700	22.6	12.9	790	28.1	78.5	19.4	11.8
36 003	Allegany	82.3	8.4	18,574	73.7	62,500	21.9	14.5	549	29.9	71.7	21.6	7.7
36 005	Bronx	88.3	2.2	468,735	21.5	358,700	32.4	12.5	844	32.8	25.0	41.2	59.1
36 007	Broome	84.3	6.3	80,870	66.7	91,800	20.6	14.6	565	28.6	80.9	18.7	10.3
36 009	Cattaraugus	85.3	6.5	32,394	72.3	73,800	22.2	13.8	558	27.9	78.2	20.8	8.1
36 011	Cayuga	85.6	6.6	31,438	73.8	93,100	22.3	15.7	599	27.8	79.3	22.0	8.6
36 013	Chautauqua	86.0	5.6	54,351	69.0	75,900	21.7	14.7	536	30.9	79.9	17.3	10.5
36 015	Chemung	82.5	6.7	34,767	67.5	78,300	21.4	14.1	597	32.6	81.0	19.6	8.6
36 017	Chenango	87.5	4.7	19,783	77.6	81,500	22.2	14.0	536	25.2	78.6	23.0	6.5

Table C-2. Counties — Where: Migration, Housing, and Transportation, 2005–2007—*Continued*

STATE County code	STATE County	Percent who lived in the same house one year ago	Percent who did not live in county one year ago	Total occupied housing units	Percent owner-occupied housing units	Median value of owner-occupied housing units (dollars)	Median selected monthly owner costs as a percentage of household income		Median gross rent (dollars)	Median gross rent as a percentage of household income	Percent of workers who drove alone to work	Mean travel time to work (minutes)	Percent of occupied housing units with no vehicle available
							With a mortgage	Without a mortgage					
	ACS table number:	C07204	C07204	B25003	B25003	B25077	B25092	B25092	B25064	B25071	C08301	B08013/ C08012	C25045
		1	2	3	4	5	6	7	8	9	10	11	12
	New York—Cont.												
36 019	Clinton	82.7	7.0	30,088	71.4	108,800	21.8	14.0	605	29.1	77.1	18.5	8.6
36 021	Columbia	86.3	7.2	25,275	73.1	201,200	24.1	14.7	684	30.9	77.5	25.6	6.4
36 023	Cortland	82.6	10.3	18,034	66.8	89,100	21.8	14.5	609	26.5	80.9	21.0	10.5
36 025	Delaware	85.9	8.1	19,030	74.1	124,500	23.2	14.0	564	24.2	75.0	20.5	7.0
36 027	Dutchess	86.1	6.8	102,218	72.4	328,100	26.5	16.4	989	30.0	76.9	29.4	6.0
36 029	Erie	86.2	3.4	378,698	66.2	107,900	22.4	15.2	648	29.6	80.9	20.5	13.6
36 031	Essex	86.8	8.4	15,542	69.3	131,300	22.8	14.0	604	26.7	76.3	19.2	6.5
36 033	Franklin	80.2	9.9	19,071	72.5	76,600	20.4	13.7	550	32.0	75.2	18.7	9.3
36 035	Fulton	86.0	5.0	23,126	70.1	86,700	23.8	14.6	605	31.3	79.7	22.9	7.9
36 037	Genesee	87.0	5.0	22,893	73.1	95,500	24.1	14.5	665	30.8	84.7	21.4	5.9
36 039	Greene	87.8	6.9	18,609	76.1	172,600	25.9	15.4	608	26.8	81.4	25.9	5.8
36 043	Herkimer	88.9	4.0	25,238	73.7	82,600	21.2	14.4	549	27.6	79.4	22.8	8.1
36 045	Jefferson	79.6	9.8	43,512	59.3	96,300	21.1	13.7	618	27.6	79.8	20.6	7.4
36 047	Kings	90.7	2.0	877,731	31.1	533,900	33.4	16.6	930	31.6	20.8	42.1	56.1
36 049	Lewis	87.9	6.4	11,078	75.2	86,100	19.9	12.7	569	28.4	77.8	23.5	4.8
36 051	Livingston	83.9	8.5	22,644	75.4	105,600	22.7	15.4	630	30.6	79.8	23.7	3.2
36 053	Madison	86.1	8.0	25,967	77.0	98,500	21.9	14.0	650	25.1	77.0	22.7	4.7
36 055	Monroe	85.8	3.9	284,888	67.5	122,700	23.0	14.7	736	33.5	82.6	18.8	10.4
36 057	Montgomery	86.7	6.8	19,760	69.8	87,900	22.5	15.4	603	26.9	80.2	23.2	9.2
36 059	Nassau	92.4	3.0	435,464	82.6	493,400	29.9	19.3	1,334	33.6	68.5	32.8	7.1
36 061	New York	85.3	6.2	735,382	23.5	767,200	20.3	9.0	1,115	27.2	7.1	30.5	77.5
36 063	Niagara	87.7	3.8	87,249	71.4	93,300	22.4	16.3	585	28.8	85.5	20.4	9.3
36 065	Oneida	84.1	6.3	92,393	66.8	91,500	21.7	14.5	594	28.8	81.1	19.3	10.6
36 067	Onondaga	83.8	5.2	181,325	65.7	114,100	21.9	14.4	672	29.3	79.9	18.7	11.6
36 069	Ontario	84.7	6.7	40,709	73.9	118,600	22.9	14.3	660	30.0	82.0	21.7	6.5
36 071	Orange	85.8	6.7	123,112	70.2	311,700	27.7	17.2	977	33.1	73.1	32.2	9.5
36 073	Orleans	84.1	7.3	15,119	75.2	81,700	24.4	18.4	629	29.5	81.1	24.2	6.3
36 075	Oswego	84.6	4.8	46,183	72.8	81,000	21.9	14.3	617	32.0	78.7	23.3	7.4
36 077	Otsego	80.8	9.5	25,129	70.3	121,900	21.8	13.8	666	31.9	73.6	21.4	6.5
36 079	Putnam	91.1	6.2	33,513	85.3	424,400	29.1	17.2	1,138	34.2	78.2	35.9	3.9
36 081	Queens	88.4	2.6	774,251	46.4	465,200	33.3	14.6	1,090	31.6	32.1	41.7	36.0
36 083	Rensselaer	84.2	7.2	60,591	66.5	151,100	23.3	14.5	716	27.6	78.9	22.5	9.0
36 085	Richmond	91.9	1.7	166,069	71.3	461,400	28.7	14.7	1,060	32.6	53.4	42.6	16.0
36 087	Rockland	91.7	3.3	93,564	74.1	491,100	28.1	18.5	1,172	33.1	72.8	29.2	8.9
36 089	St. Lawrence	81.5	7.7	40,172	72.5	72,900	20.5	13.8	551	30.1	76.2	20.3	7.4
36 091	Saratoga	86.6	6.2	83,936	74.1	197,000	23.3	14.2	816	25.1	82.9	24.4	4.8
36 093	Schenectady	85.0	7.9	58,134	69.9	145,000	23.4	14.5	727	30.2	81.6	20.7	10.7
36 095	Schoharie	86.7	8.3	12,338	76.0	120,600	21.9	12.9	614	30.3	80.4	26.6	5.8
36 099	Seneca	84.4	9.3	11,862	78.8	86,100	23.7	14.5	621	31.5	81.4	21.3	4.2
36 101	Steuben	85.4	5.0	38,950	72.3	77,900	21.8	14.4	566	28.7	77.5	21.5	7.6
36 103	Suffolk	90.7	3.2	480,627	82.6	436,200	30.7	19.2	1,357	34.0	79.4	30.0	4.6
36 105	Sullivan	86.2	8.1	29,091	68.7	171,800	25.3	17.0	734	29.9	75.2	25.7	8.1
36 107	Tioga	89.9	3.6	19,761	78.1	89,200	22.0	13.1	575	26.7	83.3	24.0	5.0
36 109	Tompkins	69.1	13.1	37,374	52.8	147,900	22.9	12.6	799	32.8	57.4	17.8	11.6
36 111	Ulster	85.7	6.8	69,354	67.7	237,400	25.8	16.8	897	30.9	78.1	25.8	6.9
36 113	Warren	86.4	6.6	27,257	68.6	159,700	23.8	14.0	750	29.9	82.0	20.6	7.3
36 115	Washington	84.1	7.7	23,853	73.3	116,400	24.8	14.9	672	28.9	78.4	25.6	6.1
36 117	Wayne	86.3	5.5	36,171	76.3	100,100	22.8	15.7	631	29.7	84.2	24.5	6.3
36 119	Westchester	88.3	4.6	335,848	63.6	571,700	26.5	17.7	1,138	29.9	59.9	31.1	13.5
36 121	Wyoming	85.5	9.2	15,140	78.2	89,900	23.8	14.6	628	25.5	80.4	22.3	4.6
36 123	Yates	87.5	5.9	9,298	77.4	104,200	26.0	14.0	534	29.9	70.1	21.5	10.4
37 000	**North Carolina**	82.0	8.1	3,471,751	68.4	136,800	23.0	11.9	674	28.9	79.9	23.2	6.5
37 001	Alamance	79.9	7.4	56,608	68.5	131,800	24.1	11.9	684	29.1	82.0	21.8	4.7
37 003	Alexander	90.4	4.1	13,026	82.4	113,200	22.7	9.0	548	26.8	82.7	23.7	3.1
37 007	Anson	83.6	5.5	8,558	75.4	79,900	25.8	14.3	592	32.7	83.1	22.8	9.9
37 009	Ashe	91.8	4.6	11,145	78.3	132,900	21.2	11.0	496	28.9	79.6	24.7	5.7
37 013	Beaufort	83.2	7.3	18,908	75.8	94,900	23.6	14.9	542	26.1	80.0	25.8	8.1
37 017	Bladen	81.1	9.5	12,773	70.2	71,500	23.1	12.9	554	31.4	75.3	25.1	7.0
37 019	Brunswick	83.5	7.2	42,315	70.7	162,500	23.8	12.5	724	29.3	75.6	24.5	6.3
37 021	Buncombe	81.9	8.0	94,052	68.0	169,700	24.1	11.9	689	27.8	77.5	20.6	6.6
37 023	Burke	86.7	5.6	34,093	73.8	99,300	22.8	11.9	542	28.6	81.8	20.9	6.8
37 025	Cabarrus	81.7	8.0	59,766	72.2	145,800	22.2	12.6	695	24.9	83.2	26.5	5.2
37 027	Caldwell	86.2	5.6	31,032	75.6	105,500	22.2	11.5	526	26.6	86.1	21.9	5.0
37 031	Carteret	82.6	8.3	27,277	75.4	186,300	24.0	11.7	649	25.4	78.0	24.1	4.5
37 033	Caswell	88.5	9.0	8,572	77.9	90,200	23.6	14.6	465	24.7	79.9	30.2	8.1
37 035	Catawba	84.8	6.5	58,797	72.3	123,100	21.3	10.6	587	26.6	84.6	20.5	5.3
37 037	Chatham	88.8	7.0	22,499	77.7	169,800	23.1	12.4	694	32.1	76.6	26.6	4.1
37 039	Cherokee	90.4	5.5	11,019	80.6	129,500	24.4	10.9	534	25.1	86.4	20.3	5.8
37 045	Cleveland	84.8	5.7	37,206	72.6	99,000	22.9	11.7	570	28.7	85.4	22.4	7.1
37 047	Columbus	89.0	3.5	21,124	71.0	84,800	26.2	14.4	493	32.1	77.2	26.3	9.8
37 049	Craven	76.5	12.9	38,862	65.4	135,100	23.6	12.4	649	28.5	74.5	19.8	7.4
37 051	Cumberland	75.6	11.7	117,517	58.4	101,300	23.3	11.9	737	30.0	79.4	20.9	7.3
37 053	Currituck	87.6	7.6	9,203	80.7	233,800	28.7	12.7	737	26.9	77.8	33.2	2.1
37 055	Dare	86.2	7.3	15,568	68.5	347,300	29.1	13.7	961	31.0	75.2	20.0	2.0
37 057	Davidson	84.5	5.7	61,027	73.3	119,900	22.4	10.7	584	25.3	84.8	22.2	5.7

STATE County code	STATE County	Percent who lived in the same house one year ago	Percent who did not live in county one year ago	Total occupied housing units	Percent owner-occupied housing units	Median value of owner-occupied housing units (dollars)	Median selected monthly owner costs as a percentage of household income — With a mortgage	Median selected monthly owner costs as a percentage of household income — Without a mortgage	Median gross rent (dollars)	Median gross rent as a percentage of household income	Percent of workers who drove alone to work	Mean travel time to work (minutes)	Percent of occupied housing units with no vehicle available
ACS table number:		C07204	C07204	B25003	B25003	B25077	B25092	B25092	B25064	B25071	C08301	B08013/ C08012	C25045
		1	2	3	4	5	6	7	8	9	10	11	12
	North Carolina—Cont.												
37 059	Davie	88.2	5.1	15,249	82.6	144,100	21.9	10.3	632	24.6	82.0	22.9	3.4
37 061	Duplin	84.9	5.5	17,638	70.9	80,000	23.0	15.8	514	24.4	71.8	25.1	7.6
37 063	Durham	77.3	10.5	100,830	56.0	168,700	23.6	10.8	759	28.8	74.1	22.7	8.1
37 065	Edgecombe	84.3	5.6	21,313	60.4	78,100	24.7	13.5	564	36.8	79.6	19.8	13.0
37 067	Forsyth	83.1	6.1	133,900	66.2	142,400	22.3	10.1	645	28.2	82.9	20.7	7.5
37 069	Franklin	83.8	9.3	20,324	73.5	110,400	24.1	13.8	640	31.3	78.7	32.7	6.4
37 071	Gaston	82.1	7.0	75,619	69.9	111,800	23.3	13.3	632	28.7	83.4	23.4	6.9
37 077	Granville	83.0	10.2	18,915	73.9	124,500	24.0	13.4	669	28.0	88.0	26.3	4.4
37 079	Greene	84.6	11.0	6,439	68.1	80,800	20.5	18.7	567	32.2	83.6	23.1	6.5
37 081	Guilford	81.5	7.9	184,357	63.0	146,700	23.2	11.0	701	30.3	82.2	21.5	7.1
37 083	Halifax	87.5	5.5	21,391	65.9	81,400	23.3	17.6	553	34.9	83.5	22.0	13.9
37 085	Harnett	80.4	11.2	38,030	68.3	111,100	23.9	12.9	662	30.2	80.0	27.2	5.9
37 087	Haywood	86.2	5.7	24,839	73.3	143,400	21.1	10.5	611	31.3	86.7	21.0	4.7
37 089	Henderson	84.9	7.8	42,205	76.6	169,000	22.9	10.2	621	27.8	79.2	21.5	4.1
37 091	Hertford	82.7	9.5	8,478	65.4	76,900	23.2	20.2	565	33.3	82.9	21.7	11.6
37 093	Hoke	84.5	12.3	13,363	79.8	103,400	23.7	11.3	650	28.2	88.7	23.5	7.5
37 097	Iredell	83.2	7.3	55,700	73.5	151,700	23.5	10.9	653	27.3	82.1	23.2	4.9
37 099	Jackson	78.5	12.0	14,770	64.6	143,900	21.5	9.5	546	29.0	78.2	20.3	3.7
37 101	Johnston	86.0	7.2	54,695	74.2	126,400	22.7	13.0	670	27.0	79.2	29.2	4.5
37 105	Lee	87.7	5.8	21,011	72.2	122,800	22.8	13.1	565	27.9	79.7	21.9	6.2
37 107	Lenoir	85.2	5.3	24,779	59.9	90,900	25.7	13.9	556	32.1	77.6	21.7	10.9
37 109	Lincoln	87.9	5.6	27,191	78.1	124,000	23.8	10.4	601	29.1	83.3	27.4	2.1
37 111	McDowell	86.9	5.8	16,848	74.7	94,800	20.3	11.0	461	24.1	78.5	22.1	7.8
37 113	Macon	82.8	9.5	14,671	76.3	169,400	24.2	9.3	625	24.9	78.6	21.2	5.3
37 115	Madison	85.1	8.6	8,020	74.9	145,700	22.7	10.0	610	30.7	77.2	31.5	6.0
37 117	Martin	89.3	5.7	9,781	71.3	79,000	24.6	14.6	487	33.6	78.3	22.7	7.7
37 119	Mecklenburg	77.0	9.7	337,700	64.1	173,900	22.9	11.5	781	28.6	77.2	24.7	6.2
37 123	Montgomery	91.6	4.6	10,044	73.5	70,600	22.3	14.3	463	27.9	87.1	23.4	7.7
37 125	Moore	86.7	6.2	30,317	76.7	157,900	23.1	11.1	599	24.7	81.3	22.1	4.2
37 127	Nash	85.5	5.7	35,760	64.7	113,200	22.7	13.0	606	25.2	83.4	20.2	6.6
37 129	New Hanover	76.0	11.3	81,514	62.8	201,400	24.6	12.2	778	31.8	81.6	19.9	7.3
37 131	Northampton	92.0	5.0	7,954	72.0	69,600	26.2	13.5	468	31.8	86.8	23.9	14.7
37 133	Onslow	69.4	18.9	54,259	60.0	116,600	22.6	10.1	694	27.0	62.7	19.9	5.6
37 135	Orange	75.2	13.1	48,932	60.7	229,500	22.4	11.6	767	33.8	69.6	21.6	6.4
37 139	Pasquotank	83.1	8.6	14,278	67.1	155,400	25.5	12.9	646	32.6	78.4	23.5	10.6
37 141	Pender	87.3	9.4	19,107	78.3	111,600	23.9	13.1	723	30.1	78.8	29.1	5.1
37 145	Person	86.7	6.1	14,788	70.2	106,700	20.5	12.8	627	27.9	82.7	28.9	6.5
37 147	Pitt	76.0	10.1	61,572	56.7	113,700	22.9	14.3	630	35.0	82.7	19.5	9.1
37 151	Randolph	85.9	4.7	53,334	74.3	110,500	22.7	12.2	564	30.4	84.4	22.5	5.3
37 153	Richmond	90.6	4.5	18,074	68.9	67,000	23.8	14.8	480	28.6	88.7	18.6	10.9
37 155	Robeson	84.4	4.7	43,510	67.0	66,300	23.9	14.4	510	27.4	78.8	24.6	10.4
37 157	Rockingham	83.1	4.4	37,378	69.9	100,200	22.2	11.4	537	26.4	78.6	24.4	7.7
37 159	Rowan	83.9	6.3	52,027	74.2	118,500	22.2	11.2	613	28.3	83.8	22.5	6.9
37 161	Rutherford	85.4	3.4	25,926	70.7	93,900	22.3	11.1	477	26.8	80.7	23.0	9.0
37 163	Sampson	87.2	6.2	22,427	71.1	79,500	23.5	12.2	534	30.5	78.9	24.4	7.2
37 165	Scotland	83.7	9.2	12,968	67.7	78,900	25.0	15.1	493	30.9	84.4	17.1	14.8
37 167	Stanly	88.9	5.1	21,960	76.0	124,400	23.9	13.1	563	27.7	84.2	25.7	3.7
37 169	Stokes	87.6	6.1	17,478	82.6	108,600	22.4	9.3	523	26.6	85.9	28.6	3.8
37 171	Surry	88.8	4.5	28,194	75.3	96,400	21.9	11.7	507	26.4	82.0	24.1	5.8
37 175	Transylvania	82.8	10.1	12,498	75.2	166,500	23.4	8.5	574	32.0	74.0	21.2	5.7
37 179	Union	84.1	8.8	60,277	78.4	172,800	23.4	10.9	753	29.1	82.3	29.2	3.6
37 181	Vance	86.1	4.7	16,437	69.3	94,700	26.6	12.6	587	28.0	79.4	23.3	9.8
37 183	Wake	79.8	8.8	299,587	66.9	202,400	21.9	9.9	792	27.7	80.3	24.2	4.7
37 189	Watauga	71.1	12.7	18,350	58.1	190,600	24.7	9.7	633	50.1	72.3	18.8	4.2
37 191	Wayne	82.4	6.6	44,116	66.0	96,400	22.8	12.9	589	27.5	84.1	20.6	7.6
37 193	Wilkes	90.0	3.1	26,205	76.9	98,400	22.3	9.6	505	26.4	83.8	23.1	4.8
37 195	Wilson	83.3	5.7	29,586	61.2	100,900	24.2	17.2	649	31.0	79.5	19.7	10.6
37 197	Yadkin	87.8	5.6	14,728	76.1	97,100	22.6	10.5	487	27.0	80.9	24.6	3.7
38 000	**North Dakota**	82.5	7.9	271,131	66.5	97,400	20.9	11.6	513	25.1	78.5	16.0	5.5
38 015	Burleigh	84.2	8.1	31,251	68.1	131,800	22.3	11.9	524	23.9	79.7	16.0	5.5
38 017	Cass	76.1	9.2	59,718	54.1	138,900	22.3	11.9	573	27.7	82.3	16.1	7.2
38 035	Grand Forks	72.6	12.1	26,989	55.6	124,300	22.0	14.2	593	29.1	84.7	13.7	5.0
38 059	Morton	86.0	7.5	10,281	78.2	99,400	22.4	13.7	486	26.1	79.3	19.2	4.0
38 089	Stark	83.6	10.3	9,231	70.7	93,800	20.9	11.8	493	25.4	80.7	14.4	6.2
38 093	Stutsman	80.0	7.4	8,853	70.2	88,200	20.2	13.3	445	23.5	76.8	14.0	7.3
38 101	Ward	78.7	11.1	23,635	63.8	105,500	22.1	11.9	502	22.9	82.6	13.9	5.5
39 000	**Ohio**	84.2	5.5	4,500,621	70.0	134,400	23.3	13.5	645	29.3	83.1	22.4	7.8
39 001	Adams	85.1	4.6	9,853	72.3	95,200	22.9	14.0	514	31.7	72.8	33.5	7.9
39 003	Allen	83.9	5.8	40,596	71.1	99,500	20.4	12.3	555	26.3	83.5	18.2	6.6
39 005	Ashland	86.0	7.2	19,672	78.9	128,100	24.1	13.7	588	30.0	82.2	22.2	7.3
39 007	Ashtabula	83.9	6.2	39,272	71.9	117,000	24.5	15.0	586	29.9	84.7	24.5	8.0
39 009	Athens	64.0	18.5	21,970	58.9	107,000	23.0	13.9	657	50.1	66.6	21.1	7.7
39 011	Auglaize	87.0	5.2	18,163	77.5	120,600	19.9	11.6	579	22.5	86.6	17.6	4.0
39 013	Belmont	89.0	4.8	28,232	73.7	80,900	20.5	12.4	444	26.8	86.1	23.7	8.4
39 015	Brown	85.6	4.9	16,063	77.8	120,900	24.1	13.7	608	28.3	85.1	33.8	4.3

STATE County code	STATE County	Percent who lived in the same house one year ago	Percent who did not live in county one year ago	Total occupied housing units	Percent owner-occu-pied housing units	Median value of owner-occupied housing units (dollars)	Median selected monthly owner costs as a percentage of household income — With a mortgage	Median selected monthly owner costs as a percentage of household income — Without a mortgage	Median gross rent (dollars)	Median gross rent as a percentage of house-hold income	Percent of workers who drove alone to work	Mean travel time to work (minutes)	Percent of occupied housing units with no vehicle available
ACS table number:		C07204	C07204	B25003	B25003	B25077	B25092	B25092	B25064	B25071	C08301	B08013/C08012	C25045
		1	2	3	4	5	6	7	8	9	10	11	12
	Ohio—Cont.												
39 017	Butler	81.6	7.0	129,731	71.2	157,600	22.9	14.0	707	29.5	83.8	22.5	5.6
39 019	Carroll	88.8	6.0	11,197	80.5	110,000	24.0	12.5	547	26.8	82.2	29.0	3.8
39 021	Champaign	88.7	3.7	15,446	74.1	126,400	23.3	12.6	579	26.2	82.4	23.1	4.9
39 023	Clark	85.2	4.0	55,422	72.1	109,100	22.7	13.6	606	31.5	83.2	21.6	7.4
39 025	Clermont	84.3	7.9	71,769	75.4	157,000	23.2	13.2	690	27.7	85.4	27.4	4.2
39 027	Clinton	80.9	9.1	16,547	69.4	126,400	25.0	13.9	661	29.9	81.1	24.5	5.6
39 029	Columbiana	84.5	5.0	41,746	76.0	97,000	22.5	12.9	545	31.2	83.5	23.8	5.8
39 031	Coshocton	85.0	4.4	14,225	74.3	92,200	22.4	10.0	496	25.1	77.6	22.6	7.2
39 033	Crawford	83.4	5.5	18,657	74.0	91,400	22.2	12.9	563	23.8	81.4	20.2	6.6
39 035	Cuyahoga	84.9	3.7	542,856	63.7	139,300	25.1	16.0	670	30.9	79.6	23.4	13.0
39 037	Darke	85.7	4.9	20,889	76.8	114,200	22.4	12.6	556	23.0	82.8	22.5	4.0
39 039	Defiance	87.8	3.9	15,061	79.4	103,600	22.5	12.4	579	24.2	86.8	19.4	7.3
39 041	Delaware	84.2	9.5	56,607	81.2	246,600	23.7	11.7	717	27.8	84.2	24.7	2.6
39 043	Erie	87.2	5.7	31,874	73.4	135,700	22.8	13.8	626	29.4	84.6	18.4	6.3
39 045	Fairfield	84.9	6.8	51,069	77.0	167,100	23.8	11.7	691	26.4	83.4	26.9	3.9
39 047	Fayette	82.4	5.0	11,466	67.5	117,300	24.8	13.7	618	25.9	80.7	24.1	8.1
39 049	Franklin	78.5	6.3	449,236	59.6	154,600	23.7	13.5	722	29.3	82.8	20.8	7.9
39 051	Fulton	87.0	5.6	15,841	81.7	132,900	24.4	13.6	615	23.7	84.9	21.8	2.2
39 053	Gallia	84.3	4.9	11,782	72.8	88,600	22.2	12.4	483	36.7	74.3	25.2	8.7
39 055	Geauga	91.9	5.0	33,028	87.2	228,200	23.7	12.7	722	29.3	79.3	27.1	6.1
39 057	Greene	80.9	10.5	59,914	68.8	156,200	21.6	11.6	731	29.4	84.7	20.1	4.0
39 059	Guernsey	88.3	3.2	16,474	71.4	88,600	21.1	11.8	504	30.2	83.5	23.5	9.6
39 061	Hamilton	82.4	4.6	331,706	63.4	144,500	23.0	13.9	607	29.4	79.6	22.0	12.6
39 063	Hancock	79.9	7.3	30,848	73.0	124,300	22.3	12.7	591	28.4	86.0	16.9	3.8
39 065	Hardin	80.7	9.3	11,883	70.2	95,200	21.4	14.3	537	28.7	79.5	22.7	5.9
39 069	Henry	88.4	5.2	11,172	82.4	110,800	22.3	13.8	618	23.1	86.6	20.6	4.4
39 071	Highland	81.6	7.8	15,405	75.3	104,300	23.6	11.9	589	31.6	84.9	26.8	6.6
39 073	Hocking	83.4	7.1	10,730	75.4	115,200	23.0	12.4	540	23.7	81.5	31.4	5.5
39 075	Holmes	91.9	4.4	11,588	82.4	155,500	24.9	9.4	505	19.0	49.6	22.2	32.0
39 077	Huron	82.9	6.3	23,104	74.8	117,900	22.1	13.6	573	25.9	82.4	21.6	4.8
39 079	Jackson	81.8	5.1	13,017	77.0	84,200	22.7	13.4	476	32.1	83.5	25.9	8.8
39 081	Jefferson	88.1	4.8	29,535	72.8	82,700	20.7	11.5	520	30.3	84.8	21.4	9.4
39 083	Knox	84.0	6.2	21,265	75.6	123,700	24.0	12.8	631	27.5	78.0	26.6	5.5
39 085	Lake	88.9	4.3	92,949	77.8	157,600	24.3	14.0	745	29.1	86.1	23.3	4.7
39 087	Lawrence	85.6	4.9	24,657	72.9	85,900	22.4	13.2	506	29.4	86.3	23.3	8.4
39 089	Licking	82.9	6.6	59,291	75.8	149,600	23.1	12.7	657	27.1	82.7	25.6	4.4
39 091	Logan	84.7	5.3	18,886	72.5	111,300	20.9	13.3	599	27.1	85.5	21.9	5.6
39 093	Lorain	85.6	5.3	110,452	75.8	146,000	23.5	13.6	647	31.2	85.5	23.3	6.3
39 095	Lucas	83.5	4.1	178,247	66.6	123,300	23.4	14.8	616	31.5	84.5	19.8	9.9
39 097	Madison	80.5	12.1	14,480	73.5	142,300	22.6	14.2	653	26.0	82.1	25.7	4.1
39 099	Mahoning	88.3	4.1	99,678	72.5	97,800	23.1	14.9	549	31.5	87.0	20.8	8.2
39 101	Marion	79.2	8.5	24,866	71.0	95,900	22.6	14.6	609	29.8	84.1	19.9	8.6
39 103	Medina	89.6	4.8	61,084	82.8	181,600	23.6	13.3	750	30.0	86.2	26.1	3.0
39 105	Meigs	88.0	4.3	9,451	79.2	78,500	23.0	11.1	464	29.5	83.3	28.9	5.9
39 107	Mercer	87.6	3.6	15,092	80.1	121,400	21.1	12.5	592	25.8	82.7	17.8	3.0
39 109	Miami	85.4	4.6	39,306	71.6	135,800	21.8	11.9	627	26.7	85.4	19.8	6.1
39 113	Montgomery	81.9	4.6	224,650	65.5	118,800	23.1	13.8	655	30.2	83.7	20.5	8.9
39 117	Morrow	89.7	4.0	12,005	83.3	127,000	24.4	13.8	628	23.5	81.3	30.2	2.7
39 119	Muskingum	86.6	4.1	32,385	74.4	106,200	22.8	13.3	509	29.1	84.0	23.5	6.3
39 123	Ottawa	89.0	5.7	18,125	77.2	140,200	22.7	12.4	662	28.0	85.5	22.1	5.2
39 127	Perry	86.8	4.5	12,438	75.9	97,500	24.0	12.3	517	29.3	83.5	35.7	5.5
39 129	Pickaway	81.5	13.2	17,888	76.3	142,500	24.3	13.8	698	27.5	83.3	27.3	3.8
39 131	Pike	85.5	4.5	10,939	68.6	91,600	23.2	15.9	543	32.9	82.2	28.3	7.7
39 133	Portage	82.0	8.3	59,426	70.6	153,100	24.2	13.6	710	30.7	83.9	24.1	5.2
39 135	Preble	85.8	5.7	16,546	78.7	121,900	23.7	13.6	645	24.6	84.0	25.2	3.4
39 137	Putnam	91.9	3.1	12,430	85.6	127,000	20.6	10.2	553	23.5	85.3	21.7	2.3
39 139	Richland	82.7	6.6	49,720	72.1	112,300	22.3	12.9	551	27.8	84.1	19.8	8.8
39 141	Ross	81.7	7.8	27,203	74.7	103,100	22.4	12.4	572	29.3	85.9	26.3	5.3
39 143	Sandusky	87.5	4.0	23,915	74.5	116,000	22.5	13.1	525	25.1	86.0	18.7	5.9
39 145	Scioto	83.6	5.2	30,660	68.7	80,800	22.6	13.7	516	30.6	81.7	24.8	9.0
39 147	Seneca	83.6	6.1	22,311	76.8	100,300	22.1	11.3	505	25.7	83.5	19.6	5.6
39 149	Shelby	86.9	5.1	18,561	73.9	124,200	22.2	11.6	624	29.7	84.1	17.2	5.4
39 151	Stark	85.7	4.2	149,953	72.1	128,700	22.7	12.9	589	28.6	85.8	20.8	7.0
39 153	Summit	88.7	3.7	220,092	70.8	142,000	24.1	14.2	710	30.3	86.4	22.1	7.6
39 155	Trumbull	90.4	2.8	87,595	73.9	102,600	22.3	13.3	553	28.1	87.4	21.7	5.6
39 157	Tuscarawas	87.1	3.7	35,500	75.9	108,300	22.7	11.9	553	25.7	84.6	21.1	6.8
39 159	Union	82.6	12.1	16,946	77.9	169,100	22.8	10.8	758	22.9	86.3	24.1	3.5
39 161	Van Wert	83.6	5.0	11,725	80.0	86,800	21.7	10.7	556	24.7	83.9	18.5	3.9
39 165	Warren	83.8	9.1	69,694	79.1	190,400	23.0	12.6	807	25.5	86.6	24.1	2.5
39 167	Washington	87.6	5.4	25,200	73.9	106,900	21.1	10.3	520	30.6	82.1	21.5	6.4
39 169	Wayne	87.3	4.0	42,432	74.0	134,500	22.8	11.8	587	27.7	78.8	19.5	8.0
39 171	Williams	82.1	6.7	15,301	76.1	103,200	21.3	12.8	565	24.4	84.2	17.4	4.2
39 173	Wood	79.0	11.2	48,712	70.3	149,000	22.7	13.6	617	29.0	85.3	19.3	4.3
39 175	Wyandot	87.8	5.6	9,043	75.2	104,900	22.4	10.6	533	20.2	81.6	19.9	3.6

Table C-2. Counties — Where: Migration, Housing, and Transportation, 2005–2007—*Continued*

STATE County code	STATE County	Percent who lived in the same house one year ago	Percent who did not live in county one year ago	Total occupied housing units	Percent owner-occupied housing units	Median value of owner-occupied housing units (dollars)	Median selected monthly owner costs as a percentage of household income		Median gross rent (dollars)	Median gross rent as a percentage of household income	Percent of workers who drove alone to work	Mean travel time to work (minutes)	Percent of occupied housing units with no vehicle available
							With a mortgage	Without a mortgage					
	ACS table number:	C07204	C07204	B25003	B25003	B25077	B25092	B25092	B25064	B25071	C08301	B08013/C08012	C25045
		1	2	3	4	5	6	7	8	9	10	11	12
40 000	**Oklahoma**	80.0	8.2	1,386,849	68.3	95,200	21.2	11.4	587	28.1	80.6	20.2	5.7
40 001	Adair	95.2	1.9	7,569	73.7	72,500	20.9	10.7	402	25.7	76.7	25.6	4.9
40 013	Bryan	83.3	7.7	15,130	67.0	82,300	21.9	12.3	507	28.9	78.9	18.9	6.9
40 015	Caddo	80.3	7.7	10,713	70.1	63,500	18.0	11.3	499	19.8	80.6	23.4	5.9
40 017	Canadian	81.1	8.5	36,150	79.0	119,000	20.9	11.4	677	24.0	84.7	21.8	2.2
40 019	Carter	84.5	3.8	18,607	69.5	76,300	21.5	11.1	507	26.0	79.6	17.9	5.8
40 021	Cherokee	83.6	9.8	16,247	64.8	88,800	19.8	11.2	484	27.8	82.9	23.3	5.7
40 027	Cleveland	77.6	10.6	89,659	67.3	123,400	21.3	10.5	672	29.1	82.1	21.7	3.2
40 031	Comanche	73.0	13.8	41,060	60.5	88,500	20.7	11.0	598	27.4	71.9	15.5	6.4
40 037	Creek	85.9	8.0	26,252	75.9	89,500	22.2	11.1	591	27.6	80.2	24.3	4.7
40 039	Custer	74.8	12.1	10,438	60.4	82,000	18.2	11.3	554	27.8	82.3	15.6	6.2
40 041	Delaware	84.9	7.1	15,372	77.6	89,200	21.8	11.6	517	26.1	74.7	23.1	3.2
40 047	Garfield	81.6	7.6	22,791	69.5	75,300	19.4	10.6	583	26.8	82.7	15.7	4.1
40 049	Garvin	88.3	5.1	10,110	78.0	68,100	17.9	13.0	479	26.6	83.2	22.0	6.2
40 051	Grady	82.1	9.5	17,847	76.3	97,900	21.3	11.8	519	23.0	80.5	25.0	4.4
40 065	Jackson	74.0	12.2	10,039	60.5	76,200	18.8	12.3	614	24.5	82.2	12.5	8.6
40 071	Kay	85.0	4.7	18,541	72.6	68,800	20.6	12.9	553	27.0	82.4	14.9	5.4
40 079	Le Flore	81.5	8.3	17,873	72.5	65,000	20.5	10.9	473	27.4	79.8	19.3	5.6
40 081	Lincoln	85.6	6.8	12,497	76.4	80,900	20.7	11.6	496	24.3	80.6	29.9	3.4
40 083	Logan	81.8	12.1	12,759	79.5	102,500	21.0	12.2	600	25.8	79.6	28.1	5.0
40 087	McClain	85.3	10.3	10,900	80.4	103,600	17.6	11.5	536	26.1	78.1	27.7	2.2
40 089	McCurtain	81.3	4.2	13,862	67.6	71,000	21.5	10.8	473	27.5	76.4	20.1	9.8
40 097	Mayes	83.2	7.1	15,427	76.9	85,900	21.2	10.0	490	26.4	79.4	22.9	4.9
40 101	Muskogee	79.9	6.6	26,303	70.0	77,600	20.9	11.7	513	28.5	79.7	19.0	9.7
40 109	Oklahoma	77.2	7.2	279,582	61.9	107,000	22.1	11.6	624	28.8	80.6	19.4	6.6
40 111	Okmulgee	82.7	8.0	15,479	69.5	70,700	22.6	12.2	541	33.8	81.2	26.5	7.0
40 113	Osage	86.7	6.9	16,880	78.4	96,000	19.9	11.7	498	28.8	84.0	23.3	4.3
40 115	Ottawa	79.0	4.9	12,825	73.9	73,300	20.7	11.1	446	26.2	78.9	19.4	5.3
40 119	Payne	67.8	14.5	26,484	57.9	105,000	22.1	10.6	561	34.5	76.2	16.1	6.0
40 121	Pittsburg	82.2	7.6	18,278	72.1	76,400	20.3	12.3	543	26.1	84.2	18.8	6.1
40 123	Pontotoc	80.8	6.6	14,466	65.4	83,600	19.0	10.8	475	30.0	86.5	15.9	6.7
40 125	Pottawatomie	82.1	8.8	24,772	69.6	88,200	21.6	10.7	525	31.2	80.9	23.4	7.6
40 131	Rogers	82.9	8.8	28,231	81.7	127,100	21.0	10.2	660	27.0	85.3	24.2	2.7
40 133	Seminole	78.8	6.5	9,204	69.4	60,400	19.3	11.9	492	29.4	79.1	20.7	8.2
40 135	Sequoyah	84.5	7.1	14,785	72.3	73,800	19.8	11.1	527	26.0	83.7	23.6	6.0
40 137	Stephens	80.1	9.7	17,466	72.7	74,600	18.7	12.0	511	24.5	82.2	18.9	5.4
40 139	Texas	80.0	12.2	6,980	72.4	71,200	21.7	14.8	577	20.6	77.8	14.5	7.5
40 143	Tulsa	78.5	6.9	233,204	62.8	116,700	22.1	11.7	645	28.8	81.5	18.6	6.7
40 145	Wagoner	85.0	8.7	24,838	80.1	123,100	22.3	10.8	644	28.6	81.4	24.0	2.3
40 147	Washington	84.1	5.8	19,878	79.1	89,000	19.9	12.0	553	26.1	78.4	17.6	4.4
41 000	**Oregon**	79.7	8.4	1,447,409	64.7	232,000	25.9	12.3	735	29.9	72.5	22.0	7.4
41 003	Benton	71.1	14.2	32,517	57.0	233,200	23.2	10.2	698	33.4	67.0	17.4	7.6
41 005	Clackamas	83.4	8.7	139,137	71.3	310,200	26.4	12.2	821	29.3	75.5	25.7	5.1
41 007	Clatsop	77.4	10.1	16,076	63.2	218,000	27.3	13.0	643	32.5	71.9	18.7	9.5
41 009	Columbia	86.1	7.2	18,182	79.1	201,200	24.5	12.1	675	22.9	75.8	31.5	4.6
41 011	Coos	79.6	7.4	27,364	67.4	179,400	24.0	13.4	579	28.5	74.8	18.0	8.9
41 013	Crook	82.5	7.9	8,927	69.5	197,600	25.2	11.7	675	24.6	72.5	21.7	2.9
41 015	Curry	83.7	6.8	10,364	67.7	281,200	25.9	11.6	726	29.5	72.8	13.4	5.8
41 017	Deschutes	80.7	8.1	60,302	69.2	313,800	27.2	12.3	843	27.2	77.3	18.7	3.4
41 019	Douglas	81.4	6.9	42,024	69.4	168,800	25.9	11.2	637	27.7	77.3	20.1	6.1
41 027	Hood River	85.5	4.8	7,706	67.2	271,300	25.3	10.3	660	29.4	70.2	16.4	7.4
41 029	Jackson	77.7	8.4	80,058	64.2	275,800	27.9	13.4	756	31.1	77.0	18.5	6.1
41 031	Jefferson	79.3	10.1	7,368	70.5	168,100	29.9	11.1	531	25.8	70.0	20.7	2.8
41 033	Josephine	82.8	7.1	33,545	69.7	253,200	28.4	11.1	680	33.4	80.3	19.9	5.2
41 035	Klamath	80.4	6.4	26,048	69.1	151,400	23.0	12.0	598	29.2	78.6	16.8	5.3
41 039	Lane	76.8	7.9	137,630	62.4	207,100	26.1	12.1	714	31.9	72.5	19.5	7.6
41 041	Lincoln	84.1	8.4	19,623	66.1	205,600	27.0	13.4	625	30.7	71.6	17.8	7.7
41 043	Linn	78.1	8.9	42,994	68.1	163,100	24.7	12.0	673	31.9	77.0	22.5	6.3
41 045	Malheur	79.7	10.2	10,413	66.2	112,600	22.4	10.2	511	22.9	74.6	16.1	5.4
41 047	Marion	78.5	7.6	110,417	63.1	183,900	25.9	13.1	681	29.5	72.0	22.7	5.9
41 051	Multnomah	79.4	7.7	286,953	58.2	248,300	27.3	13.8	746	32.0	64.2	24.0	13.3
41 053	Polk	78.0	10.8	25,586	71.3	200,400	26.2	12.6	671	32.2	77.8	25.3	5.7
41 057	Tillamook	88.5	6.2	10,792	69.6	197,700	25.2	12.0	658	31.9	76.8	18.2	7.8
41 059	Umatilla	79.1	8.4	26,065	64.6	124,800	22.1	10.7	587	24.6	77.3	16.9	7.2
41 061	Union	80.8	7.5	9,782	65.2	135,100	21.4	12.5	565	26.8	76.8	15.3	7.0
41 065	Wasco	86.6	7.2	9,002	68.3	170,600	24.1	11.4	574	25.9	74.8	17.4	5.3
41 067	Washington	79.5	9.2	189,280	63.8	283,900	24.7	11.2	823	27.9	74.2	23.8	5.2
41 071	Yamhill	77.9	11.3	32,833	68.9	215,300	26.1	12.0	767	28.9	74.5	24.2	6.0
42 000	**Pennsylvania**	86.9	5.3	4,858,509	71.7	144,100	23.5	14.0	682	28.7	76.6	25.1	11.2
42 001	Adams	86.3	8.0	37,131	77.2	178,300	25.4	12.4	644	25.7	82.4	26.2	3.6
42 003	Allegheny	86.7	4.0	520,849	68.2	107,900	22.5	14.6	655	29.6	71.9	24.5	14.3
42 005	Armstrong	89.4	4.1	28,803	75.1	86,300	21.8	13.8	513	26.2	80.3	27.1	7.5
42 007	Beaver	88.2	3.9	71,290	75.7	108,400	23.1	14.5	534	26.0	84.5	24.4	7.0
42 009	Bedford	90.6	3.7	19,956	78.6	105,300	23.2	12.7	511	24.9	81.4	27.2	5.8
42 011	Berks	85.7	5.2	149,410	74.1	153,100	23.8	14.4	680	28.0	79.6	23.3	8.3

STATE County code	STATE County	Percent who lived in the same house one year ago	Percent who did not live in county one year ago	Total occupied housing units	Percent owner-occu-pied housing units	Median value of owner-occupied housing units (dollars)	Median selected monthly owner costs as a percentage of household income — With a mortgage	Median selected monthly owner costs as a percentage of household income — Without a mortgage	Median gross rent (dollars)	Median gross rent as a percentage of house-hold income	Percent of workers who drove alone to work	Mean travel time to work (minutes)	Percent of occupied housing units with no vehicle available
ACS table number:		C07204	C07204	B25003	B25003	B25077	B25092	B25092	B25064	B25071	C08301	B08013/ C08012	C25045
		1	2	3	4	5	6	7	8	9	10	11	12
	Pennsylvania—Cont.												
42 013	Blair	87.2	4.2	51,384	72.6	91,100	21.2	13.4	529	27.7	81.4	20.1	9.8
42 015	Bradford	88.3	3.8	24,853	74.5	90,600	23.4	14.3	515	25.3	78.8	22.4	6.2
42 017	Bucks	91.2	4.1	227,650	78.5	315,700	25.7	15.0	944	29.9	82.8	28.2	4.2
42 019	Butler	87.6	5.7	70,878	77.6	146,300	22.5	12.2	654	28.3	83.1	25.9	5.2
42 021	Cambria	87.8	5.1	59,305	73.7	80,500	20.2	13.3	471	26.4	81.6	22.5	10.3
42 025	Carbon	89.0	3.6	24,781	78.1	116,400	23.5	13.8	572	26.5	80.6	29.3	6.3
42 027	Centre	71.3	16.6	51,319	61.5	157,600	23.5	12.2	705	37.2	66.1	19.0	8.7
42 029	Chester	87.1	6.8	173,518	77.8	324,900	24.1	13.5	990	26.4	80.8	27.5	4.5
42 031	Clarion	82.9	9.1	15,969	71.9	90,100	21.0	12.4	510	32.4	79.7	21.6	8.9
42 033	Clearfield	86.4	6.7	33,214	75.7	80,000	22.6	14.2	491	27.2	82.7	24.3	6.6
42 035	Clinton	82.9	8.1	14,971	72.2	94,400	23.5	14.1	550	28.9	76.5	23.2	6.2
42 037	Columbia	85.7	6.9	25,589	71.8	103,800	23.3	13.6	551	28.1	83.0	21.1	7.5
42 039	Crawford	86.7	5.2	34,847	75.6	91,500	23.7	14.5	520	27.5	73.9	20.6	9.8
42 041	Cumberland	84.5	9.0	89,331	73.0	160,800	21.6	11.6	711	26.0	81.8	20.3	4.9
42 043	Dauphin	84.6	5.3	104,500	67.0	137,700	22.8	12.5	689	27.1	78.9	20.6	10.3
42 045	Delaware	88.4	5.7	204,448	72.7	217,500	24.7	16.3	854	29.7	74.1	27.0	10.2
42 047	Elk	93.2	2.4	13,803	78.9	85,000	20.7	13.3	500	23.4	83.6	16.9	6.8
42 049	Erie	82.7	4.5	107,218	70.0	102,600	22.9	13.3	571	29.0	80.4	18.4	9.8
42 051	Fayette	87.3	5.7	58,801	71.2	79,400	22.3	13.3	477	27.9	86.4	24.1	10.0
42 055	Franklin	85.5	6.2	56,376	74.0	158,600	22.7	10.9	603	23.6	79.5	22.9	5.4
42 059	Greene	85.6	6.7	14,509	77.0	76,000	20.0	12.0	468	29.2	82.4	26.8	7.5
42 061	Huntingdon	84.3	9.7	16,717	76.8	96,400	21.6	11.5	466	23.4	75.2	26.9	6.2
42 063	Indiana	81.3	9.7	34,699	72.7	88,800	21.0	12.3	546	37.1	77.1	22.6	7.3
42 065	Jefferson	90.3	3.8	18,792	75.7	74,400	19.9	13.0	470	27.4	83.4	20.2	7.6
42 067	Juniata	90.0	3.5	8,862	75.0	114,200	22.3	11.2	484	19.4	70.8	29.8	6.4
42 069	Lackawanna	86.6	4.9	86,218	65.6	122,700	23.7	16.0	583	27.0	79.8	19.6	10.8
42 071	Lancaster	87.0	4.5	185,001	70.4	169,500	23.7	12.1	737	27.2	78.7	21.7	9.8
42 073	Lawrence	90.3	3.2	36,349	78.5	90,200	22.4	14.5	566	28.8	82.2	20.8	8.4
42 075	Lebanon	87.0	5.2	49,465	74.7	140,800	22.5	11.7	595	25.1	82.6	22.1	7.2
42 077	Lehigh	85.5	6.3	129,391	70.3	184,000	24.1	14.2	769	30.0	82.2	23.7	9.0
42 079	Luzerne	87.0	4.6	129,840	70.9	103,700	22.6	14.8	561	27.8	81.7	21.5	10.2
42 081	Lycoming	85.1	5.1	47,719	68.1	108,700	23.1	14.5	575	28.4	78.5	19.3	8.5
42 083	McKean	85.9	5.8	17,376	74.2	67,600	20.6	13.4	533	27.8	81.3	18.7	9.6
42 085	Mercer	85.9	5.9	46,671	75.5	95,800	22.3	13.7	584	28.8	81.9	19.5	7.4
42 087	Mifflin	87.8	4.6	18,927	72.0	87,400	22.8	14.6	472	23.6	73.9	21.1	9.8
42 089	Monroe	87.2	7.7	59,036	78.1	195,200	26.9	16.6	859	27.9	76.4	38.7	3.7
42 091	Montgomery	88.5	5.7	296,231	75.8	287,000	24.0	14.3	956	28.0	79.8	26.9	5.5
42 095	Northampton	84.2	7.0	109,164	75.6	206,700	24.5	15.0	770	28.8	82.0	26.9	7.1
42 097	Northumberland	88.3	5.9	38,270	73.5	83,600	22.3	12.8	486	26.3	80.7	22.3	10.1
42 099	Perry	90.1	4.8	17,282	82.2	127,500	23.6	12.0	545	23.1	77.5	31.0	5.1
42 101	Philadelphia	86.4	4.3	557,985	57.4	117,500	25.7	15.9	765	33.4	51.2	31.4	34.1
42 103	Pike	89.5	6.9	22,611	84.4	197,900	29.0	15.8	986	32.2	75.7	42.1	4.7
42 107	Schuylkill	86.3	6.3	60,311	76.7	79,800	21.8	14.5	500	24.1	78.5	24.4	9.7
42 109	Snyder	88.0	5.6	13,994	74.9	111,500	22.6	12.3	583	23.7	76.0	21.8	4.6
42 111	Somerset	89.1	4.4	30,995	78.0	85,900	21.9	13.5	476	24.9	79.9	22.7	7.2
42 115	Susquehanna	90.7	4.2	17,384	76.9	113,400	25.5	14.1	532	25.6	79.3	26.8	5.3
42 117	Tioga	86.2	5.9	16,610	74.1	91,800	24.5	14.1	523	27.4	74.2	22.5	5.8
42 119	Union	82.0	13.0	13,549	71.6	129,200	21.8	11.2	586	27.1	75.4	18.7	8.6
42 121	Venango	86.5	4.4	22,699	74.0	70,400	21.5	13.8	516	25.9	78.8	20.2	7.1
42 123	Warren	90.2	3.5	17,758	77.1	78,600	22.1	12.7	470	23.1	79.2	20.9	8.3
42 125	Washington	88.4	4.2	82,946	78.2	122,100	21.7	12.4	514	27.0	83.9	25.3	7.4
42 127	Wayne	89.5	6.9	20,552	79.2	160,900	25.3	15.2	602	27.4	76.7	26.7	5.6
42 129	Westmoreland	90.5	4.0	150,612	77.6	118,000	22.1	13.7	544	27.0	84.1	24.9	7.3
42 131	Wyoming	89.4	4.0	11,074	78.8	128,100	23.3	14.6	595	23.4	80.5	24.5	4.0
42 133	York	87.0	5.0	162,264	77.3	156,300	23.7	13.7	688	26.1	83.5	25.1	5.7
44 000	**Rhode Island**	86.6	5.4	404,549	63.3	289,400	26.7	16.0	833	29.3	80.8	22.7	8.4
44 001	Bristol	87.4	7.5	18,783	72.3	371,400	26.4	17.7	865	29.3	81.1	24.9	4.5
44 003	Kent	89.5	5.2	68,696	74.4	249,900	26.6	16.0	858	27.9	87.5	23.1	5.3
44 005	Newport	88.0	6.6	33,675	65.3	403,600	25.6	14.8	898	26.5	80.0	22.0	7.1
44 007	Providence	85.8	4.7	233,792	56.7	271,300	27.8	16.5	813	30.0	78.8	22.3	10.9
44 009	Washington	85.9	7.1	49,603	74.3	356,400	24.3	14.5	886	28.8	81.6	23.2	3.5
45 000	**South Carolina**	83.4	7.7	1,664,561	70.3	122,600	22.7	11.4	648	28.6	81.2	23.3	7.3
45 001	Abbeville	85.2	6.9	9,468	78.6	81,100	23.9	14.2	481	40.6	76.0	25.2	7.9
45 003	Aiken	86.8	5.6	58,988	74.0	106,600	19.6	10.7	594	28.7	82.1	23.5	7.1
45 007	Anderson	82.6	6.2	68,821	74.3	107,300	21.8	10.6	577	29.5	84.2	22.7	6.4
45 011	Barnwell	91.7	5.1	8,590	75.4	66,600	19.0	13.8	485	29.0	79.1	36.7	14.5
45 013	Beaufort	78.2	10.8	56,539	69.1	302,300	27.9	11.5	934	29.2	74.1	20.2	6.0
45 015	Berkeley	82.9	11.0	55,150	72.1	137,500	22.9	11.8	764	24.6	82.4	25.7	4.5
45 019	Charleston	80.9	8.7	137,878	62.8	227,000	26.1	13.7	810	29.9	79.7	21.7	8.7
45 021	Cherokee	88.1	3.2	20,532	71.2	79,400	20.9	9.6	499	25.9	84.3	22.8	8.9
45 023	Chester	91.8	3.5	12,700	75.7	81,900	23.4	12.3	489	37.1	82.1	27.1	10.6
45 025	Chesterfield	89.7	5.5	16,110	72.9	79,300	20.6	12.1	482	25.8	78.5	25.2	10.8
45 027	Clarendon	91.6	4.9	12,994	76.7	78,100	24.6	12.2	488	24.2	79.5	26.1	9.5
45 029	Colleton	87.9	4.2	14,257	75.3	86,300	23.8	13.4	537	30.4	78.6	32.8	8.6

Table C-2. Counties — Where: Migration, Housing, and Transportation, 2005–2007—*Continued*

STATE County code	STATE County	Percent who lived in the same house one year ago	Percent who did not live in county one year ago	Total occupied housing units	Percent owner-occupied housing units	Median value of owner-occupied housing units (dollars)	Median selected monthly owner costs as a percentage of household income — With a mortgage	Without a mortgage	Median gross rent (dollars)	Median gross rent as a percentage of household income	Percent of workers who drove alone to work	Mean travel time to work (minutes)	Percent of occupied housing units with no vehicle available
ACS table number:		C07204	C07204	B25003	B25003	B25077	B25092	B25092	B25064	B25071	C08301	B08013/ C08012	C25045
		1	2	3	4	5	6	7	8	9	10	11	12
	South Carolina—Cont.												
45 031	Darlington	87.1	4.0	24,122	76.7	76,700	21.8	10.2	534	26.4	79.3	22.0	6.8
45 033	Dillon	82.4	7.6	11,579	63.4	58,500	23.6	13.9	459	27.1	81.4	21.6	14.5
45 035	Dorchester	82.5	10.5	41,571	73.6	158,400	24.2	12.1	832	27.8	84.0	27.1	6.9
45 037	Edgefield	89.2	7.3	8,877	77.0	101,600	19.7	9.7	504	28.5	84.8	26.6	8.0
45 039	Fairfield	96.5	1.4	8,075	75.1	90,000	24.4	14.9	515	26.6	85.0	28.5	9.9
45 041	Florence	83.2	5.8	48,556	68.4	99,400	21.4	11.2	581	27.7	81.8	21.9	9.1
45 043	Georgetown	89.4	6.0	22,541	68.3	165,300	24.7	13.6	608	31.1	82.4	24.2	8.0
45 045	Greenville	81.1	7.6	162,936	68.3	137,600	22.1	10.7	639	27.0	82.5	21.0	6.3
45 047	Greenwood	82.6	8.0	25,726	70.3	96,600	21.6	10.2	558	26.2	85.7	20.3	6.4
45 049	Hampton	89.2	4.1	7,261	74.1	70,500	21.5	13.2	539	25.1	78.9	34.5	11.3
45 051	Horry	81.2	9.6	105,192	70.7	157,900	24.3	12.2	734	28.8	81.9	20.5	5.7
45 053	Jasper	86.1	8.8	7,306	68.0	121,400	28.3	12.6	738	31.2	77.1	30.5	7.7
45 055	Kershaw	89.5	4.5	22,082	79.4	100,900	19.8	10.8	561	25.5	82.6	26.6	6.1
45 057	Lancaster	90.0	4.8	25,393	73.9	107,200	22.5	10.9	590	27.9	85.9	27.5	6.7
45 059	Laurens	83.8	7.4	26,163	70.8	85,500	21.9	11.1	560	32.4	76.5	24.2	10.6
45 063	Lexington	83.8	8.1	93,870	75.2	127,500	21.7	10.5	685	27.6	82.9	24.5	3.9
45 067	Marion	84.5	5.3	12,684	63.8	72,800	21.9	11.5	511	29.3	76.8	23.8	10.8
45 069	Marlboro	81.0	7.4	9,685	67.9	55,700	25.0	14.6	502	33.1	78.0	21.6	16.9
45 071	Newberry	87.7	4.2	13,647	77.7	92,000	21.6	11.8	541	33.7	79.1	23.1	6.8
45 073	Oconee	87.8	4.9	28,990	79.0	113,600	20.3	10.7	519	26.5	82.7	23.4	4.3
45 075	Orangeburg	86.3	5.5	34,122	68.8	75,500	23.3	12.3	539	33.1	84.0	23.9	10.9
45 077	Pickens	81.6	9.9	43,954	70.7	116,000	20.7	9.4	593	30.5	83.4	24.2	4.9
45 079	Richland	75.8	14.0	134,542	63.1	137,700	22.7	10.9	715	29.6	74.8	21.7	8.2
45 083	Spartanburg	84.1	5.7	104,536	72.1	107,300	22.2	9.4	577	27.3	84.6	21.4	7.7
45 085	Sumter	91.2	3.6	38,817	67.2	89,900	22.1	12.1	574	27.4	83.9	22.4	8.7
45 087	Union	87.3	4.3	11,286	73.2	66,400	22.9	12.4	489	23.9	83.4	24.4	11.0
45 089	Williamsburg	92.7	2.4	12,140	58.3	62,600	23.9	13.0	398	35.2	78.8	27.8	14.4
45 091	York	81.9	7.7	74,915	72.2	147,100	22.2	10.2	706	28.6	82.2	24.7	4.6
46 000	**South Dakota**	82.9	7.6	311,644	69.1	110,900	22.0	11.9	533	25.3	77.3	16.2	5.1
46 011	Brookings	75.9	12.6	11,710	59.2	123,600	22.2	10.7	535	28.7	75.4	12.4	3.9
46 013	Brown	83.5	6.7	14,669	66.5	97,300	19.6	13.0	457	23.6	80.0	12.2	6.6
46 029	Codington	80.5	5.6	11,128	66.0	116,500	21.2	10.7	536	26.9	80.4	13.5	5.5
46 081	Lawrence	80.5	8.5	10,035	63.0	142,300	24.6	12.5	481	27.8	74.9	18.4	7.9
46 083	Lincoln	83.9	7.3	10,779	79.3	164,100	22.1	9.4	734	24.3	85.7	18.7	3.7
46 093	Meade	80.3	12.6	9,741	71.2	131,600	24.9	12.0	624	25.5	75.7	20.4	2.7
46 099	Minnehaha	80.4	6.7	67,415	67.6	136,700	22.4	12.3	628	26.7	84.7	16.4	5.2
46 103	Pennington	78.0	9.8	37,678	69.9	136,200	23.7	12.7	635	28.0	81.7	17.1	4.0
46 135	Yankton	81.9	7.3	8,716	66.7	98,300	21.5	11.7	474	24.9	76.4	13.2	7.6
47 000	**Tennessee**	82.9	6.6	2,382,975	70.1	122,500	22.8	10.7	626	28.4	83.3	23.6	6.3
47 001	Anderson	83.6	8.4	30,844	73.7	106,400	22.1	11.4	573	26.0	85.8	22.9	6.7
47 003	Bedford	83.7	5.5	15,561	67.9	104,700	22.5	11.4	568	26.7	78.6	23.6	5.4
47 009	Blount	84.3	7.0	46,279	76.9	140,800	22.2	9.3	616	25.8	84.6	23.2	4.8
47 011	Bradley	81.8	7.1	37,402	67.6	124,700	22.7	9.9	566	28.7	86.6	20.2	4.7
47 013	Campbell	89.2	3.7	15,509	74.1	75,800	23.7	13.0	442	28.5	85.5	28.0	8.6
47 017	Carroll	87.8	6.7	11,529	79.3	72,400	21.9	12.5	492	21.6	87.0	22.3	5.2
47 019	Carter	84.2	5.9	23,549	71.5	88,100	21.8	10.5	445	23.5	83.9	21.9	7.2
47 021	Cheatham	87.8	8.2	14,054	79.6	146,600	23.1	8.7	665	33.6	80.2	31.3	3.1
47 025	Claiborne	88.0	4.2	12,445	79.0	81,700	22.6	9.7	403	32.7	85.7	25.4	7.8
47 029	Cocke	91.7	2.5	14,068	74.8	84,400	23.9	10.3	471	27.1	84.7	27.8	4.5
47 031	Coffee	83.6	6.7	20,309	71.3	109,500	23.7	11.1	571	26.6	85.5	23.3	5.6
47 035	Cumberland	85.1	7.0	20,418	79.3	114,200	23.5	9.8	525	28.5	79.1	23.5	4.6
47 037	Davidson	80.7	7.4	248,006	60.3	153,000	24.1	11.5	723	28.9	81.1	23.2	7.5
47 043	Dickson	83.5	7.1	18,161	75.9	121,500	23.3	10.9	605	25.0	80.2	30.4	5.2
47 045	Dyer	84.6	3.8	14,849	66.3	85,700	21.7	13.6	552	25.3	88.9	18.5	5.8
47 047	Fayette	85.2	9.2	12,060	75.8	163,700	22.1	9.2	599	24.3	80.1	33.0	6.0
47 051	Franklin	85.0	5.5	15,747	79.3	104,500	21.9	11.8	566	24.6	83.2	22.3	4.9
47 053	Gibson	84.4	5.1	20,148	71.8	83,400	21.7	12.9	495	30.1	86.0	20.7	8.2
47 055	Giles	86.4	4.6	11,712	76.2	97,000	21.0	12.0	516	28.5	88.2	26.7	6.3
47 057	Grainger	88.4	7.8	8,186	84.8	95,400	23.3	10.7	446	19.8	81.3	30.0	6.2
47 059	Greene	85.4	4.7	26,906	72.1	91,400	22.1	9.9	460	23.6	85.0	21.9	5.0
47 063	Hamblen	83.4	5.9	24,358	68.4	109,000	21.8	8.8	532	26.8	83.3	20.6	4.6
47 065	Hamilton	82.9	6.2	132,102	67.5	137,500	22.1	9.9	613	27.4	82.8	21.1	7.6
47 069	Hardeman	86.3	6.2	9,518	74.3	78,400	27.0	13.4	471	26.4	79.6	29.1	8.4
47 071	Hardin	86.9	5.5	10,402	74.7	81,800	23.0	10.0	411	26.0	84.6	20.9	5.6
47 073	Hawkins	83.9	7.4	22,513	75.5	91,900	22.6	9.9	466	25.5	88.0	22.8	6.8
47 077	Henderson	83.4	6.0	10,582	74.6	80,100	20.5	9.9	498	25.7	83.4	23.7	5.0
47 079	Henry	84.5	6.0	13,348	75.5	88,700	22.6	9.8	483	22.8	84.1	21.8	6.4
47 081	Hickman	84.0	8.9	8,382	75.8	97,400	21.5	10.2	532	28.3	74.8	36.6	5.5
47 089	Jefferson	82.5	10.6	19,077	76.3	110,100	21.1	9.6	566	29.7	82.1	25.7	3.6
47 093	Knox	80.4	7.1	173,713	67.5	140,300	22.0	9.9	638	28.5	84.7	21.1	6.0
47 097	Lauderdale	77.4	6.5	9,225	65.3	75,000	20.3	13.3	486	31.1	86.3	23.1	8.2
47 099	Lawrence	86.1	4.2	15,131	77.8	87,200	21.9	11.8	504	25.0	85.5	26.8	5.7
47 103	Lincoln	88.5	4.7	13,236	78.2	98,200	19.9	11.3	494	24.4	83.2	27.2	5.5
47 105	Loudon	84.0	9.8	17,845	76.3	148,200	23.4	8.9	600	28.9	81.2	22.3	4.7

Table C-2. Counties — Where: Migration, Housing, and Transportation, 2005–2007—Continued

STATE County code	STATE County	Percent who lived in the same house one year ago	Percent who did not live in county one year ago	Total occupied housing units	Percent owner-occupied housing units	Median value of owner-occupied housing units (dollars)	Median selected monthly owner costs as a percentage of household income		Median gross rent (dollars)	Median gross rent as a percentage of household income	Percent of workers who drove alone to work	Mean travel time to work (minutes)	Percent of occupied housing units with no vehicle available
							With a mortgage	Without a mortgage					
	ACS table number:	C07204	C07204	B25003	B25003	B25077	B25092	B25092	B25064	B25071	C08301	B08013/ C08012	C25045
		1	2	3	4	5	6	7	8	9	10	11	12
	Tennessee—Cont.												
47 107	McMinn	83.8	7.8	20,503	72.6	98,200	21.4	11.4	502	25.3	80.9	21.3	5.1
47 109	McNairy	89.1	3.7	9,946	84.1	76,100	21.5	12.8	453	28.7	81.9	22.3	4.1
47 111	Macon	87.2	4.9	8,064	75.4	87,000	24.7	9.9	453	29.8	77.1	30.7	5.7
47 113	Madison	82.1	6.4	38,374	66.6	110,500	22.7	11.4	652	34.5	88.0	19.4	8.0
47 115	Marion	87.4	5.0	11,855	77.1	94,800	23.0	11.2	556	20.8	82.1	25.9	4.7
47 117	Marshall	84.8	7.0	11,362	73.1	101,600	23.3	10.0	572	27.3	88.7	27.6	4.8
47 119	Maury	81.7	8.4	30,989	73.3	127,200	22.8	10.4	629	27.2	84.0	27.8	4.9
47 123	Monroe	83.7	6.1	16,197	77.2	96,100	21.6	10.1	456	26.1	85.1	26.2	4.5
47 125	Montgomery	75.6	13.1	57,090	66.5	115,700	21.2	9.1	664	25.4	83.2	23.7	3.5
47 129	Morgan	90.4	5.7	7,425	83.1	70,600	23.5	11.1	561	26.1	79.6	31.4	5.7
47 131	Obion	87.1	4.4	13,014	67.2	81,100	20.2	12.1	473	23.2	80.3	19.3	7.0
47 133	Overton	87.1	6.5	8,680	76.1	90,500	22.0	11.8	429	29.8	81.5	25.9	5.4
47 141	Putnam	81.7	8.6	26,813	63.6	117,300	22.8	11.0	534	28.8	83.3	19.6	5.0
47 143	Rhea	79.7	5.9	11,718	73.4	92,800	25.4	9.9	526	26.5	80.6	22.6	5.6
47 145	Roane	86.6	4.5	21,318	80.0	106,700	22.8	10.6	528	29.5	82.9	25.9	5.7
47 147	Robertson	88.6	5.5	22,876	76.8	139,400	23.7	9.7	638	26.5	82.0	28.4	4.4
47 149	Rutherford	80.1	8.7	87,993	69.4	147,900	22.6	9.8	730	29.7	85.8	25.5	2.9
47 151	Scott	86.1	3.8	8,600	69.3	67,700	24.2	11.7	388	22.0	85.7	25.7	6.8
47 155	Sevier	80.3	9.5	31,401	70.9	140,300	23.0	8.5	623	26.1	78.3	24.0	3.7
47 157	Shelby	80.6	4.4	345,026	62.7	127,100	24.8	13.1	736	32.9	83.0	22.4	10.2
47 163	Sullivan	85.0	5.8	66,667	74.7	99,900	20.6	9.8	480	25.9	86.1	20.0	6.0
47 165	Sumner	81.0	9.5	56,519	74.9	157,900	22.7	10.2	693	26.4	82.8	27.3	3.5
47 167	Tipton	84.9	6.2	20,788	77.2	122,600	21.6	10.9	649	27.6	85.6	30.4	3.3
47 177	Warren	86.7	3.0	14,833	70.6	84,600	23.0	11.4	519	27.4	85.2	22.4	4.4
47 179	Washington	81.9	8.3	45,726	69.5	119,900	21.6	9.3	552	24.8	86.8	20.2	5.9
47 183	Weakley	81.5	8.9	13,349	69.8	77,500	19.5	10.1	496	30.6	82.5	19.7	5.6
47 185	White	86.8	3.9	9,457	75.8	86,700	23.6	11.1	468	27.4	81.0	23.2	5.9
47 187	Williamson	85.5	8.6	56,624	82.7	311,600	22.0	8.6	964	27.4	81.3	26.3	2.2
47 189	Wilson	86.5	7.6	38,816	81.4	170,800	22.6	9.2	691	25.3	86.1	27.7	3.1
48 000	**Texas**	80.2	7.8	8,095,025	65.2	113,800	23.6	13.1	725	29.3	78.7	24.7	6.2
48 001	Anderson	79.7	12.8	15,676	71.0	71,400	21.1	14.2	622	27.8	81.5	23.5	3.8
48 005	Angelina	78.0	9.1	29,985	68.1	75,100	20.4	12.4	631	29.6	78.9	20.1	6.6
48 007	Aransas	80.2	10.6	9,917	75.9	111,700	22.0	15.4	639	33.4	72.5	20.0	5.5
48 013	Atascosa	88.7	5.8	13,371	75.6	77,800	19.0	13.0	578	27.1	74.6	32.7	7.9
48 015	Austin	87.0	6.2	9,077	80.6	122,000	21.3	12.7	587	21.2	73.8	25.4	3.3
48 019	Bandera	83.2	9.2	7,323	79.7	142,500	21.7	11.8	593	35.1	71.2	26.7	4.2
48 021	Bastrop	86.9	5.8	21,345	80.9	112,400	25.3	13.0	849	29.0	72.9	32.3	4.3
48 025	Bee	72.0	17.7	9,222	64.4	67,800	21.1	13.0	573	27.5	74.8	19.4	11.0
48 027	Bell	73.2	13.8	94,849	59.9	101,700	22.6	12.3	760	27.7	82.1	18.4	4.5
48 029	Bexar	79.6	6.6	531,371	63.6	100,800	22.6	12.0	705	28.7	78.4	24.0	8.1
48 037	Bowie	79.3	9.1	34,064	66.9	77,500	19.1	11.6	601	28.6	79.6	18.3	7.4
48 039	Brazoria	79.9	9.5	97,781	74.5	127,800	22.1	12.2	742	26.0	82.4	28.8	3.5
48 041	Brazos	68.2	16.7	60,804	47.8	126,300	22.8	12.3	691	39.2	76.3	16.9	6.1
48 049	Brown	87.9	6.5	13,826	70.9	64,900	21.4	14.0	535	29.9	83.2	15.2	7.2
48 053	Burnet	81.4	9.1	15,627	76.7	128,300	26.3	12.4	641	27.0	71.8	25.5	4.8
48 055	Caldwell	74.0	16.7	11,287	68.8	90,400	23.6	13.5	676	29.1	75.7	30.6	5.6
48 057	Calhoun	83.1	8.0	7,972	71.6	74,100	20.6	11.3	596	24.2	81.3	22.6	5.4
48 061	Cameron	87.6	3.5	114,787	67.9	66,900	28.0	14.7	531	32.8	78.0	19.7	10.2
48 067	Cass	86.4	4.6	12,425	74.5	65,900	19.1	11.3	457	24.2	81.7	26.4	6.9
48 071	Chambers	85.9	9.8	11,343	79.8	117,400	22.6	13.3	626	23.0	85.0	27.0	4.0
48 073	Cherokee	85.7	4.5	15,867	74.8	65,500	22.8	13.1	541	33.8	81.0	19.4	4.5
48 085	Collin	81.5	10.1	245,691	70.6	190,900	23.5	12.8	903	26.4	81.3	28.3	2.3
48 089	Colorado	81.6	5.3	7,614	72.1	87,200	21.8	14.4	656	24.9	70.9	24.1	8.0
48 091	Comal	81.8	11.6	36,583	76.1	158,700	22.5	12.5	785	26.1	78.4	28.6	3.9
48 097	Cooke	78.7	9.5	14,003	72.4	105,800	22.3	13.6	698	36.0	74.9	25.6	4.5
48 099	Coryell	73.2	19.7	19,236	57.3	85,400	20.6	11.3	800	27.8	72.0	21.0	4.5
48 113	Dallas	79.8	5.9	819,749	56.4	127,800	26.0	14.3	779	29.5	77.2	25.8	7.4
48 121	Denton	78.0	12.1	196,453	67.7	170,900	23.7	12.8	842	28.6	82.5	27.6	2.7
48 135	Ector	81.0	5.9	45,434	71.8	58,800	19.3	12.1	571	23.2	80.7	18.6	5.8
48 139	Ellis	81.1	9.6	45,019	74.1	129,500	24.4	14.0	814	30.1	81.3	29.3	3.7
48 141	El Paso	85.2	4.7	229,655	65.0	87,600	24.4	12.5	554	31.2	78.8	21.6	9.5
48 143	Erath	76.9	12.2	12,750	60.4	104,400	23.1	15.5	576	27.3	78.6	17.9	2.7
48 147	Fannin	78.0	11.7	11,499	72.4	75,400	21.2	13.7	636	28.1	80.7	28.4	3.9
48 149	Fayette	84.0	6.6	9,232	73.9	103,100	21.2	13.2	620	26.1	79.2	21.5	5.1
48 157	Fort Bend	85.3	8.8	133,209	82.9	161,600	24.0	12.4	966	28.7	81.2	30.5	2.2
48 167	Galveston	80.4	9.2	105,249	67.1	128,400	23.2	14.5	751	28.8	80.1	25.0	6.4
48 171	Gillespie	83.8	6.8	9,154	77.8	172,000	22.4	12.3	747	26.1	68.9	21.7	3.4
48 179	Gray	81.5	9.2	8,201	74.4	49,600	16.5	12.2	527	23.8	80.6	15.5	4.2
48 181	Grayson	81.7	6.7	43,845	70.5	91,100	23.1	14.2	662	27.6	80.3	23.0	5.3
48 183	Gregg	79.4	7.7	44,083	62.9	98,700	19.3	11.8	621	27.1	82.3	19.5	5.9
48 185	Grimes	79.2	14.0	7,479	72.0	94,800	20.2	12.6	580	35.4	76.7	26.9	10.8
48 187	Guadalupe	82.7	12.3	36,322	78.2	121,500	22.2	10.9	691	28.1	81.8	23.6	4.4
48 189	Hale	74.6	12.9	11,964	63.3	66,100	20.3	12.2	490	26.7	78.8	13.9	6.0
48 199	Hardin	84.0	8.5	18,469	78.8	82,700	20.5	10.5	636	21.7	81.3	25.9	4.8
48 201	Harris	79.4	5.9	1,323,191	58.8	126,200	24.2	12.9	758	29.9	76.9	27.6	7.3

Table C-2. Counties — Where: Migration, Housing, and Transportation, 2005–2007—*Continued*

STATE County code	STATE County	Percent who lived in the same house one year ago	Percent who did not live in county one year ago	Total occupied housing units	Percent owner-occupied housing units	Median value of owner-occupied housing units (dollars)	Median selected monthly owner costs as a percentage of household income — With a mortgage	Without a mortgage	Median gross rent (dollars)	Median gross rent as a percentage of household income	Percent of workers who drove alone to work	Mean travel time to work (minutes)	Percent of occupied housing units with no vehicle available
	ACS table number:	C07204	C07204	B25003	B25003	B25077	B25092	B25092	B25064	B25071	C08301	B08013/ C08012	C25045
		1	2	3	4	5	6	7	8	9	10	11	12
	Texas—Cont.												
48 203	Harrison	84.9	8.9	23,209	76.2	84,200	21.7	12.7	569	25.8	82.0	22.6	6.3
48 209	Hays	70.2	17.1	43,153	63.7	165,000	24.0	13.3	758	34.2	77.6	28.1	3.0
48 213	Henderson	82.8	9.1	29,987	77.6	78,700	23.7	15.9	614	27.8	77.3	30.8	4.4
48 215	Hidalgo	83.5	4.8	201,366	70.4	66,200	27.5	14.2	557	34.2	75.8	20.9	8.4
48 217	Hill	84.4	6.0	12,235	75.0	82,400	22.3	15.4	587	27.2	78.1	28.8	5.9
48 219	Hockley	79.9	11.3	8,170	73.6	63,800	19.7	10.3	522	28.7	81.4	18.9	3.6
48 221	Hood	80.8	10.5	17,460	76.8	130,800	23.3	13.5	821	26.2	78.1	32.3	2.5
48 223	Hopkins	80.4	7.7	12,497	69.0	85,600	23.4	14.0	581	28.6	74.3	20.3	6.0
48 225	Houston	82.8	8.0	8,041	71.9	65,800	24.8	16.0	563	28.8	73.6	25.6	7.8
48 227	Howard	73.6	13.7	11,247	68.5	49,600	19.3	10.5	538	32.7	83.8	17.6	4.2
48 231	Hunt	81.9	7.6	29,282	71.1	85,900	22.8	12.9	659	32.6	80.7	27.4	4.2
48 233	Hutchinson	77.7	10.4	8,796	81.0	46,200	19.6	12.7	488	18.9	80.3	16.8	4.3
48 241	Jasper	85.6	7.8	13,399	79.6	69,800	23.5	12.0	530	28.8	83.5	23.8	5.6
48 245	Jefferson	82.2	6.8	90,823	64.4	79,900	20.1	13.0	622	29.3	83.5	18.9	9.3
48 249	Jim Wells	84.0	4.8	13,192	72.0	59,700	22.3	14.3	569	32.4	82.1	22.6	7.8
48 251	Johnson	82.1	9.4	46,920	77.0	104,700	23.8	13.9	753	27.8	81.9	28.9	3.2
48 257	Kaufman	80.6	11.0	27,968	77.9	125,900	24.2	14.4	780	29.4	79.9	31.6	4.0
48 259	Kendall	82.6	11.6	11,129	71.3	199,800	19.9	11.9	848	32.3	74.5	24.2	3.3
48 265	Kerr	76.0	10.3	18,931	72.5	116,500	23.7	12.2	697	28.5	79.8	16.7	3.3
48 273	Kleberg	76.5	9.0	11,016	55.2	64,900	21.1	15.6	640	31.2	76.2	19.8	9.3
48 277	Lamar	82.7	5.3	18,622	70.3	69,600	19.6	14.6	549	28.5	79.5	20.3	10.4
48 281	Lampasas	75.3	13.0	6,890	72.7	110,000	21.9	13.9	705	30.4	82.5	27.6	5.6
48 291	Liberty	80.0	12.6	23,944	76.5	76,800	22.4	11.7	630	24.2	81.8	34.5	7.1
48 293	Limestone	82.5	7.7	7,929	75.3	66,800	19.1	14.3	562	29.5	73.8	22.9	5.3
48 303	Lubbock	73.1	8.4	99,875	59.4	93,400	21.7	11.6	702	32.7	82.5	16.7	5.0
48 309	McLennan	79.5	8.2	80,973	61.8	92,800	23.2	13.4	683	33.1	80.8	18.0	6.7
48 321	Matagorda	85.1	7.4	14,172	68.1	72,400	17.8	12.8	513	26.2	73.3	22.8	9.9
48 323	Maverick	86.0	4.7	12,930	70.4	68,200	27.0	14.0	477	28.3	73.0	17.9	10.7
48 325	Medina	89.7	5.3	12,809	84.6	87,500	21.6	13.3	611	26.9	82.8	29.2	3.7
48 329	Midland	80.6	8.2	46,331	67.4	94,000	20.7	11.5	633	27.8	81.8	17.1	5.1
48 331	Milam	86.5	5.6	9,419	72.1	77,600	22.2	13.3	603	31.7	74.7	23.9	6.7
48 339	Montgomery	80.1	11.1	132,350	76.7	144,000	22.3	12.2	820	28.0	80.3	31.4	3.7
48 341	Moore	74.4	11.0	6,607	69.3	68,100	19.3	10.6	592	21.2	74.2	16.3	2.0
48 347	Nacogdoches	77.6	11.0	22,619	60.8	82,200	23.0	11.6	616	36.0	75.7	19.4	5.9
48 349	Navarro	79.5	10.0	16,261	70.6	75,200	23.9	14.1	625	30.0	76.2	24.6	8.5
48 355	Nueces	79.7	6.6	115,713	61.3	92,100	24.1	14.4	731	32.3	77.3	19.6	7.6
48 361	Orange	84.4	5.1	32,448	76.7	75,400	19.2	11.5	614	34.2	84.1	22.8	7.4
48 363	Palo Pinto	82.4	8.6	10,324	62.8	66,500	23.7	12.8	598	30.3	79.4	22.7	6.8
48 365	Panola	87.6	5.8	8,568	82.2	68,500	19.4	14.7	550	23.3	85.8	25.4	7.6
48 367	Parker	82.3	10.7	34,787	80.6	123,700	23.7	13.5	726	30.0	81.3	29.6	3.1
48 373	Polk	87.1	7.7	16,632	76.5	61,900	25.1	14.3	597	30.3	77.7	29.8	8.7
48 375	Potter	77.0	7.7	41,868	60.4	71,300	23.8	11.4	576	30.5	78.5	16.8	6.2
48 381	Randall	80.7	7.1	42,577	70.1	120,400	21.2	11.8	651	27.9	84.1	16.9	3.4
48 397	Rockwall	80.1	14.0	22,417	84.0	174,900	26.3	14.3	1,168	27.0	76.3	32.7	0.8
48 401	Rusk	81.3	10.5	17,275	78.1	82,200	19.4	11.5	552	25.5	80.2	24.3	4.5
48 407	San Jacinto	88.6	7.1	8,385	83.8	69,400	21.0	13.2	522	27.1	83.6	38.3	6.1
48 409	San Patricio	76.0	10.9	23,450	66.1	83,300	23.1	14.8	707	29.6	78.0	20.1	7.0
48 419	Shelby	89.3	4.3	9,953	79.5	52,600	21.0	12.7	462	27.1	80.3	22.1	7.2
48 423	Smith	79.1	8.2	69,168	69.5	109,700	22.5	13.5	693	33.1	80.9	20.8	5.6
48 427	Starr	86.7	4.4	14,980	75.1	50,000	22.8	15.2	442	30.6	72.2	22.2	12.6
48 439	Tarrant	79.5	7.1	591,745	63.5	127,300	24.0	14.0	776	28.8	82.5	25.2	4.7
48 441	Taylor	75.0	10.4	48,995	61.8	75,400	21.5	12.8	673	30.3	80.7	15.3	4.4
48 449	Titus	81.2	7.6	9,924	68.8	85,900	21.8	11.7	538	24.7	77.5	17.6	4.8
48 451	Tom Green	79.5	9.8	40,887	68.1	81,700	21.3	13.4	623	29.3	77.2	16.7	6.4
48 453	Travis	74.7	9.4	368,578	54.1	178,900	24.6	12.3	816	29.1	73.6	23.6	6.2
48 457	Tyler	85.0	8.9	8,267	80.4	73,100	19.7	12.4	548	37.0	82.3	32.1	6.3
48 459	Upshur	83.6	8.7	13,391	80.3	79,800	22.2	11.1	526	21.9	79.4	28.8	4.1
48 463	Uvalde	84.6	8.2	8,480	76.6	60,100	22.4	13.5	655	31.0	78.5	18.6	7.0
48 465	Val Verde	84.2	7.0	14,789	65.9	69,600	21.7	13.7	548	34.6	79.5	16.3	7.3
48 467	Van Zandt	82.6	9.3	18,991	77.8	89,300	23.0	13.6	620	28.1	80.1	34.7	3.0
48 469	Victoria	78.2	7.2	31,531	65.4	86,600	21.1	12.2	644	28.3	77.6	20.0	7.8
48 471	Walker	70.3	21.8	19,226	55.7	89,600	24.7	13.5	696	37.1	80.0	20.7	7.9
48 473	Waller	79.1	9.6	12,511	66.2	102,200	25.3	12.9	671	49.0	71.4	33.1	5.5
48 477	Washington	81.9	9.7	12,167	71.2	122,000	22.1	9.9	677	39.1	76.6	22.0	6.8
48 479	Webb	83.9	4.4	60,859	64.4	95,100	27.6	15.0	617	34.5	76.0	19.7	9.8
48 481	Wharton	87.2	5.3	15,031	69.6	81,400	22.3	13.1	604	25.2	81.2	23.7	6.1
48 485	Wichita	74.3	11.6	48,641	63.1	81,100	22.0	12.8	642	31.4	79.1	15.7	6.2
48 489	Willacy	93.0	5.3	5,836	68.5	39,700	29.2	16.7	572	21.5	-	17.3	7.6
48 491	Williamson	79.0	11.9	116,012	73.1	162,400	24.0	12.7	907	28.1	79.2	27.0	2.6
48 493	Wilson	83.3	9.1	11,502	81.3	110,900	21.1	9.4	623	19.4	78.5	29.9	2.7
48 497	Wise	85.1	9.7	17,829	80.8	110,700	22.5	12.4	744	23.8	78.4	30.3	3.0
48 499	Wood	79.3	13.1	15,054	80.5	85,500	21.5	11.9	600	24.8	72.8	29.2	3.6
49 000	**Utah**	79.5	8.3	812,604	71.9	189,700	24.2	9.3	719	27.6	75.4	20.9	4.2
49 003	Box Elder	80.7	6.0	14,789	79.5	139,800	22.8	8.4	603	23.5	73.4	20.5	2.0
49 005	Cache	74.2	11.1	31,340	66.6	159,300	23.5	8.0	613	28.9	70.9	16.3	4.4

STATE County code	STATE County	Percent who lived in the same house one year ago	Percent who did not live in county one year ago	Total occupied housing units	Percent owner-occupied housing units	Median value of owner-occupied housing units (dollars)	Median selected monthly owner costs as a percentage of household income — With a mortgage	Without a mortgage	Median gross rent (dollars)	Median gross rent as a percentage of household income	Percent of workers who drove alone to work	Mean travel time to work (minutes)	Percent of occupied housing units with no vehicle available
ACS table number:		C07204	C07204	B25003	B25003	B25077	B25092	B25092	B25064	B25071	C08301	B08013/ C08012	C25045
		1	2	3	4	5	6	7	8	9	10	11	12
	Utah—Cont.												
49 011	Davis	82.0	9.4	84,524	78.5	195,100	23.1	8.1	727	25.8	79.8	22.3	2.8
49 021	Iron	69.4	17.0	13,774	60.9	189,600	24.9	11.0	605	26.6	73.8	15.0	4.6
49 035	Salt Lake	79.8	6.4	324,945	69.5	206,400	24.8	9.9	750	28.1	75.9	21.6	5.3
49 039	Sanpete	81.4	12.0	6,886	83.1	125,000	25.9	10.3	544	25.2	69.1	19.7	2.4
49 043	Summit	85.9	9.1	11,740	78.8	448,900	24.8	8.3	951	23.6	74.7	24.2	3.7
49 045	Tooele	84.2	9.2	15,980	78.5	158,400	22.6	8.6	743	24.8	69.5	27.6	3.3
49 047	Uintah	78.9	8.6	9,143	78.1	154,900	19.1	7.4	613	25.8	78.2	19.9	2.7
49 049	Utah	77.2	9.3	125,843	69.1	209,400	25.1	8.9	705	28.5	72.0	19.8	2.4
49 051	Wasatch	79.3	10.2	6,604	77.0	255,300	24.9	11.5	942	27.1	79.0	20.4	1.4
49 053	Washington	75.1	11.9	43,121	71.4	233,900	25.8	9.8	875	29.8	75.4	18.6	3.4
49 057	Weber	80.9	7.5	73,435	75.0	147,600	23.5	9.1	662	26.0	79.1	21.7	5.0
50 000	**Vermont**	85.0	6.8	250,871	72.2	191,500	25.0	16.2	733	29.9	75.0	21.2	6.1
50 001	Addison	88.6	5.8	13,463	76.8	191,400	24.7	14.9	745	30.4	69.5	21.7	4.4
50 003	Bennington	86.5	7.0	15,420	73.5	185,600	24.1	15.6	661	28.7	77.6	17.1	5.5
50 005	Caledonia	82.5	7.1	12,622	67.7	137,300	23.5	18.6	576	26.5	77.1	21.2	8.1
50 007	Chittenden	82.0	8.0	59,159	69.4	238,500	25.0	14.9	889	32.5	73.4	19.8	6.2
50 011	Franklin	86.0	4.9	18,219	75.7	185,700	26.3	16.6	752	29.7	73.3	26.0	5.3
50 015	Lamoille	84.1	5.9	10,072	70.2	202,800	26.2	18.2	752	30.9	75.5	23.9	6.2
50 017	Orange	90.9	4.8	11,544	78.9	175,100	24.3	16.1	735	28.4	74.5	26.4	3.4
50 019	Orleans	88.2	4.6	10,540	76.8	128,600	23.3	18.2	586	31.9	80.2	21.5	6.1
50 021	Rutland	85.6	5.9	25,987	70.4	154,200	26.0	16.7	650	27.8	78.8	19.4	6.9
50 023	Washington	85.7	6.4	24,371	70.9	177,200	24.1	16.4	739	28.5	75.0	20.9	6.4
50 025	Windham	85.3	8.0	18,847	70.4	191,200	26.2	16.0	693	29.8	72.5	20.4	7.1
50 027	Windsor	84.2	9.0	24,884	73.9	194,800	26.2	16.9	748	31.0	76.2	20.4	6.1
51 000	**Virginia**	83.1	10.1	2,909,223	69.7	238,600	24.0	10.9	875	28.2	77.2	26.8	6.2
51 001	Accomack	87.5	4.9	14,921	77.6	129,400	23.0	13.1	586	21.8	75.8	18.4	7.6
51 003	Albemarle	75.7	16.2	37,012	63.8	322,700	23.1	9.3	944	27.9	75.1	21.2	4.0
51 009	Amherst	82.7	10.8	12,728	76.1	124,500	20.0	9.0	554	26.6	81.6	22.9	7.9
51 013	Arlington	79.7	12.7	89,525	51.1	585,000	23.3	10.7	1,350	26.1	54.0	25.6	11.1
51 015	Augusta	91.2	3.6	27,368	79.4	167,000	22.6	11.1	653	28.2	83.9	22.3	3.1
51 019	Bedford	89.0	7.7	27,002	82.2	165,000	21.5	8.6	550	21.0	85.2	26.6	3.2
51 023	Botetourt	91.1	4.4	12,772	89.2	177,700	20.5	9.3	603	21.7	85.8	25.7	1.8
51 027	Buchanan	94.6	2.6	9,193	81.4	62,900	19.9	9.4	410	34.3	81.0	26.9	11.8
51 031	Campbell	85.6	8.2	21,802	74.9	114,100	19.7	9.4	530	24.6	86.2	24.2	5.4
51 033	Caroline	89.4	8.3	9,729	82.6	206,100	24.2	11.3	818	32.4	73.1	35.2	4.0
51 035	Carroll	88.9	4.9	12,746	73.8	94,000	23.1	9.1	437	20.6	78.2	25.5	6.6
51 041	Chesterfield	85.7	8.2	108,690	78.9	209,400	22.3	9.0	919	27.1	85.7	24.4	2.2
51 047	Culpeper	83.5	8.9	16,344	69.9	331,900	26.4	11.5	882	30.2	77.0	37.4	5.3
51 053	Dinwiddie	-	-	9,454	79.2	137,300	22.3	10.7	786	23.0	87.5	29.7	4.3
51 059	Fairfax	84.7	9.1	365,093	74.7	554,900	24.0	10.1	1,387	28.4	72.9	31.1	3.8
51 061	Fauquier	89.0	6.5	22,118	79.7	407,800	23.5	11.2	1,025	27.9	78.0	38.2	3.0
51 065	Fluvanna	88.2	8.3	9,332	79.7	227,100	23.2	13.8	990	22.0	81.5	29.1	6.2
51 067	Franklin	85.7	7.2	20,702	81.3	142,900	24.2	8.2	536	20.1	81.7	27.4	4.0
51 069	Frederick	86.1	7.9	26,544	79.1	259,600	24.6	11.4	961	26.2	83.2	30.2	3.5
51 073	Gloucester	85.7	7.9	14,379	79.9	201,200	23.4	9.1	684	27.3	80.6	29.6	3.3
51 075	Goochland	-	-	7,027	84.0	281,800	21.7	11.0	836	22.8	80.0	31.0	1.8
51 083	Halifax	88.9	5.0	14,467	76.5	86,300	22.8	12.8	485	27.5	84.2	26.0	11.4
51 085	Hanover	90.0	6.9	35,484	83.9	245,900	22.1	9.4	896	23.8	85.4	25.4	2.7
51 087	Henrico	81.7	9.1	116,621	67.2	210,800	23.6	10.4	879	28.3	84.0	21.2	4.9
51 089	Henry	87.9	4.5	22,956	77.3	83,400	21.2	10.8	506	25.5	78.4	23.3	6.5
51 093	Isle of Wight	88.6	8.0	13,576	81.2	224,300	22.5	12.5	658	24.4	82.8	28.3	4.6
51 095	James City	82.5	12.1	24,569	75.3	310,500	23.8	9.6	946	29.6	80.7	25.2	4.2
51 099	King George	80.7	16.3	7,693	77.0	308,800	23.1	7.8	904	29.3	81.6	35.2	2.4
51 105	Lee	86.8	4.3	9,413	71.3	69,800	19.7	10.4	386	19.6	82.4	22.9	12.4
51 107	Loudoun	84.0	10.4	85,657	83.5	541,700	27.0	12.0	1,362	29.7	78.6	32.9	1.9
51 109	Louisa	89.1	6.5	12,783	77.3	191,000	24.5	12.1	746	28.6	80.6	35.4	4.6
51 117	Mecklenburg	91.0	5.7	12,755	72.9	95,800	26.0	11.9	541	23.9	81.2	23.9	7.5
51 121	Montgomery	67.5	15.6	32,106	57.0	165,400	22.2	8.7	659	34.8	75.5	17.9	5.6
51 137	Orange	83.9	10.2	12,114	75.8	248,700	25.2	10.8	779	26.0	79.1	35.3	4.1
51 139	Page	85.6	3.9	9,755	72.4	147,800	23.2	12.4	602	25.9	76.8	37.1	4.2
51 143	Pittsylvania	90.0	4.6	25,419	79.7	92,700	22.2	12.3	529	25.0	83.8	26.2	5.8
51 145	Powhatan	79.9	19.0	8,076	90.3	264,600	22.1	9.5	889	21.6	80.6	31.5	1.7
51 147	Prince Edward	82.8	10.9	6,721	64.6	127,500	25.6	11.3	634	25.9	75.8	23.0	7.0
51 149	Prince George	80.1	16.4	10,532	71.5	172,700	22.6	10.4	780	22.7	77.4	20.4	1.4
51 153	Prince William	81.3	10.4	121,993	75.1	421,300	27.1	10.4	1,227	29.4	70.4	39.0	2.9
51 155	Pulaski	85.3	6.4	14,887	71.6	98,100	19.5	10.2	484	25.1	87.4	20.9	8.0
51 161	Roanoke	86.1	10.0	36,831	79.3	165,400	21.4	9.9	681	24.4	86.7	19.9	3.1
51 163	Rockbridge	87.5	5.5	9,296	74.1	173,900	25.3	11.9	579	27.5	76.2	22.9	3.0
51 165	Rockingham	87.4	6.2	28,507	73.9	175,200	23.2	8.9	630	24.0	79.6	21.1	6.1
51 167	Russell	86.7	7.2	12,224	74.9	80,000	21.3	9.5	439	32.1	85.2	26.5	7.5
51 169	Scott	88.1	5.7	10,057	75.8	75,800	19.0	8.9	394	25.3	81.2	27.2	9.3
51 171	Shenandoah	86.5	6.7	16,749	70.2	200,300	23.7	9.8	666	22.9	81.4	30.4	5.5
51 173	Smyth	87.5	3.9	13,355	73.9	84,400	20.0	8.9	445	21.4	82.3	23.8	9.5
51 177	Spotsylvania	85.9	9.2	40,856	81.6	328,900	25.3	9.8	1,154	28.7	77.2	39.1	3.5

Table C-2. Counties — Where: Migration, Housing, and Transportation, 2005–2007—*Continued*

STATE County code	STATE County	Percent who lived in the same house one year ago	Percent who did not live in county one year ago	Total occupied housing units	Percent owner-occupied housing units	Median value of owner-occupied housing units (dollars)	Median selected monthly owner costs as a percentage of household income — With a mortgage	Without a mortgage	Median gross rent (dollars)	Median gross rent as a percentage of household income	Percent of workers who drove alone to work	Mean travel time to work (minutes)	Percent of occupied housing units with no vehicle available
ACS table number:		C07204	C07204	B25003	B25003	B25077	B25092	B25092	B25064	B25071	C08301	B08013/C08012	C25045
		1	2	3	4	5	6	7	8	9	10	11	12
	Virginia—Cont.												
51 179	Stafford	82.9	13.7	38,866	78.8	386,900	25.2	10.2	1,197	28.4	76.5	40.3	1.7
51 185	Tazewell	85.6	4.5	17,756	73.8	71,500	20.4	10.5	466	26.6	81.1	24.0	8.8
51 187	Warren	84.7	7.6	13,470	77.0	249,000	23.7	11.3	676	24.5	77.0	38.1	3.3
51 191	Washington	85.8	6.3	22,136	75.5	111,000	21.4	9.1	541	30.4	81.3	21.8	4.8
51 195	Wise	83.6	6.6	16,025	69.2	71,700	19.0	9.7	486	28.2	86.1	22.4	11.0
51 197	Wythe	84.7	5.9	11,986	73.7	92,500	20.8	9.1	498	25.1	78.2	21.9	5.1
51 199	York	82.4	13.2	22,816	76.9	309,000	21.9	10.0	1,057	24.1	77.4	22.2	1.8
51 510	Alexandria city	79.1	15.3	62,309	47.5	527,300	24.5	12.2	1,211	27.0	63.4	28.9	10.9
51 540	Charlottesville city	68.1	26.2	16,694	46.0	242,700	28.3	14.6	791	34.6	60.5	15.2	14.7
51 550	Chesapeake city	85.3	9.7	77,808	75.1	241,600	25.6	11.6	903	28.7	84.9	23.7	4.3
51 590	Danville city	81.0	9.4	19,972	55.6	84,200	21.8	12.8	527	29.4	80.2	16.1	17.6
51 600	Fairfax city	86.5	10.4	8,311	76.6	523,100	24.8	8.5	1,430	27.5	76.2	30.6	4.5
51 630	Fredericksburg city	74.6	18.7	8,560	37.5	301,800	23.0	9.3	954	34.8	70.1	27.9	13.3
51 650	Hampton city	81.8	10.4	54,650	60.4	164,900	25.0	13.6	825	28.5	81.4	22.2	6.8
51 660	Harrisonburg city	62.0	36.2	13,920	39.2	181,200	21.5	9.3	694	30.4	73.2	14.1	8.5
51 670	Hopewell city	82.6	10.3	8,740	51.4	108,200	22.9	11.5	691	25.8	82.6	21.2	13.3
51 680	Lynchburg city	77.4	14.4	25,903	59.4	120,800	22.6	11.7	603	26.8	79.1	16.6	14.6
51 683	Manassas city	80.2	17.6	11,703	69.7	377,600	24.8	12.3	1,153	34.7	74.3	32.1	4.5
51 700	Newport News city	76.2	13.7	73,274	52.6	172,700	24.6	12.1	808	30.0	78.8	21.9	10.0
51 710	Norfolk city	75.7	13.2	85,129	47.0	181,400	27.1	14.2	765	29.9	67.5	21.3	11.9
51 730	Petersburg city	87.1	6.1	12,447	51.0	97,200	23.0	15.1	707	27.7	78.6	19.6	15.2
51 740	Portsmouth city	80.9	11.8	38,848	62.2	155,200	28.2	14.7	813	30.9	77.8	23.0	9.6
51 760	Richmond city	78.1	11.1	81,611	47.7	179,100	25.9	15.1	742	31.3	71.8	20.8	19.0
51 770	Roanoke city	81.4	8.7	41,822	59.2	116,000	23.7	13.4	601	28.1	81.3	18.1	12.6
51 775	Salem city	80.5	14.6	9,680	69.6	146,100	21.9	10.8	663	25.6	83.5	17.8	5.4
51 790	Staunton city	78.7	19.3	9,712	59.5	141,200	22.3	11.2	581	28.5	80.4	18.8	7.7
51 800	Suffolk city	83.5	9.4	29,858	71.3	229,900	24.5	11.6	720	29.8	81.9	27.4	6.5
51 810	Virginia Beach city	80.3	10.3	161,814	68.6	253,500	25.5	11.9	1,054	29.8	80.8	22.5	3.1
51 820	Waynesboro city	81.6	13.8	8,595	61.5	153,300	21.9	8.4	611	29.3	84.4	19.8	8.5
51 840	Winchester city	77.8	18.6	10,026	50.8	247,200	23.1	12.8	852	27.9	79.0	19.7	7.9
53 000	**Washington**	80.0	7.9	2,472,477	65.6	261,200	26.1	12.1	799	29.1	73.1	25.3	6.5
53 003	Asotin	82.6	6.6	8,561	71.1	137,100	24.4	9.9	604	32.9	80.4	15.2	6.9
53 005	Benton	78.9	9.2	56,720	71.0	154,600	22.2	9.4	705	29.0	79.7	21.1	4.6
53 007	Chelan	82.7	7.4	25,901	68.2	194,000	24.1	10.2	598	26.5	74.5	17.8	5.9
53 009	Clallam	82.9	7.8	30,593	69.8	214,800	24.8	12.3	732	30.6	73.1	19.3	6.4
53 011	Clark	80.1	7.9	147,270	70.0	249,000	26.2	12.2	809	29.9	78.5	25.1	4.6
53 015	Cowlitz	79.5	8.0	37,931	67.4	168,100	25.0	10.9	634	29.1	80.0	23.0	6.5
53 017	Douglas	84.9	8.4	13,177	71.0	162,900	23.3	10.2	619	28.3	78.1	18.8	2.7
53 021	Franklin	84.0	8.8	19,766	67.6	135,700	23.9	10.5	575	28.2	70.8	20.7	4.5
53 025	Grant	82.2	7.2	27,484	64.0	121,700	23.7	9.3	530	24.9	74.6	18.8	6.0
53 027	Grays Harbor	80.2	7.6	27,786	65.3	141,000	23.6	12.6	604	25.7	79.2	21.8	7.7
53 029	Island	78.7	12.2	30,360	76.9	273,900	28.3	12.6	852	29.7	65.4	25.1	2.4
53 031	Jefferson	86.2	8.1	12,778	78.8	275,800	28.1	12.5	716	28.3	72.2	24.2	4.5
53 033	King	80.3	7.2	753,780	61.9	389,200	26.5	12.9	900	28.2	67.5	26.5	9.1
53 035	Kitsap	80.9	8.9	91,579	69.3	260,700	25.8	11.7	834	28.8	68.1	29.2	5.0
53 037	Kittitas	71.9	14.1	15,669	57.7	227,900	27.0	13.3	674	48.6	67.6	18.8	8.8
53 039	Klickitat	80.9	10.1	8,193	66.7	183,600	27.0	11.7	578	24.7	75.7	21.2	6.2
53 041	Lewis	80.8	7.0	27,791	73.3	169,400	24.6	11.3	681	28.5	77.2	25.7	5.2
53 045	Mason	83.9	10.3	19,909	78.1	180,900	25.6	11.7	726	26.8	75.9	33.1	4.9
53 047	Okanogan	89.4	4.1	15,689	65.9	124,700	22.4	10.4	521	30.8	75.3	18.9	5.1
53 049	Pacific	84.7	6.8	9,752	70.9	154,000	25.2	10.9	599	29.3	77.7	18.5	6.1
53 053	Pierce	77.9	8.6	285,724	64.1	248,900	26.9	13.0	819	29.7	76.8	28.5	5.4
53 057	Skagit	80.5	8.2	42,982	68.6	241,900	27.4	13.4	849	29.3	78.0	24.6	5.0
53 061	Snohomish	80.3	7.8	255,031	68.2	319,400	28.0	13.5	895	28.8	75.1	30.2	4.5
53 063	Spokane	78.6	7.2	178,952	65.5	163,700	24.2	11.2	649	30.4	78.0	20.6	7.2
53 065	Stevens	84.3	7.6	15,459	77.9	156,700	25.6	9.5	549	27.2	73.9	27.9	5.2
53 067	Thurston	80.1	8.1	91,918	65.8	236,100	24.8	11.4	835	30.4	78.0	23.9	5.0
53 071	Walla Walla	76.6	13.2	20,817	62.0	161,600	24.2	11.7	588	31.0	71.6	14.8	6.8
53 073	Whatcom	81.1	8.2	74,831	62.8	277,700	26.7	12.5	755	33.0	74.1	19.7	6.5
53 075	Whitman	62.5	22.6	15,772	47.4	156,700	21.5	10.1	592	42.2	61.6	15.8	6.0
53 077	Yakima	80.4	4.9	76,698	65.0	134,800	24.8	11.6	602	28.4	77.0	18.6	5.8
54 000	**West Virginia**	86.9	5.7	738,943	74.9	89,500	20.1	9.8	516	28.6	80.8	25.3	9.1
54 003	Berkeley	86.6	6.3	37,329	76.4	194,900	21.8	10.8	687	27.9	80.5	29.2	5.9
54 005	Boone	90.1	3.8	10,317	79.4	74,200	17.6	8.3	433	25.8	84.3	30.6	8.6
54 009	Brooke	90.5	3.1	9,953	74.5	82,300	19.9	10.6	510	22.8	85.1	24.3	7.5
54 011	Cabell	81.2	7.0	39,236	66.5	92,300	19.1	9.5	554	31.4	79.8	20.4	13.2
54 019	Fayette	86.1	6.0	18,848	75.4	64,300	21.0	10.5	432	27.7	80.0	30.3	11.3
54 025	Greenbrier	87.0	7.2	15,342	74.7	89,800	21.6	9.2	496	26.7	82.3	23.5	8.2
54 027	Hampshire	87.4	4.9	8,364	81.6	129,500	23.0	10.8	488	35.9	77.4	37.6	7.5
54 029	Hancock	90.0	3.8	13,588	73.5	82,000	19.7	10.7	539	29.4	78.8	22.7	7.5
54 033	Harrison	88.0	5.1	28,028	74.8	87,100	19.5	11.9	527	31.2	84.0	20.9	8.7
54 035	Jackson	90.9	3.8	11,363	77.1	96,800	18.4	8.5	499	27.4	85.5	29.7	6.7
54 037	Jefferson	90.2	5.6	18,704	76.7	277,900	23.1	9.3	748	24.9	74.2	36.5	3.4
54 039	Kanawha	86.2	5.0	82,401	70.4	94,400	19.0	9.8	563	25.9	79.9	20.5	12.2
54 043	Lincoln	85.3	5.9	8,601	76.9	64,200	20.7	9.5	401	29.0	79.3	36.2	11.6
54 045	Logan	87.1	4.7	14,894	70.3	74,200	19.2	8.2	431	28.3	85.8	24.2	11.2

Table C-2. Counties — Where: Migration, Housing, and Transportation, 2005–2007—*Continued*

STATE County code	STATE County	Percent who lived in the same house one year ago	Percent who did not live in county one year ago	Total occupied housing units	Percent owner-occupied housing units	Median value of owner-occupied housing units (dollars)	Median selected monthly owner costs as a percentage of household income — With a mortgage	Without a mortgage	Median gross rent (dollars)	Median gross rent as a percentage of household income	Percent of workers who drove alone to work	Mean travel time to work (minutes)	Percent of occupied housing units with no vehicle available
ACS table number:		C07204	C07204	B25003	B25003	B25077	B25092	B25092	B25064	B25071	C08301	B08013/C08012	C25045
		1	2	3	4	5	6	7	8	9	10	11	12
	West Virginia—Cont.												
54 047	McDowell	92.9	1.8	9,296	82.5	32,000	24.3	9.9	346	29.5	84.4	28.3	17.0
54 049	Marion	86.9	5.1	22,813	74.1	81,900	20.2	11.3	526	29.5	83.3	24.1	8.0
54 051	Marshall	89.3	3.6	14,102	74.2	75,500	21.2	9.7	449	26.0	85.8	22.7	8.8
54 053	Mason	90.0	2.9	11,038	79.9	79,100	19.0	10.8	427	30.5	88.9	29.0	7.9
54 055	Mercer	86.1	4.2	25,606	75.1	73,800	20.0	9.0	451	28.1	83.5	22.6	9.1
54 057	Mineral	85.5	9.1	11,065	74.9	102,700	20.1	10.7	528	37.7	80.3	28.5	9.0
54 059	Mingo	87.3	3.1	11,408	76.6	68,700	20.4	8.4	398	26.0	-	26.7	11.1
54 061	Monongalia	77.0	13.1	31,378	64.4	129,800	21.0	9.7	602	33.8	77.2	21.5	7.1
54 067	Nicholas	92.2	3.0	10,149	80.7	73,000	21.1	10.9	414	24.8	84.3	25.8	8.6
54 069	Ohio	86.0	4.9	20,037	69.1	89,700	18.3	9.8	475	30.2	79.6	19.0	13.2
54 077	Preston	89.0	5.8	11,543	79.8	81,800	19.1	10.4	448	24.0	76.0	30.0	6.2
54 079	Putnam	91.3	5.9	21,090	85.4	122,500	19.2	8.8	622	32.3	86.6	26.1	4.3
54 081	Raleigh	85.8	7.1	31,642	74.8	89,500	19.0	9.6	517	24.9	82.3	23.8	8.7
54 083	Randolph	88.8	6.8	11,336	76.1	94,200	21.0	10.7	365	28.8	78.9	20.8	10.6
54 097	Upshur	85.5	6.1	9,547	77.4	94,500	21.6	8.7	437	27.5	80.3	22.9	9.3
54 099	Wayne	86.6	4.3	16,639	77.8	80,700	22.2	9.2	461	31.1	81.1	25.1	8.3
54 107	Wood	84.1	5.6	37,005	71.8	95,600	21.0	10.4	549	34.7	81.1	20.7	9.3
54 109	Wyoming	91.1	3.3	9,823	83.7	60,800	23.9	8.2	394	29.9	84.7	26.9	8.3
55 000	**Wisconsin**	84.3	5.8	2,235,246	70.3	162,000	24.4	14.1	675	27.9	80.1	20.9	6.5
55 001	Adams	85.3	8.0	9,306	80.4	120,500	26.8	16.2	607	28.8	77.1	25.9	3.2
55 005	Barron	86.2	6.1	19,590	73.1	124,200	24.3	14.0	558	28.9	77.0	19.2	5.5
55 009	Brown	84.1	5.6	95,165	66.3	155,400	23.5	13.5	657	26.7	85.0	17.8	5.4
55 015	Calumet	86.4	6.4	17,364	81.9	145,100	23.8	13.3	588	23.4	83.9	19.8	2.5
55 017	Chippewa	86.5	5.8	23,435	76.5	137,200	24.3	13.4	572	28.0	79.8	21.7	4.0
55 019	Clark	90.7	4.1	12,518	80.5	103,300	24.3	13.4	469	22.1	69.6	19.6	7.4
55 021	Columbia	85.1	7.6	22,304	76.1	168,400	26.1	14.7	660	26.0	81.4	26.3	3.9
55 025	Dane	78.4	7.0	187,852	63.4	222,200	24.9	12.3	795	29.1	74.3	19.8	6.9
55 027	Dodge	82.7	9.3	33,596	73.3	149,700	24.5	14.4	667	24.9	80.9	22.9	3.8
55 029	Door	88.6	3.3	13,464	77.8	175,200	28.4	14.2	620	27.5	77.7	18.0	3.9
55 031	Douglas	85.0	7.8	18,244	72.9	118,800	22.3	14.3	548	28.5	82.0	20.6	5.9
55 033	Dunn	78.1	11.4	15,439	72.7	140,100	24.0	14.0	675	29.9	75.7	21.3	3.6
55 035	Eau Claire	79.6	8.6	38,661	66.7	139,500	23.1	12.6	614	29.2	79.6	18.1	6.2
55 039	Fond du Lac	84.7	5.2	39,184	73.4	134,600	23.5	13.6	602	27.4	80.9	19.7	6.2
55 043	Grant	83.0	8.0	19,093	74.8	114,500	23.4	13.6	528	28.2	72.4	21.1	5.1
55 045	Green	87.4	5.3	14,591	77.7	138,400	25.1	14.0	608	23.7	80.5	23.2	3.8
55 049	Iowa	88.6	6.0	9,555	76.6	151,300	25.5	14.8	650	23.3	74.1	25.5	3.7
55 055	Jefferson	86.4	6.2	30,801	71.7	172,200	25.4	13.9	684	26.4	79.6	22.7	5.0
55 057	Juneau	82.1	8.0	11,103	75.3	107,800	24.6	14.3	563	21.8	77.3	21.5	3.4
55 059	Kenosha	84.5	5.3	59,838	68.9	176,400	25.6	16.2	750	28.9	81.4	25.9	6.6
55 061	Kewaunee	91.2	3.6	8,272	83.3	134,100	23.7	15.8	569	26.2	79.4	22.3	5.0
55 063	La Crosse	79.4	7.2	44,452	67.5	139,500	23.3	13.9	592	27.3	80.3	17.3	6.9
55 067	Langlade	91.1	3.4	8,565	83.8	104,400	25.8	14.2	482	31.8	78.1	20.4	5.2
55 069	Lincoln	88.9	5.6	12,753	74.6	121,900	22.9	13.8	552	19.9	80.0	21.6	6.4
55 071	Manitowoc	88.4	4.1	33,704	77.6	118,300	22.2	14.3	526	24.8	81.6	18.7	5.7
55 073	Marathon	87.8	4.7	52,251	77.2	131,700	22.5	13.4	609	24.6	82.3	18.2	4.3
55 075	Marinette	86.9	5.6	18,814	76.5	107,100	23.3	14.3	505	25.5	81.2	20.9	4.6
55 079	Milwaukee	81.4	4.1	377,310	56.0	160,100	25.7	16.4	709	30.7	77.1	21.2	13.6
55 081	Monroe	87.6	4.9	17,411	73.1	115,100	24.0	13.6	527	24.2	78.1	19.3	5.9
55 083	Oconto	90.0	5.5	15,975	82.7	139,900	25.6	15.0	528	26.0	79.3	25.7	2.7
55 085	Oneida	81.4	8.7	17,494	75.3	161,400	24.0	15.2	593	26.3	85.7	18.0	4.4
55 087	Outagamie	85.8	6.9	67,707	73.6	146,100	23.0	12.6	644	27.2	85.3	18.4	4.8
55 089	Ozaukee	88.2	6.6	33,385	78.2	244,400	24.1	13.3	733	23.5	85.7	22.4	3.2
55 093	Pierce	80.9	9.4	14,706	75.8	203,600	26.0	14.6	681	26.9	75.9	25.9	3.3
55 095	Polk	90.2	4.0	17,569	82.7	169,300	27.1	15.1	607	27.1	77.9	28.2	3.5
55 097	Portage	79.9	6.9	26,459	72.5	135,300	22.5	12.1	617	27.6	78.5	17.9	3.3
55 101	Racine	87.3	4.8	75,140	70.8	169,000	24.9	13.9	679	28.8	85.1	21.8	6.0
55 105	Rock	86.3	4.4	62,035	74.0	129,700	23.7	14.1	653	27.5	83.5	20.9	4.9
55 109	St. Croix	85.2	7.6	30,910	76.6	223,900	25.1	13.3	777	25.4	82.4	26.7	2.9
55 111	Sauk	87.5	5.0	24,910	73.0	157,900	25.6	13.8	666	27.8	79.5	21.5	4.3
55 115	Shawano	90.3	5.0	16,884	78.6	120,400	24.8	14.0	565	24.3	77.2	23.4	4.3
55 117	Sheboygan	85.3	4.3	46,278	72.7	144,100	23.4	13.5	591	25.2	81.7	17.2	6.9
55 121	Trempealeau	91.2	4.0	11,489	74.6	125,400	24.1	13.9	502	23.9	75.6	21.1	6.0
55 123	Vernon	86.4	5.1	12,126	77.0	121,800	25.0	14.8	484	23.8	73.6	22.5	9.6
55 125	Vilas	88.2	6.8	10,849	79.8	194,200	25.3	13.4	523	29.0	75.8	22.4	3.0
55 127	Walworth	83.0	7.5	38,579	71.8	186,400	26.3	14.5	718	29.0	80.6	23.3	4.0
55 131	Washington	86.4	6.0	50,050	77.8	215,300	24.6	14.5	725	26.2	83.9	23.6	3.7
55 133	Waukesha	88.1	5.9	146,942	78.2	247,200	23.9	13.3	847	27.3	86.6	22.2	3.8
55 135	Waupaca	86.7	4.9	21,304	76.8	129,800	24.3	14.7	578	27.3	78.7	20.7	5.0
55 137	Waushara	85.5	8.0	10,423	80.5	132,400	25.5	14.9	573	24.9	76.8	26.2	4.5
55 139	Winnebago	80.3	8.9	65,897	67.5	136,200	23.2	14.4	601	26.8	84.5	17.3	6.1
55 141	Wood	86.3	4.5	31,367	77.5	110,000	22.0	12.8	530	26.0	81.2	18.3	4.4

Table C-2. Counties — Where: Migration, Housing, and Transportation, 2005–2007—*Continued*

STATE County code	STATE County	Percent who lived in the same house one year ago	Percent who did not live in county one year ago	Total occupied housing units	Percent owner-occu-pied housing units	Median value of owner-occupied housing units (dollars)	Median selected monthly owner costs as a percentage of household income With a mortgage	Without a mortgage	Median gross rent (dollars)	Median gross rent as a percentage of house-hold income	Percent of workers who drove alone to work	Mean travel time to work (minutes)	Percent of occupied housing units with no vehicle available
ACS table number:		C07204	C07204	B25003	B25003	B25077	B25092	B25092	B25064	B25071	C08301	B08013/ C08012	C25045
		1	2	3	4	5	6	7	8	9	10	11	12
56 000	**Wyoming**	80.3	8.6	205,422	70.0	150,500	21.1	9.2	607	23.3	75.1	17.9	3.5
56 001	Albany	70.4	16.2	13,890	57.7	169,600	23.1	8.1	613	32.1	66.3	12.7	3.3
56 005	Campbell	83.4	6.4	13,344	76.3	179,300	19.4	8.2	706	19.1	76.0	21.3	2.7
56 013	Fremont	84.9	5.5	14,296	74.2	127,500	19.6	10.5	481	20.4	75.0	19.1	4.0
56 021	Laramie	79.4	7.4	33,640	68.6	155,000	23.5	11.0	644	25.8	81.7	15.3	3.6
56 025	Natrona	81.7	7.1	27,359	70.5	147,000	20.4	9.1	558	25.1	82.5	16.6	4.0
56 029	Park	75.6	11.2	11,603	67.8	156,400	23.1	9.7	574	26.0	73.4	16.2	3.3
56 033	Sheridan	83.6	7.4	11,929	66.6	182,000	23.3	10.4	597	23.4	77.6	15.7	6.0
56 037	Sweetwater	78.3	8.3	15,107	76.6	144,700	18.7	7.4	624	17.2	74.0	21.6	3.2
56 039	Teton	78.5	9.2	7,942	55.5	655,500	24.1	11.2	920	24.9	68.8	15.2	2.3
56 041	Uinta	81.9	10.8	7,208	72.8	140,000	18.8	8.0	512	20.2	66.0	21.4	2.6

Metro area or division code	Area name	Percent who lived in the same house one year ago	Percent who did not live in MSA one year ago	Total occupied housing units	Percent owner-occupied housing units	Median value of owner-occupied housing units (dollars)	Median selected monthly owner costs as a percentage of household income		Median gross rent (dollars)	Median gross rent as a percentage of household income	Percent of workers who drove alone to work	Mean travel time to work (minutes)	Percent of occupied housing units with no vehicle available
							With a mortgage	Without a mortgage					
	ACS table number:	C07204	C07201	B25003	B25003	B25077	B25092	B25092	B25064	B25071	C08301	B08013/C08012	C25045
		1	2	3	4	5	6	7	8	9	10	11	12
10180	Abilene, TX.........................	76.3	10.0	60,536	65.3	70,000	21.4	12.9	662	29.4	80.3	16.6	4.5
10420	Akron, OH..........................	87.2	4.2	279,518	70.8	144,600	24.1	14.1	710	30.4	85.8	22.6	7.1
10500	Albany, GA.........................	79.4	7.2	60,574	56.8	96,400	20.4	11.6	576	27.5	80.9	19.6	11.1
10580	Albany-Schenectady-Troy, NY	85.1	5.0	337,537	66.8	168,500	23.0	13.8	766	27.7	80.3	21.7	9.2
10740	Albuquerque, NM..................	80.6	5.9	320,462	68.3	163,200	23.7	10.3	674	29.7	78.2	23.4	5.6
10780	Alexandria, LA.....................	83.6	5.5	57,460	68.7	91,100	21.1	10.9	623	32.7	83.1	22.2	8.2
10900	Allentown-Bethlehem-Easton, PA-NJ	85.7	4.9	305,867	73.4	198,600	24.7	14.8	770	29.2	81.7	26.9	7.6
11020	Altoona, PA........................	87.2	4.2	51,384	72.6	91,100	21.2	13.4	529	27.7	81.4	20.1	9.8
11100	Amarillo, TX........................	78.9	6.4	87,799	65.9	96,600	22.1	11.5	611	29.0	81.5	17.0	4.7
11180	Ames, IA...........................	67.7	15.4	31,467	57.3	150,200	21.4	10.7	690	32.0	73.2	16.3	4.8
11260	Anchorage, AK.....................	78.6	7.7	124,200	64.5	237,100	24.6	11.1	943	28.7	74.9	21.0	5.8
11300	Anderson, IN.......................	82.3	6.3	51,392	73.4	97,600	22.0	11.5	606	32.1	84.3	24.2	6.6
11340	Anderson, SC.......................	82.6	6.2	68,821	74.3	107,300	21.8	10.6	577	29.5	84.2	22.7	6.4
11460	Ann Arbor, MI......................	77.1	11.2	132,861	64.8	231,600	24.4	13.1	840	34.4	75.9	22.0	6.2
11500	Anniston-Oxford, AL................	82.6	6.6	46,849	71.6	90,100	20.5	11.3	554	27.7	88.2	23.3	6.7
11540	Appleton, WI.......................	86.0	6.2	85,071	75.3	145,900	23.2	12.8	634	26.7	85.0	18.7	4.4
11700	Asheville, NC.......................	83.4	6.2	169,116	71.2	164,300	23.4	11.1	664	28.3	79.1	21.4	5.6
12020	Athens-Clarke County, GA.........	76.1	9.9	68,554	57.6	156,100	23.5	10.7	683	33.7	77.8	20.9	6.6
12060	Atlanta-Sandy Springs-Marietta, GA......	80.3	5.9	1,820,162	69.1	186,400	24.4	11.1	869	29.8	77.9	30.8	5.9
12100	Atlantic City, NJ....................	85.0	6.3	102,672	68.3	247,000	28.8	18.9	902	31.0	73.9	23.0	14.1
12220	Auburn-Opelika, AL	74.8	13.1	52,996	61.7	125,300	21.3	11.7	586	32.8	81.4	19.9	6.0
12260	Augusta-Richmond County, GA-SC	82.3	6.2	197,580	69.2	108,400	21.8	10.5	639	28.4	79.7	22.0	7.5
12420	Austin-Round Rock, TX	75.9	8.3	560,375	60.1	167,500	24.4	12.6	822	29.2	75.2	25.3	5.1
12540	Bakersfield, CA.....................	78.4	8.2	235,842	62.0	241,100	27.5	12.5	733	30.1	74.4	22.5	7.5
12580	Baltimore-Towson, MD..............	85.2	4.3	998,382	68.7	286,900	23.8	12.1	906	29.7	75.9	28.9	11.4
12620	Bangor, ME........................	82.5	6.8	60,477	71.5	118,200	22.4	13.4	616	30.3	78.7	21.8	7.0
12700	Barnstable Town, MA...............	89.6	4.1	98,989	79.3	412,900	29.7	15.0	1,067	32.5	81.8	22.9	4.3
12940	Baton Rouge, LA...................	83.1	5.7	279,761	68.8	130,000	21.2	10.2	670	31.6	83.3	26.4	7.0
12980	Battle Creek, MI...................	84.0	4.7	54,257	73.6	115,100	23.4	13.4	611	33.6	82.6	19.2	7.1
13020	Bay City, MI........................	87.4	3.0	44,733	80.4	109,300	22.4	13.5	530	27.9	85.0	20.9	6.3
13140	Beaumont-Port Arthur, TX.....................	82.9	4.9	141,740	69.1	78,800	19.9	12.3	622	29.3	83.3	20.8	8.3
13380	Bellingham, WA....................	81.1	8.2	74,831	62.8	277,700	26.7	12.5	755	33.0	74.1	19.7	6.5
13460	Bend, OR..........................	80.7	8.1	60,302	69.2	313,800	27.2	12.3	843	27.2	77.3	18.7	3.4
13740	Billings, MT........................	80.7	7.3	59,100	70.9	152,300	23.1	12.0	505	28.5	78.9	17.5	5.6
13780	Binghamton, NY....................	85.5	5.3	100,631	69.0	91,300	20.9	14.2	567	28.4	81.4	19.8	9.3
13820	Birmingham-Hoover, AL............	83.2	3.9	429,594	72.6	131,000	22.2	11.3	678	28.7	83.7	25.9	6.3
13900	Bismarck, ND......................	84.6	5.6	41,532	70.6	122,500	22.3	12.5	516	24.5	79.6	16.8	5.2
13980	Blacksburg-Christiansburg-Radford, VA.....	72.7	12.1	59,507	62.1	133,800	21.1	9.4	605	33.5	78.3	19.3	6.4
14020	Bloomington, IN....................	72.8	11.8	68,901	64.2	119,000	21.3	11.4	646	36.7	77.6	21.3	5.9
14060	Bloomington-Normal, IL............	77.2	10.2	61,177	68.4	143,200	21.8	12.0	674	29.7	77.7	17.4	4.7
14260	Boise City-Nampa, ID	77.3	7.5	212,275	71.6	181,100	23.9	10.7	704	27.5	78.9	21.6	4.2
14460	Boston-Cambridge-Quincy, MA-NH........	85.4	3.8	1,684,779	64.6	398,400	26.9	15.9	1,074	30.3	70.5	28.4	12.5
14460 14484	•Boston-Quincy, MA Division	83.8	4.2	696,066	60.7	403,100	27.4	15.8	1,097	31.0	63.6	30.0	17.2
14460 15764	•Cambridge-Newton-Framingham, MA Division..........................	85.8	4.1	556,748	65.3	440,600	26.2	15.4	1,147	28.9	71.4	27.4	10.2
14460 37764	•Peabody, MA Division...............	87.9	2.3	273,755	66.4	387,700	27.4	16.3	957	32.0	78.1	27.0	10.0
14460 40484	•Rockingham County-Strafford County, NH Division.......................	86.9	4.1	158,210	75.5	294,800	26.6	16.8	943	29.7	83.5	27.7	4.4
14500	Boulder, CO........................	76.2	11.3	113,419	66.0	342,400	24.6	10.4	946	34.7	67.8	21.3	4.8
14540	Bowling Green, KY	77.7	9.8	44,622	65.8	123,900	21.6	9.6	588	27.5	81.4	20.4	6.7
14740	Bremerton-Silverdale, WA	80.9	8.9	91,579	69.3	260,700	25.8	11.7	834	28.8	68.1	29.2	5.0
14860	Bridgeport-Stamford-Norwalk, CT.........	87.6	4.7	324,360	71.7	495,200	27.4	17.3	1,150	30.9	73.9	28.1	7.9
15180	Brownsville-Harlingen, TX	87.6	3.5	114,787	67.9	66,900	28.0	14.7	531	32.8	78.0	19.7	10.2
15260	Brunswick, GA......................	82.5	7.8	39,019	66.7	137,700	21.9	9.9	703	26.6	81.7	21.4	5.6
15380	Buffalo-Niagara Falls, NY...........	86.5	2.9	465,947	67.2	104,500	22.4	15.5	637	29.5	81.8	20.5	12.8
15500	Burlington, NC.....................	79.9	7.4	56,608	68.5	131,800	24.1	11.9	684	29.1	82.0	21.8	4.7
15540	Burlington-South Burlington, VT	83.1	6.0	80,394	71.3	225,200	25.4	15.3	852	32.0	73.5	21.5	5.9
15940	Canton-Massillon, OH..............	85.9	4.0	161,150	72.6	127,500	22.7	12.9	587	28.5	85.6	21.4	6.8
15980	Cape Coral-Fort Myers, FL..........	81.0	8.6	243,673	73.9	242,700	29.0	14.3	970	31.7	78.8	25.4	4.5
16180	Carson City, NV....................	79.5	8.3	21,330	63.6	298,700	27.5	11.5	842	29.7	79.1	16.5	6.1
16220	Casper, WY........................	81.7	7.1	27,359	70.5	147,000	20.4	9.1	558	25.1	82.5	16.6	4.0
16300	Cedar Rapids, IA...................	82.6	5.4	102,404	73.4	125,000	22.0	12.6	578	25.9	81.8	18.5	5.9
16580	Champaign-Urbana, IL..............	73.9	11.2	87,476	59.5	130,400	21.8	11.3	670	33.8	70.8	17.3	8.0
16620	Charleston, WV....................	87.6	3.8	126,252	74.4	93,400	18.9	9.4	545	26.7	81.4	23.5	10.5
16700	Charleston-North Charleston, SC	81.7	7.4	234,599	66.9	179,200	24.8	12.8	805	28.7	81.2	23.7	7.4
16740	Charlotte-Gastonia-Concord, NC-SC	79.6	7.3	616,835	68.1	158,300	22.8	11.8	743	28.4	79.7	25.2	5.8
16820	Charlottesville, VA..................	78.3	10.9	76,147	64.9	251,300	23.7	11.1	883	29.2	73.1	22.7	6.8
16860	Chattanooga, TN-GA................	83.1	5.1	202,514	70.2	125,900	22.1	10.1	604	26.7	82.4	22.5	6.7
16940	Cheyenne, WY.....................	79.4	7.4	33,640	68.6	155,000	23.5	11.0	644	25.8	81.7	15.3	3.6
16980	Chicago-Naperville-Joliet, IL-IN-WI.......	85.4	2.7	3,385,546	69.0	247,500	27.4	14.8	851	30.4	71.5	30.9	11.4
16980 16974	•Chicago-Naperville-Joliet, IL Division......	85.4	2.6	2,829,188	67.8	263,000	27.9	14.9	861	30.7	69.7	31.4	12.6
16980 23844	•Gary, IN Division..................	85.7	2.4	262,903	72.6	135,000	22.9	14.0	717	29.4	83.3	26.6	7.3

Table C-3. Metropolitan Areas — Where: Migration, Housing, and Transportation, 2005–2007—*Continued*

Metro area or division code	Area name	Percent who lived in the same house one year ago	Percent who did not live in MSA one year ago	Total occupied housing units	Percent owner-occupied housing units	Median value of owner-occupied housing units (dollars)	Median selected monthly owner costs as a percentage of household income		Median gross rent (dollars)	Median gross rent as a percentage of household income	Percent of workers who drove alone to work	Mean travel time to work (minutes)	Percent of occupied housing units with no vehicle available
							With a mortgage	Without a mortgage					
	ACS table number:	C07204	C07201	B25003	B25003	B25077	B25092	B25092	B25064	B25071	C08301	B08013/ C08012	C25045
		1	2	3	4	5	6	7	8	9	10	11	12
16980 29404	•Lake County-Kenosha County, IL-WI Division	85.6	3.3	293,455	77.4	251,100	26.7	15.2	868	29.1	79.1	29.7	4.4
17020	Chico, CA	76.4	8.7	84,607	59.1	273,500	27.9	12.8	807	35.9	75.9	20.8	7.1
17140	Cincinnati-Middletown, OH-KY-IN	83.1	3.6	803,129	69.6	150,300	22.7	13.2	651	28.4	82.4	23.4	8.3
17300	Clarksville, TN-KY	77.2	10.9	92,608	66.0	105,700	21.0	9.8	653	26.4	81.4	22.4	5.2
17420	Cleveland, TN	82.6	6.2	44,083	68.7	121,000	22.6	10.2	557	28.1	84.5	21.1	4.8
17460	Cleveland-Elyria-Mentor, OH	86.1	2.8	840,369	69.2	149,500	24.5	14.8	681	30.7	81.8	23.8	10.2
17660	Coeur d'Alene, ID	82.1	7.0	50,628	71.4	214,600	27.2	12.3	734	30.0	78.6	22.2	3.3
17780	College Station-Bryan, TX	70.7	14.6	73,853	52.6	115,900	22.8	12.3	672	37.3	76.4	18.5	6.4
17820	Colorado Springs, CO	76.1	10.5	226,360	68.4	206,000	24.8	9.1	772	29.1	77.2	22.2	4.8
17860	Columbia, MO	74.2	9.9	66,342	60.2	139,400	21.2	10.2	672	30.6	77.5	17.8	5.9
17900	Columbia, SC	81.0	8.0	271,279	69.7	126,100	22.0	11.0	694	28.8	78.6	23.7	6.7
17980	Columbus, GA-AL	76.4	11.8	108,447	60.3	115,600	22.8	10.7	645	29.9	73.5	20.2	10.1
18020	Columbus, IN	83.9	4.7	27,992	73.8	123,600	20.0	10.1	718	29.2	85.5	19.5	4.1
18140	Columbus, OH	80.4	5.0	677,522	65.7	161,300	23.6	13.0	715	28.6	83.0	22.6	6.5
18580	Corpus Christi, TX	79.1	6.6	149,080	63.0	91,000	23.8	14.6	726	31.8	77.2	19.7	7.4
18700	Corvallis, OR	71.1	14.8	32,517	57.0	233,200	23.2	10.2	698	33.4	67.0	17.4	7.6
19060	Cumberland, MD-WV	84.4	7.2	40,370	71.3	94,900	20.2	12.0	489	27.5	81.2	22.6	10.9
19100	Dallas-Fort Worth-Arlington, TX	80.0	5.0	2,080,056	63.4	140,300	24.4	13.9	795	28.8	80.1	26.6	5.1
19100 19124	•Dallas-Plano-Irving, TX Division	80.0	5.0	1,388,775	62.3	148,300	24.7	13.9	805	28.9	79.0	26.9	5.4
19100 23104	•Fort Worth-Arlington, TX Division	80.0	5.0	691,281	65.7	124,700	24.0	13.9	773	28.7	82.2	25.8	4.5
19140	Dalton, GA	85.9	3.7	44,878	70.5	114,100	22.1	9.2	573	28.7	83.7	20.0	4.8
19180	Danville, IL	87.3	4.4	32,857	71.0	71,700	20.0	12.4	573	29.9	82.1	20.4	9.9
19260	Danville, VA	86.1	4.3	45,391	69.1	89,100	22.1	12.5	528	28.3	82.4	22.3	11.0
19340	Davenport-Moline-Rock Island, IA-IL	84.5	4.5	151,011	72.9	111,400	21.3	12.2	590	27.3	83.5	19.0	6.3
19380	Dayton, OH	82.3	4.3	340,416	67.4	127,000	22.7	13.2	664	29.6	84.1	20.6	7.5
19460	Decatur, AL	84.6	4.4	58,878	76.3	101,100	20.6	10.4	518	25.7	84.8	23.2	5.4
19500	Decatur, IL	82.0	5.3	46,343	71.9	86,900	19.4	11.5	555	28.2	86.8	17.6	9.5
19660	Deltona-Daytona Beach-Ormond Beach, FL	83.7	7.5	201,368	75.1	189,900	27.4	14.7	844	35.2	80.6	23.9	5.8
19740	Denver-Aurora, CO	81.2	5.2	941,502	68.3	242,700	26.1	10.8	818	29.8	76.1	26.2	6.3
19780	Des Moines-West Des Moines, IA	81.4	5.9	214,297	73.0	144,200	22.2	13.2	688	27.0	82.6	19.5	5.0
19820	Detroit-Warren-Livonia, MI	86.8	2.3	1,689,695	74.5	171,800	24.9	14.6	753	31.3	85.1	25.9	7.7
19820 19804	•Detroit-Livonia-Dearborn, MI Division	85.5	2.1	716,137	68.4	138,200	26.2	15.0	729	34.4	82.7	24.6	12.1
19820 47644	•Warren-Troy-Farmington Hills, MI Division	87.8	2.5	973,558	79.0	197,400	24.4	14.2	780	28.6	86.7	26.8	4.5
20020	Dothan, AL	85.5	5.2	53,191	72.5	91,900	20.0	9.8	537	27.8	86.3	20.1	6.2
20100	Dover, DE	84.1	6.4	55,685	72.8	189,500	24.4	12.4	840	29.8	81.3	23.1	6.5
20220	Dubuque, IA	87.0	4.9	36,520	75.8	125,300	22.2	12.2	538	26.6	82.2	15.5	6.0
20260	Duluth, MN-WI	84.0	6.0	116,391	74.8	133,100	22.8	11.9	588	30.1	80.1	19.8	8.2
20500	Durham, NC	78.9	8.9	187,049	61.0	172,600	23.0	11.6	751	29.9	73.8	23.4	7.1
20740	Eau Claire, WI	82.2	6.5	62,096	70.4	138,700	23.5	12.9	603	28.8	79.7	19.5	5.4
20940	El Centro, CA	84.2	7.4	45,561	55.3	224,600	29.4	12.3	643	31.8	78.7	18.0	10.3
21060	Elizabethtown, KY	81.0	9.7	42,038	69.0	116,900	20.9	9.3	555	24.1	82.5	21.0	3.9
21140	Elkhart-Goshen, IN	81.9	5.2	70,835	70.8	123,000	22.0	11.3	678	27.4	79.4	17.8	6.8
21300	Elmira, NY	82.5	6.7	34,767	67.5	78,300	21.4	14.1	597	32.6	81.0	19.6	8.6
21340	El Paso, TX	85.2	4.7	229,655	65.0	87,600	24.4	12.5	554	31.2	78.8	21.6	9.5
21500	Erie, PA	82.7	4.5	107,718	70.0	102,600	22.9	13.3	571	29.0	80.4	18.4	9.8
21660	Eugene-Springfield, OR	76.8	7.9	137,630	62.4	207,100	26.1	12.1	714	31.9	72.5	19.5	7.6
21780	Evansville, IN-KY	84.8	3.8	141,508	72.7	108,600	20.3	11.2	583	28.2	85.4	20.2	7.1
21820	Fairbanks, AK	75.4	13.0	32,550	59.8	188,200	23.7	9.9	859	26.5	70.4	17.8	6.6
22020	Fargo, ND-MN	77.5	7.8	80,333	58.9	136,500	22.2	11.8	574	28.7	81.4	16.4	6.7
22140	Farmington, NM	85.7	5.5	38,466	75.3	125,800	20.6	8.8	638	25.4	84.7	23.0	5.8
22180	Fayetteville, NC	76.6	10.8	130,880	60.6	101,600	23.4	12.4	732	29.9	80.4	21.2	7.3
22220	Fayetteville-Springdale-Rogers, AR-MO	77.0	8.0	158,750	65.4	145,700	21.4	10.4	654	27.0	79.1	21.1	4.2
22380	Flagstaff, AZ	78.9	9.7	43,286	61.9	258,200	24.1	8.7	839	30.1	68.3	17.6	5.7
22420	Flint, MI	85.1	3.7	173,622	73.2	129,600	24.0	13.7	620	31.4	85.0	25.0	7.2
22500	Florence, SC	84.5	4.2	72,678	71.2	90,600	21.5	10.8	566	27.4	81.0	21.9	8.3
22520	Florence-Muscle Shoals, AL	83.3	5.9	58,668	73.1	91,600	21.4	11.0	512	29.4	85.4	23.5	6.6
22540	Fond du Lac, WI	84.7	5.3	39,184	73.4	134,600	23.5	13.6	602	27.4	80.9	19.7	6.2
22660	Fort Collins-Loveland, CO	75.6	9.4	111,524	68.5	239,700	25.3	10.8	791	32.8	76.4	21.8	3.7
22900	Fort Smith, AR-OK	81.2	5.2	107,262	68.4	83,800	20.6	11.0	531	27.8	82.1	20.3	6.5
23020	Fort Walton Beach-Crestview-Destin, FL	79.0	10.8	74,771	67.6	212,800	23.4	10.6	867	28.0	82.1	21.6	4.1
23060	Fort Wayne, IN	86.1	3.8	159,348	72.6	110,500	20.6	10.6	604	26.4	85.6	20.7	5.3
23420	Fresno, CA	82.5	4.3	276,929	56.0	284,800	27.1	11.6	761	32.2	75.5	21.1	8.8
23460	Gadsden, AL	82.4	6.7	43,059	72.9	88,900	20.7	12.8	518	28.8	83.4	23.4	5.9
23540	Gainesville, FL	74.0	11.6	101,425	55.4	168,800	23.9	10.8	762	35.1	75.3	21.5	6.8
23580	Gainesville, GA	82.9	7.2	54,184	70.8	168,000	24.3	11.6	784	28.6	78.5	26.3	6.1
24020	Glens Falls, NY	85.3	5.6	51,110	70.8	137,600	24.3	14.4	719	29.5	80.3	23.0	6.8
24140	Goldsboro, NC	82.4	6.6	44,116	66.0	96,400	22.8	12.9	589	27.5	84.1	20.6	7.6
24220	Grand Forks, ND-MN	75.2	11.1	39,388	61.8	115,800	21.3	13.5	566	29.8	81.9	14.4	5.9
24300	Grand Junction, CO	75.3	8.3	53,533	71.3	188,700	24.2	10.0	745	28.5	75.3	20.3	4.6
24340	Grand Rapids-Wyoming, MI	83.4	5.2	288,574	74.6	145,100	23.9	13.0	652	29.2	82.2	21.8	5.3

Table C-3. Metropolitan Areas — Where: Migration, Housing, and Transportation, 2005–2007—*Continued*

Metro area or division code	Area name	Percent who lived in the same house one year ago	Percent who did not live in MSA one year ago	Total occupied housing units	Percent owner-occupied housing units	Median value of owner-occupied housing units (dollars)	Median selected monthly owner costs as a percentage of household income — With a mortgage	Median selected monthly owner costs as a percentage of household income — Without a mortgage	Median gross rent (dollars)	Median gross rent as a percentage of household income	Percent of workers who drove alone to work	Mean travel time to work (minutes)	Percent of occupied housing units with no vehicle available
	ACS table number:	C07204	C07201	B25003	B25003	B25077	B25092	B25092	B25064	B25071	C08301	B08013/C08012	C25045
		1	2	3	4	5	6	7	8	9	10	11	12
24500	Great Falls, MT............................	81.5	7.2	32,190	67.9	128,100	22.8	12.1	531	24.9	83.2	15.0	6.9
24540	Greeley, CO...............................	80.9	8.7	81,024	71.1	197,200	26.6	12.9	717	30.4	79.3	23.6	4.3
24580	Green Bay, WI............................	85.3	4.7	119,412	69.6	152,200	23.8	14.0	645	26.6	83.9	19.1	5.0
24660	Greensboro-High Point, NC...........	82.6	5.8	275,069	66.1	131,900	23.0	11.4	660	29.6	82.2	22.1	6.9
24780	Greenville, NC...........................	77.0	9.8	68,011	57.7	107,700	22.7	14.7	625	34.8	82.8	19.9	8.8
24860	Greenville-Mauldin-Easley, SC	81.5	7.0	233,053	69.1	127,200	21.8	10.4	621	28.0	82.0	21.9	6.5
25060	Gulfport-Biloxi, MS.....................	76.0	8.4	91,367	68.2	124,200	23.5	11.2	739	29.4	80.3	23.8	4.1
25180	Hagerstown-Martinsburg, MD-WV.....	86.2	5.6	99,509	70.3	210,800	23.2	10.5	694	27.0	81.1	27.8	6.9
25260	Hanford-Corcoran, CA..................	78.1	12.8	38,808	57.2	220,500	26.7	10.0	719	30.0	71.8	20.3	6.8
25420	Harrisburg-Carlisle, PA................	85.0	5.8	211,113	70.8	146,500	22.3	12.1	691	26.4	80.1	21.3	7.6
25500	Harrisonburg, VA........................	77.9	11.3	42,427	62.5	176,700	22.9	9.0	668	27.4	77.5	18.8	6.9
25540	Hartford-West Hartford-East Hartford, CT.............................	86.9	3.8	455,433	69.4	243,000	24.4	15.3	849	28.6	82.5	22.5	8.0
25620	Hattiesburg, MS.........................	79.1	8.6	49,040	65.7	98,400	22.3	12.3	614	30.2	84.5	22.2	5.3
25860	Hickory-Lenoir-Morganton, NC......	86.2	4.3	136,948	74.4	112,900	22.0	11.0	562	27.1	84.0	21.2	5.4
25980	Hinesville-Fort Stewart, GA	68.3	20.6	24,081	51.3	95,300	21.7	10.7	703	26.8	77.9	21.7	5.7
26100	Holland-Grand Haven, MI	86.6	6.7	90,396	81.9	164,200	23.2	12.5	708	26.2	84.5	19.8	2.4
26180	Honolulu, HI.............................	83.5	6.9	301,189	56.9	521,500	27.5	8.7	1,161	32.1	65.3	26.8	10.3
26300	Hot Springs, AR.........................	80.4	7.9	38,796	68.1	118,300	22.9	11.3	599	32.0	76.9	21.9	8.1
26380	Houma-Bayou Cane-Thibodaux, LA.......	87.7	2.7	70,932	73.9	102,100	19.2	10.0	578	26.1	81.5	24.5	8.6
26420	Houston-Sugar Land-Baytown, TX.......	80.1	5.1	1,857,040	63.7	129,900	23.8	12.8	763	29.6	78.0	28.2	6.4
26580	Huntington-Ashland, WV-KY-OH........	84.1	4.5	114,923	72.6	86,800	20.3	10.5	523	30.1	83.6	21.7	9.8
26620	Huntsville, AL...........................	81.5	7.0	147,283	71.7	134,700	19.7	8.6	605	25.8	85.2	21.3	4.2
26820	Idaho Falls, ID..........................	80.6	8.5	40,910	74.0	130,800	22.1	9.3	610	25.9	74.6	20.8	4.1
26900	Indianapolis-Carmel, IN	81.7	4.5	651,395	69.5	139,500	22.2	11.5	701	28.8	83.7	23.6	5.6
26980	Iowa City, IA............................	73.8	11.6	58,529	62.9	161,400	22.6	10.6	688	34.9	68.9	17.8	6.0
27060	Ithaca, NY...............................	69.1	13.1	37,374	52.8	147,900	22.9	12.6	799	32.8	57.4	17.8	11.6
27100	Jackson, MI..............................	83.5	6.5	60,667	76.8	138,800	24.0	13.1	665	34.3	84.9	22.9	6.5
27140	Jackson, MS..............................	82.7	4.8	193,661	69.2	113,300	22.2	11.7	716	31.1	84.5	23.4	6.3
27180	Jackson, TN..............................	82.6	6.2	44,360	67.5	106,200	23.0	11.5	642	34.2	86.7	19.9	7.6
27260	Jacksonville, FL.........................	80.6	6.2	498,655	68.7	185,400	24.2	10.3	824	29.8	81.2	25.4	6.3
27340	Jacksonville, NC........................	69.4	18.9	54,259	60.0	116,600	22.6	10.1	694	27.0	62.7	19.9	5.6
27500	Janesville, WI...........................	86.3	4.4	62,035	74.0	129,700	23.7	14.1	653	27.5	83.5	20.9	4.9
27620	Jefferson City, MO......................	82.3	7.0	54,568	71.7	116,900	20.1	8.8	537	23.1	79.1	20.0	4.6
27740	Johnson City, TN........................	83.2	6.1	76,443	70.6	104,900	21.6	9.9	500	24.3	86.0	20.7	6.1
27780	Johnstown, PA...........................	87.8	5.1	59,305	73.7	80,500	20.2	13.3	471	26.4	81.6	22.5	10.3
27860	Jonesboro, AR...........................	79.1	7.6	44,114	64.3	90,500	20.4	10.7	537	30.5	81.7	18.2	5.9
27900	Joplin, MO...............................	81.7	5.2	64,286	69.2	88,300	21.0	10.5	559	29.4	80.3	18.5	6.3
28020	Kalamazoo-Portage, MI................	80.0	6.2	127,037	69.4	140,200	23.0	12.8	633	32.1	82.1	19.7	6.3
28100	Kankakee-Bradley, IL...................	82.3	7.6	40,249	70.5	132,700	24.1	14.6	682	27.4	81.4	22.5	7.2
28140	Kansas City, MO-KS.....................	82.3	4.3	767,120	69.7	152,500	22.7	12.4	722	28.1	83.6	22.6	5.7
28420	Kennewick-Richland-Pasco, WA	80.4	7.1	76,486	70.1	148,600	22.6	9.6	682	28.8	77.2	21.0	4.6
28660	Killeen-Temple-Fort Hood, TX........	73.3	14.0	120,975	60.2	99,100	22.2	12.2	760	27.8	80.1	19.4	4.5
28700	Kingsport-Bristol-Bristol, TN-VA.....	84.7	4.6	129,524	74.5	96,700	21.1	9.7	486	26.4	84.9	21.1	6.7
28740	Kingston, NY............................	85.7	6.8	69,354	67.7	237,400	25.8	16.8	897	30.9	78.1	25.8	6.9
28940	Knoxville, TN............................	81.9	5.7	276,343	70.6	134,600	22.2	9.9	623	27.9	84.6	22.0	5.8
29020	Kokomo, IN..............................	82.8	3.7	41,471	71.0	110,000	20.7	10.7	623	26.9	84.4	18.5	7.0
29100	La Crosse, WI-MN.......................	81.2	6.3	52,240	69.7	139,600	23.1	13.3	584	27.1	79.7	17.7	6.5
29140	Lafayette, IN............................	72.1	11.9	72,091	58.8	123,200	21.8	10.3	679	35.1	76.9	19.0	7.3
29180	Lafayette, LA............................	84.1	6.5	99,436	67.5	123,400	20.2	9.2	604	28.1	84.3	23.9	7.5
29340	Lake Charles, LA........................	79.4	5.5	74,958	69.9	93,900	19.3	10.2	608	29.5	82.2	20.5	7.5
29420	Lake Havasu City-Kingman, AZ	78.0	10.8	75,033	70.2	185,500	25.9	11.3	772	31.0	76.0	19.0	3.3
29460	Lakeland, FL.............................	79.0	8.2	222,196	71.6	132,400	25.8	12.7	770	28.9	80.8	25.0	5.5
29540	Lancaster, PA............................	87.0	4.5	185,001	70.4	169,500	23.7	12.1	737	27.2	78.7	21.7	9.8
29620	Lansing-East Lansing, MI..............	82.6	6.5	177,581	69.3	153,600	23.6	12.7	680	31.5	81.7	21.2	5.9
29700	Laredo, TX...............................	83.9	4.4	60,859	64.4	95,100	27.6	15.0	617	34.5	76.0	19.7	9.8
29740	Las Cruces, NM..........................	78.4	8.1	68,164	64.9	118,200	23.1	11.9	597	33.9	76.1	18.5	6.2
29820	Las Vegas-Paradise, NV	77.2	7.3	662,025	59.4	307,300	29.1	11.7	973	30.4	78.2	24.4	7.6
29940	Lawrence, KS.............................	70.7	12.5	42,996	57.0	168,300	23.5	12.2	729	33.5	77.0	19.6	5.4
30020	Lawton, OK..............................	73.0	13.8	41,060	60.5	88,500	20.7	11.0	598	27.4	71.9	15.5	6.4
30140	Lebanon, PA.............................	87.0	5.2	49,465	74.7	140,800	22.5	11.7	595	25.1	82.6	22.1	7.2
30300	Lewiston, ID-WA........................	79.6	6.7	24,405	69.3	136,700	23.6	10.3	554	29.3	80.8	15.3	4.9
30340	Lewiston-Auburn, ME..................	79.1	7.3	43,450	66.5	144,800	23.5	15.8	602	28.1	79.0	23.2	8.6
30460	Lexington-Fayette, KY..................	77.4	7.3	181,595	62.2	148,500	21.4	10.2	635	28.6	80.1	20.3	6.9
30620	Lima, OH.................................	83.9	5.8	40,596	71.1	99,500	20.4	12.3	555	26.3	83.5	18.2	6.6
30700	Lincoln, NE..............................	77.6	7.6	114,228	63.4	140,700	22.6	11.6	632	28.1	80.2	18.0	5.4
30780	Little Rock-North Little Rock-Conway, AR.............................	80.1	5.9	259,043	67.1	117,200	20.3	10.7	673	28.7	81.9	21.6	5.8
30860	Logan, UT-ID............................	74.9	10.7	35,397	67.3	157,200	23.5	8.4	608	28.8	70.8	16.8	4.3
30980	Longview, TX............................	80.6	7.0	74,749	69.5	91,300	19.7	11.6	606	26.5	81.3	22.2	5.3
31020	Longview, WA...........................	79.5	8.0	37,931	67.4	168,100	25.0	10.9	634	29.1	80.0	23.0	6.5
31100	Los Angeles-Long Beach-Santa Ana, CA.........................	86.3	3.0	4,148,481	52.3	583,300	31.1	11.0	1,070	32.9	73.5	28.3	8.4

Metro area or division code	Area name	Percent who lived in the same house one year ago	Percent who did not live in MSA one year ago	Total occupied housing units	Percent owner-occupied housing units	Median value of owner-occupied housing units (dollars)	Median selected monthly owner costs as a percentage of household income		Median gross rent (dollars)	Median gross rent as a percentage of household income	Percent of workers who drove alone to work	Mean travel time to work (minutes)	Percent of occupied housing units with no vehicle available
							With a mortgage	Without a mortgage					
ACS table number:		C07204	C07201	B25003	B25003	B25077	B25092	B25092	B25064	B25071	C08301	B08013/C08012	C25045
		1	2	3	4	5	6	7	8	9	10	11	12
31100 31084	•Los Angeles-Long Beach-Glendale, CA Division	86.9	2.8	3,176,441	49.3	550,000	31.7	11.3	1,002	33.0	72.3	29.1	9.5
31100 42044	•Santa Ana-Anaheim-Irvine, CA Division	84.5	3.5	972,040	62.3	656,600	29.8	10.1	1,343	32.5	77.4	26.1	4.6
31140	Louisville-Jefferson County, KY-IN	84.3	4.0	489,689	70.8	137,800	22.5	11.3	625	28.4	82.9	22.7	7.6
31180	Lubbock, TX	73.4	8.1	102,286	59.6	92,200	21.7	11.6	699	32.4	82.5	16.7	5.0
31340	Lynchburg, VA	83.9	6.3	95,650	73.0	132,600	21.1	9.7	565	25.6	82.8	22.5	7.9
31420	Macon, GA	81.9	6.4	84,844	66.3	107,900	22.8	12.3	637	31.5	82.5	22.2	9.4
31460	Madera, CA	81.1	8.5	41,849	63.6	328,100	28.6	12.5	752	30.7	73.3	27.4	6.1
31540	Madison, WI	79.5	6.5	219,711	65.2	214,300	25.1	12.8	782	28.8	75.0	20.6	6.5
31700	Manchester-Nashua, NH	85.2	5.7	149,761	70.2	276,300	26.5	15.8	979	29.1	82.8	25.1	5.1
31900	Mansfield, OH	82.7	6.6	49,720	72.1	112,300	22.3	12.9	551	27.8	84.1	19.8	8.8
32580	McAllen-Edinburg-Mission, TX	83.5	4.8	201,366	70.4	66,200	27.5	14.2	557	34.2	75.8	20.9	8.4
32780	Medford, OR	77.7	8.4	80,058	64.2	275,800	27.9	13.4	756	31.1	77.0	18.5	6.1
32820	Memphis, TN-MS-AR	81.3	3.8	475,835	65.8	125,400	24.1	12.7	726	32.0	82.9	23.5	8.8
32900	Merced, CA	80.6	5.3	72,599	57.5	333,300	31.3	11.6	799	33.4	72.9	24.2	8.2
33100	Miami-Fort Lauderdale-Pompano Beach, FL	83.8	4.1	2,015,132	67.4	292,100	32.3	17.7	981	35.7	78.5	28.2	8.6
33100 22744	•Fort Lauderdale-Pompano Beach-Deerfield Beach, FL Division	82.7	4.4	676,384	71.2	283,700	31.4	18.6	1,057	34.5	79.9	27.0	7.1
33100 33124	•Miami-Miami Beach-Kendall, FL Division	84.7	3.4	830,844	59.7	291,900	34.2	18.1	915	37.2	77.3	30.6	11.1
33100 48424	•West Palm Beach-Boca Raton-Boynton Beach, FL Division	83.8	4.8	507,904	74.8	304,100	30.5	16.8	1,067	33.8	78.7	25.3	6.4
33140	Michigan City-La Porte, IN	84.6	6.1	41,694	75.5	117,500	22.3	12.0	604	27.2	82.9	20.6	5.5
33260	Midland, TX	80.6	8.2	46,331	67.4	94,000	20.7	11.5	633	27.8	81.8	17.1	5.1
33340	Milwaukee-Waukesha-West Allis, WI	83.9	3.3	607,687	64.4	194,800	24.8	14.9	729	29.5	80.8	21.8	9.0
33460	Minneapolis-St. Paul-Bloomington, MN-WI	84.9	3.6	1,233,149	74.7	241,000	24.8	12.1	802	29.4	78.7	24.1	6.8
33540	Missoula, MT	77.0	8.6	40,636	62.4	214,200	25.3	12.6	673	32.0	73.1	17.9	5.8
33660	Mobile, AL	84.7	4.1	150,853	68.6	105,700	22.5	12.1	628	30.6	83.9	24.0	7.0
33700	Modesto, CA	81.0	5.2	158,836	63.9	359,100	30.9	12.7	883	34.0	79.2	26.5	7.0
33740	Monroe, LA	85.0	4.6	63,125	66.0	94,700	21.2	11.3	583	32.4	84.3	21.2	9.0
33780	Monroe, MI	89.4	4.8	57,946	80.9	168,500	24.0	14.2	696	27.1	87.9	24.3	4.8
33860	Montgomery, AL	81.5	7.1	136,874	68.4	111,700	21.4	10.2	666	29.5	83.8	22.0	7.6
34060	Morgantown, WV	80.1	10.7	42,921	68.6	109,800	20.4	10.0	581	32.2	76.9	23.5	6.9
34100	Morristown, TN	83.9	6.1	51,621	73.9	106,500	21.7	9.5	541	27.0	82.5	24.0	4.5
34580	Mount Vernon-Anacortes, WA	80.5	8.2	42,982	68.6	241,900	27.4	13.4	849	29.3	78.0	24.6	5.0
34620	Muncie, IN	75.5	8.5	46,513	66.2	91,200	21.8	12.3	605	33.7	77.5	18.6	7.7
34740	Muskegon-Norton Shores, MI	84.6	5.4	65,259	79.4	116,700	24.2	12.8	555	33.3	84.2	19.5	7.3
34820	Myrtle Beach-Conway-North Myrtle Beach, SC	81.2	9.6	105,192	70.7	157,900	24.3	12.2	734	28.8	81.9	20.5	5.7
34900	Napa, CA	83.0	7.5	48,312	66.3	638,600	31.4	13.5	1,121	29.4	73.4	24.0	5.4
34940	Naples-Marco Island, FL	85.0	6.4	119,883	75.7	409,000	30.4	14.9	1,061	32.3	75.0	25.1	3.8
34980	Nashville-Davidson–Murfreesboro–Franklin, TN	82.5	5.0	574,448	69.3	158,200	23.2	10.3	714	28.4	82.3	25.7	5.1
35300	New Haven-Milford, CT	86.9	4.4	322,561	66.3	264,800	26.4	18.2	908	31.9	80.9	23.8	10.7
35380	New Orleans-Metairie-Kenner, LA	79.9	5.6	392,659	65.8	162,900	23.7	10.8	772	31.6	77.0	25.8	10.0
35620	New York-Northern New Jersey-Long Island, NY-NJ-PA	89.1	2.1	6,717,007	53.7	450,200	29.0	17.3	1,016	30.5	50.5	34.3	30.3
35620 20764	•Edison, NJ Division	89.0	2.0	836,032	75.8	370,300	27.7	18.2	1,120	30.2	76.4	31.5	7.1
35620 35004	•Nassau-Suffolk, NY Division	91.5	1.3	916,091	82.6	464,900	30.3	19.3	1,347	33.8	74.3	31.3	5.8
35620 35084	•Newark-Union, NJ-PA Division	88.0	2.2	759,711	64.1	412,400	28.1	18.1	977	29.9	70.7	30.4	13.0
35620 35644	•New York-White Plains-Wayne, NY-NJ Division	88.8	2.4	4,205,173	41.2	483,500	29.3	15.7	992	30.4	35.3	36.4	43.4
35660	Niles-Benton Harbor, MI	85.4	4.5	63,400	73.1	132,600	22.4	12.4	550	29.9	83.7	18.6	7.0
35980	Norwich-New London, CT	83.5	7.2	104,132	69.5	252,400	24.8	14.2	910	28.5	79.6	21.7	5.8
36100	Ocala, FL	82.0	9.1	127,764	78.2	142,900	25.7	12.3	732	29.4	81.2	24.1	4.3
36140	Ocean City, NJ	87.4	6.3	47,229	74.0	328,600	28.4	18.5	944	31.3	79.0	20.6	8.8
36220	Odessa, TX	81.0	6.0	45,434	71.8	58,800	19.3	12.1	571	23.2	80.7	18.6	5.8
36260	Ogden-Clearfield, UT	81.7	6.2	160,434	77.1	173,800	23.3	8.6	698	25.7	79.5	22.1	3.8
36420	Oklahoma City, OK	78.4	5.7	459,394	66.1	111,200	21.6	11.4	629	28.3	81.2	21.1	5.3
36500	Olympia, WA	80.1	8.1	91,918	65.8	236,100	24.8	11.4	835	30.4	78.0	23.9	5.0
36540	Omaha-Council Bluffs, NE-IA	82.1	4.4	317,650	68.0	139,300	22.9	13.0	693	27.2	82.8	19.3	5.7
36740	Orlando-Kissimmee, FL	79.8	7.3	752,280	66.8	229,400	27.1	12.4	937	32.9	80.2	26.8	4.9
36780	Oshkosh-Neenah, WI	80.3	9.0	65,897	67.5	136,200	23.2	14.4	601	26.8	84.5	17.3	6.1
36980	Owensboro, KY	83.0	5.0	45,945	71.3	98,000	19.7	9.9	506	28.1	85.8	19.4	5.9
37100	Oxnard-Thousand Oaks-Ventura, CA	86.1	5.2	255,527	68.5	631,000	29.6	11.4	1,299	32.1	78.9	26.1	3.9
37340	Palm Bay-Melbourne-Titusville, FL	84.8	6.4	217,708	76.7	206,300	26.4	13.0	841	32.5	83.5	23.3	4.3
37380	Palm Coast, FL	83.1	12.5	37,601	75.9	235,000	29.5	13.2	992	34.2	82.4	22.4	3.1
37460	Panama City-Lynn Haven, FL	77.0	9.6	71,417	64.8	176,500	24.3	11.2	781	28.2	80.1	21.0	5.0
37620	Parkersburg-Marietta-Vienna, WV-OH	85.9	3.8	67,453	73.1	98,100	20.7	10.3	532	32.9	81.6	21.5	8.2
37700	Pascagoula, MS	82.8	6.7	55,071	74.1	106,900	21.8	11.1	723	29.6	84.6	24.9	4.7
37860	Pensacola-Ferry Pass-Brent, FL	78.6	9.1	168,016	71.3	150,800	24.3	11.4	749	31.1	76.6	24.1	5.9
37900	Peoria, IL	85.1	4.5	148,604	73.7	116,300	21.3	12.4	623	25.6	85.0	20.2	7.0

Metro area or division code	Area name	Percent who lived in the same house one year ago	Percent who did not live in MSA one year ago	Total occupied housing units	Percent owner-occupied housing units	Median value of owner-occupied housing units (dollars)	Median selected monthly owner costs as a percentage of household income		Median gross rent (dollars)	Median gross rent as a percentage of household income	Percent of workers who drove alone to work	Mean travel time to work (minutes)	Percent of occupied housing units with no vehicle available
							With a mortgage	Without a mortgage					
ACS table number:		C07204	C07201	B25003	B25003	B25077	B25092	B25092	B25064	B25071	C08301	B08013/ C08012	C25045
		1	2	3	4	5	6	7	8	9	10	11	12
37980	Philadelphia-Camden-Wilmington, PA-NJ-DE-MD...	87.6	3.2	2,169,515	70.7	228,200	24.8	15.1	858	30.5	73.8	28.0	13.6
37980 15804	•Camden, NJ Division ...	88.4	3.1	455,256	75.6	227,500	25.9	17.7	887	30.5	79.6	27.3	7.2
37980 37964	•Philadelphia, PA Division...	88.0	3.0	1,459,832	69.0	227,800	24.8	15.1	845	30.7	70.5	28.7	16.8
37980 48864	•Wilmington, DE-MD-NJ Division ...	84.1	4.4	254,427	72.3	231,000	23.2	11.2	884	29.4	80.4	25.6	6.9
38060	Phoenix-Mesa-Scottsdale, AZ ...	78.1	6.4	1,421,271	68.8	243,500	25.1	10.8	838	29.6	74.8	26.6	6.2
38220	Pine Bluff, AR...	82.3	6.5	38,057	65.8	65,900	19.4	11.8	578	33.1	84.3	20.5	9.9
38300	Pittsburgh, PA ...	87.7	2.8	984,179	72.1	110,600	22.4	14.0	607	28.6	77.6	24.8	11.0
38340	Pittsfield, MA ...	87.9	3.8	55,127	68.0	184,900	23.4	14.2	642	27.8	78.7	18.6	8.9
38540	Pocatello, ID...	77.8	9.0	31,690	70.5	113,900	21.0	11.6	538	29.5	79.3	17.2	4.1
38860	Portland-South Portland-Biddeford, ME...	85.4	4.8	207,652	72.2	234,500	25.3	14.8	797	29.3	78.3	23.1	5.9
38900	Portland-Vancouver-Beaverton, OR-WA	80.4	5.6	817,906	64.8	262,600	26.2	12.5	786	30.0	72.0	24.6	7.9
38940	Port St. Lucie, FL ...	84.2	7.7	157,673	77.1	230,000	29.6	14.3	983	32.2	81.8	25.9	4.1
39100	Poughkeepsie-Newburgh-Middletown, NY ...	85.9	6.4	225,330	71.2	319,500	27.2	16.8	982	31.7	74.8	31.0	7.9
39140	Prescott, AZ ...	82.3	8.1	84,352	72.1	229,800	26.6	11.7	791	30.5	76.3	20.8	4.2
39300	Providence-New Bedford-Fall River, RI-MA ...	86.8	3.7	613,430	63.5	301,600	26.6	15.6	805	29.2	81.0	23.6	8.8
39340	Provo-Orem, UT ...	77.3	9.2	128,810	69.4	207,500	25.0	8.9	703	28.5	72.0	20.0	2.4
39380	Pueblo, CO ...	82.1	6.0	58,819	69.8	131,400	25.9	12.1	610	33.3	79.1	20.6	7.3
39460	Punta Gorda, FL ...	83.4	8.8	70,376	83.4	202,600	29.9	14.8	935	31.4	82.8	21.7	4.1
39540	Racine, WI ...	87.3	4.8	75,140	70.8	169,000	24.9	13.9	679	28.8	85.1	21.8	6.0
39580	Raleigh-Cary, NC ...	81.0	7.9	374,606	68.4	181,100	22.1	10.9	775	27.7	80.1	25.4	4.8
39660	Rapid City, SD ...	78.5	8.8	47,419	70.1	135,200	23.9	12.6	633	27.7	80.5	17.7	3.8
39740	Reading, PA ...	85.7	5.2	149,410	74.1	153,100	23.8	14.4	680	28.0	79.6	23.3	8.3
39820	Redding, CA ...	83.6	5.4	68,762	64.7	263,000	27.8	11.9	786	32.4	80.1	18.9	6.6
39900	Reno-Sparks, NV ...	79.1	7.2	157,000	60.3	345,900	27.9	12.5	878	29.1	75.7	21.3	6.9
40060	Richmond, VA ...	84.1	5.1	459,039	69.4	199,900	23.2	10.9	814	28.4	81.8	24.1	6.8
40140	Riverside-San Bernardino-Ontario, CA....	81.7	6.7	1,227,896	67.6	379,700	31.0	12.7	1,006	33.8	76.0	30.7	4.7
40220	Roanoke, VA ...	84.7	5.0	123,888	73.1	145,300	22.3	10.2	625	25.8	83.8	21.5	6.5
40340	Rochester, MN ...	87.0	5.2	70,452	78.8	166,300	22.5	10.5	659	25.0	77.7	17.5	5.4
40380	Rochester, NY ...	85.5	3.6	399,531	69.7	117,500	23.0	14.9	716	32.7	82.5	20.1	9.1
40420	Rockford, IL ...	84.9	5.0	126,794	73.6	120,200	24.2	14.2	644	29.6	84.1	22.9	7.2
40580	Rocky Mount, NC ...	85.1	5.1	57,073	63.1	96,400	23.4	13.2	592	29.3	82.1	20.0	9.0
40660	Rome, GA ...	82.9	6.5	34,506	69.4	113,700	23.4	11.2	614	31.9	80.1	21.3	8.8
40900	Sacramento–Arden-Arcade–Roseville, CA ...	80.4	5.8	756,162	63.4	407,800	29.2	11.2	955	32.3	75.4	25.7	6.0
40980	Saginaw-Saginaw Township North, MI ...	86.1	3.8	77,707	75.8	114,400	23.0	13.5	618	34.4	86.2	21.1	8.0
41060	St. Cloud, MN...	82.3	7.9	69,272	73.5	175,600	24.0	12.1	639	28.6	78.1	20.7	5.6
41100	St. George, UT ...	75.1	11.9	43,121	71.4	233,900	25.8	9.8	875	29.8	75.4	18.6	3.4
41140	St. Joseph, MO-KS ...	80.1	6.8	46,675	69.8	101,300	20.9	10.6	542	28.4	82.7	19.3	7.5
41180	St. Louis, MO-IL ...	85.2	3.2	1,090,503	73.3	150,700	22.4	12.2	683	29.0	82.7	24.7	7.3
41420	Salem, OR ...	78.4	7.6	136,003	64.6	187,500	26.0	12.9	680	29.8	73.0	23.2	5.9
41500	Salinas, CA ...	81.3	7.3	124,146	54.4	662,300	33.9	10.1	1,069	30.5	69.3	21.8	6.8
41540	Salisbury, MD ...	80.7	8.2	43,669	65.6	168,400	23.7	13.3	793	27.8	78.6	21.5	8.6
41620	Salt Lake City, UT ...	80.2	6.2	352,665	70.2	206,200	24.6	9.8	751	27.9	75.6	22.0	5.1
41660	San Angelo, TX ...	79.6	9.7	41,514	68.3	81,400	21.2	13.4	622	29.2	77.4	17.0	6.3
41700	San Antonio, TX...	80.5	6.1	660,410	66.4	106,100	22.4	11.9	706	28.5	78.5	24.6	7.4
41740	San Diego-Carlsbad-San Marcos, CA......	80.6	6.4	1,041,790	57.3	559,400	31.0	11.3	1,155	32.9	75.2	25.2	6.1
41780	Sandusky, OH ...	87.2	5.7	31,874	73.4	135,700	22.8	13.8	626	29.4	84.6	18.4	6.3
41860	San Francisco-Oakland-Fremont, CA	84.1	4.5	1,556,247	58.1	687,900	30.9	11.0	1,204	29.6	63.0	28.5	11.8
41860 36084	•Oakland-Fremont-Hayward, CA Division ...	83.5	4.3	881,418	63.1	627,100	31.0	11.1	1,144	31.4	68.7	29.3	7.7
41860 41884	•San Francisco-San Mateo-Redwood City, CA Division ...	84.9	4.7	674,829	51.6	818,300	30.9	10.9	1,289	28.2	55.6	27.3	17.1
41940	San Jose-Sunnyvale-Santa Clara, CA	82.7	5.3	598,755	60.8	723,600	29.8	9.7	1,282	28.4	77.1	24.5	5.1
42020	San Luis Obispo-Paso Robles, CA ...	76.2	9.8	103,026	59.2	562,400	31.5	11.5	1,077	35.5	73.3	19.7	4.0
42060	Santa Barbara-Santa Maria-Goleta, CA....	77.9	7.9	140,137	54.5	653,400	31.9	11.1	1,194	35.8	66.8	19.6	5.9
42100	Santa Cruz-Watsonville, CA ...	80.4	7.4	93,518	60.0	718,700	32.6	12.2	1,197	34.0	70.7	25.4	5.6
42140	Santa Fe, NM ...	81.6	9.0	52,956	72.2	281,500	25.3	10.3	889	31.4	71.6	21.6	3.8
42220	Santa Rosa-Petaluma, CA...	84.1	4.5	177,331	63.1	611,300	32.2	12.3	1,162	32.6	73.8	24.7	5.4
42260	Sarasota-Bradenton-Venice, FL ...	82.2	6.8	299,995	75.7	243,700	28.8	14.3	943	32.8	79.1	22.3	4.9
42340	Savannah, GA ...	82.6	6.6	123,263	63.5	153,100	23.8	12.2	809	32.7	80.7	23.4	8.3
42540	Scranton–Wilkes-Barre, PA ...	87.0	4.1	227,132	69.2	112,100	23.0	15.2	573	27.3	80.9	20.9	10.1
42660	Seattle-Tacoma-Bellevue, WA ...	79.7	5.9	1,294,535	63.6	341,700	26.9	13.1	881	28.6	71.0	27.7	7.4
42660 42644	•Seattle-Bellevue-Everett, WA Division ...	80.3	5.7	1,008,811	63.5	367,800	27.0	13.1	899	28.4	69.4	27.5	7.9
42660 45104	•Tacoma, WA Division ...	77.9	6.5	285,724	64.1	248,900	26.9	13.0	819	29.7	76.8	28.5	5.4
42680	Sebastian-Vero Beach, FL ...	82.7	9.1	58,175	75.5	211,400	27.8	15.1	927	35.6	83.6	21.9	5.2
43100	Sheboygan, WI ...	85.3	4.3	46,278	72.7	144,100	23.4	13.5	591	25.2	81.7	17.2	6.9
43300	Sherman-Denison, TX ...	81.7	6.7	43,845	70.5	91,100	23.1	14.2	662	27.6	80.3	23.0	5.3
43340	Shreveport-Bossier City, LA...	81.4	5.9	148,406	65.5	101,300	21.6	9.9	605	29.1	82.8	20.2	9.6
43580	Sioux City, IA-NE-SD ...	81.3	5.4	54,302	70.4	92,600	21.4	12.5	590	27.2	79.1	16.8	6.0
43620	Sioux Falls, SD ...	81.6	5.6	83,973	69.7	137,300	22.3	11.9	632	26.2	84.1	17.2	4.8

Metro area or division code	Area name	Percent who lived in the same house one year ago	Percent who did not live in MSA one year ago	Total occupied housing units	Percent owner-occupied housing units	Median value of owner-occupied housing units (dollars)	Median selected monthly owner costs as a percentage of household income — With a mortgage	Without a mortgage	Median gross rent (dollars)	Median gross rent as a percentage of household income	Percent of workers who drove alone to work	Mean travel time to work (minutes)	Percent of occupied housing units with no vehicle available
ACS table number:		C07204	C07201	B25003	B25003	B25077	B25092	B25092	B25064	B25071	C08301	B08013/C08012	C25045
		1	2	3	4	5	6	7	8	9	10	11	12
43780	South Bend-Mishawaka, IN-MI	85.4	5.6	121,616	73.5	114,600	21.8	12.2	675	28.1	82.3	20.4	6.6
43900	Spartanburg, SC	84.1	5.7	104,536	72.1	107,300	22.2	9.4	577	27.3	84.6	21.4	7.7
44060	Spokane, WA	78.6	7.2	178,952	65.5	163,700	24.2	11.2	649	30.4	78.0	20.6	7.2
44100	Springfield, IL	84.1	4.5	86,365	71.2	112,200	21.7	11.7	614	28.3	83.6	19.1	6.5
44140	Springfield, MA	84.6	4.7	261,819	64.5	203,700	24.4	14.7	718	31.0	81.2	22.1	10.5
44180	Springfield, MO	77.9	8.1	164,626	67.6	120,200	22.3	10.3	592	28.3	81.5	22.1	6.0
44220	Springfield, OH	85.2	4.0	55,422	72.1	109,100	22.7	13.6	606	31.5	83.2	21.6	7.4
44300	State College, PA	71.3	16.6	51,319	61.5	157,600	23.5	12.2	705	37.2	66.1	19.0	8.7
44700	Stockton, CA	80.5	6.0	207,792	63.0	401,100	31.5	12.1	908	33.6	75.9	29.6	6.1
44940	Sumter, SC	91.2	3.6	38,817	67.2	89,900	22.1	12.1	574	27.4	83.9	22.4	8.7
45060	Syracuse, NY	84.2	4.7	253,475	68.1	104,400	21.9	14.3	663	29.2	79.4	20.0	10.1
45220	Tallahassee, FL	76.8	7.9	138,401	61.7	162,700	23.8	10.6	790	34.7	79.9	22.5	6.2
45300	Tampa-St. Petersburg-Clearwater, FL	81.4	5.9	1,110,157	70.9	188,300	27.1	14.2	833	31.4	80.3	25.6	6.6
45460	Terre Haute, IN	82.8	5.5	66,964	70.5	83,600	19.9	12.6	554	29.4	83.9	21.8	6.4
45500	Texarkana, TX-Texarkana, AR	78.9	6.9	50,597	66.2	77,800	18.8	11.4	578	28.4	80.6	18.6	7.5
45780	Toledo, OH	83.2	4.2	260,925	69.0	130,900	23.3	14.3	619	30.3	84.8	20.0	8.0
45820	Topeka, KS	82.4	5.1	93,869	70.6	108,300	21.9	11.9	588	27.8	81.5	20.1	5.7
45940	Trenton-Ewing, NJ	86.0	6.7	127,253	69.5	304,600	25.8	16.5	971	30.6	72.9	26.8	10.6
46060	Tucson, AZ	77.8	7.2	370,126	65.3	194,500	24.4	10.7	686	30.7	75.2	23.7	8.3
46140	Tulsa, OK	80.6	5.0	350,732	67.8	112,300	21.9	11.5	633	28.8	81.7	20.6	5.8
46220	Tuscaloosa, AL	80.1	8.6	80,443	63.0	129,600	21.8	10.9	617	32.9	83.9	20.6	8.6
46340	Tyler, TX	79.1	8.2	69,168	69.5	109,700	22.5	13.5	693	33.1	80.9	20.8	5.6
46540	Utica-Rome, NY	85.1	5.1	117,631	68.3	89,100	21.6	14.5	587	28.6	80.7	20.1	10.1
46660	Valdosta, GA	77.2	9.3	48,739	60.9	106,100	21.9	10.8	626	28.4	82.3	18.5	6.6
46700	Vallejo-Fairfield, CA	82.3	6.9	135,704	66.8	472,500	30.9	11.3	1,127	34.0	76.0	29.5	5.4
47020	Victoria, TX	80.0	6.4	42,288	67.9	84,400	20.8	11.9	634	27.4	78.3	20.9	7.2
47220	Vineland-Millville-Bridgeton, NJ	87.9	5.0	50,165	68.4	156,500	25.6	16.2	788	32.0	81.2	25.0	10.7
47260	Virginia Beach-Norfolk-Newport News, VA-NC	80.7	6.9	620,138	65.0	219,300	25.1	12.2	864	29.5	79.0	23.3	6.3
47300	Visalia-Porterville, CA	86.6	4.3	121,457	59.7	223,600	27.2	11.3	668	28.9	73.9	21.3	7.5
47380	Waco, TX	79.5	8.2	80,973	61.8	92,800	23.2	13.4	683	33.1	80.8	18.0	6.7
47580	Warner Robins, GA	78.2	9.1	48,519	67.7	120,900	20.6	9.2	687	28.0	85.6	20.5	6.3
47900	Washington Arlington-Alexandria, DC-VA-MD-WV	83.6	5.2	1,949,715	67.4	439,800	25.0	10.7	1,160	28.7	66.4	33.3	9.8
47900 13644	•Bethesda-Gaithersburg-Frederick, MD Division	84.8	5.1	422,977	71.3	469,200	24.4	10.4	1,256	29.4	68.9	33.2	6.6
47900 47894	•Washington-Arlington-Alexandria, DC-VA-MD-WV Division	83.2	5.2	1,526,738	66.3	430,700	25.2	10.8	1,136	28.6	65.7	33.3	10.7
47940	Waterloo-Cedar Falls, IA	80.2	6.9	65,857	72.4	112,100	21.3	12.2	583	31.3	81.4	16.2	6.1
48140	Wausau, WI	87.8	4.7	52,251	77.2	131,700	22.5	13.4	609	24.6	82.3	18.2	4.3
48260	Weirton-Steubenville, WV-OH	89.0	3.5	53,076	73.3	82,500	20.2	11.1	523	28.3	83.3	22.3	8.6
48300	Wenatchee, WA	83.4	5.8	39,078	69.2	181,600	23.8	10.2	604	26.8	75.7	18.2	4.8
48540	Wheeling, WV-OH	88.2	3.4	62,371	72.3	81,400	19.7	10.9	459	28.1	84.0	22.0	10.0
48620	Wichita, KS	80.2	4.7	230,159	69.3	107,000	20.8	11.5	602	28.1	84.0	18.4	5.7
48660	Wichita Falls, TX	76.2	10.1	56,573	65.7	80,700	21.7	12.9	640	30.5	79.1	16.6	5.7
48700	Williamsport, PA	85.1	5.1	47,719	68.1	108,700	23.1	14.5	575	28.4	78.5	19.3	8.5
48900	Wilmington, NC	79.8	8.1	142,936	67.2	177,500	24.2	12.4	756	31.0	79.6	22.4	6.7
49020	Winchester, VA-WV	84.6	6.7	44,934	73.2	227,500	24.1	11.5	867	27.6	81.4	29.0	5.2
49180	Winston-Salem, NC	84.4	5.0	181,355	69.9	135,700	22.3	10.1	629	28.0	83.0	22.0	6.5
49340	Worcester, MA	88.0	4.2	287,535	68.7	289,600	25.0	15.0	811	29.1	82.7	26.8	7.7
49420	Yakima, WA	80.4	4.9	76,698	65.0	134,800	24.8	11.6	602	28.4	77.0	18.6	5.8
49620	York-Hanover, PA	87.0	5.0	162,264	77.3	156,300	23.7	13.7	688	26.1	83.5	25.1	5.7
49660	Youngstown-Warren-Boardman, OH-PA	88.6	3.2	233,944	73.6	99,100	22.6	14.0	554	29.5	86.1	20.9	7.0
49700	Yuba City, CA	80.4	8.4	54,232	61.9	292,600	28.5	11.4	755	31.2	74.9	27.6	5.8
49740	Yuma, AZ	79.1	9.2	68,857	70.3	124,700	24.5	9.9	647	28.6	74.4	19.1	6.1

Table C-4. Cities — Where: Migration, Housing, and Transportation, 2005–2007

STATE Place code	STATE City	Percent who lived in the same house one year ago	Percent who did not live in city one year ago	Total occupied housing units	Percent owner-occupied housing units	Median value of owner-occupied housing units (dollars)[1]	Median selected monthly owner costs as a percentage of household income		Median gross rent (dollars)	Median gross rent as a percentage of household income[2]	Percent of workers who drove alone to work	Mean travel time to work (minutes)	Percent of occupied housing units with no vehicle available
							With a mortgage	Without a mortgage					
	ACS table number:	C07204	C07204	B25003	B25003	B25077	B25092	B25092	B25064	B25071	C08301	B08013/C08012	C25045
		1	2	3	4	5	6	7	8	9	10	11	12
00 00000	**United States**	83.4	11.4	111,609,629	67.3	181,800	24.7	12.7	781	29.8	76.1	25.1	8.8
01 00000	**Alabama**	83.3	11.9	1,798,304	71.3	106,800	21.5	11.2	586	28.7	83.6	23.6	6.7
01 00820	Alabaster	85.9	11.0	10,380	86.6	155,400	21.2	11.2	821	22.2	86.5	30.7	2.4
01 01852	Anniston	78.9	9.4	10,241	58.8	92,600	23.5	13.5	573	28.7	88.1	21.7	11.4
01 02956	Athens	81.0	11.1	8,249	58.4	106,000	20.5	12.2	514	24.1	85.2	21.1	6.5
01 03076	Auburn	63.7	21.1	21,965	45.9	174,200	21.5	12.0	603	36.5	80.2	16.8	5.9
01 05980	Bessemer	83.7	7.1	11,490	60.5	84,000	23.3	16.6	546	32.1	85.2	23.7	13.7
01 07000	Birmingham	76.9	8.1	90,641	53.0	81,500	25.9	14.7	631	33.7	78.3	21.9	14.1
01 20104	Decatur	81.0	9.2	22,268	67.0	111,500	18.9	9.1	515	26.8	85.6	19.2	7.3
01 21184	Dothan	83.0	8.2	24,611	64.2	119,000	19.6	9.1	557	28.1	86.3	17.1	7.9
01 24184	Enterprise	72.4	18.1	9,029	65.0	121,900	19.8	8.2	608	24.1	83.9	18.0	7.0
01 26896	Florence	78.7	13.9	15,677	62.1	93,500	21.6	11.4	485	35.1	81.5	18.7	13.2
01 28696	Gadsden	76.2	11.3	16,531	60.5	67,200	23.9	15.3	488	31.9	81.3	19.4	9.8
01 35800	Homewood	73.1	22.6	11,048	58.0	282,000	24.3	14.1	822	28.5	85.5	16.3	6.2
01 35896	Hoover	77.0	16.9	29,676	69.6	240,900	21.5	8.7	863	26.2	85.7	24.2	2.7
01 37000	Huntsville	77.5	10.4	69,229	61.4	132,200	19.4	7.9	602	27.2	83.8	17.5	6.1
01 45784	Madison	82.6	12.9	13,875	70.4	192,600	18.6	7.9	701	23.2	88.2	19.8	1.4
01 50000	Mobile	82.7	7.2	74,912	59.7	103,000	22.8	12.7	626	30.9	84.2	21.1	8.3
01 51000	Montgomery	80.1	7.8	80,441	61.1	107,600	21.6	9.6	671	30.4	83.5	18.2	9.0
01 51696	Mountain Brook	87.6	9.7	8,028	90.3	547,300	20.2	9.9	803	30.3	-	16.3	1.3
01 55200	Northport	79.4	17.1	9,347	59.7	141,300	19.9	8.4	600	35.4	91.6	17.4	9.3
01 57048	Opelika	78.8	11.3	10,916	61.3	96,600	21.8	12.0	541	29.7	82.6	16.0	11.1
01 57576	Oxford	80.1	12.6	8,570	74.0	102,400	19.6	9.8	589	19.6	91.1	21.2	5.3
01 58848	Pelham	77.5	17.0	7,614	86.5	155,400	21.8	11.7	843	36.0	85.2	24.0	0.9
01 59472	Phenix	78.3	10.2	12,869	53.0	103,800	21.9	10.4	532	33.0	80.0	18.3	12.4
01 62328	Prattville	83.5	9.7	10,705	72.4	131,000	20.5	8.7	750	28.7	86.5	21.6	5.6
01 62496	Prichard	85.5	11.8	9,327	58.9	61,400	28.8	15.8	571	37.4	82.4	21.7	17.1
01 77256	Tuscaloosa	72.2	16.6	33,039	46.9	142,300	24.3	11.0	619	34.8	79.8	16.0	10.6
01 78552	Vestavia Hills	85.4	13.8	13,973	75.3	290,900	19.5	9.9	895	32.5	86.8	19.8	3.7
02 00000	**Alaska**	78.6	12.6	233,861	63.7	213,400	23.9	10.5	898	27.2	66.6	18.0	10.1
02 03000	Anchorage municipality	77.5	8.7	102,476	61.0	248,800	24.6	11.6	949	28.5	76.0	17.9	6.4
02 24230	Fairbanks	67.3	20.7	11,320	37.8	176,700	25.4	12.9	849	28.7	60.0	13.6	13.5
02 36400	Juneau city and borough	77.9	10.7	11,618	66.3	276,100	24.4	11.5	912	28.4	60.2	14.9	8.0
04 00000	**Arizona**	78.7	13.3	2,215,761	68.6	221,800	24.9	10.6	786	29.6	74.8	25.0	6.4
04 02830	Apache Junction	81.7	13.2	19,542	77.6	125,300	27.1	11.4	643	28.4	74.9	32.0	12.7
04 04720	Avondale	76.4	18.3	19,505	69.1	243,100	25.5	10.9	1066	29.8	75.7	26.5	5.1
04 07940	Buckeye town	63.6	31.3	7,357	70.2	235,100	27.5	14.6	899	26.9	70.2	34.0	5.7
04 08220	Bullhead	74.7	12.9	16,449	61.6	156,300	27.9	11.8	758	29.4	76.5	18.2	3.8
04 10530	Casa Grande	71.9	14.5	16,384	58.6	166,900	23.8	11.0	736	28.1	76.3	19.0	9.3
04 10670	Casas Adobes CDP	80.4	19.6	23,565	65.2	234,500	23.0	11.4	892	31.5	81.7	25.4	5.9
04 11230	Catalina Foothills CDP	84.6	15.4	24,558	74.8	460,000	22.8	9.8	843	27.5	79.5	23.0	2.3
04 12000	Chandler	76.7	16.5	82,288	69.9	292,800	23.5	9.5	1005	27.0	77.8	25.5	2.8
04 20540	Drexel Heights CDP	-	-	8,265	81.2	148,500	26.0	11.7	856	28.7	80.5	30.1	3.8
04 22220	El Mirage	82.2	15.1	8,699	79.4	208,400	28.0	12.5	1037	28.5	79.3	31.0	3.5
04 23620	Flagstaff	69.7	15.4	22,256	51.6	305,700	23.6	9.1	891	33.4	67.5	15.8	5.7
04 25030	Fortuna Foothills CDP	79.6	20.4	12,369	87.5	130,800	26.0	8.0	851	31.4	-	20.6	3.1
04 25300	Fountain Hills town	84.0	9.6	10,364	87.1	456,100	25.1	11.8	1237	33.7	79.7	26.8	3.4
04 27400	Gilbert town	79.2	16.3	57,609	80.6	343,600	24.2	9.2	1148	29.8	80.2	28.7	1.4
04 27820	Glendale	78.1	16.3	77,990	64.4	227,300	24.6	10.6	769	30.5	73.4	27.1	7.6
04 28380	Goodyear	74.3	22.5	16,032	82.4	325,500	25.9	9.2	1181	27.3	80.4	30.2	1.0
04 29710	Green Valley CDP	86.5	9.8	12,775	85.9	185,200	25.5	7.8	858	39.8	-	22.6	4.3
04 37620	Kingman	67.0	21.7	11,011	63.2	181,900	24.1	10.5	822	30.9	78.5	13.5	3.6
04 39370	Lake Havasu	82.8	7.6	21,869	72.2	248,000	27.8	11.7	819	32.3	78.5	19.0	3.4
04 44270	Marana town	74.8	23.6	9,847	78.1	280,900	25.6	7.7	1016	25.2	80.5	28.5	2.5
04 44410	Maricopa	58.8	38.3	7,491	83.2	261,000	28.8	7.0	1322	29.0	74.8	33.9	1.5
04 46000	Mesa	80.9	10.6	170,023	67.2	210,600	24.4	11.3	816	29.5	73.2	25.9	6.7
04 49360	New River CDP	83.7	16.1	8,903	90.7	433,700	26.4	9.2	1316	21.9	78.7	31.7	1.0
04 51600	Oro Valley town	85.5	11.5	16,058	83.4	329,100	22.8	9.1	920	27.8	83.1	27.0	1.6
04 54050	Peoria	83.2	12.6	51,333	79.4	259,900	24.9	11.8	1107	34.3	80.2	27.4	4.9
04 55000	Phoenix	76.8	9.8	483,915	60.9	230,300	25.9	11.6	778	29.9	72.7	26.0	8.3
04 57380	Prescott	78.4	12.1	19,079	67.2	324,400	25.9	10.5	801	33.5	80.2	16.4	4.4
04 57450	Prescott Valley town	83.7	11.4	14,061	66.2	215,000	25.4	11.7	797	27.7	79.7	19.9	3.1
04 58150	Queen Creek town	69.0	28.8	11,192	86.1	308,000	30.3	15.7	1173	29.9	79.1	41.2	0.3
04 63470	San Luis	-	-	3,622	77.0	105,300	26.8	13.7	519	38.6	64.7	30.4	12.4
04 65000	Scottsdale	81.7	10.7	95,783	72.6	481,000	25.1	11.0	1043	27.6	78.4	22.5	3.8
04 66820	Sierra Vista	67.6	24.5	15,716	56.3	189,300	21.7	8.3	725	28.9	74.9	14.5	5.3
04 66845	Sierra Vista Southeast CDP	85.1	14.9	6,879	84.3	175,200	25.6	7.6	935	27.8	77.8	20.8	2.0
04 70320	Sun CDP	86.0	12.1	24,383	86.4	158,400	24.6	11.2	990	42.8	88.7	23.9	7.0
04 70355	Sun West CDP	90.3	7.1	15,383	91.1	218,700	24.3	8.3	968	49.4	74.5	23.7	3.3
04 71510	Surprise	73.7	22.0	37,324	85.6	266,300	26.9	9.2	1076	29.4	75.3	33.0	2.4
04 73000	Tempe	72.9	18.1	60,024	49.2	241,500	22.0	9.0	834	30.9	72.4	21.1	7.2
04 77000	Tucson	73.7	9.3	205,563	54.2	167,500	25.0	12.1	647	31.4	72.0	21.5	11.3
04 85540	Yuma	76.0	12.2	36,235	61.5	146,000	24.4	10.5	680	27.6	75.6	17.1	6.5

1. $1,000,001 is the top code symbolizing a median value over one million dollars.
2. 50.1 is the top code symbolizing a median gross rent as a percentage of household income of 50.1 percent or more.

STATE Place code	STATE City	Percent who lived in the same house one year ago	Percent who did not live in city one year ago	Total occupied housing units	Percent owner-occupied housing units	Median value of owner-occupied housing units (dollars)[1]	Median selected monthly owner costs as a percentage of household income With a mortgage	Without a mortgage	Median gross rent (dollars)	Median gross rent as a percentage of household income[2]	Percent of workers who drove alone to work	Mean travel time to work (minutes)	Percent of occupied housing units with no vehicle available
ACS table number:		C07204	C07204	B25003	B25003	B25077	B25092	B25092	B25064	B25071	C08301	B08013/ C08012	C25045
		1	2	3	4	5	6	7	8	9	10	11	12
05 00000	**Arkansas**	80.7	13.0	1,096,622	68.0	93,700	20.6	11.3	578	28.8	80.7	20.8	6.6
05 05290	Benton	78.9	12.2	9,741	63.1	104,100	20.4	11.0	686	29.2	77.0	20.7	5.1
05 05320	Bentonville	69.7	24.8	10,717	61.4	162,100	20.7	10.7	713	26.4	79.6	15.1	4.9
05 10300	Cabot	73.1	19.0	7,582	70.2	132,300	20.6	11.3	682	24.2	84.7	27.5	4.2
05 15190	Conway	70.1	17.1	19,918	54.4	136,500	19.1	10.8	620	29.7	80.5	20.6	4.1
05 23290	Fayetteville	63.5	19.5	29,564	41.1	166,100	20.9	11.0	627	27.8	80.8	17.4	7.1
05 24550	Fort Smith	77.3	9.5	32,924	55.9	100,700	20.5	11.5	534	28.0	83.0	14.7	8.0
05 33400	Hot Springs	74.7	12.8	16,261	53.0	91,900	23.6	13.1	564	33.3	73.9	16.9	14.2
05 34750	Jacksonville	72.3	19.9	10,693	48.7	92,500	20.1	8.3	623	26.5	80.7	17.8	6.7
05 35710	Jonesboro	74.8	12.4	23,418	58.7	120,000	20.4	9.0	561	32.6	80.3	15.7	7.0
05 41000	Little Rock	77.7	8.7	79,573	59.7	134,500	21.6	12.0	707	29.6	82.2	17.2	8.5
05 50450	North Little Rock	81.7	10.6	25,538	59.2	101,400	19.6	11.7	683	34.7	84.2	18.0	8.7
05 53390	Paragould	76.7	10.5	9,731	60.9	80,800	20.1	11.0	547	30.0	84.9	18.8	9.1
05 55310	Pine Bluff	79.2	9.9	19,245	56.0	58,300	19.6	13.2	597	35.7	85.3	16.6	13.4
05 60410	Rogers	76.7	13.6	16,924	62.6	150,400	21.9	12.1	689	28.3	79.6	16.3	5.0
05 61670	Russellville	72.1	16.7	10,382	54.8	96,000	19.7	8.8	512	26.4	88.9	13.4	3.1
05 63020	Searcy	67.9	20.8	7,691	54.5	98,500	17.7	12.6	537	24.6	74.7	15.9	6.7
05 63800	Sherwood	84.1	11.7	10,016	73.6	129,800	22.2	8.1	724	25.7	88.0	19.4	2.4
05 66080	Springdale	73.0	13.1	21,653	59.4	144,400	21.5	10.5	672	27.8	76.4	18.2	5.1
05 68810	Texarkana	74.7	12.8	11,933	57.0	80,700	18.5	12.1	563	20.0	84.8	16.8	8.9
05 71480	Van Buren	75.7	12.0	7,443	63.2	93,600	20.9	10.6	631	30.9	83.4	21.3	6.7
05 74540	West Memphis	72.8	11.4	10,847	53.1	80,800	23.4	15.2	606	33.9	81.8	19.1	10.2
06 00000	**California**	83.5	10.6	12,140,888	58.4	513,200	30.5	11.5	1058	32.2	73.1	27.0	7.5
06 00296	Adelanto	63.6	29.1	6,576	60.6	262,800	33.8	16.8	982	40.6	70.3	36.7	10.3
06 00394	Agoura Hills	88.3	9.1	7,108	78.9	793,700	27.7	10.8	1893	31.6	83.3	28.0	1.8
06 00562	Alameda	83.2	11.1	29,287	49.7	669,300	28.8	11.0	1162	26.8	63.5	26.4	8.5
06 00884	Alhambra	88.0	9.5	28,535	44.3	494,200	31.1	9.6	1027	29.6	75.9	29.8	8.4
06 00947	Aliso Viejo	82.9	14.3	18,009	62.6	615,500	29.9	12.6	1730	29.8	78.9	28.4	3.2
06 01290	Altadena CDP	91.3	6.8	14,559	72.1	653,500	28.4	9.7	1099	29.1	77.5	27.4	3.6
06 02000	Anaheim	83.1	9.7	96,930	50.6	585,500	30.5	9.8	1174	35.5	73.0	26.6	6.0
06 02252	Antioch	84.1	8.6	32,217	72.9	501,500	33.1	9.3	1160	38.4	70.9	40.7	4.3
06 02364	Apple Valley town	83.7	10.3	22,697	71.5	312,200	29.5	14.7	976	40.9	77.1	32.8	5.0
06 02462	Arcadia	87.5	8.3	19,618	64.8	773,000	29.7	11.3	1184	30.5	78.1	28.1	4.2
06 02553	Arden-Arcade CDP	78.0	22.0	41,184	50.6	395,800	26.2	8.7	824	31.5	76.1	22.8	9.1
06 02980	Ashland CDP	-	-	6,623	35.5	513,800	32.3	10.1	1014	32.3	55.3	30.2	13.3
06 03064	Atascadero	79.1	9.4	10,531	60.7	465,700	29.6	11.9	965	30.6	72.1	21.0	5.6
06 03162	Atwater	74.6	11.6	9,187	58.7	299,600	31.5	12.0	850	29.0	72.4	19.2	7.2
06 03386	Azusa	79.5	13.4	13,123	53.9	410,300	29.5	9.8	1100	33.4	70.3	28.0	6.1
06 03526	Bakersfield	79.0	8.6	100,108	60.9	295,900	28.3	12.4	824	31.0	79.0	21.5	6.9
06 03666	Baldwin Park	90.6	6.6	17,557	65.6	413,800	33.6	8.6	1032	34.0	70.8	29.3	5.1
06 03820	Banning	79.1	14.3	11,048	72.4	265,800	28.8	14.8	925	34.7	75.2	25.5	3.9
06 04030	Barstow	75.2	10.1	8,158	48.9	156,500	21.9	12.3	719	30.9	72.8	24.8	11.0
06 04415	Bay Point CDP	77.3	17.3	6,370	70.2	411,100	30.5	10.3	989	35.0	67.5	32.6	6.9
06 04758	Beaumont	80.3	13.5	6,612	61.3	340,800	32.1	9.9	776	29.6	76.7	33.1	5.3
06 04870	Bell	87.2	10.7	8,869	31.2	398,500	32.5	13.1	901	33.8	69.1	28.3	13.9
06 04982	Bellflower	84.6	12.4	23,701	39.7	489,200	32.3	9.7	977	32.7	74.9	26.0	6.2
06 04996	Bell Gardens	88.3	8.3	9,741	23.4	433,300	38.2	11.6	936	32.0	71.9	27.9	7.9
06 05108	Belmont	83.5	12.7	10,490	62.5	904,600	27.8	9.8	1243	26.4	76.9	24.4	4.7
06 05290	Benicia	85.8	9.1	9,882	73.4	619,600	26.3	9.3	1197	31.7	79.2	29.6	4.7
06 06000	Berkeley	73.1	18.0	43,132	46.0	736,200	30.7	11.8	1057	36.6	46.6	25.3	15.8
06 06308	Beverly Hills	90.3	6.8	14,557	48.0	1,000,001	44.2	13.2	1678	33.9	71.1	25.2	8.5
06 07064	Bloomington CDP	86.5	12.7	5,276	77.9	325,800	30.3	10.5	931	28.1	69.6	28.4	3.8
06 07218	Blythe	69.8	22.5	4,712	48.6	162,300	25.0	8.7	616	29.5	70.8	15.0	11.3
06 08058	Brawley	82.1	9.2	7,367	51.9	203,000	24.0	12.3	617	30.2	76.0	15.5	12.4
06 08100	Brea	87.1	10.2	14,415	69.6	656,900	29.4	9.3	1292	30.9	86.4	26.2	3.5
06 08142	Brentwood	87.2	8.3	14,001	84.8	623,700	34.6	14.9	1040	34.2	78.6	43.2	1.4
06 08786	Buena Park	86.0	10.4	23,641	60.6	573,000	30.2	9.4	1257	34.2	79.9	28.0	3.5
06 08954	Burbank	86.7	10.2	40,930	43.8	626,700	31.8	12.5	1149	29.7	81.3	25.6	5.7
06 09066	Burlingame	86.1	11.2	12,221	48.7	1,000,001	32.9	12.7	1214	23.7	72.4	25.8	5.6
06 09598	Calabasas	87.9	9.3	7,814	74.0	1,000,001	31.3	12.5	1774	36.8	83.2	30.1	0.9
06 09710	Calexico	-	-	8,688	52.0	254,500	32.9	16.5	706	36.0	78.4	21.4	11.3
06 10046	Camarillo	82.9	9.0	22,581	73.0	624,900	28.6	10.5	1427	30.7	81.9	21.2	4.1
06 10345	Campbell	86.0	13.1	15,541	54.8	705,800	30.6	9.6	1235	30.0	85.2	22.9	4.9
06 11194	Carlsbad	84.4	11.7	37,759	69.1	699,100	30.4	9.6	1450	33.0	77.6	29.0	2.8
06 11390	Carmichael CDP	81.7	14.3	20,507	58.6	422,100	26.8	9.1	931	35.7	76.5	23.1	7.9
06 11530	Carson	91.7	6.6	25,425	78.4	480,400	29.2	10.3	1051	27.7	81.1	25.1	2.6
06 11964	Castro Valley CDP	86.7	11.0	20,834	70.9	654,900	29.1	11.7	1203	30.6	74.8	28.0	5.2
06 12048	Cathedral	85.7	8.2	16,371	67.6	347,900	35.6	19.5	964	39.5	74.5	18.7	5.4
06 12524	Ceres	77.7	18.5	11,845	67.0	354,700	34.7	12.9	872	34.4	78.4	26.4	3.4
06 12552	Cerritos	91.0	6.9	15,889	83.9	649,800	26.5	8.3	1685	32.7	83.2	29.3	2.4
06 13014	Chico	62.1	17.2	33,401	40.6	326,500	27.2	13.2	863	39.6	72.5	16.7	8.6
06 13210	Chino	80.1	17.1	19,661	70.4	488,400	30.6	10.5	1136	31.7	82.1	30.7	3.5
06 13214	Chino Hills	87.9	9.0	22,801	83.5	594,200	28.6	7.9	1684	30.2	82.1	36.6	1.5
06 13392	Chula Vista	82.5	11.4	71,189	60.0	563,500	35.1	9.6	1076	36.4	78.1	27.6	6.0
06 13588	Citrus Heights	80.5	15.0	33,903	58.2	342,000	30.1	12.4	956	30.1	78.5	26.0	4.8

1. $1,000,001 is the top code symbolizing a median value over one million dollars.
2. 50.1 is the top code symbolizing a median gross rent as a percentage of household income of 50.1 percent or more.

STATE Place code	STATE City	Percent who lived in the same house one year ago	Percent who did not live in city one year ago	Total occupied housing units	Percent owner-occupied housing units	Median value of owner-occupied housing units (dollars)[1]	Median selected monthly owner costs as a percentage of household income		Median gross rent (dollars)	Median gross rent as a percentage of household income[2]	Percent of workers who drove alone to work	Mean travel time to work (minutes)	Percent of occupied housing units with no vehicle available
							With a mortgage	Without a mortgage					
	ACS table number:	C07204	C07204	B25003	B25003	B25077	B25092	B25092	B25064	B25071	C08301	B08013/C08012	C25045
		1	2	3	4	5	6	7	8	9	10	11	12
	California—Cont.												
06 13756	Claremont	82.9	13.5	11,230	69.2	617,100	26.2	10.4	1073	29.7	72.4	28.7	4.6
06 14218	Clovis	83.9	12.2	30,024	62.6	359,400	26.9	12.0	874	33.4	84.9	20.4	5.6
06 14260	Coachella	85.1	9.7	7,529	57.7	273,400	32.7	12.8	734	32.3	69.7	21.5	2.4
06 14890	Colton	81.9	15.0	15,842	54.6	282,100	32.6	14.5	973	35.6	79.9	25.2	4.5
06 15044	Compton	89.1	8.2	23,180	58.2	368,200	34.3	11.4	791	36.9	72.0	28.3	7.1
06 16000	Concord	81.3	11.3	43,909	63.0	565,700	31.8	11.2	1142	34.2	67.1	29.2	6.0
06 16224	Corcoran	71.4	25.4	3,473	58.9	150,500	25.7	8.0	609	39.7	69.0	25.1	12.1
06 16350	Corona	82.5	12.4	45,368	70.7	532,600	31.8	11.0	1188	32.4	75.2	32.2	3.8
06 16378	Coronado	71.6	22.6	7,373	53.6	1,000,001	30.8	15.7	1400	28.3	52.1	16.5	4.4
06 16532	Costa Mesa	80.4	12.1	38,665	40.8	690,500	30.4	9.3	1364	32.1	74.6	22.8	6.2
06 16742	Covina	83.8	13.2	16,395	57.4	487,000	29.6	9.7	1120	35.1	81.1	31.4	7.1
06 17498	Cudahy	84.7	13.5	5,515	19.8	400,800	34.9	14.2	947	29.8	72.3	31.6	11.2
06 17568	Culver	89.6	8.1	16,802	57.9	586,700	29.0	14.7	1213	29.0	80.1	25.4	7.3
06 17610	Cupertino	87.6	10.1	18,753	66.0	948,200	27.9	10.1	1765	22.5	80.7	23.5	3.2
06 17750	Cypress	87.2	9.7	16,031	68.3	626,100	28.4	8.8	1362	31.2	83.1	27.6	3.5
06 17918	Daly	83.8	11.0	29,843	60.5	643,000	34.6	9.3	1314	29.7	58.5	28.8	7.5
06 17946	Dana Point	85.4	11.9	13,720	64.1	880,400	32.9	10.3	161/	33.4	78.5	28.8	3.0
06 17988	Danville town	92.0	5.3	15,246	88.8	973,100	29.4	10.4	1764	32.8	78.3	27.4	1.7
06 18100	Davis	66.6	16.9	24,333	43.5	597,300	24.4	8.2	1152	36.8	61.9	20.1	7.1
06 18394	Delano	74.5	19.0	9,663	55.7	200,000	30.7	10.9	617	30.7	63.0	23.5	9.5
06 18996	Desert Hot Springs	73.9	16.5	7,396	50.4	255,300	30.1	13.6	804	32.8	70.0	29.5	10.4
06 19192	Diamond Bar	93.0	5.7	17,867	83.7	598,300	28.6	9.9	1704	37.1	82.6	35.7	1.4
06 19318	Dinuba	87.3	5.3	5,092	60.0	213,300	26.0	10.5	703	30.3	73.9	19.9	4.2
06 19766	Downey	86.9	9.9	34,119	54.5	593,300	31.4	9.9	1041	32.6	81.7	26.7	4.0
06 19990	Duarte	85.0	13.6	6,836	67.2	479,500	31.3	11.9	993	27.8	75.1	29.3	8.6
06 20018	Dublin	77.3	19.9	12,809	65.4	723,600	30.5	8.5	1521	24.2	77.3	27.3	2.5
06 20802	East Los Angeles CDP	93.1	6.8	30,392	35.4	386,800	34.3	10.0	790	32.2	62.5	28.8	17.2
06 20956	East Palo Alto	82.1	10.3	6,648	50.4	635,000	47.1	21.1	1028	34.1	72.7	20.1	8.1
06 21712	El Cajon	79.7	13.4	32,312	45.7	445,600	32.4	10.9	960	33.6	77.3	24.3	8.9
06 21782	El Centro	85.3	8.4	13,971	50.4	241,600	30.8	11.8	662	31.1	80.8	15.1	12.4
06 21796	El Cerrito	82.9	14.8	10,362	65.9	628,700	27.5	12.5	1286	28.7	59.8	30.8	6.5
06 21880	El Dorado Hills CDP	82.4	13.2	10,813	84.8	687,000	28.3	9.8	1555	29.0	79.1	31.5	0.3
06 22020	Elk Grove	82.7	12.4	43,582	81.0	452,000	29.5	10.0	1348	31.9	78.7	32.0	2.4
06 22230	El Monte	87.9	7.3	27,365	41.1	414,100	36.3	10.8	966	36.8	78.7	26.3	9.4
06 22300	El Paso de Robles (Paso Robles)	78.6	11.5	10,876	61.6	452,800	31.9	12.2	983	33.7	71.0	21.1	7.2
06 22678	Encinitas	84.9	12.2	22,875	64.7	762,400	29.8	9.7	1454	32.2	76.3	24.6	2.4
06 22804	Escondido	80.9	8.9	44,988	56.0	463,200	32.3	13.6	1041	35.8	73.3	27.6	8.1
06 23042	Eureka	75.6	12.6	11,304	44.4	278,600	28.2	9.0	662	33.3	69.6	14.3	9.8
06 23182	Fairfield	80.2	10.9	33,330	63.1	470,300	31.2	11.7	1122	34.5	75.0	29.2	5.5
06 23294	Fair Oaks CDP	85.3	12.4	11,044	72.5	502,900	25.2	8.9	933	30.3	75.9	25.3	3.1
06 23462	Fallbrook CDP	83.9	10.5	10,120	64.5	569,500	35.4	13.4	925	32.0	75.0	31.7	5.8
06 24477	Florence-Graham CDP	89.8	10.2	14,337	39.4	373,400	38.5	8.1	829	39.1	64.3	28.3	14.6
06 24498	Florin CDP	78.5	21.5	8,700	61.0	254,700	32.2	13.6	930	36.7	73.6	26.8	9.5
06 24638	Folsom	80.7	13.9	23,610	74.2	512,800	27.1	13.2	1185	28.3	78.2	25.2	4.6
06 24680	Fontana	83.5	11.7	45,602	72.3	420,800	33.4	10.2	976	33.3	74.7	31.6	4.0
06 25338	Foster	82.0	15.6	11,967	60.6	790,500	28.5	11.3	1777	23.9	78.9	25.1	3.0
06 25380	Fountain Valley	90.6	7.9	18,685	72.9	684,100	30.1	8.4	1396	34.5	84.6	24.3	1.2
06 26000	Fremont	82.3	10.5	68,264	66.2	658,700	28.2	9.6	1393	26.4	76.2	29.0	2.8
06 27000	Fresno	79.0	6.7	152,113	49.7	270,700	27.9	12.2	778	33.3	76.6	20.1	3.9
06 28000	Fullerton	82.3	11.7	45,697	55.1	630,800	29.6	9.1	1189	34.4	78.7	25.8	10.8
06 28112	Galt	-	-	6,739	83.6	362,200	34.2	15.9	906	31.1	78.0	28.4	4.8
06 28168	Gardena	89.9	7.8	20,263	49.5	464,500	30.5	12.2	925	35.5	76.4	24.8	4.1
06 29000	Garden Grove	85.1	10.4	46,160	61.6	547,400	31.3	9.0	1183	35.8	80.1	27.4	5.9
06 29504	Gilroy	82.5	7.9	13,740	64.8	684,800	33.9	11.0	1175	41.6	67.6	29.0	5.4
06 30000	Glendale	88.5	6.1	70,771	39.3	667,100	32.4	12.8	1127	35.8	78.6	25.4	7.8
06 30014	Glendora	89.4	8.6	16,744	74.5	573,500	29.1	11.6	1168	31.4	76.1	28.6	12.0
06 30378	Goleta	84.0	16.0	10,576	57.0	815,800	32.9	9.5	1489	32.8	70.5	16.2	4.1
06 30693	Granite Bay CDP	90.5	6.3	7,286	91.4	807,400	27.3	10.4	1461	30.3	79.3	28.8	4.4
06 31596	Hacienda Heights CDP	91.5	6.9	15,334	80.1	544,900	29.1	11.0	1277	42.5	80.2	33.4	1.8
06 31960	Hanford	81.8	9.7	15,916	57.1	236,500	26.2	11.0	759	30.0	79.2	20.2	5.5
06 32548	Hawthorne	88.6	8.6	29,277	27.5	560,700	38.3	10.8	898	30.9	76.8	29.3	8.0
06 33000	Hayward	81.5	11.5	41,870	58.3	551,000	33.3	9.4	1174	33.0	71.3	27.0	10.0
06 33182	Hemet	71.2	17.8	29,975	61.3	207,400	33.3	15.5	904	38.0	72.3	34.0	6.2
06 33308	Hercules	91.2	6.8	7,841	86.2	622,500	35.0	12.0	1798	33.5	68.7	36.6	11.0
06 33434	Hesperia	82.1	12.3	24,573	75.0	320,200	32.8	12.7	963	36.6	75.0	40.3	3.6
06 33588	Highland	83.8	13.5	15,631	67.6	365,700	28.0	12.1	909	42.2	79.1	27.5	2.7
06 34120	Hollister	-	-	10,116	62.3	604,800	33.5	13.0	1087	31.7	74.1	27.5	5.5
06 36000	Huntington Beach	86.4	9.0	73,781	61.7	739,800	28.5	10.0	1412	28.5	81.7	26.5	6.2
06 36056	Huntington Park	92.5	5.5	14,808	28.4	422,100	39.4	8.9	778	33.3	61.0	28.9	3.3
06 36294	Imperial Beach	71.3	22.0	8,946	34.7	530,500	32.6	8.3	992	33.5	66.4	28.1	19.4
06 36448	Indio	78.8	11.6	20,574	60.5	343,000	33.4	11.0	854	34.3	77.6	19.6	8.9
06 36546	Inglewood	88.3	8.9	37,606	36.4	462,200	37.3	13.4	915	32.6	72.0	29.2	4.3
06 36770	Irvine	75.9	18.2	65,999	57.2	716,300	28.5	9.4	1746	29.6	78.7	22.5	9.5
06 39003	La Canada Flintridge	-	-	6,780	89.8	1,000,001	29.6	8.8	2001	29.0	85.8	24.5	3.3
													1.9

1. $1,000,001 is the top code symbolizing a median value over one million dollars.
2. 50.1 is the top code symbolizing a median gross rent as a percentage of household income of 50.1 percent or more.

Table C-4. Cities — Where: Migration, Housing, and Transportation, 2005–2007—*Continued*

STATE Place code	STATE City	Percent who lived in the same house one year ago	Percent who did not live in city one year ago	Total occupied housing units	Percent owner-occupied housing units	Median value of owner-occupied housing units (dollars)[1]	Median selected monthly owner costs as a percentage of household income		Median gross rent (dollars)	Median gross rent as a percentage of household income[2]	Percent of workers who drove alone to work	Mean travel time to work (minutes)	Percent of occupied housing units with no vehicle available
							With a mortgage	Without a mortgage					
	ACS table number:	C07204	C07204	B25003	B25003	B25077	B25092	B25092	B25064	B25071	C08301	B08013/C08012	C25045
		1	2	3	4	5	6	7	8	9	10	11	12
	California—Cont.												
06 39122	Lafayette	89.4	8.0	8,998	75.4	1,000,001	27.0	9.5	1384	28.1	72.1	27.6	1.2
06 39178	Laguna Beach	83.8	13.5	11,012	60.9	1,000,001	31.3	11.5	1507	30.1	80.6	28.6	2.2
06 39220	Laguna Hills	87.5	10.8	10,319	77.3	716,200	29.0	8.5	1667	43.4	77.5	25.4	3.2
06 39248	Laguna Niguel	88.3	9.3	23,940	75.5	825,200	28.9	11.6	1697	34.5	81.6	26.7	2.6
06 39290	La Habra	83.1	12.4	18,819	56.8	548,500	27.6	11.1	1160	32.3	78.6	27.9	5.1
06 39486	Lake Elsinore	79.6	16.1	11,948	68.2	413,300	35.5	13.4	959	37.6	77.0	38.8	3.5
06 39496	Lake Forest	85.7	9.6	25,716	74.8	636,100	28.2	12.6	1651	30.0	79.4	26.0	2.3
06 39892	Lakewood	90.7	8.4	26,706	73.7	565,400	28.9	9.0	1213	29.2	83.2	27.3	3.7
06 40004	La Mesa	78.8	17.6	23,612	49.4	492,900	30.0	10.1	1086	34.8	79.3	22.5	9.9
06 40032	La Mirada	90.4	8.2	14,861	83.0	578,300	26.8	10.0	1213	37.2	83.9	30.0	4.2
06 40130	Lancaster	81.2	11.1	43,977	61.9	310,800	30.7	13.1	989	38.9	74.7	32.7	7.0
06 40326	La Presa CDP	89.3	10.7	10,524	64.9	445,300	32.9	7.8	1112	41.0	80.8	27.5	3.8
06 40340	La Puente	83.8	9.0	9,824	58.5	430,800	35.1	12.3	1013	34.4	73.7	29.6	5.1
06 40354	La Quinta	83.1	13.4	12,484	76.8	487,800	28.4	13.5	1317	31.2	79.9	21.0	3.8
06 40830	La Verne	89.0	8.6	11,143	77.7	525,800	28.1	11.4	1151	26.2	79.7	29.4	3.5
06 40886	Lawndale	89.9	6.7	9,393	35.6	465,300	30.1	10.5	1108	34.8	76.5	23.2	7.3
06 41124	Lemon Grove	88.9	9.8	7,967	61.9	448,500	29.5	13.6	1068	33.8	80.8	26.9	6.3
06 41152	Lemoore	79.6	14.3	7,759	60.3	235,100	27.1	9.3	810	26.0	80.6	21.0	2.7
06 41180	Lennox CDP	-	-	5,607	27.3	449,500	40.2	9.8	901	37.2	67.0	28.9	8.3
06 41474	Lincoln	82.0	13.6	13,717	75.0	458,200	32.4	12.7	985	38.0	80.9	31.2	2.3
06 41992	Livermore	86.9	8.1	27,601	71.4	663,500	28.8	9.1	1300	26.4	79.7	26.9	3.3
06 42202	Lodi	81.8	8.0	21,887	55.4	379,200	28.2	13.4	929	35.4	78.6	22.9	5.7
06 42370	Loma Linda	76.8	19.6	8,703	40.6	363,300	29.9	12.5	1065	30.6	70.8	19.5	8.7
06 42468	Lomita	-	-	7,622	44.3	554,700	27.3	9.2	1128	28.0	83.5	22.8	4.0
06 42524	Lompoc	75.0	13.0	13,343	50.3	405,200	31.8	9.1	928	33.3	64.1	26.3	6.0
06 43000	Long Beach	81.9	9.4	161,229	42.2	555,500	31.3	9.3	939	32.8	72.8	28.1	12.0
06 43280	Los Altos	90.9	8.4	10,575	85.3	1,000,001	27.2	10.6	2001	27.0	80.6	20.8	2.5
06 44000	Los Angeles	86.5	5.2	1,274,791	39.9	594,900	33.9	12.7	962	33.9	67.3	29.4	12.9
06 44028	Los Banos	84.0	8.2	9,626	66.8	405,000	35.2	11.9	959	43.6	72.6	41.8	7.7
06 44112	Los Gatos town	86.2	11.6	12,015	67.7	1,000,001	28.6	8.8	1390	26.7	81.7	24.7	3.6
06 44574	Lynwood	85.2	12.0	14,854	52.0	433,200	34.5	11.8	881	35.6	69.6	26.8	7.3
06 45022	Madera	79.3	7.1	14,642	50.9	301,400	28.6	11.1	728	29.6	67.5	25.8	10.0
06 45400	Manhattan Beach	86.5	9.9	13,932	72.0	1,000,001	28.0	8.5	1871	25.1	80.8	29.9	2.4
06 45484	Manteca	82.0	12.2	19,572	65.3	429,500	31.6	13.9	970	29.0	77.0	33.1	4.0
06 46114	Martinez	87.0	9.4	13,872	71.5	603,100	28.7	10.0	1100	30.2	77.0	26.9	4.7
06 46492	Maywood	90.7	6.4	6,669	29.8	383,100	36.8	8.4	876	32.9	65.4	28.4	11.9
06 46870	Menlo Park	86.0	12.0	11,908	63.8	1,000,001	29.1	8.6	1596	23.9	70.4	20.4	5.0
06 46898	Merced	72.8	8.3	22,993	43.7	321,100	27.6	12.8	770	37.0	72.0	19.6	12.3
06 47486	Millbrae	89.6	7.7	7,941	64.2	935,500	31.4	12.2	1379	32.7	64.6	26.2	7.3
06 47766	Milpitas	80.4	15.4	18,147	66.2	652,400	30.1	8.6	1408	28.8	81.1	21.3	5.1
06 47976	Mira Loma CDP	-	-	5,384	74.2	464,800	31.8	11.1	1188	33.9	77.3	31.4	1.5
06 48256	Mission Viejo	89.7	8.4	33,726	79.9	679,500	28.2	11.7	1625	33.4	80.4	26.0	2.9
06 48354	Modesto	81.0	7.7	68,441	61.0	348,900	29.9	12.6	933	34.7	82.3	25.3	8.2
06 48648	Monrovia	82.6	13.9	13,613	50.4	560,400	28.5	12.3	1103	31.2	71.2	27.0	6.2
06 48788	Montclair	86.2	10.4	9,043	58.5	397,600	29.6	14.8	991	29.8	70.6	30.3	2.7
06 48816	Montebello	88.6	8.4	19,310	45.9	472,600	31.8	10.4	972	28.9	74.8	26.9	8.0
06 48872	Monterey	71.8	24.8	12,132	36.7	810,200	28.5	9.6	1184	30.6	57.4	14.7	6.8
06 48914	Monterey Park	93.4	4.7	20,017	53.1	496,200	33.2	10.6	988	30.0	78.4	28.5	10.1
06 49138	Moorpark	93.9	4.3	9,398	82.8	644,000	30.0	11.3	1542	36.1	81.1	30.1	1.9
06 49270	Moreno Valley	85.9	8.7	47,554	70.6	367,900	34.0	13.1	1155	40.4	78.1	35.9	4.7
06 49278	Morgan Hill	82.5	12.8	11,378	79.6	762,300	28.0	8.2	1212	35.3	76.7	29.2	2.4
06 49670	Mountain View	79.9	15.3	31,508	41.9	727,600	26.3	9.6	1338	25.3	76.9	21.4	5.0
06 50076	Murrieta	83.4	12.1	28,838	76.9	472,500	33.5	13.8	1265	33.1	77.3	35.2	2.1
06 50258	Napa	80.5	9.1	28,109	59.9	612,200	31.6	13.3	1105	30.3	75.4	23.6	7.1
06 50398	National	80.4	13.8	14,474	34.4	435,300	40.5	10.3	840	34.0	56.5	25.0	15.9
06 50916	Newark	88.9	7.3	12,757	75.1	610,500	32.0	9.3	1296	29.7	78.4	25.2	3.2
06 51182	Newport Beach	83.7	10.9	36,748	60.9	1,000,001	29.4	9.5	1840	26.2	81.3	23.4	2.1
06 51560	Norco	75.7	22.2	6,797	81.6	610,300	29.3	10.6	1560	41.0	75.0	32.5	3.4
06 51924	North Highlands CDP	79.7	17.7	15,365	55.0	266,200	34.2	14.6	939	34.4	72.5	25.7	7.3
06 52379	North Tustin CDP	93.5	6.5	8,549	94.3	933,700	29.6	8.0	2001	23.5	86.2	22.6	1.3
06 52526	Norwalk	89.7	7.5	27,720	68.4	452,300	33.1	9.6	1129	33.7	76.3	27.8	6.0
06 52582	Novato	82.1	11.6	19,732	69.5	729,700	33.0	11.4	1438	38.2	71.4	32.0	5.9
06 53000	Oakland	81.6	8.6	145,409	44.9	558,200	34.5	13.4	947	32.4	58.9	27.4	17.0
06 53070	Oakley	89.7	8.3	8,962	80.3	484,400	33.8	12.6	1532	40.7	75.8	39.0	1.8
06 53322	Oceanside	80.6	11.4	59,615	64.2	502,300	32.7	12.4	1213	31.5	75.1	29.3	6.1
06 53448	Oildale CDP	67.1	32.9	12,199	50.1	187,300	27.3	13.3	763	31.0	77.3	19.6	9.6
06 53896	Ontario	84.2	9.3	45,269	59.1	405,000	30.3	10.8	1078	29.5	76.6	27.4	4.4
06 53980	Orange	83.3	10.9	42,350	65.3	642,800	30.4	9.8	1273	31.2	76.6	25.3	3.8
06 54092	Orangevale CDP	84.7	11.7	9,644	74.1	399,600	29.4	10.6	1067	28.7	79.6	27.1	2.5
06 54120	Orcutt CDP	87.7	11.9	10,226	79.2	472,800	28.0	11.3	1470	31.1	81.0	19.6	2.3
06 54652	Oxnard	84.8	7.4	47,126	59.2	573,700	32.9	10.5	1144	35.1	71.5	25.7	5.7
06 54806	Pacifica	87.1	8.8	14,004	70.4	708,900	29.9	9.2	1486	30.8	72.9	28.8	4.2
06 55156	Palmdale	85.5	9.1	38,914	71.3	353,900	31.9	13.0	981	41.3	72.4	40.2	3.9
06 55184	Palm Desert	78.6	16.9	22,563	66.2	403,300	28.3	14.9	1048	33.0	79.3	20.7	3.3
06 55254	Palm Springs	79.9	14.3	20,347	59.9	398,300	34.7	17.0	925	33.5	75.3	20.0	8.4

1. $1,000,001 is the top code symbolizing a median value over one million dollars.
2. 50.1 is the top code symbolizing a median gross rent as a percentage of household income of 50.1 percent or more.

STATE Place code	STATE City	Percent who lived in the same house one year ago	Percent who did not live in city one year ago	Total occupied housing units	Percent owner-occupied housing units	Median value of owner-occupied housing units (dollars)[1]	Median selected monthly owner costs as a percentage of household income		Median gross rent (dollars)	Median gross rent as a percentage of house-hold income[2]	Percent of workers who drove alone to work	Mean travel time to work (minutes)	Percent of occupied housing units with no vehicle available
							With a mortgage	Without a mortgage					
ACS table number:		C07204	C07204	B25003	B25003	B25077	B25092	B25092	B25064	B25071	C08301	B08013/C08012	C25045
		1	2	3	4	5	6	7	8	9	10	11	12
	California—Cont.												
06 55282	Palo Alto	83.3	12.2	25,486	60.1	1,000,001	25.5	7.9	1579	23.9	71.9	20.6	6.9
06 55520	Paradise town	85.4	8.5	11,671	71.2	245,000	30.3	13.3	691	33.4	80.4	21.0	7.4
06 55618	Paramount	86.9	8.6	14,366	45.5	356,800	37.7	13.3	1009	35.4	71.5	26.9	5.4
06 55837	Parkway-South Sacramento CDP	-	-	10,557	42.8	273,100	33.5	10.4	751	38.9	57.0	22.7	15.0
06 56000	Pasadena	83.2	11.0	51,973	47.6	663,900	28.7	10.0	1101	30.9	73.0	25.6	10.0
06 56700	Perris	78.9	14.2	14,029	65.1	330,500	36.2	13.1	1064	35.0	72.5	36.2	4.4
06 56784	Petaluma	86.7	8.2	21,081	68.5	615,800	31.4	12.0	1259	32.2	70.7	29.2	5.8
06 56924	Pico Rivera	91.2	7.6	17,270	68.8	451,800	28.4	8.8	1055	33.7	76.2	28.9	5.9
06 57456	Pittsburg	79.1	10.2	19,308	62.5	459,300	33.0	14.1	1093	38.0	63.6	35.3	6.7
06 57526	Placentia	89.0	7.7	16,022	67.4	615,900	29.0	8.4	1295	33.2	77.9	26.6	3.2
06 57764	Pleasant Hill	82.6	13.3	13,673	64.8	658,900	29.1	12.7	1245	29.1	74.8	27.8	7.1
06 57792	Pleasanton	85.7	9.7	24,917	71.8	820,000	27.8	9.4	1439	23.9	78.0	27.4	2.1
06 58072	Pomona	83.1	10.3	38,643	59.9	397,800	32.9	11.9	981	36.9	69.2	29.7	7.5
06 58240	Porterville	85.0	6.9	15,151	56.8	206,700	28.0	12.7	642	30.2	69.7	21.8	9.9
06 58296	Port Hueneme	77.4	19.0	7,267	56.3	459,800	33.9	16.8	1165	32.7	70.1	21.5	4.6
06 58520	Poway	87.6	9.9	16,147	77.2	664,800	26.8	10.7	1240	29.0	81.4	25.7	2.7
06 59444	Rancho Cordova	78.2	14.4	21,801	52.9	320,300	29.5	9.5	894	33.1	75.2	27.4	8.2
06 59451	Rancho Cucamonga	84.4	12.2	50,890	67.7	508,100	28.5	11.6	1345	32.9	82.3	29.7	3.1
06 59514	Rancho Palos Verdes	90.5	7.6	16,061	77.5	1,000,001	30.2	8.8	2001	28.7	83.0	33.1	1.9
06 59550	Rancho San Diego CDP	84.7	15.3	7,166	80.1	648,200	30.3	10.6	1459	28.0	-	26.1	0.9
06 59587	Rancho Santa Margarita	87.0	9.7	16,658	77.3	664,400	31.6	13.7	1636	30.9	84.2	27.1	3.3
06 59920	Redding	79.6	9.3	35,621	55.4	274,900	26.4	12.5	807	32.8	79.9	16.2	8.2
06 59962	Redlands	80.9	11.2	25,468	61.5	415,700	27.5	9.8	1063	33.7	78.7	23.1	4.3
06 60018	Redondo Beach	84.4	12.5	28,634	51.4	788,000	26.8	9.6	1423	25.4	77.7	27.5	4.1
06 60102	Redwood	83.5	10.3	27,423	54.3	820,900	29.2	10.8	1323	31.3	73.3	22.9	5.0
06 60242	Reedley	89.1	8.8	6,350	62.8	236,200	27.0	10.1	706	33.5	57.4	22.5	13.3
06 60466	Rialto	82.4	13.4	25,781	69.7	356,400	32.9	11.6	980	38.7	74.2	33.1	6.0
06 60620	Richmond	81.8	12.1	33,997	57.7	470,800	36.4	11.3	1051	34.9	62.6	32.4	11.6
06 60704	Ridgecrest	75.2	16.1	10,331	62.1	187,000	18.4	9.0	664	25.5	70.3	16.5	6.5
06 61068	Riverbank	83.5	8.6	5,958	71.2	352,800	32.5	12.7	997	29.8	80.7	28.7	5.2
06 62000	Riverside	79.0	10.7	91,780	57.2	406,800	30.3	9.8	1026	32.9	72.8	29.8	6.0
06 62364	Rocklin	79.8	14.3	19,851	67.5	487,300	29.6	13.7	1173	32.2	80.0	25.8	3.0
06 62546	Rohnert Park	79.7	12.5	15,665	56.5	488,400	33.7	15.7	1190	32.6	79.3	27.2	6.9
06 62896	Rosemead	93.6	5.0	14,110	54.0	467,300	32.2	11.0	1021	39.8	74.9	26.6	8.9
06 62910	Rosemont CDP	75.8	24.2	8,660	55.5	330,900	28.8	7.8	951	34.5	78.7	24.5	7.7
06 62938	Roseville	79.2	12.6	43,353	64.8	457,900	27.9	12.0	1069	29.9	78.6	25.6	4.3
06 63218	Rowland Heights CDP	85.5	11.7	14,518	67.0	605,700	29.4	9.1	1238	34.6	72.6	32.9	5.4
06 63260	Rubidoux CDP	82.1	17.7	9,439	66.0	348,100	27.5	9.8	875	31.7	71.8	29.2	4.8
06 64000	Sacramento	77.6	9.8	169,544	52.5	354,300	29.8	10.6	916	32.2	71.3	23.6	9.9
06 64224	Salinas	80.9	6.5	40,426	49.6	584,800	36.5	9.2	967	30.1	68.7	22.3	8.7
06 65000	San Bernardino	78.9	12.9	61,617	52.6	300,800	31.7	11.8	850	36.2	75.7	27.8	9.9
06 65028	San Bruno	84.3	15.0	15,486	63.2	671,700	33.0	10.6	1447	29.2	72.0	22.3	4.3
06 65042	San Buenaventura (Ventura)	82.3	9.8	39,476	58.0	602,500	28.8	9.8	1238	31.5	80.4	22.3	4.9
06 65070	San Carlos	90.1	7.5	11,607	76.1	927,200	27.5	11.6	1401	34.7	79.6	25.5	6.3
06 65084	San Clemente	88.4	7.3	22,971	69.5	883,100	32.5	10.0	1370	31.2	78.5	25.5	4.2
06 66000	San Diego	78.6	9.8	464,555	50.5	567,100	29.7	10.3	1184	32.1	75.1	23.0	7.2
06 66070	San Dimas	89.1	9.5	12,727	75.2	543,100	29.4	9.7	1231	28.1	80.8	30.1	5.2
06 66140	San Fernando	-	-	5,838	51.8	448,500	37.3	9.3	919	35.1	69.3	24.7	9.8
06 67000	San Francisco	84.3	7.0	321,692	38.4	789,400	30.6	11.3	1197	27.3	39.6	29.1	29.7
06 67042	San Gabriel	87.0	10.2	12,430	47.8	556,000	30.6	9.3	1098	33.5	72.5	26.8	4.3
06 67056	Sanger	82.6	9.4	6,369	63.3	232,600	27.9	14.6	668	25.2	77.7	24.8	7.3
06 67112	San Jacinto	78.6	13.0	11,687	65.8	287,300	32.6	13.0	873	40.5	77.2	32.6	5.5
06 68000	San Jose	83.0	6.2	286,965	61.6	665,200	30.8	10.9	1227	30.5	77.6	25.5	5.5
06 68028	San Juan Capistrano	89.9	7.4	11,460	82.7	647,000	32.5	14.4	1416	33.8	75.9	22.8	3.7
06 68084	San Leandro	87.9	9.1	30,805	62.2	583,400	31.0	10.4	1068	29.6	69.3	26.8	6.3
06 68112	San Lorenzo CDP	91.7	7.8	7,643	73.3	577,500	29.4	10.4	1381	30.4	73.6	26.8	5.8
06 68154	San Luis Obispo	63.1	18.1	21,510	36.9	584,300	30.2	11.0	1113	50.1	71.2	14.3	5.1
06 68196	San Marcos	83.2	11.9	24,220	68.1	521,400	30.4	14.2	1173	35.1	74.5	27.8	4.5
06 68252	San Mateo	83.8	10.2	36,501	55.2	783,900	31.4	11.0	1394	28.3	73.4	23.4	7.4
06 68294	San Pablo	81.9	13.3	9,277	54.8	432,700	33.8	16.1	997	39.9	59.2	29.5	13.6
06 68364	San Rafael	79.7	14.2	22,466	54.0	847,600	31.4	12.2	1302	35.1	62.1	26.0	9.5
06 68378	San Ramon	82.8	10.9	21,097	73.9	806,900	30.8	10.9	1509	25.9	78.3	29.5	2.8
06 69000	Santa Ana	82.1	7.9	73,863	50.3	537,100	34.2	8.6	1158	33.3	63.5	25.9	8.3
06 69070	Santa Barbara	77.2	10.5	35,455	42.6	1,000,001	32.9	11.4	1285	37.2	63.8	16.8	9.7
06 69084	Santa Clara	76.0	18.4	40,665	47.5	656,500	28.4	8.1	1252	26.4	79.7	20.6	5.9
06 69088	Santa Clarita	85.2	13.6	58,144	74.8	540,800	29.5	11.7	1403	34.0	75.3	33.2	3.7
06 69112	Santa Cruz	67.6	18.0	21,222	47.8	777,800	31.7	11.2	1224	34.5	61.4	22.0	9.1
06 69196	Santa Maria	78.8	7.1	25,116	52.1	433,100	32.6	12.2	954	35.6	66.0	22.0	6.7
06 70000	Santa Monica	82.8	13.9	46,357	29.5	950,900	28.8	10.9	1248	28.2	71.8	24.3	10.0
06 70042	Santa Paula	88.5	4.5	8,408	60.4	498,700	28.7	12.2	954	36.9	74.6	27.2	5.5
06 70098	Santa Rosa	82.2	7.3	58,637	56.6	574,900	31.0	12.2	1125	33.7	74.3	21.2	6.8
06 70224	Santee	84.9	12.5	18,827	71.8	447,000	29.6	14.0	1148	30.9	80.5	25.7	3.6
06 70280	Saratoga	92.0	5.8	10,826	85.1	1,000,001	30.2	8.7	2001	26.3	85.8	24.2	3.7
06 70686	Seal Beach	90.1	7.7	12,747	79.2	334,200	30.3	12.6	1436	28.0	87.8	29.8	11.0

1. $1,000,001 is the top code symbolizing a median value over one million dollars.
2. 50.1 is the top code symbolizing a median gross rent as a percentage of household income of 50.1 percent or more.

STATE Place code	STATE City	Percent who lived in the same house one year ago	Percent who did not live in city one year ago	Total occupied housing units	Percent owner-occupied housing units	Median value of owner-occupied housing units (dollars)[1]	Median selected monthly owner costs as a percentage of household income		Median gross rent (dollars)	Median gross rent as a percentage of household income[2]	Percent of workers who drove alone to work	Mean travel time to work (minutes)	Percent of occupied housing units with no vehicle available
							With a mortgage	Without a mortgage					
ACS table number:		C07204	C07204	B25003	B25003	B25077	B25092	B25092	B25064	B25071	C08301	B08013/C08012	C25045
		1	2	3	4	5	6	7	8	9	10	11	12
	California—Cont.												
06 70742	Seaside	73.4	16.9	9,962	42.3	629,200	31.4	8.1	1287	32.6	61.1	22.0	8.8
06 70882	Selma	84.7	7.9	6,294	62.0	252,700	27.0	11.7	651	33.0	70.0	22.4	8.1
06 72016	Simi Valley	89.3	6.3	39,696	77.6	617,300	29.5	11.9	1463	30.1	85.3	31.9	3.2
06 72520	Soledad	76.4	16.7	3,478	66.6	521,100	38.4	12.3	943	33.2	70.0	27.1	11.1
06 72996	South El Monte	-	-	4,819	43.0	412,600	32.4	12.5	915	34.0	67.1	25.2	12.0
06 73080	South Gate	89.5	8.1	24,222	46.8	433,600	35.6	11.5	871	33.4	72.6	27.7	10.2
06 73108	South Lake Tahoe	75.2	11.8	9,429	39.3	405,100	33.3	17.1	893	32.3	65.8	16.6	8.5
06 73220	South Pasadena	82.6	14.6	10,441	45.5	785,200	27.4	14.4	1193	24.2	77.8	28.7	2.5
06 73262	South San Francisco	89.2	8.0	20,118	62.7	680,700	30.7	8.9	1312	31.1	65.9	24.5	8.4
06 73430	South Whittier CDP	87.4	12.6	15,312	65.3	468,800	29.4	11.1	1103	29.4	77.6	29.8	3.9
06 73696	Spring Valley CDP	86.2	11.7	9,344	65.4	505,700	33.1	12.4	1355	36.4	85.0	26.2	4.2
06 73962	Stanton	83.9	13.5	10,652	52.9	404,300	31.5	14.5	1166	36.0	72.6	29.1	9.1
06 75000	Stockton	78.0	6.0	89,867	55.1	363,900	32.4	10.8	868	34.2	74.6	26.7	9.3
06 75630	Suisun	84.5	13.6	8,184	73.5	445,000	34.0	9.7	1169	33.2	76.1	34.0	1.4
06 75826	Sun CDP	84.1	13.2	9,954	88.7	239,600	34.1	13.4	1019	37.8	-	40.0	4.3
06 77000	Sunnyvale	81.6	12.8	52,492	49.1	705,200	27.0	8.8	1319	23.5	76.2	21.9	3.9
06 78120	Temecula	82.5	13.7	29,185	71.2	468,000	31.5	11.7	1363	35.0	77.4	34.0	2.6
06 78148	Temple	88.6	10.2	11,277	66.6	570,000	30.1	9.6	1107	27.2	79.9	29.0	2.7
06 78582	Thousand Oaks	86.7	8.0	44,065	75.6	724,600	27.9	12.1	1600	28.8	81.6	24.9	2.3
06 80000	Torrance	88.3	8.1	54,379	57.6	669,600	27.7	10.6	1276	28.7	82.8	25.8	4.5
06 80238	Tracy	82.0	11.8	24,208	73.0	548,900	32.5	12.3	1237	36.9	74.8	43.8	2.2
06 80644	Tulare	82.2	9.4	16,223	59.9	218,700	26.1	11.0	778	29.6	80.0	19.5	5.9
06 80812	Turlock	79.5	11.0	21,934	58.1	368,100	29.3	10.7	870	33.8	77.2	21.5	6.6
06 80854	Tustin	81.6	13.2	24,314	52.4	607,600	28.8	12.5	1345	30.2	80.7	22.6	3.5
06 80994	Twentynine Palms	58.8	32.8	7,570	43.8	149,300	20.4	13.1	731	26.4	53.4	12.2	4.4
06 81204	Union	88.9	8.4	19,152	73.4	617,600	31.4	8.5	1226	29.5	73.6	30.1	3.4
06 81344	Upland	83.4	11.1	26,079	58.4	529,900	27.8	10.1	1111	31.6	83.6	27.8	4.0
06 81554	Vacaville	81.0	11.5	29,669	66.8	463,400	29.1	11.2	1163	33.9	81.1	27.5	5.1
06 81638	Valinda CDP	-	-	5,105	69.2	450,300	35.3	11.8	1383	39.4	79.7	32.5	1.5
06 81666	Vallejo	83.3	7.5	39,033	64.7	451,500	33.5	11.8	1089	35.1	71.8	31.6	7.4
06 82590	Victorville	77.1	18.4	28,869	66.2	296,700	31.3	12.5	896	40.8	74.3	33.6	6.0
06 82852	Vineyard CDP	83.4	16.6	6,290	85.5	447,000	30.1	10.0	1522	42.2	81.8	31.1	1.4
06 82954	Visalia	87.5	6.6	37,616	61.9	251,400	25.6	12.1	795	30.6	80.3	20.6	8.5
06 82996	Vista	78.5	15.5	28,955	54.7	491,500	31.4	14.5	1171	34.5	71.3	26.7	2.9
06 83332	Walnut	95.1	4.3	8,306	90.9	657,900	27.7	8.5	1893	34.5	78.2	36.5	2.3
06 83346	Walnut Creek	81.2	13.1	30,700	70.4	666,400	27.8	13.6	1305	25.9	69.5	27.0	7.1
06 83542	Wasco	67.5	24.6	4,922	52.4	187,400	28.7	12.8	524	28.4	61.7	22.8	13.4
06 83668	Watsonville	85.3	5.1	12,103	49.1	586,500	38.0	10.8	984	36.5	71.0	24.0	9.9
06 84144	West Carson CDP	-	-	6,933	74.4	470,500	24.4	14.8	1130	25.5	79.8	27.4	3.5
06 84200	West Covina	86.3	11.0	32,289	66.0	509,800	30.1	10.0	1211	37.4	78.9	30.9	5.4
06 84410	West Hollywood	84.0	13.6	22,227	22.7	657,600	33.2	24.2	1085	29.9	72.1	27.2	15.2
06 84550	Westminster	87.3	9.2	26,881	57.4	572,200	30.1	9.6	1192	36.2	80.8	26.6	6.8
06 84592	Westmont CDP	-	-	9,584	34.2	413,900	39.1	13.0	863	47.3	70.8	33.7	14.0
06 84774	West Puente Valley CDP	89.7	10.3	5,017	80.6	442,600	31.8	9.9	1383	29.5	79.0	29.4	7.4
06 84816	West Sacramento	80.4	11.6	15,339	62.1	350,900	30.6	13.4	797	33.3	78.4	22.4	9.0
06 84921	West Whittier-Los Nietos CDP	-	-	6,702	70.4	463,700	32.8	9.5	1139	40.0	79.0	28.7	5.1
06 85292	Whittier	85.9	7.6	28,951	58.9	567,100	29.0	9.2	959	31.2	77.9	29.4	6.1
06 85446	Wildomar CDP	-	-	6,842	85.7	402,400	35.5	8.8	901	36.1	73.0	39.4	3.3
06 85614	Willowbrook CDP	89.4	10.6	8,231	51.7	342,000	40.6	13.3	843	38.3	72.4	29.4	10.8
06 85922	Windsor town	85.0	10.4	8,364	71.4	605,000	31.6	16.0	1657	26.5	82.4	23.6	3.5
06 86328	Woodland	81.7	9.7	17,907	62.7	395,800	29.4	8.9	857	30.3	78.4	19.0	7.3
06 86832	Yorba Linda	90.7	6.9	21,047	83.9	837,100	26.0	8.8	1522	32.2	86.2	30.1	3.9
06 86972	Yuba	79.9	12.9	20,293	61.5	297,000	28.0	12.8	805	31.5	72.4	26.2	8.3
06 87042	Yucaipa	84.9	10.2	17,301	76.4	336,300	27.0	15.7	928	31.9	81.5	30.9	4.3
06 87056	Yucca Valley town	83.7	12.3	7,747	68.4	219,700	26.0	18.9	726	31.1	77.5	29.8	7.6
08 00000	**Colorado**	79.6	13.7	1,838,303	68.7	230,400	25.6	10.8	797	30.0	75.0	23.8	5.5
08 03455	Arvada	84.3	11.0	40,405	76.9	240,100	24.8	11.1	837	30.4	79.2	25.9	4.2
08 04000	Aurora	79.7	10.5	112,759	64.3	195,000	27.6	9.9	784	31.6	78.0	27.2	6.5
08 07850	Boulder	63.4	20.3	37,174	50.7	452,700	24.8	10.1	957	41.2	54.6	17.8	8.2
08 08675	Brighton	76.3	15.9	9,591	74.9	210,000	27.0	12.5	792	33.5	74.7	26.4	3.6
08 09280	Broomfield	80.6	15.3	17,507	75.1	245,600	24.1	13.9	972	27.4	76.1	26.8	1.9
08 12415	Castle Rock town	77.4	18.2	13,234	78.3	268,500	25.7	10.5	955	28.7	80.2	26.3	1.5
08 12815	Centennial	87.8	12.2	38,127	84.6	288,300	24.0	8.4	1150	29.1	79.8	24.8	1.6
08 15165	Clifton CDP	73.3	25.1	7,398	71.5	133,200	24.8	13.1	683	24.9	74.9	20.9	2.4
08 16000	Colorado Springs	75.1	11.5	155,741	63.6	201,300	24.5	9.1	736	28.9	79.2	20.6	5.9
08 16110	Columbine CDP	88.9	11.1	9,011	88.3	275,100	24.0	11.0	1320	38.0	83.1	25.9	1.9
08 16495	Commerce	83.1	13.5	11,306	72.5	204,900	31.0	12.1	807	37.5	71.0	27.2	4.1
08 20000	Denver	78.7	10.0	244,261	55.6	234,200	27.5	11.6	734	30.0	70.2	23.7	12.5
08 24785	Englewood	80.3	16.2	14,091	50.4	208,900	27.3	13.3	779	29.2	72.5	23.9	12.6
08 27425	Fort Collins	68.1	15.3	53,122	57.6	233,800	24.6	9.9	785	34.9	73.8	19.5	4.5
08 31660	Grand Junction	71.6	13.5	22,355	62.5	187,300	24.7	10.7	655	29.9	74.1	16.4	7.8
08 32155	Greeley	74.0	12.6	31,035	59.3	171,500	25.9	13.4	642	31.2	79.2	19.3	7.8
08 36410	Highlands Ranch CDP	82.5	14.5	31,013	84.9	318,600	22.7	8.1	1111	26.5	81.5	25.7	1.0
08 40377	Ken Caryl CDP	88.0	12.0	12,661	85.1	247,900	24.7	11.5	1076	27.9	82.2	28.3	2.4
08 41835	Lafayette	81.8	12.9	9,695	76.3	246,500	25.9	15.0	915	32.1	74.1	23.1	2.1

1. $1,000,001 is the top code symbolizing a median value over one million dollars.
2. 50.1 is the top code symbolizing a median gross rent as a percentage of household income of 50.1 percent or more.

STATE Place code	STATE City	Percent who lived in the same house one year ago	Percent who did not live in city one year ago	Total occupied housing units	Percent owner-occupied housing units	Median value of owner-occupied housing units (dollars)[1]	Median selected monthly owner costs as a percentage of household income With a mortgage	Without a mortgage	Median gross rent (dollars)	Median gross rent as a percentage of household income[2]	Percent of workers who drove alone to work	Mean travel time to work (minutes)	Percent of occupied housing units with no vehicle available
ACS table number:		C07204	C07204	B25003	B25003	B25077	B25092	B25092	B25064	B25071	C08301	B08013/C08012	C25045
		1	2	3	4	5	6	7	8	9	10	11	12
	Colorado—Cont.												
08 43000	Lakewood	76.7	16.4	62,037	61.8	237,000	25.7	10.3	820	30.6	77.3	24.4	7.0
08 45255	Littleton	82.1	12.2	18,200	66.2	266,800	24.0	10.4	772	29.8	77.7	23.5	7.5
08 45970	Longmont	79.7	10.9	32,079	65.7	237,300	24.6	10.4	883	31.5	76.0	22.0	4.8
08 46465	Loveland	78.9	10.0	25,047	70.9	214,300	25.5	11.8	793	27.8	81.8	23.4	4.4
08 54330	Northglenn	79.9	17.1	13,574	59.6	197,400	28.9	9.6	875	27.3	78.2	27.6	3.6
08 57630	Parker town	73.5	19.4	13,350	76.7	275,500	25.0	10.6	1044	27.7	79.6	26.1	2.0
08 62000	Pueblo	80.7	6.6	41,438	64.3	114,800	26.3	12.9	576	34.7	77.0	18.0	9.5
08 62220	Pueblo West CDP	83.3	15.0	8,632	82.6	172,800	25.0	8.6	900	24.5	83.1	25.8	1.4
08 68847	Security-Widefield CDP	84.1	15.6	10,976	84.9	167,300	24.4	10.3	1079	25.0	85.5	22.4	2.2
08 77290	Thornton	82.8	12.1	37,790	74.2	218,600	26.5	12.5	959	30.0	80.3	28.4	3.2
08 83835	Westminster	81.4	13.9	40,362	70.4	227,300	25.8	11.6	892	28.6	80.9	25.8	4.6
08 84440	Wheat Ridge	78.6	15.8	14,265	58.6	228,200	28.6	11.8	790	29.2	72.8	23.5	6.4
09 00000	**Connecticut**	86.9	9.4	1,323,431	69.7	294,100	25.8	16.3	910	29.8	79.7	24.5	8.2
09 08000	Bridgeport	82.7	7.8	48,037	46.6	232,200	36.1	22.0	940	34.5	67.3	26.9	21.1
09 08420	Bristol	87.5	6.0	25,120	65.9	207,600	24.3	15.1	754	27.1	86.5	22.4	6.2
09 13435	Central Manchester CDP	85.9	14.1	12,826	56.9	179,700	25.5	20.2	888	30.2	81.8	20.5	9.9
09 18430	Danbury	84.2	9.7	29,303	61.5	356,800	28.8	15.7	1169	28.7	75.8	25.7	8.2
09 18920	Darien CDP	88.0	4.4	6,791	86.3	1,000,001	21.6	16.6	2001	34.9	59.8	37.2	2.7
09 22700	East Hartford CDP	84.4	9.4	19,118	59.1	184,100	27.2	18.1	823	27.7	78.9	21.5	10.8
09 22980	East Haven CDP	91.9	5.4	11,285	78.7	231,500	26.8	22.9	909	33.9	85.4	22.3	8.6
09 37000	Hartford	76.8	9.8	43,407	25.5	182,000	29.7	17.6	722	33.8	59.8	20.7	33.2
09 46450	Meriden	86.9	4.3	23,499	62.0	202,300	25.1	16.5	825	30.8	80.9	20.3	12.6
09 47290	Middletown	81.7	10.6	19,727	54.6	221,400	24.3	17.4	845	26.7	80.4	21.1	8.2
09 47515	Milford (balance)	90.0	6.6	20,265	78.8	348,100	26.9	18.7	1142	27.1	83.9	26.3	4.9
09 49880	Naugatuck borough	87.5	8.5	11,518	70.5	221,100	25.3	18.3	813	28.6	84.1	27.3	5.2
09 50370	New Britain	84.5	9.3	26,528	45.4	169,700	30.5	20.9	749	30.0	80.9	20.0	14.0
09 52000	New Haven	75.1	12.8	46,302	31.9	215,700	29.6	20.7	927	34.2	59.6	20.6	26.9
09 52210	Newington CDP	91.7	7.6	11,945	83.1	225,500	24.8	14.2	953	26.4	89.0	20.1	4.2
09 52280	New London	75.1	14.4	10,387	37.4	209,800	28.0	17.2	876	28.0	65.4	18.2	14.7
09 54940	North Haven CDP	94.2	4.8	9,091	83.4	340,300	24.6	15.7	1162	27.3	87.0	22.1	3.3
09 55990	Norwalk	86.8	7.5	31,844	65.6	490,600	28.2	19.5	1203	32.7	74.7	24.2	7.1
09 56200	Norwich	78.8	10.9	15,129	55.9	201,900	24.9	18.2	820	30.7	74.1	20.3	10.6
09 68100	Shelton	91.3	5.8	14,473	84.8	384,700	24.2	14.7	1075	28.8	88.2	26.0	4.4
09 73000	Stamford	85.6	6.3	46,184	59.6	598,000	29.4	17.3	1349	29.7	69.0	25.3	11.3
09 74260	Stratford CDP	91.5	6.6	19,823	80.8	321,800	30.3	19.5	975	29.5	81.9	27.4	6.7
09 76500	Torrington	87.5	6.1	15,133	66.1	179,000	28.6	16.2	702	30.4	83.2	23.6	11.9
09 77270	Trumbull CDP	95.5	2.9	12,178	92.8	484,400	25.9	20.1	1232	37.7	85.3	29.8	3.5
09 80000	Waterbury	84.5	5.3	41,939	50.6	155,900	27.7	19.8	810	33.7	82.5	22.9	16.9
09 82660	West Hartford CDP	88.3	8.5	24,325	74.3	313,800	24.5	15.1	995	27.7	81.2	21.2	7.1
09 82800	West Haven	84.1	10.9	20,826	63.8	231,900	30.7	21.3	935	32.0	83.0	22.7	7.2
09 83570	Westport CDP	91.8	5.3	8,998	89.1	1,000,001	26.5	19.1	1117	27.9	62.6	36.7	1.9
09 84970	Wethersfield CDP	92.8	5.9	11,204	79.5	259,500	24.6	17.8	825	25.6	80.5	20.4	6.1
10 00000	**Delaware**	84.5	13.4	321,748	73.6	225,200	23.4	11.0	868	29.3	80.1	23.8	6.5
10 21200	Dover	75.0	14.0	12,933	55.3	167,200	25.8	12.4	813	28.3	76.0	18.1	10.6
10 50670	Newark	57.1	23.8	8,489	58.0	259,400	21.8	8.2	938	44.9	61.6	19.4	8.9
10 77580	Wilmington	79.3	10.6	26,690	48.8	165,600	23.7	12.7	817	32.6	67.9	20.1	25.1
11 00000	**District Of Columbia**	79.4	10.3	249,805	44.1	424,200	24.6	11.1	906	29.4	36.3	29.4	36.5
11 50000	Washington	79.4	10.3	249,805	44.1	424,200	24.6	11.1	906	29.4	36.3	29.4	36.5
12 00000	**Florida**	81.9	14.3	7,077,123	70.3	217,800	28.0	14.0	892	32.9	79.5	25.9	6.4
12 00950	Altamonte Springs	72.6	20.9	17,884	48.4	212,300	26.8	13.0	957	28.2	81.5	23.0	5.0
12 01700	Apopka	82.8	12.9	13,274	79.0	231,600	25.1	14.3	871	30.9	77.6	30.5	2.9
12 02681	Aventura	84.1	12.4	15,006	76.8	372,300	37.7	24.2	1586	38.5	78.5	32.2	10.2
12 04162	Bayonet Point CDP	81.2	18.8	11,293	78.6	133,300	29.2	15.1	843	32.6	-	25.8	9.2
12 05462	Bellview CDP	83.5	16.5	9,257	77.2	128,200	24.4	10.0	800	29.6	80.9	21.5	3.5
12 06875	Bloomingdale CDP	88.0	12.0	6,767	91.6	244,100	23.3	10.5	1432	23.4	77.9	29.7	2.6
12 07235	Boca Del Mar CDP	80.3	19.7	10,530	60.9	347,300	27.4	14.8	1372	39.7	79.9	20.6	10.9
12 07300	Boca Raton	83.3	9.5	34,381	74.5	465,000	31.7	16.0	1305	33.9	75.7	20.8	5.0
12 07525	Bonita Springs	82.5	12.8	19,145	81.1	312,100	30.4	12.7	1101	31.6	77.2	23.5	3.4
12 07875	Boynton Beach	85.3	11.2	26,429	72.6	232,200	31.8	16.2	1112	36.0	85.3	22.6	6.4
12 07950	Bradenton	79.7	11.9	23,102	57.8	191,100	29.7	14.0	881	32.3	79.8	21.3	6.5
12 08150	Brandon CDP	78.8	17.6	34,621	66.6	195,600	25.8	12.7	980	30.1	83.9	26.0	4.2
12 08300	Brent CDP	78.3	21.7	7,685	64.9	88,800	26.7	11.4	604	30.2	59.1	19.1	9.2
12 10275	Cape Coral	83.1	9.8	57,429	75.1	272,800	30.3	17.5	1080	31.8	82.8	24.7	3.1
12 11050	Casselberry	80.7	16.4	10,724	64.3	180,800	27.9	14.3	945	31.6	81.6	26.4	3.7
12 12425	Citrus Park CDP	83.1	16.9	9,302	72.0	232,100	25.9	13.1	991	35.1	81.7	25.8	3.6
12 12875	Clearwater	83.2	10.2	46,282	62.6	197,500	28.6	18.3	866	33.9	73.6	23.3	8.8
12 13275	Coconut Creek	84.2	12.9	20,863	77.6	225,900	30.5	22.8	1193	33.4	81.6	24.7	6.8
12 14125	Cooper	92.0	6.8	9,741	94.3	407,200	28.6	11.3	1205	31.3	85.4	25.3	1.2
12 14250	Coral Gables	80.0	17.7	16,994	70.3	748,000	29.0	17.5	1069	30.9	78.0	24.4	5.2
12 14400	Coral Springs	83.0	11.3	42,242	68.8	409,200	30.3	14.2	1210	32.5	83.0	27.8	4.0
12 14412	Coral Terrace CDP	-	-	7,929	72.2	338,800	31.7	27.3	892	38.1	82.4	26.8	7.8
12 14895	Country Club CDP	85.4	14.6	12,373	56.6	251,800	32.6	13.5	999	36.7	87.3	32.0	3.6
12 15968	Cutler Bay town	89.9	9.7	12,163	77.9	308,400	33.6	13.5	852	32.3	82.0	34.6	7.9

1. $1,000,001 is the top code symbolizing a median value over one million dollars.
2. 50.1 is the top code symbolizing a median gross rent as a percentage of household income of 50.1 percent or more.

318 The Who, What, and Where of America

Table C-4. Cities — Where: Migration, Housing, and Transportation, 2005–2007—*Continued*

STATE Place code	STATE City	Percent who lived in the same house one year ago	Percent who did not live in city one year ago	Total occupied housing units	Percent owner-occupied housing units	Median value of owner-occupied housing units (dollars)[1]	Median selected monthly owner costs as a percentage of household income — With a mortgage	Without a mortgage	Median gross rent (dollars)	Median gross rent as a percentage of household income[2]	Percent of workers who drove alone to work	Mean travel time to work (minutes)	Percent of occupied housing units with no vehicle available
ACS table number:		C07204	C07204	B25003	B25003	B25077	B25092	B25092	B25064	B25071	C08301	B08013/ C08012	C25045
		1	2	3	4	5	6	7	8	9	10	11	12
	Florida—Cont.												
12 16335	Dania Beach	78.2	21.3	12,691	56.5	217,400	33.2	16.4	989	32.8	79.2	24.8	9.0
12 16475	Davie town	81.5	14.8	34,893	78.0	292,600	29.8	17.9	1030	33.4	81.8	27.2	4.6
12 16525	Daytona Beach	75.6	17.7	27,243	49.8	167,400	29.5	14.8	743	35.7	76.4	19.4	12.9
12 16725	Deerfield Beach	81.0	15.5	33,078	69.0	198,600	32.5	18.5	1089	33.9	79.4	23.5	11.9
12 16875	De Land	75.8	16.7	10,215	55.1	169,100	25.7	13.0	763	42.3	76.0	21.6	13.4
12 17100	Delray Beach	79.8	13.6	26,811	68.3	275,000	31.4	16.7	1202	35.6	81.5	20.5	8.3
12 17200	Deltona	85.0	9.7	30,610	85.7	184,200	28.6	12.7	1062	37.4	83.1	30.7	3.2
12 17935	Doral	75.5	21.5	12,823	58.1	368,900	34.2	15.6	1632	35.2	86.5	27.1	0.9
12 18575	Dunedin	82.6	12.1	17,842	70.5	195,300	28.5	14.9	813	32.8	83.0	23.0	9.0
12 19206	East Lake CDP	85.5	14.5	13,599	79.9	350,300	26.3	14.4	1126	22.9	85.8	29.6	2.4
12 19825	Edgewater	80.7	13.3	8,835	79.9	181,700	27.6	14.9	923	32.3	75.9	24.7	3.5
12 20108	Egypt Lake-Leto CDP	72.4	27.6	13,715	48.3	164,400	29.2	14.6	842	32.1	77.6	24.9	8.9
12 22275	Ferry Pass CDP	74.2	25.8	12,770	54.5	151,000	23.3	10.6	830	31.4	86.0	23.2	8.7
12 24000	Fort Lauderdale	79.4	10.6	71,357	61.4	362,700	31.5	17.6	909	33.4	74.8	24.7	8.3
12 24125	Fort Myers	74.1	11.8	24,177	41.7	190,100	27.8	14.5	853	33.5	67.5	24.6	11.2
12 24300	Fort Pierce	80.9	7.9	14,331	53.1	137,300	33.5	17.0	825	35.8	69.5	23.5	11.1
12 24562	Fountainbleau CDP	78.4	21.6	22,004	55.2	212,000	37.6	17.6	1121	38.7	79.1	29.5	9.1
12 24581	Four Corners CDP	70.9	29.1	8,576	62.3	211,700	30.6	12.7	896	28.6	78.8	26.8	2.4
12 24925	Fruit Cove CDP	87.4	12.6	9,254	91.4	329,200	22.7	12.9	1145	31.1	88.6	30.3	1.4
12 25175	Gainesville	64.5	18.1	46,860	42.1	156,600	26.1	10.4	736	38.6	70.8	17.8	9.3
12 26300	Golden Gate CDP	84.3	15.7	7,002	44.5	294,900	37.6	9.5	1004	34.7	68.8	25.9	4.5
12 26375	Golden Glades CDP	85.4	14.6	10,798	55.5	267,200	33.1	12.6	872	36.2	79.4	28.3	8.5
12 27313	Greater Carrollwood CDP	81.7	18.3	13,965	73.8	221,800	25.4	12.1	977	27.7	82.8	25.3	3.2
12 27317	Greater Northdale CDP	86.5	13.5	8,897	72.3	247,400	27.6	10.5	1010	23.8	-	27.7	1.5
12 27322	Greenacres	82.6	15.9	13,370	71.2	189,300	27.8	18.6	1057	30.1	77.3	28.7	3.8
12 28452	Hallandale Beach	78.9	16.5	17,177	64.4	216,100	33.3	20.8	930	40.3	70.8	28.3	15.2
12 30000	Hialeah	87.4	6.4	72,215	52.0	228,000	38.1	20.8	850	40.7	79.4	26.4	13.0
12 31075	Holiday CDP	77.5	20.1	10,814	73.3	121,500	28.0	13.5	794	29.0	80.2	28.0	7.1
12 32000	Hollywood	79.4	12.9	57,751	63.3	273,900	30.4	17.6	917	36.7	78.1	27.2	9.4
12 32275	Homestead	80.3	12.8	15,578	43.6	226,100	34.7	20.5	855	41.2	63.5	33.4	14.4
12 35000	Jacksonville	79.7	7.0	316,400	64.3	165,300	24.1	10.1	798	30.0	80.2	23.7	7.6
12 35050	Jacksonville Beach	82.8	14.2	9,565	68.8	327,300	24.2	12.8	933	34.2	80.2	21.5	7.5
12 35350	Jasmine Estates CDP	80.8	19.2	8,357	62.6	133,900	31.6	14.8	831	40.4	80.2	27.4	6.6
12 35875	Jupiter town	81.6	10.5	20,264	75.8	362,200	29.1	14.7	1205	25.9	72.8	23.0	5.4
12 36062	Kendale Lakes CDP	90.0	10.0	19,520	76.8	252,400	32.9	16.1	1166	40.7	85.0	35.7	2.6
12 36100	Kendall CDP	84.2	15.8	29,572	68.2	359,100	29.7	16.4	1128	35.5	80.4	32.6	4.8
12 36121	Kendall West CDP	81.3	18.7	12,709	67.1	242,100	34.2	19.6	1153	34.8	80.8	38.1	6.6
12 36462	Keystone CDP	84.9	15.1	7,572	92.2	396,300	24.2	10.3	1697	41.3	81.0	34.6	1.7
12 36550	Key West	78.3	9.1	9,671	49.3	744,700	47.2	16.6	1228	35.4	52.7	11.2	18.9
12 36950	Kissimmee	74.9	17.6	21,922	45.2	209,400	30.5	12.6	917	36.4	75.8	28.1	8.4
12 38250	Lakeland	72.2	14.3	40,968	56.3	133,000	25.1	14.5	828	30.0	80.1	22.1	9.2
12 38350	Lake Magdalene CDP	80.3	19.6	12,778	71.8	203,100	23.6	13.0	820	32.4	81.7	26.7	5.1
12 38813	Lakeside CDP	84.2	15.8	11,954	80.4	174,700	23.1	10.1	939	25.7	83.4	33.2	1.9
12 39075	Lake Worth	78.4	13.1	12,538	50.4	211,800	33.8	16.5	882	31.4	57.1	30.6	11.5
12 39200	Land O' Lakes CDP	84.1	14.3	10,887	88.8	247,000	24.0	12.3	1081	20.2	82.7	29.6	1.3
12 39425	Largo	81.3	13.6	36,675	63.3	131,400	27.1	15.4	813	32.3	80.8	21.4	9.2
12 39525	Lauderdale Lakes	82.2	15.6	11,478	67.1	156,700	36.5	18.1	916	35.7	74.8	27.9	11.9
12 39550	Lauderhill	80.7	15.9	24,760	60.9	176,500	34.3	20.3	930	39.1	75.6	28.2	11.8
12 39875	Leesburg	81.9	12.9	8,112	58.8	131,900	24.9	12.7	742	31.5	74.1	18.8	7.3
12 39925	Lehigh Acres CDP	78.1	18.3	22,043	76.2	203,800	32.6	14.0	1037	31.1	80.3	31.7	3.9
12 41775	Lutz CDP	88.9	10.4	7,056	85.4	247,500	23.8	12.6	936	35.0	-	29.8	1.8
12 43125	Margate	83.8	14.2	22,552	76.6	204,300	33.2	19.5	1157	35.2	81.7	27.7	7.6
12 43975	Melbourne	81.0	11.4	32,907	63.7	179,700	26.0	12.0	833	34.0	81.8	20.1	6.9
12 44275	Merritt Island CDP	84.3	12.2	14,505	74.7	249,900	26.5	14.0	869	29.6	84.0	24.5	5.3
12 45000	Miami	80.6	6.0	135,902	36.4	298,500	37.3	21.0	784	37.1	68.7	28.5	20.6
12 45025	Miami Beach	77.7	15.1	43,319	43.6	382,300	33.2	23.0	936	42.3	61.8	26.2	25.9
12 45060	Miami Gardens	91.5	8.4	31,509	70.3	202,200	37.4	16.5	881	38.5	81.9	29.5	10.9
12 45100	Miami Lakes town	84.6	11.6	10,704	67.5	408,000	31.2	14.1	1140	32.1	85.7	30.6	3.5
12 45975	Miramar	83.2	14.1	34,113	79.1	337,800	33.9	16.7	1260	34.8	82.0	32.1	2.4
12 47625	Naples	89.3	7.6	9,525	80.3	916,300	32.2	15.6	1090	32.9	77.7	18.6	5.3
12 48625	New Smyrna Beach	80.8	10.2	10,145	75.3	236,300	26.3	15.6	851	36.2	76.2	21.2	5.0
12 49350	North Fort Myers CDP	86.4	10.6	21,381	85.5	105,800	27.8	14.7	721	29.7	76.8	24.3	6.7
12 49425	North Lauderdale	81.1	16.4	13,224	67.8	215,900	36.9	18.0	1110	36.8	82.9	28.2	2.6
12 49450	North Miami	79.4	17.6	19,698	53.1	231,900	38.3	16.1	885	35.0	71.2	32.4	10.4
12 49475	North Miami Beach	83.2	12.5	14,490	60.8	241,400	38.0	14.6	907	33.7	74.4	30.8	9.6
12 49675	North Port	80.5	15.6	17,891	82.0	206,700	28.6	13.8	997	31.3	81.9	28.0	3.8
12 50575	Oakland Park	78.7	19.9	16,981	61.5	259,700	30.5	17.8	975	33.8	70.9	24.2	7.3
12 50638	Oak Ridge CDP	74.0	26.0	7,348	40.7	170,700	30.3	10.8	845	32.2	69.3	24.6	6.7
12 50750	Ocala	73.7	15.7	21,583	54.3	135,800	26.4	15.1	768	30.7	80.7	18.8	9.6
12 51075	Ocoee	80.7	17.1	10,690	80.0	240,200	24.5	13.1	1091	32.9	82.0	28.0	3.2
12 53000	Orlando	71.4	14.4	92,509	41.5	233,600	27.2	13.0	917	33.6	76.9	24.3	9.9
12 53150	Ormond Beach	89.1	7.6	17,064	81.5	229,900	26.6	17.6	1004	40.0	85.8	20.2	4.9
12 53575	Oviedo	82.5	14.4	9,596	82.7	291,000	24.2	7.5	1266	37.2	86.1	29.3	0.7
12 54000	Palm Bay	84.5	9.7	34,995	78.8	184,600	28.1	14.3	880	33.9	82.9	25.3	3.1
12 54075	Palm Beach Gardens	83.0	13.5	19,020	74.5	386,100	27.7	13.7	1209	29.0	86.2	19.3	5.4

1. $1,000,001 is the top code symbolizing a median value over one million dollars.
2. 50.1 is the top code symbolizing a median gross rent as a percentage of household income of 50.1 percent or more.

STATE Place code	STATE City	Percent who lived in the same house one year ago	Percent who did not live in city one year ago	Total occupied housing units	Percent owner-occupied housing units	Median value of owner-occupied housing units (dollars)[1]	Median selected monthly owner costs as a percentage of household income		Median gross rent (dollars)	Median gross rent as a percentage of house-hold income[2]	Percent of workers who drove alone to work	Mean travel time to work (minutes)	Percent of occupied housing units with no vehicle available
							With a mortgage	Without a mortgage					
ACS table number:		C07204	C07204	B25003	B25003	B25077	B25092	B25092	B25064	B25071	C08301	B08013/ C08012	C25045
		1	2	3	4	5	6	7	8	9	10	11	12
	Florida—Cont.												
12 54175	Palm CDP	88.1	9.8	9,044	84.8	388,400	27.2	13.1	1218	30.6	81.0	25.9	2.3
12 54200	Palm Coast	81.8	14.2	28,498	75.1	233,000	29.6	12.8	1042	35.4	83.4	22.5	2.4
12 54275	Palmetto Bay village	-	-	8,026	87.7	556,100	30.2	13.7	957	37.9	79.7	36.4	2.5
12 54350	Palm Harbor CDP	85.8	11.2	24,848	80.8	215,400	26.2	15.0	965	32.4	82.6	25.8	4.3
12 54387	Palm River-Clair Mel CDP	82.8	17.2	7,727	67.0	132,200	26.2	10.2	842	36.5	81.1	24.0	4.9
12 54525	Palm Valley CDP	84.8	15.2	8,002	76.8	473,700	25.6	13.2	1243	25.1	85.0	23.0	2.6
12 54700	Panama	75.4	15.9	16,559	54.2	157,000	26.6	12.5	764	29.0	77.8	16.5	7.7
12 55125	Parkland	84.4	14.3	6,831	82.8	650,900	30.6	14.3	2001	41.6	81.4	27.0	6.0
12 55775	Pembroke Pines	88.1	9.3	56,240	81.0	314,400	29.6	20.5	1308	34.8	85.0	30.3	5.0
12 55925	Pensacola	80.3	11.2	23,953	65.6	162,100	24.4	11.9	779	30.1	82.3	18.0	6.6
12 56825	Pine Hills CDP	78.7	21.3	13,466	56.7	155,700	31.4	12.5	865	32.6	73.6	29.9	8.8
12 56975	Pinellas Park	83.9	12.9	20,620	72.2	152,200	28.8	17.1	777	28.2	80.2	19.6	8.5
12 57425	Plantation	83.7	12.4	32,670	74.7	351,300	28.7	14.7	1261	33.7	83.7	25.0	4.7
12 57550	Plant	86.5	8.0	12,155	67.4	168,000	25.8	13.4	798	32.6	69.4	22.1	9.2
12 57900	Poinciana CDP	78.9	21.1	8,393	82.3	217,300	33.5	11.1	1086	28.0	-	44.0	3.7
12 58050	Pompano Beach	80.4	12.2	43,411	64.9	241,800	32.6	17.1	983	34.4	76.1	24.8	7.9
12 58350	Port Charlotte CDP	85.2	9.4	21,248	82.6	172,800	31.4	13.8	949	38.0	83.3	20.7	6.4
12 58575	Port Orange	86.4	9.2	22,490	80.8	192,600	27.2	14.6	924	38.0	87.4	21.9	4.1
12 58715	Port St. Lucie	83.9	10.2	52,860	79.6	235,900	32.6	16.0	1188	33.0	86.8	29.1	2.8
12 60230	Richmond West CDP	-	-	8,656	91.5	346,400	35.0	15.2	1696	50.1	80.4	38.9	0.8
12 60975	Riviera Beach	77.9	19.7	12,039	60.1	233,000	34.5	18.3	952	36.2	80.1	21.1	8.5
12 61500	Rockledge	86.2	12.1	9,491	85.2	211,700	25.3	9.7	920	35.3	85.5	23.5	5.6
12 62100	Royal Palm Beach village	89.0	8.5	10,965	87.6	314,000	31.0	17.2	1317	32.7	83.3	30.0	3.3
12 62625	St. Cloud	83.8	11.4	11,360	73.3	195,800	28.0	13.8	823	34.8	86.2	30.4	7.3
12 63000	St. Petersburg	82.8	8.0	105,116	65.4	185,300	28.0	15.2	771	32.4	80.1	22.2	10.3
12 63650	Sanford	75.6	17.3	17,975	53.1	164,300	27.4	11.4	846	32.1	75.6	24.6	7.9
12 64175	Sarasota	73.3	13.6	22,294	58.0	247,400	33.5	15.5	925	33.4	71.1	19.5	10.6
12 64825	Sebastian	89.0	8.2	8,479	84.5	198,200	28.0	14.4	919	33.9	86.9	26.8	3.8
12 67258	South Bradenton CDP	75.9	24.1	11,100	55.9	104,000	35.5	13.5	833	30.8	76.7	23.4	7.5
12 67575	South Miami Heights CDP	82.9	17.1	10,922	61.1	254,200	36.4	17.3	823	39.9	68.0	36.0	15.4
12 68350	Spring Hill CDP	82.5	13.1	35,639	84.2	175,300	28.3	13.7	888	28.3	82.9	28.0	3.5
12 69700	Sunrise	85.9	11.1	33,412	76.1	235,700	31.9	22.4	1147	32.6	81.4	26.7	8.6
12 70600	Tallahassee	66.3	14.3	70,467	45.2	179,200	24.8	10.5	799	37.0	81.0	18.0	7.3
12 70675	Tamarac	83.5	13.3	29,780	81.7	205,900	34.2	22.5	1094	40.7	84.2	27.5	8.1
12 70700	Tamiami CDP	90.5	9.5	17,096	83.9	316,200	33.7	18.5	1175	42.2	85.3	32.8	4.5
12 71000	Tampa	76.0	9.7	131,532	56.9	200,100	27.0	14.0	799	32.4	77.8	23.4	10.2
12 71150	Tarpon Springs	85.0	12.3	10,014	80.9	205,900	28.0	15.9	680	34.1	79.5	27.0	6.6
12 71400	Temple Terrace	75.5	22.4	10,058	55.7	195,600	25.7	13.1	914	29.8	85.2	23.2	4.7
12 71567	The Crossings CDP	83.0	17.0	8,682	73.6	303,700	28.8	14.9	1300	31.7	79.1	35.4	3.1
12 71569	The Hammocks CDP	84.1	15.9	16,966	66.2	315,500	30.5	11.8	1181	35.9	81.6	39.1	3.1
12 71900	Titusville	80.5	12.1	18,607	70.9	160,400	24.2	12.1	721	34.7	84.9	23.8	5.9
12 72145	Town 'n' Country CDP	76.8	23.2	30,609	67.9	182,400	28.8	14.1	920	31.1	83.0	25.7	4.9
12 73163	University CDP	63.1	36.9	13,613	11.1	117,000	26.7	12.0	709	36.6	64.2	25.9	24.1
12 73287	University Park CDP	84.2	15.8	8,862	65.5	364,900	33.8	20.0	1051	37.0	86.0	29.3	6.0
12 73900	Venice	85.6	11.7	11,162	75.0	239,800	28.5	15.9	891	39.8	85.1	19.6	8.4
12 74200	Vero Beach South CDP	82.2	17.8	10,689	75.6	204,800	28.0	12.2	889	37.1	83.1	17.4	2.5
12 75725	Wekiwa Springs CDP	85.3	14.7	9,145	79.6	337,200	24.3	12.4	1157	30.2	-	25.2	0.7
12 75812	Wellington village	85.1	10.6	17,813	80.6	409,600	28.8	16.1	1378	33.1	82.7	30.2	0.6
12 75912	West and East Lealman CDP	-	-	10,880	63.7	110,000	24.8	18.4	720	34.2	80.5	18.2	9.4
12 76062	Westchase CDP	80.9	19.1	7,870	73.1	348,300	24.2	12.6	1231	25.9	82.2	29.9	2.1
12 76075	Westchester CDP	-	-	9,996	63.9	347,600	35.2	17.2	1058	45.4	81.2	30.0	6.6
12 76487	West Little River CDP	-	-	9,746	62.6	173,400	43.2	15.4	657	42.3	69.0	29.3	19.1
12 76582	Weston	85.2	10.5	21,168	80.7	482,200	28.8	15.8	1607	32.5	81.8	28.4	1.3
12 76600	West Palm Beach	79.4	13.4	36,703	55.3	275,600	31.9	16.5	947	34.7	74.4	23.0	11.7
12 76675	West Pensacola CDP	73.8	26.2	9,584	53.2	81,900	30.4	12.8	665	37.7	73.8	19.3	13.7
12 78250	Winter Garden	80.9	14.2	9,468	73.7	255,700	25.1	13.2	914	31.4	80.0	27.2	4.9
12 78275	Winter Haven	75.1	14.4	13,309	58.3	111,300	28.0	13.8	697	34.3	83.5	23.8	12.6
12 78300	Winter Park	80.1	15.7	12,380	68.6	404,200	25.1	10.8	945	35.0	82.2	20.2	7.4
12 78325	Winter Springs	86.8	10.0	13,078	78.3	259,600	24.8	11.3	1107	29.0	85.2	28.6	1.6
12 78800	Wright CDP	79.4	20.6	10,276	57.3	185,300	24.7	12.8	833	29.8	82.2	16.8	7.0
12 78975	Yeehaw Junction CDP	78.9	21.1	8,324	73.7	212,200	37.6	15.4	1144	40.6	-	29.2	2.7
13 00000	**Georgia**	81.0	15.6	3,364,749	67.9	156,300	23.7	11.3	756	29.5	78.7	27.1	6.7
13 01052	Albany	72.8	13.1	29,481	42.1	97,700	20.1	12.5	580	29.3	78.7	17.0	15.7
13 01696	Alpharetta	81.4	14.9	23,562	70.9	321,800	23.4	10.9	979	21.7	81.7	27.1	2.8
13 03440	Athens-Clarke County (balance)	68.7	15.1	42,033	45.1	158,700	24.7	10.6	684	34.6	74.2	19.1	8.3
13 04000	Atlanta	76.2	11.9	168,252	50.3	235,200	26.7	14.5	821	32.1	67.3	26.1	18.6
13 04204	Augusta-Richmond County (balance)	74.9	12.4	73,453	57.0	94,100	23.2	12.3	660	29.1	74.6	18.7	9.8
13 12834	Candler-McAfee CDP	77.4	22.6	9,418	54.4	143,400	32.7	13.3	834	34.0	65.8	37.9	13.5
13 12988	Canton	77.1	14.0	5,210	50.7	165,500	32.0	18.6	746	36.1	-	28.6	10.6
13 13492	Carrollton	62.3	22.5	8,856	39.0	151,800	22.5	18.8	667	30.2	80.0	25.9	9.8
13 17776	College Park	66.6	25.1	5,924	27.7	162,000	24.8	18.8	719	34.8	50.5	26.9	27.4

1. $1,000,001 is the top code symbolizing a median value over one million dollars.
2. 50.1 is the top code symbolizing a median gross rent as a percentage of household income of 50.1 percent or more.

Table C-4. Cities — Where: Migration, Housing, and Transportation, 2005–2007—*Continued*

STATE Place code	STATE City	Percent who lived in the same house one year ago	Percent who did not live in city one year ago	Total occupied housing units	Percent owner-occupied housing units	Median value of owner-occupied housing units (dollars)[1]	Median selected monthly owner costs as a percentage of household income With a mortgage	Without a mortgage	Median gross rent (dollars)	Median gross rent as a percentage of household income[2]	Percent of workers who drove alone to work	Mean travel time to work (minutes)	Percent of occupied housing units with no vehicle available
ACS table number:		C07204	C07204	B25003	B25003	B25077	B25092	B25092	B25064	B25071	C08301	B08013/C08012	C25045
		1	2	3	4	5	6	7	8	9	10	11	12
	Georgia—Cont.												
13 19000	Columbus	75.6	13.0	71,365	57.3	119,600	22.8	9.7	679	29.4	72.6	18.4	10.5
13 21380	Dalton	77.4	10.6	10,316	53.4	140,000	24.5	10.9	576	27.1	76.9	14.7	7.9
13 23900	Douglasville	70.3	21.7	9,153	48.5	167,100	26.7	8.6	819	32.3	81.7	32.9	8.3
13 24600	Duluth	76.2	20.0	10,115	56.4	195,500	23.1	8.4	962	24.7	79.5	28.5	2.4
13 24768	Dunwoody CDP	83.2	15.9	16,174	66.2	393,700	21.1	9.6	1098	25.8	80.7	23.2	3.1
13 25720	East Point	78.5	17.9	12,064	49.5	155,700	26.8	14.4	848	33.1	58.4	33.0	16.5
13 30536	Forest Park	70.7	27.1	6,087	59.1	101,100	28.6	11.1	757	35.2	70.7	30.0	10.2
13 31908	Gainesville	71.9	16.1	9,481	41.0	185,800	20.8	15.3	771	28.7	63.2	23.7	14.0
13 35324	Griffin	75.4	9.5	7,956	43.6	130,000	24.2	12.5	741	34.6	72.6	25.9	15.2
13 38964	Hinesville	67.4	18.5	11,042	50.0	98,200	21.5	9.8	681	26.9	80.7	19.8	7.8
13 42425	Johns Creek	88.3	9.9	26,400	85.5	335,900	22.9	9.5	1155	24.1	78.5	30.5	1.0
13 43192	Kennesaw	75.8	18.7	9,993	73.8	175,300	24.8	11.0	1035	29.8	83.9	30.6	1.9
13 44340	LaGrange	68.2	13.9	10,492	47.2	99,600	25.3	11.8	621	29.9	72.8	17.9	14.4
13 45488	Lawrenceville	75.4	13.9	9,442	54.9	154,700	24.9	9.6	817	29.3	72.7	32.8	5.5
13 48288	Mableton CDP	83.5	14.5	13,167	80.3	164,800	26.7	8.1	909	38.5	81.3	31.8	2.0
13 49000	Macon	76.2	9.4	35,960	50.8	85,900	25.6	13.2	567	34.6	78.6	18.9	17.3
13 49756	Marietta	73.8	18.4	22,111	45.6	215,100	25.7	10.4	824	31.6	71.2	26.3	8.3
13 50036	Martinez CDP	84.2	13.9	10,116	81.1	137,700	21.5	7.4	807	27.0	87.5	19.8	1.7
13 51492	Milledgeville	70.6	18.7	4,470	51.2	103,600	22.2	12.5	637	37.6	82.2	13.3	14.5
13 55020	Newnan	68.3	19.8	8,223	48.5	175,500	23.3	10.4	810	25.3	79.2	31.6	7.5
13 56000	North Atlanta CDP	64.5	30.0	15,709	41.9	396,200	24.3	12.5	909	30.5	65.7	29.9	12.8
13 56168	North Druid Hills CDP	68.5	31.5	9,361	42.5	299,400	22.2	12.0	972	27.1	77.0	22.6	9.6
13 59724	Peachtree	83.9	11.6	12,277	80.2	266,800	22.6	9.8	963	28.3	83.4	27.3	0.9
13 63952	Redan CDP	84.4	15.6	12,868	68.3	137,500	27.3	10.0	956	30.4	80.0	36.2	5.9
13 66668	Rome	80.6	9.8	13,167	55.9	116,900	23.5	12.5	544	34.1	76.3	17.4	15.3
13 67284	Roswell	84.5	11.9	35,228	73.6	294,100	23.6	10.9	955	29.1	78.8	28.0	3.6
13 68516	Sandy Springs	73.1	26.7	40,279	53.9	451,200	22.0	11.9	935	26.3	77.5	23.8	6.5
13 69000	Savannah	82.3	7.8	51,732	49.2	125,200	26.1	14.1	754	36.7	76.9	20.0	15.7
13 71492	Smyrna	77.0	15.6	20,493	57.7	205,400	23.7	11.8	859	27.8	81.5	26.9	3.4
13 71604	Snellville	85.5	12.2	6,259	88.5	173,100	24.2	10.6	1075	29.4	-	33.9	2.4
13 73256	Statesboro	50.5	30.2	8,751	29.5	94,600	25.2	8.4	536	43.1	76.4	17.2	6.3
13 77652	Tucker CDP	83.2	15.3	11,668	77.5	215,000	23.2	12.4	947	30.0	79.6	24.4	3.2
13 78800	Valdosta	70.4	14.5	18,760	41.2	119,000	22.7	11.5	632	28.6	81.8	15.4	10.2
13 80508	Warner Robins	75.5	12.7	22,954	56.8	101,600	21.3	8.9	704	31.1	87.5	20.4	8.7
13 84176	Woodstock	77.0	15.8	7,624	68.9	188,200	28.4	11.4	926	25.1	79.5	31.7	1.9
15 00000	**Hawaii**	83.8	12.5	433,664	58.9	510,500	27.7	8.9	1144	31.0	67.4	25.7	8.6
15 14650	Hilo CDP	82.6	9.1	17,977	64.1	306,600	21.1	7.6	863	28.3	69.0	20.8	8.9
15 17000	Honolulu CDP	85.3	7.5	141,535	50.0	557,200	28.1	9.2	1007	32.0	59.6	22.8	16.1
15 22700	Kahului CDP	86.5	9.4	6,336	59.8	603,000	34.8	9.8	803	29.3	73.9	20.7	8.6
15 23150	Kailua CDP (Honolulu County)	88.5	8.4	11,975	71.0	771,200	26.7	10.1	1569	28.7	70.4	27.6	3.7
15 28250	Kaneohe CDP	87.8	9.1	11,406	67.5	583,600	28.1	8.2	1482	27.6	72.4	27.3	6.2
15 36500	Kihei CDP	77.4	11.3	7,604	48.1	574,800	37.4	12.3	1297	29.4	67.3	21.2	3.1
15 51050	Mililani Town CDP	86.4	10.5	9,433	76.5	478,600	27.5	6.5	1656	30.8	77.1	32.3	3.7
15 62600	Pearl CDP	85.0	13.7	9,141	64.5	499,200	25.4	7.5	1494	33.9	69.4	28.2	6.2
15 77750	Waimalu CDP	87.1	12.9	10,460	63.2	427,100	24.6	8.6	1376	28.8	74.0	26.2	2.9
15 79700	Waipahu CDP	87.5	9.4	7,961	59.7	503,000	30.0	7.1	976	29.2	56.4	28.7	11.9
16 00000	**Idaho**	79.1	14.2	545,171	71.6	158,600	23.7	10.5	644	27.3	76.6	20.1	3.9
16 08830	Boise	74.5	11.9	84,734	62.5	193,900	23.2	10.6	698	28.0	78.5	17.8	5.4
16 12250	Caldwell	78.9	13.8	11,439	70.7	120,300	27.2	13.9	556	25.9	74.4	22.4	4.4
16 16750	Coeur d'Alene	75.8	15.1	16,984	55.6	186,900	28.1	17.1	727	31.2	78.4	18.2	5.4
16 39700	Idaho Falls	77.7	12.0	20,178	68.1	119,500	21.9	10.1	604	28.2	74.6	18.5	5.9
16 46540	Lewiston	76.5	12.4	13,158	66.1	134,600	22.6	11.7	532	28.6	80.8	13.8	4.3
16 52120	Meridian	77.9	15.8	20,502	80.2	204,500	23.0	11.3	847	26.4	86.2	21.6	2.7
16 54550	Moscow	51.0	26.8	8,081	41.3	171,100	22.9	9.4	627	34.4	58.4	12.3	9.8
16 56260	Nampa	71.5	16.5	26,198	66.8	137,700	24.0	13.0	721	30.9	77.7	25.3	6.3
16 64090	Pocatello	74.7	11.3	19,823	67.0	109,800	20.9	12.3	525	29.2	81.9	15.5	3.9
16 64810	Post Falls	81.0	14.0	9,307	68.5	194,200	26.3	12.7	867	35.8	79.5	22.0	3.1
16 67420	Rexburg	45.0	30.9	5,784	42.0	157,400	24.2	7.7	584	34.8	59.1	12.2	3.3
16 82810	Twin Falls	75.4	12.5	15,686	60.2	127,400	23.3	11.1	615	24.1	84.5	13.3	4.1
17 00000	**Illinois**	84.9	9.2	4,724,462	70.1	198,100	25.5	13.8	780	29.8	74.1	28.0	10.1
17 00243	Addison village	89.2	6.6	11,892	73.3	282,100	29.1	16.7	833	35.8	79.7	24.4	4.7
17 00685	Algonquin village	92.1	6.7	9,786	94.3	299,200	24.6	14.1	880	41.4	85.9	37.8	2.6
17 01114	Alton	80.5	9.1	11,562	64.6	77,700	21.3	13.2	631	32.5	85.7	22.7	10.1
17 02154	Arlington Heights village	89.9	6.8	30,865	79.3	364,700	23.9	15.2	971	27.2	79.7	28.3	6.7
17 03012	Aurora	83.6	9.5	57,614	72.9	199,200	28.7	14.7	974	32.4	74.7	30.0	5.3
17 04013	Bartlett village	88.0	10.8	13,373	94.6	312,100	28.0	17.0	931	29.3	86.2	32.2	1.9
17 04078	Batavia	90.9	7.5	9,408	79.6	323,500	25.1	13.2	931	28.4	79.1	29.2	4.9
17 04845	Belleville	83.1	11.3	17,647	62.6	95,400	22.1	13.0	656	29.7	81.3	23.5	9.0
17 05092	Belvidere	82.3	10.7	8,379	69.7	139,700	29.2	16.6	596	31.3	79.9	27.8	9.0
17 05248	Bensenville village	85.1	8.5	7,212	54.4	250,600	31.5	16.9	940	27.9	79.2	23.8	4.9
17 05573	Berwyn	84.4	11.1	18,971	63.8	238,700	31.7	15.8	810	30.0	69.8	29.7	9.9
17 06587	Bloomingdale village	84.4	12.5	7,985	73.1	325,800	28.2	13.6	1161	27.0	82.4	26.7	3.9

1. $1,000,001 is the top code symbolizing a median value over one million dollars.
2. 50.1 is the top code symbolizing a median gross rent as a percentage of household income of 50.1 percent or more.

Table C-4. Cities — Where: Migration, Housing, and Transportation, 2005–2007—Continued

STATE Place code	STATE City	Percent who lived in the same house one year ago	Percent who did not live in city one year ago	Total occupied housing units	Percent owner-occupied housing units	Median value of owner-occupied housing units (dollars)[1]	Median selected monthly owner costs as a percentage of household income		Median gross rent (dollars)	Median gross rent as a percentage of household income[2]	Percent of workers who drove alone to work	Mean travel time to work (minutes)	Percent of occupied housing units with no vehicle available
							With a mortgage	Without a mortgage					
ACS table number:		C07204	C07204	B25003	B25003	B25077	B25092	B25092	B25064	B25071	C08301	B08013/C08012	C25045
		1	2	3	4	5	6	7	8	9	10	11	12
	Illinois—Cont.												
17 06613	Bloomington	78.6	11.0	28,607	66.2	147,000	21.8	11.8	679	26.3	80.5	15.4	6.7
17 06704	Blue Island	-	-	8,176	58.0	156,600	26.6	16.2	737	27.5	68.9	29.7	12.5
17 07133	Bolingbrook village	87.5	10.4	21,241	86.9	242,100	28.6	14.3	934	34.0	78.7	32.9	2.3
17 09447	Buffalo Grove village	90.5	8.3	16,450	85.0	341,000	28.0	16.3	1177	27.3	84.0	29.5	2.9
17 09642	Burbank	90.0	7.4	9,314	84.2	236,000	31.4	14.8	905	30.8	80.3	30.2	6.7
17 10487	Calumet	80.6	16.2	15,460	57.5	132,900	28.9	16.9	808	28.7	70.4	36.0	8.6
17 11163	Carbondale	56.3	30.9	10,541	26.1	101,800	22.2	10.6	505	48.2	72.3	12.7	15.9
17 11332	Carol Stream village	87.2	9.5	13,977	73.3	246,500	25.8	13.6	877	27.3	83.7	28.6	3.9
17 11358	Carpentersville village	83.1	8.2	11,126	82.0	180,300	31.6	16.2	886	27.4	80.9	29.8	1.8
17 12385	Champaign	64.4	21.2	30,072	48.5	140,200	22.6	11.1	713	38.6	64.8	14.4	10.5
17 12567	Charleston	50.2	28.9	7,785	41.0	89,900	20.8	10.4	633	50.1	71.4	14.5	8.5
17 14000	Chicago	82.8	4.9	1,014,120	49.3	270,700	30.4	15.6	830	31.9	52.2	34.0	25.6
17 14026	Chicago Heights	83.8	11.6	10,235	67.0	132,400	29.6	15.3	755	44.6	78.4	28.9	11.6
17 14351	Cicero town	81.4	11.8	21,533	56.2	230,800	39.1	20.2	745	31.7	59.4	31.4	10.4
17 15599	Collinsville	84.9	9.9	10,730	66.9	122,700	22.4	12.9	641	24.1	87.7	23.8	4.5
17 17458	Crest Hill	82.2	16.9	6,840	75.7	190,000	29.1	19.0	839	26.9	-	31.6	5.4
17 17887	Crystal Lake	87.8	7.1	13,976	77.5	240,600	25.1	16.7	1124	31.1	81.9	32.2	5.4
17 18563	Danville	82.7	8.8	13,360	57.4	64,600	20.5	13.4	588	35.1	82.0	16.0	15.6
17 18628	Darien	87.9	9.9	9,028	84.2	329,700	25.2	14.0	996	25.2	87.2	31.3	3.0
17 18823	Decatur	79.1	7.4	33,018	65.7	75,700	20.0	11.9	558	29.5	85.5	16.2	12.5
17 19161	DeKalb	56.1	23.2	14,278	45.9	174,800	25.5	15.1	747	34.1	76.6	20.8	5.3
17 19642	Des Plaines	92.2	4.5	22,018	83.0	294,600	29.1	16.0	869	33.2	77.8	25.5	8.0
17 20292	Dolton village	87.2	10.1	8,910	76.6	137,700	30.8	18.4	891	31.7	78.3	36.7	7.1
17 20591	Downers Grove village	89.5	8.3	18,732	80.0	350,500	25.8	13.4	914	28.6	75.0	27.6	6.6
17 22073	East Moline	84.5	11.0	8,910	67.4	96,200	20.9	14.1	495	30.9	80.8	18.3	11.6
17 22164	East Peoria	86.3	10.5	10,167	79.7	117,600	21.9	12.2	568	31.0	-	19.8	7.5
17 22255	East St. Louis	85.1	6.3	10,691	53.1	57,400	32.2	14.3	386	35.2	65.6	22.0	27.8
17 22697	Edwardsville	73.8	18.2	8,639	68.0	158,400	21.5	11.8	762	38.2	77.0	23.1	4.2
17 23074	Elgin	81.2	9.3	33,486	69.1	211,300	30.3	16.2	833	29.8	78.2	27.5	6.4
17 23256	Elk Grove Village village	90.3	8.0	13,531	79.3	297,100	24.8	11.8	925	28.6	87.5	24.3	3.7
17 23620	Elmhurst	88.3	8.4	15,531	84.1	395,600	26.9	15.1	1141	27.5	78.2	25.7	3.9
17 23724	Elmwood Park village	91.5	5.7	9,438	67.7	313,000	33.5	18.3	859	35.9	71.5	30.5	14.9
17 24582	Evanston	76.8	13.7	27,419	60.0	405,100	27.8	15.2	1010	32.2	53.4	27.7	15.2
17 27884	Freeport	78.5	5.7	10,568	66.0	77,900	24.1	14.1	516	28.6	78.6	17.5	14.0
17 28326	Galesburg	86.0	8.5	13,171	60.3	68,000	21.0	13.1	477	29.0	82.3	14.7	12.3
17 28872	Geneva	87.6	10.3	8,034	87.0	327,100	25.2	14.9	1043	26.6	82.8	28.8	1.9
17 29730	Glendale Heights village	81.6	14.4	11,751	72.5	219,000	30.2	13.9	974	29.6	84.7	27.4	3.3
17 29756	Glen Ellyn village	89.9	6.7	10,009	78.3	420,400	25.9	17.2	850	25.7	69.1	30.1	3.3
17 29938	Glenview village	90.8	6.6	16,766	90.1	546,400	25.8	14.4	1500	29.1	75.8	28.5	3.0
17 30926	Granite	85.6	6.2	12,478	73.2	78,700	22.0	14.2	597	28.8	83.5	21.4	7.6
17 31121	Grayslake village	90.1	7.6	7,448	86.2	276,000	26.1	19.5	850	30.5	82.6	35.8	2.1
17 32018	Gurnee village	82.9	11.9	11,054	78.1	294,500	25.4	17.0	1024	28.3	85.6	29.4	3.3
17 32746	Hanover Park village	85.7	10.6	11,880	81.2	222,800	28.9	11.8	975	41.2	80.3	28.9	4.9
17 33383	Harvey	78.2	17.2	9,033	50.0	100,700	24.8	17.0	853	38.5	68.0	31.7	20.1
17 34722	Highland Park	91.6	5.5	10,542	84.3	603,900	25.3	15.5	1086	29.7	70.5	26.6	1.9
17 35411	Hoffman Estates village	85.6	11.7	18,541	80.0	307,500	26.3	11.5	1001	25.2	85.4	28.8	4.1
17 35835	Homer Glen village	90.6	9.4	7,487	96.7	349,900	27.3	14.0	1580	28.8	85.6	33.8	4.4
17 36750	Huntley village	87.7	11.2	8,082	92.4	287,400	29.1	18.8	937	31.1	81.3	37.2	2.5
17 38570	Joliet	83.9	9.1	44,188	75.5	193,800	27.0	13.3	754	32.2	80.5	31.4	6.6
17 38934	Kankakee	80.5	8.5	9,690	54.6	87,300	26.4	15.6	613	37.4	74.8	18.0	16.3
17 41105	Lake Forest	90.8	5.7	6,749	91.0	869,200	27.2	12.0	1187	36.9	69.4	31.5	3.1
17 41183	Lake in the Hills village	91.7	6.5	9,473	93.5	252,500	27.7	18.4	981	40.4	81.0	38.7	2.3
17 41742	Lake Zurich village	88.9	8.2	6,488	87.3	349,500	24.5	14.1	1077	20.5	88.4	30.8	0.3
17 42028	Lansing village	89.9	8.7	10,948	77.0	150,600	26.0	13.2	855	33.2	82.5	33.6	5.1
17 43250	Libertyville village	89.2	8.0	7,400	82.0	455,100	24.7	14.6	905	29.1	83.1	25.8	5.1
17 43939	Lisle village	80.7	15.8	9,087	64.1	325,200	27.6	13.0	943	24.4	74.5	28.9	5.4
17 44225	Lockport	85.1	11.4	7,704	84.2	238,600	28.5	14.7	833	30.7	80.2	34.1	3.1
17 44407	Lombard village	88.6	9.3	17,204	80.4	260,800	26.2	15.0	1029	26.3	82.8	27.0	5.0
17 45031	Loves Park	82.7	13.9	9,813	72.2	113,900	22.5	12.6	689	25.9	86.3	19.7	3.9
17 45694	McHenry	84.0	6.5	9,213	72.2	224,000	24.7	16.6	935	29.2	87.9	27.5	5.4
17 45726	Machesney Park village	86.9	9.8	8,004	84.0	111,600	22.4	13.4	842	32.4	86.4	21.9	3.5
17 47774	Maywood village	86.9	11.2	7,628	65.3	176,600	30.0	19.8	747	35.8	74.6	30.1	14.4
17 48242	Melrose Park village	77.7	16.1	7,723	54.0	276,600	38.2	17.2	790	29.8	66.1	26.6	14.2
17 49867	Moline	81.8	12.0	18,857	68.6	101,100	22.7	10.5	605	26.3	81.8	16.9	5.8
17 50647	Morton Grove village	93.8	5.3	8,286	93.4	372,900	32.1	15.0	940	40.0	78.4	28.3	3.8
17 51089	Mount Prospect village	87.2	9.6	20,956	75.0	346,400	26.5	16.7	833	25.0	77.3	27.5	4.8
17 51349	Mundelein village	86.0	9.5	9,891	82.0	238,900	27.6	13.3	956	28.0	77.0	27.5	3.2
17 51622	Naperville	87.7	9.6	47,975	80.5	400,400	23.9	13.8	1040	25.0	76.1	33.5	1.8
17 52584	New Lenox village	91.5	7.7	7,345	91.1	290,700	26.6	17.6	1049	29.2	83.2	34.8	-
17 53000	Niles village	91.1	5.6	11,927	75.2	335,400	31.0	18.0	907	28.0	81.9	26.9	11.8
17 53234	Normal town	64.4	22.3	17,352	57.0	144,000	21.7	9.8	673	37.9	72.1	16.3	4.0
17 53481	Northbrook village	90.6	5.1	12,413	92.5	591,000	24.8	12.8	1622	31.2	75.1	29.0	2.7
17 53559	North Chicago	62.5	33.9	6,881	45.4	150,200	31.6	17.1	987	32.1	44.4	19.6	7.9
17 54638	Oak Forest	84.1	12.9	10,016	82.4	216,300	25.5	13.1	838	34.3	79.0	31.4	4.8

1. $1,000,001 is the top code symbolizing a median value over one million dollars.
2. 50.1 is the top code symbolizing a median gross rent as a percentage of household income of 50.1 percent or more.

Table C-4. Cities — Where: Migration, Housing, and Transportation, 2005–2007—*Continued*

STATE Place code	STATE City	Percent who lived in the same house one year ago	Percent who did not live in city one year ago	Total occupied housing units	Percent owner-occupied housing units	Median value of owner-occupied housing units (dollars)[1]	Median selected monthly owner costs as a percentage of household income		Median gross rent (dollars)	Median gross rent as a percentage of household income[2]	Percent of workers who drove alone to work	Mean travel time to work (minutes)	Percent of occupied housing units with no vehicle available
							With a mortgage	Without a mortgage					
	ACS table number:	C07204	C07204	B25003	B25003	B25077	B25092	B25092	B25064	B25071	C08301	B08013/C08012	C25045
		1	2	3	4	5	6	7	8	9	10	11	12
	Illinois—Cont.												
17 54820	Oak Lawn village	89.9	8.4	22,199	82.2	225,500	26.1	18.0	860	35.2	79.4	31.1	7.8
17 54885	Oak Park village	87.1	9.9	22,120	62.1	388,800	25.5	14.4	875	27.0	59.4	30.1	14.2
17 55249	O'Fallon	81.6	16.4	10,424	69.9	171,400	21.9	11.4	793	24.7	86.4	22.4	5.2
17 56640	Orland Park village	91.8	6.1	21,939	90.0	321,100	26.6	15.4	936	25.1	83.2	33.0	2.8
17 56887	Oswego village	79.1	19.0	7,323	90.0	276,900	29.3	16.8	1218	31.9	85.9	33.7	1.1
17 57225	Palatine village	84.0	12.4	26,542	73.0	318,300	26.8	15.2	974	27.3	82.1	26.9	4.7
17 57732	Park Forest village	85.0	9.7	9,558	70.6	113,000	26.2	14.5	841	38.0	74.8	32.7	5.9
17 57875	Park Ridge	92.5	5.4	13,884	87.2	480,600	26.9	16.4	1046	26.0	72.9	27.8	4.1
17 58447	Pekin	80.3	9.5	13,436	67.7	97,500	20.6	12.8	528	28.7	83.9	19.9	8.1
17 59000	Peoria	80.1	8.3	46,255	60.9	108,800	21.7	12.9	643	28.1	81.1	16.5	13.0
17 60287	Plainfield village	84.9	12.0	9,372	93.1	329,700	26.7	11.8	1104	29.3	84.2	39.8	0.8
17 62367	Quincy	81.9	7.4	17,125	63.4	84,700	20.2	12.2	516	28.1	82.4	12.3	9.7
17 65000	Rockford	82.4	7.1	57,032	62.7	99,000	25.8	14.8	627	31.7	81.6	20.6	11.4
17 65078	Rock Island	81.2	9.6	15,077	69.0	90,500	22.0	12.7	516	31.2	82.1	16.0	11.1
17 65338	Rolling Meadows	86.1	10.9	8,750	78.1	270,900	28.1	16.3	943	29.6	75.3	23.7	6.2
17 65442	Romeoville village	84.7	10.9	11,904	89.4	206,600	31.5	15.2	1151	30.6	77.6	36.9	1.3
17 65806	Roselle village	89.2	7.2	8,836	84.3	288,500	28.0	12.8	997	24.7	84.3	29.6	2.8
17 66040	Round Lake Beach village	88.7	8.7	8,160	87.2	171,400	27.5	12.7	1006	34.1	78.6	37.6	3.3
17 66703	St. Charles	88.3	7.9	13,082	75.0	310,900	24.8	14.7	955	30.3	82.6	27.4	5.4
17 68003	Schaumburg village	83.9	12.3	31,630	68.8	258,800	25.7	13.8	1089	27.9	83.2	27.6	5.5
17 70122	Skokie village	85.7	11.5	23,228	74.3	374,100	31.5	15.1	1051	31.6	72.9	27.5	6.9
17 70720	South Elgin village	85.2	13.9	7,048	90.6	245,100	27.6	14.5	1021	35.4	83.9	29.3	1.1
17 70850	South Holland village	89.8	8.7	7,845	89.4	180,800	29.1	14.6	1404	49.4	70.1	35.6	6.2
17 72000	Springfield	81.5	8.0	49,391	63.0	107,100	21.4	11.3	607	29.5	82.8	17.1	9.2
17 73157	Streamwood village	84.8	12.2	13,155	92.1	231,600	28.1	16.1	1298	50.1	84.3	31.0	0.4
17 75484	Tinley Park village	90.2	8.5	21,667	88.7	246,100	24.9	16.9	856	28.8	79.8	34.7	3.2
17 77005	Urbana	59.0	29.9	14,417	39.6	135,200	22.2	8.9	667	39.1	51.2	14.4	14.9
17 77694	Vernon Hills village	82.0	13.9	8,989	75.6	364,700	26.6	14.5	1150	29.7	79.0	20.0	6.1
17 77993	Villa Park village	86.8	9.2	8,000	78.4	257,100	27.1	14.2	936	32.9	77.6	24.8	3.9
17 79293	Waukegan	81.6	8.8	27,692	56.0	165,200	30.8	14.8	775	27.9	73.5	26.5	9.0
17 80060	West Chicago	86.9	7.8	7,281	75.2	249,200	28.8	12.3	786	26.8	77.7	24.0	3.0
17 80645	Westmont village	84.8	10.8	9,267	59.4	301,600	25.1	14.0	851	29.0	77.2	28.5	5.4
17 81048	Wheaton	84.8	10.1	18,930	78.0	357,000	24.0	13.9	976	27.2	74.5	27.7	4.1
17 81087	Wheeling village	79.1	13.3	14,407	63.5	243,400	30.8	15.4	974	30.9	78.3	25.5	5.3
17 82075	Wilmette village	94.4	4.1	10,056	87.1	677,400	25.5	14.5	1493	21.1	65.5	31.8	3.9
17 83245	Woodridge village	84.7	13.5	12,569	71.4	268,300	28.1	12.1	941	28.8	82.5	30.4	1.7
17 83349	Woodstock	83.0	11.9	8,136	68.2	192,900	25.8	19.0	853	33.3	75.7	28.1	7.3
17 84220	Zion	80.9	10.4	7,928	62.1	163,400	28.9	19.0	837	33.6	75.8	30.6	10.8
18 00000	**Indiana**	83.2	10.4	2,447,887	72.1	119,400	21.8	11.8	646	28.6	82.6	22.4	6.2
18 01468	Anderson	76.7	9.5	23,932	63.6	78,500	24.5	13.2	583	34.6	82.6	22.7	10.3
18 05860	Bloomington	53.0	24.6	26,733	37.6	155,400	21.7	11.9	683	42.8	69.2	14.4	9.3
18 10342	Carmel	85.9	10.3	22,934	79.0	251,400	19.9	8.5	918	25.4	84.3	23.4	1.5
18 12934	Clarksville town	78.9	16.9	9,538	60.0	107,000	23.3	10.1	616	31.7	78.4	19.9	11.1
18 14734	Columbus	79.3	8.8	16,303	63.2	133,200	19.9	11.0	718	29.5	85.9	16.7	5.8
18 16138	Crown Point	83.6	12.1	8,604	75.7	163,100	23.3	14.4	750	27.5	81.9	24.7	5.5
18 19486	East Chicago	84.3	10.1	11,148	45.7	81,000	24.4	21.4	581	32.9	79.5	21.1	23.3
18 20728	Elkhart	73.0	10.3	20,032	52.9	88,900	25.3	12.0	615	27.6	75.4	16.6	9.9
18 22000	Evansville	78.9	6.6	49,733	60.0	87,400	21.9	13.0	593	32.0	82.1	17.0	11.4
18 23278	Fishers town	83.4	12.2	22,188	80.4	193,900	19.9	10.0	924	23.2	87.2	25.9	1.4
18 25000	Fort Wayne	83.8	6.0	101,243	64.2	98,300	20.3	10.5	603	26.6	86.1	19.7	6.3
18 25450	Franklin	77.5	13.0	8,432	66.3	116,300	22.2	9.5	782	28.4	84.3	22.6	6.2
18 27000	Gary	81.5	7.4	33,637	54.2	68,300	25.4	18.0	623	34.7	83.3	23.8	18.9
18 28386	Goshen	79.9	10.3	11,562	64.1	107,200	23.4	13.4	691	29.4	79.7	17.7	6.0
18 28800	Granger CDP	91.0	7.1	10,285	98.0	195,600	20.4	7.6	1378	31.3	90.1	21.2	0.9
18 29898	Greenwood	77.0	16.0	18,941	64.7	133,500	22.1	10.5	730	28.4	85.2	24.2	4.2
18 31000	Hammond	83.8	10.3	28,994	64.6	95,900	26.8	14.9	711	33.3	79.9	25.4	10.7
18 33466	Highland town	87.1	10.4	10,057	79.2	146,000	21.8	13.3	797	22.1	82.3	26.1	3.3
18 34114	Hobart	85.1	10.3	11,072	78.4	126,600	23.6	14.6	852	25.4	88.1	26.0	2.3
18 36003	Indianapolis (balance)	78.8	6.6	323,756	60.5	121,200	22.8	12.0	677	29.6	81.7	21.8	8.3
18 38358	Jeffersonville	79.2	13.8	12,499	61.0	112,400	21.6	12.5	603	27.2	85.2	20.0	8.9
18 40392	Kokomo	79.0	7.2	20,256	59.8	88,400	20.8	12.5	599	27.9	85.4	16.8	12.2
18 40788	Lafayette	71.0	13.1	27,209	53.7	102,400	22.5	10.3	667	31.3	78.0	16.9	9.8
18 42246	La Porte	83.7	11.1	8,841	63.8	93,600	21.0	13.6	570	26.9	81.9	17.8	8.8
18 42426	Lawrence	85.5	14.0	16,594	77.0	133,100	21.7	12.1	690	28.2	84.0	23.4	3.4
18 46908	Marion	79.2	8.8	12,019	61.3	67,600	23.2	13.1	492	28.6	79.1	16.2	10.3
18 48528	Merrillville town	86.8	9.4	12,931	65.5	128,000	25.1	15.0	819	33.5	84.6	27.6	8.4
18 48798	Michigan City	79.9	7.5	12,182	59.8	87,700	24.6	11.8	598	29.9	78.6	17.8	9.2
18 49932	Mishawaka	82.8	10.8	20,311	54.8	93,900	20.6	14.2	668	27.9	84.2	19.5	7.8
18 51876	Muncie	65.9	14.2	26,427	53.3	68,100	23.0	13.9	589	40.4	70.8	16.2	12.0
18 51912	Munster town	92.2	4.6	9,008	88.6	199,500	24.4	13.0	810	25.2	84.4	27.2	4.7
18 52326	New Albany	84.2	10.7	15,099	61.2	109,600	22.5	11.9	623	27.1	84.4	18.6	10.6
18 54180	Noblesville	82.0	12.2	15,765	76.3	169,200	22.6	10.6	748	27.7	86.9	27.1	1.1
18 60246	Plainfield town	76.5	17.8	8,905	68.5	136,800	22.4	11.7	770	28.9	-	22.1	4.3
18 61092	Portage	86.4	8.7	14,095	70.2	126,900	21.3	15.6	764	29.8	87.9	25.3	3.8
18 64260	Richmond	75.1	8.3	15,031	60.6	86,300	21.2	16.0	560	28.2	78.5	16.6	13.5

1. $1,000,001 is the top code symbolizing a median value over one million dollars.
2. 50.1 is the top code symbolizing a median gross rent as a percentage of household income of 50.1 percent or more.

Table C-4. Cities — Where: Migration, Housing, and Transportation, 2005–2007—Continued

STATE Place code	STATE City	Percent who lived in the same house one year ago	Percent who did not live in city one year ago	Total occupied housing units	Percent owner-occupied housing units	Median value of owner-occupied housing units (dollars)[1]	Median selected monthly owner costs as a percentage of household income With a mortgage	Without a mortgage	Median gross rent (dollars)	Median gross rent as a percentage of household income[2]	Percent of workers who drove alone to work	Mean travel time to work (minutes)	Percent of occupied housing units with no vehicle available
ACS table number:		C07204	C07204	B25003	B25003	B25077	B25092	B25092	B25064	B25071	C08301	B08013/ C08012	C25045
		1	2	3	4	5	6	7	8	9	10	11	12
	Indiana—Cont.												
18 68220	Schererville town	88.1	8.5	11,198	79.0	197,500	22.2	11.0	752	21.3	82.6	32.3	2.6
18 71000	South Bend	83.4	8.2	39,718	62.9	84,300	23.5	13.6	672	29.8	79.4	18.7	11.5
18 75428	Terre Haute	75.4	10.5	22,587	57.4	73,300	20.1	14.6	544	33.7	79.7	16.4	11.7
18 78326	Valparaiso	76.4	12.1	12,243	55.3	156,000	21.7	12.8	743	29.4	78.0	22.4	4.5
18 82700	Westfield town	82.8	14.3	9,629	80.9	209,200	21.7	12.5	872	22.8	83.6	24.1	1.0
18 82862	West Lafayette	57.2	18.9	10,928	33.5	168,000	19.8	8.8	713	50.1	58.5	14.4	10.1
19 00000	**Iowa**	83.1	10.4	1,206,848	73.3	112,600	21.5	12.4	587	26.9	78.8	18.2	5.3
19 01855	Ames	57.9	21.2	20,106	46.1	164,300	21.3	8.8	703	33.9	69.4	14.5	4.6
19 02305	Ankeny	77.1	15.4	15,521	77.8	168,100	21.3	13.9	722	26.2	81.4	20.2	1.5
19 06355	Bettendorf	85.6	9.5	13,307	79.6	160,100	20.2	9.4	689	25.2	88.6	17.0	3.9
19 09550	Burlington	82.0	8.3	11,068	71.9	75,600	20.7	13.8	565	31.1	85.2	14.6	7.7
19 11755	Cedar Falls	68.9	18.1	13,848	63.7	140,500	20.2	11.2	636	38.5	79.8	12.7	4.7
19 12000	Cedar Rapids	80.2	9.0	53,704	68.4	119,700	21.9	13.5	599	26.3	81.9	16.3	7.9
19 14430	Clinton	81.3	6.3	11,783	69.1	78,900	20.7	14.6	499	29.2	83.3	16.2	9.7
19 16860	Council Bluffs	76.2	10.2	24,205	65.2	107,000	22.9	13.8	688	27.7	82.4	16.7	6.6
19 19000	Davenport	80.7	9.8	39,066	65.7	110,500	22.2	12.7	620	29.5	81.8	17.5	7.2
19 21000	Des Moines	79.7	8.4	82,567	67.1	112,300	23.7	14.7	641	29.7	81.1	18.1	8.1
19 22395	Dubuque	83.2	7.0	23,651	70.1	115,100	22.4	12.6	538	27.1	83.5	12.8	8.1
19 28515	Fort Dodge	83.2	4.4	10,664	65.6	83,600	19.6	13.8	512	26.3	83.7	13.4	5.8
19 38595	Iowa	62.2	20.0	26,564	51.1	166,400	23.1	10.2	685	42.2	61.2	15.9	8.5
19 49485	Marion	84.3	11.9	12,732	73.7	126,500	22.0	13.2	547	26.3	89.0	19.0	5.7
19 49755	Marshalltown	84.0	7.7	10,411	72.5	91,300	21.9	13.8	581	27.2	76.3	14.8	6.7
19 50160	Mason	82.4	8.3	11,962	70.5	98,800	20.9	12.1	572	29.2	78.7	13.9	6.0
19 55110	Muscatine	85.5	7.6	8,875	71.7	100,200	21.9	12.7	559	30.9	85.4	13.7	7.2
19 60465	Ottumwa	79.4	10.9	10,291	71.6	65,500	21.1	15.2	544	27.1	74.4	15.1	7.4
19 73335	Sioux	80.6	7.2	31,388	66.6	87,500	21.4	12.9	587	29.1	78.8	15.8	7.9
19 79950	Urbandale	87.1	11.4	14,275	80.3	183,000	21.5	9.1	740	24.4	88.4	17.7	3.6
19 82425	Waterloo	79.6	9.2	28,072	68.6	93,000	22.1	13.6	580	33.0	83.2	16.0	8.8
19 83910	West Des Moines	78.6	19.1	23,158	65.2	178,000	21.0	11.2	804	24.0	87.6	16.7	4.9
20 00000	**Kansas**	81.1	11.0	1,083,868	70.0	114,400	21.6	12.1	626	27.3	81.6	18.5	5.0
20 17800	Derby	85.0	8.3	7,490	80.2	133,900	20.9	12.4	816	22.7	86.9	18.8	1.1
20 18250	Dodge	78.1	9.9	8,390	61.1	81,200	23.5	11.8	573	29.3	79.8	13.1	6.9
20 21275	Emporia	67.6	17.9	10,672	52.2	82,700	22.9	11.8	540	32.9	77.1	13.3	9.7
20 25325	Garden	79.8	6.3	8,566	68.0	92,900	22.1	10.6	581	27.1	80.0	12.9	7.2
20 31100	Hays	73.5	11.7	8,419	60.6	121,500	20.2	11.2	616	31.0	86.9	12.2	8.7
20 33625	Hutchinson	79.9	11.0	16,852	69.2	79,800	21.6	13.6	540	24.8	83.7	14.6	5.3
20 36000	Kansas	82.4	8.3	53,730	63.9	90,100	26.4	15.4	677	31.7	79.7	20.3	9.1
20 38900	Lawrence	66.3	14.9	34,951	50.7	164,700	23.2	12.5	726	34.4	75.9	18.8	6.3
20 39000	Leavenworth	66.3	25.5	11,849	53.9	118,100	20.2	11.6	695	29.0	76.7	17.8	7.6
20 39075	Leawood	90.6	6.5	11,718	94.1	359,700	21.7	9.9	1197	33.9	85.9	20.4	2.1
20 39350	Lenexa	80.2	15.3	17,189	65.7	213,400	21.2	9.9	821	27.8	86.5	19.8	3.5
20 39825	Liberal	75.0	12.9	6,711	62.4	76,300	21.0	13.0	554	22.8	73.2	12.8	5.2
20 44250	Manhattan	63.5	21.5	17,913	47.0	150,400	23.0	9.6	672	32.8	73.7	13.9	4.8
20 52575	Olathe	82.8	11.7	40,008	74.5	186,400	22.2	10.5	741	25.7	84.8	20.5	2.7
20 53775	Overland Park	82.3	12.4	66,420	67.4	215,900	21.3	10.9	869	24.7	86.1	19.6	2.7
20 57575	Prairie Village	86.9	9.9	9,752	84.3	194,100	22.9	11.3	1028	26.3	88.3	18.8	3.6
20 62700	Salina	79.5	8.4	18,852	64.6	99,300	21.6	11.5	521	28.7	82.1	13.4	7.8
20 64500	Shawnee	80.7	13.0	22,537	73.5	190,800	22.1	10.7	755	24.4	87.6	21.2	2.1
20 71000	Topeka	76.8	7.8	53,100	60.9	88,500	21.7	12.5	583	28.9	81.5	17.0	8.0
20 79000	Wichita	77.4	6.9	145,140	63.4	103,400	21.0	11.6	595	28.9	83.5	17.0	7.1
21 00000	**Kentucky**	83.3	11.7	1,654,119	70.8	109,700	21.5	10.7	560	27.8	81.7	22.3	7.8
21 02368	Ashland	83.1	12.1	9,359	63.7	88,500	17.9	11.0	499	27.2	86.0	15.8	10.0
21 08902	Bowling Green	66.2	17.4	21,579	46.1	127,700	22.6	9.6	586	28.6	77.1	16.6	10.6
21 17848	Covington	75.7	15.0	17,825	55.6	94,800	22.4	12.2	545	29.5	77.0	19.7	10.6
21 24274	Elizabethtown	83.5	9.9	10,224	62.1	135,000	19.8	9.7	546	25.0	86.5	18.0	6.2
21 27982	Florence	73.9	17.4	11,861	50.8	133,900	20.8	11.3	715	25.6	86.6	21.0	8.3
21 28900	Frankfort	75.2	10.0	12,232	56.1	120,000	20.3	11.4	536	26.8	76.1	15.8	10.6
21 30700	Georgetown	74.3	13.5	8,896	63.5	133,500	19.3	8.1	593	26.7	76.5	18.5	6.6
21 35866	Henderson	78.6	12.2	11,901	58.6	90,500	19.9	9.6	509	27.6	86.2	16.3	12.3
21 37918	Hopkinsville	78.9	9.7	13,036	57.5	87,300	19.5	11.1	567	25.0	82.8	16.3	10.4
21 39142	Independence	90.9	7.7	6,660	87.2	151,800	23.5	11.2	555	25.2	84.3	25.9	2.3
21 40222	Jeffersontown	85.6	13.9	11,026	71.0	158,300	22.5	10.5	756	29.4	81.6	19.8	4.0
21 46027	Lexington-Fayette urban county	75.5	9.8	117,478	59.1	152,400	21.5	9.7	639	28.8	80.6	19.6	7.5
21 48006	Louisville/Jefferson County (balance)	83.1	5.4	231,425	65.3	131,200	22.8	12.2	612	29.3	81.6	21.1	10.8
21 56136	Nicholasville	80.0	11.2	9,599	60.9	120,000	22.6	15.3	666	30.1	80.0	21.8	5.5
21 58620	Owensboro	78.8	8.4	24,541	58.4	96,000	20.2	11.1	513	28.9	86.3	15.8	8.1
21 58836	Paducah	76.9	13.8	11,489	53.9	82,000	23.3	13.3	471	29.9	79.3	15.1	13.5
21 63912	Radcliff	75.4	19.1	8,532	57.7	107,400	21.2	9.0	509	20.7	-	19.4	3.4
21 65226	Richmond	65.4	18.1	11,008	42.4	126,200	21.8	11.2	496	28.5	75.3	19.8	10.4
22 00000	**Louisiana**	82.6	12.2	1,605,203	68.1	113,500	21.4	10.5	629	30.3	80.9	24.9	9.0
22 00975	Alexandria	78.9	8.1	18,066	57.3	95,900	25.4	14.1	653	41.9	84.6	15.5	14.4
22 05000	Baton Rouge	76.6	10.0	89,468	52.3	130,800	22.9	11.7	680	34.6	78.7	21.4	9.9
22 08920	Bossier	75.3	14.9	24,039	56.8	114,000	20.7	8.1	665	25.3	84.7	17.2	6.7

1. $1,000,001 is the top code symbolizing a median value over one million dollars.
2. 50.1 is the top code symbolizing a median gross rent as a percentage of household income of 50.1 percent or more.

STATE Place code	STATE City	Percent who lived in the same house one year ago	Percent who did not live in city one year ago	Total occupied housing units	Percent owner-occupied housing units	Median value of owner-occupied housing units (dollars)[1]	Median selected monthly owner costs as a percentage of household income With a mortgage	Median selected monthly owner costs as a percentage of household income Without a mortgage	Median gross rent (dollars)	Median gross rent as a percentage of household income[2]	Percent of workers who drove alone to work	Mean travel time to work (minutes)	Percent of occupied housing units with no vehicle available
	ACS table number:	C07204	C07204	B25003	B25003	B25077	B25092	B25092	B25064	B25071	C08301	B08013/ C08012	C25045
		1	2	3	4	5	6	7	8	9	10	11	12
	Louisiana—Cont.												
22 33245	Harvey CDP	76.6	18.8	7,591	62.8	129,200	26.1	9.2	794	39.3	77.0	24.9	8.5
22 36255	Houma	85.9	6.6	12,281	65.2	132,000	19.5	11.3	569	30.5	84.9	19.8	13.9
22 39475	Kenner	80.8	12.5	22,991	60.2	164,900	24.2	10.5	817	30.3	79.0	26.1	8.1
22 40735	Lafayette	81.6	9.7	47,481	58.7	144,500	20.2	9.7	630	27.6	82.3	21.0	8.9
22 41155	Lake Charles	75.7	9.5	28,608	57.3	97,400	20.5	11.7	597	31.9	79.5	16.5	11.4
22 42030	Laplace CDP	86.0	9.8	10,588	83.2	143,500	22.7	9.3	634	29.2	86.4	26.9	4.8
22 48785	Marrero CDP	82.3	12.1	11,209	66.5	113,000	23.3	11.7	645	42.2	75.9	23.0	11.6
22 50115	Metairie CDP	82.7	11.5	54,163	65.7	199,300	22.5	10.5	768	30.6	80.4	22.1	5.8
22 51410	Monroe	83.7	6.6	17,661	52.1	94,500	21.0	13.2	546	33.5	81.0	16.4	16.8
22 54035	New Iberia	83.1	7.2	11,632	62.2	82,100	22.8	11.6	590	27.1	83.4	19.8	13.3
22 55000	New Orleans	71.9	12.3	101,221	50.1	166,500	27.6	12.4	753	34.7	64.9	23.8	21.8
22 58045	Opelousas	83.1	6.3	9,107	55.1	84,900	24.8	13.0	426	39.5	78.1	22.2	21.5
22 66655	Ruston	64.4	23.8	7,916	44.8	114,200	19.4	12.7	581	50.0	76.3	14.1	13.2
22 70000	Shreveport	80.3	7.3	77,562	60.1	98,800	22.7	11.6	606	32.0	80.6	17.8	12.3
22 70805	Slidell	84.6	11.5	9,252	78.5	148,600	22.6	11.7	925	34.5	78.8	27.0	5.9
22 75180	Terrytown CDP	77.5	20.9	7,547	55.8	152,900	22.9	11.3	804	36.9	83.3	22.4	10.9
23 00000	**Maine**	85.2	11.7	542,424	72.9	167,700	23.7	13.8	650	28.8	78.5	22.6	6.3
23 02060	Auburn	79.1	16.7	9,826	59.8	148,000	25.3	19.0	582	27.7	82.2	19.6	9.1
23 02795	Bangor	73.7	17.3	13,457	49.7	132,200	23.0	18.2	628	28.6	75.6	16.2	14.2
23 04860	Biddeford	81.1	11.2	9,518	54.1	219,700	26.4	16.3	727	29.0	74.7	19.7	8.6
23 38740	Lewiston	71.1	12.4	15,644	51.2	138,900	24.7	16.7	580	29.0	74.0	21.9	14.3
23 60545	Portland	76.1	12.5	28,515	44.7	248,500	26.2	16.3	803	29.5	69.9	16.9	16.4
23 71990	South Portland	85.8	9.1	10,377	67.3	220,400	26.9	14.9	858	31.7	80.3	19.0	7.8
24 00000	**Maryland**	84.9	12.2	2,082,573	69.4	323,400	24.4	11.7	977	29.2	73.3	30.8	9.2
24 01600	Annapolis	81.1	12.2	15,039	57.5	412,100	24.0	10.5	1126	27.1	66.3	26.7	10.4
24 01975	Arbutus CDP	80.9	17.3	8,133	68.4	227,400	24.6	13.7	777	26.3	81.3	24.2	9.6
24 02275	Arnold CDP	89.2	9.8	8,468	89.4	425,100	23.8	10.6	1310	24.9	85.6	28.3	6.1
24 02825	Aspen Hill CDP	80.0	16.9	17,520	67.8	448,900	26.2	9.5	1282	31.8	65.9	34.6	7.6
24 04000	Baltimore	83.0	5.7	235,734	51.1	130,900	24.8	15.3	745	32.0	58.6	28.5	30.4
24 05825	Bel Air North CDP	88.7	11.3	10,184	88.5	325,600	21.0	13.0	1161	30.0	88.2	33.5	2.6
24 05950	Bel Air South CDP	85.1	14.8	17,693	82.2	280,000	22.6	9.1	874	27.1	83.7	31.6	4.5
24 07125	Bethesda CDP	84.5	12.6	23,900	68.4	761,500	20.7	11.1	1440	27.3	57.9	26.8	7.8
24 08775	Bowie	89.6	7.9	20,597	88.2	364,900	23.8	10.7	1495	29.4	75.1	36.8	2.4
24 13325	Carney CDP	84.2	15.6	12,351	61.1	223,700	22.8	9.0	1033	29.2	85.4	26.1	8.2
24 14125	Catonsville CDP	84.5	13.7	15,333	69.4	300,700	23.1	9.7	1000	30.6	81.9	25.6	11.5
24 16875	Chillum CDP	70.3	29.7	11,054	39.9	336,000	30.6	12.1	1000	30.7	48.4	35.1	19.3
24 17900	Clinton CDP	93.4	6.4	9,370	90.3	339,900	26.6	10.2	1177	24.6	69.5	41.7	3.0
24 18250	Cockeysville CDP	75.4	21.6	9,388	37.8	336,500	22.4	10.4	941	24.4	77.8	26.1	5.7
24 18750	College Park	61.6	29.9	5,584	57.4	347,900	22.9	10.7	1356	50.1	45.3	24.5	4.7
24 19125	Columbia CDP	82.9	12.8	35,883	69.2	390,000	23.0	8.2	1251	26.8	78.4	29.4	4.1
24 20875	Crofton CDP	84.1	9.3	7,352	79.3	415,800	23.7	8.2	1321	24.3	82.3	31.6	1.0
24 21325	Cumberland	82.6	7.9	9,613	58.9	83,000	22.6	15.3	481	27.9	77.2	17.9	21.2
24 23975	Dundalk CDP	84.5	12.6	24,823	66.3	141,100	23.5	13.7	789	32.0	75.3	25.6	15.0
24 25150	Edgewood CDP	82.5	11.9	8,958	70.9	172,400	23.6	12.5	891	30.4	70.0	29.5	7.9
24 25575	Eldersburg CDP	91.1	8.4	10,301	87.0	385,200	23.3	11.7	891	31.7	84.2	33.2	2.3
24 25750	Elkridge CDP	87.1	12.3	8,743	81.7	354,400	24.1	9.2	1206	28.1	86.0	25.9	1.7
24 26000	Ellicott CDP	88.2	9.1	22,658	74.5	522,500	23.2	9.8	1218	30.3	80.8	29.7	4.8
24 26600	Essex CDP	81.4	15.4	15,816	56.1	193,700	24.0	14.9	814	28.5	78.0	30.3	13.6
24 27250	Fairland CDP	77.8	22.2	8,510	53.8	398,200	28.4	14.5	1308	34.3	71.4	38.1	10.0
24 29525	Fort Washington CDP	85.5	13.6	8,339	88.3	390,500	24.2	9.1	1232	28.5	69.9	42.5	2.7
24 30325	Frederick	75.5	14.7	24,399	57.2	317,400	26.3	14.4	1013	28.1	74.9	30.8	7.3
24 31175	Gaithersburg	79.9	14.2	21,368	56.7	413,400	26.1	9.3	1275	32.0	68.4	31.4	7.3
24 32025	Germantown CDP	80.4	15.2	21,751	71.9	346,100	26.6	8.0	1259	31.9	71.3	34.7	5.4
24 32650	Glen Burnie CDP	83.4	11.5	15,036	66.8	244,100	25.3	12.1	962	31.9	79.5	23.7	9.0
24 34711	Greater Landover CDP	77.7	22.3	7,534	50.1	198,800	31.1	11.7	1078	32.6	50.9	32.9	17.8
24 34712	Greater Upper Marlboro CDP	85.7	14.3	7,793	83.7	366,500	27.3	9.2	1345	30.5	78.5	39.1	2.9
24 34775	Greenbelt	80.4	16.0	9,542	52.0	227,000	23.2	8.3	1106	27.4	64.3	32.3	11.4
24 36075	Hagerstown	82.1	9.4	16,589	45.0	166,900	25.7	17.8	663	29.2	77.3	23.9	15.9
24 45612	Lanham-Seabrook CDP	84.9	14.9	7,036	76.3	334,300	26.2	8.4	1073	23.0	66.5	32.9	3.5
24 45900	Laurel	76.1	16.4	9,924	52.7	282,700	26.6	9.9	1036	26.8	69.3	32.5	9.5
24 47450	Lochearn CDP	85.2	14.8	9,720	68.2	197,900	27.8	11.5	918	32.5	71.3	29.6	8.6
24 52300	Middle River CDP	83.3	14.0	9,038	66.7	143,300	22.9	14.2	869	26.9	75.9	25.2	6.8
24 52562	Milford Mill CDP	80.9	19.1	10,891	45.7	216,800	28.5	12.2	995	27.4	78.7	30.1	7.3
24 53325	Montgomery Village CDP	82.0	16.3	14,457	75.4	367,100	24.0	8.1	1259	25.8	64.8	34.3	5.8
24 56337	North Bethesda CDP	78.9	20.3	17,803	62.3	515,900	25.7	10.6	1474	28.2	61.7	27.1	6.9
24 56875	North Potomac CDP	86.9	12.8	8,075	82.1	641,600	20.7	8.1	1779	31.6	73.5	34.4	2.0
24 58300	Odenton CDP	84.8	13.9	9,735	79.9	351,000	24.4	13.8	1489	25.0	84.1	29.4	1.4
24 58900	Olney CDP	92.3	6.8	11,292	90.0	562,000	23.9	9.6	1329	30.5	79.9	35.3	1.9
24 59425	Owings Mills CDP	75.1	21.1	11,914	49.8	249,600	26.6	10.5	1135	25.5	80.2	32.7	3.1
24 59505	Oxon Hill-Glassmanor CDP	84.5	11.4	14,346	47.1	256,400	31.1	14.6	977	27.8	61.7	38.8	11.8
24 60275	Parkville CDP	88.5	10.7	12,860	66.0	187,300	23.4	12.5	869	34.6	75.2	26.6	10.5
24 60975	Perry Hall CDP	89.5	9.1	11,615	81.0	248,300	21.8	12.2	1077	23.7	86.6	28.8	4.0
24 61400	Pikesville CDP	87.8	10.4	13,250	69.1	314,200	22.0	10.5	980	30.5	76.0	25.3	10.6

1. $1,000,001 is the top code symbolizing a median value over one million dollars.
2. 50.1 is the top code symbolizing a median gross rent as a percentage of household income of 50.1 percent or more.

STATE Place code	STATE City	Percent who lived in the same house one year ago	Percent who did not live in city one year ago	Total occupied housing units	Percent owner-occupied housing units	Median value of owner-occupied housing units (dollars)[1]	Median selected monthly owner costs as a percentage of household income		Median gross rent (dollars)	Median gross rent as a percentage of household income[2]	Percent of workers who drove alone to work	Mean travel time to work (minutes)	Percent of occupied housing units with no vehicle available
							With a mortgage	Without a mortgage					
	ACS table number:	C07204	C07204	B25003	B25003	B25077	B25092	B25092	B25064	B25071	C08301	B08013/ C08012	C25045
		1	2	3	4	5	6	7	8	9	10	11	12
	Maryland—Cont.												
24 63300	Potomac CDP	88.0	10.0	16,286	86.0	874,900	22.3	9.2	1502	32.3	76.0	30.7	2.5
24 64950	Randallstown CDP	84.5	13.0	11,313	72.3	238,400	26.9	9.7	969	31.6	78.6	30.4	6.3
24 65600	Reisterstown CDP	85.5	11.7	9,345	64.2	243,900	24.0	9.0	875	29.1	79.6	31.5	7.5
24 67675	Rockville	82.3	14.3	20,328	64.9	501,600	24.8	10.3	1437	28.1	61.1	30.1	7.1
24 69350	St. Charles CDP	86.3	13.7	13,149	68.7	308,400	25.7	7.7	1112	29.7	77.1	38.0	6.5
24 69925	Salisbury	68.7	18.1	10,034	37.5	150,000	27.0	14.4	836	27.0	70.6	19.8	15.9
24 71150	Severn CDP	80.4	18.0	13,884	75.6	360,900	23.3	10.7	1192	29.1	82.7	27.7	4.9
24 71200	Severna Park CDP	92.2	6.4	9,980	90.9	540,000	23.2	9.1	1618	31.0	85.9	27.0	1.8
24 72450	Silver Spring CDP	81.3	13.7	29,448	45.2	464,100	24.8	9.7	1179	28.8	51.7	35.1	16.1
24 73550	South Gate CDP	78.8	21.2	12,204	50.3	278,700	23.2	10.7	998	30.3	78.2	27.2	4.6
24 75762	Suitland-Silver Hill CDP	80.1	15.6	12,901	32.7	238,100	27.4	12.5	958	25.6	55.0	33.3	16.2
24 78425	Towson CDP	77.2	18.6	20,885	59.3	326,700	20.6	9.3	999	35.9	77.3	23.3	9.2
24 81175	Waldorf CDP	87.4	8.9	8,955	78.3	348,600	24.8	10.9	1247	27.1	76.6	36.5	1.6
24 83837	Wheaton-Glenmont CDP	85.5	14.0	19,497	67.5	402,800	27.4	10.0	1252	30.0	59.1	34.8	8.3
24 84375	White Oak CDP	82.9	17.1	7,473	45.8	473,100	27.3	8.6	1245	28.1	66.3	37.8	10.4
24 86475	Woodlawn CDP (Baltimore County)	86.4	13.0	14,297	66.5	216,300	24.7	11.6	936	29.8	78.6	26.1	6.6
25 00000	**Massachusetts**	85.9	9.4	2,448,608	65.0	366,200	26.5	15.3	952	30.1	73.6	27.0	11.5
25 00765	Agawam	90.8	6.8	11,201	76.2	215,300	23.5	13.9	764	28.4	90.3	21.0	5.6
25 01640	Arlington CDP	87.5	10.3	18,192	61.6	488,400	24.5	18.0	1244	27.2	66.2	28.0	10.8
25 02690	Attleboro	86.7	6.5	16,403	71.1	323,400	25.7	13.7	879	29.2	78.7	26.9	6.5
25 03690	Barnstable Town	86.7	9.0	20,176	76.2	399,700	31.8	14.9	1213	33.2	79.7	22.1	5.6
25 05105	Belmont CDP	86.4	11.0	9,552	63.0	640,300	26.5	14.2	1491	30.4	69.8	26.2	4.4
25 05595	Beverly	87.0	8.9	15,182	61.6	399,100	27.0	18.2	1000	28.5	78.1	24.8	6.2
25 07000	Boston	76.0	11.2	232,099	38.2	426,100	29.1	16.4	1110	31.6	41.0	29.1	35.5
25 07700	Braintree CDP	90.5	6.6	12,845	75.2	384,700	25.0	13.8	1205	28.2	78.1	29.1	6.4
25 09000	Brockton	82.4	9.7	33,324	58.2	299,800	31.6	16.8	936	32.8	76.0	29.0	12.1
25 09210	Brookline CDP	80.2	14.4	25,591	53.3	664,700	24.6	13.2	1638	30.2	41.4	27.2	22.4
25 09875	Burlington CDP	86.7	10.9	8,619	77.2	444,000	25.6	14.1	1542	24.1	85.3	27.3	3.7
25 11000	Cambridge	73.2	19.5	41,174	39.2	560,400	26.5	15.7	1325	30.9	33.3	24.4	31.3
25 13205	Chelsea	79.8	7.6	11,564	35.4	357,200	37.8	32.7	975	32.1	49.4	27.5	30.0
25 13660	Chicopee	84.2	9.7	23,427	58.7	164,800	24.3	17.5	666	28.1	87.7	18.0	10.4
25 16285	Danvers CDP	94.8	3.1	9,476	79.2	405,400	25.7	14.8	1120	28.4	85.8	24.7	6.1
25 16530	Dedham CDP	91.5	6.4	8,786	82.9	413,300	27.7	18.2	1119	31.2	76.9	29.4	4.1
25 21990	Everett	82.5	10.2	14,958	45.4	400,700	35.9	19.6	1069	28.6	61.9	27.9	16.3
25 23000	Fall River	82.8	7.1	38,538	35.5	274,800	29.1	15.0	637	27.2	78.9	21.1	16.8
25 23875	Fitchburg	83.1	11.0	14,918	56.0	226,500	27.9	18.1	759	33.0	81.5	24.3	15.3
25 24960	Framingham CDP	84.9	10.1	25,076	59.5	377,700	26.5	16.4	1070	31.1	74.1	27.1	7.5
25 25100	Franklin	89.7	7.2	10,768	84.1	390,900	25.2	14.6	1141	33.2	81.5	33.0	5.1
25 25485	Gardner	82.7	11.8	8,073	56.9	217,100	24.7	15.6	671	27.5	76.5	23.7	8.4
25 26150	Gloucester	92.2	4.3	11,865	65.0	407,300	27.3	17.8	930	28.6	76.8	23.6	8.6
25 29405	Haverhill	84.9	9.2	22,494	64.7	310,900	26.3	16.4	973	31.1	82.3	27.5	10.1
25 30840	Holyoke	79.2	10.1	14,938	43.2	181,300	24.5	14.2	655	32.7	82.0	17.9	20.0
25 34550	Lawrence	80.0	5.5	24,358	36.9	274,100	40.0	16.9	922	38.6	64.8	22.3	23.5
25 35075	Leominster	88.8	5.5	16,685	62.2	259,500	25.2	16.0	772	30.7	83.6	24.8	10.4
25 35250	Lexington CDP	91.3	7.3	10,936	83.2	677,200	23.0	14.6	1700	26.2	77.1	26.7	3.6
25 37000	Lowell	83.4	5.5	36,943	48.2	274,600	28.7	17.9	905	29.6	78.8	25.5	14.8
25 37490	Lynn	84.6	5.3	32,339	48.9	315,200	30.1	18.3	884	33.3	72.7	27.4	18.4
25 37875	Malden	82.4	12.6	22,682	47.1	369,000	33.6	15.8	1107	31.4	58.2	29.2	22.0
25 38435	Marblehead CDP	90.3	4.6	8,209	77.6	639,100	28.7	14.0	1041	25.8	75.6	30.2	3.2
25 38715	Marlborough	87.5	7.3	14,776	61.3	360,000	24.7	18.3	1000	27.2	81.2	28.2	9.6
25 39835	Medford	79.6	14.9	21,354	63.5	432,400	28.6	17.7	1165	29.2	66.4	26.5	11.0
25 40115	Melrose	89.9	7.5	10,864	67.9	441,500	24.0	15.0	902	28.1	72.9	27.2	8.2
25 40710	Methuen	89.5	7.3	16,567	76.0	328,300	27.1	20.9	862	33.6	85.1	24.9	8.6
25 41200	Milford CDP	87.3	7.5	9,495	64.2	330,600	25.0	19.4	970	29.6	78.5	26.1	6.2
25 41725	Milton CDP	88.5	9.5	9,058	82.9	495,900	25.9	18.5	1501	35.5	77.9	28.8	6.6
25 44140	Needham CDP	87.9	8.4	10,424	85.0	658,200	24.4	15.7	1360	35.3	73.6	27.5	6.8
25 45000	New Bedford	83.8	6.2	38,019	45.6	252,900	30.0	19.7	680	30.6	76.7	22.7	19.7
25 45560	Newton	82.0	12.7	31,873	70.6	693,500	25.1	15.1	1412	27.0	66.3	27.0	6.1
25 46330	Northampton	78.4	17.5	12,108	55.8	248,700	24.9	16.7	797	32.0	68.9	19.5	10.1
25 50285	Norwood CDP	82.1	10.2	11,569	56.4	394,500	25.1	14.1	1186	27.3	80.5	26.3	6.8
25 52490	Peabody	90.3	7.3	19,286	69.2	382,800	25.6	14.5	1033	33.3	85.4	24.3	10.2
25 53960	Pittsfield	88.3	4.2	19,989	60.7	155,700	21.9	14.7	622	28.5	78.9	15.9	12.1
25 55745	Quincy	81.2	11.5	37,903	51.9	372,700	27.8	17.0	1101	29.4	60.2	30.4	13.8
25 55990	Randolph CDP	86.9	9.3	11,000	74.1	344,100	28.5	15.4	1084	26.9	75.8	29.7	9.1
25 56165	Reading CDP	93.6	4.8	8,954	87.0	461,500	24.2	16.3	862	27.2	83.5	29.5	6.3
25 56585	Revere	84.4	9.5	20,176	51.6	355,400	30.7	19.5	986	31.4	63.9	27.1	11.7
25 59105	Salem	84.8	8.3	17,332	55.0	353,400	28.9	17.7	1012	32.5	70.4	29.0	13.5
25 60050	Saugus CDP	92.8	4.4	9,983	77.3	380,200	26.1	16.0	1067	31.5	83.2	24.3	7.1
25 62535	Somerville	77.6	16.2	29,057	35.0	473,800	29.5	16.4	1266	29.3	40.8	28.1	25.3
25 67000	Springfield	82.0	6.4	55,363	49.6	150,500	26.7	16.6	680	33.4	77.3	20.7	20.9
25 67700	Stoneham CDP	92.5	5.1	8,809	69.2	436,200	27.8	17.3	1126	30.8	84.5	24.8	7.3
25 69170	Taunton	84.8	8.8	22,187	62.0	304,500	27.1	16.3	879	29.1	80.5	27.8	7.2
25 72250	Wakefield CDP	89.3	5.4	9,408	72.2	427,400	25.0	13.3	1033	24.7	77.3	27.6	6.0
25 72600	Waltham	79.2	15.3	22,778	48.9	441,900	27.9	15.7	1217	30.7	70.0	22.9	8.9
25 73440	Watertown	85.3	10.6	13,817	52.1	435,600	30.0	17.7	1340	25.9	67.7	25.9	8.2

1. $1,000,001 is the top code symbolizing a median value over one million dollars.
2. 50.1 is the top code symbolizing a median gross rent as a percentage of household income of 50.1 percent or more.

STATE Place code	STATE City	Percent who lived in the same house one year ago	Percent who did not live in city one year ago	Total occupied housing units	Percent owner-occupied housing units	Median value of owner-occupied housing units (dollars)[1]	Median selected monthly owner costs as a percentage of household income — With a mortgage	Without a mortgage	Median gross rent (dollars)	Median gross rent as a percentage of household income[2]	Percent of workers who drove alone to work	Mean travel time to work (minutes)	Percent of occupied housing units with no vehicle available
ACS table number:		C07204	C07204	B25003	B25003	B25077	B25092	B25092	B25064	B25071	C08301	B08013/C08012	C25045
		1	2	3	4	5	6	7	8	9	10	11	12
	Massachusetts—Cont.												
25 74210	Wellesley CDP	84.7	10.7	9,430	78.7	910,900	24.9	11.2	1313	25.8	61.8	25.8	4.6
25 76030	Westfield	81.1	10.3	15,170	65.6	214,100	23.0	15.0	788	29.7	87.2	23.2	7.3
25 77850	West Springfield	86.3	7.5	11,798	59.1	199,800	24.8	16.8	719	27.1	85.4	20.7	8.7
25 78900	Weymouth CDP	88.1	7.7	21,835	69.9	351,700	25.7	15.8	1104	29.1	79.8	29.3	4.9
25 80195	Wilmington CDP	94.4	4.9	7,376	87.4	412,200	26.2	12.4	1228	32.8	85.9	28.1	3.9
25 80545	Winchester CDP	91.0	6.5	7,962	83.2	696,300	23.5	18.2	1354	28.9	75.5	27.4	3.6
25 80965	Winthrop CDP	89.6	7.9	7,874	60.9	422,400	27.8	16.6	1059	35.5	65.0	29.3	10.1
25 81035	Woburn	88.0	6.6	14,834	64.8	397,900	27.9	15.7	1143	27.1	83.8	23.0	7.0
25 82000	Worcester	84.8	6.7	64,535	49.0	254,500	27.4	19.4	807	30.0	78.6	22.8	15.9
26 00000	**Michigan**	85.4	10.5	3,864,307	75.1	152,200	24.3	13.6	689	31.0	83.2	23.6	6.6
26 00440	Adrian	78.5	11.2	8,079	62.3	103,500	25.3	13.6	616	29.0	71.4	19.1	10.0
26 01380	Allen Park	93.0	4.2	11,615	90.6	149,100	23.2	15.4	738	24.3	90.0	20.9	5.2
26 03000	Ann Arbor	67.2	18.8	44,559	48.9	245,100	23.9	13.2	938	36.2	61.3	18.5	9.3
26 04105	Auburn Hills	72.3	22.3	8,186	50.3	159,000	25.0	13.0	854	28.8	83.0	20.5	1.5
26 05920	Battle Creek	80.9	5.4	20,599	65.8	99,500	23.5	13.7	646	36.2	80.6	16.4	10.4
26 06020	Bay	80.6	5.8	14,613	71.7	85,500	23.4	16.7	494	29.1	82.9	19.0	11.1
26 09190	Bloomfield Township CDP	94.0	5.9	16,377	92.2	443,100	23.0	11.7	1017	22.2	88.4	23.6	1.6
26 12060	Burton	85.4	12.0	12,313	76.2	115,600	23.9	13.2	565	29.1	82.7	24.4	7.7
26 13110	Canton CDP	86.2	11.1	31,992	79.9	240,200	23.5	13.4	886	25.9	89.4	26.9	2.1
26 16510	Clinton CDP	84.0	13.2	40,991	71.4	165,700	24.8	15.6	697	30.1	88.8	26.2	4.4
26 21000	Dearborn	86.1	6.4	34,687	72.3	162,000	27.1	14.0	908	37.3	86.7	20.0	7.4
26 21020	Dearborn Heights	88.9	8.0	22,393	83.1	143,800	26.6	14.5	840	30.1	86.4	24.0	5.8
26 22000	Detroit	83.5	3.3	285,912	55.3	89,500	31.4	17.6	717	39.7	73.5	26.3	20.7
26 24120	East Lansing	54.1	29.4	14,040	34.8	206,000	21.8	11.8	742	50.1	58.1	14.5	10.2
26 24290	Eastpointe	90.7	6.8	13,530	83.5	127,800	25.5	17.3	686	29.9	87.6	24.9	5.0
26 27440	Farmington Hills	84.6	11.2	33,623	68.1	271,700	23.0	16.3	933	27.2	86.5	24.4	4.2
26 27880	Ferndale	87.7	10.7	9,350	76.9	145,800	24.9	20.5	789	31.8	82.6	22.3	6.2
26 29000	Flint	79.2	6.9	43,773	57.0	65,100	24.7	14.6	619	37.7	78.9	21.7	14.7
26 29580	Forest Hills CDP	90.4	9.6	8,390	96.3	254,000	21.5	13.1	-	24.0	83.6	19.5	1.5
26 31420	Garden	90.0	8.8	11,280	83.7	146,300	26.4	13.8	682	31.7	86.2	25.3	7.8
26 34000	Grand Rapids	77.2	10.7	73,360	61.9	124,200	24.7	12.6	674	33.4	76.3	18.6	10.8
26 36280	Hamtramck	80.1	12.4	6,446	50.5	92,800	43.7	17.6	603	35.7	72.0	27.5	19.6
26 36810	Harrison CDP	87.8	10.2	10,178	75.0	187,400	22.7	14.3	742	25.8	84.7	28.7	4.0
26 38640	Holland	79.7	11.0	11,401	68.2	139,400	25.6	12.8	649	27.5	79.9	15.2	4.4
26 40680	Inkster	75.9	18.1	10,188	54.1	101,900	25.2	14.8	711	29.3	80.8	23.1	14.9
26 41420	Jackson	77.1	7.7	13,798	59.8	96,900	25.6	14.3	635	39.4	79.5	18.6	14.7
26 42160	Kalamazoo	64.6	17.6	27,790	47.5	108,300	24.2	13.1	624	35.8	76.0	17.6	13.1
26 42820	Kentwood	80.7	16.2	19,163	64.3	143,900	24.1	14.1	673	26.2	85.7	18.6	4.2
26 46000	Lansing	81.6	8.6	47,792	59.1	109,000	24.9	14.8	620	32.2	81.7	19.0	10.2
26 47800	Lincoln Park	87.4	9.1	15,265	79.1	116,800	25.9	14.6	603	29.8	83.8	21.1	8.0
26 49000	Livonia	92.8	5.0	37,791	90.1	200,800	23.1	12.9	820	32.5	90.2	23.2	4.3
26 50560	Madison Heights	87.4	9.4	12,826	74.2	140,600	24.1	15.5	660	28.9	86.7	22.8	8.2
26 51900	Marquette	71.7	20.6	7,605	54.3	133,900	20.5	14.3	510	36.6	78.5	11.7	8.5
26 53780	Midland	81.6	11.0	16,908	67.6	141,500	18.9	11.9	573	33.3	84.3	16.2	6.3
26 55020	Monroe	85.4	6.9	8,887	61.1	158,200	25.2	17.3	618	26.1	84.1	21.6	9.5
26 56020	Mount Pleasant	47.8	27.5	7,958	34.2	133,100	24.7	9.8	616	33.8	69.9	12.0	10.2
26 56320	Muskegon	72.0	16.5	13,974	58.3	80,600	26.9	12.5	508	35.9	80.3	15.9	13.9
26 59140	Norton Shores	87.2	12.2	9,935	85.6	137,400	22.3	12.9	826	26.9	89.0	16.7	2.9
26 59440	Novi	85.1	12.9	21,316	69.6	287,700	23.0	14.4	941	23.0	91.2	26.2	3.5
26 59920	Oak Park	84.0	14.0	11,322	73.1	151,700	25.8	19.4	786	34.9	83.7	25.2	7.2
26 60340	Okemos CDP	84.4	14.0	8,724	69.4	233,700	19.4	10.7	813	28.9	79.5	20.9	4.5
26 65085	Plymouth Township CDP	91.4	8.5	11,252	84.8	292,200	21.1	11.9	728	27.0	91.1	24.9	4.4
26 65440	Pontiac	76.1	10.8	23,180	52.6	105,000	29.2	16.3	723	37.0	76.3	22.5	14.6
26 65560	Portage	84.3	10.6	19,378	69.4	155,300	22.2	11.7	651	30.5	87.6	17.4	4.8
26 65820	Port Huron	78.8	12.2	12,921	58.8	112,000	24.1	17.3	658	32.5	79.5	17.2	10.9
26 67620	Redford CDP	87.0	9.8	19,360	89.9	135,700	24.9	15.2	933	33.1	88.7	23.3	4.2
26 69035	Rochester Hills	88.5	9.6	27,252	79.3	275,500	22.7	13.1	975	28.7	86.8	26.0	3.4
26 69420	Romulus	82.4	14.6	9,144	68.8	135,400	27.9	18.7	684	29.7	84.8	25.6	6.2
26 69800	Roseville	89.7	7.8	19,218	74.0	125,000	26.0	14.7	712	31.3	86.4	24.0	6.9
26 70040	Royal Oak	85.5	11.0	27,759	74.5	196,300	22.9	12.9	751	25.7	87.1	22.3	6.1
26 70520	Saginaw	83.8	5.1	20,067	64.3	63,900	25.2	17.0	574	43.2	81.1	17.3	18.0
26 70545	Saginaw Township North CDP	78.2	21.8	10,800	65.1	137,900	21.4	10.9	640	30.2	91.0	18.4	6.3
26 70760	St. Clair Shores	90.2	6.7	26,818	84.3	152,100	25.5	15.7	670	26.1	89.9	24.5	6.2
26 72818	Shelby CDP	87.3	10.9	27,591	81.3	230,100	24.9	14.8	795	24.5	86.8	28.0	3.0
26 74900	Southfield	82.6	11.2	31,611	57.9	188,700	28.8	16.3	897	31.2	84.8	22.8	7.4
26 74960	Southgate	87.8	8.7	13,109	68.2	142,800	23.7	15.0	735	28.7	90.3	21.5	9.0
26 76460	Sterling Heights	88.2	8.1	49,429	79.1	191,400	23.5	13.7	756	26.8	89.8	25.1	5.7
26 79000	Taylor	84.8	12.1	24,233	72.4	130,600	26.1	14.4	730	28.4	86.2	21.4	6.1
26 80700	Troy	90.1	7.0	31,159	78.2	274,200	23.0	12.4	947	22.1	87.8	24.0	3.8
26 82960	Walker	78.6	20.1	9,387	66.7	155,700	21.9	11.7	591	27.2	86.4	19.2	2.5
26 84000	Warren	88.0	8.1	54,157	80.1	147,400	24.5	14.7	718	30.5	84.7	23.4	5.9
26 84220	Waterford CDP	85.1	10.2	30,516	76.2	176,300	24.5	13.4	716	28.2	86.7	27.8	5.3
26 85510	West Bloomfield Township CDP	91.8	5.7	24,387	86.6	338,300	25.7	14.6	1241	35.3	88.8	28.5	2.6

1. $1,000,001 is the top code symbolizing a median value over one million dollars.
2. 50.1 is the top code symbolizing a median gross rent as a percentage of household income of 50.1 percent or more.

Table C-4. Cities — Where: Migration, Housing, and Transportation, 2005–2007—Continued

STATE Place code	STATE City	Percent who lived in the same house one year ago	Percent who did not live in city one year ago	Total occupied housing units	Percent owner-occupied housing units	Median value of owner-occupied housing units (dollars)[1]	Median selected monthly owner costs as a percentage of household income		Median gross rent (dollars)	Median gross rent as a percentage of household income[2]	Percent of workers who drove alone to work	Mean travel time to work (minutes)	Percent of occupied housing units with no vehicle available
							With a mortgage	Without a mortgage					
	ACS table number:	C07204	C07204	B25003	B25003	B25077	B25092	B25092	B25064	B25071	C08301	B08013/ C08012	C25045
		1	2	3	4	5	6	7	8	9	10	11	12
	Michigan—Cont.												
26 86000	Westland	84.3	10.8	34,331	67.4	150,500	24.9	14.5	743	27.7	87.0	23.3	6.6
26 88900	Wyandotte	87.2	8.3	11,654	75.3	142,800	24.5	14.4	727	27.1	88.1	21.9	8.2
26 88940	Wyoming	80.0	13.4	26,717	68.8	121,700	24.4	13.9	661	29.4	85.0	19.9	3.7
26 89140	Ypsilanti	61.4	23.8	8,541	44.9	179,200	25.8	20.2	711	34.5	70.5	19.7	13.6
27 00000	**Minnesota**	85.2	10.4	2,041,466	75.8	207,200	24.2	11.9	719	29.0	78.1	22.1	6.5
27 01486	Andover	92.9	5.8	9,489	97.1	281,100	24.1	9.0	943	26.1	84.7	29.0	2.2
27 01900	Apple Valley	87.6	9.7	18,419	86.0	247,900	23.5	10.9	992	32.0	82.7	24.7	3.6
27 02908	Austin	87.2	5.6	9,820	74.2	94,800	20.2	12.2	532	28.9	80.5	15.1	8.7
27 06382	Blaine	87.7	10.2	20,448	91.7	222,000	24.0	12.4	828	28.4	83.8	26.9	2.3
27 06616	Bloomington	83.8	10.7	35,347	70.7	244,200	23.9	13.1	876	29.0	79.7	21.4	5.8
27 07948	Brooklyn Center	78.2	20.3	10,859	66.9	191,900	29.3	14.6	827	33.0	78.0	22.7	9.4
27 07966	Brooklyn Park	85.4	10.7	25,695	74.8	231,500	26.3	12.1	777	30.1	79.8	24.0	5.7
27 08794	Burnsville	82.0	13.0	24,475	66.5	242,900	24.2	10.4	875	30.3	81.8	23.3	5.5
27 10846	Champlin	94.5	4.1	8,309	90.2	239,400	24.6	8.4	720	37.0	84.2	25.8	2.4
27 10918	Chanhassen	89.2	10.3	8,488	88.3	345,400	23.7	9.5	880	22.2	82.8	23.5	2.0
27 10972	Chaska	83.6	12.8	8,281	74.9	240,600	25.1	9.6	872	26.2	82.1	24.2	2.0
27 13114	Coon Rapids	86.4	10.1	23,451	79.5	210,500	24.8	12.5	870	29.6	82.4	24.2	3.4
27 13456	Cottage Grove	91.2	5.9	11,220	91.5	231,400	25.0	11.4	1028	27.7	85.3	25.6	1.2
27 14158	Crystal	88.1	11.1	9,468	79.4	195,800	25.2	13.9	765	25.0	84.9	20.2	6.2
27 17000	Duluth	75.6	12.0	35,619	64.7	146,500	23.1	12.8	660	32.8	78.3	16.3	13.2
27 17288	Eagan	86.7	9.5	24,997	76.3	263,000	22.9	8.3	927	25.4	83.9	22.5	2.0
27 18116	Eden Prairie	86.5	10.3	23,106	78.3	340,700	22.0	9.4	988	24.7	82.9	20.9	2.7
27 18188	Edina	87.3	8.1	21,347	78.2	398,700	23.4	12.4	969	26.9	80.0	18.9	6.9
27 18674	Elk River	88.7	8.6	7,517	87.1	244,300	27.7	12.0	778	25.0	81.9	28.6	2.3
27 20546	Faribault	81.5	8.6	7,672	73.7	162,700	26.7	9.7	612	27.3	78.6	19.7	8.7
27 22814	Fridley	83.2	13.8	10,996	64.5	211,800	23.7	12.4	775	25.4	82.9	20.6	6.6
27 24308	Golden Valley	86.2	11.5	8,949	80.4	283,300	23.6	12.1	900	27.2	80.4	18.1	4.6
27 27530	Hastings	90.2	7.4	7,721	78.8	219,300	26.3	13.1	801	33.4	86.2	22.6	7.0
27 31076	Inver Grove Heights	87.0	9.7	12,894	80.2	228,800	23.1	9.7	798	26.1	86.6	21.1	3.4
27 35180	Lakeville	90.0	8.4	17,508	93.1	296,500	23.3	9.7	944	36.6	84.1	25.0	1.5
27 39878	Mankato	66.6	19.6	13,943	59.9	153,100	24.4	12.7	601	32.7	76.8	14.6	10.3
27 40166	Maple Grove	92.0	7.2	21,558	91.0	278,500	22.9	8.3	1110	32.6	83.3	24.6	1.8
27 40382	Maplewood	86.4	11.5	14,328	75.7	229,200	24.3	11.4	838	30.1	80.4	21.3	6.0
27 43000	Minneapolis	74.5	13.0	155,155	53.8	230,500	25.9	14.7	729	31.4	61.8	21.6	17.6
27 43252	Minnetonka	88.3	10.5	22,173	74.8	327,000	23.6	12.3	1017	27.0	82.3	19.8	2.4
27 43864	Moorhead	73.5	15.3	12,827	65.5	128,000	22.0	12.0	596	37.0	78.0	14.4	7.1
27 45430	New Brighton	85.4	13.2	9,271	71.8	233,500	23.4	12.9	787	28.2	83.0	20.7	6.0
27 45628	New Hope	84.0	12.4	8,320	57.6	227,500	23.2	12.2	767	31.5	82.0	22.4	15.2
27 47680	Oakdale	91.0	8.4	11,205	80.3	228,100	25.8	11.8	720	36.2	86.9	22.8	3.9
27 49300	Owatonna	82.7	10.7	9,325	75.3	147,800	25.0	12.4	665	28.1	81.0	14.8	5.3
27 51730	Plymouth	85.2	12.1	27,801	77.0	324,600	23.0	10.6	973	28.1	82.7	22.0	2.9
27 52594	Prior Lake	90.0	5.7	6,955	89.9	298,500	23.7	10.0	861	24.8	84.3	26.2	2.4
27 53026	Ramsey	92.5	5.8	6,955	95.2	236,900	25.3	9.6	1250	30.2	87.2	27.8	0.4
27 54214	Richfield	88.2	9.7	14,435	67.8	223,600	25.8	13.8	727	32.3	77.6	19.8	9.8
27 54880	Rochester	84.6	7.5	39,203	73.1	160,500	22.3	9.4	675	24.7	76.5	14.9	6.6
27 55726	Rosemount	86.8	10.6	7,038	91.9	258,000	24.0	11.9	989	29.0	83.0	24.8	2.0
27 55852	Roseville	84.5	13.3	14,451	69.5	240,300	23.6	12.6	798	29.3	81.3	20.0	8.0
27 56896	St. Cloud	69.7	18.8	24,580	55.7	156,800	23.3	11.2	634	31.6	76.7	17.7	8.9
27 57220	St. Louis Park	80.0	16.2	20,652	63.8	238,500	24.1	12.3	859	26.5	79.0	19.5	8.9
27 58000	St. Paul	79.4	10.4	107,237	57.7	208,500	26.7	12.0	746	31.4	68.9	21.5	14.4
27 58738	Savage	89.5	9.4	8,561	90.1	291,300	23.3	11.7	985	26.5	85.5	25.4	0.8
27 59350	Shakopee	84.4	11.6	12,105	78.7	238,800	25.0	10.2	842	26.4	78.9	25.7	3.1
27 59998	Shoreview	91.2	7.6	10,734	86.4	248,300	22.7	11.7	869	28.8	83.7	24.0	2.3
27 69970	White Bear Lake	89.7	8.6	10,488	75.4	225,500	26.7	9.2	856	32.1	87.1	23.5	6.1
27 71032	Winona	71.6	17.9	10,487	58.1	142,200	23.2	10.8	531	33.4	70.8	12.9	12.5
27 71428	Woodbury	87.9	9.4	20,464	85.5	311,700	23.3	9.2	1109	24.5	82.8	25.6	2.1
28 00000	**Mississippi**	82.9	12.4	1,079,584	70.9	88,100	22.9	12.4	591	30.6	82.0	23.7	7.1
28 06220	Biloxi	72.8	15.6	17,042	57.5	144,900	22.6	9.2	759	28.2	74.9	19.2	6.0
28 08300	Brandon	85.0	9.4	7,558	76.4	159,500	21.4	8.3	727	27.9	86.2	24.5	1.0
28 14420	Clinton	77.3	13.5	10,112	71.9	127,300	22.0	8.1	742	26.9	88.2	20.0	1.1
28 15380	Columbus	75.0	13.7	9,343	55.2	86,400	24.3	12.2	542	33.1	80.1	15.6	8.8
28 29180	Greenville	79.9	5.9	14,495	56.4	65,600	27.0	14.0	595	32.9	83.6	16.3	14.0
28 29700	Gulfport	74.1	15.6	26,208	63.4	110,500	23.8	13.0	745	32.9	79.2	21.6	5.8
28 31020	Hattiesburg	67.3	16.9	18,876	42.0	92,600	23.2	14.3	582	32.1	85.2	17.2	9.2
28 33700	Horn Lake	78.6	16.8	7,999	70.6	94,600	24.0	12.1	923	27.9	81.7	25.6	3.9
28 36000	Jackson	78.9	7.2	63,674	56.1	84,300	24.1	13.8	707	34.7	82.7	19.9	9.7
28 46640	Meridian	78.6	10.6	15,946	51.5	73,000	25.0	13.2	544	32.5	84.3	15.4	15.9
28 54040	Olive Branch	90.1	8.2	10,719	87.1	157,900	23.2	9.4	807	31.7	85.7	23.9	3.1
28 55360	Pascagoula	70.9	14.1	8,388	52.5	94,700	19.8	11.6	631	31.7	83.8	15.2	8.4
28 55760	Pearl	83.2	15.4	9,368	64.9	100,300	20.9	9.0	708	37.5	87.7	17.4	4.6
28 62520	Ridgeland	71.9	23.9	11,099	45.6	160,400	19.2	9.6	806	24.6	-	19.9	5.1
28 69280	Southaven	75.6	18.0	15,900	67.1	124,100	23.3	9.7	815	26.2	85.3	23.9	1.4
28 70240	Starkville	66.6	18.7	9,858	39.8	120,600	19.9	8.6	578	48.8	75.0	12.9	6.5
28 74840	Tupelo	76.9	15.2	13,258	61.9	115,100	20.7	11.0	514	33.2	87.7	15.7	8.8
28 76720	Vicksburg	81.8	9.1	10,461	52.5	86,300	24.3	17.6	579	37.0	81.8	18.8	10.9

1. $1,000,001 is the top code symbolizing a median value over one million dollars.
2. 50.1 is the top code symbolizing a median gross rent as a percentage of household income of 50.1 percent or more.

Table C-4. Cities — Where: Migration, Housing, and Transportation, 2005–2007—*Continued*

STATE Place code	STATE City	Percent who lived in the same house one year ago	Percent who did not live in city one year ago	Total occupied housing units	Percent owner-occupied housing units	Median value of owner-occupied housing units (dollars)[1]	Median selected monthly owner costs as a percentage of household income — With a mortgage	Median selected monthly owner costs as a percentage of household income — Without a mortgage	Median gross rent (dollars)	Median gross rent as a percentage of household income[2]	Percent of workers who drove alone to work	Mean travel time to work (minutes)	Percent of occupied housing units with no vehicle available
	ACS table number:	C07204	C07204	B25003	B25003	B25077	B25092	B25092	B25064	B25071	C08301	B08013/ C08012	C25045
		1	2	3	4	5	6	7	8	9	10	11	12
29 00000	**Missouri**	82.6	12.4	2,300,211	70.7	131,100	22.2	11.4	623	28.4	80.8	23.1	6.9
29 00280	Affton CDP	84.5	14.2	9,112	84.5	148,500	22.1	15.2	643	30.7	81.4	22.3	3.7
29 01972	Arnold	89.6	6.8	7,705	84.0	145,800	21.2	11.0	725	21.0	86.8	26.8	3.9
29 03160	Ballwin	88.8	8.6	11,733	82.7	226,000	21.2	10.1	885	28.1	86.8	25.0	1.4
29 04384	Belton	76.2	14.2	8,511	68.7	128,100	23.2	11.8	892	32.6	81.2	25.3	3.6
29 06652	Blue Springs	86.2	7.6	19,307	75.7	146,100	20.6	11.7	779	25.1	87.5	25.6	2.8
29 11242	Cape Girardeau	70.9	17.1	15,325	55.8	119,500	20.1	11.2	570	33.5	81.9	15.9	7.8
29 13600	Chesterfield	92.1	5.7	19,225	83.3	347,600	21.6	12.0	936	28.5	83.6	23.0	3.2
29 15670	Columbia	67.4	15.8	40,155	49.4	153,900	21.0	10.8	681	33.3	75.5	15.5	8.1
29 23986	Ferguson	-	-	8,494	69.3	92,100	25.3	13.9	694	43.7	80.3	25.3	11.3
29 24778	Florissant	88.0	8.8	21,058	76.0	115,700	22.8	11.4	711	28.2	86.0	23.2	5.3
29 27190	Gladstone	83.6	14.5	10,813	69.8	142,900	24.8	11.5	686	24.9	90.3	20.0	2.0
29 28324	Grandview	86.5	9.3	9,703	62.5	112,200	24.8	14.3	665	30.1	83.3	23.9	10.4
29 31276	Hazelwood	81.2	15.3	11,131	67.1	125,300	21.7	11.1	734	27.4	86.7	21.5	3.5
29 35000	Independence	81.7	10.3	49,133	69.2	106,800	24.0	13.0	667	27.9	83.2	23.6	5.9
29 37000	Jefferson	76.8	13.7	16,806	57.2	123,100	19.8	8.0	510	22.3	82.6	14.9	7.3
29 37592	Joplin	75.1	11.1	19,829	60.1	80,000	20.4	11.8	584	33.3	82.0	15.7	9.1
29 38000	Kansas	79.4	8.9	184,172	58.8	129,900	22.9	13.4	682	29.4	80.4	20.8	10.7
29 39044	Kirkwood	88.1	9.5	11,702	79.4	236,200	21.6	13.6	813	25.9	86.2	18.6	5.4
29 41348	Lee's Summit	84.6	10.2	33,160	78.2	179,300	22.1	12.3	894	34.5	87.0	24.7	4.1
29 42032	Liberty	80.5	13.3	10,261	73.9	167,100	23.2	11.7	682	28.2	89.2	21.1	3.2
29 46586	Maryland Heights	77.7	19.3	17,087	63.0	159,200	20.8	9.5	741	21.3	84.8	20.5	1.7
29 47180	Mehlville CDP	86.2	13.1	12,456	70.7	155,000	24.0	12.7	655	22.5	84.1	22.4	5.8
29 53876	Oakville CDP	93.1	6.7	13,561	87.1	209,600	19.9	10.4	712	25.4	89.0	27.1	0.9
29 54074	O'Fallon	86.0	12.1	24,238	88.7	196,700	22.4	11.9	834	24.1	89.4	26.0	1.5
29 60788	Raytown	86.0	11.9	12,713	75.0	114,700	23.1	13.3	742	29.8	87.3	21.9	5.2
29 64082	St. Charles	79.4	14.7	25,475	65.8	172,800	21.3	12.0	751	27.6	87.6	20.8	4.6
29 64550	St. Joseph	76.2	9.2	28,489	65.2	96,100	21.0	10.7	538	30.1	82.3	16.1	10.2
29 65000	St. Louis	80.1	7.3	140,934	50.7	115,700	24.9	13.9	609	31.3	71.1	23.7	21.7
29 65126	St. Peters	88.3	9.7	20,171	82.9	165,800	21.6	12.4	835	26.1	86.9	23.8	3.3
29 66440	Sedalia	78.9	11.7	8,411	63.8	73,600	23.1	13.4	565	27.3	81.4	18.7	6.6
29 69266	Spanish Lake CDP	77.0	21.7	8,387	52.8	113,900	24.1	17.1	683	36.3	84.3	26.9	6.7
29 70000	Springfield	72.3	14.1	68,354	53.6	97,800	22.4	10.9	581	29.7	80.4	18.3	8.7
29 75220	University	79.9	17.5	15,366	58.4	216,700	24.4	12.8	785	31.1	76.3	18.0	12.2
29 78154	Webster Groves	90.1	8.0	9,369	86.0	219,800	23.0	14.4	893	43.9	86.2	20.9	4.3
29 78442	Wentzville	89.2	8.7	6,082	84.8	202,000	24.7	11.6	568	25.1	85.7	30.8	2.3
29 79820	Wildwood	90.2	9.3	11,973	90.0	348,200	21.2	8.4	886	26.6	83.3	29.4	1.4
30 00000	**Montana**	81.7	12.3	369,329	70.1	152,300	23.8	12.1	582	27.4	73.9	17.4	4.9
30 06550	Billings	77.3	10.6	40,056	65.8	150,100	23.1	12.1	589	29.0	80.6	15.6	7.0
30 08950	Bozeman	58.4	24.3	13,013	46.7	251,300	24.6	11.5	779	31.5	64.3	15.0	5.4
30 11397	Butte-Silver Bow (balance)	78.8	7.7	13,972	67.1	94,900	23.4	13.6	508	28.4	77.6	16.3	7.6
30 32800	Great Falls	81.3	7.5	23,810	66.9	126,100	23.4	12.2	514	25.0	84.3	13.7	8.3
30 35600	Helena	70.2	19.4	11,317	57.1	160,800	23.1	12.4	586	27.4	69.6	12.9	6.1
30 40075	Kalispell	86.1	10.1	7,122	63.1	173,200	25.5	13.3	622	32.1	74.5	16.6	8.5
30 50200	Missoula	71.0	11.9	25,638	50.9	216,800	25.0	14.2	648	33.1	69.0	15.1	8.1
31 00000	**Nebraska**	82.3	9.7	698,163	68.5	118,200	22.3	13.0	610	26.4	79.8	17.7	5.2
31 03950	Bellevue	84.7	8.6	17,047	64.8	130,700	22.9	12.1	684	24.7	85.9	18.2	2.2
31 10110	Columbus	86.0	6.6	8,845	70.0	103,400	20.1	10.8	483	25.1	87.2	12.1	6.0
31 17670	Fremont	82.3	7.8	10,209	62.3	118,800	20.4	12.4	605	31.7	85.7	16.1	5.6
31 19595	Grand Island	77.8	8.5	16,938	63.9	95,700	22.8	12.8	549	24.9	81.0	14.2	5.5
31 21415	Hastings	80.7	8.4	10,128	67.6	87,400	22.0	12.6	541	26.1	77.1	14.1	6.1
31 25055	Kearney	72.0	13.8	11,411	59.4	122,600	22.3	13.8	580	26.0	82.0	11.6	5.0
31 28000	Lincoln	76.0	8.7	98,577	60.5	137,400	22.5	11.3	635	28.3	80.7	14.7	6.1
31 34615	Norfolk	80.2	12.5	9,371	65.8	96,100	21.3	14.0	496	25.2	80.0	14.7	8.1
31 35000	North Platte	77.4	11.5	10,384	62.6	85,800	22.5	14.2	581	24.0	83.4	13.5	3.4
31 37000	Omaha	79.8	6.4	152,940	59.1	125,800	23.3	13.4	675	28.4	80.7	17.7	8.7
31 38295	Papillion	83.8	14.3	6,718	71.4	163,900	21.4	12.4	793	23.5	87.6	19.0	3.8
32 00000	**Nevada**	78.3	15.8	932,715	61.0	302,600	28.3	11.7	944	29.8	77.5	23.6	7.0
32 09700	Carson	79.5	8.3	21,330	63.6	298,700	27.5	11.5	842	29.7	79.1	16.5	6.1
32 23770	Enterprise CDP	64.0	36.0	24,277	64.9	382,700	31.1	8.1	1300	28.9	82.2	23.7	3.0
32 31900	Henderson	79.4	13.6	92,431	68.1	365,300	27.3	10.5	1134	29.5	84.0	22.9	3.2
32 40000	Las Vegas	78.6	9.7	207,313	59.7	300,400	28.6	11.9	941	31.1	77.8	25.3	8.6
32 51800	North Las Vegas	73.4	22.5	59,139	64.6	282,800	31.6	12.9	1023	31.4	78.3	27.6	8.1
32 53800	Pahrump CDP	82.8	9.2	11,556	79.4	187,100	28.7	13.1	829	29.1	68.2	29.5	1.5
32 54600	Paradise CDP	77.8	22.2	84,725	45.6	296,800	28.5	11.6	889	31.2	73.7	21.8	12.6
32 60600	Reno	73.0	12.1	86,506	48.1	339,100	27.7	12.9	829	29.5	72.3	19.3	10.2
32 68400	Sparks	82.3	11.5	29,798	63.5	323,600	28.1	14.7	963	28.6	78.4	21.3	4.9
32 68585	Spring Valley CDP	78.0	22.0	64,497	55.7	328,500	29.9	11.4	1094	29.9	80.2	21.9	5.8
32 71400	Sunrise Manor CDP	77.6	22.4	63,820	60.5	227,900	29.9	14.9	912	31.5	75.2	27.8	7.6
32 71600	Sun Valley CDP	80.0	18.7	6,678	71.1	185,900	30.7	12.6	970	26.4	74.6	22.6	2.4
32 83800	Whitney CDP	81.8	18.2	8,783	62.6	199,500	31.4	11.4	884	32.8	77.4	24.7	6.9
32 84600	Winchester CDP	-	-	11,427	44.0	225,700	30.0	12.9	816	30.9	69.2	21.8	13.9
33 00000	**New Hampshire**	85.7	10.8	500,671	73.2	250,700	26.3	16.0	892	28.7	81.6	25.0	5.0
33 14200	Concord	79.8	12.5	16,851	53.9	223,200	26.6	20.8	899	28.9	79.8	20.2	11.8
33 17860	Derry CDP	85.9	7.7	8,927	59.5	239,200	29.8	23.2	1014	25.3	84.8	30.0	3.5

1. $1,000,001 is the top code symbolizing a median value over one million dollars.
2. 50.1 is the top code symbolizing a median gross rent as a percentage of household income of 50.1 percent or more.

STATE Place code	STATE City	Percent who lived in the same house one year ago	Percent who did not live in city one year ago	Total occupied housing units	Percent owner-occupied housing units	Median value of owner-occupied housing units (dollars)[1]	Median selected monthly owner costs as a percentage of household income		Median gross rent (dollars)	Median gross rent as a percentage of household income[2]	Percent of workers who drove alone to work	Mean travel time to work (minutes)	Percent of occupied housing units with no vehicle available
							With a mortgage	Without a mortgage					
	ACS table number:	C07204	C07204	B25003	B25003	B25077	B25092	B25092	B25064	B25071	C08301	B08013/C08012	C25045
		1	2	3	4	5	6	7	8	9	10	11	12
	New Hampshire—Cont.												
33 18820	Dover	81.2	11.5	11,920	59.5	259,800	26.9	18.0	834	29.2	82.4	22.6	8.1
33 39300	Keene	75.0	14.1	8,872	60.9	190,100	24.3	19.0	877	28.5	73.4	14.4	8.8
33 45140	Manchester	77.2	10.3	43,992	51.1	235,500	26.9	17.1	929	29.9	81.3	21.3	8.7
33 50260	Nashua	83.5	8.5	34,526	61.5	274,800	26.7	16.7	1062	28.7	82.1	24.2	7.0
33 62900	Portsmouth	77.9	14.3	9,960	49.3	339,600	25.6	20.3	1060	29.7	83.6	20.9	5.4
33 65140	Rochester	83.5	10.8	11,849	66.7	183,900	27.4	16.2	835	30.2	82.1	26.3	10.3
34 00000	**New Jersey**	88.3	8.7	3,143,408	67.4	358,400	27.7	18.3	1002	30.2	72.1	29.4	11.4
34 02080	Atlantic	85.5	8.0	15,977	29.1	218,000	29.4	22.7	753	30.0	39.7	19.7	48.0
34 03580	Bayonne	87.5	4.9	24,161	38.6	370,500	28.3	24.7	898	29.5	55.9	30.4	27.9
34 04690	Belleville CDP	85.7	8.2	13,083	58.3	326,800	36.1	22.2	996	30.7	71.4	27.7	9.6
34 05170	Bergenfield borough	90.8	8.6	9,057	70.3	388,700	31.5	19.7	1063	27.6	63.8	33.1	9.5
34 06250	Bloomfield CDP	88.7	7.2	18,383	55.2	364,700	30.0	18.5	1027	28.1	72.4	28.4	12.2
34 07600	Bridgeton	80.3	11.5	6,146	46.9	100,000	28.5	19.0	744	41.6	62.7	26.8	23.1
34 10000	Camden	84.2	5.4	23,700	41.5	71,900	25.0	19.8	712	38.6	48.7	24.6	37.5
34 10750	Carteret borough	91.1	7.8	7,061	65.1	322,800	33.8	19.8	737	27.1	71.0	26.1	15.5
34 13570	Cliffside Park borough	88.4	7.3	9,614	49.8	469,200	32.0	28.6	1197	29.8	56.7	30.0	14.9
34 13690	Clifton	90.7	6.4	29,480	61.1	380,600	33.1	23.3	1059	32.1	74.9	25.7	9.0
34 15670	Cranford CDP	94.6	4.4	8,115	87.0	472,500	23.6	19.6	1233	25.8	80.2	30.8	4.0
34 18970	East Brunswick CDP	91.8	6.4	16,063	87.0	415,400	26.7	14.7	1253	31.9	76.0	35.9	3.2
34 19390	East Orange	81.8	10.0	24,279	26.1	239,100	39.4	24.0	859	31.9	56.1	29.8	36.9
34 20260	Edison CDP	81.7	13.2	34,666	63.3	379,100	27.5	15.6	1240	24.3	69.2	35.2	6.3
34 21000	Elizabeth	82.4	5.7	41,616	29.5	390,300	38.3	26.9	922	30.0	53.9	24.4	26.9
34 21480	Englewood	90.9	6.3	9,572	60.9	440,500	28.5	20.5	1051	30.8	65.1	29.3	16.2
34 22180	Ewing CDP	83.6	13.6	12,895	70.4	247,500	25.6	19.1	977	27.2	82.9	23.1	6.1
34 22470	Fair Lawn borough	91.0	7.2	12,582	75.9	425,200	26.4	18.1	1188	30.5	73.9	27.7	4.7
34 24420	Fort Lee borough	85.3	11.6	16,654	61.4	349,500	29.0	16.8	1406	27.1	57.6	34.4	12.9
34 25770	Garfield	83.2	12.5	10,974	36.1	365,000	37.8	26.1	1086	30.7	71.4	22.2	13.0
34 28680	Hackensack	82.7	12.3	18,996	39.0	361,200	34.0	22.6	1158	29.6	61.6	28.9	15.2
34 32250	Hoboken	76.5	14.9	20,755	32.3	561,100	21.3	21.0	1507	23.0	29.0	36.7	36.0
34 34440	Irvington CDP	79.3	12.3	20,695	29.6	227,000	32.1	16.1	909	27.9	58.0	32.5	25.5
34 36000	Jersey	85.1	7.2	87,919	32.6	355,000	33.2	20.8	960	29.3	35.4	33.1	39.3
34 36510	Kearny town	90.5	6.3	12,774	49.6	355,300	32.4	18.5	1016	28.3	65.9	27.5	15.1
34 38580	Lakewood CDP	84.2	5.9	10,507	36.4	409,500	38.2	30.0	1125	46.5	52.1	26.1	16.9
34 40350	Linden	85.4	8.2	14,924	59.8	330,400	31.7	17.7	1019	30.7	74.4	24.5	10.6
34 40920	Livingston CDP	91.2	7.6	9,563	93.2	604,500	23.6	15.2	1712	43.2	75.9	30.5	2.9
34 41100	Lodi borough	86.7	10.1	9,321	45.4	429,200	41.3	28.4	1094	31.8	75.4	21.6	6.6
34 41310	Long Branch	78.9	10.7	12,426	43.8	429,400	36.4	21.0	1094	31.0	55.6	26.7	17.1
34 43830	Maplewood CDP	93.5	6.3	8,406	81.9	467,000	27.5	18.3	1297	29.0	63.5	33.4	8.3
34 45495	Mercerville-Hamilton Square CDP	92.7	6.5	9,293	91.5	324,200	24.5	18.2	962	28.0	86.0	24.9	4.2
34 46680	Millville	90.1	7.3	9,978	59.1	157,400	24.8	17.8	716	30.9	82.9	26.9	14.9
34 47490	Montclair CDP	89.1	6.8	14,465	61.8	599,300	26.0	21.4	1148	27.3	55.8	33.8	8.3
34 51000	Newark	79.6	9.6	91,491	25.4	285,500	39.1	22.8	818	31.0	46.4	31.2	40.6
34 51210	New Brunswick	70.2	9.1	12,483	28.1	294,800	29.3	24.3	1186	34.0	47.6	23.4	27.6
34 52605	North Brunswick Township CDP	87.9	10.9	13,927	64.1	345,800	27.7	14.6	1229	28.8	77.1	31.8	7.5
34 53280	North Plainfield borough	91.0	5.0	6,891	63.7	322,200	32.7	18.8	1094	28.7	73.1	25.7	6.4
34 53670	Nutley CDP	93.8	4.3	10,898	72.0	419,800	27.1	23.2	1074	26.1	75.2	26.8	5.4
34 54690	Old Bridge CDP	91.9	6.9	6,946	96.2	371,300	26.9	15.0	932	32.7	75.1	35.3	2.6
34 55020	Orange CDP	86.5	9.3	11,468	31.5	274,600	33.2	22.3	882	29.7	60.1	29.3	28.2
34 55950	Paramus borough	91.0	7.0	8,371	88.8	587,300	29.1	15.6	2001	27.4	76.8	29.4	3.3
34 56550	Passaic	91.7	4.1	19,405	26.0	352,800	39.1	20.1	943	44.2	44.4	24.6	38.3
34 57000	Paterson	90.2	3.6	44,069	30.3	334,200	38.7	24.6	970	39.9	62.5	24.8	26.6
34 57690	Pennsauken CDP	90.0	6.5	12,535	84.1	175,100	27.8	16.0	739	34.7	73.7	23.6	9.3
34 58200	Perth Amboy	89.6	3.4	15,008	39.2	325,300	31.0	18.4	1012	32.3	65.2	21.4	22.0
34 59190	Plainfield	87.0	6.7	15,050	52.3	313,500	34.0	19.3	987	46.2	65.7	28.5	14.8
34 61530	Rahway	90.7	4.7	9,877	63.7	316,500	30.4	21.1	1044	32.4	76.1	27.3	9.9
34 63000	Ridgewood village	90.6	7.1	8,605	82.5	708,000	27.7	17.6	1422	27.1	66.9	32.0	7.1
34 64620	Roselle borough	90.8	6.6	7,495	65.4	296,400	36.6	20.1	949	33.1	69.6	29.6	11.1
34 65790	Sayreville borough	91.6	5.9	15,651	66.0	342,100	25.4	16.3	990	26.1	78.5	29.9	6.7
34 66090	Scotch Plains CDP	92.4	5.8	7,885	80.9	503,800	26.4	16.5	1249	25.5	77.7	30.2	4.2
34 68370	Somerset CDP	87.4	7.2	8,174	73.9	333,100	29.5	15.7	1141	29.0	77.5	29.3	5.4
34 69390	South Plainfield borough	91.9	7.1	7,588	86.0	352,200	25.3	14.0	1248	22.8	83.6	26.8	4.5
34 71430	Summit	93.7	4.5	7,441	73.7	726,400	23.3	13.4	1521	27.9	60.1	32.1	3.4
34 72390	Teaneck CDP	89.9	7.0	14,194	78.4	431,500	27.1	17.6	1126	36.4	63.8	31.5	7.9
34 73110	Toms River CDP	90.8	5.6	33,247	84.1	334,300	27.5	18.4	1110	33.8	82.4	29.5	5.7
34 74000	Trenton	81.1	7.1	26,488	43.9	120,000	25.7	16.7	846	34.0	55.1	24.0	29.9
34 74510	Union CDP	89.6	8.5	19,403	76.2	359,900	30.9	21.1	1130	28.1	75.9	26.7	6.2
34 74630	Union	92.1	3.6	22,080	22.4	404,600	42.2	24.9	895	31.8	32.2	28.1	44.7
34 76070	Vineland	90.6	3.9	20,807	71.4	168,100	26.5	16.7	808	32.0	82.0	24.0	8.8
34 77870	Wayne CDP	91.2	5.9	17,520	82.3	532,100	27.4	18.7	1193	33.7	80.9	26.3	3.8
34 79040	Westfield town	96.1	2.9	9,954	81.5	643,100	21.8	14.9	1410	28.7	70.8	32.3	4.7
34 79430	West Milford CDP	90.2	7.2	8,976	90.2	346,900	28.0	23.0	1129	35.1	84.7	35.2	2.0
34 79610	West New York town	83.4	11.1	17,906	23.5	376,000	32.3	17.5	951	29.7	36.0	31.4	36.9
34 79790	West Orange CDP	91.2	5.7	16,476	71.4	428,000	28.7	20.0	1110	27.5	70.5	30.4	9.0

1. $1,000,001 is the top code symbolizing a median value over one million dollars.
2. 50.1 is the top code symbolizing a median gross rent as a percentage of household income of 50.1 percent or more.

STATE Place code	STATE City	Percent who lived in the same house one year ago	Percent who did not live in city one year ago	Total occupied housing units	Percent owner-occupied housing units	Median value of owner-occupied housing units (dollars)[1]	Median selected monthly owner costs as a percentage of household income		Median gross rent (dollars)	Median gross rent as a percentage of household income[2]	Percent of workers who drove alone to work	Mean travel time to work (minutes)	Percent of occupied housing units with no vehicle available
							With a mortgage	Without a mortgage					
ACS table number:		C07204	C07204	B25003	B25003	B25077	B25092	B25092	B25064	B25071	C08301	B08013/C08012	C25045
		1	2	3	4	5	6	7	8	9	10	11	12
35 00000	**New Mexico**	82.3	10.4	728,508	69.6	140,100	22.9	10.2	630	29.2	77.2	21.2	5.6
35 01780	Alamogordo	78.1	13.0	14,532	61.7	89,500	22.4	9.6	604	28.5	82.6	16.2	4.5
35 02000	Albuquerque	78.5	7.4	209,324	61.9	167,800	23.6	10.7	657	29.6	78.4	21.0	6.5
35 12150	Carlsbad	77.5	8.0	10,239	69.7	75,500	20.7	9.4	563	26.1	76.4	17.0	3.6
35 16420	Clovis	78.4	10.1	13,731	62.8	90,000	21.6	10.6	510	26.8	83.7	14.0	6.6
35 25800	Farmington	81.6	10.0	15,290	67.1	150,300	21.5	9.1	669	27.3	83.6	17.5	4.1
35 32520	Hobbs	81.6	10.1	10,458	66.5	78,300	19.2	9.1	552	21.9	80.0	17.2	6.5
35 39380	Las Cruces	70.3	12.4	35,208	55.2	134,200	23.0	12.6	635	34.0	75.2	16.3	7.2
35 63460	Rio Rancho	79.9	14.7	24,767	80.3	161,300	24.1	9.0	922	32.9	79.9	28.1	3.6
35 64930	Roswell	78.6	9.0	17,477	68.1	72,400	19.5	10.5	529	26.2	70.1	14.4	4.6
35 70500	Santa Fe	77.0	10.9	26,688	63.3	302,000	26.3	10.2	912	33.1	71.8	18.4	6.0
35 74520	South Valley CDP	89.1	10.9	13,421	72.6	129,600	24.7	12.2	688	35.9	77.0	25.6	5.9
36 00000	**New York**	87.8	6.9	7,096,035	55.6	293,400	26.0	15.4	898	30.4	54.3	31.2	28.3
36 01000	Albany	76.0	13.5	38,195	41.2	156,600	23.2	13.8	740	32.0	64.6	18.0	24.6
36 03078	Auburn	80.2	9.6	10,672	50.7	83,500	22.6	17.4	588	29.2	77.1	17.9	17.6
36 04143	Baldwin CDP	87.2	8.6	7,212	79.8	438,900	33.2	15.8	1157	43.6	70.1	30.7	6.8
36 04935	Bay Shore CDP	75.4	19.7	7,989	68.1	367,800	31.5	20.0	1256	36.7	78.6	23.8	7.5
36 06607	Binghamton	80.3	10.1	20,305	46.7	79,100	20.7	17.4	523	32.8	73.9	16.0	20.9
36 08026	Brentwood CDP	87.4	7.0	13,043	76.7	357,100	35.8	16.5	1147	35.7	74.5	26.6	8.3
36 08257	Brighton CDP	80.4	17.9	15,460	61.4	155,000	22.7	13.7	817	27.2	81.0	15.6	7.2
36 11000	Buffalo	79.8	6.0	113,429	43.9	61,200	22.2	14.7	605	32.8	65.9	19.9	30.3
36 13376	Centereach CDP	94.4	4.9	8,685	89.4	394,100	31.5	14.8	1662	36.2	84.4	30.7	4.3
36 13552	Central Islip CDP	86.7	11.2	9,949	71.3	335,000	34.5	22.6	1507	35.9	69.9	31.6	10.0
36 15000	Cheektowaga CDP	87.4	9.8	33,915	72.3	89,700	23.0	17.8	699	26.1	87.0	18.6	7.8
36 17530	Commack CDP	95.4	4.4	11,549	93.0	548,500	28.5	20.1	1610	36.8	81.2	31.4	3.1
36 18146	Copiague CDP	91.0	7.3	7,235	82.4	377,400	39.2	20.7	1227	29.0	78.6	26.6	7.8
36 18157	Coram CDP	88.6	10.9	13,381	76.2	364,600	31.6	24.3	1401	30.1	82.0	35.6	4.0
36 19972	Deer Park CDP	95.8	3.2	9,704	77.5	413,500	32.3	23.7	1331	39.9	75.3	37.0	4.9
36 20687	Dix Hills CDP	-	-	7,460	98.0	763,700	29.9	19.8	1952	38.8	75.3	37.0	2.0
36 21809	Eastchester CDP	-	-	7,796	81.5	574,100	23.6	13.9	1213	28.1	64.8	30.9	9.3
36 22502	East Meadow CDP	90.2	9.2	11,735	90.6	450,900	30.7	19.1	822	25.2	74.9	29.8	7.3
36 22612	East Northport CDP	92.0	6.9	6,795	87.3	486,500	29.4	18.9	1534	42.7	79.6	30.2	0.7
36 22733	East Patchogue CDP	-	-	8,303	64.2	380,300	31.2	19.0	1205	33.7	80.0	24.5	5.3
36 24229	Elmira	77.5	14.2	11,005	48.5	61,700	23.0	14.5	556	34.2	72.3	16.0	18.4
36 24273	Elmont CDP	92.7	5.4	9,313	81.6	422,400	36.6	19.8	1291	28.0	62.2	38.0	7.7
36 27309	Franklin Square CDP	93.4	6.1	10,381	85.5	480,400	33.8	21.8	1241	31.4	73.8	30.9	7.8
36 27485	Freeport village	83.1	7.1	13,373	69.5	394,900	32.1	18.6	1209	41.9	63.5	29.2	12.0
36 28178	Garden village	94.4	3.9	6,760	95.7	856,200	23.4	20.5	1881	36.8	59.0	36.4	2.1
36 29113	Glen Cove	92.4	5.1	9,475	62.1	555,200	30.9	21.4	1425	32.6	69.5	25.5	10.0
36 32402	Harrison village	81.0	17.1	8,726	66.4	915,700	29.3	17.4	1737	29.3	62.5	26.9	5.7
36 32732	Hauppauge CDP	91.4	7.2	7,401	82.2	552,500	29.8	17.0	1525	29.6	85.9	29.3	2.1
36 33139	Hempstead village	82.0	11.0	15,007	44.6	357,100	36.5	25.4	1179	37.8	51.5	33.9	25.2
36 34374	Hicksville CDP	92.8	5.9	13,517	86.5	450,500	29.6	18.4	1425	31.2	72.4	29.1	6.6
36 35056	Holbrook CDP	89.3	9.1	8,746	81.2	427,000	26.1	17.4	1478	25.4	83.7	26.8	2.4
36 37044	Huntington Station CDP	93.3	5.7	9,657	73.0	423,700	31.3	18.3	1344	35.5	74.9	27.2	8.5
36 37737	Irondequoit CDP	92.3	7.6	22,107	82.0	104,800	24.2	14.3	715	33.2	87.0	18.0	7.2
36 38077	Ithaca	48.7	23.0	10,908	25.7	162,300	22.6	13.1	786	39.2	32.3	15.0	23.5
36 38264	Jamestown	80.1	7.6	13,264	48.9	61,300	19.9	15.2	503	31.3	77.0	14.7	19.1
36 39727	Kingston	79.6	11.3	10,112	42.4	193,000	26.8	15.4	846	31.7	75.6	19.2	20.6
36 39853	Kiryas Joel village	-	-	2,756	33.1	352,500	49.4	50.1	1030	50.1	23.9	31.8	62.9
36 42081	Levittown CDP	94.2	4.9	17,253	91.9	409,100	31.5	20.0	1478	29.6	79.3	29.2	5.1
36 42554	Lindenhurst village	-	-	8,981	88.9	410,500	32.3	20.3	1454	33.6	79.8	30.8	4.2
36 43082	Lockport	83.5	6.0	9,425	58.5	76,700	22.8	19.7	596	30.0	76.1	20.2	14.2
36 43335	Long Beach	90.1	5.7	14,200	59.0	516,900	28.4	19.1	1516	31.8	59.8	40.3	11.6
36 45986	Massapequa CDP	95.6	2.5	6,805	95.7	576,000	29.5	18.9	1567	33.8	76.5	34.5	1.2
36 46404	Medford CDP	93.2	6.0	7,094	88.3	353,500	28.0	17.6	1198	31.4	79.8	31.0	4.5
36 46668	Merrick CDP	-	-	7,282	96.9	568,000	29.5	15.5	1476	29.6	70.6	31.6	2.5
36 47042	Middletown	78.5	13.8	9,124	53.4	220,300	27.3	17.3	952	36.7	66.6	27.4	14.1
36 49121	Mount Vernon	91.1	4.7	24,073	37.6	416,000	30.4	19.7	1056	31.9	52.0	29.3	30.7
36 50034	Newburgh	71.1	8.4	9,449	29.1	205,200	33.6	19.2	962	38.4	52.0	20.5	31.7
36 50100	New CDP	95.6	3.4	10,883	93.0	587,900	25.8	15.3	1156	27.3	80.1	32.8	1.6
36 50617	New Rochelle	90.0	5.8	25,049	55.2	586,700	27.5	20.7	1134	28.7	53.5	28.6	16.6
36 51000	New York	88.7	3.0	3,022,151	33.9	492,400	29.9	14.0	973	30.4	23.3	39.3	54.4
36 51055	Niagara Falls	87.0	5.5	21,426	58.8	62,000	23.0	18.2	547	34.5	80.9	15.3	18.9
36 53682	North Tonawanda	89.5	6.5	13,827	66.8	90,500	22.8	16.2	588	23.9	87.1	21.0	6.4
36 54441	Oceanside CDP	-	-	11,400	88.4	491,500	28.0	17.1	1128	30.7	75.2	31.2	6.0
36 55530	Ossining village	85.8	9.1	8,076	55.7	438,500	30.3	17.7	1259	32.4	64.3	30.5	13.9
36 56979	Peekskill	83.9	6.2	8,938	54.0	353,100	30.1	20.3	1226	36.8	59.0	29.2	12.8
36 58442	Plainview CDP	97.3	1.6	8,712	91.4	576,700	26.5	20.9	904	25.9	71.9	33.0	5.6
36 59223	Port Chester village	80.6	5.7	9,521	47.4	483,900	32.1	34.7	1184	33.3	56.0	22.1	16.6
36 59641	Poughkeepsie	77.8	8.8	11,821	43.5	269,600	29.8	17.3	892	34.9	63.6	23.7	20.4
36 63000	Rochester	78.0	6.6	80,803	41.8	66,500	23.9	17.4	693	39.1	72.7	17.9	24.1
36 63264	Rockville Centre village	94.1	4.9	8,876	78.8	636,600	25.4	17.7	1111	34.0	65.0	34.9	8.1
36 63418	Rome	80.4	9.4	14,338	54.9	76,100	22.7	17.3	556	26.4	80.1	18.1	15.0
36 63473	Ronkonkoma CDP	90.5	8.6	6,609	81.8	392,900	28.1	15.8	1499	37.2	83.2	29.4	2.3
36 63924	Rotterdam CDP	91.1	7.5	8,621	84.2	136,100	23.6	14.3	756	28.0	89.7	19.2	6.5

1. $1,000,001 is the top code symbolizing a median value over one million dollars.
2. 50.1 is the top code symbolizing a median gross rent as a percentage of household income of 50.1 percent or more.

Table C-4. Cities — Where: Migration, Housing, and Transportation, 2005–2007—Continued

STATE Place code	STATE City	Percent who lived in the same house one year ago	Percent who did not live in city one year ago	Total occupied housing units	Percent owner-occupied housing units	Median value of owner-occupied housing units (dollars)[1]	Median selected monthly owner costs as a percentage of household income		Median gross rent (dollars)	Median gross rent as a percentage of household income[2]	Percent of workers who drove alone to work	Mean travel time to work (minutes)	Percent of occupied housing units with no vehicle available
							With a mortgage	Without a mortgage					
ACS table number:		C07204	C07204	B25003	B25003	B25077	B25092	B25092	B25064	B25071	C08301	B08013/C08012	C25045
		1	2	3	4	5	6	7	8	9	10	11	12
	New York—Cont.												
36 65255	Saratoga Springs	78.0	18.5	11,064	59.3	260,700	24.3	20.1	851	28.2	76.0	21.6	9.3
36 65508	Schenectady	78.3	11.0	24,069	50.9	98,100	25.7	16.7	699	31.3	71.9	20.5	18.7
36 66212	Selden CDP	88.1	11.3	6,936	83.4	352,400	34.7	18.8	1329	26.8	-	31.6	4.7
36 67070	Shirley CDP	94.2	4.3	7,648	84.2	332,600	30.5	15.0	1691	50.1	84.9	32.3	1.7
36 67851	Smithtown CDP	93.5	5.5	8,361	88.6	570,000	28.0	18.4	1086	31.9	80.0	29.3	7.1
36 70420	Spring Valley village	86.4	5.0	6,834	33.8	248,000	38.9	21.9	1086	31.9	55.8	25.4	22.4
36 73000	Syracuse	71.1	11.6	55,317	40.7	77,800	23.3	17.7	631	35.5	65.6	16.9	25.5
36 74183	Tonawanda CDP	89.4	10.3	26,345	73.3	101,000	22.7	14.6	697	28.6	84.6	18.3	8.8
36 75484	Troy	72.2	13.6	19,177	42.9	118,100	23.8	16.3	702	30.1	64.7	21.0	19.8
36 76089	Uniondale CDP	88.2	9.7	6,529	80.7	383,000	36.0	22.2	1338	34.1	66.1	31.1	13.5
36 76540	Utica	79.5	9.4	24,952	46.9	73,000	22.2	15.7	584	32.3	75.6	17.8	20.1
36 76705	Valley Stream village	93.1	4.5	12,424	81.4	438,000	33.7	22.5	1269	36.1	62.6	34.1	6.2
36 78608	Watertown	77.0	14.1	11,821	45.5	87,700	21.8	15.4	568	28.1	76.1	15.4	16.4
36 79246	West Babylon CDP	91.1	7.5	13,699	75.7	396,400	33.0	20.1	1264	41.4	78.0	30.5	4.7
36 80302	West Islip CDP	95.8	3.4	8,264	94.8	466,400	30.4	20.8	1214	24.4	78.6	28.5	2.1
36 80907	West Seneca CDP	92.4	6.2	18,803	78.3	113,200	23.1	14.9	668	26.7	89.1	20.1	4.7
36 81677	White Plains	84.1	9.2	21,410	55.7	508,400	25.4	15.1	1163	28.7	56.7	26.0	17.9
36 84000	Yonkers	88.6	5.4	72,616	48.0	433,900	26.2	16.7	994	30.3	55.8	30.8	23.4
37 00000	**North Carolina**	82.0	13.1	3,471,751	68.4	136,800	23.0	11.9	674	28.9	79.9	23.2	6.5
37 01520	Apex town	85.0	10.6	11,573	80.3	225,100	22.2	11.5	846	23.0	80.6	25.5	1.8
37 02080	Asheboro	78.3	11.8	9,624	50.8	102,500	23.2	16.1	568	31.3	82.1	18.4	8.3
37 02140	Asheville	75.6	14.0	33,725	54.9	174,800	27.1	13.7	719	28.9	75.1	17.6	10.5
37 09060	Burlington	73.5	16.1	19,631	58.1	119,900	24.9	12.6	676	26.0	78.9	19.3	5.0
37 10740	Cary town	82.8	12.8	42,553	70.4	253,700	20.7	8.2	844	24.6	81.9	22.5	1.9
37 11800	Chapel Hill town	68.0	20.7	20,961	48.4	324,400	21.5	9.3	786	37.9	63.2	19.7	9.0
37 12000	Charlotte	75.5	10.7	265,874	60.4	166,300	23.0	11.9	772	28.9	76.2	24.1	7.3
37 14100	Concord	78.0	10.1	25,483	65.5	143,200	22.3	13.7	708	23.2	81.4	25.4	6.1
37 14700	Cornelius town	81.3	16.0	8,992	76.0	267,000	21.2	12.8	980	23.8	81.5	29.2	1.3
37 19000	Durham	75.8	11.4	84,894	51.0	168,100	24.1	12.0	752	29.1	72.9	21.8	9.3
37 22920	Fayetteville	77.5	12.2	71,704	56.4	100,500	23.4	12.5	741	29.8	83.3	20.4	8.0
37 24260	Fort Bragg CDP	37.4	56.1	3,573	0.3	-	-	-	945	27.3	37.4	10.9	-
37 25480	Garner town	81.0	16.1	8,047	69.2	144,100	23.4	12.6	784	28.4	78.4	25.5	4.7
37 25580	Gastonia	77.6	12.5	26,573	57.5	125,600	24.3	14.5	648	29.0	80.3	21.9	11.0
37 26880	Goldsboro	75.6	13.3	14,056	43.8	109,500	23.9	12.8	549	29.1	82.3	16.3	14.1
37 28000	Greensboro	78.3	11.2	98,318	53.3	139,100	23.6	11.9	705	31.4	80.5	20.2	8.3
37 28080	Greenville	62.9	20.1	30,393	36.9	127,500	24.0	13.1	634	36.0	79.9	16.6	12.2
37 30120	Havelock	60.7	31.6	5,834	49.8	123,900	24.0	8.1	715	24.7	64.1	13.5	7.2
37 31060	Hickory	76.4	13.0	16,174	54.9	143,700	20.9	13.5	584	26.6	82.5	20.8	6.8
37 31400	High Point	79.1	11.0	38,615	60.4	137,000	24.3	12.9	689	29.9	80.7	20.2	10.1
37 33120	Huntersville town	82.1	13.1	15,864	80.0	231,400	21.8	10.9	867	25.5	81.4	26.1	1.4
37 34200	Jacksonville	57.6	36.9	17,597	43.3	115,900	23.8	8.6	766	26.0	48.2	14.0	6.9
37 35200	Kannapolis	83.2	10.9	15,899	63.7	101,700	24.6	14.0	671	31.1	80.2	23.1	9.9
37 35600	Kernersville town	82.6	11.7	9,281	62.8	162,000	24.0	11.2	609	25.1	88.5	19.4	3.2
37 35920	Kinston	79.4	9.1	10,047	46.8	100,100	28.0	17.0	569	39.2	74.4	16.8	18.1
37 38060	Lexington	71.8	16.6	7,592	46.0	103,000	25.3	14.6	538	30.0	77.4	21.6	14.0
37 39700	Lumberton	79.0	13.2	8,548	49.2	85,100	23.0	13.2	496	28.6	81.4	18.0	16.6
37 41960	Matthews town	87.3	10.8	10,495	81.1	199,300	20.3	10.5	811	27.1	78.9	26.8	3.2
37 43920	Monroe	80.1	12.4	11,731	53.4	148,000	24.3	12.4	708	31.3	73.7	24.7	8.1
37 44220	Mooresville town	73.0	17.4	10,839	63.0	186,000	23.5	11.4	709	26.9	82.5	24.4	3.7
37 46340	New Bern	76.0	14.9	12,554	53.6	136,600	24.1	15.1	595	31.5	78.5	18.0	15.0
37 55000	Raleigh	73.9	13.5	136,993	55.0	190,500	22.3	10.2	780	29.4	78.4	22.1	7.0
37 57500	Rocky Mount	82.0	6.6	21,928	53.2	106,900	25.8	14.4	630	29.6	83.1	17.5	11.9
37 58860	Salisbury	75.8	14.2	11,521	56.2	128,300	22.4	13.3	610	31.4	78.9	18.6	11.7
37 59280	Sanford	85.0	8.8	9,594	60.0	119,900	22.9	13.9	556	28.9	75.5	19.4	10.5
37 61200	Shelby	80.7	8.1	7,992	58.5	109,300	24.1	12.8	596	31.9	84.9	20.2	13.2
37 64740	Statesville	74.8	9.6	9,850	54.0	116,400	25.0	13.0	609	28.8	79.5	18.1	12.5
37 67420	Thomasville	80.6	9.2	10,287	59.9	101,300	22.3	11.5	591	28.5	79.7	19.9	11.2
37 70540	Wake Forest town	74.9	23.8	7,761	71.3	215,200	23.9	13.1	838	24.6	78.2	28.1	5.5
37 74440	Wilmington	71.1	14.6	45,016	51.2	198,400	26.3	14.1	755	33.7	80.2	18.3	11.4
37 74540	Wilson	80.2	8.0	18,112	51.2	122,600	23.7	18.3	651	33.0	77.5	18.0	14.9
37 75000	Winston-Salem	81.2	7.7	87,371	58.2	134,500	22.9	11.1	645	28.9	80.5	19.8	9.9
38 00000	**North Dakota**	82.5	10.3	271,131	66.5	97,400	20.9	11.6	513	25.1	78.5	16.0	5.5
38 07200	Bismarck	82.3	9.2	25,732	62.9	124,900	22.3	12.7	525	24.2	81.0	14.8	6.5
38 25700	Fargo	71.6	12.7	44,136	45.3	134,400	22.4	12.4	577	28.0	81.5	15.0	9.0
38 32060	Grand Forks	69.2	14.0	21,356	51.2	131,000	22.2	14.6	594	30.0	85.4	12.7	5.8
38 53380	Minot	78.0	12.5	16,624	61.4	108,100	22.9	12.8	502	23.1	84.2	13.4	7.3
38 84780	West Fargo	81.2	12.7	8,293	72.0	138,700	22.9	14.5	530	26.2	89.6	15.8	3.3
39 00000	**Ohio**	84.2	10.6	4,500,621	70.0	134,400	23.3	13.5	645	29.3	83.1	22.4	7.8
39 01000	Akron	84.7	5.7	83,935	58.7	94,600	25.6	15.7	652	32.4	81.9	20.9	12.5
39 01420	Alliance	79.6	12.1	8,313	58.0	86,100	21.9	13.9	539	29.6	79.4	17.3	9.3
39 02568	Ashland	76.6	12.0	8,134	66.8	104,300	23.4	15.7	550	31.8	80.5	15.5	8.6
39 02736	Athens	34.8	40.1	6,045	32.1	152,300	21.8	11.5	763	50.1	41.2	12.4	9.7
39 03184	Austintown CDP	85.7	9.9	13,895	68.3	96,100	24.2	14.9	538	27.6	90.1	20.9	5.2
39 03464	Avon Lake	90.0	7.9	8,117	88.0	221,900	21.9	12.2	769	30.8	88.7	24.9	3.8

1. $1,000,001 is the top code symbolizing a median value over one million dollars.
2. 50.1 is the top code symbolizing a median gross rent as a percentage of household income of 50.1 percent or more.

Table C-4. Cities — Where: Migration, Housing, and Transportation, 2005–2007—Continued

STATE Place code	STATE City	Percent who lived in the same house one year ago	Percent who did not live in city one year ago	Total occupied housing units	Percent owner-occupied housing units	Median value of owner-occupied housing units (dollars)[1]	Median selected monthly owner costs as a percentage of household income — With a mortgage	Without a mortgage	Median gross rent (dollars)	Median gross rent as a percentage of household income[2]	Percent of workers who drove alone to work	Mean travel time to work (minutes)	Percent of occupied housing units with no vehicle available
ACS table number:		C07204	C07204	B25003	B25003	B25077	B25092	B25092	B25064	B25071	C08301	B08013/C08012	C25045
		1	2	3	4	5	6	7	8	9	10	11	12
	North Dakota—Cont.												
39 03828	Barberton	89.9	6.0	11,547	67.2	96,200	26.4	13.4	549	28.3	85.5	20.2	11.9
39 04720	Beavercreek	84.7	12.1	16,577	78.6	175,700	20.5	11.6	935	25.2	91.4	18.8	0.9
39 07454	Boardman CDP	90.8	6.8	15,739	69.9	116,300	23.4	13.7	568	29.3	92.3	18.1	6.5
39 07972	Bowling Green	53.4	29.1	11,155	39.9	163,900	21.7	10.2	565	35.7	73.7	14.2	7.9
39 09680	Brunswick	89.2	6.6	13,051	81.4	164,700	23.1	14.2	751	29.1	91.4	27.1	2.3
39 12000	Canton	80.6	8.2	31,390	56.9	81,800	24.5	14.0	499	31.5	80.7	19.0	16.2
39 13190	Centerville	87.1	10.6	10,208	78.7	177,100	20.7	12.5	753	36.2	89.6	20.3	3.7
39 14184	Chillicothe	78.8	12.4	8,734	62.6	97,600	21.6	12.2	567	33.5	86.6	21.3	11.1
39 15000	Cincinnati	73.7	9.0	128,357	42.6	125,900	24.5	15.2	550	30.3	70.2	21.5	23.6
39 16000	Cleveland	81.4	5.9	168,557	47.7	88,900	28.6	16.6	610	33.4	69.5	23.8	24.0
39 16014	Cleveland Heights	82.8	11.2	19,419	60.6	145,500	25.8	15.2	742	31.0	73.2	23.9	13.8
39 18000	Columbus	74.9	11.0	303,031	51.7	137,400	24.0	13.4	709	29.7	81.6	20.6	9.5
39 19778	Cuyahoga Falls	92.5	4.6	21,237	68.7	131,300	22.9	14.9	669	28.5	90.7	20.4	6.5
39 21000	Dayton	74.8	8.9	61,271	51.8	80,800	24.1	15.4	580	34.7	73.9	20.1	19.5
39 21434	Delaware	78.4	13.1	12,571	60.8	166,500	24.9	11.1	687	30.8	81.7	24.0	7.1
39 22694	Dublin	81.2	12.8	14,472	81.5	324,000	22.1	9.9	945	22.9	85.2	22.9	0.6
39 23380	East Cleveland	72.9	21.5	8,685	33.4	83,000	36.2	22.5	631	32.3	70.0	27.4	31.2
39 25256	Elyria	83.6	8.0	21,827	65.7	113,100	23.8	14.2	630	29.9	86.1	20.8	10.1
39 25704	Euclid	82.0	12.7	23,614	57.7	111,300	24.8	16.8	671	31.1	79.4	25.8	15.7
39 25914	Fairborn	69.8	19.4	14,548	45.0	107,900	20.4	10.6	678	30.8	80.3	19.0	6.2
39 25970	Fairfield	83.0	12.4	16,637	69.8	145,700	22.1	13.5	777	25.3	85.7	22.7	2.7
39 27048	Findlay	74.8	11.8	17,844	66.0	117,500	22.2	12.9	582	29.4	84.3	14.4	5.2
39 29106	Gahanna	88.7	8.6	12,928	79.4	184,000	22.0	11.3	799	26.2	85.7	20.6	2.8
39 29428	Garfield Heights	86.1	10.8	11,789	75.8	107,400	23.7	20.4	700	36.1	83.4	21.2	8.6
39 31860	Green	91.7	8.0	9,679	79.2	170,700	22.4	13.1	751	29.2	85.1	22.8	4.7
39 32592	Grove	83.2	10.3	12,628	72.4	169,600	24.0	13.5	768	30.4	87.1	21.1	3.6
39 33012	Hamilton	78.4	9.2	23,564	57.2	110,000	24.6	14.6	664	30.2	80.7	21.8	10.7
39 35476	Hilliard	83.3	14.4	10,727	77.5	215,700	23.5	12.1	842	27.5	87.8	21.0	3.3
39 36610	Huber Heights	85.2	8.6	14,188	74.5	115,500	21.8	14.3	755	28.8	88.6	21.4	3.8
39 36651	Hudson	93.4	4.9	7,861	91.5	306,200	21.1	12.8	2001	50.1	85.5	25.0	1.8
39 39872	Kent	61.9	26.5	9,963	38.8	141,700	23.5	12.9	684	38.8	75.1	19.1	8.2
39 40040	Kettering	85.1	10.6	25,125	68.6	133,200	23.1	12.8	646	26.7	85.2	19.4	5.4
39 41664	Lakewood	80.3	12.7	24,898	48.1	143,700	23.4	16.1	658	27.1	75.2	22.6	13.4
39 41720	Lancaster	81.8	7.6	15,582	58.7	121,200	23.6	12.0	657	28.0	80.9	24.1	8.4
39 42364	Lebanon	79.5	10.5	6,598	69.1	165,100	22.2	13.5	725	26.1	88.6	23.0	2.0
39 43554	Lima	77.9	10.3	14,695	53.8	69,200	20.3	12.2	531	28.9	79.1	16.8	11.5
39 44856	Lorain	81.3	7.0	24,557	61.5	104,800	23.7	13.3	599	33.3	82.5	23.3	11.8
39 47138	Mansfield	76.6	10.8	19,521	58.8	84,800	23.5	13.5	520	29.1	79.2	18.1	15.2
39 47306	Maple Heights	89.4	9.8	10,379	79.3	101,300	27.0	17.6	714	35.0	84.6	22.1	9.9
39 47754	Marion	75.3	13.4	13,099	60.9	77,900	23.1	15.6	578	32.2	81.3	18.3	13.8
39 48188	Mason	86.1	10.6	10,216	87.5	216,400	22.1	14.2	837	26.9	84.8	25.4	2.5
39 48244	Massillon	83.6	9.1	12,664	68.0	98,700	22.3	13.9	582	31.0	80.6	20.7	9.8
39 48790	Medina	85.3	9.7	10,649	69.9	167,500	23.4	12.9	706	33.9	86.4	25.3	5.5
39 49056	Mentor	90.5	7.1	18,969	87.7	172,900	23.7	14.4	869	29.2	87.9	23.9	3.4
39 49840	Middletown	76.2	8.6	20,172	58.0	107,200	24.2	16.6	639	28.9	82.9	19.5	11.0
39 54040	Newark	75.1	10.7	19,060	59.2	109,500	23.3	12.6	594	28.8	81.0	22.1	9.2
39 56882	North Olmsted	89.1	9.5	13,446	78.9	159,600	24.7	15.7	727	26.5	84.7	21.9	3.0
39 56966	North Ridgeville	90.7	6.9	9,951	89.7	161,600	23.0	14.0	647	25.3	88.9	23.6	1.7
39 57008	North Royalton	88.7	9.3	12,299	73.3	209,500	24.8	13.6	699	21.5	88.0	25.6	1.6
39 57386	Norwood	77.1	15.9	8,162	62.4	115,300	23.3	17.2	542	32.8	88.4	19.5	11.9
39 59234	Oxford	35.7	31.7	5,698	30.0	193,000	19.6	12.4	683	50.1	53.9	12.3	11.7
39 61000	Parma	88.8	7.6	33,609	77.2	133,900	24.2	15.4	659	27.9	86.0	23.2	6.3
39 62848	Piqua	79.2	9.0	8,305	60.0	99,500	22.2	14.5	618	28.1	84.8	17.1	11.5
39 64304	Portsmouth	72.8	14.9	8,707	51.1	67,500	23.0	15.7	492	32.4	78.2	18.0	17.7
39 66390	Reynoldsburg	82.3	12.1	13,696	63.0	148,400	22.6	13.5	777	27.8	83.8	23.2	5.2
39 67468	Riverside	81.1	16.9	10,431	58.5	97,200	23.4	13.2	680	24.0	87.4	17.1	5.9
39 70380	Sandusky	81.8	7.3	11,333	58.9	89,500	22.4	14.0	532	34.7	84.9	16.6	10.6
39 71682	Shaker Heights	87.4	9.4	11,723	68.5	228,100	23.1	18.1	864	33.2	73.6	26.8	5.6
39 72424	Sidney	79.3	10.0	8,311	57.9	102,700	22.4	11.8	628	32.7	80.9	14.0	9.4
39 72928	Solon	91.0	7.2	8,094	88.0	280,100	22.9	11.5	948	31.5	88.4	23.1	2.2
39 73264	South Euclid	88.7	9.8	9,269	83.9	136,900	25.7	19.2	994	47.9	82.8	22.0	4.8
39 74118	Springfield	80.3	7.1	24,493	57.7	84,700	23.8	15.2	608	34.8	77.4	18.1	12.6
39 74944	Stow	90.9	7.1	13,922	69.2	170,900	22.2	12.8	833	24.4	90.9	22.2	4.4
39 75098	Strongsville	91.7	6.2	17,627	83.6	207,400	23.4	12.3	715	25.6	84.8	27.1	3.9
39 77000	Toledo	80.6	6.0	119,248	59.4	98,000	23.7	15.9	598	33.3	81.9	19.3	12.5
39 77504	Trotwood	77.7	14.7	10,674	61.5	86,500	25.6	17.1	692	30.7	83.2	22.0	10.7
39 77588	Troy	77.6	10.3	9,546	58.9	122,400	22.2	11.3	608	28.4	87.3	17.8	9.0
39 79002	Upper Arlington	89.3	9.5	13,929	81.3	311,000	22.9	14.1	1005	26.6	85.0	18.4	3.0
39 80304	Wadsworth	88.8	6.3	7,424	79.2	154,300	22.9	13.0	705	28.0	84.1	21.7	4.7
39 80892	Warren	86.2	6.6	17,980	57.0	72,600	23.1	13.9	552	32.5	87.2	21.0	8.3
39 83342	Westerville	86.4	10.9	13,510	79.0	210,800	22.9	12.9	719	27.9	83.6	25.3	5.5
39 83622	Westlake	88.4	9.2	13,317	74.0	226,500	23.8	16.1	884	30.6	85.0	24.0	5.8
39 85484	Willoughby	87.1	10.2	10,744	60.1	152,700	24.2	13.9	768	25.3	86.4	21.1	7.1
39 86548	Wooster	79.6	9.7	10,464	59.6	121,900	24.5	12.3	570	28.8	72.8	17.1	8.0

1. $1,000,001 is the top code symbolizing a median value over one million dollars.
2. 50.1 is the top code symbolizing a median gross rent as a percentage of household income of 50.1 percent or more.

Table C-4. Cities — Where: Migration, Housing, and Transportation, 2005–2007—*Continued*

STATE Place code	STATE City	Percent who lived in the same house one year ago	Percent who did not live in city one year ago	Total occupied housing units	Percent owner-occupied housing units	Median value of owner-occupied housing units (dollars)[1]	Median selected monthly owner costs as a percentage of household income		Median gross rent (dollars)	Median gross rent as a percentage of household income[2]	Percent of workers who drove alone to work	Mean travel time to work (minutes)	Percent of occupied housing units with no vehicle available
							With a mortgage	Without a mortgage					
ACS table number:		C07204	C07204	B25003	B25003	B25077	B25092	B25092	B25064	B25071	C08301	B08013/C08012	C25045
		1	2	3	4	5	6	7	8	9	10	11	12
	North Dakota—Cont.												
39 86772	Xenia	86.0	4.8	9,444	65.3	96,700	23.8	11.4	638	32.7	84.8	20.9	10.0
39 88000	Youngstown	84.3	7.2	27,930	60.4	50,300	23.5	16.9	524	40.2	77.5	20.1	17.2
39 88084	Zanesville	83.3	9.3	9,978	59.9	82,200	25.7	14.9	499	31.3	84.5	18.3	12.1
40 00000	**Oklahoma**	80.0	12.1	1,386,849	68.3	95,200	21.2	11.4	587	28.1	80.6	20.2	5.7
40 02600	Ardmore	78.7	8.6	10,205	62.6	74,000	21.8	12.4	511	26.9	81.8	15.2	8.6
40 04450	Bartlesville	83.0	7.8	14,148	76.2	87,800	20.3	12.3	543	24.6	76.5	15.7	5.8
40 06400	Bixby	84.4	11.7	6,438	80.3	145,500	21.1	12.3	674	24.1	80.2	22.3	2.6
40 09050	Broken Arrow	85.4	9.5	32,906	80.9	135,400	22.1	11.3	763	27.3	85.7	20.2	1.6
40 19900	Del	81.1	15.7	8,945	67.0	68,800	21.9	12.2	548	26.4	84.7	17.9	7.9
40 21900	Duncan	72.9	16.8	9,927	64.7	73,500	18.7	12.1	519	23.9	82.1	17.5	5.8
40 23200	Edmond	78.8	11.6	30,175	72.3	169,100	22.1	9.0	755	30.5	83.4	19.3	3.3
40 23950	Enid	79.4	8.7	18,720	66.0	73,100	19.3	10.7	584	27.6	81.9	14.3	4.5
40 41850	Lawton	69.2	19.0	32,171	55.3	85,700	21.5	11.9	604	27.5	69.2	14.2	7.4
40 48350	Midwest	79.2	13.7	22,960	62.9	86,800	21.5	10.6	617	24.3	84.9	18.9	4.9
40 49200	Moore	81.3	14.4	17,752	72.5	98,800	21.5	9.9	766	24.6	87.6	21.8	2.6
40 50050	Muskogee	77.6	7.8	15,646	62.6	72,900	21.8	12.4	514	29.3	79.4	15.9	13.0
40 52500	Norman	71.0	14.9	42,147	55.7	132,800	21.4	10.5	651	33.7	78.1	20.3	4.4
40 55000	Oklahoma	77.1	10.0	217,431	61.5	112,500	22.1	12.1	618	28.8	80.1	19.4	6.8
40 56650	Owasso	83.3	13.4	9,562	68.8	132,400	20.6	10.4	696	26.2	80.7	20.2	6.7
40 59850	Ponca	82.1	6.8	10,470	68.7	72,500	19.8	14.0	587	27.5	84.0	12.7	7.2
40 65400	Sapulpa	81.0	12.3	8,419	69.9	96,200	24.2	12.2	752	29.0	84.5	20.1	4.9
40 66800	Shawnee	76.6	13.5	11,433	59.5	84,700	21.2	10.6	514	30.8	80.3	19.3	11.4
40 70300	Stillwater	59.3	20.6	15,222	44.1	125,600	23.0	9.8	555	38.5	73.5	13.5	7.9
40 75000	Tulsa	75.1	9.7	163,394	55.4	109,000	22.4	12.0	632	29.3	80.2	17.3	8.4
40 82950	Yukon	80.8	8.7	8,480	72.6	109,500	20.5	11.8	635	26.4	85.4	20.5	2.2
41 00000	**Oregon**	79.7	13.8	1,447,409	64.7	232,000	25.9	12.3	735	29.9	72.5	22.0	7.4
41 01000	Albany	74.2	12.0	18,466	60.4	168,900	24.6	12.2	661	32.1	77.3	18.8	7.0
41 01650	Aloha CDP	82.5	15.2	16,396	69.4	227,400	27.2	9.6	866	31.4	75.7	25.7	3.7
41 01850	Altamont CDP	-	-	7,823	74.3	137,300	23.3	11.3	620	29.0	81.3	14.3	3.8
41 03050	Ashland	68.7	19.2	9,147	50.1	409,100	28.3	14.8	783	38.2	66.5	14.8	8.3
41 05350	Beaverton	77.5	15.5	33,306	54.0	284,900	26.0	13.8	807	26.1	72.3	23.8	6.7
41 05800	Bend	76.0	12.6	29,290	60.8	334,500	27.6	12.4	862	27.9	78.4	15.7	4.6
41 15800	Corvallis	61.7	21.1	21,079	44.8	223,300	24.1	10.4	697	36.9	61.7	15.0	10.4
41 23850	Eugene	69.4	15.5	62,486	51.8	220,600	25.9	13.2	733	33.9	66.9	16.6	10.5
41 26200	Forest Grove	74.9	16.0	7,048	58.6	194,400	23.7	13.1	679	30.2	72.9	22.0	10.2
41 30550	Grants Pass	78.1	12.0	14,167	55.8	239,100	28.1	13.2	679	35.5	83.9	16.3	10.2
41 31250	Gresham	78.2	14.2	36,959	57.9	220,000	27.0	15.3	734	30.7	71.1	25.7	8.3
41 32850	Hayesville CDP	72.7	27.3	7,570	51.4	166,500	23.2	13.5	653	33.0	69.0	23.0	8.2
41 34100	Hillsboro	73.3	18.7	29,632	53.5	242,600	25.5	10.8	894	29.8	71.7	23.7	6.1
41 38500	Keizer	78.8	17.8	13,663	63.8	190,600	24.8	14.2	678	27.1	77.3	20.8	5.1
41 40550	Lake Oswego	83.6	12.7	15,647	74.6	507,800	26.0	12.3	982	29.5	78.5	22.0	3.3
41 45000	McMinnville	71.7	17.3	11,060	61.1	181,700	26.0	15.2	676	29.9	78.0	21.2	10.0
41 47000	Medford	74.9	12.9	29,476	54.8	251,400	27.5	12.3	742	30.9	78.0	16.2	9.5
41 48650	Milwaukie	87.9	8.3	8,569	59.9	227,000	30.1	12.1	732	32.8	75.0	23.4	8.3
41 52100	Newberg	75.4	16.3	6,837	65.0	204,100	28.3	13.7	757	27.3	71.8	21.1	9.1
41 55200	Oregon	76.8	16.4	10,743	67.5	251,300	26.9	13.7	782	32.4	75.4	25.4	7.0
41 59000	Portland	79.1	9.1	233,398	57.0	257,100	27.4	13.8	743	32.4	62.0	23.6	14.9
41 61200	Redmond	77.4	13.0	8,548	59.7	222,400	27.4	14.0	778	27.2	78.7	19.2	4.0
41 63650	Roseburg	74.4	14.6	9,216	51.0	185,900	22.7	9.3	635	29.8	78.6	15.0	14.2
41 64900	Salem	74.4	12.4	54,946	58.5	176,600	26.2	13.8	656	30.4	73.3	22.4	7.6
41 69600	Springfield	79.0	10.7	22,353	54.9	159,900	25.1	13.6	650	30.3	78.2	20.8	9.6
41 73650	Tigard	80.0	13.3	18,435	60.8	301,300	24.2	9.9	790	29.6	76.5	22.4	5.3
41 74950	Tualatin	81.5	14.4	9,878	57.3	323,300	25.2	10.1	824	28.5	77.9	21.5	7.0
41 80150	West Linn	86.6	10.2	9,563	79.0	435,300	24.2	11.0	1114	27.6	72.1	24.1	1.7
41 83750	Woodburn	85.3	6.5	7,301	65.2	157,500	30.0	13.7	745	28.3	58.7	26.8	5.4
42 00000	**Pennsylvania**	86.9	9.8	4,858,509	71.7	144,100	23.5	14.0	682	28.7	76.6	25.1	11.2
42 02000	Allentown	76.6	12.0	40,838	50.7	126,400	25.9	15.7	738	32.2	72.7	22.4	18.2
42 02184	Altoona	84.3	7.7	19,760	65.1	74,700	22.5	13.8	482	28.7	79.2	18.1	15.3
42 03714	Back Mountain CDP	87.9	11.3	8,856	85.8	152,000	22.7	13.8	593	24.5	87.4	23.3	3.1
42 06064	Bethel Park municipality	92.8	6.2	14,055	80.3	141,400	22.5	15.6	775	25.9	78.9	28.0	5.1
42 06088	Bethlehem	76.4	12.0	27,984	58.1	165,300	24.2	15.4	754	30.3	79.6	22.4	13.3
42 13208	Chester	79.6	11.9	10,710	44.0	58,900	25.0	18.3	672	34.9	57.0	23.2	35.8
42 19920	Drexel Hill CDP	88.4	9.7	11,610	63.7	190,400	24.1	17.0	872	24.7	73.2	29.6	8.0
42 21648	Easton	63.6	17.3	8,984	50.1	128,400	23.8	21.7	737	28.5	74.4	27.2	15.1
42 24000	Erie	77.7	7.2	38,929	56.7	77,200	23.9	15.6	541	30.0	75.0	16.2	17.1
42 32800	Harrisburg	75.1	8.4	19,121	41.6	72,100	23.2	13.9	609	29.4	62.3	17.9	30.7
42 33408	Hazleton	83.3	10.9	9,491	61.4	88,800	24.0	15.9	558	33.6	75.8	19.2	18.7
42 38288	Johnstown	84.0	6.8	10,042	49.5	39,600	19.7	14.5	450	28.5	75.1	17.0	26.3
42 41216	Lancaster	77.8	10.0	21,031	43.7	86,800	24.1	15.0	621	33.3	68.8	19.6	25.4
42 42168	Lebanon	82.0	9.6	9,629	47.2	79,400	20.1	10.7	497	28.1	72.7	19.5	20.7
42 42928	Levittown CDP	93.2	4.2	18,465	81.7	226,700	27.5	14.9	928	33.5	85.3	25.8	3.4
42 45904	McCandless Township CDP	90.9	9.1	11,394	79.4	177,700	21.3	13.7	771	27.4	83.8	23.3	4.5
42 46256	McKeesport	81.8	6.6	8,724	56.2	42,600	25.3	14.7	516	32.3	65.0	24.2	32.2

1. $1,000,001 is the top code symbolizing a median value over one million dollars.
2. 50.1 is the top code symbolizing a median gross rent as a percentage of household income of 50.1 percent or more.

334 The Who, What, and Where of America

Table C-4. Cities — Where: Migration, Housing, and Transportation, 2005–2007—*Continued*

STATE Place code	STATE City	Percent who lived in the same house one year ago	Percent who did not live in city one year ago	Total occupied housing units	Percent owner-occupied housing units	Median value of owner-occupied housing units (dollars)[1]	Median selected monthly owner costs as a percentage of household income — With a mortgage	Without a mortgage	Median gross rent (dollars)	Median gross rent as a percentage of household income[2]	Percent of workers who drove alone to work	Mean travel time to work (minutes)	Percent of occupied housing units with no vehicle available
	ACS table number:	C07204	C07204	B25003	B25003	B25077	B25092	B25092	B25064	B25071	C08301	B08013/ C08012	C25045
		1	2	3	4	5	6	7	8	9	10	11	12
	Pennsylvania—Cont.												
42 50528	Monroeville municipality	90.5	7.9	11,998	71.8	119,200	20.6	13.4	765	27.4	79.5	25.9	6.9
42 51704	Mount Lebanon CDP	87.9	9.9	13,620	77.7	187,300	21.5	14.3	671	27.0	68.9	27.0	7.1
42 53368	New Castle	83.8	4.8	9,646	67.1	58,500	23.7	16.2	498	31.8	77.3	17.7	14.6
42 54656	Norristown borough	78.5	8.4	12,208	42.1	141,100	26.4	17.3	884	31.5	57.6	23.5	20.1
42 59040	Penn Hills CDP	88.5	9.6	18,791	79.7	84,100	22.8	16.4	669	31.1	74.9	26.7	8.6
42 60000	Philadelphia	86.4	4.3	557,985	57.4	117,500	25.7	15.9	765	33.4	51.2	31.4	34.1
42 61000	Pittsburgh	78.9	10.5	132,054	53.1	78,400	23.5	16.0	653	32.7	54.3	21.8	26.3
42 61536	Plum borough	91.8	6.6	10,473	78.8	120,000	22.3	11.6	757	24.8	85.3	27.7	3.0
42 62416	Pottstown borough	83.4	7.8	9,199	59.8	131,200	26.8	22.0	731	32.9	78.3	26.7	14.7
42 63268	Radnor Township CDP	78.0	18.4	10,040	65.5	603,500	24.3	12.9	1152	35.8	69.2	24.4	6.6
42 63624	Reading	75.8	9.2	29,471	45.3	54,500	24.7	15.0	610	33.3	56.9	23.0	26.7
42 66356	Ross Township CDP	91.9	8.1	13,193	79.1	134,600	21.7	14.4	732	24.4	79.6	23.0	6.5
42 69000	Scranton	81.5	9.8	30,069	53.4	98,100	25.5	19.6	564	28.5	73.1	17.2	15.2
42 69596	Shaler Township CDP	93.2	5.2	11,831	87.1	126,600	22.4	15.3	674	24.7	82.3	25.7	5.3
42 73040	Springfield CDP	94.7	4.3	8,581	93.0	287,800	24.1	16.8	946	29.7	83.6	27.5	3.8
42 73808	State College borough	42.0	38.6	11,185	21.2	225,800	20.9	9.7	711	50.1	34.0	13.2	19.7
42 79277	Upper St. Clair CDP	93.0	5.3	7,102	90.8	223,500	22.1	10.0	1500	23.8	79.6	28.7	3.6
42 83512	West Mifflin borough	93.0	5.1	9,202	77.4	84,000	23.5	15.0	583	24.4	78.5	23.7	12.0
42 85152	Wilkes-Barre	75.8	16.7	16,462	53.4	74,600	24.5	16.7	540	31.4	69.4	19.4	20.9
42 85312	Williamsport	75.9	12.2	12,214	42.0	80,000	24.1	18.1	556	33.0	67.6	14.3	17.1
42 87048	York	73.8	11.0	15,645	45.6	69,500	28.6	16.1	564	28.8	67.1	18.9	23.7
44 00000	**Rhode Island**	86.6	9.2	404,549	63.3	289,400	26.7	16.0	833	29.3	80.8	22.7	8.4
44 09460	Bristol CDP	83.6	10.6	8,306	66.2	354,200	26.4	18.0	882	30.3	78.4	22.9	4.9
44 19180	Cranston	86.9	9.9	30,436	69.6	274,700	28.3	19.4	903	28.4	84.8	20.0	5.5
44 22960	East Providence	88.8	5.7	19,676	60.7	248,800	27.1	14.1	754	28.1	81.9	21.7	7.1
44 49960	Newport	79.9	12.8	9,765	47.6	416,500	26.9	16.0	858	26.5	69.6	18.7	13.6
44 51940	North Providence CDP	89.5	6.5	14,212	66.4	251,500	27.3	16.1	856	29.5	86.3	23.6	7.7
44 54640	Pawtucket	84.7	8.2	28,229	47.3	237,700	29.9	17.2	786	28.5	78.2	21.9	14.0
44 59000	Providence	76.3	11.8	59,064	37.8	256,500	31.3	18.0	846	33.0	64.0	21.6	18.6
44 74300	Warwick	90.0	6.8	35,757	75.2	239,500	26.3	16.1	965	27.6	86.9	23.0	5.0
44 78260	West Warwick CDP	86.7	10.8	12,775	58.4	237,400	29.6	17.3	746	27.8	85.3	19.9	8.2
44 80780	Woonsocket	87.4	4.8	17,560	40.9	242,000	27.8	15.1	741	29.4	83.2	23.4	12.7
45 00000	**South Carolina**	83.4	14.3	1,664,561	70.3	122,600	22.7	11.4	648	28.6	81.2	23.3	7.3
45 00550	Aiken	85.5	8.5	11,704	67.0	158,000	19.1	10.5	610	29.4	79.5	20.7	8.6
45 01360	Anderson	82.5	10.0	9,699	54.2	113,400	21.7	10.7	533	36.8	82.2	17.8	14.1
45 13330	Charleston	77.4	13.8	47,049	55.1	247,100	26.1	13.9	796	31.7	77.0	21.0	11.5
45 16000	Columbia	63.9	27.7	42,576	48.2	148,800	23.2	11.2	671	31.7	60.1	18.0	14.7
45 21985	Easley	85.3	9.2	7,986	64.8	132,700	21.5	12.0	626	24.5	84.8	25.2	7.6
45 25810	Florence	81.3	10.1	13,127	60.8	129,200	21.6	11.2	597	30.2	80.2	18.5	12.6
45 29815	Goose Creek	77.9	19.7	10,238	71.1	169,700	22.3	8.1	875	26.3	78.5	21.5	1.5
45 30850	Greenville	73.7	13.9	24,330	48.1	154,700	21.8	13.1	588	28.6	75.6	16.8	14.4
45 30895	Greenwood	77.7	12.8	7,975	49.5	79,200	22.3	14.6	560	26.7	-	17.9	9.9
45 30985	Greer	76.5	17.5	9,051	60.9	108,600	24.4	12.5	599	27.9	84.2	20.7	10.9
45 34045	Hilton Head Island town	85.7	9.1	15,445	75.9	517,800	29.1	11.8	1100	29.1	74.5	16.2	6.0
45 45115	Mauldin	80.8	17.7	8,042	63.5	145,200	20.7	7.4	740	24.3	-	18.3	3.5
45 48535	Mount Pleasant town	82.9	11.2	26,148	74.7	355,900	24.3	11.7	1122	25.6	83.3	20.6	2.2
45 49075	Myrtle Beach	79.8	13.3	11,345	57.8	160,200	28.5	13.2	722	29.9	76.7	14.8	8.6
45 50695	North Augusta	84.3	10.4	8,554	65.2	115,100	19.9	10.6	657	25.0	86.3	20.5	8.6
45 50875	North Charleston	77.0	18.7	32,438	48.2	121,600	27.5	14.5	744	31.3	77.1	21.0	12.3
45 61405	Rock Hill	74.0	13.2	22,574	54.4	130,100	23.7	12.3	731	31.5	77.7	20.4	7.6
45 62395	St. Andrews CDP	64.8	35.2	10,844	33.5	102,900	24.9	9.8	679	26.5	79.4	18.2	6.8
45 68290	Spartanburg	80.2	9.9	15,192	52.2	105,400	24.0	11.7	573	28.8	76.2	17.4	20.5
45 70270	Summerville town	80.0	14.9	13,007	68.4	170,900	24.5	12.4	842	25.5	85.7	27.7	4.6
45 70405	Sumter	87.9	7.8	14,810	53.3	99,500	22.4	12.9	597	28.3	82.7	17.9	14.7
45 71395	Taylors CDP	81.3	16.0	8,297	63.9	133,800	19.8	10.5	654	21.8	80.9	21.1	3.1
45 73870	Wade Hampton CDP	75.3	24.7	9,460	61.0	153,500	22.0	9.8	641	27.8	82.5	18.2	3.8
46 00000	**South Dakota**	82.9	10.1	311,644	69.1	110,900	22.0	11.9	533	25.3	77.3	16.2	5.1
46 00100	Aberdeen	79.1	9.2	10,388	59.6	96,500	19.9	13.2	447	23.0	81.2	10.4	8.2
46 52980	Rapid	74.7	12.5	25,352	61.4	135,500	23.5	12.2	632	27.9	82.5	15.5	5.4
46 59020	Sioux Falls	77.6	8.7	57,967	63.5	134,800	22.0	12.3	641	26.7	85.7	15.4	5.7
46 69300	Watertown	77.1	7.4	9,016	61.4	111,600	21.0	10.5	537	27.2	83.4	12.6	6.7
47 00000	**Tennessee**	82.9	11.1	2,382,975	70.1	122,500	22.8	10.7	626	28.4	83.3	23.6	6.3
47 03440	Bartlett	91.1	7.9	17,729	93.2	164,600	22.8	10.5	980	30.9	89.3	23.9	0.8
47 08280	Brentwood	91.8	6.4	10,839	95.2	445,800	20.3	9.9	1939	36.4	80.9	23.4	1.6
47 08540	Bristol	80.3	11.0	11,086	67.8	94,000	21.9	11.7	453	22.6	83.2	18.9	9.1
47 14000	Chattanooga	79.2	8.9	67,082	56.8	121,100	23.1	11.6	609	28.3	80.4	18.4	12.6
47 15160	Clarksville	72.6	16.3	42,642	60.7	111,100	21.4	8.5	672	24.6	82.6	22.4	4.0
47 15400	Cleveland	73.4	13.1	16,041	50.7	139,800	23.5	10.7	570	28.0	87.0	16.1	7.9
47 16420	Collierville town	83.8	12.9	14,477	82.6	255,400	22.4	9.9	917	28.4	87.4	24.6	3.2
47 16540	Columbia	78.4	14.2	14,489	60.8	113,900	23.0	13.3	633	28.6	83.5	26.1	7.3
47 16920	Cookeville	75.9	13.3	11,187	46.2	131,900	23.5	9.7	531	28.8	79.7	17.5	6.1
47 25760	Farragut town	89.5	9.7	7,156	92.8	273,700	21.3	8.3	899	36.0	89.1	21.2	2.4
47 27740	Franklin	76.7	16.2	20,862	68.1	277,200	22.3	9.8	979	27.1	80.1	23.0	3.6
47 28540	Gallatin	74.6	17.3	10,571	58.5	137,200	22.3	11.5	638	25.0	76.7	21.9	7.8

1. $1,000,001 is the top code symbolizing a median value over one million dollars.
2. 50.1 is the top code symbolizing a median gross rent as a percentage of household income of 50.1 percent or more.

Table C-4. Cities — Where: Migration, Housing, and Transportation, 2005–2007—*Continued*

STATE Place code	STATE City	Percent who lived in the same house one year ago	Percent who did not live in city one year ago	Total occupied housing units	Percent owner-occupied housing units	Median value of owner-occupied housing units (dollars)[1]	Median selected monthly owner costs as a percentage of household income		Median gross rent (dollars)	Median gross rent as a percentage of household income[2]	Percent of workers who drove alone to work	Mean travel time to work (minutes)	Percent of occupied housing units with no vehicle available
							With a mortgage	Without a mortgage					
ACS table number:		C07204	C07204	B25003	B25003	B25077	B25092	B25092	B25064	B25071	C08301	B08013/ C08012	C25045
		1	2	3	4	5	6	7	8	9	10	11	12
	Tennessee—Cont.												
47 28960	Germantown	89.4	8.5	14,641	90.2	278,800	20.0	8.3	1036	24.1	89.3	21.3	1.4
47 33280	Hendersonville	81.0	13.9	18,533	70.3	174,900	22.8	10.5	729	26.7	86.1	27.7	2.6
47 37640	Jackson	78.2	9.4	24,999	55.7	107,800	24.0	12.8	653	35.2	86.2	17.7	10.6
47 38320	Johnson	75.7	12.8	24,266	58.9	125,700	21.7	10.6	544	25.4	84.3	16.0	7.9
47 39560	Kingsport	84.3	7.9	21,361	63.1	99,900	19.8	9.8	483	27.5	87.1	17.4	8.7
47 40000	Knoxville	72.6	11.2	79,868	51.3	102,300	23.3	12.2	600	30.0	81.4	18.9	10.1
47 41200	La Vergne	86.3	12.5	9,673	84.3	124,100	23.6	12.2	882	28.3	87.5	27.1	1.0
47 41520	Lebanon	84.6	8.9	9,862	61.0	145,300	23.2	9.3	648	28.4	87.4	22.5	6.8
47 46380	Maryville	83.2	13.3	9,864	68.3	165,600	22.3	9.9	563	25.8	80.0	20.2	7.2
47 48000	Memphis	78.3	5.5	253,833	54.6	91,800	26.6	14.2	716	33.6	80.3	21.4	13.0
47 50280	Morristown	76.8	8.6	11,249	52.1	87,300	21.0	10.8	508	27.7	79.3	20.3	7.8
47 50780	Mount Juliet	83.0	15.6	6,310	87.7	175,700	20.9	8.7	823	30.5	-	28.5	0.7
47 51560	Murfreesboro	70.9	13.8	36,265	53.3	160,600	22.0	11.3	731	31.0	84.9	23.0	4.0
47 52006	Nashville-Davidson (balance)	80.7	7.5	237,321	59.5	150,400	24.2	11.6	722	29.0	80.9	23.2	7.7
47 55120	Oak Ridge	83.7	9.1	12,580	72.3	120,100	22.6	10.4	597	26.6	88.4	18.9	6.2
47 69420	Smyrna town	83.1	11.2	13,096	68.2	147,000	21.9	12.7	670	28.9	87.8	24.7	4.0
47 70580	Spring Hill	83.0	15.3	5,874	89.6	193,100	23.9	8.9	955	22.9	83.4	33.2	-
48 00000	**Texas**	80.2	11.9	8,095,075	65.2	113,800	23.6	13.1	725	29.3	78.7	24.7	6.2
48 01000	Abilene	73.0	13.0	42,510	58.6	73,800	21.9	12.7	674	30.9	79.9	14.7	4.8
48 01924	Allen	85.2	10.9	23,301	84.3	181,600	22.6	11.5	1089	27.6	83.7	28.7	1.2
48 02272	Alvin	77.4	14.9	8,030	58.0	95,100	23.6	16.3	655	26.6	78.3	28.1	8.6
48 03000	Amarillo	78.8	7.6	68,624	63.7	94,500	22.2	11.9	607	29.1	81.1	15.7	5.0
48 04000	Arlington	77.3	11.0	128,277	58.0	127,200	24.2	13.5	762	28.8	83.1	25.2	4.1
48 04462	Atascocita CDP	84.1	15.9	18,180	86.9	149,000	23.6	13.9	1173	28.0	85.5	32.0	1.0
48 05000	Austin	71.7	11.1	294,716	47.0	178,800	24.6	12.5	810	29.0	72.7	22.4	7.3
48 06128	Baytown	76.8	12.2	24,928	59.8	91,600	23.7	13.6	690	26.7	83.4	22.3	6.1
48 07000	Beaumont	79.2	8.2	43,788	57.8	88,100	21.6	13.0	649	32.0	82.1	18.8	11.1
48 07132	Bedford	75.9	19.5	20,429	56.6	148,400	22.2	13.4	819	26.6	87.6	23.2	3.1
48 07552	Benbrook	84.7	13.0	9,021	67.3	123,100	22.7	13.3	853	25.9	87.7	22.8	3.3
48 08236	Big Spring	69.9	17.4	8,059	64.3	44,300	19.7	11.8	533	32.2	84.3	13.9	5.6
48 10768	Brownsville	85.1	4.0	49,413	62.4	71,500	28.8	14.8	504	35.9	75.6	19.6	12.5
48 10897	Brushy Creek CDP	82.9	15.6	6,042	84.0	202,600	20.4	9.5	1443	29.4	84.2	27.0	1.2
48 10912	Bryan	72.7	17.8	24,598	54.4	95,900	24.8	13.3	662	35.3	75.6	16.8	7.3
48 11428	Burleson	82.0	13.7	9,948	80.1	117,100	24.5	14.2	917	27.3	85.3	26.4	2.7
48 13024	Carrollton	80.7	13.2	40,249	65.7	158,000	23.7	12.0	904	28.0	82.6	23.6	2.7
48 13492	Cedar Hill	86.5	10.0	13,719	83.1	130,700	27.1	15.5	1054	35.1	80.1	30.6	3.4
48 13552	Cedar Park	79.5	16.5	13,475	71.2	166,500	24.6	14.6	910	31.5	78.6	28.1	2.6
48 14236	Channelview CDP	84.1	10.4	11,254	74.1	89,000	28.3	12.1	769	28.8	78.8	23.7	5.2
48 15364	Cleburne	76.2	13.7	9,990	63.3	86,500	23.9	14.1	752	29.8	76.3	24.7	8.1
48 15628	Cloverleaf CDP	-	-	6,601	60.5	101,700	22.6	13.2	655	33.2	-	24.3	6.6
48 15976	College Station	60.4	24.6	28,541	33.8	151,700	22.2	11.7	696	42.2	76.3	15.9	5.8
48 15988	Colleyville	91.6	7.0	7,242	97.3	372,400	22.7	15.6	1695	25.1	85.9	25.0	-
48 16432	Conroe	69.2	16.8	15,904	53.3	112,700	23.9	13.2	725	26.7	71.4	23.2	8.8
48 16612	Coppell	87.2	10.7	13,913	77.4	244,700	22.5	10.4	1017	24.0	84.6	22.9	1.8
48 16624	Copperas Cove	77.8	14.2	9,702	57.2	86,700	20.7	12.2	768	28.6	79.7	22.2	5.6
48 16696	Corinth	84.2	15.3	5,903	89.7	169,200	22.1	9.6	1386	26.0	82.1	31.5	0.5
48 17000	Corpus Christi	78.6	7.1	103,788	59.4	95,000	24.2	14.6	736	32.1	77.6	19.4	7.8
48 17060	Corsicana	75.5	12.8	8,606	60.6	72,000	24.4	14.9	618	31.3	74.5	18.5	12.2
48 19000	Dallas	77.4	8.6	440,633	47.0	128,200	26.6	14.9	738	29.4	74.1	25.5	10.1
48 19624	Deer Park	84.8	11.2	10,490	80.5	123,900	20.3	11.1	909	31.1	90.8	24.3	3.3
48 19792	Del Rio	84.5	6.6	11,463	65.0	71,700	21.6	14.0	540	35.7	79.5	16.3	7.2
48 19900	Denison	78.2	11.5	9,354	60.7	72,800	23.6	15.5	612	31.7	81.4	19.7	6.2
48 19972	Denton	66.6	20.9	34,146	51.1	135,200	25.6	12.4	741	36.7	78.0	23.3	5.9
48 20092	DeSoto	86.8	11.7	15,899	72.8	149,200	27.1	12.8	829	32.7	82.0	29.6	3.8
48 21628	Duncanville	81.1	12.6	13,091	73.7	115,300	27.8	14.9	925	33.4	78.7	26.7	4.6
48 21892	Eagle Pass	83.8	7.8	7,151	62.6	87,200	25.0	14.3	464	27.0	74.5	16.2	16.2
48 22660	Edinburg	79.7	12.0	20,059	56.2	85,900	25.6	14.4	583	35.9	76.3	19.8	8.7
48 24000	El Paso	84.8	4.7	196,788	62.6	91,600	24.2	12.2	557	31.0	79.7	21.3	10.2
48 24768	Euless	72.4	19.9	21,088	44.6	132,100	23.8	13.5	834	26.2	83.0	21.8	2.6
48 25452	Farmers Branch	86.8	12.1	10,239	70.4	135,500	23.9	14.2	914	32.5	82.9	20.3	2.0
48 26232	Flower Mound town	85.6	10.7	19,813	92.7	232,600	22.8	13.0	1327	29.6	82.1	27.9	0.6
48 26736	Fort Hood CDP	46.4	50.4	6,012	0.3	-	-	-	905	30.7	57.1	11.5	-
48 27000	Fort Worth	78.3	10.9	222,346	59.3	107,900	24.6	14.3	733	29.8	80.0	24.7	7.2
48 27648	Friendswood	81.9	13.9	12,477	79.7	186,600	22.2	10.9	900	29.5	85.4	28.5	2.6
48 27684	Frisco	78.5	16.4	28,494	79.6	231,300	23.5	11.3	996	27.4	80.5	31.1	2.3
48 28068	Galveston	70.1	14.6	23,710	42.9	113,300	25.7	17.8	717	29.7	67.8	17.3	12.3
48 29000	Garland	81.9	11.2	75,041	66.9	117,400	26.6	14.1	857	29.8	79.7	27.5	4.0
48 29336	Georgetown	78.6	14.9	14,093	74.6	173,600	24.7	12.4	852	30.8	70.5	24.9	3.3
48 30464	Grand Prairie	80.1	13.6	50,273	65.5	118,300	26.1	14.0	825	30.1	80.3	27.6	4.2
48 30644	Grapevine	79.3	15.2	17,259	65.5	196,000	22.9	12.3	907	24.9	85.9	22.9	2.2
48 30920	Greenville	77.3	12.4	9,208	54.0	80,900	21.6	11.5	670	24.9	84.3	19.0	4.2
48 31928	Haltom	80.5	15.5	15,297	56.7	86,000	24.3	15.5	734	27.7	80.3	22.5	5.0
48 32312	Harker Heights	75.4	20.9	7,076	70.6	154,700	24.5	10.1	755	25.3	85.0	20.1	3.2
48 32372	Harlingen	85.7	7.2	22,153	62.0	69,400	24.2	14.0	618	29.9	83.5	17.6	10.4
48 35000	Houston	76.6	8.0	738,807	47.2	119,300	24.9	13.4	740	30.3	73.2	26.3	10.4

1. $1,000,001 is the top code symbolizing a median value over one million dollars.
2. 50.1 is the top code symbolizing a median gross rent as a percentage of household income of 50.1 percent or more.

STATE Place code	STATE City	Percent who lived in the same house one year ago	Percent who did not live in city one year ago	Total occupied housing units	Percent owner-occupied housing units	Median value of owner-occupied housing units (dollars)[1]	Median selected monthly owner costs as a percentage of household income		Median gross rent (dollars)	Median gross rent as a percentage of household income[2]	Percent of workers who drove alone to work	Mean travel time to work (minutes)	Percent of occupied housing units with no vehicle available
							With a mortgage	Without a mortgage					
	ACS table number:	C07204	C07204	B25003	B25003	B25077	B25092	B25092	B25064	B25071	C08301	B08013/C08012	C25045
		1	2	3	4	5	6	7	8	9	10	11	12
	Texas—Cont.												
48 35528	Huntsville	60.1	31.6	12,109	42.4	102,500	24.9	12.9	697	42.5	78.9	17.8	8.0
48 35576	Hurst	80.5	13.0	13,858	68.5	134,000	24.1	14.7	742	29.4	82.0	24.5	2.7
48 37000	Irving	73.3	15.2	78,209	41.4	131,600	25.3	14.2	809	26.8	76.5	22.8	5.2
48 38632	Keller	85.5	12.7	12,147	89.6	245,700	23.3	13.2	1031	38.5	83.6	27.8	0.7
48 39040	Kerrville	67.5	17.4	9,081	62.5	121,000	24.1	13.0	705	28.6	79.4	13.9	4.4
48 39148	Killeen	66.4	20.7	37,738	51.2	93,500	22.9	11.3	782	27.6	83.5	18.4	3.8
48 39352	Kingsville	74.5	9.0	8,904	49.2	61,700	20.8	14.7	622	31.2	74.2	18.8	9.6
48 39952	Kyle	72.0	24.2	4,823	76.5	140,600	24.3	14.1	1199	27.9	84.6	34.7	2.5
48 40588	Lake Jackson	76.4	12.3	10,293	70.5	120,900	19.4	9.9	786	23.1	88.9	21.9	3.1
48 41212	Lancaster	85.9	9.6	10,697	68.6	111,300	28.8	19.7	795	28.8	77.1	30.0	4.1
48 41440	La Porte	84.0	11.0	11,847	77.6	112,200	21.3	13.5	886	24.1	88.1	21.8	2.6
48 41464	Laredo	83.5	4.8	57,440	63.2	99,000	27.4	15.3	620	34.4	76.4	19.0	9.9
48 41980	League	81.0	15.7	23,378	79.2	161,200	24.1	12.5	879	24.0	84.9	29.0	2.3
48 42016	Leander	79.6	16.7	6,004	85.6	136,000	25.3	15.9	1199	29.5	75.1	33.2	2.3
48 42508	Lewisville	76.4	15.6	32,046	49.2	145,800	24.4	13.4	855	27.4	85.6	25.4	3.5
48 43012	Little Elm	82.4	17.0	5,850	89.2	147,400	25.8	13.0	1296	25.9	-	37.3	0.4
48 43888	Longview	76.0	9.0	29,641	57.0	102,400	19.3	12.4	633	26.9	82.5	18.5	7.0
48 45000	Lubbock	70.5	10.7	83,759	55.4	97,600	21.8	11.9	706	33.4	82.6	15.8	5.6
48 45072	Lufkin	76.9	12.5	12,727	56.1	85,700	20.3	12.9	626	28.2	81.8	19.3	8.1
48 45384	McAllen	79.0	11.2	39,825	62.4	91,200	24.4	14.2	631	29.7	78.9	18.5	5.4
48 45744	McKinney	76.6	17.5	35,469	73.7	180,900	24.6	14.8	850	31.3	80.8	30.5	2.7
48 46452	Mansfield	86.5	9.9	14,991	83.6	170,200	24.6	14.1	953	27.8	84.8	30.3	0.9
48 46776	Marshall	81.3	11.7	8,483	65.9	66,800	23.8	13.3	522	26.9	76.9	19.5	12.0
48 47892	Mesquite	85.7	7.3	46,276	66.6	113,300	25.6	13.0	853	30.0	86.7	28.5	4.1
48 48072	Midland	78.9	10.3	38,988	64.9	97,000	20.8	11.9	651	28.6	82.9	16.4	5.9
48 48760	Mission	82.9	9.2	20,655	74.1	77,200	27.8	12.1	596	36.3	78.0	24.0	8.0
48 48772	Mission Bend CDP	89.8	9.2	9,067	85.2	119,900	25.7	9.3	1182	32.0	81.1	31.7	0.8
48 48804	Missouri	89.4	8.6	18,170	91.9	151,700	25.5	13.3	1034	31.1	82.7	31.0	1.2
48 50256	Nacogdoches	67.3	18.2	11,553	46.0	97,500	22.7	13.0	614	40.4	70.3	14.0	8.6
48 50820	New Braunfels	78.1	13.8	18,559	65.1	136,400	21.6	13.1	823	26.7	81.8	22.0	6.7
48 52356	North Richland Hills	80.6	14.6	22,585	67.5	133,800	23.5	14.3	859	26.1	85.1	25.6	2.6
48 53388	Odessa	79.7	8.3	34,671	67.8	65,500	19.1	12.7	576	23.5	81.2	16.9	6.5
48 55080	Paris	78.9	9.0	10,025	58.3	63,200	21.4	16.9	539	28.5	76.3	16.9	16.0
48 56000	Pasadena	80.8	9.5	48,080	57.2	101,900	24.6	13.5	698	27.8	78.9	25.6	5.6
48 56340	Pearland	82.9	12.5	24,753	82.8	163,500	23.0	12.6	934	26.0	84.0	31.2	2.2
48 57176	Pflugerville	84.1	14.0	11,355	82.5	166,500	24.3	10.2	893	34.6	83.1	25.5	2.7
48 57200	Pharr	81.5	10.7	17,539	65.5	59,100	30.2	15.1	577	37.9	76.3	19.1	9.8
48 57980	Plainview	76.7	9.8	7,908	59.1	70,200	20.6	11.8	484	27.9	77.5	11.4	7.1
48 58016	Plano	84.0	11.0	92,356	67.4	201,700	22.6	11.1	929	25.7	81.9	26.3	2.7
48 58820	Port Arthur	85.9	5.8	19,547	58.7	46,100	21.9	13.5	519	28.4	76.7	20.0	13.4
48 61796	Richardson	82.2	12.3	38,168	66.1	167,700	22.9	12.3	957	28.9	81.0	22.9	3.5
48 62828	Rockwall	80.6	14.2	10,159	78.8	184,800	25.3	12.6	1222	25.8	79.2	33.0	0.5
48 63284	Rosenberg	78.3	14.4	7,954	59.9	94,600	23.0	15.5	724	28.4	77.1	24.8	9.0
48 63500	Round Rock	77.4	16.8	27,407	67.8	155,900	23.7	11.9	927	28.1	81.2	24.7	2.1
48 63572	Rowlett	86.2	10.4	17,997	90.4	153,600	25.0	13.0	1148	30.5	83.6	31.5	1.6
48 64472	San Angelo	77.5	11.5	35,177	65.2	80,900	21.4	13.7	625	29.5	76.9	15.3	6.9
48 65000	San Antonio	79.3	6.6	438,703	60.6	96,100	22.6	12.4	696	28.7	78.2	23.6	9.0
48 65036	San Benito	87.5	6.7	7,949	69.4	39,200	23.1	16.7	510	27.3	71.8	19.0	8.6
48 65516	San Juan	84.1	11.8	9,121	74.3	67,400	28.9	15.3	437	30.2	81.8	18.0	5.8
48 65600	San Marcos	49.6	27.1	14,976	26.6	114,500	25.6	14.7	716	41.4	75.7	20.9	6.3
48 66128	Schertz	79.1	18.0	9,086	79.7	141,600	21.2	10.8	780	24.7	84.4	24.2	2.0
48 66644	Seguin	81.9	9.1	8,043	58.7	87,600	22.7	12.4	619	28.8	78.4	18.6	11.2
48 67496	Sherman	76.9	12.0	14,297	57.8	84,500	23.6	15.2	713	27.6	77.5	19.3	6.7
48 68636	Socorro	-	-	8,276	80.5	68,500	29.6	15.0	427	36.4	81.0	23.0	7.8
48 69032	Southlake	88.5	10.0	7,585	96.9	425,500	23.2	13.8	1577	-	79.8	28.5	0.7
48 69596	Spring CDP	84.0	13.2	15,730	82.3	109,500	23.3	12.5	1124	29.3	81.3	31.3	1.1
48 70808	Sugar Land	86.3	11.3	21,593	83.0	208,000	22.6	11.1	1179	27.4	80.8	27.8	1.6
48 72176	Temple	82.5	9.1	22,782	60.6	99,600	22.0	13.4	649	29.5	84.8	16.1	7.4
48 72368	Texarkana	73.8	15.8	14,102	54.7	82,900	19.6	12.7	620	30.0	78.9	15.2	11.1
48 72392	Texas	82.1	9.5	16,645	61.5	86,700	23.0	14.9	647	29.9	81.7	20.4	8.3
48 72530	The Colony	80.6	13.5	12,050	74.3	137,500	22.7	16.7	1083	25.4	86.5	29.6	1.2
48 72656	The Woodlands CDP	83.5	14.3	22,326	74.7	203,900	20.8	10.8	943	28.0	80.2	29.3	4.4
48 74144	Tyler	75.0	12.0	33,236	57.9	114,500	23.2	13.7	704	34.9	79.7	17.4	8.5
48 74492	University Park	79.8	20.1	7,279	77.5	838,300	27.6	12.4	1389	30.7	77.6	16.4	2.5
48 75428	Victoria	73.5	9.9	23,412	58.5	86,900	21.8	13.1	638	28.4	76.6	18.4	9.7
48 76000	Waco	75.4	11.9	41,484	48.4	77,600	23.8	14.5	677	36.0	78.0	15.9	9.2
48 76672	Watauga	84.4	15.1	7,744	80.2	98,700	22.2	13.6	1139	27.5	87.7	27.7	1.3
48 76816	Waxahachie	68.6	18.2	8,608	56.7	119,600	27.4	16.5	852	40.4	81.6	23.2	3.3
48 76864	Weatherford	82.8	10.6	8,308	67.9	113,800	25.8	13.3	748	30.0	82.4	22.4	5.3
48 77272	Weslaco	86.1	7.2	11,320	68.9	53,500	28.6	14.0	468	35.6	73.9	18.0	11.5
48 79000	Wichita Falls	72.5	14.0	38,530	59.2	84,000	22.4	13.3	643	32.6	77.8	14.8	7.4
48 80356	Wylie	81.2	13.0	9,977	82.8	147,600	25.6	19.4	993	28.3	77.5	33.0	1.3
49 00000	**Utah**	79.5	15.0	812,604	71.9	189,700	24.2	9.3	719	27.6	75.4	20.9	4.2
49 01310	American Fork	84.6	10.8	7,185	78.7	192,100	22.7	8.0	767	23.4	79.8	21.6	1.3
49 07690	Bountiful	86.6	10.4	13,966	77.6	213,200	21.9	7.6	710	23.9	78.8	20.0	2.8

1. $1,000,001 is the top code symbolizing a median value over one million dollars.
2. 50.1 is the top code symbolizing a median gross rent as a percentage of household income of 50.1 percent or more.

Table C-4. Cities — Where: Migration, Housing, and Transportation, 2005–2007—Continued

STATE Place code	STATE City	Percent who lived in the same house one year ago	Percent who did not live in city one year ago	Total occupied housing units	Percent owner-occupied housing units	Median value of owner-occupied housing units (dollars)[1]	Median selected monthly owner costs as a percentage of household income		Median gross rent (dollars)	Median gross rent as a percentage of household income[2]	Percent of workers who drove alone to work	Mean travel time to work (minutes)	Percent of occupied housing units with no vehicle available
							With a mortgage	Without a mortgage					
ACS table number:		C07204	C07204	B25003	B25003	B25077	B25092	B25092	B25064	B25071	C08301	B08013/ C08012	C25045
		1	2	3	4	5	6	7	8	9	10	11	12
	Utah—Cont.												
49 11320	Cedar	59.7	24.1	8,768	49.9	213,500	23.9	10.9	580	27.0	75.4	12.8	6.2
49 13850	Clearfield	64.8	29.8	8,605	56.1	133,000	26.0	11.5	707	30.8	79.6	21.8	7.9
49 16270	Cottonwood Heights	82.7	16.6	12,138	72.4	275,200	22.7	10.6	851	29.8	81.9	20.6	2.0
49 20120	Draper	80.8	17.9	9,677	80.5	387,300	26.1	10.5	952	27.5	80.5	21.8	1.8
49 36070	Holladay	83.3	15.3	10,019	73.6	318,600	23.5	10.5	820	23.2	80.8	20.1	4.5
49 40360	Kaysville	84.2	10.8	6,650	86.9	217,500	22.5	8.3	664	22.8	79.2	24.5	2.3
49 40470	Kearns CDP	76.1	18.8	9,991	86.4	138,800	27.1	11.0	937	27.8	75.2	25.8	1.1
49 43660	Layton	83.2	12.8	20,487	72.9	179,700	23.2	7.8	744	24.2	80.4	22.2	3.9
49 44320	Lehi	84.3	12.5	8,997	83.1	223,500	24.1	9.3	879	26.8	75.4	22.8	1.9
49 45860	Logan	59.3	21.6	14,652	45.0	143,600	23.7	7.7	589	29.0	65.7	12.1	5.9
49 47290	Magna CDP	86.0	9.5	7,192	82.0	138,600	25.4	9.6	987	31.7	74.3	23.7	3.0
49 49710	Midvale	73.4	23.0	11,538	49.0	173,800	24.2	11.9	716	25.8	72.7	20.9	6.3
49 50150	Millcreek CDP	72.6	27.2	12,543	49.0	192,100	27.4	9.7	769	24.7	72.4	21.5	8.6
49 53230	Murray	77.8	20.4	17,411	68.8	209,000	25.2	11.1	771	25.6	78.2	20.0	3.6
49 55980	Ogden	76.6	10.2	28,705	60.9	117,500	23.7	11.8	613	27.8	76.2	21.2	9.6
49 57300	Orem	84.1	10.0	25,846	63.3	193,100	23.6	9.0	712	26.0	74.0	18.2	2.2
49 60930	Pleasant Grove	81.2	15.1	8,436	77.8	223,700	25.1	7.7	769	24.4	75.2	20.9	1.8
49 62470	Provo	53.9	27.2	31,100	44.3	187,200	25.4	8.9	641	32.5	63.4	16.3	4.7
49 64340	Riverton	86.5	11.5	8,962	90.9	256,500	23.1	8.3	1127	25.2	79.1	24.6	1.2
49 65110	Roy	81.3	16.2	11,962	83.7	141,800	23.6	7.0	846	29.2	81.0	21.6	1.5
49 65330	St. George	71.6	18.3	24,415	64.8	241,100	25.2	9.7	872	29.9	77.0	16.7	4.3
49 67000	Salt Lake	74.6	12.2	72,901	52.4	205,700	24.8	11.1	661	28.3	69.8	18.9	10.9
49 67440	Sandy	86.0	10.7	27,803	83.0	243,000	22.6	8.6	856	27.5	78.8	21.5	2.3
49 70850	South Jordan	85.4	11.7	10,675	89.6	332,200	24.6	9.8	1192	26.8	80.8	23.3	1.2
49 71070	South Salt Lake	56.6	43.0	7,900	38.5	147,700	27.3	8.5	653	30.7	60.8	20.8	12.6
49 71290	Spanish Fork	79.3	12.9	7,695	75.1	186,400	24.8	10.9	782	25.9	72.6	19.1	0.8
49 72280	Springville	83.6	11.6	7,607	74.9	179,500	26.2	9.9	725	27.6	79.9	18.3	1.4
49 74810	Syracuse	83.2	16.5	5,012	91.7	225,000	23.9	8.7	1105	21.3	80.9	25.3	1.0
49 75360	Taylorsville	77.1	19.1	19,590	71.2	165,400	23.9	8.6	790	28.5	79.9	21.0	3.2
49 76680	Tooele	83.8	10.5	9,755	75.2	145,000	23.2	9.9	802	27.3	69.4	29.0	4.1
49 82950	West Jordan	84.1	12.8	27,747	80.7	196,900	26.2	8.3	857	27.3	78.9	23.6	1.9
49 83470	West Valley	78.5	17.4	35,998	69.7	156,300	25.5	10.9	762	32.0	75.8	23.0	5.5
50 00000	**Vermont**	85.0	12.4	250,871	72.2	191,500	25.0	16.2	733	29.9	75.0	21.2	6.1
50 10675	Burlington	70.0	17.9	15,142	43.7	243,700	26.6	17.7	817	34.4	55.9	16.3	12.4
51 00000	**Virginia**	83.1	13.6	2,909,223	69.7	238,600	24.0	10.9	875	28.2	77.2	26.8	6.2
51 01000	Alexandria	79.1	15.3	62,309	47.5	527,300	24.5	12.2	1211	27.0	63.4	28.9	10.9
51 01912	Annandale CDP	84.7	12.4	19,663	69.2	543,900	23.9	8.4	1364	29.8	74.4	29.7	5.4
51 03000	Arlington CDP	79.7	12.7	89,525	51.1	585,000	23.3	10.7	1350	26.1	54.0	25.6	11.1
51 04088	Bailey's Crossroads CDP	76.3	23.7	8,734	46.3	355,700	24.3	14.6	1131	29.5	55.7	31.8	15.1
51 07784	Blacksburg town	50.2	28.6	12,741	33.3	227,400	21.3	6.9	716	45.1	69.5	14.3	3.4
51 11464	Burke CDP	86.8	12.0	19,463	87.5	509,300	22.2	7.6	1819	27.3	77.2	33.7	2.0
51 13720	Cave Spring CDP	82.9	17.1	11,421	71.3	189,400	19.7	10.7	705	24.5	-	18.3	2.9
51 14440	Centreville CDP	82.2	13.0	18,241	74.2	426,400	27.4	8.6	1430	27.6	78.0	35.0	1.6
51 14744	Chantilly CDP	83.7	15.9	16,099	79.8	522,500	25.4	10.1	1481	24.0	75.2	31.9	2.6
51 14968	Charlottesville	68.1	26.2	16,694	46.0	242,700	28.3	14.6	791	34.6	60.5	15.2	14.7
51 16000	Chesapeake	85.3	9.7	77,808	75.1	241,600	25.6	11.6	903	28.7	84.9	23.7	4.3
51 16096	Chester CDP	83.8	13.8	8,005	70.9	186,600	22.8	9.4	832	27.5	86.5	22.2	2.1
51 21088	Dale CDP	82.2	15.9	21,009	77.5	367,100	29.2	8.7	1274	30.2	67.8	41.3	3.2
51 21344	Danville	81.0	9.4	19,972	55.6	84,200	21.8	12.8	527	29.4	80.2	16.1	17.6
51 26496	Fairfax	86.5	10.4	8,311	76.6	523,100	24.8	8.5	1430	27.5	76.2	30.6	4.5
51 29552	Franconia CDP	81.7	18.3	13,845	74.0	471,800	24.1	8.2	1697	26.6	70.2	34.0	3.7
51 29744	Fredericksburg	74.6	18.7	8,560	37.5	301,800	23.0	9.3	954	34.8	70.1	27.9	13.3
51 33584	Groveton CDP	80.2	19.8	7,641	61.2	463,800	26.2	14.1	1137	31.9	65.0	32.8	8.2
51 35000	Hampton	81.8	10.4	54,650	60.4	164,900	25.0	13.6	825	28.5	81.4	22.2	6.8
51 35624	Harrisonburg	62.0	36.2	13,920	39.2	181,200	21.5	9.3	694	30.4	73.2	14.1	8.5
51 36648	Herndon town	83.3	13.5	6,341	68.9	449,000	25.9	6.8	1321	38.0	67.3	24.5	11.1
51 38424	Hopewell	82.6	10.3	8,740	51.4	108,200	22.9	11.5	691	25.8	82.6	21.2	13.3
51 40584	Jefferson CDP	84.3	15.7	9,565	70.6	482,400	26.6	11.7	1248	27.4	72.7	26.6	7.2
51 43432	Lake Ridge CDP	80.5	19.2	12,128	78.5	378,000	24.3	7.4	1429	25.0	69.8	38.8	1.7
51 44984	Leesburg town	82.7	11.2	12,165	79.9	473,900	28.5	11.5	1218	32.4	82.1	30.3	3.6
51 45957	Linton Hall CDP	78.9	21.1	6,194	95.5	510,600	28.4	10.1	2001	34.2	78.3	46.3	1.4
51 47064	Lorton CDP	75.4	21.9	8,306	71.1	467,900	29.2	8.0	1496	30.3	75.5	33.2	2.7
51 47672	Lynchburg	77.4	14.4	25,903	59.4	120,800	22.6	11.7	603	26.8	79.1	16.6	14.6
51 48376	McLean CDP	90.8	6.5	14,678	89.6	863,700	22.6	12.0	2001	28.8	76.3	26.3	1.6
51 48952	Manassas	80.2	17.6	11,703	69.7	377,600	24.8	12.3	1153	34.7	74.3	32.1	4.5
51 50856	Mechanicsville CDP	87.9	9.5	13,353	79.6	220,100	22.3	9.2	942	23.5	86.7	24.6	3.9
51 54144	Mount Vernon CDP	88.5	11.5	11,077	68.1	455,800	28.8	12.0	1245	28.8	68.0	34.2	6.9
51 55752	Newington CDP	92.9	7.1	7,292	80.4	509,900	23.1	7.9	1760	24.8	70.6	34.9	1.8
51 56000	Newport News	76.2	13.7	73,274	52.6	172,700	24.6	12.1	808	30.0	78.8	21.9	10.0
51 57000	Norfolk	75.7	13.2	85,129	47.0	181,400	27.1	14.2	765	29.9	67.5	21.3	11.9
51 58472	Oakton CDP	81.0	17.8	12,488	68.0	612,800	24.0	9.9	1429	26.8	63.1	30.5	3.9
51 61832	Petersburg	87.1	6.1	12,447	51.0	97,200	23.0	15.1	707	27.7	78.6	19.6	15.2
51 64000	Portsmouth	80.9	11.8	38,848	62.2	155,200	28.2	14.7	813	30.9	77.8	23.0	9.6
51 66672	Reston CDP	83.1	12.6	23,348	71.7	487,400	23.4	10.4	1285	28.7	78.7	27.0	3.6

1. $1,000,001 is the top code symbolizing a median value over one million dollars.
2. 50.1 is the top code symbolizing a median gross rent as a percentage of household income of 50.1 percent or more.

STATE Place code	STATE City	Percent who lived in the same house one year ago	Percent who did not live in city one year ago	Total occupied housing units	Percent owner-occupied housing units	Median value of owner-occupied housing units (dollars)[1]	Median selected monthly owner costs as a percentage of household income		Median gross rent (dollars)	Median gross rent as a percentage of household income[2]	Percent of workers who drove alone to work	Mean travel time to work (minutes)	Percent of occupied housing units with no vehicle available
							With a mortgage	Without a mortgage					
	ACS table number:	C07204	C07204	B25003	B25003	B25077	B25092	B25092	B25064	B25071	C08301	B08013/C08012	C25045
		1	2	3	4	5	6	7	8	9	10	11	12
	Virginia—Cont.												
51 67000	Richmond	78.1	11.1	81,611	47.7	179,100	25.9	15.1	742	31.3	71.8	20.8	19.0
51 68000	Roanoke	81.4	8.7	41,822	59.2	116,000	23.7	13.4	601	28.1	81.3	18.1	12.6
51 70000	Salem	80.5	14.6	9,680	69.6	146,100	21.9	10.8	663	25.6	83.5	17.8	5.4
51 74592	Springfield CDP	83.5	14.2	12,000	62.9	487,400	28.8	13.2	1519	36.6	69.7	31.4	9.4
51 75216	Staunton	78.7	19.3	9,712	59.5	141,200	22.3	11.2	581	28.5	80.4	18.8	7.7
51 76432	Suffolk	83.5	9.4	29,858	71.3	229,900	24.5	11.6	720	29.8	81.9	27.4	6.5
51 79560	Tuckahoe CDP	85.0	15.0	18,660	67.8	267,700	21.6	10.0	912	25.8	81.4	22.0	4.1
51 82000	Virginia Beach	80.3	10.3	161,814	68.6	253,500	25.5	11.9	1054	29.8	80.8	22.5	3.1
51 83680	Waynesboro	81.6	13.8	8,595	61.5	153,300	21.9	8.4	611	29.3	84.4	19.8	8.5
51 84976	West Springfield CDP	85.8	14.2	10,528	85.5	488,400	24.8	10.1	1623	28.9	72.3	31.1	0.9
51 86720	Winchester	77.8	18.6	10,026	50.8	247,200	23.1	12.8	852	27.9	79.0	19.7	7.9
51 87312	Woodbridge CDP	75.5	18.8	11,371	58.9	361,500	28.8	11.9	1187	27.0	71.3	36.7	2.3
53 00000	**Washington**	80.0	14.6	2,472,477	65.6	261,200	26.1	12.1	799	29.1	73.1	25.3	6.5
53 03180	Auburn	76.2	15.5	19,430	55.6	240,400	28.5	13.9	755	31.1	74.1	29.4	11.2
53 03736	Bainbridge Island	88.5	7.7	8,929	81.1	573,400	25.7	13.6	971	31.9	45.5	41.2	4.3
53 05210	Bellevue	78.8	15.3	49,391	58.7	511,900	24.5	11.2	1059	24.9	69.7	21.9	5.7
53 05280	Bellingham	69.7	16.3	31,830	45.1	292,000	27.0	13.4	750	34.6	69.4	17.2	10.5
53 07380	Bothell	83.5	14.5	14,040	65.5	359,900	25.4	13.7	1000	28.9	73.9	26.7	6.5
53 07695	Bremerton	76.2	15.7	14,866	45.3	197,000	27.0	12.0	677	31.1	63.8	26.4	12.7
53 08850	Burien	80.8	16.5	13,104	53.6	323,700	26.5	13.8	795	30.9	73.6	25.6	11.7
53 10372	Cascade-Fairwood CDP	79.6	20.4	14,351	71.6	319,100	26.9	11.8	1064	28.9	75.5	30.9	4.0
53 14940	Cottage Lake CDP	91.6	8.4	8,450	94.0	573,600	24.5	10.7	1464	25.0	76.6	27.1	0.4
53 17635	Des Moines	75.7	19.3	10,907	66.7	290,400	27.7	12.3	846	25.8	72.8	26.4	2.6
53 19515	East Hill-Meridian CDP	85.6	14.4	10,086	78.7	304,100	26.9	12.4	966	28.9	73.3	28.1	2.9
53 20750	Edmonds	84.3	11.2	17,962	67.6	398,200	28.2	14.7	863	28.9	74.2	29.0	4.6
53 22640	Everett	71.5	15.5	39,975	46.5	256,100	29.5	17.1	782	29.4	72.9	25.4	9.5
53 23515	Federal Way	80.4	12.2	33,110	59.6	279,500	27.1	11.5	850	30.3	68.8	29.9	7.4
53 33380	Inglewood-Finn Hill CDP	80.7	19.3	9,749	77.7	411,400	26.1	12.5	992	29.0	72.7	27.3	1.9
53 33805	Issaquah	78.2	19.4	10,621	66.8	407,200	27.8	17.2	1243	27.3	75.1	26.5	5.7
53 35170	Kenmore	87.8	9.3	8,084	74.6	400,600	23.8	13.1	858	29.2	77.0	29.2	4.5
53 35275	Kennewick	74.7	14.0	22,735	63.1	144,300	22.7	10.1	711	31.2	78.2	22.2	7.4
53 35415	Kent	73.6	20.9	33,329	51.4	281,300	26.8	12.4	838	27.8	73.7	28.9	8.6
53 35940	Kirkland	78.2	15.0	22,175	59.4	491,000	26.4	17.1	1107	26.1	71.7	23.1	5.1
53 36745	Lacey	77.7	17.6	14,304	49.5	216,400	25.6	12.3	826	28.2	81.7	20.9	6.9
53 38038	Lakewood	71.4	22.9	23,989	50.7	222,800	27.1	12.1	726	27.5	75.6	24.2	7.6
53 40245	Longview	73.5	11.8	15,019	56.0	155,800	24.5	11.0	614	33.9	78.5	19.6	11.6
53 40840	Lynnwood	79.1	14.5	13,597	56.2	309,300	29.1	14.8	791	31.9	69.7	29.1	9.2
53 43955	Marysville	77.7	17.8	13,332	64.4	267,400	28.6	16.8	876	28.3	73.9	28.4	5.4
53 45005	Mercer Island	84.8	10.5	9,292	77.3	878,600	21.5	11.8	1418	29.9	71.5	21.6	4.6
53 47490	Mountlake Terrace	83.8	14.9	8,486	63.6	264,500	28.6	12.3	896	32.6	75.5	30.6	4.4
53 47560	Mount Vernon	75.7	12.7	10,573	57.0	215,600	30.3	15.8	803	29.3	75.2	21.5	8.8
53 47735	Mukilteo	80.8	13.5	7,988	70.4	432,300	23.1	11.8	963	25.8	82.3	25.9	2.6
53 49665	North Creek CDP	81.1	18.9	10,930	73.5	360,500	25.7	13.1	1160	26.8	76.8	30.3	1.4
53 49992	North Marysville CDP	88.8	11.2	7,312	82.1	258,800	29.3	12.8	1178	27.6	76.2	30.0	2.4
53 50360	Oak Harbor	74.9	15.0	7,730	55.4	220,400	27.9	12.5	841	32.8	77.2	16.8	4.3
53 51300	Olympia	73.4	13.3	19,767	50.2	238,700	24.2	13.0	799	30.8	73.5	19.5	9.3
53 52765	Paine Field-Lake Stickney CDP	69.5	30.5	10,786	44.9	229,800	31.3	13.1	869	29.3	69.4	28.0	7.3
53 53335	Parkland CDP	72.0	27.6	10,344	48.0	202,600	28.1	13.6	816	29.4	76.5	25.1	6.2
53 53545	Pasco	83.8	8.2	13,842	66.2	131,900	24.9	10.9	575	30.6	68.8	21.1	5.2
53 54215	Picnic Point-North Lynnwood CDP	74.7	25.3	10,716	58.9	331,000	27.3	12.1	1068	26.8	77.6	28.0	5.2
53 56625	Pullman	49.4	33.1	9,598	33.1	188,600	22.9	10.0	593	50.1	52.9	12.7	6.5
53 56695	Puyallup	73.8	15.9	14,475	52.5	269,300	27.0	11.9	903	29.4	78.1	27.0	7.2
53 57535	Redmond	73.3	19.7	23,544	53.6	419,900	24.7	12.4	1140	23.7	72.3	20.4	4.7
53 57745	Renton	77.2	16.9	25,524	53.4	312,500	27.4	15.7	860	28.3	72.1	28.6	7.3
53 58235	Richland	80.4	13.1	16,844	68.5	174,000	20.8	8.5	704	25.8	82.1	17.8	3.7
53 61115	Sammamish	87.0	9.5	14,875	89.6	589,400	23.8	9.3	1527	27.6	76.0	30.8	0.9
53 62288	SeaTac	78.5	16.7	8,665	56.8	257,100	29.3	14.2	723	30.1	73.3	22.8	8.8
53 63000	Seattle	77.2	10.4	260,760	51.1	439,500	27.1	13.4	860	28.3	55.5	24.5	16.0
53 63052	Seattle Hill-Silver Firs CDP	86.1	13.9	12,746	91.0	358,400	26.3	9.9	1236	26.7	75.6	31.4	2.2
53 63960	Shoreline	84.3	11.6	21,348	68.7	346,300	28.6	13.2	982	31.6	67.6	26.4	5.6
53 65922	South Hill CDP	79.9	20.1	15,837	79.2	278,000	25.3	12.3	1084	30.6	80.3	33.8	1.7
53 66255	Spanaway CDP	73.4	22.6	9,303	68.9	203,200	26.6	14.0	1044	24.8	81.7	33.8	3.2
53 67000	Spokane	75.7	9.6	86,848	57.6	142,100	24.6	12.9	626	31.0	76.4	19.1	9.7
53 67167	Spokane Valley	80.1	16.4	35,550	64.6	157,300	24.2	10.3	668	30.8	79.6	19.3	6.9
53 70000	Tacoma	77.2	11.3	77,806	54.8	224,100	28.8	14.9	763	30.9	75.5	24.7	9.9
53 73465	University Place	76.6	19.2	13,605	55.7	327,700	26.6	14.6	797	31.2	77.6	24.7	3.2
53 74060	Vancouver	76.8	11.4	62,958	55.1	225,800	26.0	12.0	786	30.2	78.5	22.5	7.3
53 75775	Walla Walla	69.7	18.9	11,339	53.1	147,600	25.3	13.1	623	32.7	71.2	12.8	9.5
53 77105	Wenatchee	78.7	9.7	11,899	61.8	169,800	25.1	13.0	615	28.1	78.2	15.5	7.9
53 80010	Yakima	75.4	9.7	30,703	55.5	132,600	25.4	12.4	606	29.6	75.4	17.6	9.3
54 00000	**West Virginia**	86.9	10.9	738,943	74.9	89,500	20.1	9.8	516	28.6	80.8	25.3	9.1
54 14600	Charleston	81.2	11.7	24,560	57.9	121,100	20.0	11.1	549	28.7	77.2	15.7	20.7
54 39460	Huntington	76.7	11.0	20,733	56.1	79,000	21.1	10.8	553	34.6	75.3	17.0	18.4

1. $1,000,001 is the top code symbolizing a median value over one million dollars.
2. 50.1 is the top code symbolizing a median gross rent as a percentage of household income of 50.1 percent or more.

Table C-4. Cities — Where: Migration, Housing, and Transportation, 2005–2007—*Continued*

STATE Place code	STATE City	Percent who lived in the same house one year ago	Percent who did not live in city one year ago	Total occupied housing units	Percent owner-occupied housing units	Median value of owner-occupied housing units (dollars)[1]	Median selected monthly owner costs as a percentage of household income		Median gross rent (dollars)	Median gross rent as a percentage of household income[2]	Percent of workers who drove alone to work	Mean travel time to work (minutes)	Percent of occupied housing units with no vehicle available
							With a mortgage	Without a mortgage					
ACS table number:		C07204	C07204	B25003	B25003	B25077	B25092	B25092	B25064	B25071	C08301	B08013/ C08012	C25045
		1	2	3	4	5	6	7	8	9	10	11	12
	West Virginia—Cont.												
54 55756	Morgantown	56.9	29.9	8,715	49.3	140,100	22.0	11.6	594	47.6	66.4	18.3	10.0
54 62140	Parkersburg	77.7	13.4	14,241	59.9	81,200	22.9	10.9	558	35.4	75.6	17.9	14.9
54 86452	Wheeling	86.3	6.6	13,816	63.9	84,200	19.6	10.5	459	29.5	74.1	16.8	17.0
55 00000	**Wisconsin**	84.3	9.7	2,235,246	70.3	162,000	24.4	14.1	675	27.9	80.1	20.9	6.5
55 02375	Appleton	81.8	9.5	28,606	70.1	133,300	23.5	12.7	599	28.7	83.7	16.7	6.1
55 06500	Beloit	83.1	6.1	13,632	65.4	85,200	24.6	17.7	637	33.8	76.0	19.2	8.6
55 10025	Brookfield	90.8	6.6	14,463	86.2	292,700	22.5	13.4	1203	28.5	86.4	19.9	1.9
55 11950	Caledonia village	88.9	10.9	9,702	82.2	198,400	25.7	12.3	776	19.7	88.1	22.6	1.7
55 19775	De Pere	83.9	12.0	9,219	62.8	163,800	23.9	13.4	720	27.4	86.2	15.2	7.2
55 22300	Eau Claire	73.8	12.0	26,072	58.7	130,800	23.3	12.9	610	29.5	80.1	16.4	6.8
55 25950	Fitchburg	78.4	20.7	9,118	57.4	283,700	24.8	9.0	801	27.5	83.0	19.7	3.5
55 26275	Fond du Lac	77.4	9.1	17,102	61.5	117,800	23.6	13.7	598	27.9	82.3	17.8	8.6
55 27300	Franklin	83.1	13.9	12,747	81.5	220,800	25.2	16.1	817	24.3	88.8	23.5	4.5
55 31000	Green Bay	82.3	6.7	40,510	58.0	129,300	24.2	13.8	604	28.4	83.3	17.8	8.3
55 31175	Greenfield	85.7	11.1	16,475	65.2	180,300	24.1	16.0	749	27.7	85.9	21.2	6.3
55 37825	Janesville	85.2	6.3	24,942	71.7	129,800	22.7	13.5	663	25.4	86.0	19.1	5.1
55 39225	Kenosha	82.0	7.0	35,564	62.0	158,700	26.3	16.6	718	29.1	80.1	23.6	8.5
55 40775	La Crosse	70.6	12.8	21,221	52.4	115,100	23.4	14.8	547	29.3	73.3	15.1	12.2
55 48000	Madison	70.3	12.1	91,807	53.0	210,300	25.6	12.4	801	30.7	65.4	18.4	11.1
55 48500	Manitowoc	84.9	7.4	14,203	68.9	102,800	22.3	13.4	518	26.0	82.5	15.8	8.6
55 51000	Menomonee Falls village	89.4	8.1	13,653	79.4	224,300	23.2	14.9	872	29.9	88.2	19.6	3.8
55 51150	Mequon	89.9	7.9	8,460	91.2	349,200	23.3	14.0	1284	28.9	83.6	23.5	2.5
55 53000	Milwaukee	78.4	6.0	224,817	49.0	133,200	27.6	17.8	690	32.2	71.7	21.3	17.8
55 54875	Mount Pleasant village	89.6	10.3	10,365	76.8	189,400	24.3	14.6	683	25.4	90.7	18.0	3.1
55 55275	Muskego	90.5	7.3	8,310	84.9	255,300	25.1	14.9	954	23.8	88.8	25.2	1.8
55 55750	Neenah	85.6	11.1	10,187	70.1	122,600	21.9	13.0	615	23.6	86.9	17.7	5.1
55 56375	New Berlin	90.1	8.0	15,189	81.3	232,900	22.5	13.3	932	24.2	87.6	22.3	3.6
55 58800	Oak Creek	85.9	10.2	13,525	63.9	206,000	23.3	14.5	827	26.5	83.7	22.6	3.1
55 60500	Oshkosh	73.6	11.7	25,669	59.2	116,500	24.0	15.0	595	28.3	79.9	16.4	8.9
55 66000	Racine	84.9	5.1	31,163	59.2	124,700	25.5	14.5	631	33.5	80.1	20.0	11.8
55 72975	Sheboygan	82.0	6.7	20,749	62.1	111,200	24.2	14.1	581	26.6	78.9	14.4	10.3
55 75125	South Milwaukee	87.4	8.0	8,839	63.2	161,800	24.3	15.5	676	27.8	81.1	23.4	7.2
55 77200	Stevens Point	64.5	17.4	9,552	55.5	108,900	23.1	12.1	615	30.7	71.1	14.3	3.7
55 78600	Sun Prairie	80.3	15.6	10,495	67.0	203,900	24.4	14.2	792	27.0	87.0	22.5	3.4
55 78650	Superior	81.7	9.8	11,480	63.9	108,200	20.5	15.2	543	29.3	85.0	15.3	8.5
55 83975	Watertown	86.2	5.5	9,029	63.7	156,100	25.3	14.4	671	29.0	83.0	20.0	5.0
55 84250	Waukesha	80.6	12.1	27,688	58.9	198,700	24.2	14.9	764	28.5	83.0	20.6	8.6
55 84475	Wausau	84.3	8.3	16,264	63.2	102,000	23.5	15.1	571	26.4	80.9	14.9	8.2
55 84675	Wauwatosa	88.4	9.8	20,832	68.8	222,300	22.8	13.3	876	29.2	85.4	17.6	6.7
55 85300	West Allis	86.3	9.9	27,447	58.9	156,100	25.2	18.4	681	28.0	85.1	20.7	11.9
55 85350	West Bend	81.5	9.8	12,530	64.1	171,800	23.4	17.3	717	28.4	82.8	23.4	6.2
56 00000	**Wyoming**	80.3	12.6	205,422	70.0	150,500	21.1	9.2	607	23.3	75.1	17.9	3.5
56 13150	Casper	81.0	9.4	20,515	68.0	147,400	20.7	9.4	563	25.2	82.7	16.2	4.8
56 13900	Cheyenne	78.7	8.8	22,929	64.4	150,000	23.3	10.5	639	25.6	85.0	13.7	4.6
56 31855	Gillette	80.1	8.1	8,441	69.9	168,800	19.4	8.0	687	18.4	77.5	20.3	3.6
56 45050	Laramie	67.5	19.6	11,787	54.5	164,300	22.8	7.9	610	33.9	64.4	11.1	3.8

1. $1,000,001 is the top code symbolizing a median value over one million dollars.
2. 50.1 is the top code symbolizing a median gross rent as a percentage of household income of 50.1 percent or more.

Appendixes

A. Glossary
B. Source Notes and Explanations
C. Geographic Concepts and Codes

APPENDIX A:
GLOSSARY

Accuracy. One of four key dimensions of survey quality. Accuracy refers to the difference between the survey estimate and the true (unknown) value. Attributes are measured in terms of sources of error (for example, coverage, sampling, nonresponse, measurement, and processing).

American Community Survey Alert. This periodic electronic newsletter informs data users and other interested parties about news, events, data releases, congressional actions, and other developments associated with the ACS. See <http://www.census.gov/acs/www/Special/Alerts/Latest.htm>.

American FactFinder (AFF). An electronic system for access to and dissemination of Census Bureau data on the Internet. AFF offers prepackaged data products and user-selected data tables and maps from Census 2000, the 1990 Census of Population and Housing, the 1997 and 2002 Economic Censuses, the Population Estimates Program, annual economic surveys, and the ACS.

Balance. A consolidated city results from the merger of a county with its principal incorporated place. The "balance" is that portion of a consolidated city minus the semi-independent places that remain.

Block group. A subdivision of a census tract (or, prior to 2000, a block numbering area), a block group is a cluster of blocks having the same first digit of their four-digit identifying number within a census tract.

Census Designated Places(CDPs). CDPs are closely settled, named, unincorporated communities that contain a mixture of residential, commercial, and retail areas similar to those found in incorporated places of similar sizes. They allow for the tabulation of data for places that would otherwise not be included.

Census geography. A collective term referring to the types of geographic areas used by the Census Bureau in its data collection and tabulation operations, including their structure, designations, and relationships to one another. See <http://www.census.gov/geo/www/index.html>.

Census tract. A small, relatively permanent statistical subdivision of a county delineated by a local committee of census data users for the purpose of presenting data. Census tract boundaries normally follow visible features, but may follow governmental unit boundaries and other nonvisible features; they always nest within counties. Designed to be relatively homogeneous units with respect to population characteristics, economic status, and living conditions at the time of establishment, census tracts average about 4,000 inhabitants.

Coefficient of variation (CV). The ratio of the standard error (square root of the variance) to the value being estimated, usually expressed in terms of a percentage (also known as the relative standard deviation). The lower the CV, the higher the relative reliability of the estimate.

Comparison profile. Comparison profiles are available from the American Community Survey for 1-year estimates beginning in 2007. These tables are available for the United States, the 50 states, the District of Columbia, and geographic areas with a population of more than 65,000.

Confidence interval. The sample estimate and its standard error permit the construction of a confidence interval that represents the degree of uncertainty about the estimate. A 90-percent confidence interval can be interpreted roughly as providing 90 percent certainty that the interval defined by the upper and lower bounds contains the true value of the characteristic.

Confidentiality. The guarantee made by law (Title 13, United States Code) to individuals who provide census information, regarding nondisclosure of that information to others.

Consolidated city. The U.S. Census Bureau refers to a governmental unit for which the functions of an incorporated place and its county or minor civil division have merged as a consolidated government. If one or more other incorporated places continue to function as separate governmental units even though they are part of a consolidated government, the Census Bureau refers to the primary incorporated place as the "balance."

Consumer Price Index (CPI). The CPI program of the Bureau of Labor Statistics produces monthly data on changes in the prices paid by urban consumers for a representative basket of goods and services.

Controlled. During the ACS weighting process, the intercensal population and housing estimates are used as survey controls. Weights are adjusted so that ACS estimates conform to these controls.

Current Population Survey (CPS). The CPS is a monthly survey of about 50,000 households conducted by the Census Bureau for the Bureau of Labor Statistics. The CPS is the primary source of information on the labor force characteristics of the U.S. population.

Current residence. The concept used in the ACS to determine who should be considered a resident of a sample address. Everyone who is currently living or staying at a sample address is considered a resident of that address, except people staying there for 2 months or less. People who have established residence at the sample unit and are away for only a short period of time are also considered to be current residents.

Custom tabulations. The Census Bureau offers a wide variety of general purpose data products from the ACS. These products are designed to meet the needs of the majority of data users and contain predefined sets of data for standard census geographic areas, including both political and statistical geography. These products are available on the American FactFinder and the ACS Web site. For users with data needs not met through the general purpose products, the Census Bureau offers "custom" tabulations on a cost-reimbursable basis, with the American Community Survey Custom Tabulation program. Custom tabulations are created by tabulating data from ACS microdata files. They vary in size, complexity, and cost depending on the needs of the sponsoring client.

Data profiles. Detailed tables that provide summaries by social, economic, and housing characteristics. There is a new ACS demographic and housing units profile that should be used if official estimates from the Population Estimates Program are not available.

Detailed tables. Approximately 1,200 different tables that contain basic distributions of characteristics. These tables provide the most detailed data and are the basis for other ACS products.

Disclosure avoidance (DA). Statistical methods used in the tabulation of data prior to releasing data products to ensure the confidentiality of responses. See Confidentiality.

Estimates. Numerical values obtained from a statistical sample and assigned to a population parameter. Data produced from the ACS interviews are collected from samples of housing units. These data are used to produce estimates of the actual figures that would have been obtained by interviewing the entire population using the same methodology.

File Transfer Protocol (FTP) site. A Web site that allows data files to be downloaded from the Census Bureau Web site.

Five-year estimates. Estimates based on 5 years of ACS data. These estimates reflect the characteristics of a geographic area over the entire 5-year period and will be published for all geographic areas down to the census block group level.

Geographic comparison tables. More than 80 single-variable tables comparing key indicators for geographies other than states.

Geographic summary level. A geographic summary level specifies the content and the hierarchical relationships of the geographic elements that are required to tabulate and summarize data. For example, the county summary level specifies the state-county hierarchy. Thus, both the state code and the county code are required to uniquely identify a county in the United States or Puerto Rico.

Group quarters (GQ) facilities. A GQ facility is a place where people live or stay that is normally owned or managed by an entity or organization providing housing and/or services for the residents. These services may include custodial or medical care, as well as other types of assistance. Residency is commonly restricted to those receiving these services. People living in GQ facilities are usually not related to each other. The ACS collects data from people living in both housing units and GQ facilities.

Group quarters (GQ) population. The number of persons residing in GQ facilities.

Item allocation rates. Allocation is a method of imputation used when values for missing or inconsistent items cannot be derived from the existing response record. In these cases, the imputation must be based on other techniques such as using answers from other people in the household, other responding housing units, or people believed to have similar characteristics. Such donors are reflected in a table referred to as an allocation matrix. The rate is the percentage of times this method is used.

Margin of error (MOE). Some ACS products provide an MOE instead of confidence intervals. An MOE is the difference between an estimate and its upper or lower confidence bounds. Confidence bounds can be created by adding the margin of error to the estimate (for the upper bound) and subtracting the margin of error from the estimate (for the lower bound). All published ACS margins of error are based on a 90-percent confidence level.

Multiyear estimates. Three- and five-year estimates based on multiple years of ACS data. Three-year estimates will be published for geographic areas with a population of 20,000 or more. Five-year estimates will be published for all geographic areas down to the census block group level.

Narrative profile. A data product that includes easy-to-read descriptions for a particular geography.

Nonsampling error. Total survey error can be classified into two categories—sampling error and nonsampling error. Nonsampling error includes measurement errors due to interviewers, respondents, instruments, and mode; nonresponse error; coverage error; and processing error.

Period estimates. An estimate based on information collected over a period of time. For ACS the period is either 1 year, 3 years, or 5 years.

Point-in-time estimates. An estimate based on one point in time. The decennial census long-form estimates for Census 2000 were based on information collected as of April 1, 2000.

Population Estimates Program. Official Census Bureau estimates of the population of the United States, states, metropolitan areas, cities and towns, and counties; also official Census Bureau estimates of housing units.

Public Use Microdata Area (PUMA). An area that defines the extent of territory for which the Census Bureau releases Public Use Microdata Sample (PUMS) records.

Public Use Microdata Sample (PUMS) files. Computerized files that contain a sample of individual records, with identifying information removed, showing the population and housing characteristics of the units, and people included on those forms.

Puerto Rico Community Survey (PRCS). The counterpart to the ACS that is conducted in Puerto Rico.

Quality measures. Statistics that provide information about the quality of the ACS data. The ACS releases four different quality measures with the annual data release: 1) initial sample size and final interviews; 2) coverage rates; 3) response rates, and; 4) item allocation rates for all collected variables. The ACS Quality Measures Web site <http://www.census.gov/acs/www/UseData/sse/> provides these statistics each year. In addition, the coverage rates are also available for males and females separately.

Reference period. Time interval to which survey responses refer. For example, many ACS questions refer to the day of the interview; others refer to "the past 12 months" or "last week."

Residence rules. The series of rules that define who (if anyone) is considered to be a resident of a sample address for purposes of the survey or census.

Sampling error. Errors that occur because only part of the population is directly contacted. With any sample, differences are likely to exist between the characteristics of the sampled population and the larger group from which the sample was chosen.

Sampling variability. Variation that occurs by chance because a sample is surveyed rather than the entire population.

Selected population profiles. An ACS data product that provides certain characteristics for a specific race or ethnic group (for example, Alaska Natives) or other population subgroup (for example, people aged 60 years and over). This data product is produced directly from the sample microdata (that is, not a derived product).

Single-year estimates. Estimates based on the set of ACS interviews conducted from January through December of a given calendar year. These estimates are published each year for geographic areas with a population of 65,000 or more.

Standard error. The standard error is a measure of the deviation of a sample estimate from the average of all possible samples.

Statistical significance. The determination of whether the difference between two estimates is not likely to be from random chance (sampling error) alone. This determination is based on both the estimates themselves and their standard errors. For ACS data, two estimates are "significantly different at the 90 percent level" if their difference is large enough to infer that there was a less than 10 percent chance that the difference came entirely from random variation.

Subject tables. Data products organized by subject area that present an overview of the information that analysts most often receive requests for from data users.

Summary files. Consist of detailed tables of Census 2000 social, economic, and housing characteristics compiled from a sample of approximately 19 million housing units (about 1 in 6 households) that received the Census 2000 long-form questionnaire.

Thematic maps. Display geographic variation in map format from the geographic ranking tables.

Three-year estimates. Estimates based on 3 years of ACS data. These estimates are meant to reflect the characteristics of a geographic area over the entire 3-year period. These estimates will be published for geographic areas with a population of 20,000 or more.

APPENDIX B:
SOURCE NOTES AND EXPLANATIONS

With one exception, all data in this book are from the 2005–2007 American Community Survey 3-year estimates. The sole exception is the population change between 2005–2007, which comes from the Census Bureau's annual population estimates and is included here as an indicator of the level of growth of each geographic area during the 3-year period of the ACS estimates.

This section of source notes is generally excerpted from: <http://www.census.gov/acs/www/Downloads/2007/usedata/Subject_Definitions.pdf>

The data were assembled from the ACS detailed tables and the following notes reference the numbers of those detailed tables. Also include with each table number and title is the table's universe, which is the total number of units (e.g., individuals, households, businesses, in the population of interest). Many of the data items can also be found in ACS profiles, subject tables, geographic comparison tables, and other formats available on the ACS Web site.

Symbols

A "-" in a cell indicates that either there were no sample cases or the number of sample cases was too small.

In several categories, including median value of owner-occupied housing units and median gross rent as a percentage of household income, top codes are used. In this publication, these codes are only present in Table C-4.

Part A — WHO

Table A-1. Who — Age, Race/Ethnicity, and Household Structure

Table A-1 presents 60 items for the United States as a whole and for each individual state and the District of Columbia

POPULATION, Item 1
Source: Table B01003. TOTAL POPULATION
Universe: TOTAL POPULATION

POPULATION CHANGE, Item 2
Source: U.S. Census Bureau—Population Estimates

The population change data for 2005–2007 are based on Census Bureau estimates of the resident population as of July 1.

RACE, Items 3–8, 10–11
Source: Table B02001. RACE; Table B02008. WHITE ALONE OR IN COMBINATION WITH ONE OR MORE OTHER RACES; Table B02009. BLACK OR AFRICAN AMERICAN ALONE OR IN COMBINATION WITH ONE OR MORE OTHER RACES; Table B02010. AMERICAN INDIAN AND ALASKA NATIVE ALONE OR IN COMBINATION WITH ONE OR MORE OTHER RACES; Table B02011. ASIAN ALONE OR IN COMBINATION WITH ONE OR MORE OTHER RACES; Table B02012. NATIVE HAWAIIAN AND OTHER PACIFIC ISLANDER ALONE OR IN COMBINATION WITH ONE OR MORE OTHER RACES; Table B02013. SOME OTHER RACE ALONE OR IN COMBINATION WITH ONE OR MORE OTHER RACES; Table B01001H. SEX BY AGE (WHITE ALONE, NOT HISPANIC OR LATINO)
Universe: TOTAL POPULATION

The concept of race, as used by the Census Bureau, reflects self-identification by people according to the race or races with which they most closely identify. These categories are socio-political constructs and should not be interpreted as being scientific or anthropological in nature. Furthermore, the race categories include both racial and national-origin groups. The racial classifications used by the Census Bureau adhere to the October 30, 1997, Federal Register Notice entitled, "Revisions to the Standards for the Classification of Federal Data on Race and Ethnicity," issued by the Office of Management and Budget (OMB). These standards govern the categories used to collect and present federal data on race and ethnicity. The OMB requires five minimum categories (White, Black or African American, American Indian or Alaska Native, Asian, and Native Hawaiian or Other Pacific Islander) for race. The race categories are described below with a sixth category, "Some other race," added with OMB approval. In addition to the five race groups, the OMB also states that respondents should be offered the option of selecting one or more races.

The **White** population includes persons having origins in any of the original peoples of Europe, the Middle East, or

North Africa. It includes people who indicate their race as "White" or report entries such as Irish, German, Italian, Lebanese, Near Easterner, Arab, or Polish.

Black population includes persons having origins in any of the Black racial groups of Africa. It includes people who indicate their race as "Black, African American, or Negro," or provide written entries such as African American, Afro-American, Kenyan, Nigerian, or Haitian.

The **American Indian or Alaska Native** population includes persons having origins in any of the original peoples of North and South America (including Central America) and who maintain tribal affiliation or community attachment. It includes people who classified themselves as Canadian Indian, French-American Indian, Spanish-American Indian, Eskimo, Aleut, Alaska Indian, or any of the American Indian or Alaska Native tribes.

The **Asian and Pacific Islander** population combines two census groupings: Asian and Native Hawaiian or Other Pacific Islander. The **Asian** population includes persons having origins in any of the original peoples of the Far East, Southeast Asia, or the Indian subcontinent including, for example, Cambodia, China, India, Japan, Korea, Malaysia, Pakistan, the Philippine Islands, Thailand, and Vietnam. It includes Asian Indian, Chinese, Filipino, Korean, Japanese, Vietnamese, and Other Asian. The **Native Hawaiian or Other Pacific Islander** population includes persons having origins in any of the original peoples of Hawaii, Guam, Samoa, or other Pacific Islands. It includes people who indicate their race as Native Hawaiian, Guamanian or Chamorro, Samoan, and Other Pacific Islander.

Some Other Race includes all other responses not included in the "White," "Black or African American," "American Indian or Alaska Native," "Asian," and "Native Hawaiian or Other Pacific Islander" race categories described above. Respondents providing write-in entries such as multiracial, mixed, interracial, or a Hispanic/Latino group (for example, Mexican, Puerto Rican, or Cuban) in the "Some other race" write-in space are included in this category.

Two or More Races. People may have chosen to provide two or more races either by checking two or more race response check boxes, by providing multiple write-in responses, or by some combination of check boxes and write-in responses.

HISPANIC ORIGIN, Item 9
Source: Table C03002. HISPANIC OR LATINO ORIGIN BY RACE
Universe: TOTAL POPULATION

The data on the **Hispanic or Latino** population, which was asked of all people, were derived from answers to Question 5. The terms "Spanish," "Hispanic," and "Latino" are used interchangeably. Some respondents identify with all three terms, while others may identify with only one of these three specific terms. Hispanics or Latinos who identify with the terms "Spanish," "Hispanic," or "Latino" are those who classify themselves in one of the specific Hispanic or Latino categories listed on the questionnaire – "Mexican," "Puerto Rican," or "Cuban" – as well as those who indicate that they are "other Spanish/Hispanic/Latino." People who do not identify with one of the specific origins listed on the questionnaire but indicate that they are "other Spanish/Hispanic/Latino" are those whose origins are from Spain, the Spanish-speaking countries of Central or South America, the Dominican Republic, or people identifying themselves generally as Spanish, Spanish-American, Hispanic, Hispano, Latino, and so on.

AGE, Items 12–21, 23–31
Source: Table B01001. SEX BY AGE; Table B01002. MEDIAN AGE BY SEX; Table B01002H. MEDIAN AGE BY SEX (WHITE ALONE, NOT HISPANIC OR LATINO); Table B01002B. MEDIAN AGE BY SEX (BLACK OR AFRICAN AMERICAN ALONE); Table B01002C. MEDIAN AGE BY SEX (AMERICAN INDIAN AND ALASKA NATIVE); Table B01002D. MEDIAN AGE BY SEX (ASIAN ALONE); Table B01002E. MEDIAN AGE BY SEX (NATIVE HAWAIIAN AND OTHER PACIFIC ISLANDER ALONE); Table B01002F. MEDIAN AGE BY SEX (SOME OTHER RACE ALONE); Table B01002G. MEDIAN AGE BY SEX (TWO OR MORE RACES); Table B01002I. MEDIAN AGE BY SEX (HISPANIC OR LATINO)
Universe: TOTAL POPULATION

The age classification is based on the age of the person in complete years at the time of interview. Both age and date of birth are used in combination to calculate the most accurate age at the time of the interview. Inconsistently reported and missing values are assigned or imputed based on the values of other variables for that person, from other people in the household, or from people in other households ("hot deck" imputation). Data on age are used to determine the applicability of other questions for a particular individual and to classify other characteristics in tabulations. Age data are needed to interpret most social and economic characteristics used to plan and analyze programs and policies. Therefore, age data are tabulated by many different age groupings, such as 5-year age groups.

The **median age** is the age that divides the population into two equal-size groups. Half of the population is older than the median age and half is younger. Median age is based on a standard distribution of the population by single years of age and is shown to the nearest tenth of a year.

PERCENT FEMALE, Item 22
Source: Table B01001. SEX BY AGE
Universe: TOTAL POPULATION

The female population is shown as a percentage of the total population.

MARITAL STATUS, Items 32–36
Source: Table B12001. SEX BY MARITAL STATUS FOR THE POPULATION 15 YEARS AND OVER
Universe: POPULATION 15 YEARS AND OVER

The **marital status** classification refers to the status at the time of interview. Data on marital status are tabulated only for people 15 years old and over. All people were asked whether they were "now married," "widowed," "divorced," "separated," or "never married." Couples who live together (unmarried people, people in common-law marriages) were allowed to report the marital status they considered the most appropriate. When marital status was not reported, it was imputed according to the relationship to the householder and sex and age of the person. Differences in the number of currently married males and females occur because there is no step in the weighting process to equalize the weighted estimates of husbands and wives.

Never married includes all people who have never been married, including people whose only marriage(s) was annulled.

Now married includes all people whose current marriage has not ended by widowhood or divorce. This category includes people defined as "separated" and "spouse absent."

Widowed includes widows and widowers who have not remarried.

Divorced includes people who are legally divorced and who have not remarried.

Differences between the number of currently married males and the number of currently married females occur because of reporting differences and because some husbands and wives have their usual residence in different areas. By definition, the numbers would be the same.

FOREIGN BORN, Item 37
Source: Table B05002. PLACE OF BIRTH BY CITIZENSHIP STATUS
Universe: TOTAL POPULATION

The **foreign-born** population includes anyone who was not a U.S. citizen or a U.S. national at birth. This includes respondents who indicated they were a U.S. citizen by naturalization or not a U.S. citizen.

LANGUAGES SPOKEN, Items 38–41
Source: Table B16002. HOUSEHOLD LANGUAGE BY LINGUISTIC ISOLATION
Universe: HOUSEHOLDS

Language spoken at home. Questions on language spoken at home were asked only of persons 5 years of age and older. Instructions mailed with the American Community Survey questionnaire instructed respondents to mark "Yes" on Question 13a if they sometimes or always spoke a language other than English at home, and "No" if a language was spoken only at school – or if speaking was limited to a few expressions or slang. For Question 13b, respondents printed the name of the non-English language they spoke at home. If the person spoke more than one non-English language, they reported the language spoken most often. If the language spoken most frequently could not be determined, the respondent reported the language learned first.

Questions 13a and 13b referred to languages spoken at home in an effort to measure the current use of languages other than English. This category excluded respondents who spoke a language other than English exclusively outside of the home.

Most respondents who reported speaking a language other than English also spoke English. The questions did not permit a determination of the primary language of persons who spoke both English and another language.

Household language. In households where one or more people spoke a language other than English, the household language assigned to all household members was the non-English language spoken by the first person with a non-English language. This assignment scheme ranked household members in the following order: householder, spouse, parent, sibling, child, grandchild, other relative, stepchild, unmarried partner, housemate or roommate, and other nonrelatives. Therefore, a person who spoke only English may have had a non-English household language assigned during tabulations by household language.

Ability to speak English. Respondents who reported speaking a language other than English were asked to indicate their English ability based on one of the following categories: "Very well," "Well," "Not well," or "Not at all." Ideally, the data on ability to speak English represented a person's perception of their own ability. However, because one household member usually completes American Community Survey questionnaires, the responses may have represented the perception of another household member. Respondents were not instructed on how to interpret the response categories in Question 13c.

Linguistic isolation. A linguistically isolated household was one in which all adults had some limitation in communicating English. A household was classified as "linguistically isolated" if, 1.) No household member age 14 years and over spoke only English, and 2.) No household member age 14 years and over who spoke another language spoke English "Very well." All members of a linguistically isolated household were tabulated as linguistically isolated, including members under 14 years old who may have spoken only English.

HOUSEHOLDS AND HOUSEHOLD TYPE, Item 42–60

Source: Table B11001. HOUSEHOLD TYPE (INCLUDING LIVING ALONE); Table B11006. HOUSEHOLDS BY PRESENCE OF PEOPLE 60 YEARS AND OVER BY HOUSEHOLD TYPE; Table C11005. HOUSEHOLDS BY PRESENCE OF PEOPLE UNDER 18 YEARS BY HOUSEHOLD TYPE; Table B25010. AVERAGE HOUSEHOLD SIZE OF OCCUPIED HOUSING UNITS BY TENURE
Universe: HOUSEHOLDS

A **household** includes all the people who occupy a housing unit. (People not living in households are classified as living in group quarters.) A housing unit is a house, an apartment, a mobile home, a group of rooms, or a single room that is occupied (or if vacant, is intended for occupancy) as separate living quarters. Separate living quarters are those in which the occupants live separately from any other people in the building and which have direct access from the outside of the building or through a common hall. The occupants may be a single family, one person living alone, two or more families living together, or any other group of related or unrelated people who share living arrangements.

A **family household** consists of a householder and one or more other people living in the same household who are related to the householder by birth, marriage, or adoption. All people in a household who are related to the householder are regarded as members of his or her family. A family household may contain people not related to the householder, but those people are not included as part of the householder's family in tabulations. Thus, the number of family households is equal to the number of families, but family households may include more members than do families. A household can contain only one family for purposes of tabulations.

A **married-couple family** is one in which the householder and his or her spouse are listed as members of the same household.

The category **male family households** includes only male-headed family households with no spouse present. Similarly, the category **female family households** includes only female-headed family households with no spouse present.

A **nonfamily household** consists of a group of unrelated people or of one person living alone.

Tables A-2, A-3, and A-4. Who — Age, Race/Ethnicity, and Household Structure

Table A-2 presents 24 items for the United States as a whole, each individual state and the District of Columbia, and 1,817 counties, county equivalents, and independent cities with a 2007 population of 20,000 or more.

Table A-3 presents 24 items for 363 Metropolitan Statistical Areas and 29 Metropolitan Divisions within the 12 largest Metropolitan Statistical Areas.

Table A-4 presents 24 items for 2,065 cities, Census Designated Places, and the principal portions of consolidated cities with a 2007 population of 20,000 or more.

POPULATION, Item 1
Source: Table B01003. TOTAL POPULATION
Universe: TOTAL POPULATION

POPULATION CHANGE, Item 2
Source: U.S. Census Bureau—Population Estimates

The population change data for 2005–2007 are based on Census Bureau estimates of the resident population as of July 1. Population estimates are not available for Census designated places (CDPs).

AGE, Items 3–9
Source: Table B01001. SEX BY AGE and Table B01002. MEDIAN AGE BY SEX
Universe: TOTAL POPULATION

The age classification is based on the age of the person in complete years at the time of interview. Both age and date of birth are used in combination to calculate the most accurate age at the time of the interview. Inconsistently reported and missing values are assigned or imputed based on the values of other variables for that person, from other people in the household, or from people in other households ("hot deck" imputation). Data on age are used to determine the applicability of other questions for a particular individual and to classify other characteristics in tabulations. Age data are needed to interpret most social and economic characteristics used to plan and analyze programs and policies. Therefore, age data are tabulated by many different age groupings, such as 5-year age groups.

The **median age** is the age that divides the population into two equal-size groups. Half of the population is older than the median age and half is younger. Median age is based on a standard distribution of the population by single years of age and is shown to the nearest tenth of a year.

RACE, Items 10–13
Source: B02008. WHITE ALONE OR IN COMBINATION WITH ONE OR MORE OTHER RACES; Table

B02009. BLACK OR AFRICAN AMERICAN ALONE OR IN COMBINATION WITH ONE OR MORE OTHER RACES; Table B02010. AMERICAN INDIAN AND ALASKA NATIVE ALONE OR IN COMBINATION WITH ONE OR MORE OTHER RACES; Table B02011. ASIAN ALONE OR IN COMBINATION WITH ONE OR MORE OTHER RACES; Table B02012. NATIVE HAWAIIAN AND OTHER PACIFIC ISLANDER ALONE OR IN COMBINATION WITH ONE OR MORE OTHER RACES; B02013. SOME OTHER RACE ALONE OR IN COMBINATION WITH ONE OR MORE OTHER RACES
Universe: TOTAL POPULATION

The concept of race, as used by the Census Bureau, reflects self-identification by people according to the race or races with which they most closely identify. These categories are socio-political constructs and should not be interpreted as being scientific or anthropological in nature. Furthermore, the race categories include both racial and national-origin groups. The racial classifications used by the Census Bureau adhere to the October 30, 1997, Federal Register Notice entitled, "Revisions to the Standards for the Classification of Federal Data on Race and Ethnicity," issued by the Office of Management and Budget (OMB). These standards govern the categories used to collect and present federal data on race and ethnicity. The OMB requires five minimum categories (White, Black or African American, American Indian or Alaska Native, Asian, and Native Hawaiian or Other Pacific Islander) for race. The race categories are described below with a sixth category, "Some other race," added with OMB approval. In addition to the five race groups, the OMB also states that respondents should be offered the option of selecting one or more races.

The **White** population includes persons having origins in any of the original peoples of Europe, the Middle East, or North Africa. It includes people who indicate their race as "White" or report entries such as Irish, German, Italian, Lebanese, Near Easterner, Arab, or Polish.

The **Black** population includes persons having origins in any of the Black racial groups of Africa. It includes people who indicate their race as "Black, African American, or Negro," or provide written entries such as African American, Afro-American, Kenyan, Nigerian, or Haitian.

The **American Indian or Alaska Native** population includes persons having origins in any of the original peoples of North and South America (including Central America) and who maintain tribal affiliation or community attachment. It includes people who classified themselves as Canadian Indian, French-American Indian, Spanish-American Indian, Eskimo, Aleut, Alaska Indian, or any of the American Indian or Alaska Native tribes.

The **Asian and Pacific Islander** population combines two census groupings: Asian and Native Hawaiian or Other Pacific Islander. The **Asian** population includes persons having origins in any of the original peoples of the Far East, Southeast Asia, or the Indian subcontinent including, for example, Cambodia, China, India, Japan, Korea, Malaysia, Pakistan, the Philippine Islands, Thailand, and Vietnam. It includes Asian Indian, Chinese, Filipino, Korean, Japanese, Vietnamese, and Other Asian. The **Native Hawaiian or Other Pacific Islander** population includes persons having origins in any of the original peoples of Hawaii, Guam, Samoa, or other Pacific Islands. It includes people who indicate their race as Native Hawaiian, Guamanian or Chamorro, Samoan, and Other Pacific Islander.

HISPANIC ORIGIN, Item 14
Source: Table C03002. HISPANIC OR LATINO ORIGIN BY RACE
Universe: TOTAL POPULATION

The data on the **Hispanic or Latino** population, which was asked of all people, were derived from answers to Question 5. The terms "Spanish," "Hispanic," and "Latino" are used interchangeably. Some respondents identify with all three terms, while others may identify with only one of these three specific terms. Hispanics or Latinos who identify with the terms "Spanish," "Hispanic," or "Latino" are those who classify themselves in one of the specific Hispanic or Latino categories listed on the questionnaire – "Mexican," "Puerto Rican," or "Cuban" – as well as those who indicate that they are "other Spanish/Hispanic/Latino." People who do not identify with one of the specific origins listed on the questionnaire but indicate that they are "other Spanish/Hispanic/Latino" are those whose origins are from Spain, the Spanish-speaking countries of Central or South America, the Dominican Republic, or people identifying themselves generally as Spanish, Spanish-American, Hispanic, Hispano, Latino, and so on.

FOREIGN BORN, Item 15
Source: Table C05002. PLACE OF BIRTH BY CITIZENSHIP STATUS
Universe: TOTAL POPULATION

The **foreign-born** population includes anyone who was not a U.S. citizen or a U.S. national at birth. This includes respondents who indicated they were a U.S. citizen by naturalization or not a U.S. citizen.

HOUSEHOLDS AND HOUSEHOLD TYPE, Item 16–24
Source: Table B11001. HOUSEHOLD TYPE (INCLUDING LIVING ALONE); Table B11006. HOUSEHOLDS BY PRESENCE OF PEOPLE 60 YEARS AND OVER BY HOUSEHOLD TYPE; Table C11005. HOUSEHOLDS BY PRESENCE OF PEOPLE UNDER 18 YEARS BY HOUSEHOLD TYPE
Universe: HOUSEHOLDS

A **household** includes all the people who occupy a housing unit. (People not living in households are classified as living in group quarters.) A housing unit is a house, an apartment, a mobile home, a group of rooms, or a single room that is occupied (or if vacant, is intended for occupancy) as separate living quarters. Separate living quarters are those in which the occupants live separately from any other people in the building and which have direct access from the outside of the building or through a common hall. The occupants may be a single family, one person living alone, two or more families living together, or any other group of related or unrelated people who share living arrangements.

A **family household** consists of a householder and one or more other people living in the same household who are related to the householder by birth, marriage, or adoption. All people in a household who are related to the householder are regarded as members of his or her family. A family household may contain people not related to the householder, but those people are not included as part of the householder's family in tabulations. Thus, the number of family households is equal to the number of families, but family households may include more members than do families. A household can contain only one family for purposes of tabulations.

A **married-couple family** is one in which the householder and his or her spouse are listed as members of the same household.

The category **male family households** includes only male-headed family households with no spouse present. Similarly, the category **female family households** includes only female-headed family households with no spouse present.

A **nonfamily household** consists of a group of unrelated people or of one person living alone.

Part B — WHAT

Table B-1. What — Education, Employment, and Income

Table B-1 presents 154 items for the United States as a whole and for each individual state and the District of Columbia.

EDUCATIONAL ATTAINMENT, Items 1–6
Source: Table C15002. SEX BY EDUCATIONAL ATTAINMENT FOR THE POPULATION 25 YEARS AND OVER
Universe: POPULATION 25 YEARS AND OVER

Data on **educational attainment** were derived from a question that asked respondents for the highest level of

school completed or the highest degree received. Persons currently enrolled in school are instructed to report the level of the previous grade attended or the highest degree received. Persons who had passed a high school equivalency examination were considered high school graduates. Schooling received in foreign schools was to be reported as the equivalent grade or years in the regular American school system.

Specifically excluded are vocational and technical training, such as barber school training; business, trade, technical, and vocational schools; or other training for a specific trade.

No high school diploma includes all persons who have not received a high school diploma.

High school graduate includes persons whose highest degree was a high school diploma or its equivalent, including those who passed a high school equivalency examination.

Some college or associate's degree includes people who attended college but did not receive a degree or received an associate's degree.

Bachelor's degree includes persons who have received bachelor's degrees.

Graduate or professional degree includes persons who have received master's degrees, professional school degrees (such as law school or medical school degrees), or doctoral degrees.

SCHOOL ENROLLMENT, Items 7–17
Source: Table C14002. SCHOOL ENROLLMENT BY LEVEL OF SCHOOL BY TYPE OF SCHOOL FOR THE POPULATION 3 YEARS AND OVER
Universe: POPULATION 3 YEARS AND OVER

People were classified as **enrolled in school** if they were attending a "regular" public or private school or college at any time during the 3 months prior to the time of interview. The question included instructions to "include only nursery or preschool, kindergarten, elementary school, and schooling which leads to a high school diploma, or a college degree" as regular school or college. Respondents who did not answer the enrollment question were assigned the enrollment status and type of school of a person with the same age, sex, race, and Hispanic or Latino origin whose residence was in the same or nearby area.

A regular school advances a person toward an elementary school certificate, a high school diploma, or a college, university, or professional school (such as law or medicine) degree. Tutoring or correspondence schools are included if credit can be obtained in a "regular school." People enrolled in "vocational, technical, or business school" were not reported as enrolled in regular school. Field interviewers were instructed to classify individuals who were home schooled as enrolled in private school. The guide sent out with the mail questionnaire does not include explicit instructions for how to classify home schoolers.

Enrolled in public and private school includes people who attended school in the reference period and indicated they were enrolled by marking one of the questionnaire categories for "public school, public college," or "private school, private college." The instruction guide defines a public school as "any school or college controlled and supported primarily by a local, county, state, or federal government." Private schools are defined as schools supported and controlled primarily by religious organizations or other private groups. Respondents who marked both the "public" and "private" boxes are edited to the first entry, "public."

Grade in which enrolled. Since 1999, in the American Community Survey, people reported to be enrolled in "public school, public college" or "private school, private college" were classified by grade or level according to responses to the question "What grade or level was this person attending?" Seven levels were identified: nursery school, preschool; kindergarten; elementary grade 1 to grade 4 or grade 5 to grade 8; high school grade 9 to grade 12; college undergraduate years (freshman to senior); and graduate or professional school (*for example: medical, dental, or law school*).

EMPLOYMENT STATUS, Items 18–40
Source: Table C20005. SEX BY WORK EXPERIENCE IN THE PAST 12 MONTHS BY EARNINGS IN THE PAST 12 MONTHS (IN 2007 INFLATION-ADJUSTED DOLLARS) FOR THE POPULATION 16 YEARS AND OVER; Table C23001. SEX BY AGE BY EMPLOYMENT STATUS FOR THE POPULATION 16 YEARS AND OVER
Universe: POPULATION 16 YEARS AND OVER

Table B23006. EDUCATIONAL ATTAINMENT BY EMPLOYMENT STATUS FOR THE POPULATION 25 TO 64 YEARS
Universe: POPULATION 25 TO 64 YEARS

Table C14005. SEX BY SCHOOL ENROLLMENT BY EDUCATIONAL ATTAINMENT BY EMPLOYMENT STATUS FOR THE POPULATION 16 TO 19 YEARS
Universe: POPULATION 16 TO 19 YEARS

Table C08202. HOUSEHOLD SIZE BY NUMBER OF WORKERS IN HOUSEHOLD
Universe: HOUSEHOLDS

Total employment includes all civilians 16 years old and over who were either (1) "at work"—those who did any work at all during the reference week as paid employees, worked in either their own business or profession, worked on their own farm, or worked 15 hours or more as unpaid workers in a family farm or business; or were (2) "with a job, but not at work"—those who had a job but were not at work that week due to illness, weather, industrial dispute, vacation, or other personal reasons.

The **labor force** consists of all persons 16 years old and over who are either employed or unemployed, including those in the armed forces

The **unemployment rate** represents the number of unemployed people as a percentage of the labor force.

Unemployment includes all persons who did not work during the survey week, made specific efforts to find a job during the previous four weeks, and were available for work during the survey week (except for temporary illness). Persons waiting to be called back to a job from which they had been laid off and those waiting to report to a new job within the next 30 days are included in unemployment figures.

Full-time, year-round includes all persons 16 years old and over who usually worked 35 hours or more per week for 50 to 52 weeks in the past 12 months.

Households with no worker. The term "worker" as used here refers to work status in the past 12 months.

Not enrolled, not high school graduate. This category includes people of compulsory school attendance age or above (ages 16 to 19) who were not enrolled in school and were not high school graduates. These people may be referred to as "high school dropouts." There is no restriction on when they "dropped out" of school; therefore, they may have dropped out before high school and never attended high school.

CHILDREN IN FAMILIES BY LIVING ARRANGEMENTS AND EMPLOYMENT STATUS OF PARENTS, Items 41–60
Source: Table C23008. AGE OF OWN CHILDREN UNDER 18 YEARS IN FAMILIES AND SUBFAMILIES BY LIVING ARRANGEMENTS BY EMPLOYMENT STATUS OF PARENTS
Universe: OWN CHILDREN UNDER 18 YEARS IN FAMILIES AND SUBFAMILIES

Table C23007. PRESENCE OF OWN CHILDREN UNDER 18 YEARS BY FAMILY TYPE BY EMPLOYMENT STATUS
Universe: FAMILIES

Table B23003. PRESENCE OF OWN CHILDREN UNDER 18 YEARS BY AGE OF OWN CHILDREN

UNDER 18 YEARS BY EMPLOYMENT STATUS FOR FEMALES 20 TO 64 YEARS
Universe: FEMALES 20 TO 64 YEARS IN HOUSEHOLDS

An **own child** is a never-married child under 18 years who is a son or daughter by birth, a stepchild, or an adopted child of the householder. Own children are further classified as living with two parents or with one parent only. Own children of the householder living with two parents are by definition found only in married-couple families. In the employment status tabulations in this book, own child refers to a never married child under the age of 18 in a family or a subfamily who is a son or daughter, by birth, marriage, or adoption, of a member of the householder's family, but not necessarily of the householder.

CLASS OF WORKER, Items 61–64
Source: Table C24080. SEX BY CLASS OF WORKER FOR THE CIVILIAN EMPLOYED POPULATION 16 YEARS AND OVER
Universe: CIVILIAN EMPLOYED POPULATION 16 YEARS AND OVER

For employed people, the data on **class of worker** refer to the person's job during the previous week. For those who worked two or more jobs, the data refer to the job where the person worked the greatest number of hours. For unemployed people, the data refer to their last job. The information on **class of worker** refers to the same job as a respondent's industry and occupation and categorizes people according to the type of ownership of the employing organization. The class of worker categories are defined as follows:

Private wage and salary workers includes people who worked for wages, salary, commission, tips, pay-in-kind, or piece rates for a private for-profit employer or a private not-for-profit, tax-exempt or charitable organization. Self-employed people whose business was incorporated are included with private wage and salary workers because they are paid employees of their own companies.

Government workers includes people who were employees of any local, state, or federal governmental unit, regardless of the activity of the particular agency. Employees of foreign governments, the United Nations, or other formal international organizations controlled by governments were classified as "federal government workers." The class of worker government categories includes all government workers, though government workers may work in different industries. For example, people who work in a public elementary or secondary school are coded as local government class of workers.

Self-employed includes people who worked for profit or fees in their own unincorporated business, profession, or trade, or who operated a farm.

Unpaid family workers includes people who worked 15 hours or more a week without pay in a business or on a farm operated by a relative.

OCCUPATION, Items 65–71
Source: Table C24060. OCCUPATION BY CLASS OF WORKER FOR THE CIVILIAN EMPLOYED POPULATION 16 YEARS AND OVER
Universe: CIVILIAN EMPLOYED POPULATION 16 YEARS AND OVER

For employed people, the data on **occupation** refer to the person's job during the previous week. For those who worked two or more jobs, the data refer to the job where the person worked the greatest number of hours. For unemployed people, the data refer to their last job.

Written responses to the occupation questions are coded using the occupational classification system developed for the 2000 census and modified in 2002. This system consists of 509 specific occupational categories, including military, for employed people, arranged into 23 major occupational groups. This classification was developed based on the *Standard Occupational Classification (SOC) Manual: 2000*, published by the Executive Office of the President, Office of Management and Budget.

INDUSTRY, Items 72–84
Source: Table C24070. INDUSTRY BY CLASS OF WORKER FOR CIVILIAN EMPLOYED POPULATION 16 YEARS AND OVER
Universe: CIVILIAN EMPLOYED POPULATION 16 YEARS AND OVER

For employed people, the data on **industry** refer to the person's job during the previous week. For those who worked two or more jobs, the data refer to the job where the person worked the greatest number of hours. For unemployed people, the data refer to their last job.

Written responses to the industry questions are coded using the industry classification system developed for Census 2000 and modified in 2002. This system consists of 270 categories for employed people, including military, classified into 20 sectors. The modified 2002 census industry classification was developed from the 2002 North American Industry Classification System (NAICS) published by the Executive Office of the President, Office of Management and Budget. The NAICS was developed to increase comparability in industry definitions between the United States, Mexico, and Canada. It provides industry classifications that group establishments into industries based on the activities in which they are primarily engaged. The NAICS was created for establishment designations and provides detail about the smallest operating establishment, while the American Community Survey data are collected from households and differ in detail and nature from those obtained from establishment surveys. Because of disclosure issues, ACS data cannot be released in great detail, and the industry classification system, while defined in NAICS terms, cannot reflect the full detail for all categories.

The industry category, "Public administration," is limited to regular government functions such as legislative, judicial, administrative, and regulatory activities. Other government organizations such as public schools, public hospitals, liquor stores, and bus lines are classified by industry according to the activity in which they are engaged.

VETERAN STATUS, Item 85
Source: Table B21002. PERIOD OF MILITARY SERVICE FOR CIVILIAN VETERANS 18 YEARS AND OVER
Universe: CIVILIAN VETERANS 18 YEARS AND OVER

A "civilian veteran" is a person 18 years old or over who has served (even for a short time), but is not now serving, on active duty in the U.S. Army, Navy, Air Force, Marine Corps, or the Coast Guard, or who served in the U.S. Merchant Marine during World War II. People who served in the National Guard or Military Reserves are classified as veterans only if they were ever called or ordered to active duty, not counting the 4–6 months for initial training or yearly summer camps. All other civilians 18 years old and over are classified as nonveterans.

HOUSEHOLD INCOME, Items 86–99, 113–138
Source: Table B19049. MEDIAN HOUSEHOLD INCOME IN THE PAST 12 MONTHS (IN 2007 INFLATION-ADJUSTED DOLLARS) BY AGE OF HOUSEHOLDER; Table B19013A THROUGH B19013I MEDIAN HOUSEHOLD INCOME IN THE PAST 12 MONTHS (IN 2007 INFLATION-ADJUSTED DOLLARS) FOR 9 RACE AND HISPANIC ORIGIN GROUPS; Table B19052. WAGE OR SALARY INCOME IN THE PAST 12 MONTHS FOR HOUSEHOLDS; Table B19053. SELF-EMPLOYMENT INCOME IN THE PAST 12 MONTHS FOR HOUSEHOLDS; Table B19054. INTEREST, DIVIDENDS, OR NET RENTAL INCOME IN THE PAST 12 MONTHS FOR HOUSEHOLDS; Table B19055. SOCIAL SECURITY INCOME IN THE PAST 12 MONTHS FOR HOUSEHOLDS; Table B19056. SUPPLEMENTAL SECURITY INCOME (SSI) IN THE PAST 12 MONTHS FOR HOUSEHOLDS; Table B19057. PUBLIC ASSISTANCE INCOME IN THE PAST 12 MONTHS FOR HOUSEHOLDS; Table B19058. PUBLIC ASSISTANCE INCOME OR FOOD STAMPS IN THE PAST 12 MONTHS FOR HOUSEHOLDS; Table B19059. RETIREMENT INCOME IN THE PAST 12 MONTHS FOR HOUSEHOLDS; Table B19060. OTHER TYPES OF INCOME IN THE PAST 12 MONTHS FOR HOUSEHOLDS
Universe: HOUSEHOLDS

Income of households includes the income of the householder and all other individuals 15 years old and over in the household, whether they are related to the householder or not. Because many households consist of only one person, average household income is usually less than average family income. Although the household income statistics cover the past 12 months, the characteristics of individuals and the composition of households refer to the time of interview. Thus, the income of the household does not include amounts received by individuals who were members of the household during all or part of the past 12 months if these individuals no longer resided in the household at the time of interview. Similarly, income amounts reported by individuals who did not reside in the household during the past 12 months but who were members of the household at the time of interview are included. However, the composition of most households was the same during the past 12 months as at the time of interview.

Income components were reported for the 12 months preceding the interview month. Monthly Consumer Price Indices (CPI) factors were used to inflation-adjust these components to a reference calendar year (January through December). For example, a household interviewed in March 2007 reports their income for March 2006 through February 2007. Their income is adjusted to the 2007 reference calendar year by multiplying their reported income by 2007 average annual CPI (January–December 2007) and then dividing by the average CPI for March 2006–February 2007.

In order to inflate income amounts from previous years, the dollar values on individual records are inflated to the latest year's dollar values by multiplying by a factor equal to the average annual CPI-U-RS factor for the current year, divided by the average annual CPI-U-RS factor for the earlier/earliest year.

Median income divides the income distribution into two equal parts, with half of all cases below the median income level and half of all cases above the median income level. For households and families, the median income is based on the distribution of the total number of households and families, including those with no income. Median income for households is computed on the basis of a standard distribution with a minimum value of less than $2,500 and a maximum value of $200,000 or more and is rounded to the nearest whole dollar.

The eight types of income reported in the American Community Survey are defined as follows:

1. **Wage or salary income:** Wage or salary income includes total money earnings received for work performed as an employee during the past 12 months. It includes wages, salary, armed forces pay, commissions, tips, piece-rate

payments, and cash bonuses earned before deductions were made for taxes, bonds, pensions, union dues, etc.

2. **Self-employment income:** Self-employment income includes both farm and non-farm self-employment income.

Farm self-employment income includes net money income (gross receipts minus operating expenses) from the operation of a farm by a person on his or her own account, as an owner, renter, or sharecropper. Gross receipts include the value of all products sold, government farm programs, money received from the rental of farm equipment to others, and incidental receipts from the sale of wood, sand, gravel, etc. Operating expenses include cost of feed, fertilizer, seed, and other farming supplies, cash wages paid to farmhands, depreciation charges, cash rent, interest on farm mortgages, farm building repairs, farm taxes (not state and federal personal income taxes), etc. The value of fuel, food, or other farm products used for family living is not included as part of net income.

Non-farm self-employment income includes net money income (gross receipts minus expenses) from one's own business, professional enterprise, or partnership. Gross receipts include the value of all goods sold and services rendered. Expenses include costs of goods purchased, rent, heat, light, power, depreciation charges, wages and salaries paid, business taxes (not personal income taxes), etc.

3. **Interest, dividends, or net rental income:** Interest, dividends, or net rental income includes interest on savings or bonds, dividends from stockholdings or membership in associations, net income from rental of property to others and receipts from boarders or lodgers, net royalties, and periodic payments from an estate or trust fund.

4. **Social Security income:** Social Security income includes Social Security pensions and survivor benefits, permanent disability insurance payments made by the Social Security Administration prior to deductions for medical insurance, and railroad retirement insurance checks from the U.S. government. Medicare reimbursements are not included.

5. **Supplemental Security Income (SSI):** Supplemental Security Income (SSI) is a nationwide U.S. assistance program administered by the Social Security Administration that guarantees a minimum level of income for needy aged, blind, or disabled individuals. The Puerto Rico Community Survey questionnaire asks about the receipt of SSI; however, SSI is not a federally-administered program in Puerto Rico. Therefore, it is probably not being interpreted by most respondents in the same manner as SSI in the United States. The only way a resident of Puerto Rico could have appropriately reported SSI would have been if they lived in the United States at any time during the past 12-month reference period and received SSI.

6. **Public assistance income:** Public assistance income includes general assistance and Temporary Assistance to Needy Families (TANF). Separate payments received for hospital or other medical care, (vendor payments) are excluded. This does not include Supplemental Security Income (SSI) or noncash benefits such as Food Stamps. The terms "public assistance income" and "cash public assistance" are used interchangeably in the 2007 ACS data products.

7. **Retirement, survivor, or disability income:** Retirement income includes: (1) retirement pensions and survivor benefits from a former employer; labor union; or federal, state, or local government; and the U.S. military; (2) disability income from companies or unions; federal, state, or local government; and the U.S. military; (3) periodic receipts from annuities and insurance; and (4) regular income from IRA and Keogh plans. This does not include Social Security income.

8. **All other income:** All other income includes unemployment compensation, Veterans' Administration (VA) payments, alimony and child support, contributions received periodically from people not living in the household, military family allotments, and other kinds of periodic income other than earnings.

Receipts from the following sources are not included as income: capital gains, money received from the sale of property (unless the recipient was engaged in the business of selling such property); the value of income "in kind" from food stamps, public housing subsidies, medical care, employer contributions for individuals, etc.; withdrawal of bank deposits; money borrowed; tax refunds; exchange of money between relatives living in the same household; gifts and lump-sum inheritances, insurance payments, and other types of lump-sum receipts.

Although receipt of **food stamps** is included in an income table, the data on Food Stamp benefits were obtained from a Housing Question in the 2007 American Community Survey. The Food Stamp Act of 1977 defines this federally-funded program as one intended to "permit low-income households to obtain a more nutritious diet" (from Title XIII of Public Law 95-113, The Food Stamp Act of 1977, declaration of policy). Food purchasing power is increased by providing eligible households with coupons or cards that can be used to purchase food. The Food and Nutrition Service (FNS) of the U.S. Department of Agriculture (USDA) administers the Food Stamp Program through state and local welfare offices. The Food Stamp Program is the major national income support program to which all low-income and low-resource households, regardless of household characteristics, are eligible.

The questions on participation in the Food Stamp Program were designed to identify households in which one or more of the current members received food stamps during the past 12 months. Once a food stamp household was identified, a question was asked about the total value of all food stamps received for the household during that 12-month period.

FAMILY INCOME, Items 100–106
Source: Table B19126. MEDIAN FAMILY INCOME IN THE PAST 12 MONTHS (IN 2007 INFLATION-ADJUSTED DOLLARS) BY FAMILY TYPE BY PRESENCE OF OWN CHILDREN UNDER 18 YEARS
Universe: FAMILIES

In compiling statistics on **family income**, the incomes of all members 15 years old and over related to the householder are summed and treated as a single amount. Although the family income statistics cover the past 12 months, the characteristics of individuals and the composition of families refer to the time of interview. Thus, the income of the family does not include amounts received by individuals who were members of the family during all or part of the past 12 months if these individuals no longer resided with the family at the time of interview. Similarly, income amounts reported by individuals who did not reside with the family during the past 12 months but who were members of the family at the time of interview are included. However, the composition of most families was the same during the past 12 months as at the time of interview.

NONFAMILY HOUSEHOLD INCOME, Items 107–109
Source: Table B19215. MEDIAN NONFAMILY HOUSEHOLD INCOME IN THE PAST 12 MONTHS (IN 2007 INFLATION-ADJUSTED DOLLARS) BY SEX OF HOUSEHOLDER BY LIVING ALONE BY AGE OF HOUSEHOLDER
Universe: NONFAMILY HOUSEHOLDS

Nonfamily household income includes the income of the householder and all other individuals 15 years old and over in the nonfamily household. Although the household income statistics cover the past 12 months, the characteristics of individuals and the composition of households refer to the time of interview. Thus, the income of the household does not include amounts received by individuals who were members of the household during all or part of the past 12 months if these individuals no longer resided in the household at the time of interview. Similarly, income amounts reported by individuals who did not reside in the household during the past 12 months but who were members of the household at the time of interview are included. However, the composition of most households was the same during the past 12 months as at the time of interview.

INCOME OF INDIVIDUALS, Items 110–111
Source: Table B19326. MEDIAN INCOME IN THE PAST 12 MONTHS (IN 2007 INFLATION-ADJUSTED DOLLARS) BY SEX BY WORK EXPERIENCE IN THE PAST 12 MONTHS FOR THE POPULATION 15 YEARS AND OVER WITH INCOME
Universe: POPULATION 15 YEARS AND OVER WITH INCOME IN THE PAST 12 MONTHS

Income of individuals. Income for individuals is obtained by summing the eight types of income for each person 15 years old and over. The characteristics of individuals are based on the time of interview even though the amounts are for the past 12 months.

PER CAPITA INCOME, Item 112
Source: Table B19301. PER CAPITA INCOME IN THE PAST 12 MONTHS (IN 2007 INFLATION-ADJUSTED DOLLARS)
Universe: TOTAL POPULATION

Per capita income is the mean income computed for every man, woman, and child in a particular group including those living in group quarters. It is derived by dividing the aggregate income of a particular group by the total population in that group. Per capita income is rounded to the nearest whole dollar.

POVERTY STATUS, Items 139–154
Source: Table C17017. POVERTY STATUS IN THE PAST 12 MONTHS BY HOUSEHOLD TYPE
Universe: HOUSEHOLDS

Table C17001. POVERTY STATUS IN THE PAST 12 MONTHS BY SEX BY AGE; C17001B, D, H, AND I. POVERTY STATUS IN THE PAST 12 MONTHS BY SEX AND AGE FOR SELECTED RACE AND HISPANIC ORIGIN GROUPS
Universe: POPULATION FOR WHOM POVERTY STATUS IS DETERMINED

The **poverty status** data were derived from data collected on the number of persons in the household, from questionnaire item 3, which provides data on each person's relationship to the householder, and items 41 and 42, the same questions used to derive the income data. The Social Security Administration (SSA) developed the original poverty definition in 1964, which federal interagency committees subsequently revised in 1969 and 1980. The Office of Management and Budget's (OMB) *Directive 14* prescribes the SSA's definition as the official poverty measure for federal agencies to use in their statistical work. Poverty statistics presented in American Community Survey products adhere to the standards defined by OMB in *Directive 14*.

The poverty thresholds vary depending on three criteria: size of family, number of children, and, for one- and two-person families, age of householder. In determining the poverty status of families and unrelated individuals, the Census Bureau uses thresholds (income cutoffs) arranged in a two-dimensional matrix. The matrix consists of family size (from one person to nine or more persons), cross-classified by presence and number of family members under 18 years old (from no children present to eight or more children present). Unrelated individuals and two-person families are further differentiated by age of reference person (under 65 years old and 65 years old and over). To determine a person's poverty status, the person's total family income in the last 12 months is compared to the poverty threshold appropriate for that person's family size and composition. If the total income of that person's family is less than the threshold appropriate for that family, then the person is considered poor or "below the poverty level," together with every member of his or her family. If a person is not living with anyone related by birth, marriage, or adoption, then the person's own income is compared with his or her poverty threshold. The average poverty threshold for a four-person family was $21,203 in 2007.

Since ACS is a continuous survey, people respond throughout the year. Because the income questions specify a period covering the last 12 months, the appropriate poverty thresholds are determined by multiplying the base-year poverty thresholds (1982) by the average of the monthly inflation factors for the 12 months preceding the data collection.

Tables B-2, B-3, and B-4. What — Education, Employment, and Income

Table B-2 presents 12 items for the United States as a whole, each individual state and the District of Columbia, and 1,817 counties, county equivalents, and independent cities with a 2007 population of 20,000 or more.

Table B-3 presents 12 items for 363 Metropolitan Statistical Areas and 29 Metropolitan Divisions within the 12 largest Metropolitan Statistical Areas.

Table B-4 presents 12 items for 2,065 cities, Census Designated Places, and the principal portions of consolidated cities with a 2007 population of 20,000 or more.

EDUCATIONAL ATTAINMENT, Items 1–3
Source: Table C15002. SEX BY EDUCATIONAL ATTAINMENT FOR THE POPULATION 25 YEARS AND OVER
Universe: POPULATION 25 YEARS AND OVER

Data on **educational attainment** were derived from a question that asked respondents for the highest level of school completed or the highest degree received. Persons currently enrolled in school are instructed to report the level of the previous grade attended or the highest degree received. Persons who had passed a high school equivalency examination were considered high school graduates. Schooling received in foreign schools was to be reported as the equivalent grade or years in the regular American school system.

Specifically excluded are vocational and technical training, such as barber school training; business, trade, technical, and vocational schools; or other training for a specific trade.

High school diploma or less. This category includes persons whose highest degree was a high school diploma or its equivalent, and those who reported any level lower than a high school diploma.

Bachelor's degree or more. This category includes persons who have received bachelor's degrees, master's degrees, professional school degrees (such as law school or medical school degrees), or doctoral degrees.

EMPLOYMENT STATUS, Items 4–8
Source: Table C20005. SEX BY WORK EXPERIENCE IN THE PAST 12 MONTHS BY EARNINGS IN THE PAST 12 MONTHS (IN 2007 INFLATION-ADJUSTED DOLLARS) FOR THE POPULATION 16 YEARS AND OVER; Table C23001. SEX BY AGE BY EMPLOYMENT STATUS FOR THE POPULATION 16 YEARS AND OVER
Universe: POPULATION 16 YEARS AND OVER

Table C08202. HOUSEHOLD SIZE BY NUMBER OF WORKERS IN HOUSEHOLD
Universe: HOUSEHOLDS

Total employment includes all civilians 16 years old and over who were either (1) "at work"—those who did any work at all during the reference week as paid employees, worked in either their own business or profession, worked on their own farm, or worked 15 hours or more as unpaid workers in a family farm or business; or were (2) "with a job, but not at work"—those who had a job but were not at work that week due to illness, weather, industrial dispute, vacation, or other personal reasons.

The **labor force** consists of all persons 16 years old and over who are either employed or unemployed, including those in the armed forces

The **unemployment rate** represents the number of unemployed people as a percentage of the labor force.

Unemployment includes all persons who did not work during the survey week, made specific efforts to find a job during the previous four weeks, and were available for work during the survey week (except for temporary illness). Persons waiting to be called back to a job from which they had been laid off and those waiting to report to a new job within the next 30 days are included in unemployment figures.

Full-time, year-round includes all persons 16 years old and over who usually worked 35 hours or more per week for 50 to 52 weeks in the past 12 months.

Households with no worker. The term "worker" as used here refers to work status in the past 12 months.

INCOME, Items 9–12
Source: B19013. MEDIAN HOUSEHOLD INCOME IN THE PAST 12 MONTHS (IN 2007 INFLATION-ADJUSTED DOLLARS);
Universe: HOUSEHOLDS

Table C17015. POVERTY STATUS IN THE PAST 12 MONTHS OF FAMILIES BY SOCIAL SECURITY INCOME BY SUPPLEMENTAL SECURITY INCOME (SSI) AND PUBLIC ASSISTANCE INCOME;
Universe: HOUSEHOLDS

Table C19001. HOUSEHOLD INCOME IN THE PAST 12 MONTHS (IN 2007 INFLATION-ADJUSTED DOLLARS)
Universe: HOUSEHOLDS

Household income includes the income of the householder and all other individuals 15 years old and over in the household, whether or not they are related to the householder. Since many households consist of only one person, average household income is usually less than average family income. Although the household income statistics cover the past 12 months, the characteristics of individuals and the composition of households refer to the time of enumeration. Thus, the income of the household does not include amounts received by individuals who were members of the household during all or part of the past 12 months if these individuals no longer resided in the household at the time of enumeration. Similarly, income amounts reported by individuals who did not reside in the household during the past 12 months but who were members of the household at the time of enumeration are included. However, the composition of most households was the same during the past 12 months as at the time of enumeration.

Median income divides the income distribution into two equal parts, with half of all cases below the median income level and half of all cases above the median income level. For households and families, the median income is based on the distribution of the total number of households and families, including those with no income. Median income for households is computed on the basis of a standard distribution with a minimum value of less than $2,500 and a maximum value of $200,000 or more and is rounded to the nearest whole dollar.

For **family income**, the incomes of all household members 15 years old and over related to the householder are summed and treated as a single amount. Although the family income statistics cover the past 12 months, the characteristics of individuals and the composition of families refer to the time of enumeration. Thus, the income of the family does not include amounts received by individuals who were members of the family during all of part of the past 12 months if these individuals no longer resided with the family at the time of enumeration. Similarly, income amounts reported by individuals who did not reside with the family during the past 12 months but who were members of the family at the time of enumeration are included. However, the composition of most families was the same during the past 12 months as at the time of enumeration.

Income in the American Community Survey is for the past 12 months as opposed to a single reference year.

The **poverty status** data were derived from data collected on the number of persons in the household, from questionnaire item 3, which provides data on each person's relationship to the householder, and items 41 and 42, the same questions used to derive the income data. The Social Security Administration (SSA) developed the original poverty definition in 1964, which federal interagency committees subsequently revised in 1969 and 1980. The Office of Management and Budget's (OMB) *Directive 14* prescribes the SSA's definition as the official poverty measure for federal agencies to use in their statistical work. Poverty statistics presented in American Community Survey products adhere to the standards defined by OMB in *Directive 14*.

The poverty thresholds vary depending on three criteria: size of family, number of children, and, for one- and two-person families, age of householder. In determining the poverty status of families and unrelated individuals, the Census Bureau uses thresholds (income cutoffs) arranged in a two-dimensional matrix. The matrix consists of family size (from one person to nine or more persons), cross-classified by presence and number of family members under 18 years old (from no children present to eight or more children present). Unrelated individuals and two-person families are further differentiated by age of reference person (under 65 years old and 65 years old and over). To determine a person's poverty status, the person's total family income in the last 12 months is compared to the poverty threshold appropriate for that person's family size and composition. If the total income of that person's family is less than the threshold appropriate for that family, then the person is considered poor or "below the poverty level," together with every member of his or her family. If a person is not living with anyone related by birth, marriage, or adoption, then the person's own income is compared with his or her poverty threshold. The average poverty threshold for a four-person family was $21,203 in 2007.

Since ACS is a continuous survey, people respond throughout the year. Because the income questions specify a period covering the last 12 months, the appropriate poverty thresholds are determined by multiplying the base-year poverty thresholds (1982) by the average of the monthly inflation factors for the 12 months preceding the data collection.

Part C — WHERE

Table C-1. Where — Migration, Housing, and Transportation

Table C-1 presents 87 items for the United States as a whole and for each individual state and the District of Columbia.

PLACE OF RESIDENCE, Items 1–7
Source: Table C07204. GEOGRAPHICAL MOBILITY IN THE PAST YEAR FOR CURRENT RESIDENCE—STATE, COUNTY AND PLACE LEVEL IN THE UNITED STATES (for states, counties, and cities)
Universe: POPULATION 1 YEAR AND OVER IN THE UNITED STATES

Residence one year ago is used in conjunction with location of current residence to determine the extent of residential mobility of the population and the resulting redistribution of the population across the various states, metropolitan areas, and regions of the country.

Same house includes all people 1 year and over who did not move during the 1 year as well as those who had moved and returned to their residence 1 year ago.

Different house in the United States includes people who lived in the United States 1 year ago but in a different house or apartment from the one they occupied at the time of interview. These movers are then further subdivided according to the type of move. Movers within the U.S. are divided into groups according to their previous residence: **Different house, same city or town; Different house, different city, same county; Different house, different county, same state; and Different state.**

Abroad includes those whose previous residence was in a foreign country, Puerto Rico, American Samoa, Guam, the Northern Marianas, or the U.S. Virgin Islands, including members of the armed forces and their dependents.

HOMEOWNERSHIP BY RACE, HISPANIC ORIGIN, AGE OF HOUSEHOLDER, AND HOUSEHOLD TYPE, Items 8–35
Source: Table B25003. TENURE; Table B25003H. TENURE (WHITE ALONE, NOT HISPANIC OR LATINO HOUSEHOLDER); Table B25003B. TENURE (BLACK OR AFRICAN AMERICAN ALONE HOUSEHOLDER); Table B25003C. TENURE (AMERICAN INDIAN AND ALASKA NATIVE ALONE HOUSEHOLDER); Table B25003D. TENURE (ASIAN ALONE HOUSEHOLDER); Table B25003E. TENURE (NATIVE HAWAIIAN AND OTHER PACIFIC ISLANDER ALONE HOUSEHOLDER); Table B25003I. TENURE (HISPANIC OR LATINO HOUSEHOLDER); Table B25007. TENURE BY AGE OF HOUSEHOLDER; Table C25115. TENURE BY HOUSEHOLD TYPE
Universe: OCCUPIED HOUSING UNITS

A **housing unit** is a house, apartment, mobile home or trailer, group of rooms, or single room occupied or, if vacant, intended for occupancy as separate living quarters. Separate living quarters are those in which the occupants do not live and eat with any other person in the structure and which have direct access from the outside of the building or through a common hall. For vacant units, the criteria of separateness and direct access are applied to the intended occupants whenever possible. If that information cannot be obtained, the criteria are applied to the previous occupants.

The occupants of a housing unit may be a single family, one person living alone, two or more families living together, or any other group of related or unrelated persons who share living arrangements. Both occupied and vacant housing units are included in the housing inventory, although recreational vehicles, tents, caves, boats, railroad cars, and the like are included only if they are occupied as a person's usual place of residence.

Occupied housing units are classified as either owner occupied or renter occupied. A housing unit is classified as occupied if it is the usual place of residence of the person or group of persons living in it at the time of enumeration, or if the occupants are only temporarily absent from the residence for two months or less, that is, away on vacation or a business trip. If all the people staying in the unit at the time of the interview are staying there for two months or less, the unit is considered to be temporarily occupied and classified as "vacant."

A housing unit is **owner occupied** if the owner or co-owner lives in the unit even if it is mortgaged or not fully paid for. The owner or co-owner must live in the unit and usually is Person 1 on the questionnaire. The unit is "Owned by you or someone in this household with a mortgage or loan" if it is being purchased with a mortgage or some other debt arrangement such as a deed of trust, trust deed, contract to purchase, land contract, or purchase agreement. The unit also is considered owned with a mortgage if it is built on leased land and there is a mortgage on the unit. Mobile homes occupied by owners with installment loan balances also are included in this category.

All occupied housing units which are not owner occupied, whether they are rented for cash rent or occupied without payment of cash rent, are classified as **renter occupied**. "No cash rent" units are separately identified in the rent tabulations. Such units are generally provided free by friends or relatives or in exchange for services such as resident manager, caretaker, minister, or tenant farmer. Housing units on military bases also are classified in the "No cash rent" category. "Rented for cash rent" includes units in continuing care, sometimes called life care arrangements. These arrangements usually involve a contract between one or more individuals and a health services provider guaranteeing the individual shelter, usually a house or apartment, and services, such as meals or transportation to shopping or recreation.

HOUSEHOLD SIZE, Items 36–38
Source: Table B25010. AVERAGE HOUSEHOLD SIZE OF OCCUPIED HOUSING UNITS BY TENURE
Universe: OCCUPIED HOUSING UNITS

Household size is based on the count of people in occupied housing units. All people occupying the housing unit are counted, including the householder, occupants related to the householder, and lodgers, roomers, boarders, and so forth.

Average household size of occupied units is obtained by dividing the number of people living in occupied housing units by the total number of occupied housing units. This measure is rounded to the nearest hundredth.

Average household size of owner-occupied units is obtained by dividing the number of people living in owner-occupied housing units by the total number of owner-occupied housing units. This measure is rounded to the nearest hundredth.

Average household size of renter-occupied units is obtained by dividing the number of people living in renter-occupied housing units by the total number of renter-occupied housing units. This measure is rounded to the nearest hundredth.

UNITS THAT ARE CROWDED OR LACKING COMPLETE PLUMBING, Item 39
Source: Table C25016. TENURE BY PLUMBING FACILITIES BY OCCUPANTS PER ROOM
Universe: OCCUPIED HOUSING UNITS

Item 39 shows the percentage of housing units in the state that are **crowded** or **lacking complete plumbing facilities.**

Occupants per room is obtained by dividing the number of people in each occupied housing unit by the number of rooms in the unit. Although the Census Bureau has no official definition of **crowded** units, many users consider units with more than one occupant per room to be crowded, the measure used in this item.

The question on plumbing facilities was asked at both occupied and vacant housing units. Complete plumbing facilities include: (1) hot and cold piped water, (2) a flush toilet, and (3) a bathtub or shower. All three facilities must be located inside the house, apartment, or mobile home, but not necessarily in the same room. Housing units are classified as **lacking complete plumbing facilities** when any of the three facilities is not present.

MEDIAN HOUSEHOLD INCOME IN THE PAST 12 MONTHS, Items 40–44
Source: Table B25119. MEDIAN HOUSEHOLD INCOME THE PAST 12 MONTHS (IN 2007 INFLATION-ADJUSTED DOLLARS) BY TENURE
Universe: OCCUPIED HOUSING UNITS

Table B25099. MORTGAGE STATUS BY MEDIAN HOUSEHOLD INCOME IN THE PAST 12 MONTHS (IN 2007 INFLATION-ADJUSTED DOLLARS)
Universe: OWNER-OCCUPIED HOUSING UNITS

The data on **mortgage status** were obtained from questions that were asked at owner-occupied units. The category **with a mortgage** refers to all forms of debt where the property is pledged as security for repayment of the debt, including deeds of trust; trust deeds; contracts to purchase; land contracts; junior mortgages; and home equity loans.

The category **without a mortgage** comprises housing units owned free and clear of debt.

HOUSING VALUES AND COSTS, Items 45–51, 54–63
Source: Table B25097. MORTGAGE STATUS BY MEDIAN VALUE (DOLLARS); Table B25081. MORTGAGE STATUS; Table B25092. MEDIAN SELECTED MONTHLY OWNER COSTS AS A PERCENTAGE OF HOUSEHOLD INCOME IN THE PAST 12 MONTHS; Table B25088. MEDIAN SELECTED MONTHLY OWNER COSTS (DOLLARS) BY MORTGAGE STATUS; Table C25093. AGE OF HOUSEHOLDER BY SELECTED MONTHLY OWNER COSTS AS A PERCENTAGE OF HOUSEHOLD INCOME IN THE PAST 12 MONTHS
Universe: OWNER-OCCUPIED HOUSING UNITS

Table: B25105. MEDIAN MONTHLY HOUSING COSTS (DOLLARS)

Universe: OCCUPIED HOUSING UNITS WITH MONTHLY HOUSING COST

Median value is the dollar amount that divides the distribution of specified owner-occupied housing units into two equal parts, with half of all units below the median value and half above the median value. Value is defined as the respondent's estimate of what the house would sell for if it were for sale. If the house or mobile home was owned or being bought, but the land on which it sits was not, the respondent was asked to estimate the combined value of the house or mobile home and the land. For vacant units, value was the price asked for the property. Value was tabulated separately for all owner-occupied and vacant-for-sale housing units, as well as owner-occupied and vacant-for-sale mobile homes.

Since value is the only dollar amount captured on the questionnaire in specified intervals (checkboxes), the category boundaries for previous years are not adjusted for inflation. However, the median value is adjusted for inflation by multiplying a factor equal to the average annual CPI-U-RS factor for the current year, divided by the average annual CPI-U-RS factor for the earlier/earliest year.

Housing cost as a percentage of income is shown separately for owners with mortgages, owners without mortgages, and renters. Selected owner costs include utilities and fuels, mortgage payments, insurance, taxes, etc. In each case, the ratio of housing cost to income is computed separately for each housing unit. The housing cost ratios for half of all units are above the median shown in this book, and half are below the median shown in the book.

The data for monthly housing costs are developed from a distribution of **selected monthly owner costs** for owner-occupied units and **gross rent** for renter-occupied units.

RENT, Items 52–53, 64–67
Source: Table B25064. MEDIAN GROSS RENT (DOLLARS); Table B25071. MEDIAN GROSS RENT AS A PERCENTAGE OF HOUSEHOLD INCOME IN THE PAST 12 MONTHS (DOLLARS)
Universe: RENTER-OCCUPIED HOUSING UNITS PAYING CASH RENT

Table C25072. AGE OF HOUSEHOLDER BY GROSS RENT AS A PERCENTAGE OF HOUSEHOLD INCOME IN THE PAST 12 MONTHS
Universe: RENTER-OCCUPIED HOUSING UNITS

Median gross rent divides the distribution of renter-occupied housing units into two equal parts: one-half of the cases falling below the median gross rent and one-half above the median.

Gross rent is the contract rent plus the estimated average monthly cost of utilities (electricity, gas, and water and sewer) and fuels (oil, coal, kerosene, wood, etc.) if these are paid by the renter (or paid for the renter by someone else). Gross rent is intended to eliminate differentials that result from varying practices with respect to the inclusion of utilities and fuels as part of the rental payment. The estimated costs of water and sewer, and fuels are reported on a 12-month basis but are converted to monthly figures for the tabulations. Renter units occupied without payment of cash rent are not included in the tabulations.

To inflate gross rent amounts from previous years, the dollar values are inflated to the latest year's dollar values by multiplying by a factor equal to the average annual Consumer Price Index (CPI-U-RS) factor for the current year, divided by the average annual CPI-U-RS factor for the earlier/earliest year.

Gross rent as a percentage of household income is a computed ratio of monthly gross rent to monthly household income (total household income divided by 12). Median gross rent divides the gross rent as a percentage of household income distribution into two equal parts: one-half of the cases falling below the median gross rent as a percentage of household income and one-half above the median.

MEANS OF TRANSPORTATION TO WORK, Items 68–75
Source: Table C08301. MEANS OF TRANSPORTATION TO WORK
Universe: WORKERS 16 YEARS AND OVER

Means of transportation to work refers to the principal mode of travel or type of conveyance that the worker usually used to get from home to work during the reference week. People who used different means of transportation on different days of the week were asked to specify the one they used most often, that is, the greatest number of days. People who used more than one means of transportation to get to work each day were asked to report the one used for the longest distance during the work trip.

The category, **car, truck, or van**, includes workers using a car (including company cars but excluding taxicabs), a truck of one-ton capacity or less, or a van. A question on vehicle occupancy was asked of people who indicated that they worked at some time during the reference week and who reported that their means of transportation to work was **car, truck, or van**. The category, **drove alone**, includes people who usually drove alone to work as well as people who were driven to work by someone who then drove back home or to a non-work destination. The category, **carpooled**, includes workers who reported that two or more people usually rode to work in the vehicle during the reference week.

The category, **public transportation**, includes workers who used a bus or trolley bus, streetcar or trolley car, subway or elevated, railroad, or ferryboat, even if each mode is not shown separately in the tabulation.. The category, "Other means," includes workers who used a mode of travel that is not identified separately within the data distribution.

MEAN TRAVEL TIME TO WORK, Items 76–81
Source: Table C08301. MEANS OF TRANSPORTATION TO WORK
Universe: WORKERS 16 YEARS AND OVER

Table B08136. AGGREGATE TRAVEL TIME TO WORK (IN MINUTES) OF WORKERS BY MEANS OF TRANS-PORTATION TO WORK;
Universe: WORKERS 16 YEARS AND OVER WHO DID NOT WORK AT HOME

Travel time to work refers to the total number of minutes that it usually took the worker to get from home to work during the reference week. The elapsed time includes time spent waiting for public transportation, picking up passengers in carpools, and time spent in other activities related to getting to work.

Mean travel time to work (in minutes) is the average travel time that workers usually took to get from home to work (one way) during the reference week. This measure is obtained by dividing the total number of minutes taken to get from home to work (the aggregate travel time) by the number of workers 16 years old and over who did not work at home.

VEHICLES AVAILABLE, Items 82–87
Source: Table B08201. HOUSEHOLD SIZE BY VEHI-CLES AVAILABLE; Table B25046. AGGREGATE NUMBER OF VEHICLES AVAILABLE BY TENURE;
Universe: OCCUPIED HOUSING UNITS

The data on vehicles available show the number of passenger cars, vans, and pickup or panel trucks of one-ton capacity or less kept at home and available for the use of household members. Vehicles rented or leased for one month or more, company vehicles, and police and government vehicles are included if kept at home and used for non-business purposes. Dismantled or immobile vehicles are excluded. Vehicles kept at home but used only for business purposes also are excluded,

Tables C-2, C-3, and C-4. Where — Migration, Housing, and Transportation

Table C-2 presents 12 items for the United States as a whole, each individual state and the District of Columbia, and 1,817 counties, county equivalents, and independent cities with a 2007 population of 20,000 or more.

Table C-3 presents 12 items for 363 Metropolitan Statistical Areas and 29 Metropolitan Divisions within the 12 largest Metropolitan Statistical Areas.

Table C-4 presents 12 items for 2,065 cities, Census Designated Places, and the principal portions of consolidated cities with a 2007 population of 20,000 or more.

PLACE OF RESIDENCE, Items 1 and 2
Source: Table C07204. GEOGRAPHICAL MOBILITY IN THE PAST YEAR FOR CURRENT RESIDENCE--STATE, COUNTY AND PLACE LEVEL IN THE UNITED STATES (for states, counties, and cities)
Universe: POPULATION 1 YEAR AND OVER IN THE UNITED STATES

Table C07201. GEOGRAPHICAL MOBILITY IN THE PAST YEAR FOR CURRENT RESIDENCE--MET-ROPOLITAN STATISTICAL AREA LEVEL IN THE UNITED STATES (for Metropolitan Areas)
Universe: POPULATION 1 YEAR AND OVER LIV-ING IN A METROPOLITAN STATISTICAL AREA IN THE UNITED STATES

Residence one year ago is used in conjunction with location of current residence to determine the extent of residential mobility of the population and the resulting redistribution of the population across the various states, metropolitan areas, and regions of the country. **Same house** includes all people 1 year old and over who, a year earlier, lived in the same house or apartment that they occupied at the time of interview.

Did not live in county/city/metropolitan area one year ago includes all persons who did not live in the listed county, city, or metropolitan area 1 year ago, whether their previous residence was in the same state, a different state, Puerto Rico, or abroad.

OCCUPIED HOUSING UNITS, Items 3–4
Source: Table B25003. TENURE
Universe: OCCUPIED HOUSING UNITS

A **housing unit** is a house, apartment, mobile home or trailer, group of rooms, or single room occupied or, if vacant, intended for occupancy as separate living quarters. Separate living quarters are those in which the occupants do not live and eat with any other person in the structure and which have direct access from the outside of the building or through a common hall. For vacant units, the criteria of separateness and direct access are applied to the intended occupants whenever possible. If that information cannot be obtained, the criteria are applied to the previous occupants.

The occupants of a housing unit may be a single family, one person living alone, two or more families living together, or any other group of related or unrelated persons who share living arrangements. Both occupied and vacant housing units are included in the housing inventory, although recreational vehicles, tents, caves, boats, railroad cars, and the like are included only if they are occupied as a person's usual place of residence.

Occupied housing units are classified as either owner occupied or renter occupied. A housing unit is classified as occupied if it is the usual place of residence of the person or group of persons living in it at the time of enumeration, or if the occupants are only temporarily absent from the residence for two months or less, that is, away on vacation or a business trip. If all the people staying in the unit at the time of the interview are staying there for two months or less, the unit is considered to be temporarily occupied and classified as "vacant."

A housing unit is **owner occupied** if the owner or co-owner lives in the unit even if it is mortgaged or not fully paid for. The owner or co-owner must live in the unit and usually is Person 1 on the questionnaire. The unit is "Owned by you or someone in this household with a mortgage or loan" if it is being purchased with a mortgage or some other debt arrangement such as a deed of trust, trust deed, contract to purchase, land contract, or purchase agreement. The unit also is considered owned with a mortgage if it is built on leased land and there is a mortgage on the unit. Mobile homes occupied by owners with installment loan balances also are included in this category.

All occupied housing units which are not owner occupied, whether they are rented for cash rent or occupied without payment of cash rent, are classified as **renter occupied**. "No cash rent" units are separately identified in the rent tabulations. Such units are generally provided free by friends or relatives or in exchange for services such as resident manager, caretaker, minister, or tenant farmer. Housing units on military bases also are classified in the "No cash rent" category. "Rented for cash rent" includes units in continuing care, sometimes called life care arrangements. These arrangements usually involve a contract between one or more individuals and a health services provider guaranteeing the individual shelter, usually a house or apartment, and services, such as meals or transportation to shopping or recreation.

HOUSING VALUES AND COSTS, Items 5–7
Source: Table B25077. MEDIAN VALUE (DOLLARS) and Table B25092. MEDIAN SELECTED MONTHLY OWNER COSTS AS A PERCENTAGE OF HOUSE-HOLD INCOME IN THE PAST 12 MONTHS
Universe: OWNER-OCCUPIED HOUSING UNITS

Median value is the dollar amount that divides the distribution of specified owner-occupied housing units into two

equal parts, with half of all units below the median value and half above the median value. Value is defined as the respondent's estimate of what the house would sell for if it were for sale. If the house or mobile home was owned or being bought, but the land on which it sits was not, the respondent was asked to estimate the combined value of the house or mobile home and the land. For vacant units, value was the price asked for the property. Value was tabulated separately for all owner-occupied and vacant-for-sale housing units, as well as owner-occupied and vacant-for-sale mobile homes. $1,000,001 is the top code symbolizing a median value over one million dollars.

Since value is the only dollar amount captured on the questionnaire in specified intervals (checkboxes), the category boundaries for previous years are not adjusted for inflation. However, the median value is adjusted for inflation by multiplying a factor equal to the average annual CPI-U-RS factor for the current year, divided by the average annual CPI-U-RS factor for the earlier/earliest year.

Housing cost as a percentage of income is shown separately for owners with mortgages, owners without mortgages, and renters. Selected owner costs include utilities and fuels, mortgage payments, insurance, taxes, etc. In each case, the ratio of housing cost to income is computed separately for each housing unit. The housing cost ratios for half of all units are above the median shown in this book, and half are below the median shown in the book.

RENT, Items 8–9
Source: Table B25064. MEDIAN GROSS RENT (DOLLARS); Table B25071. MEDIAN GROSS RENT AS A PERCENTAGE OF HOUSEHOLD INCOME IN THE PAST 12 MONTHS (DOLLARS)
Universe: RENTER-OCCUPIED HOUSING UNITS PAYING CASH RENT

Median gross rent divides the distribution of renter-occupied housing units into two equal parts: one-half of the cases falling below the median gross rent and one-half above the median.

Gross rent is the contract rent plus the estimated average monthly cost of utilities (electricity, gas, and water and sewer) and fuels (oil, coal, kerosene, wood, etc.) if these are paid by the renter (or paid for the renter by someone else). Gross rent is intended to eliminate differentials that result from varying practices with respect to the inclusion of utilities and fuels as part of the rental payment. The estimated costs of water and sewer, and fuels are reported on a 12-month basis but are converted to monthly figures for the tabulations. Renter units occupied without payment of cash rent are not included in the tabulations.

To inflate gross rent amounts from previous years, the dollar values are inflated to the latest year's dollar values by multiplying by a factor equal to the average annual Consumer Price Index (CPI-U-RS) factor for the current year, divided by the average annual CPI-U-RS factor for the earlier/earliest year.

Gross rent as a percentage of household income is a computed ratio of monthly gross rent to monthly household income (total household income divided by 12). Median gross rent divides the gross rent as a percentage of household income distribution into two equal parts: one-half of the cases falling below the median gross rent as a percentage of household income and one-half above the median. 50.1 is the top code symbolizing a median gross rent as a percentage of household income of 50.1 percent or more.

MEANS OF TRANSPORTATION TO WORK, Item 10
Source: Table C08301. MEANS OF TRANSPORTATION TO WORK
Universe: WORKERS 16 YEARS AND OVER

Means of transportation to work refers to the principal mode of travel or type of conveyance that the worker usually used to get from home to work during the reference week. People who used different means of transportation on different days of the week were asked to specify the one they used most often, that is, the greatest number of days. People who used more than one means of transportation to get to work each day were asked to report the one used for the longest distance during the work trip.

Item 10 shows the percentage of workers who drove alone to work. Other means of transportation include carpooling, public transportation, walking, taking a taxicab, motorcycling, bicycling, other means, or working at home.

MEAN TRAVEL TIME TO WORK, Item 11
Source: Table B08013. AGGREGATE TRAVEL TIME TO WORK (IN MINUTES) OF WORKERS BY SEX; Table C08012. SEX OF WORKERS BY TRAVEL TIME TO WORK
Universe: WORKERS 16 YEARS AND OVER WHO DID NOT WORK AT HOME

Travel time to work refers to the total number of minutes that it usually took the worker to get from home to work during the reference week. The elapsed time includes time spent waiting for public transportation, picking up passengers in carpools, and time spent in other activities related to getting to work.

Mean travel time to work (in minutes) is the average travel time that workers usually took to get from home to work (one way) during the reference week. This measure is obtained by dividing the total number of minutes taken to get from home to work (the aggregate travel time) by the number of workers 16 years old and over who did not work at home.

VEHICLES AVAILABLE, Item 12
Source: Table C25045. TENURE BY VEHICLES AVAILABLE BY AGE OF HOUSEHOLDER
Universe: OCCUPIED HOUSING UNITS

The data on vehicles available show the number of passenger cars, vans, and pickup or panel trucks of one-ton capacity or less kept at home and available for the use of household members. Vehicles rented or leased for one month or more, company vehicles, and police and government vehicles are included if kept at home and used for non-business purposes. Dismantled or immobile vehicles are excluded. Vehicles kept at home but used only for business purposes also are excluded.

APPENDIX C:
GEOGRAPHIC CONCEPTS AND CODES

GEOGRAPHIC AREAS COVERED

The Who, What, and Where of America presents data for the United States, all states, all metropolitan areas, counties with populations of 20,000 or more, and cities with populations of 20,000 or more. The population sizes are based on the July 1, 2007, population estimates from the Census Bureau's Population Estimates Program.

STATES AND COUNTIES

Data are presented for each of the 50 states, the District of Columbia, and the United States as a whole. The states are arranged alphabetically and counties are arranged alphabetically within each state. Data are presented for 1,817 counties and county equivalents with populations of 20,000 or more.

County equivalents

In Louisiana, the primary divisions of the state are known as parishes rather than counties. In Alaska, the county equivalents are the organized boroughs, together with the census areas that were developed for general statistical purposes by the state of Alaska and the U.S. Census Bureau. Four states—Maryland, Missouri, Nevada, and Virginia—have one or more incorporated places that are legally independent of any county and thus constitute primary divisions of their states. Within each state, independent cities are listed alphabetically following the list of counties. The District of Columbia is not divided into counties or county equivalents—data for the entire district are presented as a county equivalent. New York City contains five counties: Bronx, Kings, New York, Queens, and Richmond.

METROPOLITAN AREAS

Data are included for all 363 metropolitan statistical areas and 29 metropolitan divisions, which are located within the 11 largest metropolitan statistical areas. The metropolitan statistical areas are listed alphabetically, and the metropolitan divisions are listed alphabetically under the metropolitan statistical area of which they are components.

The U.S. Office of Management and Budget (OMB) defines metropolitan and micropolitan statistical areas according to published standards. The major purpose of defining these areas is to enable all U.S. government agencies to use the same geographic definitions in tabulating and publishing data. The general concept of a metropolitan or micropolitan statistical area is that of a core area containing a substantial population nucleus, together with adjacent communities that have a high degree of economic and social integration with the core. Currently defined metropolitan and micropolitan statistical areas are based on application of the new 2000 standards to 2000 decennial census data, updated each year according to the most recent population estimates. Current metropolitan and micropolitan statistical area definitions were announced by OMB effective November 20, 2007.

Standard definitions of metropolitan areas were first issued in 1949 by the Bureau of the Budget (the predecessor of OMB), under the designation "standard metropolitan area" (SMA). The term was changed to "standard metropolitan statistical area" (SMSA) in 1959, and to "metropolitan statistical area" (MSA) in 1983. The term "metropolitan area" (MA) was adopted in 1990 and refers collectively to metropolitan statistical areas (MSAs), consolidated metropolitan statistical areas (CMSAs), and primary metropolitan statistical areas (PMSAs). The term "core based statistical area" (CBSA) became effective in 2000 and refers collectively to metropolitan and micropolitan statistical areas.

The 2000 standards provide that each CBSA must contain at least one urban area of 10,000 or more population. Each metropolitan statistical area must have at least one urbanized area of 50,000 or more inhabitants. Each micropolitan statistical area must have at least one urban cluster of at least 10,000 but less than 50,000 people.

Under the standards, the county (or counties) in which at least 50 percent of the population resides within urban areas of 10,000 or more population, or that contain at least 5,000 people residing within a single urban area of 10,000 or more population, is identified as a "central county" (counties). Additional "outlying counties" are included in the CBSA if they meet specified requirements of commuting to or from the central counties. Counties or equivalent entities form the geographic "building blocks" for metropolitan and micropolitan statistical areas throughout the United States.

If specified criteria are met, a metropolitan statistical area containing a single core with a population of 2.5 million or more may be subdivided to form smaller groupings of counties referred to as "metropolitan divisions."

The largest city in each metropolitan statistical area is designated a "principal city." Additional cities qualify if specified requirements are met concerning population size and employment. The title of each metropolitan statistical area consists of the names of up to three of its principal cities and the name of each state into which the metropolitan statistical area extends. Titles of metropolitan divisions also typically are based on principal city names, but in certain cases consist of county names. The principal city need not be an incorporated place if it meets the requirements of population size and employment. Usually such a principal city is a Census designated place.

In view of the importance of cities and town in New England, the 2000 standards also provide for a set of geographic areas that are defined using cities and towns in the six New England states. These New England city and town areas (NECTAs) are not included in this volume.

CITIES

This book presents data for 2,065 cities with estimated populations of 20,000 or more in 2007. Corresponding data for states are also provided. The states are arranged alphabetically and the cities are ordered alphabetically within each state.

As used in this volume, the term *city* refers to *places* as defined by the Census Bureau. These include places that have been incorporated as cities, boroughs, towns, or villages under the laws of their respective states, as well as Census designated places (CDPs). CDPs are delineated by the Census Bureau, in cooperation with states and localities, as statistical counterparts of incorporated places for purposes of the decennial census and the ACS. CDPs comprise densely settled concentrations of population that are identifiable by name but are not legally incorporated places.

Included with the incorporated cities are the principal portions of seven consolidated cities. A consolidated city is an incorporated place that has combined its government functions with a county or subcounty entity but contains one or more other semi-independent incorporated places that continue to function as local governments within the consolidated government. Consolidated cities are not included in this book, but the "consolidated city (balance)" portions are treated as incorporated places in the ACS data. Consolidated city (balance) portions included in this volume are Milford, CT; Athens-Clarke County, GA; Augusta-Richmond County, GA; Indianapolis, IN; Louisville-Jefferson County, KY; Butte-Silver Bow, MT; and Nashville-Davidson, TN.

Towns in the New England states and New York are treated as minor civil divisions (MCDs) and are not included in this book.

GEOGRAPHIC CODES

The tables in this book provide a geographic code or codes for each area.

For counties, a five-digit state and county code is given for each state and county. The first two digits indicate the state; the remaining three represent the county. Within each state, the counties are listed in order, beginning with 001, with even numbers usually omitted. Independent cities follow the counties and begin with the number 510. In the state-level tables, a two-digit state code is provided. The state code is a sequential numbering, with some gaps, of the states and the District of Columbia in alphabetical order from Alabama (01) to Wyoming (56).

These codes have been established by the U.S. government as Federal Information Processing Standards and are often referred to as *FIPS codes*. They are used by U.S. government agencies and many other organizations for data presentation. The codes are provided in this volume for use in matching the data given here with other data sources in which counties are identified by FIPS code.

The metropolitan area tables provide metro area codes for each metropolitan area, as well as metropolitan division codes where appropriate.

For cities, a seven-digit state and place code is included. The first two digits identify the state and are the same as the FIPS codes described above. The remaining five digits are the place FIPS codes established by the U.S. government.

INDEPENDENT CITIES

The following independent cities are not included in any county; their data are presented separately in this volume.

MARYLAND
Baltimore (separate from Baltimore County)

MISSOURI
St. Louis (separate from St. Louis County)

NEVADA
Carson City

VIRGINIA

Alexandria	Norfolk
Charlottesville	Petersburg
Chesapeake	Portsmouth
Danville	Richmond
Fairfax	Roanoke
Fredericksburg	Salem
Hampton	Staunton
Harrisonburg	Suffolk
Hopewell	Virginia Beach
Lynchbur	Waynesboro g
Manassas	Winchester
Newport News	